CASES AND MATERIALS ON

PATENT LAW

Second Edition

By

Martin J. Adelman
Professor of Law
George Washington University

Randall R. Rader
Circuit Judge
United States Court of Appeals for the Federal Circuit
Lecturer in Law
George Washington University

John R. Thomas
Associate Professor of Law
George Washington University

Harold C. Wegner
Foley & Lardner

AMERICAN CASEBOOK SERIES®

Mat #17186906

COPYRIGHT © 1998 WEST GROUP
COPYRIGHT © 2003 By WEST GROUP
      610 Opperman Drive
      P.O. Box 64526
      St. Paul, MN 55164–0526
      1–800–328–9352

ISBN 0–314–24637–1

 TEXT IS PRINTED ON 10% POST CONSUMER RECYCLED PAPER

Acknowledgments

The authors wish to acknowledge that in the writing of this casebook we have been assisted by many colleagues. Special appreciation is due to individuals who, through classroom use or other contributions, helped improve the book. They are Steve Anzalone, Doug Baldwin, Rebecca Eisenberg, Robert Goldman, Mark Janis, Mike Kaminski, Roberta Morris, Gerald Mossinghoff, Kimberly Pace, John Paul, Kathy White and John Witherspoon. The authors gratefully recognize as well the many students at George Washington University, the United States Patent and Trademark Office Juris Masters Program, the University of Virginia, and Wayne State University who have been subjected to evolving versions of this manuscript. Their suggestions and observations have considerably advanced the efforts reflected in this final version of the book, the culmination of seven years of work on a basic patents text.

The authors also give particular thanks to support shown by their respective institutions, and in particular to their Deans, fellow faculty members and administrators. We gratefully acknowledge support offered by the Max Planck Institute for Foreign and Comparative Patent, Copyright and Competition Law of Munich, Germany, and by Finnegan, Henderson, Farabow, Garrett & Dunner, L.L.P., of Washington, D.C. Particular thanks is also due to Mr. Toyomaro Yoshida of the Institute of Intellectual Property in Tokyo, Japan, and to Dr. Paul Tauchner and his colleagues at Vossius & Partner of Munich, Germany.

Any omissions and errors that remain are, of course, the responsibility of the authors. Readers should also note that this project has been a team effort of four very independent members of the patent community, with portions presenting a strongly held view of one author that is not necessarily shared by the others. Although no single author agrees with all of the points made in this book, we felt compelled to include different points of view in order to offer a complete academic presentation.

*

Summary of Contents

*

Table of Contents

Table of Cases

The principal cases are in bold type. Cases cited or discussed in the text are roman type. References are to pages. Cases cited in principal cases and within other quoted materials are not included.

*

CASES AND MATERIALS ON

PATENT LAW

Second Edition

*

Chapter One

INTRODUCTION

Fueled both by its longstanding traditions and the extraordinary dynamism of the modern innovative community, patent law has risen from an obscure station to take a central place within the intellectual property law. Students taking a first look at patents have come at a good time. In recent years the patent law has become a more robust discipline, enriched by increasingly sophisticated legal and economic analysis; recognized as a key determinant of international trade; and marked by an expansion into a array of disciplines that span the entire range of human endeavor.

In American literary arts, Mark Twain at one point called upon Hank Morgan to comment:

> That reminds me to remark, in passing, that the very first official thing I did, in my administration–and it was on the very first day of it, too–was to start a patent office; for I knew that a country without a patent office and good patent laws was just a crab, and couldn't travel any way but sideways or backwards.

MARK TWAIN, A CONNECTICUT YANKEE AT KING ARTHUR'S COURT 92 (1889) (Justin Kaplan ed. 1971). Although Twain offered this statement in a satirical tone, now more than ever patent law is not merely for technicians. The principles underlying this regime of property rights have a broad, humanistic focus which implicate essential societal goals. At heart these goals attempt to strike a balance between the encouragement of the labors that lead to innovation and the dissemination of the fruits of those labors. As you make your way through the materials that follow, consider whether this elusive balance has been achieved.

§ 1.1 OVERVIEW OF THIS CASEBOOK

Any study of patent law must ultimately focus on the current statute, which since 1952 has been codified as Title 35 of the United States Code. The starting point is patent-eligibility as governed by 35

1

U.S.C.A. § 101. Chapter 2 of this casebook addresses the precise scope of subject matter covered by patents. Section 101 additionally requires that an invention be "useful" to receive patent protection. Chapter 3 considers this requirement.

Perhaps the core requirement of the law is that a patentable invention must be new. If the invention is *precisely* the same as earlier work in the field eligible to be considered, then the inquiry is ended as to the claim in question: it lacks novelty and denied patent protection by § 102. Chapters 4, 5, and 6 address the often intricate issues surrounding the novelty requirement under United States law.

Even though the invention may go towards novel subject matter, patentability is denied if the claimed invention is "obvious" to "a person having ordinary skill in the art." The § 103 statutory test for obviousness is judged from the viewpoint of the skilled artisan and denies patentability if the differences between the subject matter and the prior art would have rendered the subject matter obvious at the time the invention was made. The nonobviousness standard, along with the sorts of technology eligible, are addressed in Chapters 7 and 8 respectively.

Unlike some other forms of intellectual property, patents do not arise without the significant involvement of an administrative agency. In order to obtain protection, inventors must instead undertake the process of so-called "patent prosecution" at the United States Patent and Trademark Office, also called the "U.S. PTO" or simply the "PTO." Chapters 9, 10, and 11 consider the requirements of patent applications as to both their "specifications," the often lengthy description of the technical problem the inventor faced and the invention produced to solve that problem, and their "claims," the concise delineations of an invention that serve as the primary source of proprietary rights.

Chapter 12 then reviews the patent acquisition process itself, along with applicant abuses of the procedure—so-called "inequitable conduct" and "double patenting"—and their ramifications. And although a patent has issued, this event does not necessarily end its consideration by the United States Patent and Trademark Office. Chapter 13 therefore considers post-grant procedures that may yet result upon issued patents, including reissue and reexamination proceedings. Additionally, Chapter 14 addresses aspects of patent acquisition outside of the United States.

Once the Patent and Trademark Office grants a patent, its proprietor obtains the right to exclude others practicing the invention in the United States. Those who make or use the invention without the authority of the patentee commit patent infringement, a topic addressed in Chapter 15. Beyond those topics already discussed, Chapter 16 considers additional, equitable defenses that accused infringers may raise during suit. Chapter 17 then addresses available remedies under the United States patent statute. Chapters 18 and 19 expand upon topics previously addressed by considering different aspects of patent enforcement, licensing, misuse and patent-antitrust.

As you make your way through this casebook, you will note that it is *comparative*. Although certainly a tool designed to teach the patent law of the United States to the exclusion of that of other nations, this text will constantly refer to aspects of foreign patent systems as well. Where tribunals from abroad have provided more compelling reasoning to support a common legal doctrine, or are certain to have foreshadowed future developments in the United States, this casebook will unhesitatingly stress their reasoning over that of domestic fora. These comparative studies serve as an insightful focus for grasp of domestic doctrines and stimulate critical thinking about the array of alternatives which exist under varying statutory regimes.

A second rationale for the comparative approach is far more prosaic. In the current technological and economic climate, patent practitioners without an understanding of the international patent system place their clients at a significant disadvantage. It is not an overstatement to say that no patent attorney in the United States truly practices domestic patent law in our contemporary, globally-oriented economy. Further, in recent years, reform of United States patent law has largely been motivated by the global international harmonization movement. Lacking a grasp of the relevant issues and actors from without the United States, a would-be patent attorney will not possess the analytical tools to comprehend future changes domestically.

Another focus of the book is on the *historical development* of patent law doctrines. Although certainly presenting the most current law from the United States Supreme Court, Court of Appeals for the Federal Circuit, United States Patent Office and foreign sources, this casebook does not neglect their antecedents. Patent law is as much a process as a static entity; the ever-quickening reforms of patent systems worldwide render snapshot views extremely inappropriate. Only an appreciation of the contours of earlier statutes and case law allows students to chart the possibilities of future reform and place older, yet frequently cited precedent, in context. In addition, because patent law has a fundamentally *economic* orientation, this casebook will also offer perspectives from law and economics studies to articulate and explain patent law principles.

With these concentrations in mind, the student can find no better introduction to the patent law than through an historical overview.

§ 1.2 FOUNDATIONS OF THE UNITED STATES PATENT SYSTEM

BONITO BOATS, INC. v. THUNDER CRAFT BOATS, INC.

United States Supreme Court, 1989.
489 U.S. 141, 109 S.Ct. 971, 9 U.S.P.Q.2d 1847.

O'CONNOR, JUSTICE.

II

Article I, § 8, cl. 8, of the Constitution gives Congress the power "[t]o promote the Progress of Science and useful Arts, by securing for limited Times to Authors and Inventors the exclusive Right to their respective Writings and Discoveries." The Patent Clause itself reflects a balance between the need to encourage innovation and the avoidance of monopolies which stifle competition without any concomitant advance in the "Progress of Science and useful Arts." As we have noted in the past, the Clause contains both a grant of power and certain limitations upon the exercise of that power. Congress may not create patent monopolies of unlimited duration, nor may it "authorize the issuance of patents whose effects are to remove existent knowledge from the public domain, or to restrict free access to materials already available." *Graham v. John Deere Co. of Kansas City*, 383 U.S. 1, 6, 86 S.Ct. 684, 688, 15 L.Ed.2d 545 (1966).

From their inception, the federal patent laws have embodied a careful balance between the need to promote innovation and the recognition that imitation and refinement through imitation are both necessary to invention itself and the very lifeblood of a competitive economy. Soon after the adoption of the Constitution, the First Congress enacted the Patent Act of 1790, which allowed the grant of a limited monopoly of 14 years to any applicant that "hath * * * invented or discovered any useful art, manufacture, * * * or device, or any improvement therein not before known or used." 1 Stat. 109, 110. In addition to novelty, the 1790 Act required that the invention be "sufficiently useful and important" to merit the 14–year right of exclusion. Ibid. Section 2 of the Act required that the patentee deposit with the Secretary of State, a specification and if possible a model of the new invention, "which specification shall be so particular, and said models so exact, as not only to distinguish the invention or discovery from other things before known and used, but also to enable a workman or other person skilled in the art or manufacture * * * to make, construct, or use the same, to the end that the public may have the full benefit thereof, after the expiration of the patent term." Ibid.

The first Patent Act established an agency known by self-designation as the "Commissioners for the promotion of Useful Arts," composed of the Secretary of State, the Secretary of the Department of War, and the Attorney General, any two of whom could grant a patent. Thomas Jefferson was the first Secretary of State, and the driving force behind early federal patent policy. For Jefferson, a central tenet of the patent system in a free market economy was that "a machine of which we were possessed, might be applied by every man to any use of which it is susceptible." 13 WRITINGS OF THOMAS JEFFERSON 335 (Memorial ed. 1904). He viewed a grant of patent rights in an idea already disclosed to the public as akin to an ex post facto law, "obstruct[ing] others in the use of what they possessed before." *Id.*, at 326–327. Jefferson also played a large role in the drafting of our Nation's second Patent Act, which became law in 1793. The Patent Act of 1793 carried over the requirement that the subject of a patent application be "not known or used before the application." Ch. 11, 1 Stat. 318, 319. A defense to an infringement action was created where "the thing, thus secured by patent, was not originally discovered by the patentee, but had been in use, or had been described in some public work anterior to the supposed discovery of the patentee." *Id.*, at 322. Thus, from the outset, federal patent law has been about the difficult business "of drawing a line between the things which are worth to the public the embarrassment of an exclusive patent, and those which are not." 13 WRITINGS OF THOMAS JEFFERSON, *supra*, at 335.

Today's patent statute is remarkably similar to the law as known to Jefferson in 1793. Protection is offered to "[w]hoever invents or discovers any new and useful process, machine, manufacture, or composition of matter, or any new and useful improvement thereof." 35 U.S.C. § 101. Since 1842, Congress has also made protection available for "any new, original and ornamental design for an article of manufacture." 35 U.S.C. § 171. To qualify for protection, a design must present an aesthetically pleasing appearance that is not dictated by function alone, and must satisfy the other criteria of patentability. The novelty requirement of patentability is presently expressed in 35 U.S.C. §§ 102(a) and (b), which provide:

A person shall be entitled to a patent unless—

(a) the invention was known or used by others in this country, or patented or described in a printed publication in this or a foreign country, before the invention thereof by the applicant for patent, or

(b) the invention was patented or described in a printed publication in this or a foreign country or in public use or on sale in this country more than one year prior to the date of application for patent in the United States * * *.

Sections 102(a) and (b) operate in tandem to exclude from consideration for patent protection knowledge that is already available to the public. They express a congressional determination that the creation of a monopoly in such information would not only serve no socially useful purpose, but would in fact injure the public by removing existing knowledge from public use. From the Patent Act of 1790 to the present day, the public sale of an unpatented article has acted as a complete bar to federal protection of the idea embodied in the article thus placed in public commerce.

In the case of *Pennock v. Dialogue*, 2 Pet. 1, 7 L.Ed. 327 (1829), Justice Story applied these principles under the patent law of 1800. The patentee had developed a new technique for the manufacture of rubber hose for the conveyance of air and fluids. The invention was reduced to practice in 1811, but letters patent were not sought and granted until 1818. In the interval, the patentee had licensed a third party to market the hose, and over 13,000 feet of the new product had been sold in the city of Philadelphia alone. The Court concluded that the patent was invalid due to the prior public sale, indicating that, "if [an inventor] suffers the thing he invented to go into public use, or to be publicly sold for use" "[h]is voluntary act or acquiescence in the public sale and use is an abandonment of his right." *Id.*, 2 Pet., at 23–24. The Court noted that under the common law of England, letters patent were unavailable for the protection of articles in public commerce at the time of the application, id., at 20, and that this same doctrine was immediately embodied in the first patent laws passed in this country. *Id.*, at 21–22.

As the holding of *Pennock* makes clear, the federal patent scheme creates a limited opportunity to obtain a property right in an idea. Once an inventor has decided to lift the veil of secrecy from his work, he must choose the protection of a federal patent or the dedication of his idea to the public at large. As Judge Learned Hand once put it: "[I]t is a condition upon the inventor's right to a patent that he shall not exploit his discovery competitively after it is ready for patenting; he must content himself with either secrecy or legal monopoly." *Metallizing Engineering Co. v. Kenyon Bearing & Auto Parts Co.*, 153 F.2d 516, 520 (CA2), *cert. denied*, 328 U.S. 840, 66 S.Ct. 1016, 90 L.Ed. 1615 (1946).

In addition to the requirements of novelty and utility, the federal patent law has long required that an innovation not be anticipated by the prior art in the field. Even if a particular combination of elements is "novel" in the literal sense of the term, it will not qualify for federal patent protection if its contours are so traced by the existing technology in the field that the "improvement is the work of the skillful mechanic, not that of the inventor." *Hotchkiss v. Greenwood*, 11 How. 248, 267, 13 L.Ed. 683 (1851). In 1952, Congress codified this judicially developed requirement in 35 U.S.C. § 103, which refuses protection to new developments where "the differences between the subject matter sought to be patented and the prior art are such that the subject matter as a whole would have been obvious at the time the invention was made to a person of ordinary skill in the art to which said subject matter pertains." The nonobviousness requirement extends the field of unpatentable material beyond that which is known to the public under § 102, to include that which could readily be deduced from publicly available material by a person of ordinary skill in the pertinent field of endeavor. *See Graham*, 383 U.S., at 15, 86 S.Ct., at 692. Taken together, the novelty and nonobviousness requirements express a congressional determination that the purposes behind the Patent Clause are best served by free competition and exploitation of either that which is already available to the public or that which may be readily discerned from publicly available material. *See Aronson v. Quick Point Pencil Co.*, 440 U.S. 257, 262, 99 S.Ct. 1096, 1099, 59 L.Ed.2d 296 (1979) ("[T]he stringent requirements for patent protection seek to ensure that ideas in the public domain remain there for the use of the public").

The applicant whose invention satisfies the requirements of novelty, nonobviousness, and utility, and who is willing to reveal to the public the substance of his discovery and "the best mode * * * of carrying out his invention," 35 U.S.C. § 112, is granted "the right to exclude others from making, using, or selling the invention throughout the United States," for a period of [20] years. 35 U.S.C. § 154. The federal patent system thus embodies a carefully crafted bargain for encouraging the creation and disclosure of new, useful, and nonobvious advances in technology and design in return for the exclusive right to practice the invention for a period of years. "[The inventor] may keep his invention secret and reap its fruits indefinitely. In consideration of its disclosure and the consequent benefit to the community, the patent is granted. An exclusive enjoyment is guaranteed him for seventeen years, but upon expiration of that period, the knowledge of the invention inures to the people, who are thus enabled without restriction to practice it and profit by its use." *United States v. Dubilier Condenser Corp.*, 289 U.S. 178, 186–187, 53 S.Ct. 554, 557, 77 L.Ed. 1114 (1933).

The attractiveness of such a bargain, and its effectiveness in inducing creative effort and disclosure of the results of that effort, depend almost entirely on a backdrop of free competition in the exploitation of unpatented designs and innovations. The novelty and nonobviousness requirements of patentability embody a congressional understanding, implicit in the Patent Clause itself, that free exploitation of ideas will be the rule, to which the protection of a federal patent is the exception. Moreover, the ultimate goal of the patent system is to bring new designs and technologies into the public domain through disclosure. State law protection for techniques and designs whose disclosure has already been induced by market rewards may conflict with the very purpose of the patent laws by decreasing the range of ideas available as the building blocks of further innovation. The offer of federal protection from competitive exploitation of intellectual property would be rendered meaningless in a world where substantially similar state law protections were readily available. To a limited extent, the federal patent laws must determine not only what is protected, but also what is free for all to use. Cf. *Arkansas Electric Cooperative Corp. v. Arkansas Public Service Comm'n*, 461 U.S. 375, 384, 103 S.Ct. 1905, 1912, 76 L.Ed.2d 1 (1983) ("[A] federal decision to forgo regulation in a given area may imply an authoritative federal determination that the area is best left un regulated, and in that event would have as much pre-emptive force as a decision to regulate").

Notes

1. The Dual Grant. Scholars who have studied the aforementioned constitutional provision have concluded that it is really two grants of power rolled into one; first, to establish a copyright system and, second, to establish a patent system. Their conclusions have been that the constitutionally-stated purpose of granting patent rights to inventors for their discoveries is the promotion of progress in the "useful Arts," (1979) (Rich, J.), *cert. granted and appeal dismissed, Diamond v. Bergy, aff'd as to related case sub nom Diamond v. Chakrabarty*, 447 U.S. 303, 206 U.S.P.Q. 193 (1980).

2. Substantive Constitutional Patent Law. An argument is sometimes made that there is a "constitutional" standard of "invention" or that it is "unconstitutional" to have a law such as first-to-file or that a particular case should have a certain outcome to meet a "constitutional" standard. As pointed out by Judge Rich in *Bergy*, "the Constitutional clause ... neither gave to nor preserved in inventors ... any rights and set no standards for the patentability of individual inventions; it merely empowered Congress, if it elected to do so, to secure to inventors an 'exclusive right' for an unstated 'limited' time for the stated purpose of promoting useful arts.''

3. Promoting Progress. Much effort has been devoted towards the study of whether the patent system actually achieves its stated goal of promoting technology. Suppose an economic researcher is actually able to prove that within a given technological field, the patent system actually hinders technological growth. That is, suppose that given the technological patterns within a particular industry—including, for example, product cycle, barriers to market entry, specialized knowledge required to compete— patents actually contributed to market concentration and decreased innovation. Would the grant of patents in that technological field therefore be unconstitutional?

4. Patent Term. As discussed here in Chapter 12, *Prosecution*, the term of a utility patent is 20 years, measured from the date the inventor filed a patent application. Suppose, however, that Congress chooses to extend the term of patents to say, 150 years each. Would such a term run afoul of the Constitution?

5. Inventorship. Under the United States Constitution, which party may obtain a patent? Suppose an inventor is employed by a corporation, and as part of his employment contract he is obliged to assign ownership of all of his inventions, along with any resulting patents, to his employer. However, the parties suffer a falling out and the inventor refuses to apply for any patents. Under the Constitution, does the employer have any redress? Alternatively, suppose the inventor is deceased or otherwise incapacitated. Does the Constitution allow a patent to issue? The legal concept of inventorship is also addressed here in Chapter 12.

§ 1.3 ORIGINS OF THE PATENT SYSTEM

Legal historians have been quick to seize upon venerable antecedents to our contemporary patent law regime. An ancient Greek system of rewarding cooks for excellent recipes, *see* BRUCE BUGBEE, GENESIS OF AMERICAN PATENT AND COPYRIGHT LAW 166 n.5 (1967), exclusive privileges granted for innovations relating to Tyrolean mines in the Fourteenth Century, *see* ERICH KAUFER, THE ECONOMICS OF THE PATENT SYSTEM (1989), and a Florentine patent granted in 1421, *see* M. Frumkin, *The Origin of Patents*, 27 J. PAT. OFF.SOC'Y 166 (1948), have been variously cited as predecessors to the modern patent law. However, most observers consider legislation enacted on March 19, 1474, by the Venetian Republic as the first true patent statute. *See* Giulio Mandich, *Venentian Patents (1450–1550)*, 30 J. PAT. OFF. SOC'Y 166 (1948). With its requirements that the invention be new, useful, and reduced to practice; provision for a ten-year term; and registration and remedial scheme, the Venetian statute bears a remarkable resemblance to the modern law. By the Seventeenth Century, numerous European states had enacted similar legislation. *See* F.D. Prager, *A History of Intellectual Property From 1545 to 1787*, 26 J. PAT. OFF.SOC'Y 711 (1944). For purposes of the common law world, the most significant of these successors was the English Statute of Monopolies, 21 Jac.1 c. 3 (1624), an important commercial statute of the Jacobean era.

§ 1.3[a]   The Statute of Monopolies

By the start of the Seventeenth Century, the English Crown had a long history of awarding importation franchises and other exclusive rights. But this practice had become subject to abuse during the reigns of Elizabeth I and James I, as favored subjects obtained grants of supervision or control over long-established industries. Parliament responded in 1624 by enacting the Statute of Monopolies. *See* Chris R. Kyle, *'But a New Button to an Old Coat': The Enactment of the Statute of Monopolies*, 19 J. LEGAL HISTORY 203 (1998). Although the Statute was principally designed to proscribe monopolistic grants by the Crown, it did authorize the issuance of "letters patent:"

> [B]e it declared and enacted that any declaration before mentioned shall not extend to any letters patent and grants of privilege for the term of fourteen years or under, hereafter to be made of the sole working or making of any manner of new manufactures within this realm, to the true and first inventors of such manufacture....

This exception in section 6 of the Statute of Monopolies is the foundation of patent law in the common law world.

§ 1.3[b]   The U.S. Patent System

The patent tradition established by the Statute of Monopolies continued in many of the New World colonies. For example, a Connecticut statute of 1672 outlawed the award of monopolies except for "such new inventions as shall be judged profitable for the country and for such time as the general court shall judge meet." As well, many colonial governments granted individuals privileges or rewards for their inventions very early in their histories. *See* Edward C. Walterscheid, *The Early Evolution of United States Patent Law: Antecedents (Part I)*, 78 J. PAT. & TRADEMARK OFF. SOC'Y 615 (1996).

§ 1.3[b][1]   The Constitution and Early Patent Laws

By 1787, state grants of patents were at their zenith, and the delegates to the Constitutional Convention apparently realized the possibility of interstate conflicts among competing inventors. James Madison's first draft of the Constitution, introduced as the Virginia Plan, focused on the structure of national government. 1 MAX FARRAND, RECORDS OF THE FEDERAL CONSTITUTION 20–22 (1911). Due to their concentration on these structural concerns, the delegates turned to discussion of many specific national powers late in the Convention. On August 18, 1787, Charles Pinckney proposed the following powers:

> "To grant patents for useful inventions"

> "To secure to Authors exclusive rights for a certain time"

> "To establish public institutions, rewards and immunities for the promotion of agriculture, commerce, trades and manufactures"

FARRAND, Vol. 2 at 322. On the same day, Madison's records of the Convention show that he himself proposed to grant Congress power:

"To secure to literary authors their copy rights for a limited time"

"To encourage by premiums & provisions, the advancement of useful knowledge and discoveries"

FARRAND, Vol. 2 at 325. These proposals featured both exclusive rights and outright subsidies for inventive activity. The Convention referred both sets of proposals to the Committee on Detail for incorporation into the next draft of the Constitution. FARRAND, Vol. 2 at 321, 325.

The limited records of the Constitutional Convention of 1787 suggest that Charles Pinckney was the principal source of the national power to grant patents. *See* BRUCE BUGBEE, THE GENESIS OF AMERICAN PATENT AND COPYRIGHT LAW 127 (1967). Pinckney served in the South Carolina legislature in 1784 during creation of one of the more detailed colonial patent statutes. More important, Pinckney served on the Committee on Detail which received his proposal for creation of a national patent power. FARRAND, Vol. 2 at 322.

On September 5, the Committee on Detail recommended to the Convention the intellectual property language now found in the Constitution. FARRAND, Vol. 2 at 509. No doubt the convention's general inclination against direct national involvement in economic affairs inspired the Committee to limit their clause to exclusive rights alone. The Convention unanimously accepted this language. *Id.*

IN RE BERGY

Court of Customs and Patent Appeals, 1979.
596 F.2d 952, 201 U.S.P.Q. 352.

RICH, JUDGE.

THE CONSTITUTION

The grant of power to Congress to establish a patent system is in these familiar words of Article I, section 8, clauses 8 and 18:

(The Congress shall have Power) * * * (8) To promote the Progress of Science and useful Arts, by securing for limited Times to Authors and Inventors the exclusive Right to their respective Writings and Discoveries; * * * (And) (18) To make all Laws which shall be necessary and proper for carrying into Execution the foregoing Powers * * *.

Scholars who have studied this provision, its origins, and its subsequent history, have, from time to time, pointed out that it is really two grants of power rolled into one; first, to establish a copyright system and, second, to establish a patent system. See R. DEWOLF, AN OUTLINE OF COPYRIGHT LAW 15 (1925); K. Lutz, *Patents and Science. A Clarification of the Patent Clause of the Constitution,* 18 GEO.WASH.L.REV. 50 (1949); P. Federico, *Commentary on the New Patent Act,* 35 U.S.C.A. § 1 to § 110, 1, 3 (1954); G. Rich, *Principles of Patentability,* 28 GEO.WASH.L.REV. 393 (1960). Their conclusions have been that the constitutionally-stated purpose of granting patent rights to inventors for their discoveries is the promotion of progress in the "useful Arts," rather than in science. In enacting the 1952 Patent Act, both houses of Congress adopted in their reports this construction of the Constitution in identical words, as follows:

> The background, the balanced construction, and the usage current then and later, indicate that the constitutional provision is really two provisions merged into one. The purpose of the first provision is to promote the progress of Science by securing for limited times To authors the exclusive right to their Writings, the word "science" in this connection having the meaning of knowledge in general, which is one of its meanings today. The other provision is that Congress has the power to promote the Progress of useful arts by securing for limited times to inventors the exclusive right to their Discoveries. The first patent law and all patent laws up to a much later period were entitled "Acts to promote the progress of useful arts."

(H.R.Rep.No.1923, 82d Cong., 2d Sess. 4 (1952); S.Rep.No.1979, 82d Cong., 2d Sess. 3 (1952), U.S.Code Cong. & Admin.News 1952, pp. 2394, 2396.)

It is to be observed that the Constitutional clause under consideration neither gave to nor preserved in inventors (or authors) any rights and set no standards for the patentability of individual inventions; it merely empowered Congress, if it elected to do so, to secure to inventors an "exclusive right" for an unstated "limited" time for the stated purpose of promoting useful arts. We have previously pointed out that the present day equivalent of the term "useful arts" employed by the Founding Fathers is "technological arts." *In re Musgrave*, 431 F.2d 882, 893, 57 CCPA 1352, 1367, 167 U.S.P.Q. 280, 289–90 (1970).

§ 1.3[b][2] The 1790 and 1793 Acts

In his State of the Union address to Congress on January 8, 1790, President George Washington addressed intellectual property:

> The advancement of agriculture, commerce, and manufactures, by all proper means, will not, I trust, need recommendation; but I cannot forbear intimating to you the expediency of giving effectual encouragement, as well to the introduction of new and useful inventions from abroad, as to the exertions of skill and genius in producing them at home.

ANNALS OF CONGRESS, 1st Cong., 2d Sess., I, 932–33. Spurred by this reminder and numerous petitions from authors and inventors for special national protection, Congress soon enacted the first patent act. Patent Act of 1790, 1 Stat. 109–112 (April 10, 1790). The Act created a board, known as the "Commissioners for the Promotion of the Useful Arts," authorized to determine whether "the invention or discovery [was] sufficiently useful and important" to deserve a patent. The board consisted of the Secretary of State (Thomas Jefferson), Secretary of War

(Henry Knox) and the Attorney General (Edmund Randolph). *See* KEN-NETH W. DOBYNS, THE PATENT OFFICE PONY: A HISTORY OF THE EARLY PATENT OFFICE (1994).

This heroic age of patent law proved short lived, as examination duties proved too onerous for the three-member board. Congress responded by enacting the Patent Act of 1793, Act of Feb. 21, 1793, Ch. 11, 2 Stat. 318, which abandoned patent examination in favor of a registration scheme. Under the 1793 Act, the State Department was assigned the wholly administrative task of maintaining a registry of patents. Whether a registered patent was valid and enforceable was left solely to the courts.

§ 1.3[b][3]   The 1836 and 1870 Acts

Observing that the registration system of the 1793 Act had sometimes encouraged duplicative and fraudulent patents, Congress restored an examination system with the Patent Act of 1836. Act of July 4, 1836, Ch. 357, 5 Stat. 117. The 1836 Act created a Patent Office within the Department of State and provided for the filing and formal examination of patent applications. The 1870 Act largely maintained the provisions of its predecessor, Act of July 8, 1870, Ch. 230, 16 Stat. 198, but at several points stressed that patentees define their proprietary interest in a distinctly drafted claim. Litigation under these two statutes frequently culminated at the Supreme Court, resulting in opinions that established nonobviousness, enablement, experimental use and other fundamental doctrines of contemporary patent law.

§ 1.3[c]   The Paris Convention

The foundational patent harmonization treaty, the Paris Convention for the Protection of Industrial Property, was formed in 1884. 13 U.S.T. 25. As of April 15, 2002, 163 nations had signed the Paris Convention. The World Intellectual Property Organization (WIPO), a specialized agency located in Geneva, Switzerland, administers this international agreement (and a number of subsequent instruments addressing intellectual property). The Paris Convention commits its signatories to the principle of national treatment, the principle of patent independence, and a system of international priority. Through the national treatment principle, Paris Convention signatories agree to treat foreign inventors no worse than domestic inventors in their patent laws, so long as these foreign inventors are nationals of a Paris Convention signatory state. Paris Convention, Art. 2.

The Paris Convention also call for the independence of different national patents. Paris Convention, Art. 4bis. Prior to the Paris Convention, many national laws applied a principle of patent dependence against foreign inventors. As a result, domestic patents would expire at the same time any foreign patent covering the same invention lapsed, regardless of the term the patentee was ordinarily due. These provisions sometimes worked a hardship against inventors who had obtained patent protection in many countries, only to discover that marketing the invention was feasible only in some subset of them. Such an inventor would prefer to let some patent rights lapse rather than incur expensive maintenance fees. In a world where patent rights depended on one another, however, allowing one patent to lapse would amount to a global forfeiture of patent rights.

The independence principle established by the Paris Convention put an end to this situation. One significant consequence of the independence of national patents is that they must be enforced individually. Even different national patent instruments with identically drafted descriptions, drawings and claims do not stand or fall together. A competitor who succeeds in invalidating one national patent may face the prospect of repeating the effort within another set of national borders. Similarly, the successful enforcement of a patent in one forum may simply signal the start of patent litigation elsewhere.

The international priority system allows an inventor to file a patent application in one Paris Convention signatory state, which is usually the inventor's home country. Paris Convention, Art. 4. If the inventor subsequently files patent applications in any other Paris Convention signatory state within the next 12 months, overseas patent-granting authorities will treat the application as if it were filed on the first filing date. Critically, information that enters the public domain between the priority date and subsequent filing dates does not prejudice the later applications. Paris Convention priority allows inventors to preserve their original filing dates as they make arrangements to file patent applications overseas. *See generally* G.H.C. BODENHAUSEN, GUIDE TO THE PARIS CONVENTION FOR THE PROTECTION OF INDUSTRIAL PROPERTY (United International Bureau for the Protection of Intellectual Property, Geneva, Switzerland 1968).

§ 1.3[d]   Patents in the Twentieth Century

§ 1.3[d][1]   U.S. Developments

The Depression era, with all its sentiments against monopoly, brought with it a vigorous distrust of patents. Although the United States had a statutory patent system more than a century before a statutory antitrust policy, *see* Sherman Act, 15 U.S.C.A. § 2, 26 Stat. 209 (July 2, 1890), courts often treated patent licensing and enforcement as antitrust violations. *See, e.g.*, *Hensley Equip. Co. v. Esco Corp.*, 383 F.2d 252, 155 U.S.P.Q. 183 (5th Cir.1967) (license restricting licensee to use of only patented product violated Sherman Act). Additionally, federal courts including the Supreme Court created stricter and stricter tests for sufficient "inventiveness" to qualify for a patent. For example, in 1941, the Supreme Court opined: "[T]he new device [a cordless, pop-out cigarette lighter for cars], however useful it may be, must reveal the flash of creative genius." *Cuno Eng. Corp. v. The Automatic Devices Corp.*, 314 U.S. 84, 51 U.S.P.Q. 272 (1941); *see also Great Atlantic & Pacific Tea Co. v. Supermarket Equipment Corp.*, 340 U.S. 147, 87 U.S.P.Q. 303 (1950). As a workable rule of law, this standard creates more questions than answers: How much "flash" and how much "genius" suffices to show invention? How does the federal judiciary detect either the flash or the genius? The venerable Judge Learned Hand gave his pithy assessment of this legal test: "[The inventiveness test is] as fugitive, impalpable, wayward, and vague a phantom as exists in the whole paraphernalia of legal concepts." *Harries v. Air King Prod. Co.*, 183 F.2d 158, 162 (2d Cir.1950).

Thus, following the depression and the world wars, these twin foes of intellectual property—misplaced antitrust priorities and subjective inventiveness tests—eroded the incentives of the patent system. The Supreme Court's propensity to strike down patents in this era reached such proportions that Justice Jackson felt compelled to lament in dissent: "[T]he only patent that is valid is one which this Court has not been able to get its hands on." *Jungersen v. Ostby & Barton Co.*, 335 U.S. 560, 571 (1949). Throughout this era, from the advent of its jurisdiction over appeals from the United States Patent Office in 1929, the Court of Customs and Patent Appeals strove to enunciate a more consistent patent policy. Because it had no jurisdiction to hear appeals from infringement actions in the district courts, however, this court could not influence the regional circuits which marched only to the unsteady drumbeat of the Supreme Court.

World War II forced the United States to innovate and experiment. When the war came to a close, the United State found itself in a position of world economic leadership that called for continued incentives for research and development. Market demands for innovation clashed with the confusion in the courts over enforcement of patent policies. This clash produced the first general reform of the patent system since 1870. The centerpiece of the Patent Act of 1952 replaced the subjective invention test with an objective test for nonobviousness. Drawing on the language from an early Supreme Court case, *see Hotchkiss v. Greenwood*, considered here at Chapter 7, the 1952 Act directed courts to determine patentability by an objective comparison of the claimed invention and the prior art at the time of invention. 35 U.S.C.A. § 103. To preclude subjectivity and hindsight analysis, the Act required this comparison to take place from the vantage point of one of ordinary skill in the art. *Id.*

Over a decade later, the Supreme Court finally construed the pivotal language of the 1952 Act. In a trilogy of 1966 cases, reprinted here in Chapter 7, the Supreme Court applied the § 103 obviousness test as the correct test for patentability. These landmark cases should have closed the book on the amorphous invention test. Unfortunately, another Supreme Court opinion (without the careful reasoning of the 1966 trilogy) revived vestiges of the invention test: "A combination of elements may result in an effect greater than the sum of the several effects taken separately. No such synergistic result is argued here." *Anderson's–Black Rock, Inc. v. Pavement Salvage Co.*, 396 U.S. 57, 61 (1969); *see also Sakraida v. Ag Pro, Inc.*, 425 U.S. 273 (1976). Synergism? The Supreme Court's dicta reawakened the ghosts of the invention test and haunted the regional circuits for years.

Two cases in the United States Court of Appeals for the Ninth Circuit present a microcosm of more than a decade of patent law confusion. These two cases, decided within a week of each other in the same circuit, applied vastly different law and reached vastly different results on patentability. In *Reeves Instr. Corp. v. Beckman Instr., Inc.*, the Ninth Circuit applied § 103 as directed by the Supreme Court's 1966 trilogy. The result was a valid patent for an electronic test circuit for analog computers. 444 F.2d 263 (9th Cir.1971). In *Regimbal v. Scymansky*, the same court applied a vague inventiveness test. The result was an invalid patent on a new hops-picking machine. 444 F.2d 333 (9th Cir.1971). This illustration of confusion within a single circuit magnifies as the lens turns to confusion amongst the circuits in this era.

In 1972, Congress created a Commission on Revision of the Federal Court Appellate System, known as the Hruska Commission after its Chairman, Senator Roman L. Hruska (R. Neb.). The Hruska Commission studied primarily the federal judiciary's difficulty in resolving conflicts amongst regional circuit courts. This subject led the Commission to examine patent law. The Commission's patent law consultants concluded:

> Patentees now scramble to get into the 5th, 6th, and 7th circuits since the courts there are not inhospitable to patents whereas infringers scramble to get anywhere but in these circuits.... [Forum shopping of this magnitude] not only increases litigation costs inordinately and decreases one's ability to advise clients, it demeans the entire judicial process and the patent system as well.

Commission on Revision of the Federal Court Appellate System, Structure, and Internal Procedures: Recommendations for Change 152, 67 F.R.D. 195, 370 (1975) (Conclusions of Commission's consultants, Professor James B. Gambrell and Donald R. Dunner). Despite this condemnation of patent law chaos, the Hruska Commission advised against the central recommendation for reform—a specialized appeals court for patent cases.

As more years passed without resolution of the central patent law conflicts, economic pressure encouraged reconsideration of appellate court reform. By 1978, the Department of Justice had created a new Office for Improvements in the Administration of Justice (OIAJ) headed by Prof. Daniel J. Meador. After considering several models for reform, OIAJ settled on a plan to merge the Court of Claims and the Court of Customs and Patent Appeals into a single appellate court with national jurisdiction over all patent appeals. This proposal sought to resolve the conflicts and forum shopping in patent law by routing all patent appeals to a single court of appeals. This court of appeals would fashion a uniform patent policy, subject to appeal to the Supreme Court.

On March 15, 1979, the Chairman of the Senate Judiciary Committee, Edward M. Kennedy, introduced the OIAJ bill. The bill, S. 1477, passed the Senate before the close of the 96th Congress, but—due to the addition of a controversial amendment unrelated to the court reform proposal—did not pass the House. In the 97th Congress, the legislative process began anew. A few lawmakers expressed concerns that a specialized court might foster legal doctrines out of the mainstream of American jurisprudence or might fall captive to a narrow segment of the bar. This resistance gained little momentum for reasons mentioned in the House Judiciary Committee Report:

> [T]he bill creates a new intermediate appellate court markedly less specialized than either of its predecessors and provides the judges of the new court with a breadth of jurisdiction that rivals in its variety that of the regional circuits.

H.R. Rep. No. 312, 97th Cong., 1st Sess. 19 (1981). Indeed the final version of the organic act for the Federal Circuit provided jurisdiction over more than ten categories of appeals, ranging from patents to customs to taxes to government contracts and more. 28 U.S.C.A. § 1295. Finally, on April 2, 1982, President Ronald Reagan signed into law the Federal Courts Improvements Act of 1982.

Immediately after formation, the Court of Appeals for the Federal Circuit adopted the law of its predecessor courts as binding precedent for its cases as well. *South Corp. v. United States,* 690 F.2d 1368, 215 U.S.P.Q. 657 (Fed.Cir.1982). Thus the decisions of the Court of Customs and Patent Appeals continued to bind the Federal Circuit. In other respects, however, the advent of the Federal Circuit changed significantly the decisional process for patent policy. For instance, the old Court of Customs and Patent Appeals—a five-judge body—always sat *en banc.* Thus later decisions always controlled any contrary earlier pronouncements. *In re Gosteli*, 872 F.2d 1008, 1011 (Fed.Cir.1989). The Federal Circuit, with up to 12 judges, rarely sits *en banc.* When it does sit *en banc,* of course, it has authority to overrule any prior ruling of the Federal Circuit or its predecessor courts. When sitting, as it customarily does, in three-judge panels, however, the Federal Circuit lacks authority to depart from decisions of earlier panels. The court in *Newell Companies, Inc. v. Kenney Mfg. Co.*, 864 F.2d 757, 765 (Fed.Cir.1988), explained: "This court has adopted the rule that prior decisions of a panel of the court are binding precedent on subsequent panels unless and until overturned in banc. Where there is direct conflict, the precedential decision is the first."

The creation of the Federal Circuit was the first major structural change in the federal appellate system since creation of the regional circuits in 1891. The confusion in patent law reached such proportions in the late 1960s and 1970s that only a structural change of this magnitude would correct the problem. Since its creation, the Federal Circuit has sought to bring uniformity and predictability to patent law. Much of this text tests the success of that venture.

More recently, Congress enacted significant substantive and procedural changes to U.S. patent law via the American Inventors Protection Act of 1999. Pub. L. No. 106–113, 113 Stat. 1501 (Nov. 29, 1999). Among the innovations of the AIPA were the creation of an infringement defense to first inventors of business methods later patented by another; the extension of patent term in the event of processing delays at the PTO; the mandate for publication of certain pending patent applications; and the provision of optional *inter partes* reexamination procedures.

§ 1.3[d][2]   World Patent Harmonization

Following World War II, global changes to the international patent system have proceeded at an accelerated pace. Numerous new treaties followed the Paris Convention now provide inventors with a network of global rights. Among the most significant of these treaties resulted from discussion of a uniform patent system for the then-emerging European Economic Community. Following adoption of a uniform patent classification system, European states agreed to the 1963 Convention on the Unification of Certain Points of Substantive Law on Patents for Inventions. This so-called "Strasbourg Convention" set forth certain common substantive patent law principles, and formed the cornerstone of the European Patent Convention (EPC) to follow a decade later.

In addition to mandating uniform patent-eligibility criteria for member states, the EPC establishes a single patent-granting authority, the European Patent Office. The EPC therefore allows an applicant to file a single patent application at the European Patent Office which may mature into a number of individual national patents. The EPC does not displace individual national patent regimes, but exists alongside them as an alternative route to obtaining intellectual property protection. The regional model of the EPC has been emulated to some degree by contracting states in Africa and the former Soviet Union.

The United States was not entirely idle during this period of European harmonization. As something of a reaction to these efforts, the United States took a leadership position in establishing the Patent Cooperation Treaty (PCT). This treaty was ultimately formed in 1970 by representatives of world patent offices in Washington, D.C., and is open to any country which has joined the Paris Convention. Drafters of the PCT took account for the burden of duplicative patent examination proceedings in many different countries. The PCT allows certain portions of patent acquisition efforts to be completed in a single patent office and applied elsewhere, which should streamline efforts elsewhere.

Subsequently, both the North American Free Trade Agreement (NAFTA) and the Trade–Related Aspects of Intellectual Property of the World Trade Organization (TRIPS Agreement) have provided several further measures of substantive reform. NAFTA sets minimal requirements for a substantive patent law among its signatory nations. The TRIPS Agreement provides even more significant reform, both in the scope of its substantive measures and the breadth of its signatories. The treaty provides uniform legal standards for patentability in every significant aspect of a modern patent system, and further sets forth a patent term of twenty years from the filing date, as well as exclusionary rights conferred to the holder of the patent. Most of these requirements conform with prevailing United States standards.

The TRIPS Agreement is one of the most important commercial treatises in modern history. It revolutionized the treatment of intellectual property in the signatory countries. It requires, for example, that India, a country which has had a weak intellectual property regime essentially since independence, adopt a modern strong system of protection that includes protection for pharmaceutical compounds.

Future harmonization appears certain at this point, albeit the precise vehicle for achieving this result cannot be named easily. In the early 1990's, the so-called "Patent Law Treaty" or "Basic Proposal" of the World Intellectual Property Organization (WIPO) appeared the most likely prospect for future reform. The Basic Proposal contained numerous substantive provisions regarding patent law reform, although in some aspects this treaty was less comprehensive than the TRIPS Agreement. Unlike the TRIPS Agreement, however, it did contain significant measures with respect to claim interpretation and the doctrine of equivalents. *See* HAROLD C. WEGNER, PATENT HARMONIZATION (1993). The shifted emphasis upon the TRIPS Agreement as the primary intellectual property treaty, in combination with a rather abrupt announcement by the United States concerning its continuing support of a first-to-invent system, suspended negotiation at WIPO. Efforts have since begun anew on a WIPO-based international agreement on the patent law.

A second treaty, exclusively for the states of Europe, consists of the Luxembourg Community Patent Convention (CPC). The CPC provides for a true European patent, in that one administrative agency would issue a single patent effective in every signatory nation. Additionally, patent litigation fora are limited to certain national courts, a Common Appeal Court and the European Court of Justice. The CPC had such a strong start in 1975 that commentators offered varyingly optimistic predictions of the date it would come into effect, all of which have long since passed. Despite several subsequent diplomatic conferences held to promote the treaty, some European nations still have not ratified it, and possibilities for future action are uncertain. *See* JOSEPH STRAUS, THE PRESENT STATE OF THE PATENT SYSTEM IN THE EUROPEAN UNION (1997); KARA M. BONITATIBUS, *infra* at p. 902, note 4.

§ 1.4 FORMS OF PATENT PROTECTION

§ 1.4[a] Utility Patents

When lay persons use the term "patent," they are most often referring to the intellectual property right more technically known as a "utility patent." Utility patents are the usual sort of patent, pertaining generally to technological products and processes. Utility patents are governed by the Patent Act of 1952, codified in Title 35 of the U.S. Code.

Utility patent rights do not arise automatically. Inventors must prepare and submit applications to the U.S. Patent and Trademark Office ("PTO") if they wish to obtain utility patent protection. 35 U.S.C.

§ 111. PTO officials known as examiners then assess whether the application merits the award of a utility patent. 35 U.S.C. § 131.

In deciding whether to approve a utility patent application, a PTO examiner will consider whether the submitted application fully discloses and distinctly claims the invention. 35 U.S.C. § 112. The examiner will also determine whether the invention itself fulfills certain substantive standards set by the Patent Act of 1952. To be patentable, an invention must be useful, novel and nonobvious. The requirement of usefulness, or utility, is satisfied if the invention is operable and provides a tangible benefit. 35 U.S.C. § 101. To be judged novel, the invention must not be fully anticipated by a prior patent, publication or other knowledge within the public domain. 35 U.S.C. § 102. A nonobvious invention must not have been readily within the ordinary skills of a competent artisan at the time the invention was made. 35 U.S.C. § 103.

If the PTO allows the utility patent to issue, the proprietor obtains the right to exclude others from making, using, selling, offering to sell or importing into the United States the patented invention. 35 U.S.C. § 271(a). These rights are not self-enforcing. A patentee bears responsibility for monitoring its competitors to determine whether they are using the patented invention or not. Patent proprietors who wish to compel others to observe their intellectual property rights must usually commence litigation in the federal courts.

The maximum term of utility patent protection is ordinarily set at 20 years from the date the application is filed. 35 U.S.C. § 154(a)(2). The patent applicant gains no enforceable rights until such time as the application is approved for issuance as a granted patent, however. Once the utility patent expires, others may employ the patented invention without compensation to the patentee.

The following example should provide a sense of the modern utility patent instrument. As you review this document, consider the extent to which it provides the following information to members of the technological community:

- A detailed technical description of the invention.
- The extent to which the disclosed technology is regarded as proprietary.
- The basis for the examiner's decision that the patented invention presents a patentable advance over previously known technology.
- The term of the patent.
- An individual who can be contacted for purposes of licensing or obtaining further technical information.

US005190351A

United States Patent [19]

Klumpjan

[11]	Patent Number:	**5,190,351**
[45]	Date of Patent:	Mar. 2, 1993

[54] **WHEELBARROW FOR TRANSPORTING ROCKS AND STONES**

[76] Inventor: **Joe Klumpjan**, 1334 Sunset Dr. Rte. 3, Campbellsport, Wis. 53010

[21] Appl. No.: **825,881**

[22] Filed: **Jan. 27, 1992**

[51] Int. Cl.⁵ B62B 1/24
[52] U.S. Cl. 298/3; 280/47.31
[58] Field of Search 280/47.31, 47.33, 47.23; 298/2, 3

[56] **References Cited**

U.S. PATENT DOCUMENTS

48,101	6/1865	Sanford	298/3
480,670	8/1892	Radley et al.	298/2
642,569	2/1900	Baklund	280/47.31
817,677	4/1906	Smith	280/47.23
845,207	2/1907	Tripp	280/47.3
868,462	10/1907	Lorenzi	280/47.23
1,232,387	7/1917	Parker	298/3
1,305,106	5/1919	Hofer	280/47.23
1,479,223	1/1924	Carroll	280/47.33
1,544,769	7/1925	Nalder	298/3
1,754,835	4/1930	Newton	298/2
2,234,879	3/1941	Shoesmith	298/3
2,608,360	8/1952	Cootware	280/47.3

2,852,304	9/1958	Harrison	298/3
2,889,152	6/1959	Hurst et al.	280/47.31
3,092,418	6/1963	Themascus	298/3

FOREIGN PATENT DOCUMENTS

537556	5/1955	Belgium	298/2
436020	10/1935	United Kingdom	298/3

Primary Examiner—David M. Mitchell
Attorney, Agent, or Firm—Andrus, Sceales, Starke & Sawall

[57]　　　　　　**ABSTRACT**

A wheelbarrow has an enlarged wheel and a low center of gravity for transporting heavy loads. The enlarged wheel and low center of gravity increases the stability of the wheelbarrow. The wheelbarrow includes a payload bucket which is tiltable for dumping the payload. The bucket is mounted such that the dumping operation is behind the wheel of the wheelbarrow, whereby the dumping operation can be completed without substantially altering the center of gravity of the wheelbarrow, further enhancing the stability of the wheelbarrow when transporting heavy loads. The wheelbarrow bucket includes an arcuate or C-shaped bottom facilitating the dumping operation.

3 Claims, 1 Drawing Sheet

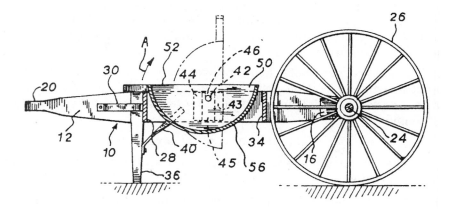

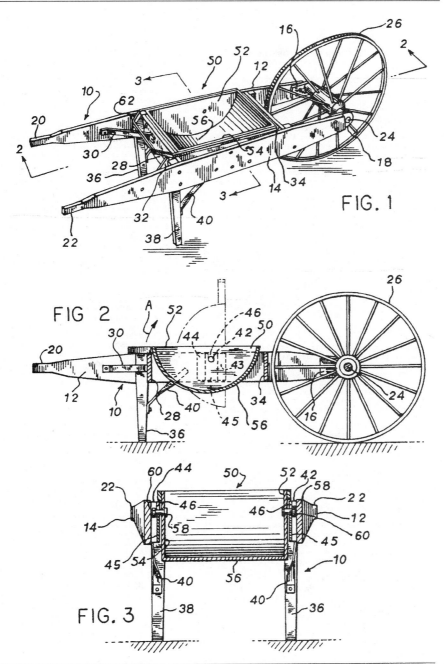

FIG. 1

FIG 2

FIG. 3

5,190,351

1

WHEELBARROW FOR TRANSPORTING ROCKS AND STONES

BACKGROUND OF THE INVENTION

1. Field of the Invention

This invention is generally related to wheelbarrows and is specifically directed to a wheelbarrow for transporting rocks and stones.

2. Description of the Prior Art

Wheelbarrows are well known. However, the wheelbarrows of the prior art are generally designed for general purpose use such as, by way of example, the wheelbarrow disclosed in U.S. Pat. No. 868,462 issued to L. Lorenzi on Oct. 15, 1907. There have also been a number of wheelbarrows designed for specific use such as the wheelbarrow of U.S. Pat. No. 642,569 issued to G. Baklund on Feb. 6, 1900. The Baklund wheelbarrow is specifically designed to carry milk cans and the like.

U.S. Pat. No. 1,479,223 issued to G. Carroll on Jan. 1, 1924 also discloses a wheelbarrow specifically designed for carrying cans but adaptable for general purpose use as well.

U.S. Pat. No. 845,207 issued to C. Tripp on Feb. 26, 1907 discloses a wheelbarrow adapted for carrying unusually large and heavy objects wherein the object such as a barrel is self-leveling and the wheelbarrow has an enlarged wheel to provide better stability.

U.S. Pat. No. 1,754,835 issued to H. B. Newton on Apr. 15, 1930 also discloses a large wheeled wheelbarrow for better distribution of weight when hauling heavy objects.

It is also known to provide dumping wheel barrows as shown, for example, in U.S. Pat. Nos. 1,544,769 issued to G. Nalder on Jul. 7, 1925; 2,234,879 issued to H. Shoesmith on Mar. 11, 1941; 2,852,304 issued to L. E. Harrison on Sep. 16, 1958; and 3,092,418 issued to J. Themascus on Jun. 4, 1963. One of the problems with each of the dumping wheelbarrows of the prior art is the weight is generally distributed above and in substantial vertical alignment with the axis of the wheel, making the wheelbarrow unstable when carrying heavy loads.

U.S. Pat. No. 1,232,387 issued to I. Parker on Jul. 3, 1917 discloses a self-leveling wheelbarrow having a pivotable bucket. However, there is not sufficient clearance between the wheelbarrow and the wheel or other frame members to provide for dumping.

None of the wheelbarrows of the prior art are specifically directed to a transportation device for picking and hauling small stones and rocks from fields which are to be tilled for growing crops. In many regions of the country such as, by way of example, northern New England and Wisconsin and other areas where prehistoric glacier movements deposited large amounts of rubble just beneath the surface and the top soil, small rocks and stones surface with each spring thaw. This provides a continuing problem when preparing fields for planting at the beginning of each growing season. Typically, the rocks and stones must be physically and manually removed from the field before tilling in order to minimize damage to plow shares and the like. Even with the development of modern mechanized equipment for preparing fields, rock and stone removal still remains a substantially manual operation. Often this is accomplished by manually taking a wheelbarrow and a rock fork to the field and physically placing the rocks and stones in the wheelbarrow for transportation to a

2

dump site. However, heretofore there have been no wheelbarrows specifically designed for this purpose. The wheelbarrows are either unstable under heavy load, difficult to manipulate, or are not well designed for the heavy loads and weight distribution generated during the rock picking activity. This requires that the wheelbarrow be used to carry lighter loads, increasing the number of trips and the amount of labor and time required to complete the task.

SUMMARY OF THE INVENTION

The subject invention is specifically directed to a wheelbarrow for picking and removing rocks from tillable fields. The wheelbarrow has a substantially oversized wheel supported on a sturdy frame. The payload bucket is supported on a plane substantially horizontal to the axis of the wheel and is adapted to be pivoted or tilted behind the wheel for dumping the rocks without disturbing the stability of the wheelbarrow. In the preferred embodiment of the invention, the bucket may be removed from the frame by lifting it out of the support channels. The handle for tilting the bucket also serves as the primary support member for supporting the bucket in a normally open, upright position during use. The axle, pivot bucket supports and handles are on a common line, minimizing back strain when lifting large loads.

The wheelbarrow has been found to be particularly well suited for removing rocks and stones from tillable fields. The enlarged wheel provides easy manipulation of the wheelbarrow and increases stability. The low center of gravity of the load increases stability and maneuverability of the wheelbarrow for this task. The low, in-line handles permit easy handling of substantially heavy loads with a minimum of back strain.

It is, therefore, an object and feature of the subject invention to provide for a wheelbarrow which is specifically designed for removing rocks and stones from tillable fields.

It is also an object and feature of the subject invention to provide for a wheelbarrow with a low center of gravity to provide stability in handling heavy loads.

It is a further object and feature of the subject invention to provide for a tiltable wheelbarrow wherein the payload is supported below the axle of the wheel, increasing stability of the wheelbarrow when transporting a heavy payload.

Other objects and features of the invention will be readily apparent from the accompanying drawings and detailed description of the preferred embodiment.

BRIEF DESCRIPTION OF THE DRAWINGS

FIG. 1 is a perspective view of a wheelbarrow made in accordance with the subject invention.

FIG. 2 is a section view of the wheelbarrow taken generally along the line 2—2 of FIG. 1.

FIG. 3 is a section view of the wheelbarrow taken generally along the line 3—3 of FIG. 1.

DETAILED DESCRIPTION OF THE PREFERED EMBODIMENT

The wheelbarrow of the subject invention is shown in FIG. 1 and includes a rigid frame 10 made of wood, steel, or other suitable material. In the preferred embodiment, the frame 10 includes two enlongated side rails 12 and 14 having an axis support such as the brackets 16, 18 at one end of the respective side rails 12, 14

5,190,351

3

and terminating in handles **20, 22** at the opposite end of respective side rails **12, 14**. An axle **24** is supported between the brackets **16** and **18** for rotatably supporting the hubbed wheel **26**. A cross brace **28** secures the side rails **12** and **14** in spaced apart relationship. In the preferred embodiment, a pair of angle brackets **30** and **32** are provided and are suitably secured to the respective side rails **12** and **14** and to the cross brace **28** to increase rigidity of the construction. Also, a second cross brace **34** may be provided just behind the wheel **26** to further increase rigidity of the assembly. In the preferred embodiment, the support legs **36** and **38** are mounted between the cross brace **28** and the respective side rails **12** and **14**. An angle bracket **40** may be attached to each leg **36, 38** and to the respective side rail **12, 14** to further increase the rigidity of the assembly.

In the preferred embodiment of the invention, a pair of support brackets **42** and **44** are secured, one each, to the respective side rails **12** and **14**. As is best shown in FIG. 2, each support bracket includes a pair of outer base plates **43** and **44** which are secured directly to the respective side rail. The center panel of the bracket includes a raised or spaced plate **45** (see FIG. 3) which includes a U-shaped channel **46**. The bucket **50** of the wheelbarrow includes a pair of outer side walls **52** and **54**. In the preferred embodiment, the side walls have an arcuate lower edge and a continuous, rounded bottom wall **56** as suitably secured thereto to make an arcuate bucket. Each side wall **52, 54** of the bucket includes a projecting mounting post **58** projecting outwardly from the side wall and having a smooth cylindrical surface adapted to be received in the U-shaped channel **46** of the respective mounting bracket **42, 44** on the side rails **12, 14**. Each mounting post **58** includes an enlarged outer head **60** to assure that the bucket does not inadvertently slip from the mounting brackets. A handle **62** is secured to the rear edge of the bucket **50** and extends toward the wheelbarrow handles **20** and **22**. The handle **62** facilitates in dumping or tilting the bucket, as indicated by arrow A in FIG. 2 and also provides the stop or support member for supporting the bucket in its normal position, by resting on the cross brace **28**.

In the preferred embodiment, the wheel **26** of the wheel barrow is approximately 30 inches in diameter, greatly increasing the stability of the wheelbarrow over the prior art, particularly when carrying substantially heavy loads such as rocks and stones. Also, as can be seen in FIG. 2, the bucket **50** can be moved to the dump position without substantially altering the center of gravity of the load, further increasing the stability of the wheel barrow during a stone picking and removal operation. In addition, where desired, the bucket may be removed from the frame of the wheelbarrow by simply lifting the bucket and sliding the posts **58** upwardly in the U-shaped channels on the mounting brackets **42, 44**. The arcuate bottom **56** of the bucket greatly facilitates in a dumping operation by permitting the stones to roll

4

or slide out of the bucket without substantially altering the center of gravity during the dumping operation.

The wheelbarrow of the present invention is ideally suited for carrying heavy payloads and is particularly well suited for removing rocks and stones from tillable fields. While specific objects and features of the subject invention have been disclosed in detail herein, it will be readily understood that the invention encompasses all modifications and enhancements within the scope and spirit of the following claims.

I claim:

1. A wheelbarrow for transporting rocks and stones, comprising:

a. a frame having two elongated, spaced side rails, each with opposite ends, one end of each rail defining a handle and the other end of each rail defining a forward axle support, and at least one cross brace spanning the spaced side rails and securing them in rigid assembly;

b. an axle mounted in the axle supports;

c. a wheel mounted on said axle for rotation relative to said frame, wherein the wheel is of a minimum diameter of 30 inches;

d. a pair of mounting brackets, one each mounted on each side rail intermediately of the opposite ends;

e. a box having a semicylindrical closed bottom, upstanding side walls having a C-shaped bottom edge and an open top, said box including a pair of axially aligned pivot posts extending from said side walls forwardly of the axis of said semicylindrical bottom to position the center of gravity of said box rearwardly of the axis of said pivot posts, each post adapted to be removably received in one of said brackets for tiltably supporting the box relative to said frame, whereby the box is movable between an upwardly opening filling position with the forward edge of the open top positioned rearwardly of the wheel and a dump position in which the contents of the box are discharged to the rear of the wheel, and wherein said cross brace defines a support for holding the box in the filling position; and

f. a support secured to and extending downwardly from said frame between the handles and the box for supporting the frame and the box above the ground.

2. The wheelbarrow of claim **1** further including a handle mounted on the continuous member adjacent one end and adapted for engaging the cross-brace when the box is in the normal position.

3. The wheelbarrow of claim **2**, wherein the side rails are substantially parallel and the side walls of the box are substantially parallel to the side rails, each mounting bracket further including a substantially U-shaped channel with an open upper end and wherein each post is of cylindrical cross-section, whereby the post may be rotated relative to the base for moving the box from the normal position to the dump position.

* * * * *

60

65

§ 1.4[b] Design Patents

Title 35 of the United States Code provides for design patents in a short series of provisions codified at §§ 171–173. Design patents may be awarded for "any new, original and ornamental design for an article of manufacture." 35 U.S.C. § 171. The surface ornamentation, configuration or shape of an object form the most typical subjects of design patents. The design may be patented only if it is embodied in an article of manufacture, such as furniture, tools or athletic footwear. The chief limitation on the patentability of designs is that they must be primarily ornamental in character. If the design is dictated by the performance of the article, then it is judged "primarily functional" and ineligible for design patent protection. *See Best Lock Corp. v. Ilco Unican Corp.*, 94 F.3d 1563, 40 U.S.P.Q.2d 1048 (Fed.Cir.1996).

An inventor must file an application at the PTO in order to obtain design patent protection. design patents are generally subject to all provisions applicable to utility patents, including originality and novelty. The design must also fulfill the requirement of nonobviousness, which is judged from the perspective of "the designer of ordinary capability who designs articles of the type presented in the application." In Re Nalbandian, 661 F.2d 1214, 211 U.S.P.Q. 782 (CCPA 1981). If the application matures into an issued design patent, the resulting design patent instrument is relatively straightforward. it principally consists of one or more drawings illustrating the proprietary design. the term of a design patent is fourteen years. 35 U.S.C. § 173.

§ 1.4[c] Plant Patents

The availability of utility patents for plants was for many years the subject of legal uncertainty. Congress responded by enacting the Townsend–Purcell Plant Patent Act. Act of May 23, 1930, 46 Stat. 376. This statute allows plant patent to issue for distinct and new varieties of plants that have been asexually reproduced. Asexual reproduction results in a plant that is genetically identical to its parent. 35 U.S.C. § 161. Typical asexual reproduction techniques include grafting, budding, the use of cuttings, layering and other methods. Plants that are produced through seeds, which involves sexual reproduction, are excluded. Also excluded from the Plant Patent Act are tuberpropagated plants or plants found in an uncultivated state. *Id.*

The acquisition and enforcement of plant patents is accomplished in a manner very similar to utility patents. Plant patents are issued by the PTO provided that the novelty and nonobviousness requirements are met. Applicants must submit an application featuring color drawings that disclose all the distinctive characteristics of the plant capable of visual representation. If approved, a plant patent enjoys a term of twenty years from the date of filing. Plant patents are infringed if another asexually reproduces the plant, or uses or sells the plant so reproduced. 35 U.S.C. § 163.

For more details on plant patents, see *J.E.M. AG Supply, Inc. v. Pioneer Hi–Bred International, Inc.*, 534 U.S. 124, 60 U.S.P.Q.2d 1865 (2001) (reprinted here in Chapter Two); and *Imazio Nursery, Inc. v. Dania Greenhouses*, 69 F.3d 1560, 36 U.S.P.Q.2d 1673 (Fed.Cir.1995).

§ 1.4[d] Patent–Like Plant Variety Protection

Another intellectual property possibility for plants is the Plant Variety Protection Act, or PVPA. This statute may be found in 7 U.S.C. § 2321 and subsequent sections. The PVPA allows the United States to comply with the International Convention for the Protection of New Varieties of Plants, an agreement the United States joined in 1981. The PVPA provides for the issuance of plant variety protection certificates that act similarly to utility and plant patents. Plant variety protection certificates exclusively pertain to sexually reproduced plants, however, including most seed-bearing plants. Fungi and bacteria are ineligible for certification. The plant must be clearly distinguishable from known varieties and stable, in that its distinctive characteristics must breed true with a reasonable degree of reliability. 7 U.S.C. § 2402(a).

A key distinction between the plant patent and plant variety protection regimes is the manner in which the inventor has reproduced the protected plant. Asexual reproduction, which results in a plant genetically identical to its parent, forms the basis of plant patent protection. Certification under the PVPA instead depends upon sexual reproduction, which results in a distinct plant that combines the characteristics of its parents.

Unlike utility and plant patents, which are issued by the PTO, plant variety protection certificates are administered by the Department of Agriculture. To be entitled to a certificate, the plant must be new, distinct, uniform and stable. If allowed to issue by the Department of Agriculture, the term of a plant variety protection certificate is twenty years (twenty-five years for trees and vines). 7 U.S.C. § 2483(b). The holder of a plant variety certificate obtains the right to "exclude others from selling the variety, or offering it for sale, or reproducing it, importing it, or exporting it, or using it in producing (as distinguished from developing) a hybrid or different variety therefrom." 7 U.S.C. § 2483(a).

An important distinction between the utility and plant patents, on one hand, and plant variety protection certificates, on the other, is the availability of two infringement exemptions under the PVPA. The PVPA includes an exemption that broadly states that the "use and reproduction of a protected variety for plant breeding or other bona fide research shall not constitute an infringement." 7 U.S.C. § 2544. In addition, the PVPA grants farmers the right to plant new crops of seeds descended from protected seeds that were legitimately purchased. 7 U.S.C. § 2543. In contrast, neither the utility nor the plant patent statutes contain these exemptions. Such activities may constitute infringements that may expose researchers and farmers to legal liability, including damages and an injunction.

J.E.M. AG Supply, Inc. v. Pioneer Hi–Bred International, Inc., 534 U.S. 124, 60 U.S.P.Q.2d 1865 (2001), reprinted in Chapter Two of this casebook, provides more information on plant variety protection certificates and their relationship with utility patents.

§ 1.5 THE NATURE AND FUNCTION OF THE PATENT SYSTEM

§ 1.5[a] Economic Rationales

The literature relating the patent system to economic theory is enormous. Perhaps the most complete review of the various theories regarding patents was prepared by Professor Fritz Machlup of Johns Hopkins University and published as Subcomm. on Patents, Trademarks, and Copyrights, & Senate Comm. on the Judiciary, 85th Cong., 2d Sess., AN ECONOMIC REVIEW OF THE PATENT SYSTEM (Comm. Print 1958). The following passage comprises a contemporary overview of some of the most current economic theories relating to patents written by Professor Rebecca S. Eisenberg.

§ 1.5[a][1]

SELECTIONS FROM REBECCA S. EISENBERG, PATENTS AND THE PROGRESS OF SCIENCE: EXCLUSIVE RIGHTS AND EXPERIMENTAL USE

56 U. CHI. L. REV. 1017 (1989).

The United States Constitution posits an instrumental justification for patents, allowing Congress to enact patent legislation for the specific purpose of promoting scientific progress.[1] In analyzing how patents promote scientific progress, the courts have emphasized two mechanisms: first, the prospect of obtaining a patent monopoly provides an incentive to invest in research to make new inventions; and second, the patent system promotes disclosure of new inventions and thereby enlarges the public storehouse of knowledge.[2] Both of these theories have been elaborated and challenged in the economics literature.[3]

---

1. U.S. Const., Art. I, § 8, cl. 8. This instrumental justification is distinct from moral arguments for patent protection advanced in some European countries, notably France, in the nineteenth century, such as the argument that inventors have a natural property right in their ideas that society is morally obligated to recognize. *See generally* Fritz Machlup and Edith Penrose, *The Patent Controversy in the Nineteenth Century*, 10 J. ECON. HIST. 1, 10–20 (1950). The framers of the United States Constitution rejected the notion that inventors have a natural property right in their inventions. Thus Thomas Jefferson wrote:

Inventions then cannot, in nature, be a subject of property. Society may give an exclusive right to the profits arising from

them, as an encouragement to men to pursue ideas which may produce utilities, but this may or may not be done according to the will and convenience of society, without claim or complaint from anybody.

See WALTER HAMILTON, INVESTIGATION OF CONCENTRATION OF ECONOMIC POWER: PATENTS & FREE ENTERPRISE 21 (TNEC Monograph No. 31) (GPO, 1941) (quoting Thomas Jefferson).

2. *Kewanee Oil Co. v. Bicron*, 416 U.S. 470, 480–81 (1974).

3. A third theory, that patents promote "innovation" or investment in the commercial development of inventions, has been

1. INCENTIVE TO INVENT.

The incentive to invent theory holds that too few inventions will be made in the absence of patent protection because inventions once made are easily appropriated by competitors of the original inventor who have not shared in the costs of invention.[4] If successful inventions are quickly imitated by free riders, competition will drive prices down to a point where the inventor receives no return on the original investment in research and development.[5] As a result, the original inventor may be unable to appropriate enough of the social value of the invention to justify the initial research and development expenditures.[6] The high risk involved in research compounds the likelihood of underinvestment in invention.[7] Thus inventions with potentially great social benefits might never come about, or at least might be significantly delayed, unless private returns to invention were increased above their free market levels. Patents serve to bring the private benefits of inventions in line with their social value by allowing inventors to use their monopoly positions to extract a price that more closely approaches the value that users receive from inventions.[8]

advanced by some commentators but has received little attention from the courts.

4. *See* WARD S. BOWMAN, JR., PATENT AND ANTITRUST LAW 2–3 (Chicago, 1973); FREDERIC M. SCHERER, INDUSTRIAL MARKET STRUCTURE AND ECONOMIC PERFORMANCE 379–99 (Rand McNally, 1970); John S. McGee, *Patent Exploitation: Some Economic and Legal Problems*, 9 J L & ECON 135 (1966); Dan Usher, *The Welfare Economics of Invention*, 31 ECONOMICA 279 (1964); Kenneth J. Arrow, *Economic Welfare and the Allocation of Resources for Invention*, *in* RATE AND DIRECTION OF INVENTIVE ACTIVITY at 609; Richard R. Nelson, *The Economics of Invention: A Survey of the Literature*, 32 J. BUS. 101 (1959); FRITZ MACHLUP, AN ECONOMIC REVIEW OF THE PATENT SYSTEM, Subcomm on Patents, Trademarks, and Copyrights of the Senate Comm on the Judiciary, Study No. 15, 85th Cong., 2d Sess. (GPO, 1958); Michael Polanyi, *Patent Reform*, 11 REV. OF ECON. STUDIES 61 (1944); Arnold Plant, *The Economic Theory Concerning Patents for Inventions*, 1 ECONOMICA 30 (1934).

5. The costs of research and development leading to a new invention are one-time, "sunk" costs. Once the invention has been made and disclosed, the marginal cost of using more intensively the knowledge gained through prior research is zero. There may still be other variable costs associated with producing goods and services through use of the invention, such as costs for labor and materials, but the invention cost is fixed in the past and need not be incurred again no matter how intensively the invention is used. In a competitive market in which anyone is free to use the

invention to produce goods without obligation to the inventor, the cost of the goods sold will be driven down to a price approaching the marginal cost of their production, and thus the selling price will not allow for any return on the sunk cost of the research and development necessary to make the invention in the first place. *See* Machlup, Subcomm on Patents, Study No 15 at 58–59.

6. *See* SCHERER, INDUSTRIAL MARKET STRUCTURE at 384; William F. Baxter, *Legal Restrictions on Exploitation of the Patent Monopoly: An Economic Analysis*, 76 YALE L. J. 267, 268–69 (1966); Machlup, Subcomm on Patents, Study No. 15 at 57–58.

7. Arrow, Economic Welfare at 614–15; Richard R. Nelson, *The Simple Economics of Basic Scientific Research*, 67 J. POL. ECON. 297 (1959). Arrow suggests that since the output of inventive effort is uncertain, and since there is no adequate market mechanism for shifting this risk, risk aversion can be expected to lead to underinvestment in invention. Arrow, *Economic Welfare* at 611–14, 616. McGee argues that inventors may display risk preference and therefore overinvest in inventive activity. McGee, 9 J. L. ECON. at 136. *See* EDWIN MANSFIELD, ET AL, RESEARCH AND INNOVATION IN THE MODERN CORPORATION 18–63 (Norton, 1971) (finding that firms tend to invest only in R & D projects with high estimated probability of success, but that firms tend to overpredict success).

8. See Baxter, 76 YALE L. J. at 270. An extreme version of this argument (attributed to John Stuart Mill) is that a patent holder can never use the patent monopoly to extract more than the value of the inven-

↓ Social benefits

Challenges to the incentive to invent justification for patents have taken a variety of forms. The most fundamental objection is that subjecting new inventions to monopoly control restricts their use and thereby reduces the social benefits of patented inventions. It is open to question whether it is necessary to endure the output-restricting effects of patent monopolies in order to stimulate invention.[9] In some cases the head start advantage gained by being first in the market with a new invention may provide a sufficient incentive to promote investment in research.[10] Similarly, the need to keep up with the technological progress of market rivals might stimulate invention without further incentives, or non-patent barriers to market entry may give enough protection from competition to make research and development profitable without patents.[11]

alternatives

Another objection to the incentive to invent justification is that patent incentives may distort economic activity in ways that undermine efficiency. For example, competing firms hoping to make patentable inventions ahead of their rivals in order to win lucrative patents may spend too much money trying to develop inventions quickly, when the same result could be achieved at less social cost through a less accelerated research effort.[12] The patent system may divert too many resources

promotes overspending => richer development

Tech. parks?

tor's efforts to society, since consumers will pay the patent holder no more than the invention is worth to them. See Machlup and Penrose, 10 J. Econ. Hist. at 20. This argument rests on the often dubious assumption that the invention would never have been made were it not for the efforts of the inventor who patented it. If instead one assumes that somebody else would eventually have made the same invention, it is no longer clearly appropriate to attribute the full social value of the invention to the efforts of the first inventor. See Bowman, Patent and Antitrust Law at 17.

9. Some critics of the patent system have suggested that government could stimulate invention at less social cost by awarding prizes to inventors in lieu of patents. See, for example, Polanyi, 11 Rev. of Econ. Studies at 65. Machlup states that such proposals for alternatives to patents are almost as old as the patent system, and notes that James Madison proposed a system of prizes and bonuses to inventors in lieu of patents at the Constitutional Convention in 1787. Machlup, Subcomm on Patents, Study No. 15 at 15 n. 83; see also Hamilton, Patents and Free Enterprise at 24–25.

Others have argued that inventions arise inevitably with or without government incentives when the state of basic knowledge and other social conditions become favorable. See Abbott P. Usher, A History of Mechanical Inventions 1–31 (McGraw Hill,

1929); S.C. Gilfillan, The Sociology of Invention 71–78 (Follett, 1935); William F. Ogburn, Social Change 86 (Huebsch, 1923); Machlup, Subcomm on Patents, Study No. 15 at 23 n. 120, 24 n. 127; Alfred E. Kahn, *Fundamental Deficiencies of the American Patent Law*, 30 Am. Econ. Rev. 475, 479–81 (1940).

10. Scherer, Industrial Market Structure at 384–87; Machlup, Subcomm on Patents, Study No. 15 at 23 n. 121, 24 n. 128, 38–39 and sources cited therein. *See generally* Jack Hirshleifer, *The Private and Social Value of Information and the Reward to Inventive Activity*, 61 Am. Econ. Rev. 561 (1971) (arguing that apart from the profits obtained from patents, innovators may profit by using their advance knowledge, or "foreknowledge," of new technologies to speculate in assets whose value will be affected by the release of the new technology).

11. Scherer, Industrial Market Structure at 387; see Arrow, *Economic Welfare* at 619–22 (arguing that if the problem of appropriability is ignored, firms in a competitive market will have a greater incentive to invent than would a monopolist because the competitive firm's incentive is equal to the full cost reduction on the competitive output, while the monopolist's incentive is diminished by the set-off of preinvention monopoly profits).

12. Richard Posner, Economic Analysis of Law 54 (Little, Brown, 2d ed 1977); Yoram

away from productive activities in which returns are limited by the forces of competition, or it may divert resources from research in fields where patent protection is unavailable to research that is more likely to yield profitable patent monopolies.

Finally, some writers have argued that the patent system may hinder progress through its effects on the research efforts of persons other than the patent holder. The existence of a patent may undermine the incentives of these other persons to make improvements in patented technologies.[13] Worse yet, it may force competitors of the patent holder to waste time and effort finding duplicative solutions to technological problems in order to avoid infringement.[14]

2. INCENTIVE TO DISCLOSE.

The incentive to disclose argument, which has been more popular with the courts than with commentators, rests on the premise that in the absence of patent protection inventors would keep their inventions

Barzel, *The Optimal Timing of Innovations*, 50 REV. ECON. & STAT. 348 (1968).

13. SCHERER, INDUSTRIAL MARKET STRUCTURE at 392; Baxter, 76 YALE L. J. at 270; Machlup, Subcomm on Patents, Study No. 15 at 64; Kahn, 30 AM. ECON. REV. at 482; PLANT, 1 ECONOMICA at 46. Edmund Kitch argues that this particular effect of the patent monopoly promotes efficiency in research.

The essence of the argument that patents undermine the incentives of persons other than the patent holders to make improvements in patented inventions is that once an invention is patented, only the patent holder and her licensees are able to reap rewards in the market for research leading to further refinements in the invention, while in the absence of patents competitors would also stand to benefit from such research. This argument overlooks the fact that the value of the improvement to the patent holder and her licensees might still give other researchers an incentive to develop it.

14. Judicial opinions often cite the incentive to invent around patents as a positive benefit of the patent system, reasoning that inventing around patents requires further research and thus stimulates further progress. *See, for example, Yarway Corp. v. Eur–Control U.S.A.*, 775 F.2d 268, 277 (Fed.Cir.1985); *State Indus. v. A.O. Smith Corp.*, 751 F.2d 1226, 1236 (Fed.Cir.1985); *Kimberly-Clark Corp. v. Johnson & Johnson*, 745 F.2d 1437 (Fed.Cir.1984). *See also* John C. Stedman, *Invention and Public Policy*, 12 J. L. & CONTEMP. PROBS 649, 662 (1947).

But some commentators argue that inventing around patents is socially wasteful in that it diverts resources from other productive uses to the task of finding redundant solutions to already solved problems. See, for example, Donald F. Turner, *The Patent System and Competitive Policy*, 44 N.Y.U. L. REV. 449, 455 (1969); Machlup, Subcomm on Patents, Study No 15 at 51. Machlup argues that research to find duplicative solutions to problems is particularly wasteful when done by the holder of the patent on the first solution in order to prevent competitors from inventing around the patent. Id. See BOWMAN, PATENT AND ANTITRUST LAW at 21–22 (arguing that inventing around patents is not necessarily socially wasteful if it leads to the development of superior products or processes, and that it is reasonable to assume that those who incur the costs of inventing around patents foresee inventing superior substitutes); SCHERER, INDUSTRIAL MARKET STRUCTURE at 386–87 (noting that although the pace of technological advance has probably been accelerated in some fields by efforts to invent around patented technologies, resources devoted to circumventing patents might otherwise be allocated to activities with "higher social incremental payoffs"); Martin J. Adelman, *The Supreme Court, Market Structure and Innovation: Chakrabarty, Rohm and Haas*, 27 ANTITRUST BULL. 457, 464 (1982) (arguing that efforts to invent around patent are unlikely to occur unless competitor and patent holder have different views of cost of developing alternative technology and thus are unable to agree on royalty for use of patented technology that makes it uneconomic to develop an alternative).

Secrecy

secret in order to prevent competitors from exploiting them.[15] Secrecy prevents the public from gaining the full benefit of new knowledge and leads to wasteful duplicative research.[16]

Economists have questioned whether patents in fact promote disclosure of inventions that would otherwise be kept secret.[17] Secrecy is not always a practical strategy for protection,[18] and often secret technologies can eventually be uncovered through reverse engineering.[19] Where long term secrecy is feasible, patent protection for a mere seventeen years might not be an attractive alternative.[20] Moreover, any technology that can be exploited in secrecy by its inventor can probably also be exploited in secrecy by an infringer, making a patent on such an invention difficult to enforce. Finally, some people have questioned whether patent disclosures in fact convey enough information to be useful to the public.[21] The proposition that patents promote disclosure of new inventions by rewarding those who disclose their inventions in patent applications is thus open to doubt on a number of grounds.

Nonetheless, it seems likely that the patent system at least facilitates disclosure by creating rights in inventions that survive disclosure. Secrecy makes it difficult for inventors to sell or license their inventions to others because it is difficult to persuade someone to pay for an idea without disclosing it, yet once the invention is disclosed, the inventor has nothing left to sell. The patent system solves this problem by permitting

---

15. *Universal Oil Prods. Co. v. Globe Oil & Ref. Co.*, 322 U.S. 471, 484 (1944); *Grant v. Raymond*, 31 U.S. 218, 247 (1832); *Sinclair & Carroll Co. v. Interchemical Corp.*, 325 U.S. 327, 331 (1945); *Cross v. Iizuka*, 753 F.2d 1040, 1046 (Fed.Cir.1985); *Flick-Reedy Corp. v. Hydro–Line Mfg. Co.*, 351 F.2d 546, 550–51 (7th Cir.1965); Bowman, Patent and Antitrust Law at 12–13; S. C. Gilfillan, *The Root of Patents, or Squaring Patents by Their Roots*, 31 J. Pat. Off. Soc'y 611, 612 (1949) (deriding "disclosure incentive" as "minor motive" for granting patents and one falling "outside the root of patents").

16. Martin J. Adelman, *Property Rights Theory and Patent–Antitrust: The Role of Compulsory Licensing*, 52 N.Y.U. L. Rev. 977, 982 (1977).

17. *See* Scherer, Industrial Market Structure at 381; Machlup, Subcomm on Patents, Study No. 15 at 32–33, 53, 76. *See also* Canada Dep't. of Consumer & Corp. Affairs, Working Paper on Patent Law Revision 40–42 (1976) ("Canada Working Paper").

18. Secrecy is impractical when efficient exploitation of the invention requires communication to a large number of firms. See Bowman, Patent and Antitrust Law at 13.

19. Plant, 1 Economica at 44. *See generally Paulik v. Rizkalla*, 760 F.2d 1270, 1276 (Fed.Cir.1985) ("[I]t is a rare invention that cannot be deciphered more readily from its commercial embodiment than from the printed patent").

20. Bowman, Patent and Antitrust Law at 13.

21. Critics of the patent system charge that patent applicants often deliberately withhold important information from patent specifications so that they may continue to protect their "know-how" through trade secrecy. *See, for example, Brenner v. Manson*, 383 U.S. 519, 533–34 (1966). See also Canada Working Paper, at 50–53; Machlup, Subcomm on Patents, Study No. 15 at 32–33; William D. Nordhaus, Invention, Growth, and Welfare: A Theoretical Treatment of Technological Change 89 (MIT, 1969) ("It is well known that a firm tries not to disclose key parts of the invention in order to reduce the chance of imitation, thereby reducing the effective diffusion of knowledge"); S.C. Gilfillan, Invention and the Patent System 61 (GPO, 1964) ("The information disclosed in patents is often not enough, taken by itself, to be of much use to the receiver"); Barkev S. Sanders, Joseph Rossman, and L. James Harris, *Attitudes of Assignees Toward Patented Inventions*, 2 Pat., Trademark & Copyright J. Res. & Educ. 463, 467–68 (Dec. 1958) (estimating that about one-half of patented inventions cannot be used without supplementary know-how).

inventors to disclose their patented inventions to potential users without losing their exclusive rights. If persons receiving disclosure use patented inventions without permission, the patent holders may sue them for infringement.[22]

* * *

There is considerable empirical evidence suggesting that technological change has been an extremely important source of economic growth over time,[23] and that levels of invention are responsive to economic stimuli.[24] But it does not necessarily follow that patent protection is necessary to preserve adequate economic incentives for invention and innovation.

Eric Schiff has compared the historical record of industrial development of countries with and without patent systems during the late nineteenth and early twentieth centuries, finding little evidence that the lack of a patent system hampered industrialization.[25] But the two countries he studied that did not have patent systems—the Netherlands and Switzerland—may have been free riding on domestic and foreign inventions that were stimulated by patent protection abroad.[26] Other

22.   Polanyi, 11 REV. OF ECON. STUDIES at 64. *See also* Edmund W. Kitch, *The Nature and Function of the Patent System*, 20 J. L. & ECON. 265, 277–78 (1977) (asserting that patent law defines a framework of legal relations among firms to facilitate disclosure, licensing, etc.).

23.   See, for example, Moses Abramovitz, *Resource and Output Trends in the U.S. Since 1870*, 46 AM. ECON. REV. 5 (1956) (Amer Econ Assoc Papers and Proceedings); Robert M. Solow, *Technological Change and the Aggregate Production Function*, 39 REV. ECON. & STAT. 312, 320 (1957) (estimating that approximately 80 percent of the growth in nonfarm output per worker in the United States between 1909 and 1949 was attributable to technological change rather than increased capital intensity); EDWARD F. DENISON, THE SOURCES OF ECONOMIC GROWTH IN THE UNITED STATES AND THE ALTERNATIVES BEFORE US 271–72 (Brookings Inst., 1962) (estimating that 36 percent of the rise in output per worker between 1929 and 1957 was attributable to the advance of scientific and technological knowledge); EDWARD F. DENISON, ACCOUNTING FOR UNITED STATES ECONOMIC GROWTH, 1929–69 128 (Brookings Inst, 1974) (estimating that 27 percent of U.S. economic growth between 1929 and 1969 was attributable to advances in knowledge); Frederic M. Scherer, *Inter-Industry Technology Flows and Productivity Growth*, 64 REV. ECON. & STAT. 627 (1982) (estimating that in the post-War era R & D has added to the rate of growth by about one percentage point per year, or about half of the annual rate of growth in productivity).

24.   *See generally* JACOB SCHMOOKLER, INVENTION AND ECONOMIC GROWTH (Harvard, 1966) (finding strong correlation between level of invention as measured by patent statistics and level of investment in capital goods, with peaks and troughs in invention tending to precede rather than to follow peaks and troughs in investment, and concluding that patented inventions are made in response to rising demand in an industry); EDWIN MANSFIELD, ET AL, RESEARCH AND INNOVATION (showing correlation between research and development funds expended and expected success of a research project and profitability of its results, and showing that timing of research and development and innovation are responsive to profit expectations.)

25.   ERIC SCHIFF, INDUSTRIALIZATION WITHOUT NATIONAL PATENTS 34–41, 96–106 (Princeton, 1971). Schiff's study focuses on the experiences of the Netherlands, which abolished its patent system in 1869 and did not replace it until 1912, and Switzerland, which did not introduce a comprehensive patent system until 1907.

26.   Id. at 23–24, 102–04. During the period under study, citizens of both Switzerland and the Netherlands were eligible for foreign patent protection under the national patent laws of other countries. Id. at 21–23. Schiff found a marked increase in the number of foreign patent applications filed by Dutch citizens after the Nether-

studies have attempted to determine, through interviews and questionnaires, the impact of patent incentives on research and development (R & D) decision making in firms. C. T. Taylor and Z. A. Silberston, in their study of the economic impact of the patent system in the United Kingdom, found that the importance of patent protection to the R & D decision making of firms varied across industries.[27] They found that patent protection had a strong influence on the willingness of pharmaceutical firms to invest in research and development, but had no more than a marginal impact on R & D expenditures in the basic chemicals industry.[28] In a similar study of U.S. firms, F. M. Scherer found that respondents did not consider patents to be particularly important in R & D decision making—except when patent lawyers prepared the responses.[29] Nonetheless, the authors of both studies interpreted their results to suggest that weakening patent protection by providing for compulsory licensing of patented inventions on reasonable terms would lead to greater reliance by firms on secrecy instead of patent protection.

Another empirical approach to determining the adequacy of the current level of patent incentives is to measure the difference between private and social rates of return to investments in research and development. In case studies of seventeen industrial innovations, Edwin Mansfield and his colleagues found that the median estimated social rate of return to investment in R & D was 56 percent, while the median private rate of return was about 25 percent.[30] According to the study, "in about 30% of the cases, the private rate of return was so low that with the benefit of hindsight no firm would have invested in the innovation, but the social rate of return was so high that from society's standpoint the investment was entirely worthwhile."[31] While the authors caution against drawing any inferences about the extent of underinvestment in research and development from their results, the data are certainly consistent with the view that the current level of incentives to make and disclose new inventions is if anything too low. Other studies have tentatively suggested that private rates of return from investments in

lands introduced its own patent system, which he interprets as evidence that the availability of patent protection in the Netherlands stimulated an increase in domestic inventive efforts. Id. at 42–51. Scherer suggests a different interpretation of Schiff's data: the passage of a Dutch patent law may have made Dutch citizens more patent-conscious and induced the growth of patent law firms, leading to more patenting abroad of inventions that might have been made with or without patent protection. FREDERIC M. SCHERER, THE ECONOMIC EFFECTS OF COMPULSORY LICENSING 36–37 (N.Y.U., 1977).

27. C. T. TAYLOR AND Z. A. SILBERSTON, THE ECONOMIC IMPACT OF THE PATENT SYSTEM 331–50 (Cambridge, 1973).

28. Attempting to explain this difference, they noted that research expenditures are higher relative to sales volume in the pharmaceutical industry than in the chemical industry, that there are more non-patent barriers to competition in the chemical industry, that patents provide stronger protection in the pharmaceutical field than in the chemical field because of the relative ease of inventing around chemical patents, and that secrecy is not practical in the pharmaceutical industry. Id. at 332–36.

29. SCHERER, COMPULSORY LICENSING at 52–62.

30. Edwin Mansfield, et al, *Social and Private Rates of Return from Industrial Innovations*, 91 Q J ECON 221, 233–34 (1977).

31. Id at 235. The gap between social and private rates of return was larger for more important innovations and for innovations that could be imitated at small cost by competitors. Id. at 237.

research and development are significantly higher than returns available on other investments,[32] offering further evidence that firms underinvest in research and development.

* * *

C. Incentive to Innovate and the Prospect Theory

Although the courts have relied primarily on the incentive to invent and incentive to disclose arguments in support of the patent system,[33] commentators have offered the additional argument that a patent monopoly is necessary to induce firms to invest in "innovation"—i.e., putting existing inventions to practical use. Even after an invention has been made, considerable further investment is often necessary before it is ready for commercial exploitation. Further research and development may be needed to establish the commercial feasibility of the invention and to bring it into large scale production. Use of the invention may call for the construction of new plant and equipment. A new product invention may require further refinements to suit the tastes of consumers, as well as promotion and advertising expenditures to persuade consumers to buy it. These additional investments may dwarf the initial research expenditures in making the invention.[34] The protection of a patent monopoly enhances the likelihood that a firm will be willing to undertake these investments.

Like the incentive to invent and incentive to disclose theories, the incentive to innovate theory holds that the patent system achieves its objectives by offering monopoly profits as a lure to promote desired behavior. But it differs from these other theories with respect to the time frame in which the incentive matters. The incentive to invent and incentive to disclose theories are concerned with incentives that operate before a patent issues. These theories assume that the patent monopoly has already served its social function of promoting invention and disclosure as soon as the patent issues, and that enforcement of the patent thereafter is simply the regrettable price that society must pay in order to live up to its end of the bargain.[35] Reducing the strength of existing

32. *See, for example,* EDWIN MANSFIELD, INDUSTRIAL RESEARCH AND TECHNOLOGICAL INNOVATION 65–80 (Norton, 1968).

33. A rare possible exception is the concurring opinion of Judge Frank in Picard v. United Aircraft Corp., 128 F.2d 632 (2d Cir.1942), in which he states: "The controversy between the defenders and assailants of our patent system may be about a false issue—the stimulus to invention. The real issue may be the stimulus to investment." Id. at 643. This statement suggests a view of the patent system as promoting innovation as well as invention. *See also SCM v. Xerox,* 645 F.2d 1195, 1206 n. 9 (2d Cir. 1981).

34. EDWIN MANSFIELD, ET AL, THE PRODUCTION AND APPLICATION OF NEW INDUSTRIAL TECH-

NOLOGY (Norton, 1977); Scherer, Industrial Market Structure at 381 (noting that development outlays constitute more than three fourths of all industrial R & D expenditures); JOHN JEWKES, DAVID SAWERS, AND RICHARD STILLERMAN, THE SOURCES OF INVENTION 212–17 (MacMillan, 2d ed 1969). *See also* FREDERIC M. SCHERER, INNOVATION AND GROWTH: SCHUMPETERIAN PERSPECTIVES 3–7 (MIT, 1984) (explaining that firms are more willing to invest large sums in development than in invention because of the unpredictability of initial technical breakthroughs).

35. As Machlup explains:

If one accepts the theory that patent protection has the social function of serving as an incentive for inventive activity, one

patents would thus presumably offer short run social benefits by increasing the use of already patented inventions, although in the long run it would reduce incentives to make and disclose new inventions. By contrast, the incentive to innovate theory gives existing patents an ongoing role in preserving the incentives of patent holders to invest in development during the patent term. Reducing the strength of existing patent monopolies might thus have the effect of undermining incentives to put existing technologies into use.[36]

1. THE SCHUMPETERIAN THEORY.

The thesis that monopolies are conducive to innovation is generally associated with the work of Joseph Schumpeter on economic development.[37] While Schumpeter does not focus exclusively on either technological innovations or the patent system, his analysis suggests how patent monopolies might promote technological innovation.[38] He emphatically distinguishes innovation from invention, noting that invention itself produces "no economically relevant effect at all."[39] Innovation, on the other hand, brings about incessant revolutionary changes in the economic system through what Schumpeter calls "a process of creative destruc-

accepts, by implication, that the beneficial effects of this incentive system must flow, not from existing patents, but from the hope for future profits from future patents; this hope may induce people to undertake certain risky investments and useful activities—to wit, financing and arranging industrial research—which they might not undertake otherwise.... [E]xisting patents impose a burden on society, a burden which it has decided to carry in order to hold out to people the chance of obtaining future profits from future patents on future inventions. Machlup, Subcomm on Patents, Study No. 15 at 55.

36. While Machlup notes the emergence of "incentive to innovate" arguments and acknowledges that existing patents would play an ongoing role in stimulating post-patent innovation as opposed to pre-patent invention, he does not analyze these arguments beyond stating that they require demonstrating "that innovations based on patentable inventions are socially more desirable than other innovations, and that the free-enterprise system would not, without monopoly incentives, generate investment opportunities to an adequate extent." Id. at 56. He also suggests, without elaboration, that the use of patents to promote innovation rather than invention might not be properly subsumed in the Constitutional goal of promoting "the Progress of Science and useful Arts." Id.

37. JOSEPH SCHUMPETER, CAPITALISM, SOCIALISM AND DEMOCRACY 81–110 (Harper & Row, 3d ed 1950); JOSEPH SCHUMPETER, 1

BUSINESS CYCLES 84–192 (McGraw Hill, 1939); JOSEPH SCHUMPETER, THE THEORY OF ECONOMIC DEVELOPMENT 61–94 (Transaction reprint, Redvers Opie trans 1983). *See also, generally,* Scherer, Schumpeterian Perspective; Morton I. Kamien and Nancy L. Schwartz, MARKET STRUCTURE AND INNOVATION (Cambridge, 1982); Vernon W. Ruttan, *Usher and Schumpeter on Invention, Innovation, and Technological Change*, 73 Q. J. ECON. 596 (1959); Carolyn S. Solo, *Innovation in the Capitalist Process: A Critique of the Schumpeterian Theory*, 65 Q. J. ECON. 417 (1951).

38. Schumpeter defines innovation broadly to include not only putting new technological inventions into practice, but also carrying out any new combination of productive resources that amounts to "the setting up of a new production function." Schumpeter, 1 Business Cycles at 87. In Schumpeter's usage the term innovation includes the development of new consumer goods, new methods of production, new markets, and new forms of industrial organization. Id. at 84; SCHUMPETER, CAPITALISM, SOCIALISM & DEMOCRACY at 82–83.

39. SCHUMPETER, 1 BUSINESS CYCLES at 84. See also Schumpeter, The Theory of Economic Development at 88–89 ("As long as they are not carried into practice, inventions are economically irrelevant. And to carry any improvement into effect is a task entirely different from the inventing of it.").

tion.''[40] In this process, new firms continually arise to carry out new innovations, driving out old firms that provide obsolete goods and services. Competition from new commodities and new technologies is far more significant in this model than price competition among firms offering similar goods and services.

competition

Schumpeter argues that in a dynamic model of the capitalist system, monopoly conditions may promote innovation and growth more effectively than competition. He bases this view primarily on "the tritest common sense," although he also notes as a matter of casual observation that economic advances are more frequently traced to big business than to firms in atomistically competitive industries.[41] He reasons that in the rapidly changing conditions of a capitalist economy, investment in innovation requires some sort of hedge against losses. Protection from competition also allows firms "to gain the time and space for further developments." Finally, and perhaps most important, the prospect of earning more than an ordinary return permits innovators to secure the financial backing of capitalists and to bid productive resources away from their current uses. A monopoly position secured through patent protection thus may increase rather than restrict the use of known technologies by facilitating the commercial introduction of such technologies by innovating firms.

2. THE PROSPECT THEORY.

Edmund Kitch offers a more elaborate analysis of the role of patents in post-invention innovation in what he calls the "prospect theory" of patent protection. According to this theory, the patent system promotes efficiency in the allocation of resources to the development of existing inventions by awarding exclusive, publicly recorded ownership in new technological "prospects" shortly after their discovery. The term "prospect theory" highlights an analogy between the functions of patent monopolies and awards of exclusive mineral claims in government owned lands in the American West.[42]

40. SCHUMPETER, CAPITALISM, SOCIALISM & DEMOCRACY at 83.

41. Id at 82. For other perspectives, see generally Arrow, Economic Welfare (arguing that incentive to innovate should be greater for competitive firms than for monopolists); Henry Villard, *Competition, Oligopoly and Research*, 66 J POL ECON 483 (1958) (arguing that "competitive oligopoly," characterized by a small number of big firms, promotes research better than either pure competition or monopoly).

Subsequent empirical studies to test Schumpeter's impression that monopoly conditions are more conducive to innovation than competition have been inconclusive. Scherer, Schumpeterian Perspectives at 169–255 and sources cited therein; Kam-

ien and Schwartz, Market Structure at 49–104 and sources cited therein; Scherer, Industrial Market Structure at 363–64 and sources cited therein.

42. The analogy between patents and mineral claims was foreshadowed by George Frost in a footnote in a 1946 article. George Frost, *Legal Incidents of Non–Use of Patented Inventions Reconsidered*, 14 GEO. WASH. L. REV. 273, 279 n. 24 (1946) ("An interesting analogy may be drawn between the law relating to patents for inventions and the mining law, an analogy which emphasizes the fact that patents are only one of the many situations where an exclusive grant is provided to encourage effort and capital investment.").

The prospect theory offers a justification for patents that is in keeping with broader theories of property rights elaborated by Harold Demsetz[43] and Richard Posner.[44] These commentators argue that private property rights promote greater efficiency in the use of resources than communal ownership because individuals can be expected to exploit communally owned resources too quickly in order to appropriate the resources for themselves before other community members deplete them. The result will be an exhaustion of resources by individuals in the present, with the costs to be borne by the community as a whole in the future. Private ownership avoids this problem by placing property owners in a position to realize the full costs as well as the benefits of exploitation, thereby internalizing what would be external costs in a system of communal ownership.

The analogy between patents and other types of property[45] is not immediately apparent because inventions that can be used to an unlimited extent without exhaustion do not seem to present the same problems of scarcity and depletion as tangible resources. Kitch clarifies the analogy by noting that while information may be used without exhausting it, resources available to use information are scarce, and property rights in inventions can improve the efficiency with which these resources are managed.

Kitch contends that patents promote efficiency in the use of resources to develop patented inventions in part by putting patent owners in a position to coordinate subsequent research and development efforts.[46] Since the owner of a patent has the exclusive right to exploit the technology defined in the patent claims, no one else is likely to invest in developing this technology without first making arrangements with the patent owner; otherwise, the subsequent researchers might ultimately be unable to benefit from their own investment in development for lack of a license to the underlying patented technology. The patent owner is thus in a position to cause researchers to share information and thereby avoid duplicative research efforts. In the absence of a patent, different investigators might try independently to develop the same invention in secrecy,

43. Harold Demsetz, *Toward a Theory of Property Rights*, 57 Am. Econ. Rev. 347 (1967) (Am Econ Assoc Papers & Proceedings).

44. Posner, Economic Analysis of the Law at 27–31.

45. While judicial decisions often speak of patent rights as a species of "property," economists studying the patent system for the most part have not drawn on property rights theory. Indeed, Fritz Machlup argues that the characterization of patents as creating "property rights" in inventions reflects confusion as to the difference between "property" and "monopoly." Machlup, Subcomm on Patents, Study No. 15 at 53–54. Machlup and Penrose trace this confusion to a deliberate "political ruse" advanced by nineteenth century advocates of the patent system in order to claim for their cause the respectable connotations of the word "property" in place of the less favorable connotations of the word "privilege." Machlup and Penrose, 10 J Econ Hist at 16–17.

46. Id. at 276. Kitch also asserts that patents promote efficiency in the development of technological prospects by preserving the incentives of patent holders to develop their inventions without fear that the results of these efforts will be appropriated by competitors and by allowing patent holders to disclose their technological achievements to other firms without losing their exclusive rights, thereby facilitating the transfer of technology among firms and reducing the amount of duplicative research efforts. Id. at 276–79.

each working without the benefit of the knowledge gained through the efforts of the others. Exclusive rights in technological prospects thus promote efficiency in research after the patent issues by putting the patent holder in a position to monitor and control such research.

Kitch finds support for the thesis that patent rights play a significant role in the ongoing development of patented inventions in two features of the patent system. First, the patent statute authorizes and promotes patent protection at an early stage in the development of new inventions,[47] making it likely that further research will remain to be done in order to develop an invention during the term of the patent. According to Kitch, inventions are commonly patented long before it becomes commercially feasible to exploit them.[48] The inventor who delays filing a patent application while continuing to develop the invention may lose the right to patent protection entirely if in the interim the inventor makes a public use of the invention[49] or begins to exploit it commercially in secrecy;[50] if the invention is described in the literature or used by others; if intervening progress in the field makes the invention obvious; or if a competitor files an earlier patent application on the same invention.[51]

Second, Kitch asserts that the patent monopoly is generally not limited to the primitive version of the invention described in the patent application, but extends to subsequent refinements as well.[52] Subsequent

47. In order to obtain a patent, an applicant need only show that the invention works—i.e., that it is capable of performing some useful function. The applicant need not show that the invention works better than other means of accomplishing the same purpose, nor even that it works well. All that is necessary is a written disclosure of the invention sufficient to enable someone skilled in the field to reduce the invention to practice—i.e., to make and use it. 35 U.S.C.A. §§ 102(g), 112 (1982). The applicant does not have to describe every possible embodiment of the invention, although § 112 does require disclosure of the "best mode" of practicing the invention known to the inventor at the time the patent application is filed.

48. Empirical evidence contradicts Kitch on this point. Barkev Sanders, in a study of assigned patents issued in 1938, 1948, and 1952, found that of the estimated 10 percent of patented inventions ever put to commercial use, about 40 percent were first put to use before the patent application was filed, about 50 percent were first put to use while the application was pending, and only about 10 percent were first put to use after issuance of the patent. Barkev Sanders, Speedy Entry of Patented Inventions into Commercial Use, 6 Pat, Trademark & Copyright J of Research & Educ 87 (1962). See also Scherer, Compulsory Licensing at 9–10 and sources cited

therein (indicating that the making of a patentable invention accompanies or follows commercial development more frequently than it precedes a lengthy period of subsequent development).

49. 35 U.S.C. § 102(b) (1982); Egbert v. Lippmann, 104 U.S. 333 (1881).

50. *See generally Pennock v. Dialogue*, 27 U.S. (2 Pet) 1 (1829); *Metallizing Engineering Co. v. Kenyon Bearing & Auto Parts Co.*, 153 F.2d 516 (2d Cir.1946).

51. Although in the U.S. patent system patent priority is awarded to the first inventor rather than to the first to file a patent application, the date of the patent application is presumed to be the same as the applicant's date of invention unless the inventor is able to prove an earlier invention date. See 35 U.S.C.A. § 102(g) (1982); *Lacotte v. Thomas*, 758 F.2d 611 (Fed.Cir. 1985).

52. Kitch, 20 J L & Econ at 268–69. As an empirical matter, this assertion is also subject to doubt. The scope of patent claims will often have to be quite narrow in order to distinguish the patented invention from the prior art. *See generally* Robert P. Merges, *Commercial Success and Patent Standards: Economic Perspectives on Innovation*, 76 Cal. L. Rev. 803, 840–41 (1988) and sources cited therein.

improved versions of the invention falling within the scope of the patent claims and newly discovered uses for the invention, although the product of further research by others, will still be subject to the control of the patent holder until the patent expires.[53] The patent holder will therefore stand to benefit from subsequent research to improve the invention, while other researchers will have little incentive to pursue further research on a patented invention without first arranging for a license to the underlying patent. Kitch argues that taken together, these features of the patent system tend to promote control over subsequent research on patented inventions by patent holders and their licensees, and that such control promotes efficiency.

§ 1.5[a][2]   Additional Theories

Two other theories relating to the patent law have been discussed in the literature: the "rent dissipation theory" articulated in Mark F. Grady & Jay I. Alexander, *Patent Law and Rent Dissipation,* 78 VA. L. REV. 305 (1992), and the "race to invent" theory set forth in Robert P. Merges & Richard R. Nelson, *On the Complex Economics of Patent Scope,* 90 COLUM. L. REV. 839 (1990). The Merges and Nelson article is part of the burgeoning literature discussing the appropriate way to treat basic and improvement inventions. *See generally* Peter S. Menell, *Intellectual Property: General Theories,* ENCYCLOPEDIA OF LAW & ECONOMICS (2000).

As explained by Professor Eisenberg, one important economic aspect of the patent system that is generally overlooked concerns the extensive literature on the relationship between industrial structure and inventive activity. However, while the precise relationship between market structure and innovation is difficult to quantify, a strong patent system should reduce any disparity in incentives to innovate with respect to different market structures. In effect the existence of a patent system makes the industrial structure of a particular industry essentially irrelevant to the innovation process. This may be the most important practical effect of any patent system. *See* Martin J. Adelman, *The Supreme Court, Market Structure and Innovation: Chakrabarty, Rohm and Haas,* 27 ANTITRUST BULL. 457–61 (1982).

§ 1.5[b]   Philosophical Rationales

In addition to economical studies, legal scholars have frequently, and productively, employed philosophical studies as a prism for critical thinking about the patent laws. In doing so, they have stressed the patent regime as one of property. Certainly the foundational philosophical text for these studies is John Locke's SECOND TREATISE OF GOVERN-

---

53. The subsequent inventor might be entitled to a patent on her improvement or new use of the earlier invention, but would not be able to exploit this patent without the permission of the holder of the patent on the underlying invention. The patent on the improvement or new use would enable the subsequent inventor to prevent the un-derlying patent holder from using this later invention. Thus no one could use the improvement without the permission of both patent holders. *See, for example, Marconi Wireless Tel. Co. v. DeForest Radio Tel. & Tel. Co.,* 236 F. 942 (S.D.N.Y.1916), *aff'd,* 243 F. 560 (2d Cir.1917).

MENT. *See* JOHN LOCKE, THE SECOND TREATISE OF GOVERNMENT ¶ 27 (1690), in TWO TREATISES OF GOVERNMENT (Peter Laslett ed. 1960). Commentators have turned with less enthusiasm to Georg Wilhelm Friedrich Hegel, who acknowledged intellectual property laws explicitly in his most important political text, THE PHILOSOPHY OF RIGHT. *See* HEGEL'S PHILOSOPHY OF RIGHT (T. M. Knox trans. 1952).

The crux of Locke's celebrated argument concerning property is that divine authority created the world as a universal common, in which all individuals possessed an equal right. An exception to this rule lies in the body of each individual, over which each individual enjoys a property right. Not only is an individual's person his own, but "the labor of his body and the work of his hands, we may say, are properly his," as the immediate extension of his person. A significant condition qualifies this labor-based property right: whenever an individual removes something from the common, there must remain "enough and as good left in the common for others." Applied to the invention of technique and technological artifacts, Locke's theory provides a compelling rationale for the patent system.

In contrast, Hegel reasoned that property results from the expression of individual will. To Hegel, human personality results from the will's continuous effort to impose itself upon the world. Hegel recognized that the interaction of the human will with the external world occurs in part through the occupation and embodiment of external, enduring objects, which society recognizes as property. Importantly for students of the patent law, however, Hegel realized that physical objects need not be the only subject of patent protection; creative expression and the embodiment of ideas are also worthy of protection through a system of exclusive rights. As manifested in intellectual property schemes such as patent protection, Hegelian notions of property provide a suitable mechanism for self-actualization, personal expression, and recognition of the dignity and worth of the individual.

Despite this focus on its place as a species of property, the patent law remains first and foremost a regime of technological evaluation. The writings of those thinkers who have contemplated the nature of technology itself therefore also present a relatively untapped lodestar for those who would assess the patent system. Although the philosophy of technology is a nascent field of study, such seminal figures as John Dewey, Martin Heidegger and Karl Marx have presented mature thought on technological growth, the ethical context of technique and technological artifacts, and the relationship between man and the made world in which he exists. It is in minds such as these that students can find alternatives to the quantitatively rigid, yet morally ambiguous path of patent law and economics.

Further Reading. Recommended starting points are the scholarly analyses presented in PETER DRAHOS, A PHILOSOPHY OF INTELLECTUAL PROPERTY (1996); Wendy Gordon, *A Property Right in Self–Expression: Equality and Individualism in the Natural Law of Intellectual Property,*

102 YALE L.J. 1533 (1993); and Justin Hughes, *The Philosophy of Intellectual Property*, 77 GEO. L.J. 287 (1988).

§ 1.6 OTHER FORMS OF INTELLECTUAL PROPERTY PROTECTION

Other areas encompassed by the term intellectual property include trademarks, copyrights, semiconductor chip protection and trade secrets. Although a full description of these and related disciplines—including such disparate regimes as industrial design and database registration, anti-counterfeiting measures, and indications of origin—exceeds the scope of this casebook, the following brief review should inform a consideration of the patent law.

§ 1.6[a] Trademarks

The fundamental federal legislation in this field, the Lanham Act, defines a trademark as "any word, name, symbol, or device, or any combination thereof [used] to identify and distinguish his or her goods, including a unique product, from those manufactured or sold by others and to indicate the source of the goods, even if that source is unknown." 15 U.S.C. § 1127. Related concepts include trade names, used to identify a business or vocation, and service marks, used in connection with services, such as those provided by the hotel or restaurant industry. *Id.* Trademark law serves to benefit consumers by allowing them to establish a vocabulary upon which selections among various goods and services can be made.

The determination of whether a mark qualifies for trademark protection depends in part upon its classification as generic, descriptive, suggestive, or arbitrary. *See Abercrombie & Fitch Co. v. Hunting World, Inc.*, 537 F.2d 4, 189 U.S.P.Q. 769 (2d Cir.1976). Generic terms are defined as the ordinary name for that sort of marked product, such as "bread" or "sugar," and can never receive trademark protection. Marks which are ordinarily and naturally used to characterize a product—referred to as descriptive marks—may also not be protected unless they have acquired a certain level of distinctiveness. This distinctiveness, so-called "secondary meaning," refers to an acquired meaning of the mark, typically through exclusive use over a lengthy period, so that it comes to refer to the origin of the goods or services, rather than those goods or services themselves. Thus, terms which merely describe the function of a service, such as "vision center" for optical clinics, or indicate a product's desirable characteristic, such as "honey-baked ham," cannot be valid trademarks absent a further showing of secondary meaning.

Suggestive marks—those which do more than describe, but require some additional thought to indicate the product—are inherently distinctive and therefore subject to protection without the need to prove secondary meaning. Such terms as "Skinvisible" for transparent medical adhesive tape and "Orange Crush" for orange-flavored soft drinks have been held to be suggestive. Arbitrary marks such as "Camel" applied to cigarettes, or coined words like "Kodak" which lack a dictionary meaning, are also considered inherently distinctive.

Importantly when considered in the context of patents, trademark protection can never extend to the functional features of a product. *See Crescent Tool Co. v. Kilborn & Bishop Co.*, 247 F. 299 (2d Cir.1917). Whether a feature is considered functional depends upon its affect upon the cost or quality of the article, as well as the availability of alternative designs. This doctrine is founded on the public interest in preventing a monopoly in useful design features, thereby hindering competitors.

Trademark infringement occurs when another person markets goods bearing a mark sufficiently similar to the trademark that a likelihood of confusion exists as to the source of the goods. 15 U.S.C. § 1125. Factors that inform the likelihood of confusion inquiry include the similarity of appearance of the marks, the strength of the trademark, consumer sophistication, competition between the goods, similarity of sales and distribution channels, the intent of the defendant, and the existence of actual consumer confusion. *See Polaroid Corp. v. Polarad Electronics Corp.*, 287 F.2d 492, 128 U.S.P.Q. 411 (2d Cir.1961).

In contrast to most trademark regimes overseas, the U.S. trademark law allows ownership to result from public use, rather than registration. However, trademarks may be registered with the United States Patent and Trademark Office when they are employed in interstate commerce, providing both evidentiary and substantive advantages in subsequent disputes. 15 U.S.C. § 1051. Trademarks are of potentially perpetual duration but may be extinguished through non-use or loss of distinctiveness. For example, use of the mark may become so widespread that it loses its ability to identify a particular product, becoming generic in the fashion of terms like *aspirin* or *escalator*, or the owner may abandon the mark or license it without the ability to maintain product quality. *See* RESTATEMENT (THIRD) OF UNFAIR COMPETITION §§ 30, 33 (1995).

§ 1.6[b]   Copyrights

Under the Copyright Act of 1976, copyright may extend to any work of authorship. 17 U.S.C. § 102(a). Exemplary of the works of authorship amenable to copyright protection are literary, musical, dramatic, choreographic, graphic, audiovisual, and architectural works, as well as sound recordings. Such works are eligible for copyright protection as soon as they are recorded in a sufficiently stable form, or, in the words of the copyright law, "fixed in any tangible medium of expression." *Id*. No formalities are necessary to secure protection. However, authors that register their works with the Copyright Office, 17 U.S.C. §§ 408–412, and that place a notice of copyright on copies of their works, 17 U.S.C. § § 401–406, are provided certain advantages when enforcing their copyrights.

A work must be original to be protected under the copyright law. 17 U.S.C. § 102(a). The originality requirement is a lenient one, requiring that the work was created by that author and was not copied from another, and that there be a minimal amount of creative authorship. Importantly, copyright protection extends only to the expression of an idea, not the idea itself. 17 U.S.C. § 102(b). For example, no author can obtain copyright protection on the abstract idea of a human changing into an insect. But the expression of that idea in a particular work of authorship with its own characters, plot, mood and setting—be it Franz Kafka's *The Metamorphosis* or the horror movie *The Fly*—may be accorded copyright protection.

Copyright confers a number of exclusive rights to the author or, in some circumstances, to the employer of the author under the "works made for hire" principle. 17 U.S.C. § 201. The copyright proprietor has the exclusive right to make copies of the protected work and to distribute it to the public. The 1976 Act also awards copyright owners the right to control derivative works, such as translations or screenplay adaptations, that are based upon the protected work. The proprietor further enjoys the exclusive right, with respect to most kinds of works, to display and perform the protected work publicly. 17 U.S.C. § 106.

The exclusive rights of copyright owners are restricted by a number of defenses, the most important of which is the fair use privilege. The fair use privilege allows the unauthorized use of copyrighted works in such contexts as educational activities, literary and social criticism, parody and news reporting. 17 U.S.C. § 107.

Each copyright ordinarily enjoys a term of the life of the author plus seventy years. 17 U.S.C. § 302(a). The copyright proprietor may file a suit in federal court in order to enjoin infringers and obtain monetary remedies. 17 U.S.C. §§ 501–505. Criminal penalties may also apply to copyright infringers. 17 U.S.C. § 506. A copyright, or any of the exclusive rights under a copyright, may be assigned or licensed to others. 17 U.S.C. § 201(d). Individual authors possess the right to terminate such transfers after 35 years, although the transferee may continue to exploit derivative works produced under the transfer prior to its termination. 17 U.S.C. § 203.

§ 1.6[c] Semiconductor Chip Protection

Semiconductor chip products, including microprocessors and memories, consist of often vast electronic circuits fabricated onto a single piece of semiconductor substrate. Designers of these products quickly learned that their work were not considered a work of authorship eligible for copyright protection. Similarly, patent protection was largely unavailable due to the nonobviousness requirement—although these products required considerable investment of time and design resources, they were usually the result of ordinary labors of skilled engineers, rather than invention within the meaning of the patent laws. The Semiconductor Chip Protection Act of 1984, Pub. L. 98–620, remedied this situation by allowing designers of new semiconductor chip products to register them at the Copyright Office, obtaining the exclusive right to manufacture and distribute them in the United States for ten years. The Chip Act, which is codified in chapter 9 of title 17 of the U.S. Code, has not been heavily employed and only rarely the subject of litigation. It nonetheless serves as an interesting model of an alternative scheme of protection, with similarities to both patent and copyright law, designed to encompass a new technology.

§ 1.6[d] Trade Secrets

Trade secret law protects secret, valuable business information from misappropriation by others. Subject matter ranging from marketing data to manufacturing know-how may be protected under the trade secret laws. Trade secret status is not limited to a fixed number of years, but endures so long as the information is valuable and maintained as a secret. *See United States v. Dubilier Condenser Corp.*, 289 U.S. 178, 186 (1933). A trade secret is misappropriated when it has been obtained through the abuse of a confidential relationship or improper means of acquisition. Unlike the Patent Act, trade secret law does not provide a cause of action against an individual who independently developed or reverse engineered the subject matter of the trade secret.

Trade secrecy serves as the chief alternative to the patent system and, as such, is worthy of more detailed review here. An inventor must either maintain a technology as a trade secret, seek patent protection from the PTO, or allow it to enter the public domain. The regime of trade secrets is broader than this, however, for trade secret law may also be used to protect subject matter that is unpatentable. For example, although a list of valued customers does not constitute patent eligible subject matter, it is amenable to protection as a trade secret.

Judicial opinions evince two distinct conceptions of the trade secret law. Some courts focus on trade secrecy as an intellectual property discipline. Under this view, trade secret law creates a proprietary interest just like a copyright, patent or mark. In deciding whether to grant relief for misappropriation of trade secrets, these courts stress the value and secrecy of the subject matter for which trade secret status is claimed. Other courts have viewed trade secret law as less concerned with creating property than in ensuring proper conduct. In resolving trade secret cases, these courts stress whether the accused misappropriator acquired the information at issue in a fair and ethical manner.

As Judge Posner noted in the leading opinion of *Rockwell Graphic Systems, Inc. v. DEV Industries, Inc.*, 925 F.2d 174, 17 U.S.P.Q.2d 1780 (7th Cir.1991), these conceptions are entirely complementary. The trade secret law encourages industry actors to develop valuable informational resources by protecting them from improper acquisition by others. As well, potential liability for trade secret misappropriation discourages individuals from engaging in activities that do not create wealth, but merely redistribute wealth from one individual to another.

§ 1.6[d][1] Sources of Law

The modern U.S. law of trade secrets arises from the common law tradition. The English equity courts of the early Nineteenth Century considered the misappropriation of such secret subject matter as the composition of medical compounds and dyes. Many of these cases involved breaches of confidence between partners, family members or a master and apprentice. The U.S. courts turned to this early precedent while considering the increasingly complex commercial relationships of an industrial society. Trade secret law continues as an adaptive discipline that has responded to changing technology, increasing employee mobility and heightened entrepreneurial activity.

The American Law Institute's 1939 Restatement of Torts included two sections that defined the subject matter of trade secrets and the misappropriation cause of action. Although this treatment was succinct, these definitions proved influential in the courts. However, trade secrets were not addressed in the 1978 Second Restatement of Torts. The American Law Institute concluded that trade secret law had grown "no more dependent on Tort law than it is on many other general fields of law and upon broad statutory developments," and opted not to house trade secrets there.

The Uniform Trade Secrets Act filled this breach in 1979. 14 U.L.A. 438 (1990). Published by the National Conference of Commissioners on Uniform State Law, the Uniform Act has been enacted in the majority of states. The Uniform Act generally follows the Restatement of Torts, but also relies upon subsequent case law to provide more useful and definitive legal standards.

The American Law Institute was not content to rest, however. A distinct Restatement (Third) of Unfair Competition was promulgated in 1993 with a thorough treatment of trade secrets in sections 39–45. The remainder of the work is devoted to trademarks, misappropriation, deceptive marking, the right of publicity and related doctrines. Like the Restatement of Torts and the Uniform Act, the Restatement of Unfair Competition remains faithful to the case law and does not presume to be an instrument of radical legal reform.

Trade secrets have traditionally been the subject of state law. However, the federal government firmly engaged the law of trade secrets in the Economic Espionage Act of 1996. Pub. L. No. 104–294, §§ 1831–1839, 110 Stat. 3488 (codified at 18 U.S.C. §§ 1831–39). That statute renders the misappropriation of trade secrets a federal crime. Housed in Title 18 of the United States Code, the Economic Espionage Act provides for substantial fines and imprisonment penalties, as well as criminal forfeiture of property and court order preserving confidentiality of trade secrets. Stiffer penalties are available when trade secrets are misappropriated for the benefit of a foreign government, instrumentality or agent.

That the common law has been supplemented by these four accounts of trade secrets law may seem to hold tremendous possibility for confusion. However, the substantive law of trade secrets provided in the Restatements, Uniform Act and Economic Espionage Act is largely consistent. The later sources are marked by more familiar language and a greater level of detail than their predecessors. Although judicial opinions may cite to different authorities, the core precepts of trade secret law remain intact.

§ 1.6[d][2]   Eligible Subject Matter

Perhaps due to its origins in the courts of equity, the trade secret law has never overly concerned itself with achieving an exact definition of the sorts of information that may be subjected to trade secret protection. The authorities do agree that there are two principle requirements for maintaining information as a trade secret. First and foremost, the information must have been the subject of reasonable efforts to maintain secrecy. Second, the information must derive commercial value from not being generally known or readily ascertainable by others. RESTATEMENT THIRD, UNFAIR COMPETITION § 39 (1995).

Subject to these overriding requirements of secrecy and value, the Restatements provide that formulae, patterns, devices or compilations of information may be protected as trade secrets. The case law reveals an enormous variety of information subject to the trade secret laws. This subject matter include lists of customers, marketing data, bid price information, technical designs, manufacturing know-how, computer programs and chemical formulae. In sum, any distinct, clearly identifiable information may become a trade secret provided that it has value and has been kept secret.

§ 1.6[d][3]   Secrecy

The principal gatekeeper to trade secret status is that the information must have been subjected to reasonable efforts to maintain its secrecy. Uniform Trade Secrets Act § 2, 14 U.L.A. 438 (1990). The case law provides no precise standard as to the efforts necessary to qualify the protected subject matter as a trade secret. A would-be trade secret holder need not erect an utterly impenetrable fortress around the information. On the other hand, the owner must make satisfactory efforts to identify the secret subject matter, notify others that it regards the subject matter as proprietary, and protect against reasonably foreseeable intrusions.

In deciding whether reasonable efforts have been made to maintain secrecy, courts will balance the costs of the efforts made against the benefits obtained. *See Rockwell Graphic Sys., Inc. v. DEV Industries, Inc.,* 925 F.2d 174 (7th Cir.1991). The courts do not require costly, burdensome safeguards that would overly disrupt the owner's usual commercial practices. However, if the owner did not engage in prudent precautions that would have yielded security benefits greater than their costs, the case for reasonable secrecy efforts is diminished.

The precautions the holder of commercially valuable information might take to maintain secrecy are legion. For example, employees, visitors and joint venturers could be required to sign confidentiality agreements. Signs, stamps and legends may declare that certain subject matter is proprietary. Locked doors, alarms and guards might deny access to individuals who do not need to know the information. Exit interviews may remind departing employees of their obligations to maintain the protected subject matter in confidence. Pertinent documents and laboratory samples could be destroyed on the premises. Although numerous other measures should be apparent, no absolute rule governs the degree of vigilance that the putative trade secret holder must maintain. Whether a court will find the existence of a trade secret depends upon an overall balancing of the equities of particular cases.

A number of circumstances may negate secrecy. Knowledge that may be readily gained from an inspection of a commercially available product is not secret. Similarly, information that may be found in publicly available journals, texts or other published materials may not be kept as a trade secret. Issuance of a U.S. patent or publication of a pending patent application also destroys the secrecy of any information claimed within. This result holds even if the published application does not mature into a granted patent, or if the patent is later held invalid. RESTATEMENT THIRD, UNFAIR COMPETITION § 39 cmt. c (1995).

§ 1.6[d][4]   Commercial Value

Information must be sufficiently valuable to provide an actual or potential economic advantage over others to qualify for trade secret protection. RESTATEMENT THIRD, UNFAIR COMPETITION § 39 cmt e (1995). Ordinarily the putative trade secret holder demonstrates value through direct evidence of the significance of the subject matter to its business, or its superiority as compared to public domain alternatives. Courts have also accepted evidence of the cost of developing the information and the extent of the pains taken to protect its secrecy as evidence of value.

Value is seldom a practical issue in trade secret cases. The high cost of enforcing intellectual property rights suggests that plaintiffs will only commence litigation concerning information of considerable value. One decision that did deny a claim for trade secret misappropriation based upon the value requirement was *Religious Technology Center v. Wollersheim*, 796 F.2d 1076 (9th Cir.1986). There, the Church of Scientology accused a former practitioner of misappropriating scriptural materials that addressed a person's spiritual well-being. The Court of Appeals for the Ninth Circuit denied the Church's trade secret claim, concluding that the value of the confidential materials were religious rather than commercial in character.

§ 1.6[d][5]   Misappropriation

An enterprise possessing trade secrets will be protected against misappropriation of those trade secrets by others. Some trade secret cases involve parties who initially learn of the trade secret through voluntary disclosure by the trade secret holder, and thereafter either use the secret for their commercial advantage or disclose it to others. Courts will grant relief in this latter class of cases where the defendant violated either an express or implied obligation of confidentiality.

An individual may owe another a duty of confidence through an express promise of confidentiality. Such promises are most typically made by employees, prospective buyers, visitors to a facility or joint venturers. A duty of confidence may also be implied from the relationship of the parties, even where no express contractual provision exists. If the trade secret holder was reasonable in inferring that the other person consented to an obligation of confidentiality, and the other knew or should have known the disclosure was made in confidence, the court will infer that an obligation of confidentiality existed.

A representative case implying a duty of confidentiality is *Smith v. Dravo Corp.*, 203 F.2d 369 (7th Cir.1953). Smith was in the cargo and freight container business. Dravo expressed an interest in buying Smith's business, and the two entered into negotiations. As part of these discussions Smith showed Dravo secret blueprints and patent applications concerning its innovative cargo containers. The deal fell through and shortly thereafter Dravo began to market freight containers similar to Smith's. Smith sued Dravo for trade secret misappropriation. Although the Court of Appeals for the Seventh Circuit observed that "no express promise of trust was exacted from the defendant," it held that a relationship of trust should be implied from the facts and granted relief.

Other trade secrets cases concern instances where individuals with no relationship to the trade secret holder have acquired the protected subject matter. In those cases, the dispositive legal issue is whether the trade secret was acquired by improper means. A trade secret owner may claim misappropriation if the defendant acquired the trade secret by performing illegal acts. Wiretapping, bribery, fraud, and theft of personal property are exemplary of the industrial espionage condemned under the trade secret law. However, trade secret protection is not limited to acts that are themselves violations of other laws. As demonstrated by the following decision, the courts have also condemned activities that amount to calculated attempts to overcome reasonable efforts to maintain secrecy.

E.I. duPONT deNEMOURS & CO. v. CHRISTOPHER

United States Court of Appeals, Fifth Circuit, 1970.
431 F.2d 1012, 166 U.S.P.Q. 421.
cert. denied, 400 U.S. 1024 (1971).

Before WISDOM, GOLDBERG, and INGRAHAM, CIRCUIT JUDGES.

GOLDBERG, CIRCUIT JUDGE:

This is a case of industrial espionage in which an airplane is the cloak and a camera the dagger. The defendants-appellants, Rolfe and Gary Christopher, are photographers in Beaumont, Texas. The Christophers were hired by an unknown third party to take aerial photographs of new construction at the Beaumont plant of E. I. duPont deNemours & Company, Inc. Sixteen photographs of the DuPont facility were taken from the air on March 19, 1969, and these photographs were later developed and delivered to the third party.

DuPont employees apparently noticed the airplane on March 19 and immediately began an investigation to determine why the craft was circling over the plant. By that afternoon the investigation had disclosed that the craft was involved in a photographic expedition and that the Christophers were the photographers. DuPont contacted the Christophers that same afternoon and asked them to reveal the name of the person or corporation requesting the photographs. The Christophers refused to disclose this information, giving as their reason the client's desire to remain anonymous.

Having reached a dead end in the investigation, DuPont subsequently filed suit against the Christophers, alleging that the Christophers had wrongfully obtained photographs revealing DuPont's trade secrets which they then sold to the undisclosed third party. DuPont contended that it had developed a highly secret but unpatented process for producing methanol, a process which gave DuPont a competitive advantage over other producers. This process, DuPont alleged, was a trade secret developed after much expensive and time-consuming research, and a secret which the company had taken special precautions to safeguard. The area photographed by the Christophers was the plant designed to produce methanol by this secret process, and because the plant was still under construction parts of the process were exposed to view from directly above the construction area. Photographs of that area, DuPont alleged, would enable a skilled person to deduce the secret process for making methanol. DuPont thus contended that the Christophers had wrongfully appropriated DuPont trade secrets by taking the photographs and delivering them to the undisclosed third party. In its suit DuPont asked for damages to cover the loss it had already sustained as a result of the wrongful disclosure of the trade secret and sought temporary and permanent injunctions prohibiting any further circulation of the photographs already taken and prohibiting any additional photographing of the methanol plant.

The Christophers answered with motions to dismiss for lack of jurisdiction and failure to state a claim upon which relief could be granted. Depositions were taken during which the Christophers again refused to disclose the name of the person to whom they had delivered the photographs. DuPont then filed a motion to compel an answer to this question and all related questions.

On June 5, 1969, the trial court held a hearing on all pending motions and an additional motion by the Christophers for summary judgment. The court denied the Christophers' motions to dismiss for want of jurisdiction and failure to state a claim and also denied their motion for summary judgment. The court granted DuPont's motion to compel the Christophers to divulge the name of their client. Having made these rulings, the court then granted the Christophers' motion for an interlocutory appeal under 28 U.S.C.A. § 1292(b) to allow the Christophers to obtain immediate appellate review of the court's finding that DuPont had stated a claim upon which relief could be granted. Agreeing with the trial court's determination that DuPont had stated a valid claim, we affirm the decision of that court.

This is a case of first impression, for the Texas courts have not faced this precise factual issue, and sitting as a diversity court we must sensitize our *Erie* antennae to divine what the Texas courts would do if such a situation were presented to them. The only question involved in this interlocutory appeal is whether DuPont has asserted a claim upon which relief can be granted. The Christophers argued both at trial and before this court that they committed no "actionable wrong" in photographing the DuPont facility and passing these photographs on to their client because they conducted all of their activities in public airspace, violated no government aviation standard, did not breach any confidential relation, and did not engage in any fraudulent or illegal conduct. In short, the Christophers argue that for an appropriation of trade secrets to be wrongful there must be a trespass, other illegal conduct, or breach of a confidential relationship. We disagree.

It is true, as the Christophers assert, that the previous trade secret cases have contained one or more of these elements. However, we do not think that the Texas courts would limit the trade secret protection exclusively to these elements. On the contrary, in *Hyde Corporation v. Huffines*, 1958, 314 S.W.2d 763, the Texas Supreme Court specifically adopted the rule found in the Restatement of Torts which provides:

> "One who discloses or uses another's trade secret, without a privilege to do so, is liable to the other if (a) he discovered the secret by improper means, or (b) his disclosure or use constitutes a breach of confidence reposed in him by the other in disclosing the secret to him * * *."

RESTATEMENT OF TORTS § 757 (1939).

Thus, although the previous cases have dealt with a breach of a confidential relationship, a trespass, or other illegal conduct, the rule is much broader than the cases heretofore encountered. Not limiting itself to specific wrongs, Texas adopted subsection (a) of the Restatement which recognizes a cause of action for the discovery of a trade secret by any 'improper' means.

The defendants, however, read *Furr's Inc. v. United Specialty Advertising Co.*, Tex.Civ.App.1960, 338 S.W.2d 762, as limiting the Texas rule to breach of a confidential relationship. The court in *Furr's* did make the statement that

> "The use of someone else's idea is not automatically a violation of the law. It must be something that meets the requirements of a 'trade secret' and has been obtained through a breach of confidence in order to entitle the injured party to damages and/or injunction."

338 S.W.2d at 766.

We think, however, that the exclusive rule which defendants have extracted from this statement is unwarranted. In the first place, in *Furr's* the court specifically found that there was no trade secret involved because the entire advertising scheme claimed to be the trade secret had been completely divulged to the public. Secondly, the court found that the plaintiff in the course of selling the scheme to the defendant had voluntarily divulged the entire scheme. Thus the court was dealing only with a possible breach of confidence concerning a properly discovered secret; there was never a question of any impropriety in the discovery or any other improper conduct on the part of the defendant. The court merely held that under those circumstances the defendant had not acted improperly if no breach of confidence occurred. We do not read *Furr's* as limiting the trade secret protection to a breach of confidential relationship when the facts of the case do raise the issue of some other wrongful conduct on the part of one discovering the trade secrets of another. If breach of confidence were meant to encompass the entire panoply of commercial improprieties, subsection (a) of the Restatement would be either surplusage or persiflage, an interpretation abhorrent to the traditional precision of the Restatement. We therefore find meaning in subsection (a) and think that the Texas Supreme Court clearly indicated by its adoption that there is a cause of action for the discovery of a trade secret by any "improper means."

The question remaining, therefore, is whether aerial photography of plant construction is an improper means of obtaining another's trade secret. We conclude that it is and that the Texas courts would so hold. The Supreme Court of that state has declared that "the undoubted tendency of the law has been to recognize and enforce higher standards of commercial morality in the business world." *Hyde Corporation v. Huffines, supra* 314 S.W.2d at 773. That court has quoted with approval articles indicating that the proper means of gaining possession of a competitor's secret process is "through inspection and analysis" of the product in order to create a duplicate. *K & G Tool & Service Co. v. G & G Fishing Tool Service*, 1958, 314 S.W.2d 782, 783, 788. Later another Texas court explained:

> "The means by which the discovery is made may be obvious, and the experimentation leading from known factors to presently unknown results may be simple and lying in the public domain. But these facts do not destroy the value of the discovery and will not advantage a competitor who by unfair means obtains the knowledge without paying the price expended by the discoverer."

Brown v. Fowler, Tex.Civ.App.1958, 316 S.W.2d 111, 114.

We think, therefore, that the Texas rule is clear. One may use his competitor's secret process if he discovers the process by reverse engineering applied to the finished product; one may use a competitor's process if he discovers it by his own independent research; but one may not avoid these labors by taking the process from the discoverer without his permission at a time when he is taking reasonable precautions to maintain its secrecy. To obtain knowledge of a process without spending the time and money to discover it independently is improper unless the holder voluntarily discloses it or fails to take reasonable precautions to ensure its secrecy.

In the instant case the Christophers deliberately flew over the Du Pont plant to get pictures of a process which Du Pont had attempted to keep secret. The Christophers delivered their pictures to a third party who was certainly aware of the means by which they had been acquired and who may be planning to use the information contained therein to manufacture methanol by the Du Pont process. The third party has a right to use this process only if he obtains this knowledge through his own research efforts, but thus far all information indicates that the third party has gained this knowledge solely by taking it from Du Pont at a time when Du Pont was making reasonable efforts to preserve its secrecy. In such a situation Du Pont has a valid cause of action to prohibit the Christophers from improperly discovering its trade secret and to prohibit the undisclosed third party from using the improperly obtained information.

We note that this view is in perfect accord with the position taken by the authors of the Restatement. In commenting on improper means of discovery the savants of the Restatement said:

> "f. Improper means of discovery. The discovery of another's trade secret by improper means subjects the actor to liability independently of the harm to the interest in the secret. Thus, if one uses physical force to take a secret formula from another's pocket, or breaks into another's office to steal the formula, his conduct is wrongful and subjects him to liability apart from the rule stated in this Section. Such conduct is also an improper means of procuring the secret under this rule. But means may be improper under this rule even though they do not cause any other harm than that to the interest in the trade secret. Examples of such means are fraudulent misrepresentations to induce disclosure, tapping of telephone wires, eavesdropping or other espionage. A complete catalogue of improper means is not possible. In general they are means which fall below the generally accepted standards of commercial morality and reasonable conduct."

RESTATEMENT OF TORTS § 757, comment f at 10 (1939).

In taking this position we realize that industrial espionage of the sort here perpetrated has become a popular sport in some segments of our industrial community. However, our devotion to free wheeling industrial competition must not force us into accepting the law of the jungle as the standard of morality expected in our commercial relations. Our tolerance of the espionage game must cease when the protections required to prevent another's spying cost so much that the spirit of inventiveness is dampened. Commercial privacy must be protected from espionage which could not have been reasonably anticipated or prevented. We do not mean to imply, however, that everything not in plain view is within the protected vale, nor that all information obtained through every extra optical extension is forbidden. Indeed, for our industrial competition to remain healthy there must be breathing room for observing a competing industrialist. A competitor can and must shop his competition for pricing and examine his products for quality, components, and methods of manufacture. Perhaps ordinary fences and roofs must be built to shut out incursive eyes, but we need not require the discoverer of a trade secret to guard against the unanticipated, the undetectable, or the unpreventable methods of espionage now available.

In the instant case Du Pont was in the midst of constructing a plant. Although after construction the finished plant would have protected much of the process from view, during the period of construction the trade secret was exposed to view from the air. To require Du Pont to put a roof over the unfinished plant to guard its secret would impose an enormous expense to prevent nothing more than a school boy's trick. We introduce here no new or radical ethic since our ethos has never given moral sanction to piracy. The market place must not deviate far from our mores. We should not require a person or corporation to take unreasonable precautions to prevent another from doing that which he ought not do in the first place. Reasonable precautions against predatory eyes we may require, but an impenetrable fortress is an unreasonable requirement, and we are not disposed to burden industrial inventors with such a duty in order to protect the fruits of their efforts. "Improper" will always be a word of many nuances, determined by time, place, and circumstances. We therefore need not proclaim a catalogue of commercial improprieties. Clearly, however, one of its commandments does say "thou shall not appropriate a trade secret through deviousness under circumstances in which countervailing defenses are not reasonably available."

Having concluded that aerial photography, from whatever altitude, is an improper method of discovering the trade secrets exposed during construction of the Du Pont plant, we need not worry about whether the flight pattern chosen by the Christophers violated any federal aviation regulations. Regardless of whether the flight was legal or illegal in that sense, the espionage was an improper means of discovering Du Pont's trade secret.

The decision of the trial court is affirmed and the case remanded to that court for proceedings on the merits.

Notes

1. Remedies. An adjudicated trade secret misappropriator may be enjoined and found liable for damages. The modern rule is that injunctions are appropriate only for the period of time that the subject matter of the trade secret would have remained unavailable to the defendant but for the misappropriation. This principle offers a compromise between two more extreme positions established in the case law. Some courts have followed the holding in *Shellmar Products Co. v. Allen–Qualley Co.*, 87 F.2d 104, 32 U.S.P.Q. 24 (7th Cir.1937), and concluded that permanent injunctions were an appropriate remedy for trade secret misappropriation on the ground that trade secrets have no set duration. Other opinions found more favor in

Judge Learned Hand's opinion in *Conmar Products Corp. v. Universal Slide Fastener Co.*, 172 F.2d 150, 80 U.S.P.Q. 108 (2d Cir. 1949), to the effect that once a trade secret entered into the public domain, the plaintiff could obtain no injunctive relief whatsoever.

Each of these extreme positions is now in disfavor. Contemporary courts have reasoned that the draconian *Shellmar* rule is punitive in character and undermines the public interest in legitimate competition. On the other hand, the *Conmar* rule leads to hard results in cases where the defendant engaged in egregious conduct, particularly where he exposed the trade secret to the public himself. The compromise position of the Uniform Trade Secrets Act states that "an injunction shall be terminated when the trade secret has ceased to exist, but the injunction may be continued for an additional reasonable period of time in order to eliminate commercial advantage that otherwise would be derived from the misappropriation." § 2(a), 14 U.L.A. 438 (1990).

As a result, successful plaintiffs in trade secret proceedings may obtain injunctions limited to the lead time advantage inappropriately gained by the misappropriator. In determining the length of this "head start," courts will weigh evidence as to the amount of time a person of ordinary skill would have required to discover independently or reverse engineer the subject matter of the trade secret. If the misappropriator can demonstrate that the trade secret holder's competitors have legitimately acquired the protected knowledge, then the court will likely decline to award an injunction at all.

Courts have demonstrated flexibility in fashioning monetary remedies for trade secret misappropriation. They will typically award an amount equal to either the loss suffered by the trade secret holder, or the gain realized by misappropriator, whichever is greater. Monetary damages are ordinarily limited to the time that the misappropriated information would not have been available otherwise to the defendant. *See, e.g., Engelhard Industries, Inc. v. Research Instrumental Corp.*, 324 F.2d 347 (9th Cir.1963).

2. Trade Secrets and Patents. Trade secrets and patents coexist in what can be described as an uneasy relationship. A principal purpose of the patent law is the dissemination of knowledge. This goal is realized through the publication of patent instruments that fully disclose the patented invention such that skilled artisans could practice it without undue experimentation. 35 U.S.C. § 112. A law of trade secrets that encourages the withholding of patentable inventions appears fundamentally at odds with this fundamental precept.

This tension results in a patent law that does not favor trade secret holders. One patent law principle that deleteriously impacts trade secret holders is that a later, independent inventor may patent the subject matter of an earlier inventor's trade secret. A first inventor may quickly transition from the status of a trade secret holder to an adjudicated patent infringer. *See* Albert C. Smith & Jared A. Stosberg, *Beware! Trade Secret Software May Be Patented By a Later Inventor*, 7 COMPUTER LAWYER no. 11 at 15 (Nov. 1990). The First Inventor Defense Act of 1999 did soften this traditional principle somewhat, allowing earlier inventors an infringement defense against subsequent patentees of methods of doing business. *See* 35 U.S.C. § 273.

Trade secrets perform a valuable role in the U.S. intellectual property scheme, however. Although patent law is an increasingly capacious regime, its subject matter does not extend to the full array of valuable information that may be the subject of a trade secret. Patent rights too must be affirmatively sought, and their acquisition usually entails significant costs and delays. Some inventors are not well schooled in the rather rarefied patent law regime and may wait overly long before filing a patent application. Even sophisticated enterprises may not recognize the value of an invention until they too have performed acts that defeat its patentability. The trade secret law fills these gaps by providing a modicum of protection for those who take prudent measures to protect valuable information.

Inventors who do not wish to dedicate their technologies to the public domain must choose between maintaining the technology as a trade secret or pursuing patent protection. A number of factors inform this decision. Whether the inventor can keep the technology secret is the most obvious. Many mechanical inventions betray their design upon inspection, while the composition of a chemical compound may be much easier to conceal. The costs associated with acquiring and maintaining patents are another element. A U.S. patent provides rights only within the United States, but discloses its subject matter for anyone in the world to see. Inventors should therefore also consider the expenses of obtaining a patent in each jurisdiction in which he does or wishes to do business.

The product cycle associated with the invention is also of importance. Products with a very short lifespan may be unmarketable by the time a patent issues. Inventors should also consider whether the industry in which they act is patent-intensive. If industry actors tend to invest heavily in maintaining their patent portfolios, then the inventor may well wish to patent for defense purposes or to have a bargaining chip available if he is accused of infringement himself. Legislative enactment of the First Inventor Defense Act of 1999 introduced another element into this calculation. If the invention concerns a "method of doing business" within the meaning of the Act, then the inventor may gain an infringement defense effective against the patents of others the claim that method. 35 U.S.C. § 273.

The publication of a patent application or issuance of a patent will destroy trade secret status for the subject matter that it properly discloses. Nothing prevents a patentee from maintaining an invention as a trade secret until such time, however. This strategy requires the applicant to preserve secrecy until the first of two events: (1) the publication of the application eighteen months following its filing date; or (2) when the PTO issues the patent, for those applications exempted from the publication requirement.

3. Federal Preemption. The tensions between the patent and trade secret laws have sometimes erupted into arguments that the patent statute preempts state trade secret laws. In addition to asserting that trade secrecy discourages disclosure of new inventions, commentators have also observed that the patent law reflects the policy that only new and nonobvious inventions merit proprietary patent rights. Although the requirement that a trade secret not be public knowledge has been equated to the patent law's novelty requirement, the trade secret laws do not demand that the secret subject matter be nonobvious. *See* Gale R. Peterson, *Trade Secrets in an Information Age*, 32 HOUSTON L. REV. 385 (1995).

Despite these apparent conflicts, the courts have ruled that trade secret protection may coexist alongside the patent and other intellectual property laws. In *Kewanee Oil Co. v. Bicron Corp.*, 416 U.S. 470 (1974), the Supreme Court observed that trade secret laws also serve a principal purpose of the patent laws, the promotion of innovation. The Court also considered the patent law a far more attractive option for inventors of patentable subject matter and reasoned that most inventors would opt for the patent system. The Court also noted that, as an historical matter, the two bodies of law had been in place since the earliest days of the Republic.

Trade Secrets Exercise

You work as a patent attorney in a major metropolitan area. One day, a Mr. Boulanger comes to your office seeking advice. You recognize him as the proprietor of a local bakery shop.

"I need your assistance," Mr. Boulanger says, with obvious concern in his voice. "About two years ago, I developed a formula for low-fat chocolate chip cookies. My products have a homemade taste—that is, they have a crunchy exterior, but a chewy center—but only a fraction of the calories of traditional chocolate chip cookies. I'm selling more cookies than ever before and I want to maintain our unique taste. My trouble is with my former employee, Ms. Cynthia Sisyphus. She left my company a few months ago to start her own bakery shop. Now she has begun to market her own cookies under the trade name 'Infamous Sisyphus.' The cookies taste just like mine! I'm certain that she stole my secret recipe!"

"Once I tasted one of Sisyphus' cookies, I immediately called her." Mr. Boulanger explains. "She claimed that my recipe was simply part of the general knowledge and skills associated with her employment. Her precise words were: 'I'm a baker. My entire set of professional skills consists of knowing various recipes. The only way you would get me to forget how to make chocolate chip cookies would be to perform brain surgery.' "

You ask Mr. Boulanger about the conditions surrounding his cookie recipe. He explains, "Well, I've written the recipe on an index card in my office. The card has the legend TOP SECRET written at the top. I store the index card in my desk, which is ordinarily locked. However, I have other files in my desk, so my accountant, bakers, and other employees need access. Right now I guess about five of my top people have a key to that desk. We're a small company, and I'm usually too busy tinkering with the ovens to stand guard by my desk."

Next, you ask Mr. Boulanger about the terms of the employment contract between his company and Ms. Sisyphus. He responds, "Well, we didn't have a formal contract. I think you lawyers call this arrangement 'employment-at-will' or something like that. But everyone in the bakery business should know that our recipes are confidential. That's how we distinguish ourselves from our competitors. No honest baker would walk out and take a proprietary recipe with him!"

Finally, you inquire as to the details of Mr. Boulanger's secret recipe. After swearing you to secrecy, Mr. Boulanger details a complex set of ingredients and cooking instructions. In essence, he substitutes fructose syrup, polydextrose, guar gum and various bulking agents for a portion of the more traditional cookie ingredients such as shortening and sugar. These ingredients are then mixed in a precise order and then baked at steadily increasing temperatures until the cookies are complete. "In this way, I can maintain a wonderful taste yet cut the calories and fat by nearly 20%."

"We may seem like a small company now," Mr. Boulanger continues, "but I've got big plans for us. We want to establish retail outlets to sell our cookies domestically and abroad. My market analyst has predicted that our chocolate chip cookies could generate sales of $15 million annually. We could base our entire business on it! Sales of our cookies could continue for ten years or more! Plus . . . nobody could ever guess the secret ingredients that make my cookies special! I'm wondering—is this the kind of thing I can get a patent on? And if so, should I try to get a patent on my recipe or keep it as my own secret?"

"But the most important point is my problem with Ms. Sisyphus," Mr. Boulanger concludes. "Will I be able to stop losing a lot of dough to her bakery . . . or is that just the way the cookie crumbles?"

How would you advise Mr. Boulanger concerning his chocolate chip cookie recipe?

Chapter Two

PATENT ELIGIBILITY

This chapter focuses upon the subject matter categories eligible for patent protection if the other statutory requirements are met. "Patent eligibility" describes the subject matter open to patenting, as opposed to the word "patentability." Patentability means that an invention both falls within a subject matter category eligible for an exclusive right and satisfies the statutory requisites of novelty, nonobviousness, utility, and adequate disclosure.

In large part, the subject matter categories eligible for an exclusive right are well settled. The focus of patent law is applied technology, referred to in the Constitution as "the useful arts." *Diamond v. Chakrabarty*, 447 U.S. 303, 206 U.S.P.Q. 193 (1980). An invention qualifies for patent protection only if it achieves a tangible, practical advance in the useful arts. Traditionally, discoveries in three areas do not qualify for an exclusive right—natural laws, phenomena of nature, and abstract principles. *Diamond v. Diehr,* 450 U.S. 175 (1980). Thus, speculative or abstract advances, such as new mathematical theories or inchoate ideas, do not fit within the general category of useful arts. *Fuller v. Yentzer,* 94 U.S. 288 (1877); *Burr v. Duryee,* 68 U.S. 531 (1864).

Section 101 of the Patent Act defines the subject matter that may be patented. According to the statute, a person who "invents or discovers any new and useful process, machine, manufacture, or any composition of matter, or any new and useful improvement thereof, may obtain a patent therefore, subject to the conditions and requirements of this title." An invention that falls within one of the four statutory categories—processes, machines, manufactures, and compositions of matter—is eligible to receive a so-called "utility patent" if the other requirements of the Patent Act are met.

An invention is therefore patent eligible under title 35 if it is a "process," defined as a series of acts which are performed upon subject matter to produce a given result, *Cochrane v. Deener,* 94 U.S. 780 (1877); a "machine," defined as any apparatus, *Nestle-Le Mur Co. v. Eugene, Ltd.,* 55 F.2d 854 (6th Cir.1932); a "composition of matter," defined as synthesized chemical compounds and composite articles, *Diamond v. Chakrabarty*, 447 U.S. 303, 206 U.S.P.Q. 193 (1980); or an article of "manufacture," defined in broad terms to capture almost any other useful technology, *id*. The article of manufacture category is of particular significance as the sole subject matter category in the original 1624 Statute of Monopolies. Its broad sweep continues to guide common law reasoning on the subject of patent eligibility. These definitions are not exclusive; an invention may fall into multiple categories. *Bandag, Inc. v. Al Bolser's Tire Stores, Inc.*, 750 F.2d 903, 223 U.S.P.Q. 982 (Fed.Cir. 1984).

The four categories set forth in section 101 refine the term "useful arts," the constitutional expression of the subject matter appropriate for patenting. Historically, the useful arts were contrasted with the liberal and fine arts. The patent system was perceived to be confined to inventions in the field of applied technology. Patentable inventions that employed the natural sciences to manipulate physical forces fell within the useful arts. Innovations that relied upon such things as the social sciences, commercial strategy or personal skill were often believed to be ineligible for patent protection.

In recent years, however, the patent system has demonstrated an increasing permissiveness towards patent eligible subject matter. In particular, the Court of Appeals for the Federal Circuit has reconsidered earlier case law concerning patent eligibility, ranging from computer software, to printed matter, to methods of doing business. In response to this trend, the Patent and Trademark Office has issued patents involving inventions from a broad range of disciplines, including a golf putt, teaching methods and techniques of psychological analysis.

The present state of affairs suggests that few, if any restrictions restrict the range of patentable subject matter. Once seemingly limited to natural scientists and engineers, the patent system now appears poised to embrace the broadest reaches of human experience. It is hardly an exaggeration to say that under current law, if you can name it, you can claim it. Much of this chapter will appear of historical significance, with the removal of earlier limitations upon patent eligibility by an increasingly lenient judiciary becoming a familiar pattern. Still, patent eligibility continually proves itself to be an unsettled field. To understand our current state of affairs it is helpful to know how we got here.

Before proceeding further, the reader should note that § 101 twice employs the phrase "new and useful." Despite this wording, the courts have traditionally distinguished the requirement of patent eligibility from those of novelty and utility. Thus, the inquiry of whether a particular invention is of the kind the patent laws were intended to protect has traditionally been considered a different matter from whether the invention possess novelty, and is useful, within the meaning of the patent law. Utility and novelty are addressed in Chapters 3–6 of this casebook.

It is also worth noting from the outset some important concepts from comparative and international law. In contrast to the U.S. statute, the European Patent Convention does not expressly state which sorts of inventions are patent-eligible. The Convention instead defines patent-eligibility in the negative, excluding the following categories of inventions in Article 56: (a) discoveries, scientific theories and mathematical methods; (b) aesthetic creations; (c) schemes, rules and methods for performing mental acts, playing games or doing business, and programs for computers; and (d) presentations of information. *See* Gert Kolle, *The Patentable Invention in the European Patent Convention*, 5 INT'L REV. INDUS. PROP. & COPYRIGHT L. 140 (1974). As will be seen, United States case law includes analogies to some of the excluded categories in Europe, but in general presents a more liberal approach.

A significant international instrument, the TRIPS Agreement, has further prompted reconsideration of patent eligibility standards. Article 27 of that agreement defines patentable subject matter as follows:

     1.   Subject to the provisions of paragraphs 2 and 3, patents shall be available for any inventions, whether products or processes, in all fields of technology, provided that they are new, involve an inventive step and are capable of industrial application. Subject to paragraph 4 of Article 65, paragraph 8 of Article 70 and paragraph 3 of this Article, patents shall be available and patent rights enjoyable without discrimination as to the place of invention, the field of technology and whether products are imported or locally produced.

     2.   Members may exclude from patentability inventions, the prevention within their territory of the commercial exploitation of which is necessary to protect ordre public or morality, including to protect human, animal or plant life or health or to avoid serious prejudice to the environment, provided that such exclusion is not made merely because the exploitation is prohibited by their law.

In paragraph 3, Article 27 of the TRIPS Agreement further provides that members may also exclude from patentability:

     (a) diagnostic, therapeutic and surgical methods for the treatment of humans or animals;

     (b) plants and animals other than micro-organisms, and essentially biological processes for the production of plants or animals other than non-biological and microbiological processes. However, Members shall provide for the protection of plant varieties either by patents or by an effective sui generis system or by any combination thereof. The provisions of this subparagraph shall be reviewed four years after the date of entry into force of the WTO Agreement.

The pledge that each WTO member state agreed to allow patents to issue on inventions "in all fields of technology" stands as among the most

1. "For the purposes of this Article, the terms 'inventive step' and 'capable of industrial application' may be deemed by a Member to be synonymous with the terms 'non-obvious' and 'useful' respectively."

prominent accomplishments of the TRIPS Agreement. Its principal effect was to require the amendment of numerous foreign patent laws that declared pharmaceuticals ineligible for patenting. As the deadline for full implementation Article 27 nears for the developing world, both the practical achievability and justice of the TRIPS Agreement remain controversial subjects in the international community.

§ 2.1. PROCESSES

Three of the categories of patent-eligible subject matter set forth in 35 U.S.C.A. § 101 refer to physical artifacts themselves: machines, compositions of matter and articles of manufacture. In themselves, these categories have presented scant difficulties for courts, likely due to their relatively discrete and tangible nature. The fourth possibility, "process," has proven decidedly more difficult. The Patent Act itself is not of considerable assistance in clarifying this term, as it circularly defines process to mean "process, art or method, and includes a new use of a known process, machine, manufacture, composition of matter, or method." 35 U.S.C.A. § 100(b). Following the earlier statutory use of "art," however, the term "process" extends from case law interpreting the British Statute of Monopolies. Although that statute on its face allowed patents only for "new manufactures," the courts soon extended the patent law to embrace technique as well. The primary modern test of the bounds of the broad term process occurred in relation to computer software.

Computer software, in general terms, is a set of machine-readable instructions capable of performing a particular task. The advent of computer technology strained the Patent Office and the courts to compare patent protection of software with alternatives, such as copyright law. Thus, opponents of eligibility for software argued that computer-related inventions have more in common with abstract principles and mental steps, which do not receive patent protection. On the other hand, computer engineers may design electronic circuits based on theoretical mathematical models, but those computer inventions nonetheless function as machines. Any consideration of the matter must begin, however, with the Supreme Court's initial encounter with this then-emerging technology in *Gottschalk v. Benson*.

GOTTSCHALK v. BENSON

United States Supreme Court, 1972.
409 U.S. 63, 175 U.S.P.Q. 673.

MR. JUSTICE DOUGLAS delivered the opinion of the Court.

Respondents filed in the Patent Office an application for an invention which was described as being related "to the processing of data by program and more particularly to the programmed conversion of numerical information" in general-purpose digital computers. They claimed a method for converting binary-coded decimal (BCD) numerals into pure binary numerals. [The claims at issue, numbered 8 and 13, provided as follows:

8. The method of converting signals from binary coded decimal form into binary which comprises the steps of

(1) storing the binary coded decimal signals in a reentrant shift register,

(2) shifting the signals to the right by at least three places, until there is a binary "1" in the second position of said register,

(3) masking out said binary "1" in said second position of said register,

(4) adding a binary "1" to the first position of said register,

(5) shifting the signals to the left by two positions,

(6) adding a "1" to said first position, and

(7) shifting the signals to the right by at least three positions in preparation for a succeeding binary "1" in the second position of said register.'

13. A data processing method for converting binary coded decimal number representations into binary number representations comprising the steps of

(1) testing each binary digit position "1," beginning with the least significant binary digit position, of the most significant decimal digit representation for a binary "0" or a binary "1";

(2) if a binary "0" is detected, repeating step (1) for the next least significant binary digit position of said most significant decimal digit representation;

(3) if a binary "1" is detected, adding a binary "1" at the (I + 1)th and (I + 3)th least significant binary digit positions of the next lesser significant decimal digit representation, and repeating step (1) for the next least significant binary digit position of said most significant decimal digit representation;

(4) upon exhausting the binary digit positions of said most significant decimal digit representation, repeating steps (1) through (3) for the next lesser significant decimal digit representation as modified by the previous execution of steps (1) through (3); and

(5) repeating steps (1) through (4) until the second least significant decimal digit representation has been so processed.]

The claims were not limited to any particular art or technology, to any particular apparatus or machinery, or to any particular end use. They purported to cover any use of the claimed method in a general-purpose digital computer of any type. Claims 8 and 13 were rejected by the Patent Office but sustained by the Court of Customs and Patent Appeals, 441 F.2d 682. The case is here on a petition for a writ of certiorari.

The question is whether the method described and claimed is a "process" within the meaning of the Patent Act.

A digital computer, as distinguished from an analog computer, operates on data expressed in digits, solving a problem by doing arithmetic as a person would do it by head and hand. Some of the digits are stored as components of the computer. Others are introduced into the computer in a form which it is designed to recognize. The computer operates then upon both new and previously stored data. The general-purpose computer is designed to perform operations under many different programs.

The representation of numbers may be in the form of a time series of electrical impulses, magnetized spots on the surface of tapes, drums, or discs, charged spots on cathode-ray tube screens, the presence or absence of punched holes on paper cards, or other devices. The method or program is a sequence of coded instructions for a digital computer.

The patent sought is on a method of programming a general-purpose digital computer to convert signals from binary-coded decimal form into pure binary form. A procedure for solving a given type of mathematical problem is known as an "algorithm." The procedures set forth in the present claims are of that kind; that is to say, they are a generalized formulation for programs to solve mathematical problems of converting one form of numerical representation to another. From the generic formulation, programs may be developed as specific applications.

The decimal system uses as digits the 10 symbols 0, 1, 2, 3, 4, 5, 6, 7, 8, and 9. The value represented by any digit depends, as it does in any positional system of notation, both on its individual value and on its relative position in the numeral. Decimal numerals are written by placing digits in the appropriate positions or columns of the numerical sequence, i.e., "unit" (100), "tens" (10^1), "hundreds" (10^2), "thousands" (10^3), etc. Accordingly, the numeral 1492 signifies (1 10) (4 10^2) (9 10^1) (2 10^0).

The pure binary system of positional notation uses two symbols as digits–0 and 1, placed in a numerical sequence with values based on consecutively ascending powers of 2. In pure binary notation, what would be the tens position is the twos position; what would be hundreds position is the fours position; what would be the thousands position is the eights. Any decimal number from 0 to 10 can be represented in the binary system with four digits or positions as indicated in the following table.

Shown as the sum of powers of 2

Decimal	2^3 (8)		2^2 (4)		2^1 (2)		2^0 (1)		Pure Binary
0 =	0	+	0	+	0	+	0	=	0000
1 =	0	+	0	+	0	+	2^0	=	0001
2 =	0	+	0	+	2^1	+	0	=	0010
3 =	0	+	0	+	2^1	+	2^0	=	0011

Decimal	2^3 (8)		2^2 (4)		2^1 (2)		2^0 (1)		Pure Binary
4 =	0	+	2^2	+	0	+	0	=	0100
5 =	0	+	2^2	+	0	+	2^0	=	0101
6 =	0	+	2^2	+	2^1	+	0	=	0110
7 =	0	+	2^2	+	2^1	+	2^0	=	0111
8 =	2^3	+	0	+	0	+	0	=	1000
9 =	2^3	+	0	+	0	+	2^0	=	1001
10 =	2^3	+	0	+	2^1	+	0	=	1010

The BCD system using decimal numerals replaces the character for each component decimal digit in the decimal numeral with the corresponding four-digit binary numeral, shown in the righthand column of the table. Thus decimal 53 is represented as 0101 0011 in BCD, because decimal 5 is equal to binary 0101 and decimal 3 is equivalent to binary 0011. In pure binary notation, however, decimal 53 equals binary 110101. The conversion of BCD numerals to pure binary numerals can be done mentally through use of the foregoing table. The method sought to be patented varies the ordinary arithmetic steps a human would use by changing the order of the steps, changing the symbolism for writing the multiplier used in some steps, and by taking subtotals after each successive operation. The mathematical procedures can be carried out in existing computers long in use, no new machinery being necessary. And, as noted, they can also be performed without a computer.

The Court stated in *Mackay Co. v. Radio Corp.*, 306 U.S. 86, 94, 59 S.Ct. 427, 431, 83 L.Ed. 506 that "(w)hile a scientific truth, or the mathematical expression of it, is not patentable invention, a novel and useful structure created with the aid of knowledge of scientific truth may be." That statement followed the longstanding rule that "(a)n idea of itself is not patentable." *Rubber-Tip Pencil Co. v. Howard*, 20 Wall. (87 U.S.) 498, 507, 22 L.Ed. 410. "A principle, in the abstract, is a fundamental truth; an original cause; a motive; these cannot be patented, as no one can claim in either of them an exclusive right." *Le Roy v. Tatham*, 14 How. (55 U.S.) 156, 175, 14 L.Ed. 367. Phenomena of nature, though just discovered, mental processes, and abstract intellectual concepts are not patentable, as they are the basic tools of scientific and technological work. As we stated in *Funk Bros. Seed Co. v. Kalo Co.*, 333 U.S. 127, 130, 68 S.Ct. 440, 441, 92 L.Ed. 588, "He who discovers a hitherto unknown phenomenon of nature has no claim to a monopoly of it which the law recognizes. If there is to be invention from such a discovery, it must come from the application of the law of nature to a new and useful end." We dealt there with a "product" claim, while the present case deals with a "process" claim. But we think the same principle applies.

Here the "process" claim is so abstract and sweeping as to cover both known and unknown uses of the BCD to pure binary conversion. The end use may (1) vary from the operation of a train to verification of drivers' licenses to researching the law books for precedents and (2) be performed through any existing machinery or future-devised machinery or without any apparatus.

In *O'Reilly v. Morse*, 15 How. (56 U.S.) 62, 14 L.Ed. 601, Morse was allowed a patent for a process of using electromagnetism to produce distinguishable signs for telegraphy. *Id.*, at 111, 14 L.Ed. 601. But the Court denied the eighth claim in which Morse claimed the use of "electromagnetism, however developed for marking or printing intelligible characters, signs, or letters, at any distances." *Id.*, at 112. The Court in disallowing that claim said, "If this claim can be maintained, it matters not by what process or machinery the result is accomplished. For aught that we now know, some future inventor, in the onward march of science, may discover a mode of writing or printing at a distance by means of the electric or galvanic current, without using any part of the process or combination set forth in the plaintiff's specification. His invention may be less complicated–less liable to get out of order–less expensive in construction, and in its operation. But yet, if it is covered by this patent, the inventor could not use it, nor the public have the benefit of it, without the permission of this patentee." *Id.*, at 113, 14 L.Ed. 601.

In *The Telephone Cases*, 126 U.S. 1, 534, 8 S.Ct. 778, 782, 31 L.Ed. 863, the Court explained the Morse case as follows: "The effect of that decision was, therefore, that the use of magnetism as a motive power, without regard to the particular process with which it was connected in the patent, could not be claimed, but that its use in that connection could." Bell's invention was the use of electric current to transmit vocal or other sounds. The claim was not "for the use of a current of electricity in its natural state as it comes from the battery, but for putting a continuous current, in a closed circuit, into a certain specified condition, suited to the transmission of vocal and other sounds, and using it in that condition for that purpose." *Ibid*. The claim, in other words, was not "one for the use of electricity distinct from the particular process with which it is connected in his patent." *Id.*, at 535, 8 S.Ct., at 782. The patent was for that use of electricity "both for the magneto and variable resistance methods". *Id.*, at 538, 8 S.Ct., at 784. Bell's claim, in other words, was not one for all telephonic use of electricity.

In *Corning v. Burden*, 15 How. (56 U.S.) 252, 267–268, 14 L.Ed. 683, the Court said, "One may discover a new and useful improvement in the process of tanning, dyeing, etc., irrespective of any particular form of machinery or mechanical device." The examples, given were the "arts of tanning, dyeing, making waterproof cloth, vulcanizing India rubber, smelting ores." *Id.*, at 267, 14 L.Ed. 683. Those are instances, however, where the use of chemical substances or physical acts, such as temperature control, changes articles or materials. The chemical process or the physical acts which transform the raw material are, however, sufficiently definite to confine the patent monopoly within rather definite bounds.

Cochrane v. Deener, 94 U.S. 780, 24 L.Ed. 139, involved a process for manufacturing flour so as to improve its quality. The process first separated the superfine flour and then removed impurities from the middlings by blasts of air, reground the middlings, and then combined the product with the superfine. *Id.*, at 785, 24 L.Ed. 139. The claim was not limited to any special arrangement of machinery. *Ibid*. The Court said, "That a process may be patentable, irrespective of the particular form of the instrumentalities used, cannot be disputed. If one of the steps of a process be that a certain substance is to be reduced to a powder, it may not be at all material what instrument or machinery is used to effect that object, whether a hammer, a pestle and mortar, or a mill. Either may be pointed out; but if the patent is not confined to that particular tool or machine, the use of the others would be an infringement, the general process being the same. A process is a mode of treatment of certain materials to produce a given result. It is an act, or a series of acts, performed upon the subject-matter to be transformed and reduced to a different state or thing." *Id.*, at 787–788, 24 L.Ed. 139.

Transformation and reduction of an article "to a different state or thing" is the clue to the patentability of a process claim that does not include particular machines. So it is that a patent in the process of "manufacturing fat acids and glycerine from fatty bodies by the action of water at a high temperature and pressure" was sustained in *Tilghman v. Proctor*, 102 U.S. 707, 721, 26 L.Ed. 279. The Court said, "The chemical principle or scientific fact upon which it is founded is, that the elements of neutral fat require to be severally united with an atomic equivalent of water in order to separate from each other and become free. This chemical fact was not discovered by Tilghman. He only claims to have invented a particular mode of bringing about the desired chemical union between the fatty elements and water." *Id.*, at 729, 26 L.Ed. 279.

It is argued that a process patent must either be tied to a particular machine or apparatus or must operate to change articles or materials to a "different state or thing." We do not hold that no process patent could ever qualify if it did not meet the requirements of our prior precedents. It is said that the decision precludes a patent for any program servicing a computer. We do not so hold. It is said that we have before us a program for a digital computer but extend our holding to programs for analog computers. We have, however, made clear from the start that we deal with a program only for digital computers. It is said we freeze process patents to old technologies, leaving no room for the revelations of the new, onrushing technology. Such is not our purpose. What we come down to in a nutshell is the following.

It is conceded that one may not patent an idea. But in practical effect that would be the result if the formula for converting BCD numerals to pure binary numerals were patented in this case. The mathematical formula involved here has no substantial practical application except in connection with a digital computer, which means that if the judgment below is affirmed, the patent would wholly pre-empt the mathematical formula and in practical effect would be a patent on the algorithm itself.

It may be that the patent laws should be extended to cover these programs, a policy matter to which we are not competent to speak. The

President's Commission on the Patent System[2] rejected the proposal that these programs be patentable:

If these programs are to be patentable, considerable problems are raised which only committees of Congress can manage, for broad powers of investigation are needed, including hearings which canvass the wide variety of views which those operating in this field entertain. The technological problems tendered in the many briefs before us indicate to us that considered action by the Congress is needed.

Reversed.

MR. JUSTICE STEWART, MR. JUSTICE BLACKMUN, and MR. JUSTICE POWELL took no part in the consideration or decision of this case.

Notes

1. Software Patent Policy. Consider the distinction between claims 8 and 13 in *Benson*. The former might be based upon a piece of hardware a technician might construct in an electronics circuit laboratory. But the latter claim addresses something a mathematician can do upon a piece of paper; in fact, with a pencil you can perform conduct which falls within the scope of the claim in the margin of this book at this very moment. (You may wish to do so in order to obtain a better understanding of the claimed invention in *Benson*.) In essentially equating the two sorts of claims, what policy goals does the *Benson* court fulfill? To what extent can the "algorithm" here be likened to a law of nature always "known," but never before articulated? Had the Court decided differently, would the applicant truly have gained exclusive rights in a fundamental mathematical principle, offensive to public policy?

2. The Nutshell. The famous "nutshell" of the *Benson* opinion reasons that the claimed invention was not patent eligible because its only practical application was towards digital computer technology. The nutshell is the paragraph near the end of the majority opinion that begins "It is conceded. . . ." Today that observation strikes a humorous chord. With much of the world economy controlled by digital computers, it seems almost nonsensical to suggest that the invention has no substantial application except in connection with a digital computer. Does some of the Court's problem flow from its inability to project the future usefulness of computer technology? Despite this historical anomaly, would the Court have been

---

2. "To Promote the Progress of ... Useful Arts," Report of the President's Commission on the Patent System (1966).

"Uncertainty now exists as to whether the statute permits a valid patent to be granted on programs. Direct attempts to patent programs have been rejected on the ground of nonstatutory subject matter. Indirect attempts to obtain patents and avoid the rejection, by drafting claims as a process, or a machine or components thereof programmed in a given manner, rather than as a program itself, have confused the issue further and should not be permitted. "The Patent Office now cannot examine

applications for programs because of a lack of a classification technique and the requisite search files. Even if these were available, reliable searches would not be feasible or economic because of the tremendous volume of prior art being generated. Without this search, the patenting of programs would be tantamount to mere registration and the presumption of validity would be all but nonexistent. 'It is noted that the creation of programs has undergone substantial and satisfactory growth in the absence of patent protection and that copyright protection for programs is presently available.'"

more accepting of the invention if it could be applied towards a number of different disciplines? Would the Court have been more accepting if the applicant had specifically identified the invention's end uses in digital computer technology (does it facilitate storage or speed of use)? Consider also the example of a new, high-speed, low-cost electronic circuit designed to be, and only useful as, a computer component. Is such a device patent-eligible under the language of the "nutshell"?

3. Software Patents under *Benson*. The Court indicates that its decision does not preclude the possibility of software patents. What sorts of computer programs could be eligible for patentability under the *Benson* approach?

4. The Mental Steps Doctrine. In his reasoning, Justice Douglas excludes from eligibility for patent protection "[p]henomena of nature, though just discovered, *mental processes*, and abstract intellectual concepts." (Emphasis added). At another point, the Justice describes the invention as "solving a problem by doing arithmetic as a person would do it *by head and hand*." (Emphasis added). These allusions to mental process referred to a doctrine developed by the CCPA in earlier software invention cases. *See, e.g., In re Abrams*, 188 F.2d 165, 89 U.S.P.Q. 266 (CCPA 1951) (method of detecting petroleum by computing rates of pressure change not patent eligible); *In re Shao Wen Yuan*, 188 F.2d 377, 89 U.S.P.Q. 324 (CCPA 1951) (mathematical processes to determine optimal airfoil not patent eligible). Under the CCPA "mental steps" doctrine, "[I]t [was] self-evident that thought is not patentable." *Abrams*, 188 F.2d at 168.

The CCPA later repudiated the "mental steps" doctrine: "[C]haracterizing steps of method claims as 'mental,' 'purely mental,' 'physical,' or 'purely physical' gave little certainty to the law." *In re Musgrave*, 431 F.2d 882, 891, 167 U.S.P.Q. 280, 287 (CCPA 1970). Nonetheless the Supreme Court seemed to resurrect the doctrine in *Benson*. Is there any reasoned basis for distinguishing between "mental" and "physical" steps in a process? Is there any statutory basis? Does implementing a claim inevitably involve some mental processing? How much is too much? These questions perhaps suggest why the Supreme Court's invocation of the mental steps doctrine has drifted into obscurity. *See Diamond v. Diehr*, 450 U.S. 175, 195–96, nn. 6–9 (Stevens, J., dissenting) (citing in dissent "mental step" cases). Nonetheless the vestiges of the doctrine still echoed in the *Freeman-Walter–Abele* test with its emphasis on "physical" steps.

5. Basic Tools. The *Benson* Court suggested that patents should not be awarded to inventions comprising the "basic tools of scientific and technological work." How legitimate is this rationale? Should patents be refused to inventors of otherwise patentable microscopes, voltmeters, centrifuges and other sorts of everyday equipment in the laboratories of contemporary scientists, engineers and technicians?

6. Parker v. Flook. Following *Benson*, the Court decided *Parker v. Flook*, 437 U.S. 584 (1978). Here, the inventor claimed a "method for updating alarm limits" specifically limited to the process of catalytic conversion. If any of several operating conditions such as temperature or pressure exceeded a certain "alarm limit," as maintained by the invention, a signal would indicate the presence of inefficient or dangerous conditions. The claimed process consisted of three steps: measuring the current operating conditions; redetermining the proper value of the alarm limit through use of a mathematical calculation; and adjusting the alarm limit to the updated value.

Following rejection of the application by the Patent Office, the Court of Customs and Patent Appeals reversed. After granting certiorari, the Court again reversed. Writing for the majority, Justice Stevens provided what proved to be a short-lived test for considering patent eligibility:

> The process itself, not merely the mathematical algorithm, must be new and useful. Indeed the novelty of the mathematical algorithm is not a determining factor at all. Whether the algorithm was in fact known or unknown at the time of the claimed invention, as one of the "basic tools of scientific and technological work," see *Gottschalk v. Benson*, 409 U.S. at 67, it is treated as though it were a familiar part of the prior art.

Id. at 592–91. Following this approach, the Court concluded that Flook's "process is unpatentable under § 101, not because it contains a mathematical algorithm as one component, but because once that algorithm is assumed to be within the prior art, the application, considered as a whole, contains no patentable invention." *Id.* at 594. It was not enough here that the invention was limited to the specific physical process of catalytic conversion and that the adjustment of the alarm limit constituted "post-solution activity." The Court considered the application to be of an abstract nature and wholly focused upon the calculation of alarm limit values, "comparable to a claim that the formula 2Br can be usefully applied in determining the circumference of a wheel." *Id.* at 595.

Justice Stewart filed a dissenting opinion, characterizing the issue before the Court as "whether a claimed process loses its status of subject-matter patentability simply because *one step* in the process would not be patentable subject matter if considered in isolation." *Id.* at 599 (emphasis in original). The majority opinion was accused of applying the criteria of novelty and nonobviousness towards the eligibility determination.

Three years later, however, the Court would express a dramatically different view on patent-eligible subject matter in a 5–4 decision, its last relating to software.

7. Abstractness? In *Benson*, Justice Douglas stated at one point:

> Here the "process" claim is so abstract and sweeping as to cover both known and unknown uses of the BCD to pure binary conversion.

This allusion to the classic non-statutory, and thus ineligible, category of abstract principles becomes a key to limiting *Benson* when the Supreme Court changed its direction.

DIAMOND v. DIEHR

United States Supreme Court, 1981.
450 U.S. 175, 209 U.S.P.Q. 1.

James R. Diehr II and Theodore A. Lutton claimed a method of operating molding presses during the production of rubber articles. The inventors asserted that their method ensured that articles remained within the presses for the proper amount of time. Claim 1 of their application provided:

A *method of operating a rubber-molding press for precision molded compounds with the aid of a digital computer, comprising:*

"providing said computer with a data base for said press including at least,

"natural logarithm conversion data (ln),

"the activation energy constant (c) unique to each batch of said compound being molded, and

"a constant (x) dependent upon the geometry of the particular mold of the press,

"initiating an interval timer in said computer upon the closure of the press for monitoring the elapsed time of said closure,

"constantly determining the temperature (Z) of the mold at a location closely adjacent to the mold cavity in the press during molding,

"constantly providing the computer with the temperature (Z),

"repetitively calculating in the computer, at frequent intervals during each cure, the Arrhenius equation for reaction time during the cure, which is 'ln v = CZ + x' where v is the total required cure time,

"repetitively comparing in the computer at said frequent intervals during the cure each said calculation of the total required cure time calculated with the Arrhenius equation and said elapsed time, and

"opening the press automatically when a said comparison indicates equivalence."

The patent examiner rejected the respondents' claims as being drawn to nonstatutory subject matter under 35 U.S.C. § 101. Citing Benson, *the examiner considered that the steps of the claimed process implemented in computer software comprised nonstatutory subject matter. The remaining steps–installing rubber in the press and the subsequent closing of the press–were "conventional and necessary to the process and cannot be the basis of patentability." The examiner concluded that the inventors merely claimed a computer program useful towards operating a rubber-molding press.*

The Patent and Trademark Office Board of Appeals affirmed the decision of the examiner, but the Court of Customs and Patent Appeals reversed. The CCPA concluded that the claims were not directed to a mathematical algorithm, but rather to an improved process for molding rubber articles. The Commissioner then sought review of the issue before the United States Supreme Court.

JUSTICE REHNQUIST delivered the opinion of the Court.

We granted certiorari to determine whether a process for curing synthetic rubber which includes in several of its steps the use of a mathematical formula and a programmed digital computer is patentable subject matter under 35 U.S.C. § 101.

I

The patent application at issue was filed by the respondents on August 6, 1975. The claimed invention is a process for molding raw, uncured synthetic rubber into cured precision products. The process uses a mold for precisely shaping the uncured material under heat and pressure and then curing the synthetic rubber in the mold so that the product will retain its shape and be functionally operative after the molding is completed.[3]

Respondents claim that their process ensures the production of molded articles which are properly cured. Achieving the perfect cure depends upon several factors including the thickness of the article to be molded, the temperature of the molding process, and the amount of time that the article is allowed to remain in the press. It is possible using well-known time, temperature, and cure relationships to calculate by means of the Arrhenius equation[4] when to open the press and remove the cured product. Nonetheless, according to the respondents, the industry has not been able to obtain uniformly accurate cures because the temperature of the molding press could not be precisely measured, thus making it difficult to do the necessary computations to determine cure time. Because the temperature inside the press has heretofore been viewed as an uncontrollable variable, the conventional industry practice has been to calculate the cure time as the shortest time in which all parts of the product will definitely be cured, assuming a reasonable amount of mold-opening time during loading and unloading. But the shortcoming of this practice is that operating with an uncontrollable variable inevitably led in some instances to overestimating the mold-opening time and overcuring the rubber, and in other instances to underestimating that time and undercuring the product.

Respondents characterize their contribution to the art to reside in the process of constantly measuring the actual temperature inside the mold. These temperature measurements are then automatically fed into a computer which repeatedly recalculates the cure time by use of the Arrhenius equation. When the recalculated time equals the actual time that has elapsed since the press was closed, the computer signals a device to open the press. According to the respondents, the continuous measuring of the temperature inside the mold cavity, the feeding of this information to a digital computer which constantly recalculates the cure

---

3. A "cure" is obtained by mixing curing agents into the uncured polymer in advance of molding and then applying heat over a period of time. If the synthetic rubber is cured for the right length of time at the right temperature, it becomes a usable product.

4. The equation is named after its discoverer Svante Arrhenius and has long been used to calculate the cure time in rubber-molding presses. The equation can be expressed as follows:

$$\ln v = CZ + x$$

wherein ln v is the natural logarithm of v, the total required cure time; C is the activation constant, a unique figure for each batch of each compound being molded, determined in accordance with rheometer measurements of each batch; Z is the temperature in the mold; and x is a constant dependent on the geometry of the particular mold in the press. A rheometer is an instrument to measure flow of viscous substances.

time, and the signaling by the computer to open the press, are all new in the art.

II

Last Term in *Diamond v. Chakrabarty*, 447 U.S. 303, 100 S.Ct. 2204, 65 L.Ed.2d 144 (1980), this Court discussed the historical purposes of the patent laws and in particular 35 U.S.C. § 101. As in Chakrabarty, we must here construe 35 U.S.C. § 101 which provides: "Whoever, invents or discovers any new and useful process, machine manufacture, or composition of matter, or any new and useful improvement thereof, may obtain a patent therefor, subject to the conditions and requirements of this title."

In cases of statutory construction, we begin with the language of the statute. Unless otherwise defined, "words will be interpreted as taking their ordinary, contemporary, common meaning," and, in dealing with the patent laws, we have more than once cautioned that "courts 'should not read into the patent laws limitations and conditions which the legislature has not expressed.' "

The Patent Act of 1793 defined statutory subject matter as "any new and useful art, machine, manufacture or composition of matter, or any new or useful improvement [thereof]." Act of Feb. 21, 1793, ch. 11, s 1, 1 Stat. 318. Not until the patent laws were recodified in 1952 did Congress replace the word "art" with the word "process." It is that latter word which we confront today, and in order to determine its meaning we may not be unmindful of the Committee Reports accompanying the 1952 Act which inform us that Congress intended statutory subject matter to "include anything under the sun that is made by man." S.Rep.No.1979, 82d Cong., 2d Sess., 5 (1952); H.R.Rep.No.1923, 82d Cong., 2d Sess., 6 (1952), U.S.CODE CONG. & ADMIN.NEWS 1952, pp. 2394, 2399.

Although the term "process" was not added to 35 U.S.C. § 101 until 1952 a process has historically enjoyed patent protection because it was considered a form of "art" as that term was used in the 1793 Act.

Analyzing respondents' claims, we think that a physical and chemical process for molding precision synthetic rubber products falls within *holding* the § 101 categories of possibly patentable subject matter. That respondents' claims involve the transformation of an article, in this case raw, uncured synthetic rubber, into a different state or thing cannot be disputed. The respondents' claims describe in detail a step-by-step method for accomplishing such, beginning with the loading of a mold with raw, uncured rubber and ending with the eventual opening of the press at the conclusion of the cure. Industrial processes such as this are the types which have historically been eligible to receive the protection of our patent laws.

III

Our conclusion regarding respondents' claims is not altered by the fact that in several steps of the process a mathematical equation and a programmed digital computer are used. This Court has undoubtedly recognized limits to § 101 and every discovery is not embraced within the statutory terms. Excluded from such patent protection are laws of nature, natural phenomena, and abstract ideas. "An idea of itself is not patentable," *Rubber-Tip Pencil Co. v. Howard*, 20 Wall. 498, 507, 22 L.Ed. 410 (1874). "A principle, in the abstract, is a fundamental truth; an original cause; a motive; these cannot be patented, as no one can claim in either of them an exclusive right." *Le Roy v. Tatham*, 14 How. 156, 175, 14 L.Ed. 367 (1853). Only last Term, we explained: "[A] new mineral discovered in the earth or a new plant found in the wild is not patentable subject matter. Likewise, Einstein could not patent his celebrated law that $E = mc^2$; nor could Newton have patented the law of gravity. Such discoveries are 'manifestations of . . . nature, free to all men and reserved exclusively to none.'" *Diamond v. Chakrabarty*, 447 U.S., at 309, 100 S.Ct., at 2208, *quoting Funk Bros. Seed Co. v. Kalo Inoculant Co., supra*, at 130, 68 S.Ct., at 441.

Our recent holdings in Gottschalk v. Benson, supra, and Parker v. Flook, supra, both of which are computer-related, stand for no more than these long-established principles. In Benson, we held unpatentable claims for an algorithm used to convert binary code decimal numbers to equivalent pure binary numbers. The sole practical application of the algorithm was in connection with the programming of a general purpose digital computer. We defined "algorithm" as a "procedure for solving a given type of mathematical problem," and we concluded that such an algorithm, or mathematical formula, is like a law of nature, which cannot be the subject of a patent.[5]

Parker v. Flook, supra, presented a similar situation. The claims were drawn to a method for computing an "alarm limit." An "alarm limit" is simply a number and the Court concluded that the application sought to protect a formula for computing this number. Using this formula, the updated alarm limit could be calculated if several other variables were known. The application, however, did not purport to explain how these other variables were to be determined, nor did it purport "to contain any disclosure relating to the chemical processes at work, the monitoring of process variables, or the means of setting off an alarm or adjusting an alarm system. All that it provides is a formula for computing an updated alarm limit." 437 U.S., at 586, 98 S.Ct., at 2523.

---

5. The term "algorithm" is subject to a variety of definitions. The petitioner defines the term to mean: " '1. A fixed step-by-step procedure for accomplishing a given result; usually a simplified procedure for solving a complex problem, also a full statement of a finite number of steps. 2. A defined process or set of rules that leads [sic] and assures development of a desired output from a given input. A sequence of formulas and/or algebraic/logical steps to calculate or determine a given task; processing rules.' "Brief for Petitioner in Diamond v. Bradley, O.T. 1980, No. 79–855, p. 6, n. 12, quoting C.

SIPPL & R. SIPPL, COMPUTER DICTIONARY AND HANDBOOK 23 (2d ed. 1972). This definition is significantly broader than the definition this Court employed in *Benson* and *Flook*. Our previous decisions regarding the patentability of "algorithms" are necessarily limited to the more narrow definition employed by the Court, and we do not pass judgment on whether processes falling outside the definition previously used by this Court, but within the definition offered by the petitioner, would be patentable subject matter.

In contrast, the respondents here do not seek to patent a mathematical formula. Instead, they seek patent protection for a process of curing synthetic rubber. Their process admittedly employs a well-known mathematical equation, but they do not seek to pre-empt the use of that equation. Rather, they seek only to foreclose from others the use of that equation in conjunction with all of the other steps in their claimed process. These include installing rubber in a press, closing the mold, constantly determining the temperature of the mold, constantly recalculating the appropriate cure time through the use of the formula and a digital computer, and automatically opening the press at the proper time. Obviously, one does not need a "computer" to cure natural or synthetic rubber, but if the computer use incorporated in the process patent significantly lessens the possibility of "overcuring" or "undercuring," the process as a whole does not thereby become unpatentable subject matter.

Our earlier opinions lend support to our present conclusion that a claim drawn to subject matter otherwise statutory does not become nonstatutory simply because it uses a mathematical formula, computer program, or digital computer. In *Gottschalk v. Benson*, we noted: "It is said that the decision precludes a patent for any program servicing a computer. We do not so hold." 409 U.S., at 71, 93 S.Ct., at 257. Similarly, in *Parker v. Flook*, we stated that "a process is not unpatentable simply because it contains a law of nature or a mathematical algorithm." 437 U.S., at 590, 98 S.Ct., at 2526. It is now commonplace that an application of a law of nature or mathematical formula to a known structure or process may well be deserving of patent protection. As Justice Stone explained four decades ago: "While a scientific truth, or the mathematical expression of it, is not a patentable invention, a novel and useful structure created with the aid of knowledge of scientific truth may be." *Mackay Radio & Telegraph Co. v. Radio of America*, 306 U.S. 86, 94, 59 S.Ct. 427, 431, 83 L.Ed. 506 (1939).

We think this statement in *Mackay* takes us a long way toward the correct answer in this case. Arrhenius' equation is not patentable in isolation, but when a process for curing rubber is devised which incorporates in it a more efficient solution of the equation, that process is at the very least not barred at the threshold by § 101.

In determining the eligibility of respondents' claimed process for patent protection under § 101, their claims must be considered as a whole. It is inappropriate to dissect the claims into old and new elements and then to ignore the presence of the old elements in the analysis. This is particularly true in a process claim because a new combination of steps in a process may be patentable even though all the constituents of the combination were well known and in common use before the combination was made. The "novelty" of any element or steps in a process, or even of the process itself, is of no relevance in determining whether the subject matter of a claim falls within the § 101 categories of possibly patentable subject matter.

It has been urged that novelty is an appropriate consideration under § 101. Presumably, this argument results from the language in § 101 referring to any "new and useful" process, machine, etc. Section 101, however, is a general statement of the type of subject matter that is eligible for patent protection "subject to the conditions and requirements of this title." Specific conditions for patentability follow and § 102 covers in detail the conditions relating to novelty. The question therefore of whether a particular invention is novel is "wholly apart from whether the invention falls into a category of statutory subject matter." *In re Bergy*, 596 F.2d 952, 961 (Cust. & Pat.App., 1979) (emphasis deleted).

In this case, it may later be determined that the respondents' process is not deserving of patent protection because it fails to satisfy the statutory conditions of novelty under § 102 or nonobviousness under § 103. A rejection on either of these grounds does not affect the determination that respondents' claims recited subject matter which was eligible for patent protection under § 101.

IV

We have before us today only the question of whether respondents' claims fall within the § 101 categories of possibly patentable subject matter. We view respondents' claims as nothing more than a process for molding rubber products and not as an attempt to patent a mathematical formula. We recognize, of course, that when a claim recites a mathematical formula (or scientific principle or phenomenon of nature), an inquiry must be made into whether the claim is seeking patent protection for that formula in the abstract. A mathematical formula as such is not accorded the protection of our patent laws, *Gottschalk v. Benson*, 409 U.S. 63, 93 S.Ct. 253, 34 L.Ed.2d 273 (1972), and this principle cannot be circumvented by attempting to limit the use of the formula to a particular technological environment. *Parker v. Flook*, 437 U.S. 584, 98 S.Ct. 2522, 57 L.Ed.2d 451 (1978). Similarly, insignificant post-solution activity will not transform an unpatentable principle into a patentable process. To hold otherwise would allow a competent draftsman to evade the recognized limitations on the type of subject matter eligible for patent protection. On the other hand, when a claim containing a mathematical formula implements or applies that formula in a structure or process which, when considered as a whole, is performing a function which the patent laws were designed to protect (e.g., transforming or reducing an article to a different state or thing), then the claim satisfies the requirements of § 101. Because we do not view respondents' claims as an attempt to patent a mathematical formula, but rather to be drawn to an industrial process for the molding of rubber products, we affirm the judgment of the Court of Customs and Patent Appeals.

Notes

1. Physical Steps. The majority opinion makes much of the physical and chemical processes that accompany the claimed algorithm, distinguishing *Parker v. Flook* on this ground. Did the invention here pass muster simply because its accompanying application fully described the rubber curing process, as well as claimed the opening of an oven door at its completion? To what extent should this minimal recitation make a difference? Let us suppose, as is most likely the case, that the particular set of equations described in the patent application finds its only use in curing rubber, as compared to, say, baking a cake. Would the supposedly limiting physical processes so heavily relied upon by the Court actually constrain the scope of the invention in any realistic sense, or did they merely present the only valid technical context in which the mathematics would effectively operate?

2. Something Old; Something New? The invention in *Diehr* may be seen as the combination of a number of preexisting elements: the Arrhenius equation; integral calculus for constantly calculating the cure time; and such sundry apparatus capable of measuring temperature, opening a press, and performing other tasks. Is this combination of old elements patent eligible subject matter? Does this sort of analysis properly fall within the § 101 inquiry at all, or is this a matter for the novelty requirement (detailed in Chapters 4–6 of this casebook)? What if the inventors had themselves discovered the Arrhenius equation?

3. Federal Circuit Reaction. Because the Supreme Court had not overruled *Benson*, the Court of Appeals for the Federal Circuit proceeded very carefully with questions of eligibility even after *Diehr*. As demonstrated by its decision in *Arrhythmia*, he Federal Circuit continued to apply its *Freeman-Walter–Abele* test based on the physical application regime imposed by *Benson*.

ARRHYTHMIA RESEARCH TECHNOLOGY, INC. v. CORAZONIX CORP.

United States Court of Appeals, Federal Circuit, 1992.
958 F.2d 1053, 22 U.S.P.Q.2d 1033.

Before NEWMAN, LOURIE and RADER, CIRCUIT JUDGES.

PAULINE NEWMAN, CIRCUIT JUDGE.

Arrhythmia Research Technology, Inc. appeals the grant of summary judgment by the United States District Court for the Northern District of Texas declaring United States Patent No. 4,422,459 to Michael B. Simson (the '459 or Simson patent) invalid for failure to claim statutory subject matter under 35 U.S.C. § 101. The court did not decide the question of infringement.

We conclude that the claimed subject matter is statutory in terms of section 101. The judgment of invalidity on this ground is reversed.

THE SIMSON INVENTION

The invention claimed in the '459 patent is directed to the analysis of electrocardiographic signals in order to determine certain characteristics of the heart function. In the hours immediately after a heart attack (myocardial infarction) the victim is particularly vulnerable to an acute type of heart arrhythmia known as ventricular tachycardia. Ventricular tachycardia leads quickly to ventricular fibrillation, in which the heart ceases effectively to pump blood through the body. Arrhythmia Research states that 15–25% of heart attack victims are at high risk for ventricular tachycardia. It can be treated or prevented with certain drugs, but these drugs have undesirable and sometimes dangerous side effects. Dr. Simson, a cardiologist, sought a solution to the problem of determining which heart attack victims are at high risk for ventricular tachycardia, so that these persons can be carefully monitored and appropriately treated.

Heart activity is monitored by means of an electrocardiograph device, whereby electrodes attached to the patient's body detect the heart's electrical signals in accordance with the various phases of heart activity. The signals can be displayed in wave form on a monitor and/or recorded on a chart. It was known that in patients subject to ventricular tachycardia certain anomalous waves having very low amplitude and high frequency, known as "late potentials," appear toward the end of the QRS segment of the electrocardiographic signal, that is, late in the ventricular contraction cycle. Dr. Simson's method of detecting and measuring these late potentials in the QRS complex, and associated apparatus, are the subject of the '459 patent.

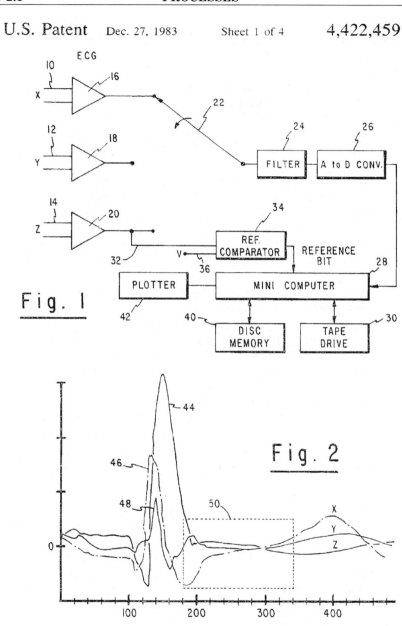

Fig. 1

Fig. 2

TIME = ms

The '459 patent specification describes these procedures. Certain of the heart attack patient's electrocardiographic signals, those obtained from electrodes designated as X, Y, and Z leads, are converted from analog to digital values, and a composite digital representation of the

QRS segment is obtained by selecting and averaging a large number of the patient's QRS waveforms. The anterior portion of the composite QRS waveform is first isolated, and then processed by a digital high pass filter in reverse time order; that is, backwards. This step of reverse time order filtering is described as the critical feature of the Simson invention, in that it enables detection of the late potentials by eliminating certain perturbations that obscure these signals. The root mean square of the reverse time filtered output is then calculated, as described in the specification, to determine the average magnitude of the anterior portion of the QRS complex. Comparison of the output, which is measured in microvolts, with a predetermined level of high frequency energy, indicates whether the patient is subject to ventricular tachycardia.

Certain steps of the invention are described as conducted with the aid of a digital computer, and the patent specification sets forth the mathematical formulae that are used to configure (program) the computer. The specification states that dedicated, specific purpose equipment or hard wired logic circuitry can also be used.

The district court held that the method and apparatus claims of the Simson patent are directed to a mathematical algorithm, and thus do not define statutory subject matter. Claim 1 is the broadest method claim: 1. A method for analyzing electrocardiograph signals to determine the presence or absence of a predetermined level of high frequency energy in the late QRS signal, comprising the steps of: converting a series of QRS signals to time segments, each segment having a digital value equivalent to the analog value of said signals at said time; applying a portion of said time segments in reverse time order to high pass filter means; determining an arithmetic value of the amplitude of the output of said filter; and comparing said value with said predetermined level. Claim 7 is a representative apparatus claim: 7. Apparatus for analyzing electrocardiograph signals to determine the level of high frequency energy in the late QRS signal comprising: means for converting X, Y, and Z lead electrocardiographic input signals to digital valued time segments; means for examining said X, Y, and Z digital valued time segments and selecting therefrom the QRS waveform portions thereof; means for signal averaging a multiplicity of said selected QRS waveforms for each of said X, Y, and Z inputs and providing composite, digital X, Y, and Z QRS waveforms; high pass filter means; means for applying to said filter means, in reverse time order, the anterior portion of each said digital X, Y, and Z waveform; and means for comparing the output of said filter means with a predetermined level to obtain an indication of the presence of a high frequency, low level, energy component in the filter output of said anterior portions. The Patent and Trademark Office had granted the patent without questioning that its claims were directed to statutory subject matter under § 101.

35 U.S.C. § 101

Whether a claim is directed to statutory subject matter is a question of law. Although determination of this question may require findings of underlying facts specific to the particular subject matter and its mode of claiming, in this case there were no disputed facts material to the issue. Thus we give plenary review to the question, with appropriate recognition of the burdens on the challenger of a duly issued United States patent. *See* 35 U.S.C. § 282 (duly issued patent is presumed valid).

A new and useful process or apparatus is patentable subject matter, as defined in 35 U.S.C. § 101: "Whoever invents or discovers any new and useful process, machine, manufacture, or composition of matter, or any new and useful improvement thereof, may obtain a patent therefor, subject to the conditions and requirements of this title." The Supreme Court has observed that Congress intended section 101 to include "anything under the sun that is made by man." *Diamond v. Chakrabarty*, 447 U.S. 303, 309, 100 S.Ct. 2204, 2208, 65 L.Ed.2d 144, 206 U.S.P.Q. 193, 197 (1980), *quoting* S.Rep. No. 1979, 82d Cong., 2d Sess., 5 (1952); H.R.Rep. No. 1923, 82d Cong., 2d Sess., 6 (1952). There are, however, qualifications to the apparent sweep of this statement. Excluded from patentability is subject matter in the categories of "laws of nature, physical phenomena, and abstract ideas". *Diamond v. Diehr*, 450 U.S. 175, 185, 101 S.Ct. 1048, 1056, 67 L.Ed.2d 155, 209 U.S.P.Q. 1, 7 (1981). A mathematical formula may describe a law of nature, a scientific truth, or an abstract idea. As courts have recognized, mathematics may also be used to describe steps of a statutory method or elements of a statutory apparatus. The exceptions to patentable subject matter derive from a lengthy jurisprudence, but their meaning was probed anew with the advent of computer-related inventions.

In *Gottschalk v. Benson*, 409 U.S. 63, 72, 93 S.Ct. 253, 257, 34 L.Ed.2d 273, 175 U.S.P.Q. 673, 676 (1972) the Court held that a patent claim that "wholly pre-empts" a mathematical formula used in a general purpose digital computer is directed solely to a mathematical algorithm, and therefore does not define statutory subject matter under section 101. The Court described the mathematical process claimed in *Benson* as "so abstract and sweeping as to cover both known and unknown uses of the BCD [binary coded decimal] to pure binary conversion", 409 U.S. at 68, 93 S.Ct. at 255, 175 U.S.P.Q. at 675, *citing O'Reilly v. Morse*, 56 U.S. (15 How.) 62, 113, 14 L.Ed. 601 (1852) for its holding that the patentee may not claim more than he has actually invented.

In *Parker v. Flook*, 437 U.S. 584, 591, 98 S.Ct. 2522, 2526, 57 L.Ed.2d 451, 198 U.S.P.Q. 193, 198 (1978) the Court explained that the criterion for patentability of a claim that requires the use of mathematical procedures is not simply whether the claim "wholly pre-empts" a mathematical algorithm, but whether the claim is directed to a new and useful process, independent of whether the mathematical algorithm required for its performance is novel. Applying these criteria the Court held nonstatutory a method claim for computer-calculating "alarm limits" for use in a catalytic conversion process, on the basis that "once that algorithm is assumed to be within the prior art, the application, considered as a whole, contains no patentable invention."

In accordance with *Flook*, the claims were analyzed to determine whether the process itself was new and useful, assuming the mathematical algorithm was "well known". As the jurisprudence developed, inventions that were implemented by the mathematically-directed performance of computers were viewed in the context of the practical application to which the computer-generated data were put. The Court of Customs and Patent Appeals observed in *In re Bradley*, 600 F.2d 807, 811–812, 202 U.S.P.Q. 480, 485 (CCPA 1979), *aff'd by an equally divided court, sub nom. Diamond v. Bradley*, 450 U.S. 381, 101 S.Ct. 1495, 67 L.Ed.2d 311 (1981): It is of course true that a modern digital computer manipulates data, usually in binary form, by performing mathematical operations, such as addition, subtraction, multiplication, division, or bit shifting, on the data. But this is only how the computer does what it does. Of importance is the significance of the data and their manipulation in the real world, i.e., *what* the computer is doing. Thus computers came to be generally recognized as devices capable of performing or implementing process steps, or serving as components of an apparatus, without negating patentability of the process or the apparatus. In *Diamond v. Diehr* the Court explained that non-statutory status under section 101 derives from the "abstract", rather than the "sweeping", nature of a claim that contains a mathematical algorithm. The Court stated: "While a scientific truth, or the mathematical expression of it, is not a patentable invention, a novel and useful structure created with the aid of knowledge of scientific truth may be." The mathematical algorithm in Diehr was the known Arrhenius equation, and the Court held that when the algorithm was incorporated in a useful process, the subject matter was statutory. The Court confirmed the rule that process steps or apparatus functions that entail computer-performed calculations, whether the calculations are described in mathematical symbols or in words, do not of themselves render a claim nonstatutory. The Court clarified its earlier holdings, stating that "[i]t is inappropriate to dissect the claims into old and new elements and then to ignore the presence of the old elements in the [section 101] analysis."

The Court thus placed the patentability of computer-aided inventions in the mainstream of the law. The ensuing mode of analysis of such inventions was summarized in *In re Meyer*, 688 F.2d 789, 795, 215 U.S.P.Q. 193, 198 (CCPA 1982): In considering a claim for compliance with 35 U.S.C. 101, it must be determined whether a scientific principle, law of nature, idea, or mental process, which may be represented by a mathematical algorithm, is included in the subject matter of the claim. If it is, it must then be determined whether such principle, law, idea, or mental process is applied in an invention of a type set forth in 35 U.S.C. § 101. The law crystallized about the principle that claims directed solely to an abstract mathematical formula or equation, including the mathematical expression of scientific truth or a law of nature, whether directly or indirectly stated, are nonstatutory under section 101; whereas claims to a specific process or apparatus that is implemented in accordance with a mathematical algorithm will generally satisfy section 101.

In applying this principle to an invention whose process steps or apparatus elements are described at least in part in terms of mathematical procedures, the mathematical procedures are considered in the context of the claimed invention as a whole. *Diehr*, 450 U.S. at 188, 101 S.Ct. at 1057, 209 U.S.P.Q. at 9. Determination of statutory subject matter has been conveniently conducted in two stages, following a protocol initiated by the Court of Customs and Patent Appeals in *In re Freeman*, 573 F.2d 1237, 197 U.S.P.Q. 464 (CCPA 1978); modified after the Court's *Flook* decision by *In re Walter*, 618 F.2d 758, 205 U.S.P.Q. 397 (CCPA 1980); and again after the Court's *Diehr* decision by *In re Abele*, 684 F.2d 902, 214 U.S.P.Q. 682 (CCPA 1982).

This analysis has been designated the *Freeman-Walter–Abele* test for statutory subject matter. It is first determined whether a mathematical algorithm is recited directly or indirectly in the claim. If so, it is next determined whether the claimed invention as a whole is no more than the algorithm itself; that is, whether the claim is directed to a mathematical algorithm that is not applied to or limited by physical elements or process steps. Such claims are nonstatutory. However, when the mathematical algorithm is applied in one or more steps of an otherwise statutory process claim, or one or more elements of an otherwise statutory apparatus claim, the requirements of section 101 are met. The court explained in *Abele*, 684 F.2d at 907, 214 U.S.P.Q. at 686: [P]atentable subject matter [is not limited] to claims in which structural relationships or process steps are defined, limited or refined by the application of the algorithm. Rather, Walter should be read as requiring no more than that the algorithm be "applied in any manner to physical elements or process steps," provided that its application is circumscribed by more than a field of use limitation or non-essential post-solution activity. As summarized by the PTO in *Ex Parte Logan*, 20 U.S.P.Q.2d 1465, 1468 (PTO Bd.Pat.App. and Interf.1991), the emphasis is "on what the claimed method steps do rather than how the steps are performed".

Although the *Freeman-Walter–Abele* analysis is not the only test for statutory subject matter, *Meyer*, 688 F.2d at 796, 215 U.S.P.Q. at 198, and this court has stated that failure to meet that test may not always defeat the claim, *In re Grams*, 888 F.2d 835, 839, 12 U.S.P.Q.2d 1824, 1827 (Fed.Cir.1989), this analytic procedure is conveniently applied to the Simson invention.

ANALYSIS

Arrhythmia Research states that the district court erred in law, and that the combination of physical, mechanical, and electrical steps that are described and claimed in the '459 patent constitutes statutory subject matter. Arrhythmia Research stresses that the claims are directed to a process and apparatus for detecting and analyzing a specific heart activity signal, and do not preempt the mathematical algorithms used in any of the procedures. Arrhythmia Research states that the patentability of such claims is now well established by law, precedent, and practice.

Corazonix states that the claims define no more than a mathematical algorithm that calculates a number. Corazonix states that in Simson's process and apparatus claims mathematical algorithms are merely presented and solved, and that Simson's designation of a field of use and post-solution activity are not essential to the claims and thus do not cure this defect. Thus, Corazonix states that the claims are not directed to statutory subject matter, and that the district court's judgment was correct.

A.   The Process Claims

Although mathematical calculations are involved in carrying out the claimed process, Arrhythmia Research argues that the claims are directed to a method of detection of a certain heart condition by a novel method of analyzing a portion of the electrocardiographically measured heart cycle. This is accomplished by procedures conducted by means of electronic equipment programmed to perform mathematical computation.

Applying the *Freeman-Walter–Abele* protocol, we accept for the purposes of this analysis the proposition that a mathematical algorithm is included in the subject matter of the process claims in that some claimed steps are described in the specification by mathematical formulae. *See In re Johnson*, 589 F.2d 1070, 1078, 200 U.S.P.Q. 199, 208 (CCPA 1978) ("Reference to the specification must be made to determine whether [claimed] terms indirectly recite mathematical calculations, formulae, or equations.") We thus proceed to the second stage of the analysis, to determine whether the claimed process is otherwise statutory; that is, we determine what the claimed steps do, independent of how they are implemented.

Simson's process is claimed as a "method for analyzing electrocardiograph signals to determine the presence or absence of a predetermined level of high-frequency energy in the late QRS signal". This claim limitation is not ignored in determining whether the subject matter as a whole is statutory, for all of the claim steps are in implementation of this method. The electrocardiograph signals are first transformed from analog form, in which they are obtained, to the corresponding digital signal. These input signals are not abstractions; they are related to the patient's heart function. The anterior portion of the QRS signal is then processed, as the next step, by the procedure known as reverse time order filtration. The digital filter design selected by Dr. Simson for this purpose, known as the Butterworth filter, is one of several known procedures for frequency filtering of digital waveforms. The filtered signal is further analyzed to determine its average magnitude, as described in the specification, by the root mean square technique. Comparison of the resulting output to a predetermined level determines whether late potentials reside in the anterior portion of the QRS segment, thus indicating whether the patient is at high risk for ventricular tachycardia. The resultant output is not an abstract number, but is a signal related to the patient's heart activity.

These claimed steps of "converting", "applying", "determining", and "comparing" are physical process steps that transform one physical, electrical signal into another. The view that "there is nothing necessarily physical about 'signals'" is incorrect. *In re Taner*, 681 F.2d 787, 790, 214 U.S.P.Q. 678, 681 (CCPA 1982) (holding statutory claims to a method of seismic exploration including the mathematically described steps of "summing" and "simulating from"). The *Freeman–Walter–Abele* standard is met, for the steps of Simson's claimed method comprise an otherwise statutory process whose mathematical procedures are applied to physical process steps.

It was undisputed that the individual mathematical procedures that describe these steps are all known in the abstract. The method claims do not wholly preempt these procedures, but limit their application to the defined process steps. In answering the question "What did the applicant invent?", *Grams*, 888 F.2d at 839, 12 U.S.P.Q.2d at 1827, the Simson method is properly viewed as a method of analyzing electrocardiograph signals in order to determine a specified heart activity. Like the court in *Abele*, which was "faced simply with an improved CAT-scan process", 684 F.2d at 909, 214 U.S.P.Q. at 688, the Simson invention is properly viewed as an electrocardiograph analysis process. The claims do not encompass subject matter transcending what Dr. Simson invented, as in *O'Reilly v. Morse*, 56 U.S. (15 How.) at 113 (claims covered any use of electric current to transmit characters at a distance); or in *Benson*, 409 U.S. at 68, 93 S.Ct. at 255, 175 U.S.P.Q. at 675 (use of claimed process could "vary from the operation of a train to verification of driver's licenses to researching the law books for precedents"); or in *Grams*, 888 F.2d at 840, 12 U.S.P.Q.2d at 1828 (invention had application to "any complex system, whether it be electrical, mechanical, chemical or biological, or combinations thereof.")

The Simson claims are analogous to those upheld in *Diehr*, wherein the Court remarked that the applicants "do not seek to patent a mathematical formula.... they seek only to foreclose from others the use of that equation in conjunction with all of the other steps in their claimed process". 450 U.S. at 187, 101 S.Ct. at 1057, 209 U.S.P.Q. at 8. Simson's claimed method is similarly limited. The process claims comprise statutory subject matter.

B. The Apparatus Claims

The Simson apparatus for analyzing electrocardiographic signals is claimed in the style of 35 U.S.C. § 112, paragraph 6, whereby functionally described claim elements are "construed to cover the corresponding structure, material, or acts described in the specification and equivalents thereof". Thus the statutory nature vel non of Simson's apparatus claims is determined with reference to the description in the '459 patent specification. *In re Iwahashi*, 888 F.2d 1370, 1375, 12 U.S.P.Q.2d 1908, 1911–12 (Fed.Cir.1989).

The apparatus claims require a means for converting the electrocardiograph signals from the analog form in which they are generated into digital form. This means is described in the specification as a specific electronic device, a conventional analog-to-digital converter. A minicomputer, configured as described in the specification, is the means of calculating composite digital time segments of the QRS waveform. The product is stored, as stated in the specification, in the form of electrical signals. The high pass filter means is described in the specification as the minicomputer configured to perform the function of reverse time order filtration of the anterior portion of the QRS waveform. The specification and drawings show a disc memory unit to store the composite QRS signals, and associated connecting leads to the computer's processing unit. The comparing means is the processing unit configured to perform the specified function of root mean square averaging of the anterior portion of the QRS complex, and comparison of the resulting output with a predetermined level to provide an indication of the presence of late potentials in the electrocardiograph signal.

The Simson apparatus claims thus define "a combination of interrelated means" for performing specified functions. The computer-performed operations transform a particular input signal to a different output signal, in accordance with the internal structure of the computer as configured by electronic instructions. "The claimed invention ... converts one physical thing into another physical thing just as any other electrical circuitry would do".

The use of mathematical formulae or relationships to describe the electronic structure and operation of an apparatus does not make it nonstatutory. When mathematical formulae are the standard way of expressing certain functions or apparatus, it is appropriate that mathematical terms be used. That Simson's claimed functions could not have been performed effectively without the speed and capability of electronic devices and components does not determine whether the claims are statutory.

Corazonix argues that the final output of the claimed apparatus (and process) is simply a number, and that Benson and Flook support the position that when the end product is a number, the claim is nonstatutory and can not be saved by claim limitations of the use to which this number is put. However, the number obtained is not a mathematical abstraction; it is a measure in microvolts of a specified heart activity, an indicator of the risk of ventricular tachycardia. That the product is numerical is not a criterion of whether the claim is directed to statutory subject matter.

The Simson apparatus claims satisfy the criteria for statutory subject matter. They are directed to a specific apparatus of practical utility and specified application, and meet the requirements of 35 U.S.C. § 101.

CONCLUSION

The judgment of invalidity on the ground that the claimed method and apparatus do not define statutory subject matter is reversed. The cause is remanded for resolution of remaining issues.

RADER, CIRCUIT JUDGE, concurring.

Nearly twenty years ago, in *Gottschalk v. Benson*, 409 U.S. 63, 93 S.Ct. 253, 34 L.Ed.2d 273 (1972), the Supreme Court dealt with a computer process for conversion of binary coded decimals into pure binary numbers. *Benson* held this mathematical algorithm ineligible for patent protection. 409 U.S. at 65, 71–72, 93 S.Ct. at 254, 257. Because computer programs rely heavily on mathematical algorithms, commentators saw dire implications in the Supreme Court's opinion for patent protection of computer software. For instance, one treatise, citing *Benson*, stated: [A] recent Supreme Court decision seemingly eliminated patent protection for computer software. DONALD S. CHISUM, PATENTS § 1.01 (1991); *see also id.* at § 1.03[6].

The court upholds the '459 patent by applying a permutation of the *Benson* algorithm rule. In reaching this result, the court adds another cord to the twisted knot of precedent encircling and confining the *Benson* rule. While fully concurring in the court's result and commending its ability to trace legal strands through the tangle of post-*Benson* case law, I read later Supreme Court opinions to have cut the Gordian knot. The Supreme Court cut the knot by strictly limiting *Benson*.

Relying on the language of the patent statute, the Supreme Court in *Diamond v. Diehr*, 450 U.S. 175, 101 S.Ct. 1048, 67 L.Ed.2d 155 (1981), turned away from the *Benson* algorithm rule. [Following *Diehr*, courts] should give "process" its literal and predictable meaning, without conjecturing about the policy implications of that literal reading. *Cf. Chakrabarty*, 447 U.S. at 316–18, 100 S.Ct. at 2211–12. If Congress wishes to remove some processes from patent protection, it can enact such an exclusion. Again, in the absence of legislated limits on the meaning of the Act, courts should not presume to construct limits.

The claims of the '459 patent define an apparatus and a process. Both are patentable subject matter within the language of section 101. To me, the Supreme Court's most recent message is clear: when all else fails (and the algorithm rule clearly has), consult the statute. On this basis, I, too, would reverse and remand.

Notes

1. Medical Discovery. The *Arrhythmia* court determined that the patent applicant invented electronic structure for transforming electrical signals. Is a better view that the inventor discovered the "scientific truth" that patients whose hearts exhibit certain electrical signals are at risk for ventricular tachycardia, and employed admittedly standard digital signal processing techniques to isolate those signals? Consider the following statement from 1 MARTIN J. ADELMAN, PATENT LAW PERSPECTIVES § 1.4[3] at n.246 (2d ed. 1992).

> Clearly doctors treating heart patients want to know which patients are likely to experience serious complications such as ventricular fibrillation after a heart attack. Suppose, a doctor discovered that certain heart sounds are associated with a substantial increase in the risk of ventricu-

lar fibrillation. Unless the doctor's discovery can be the basis for a statutory process or some product such as an automatic device for detecting such heart sounds, the doctor has simply made an unpatentable discovery. Much of the science of medicine is based on such unpatentable discoveries.

There are two possible attitudes toward doctors who make unpatentable discoveries. One is that it is both wrong and unprofessional for doctors to try to profit from the making of useful medical discoveries. They should simply publish them so that humanity can benefit from their use. Therefore, any doctor who first detected a particular heart sound and associated it with an increased risk of ventricular fibrillation and who promptly publishes that knowledge would have made an important contribution to mankind because doctors the world over could now select out those post-myocardial infarction patients at increased risk and provide them with preventive treatments secure in the knowledge that the risk of the treatments is less than the risk of ventricular fibrillation. The other attitude is that it is too bad that the doctor who contributed this important discovery to the world is unable to collect any royalties from all the other doctors who now recognize this specific sound and correlate it with the risk of ventricular fibrillation and who collect substantial fees for their efforts. Those whose attitudes more closely follow the latter approach would look for ways to compensate the doctor, if possible. Today it is this second attitude which prevails and governs the approach of patent law. Therefore, we would expect that if the doctor had designed a machine to detect the special heart sound and indicate its presence or absence, that machine would be statutory either claimed as a machine or a process. This would be so even if the machine itself were the result of routine engineering. Of course, once the law adopts this approach, then even if the designer of the machine did not discover the relationship between the heart sound and ventricular fibrillation, the process or machine would remain statutory although perhaps unpatentable for obviousness.

2. Physical Signals. In *Arrhythmia*, the court applied the *Freeman–Walter–Abele* test to detect physical steps which transform the mathematical algorithm into subject matter eligible for patent protection. *Freeman* and *Walter* occurred before *Diehr*, *Abele* after. Did *Diehr* perpetuate or depart from the search for physical steps? In any event, this post? *Diehr* opinion asserts that electrical signals are necessarily physical, in keeping with the transformation standard mentioned in *Diamond v. Diehr*. Should the mere presence of electrical signals indicate the close of the patent eligibility inquiry? Suppose an inventor claims a method for solving square roots for use in a standard computer; like all digital electronic computers, the invention employs physical electrical signals as part of its internal operation. Is such an invention eligible for patent protection?

3. *En Banc* Review. Legal uncertainties over the possibility of patent protection for computer-related inventions made the issue ripe for *in banc* review by the Federal Circuit. The result was *In re Alappat,* 33 F.3d 1526, 31 U.S.P.Q.2d 1545. In 1994, the Federal Circuit examined an invention that creates a smooth waveform display in a digital oscilloscope. An expanded Board of Patent Appeals and Interferences rejected the application as an ineligible mathematical algorithm. Although the invention employed mathematical principles, the *en banc* court reasoned:

> Because claim 15 is directed to a machine, which is one of the four categories of patentable subject matter enumerated in § 101, claim 15 appears on its face to be directed to § 101 subject matter.
>
> This does not quite end the analysis, however, because the Board majority argues that the claimed subject matter falls within a judicially created exception to § 101 which the majority refers to as the "mathematical algorithm" exception.
>
> In *Diamond v. Diehr*, 450 U.S. 175, 101 S.Ct. 1048, 67 L.Ed.2d 155 (1981), its most recent case addressing § 101, the Supreme Court explained that there are three categories of subject matter for which one may not obtain patent protection, namely "laws of nature, natural phenomena, and abstract ideas." *Diehr*, 450 U.S. at 185, 101 S.Ct. at 1056. Of relevance to this case, the Supreme Court also has held that certain mathematical subject matter is not, standing alone, entitled to patent protection. A close analysis of *Diehr, Flook*, and *Benson* reveals that the Supreme Court never intended to create an overly broad, fourth category of subject matter excluded from § 101. Rather, at the core of the Court's analysis in each of these cases lies an attempt by the Court to explain a rather straightforward concept, namely, that certain types of mathematical subject matter, standing alone, represent nothing more than abstract ideas until reduced to some type of practical application, and thus that subject matter is not, in and of itself, entitled to patent protection.
>
> Given the foregoing, the proper inquiry in dealing with the so-called mathematical subject matter exception to § 101 alleged herein is to see whether the claimed subject matter as a whole is a disembodied mathematical concept, whether categorized as a mathematical formula, mathematical equation, mathematical algorithm, or the like, which in essence represents nothing more than a "law of nature," "natural phenomenon," or "abstract idea." If so, *Diehr* precludes the patenting of that subject matter. That is not the case here.

Alappat continued to limit obstacles to patenting computer-related inventions. Did *Alappat* also chart a course to claim any software invention, namely claim in terms of the machine components that the software manipulates to perform its function?

4. Interchangeable Hardware and Software: The Federal Circuit determined that Alappat's invention was a "machine" within the meaning of section 101. Two judges (Archer and Nies) in dissent protested this characterization: "[The circuitry elements of the claimed rasterizer] are only a convenient and basic way of electrically representing the mathematical operations to be performed, that is, converting vector data into matrix or raster data." The Federal Circuit responded:

> Although many, or arguably even all, of the ... elements recited in claim 15 represent circuitry elements that perform mathematical calculations, which is essentially true of all digital electrical circuits, the claimed invention as a whole is directed to a combination of interrelated

elements which combine to form a machine for converting discrete waveform data samples into anti-aliased pixel illumination intensity data to be displayed on a display means. This is not a disembodied mathematical concept which may be characterized as an "abstract idea," but rather a specific machine to produce a useful, concrete, and tangible result.

This language suggested that *Alappat* confined the Supreme Court's *Benson* case to deny patents on nothing more than disembodied mathematical concepts. More importantly, the debate between majority and dissent in *Alappat* resolved a central issue about claiming computer inventions. Computer inventions feature hardware and software. In modern computer technology, these seemingly different elements are fully, and almost instantly, interchangeable. In light of the above discussion, does the act of "programming" software into a computer's hardware transform that hardware into a new machine? Actually the CCPA had already answered that question:

> [I]f a machine is programmed in a certain new and unobvious way, it is physically different from the machine without that program; its memory elements are differently arranged. The fact that these physical changes are invisible to the eye should not tempt us to conclude that the machine has not been changed.

In re Bernhart, 417 F.2d 1395, 1400, 163 U.S.P.Q. 611 (CCPA 1969); *see also In re Prater*, 415 F.2d 1393, 1404 n. 29, 162 U.S.P.Q. 541 (CCPA 1969). Apparently, after *Alappat*, every software invention can overcome patent eligibility problems if claimed in terms of its interchangeable hardware elements. If so, why not permit direct claiming of software? Why the subterfuge of claiming in terms of hardware? Is the hardware claim necessary to give understandable form to software inventions?

In *Alappat*, the Federal Circuit did not apply the *Freeman-Walter–Abele* test or any other vestiges of the *Benson* era, but instead limited *Benson* to a case about abstractness and construed the statutory categories of patent eligibility very broadly. Does this reasoning shift the focus for computer-related inventions away from section 101 patent eligibility questions to the patentability requirements of sections 102, 103, and 112? The next major Federal Circuit case answered that question.

STATE STREET BANK & TRUST CO. v. SIGNATURE FINANCIAL GROUP, INC.

United States Court of Appeals, Federal Circuit, 1998.
149 F.3d 1368, 47 U.S.P.Q.2d 1596.

Before RICH, PLAGER, and BRYSON, Circuit Judges.

RICH, CIRCUIT JUDGE.

Signature Financial Group, Inc. (Signature) appeals from the decision of the United States District Court for the District of Massachusetts granting a motion for summary judgment in favor of State Street Bank & Trust Co. (State Street), finding U.S. Patent No. 5,193,056 (the '056 patent) invalid on the ground that the claimed subject matter is not encompassed by 35 U.S.C. § 101 (1994). We reverse and remand because we conclude that the patent claims are directed to statutory subject matter.

Background

Signature is the assignee of the '056 patent which is entitled "Data Processing System for Hub and Spoke Financial Services Configuration. "The '056 patent is generally directed to a data processing system (the system) for implementing an investment structure which was developed for use in Signature's business as an administrator and accounting agent for mutual funds. In essence, the system, identified by the proprietary name Hub and Spoke (R), facilitates a structure whereby mutual funds (Spokes) pool their assets in an investment portfolio (Hub) organized as a partnership. This investment configuration provides the administrator of a mutual fund with the advantageous combination of economies of scale in administering investments coupled with the tax advantages of a partnership.

State Street and Signature are both in the business of acting as custodians and accounting agents for multi-tiered partnership fund financial services. State Street negotiated with Signature for a license to use its patented data processing system described and claimed in the '056 patent. When negotiations broke down, State Street brought a declaratory judgment action asserting invalidity, unenforceability, and noninfringement in Massachusetts district court, and then filed a motion for partial summary judgment of patent invalidity for failure to claim statutory subject matter under § 101. The motion was granted and this appeal followed.

Discussion

The substantive issue at hand, whether the '056 patent is invalid for failure to claim statutory subject matter under § 101, is a matter of both claim construction and statutory construction. We hold that declaratory judgment plaintiff State Street was not entitled to the grant of summary judgment of invalidity of the '056 patent under § 101 as a matter of law, because the patent claims are directed to statutory subject matter.

The patented invention relates generally to a system that allows an administrator to monitor and record the financial information flow and make all calculations necessary for maintaining a partner fund financial services configuration. As previously mentioned, a partner fund financial services configuration essentially allows several mutual funds, or "Spokes," to pool their investment funds into a single portfolio, or "Hub," allowing for consolidation of, inter alia, the costs of administering the fund combined with the tax advantages of a partnership. In particular, this system provides means for a daily allocation of assets for two or more Spokes that are invested in the same Hub. The system determines the percentage share that each Spoke maintains in the Hub, while taking into consideration daily changes both in the value of the Hub's investment securities and in the concomitant amount of each Spoke's assets.

In determining daily changes, the system also allows for the allocation among the Spokes of the Hub's daily income, expenses, and net realized and unrealized gain or loss, calculating each day's total investments based on the concept of a book capital account. This enables the determination of a true asset value of each Spoke and accurate calculation of allocation ratios between or among the Spokes. The system additionally tracks all the relevant data determined on a daily basis for the Hub and each Spoke, so that aggregate year end income, expenses, and capital gain or loss can be determined for accounting and for tax purposes for the Hub and, as a result, for each publicly traded Spoke.

It is essential that these calculations are quickly and accurately performed. In large part this is required because each Spoke sells shares to the public and the price of those shares is substantially based on the Spoke's percentage interest in the portfolio. In some instances, a mutual fund administrator is required to calculate the value of the shares to the nearest penny within as little as an hour and a half after the market closes. Given the complexity of the calculations, a computer or equivalent device is a virtual necessity to perform the task.

The '056 patent application was filed 11 March 1991. It initially contained six "machine" claims, which incorporated means-plus-function clauses, and six method claims. According to Signature, during prosecution the examiner contemplated a § 101 rejection for failure to claim statutory subject matter. However, upon cancellation of the six method claims, the examiner issued a notice of allowance for the remaining present six claims on appeal. Only claim 1 is an independent claim.

The district court began its analysis by construing the claims to be directed to a process, with each "means" clause merely representing a step in that process. However, "machine" claims having "means" clauses may only be reasonably viewed as process claims if there is no supporting structure in the written description that corresponds to the claimed "means" elements. *See In re Alappat*, 33 F.3d 1526, 1540–41, 31 USPQ2d 1545, 1554 (Fed.Cir.1994) (*in banc*). This is not the case now before us.

When independent claim 1 is properly construed in accordance with § 112, ¶ 6, it is directed to a machine, as demonstrated below, where representative claim 1 is set forth, the subject matter in brackets stating the structure the written description discloses as corresponding to the respective "means" recited in the claims.

1. A data processing system for managing a financial services configuration of a portfolio established as a partnership, each partner being one of a plurality of funds, comprising:

    (a) computer processor means [a personal computer including a CPU] for processing data;

    (b) storage means [a data disk] for storing data on a storage medium;

(c) first means [an arithmetic logic circuit configured to prepare the data disk to magnetically store selected data] for initializing the storage medium;

(d) second means [an arithmetic logic circuit configured to retrieve information from a specific file, calculate incremental increases or decreases based on specific input, allocate the results on a percentage basis, and store the output in a separate file] for processing data regarding assets in the portfolio and each of the funds from a previous day and data regarding increases or decreases in each of the funds, [sic, funds'] assets and for allocating the percentage share that each fund holds in the portfolio;

(e) third means [an arithmetic logic circuit configured to retrieve information from a specific file, calculate incremental increases and decreases based on specific input, allocate the results on a percentage basis and store the output in a separate file] for processing data regarding daily incremental income, expenses, and net realized gain or loss for the portfolio and for allocating such data among each fund;

(f) fourth means [an arithmetic logic circuit configured to retrieve information from a specific file, calculate incremental increases and decreases based on specific input, allocate the results on a percentage basis and store the output in a separate file] for processing data regarding daily net unrealized gain or loss for the portfolio and for allocating such data among each fund; and

(g) fifth means [an arithmetic logic circuit configured to retrieve information from specific files, calculate that information on an aggregate basis and store the output in a separate file] for processing data regarding aggregate year-end income, expenses, and capital gain or loss for the portfolio and each of the funds.

Each claim component, recited as a "means" plus its function, is to be read, of course, pursuant to § 112, ¶ 6, as inclusive of the equivalents of the structures disclosed in the written description portion of the specification. Thus, claim 1, properly construed, claims a machine, namely, a data processing system for managing a financial services configuration of a portfolio established as a partnership, which machine is made up of, at the very least, the specific structures disclosed in the written description and corresponding to the means-plus-function elements (a)-(g) recited in the claim. A "machine" is proper statutory subject matter under 101. We note that, for the purposes of a 101 analysis, it is of little relevance whether claim 1 is directed to a machine or a process, as long as it falls within at least one of the four enumerated categories of patentable subject matter, "machine" and "process" being such categories.

This does not end our analysis, however, because the court concluded that the claimed subject matter fell into one of two alternative judicially-created exceptions to statutory subject matter. The court refers to the first exception as the "mathematical algorithm" exception and the second exception as the "business method" exception. Section 101 reads:

> Whoever invents or discovers any new and useful process, machine, manufacture, or composition of matter, or any new and useful improvement thereof, may obtain a patent therefor, subject to the conditions and requirements of this title.

The plain and unambiguous meaning of § 101 is that any invention falling within one of the four stated categories of statutory subject matter may be patented, provided it meets the other requirements for patentability set forth in Title 35, i.e., those found in §§ 102, 103, and 112, ¶ 2.

The repetitive use of the expansive term "any" in § 101 shows Congress's intent not to place any restrictions on the subject matter for which a patent may be obtained beyond those specifically recited in § 101. Indeed, the Supreme Court has acknowledged that Congress intended § 101 to extend to "anything under the sun that is made by man." *Diamond v. Chakrabarty*, 447 U.S. 303, 309, 100 S.Ct. 2204, 65 L.Ed.2d 144 (1980). Thus, it is improper to read limitations into § 101 on the subject matter that may be patented where the legislative history indicates that Congress clearly did not intend such limitations. *See Chakrabarty*, 447 U.S. at 308, 100 S.Ct. 2204 ("We have also cautioned that courts 'should not read into the patent laws limitations and conditions which the legislature has not expressed.'"(citations omitted)).

The "Mathematical Algorithm" Exception

The Supreme Court has identified three categories of subject matter that are unpatentable, namely "laws of nature, natural phenomena, and abstract ideas." *Diehr*, 450 U.S. at 185, 101 S.Ct. 1048. Of particular relevance to this case, the Court has held that mathematical algorithms are not patentable subject matter to the extent that they are merely abstract ideas. *See Diehr*, 450 U.S. 175, 101 S.Ct. 1048, *passim*; *Parker v. Flook*, 437 U.S. 584, 98 S.Ct. 2522, 57 L.Ed.2d 451 (1978); *Gottschalk v. Benson*, 409 U.S. 63, 93 S.Ct. 253, 34 L.Ed.2d 273 (1972). In *Diehr*, the Court explained that certain types of mathematical subject matter, standing alone, represent nothing more than abstract ideas until reduced to some type of practical application, i.e., "a useful, concrete and tangible result." *Alappat*, 33 F.3d at 1544, 31 USPQ2d at 1557.

This has come to be known as the mathematical algorithm exception. This designation has led to some confusion, especially given the *Freeman-Walter–Abele* analysis. By keeping in mind that the mathematical algorithm is unpatentable only to the extent that it represents an abstract idea, this confusion may be ameliorated.

Unpatentable mathematical algorithms are identifiable by showing they are merely abstract ideas constituting disembodied concepts or truths that are not "useful." From a practical standpoint, this means that to be patentable an algorithm must be applied in a "useful" way. In Alappat, we held that data, transformed by a machine through a series of mathematical calculations to produce a smooth waveform display on a rasterizer monitor, constituted a practical application of an abstract idea (a mathematical algorithm, formula, or calculation), because it produced "a useful, concrete and tangible result"—the smooth waveform.

Today, we hold that the transformation of data, representing discrete dollar amounts, by a machine through a series of mathematical calculations into a final share price, constitutes a practical application of a mathematical algorithm, formula, or calculation, because it produces "a useful, concrete and tangible result"—a final share price momentarily fixed for recording and reporting purposes and even accepted and relied upon by regulatory authorities and in subsequent trades.

The district court erred by applying the *Freeman-Walter–Abele* test to determine whether the claimed subject matter was an unpatentable abstract idea. The *Freeman-Walter–Abele* test was designed by the Court of Customs and Patent Appeals, and subsequently adopted by this court, to extract and identify unpatentable mathematical algorithms in the aftermath of *Benson* and *Flook*. The test has been thus articulated:

> First, the claim is analyzed to determine whether a mathematical algorithm is directly or indirectly recited. Next, if a mathematical algorithm is found, the claim as a whole is further analyzed to determine whether the algorithm is "applied in any manner to physical elements or process steps," and, if it is, it "passes muster under 101."

In re Pardo, 684 F.2d 912, 915, 214 USPQ 673, 675–76 (CCPA 1982).

After *Diehr* and *Chakrabarty*, the *Freeman-Walter–Abele* test has little, if any, applicability to determining the presence of statutory subject matter. As we pointed out in *Alappat*, 33 F.3d at 1543, 31 USPQ2d at 1557, application of the test could be misleading, because a process, machine, manufacture, or composition of matter employing a law of nature, natural phenomenon, or abstract idea is patentable subject matter even though a law of nature, natural phenomenon, or abstract idea would not, by itself, be entitled to such protection. The test determines the presence of, for example, an algorithm. Under *Benson*, this may have been a sufficient indicium of nonstatutory subject matter. However, after *Diehr* and *Alappat*, the mere fact that a claimed invention involves inputting numbers, calculating numbers, outputting numbers, and storing numbers, in and of itself, would not render it nonstatutory subject matter, unless, of course, its operation does not produce a "useful, concrete and tangible result." *Alappat*, 33 F.3d at 1544. After all, as we have repeatedly stated,

> every step-by-step process, be it electronic or chemical or mechanical, involves an algorithm in the broad sense of the term. Since § 101 expressly includes processes as a category of inventions which may be patented and § 100(b) further defines the word "process" as meaning process, art or method, and includes a new use of a known process, machine, manufacture, composition of matter, or material," it follows that it is no ground for holding a claim is directed to

nonstatutory subject matter to say it includes or is directed to an algorithm. This is why the proscription against patenting has been limited to *mathematical* algorithms....

In re Iwahashi, 888 F.2d 1370, 1374, 12 USPQ2d 1908, 1911 (Fed.Cir. 1989) (emphasis in the original).

The question of whether a claim encompasses statutory subject matter should not focus on *which* of the four categories of subject matter a claim is directed to—process, machine, manufacture, or composition of matter—but rather on the essential characteristics of the subject matter, in particular, its practical utility. Section 101 specifies that statutory subject matter must also satisfy the other "conditions and requirements" of Title 35, including novelty, nonobviousness, and adequacy of disclosure and notice. *See In re Warmerdam*, 33 F.3d 1354, 1359, 31 USPQ2d 1754, 1757–58 (Fed.Cir.1994). For purpose of our analysis, as noted above, claim 1 is directed to a machine programmed with the Hub and Spoke software and admittedly produces a "useful, concrete, and tangible result." *Alappat*, 33 F.3d at 1544, 31 USPQ2d at 1557. This renders it statutory subject matter, even if the useful result is expressed in numbers, such as price, profit, percentage, cost, or loss.

The Business Method Exception

As an alternative ground for invalidating the '056 patent under § 101, the court relied on the judicially-created, so-called "business method" exception to statutory subject matter. We take this opportunity to lay this ill-conceived exception to rest. Since its inception, the "business method" exception has merely represented the application of some general, but no longer applicable legal principle, perhaps arising out of the "requirement for invention"—which was eliminated by § 103. Since the 1952 Patent Act, business methods have been, and should have been, subject to the same legal requirements for patentability as applied to any other process or method.

The business method exception has never been invoked by this court, or the CCPA, to deem an invention unpatentable. Application of this particular exception has always been preceded by a ruling based on some clearer concept of Title 35 or, more commonly, application of the abstract idea exception based on finding a mathematical algorithm. Illustrative is ... *In re Schrader*, 22 F.3d 290, 30 USPQ2d 1455 (Fed.Cir.1994), while making reference to the business method exception, turned on the fact that the claims implicitly recited an abstract idea in the form of a mathematical algorithm and there was no "transformation or conversion of subject matter representative of or constituting physical activity or objects." 22 F.3d at 294, 30 USPQ2d at 1459 (emphasis omitted).

Even the case frequently cited as establishing the business method exception to statutory subject matter, *Hotel Security Checking Co. v. Lorraine Co.*, 160 F. 467 (2d Cir.1908), did not rely on the exception to strike the patent. In that case, the patent was found invalid for lack of novelty and "invention," not because it was improper subject matter for a patent. The court stated "the fundamental principle of the system is as old as the art of bookkeeping, i.e., charging the goods of the employer to the agent who takes them." *Id.* at 469. "If at the time of [the patent] application, there had been no system of bookkeeping of any kind in restaurants, we would be confronted with the question whether a new and useful system of cash registering and account checking is such an art as is patentable under the statute." *Id.* at 472.

This case is no exception. The district court announced the precepts of the business method exception as set forth in several treatises, but noted as its primary reason for finding the patent invalid under the business method exception as follows:

> If Signature's invention were patentable, any financial institution desirous of implementing a multi-tiered funding complex modelled (sic) on a Hub and Spoke configuration would be required to seek Signature's permission before embarking on such a project. *This is so because the '056 Patent is claimed [sic] sufficiently broadly to foreclose virtually any computer-implemented accounting method necessary to manage this type of financial structure.*

927 F.Supp. 502, 516, 38 USPQ2d 1530, 1542 (emphasis added). Whether the patent's claims are too broad to be patentable is not to be judged under 101, but rather under §§ 102, 103 and 112. Assuming the above statement to be correct, it has nothing to do with whether what is claimed is statutory subject matter.

In view of this background, it comes as no surprise that in the most recent edition of the Manual of Patent Examining Procedures (MPEP) (1996), a paragraph of § 706.03(a) was deleted. In past editions it read:

> Though seemingly within the category of process or method, a method of doing business can be rejected as not being within the statutory classes. *See Hotel Security Checking Co. v. Lorraine Co.*, 160 F. 467 (2d Cir.1908) and *In re Wait*, 24 USPQ 88, 22 C.C.P.A. 822, 73 F.2d 982 (1934).

MPEP § 706.03(a) (1994). This acknowledgment is buttressed by the U.S. Patent and Trademark 1996 Examination Guidelines for Computer Related Inventions which now read:

> Office personnel have had difficulty in properly treating claims directed to methods of doing business. Claims should not be categorized as methods of doing business. Instead such claims should be treated like any other process claims.

Examination Guidelines, 61 FED.REG. 7478, 7479 (1996). We agree that this is precisely the manner in which this type of claim should be treated. Whether the claims are directed to subject matter within 101 should not turn on whether the claimed subject matter does _business_ instead of something else.

REVERSED AND REMANDED

Notes

1. Claiming as a "machine"? Standard advice after the *Alappat* case was to claim software inventions with repeated references to arithmetic logic units, barrel shifters, and ROM—the usual hardware components of personal computers. By invoking those terms, the advice continued, the invention could be characterized as a machine and fall within the patent eligibility rules set by *Alappat*. At one point the *State Street* opinion notes that patent eligibility does not focus on which of the four categories of subject matter a claim is directed to ... but rather on ... its practical utility. Does this mean that a claim drafter for software inventions need no longer employ the fiction of invoking machine terms? Is this "practical utility" requirement the same as the utility standard discussed in Chapter 3 of this casebook?

2. Farewell to *Freeman-Walter–Abele*. The *Arrhythmia* decision, among others, used the *Freeman-Walter–Abele* test for patent eligibility. This test essentially recognized that the *Benson* algorithm exception (among other rationales in the wandering opinion) rested on the principle that mental processes or head and hand processes were not eligible for patenting. Thus, the *Freeman-Walter–Abele* test sought physical steps to avoid the mental processes trap. *State Street's* rejection of the *Freeman-Walter–Abele* test thus repudiates one of the underpinnings of the *Benson* opinion. Does rejection of the *Freeman-Walter–Abele* test mean that the Federal Circuit has essentially adopted the view of the concurrence in *Arrythmia* that *Freeman-Walter–Abele* was an outdated vestige of past errors in interpreting section 101?

3. *State Street* applied to claimed processes. In *State Street,* the court classified the invention as a machine because the means claims may only be reasonably viewed as process claims if there is no supporting structure in the written description. Within a few months of *State Street,* the Federal Circuit had already applied its rule to process claims. In *AT&T Corp. v. Excel Communications, Inc.,* 172 F.3d 1352, 50 U.S.P.Q.2d 1447 (Fed.Cir.1999), a case reviewing the patent eligibility of a method of billing long distance telephone calls, Judge Plager explained for the court:

> In the case before us, AT & T did not charge Excel with infringement of its apparatus claims, but limited its infringement charge to the specified method or process claims ... [W]e consider the scope of section 101 to be the same regardless of the form—machine or process—in which a particular claim is drafted ... Thus, we are comfortable in applying our reasoning in *Alappat* and *State Street* to the method claims at issue in this case

The invention in *AT&T* went towards a method of inserting data into a long distance call record in order to enable proper billing of the call. Thus, for instance, the data might enable the long distance call company to provide a discount when both the caller and the recipient of the call use the same phone company. This invention solely involved information exchange, not a physical transformation as suggested in some earlier cases, yet the Federal Circuit upheld its patent eligibility as a useful invention. Have these cases really brought patent law into the information age in the sense that information alone (a method of efficiently communicating) seems to be patent eligible? What difficulties will the PTO face in acquiring prior art to examine technologies that in the past were not subject to patent protection and thus were held as trade secrets?

4.   Abstractness the last obstacle to eligibility. In referring to *In re Schrader,* the *State Street* court made it clear that a claim could still be ineligible due to abstractness. Similarly, the *AT&T* court explained that the result in the earlier *Warmerdam* opinion was a straightforward application of the basic principle that mere abstract ideas are not within the categories of inventions of discoveries that may be patented. *State Street* concludes rather summarily that a useful concrete and tangible result is not abstract. Where is the dividing line between useful and abstract? What neutral principle separates the useful from the abstract? Is the *State Street* reasoning just shifting the arbitrary decision of patent eligibility to a new ground— utility vs. abstractness? Even if you answer yes to this last question, has the new arbitrary decision (useful vs. abstract) advanced the ball in terms of counting more valuable technologies as eligible over the last arbitrary decision (algorithm vs physical transformation)?

5.   The Guidelines Vindicated. In the closing paragraph of *State Street*, the court blesses the 1996 PTO guidelines on computer related inventions. Will the guidelines and the new *State Street* utility test, now approved by the Federal Circuit, answer most eligibility questions or just create new litigation over the meaning of new terminology?

6.   Criticizing *State Street*. In *The Patenting of the Liberal Professions,* 40 BOSTON COLLEGE L. REV. 1139 (1999), Professor Thomas subjects the State *Street* opinion to severe criticism:

> The State *Street* court also squarely stated that the district court had erred by applying the *Freeman-Walter–Abele* test. According to the court, "[a]fter *Diehr* and *Chakrabarty,* the *Freeman-Walter–Abele* test has little, if any, applicability to determining the presence of statutory subject matter." As a matter of chronology this statement is plainly false: the Supreme Court issued *Chakrabarty* in 1980 and *Diehr* in 1981. The Court of Customs and Patent Appeals authored *Abele* in 1982.
>
> This aberrant reinterpretation of *Diehr* and *Chakrabarty* also does a disservice to any number of Federal Circuit opinions which applied the *Freeman-Walter–Abele* test in patent eligibility determinations. It further seems to misread *Chakrabarty.* There the Court expressly stated that a "claim for an improved method of calculation even when tied to a specific end use, is unpatentable subject matter under § 101." This standard appears to provide ample basis for striking down Signature's claimed system, which does nothing more than maintain the accounting books for a particular financial product.
>
> In perhaps the most telling line of the opinion, the State *Street* opinion further told us that the key inquiry concerning statutory subject matter involves "the essential characteristics of the subject matter, in particular, its practical utility." This remark appears to collapse the subject matter inquiry into another patentability requisite, that of utility. The utility standard has always been a minimal one, requiring

only that the invention confer a specific benefit in currently available form. The difficulty with this approach is that, since the early Nineteenth Century, the utility standard has been understood to present a distinct additional hurdle to patentability. Not only does this dramatic reinterpretation of § 101 seem to relegate that statute's recitation of categories of patentable subject matter into little more than claim formatting protocols, it also presents an extremely vitiated gatekeeper to the patent system.

Last, we have good reason to doubt whether such innovations lie within the useful arts, the constitutional stricture concerning patentable subject matter. The sparse materials we possess regarding this term suggests that the Framers were unlikely to see every created thing as encompassed within it. They undoubtedly contemplated the industrial, mechanical, and manual arts of the late Eighteenth Century in contrast to the seven liberal arts and the four fine arts of classical learning. The Framers were also likely aware of the English experience leading to the Statute of Monopolies. The principal aim of that legislation was to proscribe grants of monopolies except for any letters patent providing the exclusive right of the sole working or making of "any manner of new manufactures within this realm, to the true and first inventor...."

In a passage especially worthy of consideration following *State Street,* the Court of Customs and Patent Appeals explained that the inclusion of the patent and copyright clause in the Constitution "doubtlessly was due to the fact that those who formulated the Constitution were familiar with the long struggle over monopolies so prominent in English history, where exclusive rights to engage even in *ordinary business activities* were granted so frequently by the Crown." *In re Shao Wen Yuan,* 188 F.2d 377, 380, 89 U.S.P.Q. 324, 327 (CCPA 1951) (emphasis added). Whether the *State Street* panel has respected the policy concerns that animated the Statute of Monopolies remains questionable.

7.   Software and Business Methods in Europe. Article 52(2) of the European Patent Convention explicitly places "programs for computers," "mathematical methods," and "presentations of information" without the scope of patent eligibility. But despite these seeming prohibitions, the European Patent Office has granted patents to a wide variety of computer-related inventions. The Guidelines for Examination in the European Patent Office indicate that:

> A computer program claimed by itself or as a record on a carrier, is not patentable irrespective of its content. The situation is not normally changed when the computer program is loaded into a known computer. If however the subject-matter as claimed makes a technical contribution to the known art, patentability should not be denied merely on the ground that a computer program is involved in its implementation. This means, for example, that program-controlled machines and program-controlled manufacturing and control processes should normally be regarded as patentable subject-matter. It follows also that, where the claimed subject-matter is concerned only with the program-controlled internal working of a known computer, the subject-matter could be patentable if it provides a technical effect. As an example consider the

case of a known data-processing system with a small fast working memory and a larger but slower further memory. Suppose that the two memories are organized under program control, in such a way that a process which needs more address space than the capacity of the fast working memory can be executed at substantially the same speed as if the process data were loaded entirely in that fast memory. The effect of the program in virtually extending the working memory is of a technical character and might therefore support patentability.

The seminal decision of the EPO Technical Board of Appeal in *Computer-related Invention/VICOM*, T 208/84, 1987 OJ EPO 14 (1986), concerned a claimed method and apparatus for digitally processing images in the form of a two-dimensional data array. The Board held that the invention was related to a technical process rather than a mathematical algorithm as such. According to the Board, the claimed process did not merely manipulate numbers to reach a numerical result; a technical means implemented a method leading to a change in a physical entity. For an extensive discussion of *VICOM* by the English Court of Appeal see *In re Matter of Application No. 9204959.2 by FUJITSU Ltd., see also X-ray Apparatus/Koch & Sterzel*, T 26/86, 1988 OJ EPO 19 (1987). The German courts have followed an approach centering upon the invention's technical effect as well. *See, e.g., Tauchcomputer* ("Diving Computer"), X ZR 43/91 (1992) (English translation available in 1993 OJ EPO 250); *Chinesische Schriftzeichen* ("Chinese Characters"), X ZB 24/89 (1991) (English translation available in 1992 OJ EPO 798).

The leading EPO "business methods" case is *Pension Benefit Systems*, 2001 OJ EPO 413. The application at issue there claimed a method and apparatus for controlling a pension benefits program. The Technical Board of Appeal affirmed the examiner's rejection of the method claims as reciting unpatentable subject matter. The Board concluded that "methods only involving economic concepts and practices of doing business are not inventions within the meaning of Article 52(1) EPC. A feature of a method which concerns the use of technical means for a purely non-technical purpose and/or for processing purely non-technical information does not necessarily confer a technical character on such a method." Although the Board conceded that "an apparatus constituting a physical entity or concrete product, suitable for performing or supporting an economic activity, is [a patentable] invention," it concluded that the claimed subject matter did not present an advance sufficient to fulfill the requirement of inventive step (the European analogue to the U.S. nonobviousness requirement).

More recently, the European Commission has proposed a Directive on the Patentability of Computer–Implemented Inventions. The current form of the Directive, which issued on February 20, 2002, would appear to liberalize the requirements for patenting computer software in Europe. Most notable is Article 4 of the Directive, which reads:

Conditions for patentability

1. Member States shall ensure that a computer-implemented invention is patentable on the condition that it is susceptible of industrial application, is new, and involves an inventive step.

2.   Member States shall ensure that it is a condition of involving an inventive step that a computer-implemented invention must make a technical contribution.

3.   The technical contribution shall be assessed by consideration of the difference between the scope of the patent claim considered as a whole, elements of which may comprise both technical and non-technical features, and the state of the art.

Somewhat unhelpfully, the draft Directive defines the crucial term "technical contribution" as "a contribution to the state of the art in a technical field which is not obvious to a person skilled in the art." Article 2(b). Discussion over the draft Directive proceeds as this casebook goes to press.

   8.   Software and Business Methods in Japan. Japanese patent law is generally permissive of patents upon software. Unless they can be successfully characterized as computer programs, however, business methods have fared less well. General notions of patent eligibility are founded in Article 2(1) of the Japanese Patent Act, which defines "invention" as the "highly advanced creation of technical ideas by which a law of nature is utilized." A patent application which claims a natural law itself will thus be rejected as nonstatutory. Within the computer arts, inventions which control hardware processes or process information based upon the physical or technical qualities of an object may receive patent protection; patent ineligible inventions are those which perform "information processing . . . based on mathematical methods, schemes, rules or methods for doing business or performing mental activities." *See generally Examination Guidelines for Patent and Utility Model in Japan* (AIPPI Japan).

§ 2.2   COMPOSITIONS OF MATTER—BIOTECHNOLOGY

Since the late 1970s, scientists have been able to cause living organisms to express genetic material from outside their own species, with extraordinary results. New strains of plants produce higher yields, resist viruses and pests, and are productive in formerly inhospitable climates. So-called "transgenic" animals currently produce an array of human pharmaceutical compounds that would otherwise be unavailable due to expense or insufficient sources of supply. Others serve as potent research tools, allowing scientists to explore human diseases for which inadequate, or even no natural animal subjects exist. The prospect of human consumption of superior transgenic livestock, the elimination of certain genetic diseases and other advances seemingly out of the realm of speculative fiction appear not so distant. *See generally* Reid G. Adler, *Controlling the Application of Biotechnology: A Critical Analysis of the Proposed Moratorium on Animal Patenting*, 1 HARV. J. L. & TECHNOLOGY 1 (1988).

In what may be the only predictable element of this dramatic technical field, applicants quickly sought patent protection for their biotechnology advances. The prospect of patents on "living inventions" ultimately provoked a tremendous outcry, with intense public concern overly a field of law often considered obscure. As you review these materials, consider whether the patent law is itself an appropriate vehicle to resolve the social issues of technical advance.

DIAMOND, COMMISSIONER OF PATENTS AND TRADEMARKS v. CHAKRABARTY

United States Supreme Court, 1980.
447 U.S. 303, 206 U.S.P.Q. 193.

Dr. Ananda N. Chakrabarty artificially created an oil-eating bacterium and filed a patent application with three sorts of claims. Two of them were in method format–the method of making the bacterium and the method of using the bacterium to consume oil. The third claim category was directed towards the bacterium itself, providing:

> 7. *A bacterium from the genus Pseudomonas containing therein at least two stable energy-generating plasmids, each of said plasmids providing a separate hydrocarbon degradative pathway.*

The PTO rejected this latter claim on the ground that the bacterium was a product of nature, or, alternatively, that it was a living thing and therefore outside the purview of Title 35. The Supreme Court ultimately took up the matter and overturned the examiner's rejection in the following opinion.

BURGER, CHIEF JUSTICE.

II

The Constitution grants Congress broad power to legislate to "promote the Progress of Science and useful Arts, by securing for limited Times to Authors and Inventors the exclusive Right to their respective Writings and Discoveries." Art. I, § 8, cl. 8. The patent laws promote this progress by offering inventors exclusive rights for a limited period as an incentive for their inventiveness and research efforts. *Kewanee Oil Co. v. Bicron Corp.*, 416 U.S. 470, 480–481, 94 S.Ct. 1879, 1885–1886, 40 L.Ed.2d 315 (1974); *Universal Oil Co. v. Globe Co.*, 322 U.S. 471, 484, 64 S.Ct. 1110, 1116, 88 L.Ed. 1399 (1944). The authority of Congress is exercised in the hope that "[t]he productive effort thereby fostered will have a positive effect on society through the introduction of new products and processes of manufacture into the economy, and the emanations by way of increased employment and better lives for our citizens." *Kewanee, supra*, 416 U.S., at 480, 94 S.Ct., at 1885–86.

The question before us in this case is a narrow one of statutory interpretation requiring us to construe 35 U.S.C. § 101. . . . Specifically, we must determine whether respondent's micro-organism constitutes a "manufacture" or "composition of matter" within the meaning of the statute.

III

In cases of statutory construction we begin, of course, with the language of the statute. And "unless otherwise defined, words will be interpreted as taking their ordinary, contemporary common meaning." *Perrin v. United States*, 444 U.S. 37, 42, 100 S.Ct. 311, 314, 62 L.Ed.2d 199 (1979). We have also cautioned that courts "should not read into the patent laws limitations and conditions which the legislature has not expressed." *United States v. Dubilier Condenser Corp.*, 289 U.S. 178, 199, 53 S.Ct. 554, 561, 77 L.Ed. 1114 (1933).

Guided by these canons of construction, this Court has read the term "manufacture" in § 101 in accordance with its dictionary definition to mean "the production of articles for use from raw or prepared materials by giving to these materials new forms, qualities, properties, or combinations, whether by hand-labor or by machinery." *American Fruit Growers, Inc. v. Brogdex Co.*, 283 U.S. 1, 11, 51 S.Ct. 328, 330, 75 L.Ed. 801 (1931). Similarly, "composition of matter" has been construed consistent with its common usage to include "all compositions of two or more substances and ... all composite articles, whether they be the results of chemical union, or of mechanical mixture, or whether they be gases, fluids, powders or solids." *Shell Development Co. v. Watson*, 149 F.Supp. 279, 280 (D.C.1957) (citing 1 A. DELLER, WALKER ON PATENTS § 14, p. 55 (1st ed. 1937)). In choosing such expansive terms as "manufacture" and "composition of matter," modified by the comprehensive "any," Congress plainly contemplated that the patent laws would be given wide scope.

The relevant legislative history also supports a broad construction. The Patent Act of 1793, authored by Thomas Jefferson, defined statutory subject matter as "any new and useful art, machine, manufacture, or composition of matter, or any new or useful improvement [thereof]." Act of Feb. 21, 1793, § 1, 1 Stat. 319. The Act embodied Jefferson's philosophy that "ingenuity should receive a liberal encouragement." 5 WRITINGS OF THOMAS JEFFERSON 75–76 (Washington ed. 1871). See *Graham v. John Deere Co.*, 383 U.S. 1, 7–10, 86 S.Ct. 684, 688–690, 15 L.Ed.2d 545 (1966). Subsequent patent statutes in 1836, 1870, and 1874 employed this same broad language. In 1952, when the patent laws were recodified, Congress replaced the word "art" with "process," but otherwise left Jefferson's language intact. The Committee Reports accompanying the 1952 Act inform us that Congress intended statutory subject matter to "include anything under the sun that is made by man." S.Rep.No.1979, 82d Cong., 2d Sess., 5 (1952); H.R.Rep.No.1923, 82d Cong., 2d Sess., 6 (1952).

This is not to suggest that § 101 has no limits or that it embraces every discovery. The laws of nature, physical phenomena, and abstract ideas have been held not patentable. See *Parker v. Flook*, 437 U.S. 584, 98 S.Ct. 2522, 57 L.Ed.2d 451 (1978); *Gottschalk v. Benson*, 409 U.S. 63, 67, 93 S.Ct. 253, 255, 34 L.Ed.2d 273 (1972); *Funk Brothers Seed Co. v. Kalo Inoculant Co.*, 333 U.S. 127, 130, 68 S.Ct. 440, 441, 92 L.Ed. 588 (1948); *O'Reilly v. Morse*, 15 How. 62, 112–121, 14 L.Ed. 601 (1854); *Le Roy v. Tatham*, 14 How. 156, 175, 14 L.Ed. 367 (1853). Thus, a new mineral discovered in the earth or a new plant found in the wild is not patentable subject matter. Likewise, Einstein could not patent his celebrated law that E=mc 2; nor could Newton have patented the law of gravity. Such discoveries are "manifestations of . . . nature, free to all men and reserved exclusively to none." *Funk, supra*, 333 U.S., at 130, 68 S.Ct., at 441.

Judged in this light, respondent's micro-organism plainly qualifies as patentable subject matter. His claim is not to a hitherto unknown natural phenomenon, but to a nonnaturally occurring manufacture or composition of matter—a product of human ingenuity "having a distinctive name, character [and] use." *Hartranft v. Wiegmann*, 121 U.S. 609, 615, 7 S.Ct. 1240, 1243, 30 L.Ed. 1012 (1887). The point is underscored dramatically by comparison of the invention here with that in *Funk*. There, the patentee had discovered that there existed in nature certain species of root-nodule bacteria which did not exert a mutually inhibitive effect on each other. He used that discovery to produce a mixed culture capable of inoculating the seeds of leguminous plants. Concluding that the patentee had discovered "only some of the handiwork of nature," the Court ruled the product nonpatentable:

> "Each of the species of root-nodule bacteria contained in the package infects the same group of leguminous plants which it always infected. No species acquires a different use. The combination of species produces no new bacteria, no change in the six species of bacteria, and no enlargement of the range of their utility. Each species has the same effect it always had. The bacteria perform in their natural way. Their use in combination does not improve in any way their natural functioning. They serve the ends nature originally provided and act quite independently of any effort of the patentee." 333 U.S., at 131, 68 S.Ct., at 442.

Here, by contrast, the patentee has produced a new bacterium with markedly different characteristics from any found in nature and one having the potential for significant utility. His discovery is not nature's handiwork, but his own; accordingly it is patentable subject matter under § 101.

IV

Two contrary arguments are advanced, neither of which we find persuasive.

(A)

The petitioner's first argument rests on the enactment of the 1930 Plant Patent Act, which afforded patent protection to certain asexually reproduced plants, and the 1970 Plant Variety Protection Act, which authorized protection for certain sexually reproduced plants but excluded bacteria from its protection. In the petitioner's view, the passage of these Acts evidences congressional understanding that the terms "manufacture" or "composition of matter" do not include living things; if they did, the petitioner argues, neither Act would have been necessary.

We reject this argument. Prior to 1930, two factors were thought to remove plants from patent protection. The first was the belief that plants, even those artificially bred, were products of nature for purposes of the patent law. This position appears to have derived from the decision of the patent office in *Ex parte Latimer*, 1889 Dec.Com.Pat. 123, in which a patent claim for fiber found in the needle of the *Pinus australis* was rejected. The Commissioner reasoned that a contrary result would permit "patents [to] be obtained upon the trees of the forest and the plants of the earth, which of course would be unreasonable and impossible." *Id.*, at 126. The *Latimer* case, it seems, came to "se[t] forth the general stand taken in these matters" that plants were natural products not subject to patent protection. Thorne, *Relation of Patent Law to Natural Products*, 6 J. PAT.OFF.SOC. 23, 24 (1923). The second obstacle to patent protection for plants was the fact that plants were thought not amenable to the "written description" requirement of the patent law. See 35 U.S.C. § 112. Because new plants may differ from old only in color or perfume, differentiation by written description was often impossible. See Hearings on H.R.11372 before the House Committee on Patents, 71st Cong., 2d Sess. 7 (1930) (memorandum of Patent Commissioner Robertson).

In enacting the Plant Patent Act, Congress addressed both of these concerns. It explained at length its belief that the work of the plant breeder "in aid of nature" was patentable invention. S.Rep.No.315, 71st Cong., 2d Sess., 6–8 (1930); H.R.Rep.No.1129, 71st Cong., 2d Sess., 7–9 (1930). And it relaxed the written description requirement in favor of "a description ... as complete as is reasonably possible." 35 U.S.C. § 162. No Committee or Member of Congress, however, expressed the broader view, now urged by the petitioner, that the terms "manufacture" or "composition of matter" exclude living things. The sole support for that position in the legislative history of the 1930 Act is found in the conclusory statement of Secretary of Agriculture Hyde, in a letter to the Chairmen of the House and Senate Committees considering the 1930 Act, that "the patent laws ... at the present time are understood to cover only inventions or discoveries in the field of inanimate nature." See S.Rep.No.315, *supra*, at Appendix A; H.R.Rep.No.1129, *supra*, at Appendix A. Secretary Hyde's opinion, however, is not entitled to controlling weight. His views were solicited on the administration of the new law and not on the scope of patentable subject matter—an area beyond his competence. Moreover, there is language in the House and Senate Committee Reports suggesting that to the extent Congress considered the matter it found the Secretary's dichotomy unpersuasive. The Reports observe:

> "There is a clear and logical distinction *between the discovery of a new variety of plant and of certain inanimate things*, such, for example, as a new and useful natural mineral. The mineral is created wholly by nature unassisted by man.... On the other hand, a plant discovery resulting from cultivation is unique, isolated, and is not repeated by nature, nor can it be reproduced by nature

unaided by man. . . ." S.Rep.No.315, *supra*, at 6; H.R.Rep.No.1129, *supra*, at 7 (emphasis added).

Congress thus recognized that the relevant distinction was not between living and inanimate things, but between products of nature, whether living or not, and human-made inventions. Here, respondent's micro-organism is the result of human ingenuity and research. Hence, the passage of the Plant Patent Act affords the Government no support.

Nor does the passage of the 1970 Plant Variety Protection Act support the Government's position. As the Government acknowledges, sexually reproduced plants were not included under the 1930 Act because new varieties could not be reproduced true-to-type through seedlings. Brief for Petitioner 27, n. 31. By 1970, however, it was generally recognized that true-to-type reproduction was possible and that plant patent protection was therefore appropriate. The 1970 Act extended that protection. There is nothing in its language or history to suggest that it was enacted because § 101 did not include living things.

In particular, we find nothing in the exclusion of bacteria from plant variety protection to support the petitioner's position. The legislative history gives no reason for this exclusion. As the Court of Customs and Patent Appeals suggested, it may simply reflect congressional agreement with the result reached by that court in deciding *In re Arzberger*, 27 C.C.P.A. (Pat.) 1315, 112 F.2d 834 (1940), which held that bacteria were not plants for the purposes of the 1930 Act. Or it may reflect the fact that prior to 1970 the Patent Office had issued patents for bacteria under § 101. In any event, absent some clear indication that Congress "focused on [the] issues ... directly related to the one presently before the Court," *SEC v. Sloan*, 436 U.S. 103, 120–121, 98 S.Ct. 1702, 1713, 56 L.Ed.2d 148 (1978), there is no basis for reading into its actions an intent to modify the plain meaning of the words found in § 101.

(B)

The petitioner's second argument is that micro-organisms cannot qualify as patentable subject matter until Congress expressly authorizes such protection. His position rests on the fact that genetic technology was unforeseen when Congress enacted § 101. From this it is argued that resolution of the patentability of inventions such as respondent's should be left to Congress. The legislative process, the petitioner argues, is best equipped to weigh the competing economic, social, and scientific considerations involved, and to determine whether living organisms produced by genetic engineering should receive patent protection. In support of this position, the petitioner relies on our recent holding in *Parker v. Flook*, 437 U.S. 584, 98 S.Ct. 2522, 57 L.Ed.2d 451 (1978), and the statement that the judiciary "must proceed cautiously when ... asked to extend patent rights into areas wholly unforeseen by Congress." *Id.*, at 596, 98 S.Ct. at 2529.

It is, of course, correct that Congress, not the courts, must define the limits of patentability; but it is equally true that once Congress has spoken it is "the province and duty of the judicial department to say what the law is." *Marbury v. Madison*, 1 Cranch 137, 177, 2 L.Ed. 60 (1803). Congress has performed its constitutional role in defining patentable subject matter in § 101; we perform ours in construing the language Congress has employed. In so doing, our obligation is to take statutes as we find them, guided, if ambiguity appears, by the legislative history and statutory purpose. Here, we perceive no ambiguity. The subject-matter provisions of the patent law have been cast in broad terms to fulfill the constitutional and statutory goal of promoting "the Progress of Science and the useful Arts" with all that means for the social and economic benefits envisioned by Jefferson. Broad general language is not necessarily ambiguous when congressional objectives require broad terms.

Nothing in Flook is to the contrary. That case applied our prior precedents to determine that a "claim for an improved method of calculation, even when tied to a specific end use, is unpatentable subject matter under § 101." 437 U.S., at 595, n. 18, 98 S.Ct., at 2528, n. 18. The Court carefully scrutinized the claim at issue to determine whether it was precluded from patent protection under "the principles underlying the prohibition against patents for 'ideas' or phenomena of nature." *Id.*, at 593, 98 S.Ct. at 2527. We have done that here. Flook did not announce a new principle that inventions in areas not contemplated by Congress when the patent laws were enacted are unpatentable per se.

To read that concept into Flook would frustrate the purposes of the patent law. This Court frequently has observed that a statute is not to be confined to the "particular application[s] ... contemplated by the legislators." *Barr v. United States*, 324 U.S. 83, 90, 65 S.Ct. 522, 525, 89 L.Ed. 765 (1945). This is especially true in the field of patent law. A rule that unanticipated inventions are without protection would conflict with the core concept of the patent law that anticipation undermines patentability. *See Graham v. John Deere Co.*, 383 U.S., at 12–17, 86 S.Ct., at 691–693. Mr. Justice Douglas reminded that the inventions most benefiting mankind are those that "push back the frontiers of chemistry, physics, and the like." *Great A. & P. Tea Co. v. Supermarket Corp.*, 340 U.S. 147, 154, 71 S.Ct. 127, 131, 95 L.Ed. 162 (1950) (concurring opinion). Congress employed broad general language in drafting § 101 precisely because such inventions are often unforeseeable.

To buttress his argument, the petitioner, with the support of amicus, points to grave risks that may be generated by research endeavors such as respondent's. The briefs present a gruesome parade of horribles. Scientists, among them Nobel laureates, are quoted suggesting that genetic research may pose a serious threat to the human race, or, at the very least, that the dangers are far too substantial to permit such research to proceed apace at this time. We are told that genetic research and related technological developments may spread pollution and disease, that it may result in a loss of genetic diversity, and that its practice may tend to depreciate the value of human life. These arguments are forcefully, even passionately, presented; they remind us that, at times, human ingenuity seems unable to control fully the forces it creates–that with Hamlet, it is sometimes better "to bear those ills we have than fly to others that we know not of."

It is argued that this Court should weigh these potential hazards in considering whether respondent's invention is patentable subject matter under § 101. We disagree. The grant or denial of patents on micro-organisms is not likely to put an end to genetic research or to its attendant risks. The large amount of research that has already occurred when no researcher had sure knowledge that patent protection would be available suggests that legislative or judicial fiat as to patentability will not deter the scientific mind from probing into the unknown any more than Canute could command the tides. Whether respondent's claims are patentable may determine whether research efforts are accelerated by the hope of reward or slowed by want of incentives, but that is all.

What is more important is that we are without competence to entertain these arguments–either to brush them aside as fantasies generated by fear of the unknown, or to act on them. The choice we are urged to make is a matter of high policy for resolution within the legislative process after the kind of investigation, examination, and study that legislative bodies can provide and courts cannot. That process involves the balancing of competing values and interests, which in our democratic system is the business of elected representatives. Whatever their validity, the contentions now pressed on us should be addressed to the political branches of the Government, the Congress and the Executive, and not to the courts.

We have emphasized in the recent past that "[o]ur individual appraisal of the wisdom or unwisdom of a particular [legislative] course . . . is to be put aside in the process of interpreting a statute." *TVA v. Hill*, 437 U.S., at 194, 98 S.Ct., at 2302. Our task, rather, is the narrow one of determining what Congress meant by the words it used in the statute; once that is done our powers are exhausted. Congress is free to amend § 101 so as to exclude from patent protection organisms produced by genetic engineering. *Cf.* 42 U.S.C.A. § 2181(a), exempting from patent protection inventions "useful solely in the utilization of special nuclear material or atomic energy in an atomic weapon." Or it may chose to craft a statute specifically designed for such living things. But, until Congress takes such action, this Court must construe the language of § 101 as it is. The language of that section fairly embraces respondent's invention.

Notes

1. More a Signal Than a Result. While even if the holding in *Chakrabarty* had been that Dr. Chakrabarty's oil-eating Pseudomonas was not patent-eligible, this would have not have impacted the patentability of claims to products made through genetic engineering, nor the patentability of claims to the method of expression of new or transfected microorganisms or other host cells. Nevertheless *Chakrabarty* was a clear signal that patenting was broadly available in the biotechnology field, and this ruling opened the coffers of Wall Street to the biotechnology industry. *See generally* Albert P. Halluin, *Patenting the Results of Genetic Engineering Research: An Overview*, in BANBURY REP. 10: PATENTING OF LIFE FORMS, *at* 67–126 (Cold Spring Harbor Laboratories 1982).

    2. European Patents on Biotechnology. Developments in Europe undertook a more curious route than in the United States. The German *Bundesgerichtshof* ("Federal Supreme Court") issued its seminal dicta in the 1969 *Rote Taube* case ("Red Dove"), *Ex parte Schreiner*, 1969 *GRUR* 672, 1 INT'L REV. INDUS. PROP. & COPYRIGHT L. 136 (1970), opening the door to patenting the inventions of modern technology. Here, the court affirmed the German Patent Office's rejection of an application claiming a method for breeding doves with red plumage based on the method's lack of repeatability. The court denied that biological manipulation lacked a technical character, however, asserting that "no sufficient reason is apparent for excluding methodical utilization of natural biological forces and phenomenon from patent protection in principle."

    The more comprehensive opinion in *Bäckerhefe* ("Baker's Yeast") followed. *In re Koninklijke Nederlandsche Gist-en Spiritusfabriek N.V.*, 1975 *GRUR* 430, 6 INT'L REV. INDUS. PROP. & COPYRIGHT L. 207 (Bundesgerichtshof 1975). Issued a full five years before *Chakrabarty*, the court held that patent protection for a new microorganism is possible, if the inventor shows a reproducible way to generate the new microorganism. *See* Harold C. Wegner, *Patenting Nature's Secrets: Microorganisms*, 7 INT'L REV. INDUS. PROP. & COPYRIGHT L. 235 (1976).

    While Continental Europe of the 1970's created a positive view on the patenting of biotechnology inventions, law promulgated a decade before shackled the future European patent system with a narrow treaty language with respect to some living inventions. Political reasons resulted in the Strasbourg Convention of 1963 serving as the underlying basis for the substantive points of the European Patent Convention of 1973. Among them were the notorious restrictions of Article 53(b), which excludes patent protection for "plant or animal varieties or essentially biological processes for the production of plants or animals," but expressly does not prohibit the patenting of "microbiological processes or the products thereof." *See generally* Noel Byrne, *Plants, Animals and Industrial Patents*, 16 INT'L REV. INDUS. PROP. & COPYRIGHT L. 1 (1985).

    The European Parliament subsequently engaged in a rancorous debate concerning the propriety of patent protection for biotechnologies. A 1993 European Parliament resolution attacked the Onco-mouse patent and affirmed the Parliament's opposition to the patenting of living things. The tide shifted somewhat in the mid–1990's however, such that on July 16, 1997, the European Parliament adopted a Directive on the Protection of Biotechnology Inventions. The Directive is more favorable to patenting than might have been anticipated, allowing the patenting of human genes and tissues among others. *See* Lydia Nenow, *To Patent or Not to Patent: The European Union's New Biotech Directive*, 23 HOUSTON J. INT'L L. 569 (2001).

    3. Subsequent U.S. Developments. In the wake of *Chakrabarty*, applicants soon turned to the United States Patent and Trademark Office with inventions for living organisms, including mammalian animals. In *Ex* *parte Allen*, 2 U.S.P.Q.2d 1425 (BPAI 1987), the Board held that the claimed polyploid oysters were nonnaturally occurring manufactures or compositions of matter under § 101. The Federal Circuit subsequently dismissed a suit brought by various animal and farmers rights groups, including the American Society for the Prevention of Cruelty to Animals, the Wisconsin Family Farm Defense Fund, and the People for the Ethical Treatment of Animals, for lack of standing. These groups had filed suit in district court under the Administrative Procedure Act, 5 U.S.C.A. §§ 701–706, challenging a Patent and Trademark Office Notice which provided that the PTO "now considers non-naturally occurring, non-human multicellular organisms, including animals, to be patentable subject matter within the scope of 35 U.S.C. § 101." The court reasoned that:

> Here appellants assert no adverse effect on any individual's rights to benefits under the patent statute. Rather, they assert that the general public has an interest in the statutory limitations to patentability. Essentially, appellants assert a right, as members of the public particularly interested in animals, to sue for what they perceive to be an unwarranted interference with the discretionary judgment of an examiner. However, it must be noted that whether patents are allowable for animal life forms is not a matter of discretion but of law. . . .

> [T]he farmers' alleged injuries are (1) having to pay increased costs in the form of royalties on patented animals and (2) suffering decreased profits because of competition from more productive non-naturally occurring animals. With respect to the alleged "royalties" injury, farmers cannot be forced to purchase improved animals and pay the premium (i.e., "royalty") which the farmers say is likely to be asked. Indeed, their allegation that their costs of operation will increase by reason of "royalties" is at best speculative. The motivation to purchase normally arises from the prospect of an economic advantage. Further, the ability of a market participant to affect price, i.e., exert market power, depends on whether competitive patented or non-patented animals are available. This in turn depends on the speculative activities of third party competitors whose market actions would determine the existence and extent of acceptable, noninfringing substitutes in the relevant product market. Such speculation as to market actors and their activities further beclouds the issue of causation as it concerns the farmers' alleged economic injury.

> Similarly, the farmers' alleged injury from increased competition can only result from the development and commercialization of genetically improved animals–not from the grant of a patent. We do not denigrate the stimulation of invention that the possibility of patent protection provides. However, were we to enjoin issuance of patents for non-naturally occurring animals, the requested relief would not prevent the development of such animals. It should hardly need saying that the issuance of a patent gives no right to make, use or sell a patented invention, or that the absence of a patent creates no legal prohibition against continued research or development.

Animal Legal Defense Fund v. Quigg, 932 F.2d 920, 18 U.S.P.Q.2d 1677 (Fed.Cir.1991). In any event, the Supreme Court did not revisit the patent eligibility arena for many years, when in 2002 the Court at last turned to another biotechnology patent case.

J.E.M. AG SUPPLY, INC. v. PIONEER HI–BRED INTERNATIONAL, INC.

534 U.S. 124, United States Supreme Court, 2001.

THOMAS, J., delivered the opinion of the Court, in which REHNQUIST, C. J., and SCALIA, KENNEDY, SOUTER, and GINSBURG, JJ., joined. SCALIA, J., filed a concurring opinion. BREYER, J., filed a dissenting opinion, in which STEVENS, J., joined. O'CONNOR, J., took no part in the consideration or decision of the case.

JUSTICE THOMAS.

This case presents the question whether utility patents may be issued for plants under 35 U.S.C. 101, or whether the Plant Variety Protection Act, 7 U.S.C. § 2321 et seq., and the Plant Patent Act of 1930, 35 U.S.C. §§ 161–164, are the exclusive means of obtaining a federal statutory right to exclude others from reproducing, selling, or using plants or plant varieties. We hold that utility patents may be issued for plants.

I

The United States Patent and Trademark Office (PTO) has issued some 1,800 utility patents for plants, plant parts, and seeds pursuant to 35 U.S.C. § 101. Seventeen of these patents are held by respondent Pioneer Hi–Bred International, Inc. (Pioneer). Pioneer's patents cover the manufacture, use, sale, and offer for sale of the company's inbred and hybrid corn seed products. A patent for an inbred corn line protects both the seeds and plants of the inbred line and the hybrids produced by crossing the protected inbred line with another corn line. Pedigree inbred corn plants are developed by crossing corn plants with desirable characteristics and then inbreeding the resulting plants for several generations until the resulting plant line is homogeneous. Inbreds are often weak and have a low yield; their value lies primarily in their use for making hybrids.

Hybrid seeds are produced by crossing two inbred corn plants and are especially valuable because they produce strong and vibrant hybrid plants with selected highly desirable characteristics. For instance, Pioneer's hybrid corn plant 3394 is "characterized by superior yield for maturity, excellent seedling vigor, very good roots and stalks, and exceptional stay green." U.S. Patent No. 5,491,295. Hybrid plants, however, generally do not reproduce true-to-type, i.e., seeds produced by a hybrid plant do not reliably yield plants with the same hybrid characteristics. Thus, a farmer who wishes to continue growing hybrid plants generally needs to buy more hybrid seed.

Pioneer sells its patented hybrid seeds under a limited label license that provides: "License is granted solely to produce grain and/or forage."

Id., at 51. The license "does not extend to the use of seed from such crop or the progeny thereof for propagation or seed multiplication." *Ibid*. It strictly prohibits "the use of such seed or the progeny thereof for propagation or seed multiplication or for production or development of a hybrid or different variety of seed." *Ibid*.

Petitioner J.E.M. Ag Supply, Inc., doing business as Farm Advantage, Inc., purchased patented hybrid seeds from Pioneer in bags bearing this license agreement. Although not a licensed sales representative of Pioneer, Farm Advantage resold these bags. Pioneer subsequently brought a complaint for patent infringement against Farm Advantage and several other corporations and residents of the State of Iowa who are distributors and customers for Farm Advantage (referred to collectively as Farm Advantage or petitioners). Pioneer alleged that Farm Advantage has "for a long-time past been and still [is] infringing one or more [Pioneer patents] by making, using, selling, or offering for sale corn seed of the . . . hybrids in infringement of these patents-in-suit."

Farm Advantage answered with a general denial of patent infringement and entered a counterclaim of patent invalidity, arguing that patents that purport to confer protection for corn plants are invalid because sexually reproducing plants are not patentable subject matter within the scope of 35 U.S.C. § 101. Farm Advantage maintained that the Plant Patent Act of 1930 (PPA) and the Plant Variety Protection Act (PVPA) set forth the exclusive statutory means for the protection of plant life because these statutes are more specific than § 101, and thus each carves out subject matter from § 101 for special treatment.

The District Court granted summary judgment to Pioneer. Relying on this Court's broad construction of § 101 in *Diamond v. Chakrabarty*, 447 U.S. 303, the District Court held that the subject matter covered by § 101 clearly includes plant life. It further concluded that in enacting the PPA and the PVPA Congress neither expressly nor implicitly removed plants from 101's subject matter. *Id.*, at 1819. In particular, the District Court noted that Congress did not implicitly repeal § 101 by passing the more specific PVPA because there was no irreconcilable conflict between the PVPA and § 101. The United States Court of Appeals for the Federal Circuit affirmed the judgment and reasoning of the District Court. We granted certiorari, and now affirm.

II

The question before us is whether utility patents may be issued for plants pursuant to 35 U.S.C. § 101. As this Court recognized over 20 years ago in *Chakrabarty*, 447 U.S., at 308, the language of § 101 is extremely broad. "In choosing such expansive terms as 'manufacture' and 'composition of matter,' modified by the comprehensive 'any,' Congress plainly contemplated that the patent laws would be given wide scope." This Court thus concluded in *Chakrabarty* that living things were patentable under § 101, and held that a manmade micro-organism fell within the scope of the statute. As Congress recognized, _the relevant distinction was not between living and inanimate things, but between products of nature, whether living or not, and human-made inventions."

In *Chakrabarty*, the Court also rejected the argument that Congress must expressly authorize protection for new patentable subject matter:

> It is, of course, correct that Congress, not the courts, must define the limits of patentability; but it is equally true that once Congress has spoken it is 'the province and duty of the judicial department to say what the law is.' *Marbury v. Madison*, 1 Cranch 137, 177 [2 L.Ed. 60] (1803). Congress has performed its constitutional role in defining patentable subject matter in § 101; we perform ours in construing the language Congress has employed.... The subject-matter provisions of the patent law have been cast in broad terms to fulfill the constitutional and statutory goal of promoting 'the Progress of Science and the useful Arts' with all that means for the social and economic benefits envisioned by Jefferson.

Thus, in approaching the question presented by this case, we are mindful that this Court has already spoken clearly concerning the broad scope and applicability of § 101.

Several years after *Chakrabarty*, the PTO Board of Patent Appeals and Interferences held that plants were within the understood meaning of "manufacture" or "composition of matter" and therefore were within the subject matter of § 101. *In re Hibberd*, 227 USPQ 443, 444(1985). It has been the unbroken practice of the PTO since that time to confer utility patents for plants. To obtain utility patent protection, a plant breeder must show that the plant he has developed is new, useful, and non-obvious. In addition, the plant must meet the specifications of § 112, which require a written description of the plant and a deposit of seed that is publicly accessible.

Petitioners do not allege that Pioneer's patents are invalid for failure to meet the requirements for a utility patent. Nor do they dispute that plants otherwise fall within the terms of § 101's broad language that includes "manufacture" or "composition of matter." Rather, petitioners argue that the PPA and the PVPA provide the exclusive means of protecting new varieties of plants, and so awarding utility patents for plants upsets the scheme contemplated by Congress. We disagree. Considering the two plant specific statutes in turn, we find that neither forecloses utility patent coverage for plants.

A

The 1930 PPA conferred patent protection to asexually reproduced plants. Significantly, nothing within either the original 1930 text of the statute or its recodified version in 1952 indicates that the PPA's protection for asexually reproduced plants was intended to be exclusive.

Plants were first explicitly brought within the scope of patent protection in 1930 when the PPA included "plants" among the useful things subject to patents. Thus the 1930 PPA amended the general utility patent provision to provide:

> Any person who has invented or discovered any new and useful art, machine, manufacture or composition of matter, or any new and useful improvements thereof, or who has invented or discovered and asexually reproduced any distinct and new variety of plant, other than a tuber-propagated plant, not known or used by others in this country, before his invention or discovery thereof, ... may ... obtain a patent therefor.

This provision limited protection to the asexual reproduction of the plant. Asexual reproduction occurs by grafting, budding, or the like, and produces an offspring with a genetic combination identical to that of the single parent—essentially a clone. By contrast, sexual reproduction occurs by seed and sometimes involves two different plants.

In 1952, Congress revised the patent statute and placed the plant patents into a separate chapter 15 of Title 35 entitled, "Patents for plants." 35 U.S.C. §§ 161–164. This was merely a housekeeping measure that did nothing to change the substantive rights or requirements for a plant patent. A "plant patent" continued to provide only the exclusive right to asexually reproduce a protected plant, § 163, and the description requirement remained relaxed, § 162. Plant patents under the PPA thus have very limited coverage and less stringent requirements than § 101 utility patents.

Importantly, chapter 15 nowhere states that plant patents are the exclusive means of granting intellectual property protection to plants. Although unable to point to any language that requires, or even suggests, that Congress intended the PPA's protections to be exclusive, petitioners advance three reasons why the PPA should preclude assigning utility patents for plants. We find none of these arguments to be persuasive.

First, petitioners argue that plants were not covered by the general utility patent statute prior to 1930. In advancing this argument, petitioners overlook the state of patent law and plant breeding at the time of the PPA's enactment. The Court in *Chakrabarty* explained the realities of patent law and plant breeding at the time the PPA was enacted: "Prior to 1930, two factors were thought to remove plants from patent protection. The first was the belief that plants, even those artificially bred, were products of nature for purposes of the patent law. ... The second obstacle to patent protection for plants was the fact that plants were thought not amenable to the 'written description' requirement of the patent law." 447 U.S., at 311–312, 100 S.Ct. 2204. Congress addressed these concerns with the 1930 PPA, which recognized that the work of a plant breeder was a patentable invention and relaxed the written description requirement. The PPA thus gave patent protection to breeders who were previously unable to overcome the obstacles described in *Chakrabarty*.

This does not mean, however, that prior to 1930 plants could not have fallen within the subject matter of § 101. Rather, it illustrates only that in 1930 Congress believed that plants were not patentable under

§ 101, both because they were living things and because in practice they could not meet the stringent description requirement. Yet these premises were disproved over time. As this Court held in *Chakrabarty*, "the relevant distinction" for purposes of § 101 is not "between living and inanimate things, but between products of nature, whether living or not, and human-made inventions." 447 U.S., at 313. In addition, advances in biological knowledge and breeding expertise have allowed plant breeders to satisfy § 101's demanding description requirement.

Whatever Congress may have believed about the state of patent law and the science of plant breeding in 1930, plants have always had the potential to fall within the general subject matter of § 101, which is a dynamic provision designed to encompass new and unforeseen inventions. "A rule that unanticipated inventions are without protection would conflict with the core concept of the patent law that anticipation undermines patentability." *Id.*, at 316.

Petitioners essentially ask us to deny utility patent protection for sexually reproduced plants because it was unforeseen in 1930 that such plants could receive protection under § 101. Denying patent protection under § 101 simply because such coverage was thought technologically infeasible in 1930, however, would be inconsistent with the forward-looking perspective of the utility patent statute. As we noted in *Chakrabarty*, "Congress employed broad general language in drafting § 101 precisely because [new types of] inventions are often unforeseeable." *Ibid.*

Second, petitioners maintain that the PPA's limitation to asexually reproduced plants would make no sense if Congress intended § 101 to authorize patents on plant varieties that were sexually reproduced. But this limitation once again merely reflects the reality of plant breeding in 1930. At that time, the primary means of reproducing bred plants true-to-type was through asexual reproduction. Congress thought that sexual reproduction through seeds was not a stable way to maintain desirable bred characteristics. Thus, it is hardly surprising that plant patents would protect only asexual reproduction, since this was the most reliable type of reproduction for preserving the desirable characteristics of breeding. In short, there is simply no evidence, let alone the overwhelming evidence needed to establish repeal by implication, *see Matsushita Elec. Industrial Co. v. Epstein*, 516 U.S. 367, 381, (1996), that Congress, by specifically protecting asexually reproduced plants through the PPA, intended to preclude utility patent protection for sexually reproduced plants.

Third, petitioners argue that in 1952 Congress would not have moved plants out of the utility patent provision and into § 161 if it had intended § 101 to allow for protection of plants. Petitioners again rely on negative inference because they cannot point to any express indication that Congress intended § 161 to be the exclusive means of patenting plants. But this negative inference simply does not support carving out subject matter that otherwise fits comfortably within the expansive language of § 101, especially when § 101 can protect different attributes and has more stringent requirements than does § 161.

This is especially true given that Congress in 1952 did nothing to change the substantive rights or requirements for obtaining a plant patent. Absent a clear intent to the contrary, we are loath to interpret what was essentially a housekeeping measure as an affirmative decision by Congress to deny sexually reproduced plants patent protection under § 101.

B

By passing the PVPA in 1970, Congress specifically authorized limited patent-like protection for certain sexually reproduced plants. Petitioners therefore argue that this legislation evidences Congress' intent to deny broader § 101 utility patent protection for such plants. Petitioners' argument, however, is unavailing for two reasons. First, nowhere does the PVPA purport to provide the exclusive statutory means of protecting sexually reproduced plants. Second, the PVPA and § 101 can easily be reconciled. Because it is harder to qualify for a utility patent than for a Plant Variety Protection (PVP) certificate, it only makes sense that utility patents would confer a greater scope of protection.

The PVPA provides plant variety protection for:

> The breeder of any sexually reproduced or tuber propagated plant variety (other than fungi or bacteria) who has so reproduced the variety.... 7 U.S.C. § 2402(a).

Infringement of plant variety protection occurs, *inter alia*, if someone sells or markets the protected variety, sexually multiplies the variety as a step in marketing, uses the variety in producing a hybrid, or dispenses the variety without notice that the variety is protected.

Since the 1994 amendments, the PVPA also protects "any variety that is essentially derived from a protected variety," § 2541(c)(1), and "any variety whose production requires the repeated use of a protected variety," § 2541(c)(3). *See* Plant Variety Protection Act Amendments of 1994. Practically, this means that hybrids created from protected plant varieties are also protected; however, it is not infringement to use a protected variety for the development of a hybrid. *See* 7 U.S.C. § 2541(a)(4). It is, however, infringement of a utility patent to use a protected plant in the development of another variety.

Thus, while the PVPA creates a statutory scheme that is comprehensive with respect to its particular protections and subject matter, giving limited protection to plant varieties that are new, distinct, uniform, and stable, § 2402(a), nowhere does it restrict the scope of patentable subject matter under § 101. With nothing in the statute to bolster their view that the PVPA provides the exclusive means for protecting sexually reproducing plants, petitioners rely on the legislative history of the PVPA. They argue that this history shows the PVPA was enacted because sexually reproducing plant varieties and their seeds were not and had never been intended by Congress to be included within the classes of things patentable under Title 35.

The PVPA itself, however, contains no statement that plant variety certificates were to be the exclusive means of protecting sexually reproducing plants. The relevant statements in the legislative history reveal nothing more than the limited view of plant breeding taken by some Members of Congress who believed that patent protection was unavailable for sexually reproduced plants. This view stems from a lack of awareness concerning scientific possibilities. Furthermore, at the time the PVPA was enacted, the PTO had already issued numerous utility patents for hybrid plant processes. Many of these patents, especially since the 1950's, included claims on the products of the patented process, i.e., the hybrid plant itself. Such plants were protected as part of a hybrid process and not on their own. Nonetheless, these hybrids still enjoyed protection under § 101, which reaffirms that such material was within the scope of § 101.

For all of these reasons, it is clear that there is no _positive repugnancy_ between the issuance of utility patents for plants and PVP coverage for plants. *Radzanower v. Touche Ross & Co.*, 426 U.S. 148, 155 (1976). Nor can it be said that the two statutes "cannot mutually coexist." Indeed, "when two statutes are capable of coexistence, it is the duty of the courts, absent a clearly expressed congressional intention to the contrary, to regard each as effective." Morton, 417 U.S., at 551. Here we can plainly regard each statute as effective because of its different requirements and protections. The plain meaning of § 101, as interpreted by this Court in *Chakrabarty*, clearly includes plants within its subject matter. The PPA and the PVPA are not to the contrary and can be read alongside § 101 in protecting plants.

Petitioners also suggest that even when statutes overlap and purport to protect the same commercially valuable attribute of a thing, such "dual protection" cannot exist. Yet this Court has not hesitated to give effect to two statutes that overlap, so long as each reaches some distinct cases. *See Connecticut Nat. Bank v. Germain*, 503 U.S. 249, 253 (1992). Here, while utility patents and PVP certificates do contain some similar protections, as discussed above, the overlap is only partial.

Moreover, this Court has allowed dual protection in other intellectual property cases. "Certainly the patent policy of encouraging invention is not disturbed by the existence of another form of incentive to invention. In this respect the two systems [trade secret protection and patents] are not and never would be in conflict." *Kewanee Oil*, 416 U.S., at 484; *see also Mazer v. Stein*, 347 U.S. 201, 217 (1954) (the patentability of an object does not preclude the copyright of that object as a work of art). In this case, many plant varieties that are unable to satisfy the stringent requirements of § 101 might still qualify for the lesser protections afforded by the PVPA.

III

We also note that the PTO has assigned utility patents for plants for at least 16 years and there has been no indication from either Congress or agencies with expertise that such coverage is inconsistent with the PVPA or the PPA. The Board of Patent Appeals and Interferences, which has specific expertise in issues of patent law, relied heavily on this Court's decision in *Chakrabarty* when it interpreted the subject matter of § 101 to include plants. This highly visible decision has led to the issuance of some 1,800 utility patents for plants. Moreover, the PTO, which administers § 101 as well as the PPA, recognizes and regularly issues utility patents for plants. In addition, the Department of Agriculture's Plant Variety Protection Office acknowledges the existence of utility patents for plants.

In the face of these developments, Congress has not only failed to pass legislation indicating that it disagrees with the PTO's interpretation of § 101, it has even recognized the availability of utility patents for plants. In a 1999 amendment to 35 U.S.C. § 119, which concerns the right of priority for patent rights, Congress provided: "Applications for plant breeder's rights filed in a WTO [World Trade Organization] member country . . . shall have the same effect for the purpose of the right of priority . . . as applications for patents, subject to the same conditions and requirements of this section as apply to applications for patents." 35 U.S.C. § 119(f). Crucially, § 119(f) is part of the general provisions of Title 35, not the specific chapter of the PPA, which suggests a recognition on the part of Congress that plants are patentable under § 101.

IV

For these reasons, we hold that newly developed plant breeds fall within the terms of § 101, and that neither the PPA nor the PVPA limits the scope of § 101's coverage. As in *Chakrabarty*, we decline to narrow the reach of § 101 where Congress has given us no indication that it intends this result. Accordingly, we affirm the judgment of the Court of Appeals.

JUSTICE SCALIA, concurring.

In the present case, the only ambiguity that could have been clarified by the words added to the utility patent statute by the Plant Patent Act of 1930(PPA) is whether the term "composition of matter" included living things. Stare decisis, however, prevents us from any longer regarding as an open question—as ambiguous—whether "composition of matter" includes living things. *Diamond v. Chakrabarty* holds that it does. At this point the canon against repeal by implication comes into play, and I agree with the Court that it determines the outcome. I therefore join the opinion of the Court.

JUSTICE BREYER, with whom JUSTICE STEVENS joins, dissenting.

The question before us is whether the words "manufacture" or "compositions of matter" contained in the utility patent statute, 35

U.S.C. § 101, cover plants that also fall within the scope of two more specific statutes, the Plant Patent Act of 1930 and the Plant Variety Protection Act. I believe that the words "manufacture" or "composition of matter" do not cover these plants. That is because Congress intended the two more specific statutes to exclude patent protection under the Utility Patent Statute for the plants to which the more specific Acts directly refer. And, as the Court implicitly recognizes, this Court neither considered, nor decided, this question in *Diamond v. Chakrabarty*. Consequently, I dissent.

Respondent and the Government claim that *Chakrabarty* controls the outcome in this case. This is incorrect, for *Chakrabarty* said nothing about the specific issue before us. *Chakrabarty*, in considering the scope of the Utility Patent Statute's language "manufacture, or composition of matter," asked whether those words included such living things as bacteria—a substance to which neither of the two specific plant Acts refers. The Court held that the Utility Patent Statute language included a "new" bacterium because it was "a nonnaturally occurring manufacture or composition of matter" that was "not nature's handiwork." It quoted language from a congressional Committee Report indicating that "Congress intended statutory subject matter to 'include anything under the sun that is made by man.'" But it nowhere said or implied that this Utility Patent Statute language also includes the very subject-matter with which the two specific statutes deal, namely plants. Whether a bacterium technically speaking is, or is not, a plant, the Court considered it a "life form," and not the kind of "plant" that the two specific statutes had in mind.

Notes

1. End of the Line? Despite Justice Breyer's dissent, the Court interprets *Chakrabarty* and § 101 very broadly. The Supreme Court has now twice acknowledged the breadth of the § 101 categories. Does *J.E.M. v. Pioneer* signal an end to decades of debate about the scope of exclusions from patent eligibility? Even if this case brings some resolution to U.S. law, won't differing standards for eligibility in other nations keep this issue alive in the international marketplace?

2. Did *J.E.M. v. Pioneer* Really Matter? Experience suggests that patent attorneys are sometimes able to circumvent restrictions on patent-eligible subject matter through the artful drafting of patent applications. These drafting techniques focus upon one part of each utility patent, the specific definitions of the patented invention known as the "claims." Each utility patent application, and resulting granted utility patent instrument, must contain one or more claims. In order to maximize their scope of protection, most utility patents contain multiple claims that define the invention in different ways.

Given the ability of patent attorneys to draft a variety of claims, a utility patent directed towards a plant may have a number of claims in addition to the plant as a whole. A particular utility patent might also claim a tissue culture, a method of breeding the plant, a plant part, such as pollen or seeds, or other different aspects of the invention. Not all of these claims appear to be directed towards a plant *per se*. As a result, even if *J.E.M. v. Pioneer* had been decided differently, plant breeders might still be able to obtain substantial intellectual property protection through the utility patent system. What more general lessons does this reality suggest about the effectiveness of placing restrictions upon patentable subject matter? *See* Mark D. Janis, *Sustainable Agriculture, Patent Rights, and Plant Innovation*, 9 INDIANA JOURNAL OF GLOBAL LEGAL STUDIES 91 (2001). For more on the *J.E.M. v. Pioneer* decision, as well as more general observations about overlapping regimes of intellectual property rights, see Mark D. Janis & Jay P. Kesan, *Designing an Optimal Intellectual Property System for Plants: A Supreme Court Debate*, 19 NATURE/BIOTECH. 981 (2001).

   3. And What of the PVPA? The impact of *J.E.M. v. Pioneer* may be most immediately felt with regard to the plant variety protection regime. As utility patents offer more robust rights than plant variety protection certificates, plant breeders might decline to seek plant variety protection certificates in favor of utility patents for their more commercially important inventions. It is possible that the PVPA may be relegated to a secondary, "petty patent" regime, employed for inventions with less marketplace significance or for inventions that do not meet the more rigorous standards of the utility patent statute. Should Congress pay renewed attention to the PVPA in order to determine whether that statute remains responsive to the current needs of the agricultural industry?

§ 2.3 METHODS OF MEDICAL TREATMENT

   Consider again the patented invention involved in the *Arrhythmia* decision. Is the allowance of a patent on a medical technique appropriate? Many consider the patent law an appropriate vehicle to enforce the professional ethics of the medical profession, with which the free use of medical advances appears more consonant than an award of an exclusive property right. Or, as analyzed in the following opinion, do other strictures on patent eligibility obviate any discussion of professional responsibility?

ANAESTHETIC SUPPLIES PTY LTD. v. RESCARE LTD.

Federal Court of Australia, New South Wales District, 1994.
28 IPR 383.

Before LOCKHART, SHEPPARD, and WILCOX, JJ.

LOCKHART, J.

   The case raises questions of the patentability of the invention in suit.... The question whether the invention is patentable raises the fundamental question whether a patent may be granted in Australia for a method of treatment of disease or sickness in human beings.

   3.   The patent in suit is standard patent no. 560360 (the patent) for an invention entitled "device for treating snoring sickness". Rescare Limited, the respondent, is the present registered proprietor of the

patent. The inventor who applied for the grant was Professor C E Sullivan, Professor of Medicine at the University of Sydney, who has an international reputation for research in the field of respiratory medicine and sleep disorders.

4. Obstructive sleep apnea (OSA) is a syndrome associated with an extreme form of snoring in which the sufferer chokes on the tongue and soft palate repeatedly whilst asleep.

5. In an article published in The Lancet in 1981, Professor Sullivan and members of his unit in the Faculty of Medicine at the University of Sydney discussed OSA. The authors said that OSA was a common disorder, particularly in middle aged, overweight males. They said:

> "The underlying problem is sleep-induced occlusion of the oro-pharyngeal airway, which results in multiple apnoeic episodes during sleep. There is severe fragmentation of sleep, and as the disease progresses over months or years, greater degrees of asphyxia occur; the duration of apnea frequently exceeds two minutes and the arterial haemoglobin oxygen saturation falls below 50%. Remarkably, the patient may be unaware of his nightly struggle for breath. Rather, his major symptoms are those of excessive daytime sleepiness and snoring. The nocturnal asphyxia eventually causes a variety of clinical presentations including cardiac arrhythmias, pulmonary hypertension and right heart failure, systemic hypertension, severe morning headache, intellectual and personality changes, and polycythaemia. The true cause of these findings may not be suspected. The disease is a recognised cause of sudden 'unexpected' death.
>
> In the obese subject, weight loss may reduce the number of obstructive episodes. Other measures such as neck collars and respiratory stimulants ... are less satisfactory. The only effective treatment now available is a tracheostomy which is left open at night. This immediately results in disappearance of the excessive daytime sleepiness; and the life threatening complications of hypoxaemia, such as arrhythmias and corpulmonale, improve dramatically within days. In patients who do not have any of the immediately life-threatening complications, a decision to do a tracheostomy is invariably difficult, despite the knowledge that the disease is progressive. We describe here a method which has prevented upper airway occlusion for an entire night of sleep in each of five patients with severe obstructive sleep apnea."

METHODS OF MEDICAL TREATMENT OF THE HUMAN BODY

22. Section 100(1)(d) of the 1952 Act [of Australia] provides that a patent may be revoked on the ground "that the invention, so far as claimed in any claim of the complete specification or in the claim of the petty patent specification, as the case may be, is not an invention within the meaning of this Act". The term "invention" is defined in s. 6 of the 1952 Act as meaning: "any manner of new manufacture the subject of

letters patent and grant of privilege within section 6 of the Statute of Monopolies, and includes an alleged invention;''

Section 35(1)(a) of the 1952 Act provides that an application for a patent:

"shall be in respect of a manner of new manufacture the subject of letters patent and grant of privilege within section 6 of the Statute of Monopolies".

The appellant submitted both at the trial and on appeal that claims 9 and 11 are invalid as being methods of medical treatment of the human body and that the other claims are also invalid for the same reason because, although expressed as product claims, they are, so it was argued, in substance method or process claims.

23.   Claims 9 and 11 of the patent are as follows:

"9. A method of treating snoring and/or obstructive sleep apnea in a patient comprising: applying air through a nose piece at a pressure maintained slightly greater than atmospheric substantially continuously throughout the breathing cycle."

11.   A method of treating snoring and/or obstructive sleep apnea substantially as described with reference to the drawing."

24.   The Statute of Monopolies of 1623 declared all monopolies:

"... for the sale, buying, selling, making, working, or using of any thing within this realm ..." to be contrary to law and utterly of no effect with certain exceptions:? "Provided nevertheless ... that any declaration before-mentioned shall not extend to any letters patent and grants of privilege for the term of fourteen years ... hereafter to be made, of the sole working or making of any manner of new manufacture within this realm, to the true and first inventor and inventors of such manufactures, which others at the time of making such letters patent and grants shall not use, so as also they be not contrary to the law, nor mischievous to the state, by raising prices of commodities at home, or hurt of trade, or generally inconvenient."

25.   It was argued by the appellant that a method of medical treatment of the human body does not come within s. 6 for two reasons: first, because the whole subject matter of the medical treatment of the human body is regarded as being non-economic and thus not a "manner of new manufacture"; and secondly, because it would be "generally inconvenient" to allow monopolies in respect of the medical treatment of the human body.

26.   The primary Judge rejected these arguments. As to the argument based on non-economic grounds, his Honour referred to the cases which have rejected the requirement for a "vendible product" as the sole discrimen of a manner of manufacture and relied upon observations of Barwick CJ in *Joos v. Commissioner of Patents* (1972) 126 CLR 611 to the effect that the medical field is as economic as any other. The primary

Judge rejected the argument on the "generally inconvenient" basis because there was no essential distinction between a patent for the method of the treatment of the human body and a patent for a pharmaceutical substance, and that he was not satisfied that the grant of a patent for such a method was shown to be "generally inconvenient".

27.   There is little authority on this question in Australia, New Zealand, the United Kingdom, the United States or Canada. I shall refer to the law of each of these countries, as well as of Germany and Israel.

AUSTRALIA

32.   In *Joos*, Barwick CJ considered a process patent for the treatment of hair and nails. His Honour said at 616 that there was no decision of the High Court which answered the question whether a monopoly must be refused for a process to treat human hair or nails whilst still attached to or growing upon the human body. He referred to the fact that before [*National Research Development Corporation's Application*, [1961] RPC 134 ("*NRDC*")] it might have been held that the process claimed in *Joos* as an invention could not be the subject of a monopoly under the 1952 Act because its use did not result in, or in the improvement of, a vendible article. He approached the appeal before him on the footing that the use of the process did not produce or improve a vendible article, but that did not deny, his Honour said, that the process had economic virtue or significance in the relevant sense.

33.   Barwick CJ described the decision of the High Court in *NRDC* as "a watershed" in this respect for it was there decided that it was not essential for the grant of a monopoly for a process that the use of the process should produce or improve a vendible article; it was enough that the process has commercial application. He rejected the view that a ground for non-patentability of a method of treating the human body was because, by its nature, it was essentially non-economic. The Chief Justice said at 618 that the notion of economic interest in the product of good surgery and in the advancement of its techniques was obvious and was to be regarded as sufficiently proximate to be capable of satisfying the economic element of an invention if other elements were present and no impediments existed to the grant. The Chief Justice drew a sharp distinction between a process for treating the diseases of the body and a process for improving the cosmetic appearance of the body; a difference between, for example, an abdominal operation or a skin graft on the one hand and a face lift or hair wash on the other. He considered the question whether a process otherwise appropriate for the grant of a patent must be held not to be a proper subject for a grant simply because it was a process for treatment of a part of the human body. The Chief Justice said at 619:

> "For the purpose of deciding this question it may be granted that a process for the treatment of the human body as a means of curing or preventing a disease, correcting a malfunction or removing or ameliorating an incapacity is not a proper subject matter for the grant of a monopoly under the Act. It is not essential to the decision

of this matter to controvert that proposition or to discover and express its basis in law. But I think it significant that the concession is limited to the medical treatment of disease, malfunction or incapacity."

Important in that connexion is the consideration that the concept of treatment, where medical treatment is spoken of, is not satisfied, in my opinion, by any application of a substance to the human body or part of it. Those who apply chemical preparations to the skin to prevent sun burn in climates which enjoy sunshine and moderate air temperatures can scarcely be regarded either as, in a relevant sense, treating their bodies or as undergoing treatment. On the other hand, the application to the skin of an ointment designed and effective to remove keratoses from the skin would be an instance of medical treatment. To be treatment, in the relevant sense, it seems to me that the purpose of the application to the body whether of a substance or a process, must be the arrest or cure of a disease or diseased condition or the correction of some malfunction or the amelioration of some incapacity or disability. With that sense of 'treatment', I see no difficulty in conceding, for the purposes of the decision of this case, that a process for the medical treatment of a part of the human body is not a proper subject of letters patent."

34.   Barwick CJ said at 622–3 that a class of process claims for medical treatment of human disease, malfunction, disability or incapacity of the human body should be:

"... narrowly defined. I can find no warrant in public policy or in the decided cases for including in that class processes and methods for improving, or at any rate for changing, the appearance of the human body or of parts of it.

Such cosmetic processes and methods are, in my opinion, not of a like kind with medical prophylactic or therapeutic processes or methods.

There may, of course, be many borderline instances of processes for use upon the human body or parts of it in respect of which a decision as to whether the process constitutes medical treatment or not may prove difficult."

35.   Barwick CJ did say at 623 that it was not necessary for him to express a view about the basis for excluding claims for the medical treatment of the human body, but he tended to a view that, if he had to decide the question, as then advised, he would have regarded such processes as being excluded by the term "generally inconvenient" in the Statute of Monopolies.

36.   In *Wellcome Foundation Limited v. Commissioner of Patents* (1980) 145 CLR 520 Gibbs, Stephen, Mason, Murphy and Wilson JJ said at 528 that if a new result from a process which does not produce a new substance is "an artificially created state of affairs" providing economic utility, it may be considered a "manner of new manufacture" within s. 6

of the Statute of Monopolies. In that passage their Honours endorsed what was said in *NRDC* at 277.

NEW ZEALAND

39.   The *NRDC* Case was applied in New Zealand by Barrowclough CJ in *Swift and Co. v. Commissioner of Patents* (1960) NZLR 775.

* * *

THE UNITED KINGDOM

46.   The view taken by the English cases is accurately stated in T A BLANCO-WHITE, PATENTS FOR INVENTIONS, 5th ed., at 4–911 that methods of treating or preventing human disease or infirmity are not "manners of manufacture".

* * *

CANADA

55.   In *Tennessee Eastman Co v. Commissioner of Patents* (1972) 33 DLR 3d 459 the Supreme Court of Canada concluded that the discovery that a known adhesive substance can be used for bonding human tissue does not give rise to a valid claim The judgment of the Court, delivered by Pigeon J, observed that this result was consistent with the *NRDC* Case, the *Schering* Case and Borrowclough CJ's decision in *Swift*, none of which related to medical or surgical methods.

THE UNITED STATES

56.   It appears that a broader view is taken in the United States. In the United States, patents are now granted for processes which involve the new use of old compounds for fresh medical purposes. Although the position in the United States is not entirely clear, the better view is that methods of treating the human body are not per se unpatentable: *see Ex parte Scherer* (1954) 103 U.S.P.Q. 107 which was a majority decision of the US Patent Office Board of Appeals on a method of injecting fluids into the human body by a high pressure jet, which was held to be patentable (*c.f. Morton v. New York Eye Infirmary* (1862) 17 F. Cas 879). See also PATENT LAW FUNDAMENTALS by P D Rosenburg, (1982 Revision), Chapter 6 at 6–9 where the statement is made:

> "The law is now fairly well settled: a statutory process may be composed of any combination of physical or manipulative steps. Thus, it has been held that a surgical procedure or technique, which was properly claimed, constituted a statutory process.

> Methods of diagnosis or treatment, including a regimen of drug therapy, are deemed statutory processes, even though one or more steps thereof are performed upon a human or other living organism. To be patentable the method must be new. Although the analgesic properties of aspirin have long been recognized, it is only recently

that the effectiveness of aspirin in preventing heart attacks has been established.

If the dosages of aspirin and the intervals of its administration to ward off a heart attack are the same as that for which aspirin has been taken as an analgesic, such is but the discovery of a heretofore unrecognized benefit which however meritorious would not be patentable, as the method itself is old.''

GERMANY

58.   The Federal Supreme Court of West Germany held in the *Sitosterylglykoside* Case (1983) 14 IIC 283 that the effectiveness in the treatment of an illness of a previously known active ingredient may ground a use claim to a patent, though not a composition claim.

ISRAEL

59.   The Supreme Court of Israel in *Wellcome Foundation Limited v. Plantex Limited* (1974) RPC 514 considered an action for infringement of a patent relating to the use of a known chemical substance in the treatment of gout. The question arose as to whether the discovery of novel properties in a known substance enabling it to be used for new and therapeutic purposes warranted the granting of a patent at all. Whitkon J held that it did. Whitkon J said at 540 that he believed that injustice would not be done to the spirit of our era and to recent developments in the world as regards the policy in respect of the grant of patents if the prohibition by which no patents are granted on methods of therapeutic treatment of the human body is not abolished outright. His Honour preferred to preserve this prohibition in a restricted scope even in respect of matters to which the patent ordinance still applies. He rested his judgment on the *NRDC* Case. Kahn J reached a similar conclusion, but with a reservation. He said at 539:

"Notwithstanding the important reasons for doing away with any distinction between a therapeutic treatment of the human body and other patentable subject matter, I am not ready to agree with my honourable colleague, Whitkon J, that we are called upon now to construe that Patents Ordinance in this sense. There exist grave reasons against the creation of a monopoly by a patent in respect of medical treatment. We are confronted here with saving human life or alleviating human suffering and one should take great care lest a restriction on the freedom of action of those who treat, caused by patents, should affect human life or health. This was also the view of the Israeli legislature who laid down in s. 7 of the Patents Act 1967 that no patent shall be granted for methods of therapeutic treatment of the human body."

60.   Later, at 540, Kahn J said:

"It is therefore my conclusion that an invention by which a known substance, a known composition or a known device is used for the therapeutic treatment of the human body is patentable.

However, where a substance, composition or device has already been used for the therapeutic treatment of the human body or where it is obvious on the basis of existing knowledge that they are capable of so being used for the therapeutic treatment of humans, no patent is to be granted to an inventor who discovers a new and until then unknown use for medical treatment."

FINDINGS

61.   There are, therefore, in jurisdictions outside the United Kingdom, cases which go some distance towards recognizing the patentability of methods of treatment of human beings which are no more than an application of old compounds for new therapeutic uses.

62.   On both humanitarian and economic grounds the search for medical advance is to be encouraged. The award of limited monopolies is a standard way of helping to compensate for the expense of research. Ultimately the resolution of this question is a balancing exercise. There is on the one hand a need to encourage research in connection with methods of medical treatment and on the other hand the need not unduly to restrict the activities of those who engage in the therapy of humans.

63.   The United Kingdom decisions adopt the conservative approach of not permitting as patentable inventions, discoveries of methods of treating the human body; but it must be borne in mind that the Patents Act 1977 (U.K.) did make substantial changes to the United Kingdom law. Patents may be granted only for an invention which is capable of industrial application: § 1(1)(c); an invention of a method of treatment of the human or animal body by surgery or therapy or of diagnosis practised on the human or animal body shall not be taken to be capable of industrial application: § 4(2). These provisions follow the terms of Article 52 of the European Patent Convention signed at Munich in 1973.

64.   There is no similar provision in the Australian 1990 Act. The definition of "invention" from the 1952 Act was retained in Schedule 1. But § 18(2) of the 1990 Act provides that:

"Human beings, and the biological processes for their generation, are not patentable inventions."

The question in the present case concerns the validity of the standard patent under the 1952 Act because the 1990 Act provides by s. 233(4) that no claim is invalid on any ground that would not have been available under the 1952 Act.

65.   The decisions of the English courts base their conclusion that methods of treating the human body are to be excluded from patentability on a variety of grounds, primarily grounds of ethics rather than logic, and they are not the subject of any fully developed reasoned considerations. I agree with Davison CJ in the *New Zealand Wellcome* Case that:

"the courts have been grasping for some other ground on which to base a refusal (that is other than the basis that it was not an art of manufacture and was not a form of manufacture of trade) to exclude processes for medical treatment from patent protection".

66.   The Chief Justice also said that there was a lack of logic in any distinction which produced the result that a product for treating the human body would be patentable but not a method of treating the human body.

67.   The Australian experience with the decision in the *NRDC* Case at its helm and including the retention in the 1990 Act of the previous definition of "invention" has, I think, been to the contrary of the New Zealand experience.

* * *

69.   It is also now the long established practice of the Commissioner of Patents in Australia to accept applications in respect of inventions of the character of the present patent. There is no material before us which would suggest deleterious consequences have flowed from the implementation of the Commissioner's practice.

70.   It was also argued before us that a claim in terms of claims 9 and 11 of the patent was "generally inconvenient" within the Statute of Monopolies on a number of grounds. The primary ground was because modern medicine depends on technological innovation, and so, it was argued, it is in the public interest that this should be published and freely available.

71.   Some people have a deep seated feeling or view that the art of the physician or surgeon in alleviating human suffering does not belong to the area of economic endeavour or trade and commerce; and there is need for care lest a restriction on the freedom of action of those who treat patients endangers human life or health. I also understand the view of some people and of some judges that it is for the Parliament to decide whether and how far to extend patentability into areas where the common understanding has been that patents are not available.

* * *

75.   In my opinion, there is no justification in law or in logic to say that simply because on the one hand substances produce a cosmetic result or a functional result as opposed to a curative result, one is patentable and the other is not. I see no reason in principle why a method of treatment of the human body is any less a manner of manufacture than a method for ridding crops of weeds as in *NRDC*. Australian courts must now take a realistic view of the matter in the light of current scientific development and legal process; the law must move with changing needs and times. I agree with Davison CJ that the test enumerated in the *NRDC* Case is whether the invention is a proper subject of letters patent according to the principles which have been developed for the application of § 6 of the Statute of Monopolies.

SHEPPARD, J.

54. Claims 9 and 11 of the patent in suit here raise directly the question whether it is appropriate to grant letters patent in respect of a method of treatment of the human body which is curative of some disease or which relieves a particular abnormality or other problem. Similar considerations, so it seems to me, should apply in relation to procedures which are diagnostic in character.

55. Australia is one of a large number of countries which are fortunate enough to be served by extremely competent physicians and surgeons whose task it is to maintain and improve the health of the community. Leading members of the medical profession are usually members of one or more of the distinguished colleges of physicians or surgeons which exist in the United Kingdom, the United States, the European countries and in this country. Not infrequently—this case provides an example—they are also members of a faculty of medicine within one of the universities. The hospital in which they practise medicine is allied with the university and, for this reason, is known as a teaching hospital.

56. It is well known that the work of the medical colleges involves both research and teaching. It is probably true to say that all professions, using that expression in its true sense, develop by research and by teaching. There is a willingness on the part of members to share information about new discoveries and new methods of treatment. This is particularly so in relation to surgical procedures of innumerable kinds and in relation to the management of people who are suffering from serious disease. Whether that treatment consists of the way a patient is managed in hospital, the selection of particular drugs and the dosages of them to be administered or the subjection of patients to particular treatment, for instance by radio therapy or chemotherapy, the process is an on-going one in which members of the medical profession and those associated with them learn as they go along and thus develop and improve the quality of medical treatment in the community. Commonly, important research or discoveries become the subject of learned papers or articles or even text books which are published throughout the medical world. That was done in this case. In this way there is a wide dissemination of knowledge. This occurs also when doctors, as they commonly do, travel from one country to another to attend conferences or witness methods of treatment and surgical techniques which may help them in their treatment of patients in their own countries. Not infrequently knowledge is disseminated to medical practitioners in countries less fortunate than our own. These are sometimes visited by doctors so that they may teach local practitioners about these matters and many others.

57. The subject matter of all this, although it may have its commercial elements, is the treatment and relief of human suffering. It has a direct bearing on the well being of the nation. Medical research and treatment have a long history which is replete with distinguished examples afforded by a great many dedicated men and women.

58.   The disease in question here is life-threatening. The evidence shows that, if it is not relieved, it may lead to heart failure and death. The treatment for which letters patent are sought in claims 9 and 11 is treatment which may cure or at least relieve symptoms and signs which are highly dangerous to the human body. I think the question which one needs to ask is whether the grant of a patent in these circumstances is generally inconvenient. That was the way that the matter was approached by Barwick CJ in *Joos* and by Somers J and, to a degree, Cooke J, in the *Wellcome Foundation* case in New Zealand. My own view is that there can be only one answer to that question. The grant of a patent in these circumstances seems to me to be generally inconvenient. It is not going too far, I think, to say that the Court should not contemplate the grant of letters patent which would give to one medical practitioner, or perhaps a group of medical practitioners, a monopoly over, for example, a surgical procedure which might be greatly beneficial to mankind. Its denial might mean the death or unnecessary suffering of countless people. I cannot think that this is really what the medical profession as a whole would seek to achieve. Its whole history is a denial of the proposition.

59.   In the result, therefore, I would hold claims 9 and 11 invalid on the additional ground that they involve a method of treatment of a disease affecting the human body. The position may be different if the method of treatment were for cosmetic purposes. I express no opinion on that question. But there will sometimes be cases, for example, skin grafting after serious burning, where there will be a fine line between what is therapeutic and what is cosmetic.

Wilcox, J.

I have read in draft form the reasons for judgment of Lockhart J. I agree with those reasons but wish to add some comments.

2.   The point in the case that is of general interest is the question whether a method of medical treatment of the human body is patentable. As Lockhart J's analysis demonstrates, there are decisions on that issue in several countries. They differ in approach. In Australia, there are three cases in which High Court Justices have referred to the matter, but in no case did the Court make a decision upon it. Consequently, it would be open to this Court to reach its own conclusion, if this were necessary for the disposition of the appeal. As it happens, the appellant succeeds on its claim for revocation on another ground, fair basing. So it is not necessary to determine whether the patent is invalid, in relation to claims 9 and 11 (and any other claims that ought properly to be regarded as method claims), because those claims relate to a method of medical treatment.

3.   As will be obvious from my stated agreement with Lockhart J, if the matter did fall for decision, I would reject the appellant's argument that the law does not permit the grant of a patent in respect of a method of medical treatment. Policy arguments may be made, each way, upon the question whether the law should permit such a grant. These argu-

ments are developed in some of the cases cited by Lockhart J. I need not repeat them. The important point, it seems to me, is that the Australian Parliament has not been persuaded by the policy considerations arguing against patentability. Parliament has never excluded a method of human medical treatment from patentability or the definition of "invention"; not even in the recent statute, the Patents Act 1990, that revised Australian patent law and made a specific provision (§ 18(2)) dealing with the patentability of human beings and the biological processes for their generation. I appreciate that both this statute and its predecessor, the 1952 Act, left intact the principles developed by the courts in connection with the application of § 6 of the Statute of Monopolies: see the definition of "invention" in both Acts and § 35 of the 1952 Act and § 18(1) of the 1990 Act. However, I believe that, in the face of apparently deliberate decisions by Parliament not to build this particular exclusion into its legislation, courts should be hesitant to introduce the exclusion by reference to those very general principles.

Note

1. **U.S. Legislation.** In the mid–1990's, the American Medical Association House of Delegates condemned the patenting of medical and surgical procedures. *See* Brian McCormick, *Just Rewards or Just Plain Wrong? Specter of Royalties from Method Patents Stirs Debate*, 37 AM. MED. NEWS 3 (1994). The concerns of the AMA and other observers include the threat to public health occasioned by injunctions imposed against the use of patented medical methods; the derogation of the ethical obligations of doctors to disclose medical advances freely; the potential increase to the already extraordinary costs of health care; the interference of the patent system with the ordinary process of peer review of new medical procedures; and the possibility of the invasion of patient privacy in connection with patent enforcement efforts. Are any of these concerns peculiar, or at least peculiarly acute, to the medical profession, as opposed to technologists generally?

In response to this alarm, legislation signed into law on September 30, 1996, created a new 35 U.S.C.A. § 287(c) which deprives patentees of remedies against medical practitioners engaged in infringing "medical activity." The statute defines "medical activity" as "the performance of a medical or surgical procedure on a body." The statute expressly provides that the use of patented machine, machines, or compositions of matters, the practice of a patented use of a composition of matter, and the practice of a patented biotechnology process do not comprise "medical activity." Under § 287(c), injunctions, damages and attorney fees are unavailable from medical practitioners and related entities. *See* Cynthia M. Ho, Patents, *Patients, and Public Policy: An Incomplete Intersection at 35 U.S.C. § 287(c)*, 33 U.C. DAVIS L. REV. 601 (2000). Does any practical distinction exist between this measure and declaring medical methods not patent eligible under § 101? Does this legislation violate Article 27 of the TRIPS Agreement? *See generally* Gerald J. Mossinghoff, *Remedies Under Patents on Medical and Surgical Procedures*, 78 J. PAT. & TRADEMARK OFF. SOC'Y 789 (1996).

2. **International and Comparative Approaches.** As discussed in *Anaesthetic Supplies* and as should be apparent in *Arrhythmia*, *supra*, some

observers harbor significant reservations over the patenting of methods of medical treatment. In response to these concerns, both NAFTA Article 1709 and Article 27 of the TRIPS Agreement each allow signatories to exclude diagnostic, therapeutic and surgical methods for the treatment of humans and animals from patent eligibility. Article 54(5) of the European Patent Convention takes advantage of the TRIPS Agreement exception as follows:

> Methods for treatment of the human or animal body by surgery or therapy and diagnostic methods practised on the human or animal body shall not be regarded as inventions which are susceptible of industrial application within the meaning of paragraph 1. This provision shall not apply to products, in particular substances or compositions, for use in any of these methods.

This seeming prohibition is less restrictive in practice than it may first appear, however. EPC Article 54(5) establishes a special rule that the usual novelty provisions "shall not exclude the patentability of any substance or composition, comprised in the state of the art, for use in a method referred to in Article 52, paragraph 4, provided that its use for any method referred to in that paragraph is not comprised in the state of the art." This provision permits the patenting of an old compound so long as that compound was never used as a medicine. In addition, the Swiss Patent Office devised a way to permit the patenting of new medical indications for old drugs through the use of so-called "Swiss claims." *See, e.g., Bristol–Myers Squibb Co. v. Baker Norton Pharmaceuticals Inc.*, [2001] R.P.C. 1 (English Court of Appeal). You may wish to consider these exceptions once you have mastered the patent law concepts of novelty and claiming.

Statutory Subject Matter Exercises

Are any of the following inventions patent eligible under United States law? Does the result differ under the laws of Japan or Europe?

1. A three-dimensional cube-shaped puzzle. Each face of the puzzle consists of eight smaller cubelets of differing colors. The user attempts to solve the puzzle by rotating rows of cubelets around one of several internal axes until a preselected pattern is obtained.

2. A technique for counting playing cards that supposedly makes its user an unbeatable blackjack player.

3. As the menu at a local restaurant proudly proclaims, "Every dish comes with a wonderful complement, our patented banana hollandaise sauce."

4. A method of lifting heavy weights through a modified "clean-and-jerk" technique, suitable for use by Olympic athletes.

5. A new perfume, cologne or scent.

6. A method of preventing repetitive stress injuries during computer keyboard usage by holding one's hand, wrists and forearms in a straight and fluid line.

7. A character assessment method comprising (1) instructing the person to produce a drawing which includes a pictorial representation of a hand, eye, flower, star, half-circle and other objects; and (2) subjecting the drawing to a psychological interpretation.

8. A method of remodeling a building, comprising (1) presenting design ideas to a client; (2) allowing the client to select her favorite design; (3) taking a photograph of the building; and (4) preparing a drawing of the proposed remodeled building employing the photograph and the preferred design.

9. The "Human Wave" commonly performed by spectators at sporting events.

Chapter Three

UTILITY

In addition to setting forth the categories of patent eligible subject matter, 35 U.S.C.A. § 101 requires that an invention be "useful" in order to receive patent protection. At first blush, this requirement may appear rather trivial: determining whether particular subject matter may be put towards some useful purpose would not seem to be overly difficult. The costs associated with patent acquisition and enforcement further suggest that the inventor of something useless would likely not bother to obtain a patent, nor would there be a large number of potential infringers against which to invoke a proprietary right. This intuition is largely correct: the utility requirement is one that is rarely invoked, either by patent examiners considering an application or by accused infringers seeking to strike down an issued patent.

Nonetheless, even this seemingly straightforward provision brings forth a host of policy issues. One is the measuring stick: should the claimed invention merely be useful for some practical purpose in and of itself, or should it be superior to known technologies? Is the demonstration that an invention may lead to a further invention by itself sufficient to provide patentable utility? And should an assessment of such factors as the invention's social, economic or environmental impact accompany the decision to allow a patent to issue?

In making your way through the cases that follow, note that what amounts to a rejection of a patent under § 101 may alternatively be couched in the statutory language of 35 U.S.C.A. § 112, ¶ 1. This provision, which this casebook considers in more detail in Chapter 11, requires that patent applications include a description of how to use the invention disclosed within an application. As one may suspect, an applicant who is unaware of a use for an invention has scant ability to elaborate on this use in the patent instrument itself.

The first opinion of the chapter comes from a hand that will be frequently encountered by any student of United States patent law. Joseph Story, Associate Justice of the United States Supreme Court and Dane Professor at Harvard Law School, is best known for such opinions as *Martin v. Hunter's Lessee* and *Swift v. Tyson*, as well as a dozen volumes of legal commentary. But while riding circuit in New England, Story also built a foundation of judicial precedent which continue to shape United States patent law. Among these is *Lowell v. Lewis*, a succinct jury charge that set forth the contours of the utility requirement which persist today.

§ 3.1 GENERAL PRINCIPLES

LOWELL v. LEWIS

Circuit Court, D. Massachusetts, 1817.
15 F.Cas. 1018.

STORY, CIRCUIT JUSTICE.

To entitle the plaintiff to a verdict, he must establish, that his machine is a new and useful invention; and of these facts his patent is to be considered merely prima facie evidence of a very slight nature. He must, in the first place, establish it to be a useful invention; for the law will not allow the plaintiff to recover, if the invention be of a mischievous or injurious tendency. The defendant, however, has asserted a much more broad and sweeping doctrine; and one, which I feel myself called upon to negative in the most explicit manner. He contends, that it is necessary for the plaintiff to prove, that his invention is of general utility; so that in fact, for the ordinary purposes of life, it must supersede the pumps in common use. In short, that it must be, for the public, a better pump than the common pump; and that unless the plaintiff can establish this position, the law will not give him the benefit of a patent, even though in some peculiar cases his invention might be applied with advantage. I do not so understand the law. The patent act (Act Feb. 21, 1793, c. 11 [1 Stat. 318]) uses the phrase "useful invention" mere incidentally; it occurs only in the first section, and there it seems merely descriptive of the subject matter of the application, or of the conviction of the applicant. The language is, "when any person or persons shall allege, that he or they have invented any new and useful art, machine," & c., he or they may, on pursuing the directions of the act, obtain a patent. * * * All that the law requires is, that the invention should not be frivolous or injurious to the well-being, good policy, or sound morals of society. The word "useful," therefore, is incorporated into the act in contradistinction to mischievous or immoral. For instance, a new invention to poison people, or to promote debauchery, or to facilitate private assassination, is not a patentable invention. But if the invention steers wide of these objections, whether it be more or less useful is a circumstance very material to the interests of the patentee, but of no importance to the public. If it be not extensively useful, it will silently sink into contempt and disregard.

Notes

1. Storied Remarks. Justice Story added in a Note published at 3 Wheat App. xiii, 1818, that: "By *useful* invention, in the patent act, is meant an invention which may be applied to a beneficial use in society, in contra-distinction to an invention injurious to the morals, health or good order of society, or frivolous and insignificant." *See also Bedford v. Hunt*, 3 Fed. Cas. 37 (C.C.Mass. 1817). This definition was substantially echoed in the noted patent law treatise written by Professor William Robinson at the close of the nineteenth century. According to Professor Robinson, to satisfy the utility requirement an invention must simply be more than "a mere curiosity, a scientific process exciting wonder yet not producing physical results, or [a] frivolous or trifling article not aiding in the progress nor increasing the possession of the human race." 1 W. ROBINSON, TREATISE ON THE LAW OF PATENTS FOR USEFUL INVENTIONS 463 (1890).

2.   Modern Advertising. How many advertisements have you seen or heard trumpeting the fact that the advertised product has been patented? Now that you know more about the utility requirement, what do you think of such advertising?

3.   Examination of Useless Inventions. During the period Justice Story authored these statements, the U.S. patent system did not include a professional examining corps providing a rigorous substantive review process that it does today. Given this change, does Justice Story's assertion that no harm befalls the public if a patented invention possesses limited utility remain correct? Doesn't the public suffer the burden of lengthened examination times when notoriously overworked patent examiners must allocate scarce resources towards the extended consideration of worthless technologies?

4.   Modern Perspectives on the Utility Requirement. Justice Story's remarks in *Lowell v. Lewis* should drive home the fact that the patent system is not necessarily looking for something better; just something different. This latter goal is met through the patent law's novelty and nonobviousness requirements. For most inventions outside the fields of chemistry and biotechnology—which are taken up shortly—utility plays only a minor role as a requisite to patentability at the Patent and Trademark Office or as a defense to patent infringement in the courts.

One class of patentable subject matter has persistently been scrutinized via the utility requirement, however. Accused infringers have often invoked the utility requirement where the sole use of a patented invention is to further fraudulent or immoral conduct. The following decision presents the latest thinking on the role of the utility requirement in such cases.

U.S. Patent   Nov. 19, 1996   Sheet 1 of 3   5,575,405

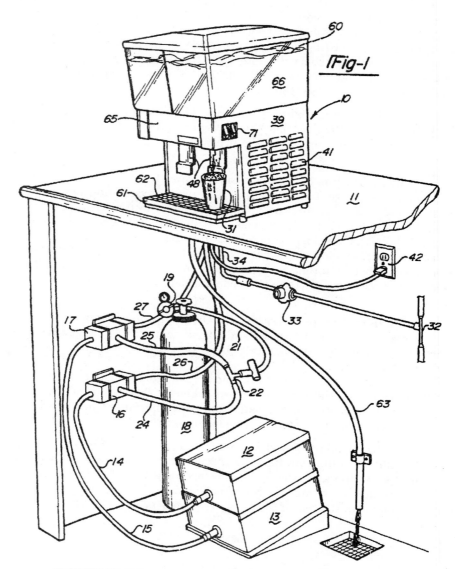

Fig-1

JUICY WHIP, INC. v. ORANGE BANG, INC.

United States Court of Appeals, Federal Circuit, 1999.
185 F.3d 1364, 51 U.S.P.Q.2d 1700.

BRYSON, CIRCUIT JUDGE.

The district court in this case held a patent invalid for lack of utility on the ground that the patented invention was designed to deceive customers by imitating another product and thereby increasing sales of a particular good. We reverse and remand.

I

Juicy Whip, Inc., is the assignee of United States Patent No. 5,575,405, which is entitled "Post–Mix Beverage Dispenser With an Associated Simulated Display of Beverage." A "post-mix" beverage dispenser stores beverage syrup concentrate and water in separate locations until the beverage is ready to be dispensed. The syrup and water are mixed together immediately before the beverage is dispensed, which is usually after the consumer requests the beverage. In contrast, in a "pre-mix" beverage dispenser, the syrup concentrate and water are pre-mixed and the beverage is stored in a display reservoir bowl until it is ready to be dispensed. The display bowl is said to stimulate impulse buying by providing the consumer with a visual beverage display. A pre-mix display bowl, however, has a limited capacity and is subject to contamination by bacteria. It therefore must be refilled and cleaned frequently.

The invention claimed in the '405 patent is a post-mix beverage dispenser that is designed to look like a pre-mix beverage dispenser. The claims require the post-mix dispenser to have a transparent bowl that is filled with a fluid that simulates the appearance of the dispensed beverage and is resistant to bacterial growth. The claims also require that the dispenser create the visual impression that the bowl is the principal source of the dispensed beverage, although in fact the beverage is mixed immediately before it is dispensed, as in conventional post-mix dispensers.

Claim 1 is representative of the claims at issue. It reads as follows:

In a post-mix beverage dispenser of the type having an outlet for discharging beverage components in predetermined proportions to provide a serving of dispensed beverage, the improvement which comprises:

a transparent bowl having no fluid connection with the outlet and visibly containing a quantity of fluid;

said fluid being resistant to organic growth and simulating the appearance of the dispensed beverage;

said bowl being positioned relative to the outlet to create the visual impression that said bowl is the reservoir and principal source of the dispensed beverage from the outlet; and

said bowl and said quantity of fluid visible within said bowl cooperating to create the visual impression that multiple servings of the dispensed beverage are stored within said bowl.

Juicy Whip sued defendants Orange Bang, Inc., and Unique Beverage Dispensers, Inc., (collectively, "Orange Bang") in the United States District Court for the Central District of California, alleging that they were infringing the claims of the '405 patent. Orange Bang moved for summary judgment of invalidity, and the district court granted Orange Bang's motion on the ground that the invention lacked utility and thus was unpatentable under 35 U.S.C. § 101.

The court concluded that the invention lacked utility because its purpose was to increase sales by deception, *i.e.,* through imitation of another product. The court explained that the purpose of the invention "is to create an illusion, whereby customers believe that the fluid contained in the bowl is the actual beverage that they are receiving, when of course it is not." Although the court acknowledged Juicy Whip's argument that the invention provides an accurate representation of the dispensed beverage for the consumer's benefit while eliminating the need for retailers to clean their display bowls, the court concluded that those claimed reasons for the patent's utility "are not independent of its deceptive purpose, and are thus insufficient to raise a disputed factual issue to present to a jury." The court further held that the invention lacked utility because it "improves the prior art only to the extent that it increases the salability of beverages dispensed from post-mix dispensers"; an invention lacks utility, the court stated, if it confers no benefit to the public other than the opportunity for making a product more salable. Finally, the court ruled that the invention lacked utility because it "is merely an imitation of the pre-mix dispenser," and thus does not constitute a new and useful machine.

II

Section 101 of the Patent Act of 1952, 35 U.S.C. § 101, provides that "[w]hoever invents or discovers any new and useful process, machine, manufacture, or composition of matter, or any new and useful improvement thereof," may obtain a patent on the invention or discovery. The threshold of utility is not high: An invention is "useful" under section 101 if it is capable of providing some identifiable benefit. *See Brenner v. Manson,* 383 U.S. 519, 534, 86 S.Ct. 1033, 16 L.Ed.2d 69 (1966); *Brooktree Corp. v. Advanced Micro Devices, Inc.,* 977 F.2d 1555, 1571 (Fed.Cir.1992) ("To violate *§ 101* the claimed device must be totally incapable of achieving a useful result"); *Fuller v. Berger,* 120 F. 274, 275 (7th Cir.1903) (test for utility is whether invention "is incapable of serving any beneficial end").

To be sure, since Justice Story's opinion in *Lowell v. Lewis,* 15 F. Cas. 1018 (C.C.D.Mass.1817), it has been stated that inventions that are "injurious to the well-being, good policy, or sound morals of society" are unpatentable. As examples of such inventions, Justice Story listed "a new invention to poison people, or to promote debauchery, or to facilitate private assassination." *Id.* at 1019. Courts have continued to recite Justice Story's formulation, *see Tol-O-Matic, Inc. v. Proma Produkt–Und Marketing Gesellschaft m.b.H.,* 945 F.2d 1546, 1552–53, 20 USPQ2d 1332, 1338 (Fed.Cir.1991); *In re Nelson,* 47 C.C.P.A. 1031, 280 F.2d 172, 178–79, 126 USPQ 242, 249 (CCPA 1960), but the principle that inventions are invalid if they are principally designed to serve immoral or illegal purposes has not been applied broadly in recent years. For example, years ago courts invalidated patents on gambling devices on the ground that they were immoral, *see e.g.*, *Brewer v. Lichtenstein,* 278 F. 512 (7th Cir.1922); *Schultze v. Holtz,* 82 F. 448 (N.D.Cal.1897); *National Automatic Device Co. v. Lloyd,* 40 F. 89 (N.D.Ill.1889), but that is no longer the law, *see In re Murphy,* 200 USPQ 801 (PTO Bd.App.1977).

In holding the patent in this case invalid for lack of utility, the district court relied on two Second Circuit cases dating from the early years of this century, *Rickard v. Du Bon,* 103 F. 868 (2d Cir.1900), and *Scott & Williams v. Aristo Hosiery Co.,* 7 F.2d 1003 (2d Cir.1925). In the *Rickard* case, the court held invalid a patent on a process for treating tobacco plants to make their leaves appear spotted. At the time of the invention, according to the court, cigar smokers considered cigars with spotted wrappers to be of superior quality, and the invention was designed to make unspotted tobacco leaves appear to be of the spotted— and thus more desirable—type. The court noted that the invention did not promote the burning quality of the leaf or improve its quality in any way; "the only effect, if not the only object, of such treatment, is to spot the tobacco, and counterfeit the leaf spotted by natural causes." Id. *at 869.*

The *Aristo Hosiery* case concerned a patent claiming a seamless stocking with a structure on the back of the stocking that imitated a seamed stocking. The imitation was commercially useful because at the time of the invention many consumers regarded seams in stockings as an indication of higher quality. The court noted that the imitation seam did not "change or improve the structure or the utility of the article," and that the record in the case justified the conclusion that true seamed stockings were superior to the seamless stockings that were the subject of the patent. *See Aristo Hosiery,* 7 F.2d at 1004. "At best," the court stated, "the seamless stocking has imitation marks for the purposes of deception, and the idea prevails that with such imitation the article is more salable." Id. That was not enough, the court concluded, to render the invention patentable.

We decline to follow *Rickard and Aristo Hosiery,* as we do not regard them as representing the correct view of the doctrine of utility under the Patent Act of 1952. The fact that one product can be altered to make it look like another is in itself a specific benefit sufficient to satisfy the statutory requirement of utility.

It is not at all unusual for a product to be designed to appear to viewers to be something it is not. For example, cubic zirconium is designed to simulate a diamond, imitation gold leaf is designed to imitate real gold leaf, synthetic fabrics are designed to simulate expensive natural fabrics, and imitation leather is designed to look like real leather. In each case, the invention of the product or process that makes such imitation possible has "utility" within the meaning of the patent statute, and indeed there are numerous patents directed toward making one product imitate another. *See, e.g.,* U.S. Pat. No. 5,762,968 (method for producing imitation grill marks on food without using heat); U.S. Pat. No. 5,899,038 (laminated flooring imitating wood); U.S. Pat. No. 5,571,545 (imitation hamburger). Much of the value of such products resides in the fact that they appear to be something they are not. Thus, in this case the claimed post-mix dispenser meets the statutory requirement of utility by embodying the features of a post-mix dispenser while imitating the visual appearance of a pre-mix dispenser.

The fact that customers may believe they are receiving fluid directly from the display tank does not deprive the invention of utility. Orange Bang has not argued that it is unlawful to display a representation of the beverage in the manner that fluid is displayed in the reservoir of the invention, even though the fluid is not what the customer will actually receive. Moreover, even if the use of a reservoir containing fluid that is not dispensed is considered deceptive, that is not by itself sufficient to render the invention unpatentable. The requirement of "utility" in patent law is not a directive to the Patent and Trademark Office or the courts to serve as arbiters of deceptive trade practices. Other agencies, such as the Federal Trade Commission and the Food and Drug Administration, are assigned the task of protecting consumers from fraud and deception in the sale of food products. *Cf. In re Watson,* 517 F.2d 465, 474–76, 186 USPQ 11, 19 (CCPA 1975) (stating that it is not the province of the Patent Office to determine, under section 101, whether drugs are safe). As the Supreme Court put the point more generally, "Congress never intended that the patent laws should displace the police powers of the States, meaning by that term those powers by which the health, good order, peace and general welfare of the community are promoted." *Webber v. Virginia,* 103 U.S. (13 Otto) 344, 347–48, 26 L.Ed. 565 (1880).

Of course, Congress is free to declare particular types of inventions unpatentable for a variety of reasons, including deceptiveness. *Cf.* 42 U.S.C. § 2181(a) (exempting from patent protection inventions useful solely in connection with special nuclear material or atomic weapons). Until such time as Congress does so, however, we find no basis in section 101 to hold that inventions can be ruled unpatentable for lack of utility simply because they have the capacity to fool some members of the public. The district court therefore erred in holding that the invention of the '405 patent lacks utility because it deceives the public through imitation in a manner that is designed to increase product sales.

REVERSED and REMANDED.

Notes

1. **Utility and Technology Assessment.** Should the patent system remain oblivious to the social, economic and environmental impacts of the technologies it embraces, remaining instead a "narrowly focused celebration of technical skill"? John R. Thomas, *The Question Concerning Patent Law and Pioneer Inventions,* 10 HIGH TECH. L.J. 35, 102 (1995). Or would we "be wise to question patent grants for inventions such as handguns, machines for processing chewing tobacco, and ozone-depleting spray canisters"? *Id.*

2. Inoperable Inventions. Courts, as well as the Patent and Trademark Office, have also employed the utility requirement to reject wholly inoperable inventions. *See, e.g., Newman v. Quigg*, 877 F.2d 1575, 11 U.S.P.Q.2d 1340 (Fed.Cir.1989) (perpetual motion machine); *In re Perrigo*, 48 F.2d 965, 9 U.S.P.Q. 152 (CCPA 1931) (method and apparatus for accumulating and transforming ether electric energy); *Ex parte Heicklen*, 16 U.S.P.Q.2d 1463 (BPAI 1989) (method to retard the aging process).

§ 3.2 THE UTILITY REQUIREMENT IN CHEMISTRY AND BIOTECHNOLOGY

Outside the chemical and biotechnological arts, utility is a scarcely questioned component of the vast majority of claimed inventions. That utility matters in these fields is largely due to the distinct technological environment in which some of these inventions arise. Rather than constructing a device directed towards a specific application, as say, an electrical engineer does while designing a new circuit, chemists and biotechnicians often synthesize new compounds without a preexisting knowledge of their precise use. They may generate the compounds based on the behavior of related ones, or may wish to explore a class of compounds for which some technical application may develop in the future. In such cases the inventor may have little more than an educated guess about what the newly created compound actually does.

The invention discussed in the Supreme Court's *Brenner v. Manson* decision arose in this fashion. The compound at issue there was a steroid. Steroids can be viewed as a "backbone" carbon rings with a variety of uses depending upon the other atoms which are joined with them. Certain contraceptives, muscle growth stimulants, and tumor inhibitors employ steroids. Chemists of the 1950's needed methods for synthesizing steroids. Yet when they sought patent protection on their results, they discover that the ordinarily dormant utility requirement posed considerable obstacles.

BRENNER, COMMISSIONER OF PATENTS v. MANSON

United States Supreme Court, 1966.
383 U.S. 519, 148 U.S.P.Q. 689.

MR. JUSTICE FORTAS delivered the opinion of the Court.

In December 1957, Howard Ringold and George Rosenkranz applied for a patent on an allegedly novel process for making certain known steroids. They claimed priority as of December 17, 1956, the date on which they had filed for a Mexican patent. United States Patent No. 2,908,693 issued late in 1959.

In January 1960, respondent Manson, a chemist engaged in steroid research, filed an application to patent precisely the same process described by Ringold and Rosenkranz. He asserted that it was he who had discovered the process, and that he had done so before December 17,

1956. Accordingly, he requested that an "interference" be declared in order to try out the issue of priority between his claim and that of Ringold and Rosenkranz.

A Patent Office examiner denied Manson's application, and the denial was affirmed by the Board of Appeals within the Patent Office. The ground for rejection was the failure "to disclose any utility for" the chemical compound produced by the process. Letter of Examiner, dated May 24, 1960. This omission was not cured, in the opinion of the Patent Office, by Manson's reference to an article in the November 1956 issue of the Journal of Organic Chemistry, 21 J. Org. Chem. 1333—1335, which revealed that steroids of a class which included the compound in question were undergoing screening for possible tumor-inhibiting effects in mice, and that a homologue[3] adjacent to Manson's steroid had proven effective in that role. Said the Board of Appeals, "It is our view that the statutory requirement of usefulness of a product cannot be presumed merely because it happens to be closely related to another compound which is known to be useful."

The Court of Customs and Patent Appeals (hereinafter CCPA) reversed, Chief Judge Worley dissenting. The court held that Manson was entitled to a declaration of interference since 'where a claimed process produces a known product it is not necessary to show utility for the product,' so long as the product 'is not alleged to be detrimental to the public interest.' Certiorari was granted to resolve this running dispute over what constitutes 'utility' in chemical process claims....

II.

Our starting point is the proposition, neither disputed nor disputable, that one may patent only that which is "useful." Suffice it to say that the concept of utility has maintained a central place in all of our patent legislation, beginning with the first patent law in 1790 and culminating in the present law's provision that

> "Whoever invents or discovers any new and useful process, machine, manufacture, or composition of matter, or any new and useful improvement thereof, may obtain a patent therefor, subject to the conditions and requirements of this title."

As is so often the case, however, a simple, everyday word can be pregnant with ambiguity when applied to the facts of life. That this is so is demonstrated by the present conflict between the Patent Office and the CCPA over how the test is to be applied to a chemical process which yields an already known product whose utility, other than as a possible object of scientific inquiry, has not yet been evidenced. It was not long ago that agency and court seemed of one mind on the question. In *[In re] Bremner*, 182 F.2d 216, 217, the court affirmed rejection by the Patent

---

3. "A homologous series is a family of chemically related compounds, the composition of which varies from member to member by CH(2) (one atom of carbon and two atoms of hydrogen) * * *. Chemists know- ing the properties of one member of a series would in general know what to expect in adjacent members." Application of Henze, 181 F.2d 196, 200—201, 37 C.C.P.A. (Pat.) 1009, 1014.

Office of both process and product claims. It noted that "no use for the products claimed to be developed by the processes had been shown in the specification." It held that "It was never intended that a patent be granted upon a product, or a process producing a product, unless such product be useful." Nor was this new doctrine in the court.

The Patent Office has remained stead-fast in this view. The CCPA, however, has moved sharply away from Bremner. The trend began in *[In re] Nelson*, 280 F.2d 172, 47 C.C.P.A. (Pat.) 1031. There, the court reversed the Patent Office's rejection of a claim on a process yielding chemical intermediates "useful to chemists doing research on steroids," despite the absence of evidence that any of the steroids thus ultimately produced were themselves "useful." The trend has accelerated, culminating in the present case where the court held it sufficient that a process produces the result intended and is not "detrimental to the public interest." 333 F.2d at 238, 52 C.C.P.A. (Pat.), at 745.

It is not remarkable that differences arise as to how the test of usefulness is to be applied to chemical processes. Even if we knew precisely what Congress meant in 1790 when it devised the "new and useful" phraseology and in subsequent re-enactments of the test, we should have difficulty in applying it in the context of contemporary chemistry where research is as comprehensive as man's grasp and where little or nothing is wholly beyond the pale of "utility"—if that word is given its broadest reach.

Respondent does not—at least in the first instance—rest upon the extreme proposition, advanced by the court below, that a novel chemical process is patentable so long as it yields the intended product and so long as the product is not itself "detrimental." Nor does he commit the outcome of his claim to the slightly more conventional proposition that any process is "useful" within the meaning of § 101 if it produces a compound whose potential usefulness is under investigation by serious scientific researchers, although he urges this position, too, as an alternative basis for affirming the decision of the CCPA. Rather, he begins with the much more orthodox argument that his process has a specific utility which would entitle him to a declaration of interference even under the Patent Office's reading of § 101. The claim is that the supporting affidavits filed pursuant to Rule 204(b), by reference to Ringold's 1956 article, reveal that an adjacent homologue of the steroid yielded by his process has been demonstrated to have tumor-inhibiting effects in mice, and that this discloses the requisite utility. We do not accept any of these theories as an adequate basis for overriding the determination of the Patent Office that the "utility" requirement has not been met.

Even on the assumption that the process would be patentable were respondent to show that the steroid produced had a tumor-inhibiting effect in mice, we would not overrule the Patent Office finding that respondent has not made such a showing. The Patent Office held that, despite the reference to the adjacent homologue, respondent's papers did not disclose a sufficient likelihood that the steroid yielded by his process would have similar tumor-inhibiting characteristics. Indeed, respondent himself recognized that the presumption that adjacent homologues have the same utility has been challenged in the steroid field because of "a greater known unpredictability of compounds in that field." In these circumstances and in this technical area, we would not overturn the finding of the Primary Examiner, affirmed by the Board of Appeals and not challenged by the CCPA.

The second and third points of respondent's argument present issues of much importance. Is a chemical process "useful" within the meaning of § 101 either (1) because it works, i.e., produces the intended product? or (2) because the compound yielded belongs to a class of compounds now the subject of serious scientific investigation? These contentions present the basic problem for our adjudication. Since we find no specific assistance in the legislative materials underlying § 101, we are remitted to an analysis of the problem in light of the general intent of Congress, the purposes of the patent system, and the implications of a decision one way or the other.

In support of his plea that we attenuate the requirement of "utility," respondent relies upon Justice Story's well-known statement that a "useful" invention is one "which may be applied to a beneficial use in society, in contradistinction to an invention injurious to the morals, health, or good order of society, or frivolous and insignificant" and upon the assertion that to do so would encourage inventors of new processes to publicize the event for the benefit of the entire scientific community, thus widening the search for uses and increasing the fund of scientific knowledge. Justice Story's language sheds little light on our subject. Narrowly read, it does no more than compel us to decide whether the invention in question is "frivolous and insignificant"—a query no easier of application than the one built into the statute. Read more broadly, so as to allow the patenting of any invention not positively harmful to society, it places such a special meaning on the word "useful" that we cannot accept it in the absence of evidence that Congress so intended. There are, after all, many things in this world which may not be considered "useful" but which, nevertheless are totally without a capacity for harm.

It is true, of course, that one of the purposes of the patent system is to encourage dissemination of information concerning discoveries and inventions. And it may be that inability to patent a process to some extent discourages disclosure and leads to greater secrecy than would otherwise be the case. The inventor of the process, or the corporate organization by which he is employed, has some incentive to keep the invention secret while uses for the product are searched out. However, in light of the highly developed art of drafting patent claims so that they disclose as little useful information as possible—while broadening the scope of the claim as widely as possible—the argument based upon the virtue of disclosure must be warily evaluated. Moreover, the pressure for secrecy is easily exaggerated, for if the inventor of a process cannot himself ascertain a "use" for that which his process yields, he has every incentive to make his invention known to those able to do so. Finally, how likely is disclosure of a patented process to spur research by others into the uses to which the product may be put? To the extent that the patentee has power to enforce his patent, there is little incentive for others to undertake a search for uses.

Whatever weight is attached to the value of encouraging disclosure and of inhibiting secrecy, we believe a more compelling consideration is that a process patent in the chemical field, which has not been developed and pointed to the degree of specific utility, creates a monopoly of knowledge which should be granted only if clearly commanded by the statute. Until the process claim has been reduced to production of a product shown to be useful, the metes and bounds of that monopoly are not capable of precise delineation. It may engross a vast, unknown, and perhaps unknowable area. Such a patent may confer power to block off whole areas of scientific development, without compensating benefit to the public. The basic quid pro quo contemplated by the Constitution and the Congress for granting a patent monopoly is the benefit derived by the public from an invention with substantial utility. Unless and until a process is refined and developed to this point—where specific benefit exists in currently available form—there is insufficient justification for permitting an applicant to engross what may prove to be a broad field.

These arguments for and against the patentability of a process which either has no known use or is useful only in the sense that it may be an object of scientific research would apply equally to the patenting of the product produced by the process. Respondent appears to concede that with respect to a product, as opposed to a process, Congress has struck the balance on the side of nonpatentability unless "utility" is shown. Indeed, the decisions of the CCPA are in accord with the view that a product may not be patented absent a showing of utility greater than any adduced in the present case. We find absolutely no warrant for the proposition that although Congress intended that no patent be granted on a chemical compound whose sole "utility" consists of its potential role as an object of use-testing, a different set of rules was meant to apply to the process which yielded the unpatentable product. That proposition seems to us little more than an attempt to evade the impact of the rules which concededly govern patentability of the product itself.

This is not to say that we mean to disparage the importance of contributions to the fund of scientific information short of the invention of something "useful," or that we are blind to the prospect that what now seems without "use" may tomorrow command the grateful attention of the public. But a patent is not a hunting license. It is not a reward for the search, but compensation for its successful conclusion. "[A] patent system must be related to the world of commerce rather than to the realm of philosophy."

Mr. Justice Douglas * * * dissents on the merits of the controversy for substantially the reasons stated by Mr. Justice Harlan.

MR. JUSTICE HARLAN, concurring in part and dissenting in part.

I cannot agree with [the Court's] resolution of the important question of patentability.

Respondent has contended that a workable chemical process, which is both new and sufficiently nonobvious to satisfy the patent statute, is by its existence alone a contribution to chemistry and "useful" as the statute employs that term. Certainly this reading of "useful" in the statute is within the scope of the constitutional grant, which states only that "[t]o promote the Progress of Science and useful Arts," the exclusive right to "Writings and Discoveries" may be secured for limited times to those who produce them. Art. I, § 8. Yet the patent statute is somewhat differently worded and is on its face open both to respondent's construction and to the contrary reading given it by the Court. In the absence of legislative history on this issue, we are thrown back on policy and practice. Because I believe that the Court's policy arguments are not convincing and that past practice favors the respondent, I would reject the narrow definition of "useful" and uphold the judgment of the Court of Customs and Patent Appeals (hereafter CCPA).

The Court's opinion sets out about half a dozen reasons in support of its interpretation. Several of these arguments seem to me to have almost no force. For instance, it is suggested that "[u]ntil the process claim has been reduced to production of a product shown to be useful, the metes and bounds of that monopoly are not capable of precise delineation" and "[i]t may engross a vast, unknown, and perhaps unknowable area". I fail to see the relevance of these assertions; process claims are not disallowed because the products they produce may be of "vast" importance nor, in any event, does advance knowledge of a specific product use provide much safeguard on this score or fix "metes and bounds" precisely since a hundred more uses may be found after a patent is granted and greatly enhance its value.

The further argument that an established product use is part of "(t)he basic quid pro quo" for the patent or is the requisite "successful conclusion" of the inventor's search appears to beg the very question whether the process is "useful" simply because it facilitates further research into possible product uses. The same infirmity seems to inhere in the Court's argument that chemical products lacking immediate utility cannot be distinguished for present purposes from the processes which create them, that respondent appears to concede and the CCPA holds that the products are nonpatentable, and that therefore the processes are nonpatentable. Assuming that the two classes cannot be distinguished, a point not adequately considered in the briefs, and assuming further that the CCPA has firmly held such products nonpatentable, this permits us to conclude only that the CCPA is wrong either as to the products or as to the processes and affords no basis for deciding whether both or neither should be patentable absent a specific product use.

More to the point, I think, are the Court's remaining, prudential arguments against patentability: namely, that disclosure induced by allowing a patent is partly undercut by patent-application drafting techniques, that disclosure may occur without granting a patent, and that a patent will discourage others from inventing uses for the product. How far opaque drafting may lessen the public benefits resulting from the issuance of a patent is not shown by any evidence in this case but, more important, the argument operates against all patents and gives no reason for singling out the class involved here. The thought that these inventions may be more likely than most to be disclosed even if patents are not allowed may have more force; but while empirical study of the industry might reveal that chemical researchers would behave in this fashion, the abstractly logical choice for them seems to me to maintain secrecy until a product use can be discovered. As to discouraging the search by others for product uses, there is no doubt this risk exists but the price paid for any patent is that research on other uses or improvements may be hampered because the original patentee will reap much of the reward. From the standpoint of the public interest the Constitution seems to have resolved that choice in favor of patentability.

What I find most troubling about the result reached by the Court is the impact it may have on chemical research. Chemistry is a highly interrelated field and a tangible benefit for society may be the outcome of a number of different discoveries, one discovery building upon the next. To encourage one chemist or research facility to invent and disseminate new processes and products may be vital to progress, although the product or process be without "utility" as the Court defines the term, because that discovery permits someone else to take a further but perhaps less difficult step leading to a commercially useful item. In my view, our awareness in this age of the importance of achieving and publicizing basic research should lead this Court to resolve uncertainties in its favor and uphold the respondent's position in this case.

This position is strengthened, I think, by what appears to have been the practice of the Patent Office during most of this century. While available proof is not conclusive, the commentators seem to be in agreement that until [In re] Bremner, 182 F.2d 216, 37 C.C.P.A. (Pat.) 1032, in 1950, chemical patent applications were commonly granted although no resulting end use was stated or the statement was in extremely broad terms. Taking this to be true, Bremner represented a deviation from established practice which the CCPA has now sought to remedy in part only to find that the Patent Office does not want to return to the beaten track. If usefulness was typically regarded as inherent during a long and prolific period of chemical research and development in this country, surely this is added reason why the Court's result should not be adopted until Congress expressly mandates it, presumably on the basis of empirical data which this Court does not possess.

Fully recognizing that there is ample room for disagreement on this problem when, as here, it is reviewed in the abstract, I believe the decision below should be affirmed.

Notes

1. **The Heightened Utility Standard of *Brenner v. Manson*.** The Supreme Court's holding provided a particularly hard result, as a utility for the claimed chemical compound had been disclosed to the public following the application's filing date. Manson did not know of the utility at the time the application was submitted to the Patent and Trademark Office, however. Of course, any chemical compound inherently possesses any useful properties that it may possess at the moment of its creation; does § 101 provide that an invention must be "useful" or that it must be "known to be useful"? Alternatively, is *Brenner v. Manson* less about the utility requirement itself (§ 101) than disclosure of that utility in a patent application (§ 112, ¶ 1)? Suppose Manson's application had indicated that, at least when present in sufficient quantities, the claimed steroid compound served as a handy paper weight? Consider also the critical remarks of Justice Fortas regarding the patent bar and claim drafting—how does this commentary have anything to do with utility?

2. **"No–Brenner" Questions.** What if at the time of Manson's invention, several thousand research groups all sought to buy steroids made by his process. Would Justice Fortas still claim that Manson's process was not useful? Also, under *Brenner v. Manson*, may an inventor obtain a patent on a new research telescope?

3. **Patenting at the Lab Bench.** Historical experience with technology demonstrate that inventors have frequently uncovered additional valuable uses of known chemical compounds. For example, iodine, originally used in the photographic and dye-making industries, and the explosive nitroglycerin found further uses in medicine, as an antiseptic and heart medication, respectively. Which way should this insight cut with respect to the utility requirement? Should courts and the Patent and Trademark Office recognize that the utility of a chemical intermediate is often a moving target? Or, should the patent law strictly uphold the utility requirement?

4. **Is Usefulness Effectiveness?** When *Brenner v. Manson* speaks of usefulness in terms of a "benefit derived by the public from an invention with substantial utility," it raises questions about inventions which do not literally advance the art because they are less effective than existing technology. Is effectiveness in this sense part of the test for utility? The Federal Circuit, speaking through Judge Edward Smith, encountered a simple invention for mud flaps on automobiles. The Circuit stated:

> Finding that an invention is an "improvement" is not a prerequisite to patentability. It is possible for an invention to be less effective than existing devices but nevertheless meet the statutory criteria for patentability.

Custom Accessories v. Jeffrey–Allan Indus., 807 F.2d 955, 960 n. 12, 1 U.S.P.Q.2d 1196, 1202 n. 12 (Fed.Cir.1986).

5.   A Note on Pharmaceutical Testing. As background for *In re Brana*, note that the testing of new pharmaceutical compounds typically occurs in three successive stages. Following the development of a likely organic molecule, scientists ordinarily perform experiments *in vitro*; that is, in the laboratory, using assays that might comprise tissue samples, membrane-bound receptors or isolated receptor sites. Those few compounds that appear to exhibit useful pharmacological properties are then the subject of more expensive *in vivo* testing in living organisms. Again, the relatively small number of successful candidates are subject to still more expensive clinical testing on human subjects. Because drug development costs are enormous, the pharmaceutical industry ordinary seeks patent protection for interesting compounds as quickly as possible. For more information on pharmaceutical testing, consult Michael Gruber, *Map the Genome, Hack the Genome*, WIRED 5.10 at 152, 193 (Oct. 1997), and Phillipe Ducor, *New Drug Discovery Technologies and Patents*, 22 RUTGERS COMP. & TECH. L.J. 369 (1996).

§ 3.3   THE UTILITY REQUIREMENT AT THE FEDERAL CIRCUIT

IN RE BRANA

United States Court of Appeals, Federal Circuit, 1995.
51 F.3d 1560, 34 U.S.P.Q.2d 1436.

Before PLAGER, LOURIE, and RADER, CIRCUIT JUDGES.

PLAGER, CIRCUIT JUDGE. Miguel F. Brana, et al. (applicants), appeal the March 19, 1993 decision of the United States Patent and Trademark Office (PTO) Board of Patent Appeals and Interferences (Board), in Appeal No. 92–1196. The Board affirmed the examiner's rejection of claims 10–13 of patent application Serial No. 533,944 under 35 U.S.C. § 112 ¶ 1 (1988). The examiner's rejection, upon which the Board relied in rendering its decision, was based specifically on a challenge to the utility of the claimed compounds and the amount of experimentation necessary to use the compounds. We conclude the Board erred, and reverse.

I.   BACKGROUND

On June 30, 1988, applicants filed patent application Serial No. 213,690 (the '690 application) directed to 5–nitrobenzo[de]isoquinoline–1,3–dione compounds, for use as antitumor substances, having the following formula:

where n is 1 or 2, R1 and R2 are identical or different and are each hydrogen, C sub1–C sub6–alkyl, C sub1–C sub6–hydroxyalkyl, pyrrolidinyl, morpholino, piperidinyl or piperacinyl, and R3 and R4 are identical or different and are each hydrogen, C sub1–C sub6–alkyl, C sub1–C sub6–acyl, C sub2–C sub7–alkoxycarbonyl, ureyl, aminocarbonyl or C sub2–C sub7–alkylaminocarbonyl. These claimed compounds differ from several prior art benzo[de]isoquinoline–1,3–dione compounds due to the presence of a nitro group (O sub2 N) at the 5–position and an amino or other amino group (NR3R4) at the 8–position of the isoquinoline ring.

The specification states that these non-symmetrical substitutions at the 5–and 8–positions produce compounds with "a better action and a better action spectrum as antitumor substances" than known benzo[de]isoquinolines, namely those in K.D. Paull et al., *Computer Assisted Structure—Activity Correlations, Drug Research*, 34(II), 1243–46 (1984) (Paull). Paull describes a computer-assisted evaluation of benzo[de]isoquinoline–1,3–diones and related compounds which have been screened for antitumor activity by testing their efficacy in vivo against two specific implanted murine (i.e., utilizing mice as test subjects) lymphocytic leukemias, P388 and L1210. These two in vivo tests are widely used by the National Cancer Institute (NCI) to measure the antitumor properties of a compound. Paull noted that one compound in particular, benzo[de]isoquinoline–1,3(2H)dione,5–amino–2(2–dimethyl-aminoethyl [sic]) (hereinafter "NSC 308847"), was found to show excellent activity against these two specific tumor models. Based on their analysis, compound NSC 308847 was selected for further studies by NCI. In addition to comparing the effectiveness of the claimed compounds with structurally similar compounds in Paull, applicants' patent specification illustrates the cytotoxicity of the claimed compounds against human tumor cells, in vitro, and concludes that these tests "had a good action."

The examiner initially rejected applicants' claims in the '690 application as obvious under 35 U.S.C. § 103 in light of U.S. Patent No. 4,614,820, issued to and referred to hereafter as Zee–Cheng et al. Zee–Cheng et al. discloses a benzo[de]isoquinoline compound for use as an antitumor agent with symmetrical substitutions on the 5–position and 8–position of the quinoline ring; in both positions the substitution was either an amino or nitro group. Although not identical to the applicants' claimed compounds, the examiner noted the similar substitution pattern (i.e., at the same positions on the isoquinoline ring) and concluded that a mixed substitution of the invention therefore would have been obvious in view of Zee–Cheng et al.

In a response dated July 14, 1989, the applicants rebutted the § 103 rejection. Applicants asserted that their mixed disubstituted compounds had unexpectedly better antitumor properties than the symmetrically substituted compounds in Zee–Cheng et al. In support of this assertion applicants attached the declaration of Dr. Gerhard Keilhauer. In his declaration Dr. Keilhauer reported that his tests indicated that applicants' claimed compounds were far more effective as antitumor agents than the compounds disclosed in Zee–Cheng et al. when tested, in vitro, against two specific types of human tumor cells, HEp and HCT–29. Applicants further noted that, although the differences between the compounds in Zee–Cheng et al. and applicants' claimed compounds were slight, there was no suggestion in the art that these improved results (over Zee–Cheng et al.) would have been expected. Although the applicants overcame the § 103 rejection, the examiner nevertheless issued a final rejection, on different grounds, on September 5, 1989.

On June 4, 1990, applicants filed a continuation application, Serial No. 533,944 (the '944 application), from the above-mentioned '690 application. Claims 10–13, the only claims remaining in the continuation application, were rejected in a final office action dated May 1, 1991. Applicants appealed the examiner's final rejection to the Board.

In his answer to the applicants' appeal brief, the examiner stated that the final rejection was based on 35 U.S.C. § 112 ¶ 1. The examiner first noted that the specification failed to describe any specific disease against which the claimed compounds were active. Furthermore, the examiner concluded that the prior art tests performed in Paull and the tests disclosed in the specification were not sufficient to establish a reasonable expectation that the claimed compounds had a practical utility (i.e. antitumor activity in humans).

In a decision dated March 19, 1993, the Board affirmed the examiner's final rejection. The three-page opinion, which lacked any additional analysis, relied entirely on the examiner's reasoning. Although noting that it also would have been proper for the examiner to reject the claims under 35 U.S.C. § 101, the Board affirmed solely on the basis of the Examiner's § 112 ¶ 1 rejection. This appeal followed.

II. Discussion

At issue in this case is an important question of the legal constraints on patent office examination practice and policy. The question is, with regard to pharmaceutical inventions, what must the applicant prove regarding the practical utility or usefulness of the invention for which patent protection is sought. This is not a new issue; it is one which we would have thought had been settled by case law years ago. We note the

Commissioner has recently addressed this question in his Examiner Guidelines for Biotech Applications, see 60 FED.REG. 97 (1995); 49 PAT. TRADEMARK & COPYRIGHT J. (BNA) No. 1210, at 234 (Jan. 5, 1995).

The requirement that an invention have utility is found in 35 U.S.C. § 101: "Whoever invents ... any new and useful ... composition of matter ... may obtain a patent therefor...." (emphasis added). It is also implicit in § 112 ¶ 1, which reads: The specification shall contain a written description of the invention, and of the manner and process of making and using it, in such full, clear, concise, and exact terms as to enable any person skilled in the art to which it pertains, or with which it is most nearly connected, to make and use the same, and shall set forth the best mode contemplated by the inventor of carrying out his invention. Obviously, if a claimed invention does not have utility, the specification cannot enable one to use it.

As noted, although the examiner and the Board both mentioned § 101, and the rejection appears to be based on the issue of whether the compounds had a practical utility, a § 101 issue, the rejection according to the Board stands on the requirements of § 112 ¶ 1. It is to that provision that we address ourselves.[12] The Board gives two reasons for the rejection; we will consider these in turn.

1.

The first basis for the Board's decision was that the applicants' specification failed to disclose a specific disease against which the claimed compounds are useful, and therefore, absent undue experimentation, one of ordinary skill in the art was precluded from using the invention. In support, the Commissioner argues that the disclosed uses in the '944 application, namely the "treatment of diseases" and "antitumor substances," are similar to the nebulous disclosure found insufficient in *In re Kirk*, 376 F.2d 936, 153 U.S.P.Q. 48 (CCPA 1967). This argument is not without merit.

In *Kirk* applicants claimed a new class of steroid compounds. One of the alleged utilities disclosed in the specification was that these compounds possessed "high biological activity." The specification, however, failed to disclose which biological properties made the compounds useful. Moreover, the court found that known specific uses of similar compounds did not cure this defect since there was no disclosure in the specification that the properties of the claimed compounds were the same as those of the known similar compounds. Furthermore, it was not alleged that one of skill in the art would have known of any specific uses, and therefore, the court concluded this alleged use was too obscure to enable one of

---

12. This court's predecessor has determined that absence of utility can be the basis of a rejection under both 35 U.S.C. § 101 and § 112 ¶ 1. In re Jolles, 628 F.2d 1322, 1326 n. 11, 206 U.S.P.Q. 885, 889 n. 11 (CCPA 1980); In re Fouche, 439 F.2d 1237, 1243, 169 U.S.P.Q. 429, 434 (CCPA 1971) ("[I]f such compositions are in fact useless, appellant's specification cannot have taught how to use them."). Since the Board affirmed the examiner's rejection based solely on § 112 ¶ 1, however, our review is limited only to whether the application complies with § 112 ¶ 1.

skill in the art to use the claimed invention. *See also Kawai v. Metlesics*, 480 F.2d 880, 178 U.S.P.Q. 158 (CCPA 1973).

Kirk would potentially be dispositive of this case were the above-mentioned language the only assertion of utility found in the '944 application. Applicants' specification, however, also states that the claimed compounds have "a better action and a better action spectrum as antitumor substances" than known compounds, specifically those analyzed in Paull. As previously noted, see supra note 4, Paull grouped various benzo[de]isoquinoline–1,3–diones, which had previously been tested in vivo for antitumor activity against two lymphocytic leukemia tumor models (P388 and L1210), into various structural classifications and analyzed the test results of the groups (i.e. what percent of the compounds in the particular group showed success against the tumor models). Since one of the tested compounds, NSC 308847, was found to be highly effective against these two lymphocytic leukemia tumor models, applicants' favorable comparison implicitly asserts that their claimed compounds are highly effective (i.e. useful) against lymphocytic leukemia. An alleged use against this particular type of cancer is much more specific than the vaguely intimated uses rejected by the courts in *Kirk* and *Kawai*. *See, e.g., Cross v. Iizuka*, 753 F.2d at 1048, 224 U.S.P.Q. at 745 (finding the disclosed practical utility for the claimed compounds—the inhibition of thromboxane synthetase in human or bovine platelet microsomes—sufficiently specific to satisfy the threshold requirement in *Kirk* and *Kawai*.)

The Commissioner contends, however, that P388 and L1210 are not diseases since the only way an animal can get sick from P388 is by a direct injection of the cell line. The Commissioner therefore concludes that applicants' reference to Paull in their specification does not provide a specific disease against which the claimed compounds can be used. We disagree.

As applicants point out, the P388 and L1210 cell lines, though technically labeled tumor models, were originally derived from lymphocytic leukemias in mice. Therefore, the P388 and L1210 cell lines do represent actual specific lymphocytic tumors; these models will produce this particular disease once implanted in mice. If applicants were required to wait until an animal naturally developed this specific tumor before testing the effectiveness of a compound against the tumor in vivo, as would be implied from the Commissioner's argument, there would be no effective way to test compounds in vivo on a large scale.   *policy*

We conclude that these tumor models represent a specific disease against which the claimed compounds are alleged to be effective. Accordingly, in light of the explicit reference to Paull, applicants' specification alleges a sufficiently specific use.

2.

The second basis for the Board's rejection was that, even if the specification did allege a specific use, applicants failed to prove that the

*test
...*

claimed compounds are useful. Citing various references, the Board found, and the Commissioner now argues, that the tests offered by the applicants to prove utility were inadequate to convince one of ordinary skill in the art that the claimed compounds are useful as antitumor agents.[13]

This court's predecessor has stated: [A] specification disclosure which contains a teaching of the manner and process of making and using the invention in terms which correspond in scope to those used in describing and defining the subject matter sought to be patented must be taken as in compliance with the enabling requirement of the first paragraph of § 112 unless there is reason to doubt the objective truth of the statements contained therein which must be relied on for enabling support. From this it follows that the PTO has the initial burden of challenging a presumptively correct assertion of utility in the disclosure. Only after the PTO provides evidence showing that one of ordinary skill in the art would reasonably doubt the asserted utility does the burden shift to the applicant to provide rebuttal evidence sufficient to convince such a person of the invention's asserted utility.

The PTO has not met this initial burden. The references cited by the Board, Pazdur and Martin, do not question the usefulness of any compound as an antitumor agent or provide any other evidence to cause one of skill in the art to question the asserted utility of applicants' compounds. Rather, these references merely discuss the therapeutic predictive value of in vivo murine tests—relevant only if applicants must prove the ultimate value in humans of their asserted utility. Likewise, we do not find that the nature of applicants' invention alone would cause one of skill in the art to reasonably doubt the asserted usefulness.

The purpose of treating cancer with chemical compounds does not suggest an inherently unbelievable undertaking or involve implausible scientific principles. Modern science has previously identified numerous successful chemotherapeutic agents. In addition, the prior art, specifically Zee Cheng et al., discloses structurally similar compounds to those claimed by the applicants which have been proven in vivo to be effective as chemotherapeutic agents against various tumor models.

Taking these facts—the nature of the invention and the PTO's proffered evidence—into consideration we conclude that one skilled in the art would be without basis to reasonably doubt applicants' asserted utility on its face. The PTO thus has not satisfied its initial burden.

We do not rest our decision there, however. Even if one skilled in the art would have reasonably questioned the asserted utility, i.e., even if the PTO met its initial burden thereby shifting the burden to the applicants to offer rebuttal evidence, applicants proffered sufficient evidence to convince one of skill in the art of the asserted utility. In particular, applicants provided through Dr. Kluge's declaration test results showing that several compounds within the scope of the claims exhibited significant antitumor activity against the L1210 standard

---

13. As noted, this would appear to be a § 101 issue, rather than § 112.

tumor model in vivo. Such evidence alone should have been sufficient to satisfy applicants' burden.

The prior art further supports the conclusion that one skilled in the art would be convinced of the applicants' asserted utility. As previously mentioned, prior art–Zee–Cheng et al. and Paull–disclosed structurally similar compounds which were proven in vivo against various tumor models to be effective as chemotherapeutic agents. Although it is true that minor changes in chemical compounds can radically alter their effects on the human body, *Kawai*, 480 F.2d at 891, 178 U.S.P.Q. at 167, evidence of success in structurally similar compounds is relevant in determining whether one skilled in the art would believe an asserted utility.

The Commissioner counters that such in vivo tests in animals are only preclinical tests to determine whether a compound is suitable for processing in the second stage of testing, by which he apparently means in vivo testing in humans, and therefore are not reasonably predictive of the success of the claimed compounds for treating cancer in humans. The Commissioner, as did the Board, confuses the requirements under the law for obtaining a patent with the requirements for obtaining government approval to market a particular drug for human consumption. *See Scott v. Finney*, 34 F.3d 1058, 1063, 32 U.S.P.Q.2d 1115, 1120 (Fed.Cir.1994) ("Testing for the full safety and effectiveness of a prosthetic device is more properly left to the Food and Drug Administration (FDA). Title 35 does not demand that such human testing occur within the confines of Patent and Trademark Office (PTO) proceedings.").

Our court's predecessor has determined that proof of an alleged pharmaceutical property for a compound by statistically significant tests with standard experimental animals is sufficient to establish utility. In concluding that similar in vivo tests were adequate proof of utility the court in *In re Krimmel* stated: We hold as we do because it is our firm conviction that one who has taught the public that a compound exhibits some desirable pharmaceutical property in a standard experimental animal has made a significant and useful contribution to the art, even though it may eventually appear that the compound is without value in the treatment in humans. Moreover, NCI apparently believes these tests are statistically significant because it has explicitly recognized both the P388 and L1210 murine tumor models as standard screening tests for determining whether new compounds may be useful as antitumor agents.

In the context of this case the Martin and Pazdur references, on which the Commissioner relies, do not convince us otherwise. Pazdur only questions the reliability of the screening tests against lung cancer; it says nothing regarding other types of tumors. Although the Martin reference does note that some laboratory oncologists are skeptical about the predictive value of in vivo murine tumor models for human therapy, Martin recognizes that these tumor models continue to contribute to an increasing human cure rate. In fact, the authors conclude that this perception (i.e. lack of predictive reliability) is not tenable in light of present information.

On the basis of animal studies, and controlled testing in a limited number of humans (referred to as Phase I testing), the Food and Drug Administration may authorize Phase II clinical studies. See 21 U.S.C. § 355(i)(1); 21 C.F.R. § 312.23(a)(5), (a)(8) (1994). Authorization for a Phase II study means that the drug may be administered to a larger number of humans, but still under strictly supervised conditions. The purpose of the Phase II study is to determine primarily the safety of the drug when administered to a larger human population, as well as its potential efficacy under different dosage regimes. See 21 C.F.R. § 312.21(b).

FDA approval, however, is not a prerequisite for finding a compound useful within the meaning of the patent laws. Usefulness in patent law, and in particular in the context of pharmaceutical inventions, necessarily includes the expectation of further research and development. The stage at which an invention in this field becomes useful is well before it is ready to be administered to humans. Were we to require Phase II testing in order to prove utility, the associated costs would prevent many companies from obtaining patent protection on promising new inventions, thereby eliminating an incentive to pursue, through research and development, potential cures in many crucial areas such as the treatment of cancer.

In view of all the foregoing, we conclude that applicants' disclosure complies with the requirements of 35 U.S.C. § 112 ¶ 1.

Notes

1. **Brenner versus Brana.** Is *Brana* consistent with *Brenner v. Manson*? If so, why does the *Brana* opinion fail to cite *Brenner*? Also, remember that in *Brenner v. Manson*, skilled artisans knew of an adjacent homologue to the claimed invention. That adjacent homologue was known to inhibit tumors in mice. Following the approach of *Brana*, would the Federal Circuit have reached the same result as the Supreme Court if presented with Manson's steroid?

2. **Patent Office Utility Guidelines.** As noted in *Brana*, the Patent and Trademark Office has recently been active in promulgating guidelines to examiners concerning the utility requirement. Interim guidelines issued in 1995 and 1999, ultimately leading to finalized Utility Examination Guidelines, 66 Fed. Reg. 1092 (Jan. 5, 2001). Under the Guidelines, "[i]f at any time during the examination, it becomes readily apparent that the claimed invention has a well-established utility, do not impose a rejection based on lack of utility. An invention has a well-established utility (1) if a person of ordinary skill in the art would immediately appreciate why the invention is useful based on the characteristics of the invention (e.g., properties or applications of a product or process), and (2) the utility is specific, substantial, and credible." The Guidelines further instruct examiners to:

Review the claims and the supporting written description to determine if the applicant has asserted for the claimed invention any specific and substantial utility that is credible:

(a) If the applicant has asserted that the claimed invention is useful for any particular practical purpose (i.e., it has a "specific and substantial utility") and the assertion would be considered credible by a person of ordinary skill in the art, do not impose a rejection based on lack of utility.

> (1) A claimed invention must have a specific and substantial utility. This requirement excludes 'throw-away,' 'insubstantial,' or 'nonspecific' utilities, such as the use of a complex invention as landfill, as a way of satisfying the utility requirement of 35 U.S.C. 101.

> (2) Credibility is assessed from the perspective of one of ordinary skill in the art in view of the disclosure and any other evidence of record (e.g., test data, affidavits or declarations from experts in the art, patents or printed publications) that is probative of the applicant's assertions. An applicant need only provide one credible assertion of specific and substantial utility for each claimed invention to satisfy the utility requirement.

(b) If no assertion of specific and substantial utility for the claimed invention made by the applicant is credible, and the claimed invention does not have a readily apparent well-established utility, reject the claim(s) under § 101 on the grounds that the invention as claimed lacks utility. . . .

(c) If the applicant has not asserted any specific and substantial utility for the claimed invention and it does not have a readily apparent well-established utility, impose a rejection under § 101, emphasizing that the applicant has not disclosed a specific and substantial utility for the invention. The § 101 [rejection shifts] the burden of coming forward with evidence to the applicant to:

> (1) Explicitly identify a specific and substantial utility for the claimed invention; and

> (2) Provide evidence that one of ordinary skill in the art would have recognized that the identified specific and substantial utility was well established at the time of filing. . . .

The examiner training materials accompanying the Utility Guidelines, available at *www.uspto.gov,* provide illuminating examples of the application of these principles to particular inventions. The consensus of the patent bar is that the Guidelines present a more rigorous utility requirement than had previously been the practice of the Patent and Trademark Office. *E.g.,* Mary Breen Smith, Comment, *An End to Gene Patents? The Human Genome Project versus the United States Patent and Trademark Office's 1999 Guidelines,* 73 U. COLO. L. REV. 747 (2002); J. Timothy Meigs, *Biotechnology Patent Prosecution in View of the PTO's Utility Examination Guidelines,* 83 J. PAT. & TRADEMARK OFF. SOC'Y 451 (2001). Commentators have questioned whether these Guidelines fully comport with the more liberal view of utility offered in the Federal Circuit's *Brana* decision.

3. Comparative Approaches. Foreign patent systems typically do not mandate that patented inventions be useful, but instead impose a parallel requirement termed "industrial applicability." Article 52(1) EPC. Article 57 EPC provides that "[a]n invention shall be considered susceptible of industrial application if it can be made or used in any kind of industry, including agriculture." The European Patent Office Guidelines indicate that the term "industry" "should be understood in its broad sense as including any physical activity of 'technical character,' i.e., an activity which belongs to the useful or practical arts as distinct from the aesthetic arts." Part C at 40. The Japanese patent law has similar standards in place. *See* Art. 29(1). Would *Brenner v. Manson* have been decided differently in Europe and Japan?

Utility Exercise

On December 18, 1997, Stuart Newman, a professor of cell biology and anatomy at New York Medical College, and Jeremy Rifkin, president of the Foundation on Economic Trends, jointly filed a patent application claiming a technique for combining human and animal embryo cells to produce a single animal-human embryo. This embryo could then be implanted in a surrogate mother to produce a "chimera," or mixture of the two species. Combinations reportedly described in the Newman–Rifkin application include mouse-human, baboon-human, chimpanzee-human and pig-human chimera. Newman and Rifkin have stated that they have no intention of producing such hybrids. They instead filed the application in order to provoke debate about the ethics of patenting life forms.

The Patent and Trademark Office responded by releasing a "media advisory" titled "Facts on Patenting Life Forms Having a Relationship to Humans." This document cited case law, including *Lowell v. Lewis*, interpreting the utility requirement as excluding patents on inventions "injurious to the well-being, good policy or sound morals of society." It further stated "that inventions directed to human/non-human chimera could, under certain circumstances, not be patentable because, among other things, they would fail to meet the public policy and morality aspects of the utility requirement." During a subsequent interview, then Patent and Trademark Office Commissioner Bruce Lehman reportedly stated that "there will be no patents on monsters, at least not while I'm commissioner."

Do you believe that the Patent and Trademark Office position accurately reflects the latest thinking on the utility requirement? For more information on this episode, see Cynthia M. Ho, *Splicing Morality and Patent Law: Issues Arising from Mixing Mice and Men*, 2 WASH. UNIV. J. L & POLICY 247 (2000); Thomas A. Magnani, Note, *The Patentability of Human–Animal Chimeras*, 14 BERKELEY TECH. L.J. 443 (1999).

Chapter Four

ANTICIPATION

Broadly stated, patent-eligible subject matter is patentable if the claimed subject matter possesses *utility*, and is both *novel* under 35 U.S.C.A. § 102 and *nonobvious* under 35 U.S.C.A. § 103. Of these four general requirements, novelty is perhaps the patent system's central value: to become eligible for the reward of a patent, an inventor must accomplish something new. Although simply expressed, the statutory basis for novelty and other patent-defeating events, including forfeitures, is among the more complex in patent law. 35 U.S.C.A. § 102 provides:

A person shall be entitled to a patent unless—

(a) the invention was known or used by others in this country, or patented or described in a printed publication in this or a foreign country, before the invention thereof by the applicant for patent, or

(b) the invention was patented or described in a printed publication in this or a foreign country or in public use or on sale in this country, more than one year prior to the date of the application for patent in the United States, or

(c) he has abandoned the invention, or

(d) the invention was first patented or caused to be patented, or was the subject of an inventor's certificate, by the applicant or his legal representatives or assigns in a foreign country prior to the date of the application for patent in this country on an application for patent or inventor's certificate filed more than twelve months before the filing of the application in the United States, or

(e) The invention was described in—

(1) an application for patent, published under section 122(b), by another filed in the United States before the invention by the applicant for patent; or

159

(2) a patent granted on an application for patent by another filed in the United States before the invention by the applicant for patent, except that an international application filed under the treaty defined in section 351(a) shall have the effects for the purposes of this subsection of an application filed in the United States only if the international application designated the United States and was published under Article 21(2) of such treaty in the English language; or

(f) he did not himself invent the subject matter sought to be patented, or

(g)(1) during the course of an interference conducted under section 135 or section 291, another inventor involved therein establishes, to the extent permitted in section 104, that before such person's invention thereof the invention was made by such other inventor and not abandoned, suppressed, or concealed, or

(2) before such person's invention thereof, the invention was made in this country by another inventor who had not abandoned, suppressed, or concealed it. In determining priority of invention under this subsection, there shall be considered not only the respective dates of conception and reduction to practice of the invention, but also the reasonable diligence of one who was first to conceive and last to reduce to practice, from a time prior to conception by the other.

Section 102 embraces a host of issues, of which two are central: the requirement of novelty, expressed in §§ 102(a), (e) and (g), and the so-called "statutory bars" of §§ 102(b) and (d). A key distinction between them is the time at which patent-defeating activity occurs. Novelty is keyed to the time the inventor completed the invention—the "invention date." The statutory bars are keyed to the day on which the inventor submitted an application to the U.S. Patent and Trademark Office—the "filing date."

The novelty sections mandate that only the first inventor of a technology can obtain a patent, regardless of whether a later inventor filed an earlier application on the same technology. These provisions are the basis of the "first to invent" priority system unique to the United States. When multiple persons claim the right to a patent on a given technology, this system allows inventors who were not the first to reach the Patent Office to establish their right to the patent by demonstrating inventive acts prior to those of their competitors.

Every other patent-issuing state currently sponsors a "race to the Patent Office" recordation system similar to that of domestic real property law. Under this "first to file" regime, the inventor who first files a patent application obtains the patent, even if another actually invented the technology first. The disparity between the United States "first to invent" system and the "first to file" regimes in the rest of the world remains of crucial importance, particularly for applicants seeking patent protection in many nations.

The statutory bars of § 102(b) are tied to the filing of a patent application. The point in time one year prior to the filing date is termed the "critical date," and statutorily specified activities such as publications or sales act to bar, or prevent, the applicant from obtaining a patent if they occur before the critical date. Section 102(b) thus produces a one-year "grace period" which allows an inventor to determine whether patent protection is desirable, and, if so, to prepare an application. If, for example, the inventor publishes an article in a scientific journal on a given date, he knows that he has one year in which to file an application. Note that the inventor has a broader range of concerns than merely his own behavior, because uses, sales, and other technical disclosures by third parties will also start the one-year clock running. Chapter 5 discusses statutory bars in more detail.

Beyond §§ 102(a) and (b), the remaining paragraphs of § 102 provide for additional patent-defeating events. Abandonment of an invention to the public amounts to a forfeiture of patent rights under § 102(c). Section 102(d) creates a statutory bar if the United States application has not been filed within one year of a foreign application on the same invention that ultimately ripened into a foreign patent right. Section 102(f) addresses the issue of derivation, denying a patent to those who have taken their technological ideas from the true inventor.

A determination of novelty requires two distinct inquiries. Section 102 requires that the current state of knowledge known to the art must be assessed as a basis for comparison. This step requires a determination of which sources from the universe of available knowledge are pertinent to the novelty inquiry. The Patent Act defines the materials—usually called "references"—that may be used to judge the novelty of the claimed invention in § 102. Typical references under § 102 include such documentary materials as patents and publications, as well as the fact of actual uses or sales of a technology within the United States. The sum of these references is denominated the "prior art."

Once we have identified all possible references that might give rise to novelty or statutory bar issues, section 102 also requires that we ask whether any one of those references fully anticipates a claim. The standard of anticipation is a strict one. Each and every element of the claimed invention must be disclosed in a single, enabling reference. This casebook takes up this standard next.

TITANIUM METALS CORP. OF AMERICA v. BANNER

United States Court of Appeals, Federal Circuit, 1985.
778 F.2d 775, 227 U.S.P.Q. 773.

Before RICH, CIRCUIT JUDGE, NICHOLS, SENIOR CIRCUIT JUDGE, and NEWMAN, CIRCUIT JUDGE.

RICH, CIRCUIT JUDGE. This appeal is from an Order of the United States District Court for the District of Columbia in a civil action brought pursuant to 35 U.S.C. § 145 against Donald W. Banner as Commissioner of Patents and Trademarks authorizing the Commissioner to issue to appellee a patent containing claims 1, 2, and 3 of patent application serial No. 598,935 for "TITANIUM ALLOY." The Commissioner has appealed. We reverse.

The inventors, Loren C. Covington and Howard R. Palmer, employees of appellee to whom they have assigned their invention and the application thereon, filed an application on March 29, 1974, serial No. 455,964, to patent an alloy they developed. The application involved on this appeal is a continuation-in-part thereof, filed July 25, 1975, containing the three claims on appeal. The alloy is made primarily of titanium (Ti) and contains small amounts of nickel (Ni) and molybdenum (Mo) as alloying ingredients to give the alloy certain desirable properties, particularly corrosion resistance in hot brine solutions, while retaining workability so that articles such as tubing can be fabricated from it by rolling, welding and other techniques. The inventors apparently also found that iron content should be limited, iron being an undesired impurity rather than an alloying ingredient. They determined the permissible ranges of the components, above and below which the desired properties were not obtained. A precise definition of the invention sought to be patented is found in the claims, set forth below, claim 3 representing the preferred composition, it being understood, however, that no iron at all would be even more preferred. 1. A titanium base alloy consisting essentially by weight of about 0.6% to 0.9% nickel, 0.2% to 0.4% molybdenum, up to 0.2% maximum iron, balance titanium, said alloy being characterized by good corrosion resistance in hot brine environments. 2. A titanium base alloy as set forth in Claim 1 having up to 0.1% iron, balance titanium. 3. A titanium base alloy as set forth in Claim 1 having 0.8% nickel, 0.3% molybdenum, up to 0.1% maximum iron, balance titanium.

The examiner's final rejection, repeated in his Answer on appeal to the Patent and Trademark Office (PTO) Board of Appeals (board), was on the grounds that claims 1 and 2 are anticipated (fully met) by, and claim 3 would have been obvious from, an article by Kalabukhova and Mikheyew, Investigation of the Mechanical Properties of Ti–Mo–Ni Alloys, Russian Metallurgy (Metally) No. 3, pages 130–133 (1970) (in the court below and hereinafter called "the Russian article") under 35 U.S.C. §§ 102 and 103, respectively. The board affirmed the examiner's rejection. However, it mistakenly proceeded on the assumption that all three claims had been rejected as anticipated under § 102 by the Russian article and ignored the obviousness rejection. On this appeal the PTO says it does not pursue the § 103 rejection further. Appellee proceeds on the basis that only the § 102 rejection is before us.

The Russian article is short (3 pages), highly technical, and contains 10 graphs as part of the discussion. As its title indicates, it relates to ternary Ti–Mo–Ni alloys, the subject of the application at bar. The examiner and the board both found that it would disclose to one skilled in the art an alloy on which at least claims 1 and 2 read, so that those claims would not be allowable under the statute because of lack of novelty of their subject matter. Since the article does not specifically disclose such an alloy in words, a little thinking is required about what it would disclose to one knowledgeable about Ti–Ni–Mo alloys. The PTO did that thinking as follows: Figure lc [a graph] shows data for the ternary titanium alloy which contains Mo and Ni in the ratio of 1:3. Amongst the actual points on the graph is one at 1% Mo + Ni. At this point, the amounts of Mo and Ni would be 0.25% and 0.75% respectively. A similar point appears on the graph shown in Figure 2 of the article. . . . Appellants do not deny that the data points are disclosed in the reference. In fact, the Hall affidavit indicates at least two specific points (at 1% and 1.25% Mo + Ni) which would represent a description of alloys falling within the scope of the instant claims.

Fig. 1. Effect of Alloy
Composition on the
Ultimate Strength,
Yield Point and
Elongation of Ti-Mo-Ni
Alloys for Mo:Ri Ratios
of 3:1, 1:1 and 1:3
(a, b and c respectively)
and for Binary Ti-Ni
Alloys (d).

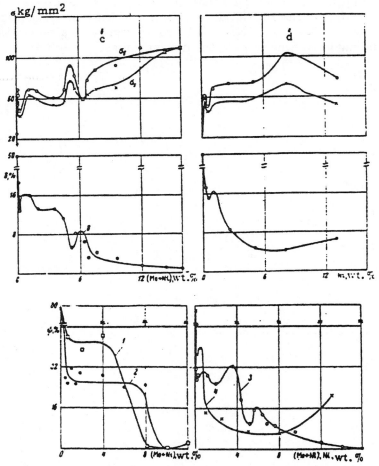

Fig. 2. Variation of the Reduction in Area of Ti-Mo-Ni Alloys
(1, 2, 3 - Alloys of Series I, II and III Respectively) and of
Ti-Ni Alloys (4) with the (Mo+Ni) Content (1-3) and the Ni
Content (4).

On that basis, the board found that the claimed alloys were not new, because they were disclosed in the prior art. It having been argued that the Russian article contains no disclosure of corrosion-resistant properties of any of the alloys, the board held: The fact that a particular property or the end use for this alloy as contemplated by appellants was not recognized in the article is of no consequence. It therefore held the Russian article to be an anticipation, noting that although the article does not discuss corrosion resistance, it does disclose other properties such as strength and ductility. The PTO further points out that the authors of the reference must have made the alloys to obtain the data points.

Being dissatisfied with the decision of the board, Titanium Metals Corporation of America, as assignee of the Covington and Palmer application, then brought an action in the District Court for the District of Columbia against the Commissioner pursuant to 35 U.S.C. § 145, its complaint alleging that the board's decision "was erroneous and contrary to law," and making profert of a certified copy of the application and all papers in the file thereof, together with a copy of the Russian article which was the sole basis of the PTO refusal to allow the claims. It prayed that the court adjudge it entitled to a patent containing claims 1–3 and authorize the Commissioner to grant such a patent. The Commissioner filed an answer denying that the applicants were the first inventors of the alloys claimed or entitled to a patent, alleging that the claims are not patentable under the law, and making profert of the Examiner's Answer, the Board of Appeals' decision, and the prior art reference.

The case came on for trial on January 24, 1980, before the Honorable John G. Penn and was concluded in two and a half hours. The testimony of one witness was heard by the court, Dr. James C. Williams, professor at Carnegie–Mellon University in Pittsburgh and an expert in titanium metallurgy. His testimony was about equally divided between direct and cross examination.

At the conclusion of the plaintiff's case, the following exchange took place between the judge and the Associate Solicitor for the PTO: THE COURT: All right. Mr. Tarring? MR. TARRING: Your Honor, generally the position of the Patent Office is we rely on the position of the tribunals below, the examiner and the Board of Appeals and their decisions are both present in the exhibit which I submitted earlier. I was not quite sure whether you would prefer that we have a post-trial brief in the matter. If that's your preference we could do that or I could make an argument on the basis of the law right now. I don't know what your preference would be. Otherwise, I'm not going to call any witnesses. THE COURT: You are not going to what? MR. TARRING: I have no intention of calling any witnesses so it's really a matter of argument at this point, I think. THE COURT: Of course, I have received your pre-trial briefs. After further discussion, it was settled that both parties would file further briefs after the hearing transcript had been prepared. They were filed in April and May, 1980. On November 16, 1984, the District Court entered the Order appealed from followed on November 28 by a supporting memorandum opinion. January 10, 1985, the PTO filed its Notice of Appeal. This court has heard oral argument and received briefs.

THE DISTRICT COURT OPINION

We are left in no doubt that the court was impressed by the totality of the evidence that the applicants for patent had discovered or invented and disclosed knowledge which is not to be found in the reference, nor do we have any doubt about that ourselves. But those facts are beside the point. The patent law imposes certain fundamental conditions for patentability, paramount among them being the condition that what is sought to be patented, as determined by the claims, be new. The basic provision of Title 35 applicable here is § 101, providing in relevant part: "Whoever invents or discovers any new ... composition of matter, or any new ... improvement thereof, may obtain a patent therefor, subject to the conditions and requirements of this title." The title of the application here involved is "Titanium Alloy," a composition of matter. Surprisingly, in all of the evidence, nobody discussed the key issue of whether the alloy was new, which is the essence of the anticipation issue, including the expert Dr. Williams. Plaintiff's counsel, bringing Dr. Williams' testimony to its climax, after he had explained the nature of the ingredients, the alloys made therefrom, and their superior corrosion resistance in hot brine, etc., repetitively asked him such questions as "Does the [Russian] article direct you as one skilled in the art to a titanium alloy having nickel present in an amount between .6 and .9 percent molybdenum in an amount between .2 and .4 percent?" (emphasis ours) followed by "Is there anything mentioned in the article about corrosion resistance?" Of course, the answers were emphatically negative. But this and like testimony does not deal with the critical question: do claims 1 and 2, to which the questions obviously relate, read on or encompass an alloy which was already known by reason of the disclosure of the Russian article?

Section 102, the usual basis for rejection for lack of novelty or anticipation, lays down certain principles for determining the novelty required by § 101, among which are the provisions in § 102(a) and (b) that the claimed invention has not been "described in a printed publication in this or a foreign country," either (a) before the invention by the applicant or (b) more than one year before the application date to which he is entitled (strictly a "loss of right" provision similar to novelty). Either provision applies in this case, the Russian article having a date some 5 years prior to the filing date and its status as "prior art" not being questioned. The PTO was never specific as to what part of § 102 applies, merely rejecting on § 102. The question, therefore, is whether claims 1 and 2 encompass and, if allowed, would enable plaintiff-appellee to exclude others from making, using, or selling an alloy described in the Russian article. *See* 35 U.S.C. § 154.

To answer the question we need only turn to the affidavit of James A. Hall, a metallurgist employed by appellee's TIMET Division, who undertook to analyze the Russian article disclosure by calculating the ingredient percentages shown in the graph data points, which he presented in tabular form. There are 15 items in his table. The second item shows a titanium base alloy containing 0.25% by weight Mo and 0.75%

Ni and this is squarely within the ranges of 0.2–0.4% Mo and 0.6–0.9% Ni of claims 1 and 2. As to that disclosed alloy of the prior art, there can be no question that claims 1 and 2 read on it and would be infringed by anyone making, using, or selling it. Therefore, the statute prohibits a patent containing them. This seems to be a case either of not adequately considering the novelty requirement of the statute, the true meaning of the correlative term "anticipation," or the meaning of the claims. By reason of the court's quotations from cases holding that a reference is not an anticipation which does not enable one skilled in the art to practice the claimed invention, it appears that the trial court thought there was some deficiency in the Russian article on that score. Enablement in this case involves only being able to make the alloy, given the ingredients and their proportions without more. The evidence here, however, clearly answers that question in two ways. Appellee's own patent application does not undertake to tell anyone how to make the alloy it describes and seeks to patent. It assumes that those skilled in the art would know how. Secondly, appellee's expert, Dr. Williams, testified on cross examination that given the alloy information in the Russian article, he would know how to prepare the alloys "by at least three techniques." Enablement is not a problem in this case.

As we read the situation, the court was misled by the arguments and evidence to the effect that the inventors here found out and disclosed in their application many things that one cannot learn from reading the Russian article and that this was sufficient in law to justify granting them a patent for their contributions—such things as what good corrosion resistance the claimed alloys have against hot brine, which possibly was not known, and the range limits of the Ni and Mo content, outside of which that resistance diminishes, which are teachings of very useful information. These things the applicants teach the art and the Russian article does not. Indeed, appellee's counsel argued in his opening statement to the trial court that the PTO's refusal of a patent was "directly contrary to the requirement of Article I, Section 8, of the Constitution," which authorizes Congress to create a patent law. But throughout the trial counsel never came to grips with the real issues: (1) what do the claims cover and (2) is what they cover new? Under the laws Congress wrote, they must be considered. Congress has not seen fit to permit the patenting of an old alloy, known to others through a printed publication, by one who has discovered its corrosion resistance or other useful properties, or has found out to what extent one can modify the composition of the alloy without losing such properties.

It is also an elementary principle of patent law that when, as by a recitation of ranges or otherwise, a claim covers several compositions, the claim is "anticipated" if one of them is in the prior art.

For all of the foregoing reasons, the court below committed clear error and legal error in authorizing the issuance of a patent on claims 1 and 2 since, properly construed, they are anticipated under § 102 by the Russian article which admittedly discloses an alloy on which these claims read.

Notes

1. A Four Corners Defense. It may be convenient to consider anticipation as a "four corners" doctrine. *Dewey & Almy Chem. Co. v. Mimex Co.*, 124 F.2d 986, 52 U.S.P.Q. 138 (2d Cir.1942). If the claimed invention can be found within the ambit of a single prior art reference, then the invention has been anticipated. References may not be combined during this inquiry, nor may elements that are analogous to the disclosure of a reference be considered.

Some earlier cases adopted a broader view of anticipation. In *Straussler v. United States*, 339 F.2d 670, 671, 143 U.S.P.Q. 443, 443–44 (Ct.Cl.1964) (emphasis added), the Court of Claims indicated:

> The test for determining if a reference anticipates a claim of a patent is whether the reference contains within its four corners adequate directions for the practice of the patent claim invalidated.... Stated another way, the reference must disclose all the elements of the claimed combination, *or their mechanical equivalents*, functioning in substantially the same way to produce substantially the same result.

Contemporary case law does not look beyond the reference itself when addressing § 102 issues. A prior art rejection may still occur based upon the proximity of a single piece of prior art to a claimed invention, but this inquiry is cast in terms of § 103 and nonobviousness.

The European view of novelty is also strict; equivalent embodiments of the disclosure of a prior art reference do not impact a novelty determination under the European Patent Convention. *See* "Fuel Injector Valve," T 167/48 (OJ EPO 1987, 369). In contrast, Japanese patent law tends to adopt a more liberal view of novelty. Its "substantial identity" test lies somewhere between the modern United States approach and what both systems refer to as "obviousness" or "inventive step." *See* Toshiko Takenaka, *The Substantial Identity Rule Under the Japanese Novelty Standard*, 9 UCLA Pac. Basin L.J. 220 (1991).

2. Genus/Species Cases. A particular problem with respect to the identity requirement of anticipation occurs when the inventor has claimed some subset of a known broader range. The inventor may have chosen a lesser number of chemical compounds, or perhaps a smaller numerical range of temperature, voltage, or some other physical quantity, than that known to the art. The patent bar often refers to the applicant's selection as a "species" chosen from out of the prior art "genus." What is the effect of such a selection upon the novelty of the applicant's claim? As suggested by *In re Kalm*, 378 F.2d 959, 154 U.S.P.Q. 10 (CCPA 1967), the applicant must demonstrate that the claimed species has improved or distinct properties over other members of the prior art genus. In holding that the applicant before it had in fact claimed a novel compound, the *Kalm* court indicated that:

> When one speaks of a "genus" in the chemical arts, one ordinarily speaks of a group of compounds closely related both in structure and in properties. Appellant has found a group of chemical compounds which possess properties diametrically opposite to the properties disclosed by Siemer [the prior art reference] for his compounds. It is quite evident

that Siemer never made the present compounds; of if he did, he never tested them to determine what effect they would have on the central nervous system, since, if he had, he could not logically have failed to report the seemingly anomalous result appellant has discovered.

While it is not necessary that a reference disclose every property or attribute of a composition of matter to be a valid anticipation, appellant has found properties for his claimed compounds which are totally incompatible and inconsistent with, not merely complementary or in addition to, those attributed by Siemer to his compounds. It is our view that [the earlier inventor] never intended to, nor does he, disclose compounds within the scope of appellant's claims.

378 F.2d at 963, 154 U.S.P.Q. at 13. The determination of whether a prior art genus anticipates a claimed species is necessarily case-by-case. 1 MARTIN J. ADELMAN, PATENT LAW PERSPECTIVES, § 2.2[4] at n.67 (2d ed. 1996) provides a list of factors which the courts have considered within the chemical arts:

(1) The number of compounds embraced by the most specific prior art description;

(2) The degree of structural similarity between the compounds of that group;

(3) The number of properties shared by compounds of that group;

(4) Whether the properties of the claimed compounds are the same as, consistent with or diametrically opposite to the properties disclosed in the prior art;

(5) The number of parameters that can be varied among the most specifically described group of prior art compounds; and

(6) Whether the claimed materials are physical mixtures or the product of chemical reactions.

What about the reverse situation, where the prior art discloses a narrow range and the claimed invention is to a broader, encompassing range? *Titanium Metals* provides the answer: "It is an elementary principle of patent law that when, as by a recitation of ranges or otherwise, a claim covers several compositions, the claim is 'anticipated' if *one* of them is in the prior art."

The European patent system addresses the novelty of genus/species inventions similarly to that of the United States. The Guidelines for Examination in the European Patent Office indicate at Part C, Chapter IV, § 7.4 that:

In considering novelty it should be borne in mind that a generic disclosure does not usually take away the novelty of any specific example falling within the terms of that disclosure, but that a specific disclosure does take away the novelty of a generic claim embracing that disclosure, e.g., a disclosure of copper takes away the novelty of metal as a generic concept, but not the novelty of any metal other than copper, and one of the rivets takes away the novelty of fastening rivets as a generic concept, but not the novelty of any fastening other than rivets.

3. More on the Enablement Requirement. To fulfill the enablement requirement of anticipation, does a prior art reference also need to disclose a use for a claimed compound? The Federal Circuit stated that it does not in *In re Schoenwald*, 964 F.2d 1122, 22 U.S.P.Q.2d 1671 (Fed.Cir. 1992). There, Schoenwald claimed the compound N-cyclohexyl-N-methyl–2– phenylethylamine as well as its pharmaceutical use. The Patent and Trade-mark Office rejected a claim to the compound as anticipated under § 102(b) by a JOURNAL OF ORGANIC CHEMISTRY article. That article specifically described the claimed compound but did not provide any use for it. Judge Mayer affirmed the PTO decision, stating that:

> So it is beyond argument that no utility need be disclosed for a reference to be anticipatory of a claim to an old compound. The compound appellants are attempting to patent is not new—the use they discovered is, and they received a method patent for that. Their complaint that this is insufficient because their reward should be consistent with the full extent of their contribution is hollow. Their contribution was finding a use for the compound, not discovering the compound itself. Therefore they are being rewarded fully for their contribution; any more would be a gratuity.

4. Comparative Approaches to Enablement. A European Patent Office Board of Appeal has interpreted Article 54 of the European Patent Convention

> in the sense that anything comprised in the state of the art can only be regarded as having been made available to the public in so far as the information given to the person skilled in the art is sufficient to enable him to practise the technical teaching which is the subject of the disclosure, taking into account the general knowledge in the field to be expected of him.

T 26/85 (OJ EPO 1990, 22, 27). Consider a reference containing technical information stored only on a microchip. The information is not readily accessible, although it could be obtained following a time-consuming, costly analysis of the microchip. Would the United States and European patent systems consider the reference enabling and thus part of the prior art? *See* T 461/88 (OJ EPO 1993, 295).

While the enablement requirement might seem self-evident to you and, indeed, is now the general rule worldwide, many English judges did not impose such a requirement. The issue of whether English patent law required an enabling disclosure was not settled until the House of Lords decided *Asahi Kasei Kogyo KK's Application,* [1991] R.P.C. 485 (H.L.), which imposed this stricture. Can you think of an argument that would support the overruled English judges?

5. Inherency. A frequently occurring fact pattern involves a prior art reference that intrinsically, rather than explicitly, discloses a subsequently claimed invention. Whether this reference should be considered patent-defeating under § 102 is addressed by the doctrine of inherency, considered in the next decision.

CONTINENTAL CAN CO. v. MONSANTO CO.

United States Court of Appeals, Federal Circuit, 1991.
948 F.2d 1264, 20 U.S.P.Q.2d 1746.

Before NEWMAN, ARCHER, and RADER, CIRCUIT JUDGES.

PAULINE NEWMAN, CIRCUIT JUDGE.

Continental Can Company USA and Continental PET Technologies (collectively "Continental") appeal the partial summary judgment of the United States District Court for the Southern District of Ohio, holding that United States Patent No. 4,108,324 (the Conobase or '324 patent) is invalid. Final judgment was entered on this issue, for the purpose of appeal.

THE PATENTED INVENTION

The '324 patent, entitled "Ribbed Bottom Structure for Plastic Container", inventors Suppayan M. Krishnakumar, Siegfried S. Roy, John F.E. Pocock, Salil K. Das, and Gautam K. Mahajan, is directed to a plastic bottle whose bottom structure has sufficient flexibility to impart improved impact resistance, combined with sufficient rigidity to resist deformation under internal pressure. The patented bottle is said to provide a superior combination of these properties. The bottom structure is illustrated as follows:

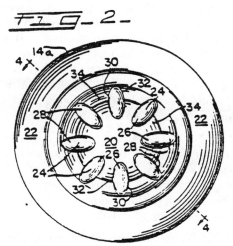

Claim 1 is the broadest claim of the '324 patent: 1. A container having a sidewall and a bottom structure closing the container at an end portion of the sidewall, the outer surface of the bottom structure comprising a central concavity, a convex heel surrounding the concavity and merging therewith and with the sidewall end portion, the lowermost points of the heel lying in a common plane, and a plurality of ribs interrupting the outer surface of the concavity and distributed in a symmetrical array, each rib extending longitudinally in the direction of the heel and downwardly from an inner portion of the concavity, whereby the outer end portion of each rib is lower than the inner end portion thereof, characterized by the feature that the ribs are hollow. Claims 2 through 5 include additional limitations, described as contributing to the structure's rigidity, flexibility, or both. Claim 2 specifies the ratios of thickness of the walls of the bottom structure to the thickness of the sidewall end portions. Claim 3 specifies that the margins of each rib merge smoothly with adjacent portions of the bottom structure. Claim 4 specifies that each rib is convex relative to the bottom structure. Claim 5 specifies that each rib is of fusiform (a gently tapered shape at the ends) configuration. Each claim carries an independent presumption of validity, 35 U.S.C. § 282, and stands or falls independent of the other claims.

Continental brought suit for patent infringement against Monsanto Company and Monsanto's successor in this business, Hoover Universal, Inc. and Hoover's parent company, Johnson Controls (collectively "Monsanto"). Monsanto moved for partial summary judgment based on issues of validity under 35 U.S.C. §§ 102 and 103.

I

35 U.S.C. § 102(A)

The statutory requirement that a patented invention be "new" is tested in accordance with 35 U.S.C. § 102(a), which provides that: § 102. A person shall be entitled to a patent unless—(a) the invention was known or used by others in this country, or patented or described in a printed publication in this or a foreign country, before the invention thereof by the applicant for patent. . . . The district court found that all the claims of the '324 patent were anticipated by U.S. Patent No. 3,468,443 (the Marcus patent). We conclude that the district court erred in claim interpretation. . . .

Anticipation under § 102(a) requires that the identical invention that is claimed was previously known to others and thus is not new. When more than one reference is required to establish unpatentability of the claimed invention anticipation under § 102 can not be found, and validity is determined in terms of § 103.

It was Monsanto's burden to show that every element of the several claims of the '324 patent was identically described in the asserted anticipating reference, the Marcus patent. The district court focused on the term "characterized by the feature that the ribs are hollow", which limits all of the '324 patent claims. Continental argues that the district court incorrectly construed this term, as a matter of law, and that the Marcus patent shows ribs that are not hollow, as that term is used in the '324 patent. Continental also points to other differences between the '324 claims and the description in the Marcus patent.

The Marcus patent rib structure is illustrated in Figure 5 and in cross-section in Figure 6:

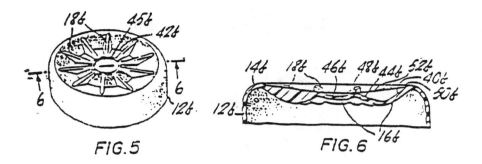

FIG.5   FIG.6

The Marcus patent does not state that its ribs are "hollow", or use a similar term. Continental's witnesses testified by deposition that the Marcus patent shows solid, not hollow, ribs. A witness (Adomaitis) had stated in an internal memorandum written at Continental in 1969, well before this litigation arose, that "the ribs of their [Marcus'] web can be made of solid beams only." Another witness, '324 co-inventor Pocock, testified that: It seems evident to me that he [Marcus] was trying to produce some kind of container integrity by the production of essentially solid ribs on the bottom of the bottle. It seems to go to great length here to illustrate them as such. Krishnakumar, another co-inventor, testified that it "is very obvious the ribs are shown solid", and that Figures 5 and 6 as well as Figures 7 through 12 of the Marcus patent all show solid ribs. However, Marcus, testifying for Monsanto, testified that his ribs were hollow, and that conventional blow molding would inherently produce hollow ribs.

The district court defined "hollow" as meaning that "the inside contour of the ribs generally follows the outside contour thereof", a definition on which the parties agreed. Continental states that the district court erred in construing "hollow", and that the phrase "characterized by the feature that the ribs are hollow" must be construed in terms of the patent in which it appears. The '324 patent explicitly distinguished the Marcus patent teachings, stating that the '324 ribs are, unlike Marcus, not filled with plastic. The '324 specification uses the term "hollow", as do the prosecution history and the claims, for this purpose. The '324 patent's usage of "hollow" is illustrated in the rib cross-section in Figure 5A:

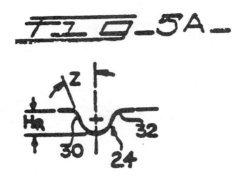

The Marcus patent's rib structure thus was explicitly differentiated by the term "hollow" as used in the '324 specification, drawings, and prosecution history. Since the claim term must be construed as used by the patentee, the district court erred in its construction of the '324 claim term "hollow". On correct claim construction, the factual question of anticipation must be decided.

Monsanto's argument is that hollow ribs were inherently produced by Marcus. Monsanto thus argues that anticipation lies because the Marcus patent's ribs are "inherently" hollow, regardless of how they are shown in the Marcus patent. Monsanto argues that because the Marcus ribs are formed by injection blow molding, which is the same process described for the Conobase '324 ribs, hollow ribs are inherently disclosed in the Marcus patent.

To serve as an anticipation when the reference is silent about the asserted inherent characteristic, such gap in the reference may be filled with recourse to extrinsic evidence. Such evidence must make clear that the missing descriptive matter is necessarily present in the thing described in the reference, and that it would be so recognized by persons of ordinary skill. *In re Oelrich*, 666 F.2d 578, 581, 212 U.S.P.Q. 323, 326 (CCPA 1981) (quoting *Hansgirg v. Kemmer*, 102 F.2d 212, 214, 40 U.S.P.Q. 665, 667 (CCPA 1939)) provides: "Inherency, however, may not be established by probabilities or possibilities. The mere fact that a certain thing may result from a given set of circumstances is not sufficient. [Citations omitted.] If, however, the disclosure is sufficient to show that the natural result flowing from the operation as taught would result in the performance of the questioned function, it seems to be well settled that the disclosure should be regarded as sufficient." This modest flexibility in the rule that "anticipation" requires that every element of the claims appear in a single reference accommodates situations where the common knowledge of technologists is not recorded in the reference; that is, where technological facts are known to those in the field of the invention, albeit not known to judges. It is not, however, a substitute for determination of patentability in terms of § 103.

Continental does not dispute the applicability of the injection blow molding process. However, Continental disputes the material fact of whether this process necessarily produced "hollow" ribs in the Marcus base structure, as the term "hollow" is used in the '324 patent. Resolution of this disputed fact adversely to Continental was improper on summary judgment. The grant of summary judgment of anticipation under § 102(a) is vacated. The issue requires trial.

Notes

1. **Accidental Uses.** One aspect of the inherency doctrine considers so-called "accidental uses." This doctrine was explained in *Tilghman v. Proctor*, 102 U.S. 707 (1880), where the patentee claimed "the manufacturing of fat acids and glycerine from fatty bodies by the action of water at a high temperature and pressure." The accused infringers pointed to several alleged anticipations of this invention, which the Supreme Court considered in turn.

We do not regard the accidental formation of fat acid in Perkins's steam cylinder from the tallow introduced to lubricate the piston (if the scum which rose on the water issuing from the ejection pipe was fat acid) as of any consequence in this inquiry. What the process was by which it was generated or formed was never fully understood. Those engaged in the art of making candles, or in any other art in which fat acids are desirable, certainly never derived from the least hint from this accidental phenomenon in regard to any practicable process for manufacturing such acids.

The accidental effects in Daniell's water barometer and in Walther's process for purifying fats and oils preparatory to soap-making, are of the same character. They revealed no process for the manufacture of fat acids. If the acids were accidentally and unwittingly produced, whilst the operators were in pursuit of other and difficult results, without exciting attention and without its even being known what was done or how it had been done, it would be absurd to say that this was an anticipation of Tilghman's discovery.

Nor do we regard the patent of Manicler, which was taken out in 1826, as anticipating the process of Tilghman. It is true that he directs a mixture of fat with about one-quarter of its weight of water to be placed in a boiler, and subjected to a heat sufficient to create a pressure equal to one atmosphere above the natural atmospheric pressure (or about 250° Fah.); the boiler being provided with a safety-valve which would secure that degree of pressure. But, subject to this pressure, the patent directed that the mixture should be made to boil, and of course that the water should be converted into steam. It is probable, therefore, that any decomposition of the fat which may have been produced by this process was due to the steam formed and passing through the mixture of the fat and water. But we have no evidence that the process was ever successful in practice.

It is unnecessary to examine in detail other alleged anticipations of Tilghman's process. We believe that we have specified the most prominent and reliable instances.

2. **Undetectable Uses.** In *In re Seaborg*, 328 F.2d 996, 140 U.S.P.Q. 662 (CCPA 1964), the applicant claimed Americium, element number 95.

Americium is formed either by bombardment of plutonium with neutrons or in a neutronic reactor operated at a high power level. The PTO rejected because element 95 must have been inherently produced in the operation of the existing Fermi reactor. The record showed that the Fermi reactor might have produced one-billionth of one gram of Americium diluted by forty tons of intensely radioactive uranium fuel. The Court of Customs and Patent Appeals reversed:

> The record before us is replete with showings that the claimed product, if it was produced in the Fermi process, was produced in such minuscule amounts and under such conditions that its presence was undetectable.

328 F.2d at 997, 140 U.S.P.Q. at 664. Does this situation differ from the undetected use in *Tilghman?*

3. Is the Skilled Artisan Always Relevant to Inherency? In *Continental Can,* the Federal Circuit stated that anticipation by inherency requires "that the missing descriptive matter is necessarily present in the thing described in the reference, and that it would be so recognized by persons of ordinary skill." At another point, the Circuit emphasized that inherency accommodates "the common knowledge of technologists ... not recorded in the reference." In a later case, *EMI Group of N. Am. Inc. v. Cypress Semiconductor Corp.,* 268 F.3d 1342, 1350–51, 60 U.S.P.Q.2d 1423, 1429–30 (Fed.Cir.2001), the Federal Circuit clarified these references:

> This requirement, that a person of ordinary skill in the art must recognize that the missing descriptive matter is necessarily present in the reference, may be sensible for claims that recite limitations of structure, compositions of matter, and method steps which could be inherently found in the prior art.... Theoretical mechanisms or rules of natural law that are recited in a claim, that themselves are not patentable, however, do not need to be recognized by one of ordinary skill in the art for a finding of inherency. A person of ordinary skill does not need to recognize that a method or structure behaves according to a law of nature in order to fully and effectively practice the method or structure.
>
> A hypothetical example clarifies this principle. Humans lit fires for thousands of years before realizing that oxygen is necessary to create and maintain a flame. The first person to discover the necessity of oxygen certainly could not have obtained a valid patent claim for "a method of making a fire by lighting a flame in the presence of oxygen." Even if prior art on lighting fires did not disclose the importance of oxygen and one of ordinary skill in the art did not know about the importance of oxygen, understanding this law of nature would not give the discoverer a right to exclude others from practicing the prior art of making fires.

4. Comparative Approaches. In litigation in Germany, England and the United States over a patent relating to the anti-histamine drug terfenadine, commonly known as Seldane, the question of whether the basic patent covering terfenadine inherently disclosed the patented metabolite was raised. In Germany and in the United States the courts avoided the issue by narrowly interpreting the claims, but this route was not taken by the House of Lords in *Merrell Dow Pharmaceuticals inc. v. H.N. Norton & Co. Ltd.,*

[1996] R.P.C. 76. Instead the House dealt directly with the issue of inherent anticipation.

Merrell Dow patented terfenadine in many countries in the 1970s. Subsequently, Merrell Dow did further work on how terfenadine functioned in humans. It discovered that it was 99.5% metabolized in the liver and then isolated the key metabolite formed in the liver, the patented acid metabolite. Merrell Dow then asserted the patent on the acid metabolite against Norton. It charged that Norton, who was selling terfenadine to people who, when they ingested terfenadine, created in their livers the patented acid metabolite. Thus, according to Merrell Dow, those who ingested terfenadine were direct infringers and Norton a contributory infringer. The House of Lords held that the acid metabolite was inherently described in the original terfenadine patent because it teaches that the ingestion of terfenadine will produce a chemical reaction in the body. Hence, it was made as a direct consequence of ingesting terfenadine. Lord Hoffmann's speech to the House of Lords included the following explanation:

In this case, knowledge of the acid metabolite was in my view made available to the public by the terfenadine specification under the description "a part of the chemical reaction in the human body produced by the ingestion of terfenadine and having an anti-histamine effect." Was this description sufficient to make the product part of the state of the art? For many purposes, obviously not. It would not enable anyone to work the invention in the form of isolating or synthesizing the acid metabolite. But for the purpose of working the invention by making the acid metabolite in the body by ingesting terfenadine, I think it plainly was. It enabled the public to work the invention by making the acid metabolite in their livers. The fact that they would not have been able to describe the chemical reaction in these terms does not mean that they were not working the invention. Whether or not a person is working a product invention is an objective fact independent of what he knows or thinks about what he is doing.

Anticipation Exercise

You are a prior art searcher working for a private firm, Skillful Searchers, Inc., located in Crystal City, Virginia. On June 1, 2002, you receive a call from Eve Klayton, a patent attorney who is a frequent client. She requests that you search through prior patents and technical literature for a description of a toothbrush with two key features:

(1) bristles fabricated from an artificial fiber, known in the trade as NYLANON, which supposedly is particularly effective at removing plaque; and

(2) a specially-shaped handle which is easy to grip.

Klayton explains that she is trying to cite references against the '123 patent, which was filed on January 19, 2001. Klayton ideally seeks an anticipating reference, and in particular one under § 102(b).

Your searches through patents and printed publication are unavailing. However, while surfing on the Internet one evening, you discover a home page entitled "Fiendish Fluoridators." The home page appears to comprise a collection of various textual files relating to the study of dental instruments, including toothbrushes. One of the files on the "Fiendish Fluoridators" home page contains the following passage:

Beyond education on the proper use of a toothbrush, one can improve the effectiveness of brushing through improved toothbrush design. Experiments have demonstrated that plaque removal rates are greatly increased where toothbrush bristles are fabricated from an artificial fiber called "NYLANON." Additionally, certain ***toothbrush handle designs*** have increased toothbrush effectiveness.

You recognize that the highlighted words comprise an invitation to employ "hypertext"; by clicking on your mouse, you can retrieve further information on the selected item. Intrigued, you move your cursor to the highlighted words and click on your mouse. Immediately, a second file appears on your computer screen. The second file originates from a different home page, which is entitled "Healthy Smiles." The second file provides diagrams and a detailed textual discussion of the precise handle design claimed in the '123 patent.

Further research indicates that "The DDS Catalog" home page was created on June 7, 1994, while the "Healthy Smiles" home page was created on May 10, 1998. Neither home page has since been modified, meaning that the files you accessed were undisputably available on the Internet as of those respective dates. You also learn that "The DDS Catalog" home page is based on a computer system in Davis, California, while the "Healthy Smiles" home page originates from a computer in Toronto, Canada.

Do your findings on the Internet constitute an anticipating reference under § 102(b)?

Chapter Five

STATUTORY BARS

The previous chapter of this casebook discussed the patent system's core value: novelty. Embedded in the statutory provision defining novelty and prior art for obviousness, 35 U.S.C.A. § 102, is a provision that creates statutory bars, namely subsection (b). This provision defeats any patent if the invention therein was "in public use or on sale in this country, more than one year prior to the filing date." Although simply stated, the policy rationales behind § 102(b) bear some discussion at the outset.

The reason for the statutory bars becomes apparent by comparing the "first to invent" patent system of the United States with the "first to file" patent systems in the rest of the world. This book discusses that contrast in more detail later, but at this juncture it suffices to note that every patent system in the world outside the United States sponsors a "race to the Patent Office" recordation system similar to that of domestic real property law. Under these "first to file" regimes, the inventor who first files a patent application obtains the patent, even if another actually invented the technology first. The United States, on the other hand, promises a patent to the first inventor, regardless of whether someone else files an application earlier claiming the same invention. In the United States, only the first inventor gets a patent, not someone who filed earlier.

With that understanding, the reason for 102(b) becomes clear by considering a hypothetical. Assume that you invent a new pill that corrects cartilage deterioration by growing new cartilage. Of course, your invention has its problems. For instance, it is expensive to make and has side effects like protruding noses and drooping ear lobes. What would you do? In a pure "first to invent" system, the answer is simple. You would wait. You would let others independently create the same invention, develop the expensive manufacturing and marketing capabilities, and solve the side effects problems. Then you would step in, claim your exclusive right as the first inventor, and demand a sizeable share of the new pharmaceutical enterprise. A "pure" first to invent system could also foster another unsavory strategy. In the same cartilage pill hypothetical, the inventor could bring the product to market and begin to reap a profit only to file for a patent many years later when competition arises. In the meantime, the inventor has prolonged indefinitely the limited time of the exclusive right. Under a pure "first to invent" system, nothing would forbid either strategy.

Because of the § 102 (b) statutory bars, the United States patent system is not a "pure" first to file regime. Instead these bars encourage timely filing and disclosure of inventive activity. Under section 102 (b), an inventor must file within a year of any public use or offer to sell the invention. Thus, the natural drive to use and profit from an invention also promotes timely patent filing. As this chapter shows, anyone, including individuals unknown to the inventor, can defeat the patent by placing the invention in public use or on sale. Thus, due to section 102 (b), inventors risk loss of their exclusive right if they attempt to adopt a waiting strategy.

Actually § 102(b) is not entirely prohibitory. It also provides a distinct advantage to inventors. The language of § 102(b) keys the patent defeating events to the filing date. The point in time one year before the filing date is termed the "critical date." Therefore, statutorily barred activities, like publishing the invention in a scientific article or offering it for sale, even a day before that critical date defeat the patent. This sounds onerous, but in practice § 102(b) provides a one-year "grace period." This grace period permits the inventor to weigh the advantages of patent protection, to perfect the invention, and to draft a patent application. Moreover, the inventor, in most instances, controls the outset of that grace period. From the time the inventor publicizes or commercializes the invention, he knows that he has one year in which to file an application. Of course, the inventor must remember that third party activities will also start the one-year clock running.

Besides setting a novelty standard, § 102 as a whole also defines the categories of prior art for obviousness determinations. With that in mind, the statutory bars of § 102 (b) correct one other defect in first-to-invent systems. This correction is described in 1 MARTIN J. ADELMAN, PATENT LAW PERSPECTIVES, § 2.3[7.§ 6] at n.36 (2d ed. 1992):

> Commentators often remark that the United States has a first-to-invent rather than a first-to-file system. However, a pure first-to-invent system makes it difficult if not impossible for a member of the public to determine the prior art against which the claimed advance must be judged at least with respect to activities within a few years of the filing date. Section 102(b) dramatically changes this situation. Thus, in reality the United States has a modified first-to-file system in that it affixes prior art status to specific activities dated more than one year before the effective United States filing date irrespective of the invention date. Of course, additional prior art may be generated by activities within the one-year period that occur before the invention date and come within the definition of 35 U.S.C.A. § 102(a). In addition, 35 U.S.C.A. §§ 102(e), (f) and (g) also

generate prior art. Nevertheless, a basic and large class of prior art is created by Section 102(b) that cannot be challenged by the inventor based on his date of invention.

As you study § 102(b) ask yourself whether this is the unspoken basis for the expansive interpretation that the courts have given to this section.

As a matter of history, the first U.S. Patent Act to contain a statutory bar was the 1836 Act. The 1836 provision, however, was actually codification of the famous case of *Pennock v. Dialogue,* 27 U.S. (2 Pet.) 1 (1829). In this case, the most renowned Supreme Court Justice in matters of patent law, Joseph Story, recognized that a first-to-invent patent system has the inherent flaws discussed above. Justice Story stated the problem in these terms:

> If an inventor should be permitted to hold back from the knowledge of the public the secrets of his invention; if he should for a long period of years retain the monopoly, and make, and sell his invention publicly, and thus gather the whole profits of it, relying upon his superior skill and knowledge of the structure; and then, and then only, when the danger of competition should force him to secure the exclusive right, he should be allowed to take out a patent, and thus exclude the public from any farther use than what should be derived under it during his fourteen years; it would materially retard the progress of science and the useful arts, and give a premium to those who should be least prompt to communicate their discoveries.

With this recognition, Justice Story also proscribed the solution to this problem:

> [I]f he [the inventor] shall put [the invention] into public use, or sell it for public use before he applies for a patent, ... this should furnish another bar to his claim.

With this famous case as the foundation, the 1836 law enacted a statutory bar. The 1839 Act clarified that a third party, unknown to the inventor, may place an invention into public use or on sale and also ameliorated the bar by enacting a 2–year grace period.

Although this introduction has emphasized the corrective function of the bars in a first to file regime, foreign systems also have statutory bars with the filing date as the trigger. These "first to file" systems, however, offer a grace period, if at all, under more limited circumstances. Due to the beneficial aspects of section 102 (b), a United States inventor can sell a commercial embodiment of his invention as long as he files an application within one year. In Europe and Japan, such a sale before filing ordinarily defeats the patent. Canada has the most enlightened grace period in a first-to-file patent system. Under the Canadian system, disclosure of an invention to the public by an applicant or by a person who obtained knowledge of the invention, directly or indirectly, from the applicant, is not patent defeating if done within a year of the filing date.

See William Lesser, *Grace Periods in First-to-File Countries*, 3 Eur. Intell. Prop. Rev. 81 (1987).

The "public use or on sale" statutory bars of § 102(b) divide into two sorts: those activities performed by the applicant, and those by third parties. This Chapter approaches the cases in that order. This Chapter will then turn to the "patented" and "printed publication" bars, as well as consider the territorial limitations set out in § 102(b).

Beyond § 102(b), the remaining paragraphs of § 102 provide for additional patent-defeating events. Abandonment of an invention to the public amounts to a forfeiture of patent rights under § 102(c). Section 102(d) creates a statutory bar if the United States application has not been filed within one year of a foreign application on the same invention that ultimately ripened into a foreign patent right.

§ 5.1 APPLICANT ACTIVITIES § 102(B)

§ 5.1[a] "Public Use"

EGBERT v. LIPPMANN

United States Supreme Court, 1881.
104 U.S. (14 Otto) 333.

Mr. Justice Woods delivered the opinion of the court.

This suit was brought for an alleged infringement of the complainant's reissued letters-patent, No. 5216, dated Jan. 7, 1873, for an improvement in corset-springs.

The original letters bear date July 17, 1866, and were issued to Samuel H. Barnes. The reissue was made to the complainant, under her then name, Frances Lee Barnes, executrix of the original patentee.

The specification for the reissue declares:

"This invention consists in forming the springs of corsets of two or more metallic plates, placed one upon another, and so connected as to prevent them from sliding off each other laterally or edgewise, and at the same time admit of their playing or sliding upon each other, in the direction of their length or longitudinally, whereby their flexibility and elasticity are greatly increased, while at the same time much strength is obtained."

The second claim is as follows:

"A pair of corset-springs, each member of the pair being composed or two or more metallic plates, placed one on another, and fastened together at their centres, and so connected at or near each end that they can move or play on each other in the direction of their length."

The bill alleges that Barnes was the original and first inventor of the improvement covered by the reissued letters-patent, and that it had not, at the time of his application for the original letters, been for more than two years in public use or on sale, with his consent or allowance.

The answer takes issue on this averment and also denies infringement. On a final hearing the court dismissed the bill, and the complainant appealed.

We have, therefore, to consider whether the defense that the patented invention had, with the consent of the inventor, been publicly used for more than two years prior to his application for the original letters, is sustained by the testimony in the record.

The sixth, seventh, and fifteenth sections of the act of July 4, 1836, c. 357 (5 Stat. 117), as qualified by the seventh section of the act of March 8, 1839, c. 88 (id. 353), were in force at the date of his application. Their effect is to render letters-patent invalid if the invention which they cover was in public use, with the consent and allowance of the inventor, for more than two years prior to his application. Since the passage of the act of 1839 it has been strenuously contended that the public use of an invention for more than two years before such application, even without his consent and allowance, renders the letters-patent therefor void.

It is unnecessary in this case to decide this question, for the alleged use of the invention covered by the letters-patent to Barnes is conceded to have been with his express consent.

The evidence on which the defendants rely to establish a prior public use of the invention consists mainly of the testimony of the complainant.

She testifies that Barnes invented the improvement covered by his patent between January and May, 1855; that between the dates named the witness and her friend Miss Cugier were complaining of the breaking of their corset-steels. Barnes, who was present, and was an intimate friend of the witness, said he thought he could make her a pair that would not break. At their next interview he presented her with a pair of corset-steels which he himself had made. The witness wore these steels a long time. In 1858 Barnes made and presented to her another pair, which she also wore a long time. When the corsets in which these steels were used wore out, the witness ripped them open and took out the steels and put them in new corsets. This was done several times.

It is admitted, and, in fact, is asserted, by complainant, that these steels embodied the invention afterwards patented by Barnes and covered by the reissued letters-patent on which this suit is brought.

Joseph H. Sturgis, another witness for complainant, testifies that in 1863 Barnes spoke to him about two inventions made by himself, one of which was a corset-steel, and that he went to the house of Barnes to see them. Before this time, and after the transactions testified to by the complainant, Barnes and she had intermarried. Barnes said his wife had a pair of steels made according to his invention in the corsets which she was then wearing, and if she would take them off he would show them to witness. Mrs. Barnes went out, and returned with a pair of corsets and a pair of scissors, and ripped the corsets open and took out the steels. Barnes then explained to witness how they were made and used.

The question for our decision is, whether this testimony shows a public use within the meaning of the statute.

We observe, in the first place, that to constitute the public use of an invention it is not necessary that more than one of the patented articles should be publicly used. The use of a great number may tend to strengthen the proof, but one well-defined case of such use is just as effectual to annul the patent as many. *McClurg v. Kingsland*, 1 How. 202; *Consolidated Fruit–Jar Co. v. Wright*, 94 U.S. 92; *Pitts v. Hall*, 2 Blatchf. 229. For instance, if the inventor of a mower, a printing-press, or a railway-car makes and sells only one of the articles invented by him, and allows the vendee to use it for two years, without restriction or limitation, the use is just as public as if he had sold and allowed the use of a great number.

We remark, secondly, that, whether the use of an invention is public or private does not necessarily depend upon the number of persons to whom its use is known. If an inventor, having made his device, gives or sells it to another, to be used by the donee or vendee, without limitation or restriction, or injunction of secrecy, and it is so used, such use is public, even though the use and knowledge of the use may be confined to one person.

We say, thirdly, that some inventions are by their very character only capable of being used where they cannot be seen or observed by the public eye. An invention may consist of a lever or spring, hidden in the running gear of a watch, or of a rachet, shaft, or cog-wheel covered from view in the recesses of a machine for spinning or weaving. Nevertheless, if its inventor sells a machine of which his invention forms a part, and allows it to be used without restriction of any kind, the use is a public one. So, on the other hand, a use necessarily open to public view, if made in good faith solely to test the qualities of the invention, and for the purpose of experiment, is not a public use within the meaning of the statute. *Elizabeth v. Pavement Company*, 97 U.S. 126; *Shaw v. Cooper*, 7 Pet. 292.

Tested by these principles, we think the evidence of the complainant herself shows that for more than two years before the application for the original letters there was, by the consent and allowance of Barnes, a public use of the invention, covered by them. He made and gave to her two pairs of corset-steels, constructed according to his device, one in 1855 and one in 1858. They were presented to her for use. He imposed no obligation of secrecy, nor any condition or restriction whatever. They were not presented for the purpose of experiment, nor to test their qualities. No such claim is set up in her testimony. The invention was at the time complete, and there is no evidence that it was afterwards changed or improved. The donee of the steels used them for years for the purpose and in the manner designed by the inventor. They were not capable of any other use. She might have exhibited them to any person, or made other steels of the same kind, and used or sold them without violating any condition or restriction imposed on her by the inventor.

According to the testimony of the complainant, the invention was completed and put into use in 1855. The inventor slept on his rights for eleven years. Letters-patent were not applied for till March, 1866. In the mean time, the invention had found its way into general, and almost universal, use. A great part of the record is taken up with the testimony of the manufacturers and venders of corset-steels, showing that before he applied for letters the principle of his device was almost universally used in the manufacture of corset-steels. It is fair to presume that having learned from this general use that there was some value in his invention, he attempted to resume, by his application, what by his acts he had clearly dedicated to the public.

"An abandonment of an invention to the public may be evinced by the conduct of the inventor at any time, even within the two years named in the law. The effect of the law is that no such consequence will necessarily follow from the invention being in public use or on sale, with the inventor's consent and allowance, at any time within the two years before his application; but that, if the invention is in public use or on sale prior to that time, it will be conclusive evidence of abandonment, and the patent will be void." *Elizabeth v. Pavement Company, supra.*

We are of opinion that the defense of two years' public use, by the consent and allowance of the inventor, before he made application for letters-patent, is satisfactorily established by the evidence.

Mr. Justice Miller dissenting.

A private use with consent, which could lead to no copy or reproduction of the machine, which taught the nature of the invention to no one but the party to whom such consent was given, which left the public at large as ignorant of this as it was before the author's discovery, was no abandonment to the public, and did not defeat his claim for a patent. If the little steep spring inserted in a single pair of corsets, and used by only one woman, covered by her outer-clothing, and in a position always withheld from public observation, is a public use of that piece of steel, I am at a loss to know the line between a private and a public use.

The opinion argues that the use was public, because, with the consent of the inventor to its use, no limitation was imposed in regard to its use in public. It may be well imagined that a prohibition to the party so permitted against exposing her use of the steel spring to public observation would have been supposed to be a piece of irony. An objection quite the opposite of this suggested by the opinion is, that the invention was incapable of a public use. That is to say, that while the statute says the right to the patent can only be defeated by a use which is public, it is equally fatal to the claim, when it is permitted to be used at all, that the article can never be used in public.

I cannot on such reasoning as this eliminate from the statute the word public, and disregard its obvious importance in connection with the remainder of the act, for the purpose of defeating a patent otherwise meritorious.

Notes

1. The Meaning of "Public." In what sense was the use by Ms. Barnes a public one? Was this use truly "public," or simply not secret, i.e., a "non-informing" use? How can a use be "public" if only a few members of the community know about it? Consider elements that might be relevant: the number of observers, the intent of the inventor, the number of uses of the invention, and the extent to which observers understand the disclosed technology. Why should a non-commercial, non-informing use be patent defeating?

2. Dissecting Disclosure. Beyond the ordinary meaning of the term "public," how does *Egbert* impact a fundamental goal of the patent system, the disclosure of technological advance? If an inventor's earlier use reveals a given technology to only an exceedingly small subset of the public that is technologically unsophisticated, and yet this public use results in the unavailability of patent protection, how will the technology be disclosed to an appreciative public in any sense? Note that a non-informing use is not patent defeating in either Europe or Japan.

3. Confidentiality Restrictions? What Form? At several points in *Egbert*, the Supreme Court noted that the invention entered use "without limitation or restriction, or injunction of secrecy...." In the first place, would the results of this case have changed if the inventor had requested confidentiality of Ms. Barnes? What form would that confidentiality agreement need to take?

In a modern public use case, the inventor of a famous cube puzzle built models of his invention as early as 1957 and used them personally. In 1968, he built a working prototype of his puzzle. He brought it to work where his boss and a few close colleagues saw it and used it. The boss liked the puzzle. In March of 1969, Nichols, the inventor, sold to his employer, Moleculon, all rights in the puzzle in exchange for a share of any proceeds. On March 3, 1970, Nichols filed a patent application on behalf of Moleculon. The patent issued two years later. In a later infringement suit, the defendant defended on the basis of public use. The Federal Circuit, speaking through Judge Baldwin, distinguished *Egbert*:

> The district court distinguished *Egbert* because here Nichols had not given over the invention for free and unrestricted use by another person. Based on the personal relationships and surrounding circumstances, the court found that Nichols at all times retained control over the puzzle's use and the distribution of information concerning it. The court characterized Nichol's use as private and for his own enjoyment. We see neither legal error in the analysis nor clear error in the findings.

> As for [the boss's] brief use of the puzzle, the court found that Nichols retained control even though he and [the boss] had not entered into any express confidentiality agreement. The court held, and we agree, that the presence or absence of such an agreement is not determinative of the public use issue.

Moleculon Research Corp. v. CBS, Inc., 793 F.2d 1261, 1266, 229 U.S.P.Q. 805 (Fed.Cir.1986). Is a confidentiality agreement as important as *Egbert* seemed to say? If close personal relationships can substitute for a confidentiality agreement, why did Egbert lose? After all, Ms. Barnes was the inventor's "intimate friend," whom he later married.

4. The Equities. Could the Court's decision have been motivated by the eleven-year delay between the filing date and the time the inventor knew of Ms. Barnes' use? Suppose a subsequent inventor of corset steels attempted to obtain a patent on the technology; would the same equities apply? Issues of third party activities are taken up in § 5.2 of this text.

METALLIZING ENGINEERING CO. v. KENYON BEARING & AUTO PARTS

Circuit Court of Appeals, Second Circuit, 1946.
153 F.2d 516, 68 U.S.P.Q. 54.
cert. denied, 328 U.S. 840 (1946).

Before L. HAND, AUGUSTUS N. HAND, and CLARK, CIRCUIT JUDGES.

L. HAND, CIRCUIT JUDGE.

The defendants appeal from the usual decree holding valid and infringed all but three of the claims of a reissued patent, issued to the plaintiff's assignor, Meduna; the original patent issued on May 25, 1943, upon an application filed on August 6, 1942. The patent is for the process of "so conditioning a metal surface that the same is, as a rule, capable of bonding thereto applied spray metal to a higher degree than is normally procurable with hitherto known practices." It is primarily useful for building up the worn metal parts of a machine.

The only question which we find necessary to decide is as to Meduna's public use of the patented process more than one year before August 6, 1942. The district judge made findings about this, which are supported by the testimony and which we accept.... The kernel of them is the following: "the inventor's main purpose in his use of the process prior to August 6, 1941, and especially in respect to all jobs for owners not known to him, was commercial, and * * * an experimental purpose in connection with such use was subordinate only." Upon this finding he concluded as matter of law that, since the use before the critical date—August 6, 1941—was not primarily for the purposes of experiment, the use was not excused for that reason. Moreover, he also concluded that the use was not public but secret, and for that reason that its predominantly commercial character did prevent it from invalidating the patent. For the last he relied upon our decisions in *Peerless Roll Leaf Co. v. Griffin & Sons*, 29 F.2d 646, and *Gillman v. Stern*, 114 F.2d 28. We think that his analysis of *Peerless Roll Leaf Co. v. Griffin & Sons*, was altogether correct, and that he had no alternative but to follow that decision; on the other hand, we now think that we were then wrong and that the decision must be overruled for reasons we shall state. *Gillman v. Stern*, supra, was, however, rightly decided.

Section one of the first and second Patent Acts, 1 Stat. 109 and 318, declared that the petition for a patent must state that the subject matter had not been "before known or used." Section six of the Act of 1836, 5 Stat. 117, changed this by providing in addition that the invention must not at the time of the application for a patent have been "in public use or on sale" with the inventor's "consent or allowance"; and Sec. 7 of the Act of 1839, 5 Stat. 353, provided that "no patent shall be held to be invalid by reason of such purchase, sale, or use prior to the application for a patent * * * except on proof of abandonment of such invention to the public; or that such purchase, sale, or prior use has been for more than two years prior to such application * * *." Section 4886 of the Revised Statutes made it a condition upon patentability that the invention shall not have been "in public use or on sale for more than two years prior to his application," and that it shall not have been "proved to have been abandoned." This is in substance the same as the Act of 1839, and is precisely the same as Sec. 31 of Title 35, U.S.C.A. except that the prior use is now limited to the United States, and to one year before the application. Sec. 1, Chap. 391, 29 Stat. 692; Sec. 1, Chap. 450, 53 Stat. 1212, 35 U.S.C.A. § 31. So far as we can find, the first case which dealt with the effect of prior use by the patentee was Pennock v. Dialogue, 2 Pet. 1, 4, 7 L.Ed. 327, in which the invention had been completed in 1811, and the patent granted in 1818 for a process of making hose by which the sections were joined together in such a way that the joints resisted pressure as well as the other parts. It did not appear that the joints in any way disclosed the process; but the patentee, between the discovery of the invention and the grant of the patent, had sold 13,000 feet of hose; and as to this the judge charged: "If the public, with the knowledge and tacit consent of the inventor, be permitted to use the invention, without opposition, it is a fraud on the public afterwards to take out a patent." The Supreme Court affirmed a judgment for the defendant, on the ground that the invention had been "known or used before the application." "If an inventor should be permitted to hold back from the knowledge of the public the secrets of his invention; if he should * * * make and sell his invention publicly, and thus gather the whole profits, * * * it would materially retard the progress of science and the useful arts" to allow him fourteen years of legal monopoly "when the danger of competition should force him to secure the exclusive right" 2 Pet. at page 19, 7 L.Ed. 327. In *Shaw v. Cooper*, 7 Pet. 292, 8 L.Ed. 689, the public use was not by the inventory, but he had neglected to prevent it after he had learned of it, and this defeated the patent. "Whatever may be the intention of the inventor, if he suffers his invention to go into public use, through any means whatsoever, without an immediate assertion of his right, he is not entitled to a patent" 7 Pet. at page 323, 8 L.Ed. 689. In *Kendall v. Winsor*, 21 How. 322, 16 L.Ed. 165, the inventor had kept the machine secret, but had sold the harness which it produced, so that the facts presented the same situation as here. Since the jury brought in a verdict for the defendant on the issue of abandonment, the case adds nothing except for the dicta on page 328 of 21 How., 16 L.Ed. 165: "the inventor who designedly, and with the view of applying it indefinitely and exclusively for his own profit, withholds his invention for the public, comes not within the policy or objects of the Constitution or acts of Congress." In *Egbert v. Lippmann*, 104 U.S. 333, 26 L.Ed. 755, although the patent was for the product which was sold, nothing could be learned about it without taking it apart, yet it was a public use within the statute. In *Hall v. Macneale*, 107 U.S. 90, 2 S.Ct. 73, 27 L.Ed. 367, the situation was the same.

In the lower courts we may begin with the often cited decision in *Macbeth-Evans Glass Co. v. General Electric Co.*, 6 Cir., 246 F. 695, which concerned a process patent for making illuminating glass. The patentee had kept the process as secret as possible, but for ten years had sold the glass, although this did not, so far as appears, disclose the process. The court held the patent invalid for two reasons, as we understand them: the first was that the delay either indicated an intention to abandon, or was of itself a forfeiture, because of the inconsistency of a practical monopoly by means of secrecy and of a later legal monopoly by means of a patent. So far, it was not an interpretation of "prior use" in the statute; but, beginning on page 702 of 246 F. 695 Judge Warrington seems to have been construing that phrase and to hold that the sales were such a use. In *Allinson Manufacturing Co. v. Ideal Filter Co.*, 8 Cir., 21 F.2d 22, the patent was for a machine for purifying gasoline: the machine was kept secret, but the gasoline had been sold for a period of six years before the application was filed. As in *Macbeth-Evans Glass Co. v. General Electric Co., supra*, 6 Cir., 246 F. 695, the court apparently invalidated the patent on two grounds: one was that the inventor had abandoned the right to a patent, or had forfeited it by his long delay. We are disposed however to read the latter part—pages 27 and 28 of 21 F.2d—as holding that the sale of gasoline was a "prior use" of the machine, notwithstanding its concealment. Certainly, the following quotation from *Pitts v. Hall*, Fed. Cas. No. 11,192, 2 Blatchf. 229, was not otherwise apposite; a patentee "is not allowed to derive any benefit from the sale or use of his machine, without forfeiting his right, except within two years prior to the time he makes his application." On the other hand in *Stresau v. Ipsen*, 77 F.2d 937, 22 C.C.P.A. (Patents) 1352, the Court of Customs and Patent Appeals did indeed decide that a process claim might be valid when the inventor had kept the process secret but had sold the product.

Coming now to our own decisions (the opinions in all of which I wrote), the first was *Grasselli Chemical Co. v. National Aniline & Chemical Co.*, 2 Cir., 26 F.2d 305, in which the patent was for a process which had been kept secret, but the product had been sold upon the market for more than two years. We held that, although the process could not have been discovered from the product, the sales constituted a "prior use," relying upon *Egbert v. Lippmann, supra*, 104 U.S. 333, 26 L.Ed. 755, and *Hall v. Macneale, supra*, 107 U.S. 90, 2 S.Ct. 73, 27 L.Ed. 367. There was nothing in this inconsistent with what we are now holding. But in *Peerless Roll Leaf Co. v. Griffin & Sons, supra*, 2 Cir., 29 F.2d 646, where the patent was for a machine, which had been kept secret, but whose output had been freely sold on the market, we sustained the patent on the ground that "the sale of the product was irrelevant, since no knowledge could possibly be acquired of the machine in that way. In this respect the machine differs from a process * * * or from any other invention necessarily contained in a product" 29 F.2d at page 649. So far as we can now find, there is nothing to support this distinction in the authorities, and we shall try to show that we misapprehended the theory on which the prior use by an inventor forfeits his right to a patent. In *Aerovox Corp. v. Polymet Manufacturing Corp., supra*, 2 Cir., 67 F.2d 860, the patent was also for a process, the use of which we held not to have been experimental, though not secret. Thus our decision sustaining the patent was right; but apparently we were by implication reverting to the doctrine of the Peerless case when we added that it was doubtful whether the process could be detected from the product, although we cited only *Hall v. Macneale, supra*, 107 U.S. 90, 2 S.Ct. 73, 27 L.Ed. 367, and *Grasselli Chemical Co. v. National Aniline Co., supra* (2 Cir., 26 F.2d 305). In *Gillman v. Stern, supra*, 2 Cir., 114 F.2d 28, it was not the inventor, but a third person who used the machine secretly and sold the product openly, and there was therefore no question either of abandonment or forfeiture by the inventor. The only issue was whether a prior use which did not disclose the invention to the art was within the statute; and it is well settled that it is not. As in the case of any other anticipation, the issue of invention must then be determined by how much the inventor has contributed any new information to the art. * * *

From the foregoing it appears that in *Peerless Roll Leaf Co. v. Griffin & Sons, supra*, 2 Cir., 29 F.2d 646, we confused two separate doctrines: (1) The effect upon his right to a patent of the inventor's competitive exploitation of his machine or of his process; (2) the contribution which a prior use by another person makes to the art. Both do indeed come within the phrase, "prior use"; but the first is a defence for quite different reasons from the second. It had its origin-at least in this country-in the passage we have quoted from *Pennock v. Dialogue, supra*, 2 Pet. 1, 7 L.Ed. 327; i.e., that it is a condition upon an inventor's right to a patent that he shall not exploit his discovery competitively after it is ready for patenting; he must content himself with either secrecy, or legal monopoly. It is true that for the limited period of two years he was allowed to do so, possibly in order to give him time to prepare an application; and even that has been recently cut down by half. But if he goes beyond that period of probation, he forfeits his right regardless of how little the public may have learned about the invention; just as he can forfeit it by too long concealment, even without exploiting the invention at all. *Woodbridge v. United States*, 263 U.S. 50, 44 S.Ct. 45, 68 L.Ed. 159; *Macbeth-Evans Glass Co. v. General Electric Co., supra*, 6 Cir., 246 F. 695. Such a forfeiture has nothing to do with abandonment, which presupposes a deliberate, though not necessarily an express, surrender of any right to a patent. Although the evidence of both may at times overlap, each comes from a quite different legal source: one, from the fact that by renouncing the right the inventor irrevocably surrenders it; the other, from the fiat of Congress that it is part of the consideration for a patent that the public shall as soon as possible begin to enjoy the disclosure.

It is indeed true that an inventor may continue for more than a year to practice his invention for his private purposes of his own enjoyment and later patent it. But that is, properly considered, not an exception to the doctrine, for he is not then making use of his secret to gain a competitive advantage over others; he does not thereby extend the period of his monopoly. Besides, as we have Seen, even that privilege has its limits, for he may conceal it so long that he will lose his right to a patent even though he does not use it at all. With that question we have not however any concern here.

Judgment reversed; complaint dismissed.

Notes

1. **Heavy Metal.** *Metallizing Engineering* is a dense piece of text that can make for difficult reading. Although one can succinctly state its holding—that secret commercial exploitation of an invention by the inventor constitutes a "public use" under § 102(b)—concise explanations of this rule of patent law seem more difficult to come by. Are you satisfied with the attempt in *D.L. Auld Co. v. Chroma Graphics Corp.*, 714 F.2d 1144, 219 U.S.P.Q. 13 (Fed.Cir.1983), providing: "The 'forfeiture' theory expressed in *Metallizing* parallels the statutory scheme of 35 U.S.C.A. § 102(b), the intent of which is to preclude the attempts by the inventor or his assignee to profit from commercial use of an invention for more than a year before an application for patent is filed." Is Judge Hand's holding a matter fairly grounded in § 102(b); the abandonment provision of § 102(c), considered later in this Chapter; or, even worse, naked public policy? Given that § 102(b) itself draws no distinction between applicants and third parties when it provides for bars based upon "public use," what policies did Judge Hand animate here?

2. **"Public" = "Secret."** Why was it so important to prevent an inventor from secretly using his invention commercially for more than a year prior to filing for a patent that Judge Hand was willing to torture the English language and hold that the word "public" really meant "secret" when modifying "use?"

3. **Federal Circuit Adoption.** The Court of Appeals for the Federal Circuit approved of Judge Learned Hand's reasoning early in its history. As discussed in *D.L. Auld Co. v. Chroma Graphics Corp.*, 714 F.2d 1144, 219 U.S.P.Q. 13 (Fed.Cir.1983):

> Where a method is kept secret, and remains secret after a sale of the product of the method, that sale will not, of course, bar another inventor from the grant of a patent on that method. The situation is different where, as here, that sale is made by the applicant for patent or his assignee. Though the magistrate referred to § 102(b), he did so in recognizing that the "activity" of [the inventor] here was that which the statute "attempts to limit to one year." In so doing, the magistrate correctly applied the concept explicated in *Metallizing*, i.e., that a party's placing of the product of a method invention on sale more than a year before that party's application filing date must act as a forfeiture of any right to the grant of a valid patent on the method to that party if

circumvention of the policy animating § 102(b) is to be avoided in respect of patents on method inventions.

5.1[b]   Experimental Use Negation

CITY OF ELIZABETH v. AMERICAN NICHOLSON PAVEMENT CO.

United States Supreme Court, 1877.
97 U.S. (7 Otto) 126.

This suit was brought by the American Nicholson Pavement Company against the city of Elizabeth, N. J., George W. Tubbs, and the New Jersey Wood–Paving Company, a corporation of New Jersey, upon a patent issued to Samuel Nicholson, dated Aug. 20, 1867, for a new and improved wooden pavement, being a second reissue of a patent issued to said Nicholson Aug. 8, 1854. The reissued patent was extended in 1868 for a further term of seven years. A copy of it is appended to the bill; and, in the specification, it is declared that the nature and object of the invention consists in providing a process or mode of constructing wooden block pavements upon a foundation along a street or roadway with facility, cheapness, and accuracy, and also in the creation and construction of such a wooden pavement as shall be comparatively permanent and durable, by so uniting and combining all its parts, both superstructure and foundation, as to provide against the slipping of the horses' feet, against noise, against unequal wear, and against rot and consequent sinking away from below. Two plans of making this pavement are specified. Both require a proper foundation on which to lay the blocks, consisting of tarred-paper or hydraulic cement covering the surface of the road-bed to the depth of about two inches, or of a flooring of boards or plank, also covered with tar, or other preventive of moisture. On this foundation, one plan is to set square blocks on end arranged like a checker-board, the alternate rows being shorter than the others, so as to leave narrow grooves or channel-ways to be filled with small broken stone or gravel, and then pouring over the whole melted tar or pitch, whereby the cavities are all filled and cemented together. The other plan is, to arrange the blocks in rows transversely across the street, separated a small space (of about an inch) by strips of board at the bottom, which serve to keep the blocks at a uniform distance apart, and then filling these spaces with the same material as before. The blocks forming the pavement are about eight inches high. The alternate rows of short blocks in the first plan and the strips of board in the second plan should not be higher than four inches.

The bill charges that the defendants infringed this patent by laying down wooden pavements in the city of Elizabeth, N. J., constructed in substantial conformity with the process patented, and prays an account of profits, and an injunction.

The defendants answered in due course. They also averred that the alleged invention of Nicholson was in public use, with his consent and allowance, for six years before he applied for a patent, on a certain avenue in Boston called the Mill-dam; and contended that said public use worked an abandonment of the pretended invention.

The question to be considered is, whether Nicholson's invention was in public use or on sale, with his consent and allowance, for more than two years prior to his application for a patent, within the meaning of the sixth, seventh, and fifteenth sections of the act of 1836, as qualified by the seventh section of the act of 1839, which were the acts in force in 1854, when he obtained his patent. It is contended by the appellants that the pavement which Nicholson put down by way of experiment, on Mill-dam Avenue in Boston, in 1848, was publicly used for the space of six years before his application for a patent, and that this was a public use within the meaning of the law.

To determine this question, it is necessary to examine the circumstances under which this pavement was put down, and the object and purpose that Nicholson had in view. It is perfectly clear from the evidence that he did not intend to abandon his right to a patent. He had filed a caveat in August, 1847, and he constructed the pavement in question by way of experiment, for the purpose of testing its qualities. The road in which it was put down, though a public road, belonged to the Boston and Roxbury Mill Corporation, which received toll for its use; and Nicholson was a stockholder and treasurer of the corporation. The pavement in question was about seventy-five feet in length, and was laid adjoining to the toll-gate and in front of the toll-house. It was constructed by Nicholson at his own expense, and was placed by him where it was, in order to see the effect upon it of heavily loaded wagons, and of varied and constant use; and also to ascertain its durability, and liability to decay. Joseph L. Lang, who was toll-collector for many years, commencing in 1849, familiar with the road before that time, and with this pavement from the time of its origin, testified as follows:

> "Mr. Nicholson was there almost daily, and when he came he would examine the pavement, would often walk over it, cane in hand, striking it with his cane, and making particular examination of its condition. He asked me very often how people liked it, and asked me a great many questions about it. I have heard him say a number of times that this was his first experiment with this pavement, and he thought that it was wearing very well. The circumstances that made this locality desirable for the purpose of obtaining a satisfactory test of the durability and value of the pavement were: that there would be a better chance to lay it there; he would have more room and a better chance than in the city; and, besides, it was a place where most everybody went over it, rich and poor. It was a great thoroughfare out of Boston. It was frequently travelled by teams having a load of five or six tons, and some larger. As these teams usually stopped at the toll-house, and started again, the stopping and starting would make as severe a trial to the pavement as it could be put to."

This evidence is corroborated by that of several other witnesses in the cause; the result of the whole being that Nicholson merely intended this piece of pavement as an experiment, to test its usefulness and durability. Was this a public use, within the meaning of the law?

An abandonment of an invention to the public may be evinced by the conduct of the inventor at any time, even within the two years named in the law. The effect of the law is, that no such consequence will necessarily follow from the invention being in public use or on sale, with the inventor's consent and allowance, at any time within two years before his application; but that, if the invention is in public use or on sale prior to that time, it will be conclusive evidence of abandonment, and the patent will be void.

But, in this case, it becomes important to inquire what is such a public use as will have the effect referred to. That the use of the pavement in question was public in one sense cannot be disputed. But can it be said that the invention was in public use? The use of an invention by the inventor himself, or of any other person under his direction, by way of experiment, and in order to bring the invention to perfection, has never been regarded as such a use. CURTIS, PATENTS, sect. 381; *Shaw v. Cooper*, 7 Pet. 292.

Now, the nature of a street pavement is such that it cannot be experimented upon satisfactorily except on a highway, which is always public.

When the subject of invention is a machine, it may be tested and tried in a building, either with or without closed doors. In either case, such use is not a public use, within the meaning of the statute, so long as the inventor is engaged, in good faith, in testing its operation. He may see cause to alter it and improve it, or not. His experiments will reveal the fact whether any and what alterations may be necessary. If durability is one of the qualities to be attained, a long period, perhaps years, may be necessary to enable the inventor to discover whether his purpose is accomplished. And though, during all that period, he may not find that any changes are necessary, yet he may be justly said to be using his machine only by way of experiment; and no one would say that such a use, pursued with a bona fide intent of testing the qualities of the machine, would be a public use, within the meaning of the statute. So long as he does not voluntarily allow others to make it and use it, and so long as it is not on sale for general use, he keeps the invention under his own control, and does not lose his title to a patent.

It would not be necessary, in such a case, that the machine should be put up and used only in the inventor's own shop or premises. He may have it put up and used in the premises of another, and the use may inure to the benefit of the owner of the establishment. Still, if used under the surveillance of the inventor, and for the purpose of enabling him to test the machine, and ascertain whether it will answer the purpose intended, and make such alterations and improvements as experience demonstrates to be necessary, it will still be a mere experimental use, and not a public use, within the meaning of the statute.

Whilst the supposed machine is in such experimental use, the public may be incidentally deriving a benefit from it. If it be a grist-mill, or a carding-machine, customers from the surrounding country may enjoy the use of it by having their grain made into flour, or their wool into rolls, and still it will not be in public use, within the meaning of the law.

But if the inventor allows his machine to be used by other persons generally, either with or without compensation, or if it is, with his consent, put on sale for such use, then it will be in public use and on public sale, within the meaning of the law.

If, now, we apply the same principles to this case, the analogy will be seen at once. Nicholson wished to experiment on his pavement. He believed it to be a good thing, but he was not sure; and the only mode in which he could test it was to place a specimen of it in a public roadway. He did this at his own expense, and with the consent of the owners of the road. Durability was one of the qualities to be attained. He wanted to know whether his pavement would stand, and whether it would resist decay. Its character for durability could not be ascertained without its being subjected to use for a considerable time. He subjected it to such use, in good faith, for the simple purpose of ascertaining whether it was what he claimed it to be. Did he do any thing more than the inventor of the supposed machine might do, in testing his invention? The public had the incidental use of the pavement, it is true; but was the invention in public use, within the meaning of the statute? We think not. The proprietors of the road alone used the invention, and used it at Nicholson's request, by way of experiment. The only way in which they could use it was by allowing the public to pass over the pavement.

Had the city of Boston, or other parties, used the invention, by laying down the pavement in other streets and places, with Nicholson's consent and allowance, then, indeed, the invention itself would have been in public use, within the meaning of the law; but this was not the case. Nicholson did not sell it, nor allow others to use it or sell it. He did not let it go beyond his control. He did nothing that indicated any intent to do so. He kept it under his own eyes, and never for a moment abandoned the intent to obtain a patent for it.

In this connection, it is proper to make another remark. It is not a public knowledge of his invention that precludes the inventor from obtaining a patent for it, but a public use or sale of it. In England, formerly, as well as under our Patent Act of 1793, if an inventor did not keep his invention secret, if a knowledge of it became public before his application for a patent, he could not obtain one. To be patentable, an invention must not have been known or used before the application; but this has not been the law of this country since the passage of the act of 1836, and it has been very much qualified in England. *Lewis v. Marling,* 10 B. & C. 22. Therefore, if it were true that during the whole period in which the pavement was used, the public knew how it was constructed, it would make no difference in the result.

It is sometimes said that an inventor acquires an undue advantage over the public by delaying to take out a patent, inasmuch as he thereby preserves the monopoly to himself for a longer period than is allowed by the policy of the law; but this cannot be said with justice when the delay is occasioned by a bona fide effort to bring his invention to perfection, or to ascertain whether it will answer the purpose intended. His monopoly only continues for the allotted period, in any event; and it is the interest of the public, as well as himself, that the invention should be perfect and properly tested, before a patent is granted for it. Any attempt to use it for a profit, and not by way of experiment, for a longer period than two years before the application, would deprive the inventor of his right to a patent.

Notes

1. **Comparison to *Egbert*.** Justice Story strove in *Pennock* to encourage early filing of an invention. Does *City of Elizabeth* undercut the policies of *Pennock*? What did Nicholson do differently from Egbert, the corset springs inventor? What evidence could Nicholson muster that Egbert could not?

2. **The Experimental Use Negation.** What statutory language dictates the result in *City of Elizabeth*? Is experimentation a "use" within the meaning of "public use" in § 102(b)? Is experimentation an exception to the public use and on sale statutory bars *or* a recognition that experimentation on an invention cannot be a public use nor an offer for sale of the invention?

A Federal Circuit opinion answers these questions. The invention was a novel orthodontic appliance for which the inventor filed a patent application on February 19, 1962. Before the critical date, the inventor used the dental device on three patients. In 1958, 1959, and 1960, the inventor used the device on one patient, but kept only "scanty records." The inventor made no commercial sales of the device until 1966. The trial court "placed a heavy burden of proof on the patent owner to prove that the inventor's use had been experimental." Judge Nies explained the district court's error:

> [I]t is incorrect to impose on the patent owner, as the trial court in this case did, the burden of proving that a "public use" was "experimental." These are not two separable issues. It is incorrect to ask: "Was it a public use?" and then, "Was it experimental?" Rather, the court is faced with a single issue: Was it public use under section 102(b)?
>
> Turning to the instant case, we note first that disclosure of the seating device to patients could not be avoided in any testing.... In any event, a pledge of confidentiality is indicative of the inventor's continued control which here is established inherently by the dentist-patient relationship of the parties.... Yet no [inventions] were offered competing orthodontists despite the fact this was one facet of the inventor's total business activity.

TP Laboratories, Inc. v. Professional Positioners, Inc., 724 F.2d 965, 971–73, 220 U.S.P.Q. 577 (Fed.Cir.1984). Does the distinction between an experimental use "exception" and a "negation" really mean anything beyond semantics? Who has the burden to prove a patent invalid and why? You will revisit this issue in connection with *Lough v. Brunswick, infra.*

3. Experimenting on the Claimed Invention or on its General Purposes? As a general rule, an experimental use only negates a statutory bar when the inventor was testing claimed features of the invention. *In re Theis,* 610 F.2d 786, 793, 204 U.S.P.Q. 188, 194 (CCPA 1979) ("It is settled law that . . . experimental sale . . . does not apply to experiments performed with respect to non-claimed features of an invention."); *LaBounty Mfg. Inc. v. United States Int'l Trade Comm'n,* 958 F.2d 1066, 1074, 22 U.S.P.Q.2d 1025, 1031 (Fed.Cir.1992); *In re Brigance,* 792 F.2d 1103, 1109, 229 U.S.P.Q. 988, 991–92 (Fed.Cir.1986). In some instances, however, the Federal Circuit has allowed an experimental use to negate a § 102 (b) bar when the testing did not focus on a claimed feature. In *Grain Processing Corp. v. American Maize–Products Co.,* 840 F.2d 902, 5 U.S.P.Q.2d 1788 (Fed.Cir.1988), a patentee sent samples of its food additive to manufacturers for testing. The Federal Circuit noted that the minimal testing was to check for adverse interactions with other food products. *Id.* at 906. The claims in *Grain Processing,* however, do not recite "food interactions" as a claimed feature. Can this result be justified as reasonable testing of the product's utility or is this a conflict in Federal Circuit application of the experimental use negation?

For another example, consider the *Manville Sales* case discussed in the next note. The inventor tested the luminaire assembly for durability in the severe winter environment, but the claims do not refer to severe conditions or durability. *See* 917 F.2d at 550. Some of the difficulty may arise from the need to test an invention for utility, i.e., to show that it works for its intended purpose. *Scott v. Finney,* 34 F.3d 1058, 1061, 32 U.S.P.Q.2d 1115, 1117 (Fed.Cir.1994). An inventor may test for the general workability of an invention and its suitability for the marketplace, for example, avoiding food interactions or durability in winter, without claiming those features which are necessary for general workability and marketability. Are utility testing and experimental use testing the same thing? If the answer is "no" because experimental use testing is more strictly confined to claimed features, does the potential overlap of utility testing and testing the claimed features explain the Federal Circuit's decision to relax the experimental use testing requirements in *Manville Sales* and *Grain Processing*?

4. Modern Experimental Use. In a modern case, the invention was an improvement in the design of lights along highways. The invention facilitated repair and maintenance of the luminaires at the top of the 150–foot pole which supported the lights. The inventor needed to test the invention in difficult weather conditions. In November, 1971, the inventor sold a prototype of his design to the State of Wyoming for installation at a rest area near Rawlins which was not yet open to the public. In March 1972, the inventor inspected the invention and determined it had survived the winter. He then authorized sales of his device. In June, 1972, the rest area opened to the public. The inventor filed for patent protection on February 3, 1973. Judge Michel delivered the decision of the Federal Circuit:

In order to determine whether an invention was on sale or in public use, we must consider how the totality of the circumstances comports with the policies underlying the on sale and public use bars.

First, Manville did nothing to lead the public to believe that its iris arm invention was in "the public domain." On the contrary, Manville conveyed to a Wyoming official that its use of the invention on one pole at one site in Wyoming was experimental. Although Manville did not advise anyone else that its use was experimental and was not intended to release its invention into the public domain, the particular circumstances made such efforts unnecessary. Manville marked its design drawing with a confidentiality notice before disclosing it to a Wyoming official, and Wyoming law prohibited officials from disclosing confidential information.

Second, Manville did not attempt to extend the patent term by commercially exploiting its invention more than one year before it filed a patent application. Manville retained ownership of the lowering device and did not notify its sales personnel about the invention, or initiate a sales campaign to market the iris arm design until March of 1972, after it first determined, based on inspecting the Fort Steele device, that the iris arms worked for their intended purpose.

Moreover, although Manville eventually received compensation for the iris arm device in fulfillment of its original contract with Wyoming, a sale that is primarily for experimental purposes, as opposed to commercial exploitation, does not raise an on sale bar. *See Baker Oil Tools, Inc. v. Geo Vann, Inc.*, 828 F.2d 1558, 1563, 4 U.S.P.Q.2d 1210, 1213 (Fed.Cir.1987).

Finally, Manville's actions are entirely consistent with the policy "favoring prompt and widespread disclosure of 'inventions.' "The iris arm device was specifically designed to withstand year around weather. Prior to its testing in the winter environment, there really was no basis for confidence by the inventor that the invention would perform as intended, and hence no proven invention to disclose.

Manville Sales Corp. v. Paramount Systems, Inc., 917 F.2d 544, 549–550, 16 U.S.P.Q.2d 1587 (Fed.Cir.1990). How important was the site chosen for this experiment—a rest area in Wyoming not yet open to the public? How about the fact that the invention was situated at the top of a 150–foot pole throughout the experimentation?

Manville also introduces the close relationship between reduction to practice, the test for completion of an invention, and the public use and on sale bars. *UMC Electronics* gives this question a different analysis.

5. Market Testing as Experimentation? In *In re Smith*, 714 F.2d 1127, 1135, 218 U.S.P.Q. 976 (Fed.Cir.1983), the Federal Circuit dealt with the question of whether market testing for consumer satisfaction qualified as an experimental use. The inventor tested the invention—a carpet deodorizer—with consumers more than a year before the application. After showing a video presentation about the product and giving several consumers samples to try in their homes, the inventor asked them about the pricing of the product, the believability of its qualities, and their purchase intent. The Federal Circuit upheld a public use bar:

> The experimental use exception, however, does not include market testing where the inventor is attempting to gauge consumer demand for his claimed invention. The purpose of such activities is commercial exploitation and not experimentation.

In re Smith, 714 F.2d at 1135. Judge Nichols dissented, noting that the line between testing the market and testing the product may be difficult to discern. Do the policies underlying the public use bar support this result? Note as well that the Federal Circuit referred loosely to the experimental use doctrine as an "exception" to public use. Is experimental use technically an "exception" or a "negation?"

LOUGH v. BRUNSWICK CORP.

United States Court of Appeals, Federal Circuit, 1996.
86 F.3d 1113, 39 U.S.P.Q.2d 1100.

Before PLAGER, LOURIE, and CLEVENGER, CIRCUIT JUDGES.

LOURIE, CIRCUIT JUDGE.

Brunswick Corporation, d/b/a Mercury Marine, appeals from the final judgment of the United States District Court for the Middle District of Florida in which the court denied Brunswick's Motion for Judgment as a Matter of Law and its Motion for New Trial after a jury verdict of infringement of U.S. Patent 4,848,775, owned by the inventor Steven G. Lough. Because the court erred in denying Brunswick's Motion for Judgment as a Matter of Law, we reverse in part and vacate in part.

BACKGROUND

Stern drives are marine propulsion devices for boats in which the engine is located inside the boat and is coupled to an outdrive, which includes a propeller located outside the boat ("inboard/outboard boat"). A typical stern drive arrangement is illustrated below.

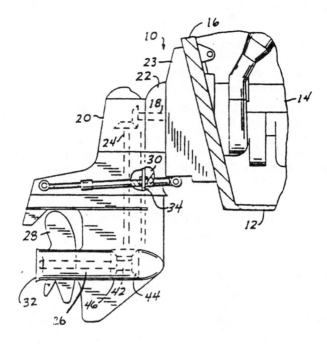

The outdrive is housed in a drive shaft housing. At the upper and lower ends of the gear shift shaft assembly, an upper seal assembly and a lower seal assembly prevent sea water and exhaust from causing corrosion by passing through the bell housing apertures provided for the shift shaft assembly. The lower seal assembly protects the gear controls at the lower end of the shift shaft , and the upper seal assembly protects the gear shift cable and user controls.

In 1986, Steven G. Lough worked as a repairman for a boat dealership in Sarasota, Florida. While repairing Brunswick inboard/outboard boats, he noticed that the upper seal assembly in the stern drives often failed due to corrosion. A typical upper seal assembly from a Brunswick motor is shown below.

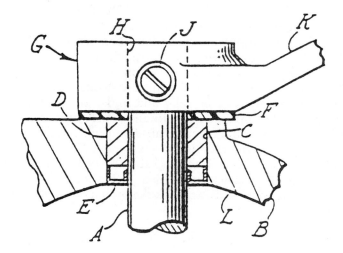

The upper seal assembly comprises a brass bushing (D) and an annular seal (E). The brass bushing (D) is forced into a bell housing aperture (C). An annular seal (E) is installed below the brass bushing (D) and is in direct contact with the aluminum bell housing (B).

Lough determined that the corrosion in the upper seal assembly occurred due to contact between the annular seal (E) and the bell housing aperture (C). He designed a new upper seal assembly that isolated the annular seal (E) from the aluminum bell housing (B) in order to prevent such corrosion.

After some trial and error with his grandfather's metal lathe, he made six usable prototypes in the spring of 1986. He installed one prototype in his own boat at home. Three months later, he gave a second prototype to a friend who installed it in his boat. He also installed prototypes in the boat of the owner of the marina where he worked and in the boat of a marina customer. He gave the remaining prototypes to longtime friends who were employees at another marina in Sarasota. Lough did not charge anyone for the prototypes. For over a year following the installation of these prototypes, Lough neither asked for nor received any comments about the operability of the prototypes. During this time, Lough did not attempt to sell any seal assemblies.

On June 6, 1988, Lough filed a patent application entitled "Liquid Seal for Marine Stern Drive Gear Shift Shafts," which issued as the '775 patent on July 18, 1989.

* * *

After learning of Lough's invention, Brunswick designed its own improved upper seal assembly.... Brunswick incorporated its new upper seal assembly in its "Alpha One" inboard/outboard boat. In addition, it sold this seal assembly as a replacement part under its "Quicksilver" line of replacement parts.

Lough sued Brunswick on June 12, 1993, alleging infringement of the '775 patent. Brunswick counterclaimed for a declaratory judgment of patent noninfringement, invalidity, and/or unenforceability. A jury found that Brunswick failed to prove that Lough's invention was in public use before the critical date on June 6, 1987, one year prior to the filing date of the '775 patent. The jury also found that Brunswick infringed claims 1–4 of the '775 patent, both literally and under the doctrine of equivalents. Based on its infringement finding, the jury awarded Lough $1,500,000 in lost profits. After trial, Brunswick filed a Motion for Judgment as a Matter of Law in which it argued, inter alia, that the claimed invention was invalid because it had been in public use before the critical date. Brunswick also filed a Motion for New Trial on damages. The court denied Brunswick's motions without any comment. Brunswick appeals.

Discussion

Brunswick challenges, inter alia, the court's denial of its motion for JMOL on the issue of public use. Brunswick argues that the district court erred in denying its motion for JMOL because the uses of Lough's prototypes prior to the critical date were not experimental. Brunswick asserts that Lough did not control the uses of his prototypes by third parties before the critical date, failed to keep records of the alleged experiments, and did not place the parties to whom the seals were given under any obligation of secrecy. Based on this objective evidence, Brunswick argues that the uses of Lough's prototypes before the critical date were not "experimental." Therefore, Brunswick contends that the jury's verdict was incorrect as a matter of law and that the court erred in denying its JMOL motion.

Lough counters that the tests performed with the six prototypes were necessary experiments conducted in the course of completing his invention. He argues that when the totality of circumstances is properly viewed, the evidence supports the jury's conclusion that those uses were experimental. Lough maintains that a number of factors support the jury's experimental use conclusion, including evidence that he received no compensation for the prototypes, he did not place the seal assemblies on sale until after he filed his patent application, and he gave the prototypes only to his friends and personal acquaintances who used them in such a manner that they were unlikely to be seen by the public. He further argues that, to verify operability of the seal assemblies, prototypes had to be installed by mechanics of various levels of skill in boats that were exposed to different conditions. Thus, he asserts that the court did not err in denying Brunswick's JMOL motion. We disagree with Lough.

One is entitled to a patent unless, inter alia, "the invention was . . . in public use . . . in this country, more than one year prior to the date of the application for patent in the United States." 35 U.S.C. § 102(b) (1994). We have defined "public use" as including "any use of [the claimed] invention by a person other than the inventor who is under no limitation, restriction or obligation of secrecy to the inventor." *In re Smith*, 714 F.2d 1127, 1134, 218 U.S.P.Q. 976, 983 (Fed.Cir.1983) (citing *Egbert v. Lippmann*, 104 U.S. 333, 336, 26 L.Ed. 755 (1881)). An evaluation of a question of public use depends on "how the totality of the circumstances of the case comports with the policies underlying the public use bar." *Tone Bros. v. Sysco Corp.*, 28 F.3d 1192, 1198, 31 U.S.P.Q.2d 1321, 1324 (Fed.Cir.1994). These policies include:

> (1) discouraging the removal, from the public domain, of inventions that the public reasonably has come to believe are freely available; (2) favoring the prompt and widespread disclosure of inventions; (3) allowing the inventor a reasonable amount of time following sales activity to determine the potential economic value of a patent; and (4) prohibiting the inventor from commercially exploiting the invention for a period greater than the statutorily prescribed time.

Id., 28 F.3d 1192, 1198, 31 U.S.P.Q.2d at 1324–25. A patentee may negate a showing of public use by coming forward with evidence that its use of the invention was experimental.

Neither party disputes that Lough's prototypes were in use before the critical date. Thus, both parties agree that the issue presented on appeal is whether the jury properly decided that the use of Lough's six prototypes in 1986, prior to the critical date, constituted experimental use so as to negate the conclusion of public use. Whether an invention was in public use prior to the critical date within the meaning of § 102(b) is a question of law.

The parties do not dispute that the five seal assemblies were used by others before June 6, 1987. The only dispute is whether these uses qualify as experimental uses. The law places the burden on Mr. Lough to come forward with convincing evidence showing that these uses were experimental uses.

"The use of an invention by the inventor himself, or of any other person under his direction, by way of experiment, and in order to bring the invention to perfection, has never been regarded as [a public] use." *City of Elizabeth v. American Nicholson Pavement Co.*, 97 U.S. 126, 134, 24 L.Ed. 1000 (1877). This doctrine is based on the underlying policy of providing an inventor time to determine if the invention is suitable for its intended purpose, in effect, to reduce the invention to practice. *See id.* at 137 ("It is sometimes said that an inventor acquires an undue advantage over the public by delaying to take out a patent ... but this cannot be said with justice when the delay is occasioned by a bona fide effort to bring his invention to perfection, or to ascertain whether it will answer the purpose intended."). If a use is experimental, it is not, as a matter of law, a public use within the meaning of section 102.

To determine whether a use is "experimental," a question of law, the totality of the circumstances must be considered, including various objective indicia of experimentation surrounding the use, such as the number of prototypes and duration of testing, whether records or progress reports were made concerning the testing, the existence of a secrecy agreement between the patentee and the party performing the testing, whether the patentee received compensation for the use of the invention, and the extent of control the inventor maintained over the testing. The last factor of control is critically important, because, if the inventor has no control over the alleged experiments, he is not experimenting. If he does not inquire about the testing or receive reports concerning the results, similarly, he is not experimenting.

In order to justify a determination that legally sufficient experimentation has occurred, there must be present certain minimal indicia. The framework might be quite formal, as may be expected when large corporations conduct experiments, governed by contracts and explicit written obligations. When individual inventors or small business units are involved, however, less formal and seemingly casual experiments can be expected. Such less formal experiments may be deemed legally sufficient to avoid the public use bar, but only if they demonstrate the presence of the same basic elements that are required validate any experimental program. Our case law sets out these elements. The question framed on this appeal is whether Lough's alleged experiments lacked enough of these required indicia so that his efforts cannot, as a matter of law, be recognized as experimental.

Here, Lough either admits or does not dispute the following facts. In the spring of 1986, he noted that the upper seal assembly in Brunswick inboard/outboard boats was failing due to galvanic corrosion between the annular seal and the aperture provided for the upper seal assembly in the aluminum bell housing. He solved this problem by isolating the annular seal from the aluminum bell housing in order to prevent corrosion. After some trial and error, Lough made six prototypes. He installed the first prototype in his own boat. Lough testified at trial that after the first prototype had been in his boat for three months and he determined that it worked, he provided the other prototypes to friends and acquaintances in order to find out if the upper seal assemblies would work as well in their boats as it had worked in his boat. Lough installed one prototype in the boat of his friend, Tom Nikla. A prototype was also installed in the boat of Jim Yow, co-owner of the dealership where Lough worked. Lough installed a fourth prototype in one of the dealership's customers who had considerable problems with corrosion in his stern drive unit. The final two prototypes were given to friends who were employed at a different marina in Florida. These friends installed one prototype in the boat of Mark Liberman, a local charter guide. They installed the other prototype in a demonstration boat at their marina. Subsequently, this boat was sold. Neither Lough nor his friends knew what happened with either the prototype or the demonstration boat after the boat was sold. After providing the five prototypes to these third parties, Lough neither asked for nor received any comments concerning the operability of these prototypes.

Accepting that the jury found these facts, which either were undisputed or were as asserted by Lough, it cannot be reasonably disputed that Lough's use of the invention was not "experimental" so as to negate a conclusion of public use. It is true that Lough did not receive any compensation for the use of the prototypes. He did not place the seal assembly on sale before applying for a patent. Lough's lack of commercialization, however, is not dispositive of the public use question in view of his failure to present objective evidence of experimentation. Lough kept no records of the alleged testing. Nor did he inspect the seal assemblies after they had been installed by other mechanics. He provided the seal assemblies to friends and acquaintances, but without any provision for follow-up involvement by him in assessment of the events occurring during the alleged experiments, and at least one seal was installed in a boat that was later sold to strangers. Thus, Lough did not maintain any supervision and control over the seals during the alleged testing.

Lough argues that other evidence supports a finding that his uses were experimental, including his own testimony that the prototypes were installed for experimental purposes and the fact that the prototypes were used in such a manner that they were unlikely to be seen by the public. However, "the expression by an inventor of his subjective intent to experiment, particularly after institution of litigation, is generally of minimal value." In addition, the fact that the prototypes were unlikely to be seen by the public does not support Lough's position. As the Supreme Court stated in *Egbert v. Lippmann:*

> [S]ome inventions are by their very character only capable of being used where they cannot be seen or observed by the public eye. An invention may consist of a lever or spring, hidden in the running gear of a watch, or of a rachet, shaft, or cog-wheel covered from view in the recesses of a machine for spinning or weaving. Nevertheless, if its inventor sells a machine of which his invention forms a part, and allows it to be used without restriction of any kind, the use is a public one.

104 U.S. at 336. Moreover, those to whom he gave the prototypes constituted "the public," in the absence of meaningful evidence of experimentation. Thus, we find Lough's reliance on this additional evidence to be of minimal value when viewed in light of the totality of the other circumstances surrounding the alleged experimentation.

We therefore hold that the jury had no legal basis to conclude that the uses of Lough's prototypes were experimental and that the prototypes were not in public use prior to the critical date. Our holding is consistent with the policy underlying the experimental use negation, that of providing an inventor time to determine if the invention is suitable for its intended purpose, i.e., to reduce the invention to practice. Lough's activities clearly were not consistent with that policy. We do not dispute that it may have been desirable in this case for Lough to have had his prototypes installed by mechanics of various levels of skill in boats that were exposed to different conditions. Moreover, Lough was free to test his invention in boats of friends and acquaintances to further verify that his invention worked for its intended purpose; however, Lough was required to maintain some degree of control and feedback over those uses of the prototypes if those tests were to negate public use. Lough's failure to monitor the use of his prototypes by his acquaintances, in addition to the lack of records or reports from those acquaintances concerning the operability of the devices, compel the conclusion that, as a matter of law, he did not engage in experimental use. Lough in effect provided the prototype seal assemblies to members of the public for their free and unrestricted use. The law does not waive statutory requirements for inventors of lesser sophistication. When one distributes his invention to members of the public under circumstances that evidence a near total disregard for supervision and control concerning its use, the absence of these minimal indicia of experimentation require a conclusion that the invention was in public use.

We conclude that the jury's determination that Lough's use of the invention was experimental so as to defeat the assertion of public use was incorrect as a matter of law. The court thus erred in denying Brunswick's JMOL motion on the validity of claims 1–4 of the '775 patent under § 102(b).

LOUGH v. BRUNSWICK CORP.

United States Court of Appeals, Federal Circuit, 1997.
103 F.3d 1517, 41 U.S.P.Q.2d 1385.

CIRCUIT JUDGES NEWMAN, PLAGER, MICHEL, and RADER issued opinions dissenting from the order denying *en banc* reconsideration of this case.

RADER, CIRCUIT JUDGE, dissenting from Order declining the suggestion for rehearing in banc.

Because I believe the *Lough* court lacks authority for this departure and complicates a quagmire of already confusing law on statutory bars, I must respectfully dissent from this court's decision to decline in banc rehearing.

* * *

A significant part of the Lough court's error is abstracting experimentation out of the public use inquiry and designating it a separate "question of law." *Lough*, 86 F.3d at 1120. This incorrect methodology flies in the face of the teaching in *TP Lab*. This court in *TP Lab*. taught that experimental use is not an exception to public use, but a negation. In other words, experimental use is not a separate exception with its own standard of review or its own multi-factored test. Instead an experimental use by definition does not abandon the invention to the public.

Disregarding *TP Lab*., the *Lough* court addressed itself to a separate doctrine of experimental use, for which it created a new standard of review separate from public use. The jury and the trial court had correctly answered the correct question: whether Lough gave his invention into public use. The *Lough* court transformed the question: "The question framed on appeal is whether Lough's alleged experiments lacked enough of these required indicia so that his efforts cannot, as a matter of law, be recognized as experimental." 86 F.3d at 1121. To reach its incorrect result, the *Lough* court had to separate experimental use from its proper context of public use, then create a separate list of required elements for a factual inquiry, and finally make the separate list a question of law to avoid the deference due to the jury verdict. Each error sent the *Lough* court fishing in deeper waters without a license.

The *Lough* court made the same mistake as the trial court in *TP Lab.*: "[I]t is incorrect to impose on the patent owner, as the trial court in this case did, the burden of proving that a 'public use' was 'experimental.'" 724 F.2d at 971. In fact, in *TP Lab.*, the inventor had used the invention nearly four years before filing, id. at 967, had kept only records that were "scanty at best," *id.* at 969, and had shown control over the invention only "inherently by the dentist-patient relationship," *id.* at 972. Yet the Federal Circuit, in a case strikingly similar to *Lough*, discerned no public use. *Id.* at 973. More important, the Federal Circuit in *TP Lab.* warned against divorcing experimentation from its public use context—the *Lough* court's initial false turn on its unauthorized fishing expedition.

* * *

Lough illustrates the arbitrariness of reapplying a factual "totality of circumstances" test on an appellate record without any deference to the fact-finding of the trial court. *Lough* lists several indicia of experimentation, including: 1) the number of prototypes and the duration of testing; 2) the attention to records or reports during testing; 3) the existence of a confidentiality arrangement; 4) the receipt of any commercial advantage by the patentee; and 5) the inventor's control over the testing. Although a brief review of prior Federal Circuit cases calls into question the sufficiency of this listing, at this point it is more important to show that the *Lough* court's application of its own indicia conflicts with binding Federal Circuit cases.

Beginning with the first indicator, *Lough* gave no analysis to its own first factor at all. The *Lough* court might have noted Lough's few prototypes or the limited duration of his testing. In fact, in view of the six years of open air testing in *City of Elizabeth*, 97 U.S. at 133, or more than a year of open display in *Moleculon*, 793 F.2d at 1263, the *Lough* court might well have followed prior cases to assess this indicator strongly in favor of experimentation. After all, Lough conducted a far more limited test than in *City of Elizabeth*, limiting his testing to six invisible prototypes over the course of one year to ensure his invention would work in the harsh marine environment.

On the second indicator, the *Lough* court weighed this harshly against Lough to undercut his experimentation claim. The Lough court declined to note that, although not keeping formal written records, Lough had taken photographs to monitor the installed seal assemblies during the experimentation period. In view of several cases that detected an experimental use despite a lack of formal record keeping on the testing, *TP Lab.*, 724 F.2d at 969 (finding experimental use with "scanty" records "at best"); *Manville Sales*, 917 F.2d at 551 (finding experimental use with one memorandum of intent to experiment, but no records of testing), the *Lough* court might well have followed prior cases in seeing this factor as no obstacle to Lough's claim of experimentation.

The *Lough* court did not analyze its own third indicator. Lough, however, testified that he only shared his experimental prototypes with a few individuals—with whom he shared a close personal or professional relationship—who he knew would maintain his secrecy. In view of Federal Circuit cases that inferred confidentiality on the basis of the close association of the patentee and the testers, *see, e.g., Moleculon*, 793 F.2d at 1266, *TP Lab.*, 724 F.2d at 972, the *Lough* court might well have weighed this indicator in favor of, rather than against, experimentation.

On the fourth indicator, the *Lough* court luke-warmly acknowledged Lough's steadfast refusal to commercially exploit his invention before filing. In view of Federal Circuit cases that attached great, perhaps dispositive weight, to this factor, *see, e.g., Ferag AG v. Quipp, Inc.*, 45 F.3d 1562, 1566, (Fed.Cir.1995) ("Foremost among these is the policy of preventing inventors from exploiting the commercial value of their inventions while deferring the beginning of the statutory term.") and *Moleculon*, 793 F.2d at 1266–67, the *Lough* court might well have given this factor considerable weight in favor of a finding of experimentation.

On the fifth indicator, the *Lough* court weighed this strongly against Lough. Once again, however, the record shows that Lough selected friends and professional associates over whom he had control by virtue of their relationship. In view of prior Federal Circuit cases permitting close relationship and notification of experimental purpose to substitute for full control, *see, e.g., Moleculon*, 793 F.2d at 1266–67, and *LaBounty Mfg. v. United States International Trade Commission*, 958 F.2d 1066, 1072 (Fed.Cir.1992) (suggesting that notification of experimental purpose may substitute for control), the *Lough* court might well have balanced this factor in favor of Lough.

Further, to buttress its own factual finding on appeal that Lough lacked control over the experiment, the *Lough* court used reasoning in conflict with other Federal Circuit cases. For instance, the *Lough* court noted that the experimental use involved Lough's associates rather than Lough himself. *Lough*, 86 F.3d at 1121–22. Other binding Federal Circuit cases have held that participation by others in the experiment does not show a lack of control. *See TP Lab.*, 724 F.2d at 972 ("routine checking of [success of invention] by one of the [inventor's associates] does not indicate the inventor's lack of control"); *Grain Processing Corp. v. American Maize–Prods. Co.*, 840 F.2d 902, 906 (Fed.Cir.1988) (submitting samples of invention to food manufacturers for determination of the product's utility did not negate experimentation). Additionally, the *Lough* court criticized the fact that one of the boats containing the experimental seal was sold at some point after the conclusion of the experiment. This indicator has also been held not to constitute a loss of control. *See Watson v. Allen,* 254 F.2d 342, 347 (D.C.Cir.1958) ("We believe the protective umbrella of the experimental use doctrine should include reasonable disposal of models and prototypes of the invention once their usefulness to the inventor has ended—reasonable in view of the nature of the device and the probability of discovery and appropriation of the invention by strangers."); *Goodwin v. Borg–Warner Corp.,* 157 F.2d 267, 273 (6th Cir.1946) (finding experimentation although automobile containing seal was later sold).

Moreover, several binding Federal Circuit cases analyze indicators the *Lough* court chose to ignore. These unacknowledged indicators further buttress Lough's case against a public use. For instance, another indicator appearing in binding precedents is the inventor's careful tailoring of the tests to the nature of the invention. The record shows Lough designed his experiments to test the invention in various kinds of boats in various marine environments. Indeed a careful assessment of this indicator might also recognize that the necessity of testing under varying circumstances militates against maintenance of full control at all times over the testing.

Still another indicator appearing in binding precedents is the hidden nature of an experiment. In determining whether an inventor intended to experiment, an invisible use may add plausibility to the inventor's explanation that he perceived little need to take further precautions to protect confidentiality. *See, e.g., Manville Sales,* 917 F.2d at 550 ("[T]he invention was mounted atop a 150–foot tall pole in a rest area still closed to the public, making it very unlikely that the public would even see the new design."); *Allied Colloids,* 64 F.3d at 1574 (public access to and knowledge of the public use is one of the factors to consider). This factor, too, if considered by the *Lough* court, would have helped Lough. In picking and choosing amongst its "totality of circumstances," the *Lough* court sadly did not consider the totality of the circumstances.

In sum, this brief comparison of the *Lough* court's assessment of the totality of the circumstances with the same assessment by prior Federal Circuit cases shows the plastic malleability of a totality of circumstances test when divorced from the discipline of a deferential standard of review. An appellate panel can pick and choose amongst malleable circumstances to reach results irreconcilable with other Federal Circuit decisions.

This comparison also shows the plausibility of the jury's unanimous verdict in Lough. For each and every indicator under the *Lough* court's abbreviated totality of circumstances analysis, this record provides factual support for the jury's conclusion.

Notes

1. Undercurrents. One theme running beneath the surface of the Federal Circuit's various views of the *Lough* case is Lough's status as a single "garage" inventor without the legal or experimental resources of a corporate laboratory. Is a legal distinction based on the inventor's status justified? How does the inventor's status affect the application of the statutory bar criteria?

2. Is the Standard of Review Issue on Statutory Bars Resolved? The dissenters from *en banc* reconsideration suggested that the *Lough* majority misapplied the standard of review: "The outcome of *Lough* turns on the standard of review applied by this court. With any level of proper deference to the fact-finding of those who heard seventeen days of evidence, this court must have affirmed. The court in *Lough*, however, purported to abandon factual inquiry." 86 F.3d at 1120. For the proposition that statutory bars should be reviewed as questions of law without deference, the *Lough* court cites *Manville Sales Corp. v. Paramount Systems, Inc.*, 917 F.2d 544, 549 (Fed.Cir.1990). *Manville*, however, does not stand for the proposition for which *Lough* cites it:

> Whether or not an invention was on sale or in public use within the meaning of section 102(b) is a question of law that this court reviews de novo; however, factual findings underlying the trial court's conclusion are subject to the clearly erroneous standard of review.

917 F.2d at 549. The *Lough* court follows the first part of the above sentence in *Manville* almost verbatim. The *Lough* court, without explanation, refuses to quote or follow the rest of the sentence in *Manville*. *Lough*, 103 F. 3d at 1532 (Rader, J., dissenting).

A few weeks after the opinions issued in *Lough*, Judge Lourie wrote for a panel consisting of himself and Judges Clevenger and Rader. The Federal Circuit determined that the district court had properly found that experimentation negated any bar on gloves made of cut-resistant yarn. Kolmes had given a limited number of gloves to a few meat-packing plants to test their workability. Kolmes also requested confidentiality and sought reports on the gloves. In stating the standard of review, the court quoted *Manville Sales* exactly:

> "Whether or not an invention was on-sale or in public use within the meaning of section 102(b) is a question of law that this court reviews de novo; however, factual findings underlying the trial court's conclusion are subject to the clearly erroneous standard."

Kolmes v. World Fibers Corp. 107 F.3d 1534, 1540, 41 U.S.P.Q.2d 1829, 1832 (Fed.Cir.1997) (citation deleted). Would application of the clearly erroneous standard, which apparently remains the law, have changed the outcome in *Lough* as the dissenters insist? Or, did the Federal Circuit in *Lough* make a legal judgment that the inventor had not qualified for the experimental use negation by failing to seek reports on his alleged experimental uses? Could the answer to both of the above questions be "yes?"

3. Experimental Use—Exception or Negation? As noted earlier, *TP Lab.* established that "it is incorrect to impose on the patent owner . . . the burden of proving that a 'public use' was 'experimental.' These are not two separate issues. It is incorrect to ask: 'Was it a public use?' and then, 'Was it experimental?' Rather the trial court is faced with a single issue: 'Was it a public use . . . ?' 724 F.2d at 971. This passage teaches that experimental use is not an exception to public use, but a negation. Is that a major flaw in *Lough*, namely the Federal Circuit sets up separate requirements for a separate doctrine of experimental use, instead of analyzing the case under the public use criteria? Didn't the jury answer the correct question: is there a public use?"

Lough performed at least one significant service. It identified the statutory bars as an area of uncertainty. The Supreme Court noticed and soon took action.

§ 5.1[c]   "On Sale"

PFAFF v. WELLS ELECTRONICS, INC.

Supreme Court of the United States, 1998.
525 U.S. 55.

JUSTICE STEVENS delivered the opinion for a unanimous court:

Section 102(b) of the Patent Act of 1952 provides that no person is entitled to patent an "invention" that has been "on sale" more than one year before filing a patent application. We granted certiorari to determine whether the commercial marketing of a newly invented product may mark the beginning of the 1–year period even though the invention has not yet been reduced to practice.

I

On April 19, 1982, petitioner, Wayne Pfaff, filed an application for a patent on a computer chip socket. Therefore, April 19, 1981, constitutes the critical date for purposes of the on-sale bar of 35 U.S.C. § 102(b); if the 1–year period began to run before that date, Pfaff lost his right to patent his invention.

Pfaff commenced work on the socket in November 1980, when representatives of Texas Instruments asked him to develop a new device for mounting and removing semiconductor chip carriers. In response to this request, he prepared detailed engineering drawings that described the design, the dimensions, and the materials to be used in making the socket. Pfaff sent those drawings to a manufacturer in February or March 1981.

Prior to March 17, 1981, Pfaff showed a sketch of his concept to representatives of Texas Instruments. On April 8, 1981, they provided Pfaff with a written confirmation of a previously placed oral purchase order for 30,100 of his new sockets for a total price of $91,155. In accord with his normal practice, Pfaff did not make and test a prototype of the new device before offering to sell it in commercial quantities.

The manufacturer took several months to develop the customized tooling necessary to produce the device, and Pfaff did not fill the order until July 1981. The evidence therefore indicates that Pfaff first reduced his invention to practice in the summer of 1981. The socket achieved substantial commercial success before Patent No. 4,491,377 ('377 patent) issued to Pfaff on January 1, 1985.

After the patent issued, petitioner brought an infringement action against respondent, Wells Electronics, Inc., the manufacturer of a competing socket. Wells prevailed on the basis of a finding of no infringement. When respondent began to market a modified device, petitioner brought this suit, alleging that the modifications infringed six of the claims in the '377 patent.

After a full evidentiary hearing before a Special Master, the District Court held that two of those claims (1 and 6) were invalid because they had been anticipated in the prior art. Nevertheless, the court concluded that four other claims (7, 10, 11, and 19) were valid and three (7, 10, and 11) were infringed by various models of respondent's sockets. Adopting the Special Master's findings, the District Court rejected respondent's § 102(b) defense because Pfaff had filed the application for the '377 patent less than a year after reducing the invention to practice.

The Court of Appeals reversed, finding all six claims invalid. 124 F.3d 1429 (C.A.Fed.1997). Four of the claims (1, 6, 7, and 10) described the socket that Pfaff had sold to Texas Instruments prior to April 8, 1981. Because that device had been offered for sale on a commercial basis more than one year before the patent application was filed on April 19, 1982, the court concluded that those claims were invalid under § 102(b). That conclusion rested on the court's view that as long as the invention was "substantially complete at the time of sale," the 1–year period began to run, even though the invention had not yet been reduced to practice. Id., at 1434. The other two claims (11 and 19) described a feature that had not been included in Pfaff's initial design, but the Court of Appeals concluded as a matter of law that the additional feature was not itself patentable because it was an obvious addition to the prior art. Given the court's § 102(b) holding, the prior art included Pfaff's first four claims.

Because other courts have held or assumed that an invention cannot be "on sale" within the meaning of § 102(b) unless and until it has been reduced to practice, *see, e.g., Timely Products Corp. v. Arron*, 523 F.2d 288, 299–302 (C.A.2 1975), and because the text of § 102(b) makes no reference to "substantial completion" of an invention, we granted certiorari. 523 U.S. 1003, 118 S.Ct. 1183, 140 L.Ed.2d 315 (1998).

II

The primary meaning of the word "invention" in the Patent Act unquestionably refers to the inventor's conception rather than to a physical embodiment of that idea. The statute does not contain any express requirement that an invention must be reduced to practice before it can be patented. Neither the statutory definition of the term in § 100 nor the basic conditions for obtaining a patent set forth in § 101 make any mention of "reduction to practice." The statute's only specific reference to that term is found in § 102(g), which sets forth the standard for resolving priority contests between two competing claimants to a patent. That subsection provides:

> "In determining priority of invention there shall be considered not only the respective dates of conception and reduction to practice of the invention, but also the reasonable diligence of one who was first to conceive and last to reduce to practice, from a time prior to conception by the other."

Thus, assuming diligence on the part of the applicant, it is normally the first inventor to conceive, rather than the first to reduce to practice, who establishes the right to the patent.

It is well settled that an invention may be patented before it is reduced to practice. In 1888, this Court upheld a patent issued to Alexander Graham Bell even though he had filed his application before constructing a working telephone. Chief Justice Waite's reasoning in that case merits quoting at length:

> "It is quite true that when Bell applied for his patent he had never actually transmitted telegraphically spoken words so that they could be distinctly heard and understood at the receiving end of his line, but in his specification he did describe accurately and with admirable clearness his process, that is to say, the exact electrical condition that must be created to accomplish his purpose, and he also described, with sufficient precision to enable one of ordinary skill in such matters to make it, a form of apparatus which, if used in the way pointed out, would produce the required effect, receive the words, and carry them to and deliver them at the appointed place. The particular instrument which he had, and which he used in his experiments, did not, under the circumstances in which it was tried, reproduce the words spoken, so that they could be clearly understood, but the proof is abundant and of the most convincing character, that other instruments, carefully constructed and made exactly in accordance with the specification, without any additions whatever, have operated and will operate successfully. A good mechanic of proper skill in matters of the kind can take the patent and, by following the specification strictly, can, without more, construct an apparatus which, when used in the way pointed out, will do all that it is claimed the method or process will do. . . ."

> "The law does not require that a discoverer or inventor, in order to get a patent for a process, must have succeeded in bringing his art to the highest degree of perfection. It is enough if he describes his method with sufficient clearness and precision to enable those skilled in the matter to understand what the process is, and if he points out some practicable way of putting it into operation." *The Telephone Cases*, 126 U.S. 1, 535–536, 8 S.Ct. 778, 31 L.Ed. 863 (1888).

When we apply the reasoning of *The Telephone Cases* to the facts of the case before us today, it is evident that Pfaff could have obtained a patent on his novel socket when he accepted the purchase order from

Texas Instruments for 30,100 units. At that time he provided the manufacturer with a description and drawings that had "sufficient clearness and precision to enable those skilled in the matter" to produce the device. The parties agree that the sockets manufactured to fill that order embody Pfaff's conception as set forth in claims 1, 6, 7, and 10 of the '377 patent. We can find no basis in the text of § 102(b) or in the facts of this case for concluding that Pfaff's invention was not "on sale" within the meaning of the statute until after it had been reduced to practice.

III

Pfaff nevertheless argues that longstanding precedent, buttressed by the strong interest in providing inventors with a clear standard identifying the onset of the 1–year period, justifies a special interpretation of the word "invention" as used in § 102(b). We are persuaded that this nontextual argument should be rejected.

As we have often explained, most recently in *Bonito Boats, Inc. v. Thunder Craft Boats, Inc.*, 489 U.S. 141, 151, 109 S.Ct. 971(1989), the patent system represents a carefully crafted bargain that encourages both the creation and the public disclosure of new and useful advances in technology, in return for an exclusive monopoly for a limited period of time. The balance between the interest in motivating innovation and enlightenment by rewarding invention with patent protection on the one hand, and the interest in avoiding monopolies that unnecessarily stifle competition on the other, has been a feature of the federal patent laws since their inception.

Consistent with these ends, § 102 of the Patent Act serves as a limiting provision, both excluding ideas that are in the public domain from patent protection and confining the duration of the monopoly to the statutory term. *See, e.g., Frantz Mfg. Co. v. Phenix Mfg. Co.*, 457 F.2d 314, 320 (C.A.7 1972).

We originally held that an inventor loses his right to a patent if he puts his invention into public use before filing a patent application. "His voluntary act or acquiescence in the public sale and use is an abandonment of his right." *Pennock v. Dialogue*, 2 Pet. 1, 24, 7 L.Ed. 327 (1829) (Story, J.). A similar reluctance to allow an inventor to remove existing knowledge from public use undergirds the on-sale bar.

Nevertheless, an inventor who seeks to perfect his discovery may conduct extensive testing without losing his right to obtain a patent for his invention—even if such testing occurs in the public eye. The law has long recognized the distinction between inventions put to experimental use and products sold commercially. *Elizabeth v. American Nicholson Pavement Co.*, 97 U.S. 126, 137 (1877).

The patent laws therefore seek both to protect the public's right to retain knowledge already in the public domain and the inventor's right to control whether and when he may patent his invention. The Patent Act of 1836, 5 Stat. 117, was the first statute that expressly included an on-sale bar to the issuance of a patent. Like the earlier holding in *Pennock*, that provision precluded patentability if the invention had been placed on sale at any time before the patent application was filed. In 1839, Congress ameliorated that requirement by enacting a 2–year grace period in which the inventor could file an application. 5 Stat. 353.

In *Andrews v. Hovey*, 123 U.S. 267, 274, 8 S.Ct. 101 (1887), we noted that the purpose of that amendment was "to fix a period of limitation which should be certain"; it required the inventor to make sure that a patent application was filed "within two years from the completion of his invention," *ibid*. In 1939, Congress reduced the grace period from two years to one year. 53 Stat. 1212.

Petitioner correctly argues that these provisions identify an interest in providing inventors with a definite standard for determining when a patent application must be filed. A rule that makes the timeliness of an application depend on the date when an invention is "substantially complete" seriously undermines the interest in certainty. Moreover, such a rule finds no support in the text of the statute. Thus, petitioner's argument calls into question the standard applied by the Court of Appeals, but it does not persuade us that it is necessary to engraft a reduction to practice element into the meaning of the term "invention" as used in § 102(b). The Federal Circuit has developed a multifactor, "totality of the circumstances" test to determine the trigger for the on-sale bar. *See, e.g., Micro Chemical, Inc. v. Great Plains Chemical Co.*, 103 F.3d 1538, 1544 (C.A.Fed.1997). As the Federal Circuit itself has noted, this test "has been criticized as unnecessarily vague." *Seal-Flex, Inc. v. Athletic Track & Court Construction*, 98 F.3d 1318, 1323, n. 2 (C.A.Fed. 1996).

The word "invention" must refer to a concept that is complete, rather than merely one that is "substantially complete." It is true that reduction to practice ordinarily provides the best evidence that an invention is complete. But just because reduction to practice is sufficient evidence of completion, it does not follow that proof of reduction to practice is necessary in every case. Indeed, both the facts of *The Telephone Cases* and the facts of this case demonstrate that one can prove that an invention is complete and ready for patenting before it has actually been reduced to practice.

We conclude, therefore, that the on-sale bar applies when two conditions are satisfied before the critical date. First, the product must be the subject of a commercial offer for sale. An inventor can both understand and control the timing of the first commercial marketing of his invention. The experimental use doctrine, for example, has not generated concerns about indefiniteness, and we perceive no reason why unmanageable uncertainty should attend a rule that measures the application of the on-sale bar of § 102(b) against the date when an invention that is ready for patenting is first marketed commercially. In this case the acceptance of the purchase order prior to April 8, 1981, makes it clear that such an offer had been made, and there is no question that the sale was commercial rather than experimental in character.

Second, the invention must be ready for patenting. That condition may be satisfied in at least two ways: by proof of reduction to practice before the critical date; or by proof that prior to the critical date the inventor had prepared drawings or other descriptions of the invention that were sufficiently specific to enable a person skilled in the art to practice the invention. In this case the second condition of the on-sale bar is satisfied because the drawings Pfaff sent to the manufacturer before the critical date fully disclosed the invention.

The evidence in this case thus fulfills the two essential conditions of the on-sale bar. As succinctly stated by Learned Hand:

> "[I]t is a condition upon an inventor's right to a patent that he shall not exploit his discovery competitively after it is ready for patenting; he must content himself with either secrecy, or legal monopoly." *Metallizing Engineering Co. v. Kenyon Bearing & Auto Parts Co.*, 153 F.2d 516, 520 (C.A.2 1946).

The judgment of the Court of Appeals finds support not only in the text of the statute but also in the basic policies underlying the statutory scheme, including § 102(b). When Pfaff accepted the purchase order for his new sockets prior to April 8, 1981, his invention was ready for patenting. The fact that the manufacturer was able to produce the socket using his detailed drawings and specifications demonstrates this fact. Furthermore, those sockets contained all the elements of the invention claimed in the '377 patent. Therefore, Pfaff's '377 patent is invalid because the invention had been on sale for more than one year in this country before he filed his patent application. Accordingly, the judgment of the Court of Appeals is affirmed.

Notes

1. **The Problem Solved by *Pfaff*.** *Pfaff* does not address at length the problem that it solved. The inventive process, of course, generally occurs in increments. As the inventor progresses slowly day by day toward solution of a problem, events may often transpire that place the emerging technology in public use or on sale. Perhaps the marketing department works independent of the engineering department. This poses a difficult question: At what point is the invention sufficiently complete to have been in public use or on sale? Despite some earlier case law suggesting a reduction to practice standard for invention completeness (invention in existence and proven to operate for its intended purpose), *Timely Prods. v. Arron*, 523 F.2d 288 (2d Cir.1975), the Federal Circuit set a confusing standard from the outset. *UMC Electronics Co. v. U.S.*, 816 F.2d 647 (Fed.Cir.1987). In *UMC*, a government contractor offered to sell the U.S. a sophisticated device for Navy aircraft. At the time of this offer to sell, the contractor had not yet completed this new device. In finding sufficient completeness to impose a bar, the Federal Circuit declined to apply the reduction to practice standard and instead invoked a confusing standard: "[T]he challenger has the burden of proving ... that the subject matter of the sale or offer to sell fully

anticipated the claimed invention or would have rendered the claimed invention obvious by its addition to the prior art." Aside from the question of how an invention becomes "prior art" against itself, this formulation offered almost no clear rule for the completeness problem. Sometimes the Federal Circuit would attempt to apply this confusing rule. *See, e.g., Envirotech Corp. v. Westech Eng'g, Inc.*, 904 F.2d 1571 (Fed.Cir.1990). Other times the Federal Circuit declined to apply the *UMC* rule in favor of other tests. *See, e.g., Micro Chem.Inc. v. Great Plains Chem. Co.*, 103 F.3d 1538 (Fed.Cir.1997)(substantially completed invention with reason to expect that it would work for its intended purpose upon completion). Did the Supreme Court's decision alleviate this competition of standards?

2.   The Federal Circuit's Application of the Supreme Court's Answer. As discussed above, before *Pfaff*, the bar would operate if the claimed invention was merely obvious in light of what was offered for sale. In *Scaltech, Inc. v. Retec/Tetra, LLC*, 156 F.3d 1193 (1998), a case initially decided before *Pfaff*, Judge Rich relied on *UMC*'s obviousness test to determine if an invention was obvious in light of the process offered for sale. When *Pfaff* issued, Judge Rich granted a petition for rehearing and revised the opinion:

> If the process that was offered for sale inherently possessed each of the claim limitations, then the process was on sale.

Inherency, of course, is a principle of anticipation requiring a showing that the process offered for sale necessarily included (though not necessarily recognized to include) each of the claim limitations. Was this reading faithful to the "ready for patenting" test?

Another case is a nearly inexplicable return to the *UMC* standard. In *Tec Air Inc. v. Denso Mfg. Michigan Inc.*, 192 F.3d 1353 (Fed.Cir.1999), Chief Judge Mayer stated:

> Denso stresses that the August 1974 drawing shows that the invention was ready for patenting, thus satisfying the second prong of *Pfaff*. However, because the offer for sale did not involve subject matter that either anticipates the invention or would have rendered it obvious, *Pfaff*'s second prong is irrelevant. *Pfaff* did not remove the requirement that the subject matter of the commercial offer for sale be something within the scope of the claim.

Fortunately, the Federal Circuit has not persisted in this apparent rejection of *Pfaff*'s second prong. In more recent cases, the Federal Circuit has faithfully applied the enablement standard in *Pfaff*'s ready-for-patenting test. *Robotic Vision Sys. v. View Eng. Inc.*, 249 F.3d 1307 (Fed.Cir.2001):

> [T]he [trial] court [correctly] concluded that the invention was ready for patenting because the inventor's disclosure was also an enabling disclosure, *i.e.*, one that was sufficiently specific to enable his co-worker, who was a person skilled in the art, to practice the invention.

3.   Sale of Patent Rights. Suppose that an inventor sells all right, title and interest in an invention—in other words, any prospective patent rights themselves—prior to the critical date. Should this offer run afoul of the statutory bar of § 102(b)? *See Moleculon Research Corp. v. CBS, Inc.*, 793 F.2d 1261, 229 U.S.P.Q. 805 (Fed.Cir.1986). As you answer this question, consider the policies underlying the statutory bar, the business realities facing the employed inventor, and the practical difficulty of distinguishing sales of an embodiment of an invention from sales of the invention itself.

4. Sales to Related Parties. The courts have sometimes struggled with the commercial environment of technology-related industry, as transactions between joint ventures and commonly controlled corporations strain the boundaries of the § 102(b) bar. In *Ferag AG v. Quipp Inc.*, 45 F.3d 1562, 33 U.S.P.Q.2d 1512 (Fed.Cir.1995), the court noted that: "A section 102(b) sale or offer must involve separate entities. Where, as in this case, the parties to an alleged sale are related, it is more difficult to determine whether the inventor is attempting to commercialize his invention; accordingly, in such cases whether there is a statutory bar depends on whether the seller so controls the purchaser that the invention remains out of the public's hands." In *Ferag*, Judge Mayer considered a patentee's sale to its exclusive U.S. distributor, of which it retained only 50% ownership, and concluded: "Because Ferag could not control Ferag, Inc.'s marketing of the invention, the two companies were separate entities for section 102(b) purposes and the transaction between them gives rise to a statutory bar."

Continental Can Co. v. Monsanto Co., 948 F.2d 1264, 20 U.S.P.Q.2d 1746 (Fed.Cir.1991), went the other way when considering a confidential manufacturer-customer development project between a third party, Admiral Plastics, and the Coca–Cola Company. Under the terms of an agreement, Admiral produced various plastic bottles and supplied them to Coca–Cola for testing; the project was ultimately terminated because the bottles failed to fulfill certain contractually specified mechanical performance requirements. The court noted that

> [T]he "on sale" bar of § 102(b) does not arise simply because the intended customer was participating in development and testing. In *Baker Oil Tools, Inc. v. Geo Vann, Inc.*, 828 F.2d 1558, 1563–65, 4 U.S.P.Q.2d 1210, 1213–15 (Fed.Cir.1987), this court summarized various factors pertinent to the "on sale" bar when there is an issue concerning the relationship between the patentee and the customer: for example, whether there was a need for testing by other than the patentee; the amount of control exercised; the stage of development of the invention; whether payments were made and the basis thereof; whether confidentiality was required; and whether technological changes were made. All of the circumstances attending the relationship must be considered in light of the public policy underlying § 102(b).

On the facts of the case, the Federal Circuit concluded that the "Marcus bottle was part of a terminated development project that never bore fruit commercially and was cloaked in confidentiality. While the line is not always bright between development and being on sale, see generally *UMC Electronics*, in this case the line was not crossed." Selected portions of the *Continental Can* decision are reprinted in this casebook in Chapter 4.

5. Reduction to Practice and Experimental Use. The *Pfaff* rule could conflict with a great deal of prior case law on application of the experimental use negation. As a negation, experimental use is not an independent test, but an application of the standard statutory bar test of

Pfaff in a setting that does not suggest that a public use or offer for sale was commercial. Under a pure ready for patenting test, however, the point of assessing application of the bar moves back along the inventive continuum to the point where the inventor enables the invention. Does this leave much room for experimenting? Experimenting is usually associated with reducing the invention to practice. Thus, does the new test swallow the experimental use negation? The Federal Circuit confronted that question in *EZ Dock v. Schafer Sys. Inc.*, 276 F.3d 1347 (Fed.Cir.2002):

> In *Pfaff*, the Supreme Court expressly preserved the experimental use or sale negation of the section 102 bars: "Nevertheless, an inventor who seeks to perfect his discovery may conduct extensive testing without losing his right to obtain a patent for his invention—even if such testing occurs in the public eye. The law has long recognized the distinction between inventions put to experimental use and products sold commercially." *Pfaff*, 525 U.S. at 64. Indeed in *Pfaff*, the Supreme Court reiterated its guidance in *City of Elizabeth v. American Nicholson Pavement Co.*, 97 U.S. 126, 137 (1877), that an inventor does not inappropriately delay filing "by a bona fide effort to bring his invention to perfection, or to ascertain whether it will answer the purpose intended." Thus, the Supreme Court and this court apply the experimental use negation without conflict with the "ready for patenting" prong of the new on-sale bar test. Indeed as noted earlier, the Supreme Court acknowledged that a litigant may show readiness for patenting with evidence of reduction to practice. Like evidence of experimentation sufficient to negate a bar, reduction to practice involves proof that an invention will work for its intended purpose. Even beyond this overlap of the experimental use negation and the ready for patenting standard, however, the Supreme Court explicitly preserved proof of experimentation as a negation of statutory bars.

Judge Linn authored a thoughtful concurrence sustaining the result in *EZ Dock*, but reading the relationship between experimenting and *Pfaff* differently:

> Because nothing in *Pfaff* altered the transitional significance of reduction to practice for experimental use negation, the heretofore complementary nature of the two tests and the symmetry that such congruence brought to the analytical framework disappeared. Traversing this new landscape now demands in each case a careful examination of the purpose of the use contemplated in a potentially barring sale, not merely that the invention then may be in an experimental stage, and signals a shift in focus from the second prong to the first in evaluating experimental use negation.

Experimental use survives *Pfaff*, but apparently on a somewhat different footing. Incidentally, the facts of *EZ Dock* are very similar to the facts of *Lough*, but the result is different. To what do you attribute the difference?

6. The "Ready for Patenting" Standard in Canada. The next chapter in this book considers the rules of determining when an invention is made for the purposes of deciding who is the first inventor or other priority questions. These rules are far more complicated than the "ready for patenting" test in *Pfaff*. The Canadian patent system had used the "ready for patenting" rule for over 100 years to determine priority questions. As you proceed to chapter 6, consider whether the Canadian (*Pfaff*) approach would serve as a better mechanism for determining priority than the approach developed in the United States?

§ 5.2 THIRD PARTY ACTIVITIES § 102(B)

Section 102 states simply: "A person shall be entitled to a patent unless ... (b) the invention was ... in public use or on sale in this country, more than one year prior to the date of the application for patent in the United States." The statutory language says nothing about how the invention is put into public use or on sale. In the cases up to this point in this Chapter, the inventors themselves took some action that arguably exploited or disclosed their invention before the critical date. The next inquiry is different: What are the implications of someone other than the inventor putting the invention into public use or on sale before the critical date?

Intuition may tell you that an inventor should not be allowed to obtain patent protection for a technology that someone else has already placed into the public domain. The other individual's open public use should dissuade any would-be inventor from seeking exclusive rights in that technology. But suppose that the other individual's use of the invention could not be readily discerned by an observer? Alternatively, suppose that an individual had maintained a technology as a secret; should such a use suffice to bar an inventor a patent even though she brought the invention into public knowledge? This casebook considers these issues by dividing third party activities into three categories: uses which themselves inform others about the invention, uses which by their nature do not inform others about the invention, and secret uses.

§ 5.2[a] Informing Uses

ELECTRIC STORAGE BATTERY CO. v. SHIMADZU

United States Supreme Court, 1939.
307 U.S. 5, 59 S.Ct. 675.

MR. JUSTICE ROBERTS delivered the opinion of the Court.

The courts below have held valid and infringed certain claims of three patents granted to Genzo Shimadzu, a citizen and resident of Japan. The earliest is for a method of forming a finely divided and, consequently, more chemically reactive, lead powder. The second is for a method or process of manufacturing a fine powder composed of lead suboxide and metallic lead and for the product of the process. The third is for an apparatus for the continuous production of lead oxides in the form of a dry fine powder. Such powder is useful in the manufacture of plates for storage batteries.

The inventions which are the basis of the patents were conceived by Shimadzu and reduced to practise in Japan not later than August 1919. He did not disclose the inventions to anyone in the United States before he applied for United States patents. Application was presented for No. 1,584,149 on January 30, 1922; for No. 1,584,150 on July 14, 1923; and for No. 1,896,020 on April 27, 1926. The inventions were not patented or described in a printed publication in this or any foreign country prior to the filing of the applications. The petitioner, without knowledge of Shimadzu's inventions, began the use of a machine, which involved both the method and the apparatus of the patents, at Philadelphia, Pennsylvania, early in 1921 and attained commercial production in June 1921. Over the objection of the petitioner the respondents were permitted by testimony, and by the introduction of contemporaneous drawings and note books, to carry the date of invention back to August 1919, and the courts below fixed that as the date of invention and reduction to practise in Japan.

If a valid patent is to issue, the invention must not have been in public use in this country for more than two years prior to the filing of the application. Such public use is an affirmative defense to be pleaded and proved. The respondents insist that the findings respecting the defense, on which the petitioner relies, are unsupported by the evidence. We cannot agree with either position. * * *

In the present case the evidence is that the petitioner, since June 1921, has continuously employed the alleged infringing machine and process for the production of lead oxide powder used in the manufacture of plates for storage batteries which have been sold in quantity. There is no finding, and we think none would have been justified, to the effect that the machine, process, and product were not well known to the employes in the plant, or that efforts were made to conceal them from anyone who had a legitimate interest in understanding them. This use, begun more than two years before Shimadzu applied for patents 1,584,-150 and 1,896,020, invalidated the claims in suit.

Notes

1. **Informing Use.** The technology in *Electric Storage Battery* was buried in a battery. On what basis did the Supreme Court decide that this technology was in "public" use? This result, of course, is consistent with *Egbert*. Thus, this public use adequately informed the public of the presence in the public domain of the invention. Does the rule change when the invention does not inform the public of invention?

2. **The Statutory Bar Period.** In 1939, Congress shortened the two-year statutory bar period discussed in *Electric Storage Battery* to its present length of one year. The Senate Report offers an explanation:

> In 1839, when the period of 2 years was first adopted, it may have been a proper length of time for an inventor to make up his mind whether or not to file a patent application for patent. Under present conditions 2 years appears unduly long and operates as a handicap to industry. Reduction of the period would serve to bring the date of patenting closer to the time when the invention is made, and would expedite applications, not only in their filing but also in their process

through the Patent Office. One year is believed to be a very fair period for all concerned.

How does a reduction in the bar period possibly bring the date of patenting close to the time the invention was made? At any rate, are you impressed with the quantitative nature of the congressional determination of the optimal grace period? Have contemporary artifacts sufficiently changed industrial conditions such that the statutory bar period should be shortened again?

§ 5.2[b] Non-informing Uses

ABBOTT LABORATORIES v. GENEVA PHARMACEUTICALS, INC.

United States Court of Appeals for the Federal Circuit, 1999.
182 F.3d 1315.

Before PLAGER, LOURIE, and BRYSON, CIRCUIT JUDGES.

LOURIE, CIRCUIT JUDGE.

Abbott Laboratories appeals from the summary judgment of the United States District Court for the Northern District of Illinois holding claim 4 of its United States Patent 5,504,207 invalid under the on-sale provision of 35 U.S.C. § 102(b) (1994). *See Abbott Labs. v. Geneva Pharms., Inc.* (N.D.Ill. Sept. 1, 1998). Because we conclude that the district court properly granted summary judgment of invalidity, we affirm.

BACKGROUND

Terazosin hydrochloride is a pharmaceutical compound used for the treatment of hypertension and benign prostatic hyperplasia. Abbott Laboratories has marketed it exclusively under the trademark Hytrin since 1987. Abbott's Hytrin tablets contain the dihydrate crystalline form of terazosin hydrochloride. Terazosin hydrochloride also exists in four anhydrous crystalline forms, and claim 4 of the '207 patent specifically claims the Form IV anhydrate. Claim 4 reads as follows: "4. The anhydrous Form IV crystalline modification of 1–(4–amino–6, 7–dimethoxy–2–quinazolinyl)–4–(2–tetrahydrofuroyl)piperazine hydrochloride characterized by principal peaks in the powder X-ray diffraction pattern at values of. . . ." The particular peaks are not important to the resolution of this case.

Abbott sued Geneva Pharmaceuticals, Inc., Novopharm Limited, and Invamed, Inc. for infringement of the '207 patent after each of them filed an Abbreviated New Drug Application (ANDA) at the United States Food and Drug Administration seeking approval to market a generic version of Hytrin containing the Form IV anhydrate. It is an act of patent infringement under certain circumstances to file an ANDA seeking approval to commercially manufacture, use, or sell a drug claimed in a patent before the expiration date of such patent. *See* 35 U.S.C. § 271(e)(2)(A) (1994). It is undisputed that such circumstances apply here. The cases were consolidated in the United States District Court for the Northern District of Illinois. The defendants each raised the affirmative defense of patent invalidity under the on-sale bar of 35 U.S.C. § 102(b), asserting that Form IV was anticipated because it was sold in the United States more than one year before the '207 patent's filing date, October 18, 1994.

It is undisputed on appeal that a company not party to this law suit, Byron Chemical Company, Inc., made at least three sales of Form IV terazosin hydrochloride anhydrate in the United States more than one year before the October 18, 1994 filing date. Byron sold a five-kilogram lot of anhydrous terazosin hydrochloride during the 1989–90 period and another lot in 1991 to defendant Geneva. Byron sold a third lot to Warner Chilcott Laboratories in 1992. Byron did not manufacture the compound itself; it bought it from two foreign manufacturers—Imhausen–Chemie GMBH in Germany and Yogodawa Pharmaceutical Company in Japan. None of these sales transactions specified which crystalline form of the anhydrous compound was being sold. Thus, at the time of the sales, the parties to the United States transactions did not know the identity of the particular crystalline form with which they were dealing. It was not until after the United States sales transactions were completed that Abbott and Geneva each tested samples from these lots and determined that the Form IV anhydrate crystal was what had been sold. Specifically, Abbott in 1995, and Geneva in 1996, each performed x-ray diffraction analyses on samples from these lots and found that the samples exhibited the pattern of principal peaks at the particular values disclosed in claim 4 that characterize the Form IV anhydrate crystal.

On defendants' motions for summary judgment, the district court held that the United States sales invalidated claim 4 under the on-sale bar. The court reasoned that Form IV was in the public domain, that buyers had come to rely on it being freely available, and that it was immaterial that the parties were unaware of the nature of that particular crystal form. Abbott timely appealed to this court.

DISCUSSION

The ultimate determination whether an invention was on sale within the meaning of § 102(b) is a question of law which we review de novo. *See Manville Sales Corp. v. Paramount Sys., Inc.*, 917 F.2d 544, 549, 16 USPQ2d 1587, 1591 (Fed.Cir.1990). A patent is invalid under § 102(b) if "the invention was . . . on sale in this country, more than one year prior to the date of the application for patent in the United States. . . ." Because Abbott filed the application for the '207 patent on October 18, 1994, the critical date for purposes of the on-sale bar is October 18, 1993. As the parties challenging the validity of a presumptively valid patent, see 35 U.S.C. § 282 (1994), the defendants bore the burden of proving the existence of an on-sale bar by clear and convincing evidence. In this case, there are no facts in dispute, leaving only the legal issue whether the § 102(b) on-sale bar invalidates the patent.

Abbott argues that claim 4 is not invalid under the on-sale bar because the "invention" was not on sale. For an "invention" to be on sale, Abbott submits, the parties must "conceive," or know precisely, the nature of the subject matter with which they are dealing. Since the parties did not know that they were dealing with Form IV, Abbott reasons, they did not "conceive" the subject matter sold and therefore there was no "invention" on sale. The defendants respond that we need only apply the two-part test for the on-sale bar recently set forth by the Supreme Court in *Pfaff v. Wells Electronics, Inc.*, and that, under this test, it is irrelevant that the parties to the sales did not know that they were dealing with Form IV rather than with another anhydrous terazosin hydrochloride crystalline form.

We agree with defendants that claim 4 is invalid and that the parties' ignorance that they were dealing with Form IV is irrelevant. The Supreme Court has recently stated a two-part test for determining when the on-sale bar applies. Before the critical date, the invention must both be the subject of a commercial sale or offer for sale and be "ready for patenting." *See Pfaff* (rejecting the "totality of the circumstances" test for determining whether an invention was on sale before the critical date). An invention may be shown to be "ready for patenting," *inter alia*, by "proof of reduction to practice before the critical date." *Id.*

The invention at issue in this case clearly meets the *Pfaff* test. Even though the parties did not know it at the time, it is undisputed that Form IV was the subject matter of at least three commercial sales in the United States before the critical date. It is also clear that the invention was "ready for patenting" because at least two foreign manufacturers had already reduced it to practice. Furthermore, the statutory on-sale bar is not subject to exceptions for sales made by third parties either innocently or fraudulently. *See Evans Cooling Sys., Inc. v. General Motors Corp.*, 125 F.3d 1448, 1453–54, 44 USPQ2d 1037, 1040–42 (Fed.Cir.1997). The fact that these sales were not made by Abbott is therefore irrelevant.

Abbott insists that there can be no on-sale bar unless conception of the invention has been proved, and that the lack of knowledge of the exact crystalline nature of the material that was sold precludes there having been a conception. We disagree that proof of conception was required. The fact that the claimed material was sold under circumstances in which no question existed that it was useful means that it was reduced to practice. In any event, this is not a priority dispute in which conception is a critical issue. The sale of the material in question obviates any need for inquiry into conception.

Abbott cites cases holding that the accidental, unintended, and unappreciated production of the product or process in question does not constitute anticipation. *See, e.g., Tilghman v. Proctor*, 102 U.S. 707, 711–12, (1881) (an accidental and incidental production of fatty acids by means not understood or appreciated did not anticipate a patented process for separating fatty bodies into fatty acids and glycerin. Those cases are all off the point because they involved the issue whether the claimed inventions were anticipated by earlier work that produced no useful or appreciated result. In contrast, the material here, having been sold, was decidedly useful and appreciated.)

Abbott argues that the invention was not on sale because those who sold the claimed product did not know all of its characteristics. We disagree. It is well settled in the law that there is no requirement that a sales offer specifically identify all the characteristics of an invention offered for sale or that the parties recognize the significance of all of these characteristics at the time of the offer. See *Scaltech Inc. v. Retec/Tetra, L.L.C.*, 178 F.3d 1378, 1384 (Fed.Cir.1999). If a product that is offered for sale inherently possesses each of the limitations of the claims, then the invention is on sale, whether or not the parties to the transaction recognize that the product possesses the claimed characteristics. *See id.*; *J.A. LaPorte, Inc. v. Norfolk Dredging Co.*, 787 F.2d 1577, 1582–83, 229 USPQ 435, 439 (Fed.Cir.1986) ("[T]he question is not whether the sale, even a third party sale, 'discloses' the invention at the time of the sale, but whether the sale relates to a device that embodies the invention.") (emphasis in original). In this case, it is undisputed that Form IV falls within the scope of claim 4. The fact that the parties to the sales transactions did not know they were dealing in Form IV at the time of the sales is therefore irrelevant to the question whether it was "on sale" before the critical date.

One of the primary purposes of the on-sale bar is to prohibit the withdrawal of inventions that have been placed into the public domain through commercialization. *See, e.g., King Instrument Corp. v. Otari Corp.*, 767 F.2d 853, 860, (Fed.Cir.1985) (the discovery of a new property of an old compound does not make claims to that compound patentable). For these reasons, we affirm the district court's judgment holding claim 4 of the '207 patent invalid.

Notes

1. Another View of Non–Informing Uses. In another case authored by Judge Lourie, *Baxter Int'l v. Cobe Labs., Inc.*, 88 F.3d 1054 (Fed.Cir. 1996), the Federal Circuit upheld a statutory bar on an inventive centrifuge device that did not damage blood platelets. The facts disclosed that an NIH laboratory had used such a centrifuge at its closed campus in Bethesda, Maryland. Judge Newman dissented:

> This new rule of law, that unpublished laboratory use after a reduction to practice is a public use, creates a new and mischievous category of "secret" prior art. I respectfully dissent from the court's ruling, for it is contrary to, and misapplies, the law of 35 U.S.C. § 102 ... the patent statute and precedent do not elevate private laboratory use after a reduction to practice to "public use" under § 102(b). When the public use is unknown and unknowable information in the possession of third persons, 35 U.S.C. § 102 accommodates such "secret prior art" only in the limited circumstances of § 102(e). This new category of internal laboratory use is immune to the most painstaking documentary search.

The court thus produces a perpetual cloud on any issued patent, defeating the objective standards and policy considerations embodied in the § 102 definitions of prior art. It is incorrect to interpret 35 U.S.C. § 102(b) to mean that laboratory use after a reduction to practice is a "public use," and thus a bar against any patent application filed, by anyone, more than a year thereafter. Section 102(b) was not intended to add to the bars based on information not published or publicly known or otherwise within the definition of prior art.

Even Judge Newman would be constrained to agree that an obscure foreign publication describing the Suaudeau centrifuge would fall within § 102(b); does such a scenario mark a substantially greater degree of dissemination than use in a private laboratory that was open at least to lab personnel? Consider as well the economics of searching for existing technology as opposed to the economics of reinventing that technology. Are there situations where the law should encourage an investigation to determine whether a particular technology exists, as opposed to the reinvention of that technology?

    2.   Theft as Prior Use. Suppose an unscrupulous individual steals an inventor's ideas and makes a commercial, informing use of them prior to the critical date. Should such activity constitute a "public use" under § 102(b)? The court in *Lorenz v. Colgate–Palmolive Peet Co.*, 167 F.2d 423, 77 U.S.P.Q. 138 (3d Cir.1948), reached a seemingly hard result on this issue:

> The prior-public-use proviso ... was enacted by Congress in the public interest. It contains no qualification or exception which limits the nature of the public use. We think that Congress intended that if an inventor does not protect his discovery by an application for a patent within the period prescribed by the Act, and an intervening public use arises from any source whatsoever, the inventor must be barred from a patent or from the fruits of his monopoly, if a patent has issued to him. There is not a single word in the statute which would tend to put an inventor, whose disclosures have been pirated, in any different position from one who has permitted the use of his process.

What do you think of this reasoning? Does any word of the statute distinguish between applicant and third party uses? Or would a contrary result provide open ground for collusion and ignore the reality that the inventor remains in control of her own destiny in such situations?

§ 5.2[c]   Secret Uses

W. L. GORE & ASSOCIATES v. GARLOCK, INC.

United States Court of Appeals, Federal Circuit, 1983.
721 F.2d 1540, 220 U.S.P.Q. 303.

Before MARKEY, CHIEF JUDGE, and DAVIS and MILLER, CIRCUIT JUDGES.

MARKEY, CHIEF JUDGE.

Appeal from a judgment of the District Court for the Northern District of Ohio holding U.S. Patents 3,953,566 ('566) and 4,187,390 ('390) invalid. We affirm in part, reverse in part, and remand for a determination of the infringement issue.

BACKGROUND

Tape of unsintered polytetrafluorethylene (PTFE) (known by the trademark TEFLON of E.I. du Pont de Nemours, Inc.) had been stretched in small increments. W.L. Gore & Associates, Inc. (Gore), assignee of the patents in suit, experienced a tape breakage problem in the operation of its "401" tape stretching machine. Dr. Robert Gore, Vice President of Gore, developed the invention disclosed and claimed in the '566 and '390 patents in the course of his effort to solve that problem. The 401 machine was disclosed and claimed in Gore's U.S. Patent 3,664,915 ('915) and was the invention of Wilbert L. Gore, Dr. Gore's father. PTFE tape had been sold as thread seal tape, i.e., tape used to keep pipe joints from leaking. The '915 patent, the application for which was filed on October 3, 1969, makes no reference to stretch rate, at 10% per second or otherwise, or to matrix tensile strength in excess of 7,300 psi.

Dr. Gore experimented with heating and stretching of highly crystalline PTFE rods. Despite slow, careful stretching, the rods broke when stretched a relatively small amount. Conventional wisdom in the art taught that breakage could be avoided only by slowing the stretch rate or by decreasing the crystallinity. In late October, 1969, Dr. Gore discovered, contrary to that teaching, that stretching the rods as fast as possible enabled him to stretch them to more than ten times their original length with no breakage. Further, though the rod was thus greatly lengthened, its diameter remained virtually unchanged throughout its length. The rapid stretching also transformed the hard, shiny rods into rods of a soft, flexible material.

Gore developed several PTFE products by rapidly stretching highly crystalline PTFE, including: (1) porous film for filters and laminates; (2) fabric laminates of PTFE film bonded to fabric to produce a remarkable material having the contradictory properties of impermeability to liquid water and permeability to water vapor, the material being used to make "breathable" rainwear and filters; (3) porous yarn for weaving or braiding into other products, like space suits and pump packing; (4) tubes used as replacements for human arteries and veins; and (5) insulation for high performance electric cables.

On May 21, 1970, Gore filed the patent application that resulted in the patents in suit. The '566 patent has 24 claims directed to processes for stretching highly crystalline, unsintered, PTFE. The processes, inter alia, include the steps of stretching PTFE at a rate above 10% per second and at a temperature between about 35 degrees C and the crystalline melt point of PTFE. The '390 patent has 77 claims directed to various products obtained by processes of the '566 patent.

SECTION 102(B) AND THE CROPPER MACHINE

In 1966 John W. Cropper (Cropper) of New Zealand developed and constructed a machine for producing stretched and unstretched PTFE thread seal tape. In 1967, Cropper sent a letter to a company in

Massachusetts, offering to sell his machine, describing its operation, and enclosing a photo. Nothing came of that letter. There is no evidence and no finding that the present inventions thereby became known or used in this country.

In 1968, Cropper sold his machine to Budd, which at some point thereafter used it to produce and sell PTFE threat seal tape. The sales agreement between Cropper and Budd provided:

ARTICLE "E"-PROTECTION OF TRADE SECRETS ETC.

1. BUDD agrees that while this agreement is in force it will not reproduce any copies of the said apparatus without the express written permission of Cropper nor will it divulge to any person or persons other than its own employees or employees of its affiliated corporations any of the said known-how or any details whatsoever relating to the apparatus. 2. BUDD agrees to take all proper steps to ensure that its employees observe the terms of Article "E" 1 and further agrees that whenever it is proper to do so it will take legal action in a Court of competent jurisdiction to enforce any one or more of the legal or equitable remedies available to a trade secret plaintiff. Budd told its employees the Cropper machine was confidential and required them to sign confidentiality agreements. Budd otherwise treated the Cropper machine like its other manufacturing equipment.

A former Budd employee said Budd made no effort to keep the secret. That Budd did not keep the machine hidden from employees legally bound to keep their knowledge confidential does not evidence a failure to maintain the secret. Similarly, that du Pont employees were shown the machine to see if they could help increase its speed does not itself establish a breach of the secrecy agreement. There is no evidence of when that viewing occurred. There is no evidence that a viewer of the machine could thereby learn anything of which process, among all possible processes, the machine is being used to practice. As Cropper testified, looking at the machine in operation does not reveal whether it is stretching, and if so, at what speed. Nor does looking disclose whether the crystallinity and temperature elements of the invention set forth in the claims are involved. There is no evidence that Budd's secret use of the Cropper machine made knowledge of the claimed process accessible to the public.

The district court held all claims of the '566 patent invalid under 102(b), supra, note 3, because "the invention" was "in public use [and] on sale" by Budd more than one year before Gore's application for patent. Beyond a failure to consider each of the claims independently, 35 U.S.C. § 282, and a failure of proof that the claimed inventions as a whole were practiced by Budd before the critical May 21, 1969 date, it was error to hold that Budd's activity with the Cropper machine, as above indicated, was a "public" use of the processes claimed in the '566 patent, that activity having been secret, not public.

Assuming, arguendo, that Budd sold tape produced on the Cropper machine before October 1969, and that that tape was made by a process set forth in a claim of the '566 patent, the issue under § 102(b) is whether that sale would defeat Dr. Gore's right to a patent on the process inventions set forth in the claims.

If Budd offered and sold anything, it was only tape, not whatever process was used in producing it. Neither party contends, and there was no evidence, that the public could learn the claimed process by examining the tape. If Budd and Cropper commercialized the tape, that could result in a forfeiture of a patent granted them for their process on an application filed by them more than a year later. *D.L. Auld Co. v. Chroma Graphics Corp.*, 714 F.2d 1144, at 1147–48 (Fed.Cir.1983); *See Metallizing Engineering Co. v. Kenyon Bearing & Auto Parts Co.*, 153 F.2d 516, 68 U.S.P.Q. 54 (2d Cir.1946). There is no reason or statutory basis, however, on which Budd's and Cropper's secret commercialization of a process, if established, could be held a bar to the grant of a patent to Gore on that process.

Early public disclosure is a linchpin of the patent system. As between a prior inventor who benefits from a process by selling its product but suppresses, conceals, or otherwise keeps the process from the public, and a later inventor who promptly files a patent application from which the public will gain a disclosure of the process, the law favors the latter. The district court therefore erred as a matter of law in applying the statute and in its determination that Budd's secret use of the Cropper machine and sale of tape rendered all process claims of the '566 patent invalid under § 102(b).

Appendix

Claims of the '566 patent discussed at trial:

1. A process for the production of a porous article of manufacture of a polymer of tetrafluoroethylene which process comprises expanding a shaped article consisting essentially of highly crystalline poly (tetrafluoroethylene) made by a paste-forming extrusion technique, after removal of lubricant, by stretching said unsintered shaped article at a rate exceeding about 10% per second and maintaining said shaped article at a temperature between about 35 degrees C. and the crystalline melt point of said tetrafluoroethylene polymer during said stretching.

3. The process of claim 1 in which the rate of stretch is about 100% per second.

17. The process of claim 1 in which the shaped article is expanded such that its final length in the direction of expansion is greater than about twice the original length.

19. The process of claim 17 in which said final length is greater than about five times the original length.

Notes

1. *Gore* **as a § 102(g) Case.** This material is so difficult that even a patent expert of Chief Judge Markey's caliber seems to have confused § 102(a) and (b). See 1 MARTIN J. ADELMAN, PATENT LAW PERSPECTIVES, § 2.3[8.–4] at n.41 (2d ed. 1992). Once you have had the opportunity to take up § 102(g) in the next chapter, consider whether the discussion of § 102(b) in *Gore* might more properly relate to that paragraph. For example, does the court draw attention to the invention date or the critical date? Does the court's description of the facts instead convince you that Budd and Cropper, the third-party inventors, concealed their invention? A further consideration of concealment under § 102(g) is taken up in this text at Chapter 5.

2. **A Potent Process?** What significance attaches to the fact that process claims were involved in *Gore v. Garlock*? Suppose the asserted claims had been to the PTFE tape itself: should the result differ?

3. **A Question of Perspective?** The facts of this case adequately show the problem with making a secret use a bar, namely Budd would get both use of the trade secret and the ability to bar Gore from attaining a patent after extensive investments to develop the technology independently. Of course, Budd could respond that as first inventor, and as such he should have the option to acquire a patent or retain his new technology as a trade secret. Gore in turn would respond that he should not be barred when Budd elected to forego patenting in favor of trade secret protection. Does this sound familiar? Budd's argument in favor of first inventor's choice is simply a restatement of problem with first-to-invent systems that Justice Story confronted in *Pennock*. Thus, this case really brings the statutory bar question full circle.

§ 5.3 PATENTS, PRINTED PUBLICATIONS, & "IN THIS COUNTRY" § 102(A) & § 102(B)

Both § 102(a) and § 102(b) refer to prior art as technology that was "patented or described in a printed publication," and further specify whether a given reference must originate from "in this country" or from overseas as well. Although the meaning of "patented" rarely creates difficulties in the domestic context, foreign intellectual property regimes sometimes offer unique forms of intellectual property protection which may strain the seemingly clear directive of this provision. So too with "printed publication"; the varying circumstances in which technological information is conveyed, the realities of educational or scientific milieux not so concerned with the precision sought by the law, and the increasing variety of communications media have also rendered the statutory term increasingly nebulous. Finally, the frequently international character of technology-based industries all too readily strains the territorial restrictions of § 102.

§ 5.3[a]   "Patented"

The next opinion involves two statutory sections, §§ 102(a) and (d), which have yet to be treated in depth in this casebook. Don't let this facet of the case concern you greatly: its discussion is fully comprehensible in the context of § 102(b).

IN RE CARLSON

United States Court of Appeals, Federal Circuit, 1992.
983 F.2d 1032, 25 U.S.P.Q.2d 1207.

Before NIES, CHIEF JUDGE, and LOURIE and CLEVENGER, CIRCUIT JUDGES.

CLEVENGER, J.

Bradley C. Carlson appeals from the January 9, 1992 decision of the U.S. Patent and Trademark Office (PTO) Board of Patent Appeals and Interferences (Board), Appeal No. 91–2823, affirming the examiner's rejection in reexamination proceeding No. 90/001,935 of the claim of U.S. Design Patent No. 289,855 (Des. 289,855) as unpatentable under 35 U.S.C. Section 103 (1988). We affirm.

I

The two issues raised in this appeal are whether the design protected by a German Geschmacksmuster constitutes an "invention ... patented ... in ... a foreign country" within the meaning of 35 U.S.C. Section 102(a) (1988) and thus may be considered prior art, and whether Des. 289,855 is unpatentable under 35 U.S.C. Section 103 (1988) as obvious in light of the pertinent prior art.

The application that culminated in issuance of Des. 289,855 on May 19, 1987 was filed with the PTO by Carlson on November 19, 1984. The claim of Des. 289,855 covers the ornamental design for a dual compartment bottle as depicted in the six figures included in the design patent.

FIG. 3

A Geschmacksmuster is a design registration obtained by an applicant from the German government after performing certain registration
procedures. Professor Chisum, in a nutshell, thus describes the registration process in effect in 1984:

> [A] person may register an industrial design or model by
> depositing with a local office an application with a drawing, photo-
> graph or sample of the article. Registration is effective on deposit,
> and lists of registered designs are published a short time after
> registration.

1 DONALD S. CHISUM, PATENTS § 3.06[2], at 3–107 (1992) (footnote omitted). Certified copies of Geschmacksmuster are available from the Amts-
gericht in which the registered designs are deposited. Such copies typically include the same information regarding the Geschmacksmuster as
provided in the Bundesanzeiger, supra, including the city of deposit, and
a copy of the drawing or photograph deposited. In the case of deposited
sample articles, certified copies of Geschmacksmuster contain photographs of the sample articles.

The Geschmacksmuster in this case embraces three different bottle
designs, Nos. 3168–3170. Only Model No. 3168 is pertinent to the design
claimed in Des. 289,855. That model is a bottle design consisting of two

attached container portions divided by a striking, asymmetrical zig-zag line of demarcation. Each container portion has an externally threaded neck with an associated screw-on cap. As translated, both the Bundesanzeiger publication referring to the Geschmacksmuster and the certified copy of the Geschmacksmuster state, in relevant part: "An open package with plastic or synthetic bottles with stoppers.... Model for plastic products." The description as "open" signifies that the deposited materials are available for public inspection. In addition, the certified copy of the Geschmacksmuster, which was supplied to the examiner as relevant prior art, includes a series of photographs of the three deposited designs taken from various orientations. The Bundesanzeiger identifies the German city of Coburg, Bavaria as the location of the registered design.

Whether a Geschmacksmuster is a foreign patent under section 102(a) is a question of first impression. That a Geschmacksmuster qualifies as a patent for section 102(d) purposes is settled law, embraced by the Solicitor, unchallenged by Carlson, and a proposition with which we do not disagree. Carlson invites this court to deny Geschmacksmuster the status of patents under section 102(a).

We do not dispute that section 102(a), relating to potential prior art in the form of patents issued in a foreign country and held by persons other than the U.S. patent applicant, serves a purpose akin to, but different from, section 102(d), which specifies the time within which the owner of a foreign patent must apply for a U.S. patent on the same invention. That distinction, however, does not suggest that a Geschmacksmuster lacks the necessary credentials to qualify as a patent under section 102(a).

Nevertheless, Carlson asserts that the correct interpretation of section 102(a) requires that a foreign patent only serve as prior art if it discloses its invention in a readily-accessible fashion. In essence, Carlson argues that the embodiment of foreign protection must take a form that fully discloses the nature of the protected design in a medium of communication capable of being widely disseminated. Because this requirement is clearly not satisfied by depositing a model in a city courthouse in a foreign land, the embodiment cannot constitute an invention patented in a foreign country for purposes of section 102(a) because it is incapable of providing detailed instruction to a large enough number of persons remote from the location of deposit. Moreover, Carlson argues, since the Bundesanzeiger entry does not explicitly refer to dual-compartment containers, it cannot provide notice of the existence of the pertinent model of the Geschmacksmuster to a designer of such containers.

Carlson correctly surmises that section 102(a) contains a requirement that a foreign patent be disclosed in order to qualify as prior art under section 102(a). The requirement, however, is only that the patent be "available to the public." *In re Ekenstam*, 256 F.2d 321, 324, 325, 118 U.S.P.Q. 349, 351, 353 (CCPA 1958) (inventions protected by secret/"private" patents do not qualify as "patented abroad" under U.S. law).

Because the description of the Geschmacksmuster in the Bundesanzeiger does not specifically refer to a multicompartment container, Carlson would have us deem the designs incorporated therein outside of the relevant field of prior art. His argument, however, represents an overly narrow view of the prior art germane to his invention. The Bundesanzeiger entry regarding the Geschmacksmuster at issue in this appeal clearly refers to a single package incorporating multiple plastic bottles, thereby alerting the public to potentially relevant designs, and directs the notified reader to proceed to Coburg to obtain the actual design. Once in Coburg, the protected design is completely "available to the public" through the certified copy of the Geschmacksmuster.

We recognize that Geschmacksmuster on display for public view in remote cities in a far-away land may create a burden of discovery for one without the time, desire, or resources to journey there in person or by agent to observe that which was registered and protected under German law. Such a burden, however, is by law imposed upon the hypothetical person of ordinary skill in the art who is charged with knowledge of all the contents of the relevant prior art.

Moreover, actual knowledge of the Geschmacksmuster is not required for the disclosure to be considered prior art. To determine patentability, a hypothetical person is presumed to know all the pertinent prior art, whether or not the applicant is actually aware of its existence. *In re Howarth*, 654 F.2d 103, 106, 210 U.S.P.Q. 689, 692 (CCPA 1981) ("Section 102 has as one objective that only the first inventor obtain a patent.... Foreign 'patents' and foreign 'printed publications' preclude the grant of a patent whether or not the information is commonly known. Under [section] 102 a conclusive presumption of knowledge of such prior art is, in effect, a statutorily required fiction.").

In conclusion, we hold that because the Geschmacksmuster fully discloses the design upon which German law conferred the exclusive rights attendant to the registration, the Geschmacksmuster qualifies as a foreign patent for purposes of section 102(a), and therefore constitutes prior art for use in the obviousness analysis under section 103.

Because the relevant prior art [including the Geschmacksmuster] renders Carlson's design obvious under section 103, the judgment of the Board is AFFIRMED.

Notes

1. Patent vs. Publication. The U.S. Patent and Trademark Office publishes all patents simultaneously with their issuance. In addition, the PTO publishes some patent applications prior to grant, approximately 18 months after they are filed. Foreign Patent Offices generally publish all pending patent applications at approximately this 18–month period, in addition to publishing all issued patents contemporaneously with their grant. Thus, the issue faced by the *Carlson* court is one that arises relatively infrequently. Patent or no, the pertinent foreign legal instrument is ordinarily published and thus prior art by reason of the "printed publication" language of §§ 102(a) and (b). When a patent specification is published the whole specification becomes prior art. However, only that part of the unpublished specification of a patent which relates to the patent claims becomes part of the prior art, see *Bendix Corp. v. Balax, Inc.,* 421 F.2d 809, 164 U.S.P.Q. 485 (7th Cir.1970).

2. Geschmacksmuster as Patent. The scope of protection of Geschmacksmuster actually has more of the flavor of copyright protection: the registrant may prevents others from copying the design, but may not enforce his rights against an independent creator. As limited as these rights to exclude are, how then could the Geschmacksmuster be considered a patent within § 102?

3. Gebrauchmuster as Patent. An alternative form of German intellectual property protection consists of a Gebrauchmuster, which the court in *Reeves Bros. v. United States Laminating Corp.,* 282 F.Supp. 118, 157 U.S.P.Q. 235 (E.D.N.Y.1968) described as follows:

> [A] Gebrauchmuster ["GM"] is registered under the German law after an application is filed in the German Patent Office. If the application meets the requirements of form and content, the GM is issued without any novelty search and is accompanied by the publication of an official notice in the German Patent Gazette that it has been so issued. There is no requirement of nonobviousness in order to obtain a GM, and its purpose is to enable the applicant to obtain a speedy protection for a new article and if desirable, to concurrently seek a regular patent, a procedure which would consume much more time. After registration the specification and claims become available to the public and anyone has free and open access to the same. The GM was not a printed publication at any time and is referred to as a utility model. It is limited to a maximum of six years instead of eighteen years, covers only articles and can never cover processes.

Is a Gebrauchmuster properly considered a patent? Is this an easier case than was presented in *Carlson?*

§ 5.3[b] "Printed Publication"

IN RE HALL

United States Court of Appeals, Federal Circuit, 1986.
781 F.2d 897, 228 U.S.P.Q. 453.

Before Baldwin, Circuit Judge, Nichols, Senior Circuit Judge, and Kashiwa, Circuit Judge.

Baldwin, Circuit Judge.

This is an appeal from the decision of the U.S. Patent and Trademark Office's (PTO) Board of Appeals, sustaining the final rejection of claims 1–25 of reissue Application No. 343,922, filed January 29, 1982, based principally on a "printed publication" bar under 35 U.S.C. § 102(b). The reference is a doctoral thesis. Because appellant concedes that his claims are unpatentable if the thesis is available as a "printed publication" more than one year prior to the application's effective filing date of February 27, 1979, the only issue is whether the thesis is available as such a printed publication. On the record before us, we affirm the board's decision.

BACKGROUND

A protest was filed during prosecution of appellant's reissue application which included in an appendix a copy of the dissertation "1,4–a-Glucanglukohydrolase ein amylotylisches Enzym ..." by Peter Foldi (Foldi thesis or dissertation). The record indicates that in September 1977, Foldi submitted his dissertation to the Department of Chemistry and Pharmacy at Freiburg University in the Federal Republic of Germany, and that Foldi was awarded a doctorate degree on November 2, 1977.

Certain affidavits from Dr. Erich Will, who is the director and manager of the Loan Department of the Library of Freiburg University, have been relied upon by the examiner and the board in reaching their decisions. One document, styled a "Declaration" and signed by Dr. Will, states that: [I]n November 1977 copies of the dissertation FOLDI ... were received in the library of Freiburg University, and in ... December 1977 copies of the said dissertation were freely made available to the faculty and student body of Freiburg University as well as to the general public. In an August 28, 1981 letter responding to an inquiry from a German corporation, Dr. Will said that the Freiburg University library was able to make the Foldi dissertation "available to our readers as early as 1977."

The examiner made a final rejection of the application claims. He said: "On the basis of the instant record it is reasonable to assume that the Foldi thesis was available (accessible) prior to February 27, 1979." He also pointed out that there was no evidence to the contrary and asked the appellant to state his "knowledge of any inquiry which may have been made regarding 'availability' beyond that presently referred to in the record." Appellant did not respond.

By letter, the PTO's Scientific Library asked Dr. Will whether the Foldi dissertation was made available to the public by being cataloged and placed in the main collection. Dr. Will replied in an October 20, 1983 letter, as translated: Our dissertations, thus also the Foldi dissertation, are indexed in a special dissertations catalogue, which is part of the general users' catalogue. In the stacks they are likewise set apart in a special dissertation section, which is part of the general stacks.

In response to a further inquiry by the PTO's Scientific Library requesting (1) the exact date of indexing and cataloging of the Foldi dissertation or (2) "the time such procedures normally take," Dr. Will replied in a June 18, 1984 letter: The Library copies of the Foldi dissertation were sent to us by the faculty on November 4, 1977. Accordingly, the dissertation most probably was available for general use toward the beginning of the month of December, 1977.

The board held that the unrebutted evidence of record was sufficient to conclude that the Foldi dissertation had an effective date as prior art more than one year prior to the filing date of the appellant's initial application. In rejecting appellant's argument that the evidence was not sufficient to establish a specific date when the dissertation became publicly available, the board said: We rely on the librarian's affidavit of express facts regarding the specific dissertation of interest and his description of the routine treatment of dissertations in general, in the ordinary course of business in his library.

On appeal, appellant raises two arguments: (1) the § 102(b) "printed publication" bar requires that the publication be accessible to the interested public, but there is no evidence that the dissertation was properly indexed in the library catalog prior to the critical date; and (2) even if the Foldi thesis were cataloged prior to the critical date, the presence of a single cataloged thesis in one university library does not constitute sufficient accessibility of the publication's teachings to those interested in the art exercising reasonable diligence.

Opinion

The statutory phrase "printed publication" has been interpreted to give effect to ongoing advances in the technologies of data storage, retrieval, and dissemination. *In re Wyer*, 655 F.2d 221, 226, 210 U.S.P.Q. 790, 794 (CCPA 1981). Because there are many ways in which a reference may be disseminated to the interested public, "public accessibility" has been called the touchstone in determining whether a reference constitutes a "printed publication" bar under 35 U.S.C. § 102(b). The § 102 publication bar is a legal determination based on underlying fact issues, and therefore must be approached on a case-by-case basis. *See id.* at 227, 210 U.S.P.Q. at 795. The proponent of the publication bar must show that prior to the critical date the reference was sufficiently accessible, at least to the public interested in the art, so that such a one by examining the reference could make the claimed invention without further research or experimentation.

Relying on *In re Bayer*, [568 F.2d 1357, 196 USPQ 670 (CCPA 1978)] appellant argues that the Foldi thesis was not shown to be accessible because Dr. Will's affidavits do not say when the thesis was indexed in the library catalog and do not chronicle the procedures for receiving and processing a thesis in the library.

As the board pointed out in its decision, the facts in Bayer differ from those here. Bayer, who was himself the author of the dissertation relied upon by the PTO, submitted a declaration from the university librarian which detailed the library's procedures for receiving, cataloging, and shelving of theses and attested to the relevant dates that Bayer's thesis was processed. The evidence showed that cataloging and shelving thesis copies routinely took many months from the time they were first received from the faculty and that during the interim the theses were accumulated in a private library office accessible only to library employees. In particular, processing of Bayer's thesis was shown to have been completed after the critical date.

On those facts the CCPA held that Bayer's thesis was not sufficiently accessible and could not give rise to the § 102(b) publication bar. But the court did not hold, as appellant would have it, that accessibility can only be shown by evidence establishing a specific date of cataloging and shelving before the critical date. While such evidence would be desirable, in lending greater certainty to the accessibility determination, the realities of routine business practice counsel against requiring such evidence. The probative value of routine business practice to show the performance of a specific act has long been recognized. Therefore, we conclude that competent evidence of the general library practice may be relied upon to establish an approximate time when a thesis became accessible.

In the present case, Dr. Will's affidavits give a rather general library procedure as to indexing, cataloging, and shelving of theses. Although no specific dates are cited (except that the thesis was received on November 4, 1977), Dr. Will's affidavits consistently maintain that inasmuch as the Foldi dissertation was received by the library in early November 1977, the dissertation "most probably was available for general use toward the beginning of the month of December, 1977." The only reasonable interpretation of the affidavits is that Dr. Will was relying on his library's general practice for indexing, cataloging, and shelving theses in estimating the time it would have taken to make the dissertation available to the interested public. Dr. Will's affidavits are competent evidence, and in these circumstances, persuasive evidence that the Foldi dissertation was accessible prior to the critical date. Reliance on an approximation found in the affidavits such as "toward the beginning of the month of December, 1977" works no injustice here because the critical date, February 27, 1978, is some two and one half months later. Moreover, it is undisputed that appellant proffered no rebuttal evidence.

Based on what we have already said concerning "public accessibility," and noting that the determination rests on the facts of each case, we reject appellant's legal argument that a single cataloged thesis in one university library does not constitute sufficient accessibility to those interested in the art exercising reasonable diligence.

We agree with the board that the evidence of record consisting of Dr. Will's affidavits establishes a prima facie case for unpatentability of the claims under the § 102(b) publication bar. It is a case which stands unrebutted.

Accordingly, the board's decision sustaining the rejection of appellant's claims is affirmed.

AFFIRMED.

Notes

1. The Printed Publication. Why should the gauge of the "printed publication" bar be public accessibility and not the demonstrated fact of actual access? How can an document in an obscure location abroad that was actually unread be considered to lie within the public domain? What other factors should be considered relevant: the author's intent, number of copies distributed, restrictions upon the extent of dissemination, or whether the applicant himself is the author?

2.   Time of Availability. The facts of *Hall* did not require that the court distinguish between the submission date of the thesis to the Library and the date of availability. Suppose, however, that the thesis was submitted prior to the critical date, but was not made available until after the critical date. What novelty-defeating effect should the thesis be accorded? Before answering too quickly, consider whether the reasoning of *Alexander Milburn*, reprinted here in Chapter 6, presents an apt analogy. *See In re Bayer*, 568 F.2d 1357, 196 U.S.P.Q. 670 (CCPA 1978).

3.   Other Cases. Should an indexed undergraduate thesis, located in a college library, be considered a printed publication? *See In re Cronyn*, 890 F.2d 1158 (Fed.Cir.1989); Comment, *In re Cronyn: Can Student Theses Bar Patent Applications*, 18 J. C. & U. L. 105 (1991). What about a typewritten paper presented at a conference overseas? *See Deep Welding, Inc. v. Sciaky Bros., Inc.*, 155 U.S.P.Q. 561 (N.D.Ill.1967). How about a foreign patent application available on microfilm? *See Phillips Electronic & Pharmaceutical Industries v. Thermal & Electronics Industries*, 311 F.Supp. 17, 165 U.S.P.Q. 185 (D.N.J.1970).

4.   Oral Disclosures. Under the European Patent Convention, but not the United States patent statute, oral disclosures may comprise prior art. Which is the better rule? Do you believe that jurisdictional variations in the availability of discovery under local procedure laws plays into this difference?

5.   Posting on the Internet Is a technical paper posted on the Internet a printed publication? Recall that under Article 29 of the Japanese patent law inventions which were described in a distributed publication or made available to the public through electric communication lines in Japan or elsewhere prior to the filing of the patent application are prior art.

§ 5.3[c]   "In This Country"

EX PARTE THOMSON

U.S. Patent and Trademark Office Board of Patent
Appeals and Interferences, 1992.
24 U.S.P.Q.2d 1618.

Before GOLDSTEIN, GOOLKASIAN, **and** KIMLIN, EXAMINERS-IN-CHIEF.

KIMLIN, EXAMINER-IN-CHIEF.

This is an appeal from the final rejection of claims 1–3, 5 and 6. Claims 1 and 2 are illustrative:

1.   A cotton cultivar having the designation Siokra (ATCC 40405).

2.   Seeds of the cotton cultivar according to Claim 1.

In the rejection of he appealed claims, the examiner relies upon the following references:

LUCKETT ET AL. (LUCKETT), NEW ZEALAND AGRONOMY SOCIETY SPECIAL PUBLICATION NO. 5, QUALITY REQUIREMENTS AND COTTON BREEDING IN AUSTRALIA, pages 276–277 (1986).

DUFF, CALIFORNIA-ARIZONA COTTON, AUSTRALIA'S SIOKRA COTTON, pages 10 and 14 (1986).

THOMSON, XEROX TELECOPIER 495, BREEDING AND PERFORMANCE ASPECTS OF SIOKRA, pages 6–8 (1987).

Appellant's claimed invention is directed to a cotton cultivar having the designation Siokra. According to appellant, Siokra "possesses the okra leaf character in combination with a high yield, high ginning out turn, good quality fiber and with resistance to 18 common races of the wide spread disease, bacterial blight." In addition, it is said that Siokra provides a good yield under a range of environmental conditions.

As noted by the examiner, appellant has not separately argued the patentability of the appealed claims with any reasonable specificity. Accordingly, all the appealed claims are considered to stand or fall together.

Appealed claims 1–3, 5 and 6 stand rejected under 35 U.S.C. § 102(b) as being clearly anticipated by either LUCKETT or DUFF in light of THOMSON.

We have thoroughly reviewed the entire record before us, which includes the well-articulated positions presented by both appellant and the examiner. In so doing, we concur with the examiner that the claimed subject matter was described in a printed publication under circumstances whereby it was in the possession of the public more than one year prior to the filing date of the present application. Accordingly, we will sustain the examiner's rejection for essentially those reasons expressed in the Answer, and add the following.

There is certainly no dispute that the claimed cotton cultivar, seeds of the cultivar, etc. are disclosed in each of the applied references, *i.e.*, LUCKETT, DUFF and THOMSON. Each discloses the commercial growth of the claimed Siokra. There is also agreement that the applicable law governing the propriety of rejections under 35 U.S.C. § 102(b) is articulated in *In re Donohue*, 766 F.2d 531, 226 USPQ 619 (Fed.Cir.1985) which explains:

> It is well settled that prior art under 35 U.S.C. § 102(b) must sufficiently describe the claimed invention to have placed the public in possession of it.... Such possession is effected if one of ordinary skill in the art could have combined the publication's description of the invention with his own knowledge to make the claimed invention.... Accordingly, even if the claimed invention is disclosed in the printed publication, that disclosure will not suffice as prior art if it was not enabling.

It is appellant's position that inasmuch as at least 12 breeding steps are necessary to arrive at the claimed Siokra cultivar, and not one of the applied references provides sufficient disclosure of such breeding steps, the references are non-enabling for the skilled artisan and, therefore, cannot anticipate the claimed invention within the meaning of 35 U.S.C. § 102. On the other hand, while the examiner acknowledges that the cited references do not disclose appellant's breeding steps, the examiner maintains that the references do disclose that the claimed Siokra, at least in Australia, was commercially available to the skilled artisan for more than one year prior to the present filing date. Therefore, the examiner concludes that both DUFF and LUCKETT are enabling disclosures since "[I]n the absence of evidence to the contrary, it is self-evident that the public was already in possession of the invention such that a person of skill in the art could obtain and reproduce the invention by seed germination without experimentation."

In upholding the examiner's rejection, we think it important to focus upon both the subject matter being claimed and the knowledge that can be reasonably attributed to one skilled in the relevant art at the time of filing the present application. In the present case, the claims on appeal are not directed to the process of breeding a specific cotton cultivar. Rather, the appealed claims define particular agricultural products, such as the cotton cultivar Siokra, as well as the seed, plants and pollen thereof. Thus, keeping in perspective the nature of the claimed subject matter, the question becomes would the skilled artisan, armed with the disclosures of the cited articles, have had the requisite knowledge to make the claimed invention, *viz.*, the Siokra cultivar and its seeds, plants and pollen.

Stated as such, we are convinced that the skilled cotton grower would have had the wherewithal, upon reading the publicly disseminated reference articles, to purchase the commercially available Siokra seeds, and employ conventional techniques to plant and nurture the seeds to maturity in order to obtain the claimed invention, *i.e.*, Siokra plants, seeds and pollen. As pointed out by the examiner, appellant has proffered no objective evidence on this record that the claimed Siokra seeds were unavailable to the skilled artisan, or that undue experimentation would have been required to reproduce Siokra by germination of the commercially available seeds.

In the absence of such evidence, the examiner's position is reasonable and in accordance with current patent jurisprudence.

Appellant contends that the examiner's position amounts to an improper and impermissible combination of the two separate and distinct bars to patentability recited in section 102(b), namely that 1) the invention was patented or described in a printed publication in this or a foreign country or 2) in public use or on sale in this country. Appellant urges that the printed publication bar is not available because the publication is not enabling, and that the "on sale" bar is not available because the on sale activities occurred in a foreign country. However, we concur with the examiner that the applied rejection does not rely upon or incorporate the public use or on sale bar of the statute. As explained above, we are satisfied that the material disclosed in each of LUCKETT, DUFF and THOMSON, when considered in conjunction with the knowledge of the skilled cotton grower, would have enabled such a skilled artisan to make the claimed Siokra cultivar, along with its seeds, plants, pollen,

etc., by purchase and planting of the requisite seeds. That is why the
Thomson declaration under 37 C.F.R. § 1.132, stating "that I am not
aware of any public use or sale of the cultivar Siokra in the United
States by others or by myself as applicant" is not relevant to the
rejection at hand. The issue is not whether the cultivar Siokra was on
public use or sale in the United States but, rather, whether Siokra seeds
were available to a skilled artisan anywhere in the world such that
he/she could attain them and make/reproduce the Siokra cultivar disclosed in the cited publications. To emphasize the evident commercial
availability of Siokra, we will quote from the cited publications. DUFF
writes "[t]aking the better part of 10 years to develop, Siokra was
introduced to the market place for the 1985–86 growing season" and
that a Michael Thomas explained that " 'the whole industry switched to
DPL90' or Siokras for the 1985–86 growing season." LUCKETT states
"Siokra is, we believe, the first okra leaf commercial variety that has
been accepted by growers for large-scale growing." In an article dated
February–April 1986, the present inventor, M.J. THOMSON, states:

> One of the two new cottons being grown this season is our (CSIRO)
> variety, Siokra. Although Siokra was made available to Cotton Seed
> Distributors (CSD) for seed increase three seasons ago, and is now
> being grown commercially on substantial areas, its formal release by
> the Federal Member for Parliament, the Honourable Tom McVeigh,
> has only recently (24–2–86) taken place.

> For this release a description of Siokra together with a summary of
> its performance in variety trials was compiled and the purpose of this
> article is to pass on this information to a wider audience.

Manifestly, it is reasonable to conclude that, at the time the cited
articles were published, skilled artisans throughout the world would
have found Siokra seeds readily available on the open market. Again,
there is no evidence of record to the contrary.

In conclusion, based on the foregoing and the reasons expressed in
the Answer, the examiner's decision rejecting the appealed claims is
affirmed.

Notes

1. Enablement in the Antipodes? Now wait a moment here. The
statutory bar applied in *Thomson* was not based upon "public use," the
Board says, but rather because the claimed cultivar had been described in a
"printed publication." Thomson argues that the cited publications are not
enabling, however, because they merely describe the plant. After all, for
mechanical, electrical or chemical technologies, diagrams or textual illustrations may fully convey the workings of the patented machine, compound or
circuit. But this technique may be less effective for plants because a drawing
or written description is often not enough—an actual sample of a plant is
needed in order to reproduce it. The Board replies, "No worries, mate—
farmers are growing Siokra down under!" Is the Board's reasoning faithful
to the wording of § 102(b)?

2. Territorial Restrictions Abroad. The policy behind the territorial restrictions included within § 102(b) is likely based upon the perceived difficulty of learning about unpublished developments overseas. By restricting the "public use" and "on sale" bars to domestic occurrences, Congress reached a judgment about what U.S. inventors should fairly be held to know. Other patent laws reflect a different conclusion. The Japanese patent law, which used to include territorial restrictions similar to the United States, removed them in favor of a regime of global prior art. The European Patent Convention also does not restrict the prior art in a territorial fashion. Do you believe that modern conveniences of communication and transportation should lead to amendments to § 102(b)?

3. A Multinational Perspective. On balance, does the presence of the words "in this country" in 102(b) help or hinder inventors domiciled in the United States as compared with those living in other countries? Why should a domestic inventor be unable to obtain a patent based upon activities that, when performed by a foreign inventor overseas, would not be pertinent to patentability? As will be seen in the discussion associated with § 102(g) presented in Chapter Six, the words "in this country" may sometimes work to the benefit of domestic inventors.

4. A Hypothetical. Suppose that an electrical engineer working for a Mexican telecommunications company develops a method useful for routing telephone calls. Her employer implements the algorithm in connection with a telephone switch located in Ensenada, Mexico. Many of the telephone calls processed by the switch originate from the United States. If the switch is employed for more than a year before an application for a United States patent is filed directed towards the method, would § 102(b) present a bar to patentability? More specifically: Does such a use constitute a "public use" under § 102(b)? If so, is the use "in this country"?

§ 5.4　ABANDONMENT § 102(c)

Review of the statutory predecessors to § 102(c) does much to explain the true impact of this provision. The Act of 1836 indicated that no patent could issue to an inventor if the claimed invention was "in public use or on sale, with his consent or allowance." Three years later, Congress changed this language by mandating that "no patent shall be held to be invalid by reason of such purchase, sale or prior use to the application of the patent . . . except on proof [1] of abandonment of such invention to the public or [2] that such purchase, sale or prior use has been for more than two years prior to such application for a patent." In 1870, language similar to that of the current statute was introduced, the grant of a patent being permissible if the invention was "not in public use or on sale for more than two years prior to such application for a patent."

As such, the current language referring to abandonment of the invention should not be read literally. Section 102(c) does not refer to the relinquishment of the invention itself; it instead refers to the surrender of an invention *to the public*. In other words, § 102(c) provides that appropriate conduct by the inventor can lead to the forfeiture of the right to obtain a patent on the invention. For instance, in an early case,

Kendall v. Winsor, 62 U.S. (21 How.) 322 (1858), the Supreme Court explained the meaning of abandonment. In this case, Winsor patented a harness-making machine. One of his employees, Aldridge left his service and began making copies of the patented machine in another state. Winsor sued for patent infringement. The defendants argued that Winsor had repeatedly stated that he preferred not to obtain a patent, but rather to maintain his technology as a trade secret and rely on the difficulty of reverse engineering the complex machine. Although Winsor later changed his mind and obtained a patent, the defendants still asserted that his statements amounted to an abandonment. The Supreme Court upheld the jury's finding of infringement. In the process it commented on abandonment:

> It is the unquestionable right of every inventor to confer gratuitously the benefits of his ingenuity upon the public, and this he may do either by express declaration or by conduct equally significant with language-such, for instance, as an acquiescence with full knowledge in the use of his invention by others; or he may forfeit his rights as an inventor by a wilful or negligent postponement of his claims, or by an attempt to withhold the benefit of his improvement from the public until a similar or the same improvement should have been made and introduced by others ... But there may be cases in which the knowledge of the invention many be surreptitiously obtained, and communicated to the public, that do not affect the right of the inventor. Under such circumstances, no presumption can arise in favor of an abandonment of the right to the inventor to the public, though an acquiescence on his part will lay the foundation for such a presumption.

Contemporary decisions rarely rely upon abandonment under § 102(c) as a basis for defeating a patent right. They instead turn to § 102(b), which provides more specified details on when the patent right is lost. In some sense, if the conditions of § 102(b) are fulfilled, then the law deems the inventor to have abandoned the right to obtain patent protection.

§ 5.5 DELAYED UNITED STATES FILING § 102(d)

Section 102(d) bars a U.S. patent when (1) an inventor files a foreign patent application more than twelve months before filing the U.S. application, and (2) a foreign patent results from that application prior to the U.S. filing date. The requirements are conjunctive: both requirements must be met in order to trigger § 102(d) and bar the issuance of a patent. By encouraging prompt filing in the United States, § 102(d) ensures that the term of U.S. patents will not appreciably extend past the expiration date of parallel foreign patents.

An example illustrates the application of § 102(d). Suppose that Orlanth, the inventor of an electric trolling motor, files an application at the Swedish Patent Office on May 25, 2003. The Swedish application matures into a granted Swedish patent on August 1, 2004. If Orlanth has not filed his U.S. patent application at the PTO as of August 1, 2004, the date of the Swedish patent grant, the § 102(d) bar would be triggered.

Commentators have often approached § 102(d) with some distaste. Because inventors may choose to file a patent application only in the United States, the policy goal of assuring that the U.S. market will become patent-free contemporaneously with foreign markets seems poorly served via the § 102(d) bar. More telling is that § 102(d) almost exclusively works against foreign inventors. Individuals based in the United States seldom encounter problems with § 102(d), for inventors the world over tend to file applications in their home patent offices first. And while this statute comports with the letter of Article 27 of the TRIPS Agreement, which requires that "patents shall be available . . . without discrimination as to the place of the invention," § 102(d) in practice derogates from the principle of national treatment of foreign inventors.

Until a decade ago, the best that could be said about § 102(d) is that it was seldom employed. Because patent prosecution almost always requires more than one year to complete, and because most foreign patent applications are published more than twelve months before their grant, the published application itself might be available as "printed publication" under § 102(b). However, a Federal Circuit opinion interpreting § 102(d), *In re Kathawala*, 9 F.3d 942 (Fed.Cir.1993), appears to have breathed new life into the statute.

Kathawala, inventor of cholesterol-inhibiting compounds, filed patent applications in the United States, Greece and Spain. The three applications included substantially the same specifications but contained differing claims. The Greek patent claimed compounds, pharmaceutical compositions, methods of use and methods of making. The U.S. patent contained all but the latter sort of claims. The Spanish patent claimed only the method of making the compound. Not only was the U.S. application filed more than one year after the Greek and Spanish applications were filed, each of these foreign applications actually led to granted patents before the U.S. filing date.

Appealing the PTO's imposition of a § 102(d) bar before the Federal Circuit, Kathawala offered two arguments worthy of note here. First, Kathawala asserted that because the Spanish patent contained only method of making claims, which were not claimed in the U.S. application, the invention claimed in the United States had not been previously "patented" in a foreign country within the meaning of § 102(d). Kathawala also urged that the claims of the Greek patent were invalid because, at the time the patent issued, the Greek patent law actually disallowed patents directed to pharmaceuticals.

The Federal Circuit had little trouble dispensing with these arguments. According to Judge Lourie, § 102(d) should not be given a constrained reading. It was enough that Kathawala's Spanish application disclosed and provided the opportunity to claim all aspects of his invention, including the compounds themselves. Allowing dilatory inventors to obtain U.S. patents on others aspect of the same "invention" patented too long ago abroad would frustrate the policy of the statute, according to the court. The court also dismissed Kathawala's arguments regarding the Greek patent, declining to speculate on the patent eligibility law of Greece. Both Greek and U.S. patents included claims towards the same subject matter because Kathawala had put them there, and their validity was irrelevant to whether the subject matter was "patented" in accordance with § 102(d).

Not only was the *Kathawala* court's unwillingness to consider Greek patent law surprising, its generous view of patented subject matter seems questionable. Few members of the patent community would say that disclosed but unclaimed subject matter is patented, for the claims are the measure of patentee rights. Perhaps *Kathawala* should have been an obviousness case. But given the robust holding in *Kathawala*, applicants should be particularly wary of foreign patent registration regimes. Under these systems, foreign patent offices do not fully examine applications for compliance with the patent law, leading to short processing times and prompt issuances of foreign patents.

STATUTORY BAR EXERCISES

Dr. Martha Bjorn works for the research and development arm of Unstrung Incorporated, a premium sports equipment manufacturer located entirely within the United States. On July 4, 2001, she invents a new process for producing tennis rackets which fulfill the standards set forth by the dominant professional tennis organization. The process results in tennis rackets identical to those made by prior art processes, but does so more quickly and cheaply. As Unstrung's patent attorney has quite a backlog of other patent applications, a United States application claiming the Bjorn process is not filed until November 14, 2002.

Would any of the following activities bar the issue of a patent to the Bjorn invention under § 102?

1. Unstrung Incorporated begins development efforts to adopt Bjorn's process to the realities of the factory production line on August 1, 2001. After modifying its existing manufacturing processes to fit the Bjorn process and working out the bugs, Unstrung judges these efforts to be successful by November 19, 2001. At that point, Unstrung then begins commercial production.

2. A few days after completing her invention, Bjorn writes an article about the process and submits it to a technical journal. The article is published on December 15, 2001.

3. Unstrung Incorporated begins shipping tennis rackets produced by the Bjorn process to distributors on February 1, 2002. Retailers makes the first sales of Bjorn-produced rackets to consumers by February 10, 2002.

4. An unrelated party located in the United States, Swish Limited, had developed a similar process to that invented by Bjorn. Swish perfected the process on October 7, 2001, and produced several dozen rackets. Ultimately, however, they decided not to employ the process on a larger scale for financial reasons. Swish maintained the process docu-

mentation and resulting rackets under lock and key, and the Swish employee-inventors maintained the pledge of confidentiality they had agreed to in their employment contracts.

5. During his September 15, 1998 retirement luncheon in Campos, Brazil, the senior engineer of a local sporting goods maker offers some advice on ways to improve the production of tennis racquets. The steps he proposes are quite similar to those ultimately suggested by Bjorn. The remarks are in Portuguese and go unrecorded.

6. Mr. Forehand is the president, chief executive officer, and sole shareholder of Unstrung Incorporated. Forehand is presented with the "Sports Manufacturing Person of the Year Award" at an elaborate industry-sponsored dinner on August 27, 2001. In a fit of largess following this acknowledgment by his peers, Forehand fully describes the Bjorn process during his acceptance speech. He then declares that "I believe this invention will transform the world of tennis and feel that all of us should participate in this dramatic possibility. I hereby dedicate our new invention to the public." The next morning, Forehand has second thoughts and orders the filing of a patent application as above.

7. Unstrung Incorporated's patent attorney contacts two foreign associates and asks them to file patent applications claiming the Bjorn process in Sweden and Germany, respectively. The Swedish application *Bar* is filed on July 15, 2001 and issues on October 13, 2002. The German *No Bar* application is filed on August 17, 2001 and issues as a granted patent on January 15, 2003.

Chapter Six

NOVELTY: PRIOR INVENTION

This Chapter turns to the second strand of issues running through the paragraphs of § 102. Section 102(a) straightforwardly states the essential first-to-invent rule which dominates United States novelty analysis. It does so by supplying a basis for rejecting patent applications which describe an invention "known or used in this country, or patented or described in a printed publication in this or a foreign country, before the invention thereof by the applicant for a patent." Section 102(a) requires some form of public knowledge of the first inventor's invention before the second inventor forms the subject matter of his patent application or patent. Section 102(e) deals with a special category of secret knowledge of a first inventor's work: a patent application, filed prior to the invention date, which has actually matured into a published application or granted patent, but which does not claim the invention.

Section 102(g) is a general provision covering secret work by a first inventor that becomes known to the public after the invention by the second inventor. Section 102(g) serves as the basis for a so-called "interference"—an intricate administrative proceeding between two or more inventors, each asserting that it was the first inventor and therefore should obtain the award of a patent. Section 102(g) has another, more humble use: simply as another category of prior art which may be used as the basis of a rejection for anticipation or nonobviousness. In this case, the party asserting the statute is not claiming the invention for itself, but arguing that the issued patent is invalid. This effort usually involves the identification of a third party which invented first. In this sense, § 102(g) acts similarly to § 102(a). But, as we shall see, § 102(g) does not embrace a first inventor whose work was secret when the second inventor/applicant made his invention.

Section 102(f) prevents a patent from issuing to an applicant who "did not himself invent the subject matter sought to be patented." If the applicant derived the invention from another, then no patent can result from his application. Although the derivation requirement could well be considered as distinct from the prior art generating provisions of

§§ 102(a), (e) and (g), it sufficiently buttresses the novelty requirement to be considered with them.

In contrast to Chapter 5, *Statutory Bars*, the novelty issues addressed in this Chapter should not be considered as fundamental to the world's patent systems. In fact, they are entirely unique to the first-to-invent system of the United States. If the United States ever adopts a first-to-file system, this Chapter could be cleanly excised from the book. As you make your way through this Chapter, consider those values which the first-to-invent system purports to foster, the extent to which it actually meets these ends, and whether the United States patent community can long afford to maintain the inherent uncertainties, high transaction costs, and legal isolation of its unique novelty regime.

§ 6.1 PRIOR INVENTION UNDER § 102(a)

WOODCOCK v. PARKER

Circuit Court, District of Massachusetts, 1813.
30 Fed.Cas. 491.

STORY, CIRCUIT JUSTICE, in summing up the cause, directed the jury as follows: The first inventor is entitled to the benefit of his invention, if he reduce it to practice and obtain a patent therefor, and a subsequent inventor cannot, by obtaining a patent therefor, oust the first inventor of his right, or maintain an action against him for the use of his own invention. In the present case, as the defendants claim their right to use the machine in controversy by a good derivative title from Samuel Parker, if the jury are satisfied that said Parker was the first and original inventor of the machine, the plaintiff cannot, under all the circumstances, maintain his action; notwithstanding he may have been a subsequent inventor, without any knowledge of the prior existence of the machine, or communication with the first inventor. It is not necessary to consider, whether if the first inventor should wholly abandon his invention and never reduce it to practice, so as to produce useful effects, a second inventor might not be entitled to the benefit of the statute patent: because here there is not the slightest evidence of such abandonment. Parker is proved to have put his machine in operation; it produced useful effects, and he followed up his invention by obtaining a patent from the department of state.

Notes

1. The "First and Original" Inventor. Although the Statute of Monopolies indicated that patents could issue to the "true and first inventor," *An Act Concerning Monopolies and Dispensations with Penal Laws, and the Forfeitures Thereof*, 21 JAC. 1, ch. 3, § 6 (1623), it did not specify whether this "first" individual was the first applicant or the first inventor in fact. Justice Story's statement in *Woodcock* is among the earliest explaining a key concept of a first-to-invent system: that potentially novelty-destroying technology is measured from the date of invention, not the filing date. The Patent Act of 1836 was the first statute explicitly to embody the concept that "known or used" applied to acts before the invention date and not the filing date:

> That any person or persons having discovered or invented any new or useful art, machine, manufacture, or composition of matter, or any new and useful improvement on any art, machine, manufacture, or composition of matter, not known or used by others before his or their discovery or invention thereof, and not, at the time of his application for a patent, in public use or on sale, with his consent or allowance, as the inventor or discoverer; and shall desire to obtain an exclusive property therein, may make application in writing to the Commissioner of Patents, expressing such desire, and the Commissioner, on due proceedings had, may grant a patent therefor.

In its modern incarnation, this rule is expressed in § 102(a) as follows:

> A person shall be entitled to a patent unless—

> (a) the invention was known or used by others in this country, or patented or described in a printed publication in this or a foreign country, before the invention thereof by the applicant for patent. . . .

See generally FRANK E. ROBBINS, THE DEFENSE OF PRIOR INVENTION: PATENT INFRINGEMENT LITIGATION (1977).

2.   Disclosure of Invention Date. It may surprise you to learn that despite the primacy of the invention date in the United States patent statute, inventors have never been required to provide their dates of invention when they file applications with the United States Patent and Trademark Office. Instead, applicants' dates of inventive activity are revealed on an *ad hoc* basis in response to references cited by the examiner via so-called "Rule 131 affidavits," discussed later in this Chapter. Why does the United States patent system act so peculiarly with regard to invention date?

3.   The Meaning of "Known or Used." This casebook has already considered the impact of the territorial limitations of § 102(a), as well as the meaning of its use of the phrase "patented or described in a printed publication," in Chapter 4. Section 102(a) employs a new term, however: the invention must be "known or used by others."

This phrase should be contrasted with the "public use" requirement of § 102(b). Chapter 4 of this casebook dealt at length with the sorts of public uses that would could create a statutory bar under § 102(b). As you may suspect, the same issues arise under § 102(a) as well. Here, of course, no distinction can be drawn between the applicant and a third party—the issue is always whether a third party's use suffices to render him the prior inventor in terms of the patent law. But the question of whether secret and noninforming uses pass muster under § 102(a) remains.

GILLMAN v. STERN

Circuit Court of Appeals, Second Circuit, 1940.
114 F.2d 28, 46 U.S.P.Q. 430.
cert. denied, 311 U.S. 718 (1941).

BEFORE L. HAND, AUGUSTUS N. HAND, and CHASE, CIRCUIT JUDGES.

L. HAND, CIRCUIT JUDGE.

Both the plaintiffs and the defendant appeal from the judgment in this action. The plaintiffs filed the usual complaint, asking an injunction for the infringement of Patent No. 1,919,674, issued on July 25, 1933, to the Sterling Airbrush Co., assignee of Laszlo Wenczel, for a pneumatic 'puffing machine.' The defendant set up a number of defenses: [including] that there had been a prior use of it by one Haas, at least as early as 1930 (the application was filed on January 21, 1931).... The judge held the patent invalid because anticipated by the prior use of Haas....

The patent was for a pneumatic machine for quilting; i.e., it blew thread or yarn "into packets formed in the fabric to stuff the same to impart a raised or embossed design".

[U]pon the issue of invalidity the defendant relies ... upon the prior use by Haas. Haas at some time undoubtedly did invent a "puffing machine" designed to perform the same work as plaintiff's machine. Further, his first "puffer" was substantially the same as the plaintiff's; and, if it had been properly proved, it might be hard to support the patent. However, not only was there no evidence as to the date of it except the work of Haas and his wife—who knew incidentally nothing of its construction—but again and again, Haas spoke of it as an unsatisfactory temporary device which he had discarded before he began to do any business. It must certainly be considered an abandoned experiment and is therefore immaterial. Haas also testified that in the autumn of 1929 he invented another "puffer" in general structure like the first, except that there was no means—as in Wenczel's machine—to vary the air pressure by changing the position of any member like the "tube, 40." The plaintiff insists that for this reason it cannot anticipate, and literally that is true; but possibly, if it could be deemed a part of the prior art, the step between it and Wenczel's disclosure would not justify a monopoly. Besides, claim one does not incorporate the "regulating valve," i.e., the "tube 40." We need not, however, pass upon this question, or indeed whether the evidence of its date of production satisfied the exacting standard set by the *Barbed Wire Patent Case*, 143 U.S. 275, 12 S.Ct. 443, 450, 36 L.Ed. 154 for it is clear that it was never in prior "public use," and that Haas was not a "first inventor." It was always kept as strictly secret as was possible, consistently with its exploitation. In general, everybody was carefully kept out of Haas' shop where the four machines were used. He testified that "no one was allowed to enter but my employees," girls he had had "for years"; and that he "had instructed my girls that if anybody should ask to get any kind of information simply tell them you don't know. In fact I have my shop door so arranged that it could only be opened from the inside." He also enjoined secrecy on his wife who testified "no one ever got into the place and no one ever saw the machine. He made everything himself." Indeed, as a condition upon even testifying in the case at bar Haas insisted, and the judge ordered, that the lawyers should be sworn to keep secret all he said about the construction of the "puffer," and that it should not be printed in the record, but typed and sealed for the inspection of the judges alone. It does not appear that the "girls" knew how the machines which they used were made, or how they operated. The only exception to this was a disclosure, such as it was, to two members of a firm going by the name of the Bona Fide Embroidery Co.—Custer and Kadison. In the same autumn of 1929 they and Haas testified that they had seen some of his quilting and were anxious to get the whole of his output. They went to his shop to satisfy themselves; Custer said that "it was very vital at that time that I should know the workings of the machine for my production of the proper designs." (By "workings he could only have meant how it performed for he never learned its construction.") After this visit the two agreed that Haas should give them his whole production and that they should sell it; they even talked about taking out a patent, but did not have the necessary money. Thus, Haas kept his machine absolutely secret from the outside world except to secure selling agents for its product, and then it was only its performance, not its construction that even they learned. Moreover, Custer and Kadison had the same motive to suppress whatever information they got that Haas had, for without a patent the secret was all that protected their market.

Such a use is clearly not a "public" one, and such an inventor is not a "first inventor." In *Gayler v. Wilder*, 10 How. 477, 481, 497, 13 L.Ed. 504, the question was whether the condition—which has always been in the statute—that the patentee must be the "first and original inventor" was defeated by anyone who had earlier conceived the same invention, or only by one who had also in some way made public his results. A majority of the court held that only the second would defeat a patent on the ground that what had not in fact enriched the art, should not count; and the doctrine is now well fixed. *Alexander Milburn Co. v. Davis–Bournonville Co.*, 270 U.S. 390, 46 S.Ct. 324, 70 L.Ed. 651. Just as a secret use is not a "public use," so a secret inventor is not a "first inventor." *Acme Flexible Clasp Co. v. Cary Mfg. Co.*, C.C., 96 F. 344; *Diamond Patent Co. v. S. E. Carr Co.*, 9 Cir., 217 F. 400, 404; *A. Schrader's Sons v. Wein Sales Corp.*, 2 Cir., 9 F.2d 306; *Peerless Roll Leaf Co. v. H. Griffin & Sons Co.*, 2 Cir., 29 F.2d 646. Haas' user was one where "the machine, process, and product were not well known to the employes in the plant," and where "efforts were made to conceal them from anyone who had a legitimate interest in understanding them," if by "legitimate interest" one means something more than curiosity or mischief. *Electric Battery Co. v. Shimadzu*, 307 U.S. 5, 20, 59 S.Ct. 675, 684, 83 L.Ed. 1071. In *E. W. Bliss Co. v. Southern Can Co.*, D.C., 251 F. 903, 908, 909, *affirmed* 4 Cir., 265 F. 1018, although people were kept out of the factory, the exclusion was not, as in Haas' case, directed to the secrecy of the supposed anticipation.

We are to distinguish between a public user which does not inform the art (*Hall v. Macneale*, 107 U.S. 90, 97, 2 S.Ct. 73, 27 L.Ed. 367) and a secret user; some confusion has resulted from the failure to do so. It is true that in each case the fund of common knowledge is not enriched, and that might indeed have been good reason originally for throwing out each as anticipations. But when the statute made any "public use" fatal to a patent, and when thereafter the court held that it was equally fatal, whether or not the patentee had consented to it, there was no escape from holding—contrary to the underlying theory of the law—that it was irrelevant whether the use informed the public so that they could profit by it. Nevertheless, it was still true that secret uses were not public uses, whether or not public uses might on occasion have no public value. Perhaps it was originally open to argument that the statute merely meant to confine prior "public uses" to the prospective patentee and to be evidence of abandonment, and that "first inventor" meant to include anyone who first conceived the thing in tangible enough form to be persuasive. But, rightly or wrongly, the law did not develop so, and it is now too late to change. Hence the anomaly that by secreting a machine one may keep it from becoming an anticipation, even though its public use would really have told nobody anything about it.

Notes

1. § 102(a) vs. § 102(b). Although Judge Learned Hand's choice of words is sometimes dated, his conclusion that secret uses do not comprise prior art under § 102(a) remains good law. What does Judge Hand say about noninforming uses? Does a comparison of third party noninforming and secret uses under § 102(a) and § 102(b) reveal consistent conclusions by the courts?

2. *Gillman* After *Metallizing*. Recall that in his later opinion in *Metallizing Engineering*, reprinted here in Chapter 4, Judge Hand conceded some prior confusion in his earlier decisions. Nonetheless, he insisted that he had properly decided *Gillman*. Given *Gillman*'s citation of statutory bar cases such as *Electric Storage Battery v. Shimadzu*, also provided in Chapter 4, are you convinced? Do § 102(a) and § 102(b) necessarily fulfill the same policies in this regard?

3. Later Holdings. Numerous subsequent cases follow *Gillman*'s insertion of the word "public" into § 102(a). *Levi Strauss & Co. v. Golden Trade, S.r.L.,* 1995 WL 710822 (S.D.N.Y.1995) provides an apt summary:

> Under section 102(a), even though the text only requires that the prior invention be "known or used," the challenger must show public knowledge or use, where the "public" means those skilled in the art. This does not require actual knowledge or use by the public, just that the prior invention was publicly accessible. Accessibility may be satisfied by work done in the open "and in the ordinary course of the activities of the employer." This public accessibility requirement is consistent with the policy that the patent system will not grant a patent for something previously done; thus the inventor is required to disclose known prior art.

National Tractor Pullers Ass'n v. Watkins, 205 U.S.P.Q. 892 (N.D.Ill.1980), presents one of the more unusual factual circumstances in which this rule was applied. There, the declaratory judgment plaintiff asserted that a patented device useful in tractor pulling contests was invalid under § 102(a). The plaintiff pointed to drawings made by a third party on the underside of a tablecloth in his mother's kitchen. The drawings had never been printed prior to their destruction, nor had the depicted device been commercialized. The court concluded that these drawings did not comprise prior art: "Prior knowledge as set forth in 35 U.S.C.A. § 102(a) must be prior public knowledge, that is knowledge which is reasonably accessible to the public."

4. The First Inventor Defense. One of the titles of the American Inventors Protection Act of 1999, the First Inventor Defense Act, created an infringement defense for an earlier inventor of a method of doing or conducting business that was later patented by another. *See* 35 U.S.C.A. § 273. The defendant must have reduced the infringing subject matter to practice one year before the effective filing date of the patent and made commercial use of that subject matter in the United States before the effective filing date. Congress enacted this legislation in response to the Federal Circuit's holding in *State Street Bank*—reprinted here in Chapter Two—and out of awareness of the prior art status of trade secrets. For more on the First Inventor Defense Act, see § 16.3 of this casebook.

5. Northern Exposure. Relative to the United States, the Canadian system was a more "pure" first-to-invent system; potentially novelty destroying technology would be that invented anywhere in the world whether secret or public prior to the invention date of the applicant. The decision of the Privy Council reaching this conclusion, *Christiana v. Rice,*[1931] A.C. 770, remains one of the great cases in patent law. *Christiana* traces the history of the Canadian patent law to the landmark 1836 Act in the United States. However, it then holds that a second inventor may not obtain a patent regardless of the circumstances surrounding the first invention. Thus, contrary to the law in the United States, *Christiana* held that a first inventor who maintains his invention in secret in a foreign country has engaged in patent defeating activity in Canada. This pure first-to-file approach was too much for the Canadian Parliament. In 1935 Parliament limited patent defeating activity to secret activity that ultimately resorted in the filing a patent application in Canada or where the information was made available to the public before the second inventor filed for his patent, *Patent Act.* R.S., c. P–4, § 61. All of this is now history since Canada abandoned the first-to-invent approach to patent law in 1989, 35–36 Elizabeth II, Chapter 41.

6. Rule 131 Practice. An important aspect of Patent Office practice is the use of Rule 131. This Rule allows applicants to declare an invention date prior to the date of a prior art reference. The need for Rule 131 arises because inventors need not attest to their date of inventive activity when they file patent applications. Instead, they reveal their invention date on an *ad hoc* basis when the examiner produces a pertinent prior art reference. Use of Rule 131 is informally known as "swearing behind" or "antedating" a reference. Rule 131 itself provides:

Code of Federal Regulations Title 37

§ 1.131 Affidavit or declaration of prior invention to overcome cited patent or publication.

> (a)(1) When any claim of an application or a patent under reexamination is rejected under 35 U.S.C.A. 102(a) or (e), or 35 U.S.C.A. 103 based on a U.S. patent to another which is prior art under 35 U.S.C.A. 102(a) or (e) and which substantially shows or describes but does not claim the same patentable invention, as defined in 37

C.F.R.§ 1.601(n), or on reference to a foreign patent or to a printed publication, the inventor of the subject matter of the rejected claim, the owner of the patent under reexamination, or the party qualified under 37 C.F.R. § 1.42, 1.43 or 1.47, may submit an appropriate oath or declaration to overcome the patent or publication. The oath or declaration must include facts showing a completion of the invention in this country or in a NAFTA or WTO member country before the filing date of the application on which the U.S. patent issued, or before the date of the foreign patent, or before the date of the printed publication. When an appropriate oath or declaration is made, the patent or publication cited shall not bar the grant of a patent to the inventor or the confirmation of the patentability of the claims of the patent, unless the date of such patent or printed publication is more than one year prior to the date on which the inventor's or patent owner's application was filed in this country.

(2) A date of completion of the invention may not be established under this section before December 8, 1993, in a NAFTA country, or before January 1, 1996, in a WTO Member country other than a NAFTA country.

(b) The showing of facts shall be such, in character and weight, as to establish reduction to practice prior to the effective date of the reference, or conception of the invention prior to the effective date of the reference coupled with due diligence from prior to said date to a subsequent reduction to practice or to the filing of the application. Original exhibits of drawings or records, or photocopies thereof, must accompany and form part of the affidavit or declaration of their absence satisfactorily explained.

* * *

Rule 131 has no applicability to statutory bars such as § 102(b), which are keyed to the filing date of the patent application. Further, the use of Rule 131 should not be confused with a true interference proceeding under § 102(g). As explained in *In re Zletz*, 893 F.2d 319, 13 U.S.P.Q.2d 1320 (Fed.Cir.1989):

> Rule 131 provides an *ex parte* mechanism whereby a patent applicant may antedate subject matter in a reference, even if the reference describes the same invention that is claimed by the applicant, provided that the same invention is not claimed in the reference when the reference is a United States patent. As explained in *In re McKellin*, 529 F.2d 1324, 1329, 188 U.S.P.Q. 428, 434 (CCPA 1976), the disclosure in a reference United States patent does not fall under 35 U.S.C.A. § 102(g) but under 35 U.S.C.A. § 102(e), and thus can be antedated in accordance with Rule 131. But when the subject matter sought to be antedated is claimed in the reference patent, Rule 131 is not available and an interference must be had to determine priority.

§ 6.2 THE ELEMENTS OF "INVENTION" UNDER § 102(g)

Section 102(g) consists of two sub-paragraphs, serving two principal purposes in the patent law. Section 102(g)(1) provides a mechanism for resolving disputes relating to so-called "priority of invention." In this class of cases, one party seeks more than merely the denial of another's entitlement to patent rights on a particular technology. It also seeks to obtain patent rights for itself.

The need to determine priority of invention should be clear. As rivals across the globe compete to develop valuable technologies, they will often develop similar or identical inventions at approximately the same time. In such circumstances, the U.S. patent system has adopted a winner-take-all policy. Only the person or persons that first developed a particular technology will be awarded a patent. This policy is implemented through the rules set forth in § 102(g), which determine which actor will be judged the first inventor in terms of the patent law. The administrative procedure through which these substantive rules are effected, a so-called "interference," is described below.

The second sub-paragraph, § 102(g)(2), expressly states the general rule of priority: "A person shall be entitled to a patent unless . . . before the applicant's invention thereof the invention was made in this country by another. . . ." Section 102(g)(2) then states an important exception to this rule. If the first inventor has "abandoned, suppressed or concealed" the technology at issue, then he has essentially forfeited his special status in accordance with § 102(g)(2). Section 102(g)(2) goes on to instruct that "[i]n determining priority of invention there shall be considered not only the respective dates of conception and reduction to practice of the invention, but also the reasonable diligence of one who was first to conceive and last to reduce to practice, from a time prior to conception by the other."

Like most of the other paragraphs of § 102, § 102(g)(2) provides a source of prior art that may be used as the basis of a rejection for anticipation or nonobviousness. In these circumstances, the party asserting a § 102(g) reference is not claiming the invention for itself, but arguing that the issued patent is invalid. This effort usually involves the identification of a third party that allegedly invented first. In this sense, then, § 102(g) functions similarly to § 102(a).

§ 6.2[a] Patent Interferences

As noted above, § 102(g) serves not only as a category of prior art, but also as the fountainhead of patent interference law. An overview of this complex proceeding, as set forth in more detail in § 135 and the Patent Office Regulations (Title 37 of the Code of Federal Regulations), should assist your understanding of the § 102(g) cases that follow.

Interferences may occur between two pending applications, or between a pending application and an issued, unexpired patent. The Patent Office will call for an interference when "an application is made for a patent which . . . would interfere with any pending application, or with any unexpired patent. . . ." 35 U.S.C.A. § 135. An examiner may declare an interference upon learning of two conflicting applications without any activity by the applicants. Alternatively, an applicant may initiate an interference upon discovering a newly issued United States patent that claims the same invention.

Patent interference procedures typically involve some particular terminology. Many cases will refer to so-called "senior" and "junior" parties: "A senior party is the party with the earliest effective filing date.... A junior party is any other party." 37 C.F.R. § 1.601(m). Interferences also make use of a concept called a "count," which corresponds to a claim which the interfering parties share. The counts of an interference define what the dispute is about; this is the subject matter which each of the parties asserts that it invented first.

The court in *Hahn v. Wong*, 892 F.2d 1028, 13 U.S.P.Q.2d 1313 (Fed.Cir.1989), described the opening phases of an interference as follows:

> Both the patent statute and the regulations of the Patent and Trademark Office authorize an interference between an application for a patent and an issued patent. 35 U.S.C.A. § 135(a) (Supp. V 1987) and 37 C.F.R. § 1.606 (1988). If the effective filing date of the application is more than three months after the effective filing date of the patent, the applicant is required to file evidence demonstrating that the "applicant is prima facie entitled to a judgment relative to the patentee," and "an explanation stating with particularity" why he "is prima facie entitled to the judgment." 37 C.F.R. § 1.608(b) (1988).
>
> When an application for an interference is filed, a primary examiner makes a preliminary determination "whether a basis upon which the applicant would be entitled to a judgment relative to the patentee is alleged and, if a basis is alleged, an interference may be declared." 37 C.F.R. § 1.608(b). As the Commissioner of Patents and Trademarks explained in his brief amicus curiae in this case, the "one and only one, purpose" of the primary examiner's examination of the application is "to determine whether the applicant alleges a date of invention prior to the effective date of the patent" (emphasis in original). See also M.P.E.P. § 2308.02, last paragraph.
>
> If the primary examiner makes a preliminary determination that the application meets that requirement, the application is referred to an examiner-in-chief to determine whether an interference should go forward. See 37 C.F.R. §§ 1.609 & 1.610(a) (1988). If the examiner-in-chief determines that a prima facie case for priority has been established, the interference proceeds. 37 C.F.R. § 1.617(a) (1988). If however, the examiner-in-chief concludes that a prima facie case has not been shown, the examiner-in-chief declares an interference but "enter[s] an order stating the reasons for the opinion and directing the applicant, within a time set in the order, to show cause why summary judgment should not be entered against the applicant." Id. If such an order to show cause issues, the applicant "may file a response to the order and state any reasons

why summary judgment should not be entered." 37 C.F.R. § 1.617(b). The rule states, however,

> Additional evidence shall not be presented by the applicant or considered by the Board unless the applicant shows good cause why any additional evidence was not initially presented with the evidence filed under § 1.608(b). Id.

A panel of the Board then determines whether (1) summary judgment should be entered against the applicant or (2) the interference should proceed. 37 C.F.R. § 1.617(g).

If the interference continues, next comes the filing of applicant preliminary statements. These statements contain allegations of the dates of various inventive activities the parties believe they can establish during an interference. After preliminary statements have been filed, the parties may submit various motions to the Board of Patent Appeals and Interferences, raising issues that will be contested during the interference. 37 C.F.R. § 1.633. These motions may address topics strictly unrelated to the interference. For example, a motion might contend that a party to the interference derived the invention from the moving party. If granted, the Patent Office would deny the nonmovant a patent under § 102(f) and dissolve the interference.

The trial phase of the interference follows. The parties are given the opportunity to present affidavits, declarations and exhibits such as laboratory notebooks and publications. After the trial comes a final hearing before a three-member panel of the Board of Patent Appeals and Interferences, consisting solely of oral argument by the parties. The Board then issues its decision, typically awarding priority of invention to one of the interfering parties.

Interferences may be resolved in other ways, however. One party may assert ordinary grounds for patent invalidity; for example, that the patent claims subject matter ineligible for patenting. This effort tends to be rather uncommon, as often a defense which invalidates one application or patent will be effective for them all; but sometimes the result that no one obtains a patent is a satisfactory solution to one of the parties to the interference. Settlement between the parties is another option, although Congress has recognized the possibility of collusive arrangements with anticompetitive effects. The result is 35 U.S.C.A. § 135(c), which requires that the parties file copies of agreements reached in contemplation of termination of an interference. The filed agreements are available for public inspection.

Sometimes the Patent Office and applicants do not become aware of interfering applications, with the result that two patents directed towards the same inventive concept issue. Section 291 of the Patent Act, entitled "Interfering Patents," addresses these hopefully rare circumstances. Owners of interfering patents may have their respective rights determined by a federal district court following the filing of a civil suit.

For more details on interference practice, the venerable multi-volume treatise CHARLES W. RIVISE & A.D. CAESAR, INTERFERENCE LAW AND PRACTICE (1940) remains the best starting point. *See also* BRUCE M. COLLINS, CURRENT PATENT INTERFERENCE PRACTICE (1992); MAURICE H. KLITZMAN, PATENT INTERFERENCE LAW AND PRACTICE (1984).

§ 6.2[b] The Rule of Priority

With this overview of interference practice complete, we next consider the workings of the United States priority regime. In *Christie v. Seybold*, 55 F. 69, 76 (6th Cir.1893), Judge (later President, later Chief Justice) Taft set forth the following statement:

> It is obvious from the foregoing that the man who first reduces an invention to practice is prima facie the first and true inventor, but that the man who first conceives, and, in a mental sense, first invents, a machine, art, or composition of matter, may date his patentable invention back to the time of its conception, if he connects the conception with its reduction to practice by reasonable diligence on his part, so that they are substantially one continuous act. The burden is on the second reducer to practice to show the prior conception, and to establish the connection between that conception and his reduction to practice by proof of due diligence. It has sometimes been held, in the decisions in the patent office, that the necessity for diligence on the part of the first conceiver does not arise until the date of the second conception; but this, we think, cannot be supported on principle. The diligence of the first reducer to practice is necessarily immaterial. It is not a race of diligence between the two inventors in the sense that the right to the patent is to be determined by comparing the diligence of the two, because the first reducer to practice, no matter what his diligence or want of it, is prior in right unless the first conceiver was using reasonable diligence at the time of the second conception and the first reduction to practice. The language of the statute, (section 4920,) in the use of the imperfect tense, "was using reasonable diligence," shows the legislative intent to confer a prior right on a first conceiver in a case where, after his mental act of invention, and pending his diligent reduction to practice, another inventor enters the field and perfects the invention before his rival. The reasonable diligence of the first conceiver must be pending at the time of the second conception, and must therefore be prior to it. Reasonable diligence by the first conceiver, beginning when his rival enters the field, could only carry his invention back to the date of the second conception, and in the race from that time the second conceiver must win because of his first reduction to practice.

Section 102(g) today states the general rule: the first inventor to reduce an invention to practice wins the priority contest. But if the inventor who is first to conceive the invention, but second to reduce the invention to practice, can show diligence from the time prior to the conception date of the first to reduce to practice, he will displace the first to reduce the invention to practice as the first inventor at law. The remaining portions of § 5.2 of this text consider the details of each of the requirements noted in § 102(g): conception, reduction to practice and diligence.

§ 6.2[c] Conception

OKA v. YOUSSEFYEH

United States Court of Appeals, Federal Circuit, 1988.
849 F.2d 581, 7 U.S.P.Q.2d 1169.

Before MARKEY, CHIEF JUDGE, RICH, CIRCUIT JUDGE, and MILLER, SENIOR CIRCUIT JUDGE.

MARKEY, CHIEF JUDGE.

The Patent and Trademark Office Board of Patent Appeals and Interferences (board), in Interference No. 101,111, awarded priority of invention to junior party Youssefyeh et al. over senior party Oka et al., who relied on their October 31, 1980 Japanese filing date under 35 U.S.C. § 119. We reverse.

BACKGROUND

The sole generic count in the interference is directed to compounds possessing angiotensin converting enzyme inhibition activity, and is set forth as follows:

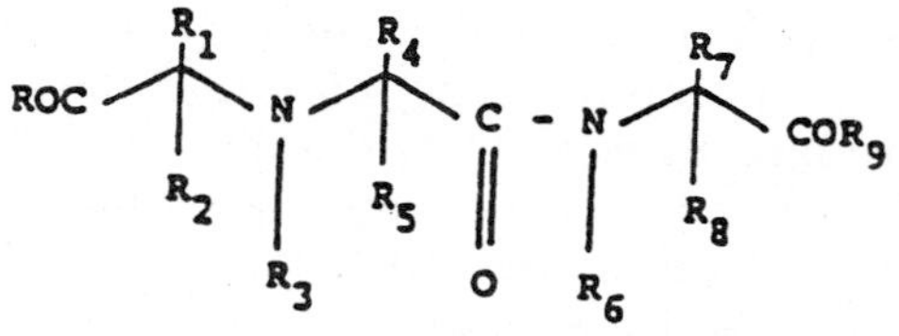

wherein: R and R sub9 are independently hydroxy or lower alkoxy; R sub1 is hydrogen, lower alkyl or aryl lower alkyl; R sub2, R sub3, R sub4, R sub5, R sub7 and R sub8 are hydrogen or lower alkyl; R sub6 is indanyl; and their pharmaceutically acceptable salts.

The compounds can be described as optionally esterified carboxyalkyl substituted dipeptides that contain two amino acid groups, one of which, typically a glycine, bears a group R sub6, defined as an "indanyl group". The indanyl glycine of the count may be a Cycloaliphatically-bonded Indanyl, typically a 2–indanyl group, or an Aromatically-bonded Indanyl, typically a 5–indanyl group.

On February 27, 1980, one of Youssefyeh's co-inventors, Suh, recorded in his notebook this structural formula, encompassing billions of compounds within the class of 2–Indanyl Glycines:

OPINION

Conception requires (1) the idea of the structure of the chemical compound, and (2) possession of an operative method of making it. Youssefyeh quotes from *Townsend v. Smith*, 36 F.2d 292, 295, 4 U.S.P.Q. 269, 271 (CCPA 1929): Conception may conveniently be considered as consisting of two parts. The first part is "the directing conception" and may be defined as the idea or conception that a certain desired result may be obtained by following a particular general plan. The directing conception is often referred to as the inventive concept, thought or idea. The second part of conception is "the selection of the means for effectively carrying out the directing conception."

When, as is often the case, a method of making a compound with conventional techniques is a matter of routine knowledge among those skilled in the art, a compound has been deemed to have been conceived when it was described, and the question of whether the conceiver was in possession of a method of making it is simply not raised. In the present case, the board itself recognized that conception required both a description, i.e., the idea, of a compound and possession of a method for making it. In denying Youssefyeh's claim of February 27, 1980, as its conception date, the board said: It is Youssefyeh's position that conception occurred on February 27, 1980, * * * because the inventors believed on that date that the compounds could be prepared in accordance with conventional techniques. However, Bernstein, a skilled Ph.D. chemist, spent over six months and was not successful in preparing the 2–indanyl compounds within the scope of the count, a circumstance which indicates that the inventors did not contemplate an operative invention, e.g., an operative method for making the compounds as of February 27, 1980.

The board made these not clearly erroneous findings: (1) because Youssefyeh had only the idea of a 2–indanyl class of compounds on February 27, 1980, it did not establish conception on that date; (2) Youssefyeh was in possession of a method of making a compound outside the scope of the interference count on October 10, 1980; (3) during the last week of October 1980, co-applicant Suh directed his assistant to use the October 10, 1980 method to prepare a species of a 5–indanyl class of compounds within the scope of the interference count; (4) the assistant successfully did so in December 1980; (5) Youssefyeh reduced the invention to practice on January 9, 1981.[1] Based on findings (2), (3), and (4), the board found that "an operative procedure was realized for preparing the 5–indanyl compound" as of October 10, 1980. That finding was clearly erroneous.

The board correctly noted that conception of a species within a genus may constitute conception of the genus. However, as Youssefyeh acknowledges, 2–indanyl compounds and 5–indanyl compounds are different species within the generic interference count. Youssefyeh did not conceive of the 2–indanyl compound as an operative invention on February 27, 1980 because it lacked at that time (and on this record never acquired) possession of a method for making it. Youssefyeh did not conceive of the 5–indanyl compound as an operative invention on October 10, 1980 because it lacked at that time the idea of the 5–indanyl compound, and the method it then possessed was a method for making something else. Thus Youssefyeh did not establish conception of either species before Oka's filing date.

That the October 10 method was found in December, after Oka's filing date, to be an effective method of making the 5–indanyl compound did not serve to move the date on which Youssefyeh had the idea of the 5–indanyl compound back to October 10, 1980. There is no evidence that that method could be used to make the 2–indanyl compound, and, given the difference between aromatically-bonded and cycloaliphatically-bonded indanyl glycines, there is no basis for a view that a description or method of making one is applicable to the other. The board made no finding that Youssefyeh had the idea of a 5–indanyl compound before the last week of October 1980. Youssefyeh does not argue, and no one testified, that it did have that idea before that time. The record would not in any event support such a finding. The board therefore erred in determining that Youssefyeh had established conception as of October 10, 1980.

Because Oka is the senior party, Youssefyeh was required to establish reduction to practice before Oka's filing date, or conception before that date coupled with reasonable diligence from just before that date to Youssefyeh's filing date. 35 U.S.C. § 102(g). The board's finding that Youssefyeh initiated preparation of a 5–indanyl compound "in the last week of October 1980" supports the conclusion that Youssefyeh failed to establish conception, much less a reduction to practice, of that class of compounds earlier than October 31, 1980. In dealing with a reduction to practice, the court in Haultain v. DeWindt, 254 F.2d 141, 117 U.S.P.Q. 278 (CCPA 1958), stated, "Further, where testimony merely places the acts within a stated time period, the inventor has not established a date for his activities earlier than the last day of the period." Id. at 142, 117

---

1. In view of our determination respecting conception, we need not and do not reach the parties' arguments on diligence and reduction to practice, except to note that neither party argues that the dual requirement for conception of an operative invention (idea plus method of making) equates conception with reduction to practice. The latter in this case would involve verification of the compound's utility as a hypotensive agent.

U.S.P.Q. at 279. That rule is equally appropriate in establishing a date of conception, nor does Youssefyeh dispute Oka's position that "the last week in October" means October 31.

Thus Youssefyeh's conception and Oka's filing date are the same, i.e., October 31, 1980. Oka, as the senior party, is presumptively entitled to an award of priority, and Youssefyeh, as the junior party in an interference between pending applications, must overcome that presumption with a preponderance of the evidence. In the event of a tie, therefore, priority must be awarded to the senior party. Because Youssefyeh, the junior party, failed to show a conception date earlier than Oka's filing date, Oka is entitled to priority. We reverse the board's award of priority to Youssefyeh.

REVERSED.

Notes

1. **And A Tie Goes to** ... Do you agree with Chief Judge Markey's conversion of the procedural assignment of the burden of proof to the junior party into a substantive rule of priority? Note that current U.S. Patent and Trademark Office practice places the burden on the junior party only to overcome the senior party's filing date in order to provoke the interference. *See* 37 C.F.R. § 1.657 (1996). The junior party need not win the entire interference at first blush, nor is the senior party's inventive activity prior to its filing date even relevant at that point. Further, once the junior party has fulfilled this burden, then any presumption should vanish under the "bursting bubble" theory of presumptions endorsed by the *en banc* Federal Circuit in *A.C. Aukerman Co. v. R.L. Chaides Construction Co*, 960 F.2d 1020, 22 U.S.P.Q.2d 1321 (Fed.Cir.1992). The *Aukerman* decision is reprinted here in part in Chapter 16.

2. **Rule of Conception.** To show conception, an inventor must present proof showing possession or knowledge of each feature of the count and communicated to a corroborating witness in sufficient detail to enable one of skill in the art to replicate the invention. *See Coleman v. Dines*, 754 F.2d 353, 359, 224 U.S.P.Q. 857 (Fed.Cir.1985). The Federal Circuit confronted a situation where proof of conception was an exchange of letters between two individuals. One of them, Coleman, claimed that the letters show his prior conception. The Federal Circuit disagreed:

> The difficulty here is that initial formation in Coleman's mind must be, but was not, firmly established. The evidence did not show that Coleman's "completed thought" was disclosed to others. [cite deleted] What was shown here, at best, was that the ideas were "intermingled," and not that Coleman was the "spark."

754 F.2d at 360. Could the letters have sufficed to show conception if they showed that Coleman was the "spark?" How should an individual inventor demonstrate her "sparkness" when more than one person contributes to the inventive process?

3. **Comparative Approaches.** The difficulty of determining which of several parties with identical priority dates should receive the patent grant is not unique to first-to-invent systems like that of the United States. In a

first-to-file regime, ties of this sort could also occur when multiple inventors simply file patent applications addressing the same invention on the same day. Article 39(2) of the Japanese Patent Act provides for this situation as follows:

> Where two or more patent applications relating to the same invention are filed on the same date, only one such applicant, agreed upon after mutual consultation among all the applicants, may obtain a patent for the invention. If no agreement is reached or no consultation is possible, none of the applicants shall obtain a patent for the invention.

Compare this approach with that set out by Article 54 of the European Patent Convention, which provides:

> (1) An invention shall be considered to be new if does not form part of the state of the art.

> (2) The state of the art shall be held to comprising everything made available to the public by means of a written or oral description, by use, or in any other way, before the date of filing of the European patent application.

> (3) Additionally, the content of European patent applications as filed, of which the dates of filing are prior to the date referred to in paragraph 2 and which were published under Article 93 on or after that date, shall be considered as comprised in the state of the art.

How does this language impact several inventors, or their assignees, who file applications to the same invention on the same day? Of the three approaches, which do you favor?

§ 6.2[d] Reduction to Practice

An inventor may reduce an invention to practice in two ways: constructively, by filing a patent application, and actually, by building and testing a physical embodiment of the invention. If the reduction to practice is to be constructive, the filed application must fully disclose the invention. As noted in *Travis v. Baker*, 137 F.2d 109, 58 U.S.P.Q. 558 (CCPA 1943), an application "must be for the same invention as that defined in the count in an interference, and it must contain a disclosure of the invention sufficiently adequate to enable one skilled in the art to practice the invention defined by the count, with all the limitations contained in the count, without the exercise of inventive facilities." As the next case indicates, the doctrine of actual reduction to practice imposes similar requirements.

SCOTT v. FINNEY

United States Court of Appeals, Federal Circuit, 1994.
34 F.3d 1058, 32 U.S.P.Q.2d 1115.

Before LOURIE, RADER, and SCHMALL, CIRCUIT JUDGES.

RADER, CIRCUIT JUDGE.

The Board of Patent Appeals and Interferences awarded priority in Interference No. 102,429 to the senior party, Dr. Roy P. Finney. The

Board held that the junior party, Dr. F. Brantley Scott and John H. Burton, did not show a reduction to practice before Dr. Finney's date of invention. Because the Board imposed an overly strict requirement for testing to show reduction to practice, this court reverses and remands.

BACKGROUND

This interference involves Dr. Finney's United States Patent No. 4,791,917, which was accorded the benefit of its May 15, 1980 parent application, and the Scott and Burton application, Serial No. 07/241,826, which was accorded the benefit of its parent application Serial No. 06/264,202, filed May 15, 1981. Although the Scott and Burton application claims a joint invention of both applicants, Dr. Scott is the sole inventor of the subject matter in interference No. 102,429.

The invention is a penile implant for men unable to obtain or maintain an erection. The prosthetic device is a self-contained unit that permits the patient to simulate an erection. The implant contains two reservoirs connected through a valve. The invention operates by shifting the inflating liquid between the two reservoirs. When the penis is flaccid, the invention maintains inflating liquid in a reservoir at the base of the penis. A simulated erection occurs when the liquid shifts through the valve into the elongated reservoir implanted in the forward section of the penis.

Prior art devices fell into two categories: flexible rods and inflatable devices. Flexible rods had the disadvantage of making the penis permanently erect. The prior inflatable devices relied on fluid from a source and pump external to the body to inflate tubes implanted in the penis. These devices also had several disadvantages.

The Interference Count at issue states:

> An implantable penile prosthesis for implanting completely within a patient's penis comprising at least one elongated member having a flexible distal forward section for implantation within the pendulous penis, said forward section being constructed to rigidize upon being filled with pressuring fluid; a proximal, rearward section adapted to be implanted within the root end of the penis, said rearward section containing a fluid reservoir chamber, externally operable pump means in said member for transferring fluid under pressure to said flexible distal forward section of said member for achieving an erection; and valve means positioned within said member which open when said pump is operated so that fluid is forced from said pump through said valve means into said flexible distal forward section of said chamber.

The parties to this interference had contested related subject matter in an earlier interference, No. 101,149. The count of 101,149 was a species of the generic count in this interference. Dr. Scott won that earlier interference.

In this interference, No. 102,429, Dr. Finney's application has an earlier filing date than Scott's application. Dr. Scott still has, however, an earlier conception date. Dr. Scott did not present evidence of diligence after conception of his invention. Rather, Dr. Scott opted to show an actual reduction to practice before Dr. Finney's date of invention.

Before the Board, Dr. Scott's primary evidence of actual reduction to practice was a videotape. The videotape showed an operation where the surgeon inserted Dr. Scott's prototype device into the penis of an anesthetized patient. The videotape showed the surgeon manipulating the implanted device. Several times the device simulated an erection when the surgeon manipulated the valve. Several times the fluid filled the forward reservoir. Several times the surgeon returned the penis to a flaccid condition by draining the fluid back into the rear reservoir. The Board found:

> It is uncontested that the penile implant used in the in-and-out procedure did rigidify the penis by pressurization of the rear chamber and did produce an erection. After the device was actuated to form the erection, the valve mechanism was manipulated to allow the device to become flaccid....

Although not part of the count, the parties agree that the invention envisions implantation of two devices—one on either side of the penis. In the videotaped demonstration, the surgeon implanted only a single prosthesis into the patient. Although using only a single prosthesis, the videotape showed a penis with enough rigidity to produce an erection. After manipulating the implanted device through the skin to simulate having and losing an erection, the surgeon removed Dr. Scott's prototype and inserted a prior art external pump mechanism.

Dr. Scott supplied other evidence as well. He presented evidence of testing for leakage, disclosed that the fabrication material was common in implanted devices, and supplied the testimony of Dr. Drogo K. Montague, an expert in the field. Dr. Montague personally handled the device at issue and viewed the videotape. He testified that the video showed, even with only a single tube, sufficient rigidity for intercourse.

In opposition, Dr. Finney testified personally about the difficulty of determining sufficient rigidity for intercourse on the basis of insertion in an anesthetized patient. Both Drs. Finney and Montague agreed that insertion of two tubes would greatly enhance rigidity.

The Board discerned insufficient evidence to show reduction to practice. Specifically, the Board determined that Dr. Scott had not shown utility, i.e., that the device would successfully operate under actual use conditions for a reasonable length of time. Thus, the Board required "testing of an implantable medical device under actual use conditions or testing under conditions that closely simulate actual use conditions for an appropriate period of time."

Because Dr. Scott had not tested his device in actual intercourse or in similar conditions to intercourse for a proper period of time, the Board determined that Dr. Scott had not reduced his invention to practice. The Board awarded the count to Dr. Finney. This appeal followed.

DISCUSSION

The issue of reduction to practice is a question of law which this court reviews de novo. This court reviews the Board's factual findings under the clearly erroneous standard.

The Scott and Burton application was copending with that of Dr. Finney. Consequently, as the junior party in this interference, Dr. Scott had the burden to show prior invention by a preponderance of evidence. To show prior invention, the junior party must show reduction to practice of the invention before the senior party, or, if the junior party reduced to practice later, conception before the senior party followed by reasonable diligence in reducing it to practice.

To show reduction to practice, the junior party must demonstrate that the invention is "suitable for its intended purpose." *Steinberg v. Seitz*, 517 F.2d 1359, 1363, 186 U.S.P.Q. 209, 212 (CCPA 1975). When testing is necessary to show proof of actual reduction to practice, the embodiment relied upon as evidence of priority must actually work for its intended purpose. Because Dr. Scott relied on such testing, this court must examine the quality and quantity of testing asserted to show a reduction to practice.

Testing sufficient to show a reduction to practice has often been at issue in interference proceedings. *Newkirk*, 825 F.2d at 1582 ("proof of actual reduction to practice requires demonstration that the embodiment relied upon as evidence of priority actually worked for its intended purpose"); *see also Kimberly–Clark Corp. v. Johnson & Johnson*, 745 F.2d 1437, 1445, 223 U.S.P.Q. 603, 607 (Fed.Cir.1984) (same); *Wiesner v. Weigert*, 666 F.2d 582, 588, 212 U.S.P.Q. 721, 726 (CCPA 1981) (same). By the same token, this court has also indicated "that '[s]ome devices are so simple and their purpose and efficacy so obvious that their complete construction is sufficient to demonstrate workability.' "*King Instrument Corp. v. Otari Corp.*, 767 F.2d 853, 861, 226 U.S.P.Q. 402, 407 (Fed.Cir.1985), *cert. denied*, 475 U.S. 1016, 106 S.Ct. 1197, 89 L.Ed.2d 312 (1986) (quoting *Eastern Rotorcraft Corp. v. United States*, 384 F.2d 429, 431, 155 U.S.P.Q. 729, 730 (Ct.Cl.1967)). Indeed, the Supreme Court, in a case featuring evidence of testing, cited approvingly three decisions of the United States Court of Appeals for the District of Columbia which stated that simple devices need no testing to show reduction to practice.

In cases requiring testing, this court's predecessor addressed many times the nature of testing necessary to show reduction to practice. Several important principles emerge from these cases. For instance, the testing requirement depends on the particular facts of each case, with the court guided by a common sense approach in weighing the sufficiency of the testing. Reduction to practice does not require "that the invention, when tested, be in a commercially satisfactory stage of development." Testing need not show utility beyond a possibility of failure, but only utility beyond a probability of failure. When reviewing the sufficiency of evidence of reduction to practice, this court applies a reasonableness standard.

Complex inventions and problems in some cases require laboratory tests that "accurately duplicate actual working conditions in practical use." *Elmore v. Schmitt*, 278 F.2d 510, 513, 125 U.S.P.Q. 653, 656 (CCPA 1960); *accord Koval v. Bodenschatz*, 463 F.2d 442, 447, 174 U.S.P.Q. 451, 455 (CCPA 1972) (testing of electrical circuit breaker did not test higher voltages); *Anderson v. Scinta*, 372 F.2d 523, 527, 152 U.S.P.Q. 584, 587 (CCPA 1967) (testing of windshield wiper blades did not simulate effect of wind on windshield); *but cf. Paivinen v. Sands*, 339 F.2d 217, 225–26, 144 U.S.P.Q. 1, 8–9 (CCPA 1964) (oscilloscope testing of magnetic switching circuit necessarily involved high speed switching). In *Elmore*, the Court of Customs and Patent Appeals noted that the various tests on a binary counter for sophisticated radar and video equipment did not account for "the resistance and character of load, nature of pulses, including voltage, duration and amplitude, and amount of capacitance used." *Elmore*, 278 F.2d at 512. The court also noted that the tests did not "reproduce[ ] the conditions of temperature, vibration, or sustained operation which would usually be encountered in a specific use." *Id. Elmore* demanded closer correlation between testing conditions and actual use conditions because the presence of many variables in that precision electronics field would otherwise raise doubts about the invention's actual capacity to solve the problem.

Less complex inventions and problems do not demand such stringent testing. In *Sellner v. Solloway*, 267 F.2d 321, 122 U.S.P.Q. 16 (CCPA 1959), for example, the inventor presented his invention, an exercise chair, at a birthday party. Because "the device involved and manner in which it is intended to operate are comparatively simple," *id.* at 323, the court sustained the sufficiency of this rudimentary testing by individuals without particular skills.

This court's predecessor well summarized many of these principles:

> A certain amount of "common sense" must be applied in determining the extent of testing required. Depending on its nature, the invention may be tested under actual conditions of use, or may be tested under "bench" or laboratory conditions which fully duplicate each and every condition of actual use, or in some cases, may be tested under laboratory conditions which do not duplicate all of the conditions of actual use. In instances where the invention is sufficiently simple, mere construction or synthesis of the subject matter may be sufficient to show that it will operate satisfactorily.

Gordon, 347 F.2d at 1006. This statement captures the underlying principle that governs the nature of testing necessary to show reduction to practice—the character of the testing varies with the character of the invention and the problem it solves.

Another predecessor to this court summarized, "the inquiry is not what kind of test was conducted, but whether the test conducted showed that the invention would work as intended in its contemplated use."

Eastern Rotorcraft Corp. v. United States, 384 F.2d 429, 431, 155 U.S.P.Q. 729, 730 (Ct.Cl.1967). Thus, the Court of Claims focused on the workability of the invention in the context of the problem it solved. The nature and complexity of the problem necessarily influence the nature and sufficiency of the testing necessary to show a reduction to practice. In any event, the testing should demonstrate "the soundness of the principles of operation of the invention." *Wolter v. Belicka*, 409 F.2d 255, 263, 161 U.S.P.Q. 335, 341 (CCPA 1969) (Rich, J., dissenting). The inventor need show only that the invention is "suitable" for its intended use.

All cases deciding the sufficiency of testing to show reduction to practice share a common theme. In each case, the court examined the record to discern whether the testing in fact demonstrated a solution to the problem intended to be solved by the invention. *See, e.g., Farrand Optical Co. v. United States*, 325 F.2d 328, 333, 139 U.S.P.Q. 249, 253 (2d Cir.1963) ("The essential inquiry here is whether the advance in the art represented by the invention . . . was embodied in a workable device that demonstrated that it could do what it was claimed to be capable of doing.") (emphasis added). In tests showing the invention's solution of a problem, the courts have not required commercial perfection nor absolute replication of the circumstances of the invention's ultimate use. Rather, they have instead adopted a common sense assessment. This common sense approach prescribes more scrupulous testing under circumstances approaching actual use conditions when the problem includes many uncertainties. On the other hand, when the problem to be solved does not present myriad variables, common sense similarly permits little or no testing to show the soundness of the principles of operation of the invention.

In the prosthetic implants field, polyurethane materials and inflatable penile prostheses were old in the art. They were tested extensively. Only the insertion and hydraulics of a manipulable valve separating two implanted reservoirs were new. Thus, Dr. Scott had the burden to show that his novel valve and dual reservoir system would simulate an erection for sexual intercourse when manipulated through the skin. Consequently, the problem presented to Dr. Scott, when viewed from the vantage point of earlier proven aspects of penile implant technology, was relatively uncomplicated.

In the videotape presentation, Dr. Scott demonstrated sufficiently the workability of his invention to solve the problems of a wholly internal penile implant. The videotaped operation showed both rigidity for intercourse and operability of the valve to inflate and deflate the device through the skin. The use of materials previously shown to work in prosthetic implants over a reasonable period of time also showed the durability of the invention for its intended purpose. In sum, Dr. Scott showed sufficient testing to establish a reasonable expectation that his invention would work under normal conditions for its intended purpose, beyond a probability of failure.

The Board erred by setting the reduction to practice standard too high. The Board erroneously suggested that a showing of reduction to practice requires human testing in actual use circumstances for a period of time. *See Engelhardt v. Judd*, 369 F.2d 408, 410–11, 151 U.S.P.Q. 732, 734 (CCPA 1966) (human testing of antihistamine and antiserotonin unnecessary in light of tests on laboratory animals). Reduction to practice, however, does not require actual use, but only a reasonable showing that the invention will work to overcome the problem it addresses. The videotape showed the rigidity and manipulability of the valve through the skin necessary for actual use. Experts testified to the invention's suitability for actual use. In the context of this art and this problem, Dr. Scott made that reasonable showing.

The Board rejected these proofs because the device was not actually used during intercourse. In this instance of a solution to a relatively simple problem, the Board required more testing than necessary to show that the device would work for its intended purpose. Even accepting the Board's conclusion that the intended purpose is to facilitate normal sexual intercourse, prior art prosthetic devices had fully tested the workability of most features of Dr. Scott's invention. Dr. Scott used the same tested and workable materials and designs of prior art implants. Only the hydraulics of a fully self-contained internal prosthesis remained to be tested for workability. Dr. Scott adequately showed the workability of these features.

Testing for the full safety and effectiveness of a prosthetic device is more properly left to the Food and Drug Administration (FDA). Title 35 does not demand that such human testing occur within the confines of Patent and Trademark Office (PTO) proceedings.

The Board's holding that Dr. Scott did not reduce his invention to practice before the May 15, 1980 filing date of Dr. Finney is reversed. Dr. Finney asserted that Dr. Scott abandoned, suppressed, or concealed the invention embodied by the count within the meaning of 35 U.S.C. § 102(g) (1988). The Board did not reach this issue in light of its holding that no reduction to practice occurred. Because the Board has not considered this issue, this court remands for a determination of whether Dr. Scott abandoned, suppressed, or concealed the invention within the meaning of § 102(g).

REVERSED AND REMANDED.

Notes

1. Constructive Reduction to Practice. Given the patent law's emphasis on tangible, material inventions, what do you think of the doctrine of constructive reduction to practice? Does it tend to confuse events which occurred in the patent office, as compared to acts in the field? In the absence of the constructive reduction to practice doctrine, one who failed to actually reduce his invention to practice before his filing date could not get an invention date earlier than his filing date. Would it be better law to give one who actually built something the opportunity to obtain an earlier filing date?

2. Continued Prosecution Required. An applicant must continue to prosecute a patent for that instrument to constitute a constructive reduction to practice. If an application is abandoned, its filing date may be used as evidence of conception of the invention. *See In re Costello*, 717 F.2d 1346, 219 U.S.P.Q. 389 (Fed.Cir.1983).

3. Standard for Proof of Actual Reduction to Practice. *Newkirk* states the classic test for reduction to practice: Does the embodiment relied upon for proof of reduction to practice actually work for its intended purpose? However, the Federal Circuit has indicated that this requirement is not always necessary:

> Our predecessor court has recognized that the invention must have been "sufficiently tested to demonstrate that it will work for its intended purpose." ... Moreover, the district court might have considered that "[s]ome devices are so simple and their purpose and efficacy so obvious that the complete construction is sufficient to demonstrate their workability." *Eastern Rotorcraft Corp. v. United States*, 384 F.2d 429, 431, 155 U.S.P.Q. 729, 730 (Ct.Cl.1967).... Accordingly, the district court did not err in inferring that the '358 invention embodied in an existing machine was sufficiently tested to constitute a reduction to practice.

King Instr. Corp. v. Otari Corp., 767 F.2d 853, 861, 226 U.S.P.Q. 402, 407 (Fed.Cir.1985). How did *Scott v. Finney* reconcile this apparent inconsistency?

4. Do You Remember When? When did you see *Scott v. Finney* cited for an important principle? The important result in the utility case, *In re Brana*, reprinted here in Chapter 3, relied principally on *Scott* for the principle that the PTO should not require human testing.

5. Simultaneous Conception and Reduction to Practice. In *Amgen, Inc. v. Chugai Pharmaceutical Co.*, 927 F.2d 1200, 18 U.S.P.Q.2d 1016 (Fed.Cir.1991), the court discussed circumstances in which conception and reduction to practice can occur simultaneously. The case concerned U.S. Patent 4,703,008, entitled "DNA Sequences Encoding Erythropoietin," which issued on October 27, 1987, to Amgen assignee Dr. Fu–Kuen Lin. The patent claimed purified and isolated DNA sequences encoding erythropoietin, as well as host cells transformed or transfected with a DNA sequence. Among the asserted claims was claim 2, which provided for: "A purified and isolated DNA sequence consisting essentially of a DNA sequence encoding human erythropoietin." Following Amgen's successful infringement suit against Chugai Pharmaceutical Co., Chugai appealed to the Federal Circuit, asserting that the '008 patent was invalid under § 102(g). The court explained:

> In some instances, an inventor is unable to establish a conception until he has reduced the invention to practice through a successful experiment. This situation results in a simultaneous conception and reduction to practice. See 3 D. CHISUM, PATENTS § 10.04[5] (1990). We agree with the district court that that is what occurred in this case.

> The invention recited in claim 2 is a "purified and isolated DNA sequence" encoding human EPO. The structure of this DNA sequence was unknown until 1983, when the gene was cloned by Lin; Fritsch was

unaware of it until 1984. As Dr. Sadler, an expert for Genetics Institute, testified in his deposition: "You have to clone it first to get the sequence." In order to design a set of degenerate probes, one of which will hybridize with a particular gene, the amino acid sequence, or a portion thereof, of the protein of interest must be known. Prior to 1983, the amino acid sequence for EPO was uncertain, and in some positions the sequence envisioned was incorrect. Thus, until Fritsch had a complete mental conception of a purified and isolated DNA sequence encoding EPO and a method for its preparation, in which the precise identity of the sequence is envisioned, or in terms of other characteristics sufficient to distinguish it from other genes, all he had was an objective to make an invention which he could not then adequately describe or define.

A gene is a chemical compound, albeit a complex one, and it is well established in our law that conception of a chemical compound requires that the inventor be able to define it so as to distinguish it from other materials, and to describe how to obtain it. Conception does not occur unless one has a mental picture of the structure of the chemical, or is able to define it by its method of preparation, its physical or chemical properties, or whatever characteristics sufficiently distinguish it. It is not sufficient to define it solely by its principal biological property, e.g., encoding human erythropoietin, because an alleged conception having no more specificity than that is simply a wish to know the identity of any material with that biological property. We hold that when an inventor is unable to envision the detailed constitution of a gene so as to distinguish it from other materials, as well as a method for obtaining it, conception has not been achieved until reduction to practice has occurred, i.e., until after the gene has been isolated.

§ 6.2[e] Diligence

GOULD v. SCHAWLOW

United States Court of Customs and Patent Appeals, 1966.
363 F.2d 908, 150 U.S.P.Q. 634.

Before WORLEY, CHIEF JUDGE, and RICH, MARTIN, SMITH AND ALMOND, JUDGES.

WORLEY, CHIEF JUDGE.

Gould appeals from the decision of the Board of Patent Interferences which awarded priority of invention of the subject matter set forth in four counts to the senior party, Schawlow and Townes (Schawlow). After reviewing a voluminous record in light of appellant's allegations of reversible error, but finding none, we affirm that decision.

The invention relates to an apparatus for light amplification by stimulated emission of radiation, better known by the acronym 'laser.'

It appears that amplification of electromagnetic radiation by stimulated emission of radiation was first realized on a practical basis by devices operating in the microwave frequency range. The laser is described in the record as an extension of the maser principle to optical wavelengths, i.e. infrared, visible and ultraviolet light. No matter in what portion of the electromagnetic spectrum it is designed to operate, it appears that the heart of a maser-like device is a working medium, generally a gas or solid, containing atoms or molecules which have one or more sets of energy levels. Unlike the situation ordinarily prevailing in a volume of matter at equilibrium, where the lower energy states of the material will be more heavily populated with atoms or molecules than the higher energy levels, the laser working medium contains material in which a higher energy level is populated by a significantly greater number of atoms than is a lower energy level of the material. A working medium in such a non-equilibrium condition is said to have an "inverted population" or "negative temperature." The means used to excite or "pump" the working medium to create an inverted population of atoms or molecules may comprise a source of electromagnetic energy, for example, a strong light of suitable wavelength directed at the working medium.

The record also shows that a medium in which a population inversion exists may be stimulated to emit its stored energy by wave energy (microwave energy in a "maser" and light energy in a "laser") of the frequency corresponding to the energy separation of the inverted pair of energy levels, thus amplifying the stimulating signal. In marked contrast to white light from the sun or an electric light bulb, which consists of a whole spectrum of colors and which is emitted in a random, non-directional manner when excited atoms spontaneously return to a lower energy level, the light radiation emerging from the laser device here under conditions of stimulated emission is both "temporally coherent" (a term used to describe the monochromatic nature of the emitted light) and "spatially coherent" (a term used to describe the tendency of the emergent light to undergo little divergence or spreading).

The counts of the interference relate to a laser comprising an active medium with the requisite energy level characteristics, means for pumping that medium, and a cavity resonator to enhance the laser operation. The cavity employed in microwave masers which characteristically has dimensions of the order of one wavelength, e.g. 1–100 centimeters, cannot be conveniently employed in light amplifiers because of the shortness ($10-(5)$—$10-(2)$ cm) of light wavelengths. Rather, a cavity is utilized which has dimensions on the order of thousands or more of light wavelengths. Typically, the cavity defined by the counts is formed by a pair of spaced, plane, parallel optical reflectors, at least one of which is partially transparent, and side members through which pumping energy is admitted and some of the spontaneous and undesired stimulated emission, deviating in its travel from an axis perpendicular to the reflecting end plates, is allowed to escape. The laser employing a pair of opposed reflectors is now termed a Fabry–Perot laser, since the structure involved is reminiscent of the so-called Fabry–Perot interferometer used by physicists for a number of years. The desired output beam of the laser is built up or amplified by repeated passes back and forth along the axis perpendicular to the reflecting end plates, ultimately passing out of the cavity through the partially transparent end reflecting member in coherent form.

With the advent of devices capable of amplifying radiation other than microwaves, the term "maser" has assumed a more general meaning—molecular amplification by stimulated emission of radiation. The Schawlow patent uses the expression "optical maser" to denote an apparatus performing the function of the "laser." As a consequence, the counts employ the expression "maser." Count 1, to which we have added numerals keyed to Fig. 2 of the Schawlow patent reproduced below, is representative:

1. A maser generator comprising a chamber (14) having end reflective parallel members (16, 17) and side members (15), a negative temperature medium disposed within said chamber, and means (20) arranged about said chamber for pumping said medium, said side members being transparent to the pumping energy and transparent to or absorptive of other energy radiated threat.

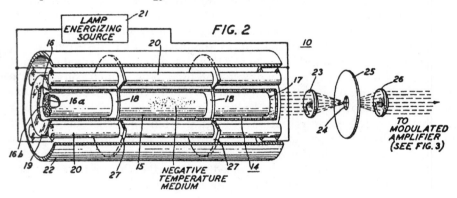

Both Schawlow and Gould rely on their filing dates of July 30, 1958, and April 6, 1959, respectively, for constructive reduction to practice of the subject matter in interference, neither party alleging an actual reduction to practice prior to those dates. Under such circumstances it is, of course, well established interference law that the junior party, here Gould, must prove by a preponderance of the evidence reasonable diligence in reducing it to practice commencing from a time just prior to July 30, 1958, to his filing date of April 6, 1959. 35 U.S.C. 102(g).

DILIGENCE

To establish reasonable diligence during the critical period from just prior to July 30, 1958, to April 6, 1959, Gould relies principally on his own testimony; that of his wife, Ruth; Exhibit 9, a notebook said to represent a 'distillation' of his efforts from November 1957 to December 1958; and the testimony of his patent attorney relating to their joint activities from December 1958 to April 1959.

Little or no question has been raised by either the board or Schawlow concerning Gould's diligence from December 1958 to his filing date of April 6, 1959. The record shows that during that time Gould's attorney prepared the present application while concurrently engaged in a 40-day patent infringement trial in Utica, New York. Under the circumstances, we do not think further discussion of the activities of Gould or his attorney during that period of time is necessary.

It appears from Gould's testimony that, shortly after recording his alleged conception in Exhibit 1, he became cognizant of the potential high cost of building his proposed device, and also became "aware of the considerable experimental difficulties in dealing with the alkali elements," the material he proposed as a working medium in that notebook. He began to consider "other possibilities that might be easier * * * to build," stating that "I was more interested in seeing it (the laser) built than trying to protect myself in my patent interests." He testified that he worked on such theoretical considerations evenings and weekends at home and in libraries, studying "a large amount of background material" and making "rough calculations in connection with that background material." As an example of some of the things he did during that period Gould stated he "conceived of a number of other pumping mechanisms besides optical pumping," and spent "maybe a hundred hours" searching the "M.I.T. wave length tables" for coincidences between strong spectral lines to find "elements that could be optically pumped." He also described the laser invention "briefly" to his patent attorney in January 1958, and was advised at that time that Columbia University would have no patent rights in that invention. The motivation for that visit to his attorney, Gould stated, was that he realized "more and more what an important development" the laser would be, having, written the notebook constituting Exhibit 1 and having made a further study of the background material.

In the belief he would not be able to do experimental work on the laser at Columbia University until he had completed his thesis, Gould simultaneously sought to locate a research facility where experimental laser work could be done. To that end he visited Stevens Institute of Technology sometime between November 1957 and February 1958, where Professor Bostick told Gould that there were insufficient funds available at Stevens to support work in the laser field. Gould stated he described the laser "in great detail" in March 1958 to his friend, Dr. Alan Berman, an individual "knowledgeable in the area of masers, generally," upon seeking employment to work on the laser at Hudson Laboratories, where Dr. Berman was associate director.

In late March 1958, Gould left Columbia University without completing his Ph.D. degree requirements, and joined the staff at TRG, Inc. According to Gould, his reason for leaving Columbia and joining TRG was to have an opportunity to do experimental work on the laser, having understood from his interviews with Dr. Daly of that company that he would have such an opportunity after completing his initial assignment on a research contract relating to a rubidium gas frequency standard, a project which occupied Gould's working time until the end of May 1958. While on that project, he disclosed his laser concept to co-worker Newstein. His next project was to write a proposal to build a rubidium maser which occupied his time until June 13; in the ensuing months through October, Gould apparently was engaged in experimental work on the rubidium maser.

During his free time from March to June 1958, Gould stated he "was busy formulating and writing down in a notebook the principles of the laser." The notebook referred to apparently is Exhibit 9, about which we will have more to say later. Gould testified he took 6 ½ days off from work at TRG in July, telling Dr. Goldmuntz, TRG's president, that he wished to finish writing his thesis. Actually, Gould stated, the real purpose of taking time off was "to get this laser notebook written," since he believed he would never finish it in a reasonable time by working on it only on weekends and evenings. Gould testified he took off two days in August, three days in September, 13 ½ days in October and 12 days in November for the same purpose. In August, Gould again talked to Dr. Berman concerning the laser, explaining, "how it worked and what its applications would be."

Toward the end of September 1958, Gould first informed Dr. Goldmuntz of his ideas concerning the laser, and was subsequently assigned to write, on company time, a proposal describing the device and methods of building it. By the middle of December 1958, the proposal was completed and submitted to various government agencies and Aerojet General Corporation for evaluation. The Advanced Research Projects Agency subsequently awarded TRG a research contract totaling nearly a million dollars for development of the subject matter of the proposal.

Summarizing his activities over the period November 1957 to December 1958, Gould estimated he spent "approximately a thousand hours" acquiring the knowledge which enabled him to devise the ideas expressed in Exhibit 9, and that there were no months or weeks during that period in which he did not "work on the laser."

In commenting on Gould's evidence of diligence, the board stated:

> * * * we do not find that a sufficient account has been made of the critical period so that we can assure ourselves that no unexplained lapse appears therein. Occurrences such as Gould's failure to participate in the reconditioning of his boat in the spring of 1958, and conversations such as those with co-worker Newstein at TRG, Inc. and with Dr. Alan Berman at beach parties in May and August, 1958 do not corroborate specific significant acts directly related to giving the invention a physical embodiment. Such evidence is far too fragmentary, and leaves to mere inference that Gould was actively engaged in reducing the invention to practice during this crucial period. We are not prepared to make this inference.

Nor are we. Even were we to disregard for the moment the necessity for corroboration and thus give Gould's testimony the full weight to which properly corroborated testimony in an interference is entitled, we find the testimony in and of itself insufficient to adequately establish what Gould did and when he did it. Little attempt has been made to identify particular activity with particular times during the critical period of concern—July to December 1958 and especially July, August and September 1958—or to establish how such activity related to reducing to practice the subject matter of the counts. In our view, Gould's testimony taken as a whole does not set forth adequate facts to support a finding of that continuity of activity which constitutes reasonable diligence. Merely stating that there were no weeks or months that he "did not work on the laser" is not enough, absent supporting facts showing specifically what that "work" consisted of and when it was performed.

Much of Gould's more detailed testimony, as summarized above, relates to the period November 1957 to March 1958. Apart form his general assertions that there were no weeks or months in 1958 that he did not work on the laser, we find the only relevant activities from July to September 1958 referred to by Gould are his acts of taking off from work at TRG in those months and his discussion with Dr. Berman in August. Gould asserts the board erred in basing its decision as to the question of diligence in part on the extent to which Gould took days off from TRG to record his ideas in Exhibit 9. While reasonable diligence does not require that one abandon his means of livelihood to further his reduction to practice, it was incumbent upon Gould, if he intends to rely on the taking of time from his normal employment as acts of diligence, to establish what was done and when it was done. Merely stating, for example, that he took off 6 ½ days in July, 2 days in August, and 3 days in September does not enable us to ascertain the extent of time gaps in his activity. The months of July and August, bracketing Schawlow's entry into the field, are critical to Gould's case, and a lapse of nearly two months would result if 6 ½ days were taken at the start of that period and the 2 days at the end. The party chargeable with diligence must account for the entire period during which diligence is required. Gould has not done so here. As in Ireland v. Smith, 97 F.2d 95, 25 CCPA 1258:

> We may surmise that appellant was probably diligent * * * but mere surmise cannot take the place of proof * * *.

Finally, Gould contends that the board has taken a "formalistic approach" to the doctrine of reasonable diligence in its statement:

> * * * we are not convinced that he was proceeding with due diligence in reducing the subject matter of the counts to practice during that portion of the critical period just prior to and after July 30, 1958, the record date of the senior party's entry into the field.

Whatever due diligence may be, Gould asserts, it would appear to reflect a particularly high standard, more than the "reasonable diligence" required by statute, and may not properly be required to establish priority. The effect of the board's holding, Gould contends, is to deny him the benefit of the principle that

> * * * An inventor who is the first to conceive an invention can prevail, no matter how limited his resources may be, and no matter

how long it should take him to complete the invention, if he devotes those resources at his command with reasonable and continuous diligence toward the actual reduction to practice of the invention.

Similar arguments have been made over the years, but the fact remains that the presence or absence of reasonable diligence must necessarily be determined by the evidence adduced in each case. Here the board held, and properly so, that Gould had failed to provide sufficient evidence to discharge his burden of proving reasonable diligence in reducing the invention to practice.

Gould would have us believe that his alleged efforts to construct a simpler and less expensive embodiment of his conception are penalized, rather than rewarded, by the patent statutes—statutes which have contributed mightily to the unprecedented advances of this country in so many fields. But such is not the case. Congress has wisely provided the same opportunity for the inventor whose attic is his laboratory as for the giants of modern industry to file a patent application and obtain the protection thereby afforded. We are aware of no valid reason why Gould could not have taken advantage of his opportunity to timely file his application and obtain the benefits of a constructive reduction to practice as did Schawlow.

Clearly it was the intent of Congress to assure the first inventor who had completed the mental act of invention that he should not be deprived of his reward by reason of delays which he could not reasonably avoid in giving his invention to the public. But we must bear in mind that it was not alone to reward the inventor that the patent monopoly was granted. The public was to get its reward and have the advantage of the inventor's discovery as early as was reasonably possible. * * * Our review of the record with due regard for Gould's arguments convinces us that the board did not err in awarding Schawlow and Townes priority of invention.

The decision is affirmed.

Notes

1. **Diligence Policy.** Why does United States patent law feature a diligence requirement? Perhaps because it recognizes that anyone can have a good idea without needing considerable funding. In contrast, reduction to practice typically requires that an inventor marshal significant resources, either to construct a working prototype or to engage the services of a patent attorney. So long as the inventor remains diligent in working towards either sort of reduction to practice, § 102(g) will preserve the privileged first inventor status. The statute may thus be seen as promoting an equality of opportunity between actors in the technological community with different levels of financial means. But is equality of opportunity worth the added complexity of a first-to-invent system?

2. **Dispelling Diligence Misconceptions.** The following points are often troublesome to students of § 102(g).

Diligence is only apposite where one party claims an earlier conception date, but a later reduction to practice date. The inventor who is both first to conceive and first to reduce an invention to practice wins the priority contest without having to show diligence. Once again, though, a holding of abandonment is possible if the inventor waits too long before filing a patent application.

Only one party's diligence is relevant in a priority contest. Section 102(g) is concerned with the diligence only of the inventor who was first to conceive, but second to reduce to practice. Competing inventors do not engage in any sort of diligence race. If the first inventor to reduce the invention to practice overly delays in bringing the invention forth, however, that delay may well be considered an abandonment.

The required period of diligence for the inventor who was first to conceive, but last to reduce to practice, begins at the time "prior to the conception by the other" and ends when the inventor who was first to conceive reduces the invention to practice. No amount of diligence which begins after the other's conception date, or occurs after reduction to practice has taken place, bears upon the priority contest.

3.   Diligence and Constructive Reduction to Practice. How does an inventor prove diligence when relying on a constructive reduction to practice—that is, when the inventor hires a patent attorney to file an application claiming the invention? Cases have recognized that other demands upon a patent attorney's workload may excuse delay in filing a particular application. In general, if the attorney takes the application up within a reasonable time, such as in the order it was received, then the inventor will be found diligent. In another case involving Gordon Gould, the court reasoned that: "The fact that Gould's patent attorney, Mr. Keegan, was able to prepare and file a 132–page patent application with 56 claims while simultaneously involved in a long infringement trial establishes diligence from at least as early as December, 1958 through the filing in April, 1959." *Gould v. General Photonics Corp.*, 534 F.Supp. 399, 404, 215 U.S.P.Q. 116, 120 (N.D.Cal.1982). The court in *Mendenhall v. Astec Industries, Inc.*, 13 U.S.P.Q.2d 1913 (E.D.Tenn.1988), *aff'd*, 887 F.2d 1094, 13 U.S.P.Q.2d 1956 (Fed.Cir.1989), was less sympathetic towards a junior practitioner. It held that diligence was not established where the patent attorney worked on client matters received following his hiring by the inventor, sat for a state bar examination, and took a vacation following that examination.

4.   *Gould*: The Rest of the Story. Gould lost this interference, but still acquired numerous patents on basic laser technology. *See Gould v. Quigg*, 822 F.2d 1074, 3 U.S.P.Q.2d 1302 (Fed.Cir.1987); *Gould v. Control Laser Corp.*, 705 F.2d 1340, 217 U.S.P.Q. 985 (Fed.Cir.1983); *In re Gould*, 673 F.2d 1385, 213 U.S.P.Q. 628 (CCPA 1982); *Gould v. Hellwarth*, 472 F.2d 1383, 176 U.S.P.Q. 515 (CCPA 1973).

§ 6.2[f]   Corroboration

An inventor may make use of the various inventive activities—conception, reduction to practice, and diligence—only if they have been corroborated.

WOODLAND TRUST v. FLOWERTREE NURSERY, INC.

United States Court of Appeals, Federal Circuit, 1998.
148 F.3d 1368, 47 U.S.P.Q.2d 1363.

Before NEWMAN, MICHEL, and CLEVENGER, CIRCUIT JUDGES.

PAULINE NEWMAN, CIRCUIT JUDGE.

Woodland Trust appeals the judgment of the United States District Court for the Middle District of Florida, holding United States Patent 4,763,440 (the '440 patent) invalid based on prior knowledge and use by others. Because uncorroborated oral testimony, particularly that of interested persons recalling long-past events, does not, of itself, provide the clear and convincing evidence required to invalidate a patent on this ground, the judgment is reversed.

BACKGROUND

The '440 patent, inventor Gregory James, is assigned to Woodland Trust. The invention is a method and apparatus for protecting a plot of foliage plants from freezing, by establishing an insulating covering of ice over ground level watering. It is described as particularly applicable to ferns grown in Florida for floral use. Claim 1 is illustrative, and describes the patented method:

1. A method for protecting a ground plot of foliage plants from freezing, said method comprising the steps of:

(a) providing ground-level sprinklers throughout said plot;

(b) covering said plot and said ground-level sprinklers with a covering of the type having openings therein;

(c) providing elevated sprinklers above said covering;

(d) sprinkling said plot with water through said ground-level sprinklers; and

(e) sprinkling said covering with water through said elevated sprinklers as the ambient temperature drops to about 32F., whereby the water from said elevated sprinklers freezes in the openings of said covering and holds heat released during operation of said ground-level sprinklers under said covering.

The patent application was filed on July 1, 1983; the patent issued on August 16, 1988. In response to Woodland's suit for patent infringement, filed in 1993, Flowertree Nursery pled several defenses, including patent invalidity under 35 U.S.C. § 102(a), § 102(b), and § 103. Under § 102(a), Flowertree stated that the method was previously known and used by each of Joseph Burke and William Hawkins (an owner of Flowertree) in the 1960s and 1970s at their nurseries in Florida, and was then discontinued by these users in 1976 and 1978. The district court found that Hawkins' system at Flowertree was reconstructed in 1988.

Four witnesses testified in support of the defense of prior knowledge and use: Mark Hawkins, Joseph Burke, Charles Hudson, and John Kaufmann. Mark Hawkins is the son of William Hawkins; he testified that his father's system, on which he worked as a child, was destroyed by a tornado in 1978, and was not reconstructed until 1988. Joseph Burke is a nursery owner who has known William Hawkins since the 1960s; he testified that he used the same system as shown in the patent, but tore it down in 1976 and did not rebuild it. Charles Hudson is a nursery owner who had worked for Joseph Burke, and John Kaufmann is a life-long friend of William Hawkins; they testified that they observed the patented system at the Burke or Hawkins nursery, before its use was discontinued. Woodland provided conflicting testimony; a witness named Marcus Crosby explained that he described the patented system to William Hawkins, his employer at Flowertree in 1988, after learning about it during his prior employment with Gregory James.

The district court credited the statements of all of the Flowertree witnesses, holding that "to discredit those witnesses in this case the court would be obliged to conclude that all four were deliberate perjurers." On the basis of this testimony the district court found that the apparatus claims of the '440 patent were anticipated under 35 U.S.C. § 102(a) by the Hawkins and Burke systems "which constitute prior art that was known publicly for many years before the filing date of the application for patent," and that the method claims of the '440 patent were anticipated under § 102(a) by the Burke method which was "openly and publicly used in the ordinary course of business" such that "the methods claimed in the patent were 'known' and 'used' by others more than one year before the filing date of the original application for the patent." The district court held the patent invalid, and did not discuss other defenses raised by Flowertree.

DISCUSSION

A

35 U.S.C. § 102(a) provides:

§ 102.   A person shall be entitled to a patent unless—

(a) the invention was known or used by others in this country, or patented or described in a printed publication in this or a foreign country, before the invention thereof by the applicant for patent. . . .

Section 102(a) establishes that a person can not patent what was already known to others. If the invention was known to or used by others in this country before the date of the patentee's invention, the later inventor has not contributed to the store of knowledge, and has no entitlement to a patent. Accordingly, in order to invalidate a patent based on prior knowledge or use, that knowledge or use must have been available to the public. *See Carella v. Starlight Archery,* 804 F.2d 135, 139, 231 U.S.P.Q. 644, 646 (Fed.Cir.1986) (the § 102(a) language "known or used by others in this country" means knowledge or use which is accessible to the public); 35 U.S.C. § 102(a) reviser's note (1952) (noting that " 'known' has been held to mean 'publicly known' " and that "no change in the language is made at this time"); P.J. Federico, *Commentary on the New Patent Act* (1954) *reprinted in* 75 J. PAT. TRADEMARK OFF. SOC'Y 161, 178 (1993) ("interpretation [of § 102(a)] by the courts excludes various kinds of private knowledge not known to the public"; these "narrowing interpretations are not changed").

Therefore, notwithstanding abandonment of the prior use—which may preclude a challenge under § 102(g)—prior knowledge or use by others may invalidate a patent under § 102(a) if the prior knowledge or use was accessible to the public.

The district court also referred to the criteria of § 102(b), which establishes a one year grace period based on publication or public use or sale, after which an inventor is barred from access to the patent system. Section 102(b), unlike § 102(a), is primarily concerned with the policy that encourages an inventor to enter the patent system promptly, while recognizing a one year period of public knowledge or use or commercial exploitation before the patent application must be filed. Thus an inventor's own prior commercial use, albeit kept secret, may constitute a public use or sale under § 102(b), barring him from obtaining a patent. *See Egbert v. Lippmann*, 104 U.S. 333, 336, 26 L.Ed. 755 (1881) (inventor's unobservable prior use was a "public use").

However, when an asserted prior use is not that of the applicant, § 102(b) is not a bar when that prior use or knowledge is not available to the public. *See W.L. Gore & Assocs., Inc. v. Garlock, Inc.*, 721 F.2d 1540, 1550, 220 U.S.P.Q. 303, 310 (Fed.Cir.1983) (third party secret commercial activity, more than one year before the patent application of another, is not a § 102(b) bar).

B

Woodland argues that the uncorroborated oral testimony of persons related to or associated with the defendant can not provide the clear and convincing evidence that precedent requires to establish prior knowledge and use, particularly in view of the many years of asserted commercial use, the passage of time after the asserted use, and the acknowledged abandonment of the system by both asserted prior users. Flowertree responds that the district court's finding of prior use turned entirely on credibility, and that the credibility assessment of the trier of fact is entitled to great respect and should not be overturned on appeal.

Although an appellate court is indeed in a poor position to assess credibility, there is a very heavy burden to be met by one challenging validity when the only evidence is the oral testimony of interested persons and their friends, particularly as to long-past events. Corroboration of oral evidence of prior invention is the general rule in patent disputes. "Throughout the history of the determination of patent rights, oral testimony by an alleged inventor asserting priority over a patentee's rights is regarded with skepticism, and as a result, such inventor testimony must be supported by some type of corroborating evidence." *Price v. Symsek,* 988 F.2d 1187, 1194, 26 U.S.P.Q.2d 1031, 1036 (Fed.Cir. 1993). In assessing corroboration, this court has endorsed the following criteria, as compiled in *In re Reuter,* 670 F.2d 1015, 1021 n. 9, 210 U.S.P.Q. 249, 255 n. 9 (Cust. & Pat.App.1981):

(1) the relationship between the corroborating witness and the alleged prior user,

(2) the time period between the event and trial,

(3) the interest of the corroborating witness in the subject matter in suit,

(4) contradiction or impeachment of the witness' testimony,

(5) the extent and details of the corroborating testimony,

(6) the witness' familiarity with the subject matter of the patented invention and the prior use,

(7) probability that a prior use could occur considering the state of the art at the time,

(8) impact of the invention on the industry, and the commercial value of its practice.

Price, 988 F.2d at 1195 n. 3, 26 U.S.P.Q.2d at 1037 n. 3. Such an analysis can be described as application of a "rule of reason" to the corroboration requirement. *See Mahurkar v. C.R. Bard, Inc.,* 79 F.3d 1572, 1577, 38 U.S.P.Q.2d 1288, 1291 (Fed.Cir.1996) (citing *Barbed Wire Patent Case,* 143 U.S. 275, 12 S.Ct. 443, 36 L.Ed. 154 (1892) and explaining that the corroboration requirement "arose out of a concern that inventors testifying in patent infringement cases would be tempted to remember facts favorable to their case by the lure of protecting their patent or defeating another's patent").

The *Barbed Wire Patent Case* litigation concerned a patent that was granted in 1874 for a barbed wire fence. Some twenty-four witnesses appeared on behalf of the accused infringers, all testifying that they had seen the same barbed wire fence exhibited by a Mr. Morley at the Delhi county fair in 1858. Witnesses testified to various events, one to having helped Morley put up the fence, another to hitching a horse to the fence and later finding the horse's nose bloodied bythe barbs, another to having received a sample of Morley barbed wire which he produced at the trial, another that a boy was thrown against the Morley fence and that scars were still visible from the barbs, and others that they were attracted to the fence and paid close attention to its construction. The patentee, in turn, presented witnesses who testified that they had attended the Delhi fair but had seen "nothing of the Morley fence," in the district court's words. The son of the witness who produced a sample of barbed wire contradicted his father's testimony. The district court deemed it extremely unlikely that all of the defendants' witnesses were lying, and held the patent invalid. *Washburn & Moen Mfg. Co. v. Beat Em All Barb–Wire Co.,* 33 F. 261 (C.C.N.D.Iowa 1888), *rev'd, Barbed*

Wire Patent Case, 143 U.S. 275, 12 S.Ct. 443, 36 L.Ed. 154 (1892). The Supreme Court, reversing, discussed the unreliability of testimony as to long-past events:

> In view of the unsatisfactory character of testimony, arising from the forgetfulness of witnesses, their liability to mistakes, their proneness to recollect things as the party calling them would have them recollect them, aside from the temptation to actual perjury, courts have not only imposed upon defendants the burden of proving such devices, but have required that the proof shall be clear, satisfactory, and beyond a reasonable doubt.

143 U.S. at 284, 12 S.Ct. 443. The Court concluded that:

> Witnesses whose memories are prodded by the eagerness of interested parties to elicit testimony favorable to themselves are not usually to be depended upon for accurate information.

Id. The Court thus required proof of prior knowledge and use that is "clear, satisfactory, and beyond a reasonable doubt." Discussing this standard, Professor Chisum observes:

> As to the exact standard of the burden of persuasion on prior use, Justice Brown in the *Barbed Wire Patent Case* did at one point refer to proof "beyond a reasonable doubt," the extremely stringent standard of criminal law. But in later cases, the Court seemed to construe the burden as one of "clear and convincing evidence," a test used in a number of areas of patent law.

1 DONALD S. CHISUM, PATENTS § 3.05[2] at 3–86 (Rel. May 1988).

In *Eibel Process Co. v. Minnesota & Ontario Paper Co.,* 261 U.S. 45, 43 S.Ct. 322, 67 L.Ed. 523 (1923) the Court cited its decision in *Barbed Wire Patent Case* as standing for the requirement of "clear and satisfactory" evidence when considering the probative value of oral evidence of prior knowledge and use of a patented invention:

> The oral evidence on this point falls far short of being enough to overcome the presumption of novelty from the granting of the patent. The temptation to remember in such cases and the ease with which honest witnesses can convince themselves after many years of having had a conception at the basis of a valuable patent, are well known in this branch of law, and have properly led to a rule that evidence to prove prior discovery must be clear and satisfactory

Eibel, 261 U.S. at 60, 43 S.Ct. 322. In that case the standard of "clear and satisfactory" evidence was held not met by the oral evidence of interested persons.

In *Radio Corp. v. Radio Engineering Laboratories,* 293 U.S. 1, 55 S.Ct. 928, 79 L.Ed. 163 (1934), the Court again discussed the issue, citing *inter alia* the *Barbed Wire Patent Case* and its criterion of "beyond a reasonable doubt." The Court explained that this was guidance, not prescription, while stressing that the burden of persuasion is heavy on an infringer who asserts that he created and used the same invention before the patentee:

> The context suggests that in these and like phrases the courts were not defining a standard in terms of scientific accuracy or literal precision, but were offering counsel and suggestion to guide the course of judgment. Through all the verbal variances, however, there runs this common core of thought and truth, that one otherwise an infringer who assails the validity of a patent fair upon its face bears a heavy burden of persuasion, and fails unless his evidence has more than a dubious preponderance.

293 U.S. at 8, 55 S.Ct. 928. This guidance, applied to this case, reinforces the heavy burden when establishing prior public knowledge and use based on long-past events. The Supreme Court's view of human nature as well as human recollection, whether deemed cynical or realistic, retains its cogency. This view is reinforced, in modern times, by the ubiquitous paper trail of virtually all commercial activity. It is rare indeed that some physical record (*e.g.*, a written document such as notes, letters, invoices, notebooks, or a sketch or drawing or photograph showing the device, a model, or some other contemporaneous record) does not exist.

In this case, despite the asserted many years of commercial and public use, we take note of the absence of any physical record to support the oral evidence. *Cf. Eibel*, 261 U.S. at 60, 43 S.Ct. 322 ("not a single written record, letter, or specification of prior date"). The asserted prior knowledge and use by Hawkins and Burke was said to have begun approximately thirty years ago and to have continued for about a decade. Hawkins testified that his prior use was terminated in 1978, and the district court found that Hawkins' system was not reconstructed until 1988. The relationship of the witnesses and the fact that the asserted prior uses ended twenty years before the trial, and were abandoned until the defendant reportedly learned of the patentee's practices, underscore the failure of this oral evidence to provide clear and convincing evidence of prior knowledge and use. The district court did not rely on the two undated photographs, and indeed their lack of detail and clarity can not have provided documentary support.

With the guidance of precedent, whose cautions stressed the frailty of memory of things long past and the temptation to remember facts favorable to the cause of one's relative or friend, we conclude that this oral evidence, standing alone, did not provide the clear and convincing evidence necessary to invalidate a patent on the ground of prior knowledge and use under § 102(a).

The judgment of invalidity on this ground is reversed. The case is remanded for further proceedings.

REVERSED AND REMANDED.

Notes

1. The Shopbook Rule. Federal Rules of Evidence 803(6) provides that:

> The following are not excluded by the hearsay rule, even though the declarant is available as a witness. A memorandum, report, record, or data compilation, in any form, of acts, events, conditions, opinions, or diagnoses, made at or near the time by, or from the information transmitted by, a person with knowledge, if kept in the course of a regularly conducted business activity, and if it was the regular practice of that business activity to make the memorandum, report, record, or data compilation, all as shown by the testimony of the custodian or other qualified witness, unless the source of information or the method or circumstances of preparation indicate lack of trustworthiness. The term "business" as used in this paragraph includes business, institution, association, profession, occupation, and calling of every kind, whether or not conducted for profit.

This provision has been held not to apply to prove dates of inventive activity. As indicated in *Horton v. Stevens*, 7 U.S.P.Q.2d 1245, 1248–49 (Bd. Pat. App. & Int'f 1988):

> The so-called Shop–Book rule does not apply to reports of scientific work in an interference proceeding. Such reports generally cannot be relied upon to prove the facts asserted therein, and therefore cannot be relied on to establish reduction to practice, since they are self-serving and not an independent corroboration of an inventor's testimony.

2. Corroboration and the Rule of Reason. The requirement of corroboration is an important restraint on claims of prior invention. In short, the rule prevents fraud. The requirement of corroboration can be very stringent. In this case, for instance, a witness testified that he had read and understood a notebook entry on a date which ensured prior reduction to practice. Senior Judge Friedman rejected this proof of corroboration:

> Those affiants' statements that by a certain date they had "read and understood" specified pages of Stephen Hahn's laboratory notebooks did not corroborate a reduction to practice. They established only that those pages existed on a certain date; they did not independently corroborate the statements made on those pages.

Hahn v. Wong, 892 F.2d 1028, 1033, 13 U.S.P.Q.2d 1313 (Fed.Cir.1989). In another instance, the Federal Circuit upheld an inventor's offer of his laboratory notebook showing his practice of the claimed invention. As corroboration, the Federal Circuit allowed (1) testimony of a co-worker that the inventor had acquired the supplies for the inventive method, (2) testimony of another co-worker that he had seen the product produced by the claimed method, and (3) general evidence that the company followed a program to record inventive activity. *Lacotte v. Thomas*, 758 F.2d 611, 225 U.S.P.Q. 633 (Fed.Cir.1985).

To ease the requirement of corroboration, *Coleman v. Dines*, 754 F.2d at 360, 224 U.S.P.Q. at 857, the Federal Circuit employs a rule of reason. This rule counsels the reasonable consideration of all evidence when weighing claims of inventorship. In one application of this rule, the Board of Patent

Appeals and Interferences had rejected corroborating evidence because the inventor did not present the testimony of the laboratory technicians who actually observed the test results showing reduction to practice. The Federal Circuit, reversed:

> Under the rule of reason, this court cannot ignore the realities of technical operations in modern day research laboratories. [cite deleted] Recognizing these realities, a junior technician performing perfunctory tasks under the supervision of a senior scientist is not generally necessary to verify the reliability of evidence about scientific methods or data. In the absence of indicia calling into question the trustworthiness of the senior scientist's testimony, the rule of reason permits the Board to rely on the trained supervisor's testimony to ascertain scientific methods or results.

Holmwood v. Sugavanam, 948 F.2d 1236, 1239, 20 U.S.P.Q.2d 1712 (Fed. Cir.1991).

§ 6.3   PATENT AWARD TO THE SECOND INVENTOR

Section 102(g) further provides that first inventors can lose that special status through their own conduct: namely, where they "abandoned, suppressed, or concealed" the invention. The following decision presents the latest thinking on this forfeiture provision.

APOTEX USA, INC. v. MERCK & CO., INC.

United States Court of Appeals, Federal Circuit, 2001.
254 F.3d 1031 59 U.S.P.Q.2d 1139.

Before LOURIE, CLEVENGER, and LINN, CIRCUIT JUDGES.

LOURIE, CIRCUIT JUDGE.

Apotex USA, Inc. appeals from the decision of the United States District Court for the Northern District of Illinois granting Merck & Co., Inc.'s motion for summary judgment that the claims of U.S. Patents 5,573,780 and 5,690,962 are invalid under 35 U.S.C. § 102(g). Because the district court did not err in granting summary judgment that the '780 and '962 patents are invalid under 35 U.S.C. § 102(g), we affirm.

BACKGROUND

Apotex is the assignee of the '780 and '962 patents, which relate to a process for making a stable solid formulation of enalapril sodium for use in the treatment of high blood pressure. Claim 1 of the '780 patent, which is representative of the claims at issue, reads as follows:

1.   A process of manufacture of a pharmaceutical solid composition comprising enalapril sodium, which process comprises the steps of:

i) a) mixing enalapril maleate with an alkaline sodium compound and at least one other excipient, adding water sufficient to moisten, and mixing to achieve a wet mass, or

b) mixing enalapril maleate with at least one excipient other than an alkaline sodium compound, adding a solution of an alkaline sodium compound in water, sufficient to moisten and mixing to achieve a wet mass; thereby to achieve a reaction without converting the enalapril maleate to a clear solution of enalapril sodium and maleic acid sodium salt in water,

ii) drying the wet mass, and

iii) further processing the dried material into tablets.

The claims of the '962 patent, which is a continuation of the application that led to the '780 patent, are identical to those found in the '780 patent except that they are not restricted to tablet form, but rather encompass any solid pharmaceutical dosage form of enalapril sodium. This distinction is not material to the resolution of this appeal.

Merck manufactures enalapril sodium under the trade name Vasotec®, and has been continuously manufacturing and commercially selling Vasotec® tablets since 1983. Merck owns both U.S. and Canadian patents covering the enalapril sodium compound, but does not own a patent covering its process of manufacturing Vasotec®. However, in 1992, Merck disclosed the ingredients utilized in its Vasotec® manufacturing process in a Canadian product monograph, and more than 30,000 copies of the monograph were distributed in 1993 alone .. Merck also disclosed the ingredients used in manufacturing Renitec® (the trademark used for its enalapril sodium product sold in various foreign countries) in the 1988 edition of the DICTIONNAIRE VIDAL, a French pharmaceutical dictionary.

In 1991, Merck and its Canadian subsidiary, Merck Frosst Canada, Inc., sued Apotex's Canadian affiliate, Apotex Canada, for infringement of Merck's Canadian patent covering the enalapril sodium compound. During the 1994 trial ("the Canadian trial"), Brian McLeod, Merck's then-vice president of marketing, performed a step-by-step narration of a videotape demonstrating Merck's process of manufacturing Vasotec®. Within days of hearing this testimony, Dr. Bernard Sherman, an Apotex official, allegedly conceived the patented process at issue.

Apotex filed the present action against Merck, alleging that Merck's process of manufacturing Vasotec® infringes all of the claims of both the '780 and '962 patents. Both parties filed cross-motions for summary judgment on the issue of infringement, and Merck cross-moved for summary judgment of invalidity under § 102(g). The district court granted Apotex's motion for summary judgment of infringement, but also granted Merck's cross-motion for summary judgment of invalidity because it found that Merck invented the process claimed in the '780 and '962 patents within the United States before Apotex, and did not abandon, suppress, or conceal that invention within the meaning of § 102(g).

Apotex thereafter filed a motion asking the court to reconsider its grant of summary judgment of invalidity, which the district court denied.

Apotex appeals from the district court's grant of summary judgment of invalidity.

DISCUSSION

Summary judgment is appropriate "if the pleadings, depositions, answers to interrogatories, and admissions on file, together with the affidavits, if any, show that there is no genuine issue as to any material fact and that the moving party is entitled to a judgment as a matter of law." FED.R.CIV.P. 56(c). For purposes of the motion, "[t]he evidence of the nonmovant is to be believed, and all justifiable inferences are to be drawn in his favor." *Anderson v. Liberty Lobby, Inc.*, 477 U.S. 242, 255, 106 S.Ct. 2505, 91 L.Ed.2d 202 (1986). We review a district court's grant of a motion for summary judgment *de novo*. *Ethicon Endo–Surgery, Inc. v. United States Surgical Corp.*, 149 F.3d 1309, 1315, 47 USPQ2d 1272, 1275 (Fed.Cir.1998).

Apotex argues that the district court improperly invalidated the '780 and '962 patents because Merck failed to prove by clear and convincing evidence that it did not suppress or conceal the patented process. Apotex contends that proof of invalidity under § 102(g) requires Merck to prove that it did not suppress or conceal the process of manufacturing Vasotec® Tablets based on its activities within the United States, and that Merck's foreign disclosures therefore cannot be used to satisfy its burden of proof. Apotex also contends that, in any event, Merck's foreign disclosures fail to prove that it did not suppress or conceal the process because nothing in the testimony from the Canadian trial, the product monograph, or the French dictionary disclosed the use of water, the occurrence of an acid-base chemical reaction between enalapril maleate and sodium bicarbonate, or the resultant enalapril sodium product. Finally, Apotex argues that the evidence demonstrates that Merck in fact suppressed or concealed its invention by failing to file a patent application on the process, by submitting misleading information in its New Drug Application ("NDA") that only disclosed the starting ingredients used to make Vasotec®, and by preventing the details of its process from circulating outside of the company.

Merck responds that § 102(g) only requires proof that the prior invention was made in the United States, and that evidence of lack of suppression or concealment can be proven by both foreign and domestic activities. Merck further argues that it did not suppress or conceal the process because it used it commercially, disclosed it in open court directly to its competitor, and published the ingredients used to make Vasotec® tablets in both the product monograph and the French dictionary. Merck also argues that the submissions it made with respect to its NDA were proper and in any event could not constitute suppression or concealment because it was the Food and Drug Administration that never made those submissions public. Finally, Merck contends that the process was not suppressed or concealed because it was obvious and Dr. Sherman admitted that Vasotec® tablets could be reverse-engineered to reveal the details of the process.

Section 102(g) operates to ensure that a patent is awarded only to the "first" inventor in law. In addition to governing priority determinations in interference proceedings in the United States Patent and Trademark Office, § 102(g) may be asserted as a basis for invalidating a patent in defense to an infringement suit. *New Idea Farm Equip. Corp. v. Sperry Corp.*, 916 F.2d 1561, 1566, 16 USPQ2d 1424, 1428 (Fed.Cir. 1990) (citation omitted). That section provides in relevant part that: "A person shall be entitled to a patent unless ... before such person's invention thereof, the invention was made in this country by another inventor who had not abandoned, suppressed, or concealed it." 35 U.S.C.A. § 102(g) (West Supp.2000). Therefore, if a patentee's invention has been made by another, prior inventor who has not abandoned, suppressed, or concealed the invention, § 102(g) will invalidate that patent.

Apotex does not dispute that Merck invented the patented process in the United States well before Dr. Sherman's alleged date of conception. Apotex also concedes that Merck did not abandon its process of manufacturing Vasotec® tablets as shown by its continuous commercial use of the process since 1983. The sole issue on appeal, therefore, is whether Merck "suppressed" or "concealed" the process within the meaning of § 102(g). Whether suppression or concealment has occurred is a question of law, which we review *de novo*.

As an initial matter, we disagree with Apotex's interpretation of § 102(g) as requiring proof negating suppression or concealment to arise from activities occurring within the United States. The plain language of § 102(g) clearly requires that the prior invention be made "in this country." However, in light of the grammatical structure of § 102(g), it would be a strained reading of that provision to interpret the language "in this country" to also modify the requirement that the prior invention was "not ... abandoned, suppressed, or concealed." A more reasonable interpretation is that it only modifies the antecedent verb "made," but not the "abandoned, suppressed, or concealed" clause that follows it. Had Congress intended the phrase "in this country" to modify "abandoned, suppressed, or concealed," it would have inserted language to that effect.

Indeed, if there were any doubt, the legislative history of § 102(g) demonstrates that Congress contemplated that precise modification, as it applied to another clause in § 102(g), and failed to adopt it. An earlier version of that provision considered in the House read as follows:

> [B]efore the applicant's invention thereof the invention was in fact made *in this country* by another who had not abandoned it and who was using reasonable diligence *in this country* in reducing it to practice or had reduced it to practice.

H.R. 3760, 82nd Cong. (1951) (emphasis added). The fact that the drafters found it desirable to emphasize that the language "in this country" applies to "using reasonable diligence" as well as to the word "made" supports the conclusion that it only modifies the verb that precedes it and not any subordinate clause that follows it. Accordingly, based upon the plain language of § 102(g) and the relevant legislative history of that provision, we conclude that the language "in this country" only applies to the country where "the invention was made," and that proof negating suppression or concealment is not limited to activities occurring within the United States.

We next turn to an issue that has not been squarely addressed by this court in considering suppression or concealment as negating prior invention in a defense to an infringement suit under § 102(g)—the burdens of proof governing such a determination. Section 282 of the Patent Act provides that "[a] patent shall be presumed valid." 35 U.S.C.A. § 282 (West Supp.2000). In order to overcome the presumption of validity, the party challenging a patent must prove facts supporting a determination of invalidity by clear and convincing evidence. *Am. Hoist & Derrick Co. v. Sowa & Sons, Inc.*, 725 F.2d 1350, 1360, 220 USPQ 763, 770 (Fed.Cir.1984). Section 282 applies with full force to a § 102(g) defense, and thus a party asserting invalidity under § 102(g) must prove facts by clear and convincing evidence establishing a prior invention that was not abandoned, suppressed, or concealed.

In *Young v. Dworkin,* one of our predecessor courts set forth the relevant burdens of proof governing a determination whether a prior invention was suppressed or concealed, in the context of an interference between co-pending applications, as follows:

> The sole remaining question is whether the board correctly held that junior party-appellant suppressed or concealed his invention within the meaning of 35 U.S.C. § 102(g). Here, the senior party-appellee bears the burden of proof by a preponderance of the evidence, notwithstanding junior party-appellant's burden on the issue of priority of invention which he has sustained.

Young v. Dworkin, 489 F.2d 1277, 1279, 180 USPQ 388, 390 (CCPA 1974). Thus, under § 102(g) interference law involving co-pending applications, once the first party to invent has established priority of invention, the second party to conceive and reduce the invention to practice has the burden of proving that the first party suppressed or concealed the invention. In such an interference, the first party to invent does not bear any burden of proof regarding suppression or concealment once it has established an earlier date of invention.

A § 102(g) prior invention defense is governed by the identical "suppressed or concealed" language applicable to priority determinations in interference proceedings. We must therefore interpret the § 102(g) defense provision consistently with established interference law. However, infringement actions implicating a § 102(g) defense differ from interferences in that a patent has been granted on the invention at issue, and therefore the presumption of validity under § 282 applies. Because the patentee (analogous to the second-to-invent in the interference context) has the benefit of the presumption of validity, that party should only be held to bear a burden of producing evidence indicating that the prior inventor may have suppressed or concealed the invention once the challenger (analogous to the first-to-invent in the interference context) has established prior invention by clear and convincing evidence. That burden bears a rough similarity to placing the burden of proving suppression or concealment on the second-to-invent under interference law, but at the same time is appropriately limited to one of production, not persuasion, giving due regard to the presumption of validity.

We therefore interpret § 102(g) as requiring that once a challenger of a patent has proven by clear and convincing evidence that "the invention was made in this country by another inventor," the burden of production shifts to the patentee to produce evidence sufficient to create a genuine issue of material fact as to whether the prior inventor has suppressed or concealed the invention. However, in accordance with the statutory presumption in 35 U.S.C. § 282, the ultimate burden of persuasion remains with the party challenging the validity of the patent. Once the patentee has satisfied its burden of production, the party alleging invalidity under § 102(g) must rebut any alleged suppression or concealment with clear and convincing evidence to the contrary.

Our case law distinguishes between two types of suppression or concealment. The first is implicated in a situation in which an inventor actively suppresses or conceals his invention from the public. *Fujikawa v. Wattanasin,* 93 F.3d 1559, 1567, 39 USPQ2d 1895, 1901 (Fed.Cir. 1996) (citing *Kendall v. Winsor,* 62 U.S. (21 How.) 322, 328, 16 L.Ed. 165 (1858)). The second involves a legal inference of suppression or concealment based upon an unreasonable delay in filing a patent application.[2] *Peeler v. Miller,* 535 F.2d 647, 655, 190 USPQ 117, 122 (1976) (holding that a four-year delay in filing a patent application after the invention was perfected was unreasonably long); *Shindelar v. Holdeman,* 628 F.2d 1337, 1342, 207 USPQ 112, 116 (1980) (finding suppression or concealment because no reasonable explanation was given for the two-year and five-month delay between reduction to practice and the filing of a patent application). The latter type is involved here.

Although a prior inventor implicated in a § 102(g) infringement defense may not have filed a patent application, in contrast to an interference contestant, that party's delay in otherwise bringing the knowledge of the invention to the public may nevertheless raise a similar inference of suppression or concealment. *See Int'l Glass Co. v. United States,* 408 F.2d 395, 403 (Ct.Cl.1969) (holding that the prior invention of a process did not invalidate a patent on the same process under § 102(g) because the prior inventor did nothing to make the invention known to the public). Even though there is no explicit disclosure requirement in § 102(g), the spirit and policy of the patent laws encourage an

---

2. A subset of the category of "inferred" suppression or concealment arises in a situation in which the first inventor is "spurred" into filing a patent application by another application, *Mason v. Hepburn,* 13 App.D.C. 86 (D.C.Cir.1898), or by the commercial activity of another, *Woofter v. Carlson,* 54 C.C.P.A. 917, 367 F.2d 436, 445–446, 151 USPQ 407, 416 (CCPA 1966). This case does not involve "spurring."

inventor to take steps to ensure that "the public has gained knowledge of the invention which will insure its preservation in the public domain" or else run the risk of being dominated by the patent of another. *Palmer v. Dudzik,* 481 F.2d 1377, 1387, 178 USPQ 608, 616 (CCPA 1973). Absent a satisfactory explanation for the delay or the presence of other mitigating facts, a prior invention will therefore be deemed suppressed or concealed within the meaning of § 102(g) "if, within a reasonable time after completion, no steps are taken to make the invention publicly known." *Int'l Glass,* 408 F.2d at 403.

In the case at hand, we find that Apotex has satisfied its burden of producing evidence sufficient to create a genuine issue of material fact that Merck suppressed or concealed its process of manufacturing enalapril sodium tablets. We emphasize at the outset that although § 102(g) prior art must be somehow made available to the public in order to defeat another patent, a § 102(g) prior inventor is under no obligation to file a patent application. Thus, while Merck's failure to file a patent application may be relevant to a determination whether it suppressed or concealed its process, especially if there were evidence that such failure was based on a decision to retain the invention as a trade secret, that failure alone does not satisfy the patentee's burden of producing evidence sufficient to create a genuine issue of material fact of suppression or concealment.

However, Apotex did allege that Merck failed to make its invention publicly known. Merck perfected its process and began commercially using the process to manufacture Vasotec® tablets no later than 1983. Although Merck argues that its process was disclosed to the public because its Vasotec® tablets could have been reverse-engineered, that argument is based on the admissions of Dr. Sherman, who drew upon the information provided in Merck's subsequent disclosures to determine the details of the process.[3] Thus, it appears that Merck took no steps to make the invention publicly known for nearly five years, when it first published the ingredients used in its process in the 1988 edition of the DICTIONNAIRE VIDAL. We find that such a delay raises an inference that Merck suppressed or concealed its invention. Accordingly, because Apotex has successfully discharged its burden of going forward with evidence creating a genuine issue of material fact of suppression or concealment, the burden shifts to Merck to rebut that showing by clear and convincing evidence to the contrary.

We conclude that Merck has succeeded in rebutting the inference of suppression or concealment created by its period of inactivity by clear and convincing evidence. In *Paulik v. Rizkalla,* we stated the rule that "the first inventor will not be barred from relying on later, resumed

---

3. It is worth noting that if it were clear that Merck's process could be reverse-engineered by one of ordinary skill through an inspection of Vasotec® tablets, Apotex could not benefit from the inference of suppression or concealment because Merck could not be said to have delayed in making the benefits of its invention known to the public. *See Palmer,* 481 F.2d at 1386–87, 178 USPQ at 615 (stating that a commercial use of an invention will preclude a finding of suppression or concealment only when such use enables the public to learn of the invention).

activity antedating an opponent's entry into the field, merely because the work done before the delay was sufficient to amount to a reduction to practice." 760 F.2d 1270, 1275, 226 USPQ 224, 228 (Fed.Cir.1985) (holding that the inference of suppression or concealment from a four-year delay between reduction to practice and the filing of a patent application was overcome by the first inventor's resumption of activity before the second inventor's date of conception). Thus, even though Merck may have suppressed or concealed the process for a period of time after it reduced it to practice in 1983, as long as it "resumed activity" (*i.e.*, made the benefits of its invention known to the public) before Apotex's entry into the field, it cannot be deemed to have suppressed or concealed the invention within the meaning of § 102(g).

Merck made several disclosures following its period of suppression or concealment that made the invention publicly known, all of which took place before Apotex's entry into the field (here, Dr. Sherman's alleged conception in April of 1994). First, Merck disclosed the ingredients used in manufacturing Vasotec® tablets in the 1988 edition of the Dictionnaire Vidal. It also widely distributed the product monograph in Canada from October 1992 through 1994, which similarly disclosed the ingredients it used in its manufacturing process. Merck also provided a step-by-step description of the process through the testimony given by Brian McLeod at the Canadian trial on March 28, 1994.

Apotex argues that these disclosures inadequately described Merck's process of manufacturing Vasotec® tablets, and therefore that the public never received the benefit of the invention. However, Dr. Sherman admitted both in his deposition in this case and in his 1994 Statement of Facts prepared for the Canadian trial that his inspection of the Vasotec® tablets that Merck sold commercially revealed that they were made using a wet granulation process. He also admitted that, after learning of the disclosed starting ingredients from the Canadian product monograph (which included sodium bicarbonate), it "immediately occurred" to him and was "obvious to any knowledgeable formulator or chemist" that the final enalapril sodium product in the Vasotec® tablets was the result of an acid-base chemical reaction between enalapril maleate and sodium bicarbonate in water. Merck's various disclosures, in conjunction with Apotex's admissions, therefore clearly and convincingly prove that Merck made the knowledge of its invention available to the public, thereby satisfying its burden of rebutting Apotex's evidence of suppression or concealment.

Moreover, Apotex's argument that Merck suppressed or concealed the process by submitting misleading information to the FDA in 1983 is irrelevant because any suppression that was implicated was overcome by Merck's subsequent activity. We therefore conclude that the district court did not err in granting summary judgment that the '780 and '962 patents are invalid under § 102(g).

Notes

1. Is this Diligence? As a technical matter, diligence plays no role in determining abandonment, suppression, or concealment. Diligence is limited to instances when an inventor is second to reduce to practice, but relies instead on proof of prior conception to show prior inventorship. Nonetheless, the acts and intentions of an applicant accused of 102(g) abandonment—sometimes referred to loosely as "diligence"—often determine the outcome of a priority issue.

2. Can I Abandon my Abandonment? In *Paulik v. Rizkalla*, 760 F.2d 1270, 226 U.S.P.Q. 224 (Fed.Cir.1985), Rizkalla was the senior party in an interference, having filed a patent application on March 10, 1975. Paulik had actually reduced the invention to practice as early as November 1970 and filed an invention disclosure form with his employer's patent department at that time. The patent department initially opted not to pursue patent protection on the invention, but began to draft an application in January or February 1975. Paulik's application was filed on June 30, 1975. The PTO Board awarded priority of invention to Rizkalla. According to the Board, Paulik's conduct fell within the language of § 102(g) denying priority of inventorship to those who have "abandoned, suppressed or concealed" the invention.

Following Paulik's appeal to the Federal Circuit, the *en banc* court reversed. The majority of the court held that an inventor, after taking no action for years, could renew inventive activities and recover from a charge of abandonment. Paulik could obtain priority if, on remand, he could "demonstrate that he had renewed activity on the invention and that he proceeded diligently to file his patent application, starting before the earliest date to which Rizkalla is entitled." Writing for the majority, Judge Newman reasoned that a contrary result would discourage inventors "from working on projects that had been 'too long' set aside, because of the impossibility of relying, in a priority contest, on either their original work or their renewed work."

A vigorous dissent authored by Judge Friedman urged that the majority's view could not be squared with the plain language of § 102(g). According to the dissent, the statute provided only that one who has abandoned, suppressed or concealed an invention has forfeited priority, with no opportunity for redemption. The dissent also questioned whether Paulik, whose deliberate suppression of the invention caused it to be the junior party, was truly deserving of priority over Rizkalla. Finally, the dissent charged the majority with adding an additional complexity to interference proceedings.

§ 6.4 DISCLOSURE IN UNITED STATES PATENT APPLICA-TIONS—§ 102(e)

ALEXANDER MILBURN CO. v. DAVIS–BOURNONVILLE CO.

United States Supreme Court, 1926.
270 U.S. 390.

MR. JUSTICE HOLMES delivered the opinion of the Court.

This is a suit for the infringement of the plaintiff's patent for an improvement in welding and cutting apparatus alleged to have been the invention of one Whitford. The suit embraced other matters but this is the only one material here. The defence is that Whitford was not the first inventor of the thing patented, and the answer gives notice that to prove the invalidity of the patent evidence will be offered that one Clifford invented the thing, his patent being referred to and identified. The application for the plaintiff's patent was filed on March 4, 1911, and the patent was issued on June 4, 1912. There was no evidence carrying Whitford's invention further back. Clifford's application was filed on January 31, 1911, before Whitford's, and his patent was issued on February 6, 1912. It is not disputed that this application gave a complete and adequate description of the thing patented to Whitford, but it did not claim it. The District Court gave the plaintiff a decree, holding that while Clifford might have added this claim to his application, yet as he did not, he was not a prior inventor. The decree was affirmed by the Circuit Court of Appeals. There is a conflict between this decision and those of other Circuit Courts of Appeal, especially the sixth. Therefore a writ of certiorari was granted by this Court.

The patent law authorizes a person who has invented an improvement like the present, "not known or used by others in this country, before his invention," etc., to obtain a patent for it. Rev. Sts. § 4886, amended by Act March 3, 1897, c. 391, § 1, 29 Stat. 692 (Comp. St. § 9430). Among the defences to a suit for infringement the fourth specified by the statute is that the patentee 'was not the original and first inventor or discoverer of any material and substantial part of the thing patented.' Rev. Sts. § 4920, amended by Act March 3, 1897, c. 391, § 2, 29 Stat. 692 (Comp. St. § 9466). Taking these words in their natural sense as they would be read by the common man, obviously one is not the first inventor if, as was the case here, somebody else has made a complete and adequate description of the thing claimed before the earliest moment to which the alleged inventor can carry his invention back. But the words cannot be taken quite so simply. In view of the gain to the public that the patent laws mean to secure we assume for purposes of decision that it would have been no bar to Whitford's patent if Clifford had written out his prior description and kept it in his portfolio uncommunicated to anyone. More than that, since the decision in the case of the Cornplanter Patent, 23 Wall. 181, it is said, at all events for many years, the Patent Office has made no search among abandoned patent applications, and by the words of the statute a previous foreign invention does not invalidate a patent granted here if it has not been patented or described in a printed publication. Rev. Sts. § 4923 (Comp. St. § 9469). *See Westinghouse Machine Co. v. General Electric Co.*, 207 F. 75, 126 C. C. A. 575. These analogies prevailed in the minds of the courts below.

On the other hand publication in a periodical is a bar. This as it seems to us is more than an arbitrary enactment, and illustrates, as does the rule concerning previous public use, the principle that, subject to the exceptions mentioned, one really must be the first inventor in order to be entitled to a patent. *Coffin v. Ogden*, 18 Wall. 120, 21 L. Ed. 821. We understand the Circuit Court of Appeals to admit that if Whitford had not applied for his patent until after the issue to Clifford, the disclosure by the latter would have had the same effect as the publication of the same words in a periodical, although not made the basis of a claim. The invention is made public property as much in the one case as in the other. But if this be true, as we think that it is, it seems to us that a sound distinction cannot be taken between that case and a patent applied for before but not granted until after a second patent is sought. The delays of the patent office ought not to cut down the effect of what has been done. The description shows that Whitford was not the first inventor. Clifford had done all that he could do to make his description public. He had taken steps that would make it public as soon as the Patent Office did its work, although, of course, amendments might be required of him before the end could be reached. We see no reason in the words or policy of the law for allowing Whitford to profit by the delay and make himself out to be the first inventor when he was not so in fact, when Clifford had shown knowledge inconsistent with the allowance of Whitford's claim, *(Webster) Loom Co. v. Higgins*, 105 U. S. 580, 26 L. Ed. 1177, and when otherwise the publication of his patent would abandon the thing described to the public unless it already was old, *McClain v. Ortmayer*, 12 S. Ct. 76, 141 U. S. 419, 424, 35 L. Ed. 800. *Underwood v. Gerber,* 13 S. Ct. 854, 149 U. S. 224, 230, 37 L. Ed. 710.

The question is not whether Clifford showed himself by the description to be the first inventor. By putting it in that form it is comparatively easy to take the next step and say that he is not an inventor in the sense of the statute unless he makes a claim. The question is whether Clifford's disclosure made it impossible for Whitford to claim the invention at a later date. The disclosure would have had the same effect as at present if Clifford had added to his description a statement that he did not claim the thing described because he abandoned it or because he believed it to be old. It is not necessary to show who did invent the thing in order to show that Whitford did not.

It is said that without a claim the thing described is not reduced to practice. But this seems to us to rest on a false theory helped out by the fiction that by a claim it is reduced to practice. A new application and a claim may be based on the original description within two years, and the original priority established notwithstanding intervening claims. *Chapman v. Wintroath*, 40 S. Ct. 234, 252 U. S. 126, 137, 64 L. Ed. 491. A description that would bar a patent if printed in a periodical or in an issued patent is equally effective in an application so far as reduction to practice goes.

As to the analogies relied upon below, the disregard of abandoned patent applications however explained cannot be taken to establish a principle beyond the rule as actually applied. As an empirical rule it no doubt is convenient if not necessary to the Patent Office, and we are not disposed to disturb it, although we infer that originally the practice of the Office was different. The policy of the statute as to foreign inventions obviously stands on its own footing and cannot be applied to domestic affairs. The fundamental rule we repeat is that the patentee must be the first inventor. The qualifications in aid of a wish to encourage improvements or to avoid laborious investigations do not prevent the rule from applying here.

Decree reversed.

Notes

1. **Statutory Codification.** The holding in *Alexander Milburn* was subsequently codified as § 102(e). As amended by the American Inventors Protection Act of 1999, § 102(e) consists of two sub-paragraphs. Section 102(e)(1) provides that a published patent application that discloses, but does not claim the invention constitutes prior art as of its filing date. Section 102(e)(2) works similarly: an issued patent that discloses, but does not claim the invention, constitutes prior art as of its filing date.

In approaching § 102(e) for the first time, one should remember procedures followed at the PTO. The PTO's current practice is to publish some of the pending patent applications eighteen months following the filing date. Not all applications are published, however. Specifically, where an applicant certifies that he will not seek foreign patent rights pertaining to that invention, the PTO will not publish the U.S. application. As a result, some patent applications are published approximately 18 months after they are filed. Other patent applications are never published at all, and their contents become publicly accessible only if the PTO allows them to issue as granted patents.

The purpose of § 102(e) is to define the point at which these published applications and issued patents serve as prior art against others. Our previous discussion of § 102(a) and (b) has shown that the patent law usually does not allow references that are not available to the public, such as trade secrets, to have patent-defeating effect. The most appropriate date for a published application or issued patent to have prior art effect might seem to be the date it actually issues from the PTO. Are you persuaded by the different conclusion of *Alexander Milburn*: that the disclosures of the patent instrument should have the status of the prior art as of their filing date?

2. **The Disclosed Invention.** What significance attaches to the fact that Clifford disclosed but did not claim the invention in Whitford's application?

3. **Secret Prior Art.** What are the equities of holding secret prior art against the patent applicant? As noted in Harold C. Wegner, *Patent Law Simplification and the Geneva Patent Convention*, 14 AM. INTELL. PROP. J. 154, 176 (1986):

> "Secret" prior art is a contradiction in terms. Prior "art" should refer to the *known* (or at least knowable) state of the art at the time the invention is made: at the time of the invention, was the sum total of knowledge from prior use, printed publications and patents *then available* such that the claimed invention would have been *at that time* [novel or] obvious to the worker with ordinary skill in the art? It stretches the bounds of credibility to say that the [prior art] may include a *secret*

disclosure in a foreign patent application not even yet filed in the United States.

Does Professor Wegner's approach comport with the first-to-invent system? In addition, even critics of secret prior art must recognize that the state of the art can be extremely difficult to determine in a world of ever-advancing technology. Surely patent applications themselves can serve as valuable, and readily accessible, indicia of the process of a technical art. How would you balance these interests?

4. The Patent Cooperation Treaty. In alluding to § 351(a) of the Patent Act, both sub-paragraphs of § 102(e) rather obliquely refer to the provisions of the Patent Cooperation Treaty (PCT). Section 102(e)(1) provides that PCT international applications designating the United States and published in the English language will have prior art effect as of their filing date. Section 102(e)(2) indicates that *Alexander Milburn* does not apply to so-called "international applications" under the PCT. Neither of these provisions changes the basic *Alexander Milburn* rule with respect to non-PCT applications filed in the United States. The PCT is discussed in greater detail in this casebook at Chapter 14.

5. Comparative Approaches. The European Patent Convention follows the same rule espoused in § 102(e), as noted in Article 54(3):

> Additionally, the content of the European patent applications as filed of which the dates of filing are prior to [the filing date] and which were published ... on or after that date, shall be considered as comprised in the state of the art.

Only the withdrawal of the prior application prior to publication excludes that application from the prior art. What are the merits of such a rule? What should be the effect upon novelty if the EPO accidentally publishes a withdrawn application? *See* European Patent Office Examination Guidelines C–IV, 6.1a; decision J 5/81, OJ EPO 1982, 115. Japan follows a similar rule to that in Europe. *See* Japanese Patent Act § 29bis.

The modern European approach replaced the earlier so-called "prior claim" approach that was employed by, among others, the English courts. A good explanation of the advantages of the whole contents approach over the prior claim approach is found in the Banks Report (THE BRITISH PATENT SYSTEM, REPORT OF THE COMMITTEE TO EXAMINE THE PATENT SYSTEM AND PATENT LAW) 87–97 (1970) (Cmnd 4407), a report that led to the Patent Act 1977. The Report at pages 87–88 describes the difference between these approaches as follows:

> There are two basic approaches to the problem. The first, which for convenience we shall refer to as the "prior claim" approach, depends upon a comparison of the *claims* of the later application with the *claims* of the earlier. The second, which we refer to as the "whole contents" approach depends upon a comparison of the *claims* of the later application with the *disclosure* or contends of the earlier one.

> The philosophical approach is different in the two cases. The prior claim approach is based upon the premise that the Crown cannot grant the same monopoly twice and since the monopoly is delineated by the claims it should be the claims of the two conflict applications which are

compared, and then only when a patent has been granted on the earlier application. With this approach it does not matter that the invention claimed in the later claim has already been disclosed, but not claimed, in the earlier application.

The philosophy behind the whole contents approach is not only that the Crown should not grant the same monopoly twice but also that it is against the public interest to grant a patent for subject matter which has already been publicly disclosed in an earlier application, notwithstanding that the disclosure was not public until after the priority date of the later application or that no patent may be finally granted on it. In other words, only the first person to take steps to disclose such subject matter to the public by means of a patent application has the right to a monopoly for it.

§ 6.5 DERIVATION—THEFT FROM A PRIOR INVENTOR— § 102(f)

Unsurprisingly, the patent law seeks not only the first, but the actual inventor. If the applicant in fact derived the invention from another, then no patent can issue. Section 102(f) thus bars a patent to an applicant who "did not himself invent the subject matter sought to be patented."

AGAWAM WOOLEN CO. v. JORDAN

United States Supreme Court, 1868.
74 U.S. (7 Wall.) 583.

MR. JUSTICE CLIFFORD delivered the opinion of the court.

The settled rule of law is, that whoever first perfects a machine is entitled to the patent, and is the real inventor, although others may have previously had the idea and made some experiments towards putting it in practice. He is the inventor and is entitled to the patent who first brought the machine to perfection and made it capable of useful operation.

No one is entitled to a patent for that which he did not invent unless he can show a legal title to the same from the inventor or by operation of law; but where a person has discovered an improved principle in a machine, manufacture, or composition of matter, and employs other persons to assist him in carrying out that principle, and they, in the course of experiments arising from that employment, make valuable discoveries ancillary to the plan and preconceived design of the employer, such suggested improvements are in general to be regarded as the property of the party who discovered the original improved principle, and may be embodied in his patent as a part of his invention.

Suggestions from another, made during the progress of such experiments, in order that they may be sufficient to defeat a patent subsequently issued, must have embraced the plan of the improvement, and must have furnished such information to the person to whom the communication was made that it would have enabled an ordinary mechanic, without the exercise of any ingenuity and special skill on his part, to construct and put the improvement in successful operation.

Persons employed, as much as employers, are entitled to their own independent inventions, but where the employer has conceived the plan of an invention and is engaged in experiments to perfect it, no suggestions from an employee, not amounting to a new method or arrangement, which, in itself is a complete invention, is sufficient to deprive the employer of the exclusive property in the perfected improvement. But where the suggestions go to make up a complete and perfect machine, embracing the substance of all that is embodied in the patent subsequently issued to the party to whom the suggestions were made, the patent is invalid, because the real invention or discovery belonged to another.

Guided by this well-established principles, the first inquiry is, what was actually done by the person who, as alleged by the respondents, was the real inventor of what is described in the reissued letters patent? They do not pretend that he invented or even suggested the entire invention, nor all of the several elements embraced in any one of the separate combinations, as expressed in the claims of the patent; and if they did, it could not for a moment be sustained, as it finds no support whatever in the evidence. None of the devices described in the specifications are new, but the claims of the patent are for the several combinations of the described elements arranged in the manner set forth, and for the purpose of working out the described results.

Regarded in that light, it is clear that the concession that the person named did not invent nor suggest the entire invention, nor any one of the separate combinations, is equivalent to an abandonment of the proposition under consideration, as it is clear to a demonstration that nothing short of that averment can be a valid defence. Respondents do not allege in the answer that the person named was a joint inventor with the original patentee, but the allegation is that he made the invention, and they deny that the assignor of the complainant ever bestowed any ingenuity upon what is described in the letters patent as his improvement. Such a defence cannot be successful unless it is proved, as common justice would forbid that any partial aid rendered under such circumstances, during the progress of experiments in perfecting the improvement, should enable the person rendering the aid to appropriate to himself the entire result of the ingenuity and toil of the originator, or put it in the power of any subsequent infringer to defeat the patent under the plea that the invention was made by the assistant and not by the originator of the plan.

The evidence shows that the original patentee was born in 1793, and that he commenced working on machinery in his youth, while he was with his father, and that, as early as the year 1812, he went into the employment of certain machinists, residing at Worcester, Massachusetts, who were engaged in constructing machinery for the manufacture of wool and cotton. While in their employment, he began experiments in woolen machinery. Those experiments were directed to the object of improving the billy, for the purpose of drawing out the carriage more accurately, and thereby making better work. Several years were spent in that business, but, in 1820, he went to Halifax, in that State, and, while there, he made numerous experiments to get rid of the billy entirely, and to dispense with short rolls, and substitute long rolls in their place. He remained there three years, and, during that time, he was constantly engaged in experiments to accomplish those objects. In the spring of 1823 he moved to Dedham, in the same State, and there hired a mill, and engaged in the manufacture of broadcloth, and also carried on the machine business, and the witness also states that he then prosecuted his experiments on a large scale.

Cans were used as a receptacle for the rovings, delivered from the doffers, before the drawing-off and winding apparatus, described in the patent, was invented. Rovings, before that invention, were spun from cans, instead of being wound upon, and spun from, spools or bobbins. Considerable importance is attached to the new method, as it was largely by that means that the use of the endless roving was made practical, and that the difficulty produced by the kinking of the roving, incident to the use of the cans, was overcome.

Theory of the respondents is, that the new method of accomplishing that function was invented by Edward Winslow, but their witness, John D. Cooper, only testifies that he made or suggested the spool and drum, which are not the only elements of that apparatus. Unaccompanied by the traverser, they would, perhaps, be better than the cans, but it is clear that the apparatus would be incomplete without that device, as it is by that means that the bobbins are evenly wound with the roving.

Testimony of that witness is, that he first suggested to Winslow that the roving must be would on a spool, else they never could make good yarn, and he proceeds to state that they procured some pasteboard, and that Winslow made a pattern for a spool and drum from that material. Explanations, in detail, are given by the witness, of the several steps taken by them in accomplishing the change in the apparatus, and the witness states that the original patentee never saw the spool and drum until he came into the mill and saw those devices in the machine. Argument for the respondents is, that the spool and drum were invented by that party while he was in the employment of the original patentee, but the complainant denies the theory of fact involved in the proposition, and insists that the statement of the witness are untrue, and that he is not entitled to credit. Further statement of the witness is, that the improvement, as soon as it was perfected, was applied to all the carding and spinning machines in the mill, and that the mills, so adjusted as to embrace that improvement, were put in successful operation during the summer and autumn of that year.

Two answers are made by the complainant to the defence founded on that testimony, both of which are sustained by the court. 1. Suppose the testimony of the witness to be all true, the complainant contends that it is not sufficiently comprehensive to support the allegations of the answer, nor even to support the proposition presented in the brief of the respondents. Taken in the strongest view for the respondents, the testimony merely shows that Winslow, or the witness Cooper, or both together, after the originator of the plan had nearly completed his great and valuable improvement, and while he was still prosecuting his experiments with the utmost diligence, suggested the spool and drum as substitutes for the cans, and that Winslow actually made those devices, and, with the aid of witness, put them into one of the machines as an experiment. When their employer first examined the arrangement, rude as it was, he expressed great satisfaction with it, but upon seeing it tried he pronounced it of no value. Neither of those opinions, however, turned out to be quite correct, as, upon further trial, when better adjusted, and by adding the traverser, so that the contrivance would wind the roving evenly on the spool, it proved to be a useful auxiliary part of the invention.

Valuable though it was and is, as aiding in the accomplishment of the desired result, it is nevertheless a great error to regard it as the invention described in the subsequent patent, or as such a material part of the same that it confers any right upon the party who made the suggestion to claim to be the inventor, or a joint inventor, of the improvement, or to suppose that the proof of what was done by that party can constitute any defence, as against the owner of the patent, to the charge of infringement.

Second answer to the defence founded on that testimony is, that the testimony is unreliable, because the witness is not entitled to credit. Hundreds of pages of the transcript are filled with proof, introduced either to assail or support the credit of that witness; but the court is of the opinion that it is not necessary to enter into those details, as the decision must be in favor of the appellee, even if every word stated by that witness is taken to be true. Entirely satisfied with our conclusion upon the merits, we are the less inclined to enter into those details, as a full analysis of the proofs within reasonable limits would be impracticable; but it is proper to say that the proofs have been carefully examined, and it is the opinion of the court that the letters patent in this case cannot be held to be invalid upon such testimony.

Notes

1. Derivation at the Federal Circuit. In 1997, the Federal Circuit had occasion to clarify a point of confusion that had crept into its case law. That court had earlier held that: "To invalidate a patent for derivation of invention, a party must demonstrate that the named inventor in the patent acquired knowledge of the claimed invention from another, or at least so much of the claimed invention as would have made it obvious to one of ordinary skill in the art." *New England Braiding Co. v. A.W. Chesterton Co.*, 970 F.2d 878, 883, 23 U.S.P.Q.2d 1622, 1626 (Fed.Cir.1992) (citing *Agawam*). That statement raised the issue of whether § 102(f) went only towards strict anticipations, or to obvious variants as will be discussed in

Chapter 8 of this casebook. In *Gambro Lundia AB v. Baxter Healthcare Corp.,* 110 F.3d 1573, 42 U.S.P.Q.2d 1378 (Fed.Cir.1997), Judge Rader addressed this issue as follows:

> Citing *New England Braiding Co. v. A.W. Chesterton Co.,* 970 F.2d 878, 23 U.S.P.Q.2d 1622 (Fed.Cir.1992), the district court concluded that Baxter did not need to prove communication of the entire conception, but rather only so much of the invention "as would have made it obvious to one of ordinary skill in the art." Based on this reasoning, the district court applied the obviousness standard in 35 U.S.C.A. § 103 (1994) to determine that the named inventors received enough information to make the invention obvious to one skilled in the dialysis art. This reasoning, however, misconstrues the dictum in *New England Braiding* and introduces incorrectly an obviousness analysis into the test for derivation.
>
> The Supreme Court announced the standard for finding communication of a prior conception over 125 years ago in *Agawam Woolen v. Jordan,* 74 U.S. (7 Wall.) 583, 19 L.Ed. 177 (1868). The Court required a showing that the communication "enabled an ordinary mechanic, without the exercise of any ingenuity and special skill on his part, to construct and put the improvement in successful operation." This court's predecessor consistently applied this Supreme Court standard.
>
> This court recognizes that the district court's incorrect derivation standard springs from dictum in this court's *New England Braiding* decision. In that case, this court noted: "To invalidate a patent for derivation of invention, a party must demonstrate that the named inventor in the patent acquired knowledge of the claimed invention from another, or at least so much of the claimed invention as would have made it obvious to one of ordinary skill in the art." *New England Braiding,* 970 F.2d at 883. This dictum did not in fact incorporate a determination of obviousness into a Section 102(f) analysis. Indeed, this court in *New England Braiding* did not apply such a test.
>
> The *New England Braiding* court upheld the denial of a preliminary injunction because the record showed a likelihood that New England Braiding's patent was invalid under 35 U.S.C.A. § 102(f). The record showed that George Champlin, the named inventor, worked for the A.W. Chesterton Co. (Chesterton) and participated in experiments that developed the invention. One Chesterton employee testified that Champlin had said, when he left to start his own company, that he wanted to patent the experimental braiding if Chesterton decided not to do so. Champlin denied these allegations. The key issue was a credibility determination between the witnesses for the two parties. The sufficiency of the communication, particularly whether the invention was obvious in light of such disclosure, was not at issue. Thus, *New England Braiding* did not incorporate an obviousness test into the § 102(f) analysis.

For consideration of § 102(f) as a source of prior art for nonobviousness determinations under § 103, see Chapter 8. For another example where the Federal Circuit arguably discounted the distinction between novelty and nonobviousness, recall *In re Kathawala*'s discussion of § 102(d), reviewed here in Chapter 5.

2.   Derivation and Inventorship. Derivation issues sometimes arise in the context of an interference. Under these circumstances, one party to the interference asserts that the other party actually acquired the idea of the invention from him. "To prove derivation in an interference proceeding, the person attacking the patent must establish prior conception of the claimed subject matter and communication of the conception to the adverse claimant." *Price v. Symsek*, 988 F.2d 1187, 26 U.S.P.Q.2d 1031 (Fed.Cir.1993). *See also Sewall v. Walters*, 21 F.3d 411, 30 U.S.P.Q.2d 1356 (Fed.Cir.1994).

3.   Patents of Importation. Early English law did not bar one who derived from a foreign inventor from obtaining a so-called "patent of importation" in England. *Edgeberry v. Stephens*, ENGLISH PATENT CASES 8 (King's Bench 1691). This possibility has since been eliminated from all modern patent regimes, although the right of the first importer to obtain an English patent remained a part of the law until the Patents Act 1977, *Easycase Inc. v. Bryan Lawrence & Co.*, [1995] F.S.R. 597 (Patents Court). Nonetheless, under contemporary United States law, consider the role that § 104 might play with regard to § 102(f). Are acts performed in countries which are not signatories to NAFTA or members of the WTO admissible as evidence of derivation? *See Hedgewick v. Akers,* 497 F.2d 905, 182 U.S.P.Q. 167 (CCPA 1974).

§ 6.6   A NOTE ON FIRST–TO–FILE VERSUS FIRST–TO–INVENT

The following excerpt from THE ADVISORY COMMISSION ON PATENT LAW REFORM, A REPORT TO THE SECRETARY OF COMMERCE 43–45 (1992), presents a thoughtful commentary on the factors guiding the adoption of a first-to-file system in the United States.

In the United States, when more than one patent application is filed claiming the same invention, the patent will be awarded to the applicant who establishes the earliest acts of invention in the United States and who has not thereafter suppressed, abandoned or concealed the invention ("first-to-invent" system). Applicants are permitted to establish a date of invention that is prior to the filing date in an interference proceeding conducted in the U.S. Patent and Trademark Office (USP-TO). In contrast, in nearly every other country which provides patent protection, priority of invention is established by the earliest effective filing date of a patent application disclosing and claiming the invention ("first-to-file").

A long-standing issue in discussions on patent law reform has been whether the United States should change its patent system to conform with the manner of awarding priority of invention in other countries. The question is again a dominant issue in discussion regarding patent law reform due to negotiations designed to achieve global harmonization of the intellectual property laws....

The principal objections raised to first-to-file by members of the public included:

• small entities might be placed at a disadvantage in the "race to the Patent Office" because of limited resources to prepare and file patent applications;

- a first-to-file system might tend to foster premature and sketchy disclosures in hastily-filed patent applications;

- the possibility of theft of an invention from the true inventor could be increased in a first-to-file system;

- the opportunity to explore commercialization possibilities prior to filing would be reduced because of the importance of early filing;

- the USPTO could be burdened with an increased volume of patent applications filed for defensive purposes.

Those members of the public responding in favor of adopting a first-to-file system raised the following points:

- most of U.S. industry is acting now on a first-to-file basis, even in the United States, to avoid forfeiture of patent rights abroad, and the first-to-invent system could be hurting the competitiveness of U.S. industry;

- a U.S. first-to-file system would encourage early filing worldwide, so that patent rights are not forfeited, and would promote the early public disclosure of inventions;

- an agreement by the United States to a harmonization treaty requiring a change to first-to-file could bring dramatic improvements in the patent systems of foreign countries for U.S. applicants seeking patents abroad;

- a first-to-file system could greatly decrease the complexity, length and expense associated with current USPTO interference procedures; and

- the first-to-file rule would provide a definite, readily determinable and legally-fixed date of priority of invention, would eliminate uncertainties associated with interferences and would provide greater reliability for U.S. patents.

From a purely statistical viewpoint there would seem to be little difference in result between a first-to-invent patent system and a first-to-file patent system. More than 99.9% of the U.S. patent applications now being filed raise no dispute as to the identity of the first inventor. Even when such disputes arise, the inventor who filed first ("senior party") is procedurally favored in the highly complex interference proceeding that follows—the senior party prevails in a significant majority of such interferences. The actual effect of a switch to a first-to-file system of priority, thus, is likely to have little or no actual significance in terms of inventors losing priority of invention to other inventors, based upon these statistical findings.

However, patents vary widely in terms of commercial importance. The public comments, as well as the experience of many Commission members, suggest that applications involved in interferences are almost always drawn to those inventions that are very important commercially. Because such inventions are often developed to answer needs in very competitive markets, the high stakes in such situations drive parties to engage in hard-fought priority contests.

The Commission feels that their recommendation to convert the U.S. system to one that measures priority based upon the first-to-file, as a whole, represents a favorable change for U.S. applicants, both large and small, in terms of ease of filing, clarification of rights, and, importantly, international competitiveness.

A short history of the development of these two systems of priority is found in P.J. Federico, *Patent Interferences in the United States Patent Office,* 2 INT'L REV. INDUS. PROP. & COPYRIGHT L. 21, 22–24 (1971). The early English practice that allowed for the possibility that the law officers of the Crown could conduct an investigation into rival claims of inventorship is described in the leading English patent treatise of its day, W.M. HINDMARCH, A TREATISE ON THE LAW RELATIVE TO Patent PRIVILEGES 503–46 (1846).

Exercises

1. Whil___
   ___ ___ laboratory, Andrea conceives of the ___ ___ semiconductor dopant on January 10, ___ ___ notebook under the heading "Dopant ___ ___ in favor of completing some other ___ ___re. Eventually, she turns again to ___ ___ efforts she fabricates a working ___ ___ immediately notifies her patent ___ ___ n is filed on October 1, 2001. ___ ___ nvention in secrecy.

   ___ provided below, will Andrea be ___ ___ se noted, assume that all

2. ___ ___pan, had described the use ___ ___ published on November 3, ___ ___pant X on June 15, 2001, and by working ___ ___ ct was able to produce the chip on September 1, ___

3. Diane developed the idea of using Dopant X on September 3, 2000. She did nothing more the project until the start of the new year, but then worked on a full-time, daily basis beginning January 3, 1996. She was at last able to construct a working chip on November 20, 2001.

4. Edward conceived of the invention on January 15, 2001, and continued work on the project for the next two months. After several false starts, he halts work on the project entirely on March 21, 2001. After spending some spare moments reflecting on his earlier work in the early summer months, he then renews his efforts on the project in late July. He successfully builds the semiconductor on August 7, 2001.

5. Felicia conceives of the a new transistor on June 20, 2000 and immediately informs her patent agent. A patent application claiming the transistor on December 1, 2000. Along with several other doping agents described as useful in implementing the transistor through semiconductor materials, the application's specification suggests the use of Dopant X. Felicia then constructs the transistor using a known dopant on June 4, 2002. Her patent is granted on April 23, 2003.

Chapter Seven

NONOBVIOUSNESS

Beyond novelty and utility, an invention must also sufficiently advance the useful arts in order to warrant the award of an exclusive right. The doctrine of obviousness compares the claimed invention with the state of the prior art to make that assessment. Novelty, the other patent doctrine that examines prior art, primarily protects the public domain by precluding patent protection if an invention is already available to the public. Obviousness, in contrast, does not apply if each and every feature of the claimed invention already appears in the public domain.

Patent law recognizes that invention is generally the conception of a new combination of several old elements. Such a combination may or may not sufficiently advance the useful arts to merit the award of a proprietary interest, however. In terms of obviousness, the new combination does not warrant a patent if, from the vantage point of one of ordinary skill in the art at the time of invention, this new combination would have been obvious.

Section 103 (a) of the Patent Act sets forth the precise parameters of the obviousness requirement:

> A patent may not be obtained though the invention is not identically disclosed or described as set forth in section 102 of this title, if the differences between the subject matter sought to be patented and the prior art are such that the subject matter as a whole would have been obvious at the time the invention was made to a person having ordinary skill in the art to which the subject matter pertains. Patentability shall not be negatived by the manner in which the invention was made.

Because obviousness is the most significant gatekeeper to patentability, this section deserves some further dissection.

At the outset, section 103 refers to inventions that are "not identically disclosed or described as set forth in section 102." This phrase distinguishes obviousness from novelty. A novelty assessment is almost quantitative. If a single prior art reference describes each feature of the claimed invention, a relatively rare occurrence, then the invention is not novel. Obviousness, on the other hand, requires a series of factual assessments culminating in an often-difficult qualitative judgment of the creative achievement involved in the invention.

Section 103 next begins to set forth the methodology of the obviousness test. Specifically, it refers to "the differences between the subject matter sought to be patented and the prior art." The "subject matter sought to be patented" is a lengthy term for the inventor's claims. The "prior art," though not expressly defined, generally refers to the references stipulated in section 102—patents, printed publications, and so forth. Thus, the same information that can defeat the novelty of a claimed invention under section 102 will, generally speaking, constitute the prior art base for evaluation under section 103. Thus, section 103 requires an assessment of the differences between the claimed invention and the entire body of prior art.

In making this assessment of differences, section 103 specifically requires consideration of the claimed invention "as a whole." As already noted, inventions are often new combinations. The "as a whole" instruction prevents evaluation of the invention part by part. Without this important requirement, an assessment might break an invention into its component parts (A + B + C), then find a prior art reference containing A, another containing B, and another containing C and on that basis alone declare the invention obvious. An analysis of this character would discount the value of combining the various elements in a new way to achieve a new result—often the central creative feature.

To avoid undervaluing the combination, section 103 requires the obviousness assessment to compare the invention as a whole to the prior art. An actual invention illustrates this principle. In the early 1980s, some scientists at 3M Corporation combined an old adhesive (seemingly useless because it did not permanently stick) with note-sized paper to create Post–It® notes. The invention replaced bulky paper clips and staples as the best way to attach a note to a page. The invention became almost instantly a worldwide commercial success. This invention, however, was merely the combination of a known glue (element A) with note-sized paper (element B). Both elements were clearly available in the prior art. Evaluating the invention part by part might have rendered this patentable invention obvious. Evaluating it "as a whole" shows that this new combination warranted an exclusive right.

Section 103 next sets forth the test for patentability. Specifically patentability depends on whether the claimed invention "would have been obvious." To understand the meaning of "obvious" in this context requires vast experience and skill in applying this legal test. Indeed many synonyms have attempted to capture the meaning of "obvious," including terms like "inventiveness," "inventive intellectual product," and, particularly overseas, "inventive step." A decision rendered over a century ago by Lindley, L.J., in *Gadd & Mason v. The Mayor of Manchester,* 9 R.P.C. 516, 524, 67 L.T. 569, 9 T.L.R. 42 (1892) provides some insight into the term:

The difficulty of saying where invention sufficient to support a patent exists and where it does not, is well known to all persons conversant with patent law. . . . If, practically speaking, there are no difficulties to be overcome in adapting an old contrivance to a new purpose, there can be no ingenuity in overcoming them, [and] there will be no invention. . . . The same rule will, I apprehend, also apply to cases in which the mode of overcoming the so-called difficulties is so obvious to every one of ordinary intelligence and acquaintance with the subject matter of the patent, as to present no difficulty to any such person. Such cases present no real difficulty to people conversant with the matter in hand, and admit of no sufficient ingenuity to support a patent. If, in these two classes of cases, patents could be supported, they would be intolerable nuisances, and would seriously impede all improvements in the practical application of common knowledge.

In sum, "obviousness" is the standard that prevents trivial advances in the useful arts from winning patent protection. Section 103 thus creates a "patent-free" zone around the state of the art, allowing skilled technicians to complete routine work such as the straightforward substitution of materials, the ordinary streamlining of parts and technical processes, and the usual marginal improvements which occur as a technology matures. Only where a claimed invention surpasses this ordinary, continuous flow of technical progress will it surmount the "obviousness" requirement.

Next, and of vital importance, section 103 makes the relevant time for assessment of obviousness "the time the invention was made." While absolutely essential to an objective assessment of obviousness, this requirement makes the legal test very difficult to implement. To apply the obviousness test properly, a patent examiner or court must enter a state of "self-induced amnesia." In literal terms, the examiner or court must forget the claimed invention and evaluate its differences from the prior art at a time before its creation. This exercise sounds easy, but is not. Inventions often change the way we view an entire problem. Consider again the Post–It® note example. In hindsight, it seems easy to combine the tacky, but non-adhesive glue with note-sized paper. Indeed, in retrospect, "anyone could do it." In fact, however, the non-adhesive glue existed for many years without a use until some creative mind conceived of the new and incredibly useful combination. Much of the case law and methodology of the obviousness requirement is designed to prevent hindsight—using the invention itself as a road map to select prior art and to evaluate the differences between the invention and the prior art.

Finally, section 103 sets the objective standard for the obviousness determination. The statute specifies that patent examiners and courts do not evaluate the invention according to their own skill and intellect. The test is not whether the invention elicits a "Gee Whiz" reaction from the examiner or court. Instead the examiner or court must make the determination from the vantage point of "a person having ordinary skill in the art." The perspective of this skilled artisan becomes the lens through which the examiner observes all the facts and makes the final judgment. Usually patent examiners and courts acquire this perspective by immersion in the prior art that provides the skilled artisan with their peculiar knowledge and understanding.

The result of this standard is that PTO examiners and judges decide whether an inventor's work product constitutes a sufficient technical advance over the state of the art to receive a patent. This determination is one of the more challenging legal feats in all of common law jurisprudence. The difficulty of framing this concept is demonstrated by the fact that the initial codification of a "novelty plus" requirement is of recent statutory vintage. Section 103 only became part of the Patent Act in 1952. The history leading up to its enactment illustrates the longstanding difficulty of finding a suitable test to measure "inventiveness."

§ 7.1   THE HISTORICAL STANDARD OF INVENTION

The development of a third significant standard of patentability alongside the novelty and utility requirements has an extraordinary history. Although early U.S. patent statutes allowed a patent to issue if the invention was deemed "sufficiently ... important," *see* Patent Act of 1790, § 1, 1 Statutes at Large 109, *reprinted in* P.J. Federico, *The First Patent Act*, 14 J. Pat. Off. Soc'y 237, 250 (1932), scant legal consequences appeared to attach to this requirement. Indeed, as noted, the 1952 Act provided the first statutory requirement for patentability beyond novelty and utility. Before 1952, the courts and early patent administrators developed certain "negative rules" for patentability determinations. *See* Hanns Ulrich, Standards of Patentability for European Inventions 60–62. For instance, mere changes in material, proportion, or form over existing technology or mere combinations of known mechanisms would not warrant a patent. *See* P.J. Federico, *Operation of the Patent Act of 1790*, 18 J. Pat. Off. Soc'y 237 (1936). The doctrinal moorings of these accepted conventions remained uncertain, however, until the Supreme Court issued its opinion in *Hotchkiss v. Greenwood*. This 1851 case began the progress toward section 103. In this case, for the first time, the Court stated that only "inventions" were patentable, and that in order to constitute an invention, a new technology must transcend the everyday efforts of a skilled mechanic.

HOTCHKISS v. GREENWOOD

United States Supreme Court, 1851.
52 U.S.(11 How.) 248.

Mr. Justice Nelson delivered the opinion of the court.

This is a writ of error to the Circuit Court of the United States for the District of Ohio.

The suit was brought against the defendants for the alleged infringement of a patent for a new and useful improvement in making door and other knobs of all kinds of clay used in pottery, and of porcelain.

The improvement consists in making the knobs of clay or porcelain, and in fitting them for their application to doors, locks, and furniture, and various other uses to which they may be adapted; but more especially in this, that of having the cavity in the knob in which the screw or shank is inserted, and by which it is fastened, largest at the bottom and in the form of dovetail, or wedge reversed, and a screw formed therein by pouring in metal in a fused state; and, after referring to drawings of the article thus made, the patentees conclude as follows:

> "What we claim as our invention, and desire to secure by letters patent, is the manufacturing of knobs, as stated in the foregoing specifications, of potter's clay, or any kind of clay used in pottery, and shaped and finished by moulding, turning, burning, and glazing; and also of porcelain."

The court charged the jury that, if knobs of the same form and for the same purposes as that claimed by the patentees, made of metal or other material, had been before known and used; and if the spindle and shank, in the form used by them, had been before known and used, and had been attached to the metallic knob by means of a cavity in the form of dovetail and infusion of melted metal, the same as the mode claimed by the patentees, in the attachment of the shank and spindle to their knob; and the knob of clay was simply the substitution of one material for another, the spindle and shank being the same as before in common use, and also the mode of connecting them by dovetail to the knob the same as before in common use, and no more ingenuity or skill required to construct the knob in this way than that possessed by an ordinary mechanic acquainted with the business, the patent was invalid, and the plaintiffs were not entitled to a verdict.

This instruction, it is claimed, is erroneous, and one for which a new trial should be granted.

The instruction assumes, and, as was admitted on the argument, properly assumes, that knobs of metal, wood, & c., connected with a shank and spindle, in the mode and by the means used by the patentees in their manufacture, had been before known, and were in public use at the date of the patent; and hence the only novelty which could be claimed on their part was the adaptation of this old contrivance to knobs of potter's clay or porcelain; in other words, the novelty consisted in the substitution of the clay knob in the place of one made of metal or wood, as the case might be. And in order to appreciate still more clearly the extent of the novelty claimed, it is proper to add, that this knob of potter's clay is not new, and therefore constitutes no part of the discovery. If it was, a very different question would arise; as it might very well be urged, and successfully urged, that a knob of a new composition of matter, to which this old contrivance had been applied, and which resulted in a new and useful article, was the proper subject of a patent.

The novelty would consist in the new composition made practically useful for the purposes of life, by the means and contrivances mentioned. It would be a new manufacture, and none the less so, within the meaning of the patent law, because the means employed to adapt the new composition to a useful purpose was old, or well known.

But in the case before us, the knob is not new, nor the metallic shank and spindle, nor the dovetail form of the cavity in the knob, nor the means by which the metallic shank is securely fastened therein. All these were well known, and in common use; and the only thing new is the substitution of a knob of a different material from that heretofore used in connection with this arrangement.

Now it may very well be, that, by connecting the clay or porcelain knob with the metallic shank in this well-known mode, an article is produced better and cheaper than in the case of the metallic or wood knob; but this does not result from any new mechanical device or contrivance, but from the fact, that the material of which the knob is composed happens to be better adapted to the purpose for which it is made. The improvement consists in the superiority of the material, and which is not new, over that previously employed in making the knob.

But this, of itself, can never be the subject of a patent. No one will pretend that a machine, made, in whole or in part, of materials better adapted to the purpose for which it is used than the materials of which the old one is constructed, and for that reason better and cheaper, can be distinguished from the old one; or, in the sense of the patent law, can entitle the manufacturer to a patent.

The difference is formal, and destitute of ingenuity or invention. It may afford evidence of judgment and skill in the selection and adaptation of the materials in the manufacture of the instrument for the purposes intended, but nothing more.

It seemed to be supposed, on the argument, that this mode of fastening the shank to the clay knob produced a new and peculiar effect upon the article, beyond that produced when applied to the metallic knob, inasmuch as the fused metal by which the shank was fastened to the knob prevented the shank from acting immediately upon the knob, it being inclosed and firmly held by the metal; that for this reason the clay or porcelain knob was not so liable to crack or be broken, but was made firm and strong, and more durable.

This is doubtless true. But the peculiar effect thus referred to is not distinguishable from that which would exist in the case of the wood knob, or one of bone or ivory, or of other materials that might be mentioned.

Now if the foregoing view of the improvement claimed in this patent be correct, it is quite apparent that there was no error in the submission of the questions presented at the trial to the jury; for unless more ingenuity and skill in applying the old method of fastening the shank and the knob were required in the application of it to the clay or porcelain knob than were possessed by an ordinary mechanic acquainted with the business, there was an absence of that degree of skill and ingenuity which constitute essential elements of every invention. In other words, the improvement is the work of the skilful mechanic, not that of the inventor.

We think, therefore, that the judgment is, and must be, affirmed.

Note

The *Hotchkiss* case has often been read as presenting the initial presentation of an additional inventiveness standard beyond that of utility and novelty. *See Graham v. John Deere Co.*, 383 U.S. 1, 3–4, 86 S.Ct. 684, 686, 15 L.Ed.2d 545 (1966) (Clark, J.) ("the 1952 [Patent] Act was intended to codify judicial precedents embracing the principle long ago announced by this Court in *Hotchkiss v. Greenwood*, 11 How. 248, 13 L.Ed. 683 (1851) * * *."); *Roanwell Corp. v. Plantronics, Inc.*, 429 U.S. 1004, 1005, 97 S.Ct. 538, 539, 50 L.Ed.2d 617, 192 U.S.P.Q. 65 (1976) (White, J., dissenting from denial of certiorari) ("This Court long ago established that the sine qua non of patentability is 'invention' and that the protection of the patent law does not extend to an 'improvement [that] is the work of the skilled mechanic, not that of the inventor.' *Hotchkiss v. Greenwood*, 52 U.S. (11 How.) 248, 267, 13 L.Ed. 683 (1851)."); *Lee v. Runge*, 404 U.S. 887, 891, 92 S.Ct. 197, 199, 30 L.Ed.2d 169, 171 U.S.P.Q. 322 (1971) (Douglas, J., dissenting from denial of certiorari).

The Supreme Court's articulation in *Hotchkiss* was not itself a pioneering invention, but a combination of pre-existing legal art. Many courts since the early nineteenth century had examined differences between the invention and the prior art. *See, e.g., Knight v. Baltimore & O. R. Co.*, 14 F.Cas. 758, No. 7882 (C.C.Md.1840) ("[i]f, before his first patent * * *, the same principle, in the same combination, which he describes as his improvement, was in public use, in ordinary carriages, upon common roads, the plaintiff was not entitled to a patent for applying the same thing to railway carriages, unless the improvement he claims contain something new *and material*, either in principle, in combination, or in the mode of operation, in order to adapt it to its new use."). *Cf. Earle v. Sawyer*, 8 F.Cas. 254, 4 Mason 1, 1 Robb.Pat.Cas. 490 (C.C.Mass.1825) (No. 4247) (Story, J.).

In any event, *Hotchkiss* articulated a doctrine that focused on the "inventiveness" of the invention. Sadly the vague and highly abstract nature of the Supreme Court's invention test caused wildly varying results and interpretations. In the Supreme Court alone, the standard for sufficient "inventiveness" took the form of "inventive effort," *Smith v. Goodyear Dental Vulcanite Co.*, 93 U.S. 486, 497 (1876); "a substantial invention or discovery," *Atlantic Works v. Brady*, 107 U.S. 192, 200 (1882); "the creative work in the inventive faculty," *Hollister v. Benedict & Burnham Mfg. Co.*, 113 U.S. 59, 73 (1885); "that impalpable something," *McClain v. Ortmayer*, 141 U.S. 419, 427 (1891); and "inventive skill," *Ansonia Brass & Copper Co. v. Electrical Supply Co.*, 144 U.S. 11, 18 (1892). One court went so far as to demand "something new, unexpected and exciting," which the disgruntled patentee protested on appeal with the comment that "there is nothing very exciting about automobile transmissions." *Thurber Corp. v. Fairchild Motor*

Corp., 269 F.2d 841, 849, 122 U.S.P.Q. 305, 311 (5th Cir.1959). As Judge Learned Hand noted, the invention standard was "as fugitive, impalpable, wayward and vague a phantom as exists in the whole paraphernalia of legal concepts." *Harries v. Air King Prods.*, 183 F.2d 158, 86 U.S.P.Q. 57 (2d Cir.1950).

In parallel with the rise of the antitrust movement, the standard of invention became increasingly difficult to satisfy, particularly at the Supreme Court. The Court's predilection for striking down patents led Justice Jackson to state "that the only patent that is valid is one which this Court has not been able to get its hands on." *Jungersen v. Ostby and Barton Co.*, 335 U.S. 560, 572 (1949). His observation had been proceeded by the standard set in *Cuno Engineering Corp. v. Automatic Devices Corp.*, 314 U.S. 84, 90 (1941), where the Court had elaborated upon the invention standard:

> We may concede that the functions performed by Mead's combination were new and useful. But that does not necessarily make the device patentable. Under the statute . . . the device must not only be "new and useful," it must also be an "invention" or discovery. " . . . It has been recognized that if an improvement is to obtain the privileged position of a patent more ingenuity must be involved than the work of a mechanic skilled in the art. . . . That is to say, the new device, *however useful it may be, must reveal the flash of creative genius, not merely the skill of the calling.* If it fails, it has not established its right to a private grant in the public domain."

The patent community considered this "flash of genius" standard as a literal declaration of war against the patent system. But the high water mark of this "war on patents" was perhaps the following decision.

GREAT A. & P. TEA CO. v. SUPERMARKET EQUIPMENT CORP.

United States Supreme Court, 1950.
340 U.S. 147, 87 U.S.P.Q. 303.

MR. JUSTICE JACKSON delivered the opinion of the Court.

Two courts below have concurred in holding three patent claims to be valid, and it is stipulated that, if valid, they have been infringed. The issue, for the resolution of which we granted certiorari, is whether they applied correct criteria of invention. We hold that they have not, and that by standards appropriate for a combination patent these claims are invalid.

Stated without artifice, the claims assert invention of a cashier's counter equipped with a three-sided frame, or rack, with no top or bottom, which, which pushed or pulled, will move groceries deposited within it by a customer to the checking clerk and leave them there when it is pushed back to repeat the operation. It is kept on the counter by guides. That the resultant device words as claimed, speeds the customer on his way, reduces checking costs for the merchant, has been widely adopted and successfully used, appear beyond dispute.

The District Court explicitly found that each element in this device was known to prior art. "However," it found, "the conception of a counter with an extension to receive a bottomless self-unloading tray with which to push the contents of the tray in front of the cashier was a decidedly novel feature and constitutes a new and useful combination." The Court of Appeals regarded this finding of invention as one of fact, sustained by substantial evidence, and affirmed it as not clearly erroneous. It identified no other new or different element to constitute invention and overcame its doubts by consideration of the need for some such device and evidence of commercial success of this one.

While this Court has sustained combination patents, it never has ventured to give a precise and comprehensive definition of the test to be applied in such cases. The voluminous literature which the subject has excited discloses no such test. It is agreed that the key to patentability of a mechanical device that brings old factors into cooperation is presence or lack of invention. In course of time the profession came to employ the term "combination" to imply its presence and the term "aggregation" to signify its absence, thus making antonyms in legal art of words which in ordinary speech are more nearly synonyms. However useful as words of art to denote in short form that an assembly of units has failed or has met the examination for invention, their employment as tests to determine invention results in nothing but confusion. The concept of invention is inherently elusive when applied to combination of old elements. This, together with the imprecision of our language, have counseled courts and text writers to be cautious in affirmative definitions or rules on the subject.

The negative rule accrued from many litigations was condensed about as precisely as the subject permits in *Lincoln Engineering Co. of Illinois v. Stewart–Warner Corp.*, 303 U.S. 545, 549, 549, 58 S.Ct. 662, 664, 82 L.Ed. 1008: "The mere aggregation of a number of old parts or elements which, in the aggregation, perform or produce no new or different function or operation than that theretofore performed or produced by them, is not patentable invention." The conjunction or concert of known elements must contribute something; only when the whole in some way exceeds the sum of its parts is the accumulation of old devices patentable. Elements may, of course, especially in chemistry or electronics, take on some new quality or function from being brought into concert, but this is not a usual result of uniting elements old in mechanics. This case is wanting in any unusual or surprising consequences from the unification of the elements here concerned, and there is nothing to indicate that the lower courts scrutinized the claims in the light of this rather severe test.

Neither court below has made any finding that old elements which made up this device perform any additional or different function in the combination than they perform out of it. This counter does what a store counter always has done-it supports merchandise at a convenient height while the customer makes his purchases and the merchant his sales. The three-sided rack will draw or push goods put within it from one place to another-just what any such a rack would do on any smooth surface-and the guide rails keep it from falling or sliding off from the counter, as guide rails have ever done. Two and two have been added together, and still they make only four.

Courts should scrutinize combination patent claims with a care proportioned to the difficulty and improbability of finding invention in an assembly of old elements. The function of a patent is to add to the sum of useful knowledge. Patents cannot be sustained when, on the contrary, their effect is to subtract from former resources freely available to skilled artisans. A patent for a combination which only unites old elements with no change in their respective functions, such as is presented here, obviously withdraws what already is known into the field of its monopoly and diminishes the resources available to skillful men. This patentee has added nothing to the total stock of knowledge, but has merely brought together segments of prior art and claims them in congregation as a monopoly.

Reversed.

MR. JUSTICE DOUGLAS, with whom MR. JUSTICE BLACK agrees, concurring.

It is worth emphasis that every patent case involving validity presents a question which requires reference to a standard written into the Constitution. Article I, § 8, contains a grant to the Congress of the power to permit patents to be issued. But unlike most of the specific powers which Congress is given, that grant is qualified. The Congress does not have free reign, for example, to decide that patents should be easily or freely given. The Congress acts under the restraint imposed by the statement of purpose in Art. I, § 8. The purpose is 'To promote the Progress of Science and useful Arts'. The means for achievement of that end is the grant for a limited time to inventors of the exclusive right to their inventions.

Every patent is the grant of a privilege of exacting tolls from the public. The Framers plainly did not want those monopolies freely granted. The invention, to justify a patent, had to serve the ends of science-to push back the frontiers of chemistry, physics, and the like; to make a distinctive contribution to scientific knowledge. That is why through the years the opinions of the Court commonly have taken "inventive genius" as the test. It is not enough that an article is new and useful. The Constitution never sanctioned the patenting of gadgets. Patents serve a higher end-the advancement of science. An invention need not be as startling as an atomic bomb to be patentable. But is has to be of such quality and distinction that masters of the scientific field in which it falls will recognize it as an advance. Mr. Justice Bradley stated in *Atlantic Works v. Brady*, 107 U.S. 192, 200, 2 S.Ct. 225, 231, 27 L.Ed. 438, the consequences of a looser standard: "It was never the object of those laws to grant a monopoly for every trifling device, every shadow of a shade of an idea, which would naturally and spontaneously occur to any skilled mechanic or operator in the ordinary progress of manufactures. Such an indiscriminate creation of exclusive privileges tends rather to obstruct than to stimulate invention. It creates a class of speculative schemers who make it their business to watch the advancing wave of improvement, and gather its foam in the form of patented monopolies, which enable them to lay a heavy tax upon the industry of the country, without contributing anything to the real advancement of the arts. It embarrasses the honest pursuit of business with fears and apprehensions of concealed liens and unknown liabilities to lawsuits and vexatious accountings for profits made in good faith."

The standard of patentability is a constitutional standard; and the question of validity of a patent is a question of law.

The attempts through the years to get a broader, looser conception of patents than the Constitution contemplates have been persistent. The Patent Office, like most administrative agencies, has looked with favor on the opportunity which the exercise of discretion affords to expand its own jurisdiction. And so it has placed a host of gadgets under the armour of patents-gadgets that obviously have had no place in the constitutional scheme of advancing scientific knowledge.

The patent involved in the present case belongs to this list of incredible patents which the Patent Office has spawned. The fact that a patent as flimsy and as spurious as this one has to be brought all the way to this Court to be declared invalid dramatically illustrates how far our patent system frequently departs from the constitutional standards which are supposed to govern.

Notes

1. Synergism. A difficulty with the Supreme Court's "synergism" standard in *Great A. & P. Tea Company* is that nearly every invention can be cast as "simply" the combination of old components, and therefore as not meeting the necessary standard of "invention." *A & P* therefore attracted great criticism as representing the culmination of subjective, hindsight-ridden and inconsistent judicial determination of inventiveness on the part of judges having no day-to-day familiarity with what would be obvious or nonobvious to a person of ordinary skill in the art as suggested by the *Hotchkiss* standard.

2. The 1952 Patent Act. Dissatisfaction with the Supreme Court's increasingly onerous standard of invention was among the reasons leading to the articulation of a statutory basis for the invention standard in the Patent Act of 1952. An individual intimately involved with the creation of the 1952 Act, the Honorable Giles S. Rich, noted the intended impact of the drafters of § 103 as follows:

1. *It put the* [invention] *requirement into the statutes for the first time, in section 103.* ... Though one may call section 103 "codification" it took a case law doctrine, expressed in hundreds of different ways, and put it into statutory language in a single form approved by Congress. In such form it became law superior to that which may be derived from any prior court opinion.

2. *The Patent Act of 1952 expresses the prerequisite to patentability without any reference to "invention" as a legal requirement.* Nowhere in the entire act is there a reference to any requirement of "invention" and the drafters did this deliberately in an effort to free the law and lawyers from bondage to that old and meaningless term. The word "invention" is used in the statute only to refer to the thing invented. That is why the requirement of "invention" should be referred to, it at all, only with respect to that which is dead.

3. *The act sets as the standard of patentability the unobviousness of the invention, at the time it was made, to person having ordinary skill in the art.* Therefore, what we have today, and have had since January 1, 1953, is a requirement of *unobviousness*, rather than a requirement of "invention."

Giles S. Rich, *The Principles of Patentability*, 42 J. Pat. Off. Soc'y 75, 89 (1960). Following the enactment of section 103, attention turned to the way the Supreme Court would interpret the statute. Unfortunately the Supreme Court was not swift to answer. Thirteen years after the effective date of the 1952 Act, the Court finally took up its pen in three cases-*Graham v. John Deere, Cook Chemical,* and *Adams*-of such importance to the patent bar that they became known merely as "The Trilogy." These decisions are probably still the most important patent cases in modern history. Certainly they are the most important cases relative to the nonobviousness requirement.

§ 7.2   THE MODERN STANDARD OF NONOBVIOUSNESS

§ 7.2[a]   The Trilogy

GRAHAM v. JOHN DEERE CO.

United States Supreme Court, 1966.
383 U.S. 1, 148 U.S.P.Q. 459.

Mr. Justice Clark delivered the opinion of the Court.

After a lapse of 15 years, the Court again focuses its attention on the patentability of inventions under the standard of Art. I, § 8, cl. 8, of the Constitution and under the conditions prescribed by the laws of the United States. Since our last expression on patent validity, *Great A. & P. Tea Co. v. Supermarket Equipment Corp.*, 340 U.S. 147, 71 S.Ct. 127, 95 L.Ed. 162 (1950), the Congress has for the first time expressly added a third statutory dimension to the two requirements of novelty and utility that had been the sole statutory test since the Patent Act of 1793. This is the test of obviousness, i.e., whether "the subject matter sought to be patented and the prior art are such that the subject matter as a whole would have been obvious at the time the invention was made to a person having ordinary skill in the art to which said subject matter pertains. Patentability shall not be negatived by the manner in which the invention was made." § 103 of the Patent Act of 1952, 35 U.S.C. § 103 (1964 ed.).

The questions, involved in each of the companion cases before us, are what effect the 1952 Act had upon traditional statutory and judicial tests of patentability and what definitive tests are now required. We have concluded that the 1952 Act was intended to codify judicial precedents embracing the principle long ago announced by this Court in *Hotchkiss v. Greenwood*, 11 How. 248, 13 L.Ed. 683 (1851), and that, while the clear language of § 103 places emphasis on an inquiry into obviousness, the general level of innovation necessary to sustain patentability remains the same.

I.

THE CASES.

(a) No. 11, *Graham v. John Deere Co.*, an infringement suit by petitioners, presents a conflict between two Circuits over the validity of a single patent on a "Clamp for vibrating Shank Plows." The invention, a combination of old mechanical elements, involves a device designed to absorb shock from plow shanks as they plow through rocky soil and thus to prevent damage to the plow. In 1955, the Fifth Circuit had held the patent valid under its rule that when a combination produces an "old result in a cheaper and otherwise more advantageous way," it is patentable. *Jeoffroy Mfg., Inc. v. Graham*, 219 F.2d 511, *cert. denied*, 350 U.S. 826, 76 S.Ct. 55, 100 L.Ed. 738. In 1964, the Eighth Circuit held, in the case at bar, that there was no new result in the patented combination and that the patent was, therefore, not valid. 333 F.2d 529, *reversing* D.C., 216 F.Supp. 272. We granted *certiorari*, 379 U.S. 956, 85 S.Ct. 652, 13 L.Ed.2d 553. Although we have determined that neither Circuit applied the correct test, we conclude that the patent is invalid under § 103 and, therefore, we affirm the judgment of the Eighth Circuit.

(b) No. 37, *Calmar, Inc. v. Cook Chemical Co.*, and No. 43, *Colgate–Palmolive Co. v. Cook Chemical Co.*, both from the Eighth Circuit, were separate declaratory judgment actions, but were filed contemporaneously. Petitioner in Calmar is the manufacturer of a finger-operated sprayer with a "hold-down" cap of the type commonly seen on grocers' shelves inserted in bottles of insecticides and other liquids prior to shipment. Petitioner in Colgate–Palmolive is a purchaser of the sprayers and uses them in the distribution of its products. Each action sought a declaration of invalidity and noninfringement of a patent on similar sprayers issued to Cook Chemical as assignee of Baxter I. Scoggin, Jr., the inventor. By cross-action, Cook Chemical claimed infringement. The actions were consolidated for trial and the patent was sustained by the District Court. 220 F.Supp. 414. The Court of Appeals affirmed, 8 Cir., 336 F.2d 110, and we granted certiorari, 380 U.S. 949, 85 S.Ct. 1082, 13 L.Ed.2d 967. We reverse.

Manifestly, the validity of each of these patents turns on the facts. The basic problems, however, are the same in each case and require initially a discussion of the constitutional and statutory provisions covering the patentability of the inventions.

II.

Congress quickly responded to the bidding of the Constitution by enacting the Patent Act of 1790 during the second session of the First Congress. It created an agency in the Department of State headed by the Secretary of State, the Secretary of the Department of War and the Attorney General, any two of whom could issue a patent for a period not exceeding 14 years to any petitioner that "hath * * * invented or discovered any useful art, manufacture, * * * or device, or any improvement therein not before known or used" if the board found that "the invention or discovery (was) sufficiently useful and important * * *." 1 Stat. 110. This group, whose members administered the patent system along with their other public duties, was known by its own designation as "Commissioners for the Promotion of Useful Arts."

Thomas Jefferson, who as Secretary of State was a member of the group, was its moving spirit and might well be called the "first administrator of our patent system." See Federico, *Operation of the Patent Act of 1790*, 18 J.PAT.OFF.SOC. 237, 238 (1936). He was not only an administrator of the patent system under the 1790 Act, but was also the author of the 1793 Patent Act. In addition, Jefferson was himself an inventor of great note. His unpatented improvements on plows, to mention but one line of his inventions, won acclaim and recognition on both sides of the Atlantic. Because of his active interest and influence in the early development of the patent system, Jefferson's views on the general nature of the limited patent monopoly under the Constitution, as well as his conclusions as to conditions for patentability under the statutory scheme, are worthy of note.

Jefferson's philosophy on the nature and purpose of the patent monopoly is expressed in a letter to Isaac McPherson (Aug. 1813), a portion of which we set out in the margin.[11] He rejected a natural-rights theory in intellectual property rights and clearly recognized the social and economic rationale of the patent system. The patent monopoly was not designed to secure to the inventor his natural right in his discover-

---

11. "Stable ownership is the gift of social law, and is given late in the progress of society. It would be curious then, if an idea, the fugitive fermentation of an individual brain, could, of natural right, be claimed in exclusive and stable property. If nature has made any one thing less susceptible than all others of exclusive property, it is the action of the thinking power called an idea, which an individual may exclusively possess as long as he keeps it to himself; but the moment it is divulged, it forces itself into the possession of every one, and the receiver cannot dispossess himself of it. Its peculiar character, too, is that no one possesses the less, because every other possesses the whole of it. He who receives an idea from me, receives instruction himself without lessening mine; as he who lights his taper at mine, receives light without darkening me. That ideas should freely spread from one to another over the globe, for the moral and mutual instruction of man, and improvement of his condition, seems to have been peculiarly and benevolently designed by nature, when she made them, like fire, expansible over all space, without lessening their density in any point, and like the air in which we breathe, move, and have our physical being, incapable of confinement or exclusive appropriation. Inventions then cannot, in nature, be a subject of property. Society may give an exclusive right to the profits arising from them, as an encouragement to men to pursue ideas which may produce utility, but this may or may not be done, according to the will and convenience of the society, without claim or complaint from anybody." VI WRITINGS OF THOMAS JEFFERSON, at 180–181 (Washington ed.).

ies. Rather, it was a reward, an inducement, to bring forth new knowledge. The grant of an exclusive right to an invention was the creation of society-at odds with the inherent free nature of disclosed ideas-and was not to be freely given. Only inventions and discoveries which furthered human knowledge, and were new and useful, justified the special inducement of a limited private monopoly. Jefferson did not believe in granting patents for small details, obvious improvements, or frivolous devices. His writings evidence his insistence upon a high level of patentability.

As a member of the patent board for several years, Jefferson saw clearly the difficulty in "drawing a line between the things which are worth to the public the embarrassment of an exclusive patent, and those which are not." The board on which he served sought to draw such a line and formulated several rules which are preserved in Jefferson's correspondence.[12] Despite the board's efforts, Jefferson saw "with what slow progress a system of general rules could be matured." Because of the "abundance" of cases and the fact that the investigations occupied "more time of the members of the board than they could spare from higher duties, the whole was turned over to the judiciary, to be matured into a system, under which every one might know when his actions were safe and lawful." Letter to McPherson, supra, at 181, 182. Apparently Congress agreed with Jefferson and the board that the courts should develop additional conditions for patentability. Although the Patent Act was amended, revised or codified some 50 times between 1790 and 1950, Congress steered clear of a statutory set of requirements other than the bare novelty and utility tests reformulated in Jefferson's draft of the 1793 Patent Act.

III.

The difficulty of formulating conditions for patentability was heightened by the generality of the constitutional grant and the statutes implementing it, together with the underlying policy of the patent system that "the things which are worth to the public the embarrassment of an exclusive patent," as Jefferson put it, must outweigh the restrictive effect of the limited patent monopoly. The inherent problem was to develop some means of weeding out those inventions which would not be disclosed or devised but for the inducement of a patent.

This Court formulated a general condition of patentability in 1851 in *Hotchkiss v. Greenwood*, 11 How. 248, 13 L.Ed. 683. The patent involved a mere substitution of materials-porcelain or clay for wood or metal in doorknobs-and the Court condemned it, holding:

---

12. "(A) machine of which we are possessed, might be applied by every man to any use of which it is susceptible." Letter to Isaac McPherson, supra, at 181. "(A) change of material should not give title to a patent. As the making a ploughshare of cast rather than of wrought iron; a comb of iron instead of horn or of ivory * * *." Ibid. "(A) mere change of form should give no right to a patent, as a high-quartered shoe instead of a low one; a round hat instead of a three-square; or a square bucket instead of a round one." Id., at 181–182. "(A combined use of old implements.) A man has a right to use a saw, an axe, a plane separately; may he not combine their uses on the same piece of wood?" Letter to Oliver Evans, (Jan. 1814), VI WRITINGS OF THOMAS JEFFERSON, at 298 (Washington ed.).

"(U)nless more ingenuity and skill * * * were required * * * than were possessed by an ordinary mechanic acquainted with the business, there was an absence of that degree of skill and ingenuity which constitute essential elements of every invention. In other words, the improvement is the work of the skilful mechanic, not that of the inventor." At p. 267.

Hotchkiss, by positing the condition that a patentable invention evidence more ingenuity and skill than that possessed by an ordinary mechanic acquainted with the business, merely distinguished between new and useful innovations that were capable of sustaining a patent and those that were not. The *Hotchkiss* test laid the cornerstone of the judicial evolution suggested by Jefferson and left to the courts by Congress. The language in the case, and in those which followed, gave birth to "invention" as a word of legal art signifying patentable inventions. Yet, as this Court has observed, "(t)he truth is, the word ('invention') cannot be defined in such manner as to afford any substantial aid in determining whether a particular device involves an exercise of the inventive faculty or not." *McClain v. Ortmayer*, 141 U.S. 419, 427, 12 S.Ct. 76, 78, 35 L.Ed. 800 (1891); *Great A. & P. Tea Co. v. Supermarket Equipment Corp., supra*, 340 U.S., at 151, 71 S.Ct. at 129. Its use as a label brought about a large variety of opinions as to its meaning both in the Patent Office, in the courts, and at the bar. The *Hotchkiss* formulation, however, lies not in any label, but in its functional approach to questions of patentability. In practice, *Hotchkiss* has required a comparison between the subject matter of the patent, or patent application, and the background skill of the calling. It has been from this comparison that patentability was in each case determined.

IV.

THE 1952 PATENT ACT.

The Act sets out the conditions of patentability in three sections. An analysis of the structure of these three sections indicates that patentability is dependent upon three explicit conditions: novelty and utility as articulated and defined in § 101 and § 102, and nonobviousness, the new statutory formulation, as set out in § 103. The first two sections, which trace closely the 1874 codification, express the "new and useful" tests which have always existed in the statutory scheme and, for our purposes here, need no clarification. The pivotal section around which the present controversy centers is § 103. It provides:

"§ 103. Conditions for patentability; non-obvious subject matter. A patent may not be obtained though the invention is not identically disclosed or described as set forth in section 102 of this title, if the differences between the subject matter sought to be patented and the prior art are such that the subject matter as a whole would have been obvious at the time the invention was made to a person having ordinary skill in the art to which said subject matter pertains. Patentability shall not be negatived by the manner in which the invention was made."

The section is cast in relatively unambiguous terms. Patentability is to depend, in addition to novelty and utility, upon the "non-obvious" nature of the "subject matter sought to be patented" to a person having ordinary skill in the pertinent art.

The first sentence of this section is strongly reminiscent of the language in *Hotchkiss*. Both formulations place emphasis on the pertinent art existing at the time the invention was made and both are implicitly tied to advances in that art. The major distinction is that Congress has emphasized "nonobviousness" as the operative test of the section, rather than the less definite "invention" language of *Hotchkiss* that Congress thought had led to "a large variety" of expressions in decisions and writings. In the title itself the Congress used the phrase "Conditions for patentability; non-obvious subject matter", thus focusing upon "nonobviousness" rather than "invention." The Senate and House Reports, S.Rep. No. 1979, 82d Cong., 2d Sess. (1952); H.R.Rep. No. 1923, 82d Cong., 2d Sess. (1952), U.S.Code Congressional and Administrative News 1952, p. 2394, reflect this emphasis in these terms:

> "Section 103, for the first time in our statute, provides a condition which exists in the law and has existed for more than 100 years, but only by reason of decisions of the courts. An invention which has been made, and which is new in the sense that the same thing has not been made before, may still not be patentable if the difference between the new thing and what was known before is not considered sufficiently great to warrant a patent. That has been expressed in a large variety of ways in decisions of the courts and in writings. Section 103 states this requirement in the title. It refers to the difference between the subject matter sought to be patented and the prior art, meaning what was known before as described in section 102. If this difference is such that the subject matter as a whole would have been obvious at the time to a person skilled in the art, then the subject matter cannot be patented. That provision paraphrases language which has often been used in decisions of the courts, and the section is added to the statute for uniformity and definiteness. This section should have a stabilizing effect and minimize great departures which have appeared in some cases.'" H.R.Rep., supra, at 7; S.Rep., supra, at 6.

It is undisputed that this section was, for the first time, a statutory expression of an additional requirement for patentability, originally expressed in *Hotchkiss*. It also seems apparent that Congress intended by the last sentence of § 103 to abolish the test it believed this Court announced in the controversial phrase "flash of creative genius," used in *Cuno Engineering Corp. v. Automatic Devices Corp.*, 314 U.S. 84, 62 S.Ct. 37, 86 L.Ed. 58 (1941).

It is contended, however, by some of the parties and by several of the amici that the first sentence of § 103 was intended to sweep away judicial precedents and to lower the level of patentability. Others contend that the Congress intended to codify the essential purpose reflected in existing judicial precedents-the rejection of insignificant variations and innovations of a commonplace sort-and also to focus inquiries under § 103 upon nonobviousness, rather than upon "invention," as a means of achieving more stability and predictability in determining patentability and validity.

The Reviser's Note to this section, with apparent reference to Hotchkiss, recognizes that judicial requirements as to "lack of patentable novelty (have) been followed since at least as early as 1850." The note indicates that the section was inserted because it "may have some stabilizing effect, and also to serve as a basis for the addition at a later time of some criteria which may be worked out." To this same effect are the reports of both Houses, supra, which state that the first sentence of the section "paraphrases language which has often been used in decisions of the courts, and the section is added to the statute for uniformity and definiteness."

We believe that this legislative history, as well as other sources, shows that the revision was not intended by Congress to change the general level of patentable invention. We conclude that the section was intended merely as a codification of judicial precedents embracing the Hotchkiss condition, with congressional directions that inquiries into the obviousness of the subject matter sought to be patented are a prerequisite to patentability.

V.

Approached in this light, the § 103 additional condition, when followed realistically, will permit a more practical test of patentability. The emphasis on non-obviousness is one of inquiry, not quality, and, as such, comports with the constitutional strictures.

While the ultimate question of patent validity is one of law, *Great A. & P. Tea Co. v. Supermarket Equipment Corp., supra*, 340 U.S. at 155, 71 S.Ct. at 131, the § 103 condition, which is but one of three conditions, each of which must be satisfied, lends itself to several basic factual inquiries. Under § 103, the scope and content of the prior art are to be determined; differences between the prior art and the claims at issue are to be ascertained; and the level of ordinary skill in the pertinent art resolved. Against this background, the obviousness or nonobviousness of the subject matter is determined. Such secondary considerations as commercial success, long felt but unsolved needs, failure of others, etc., might be utilized to give light to the circumstances surrounding the origin of the subject matter sought to be patented. As indicia of obviousness or nonobviousness, these inquiries may have relevancy. See Note, *Subtests of "Nonobviousness": A Nontechnical Approach to Patent Validity*, 112 U.PA.L.REV. 1169 (1964).

This is not to say, however, that there will not be difficulties in applying the nonobviousness test. What is obvious is not a question upon which there is likely to be uniformity of thought in every given factual context. The difficulties, however, are comparable to those encountered daily by the courts in such frames of reference as negligence and scienter, and should be amenable to a case-by-case development. We believe that strict observance of the requirements laid down here will result in that uniformity and definiteness which Congress called for in the 1952 Act.

While we have focused attention on the appropriate standard to be applied by the courts, it must be remembered that the primary responsibility for sifting out unpatentable material lies in the Patent Office. To await litigation is-for all practical purposes-to debilitate the patent system. We have observed a notorious difference between the standards applied by the Patent Office and by the courts. While many reasons can be adduced to explain the discrepancy, one may well be the free rein often exercised by Examiners in their use of the concept of "invention." In this connection we note that the Patent Office is confronted with a most difficult task. Almost 100,000 applications for patents are filed each year. Of these, about 50,000 are granted and the backlog now runs well over 200,000. 1965 ANNUAL REPORT OF THE COMMISSION OF PATENTS 13–14. This is itself a compelling reason for the Commissioner to strictly adhere to the 1952 Act as interpreted here. This would, we believe, not only expedite disposition but bring about a closer concurrence between administrative and judicial precedent.

Although we conclude here that the inquiry which the Patent Office and the courts must make as to patentability must be beamed with greater intensity on the requirements of § 103, it bears repeating that we find no change in the general strictness with which the overall test is to be applied. We have been urged to find in § 103 a relaxed standard, supposedly a congressional reaction to the "increased standard" applied by this Court in its decisions over the last 20 or 30 years. The standard has remained invariable in this Court. Technology, however, has advanced-and with remarkable rapidity in the last 50 years. Moreover, the ambit of applicable art in given fields of science has widened by disciplines unheard of a half century ago. It is but an evenhanded application to require that those persons granted the benefit of a patent monopoly be charged with an awareness of these changed conditions. The same is true of the less technical, but still useful arts. He who seeks to build a better mousetrap today has a long path to tread before reaching the Patent Office.

VI.

We now turn to the application of the conditions found necessary for patentability to the cases involved here:

A. The Patent in Issue in No. 11, Graham v. John Deere Co.

This patent, No. 2,627,798 (hereinafter called the '798 patent) relates to a spring clamp which permits plow shanks to be pushed upward when they hit obstructions in the soil, and then springs the shanks back into normal position when the obstruction is passed over. The device, which we show diagrammatically in the accompanying sketches (Appendix, Fig. 1), is fixed to the plow frame as a unit. The mechanism around which the controversy center is basically a hinge. The top half of it, known as the upper plate (marked 1 in the sketches), is a heavy metal piece clamped to the plow frame (2) and is stationary relative to the plow frame. The lower half of the hinge, known as the hinge plate (3), is connected to the rear of the upper plate by a hinge pin (4) and rotates downward with respect to it. The shank (5), which is bolted to the forward end of the hinge plate (at 6), runs beneath the plate and parallel to it for about nine inches, passes through a stirrup (7), and then continues backward for several feet curving down toward the ground. The chisel (8), which does the actual plowing, is attached to the rear end of the shank. As the plow frame is pulled forward, the chisel rips through the soil, thereby plowing it. In the normal position, the hinge plate and the shank are kept tight against the upper plate by a spring (9), which is atop the upper plate. A rod (10) runs through the center of the spring, extending down through holes in both plates and the shank. Its upper end is bolted to the top of the spring while its lower end is hooked against the underside of the shank.

When the chisel hits a rock or other obstruction in the soil, the obstruction forces the chisel and the rear portion of the shank to move upward. The shank is pivoted (at 11) against the rear of the hinge plate and pries open the hinge against the closing tendency of the spring. (See sketch labeled "Open Position," Appendix, Fig. 1.) This closing tendency is caused by the fact that, as the hinge is opened, the connecting rod is pulled downward and the spring is compressed. When the obstruction is passed over, the upward force on the chisel disappears and the spring pulls the shank and hinge plate back into their original position. The lower, rear portion of the hinge plate is constructed in the form of a stirrup (7) which brackets the shank, passing around and beneath it. The shank fits loosely into the stirrup (permitting a slight up and down play). The stirrup is designed to prevent the shank from recoiling away from the hinge plate, and thus prevents excessive strain on the shank near its bolted connection. The stirrup also girds the shank, preventing it from fishtailing from side to side.

In practical use, a number of spring-hinge-shank combinations are clamped to a plow frame, forming a set of ground-working chisels capable of withstanding the shock of rocks and other obstructions in the soil without breaking the shanks.

BACKGROUND OF THE PATENT. → State of the art

Chisel plows, as they are called, were developed for plowing in areas where the ground is relatively free from rocks or stones. Originally, the shanks were rigidly attached to the plow frames. When such plows were used in the rocky, glacial soils of some of the Northern States, they were found to have serious defects. As the chisels hit buried rocks, a vibratory motion was set up and tremendous forces were transmitted to the shank near its connection to the frame. The shanks would break. Graham, one of the petitioners, sought to meet that problem, and in 1950 obtained a patent, U.S. No. 2,493,811 (hereinafter '811), on a spring clamp where solved some of the difficulties. Graham and his companies manufactured and sold the '811 clamps. In 1950, Graham modified the '811 structure and filed for a patent. That patent, the one in issue, was granted in 1953. This suit against competing plow manufacturers resulted from charges by petitioners that several of respondents' devices infringed the '798 patent.

THE PRIOR ART. = 2 Differences

We confine our discussion to the prior patent of Graham, '811, and to the Glencoe clamp device, both among the references asserted by respondents. The Graham '811 and '798 patent devices are similar in all elements, save two: (1) the stirrup and the bolted connection of the shank to the hinge plate do not appear in '811; and (2) the position of the shank is reversed, being placed in patent '811 above the hinge plate, sandwiched between it and the upper plate. The shank is held in place by the spring rod which is hooked against the bottom of the hinge plate passing through a slot in the shank. Other differences are of no consequence to our examination. In practice the '811 patent arrangement permitted the shank to wobble or fishtail because it was not rigidly fixed to the hinge plate; moreover, as the hinge plate was below the shank, the latter caused wear on the upper plate, a member difficult to repair or replace.

Graham's '798 patent application contained 12 claims. All were rejected as not distinguished from the Graham '811 patent. The inverted position of the shank was specifically rejected as was the bolting of the shank to the hinge plate. The Patent Office examiner found these to be "matters of design well within the expected skill of the art and devoid of invention." Graham withdrew the original claims and substituted the two new ones which are substantially those in issue here. His contention was that wear was reduced in patent '798 between the shank and the heel or rear of the upper plate.[13] He also emphasized several new features, the relevant one here being that the bolt used to connect the hinge plate and shank maintained the upper face of the shank in continuing and constant contact with the underface of the hinge plate.

Graham did not urge before the Patent Office the greater "flexing" qualities of the '798 patent arrangement which he so heavily relied on in the courts. The sole element in patent '798 which petitioners argue before us is the interchanging of the shank and hinge plate and the consequences flowing from this arrangement. The contention is that this arrangement-which petitioners claim is not disclosed in the prior art-

---

13. In '811, where the shank was above the hinge plate, an upward movement of the chisel forced the shank up against the underside of the rear of the upper plate. The upper plate thus provided the fulcrum about which the hinge was pried open. Because of this, as well as the location of the hinge pin, the shank rubbed against the heel of the upper plate causing wear both to the plate and to the shank. By relocating the hinge pin and by placing the hinge plate between the shank and the upper plate, as in '798, the rubbing was eliminated and he wear point was changed to the hinge plate, a member more easily removed or replaced for repair.

permits the shank to flex under stress for its entire length. As we have sketched (see sketch, "Graham '798 Patent" in Appendix, Fig. 2), when the chisel hits an obstruction the resultant force (A) pushes the rear of the shank upward and the shank pivots against the rear of the hinge plate at (C). The natural tendency is for that portion of the shank between the pivot point and the bolted connection (i.e., between C and D) to bow downward and away from the hinge plate. The maximum distance (B) that the shank moves away from the plate is slight-for emphasis, greatly exaggerated in the sketches. This is so because of the strength of the shank and the short-nine inches or so-length of that portion of the shank between (C) and (D). On the contrary, in patent '811 (see sketch, "Graham '811 Patent" in Appendix, Fig. 2), the pivot point is the upper plate at point (c); and while the tendency for the shank to bow between points (c) and (d) is the same as in '798, the shank is restricted because of the underlying hinge plate and cannot flex as freely. In practical effect, the shank flexes only between points (a) and (c), and not along the entire length of the shank, as in '798. Petitioners say that this difference in flex, though small, effectively absorbs the tremendous forces of the shock of obstructions whereas prior art arrangements failed.

The Obviousness of the Differences.

We cannot agree with petitioners. We assume that the prior art does not disclose such an arrangement as petitioners claim in patent '798. Still we do not believe that the argument on which petitioners' contention is bottomed supports the validity of the patent. The tendency of the shank to flex is the same in all cases. If free-flexing, as petitioners now argue, is the crucial difference above the prior art, then it appears evident that the desired result would be obtainable by not boxing the shank within the confines of the hinge. The only other effective place available in the arrangement was to attach it below the hinge plate and run it through a stirrup or bracket that would not disturb its flexing qualities. Certainly a person having ordinary skill in the prior art, given the fact that the flex in the shank could be utilized more effectively if allowed to run the entire length of the shank, would immediately see that the thing to do was what Graham did, i.e., invert the shank and the hinge plate.

Petitioners' argument basing validity on the free-flex theory raised for the first time on appeal is reminiscent of *Lincoln Engineering Co. of Illinois v. Stewart–Warner Corp.*, 303 U.S. 545, 58 S.Ct. 662, 82 L.Ed. 1008 (1938), where the Court called such an effort "an afterthought. No such function * * * is hinted at in the specifications of the patent. If this were so vital an element in the functioning of the apparatus, it is strange that all mention of it was omitted." At p. 550, 58 S.Ct. at p. 665. No "flexing" argument was raised in the Patent Office. Indeed, the trial judge specifically found that "flexing is not a claim of the patent in suit * * * "and would not permit interrogation as to flexing in the accused devices. Moreover, the clear testimony of petitioners' experts shows that the flexing advantages flowing from the '798 arrangement are not, in fact, a significant feature in the patent.

We find no nonobvious facets in the '798 arrangement. The wear and repair claims were sufficient to overcome the patent examiner's original conclusions as to the validity of the patent. However, some of the prior art, notably Glencoe, was not before him. There the hinge plate is below the shank but, as the courts below found, all of the elements in the '798 patent are present in the Glencoe structure. Furthermore, even though the position of the shank and hinge plate appears reversed in Glencoe, the mechanical operation is identical. The shank there pivots about the underside of the stirrup, which in Glencoe is above the shank. In other words, the stirrup in Glencoe serves exactly the same function as the heel of the hinge plate in '798. The mere shifting of the wear point to the heel of the '798 hinge plate from the stirrup of Glencoe-itself a part of the hinge plate-presents no operative mechanical distinctions, much less nonobvious differences.

B. The Patent in Issue in No. 37, Calmar, Inc. v. Cook Chemical Co., and in No. 43, Colgate–Palmolive Co. v. Cook Chemical Co.

The single patent[14] involved in these cases relates to a plastic finger sprayer with a "hold-down" lid used as a built-in dispenser for containers or bottles packaging liquid products, principally household insecticides. Only the first two of the four claims in the patent are involved here and we, therefore, limit our discussion to them. We do not set out those claims here since they are printed in 220 F.Supp., at 417–418.

In essence the device here combines a finger-operated pump sprayer, mounted in a container or bottle by means of a container cap, with a plastic overcap which screws over the top of and depresses the sprayer (see Appendix, Fig. 3). The pump sprayer passes through the container cap and extends down into the liquid in the container; the overcap fits over the pump sprayer and screws down on the outside of a collar mounting or retainer which is molded around the body of the sprayer. When the overcap is screwed down on this collar mounting a seal is formed by the engagement of a circular ridge or rib located above the threads on the collar mounting with a mating shoulder located inside the overcap above its threads. The overcap, as it is screwed down, depresses the pump plunger rendering the pump inoperable and when the seal is effected, any liquid which might seep into the overcap through or around the pump is prevented from leaking out of the overcap. The overcap serves also to protect the sprayer head and prevent damage to it during shipment or merchandising. When the overcap is in place it does not reach the cap of the container or bottle and in no way engages it since a slight space is left between those two pieces.

---

14. The patent is U.S. No. 2,870,943 issued in 1959 to Cook Chemical Co. as assignee of Baxter I. Scoggin, Jr., the inventor. In No. 37, Calmar is the manufacturer of an alleged infringing device, and, in No. 43, Colgate is a customer of Calmar and user of its device.

The device, called a shipper-sprayer in the industry, is sold as an integrated unit with the overcap in place enabling the insecticide manufacturer to install it on the container or bottle of liquid in a single operation in an automated bottling process. The ultimate consumer simply unscrews and discards the overcap, the pump plunger springs up and the sprayer is ready for use.

THE BACKGROUND OF THE PATENT.

For many years manufacturers engaged in the insecticide business had faced a serious problem in developing sprayers that could be integrated with the containers or bottles in which the insecticides were marketed. Originally, insecticides were applied through the use of tin sprayers, not supplied by the manufacturer. In 1947, Cook Chemical, an insecticide manufacturer, began to furnish its customers with plastic pump dispensers purchased from Calmar. The dispenser was an unpatented finger-operated device mounted in a perforated cardboard holder and hung over the neck of the bottle or container. It was necessary for the ultimate consumer to remove the cap of the container and insert and attach the sprayer to the latter for use.

Hanging the sprayer on the side of the container or bottle was both expensive and troublesome. Packaging for shipment had to be a hand operation, and breakage and pilferage as well as the loss of the sprayer during shipment and retail display often occurred. Cook Chemical urged Calmar to develop an integrated sprayer that could be mounted directly in a container or bottle during the automated filling process and that would not leak during shipment or retail handling. Calmar did develop some such devices but for various reasons they were not completely successful. The situation was aggravated in 1954 by the entry of Colgate–Palmolive into the insecticide trade with its product marketed in aerosol spray cans. These containers, which used compressed gas as a propellent to dispense the liquid, did not require pump sprayers.

During the same year Calmar was acquired by the Drackett Company. Cook Chemical became apprehensive of its source of supply for pump sprayers and decided to manufacture its own through a subsidiary, Bakan Plastics, Inc. Initially, it copied its design from the unpatented Calmar sprayer, but an officer of Cook Chemical, Scoggin, was assigned to develop a more efficient device. By 1956 Scoggin had perfected the shipper-sprayer in suit and a patent was granted in 1959 to Cook Chemical as his assignee. In the interim Cook Chemical began to use Scoggin's device and also marketed it to the trade. The device was well received and soon became widely used.

In the meanwhile, Calmar employed two engineers, Corsette and Cooprider, to perfect a shipper-sprayer and by 1958 it began to market its SS–40, a device very much similar to Scoggin's. When the Scoggin patent issued, Cook Chemical charged Calmar's SS–40 with infringement and this suit followed.

The Opinions of the District Court and the Court of Appeals.

At the outset it is well to point up that the parties have always disagreed as to the scope and definition of the invention claimed in the patent in suit. Cook Chemical contends that the invention encompasses a unique combination of admittedly old elements and that patentability is found in the result produced. Its expert testified that the invention was "the first commercially successful, inexpensive integrated shipping closure pump unit which permitted automated assembly with a container of household insecticide or similar liquids to produce a practical, ready-to-use package which could be shipped without external leakage and which was so organized that the pump unit with its hold-down cap could be itself assembled and sealed and then later assembled and sealed on the container without breaking the first seal." Cook Chemical stresses the long-felt need in the industry for such a device; the inability of others to produce it; and its commercial success-all of which, contends Cook, evidences the nonobvious nature of the device at the time it was developed. On the other hand, Calmar says that the differences between Scoggin's shipper-sprayer and the prior art relate only to the design of the overcap and that the differences are so inconsequential that the device as a whole would have been obvious at the time of its invention to a person having ordinary skill in the art.

Both courts accepted Cook Chemical's contentions. While the exact basis of the District Court's holding is uncertain, the court did find the subject matter of the patent new, useful and nonobvious. It concluded that Scoggin "had produced a sealed and protected sprayer unit which the manufacturer need only screw onto the top of its container in much the same fashion as a simple metal cap." 220 F.Supp., at 418. Its decision seems to be bottomed on the finding that the Scoggin sprayer solved the long-standing problem that had confronted the industry. The Court of Appeals also found validity in the "novel" marriage "of the sprayer with the insecticide container" which took years in discovery and in "the immediate commercial success" which it enjoyed. While finding that the individual elements of the invention were "not novel per se" the court found "nothing in the prior art suggesting Scoggin's unique combination of these old features * * * as would solve the * * * problems which for years beset the insecticide industry." It concluded that "the * * * (device) meets the exacting standard required for a combination of old elements to rise to the level of patentable invention by fulfilling the long-felt need with an economical, efficient, utilitarian apparatus which achieved novel results and immediate commercial success." 336 F.2d, at 114.

The Prior Art.

Only two of the five prior art patents cited by the Patent Office Examiner in the prosecution of Scoggin's application are necessary to our discussion, i.e., Lohse U.S. Patent No. 2,119,884 (1938) and Mellon U.S. Patent No. 2,586,687 (1952). Others are cited by Calmar that were not before the Examiner, but of these our purposes require discussion of only the Livingstone U.S. Patent No. 2,715,480 (1953). Simplified drawings of each of these patents are reproduced in the Appendix, Figs. 4–6, for comparison and description.

The Lohse patent (Fig. 4) is a shipper-sprayer designed to perform the same function as Scoggin's device. The differences, recognized by the District Court, are found in the overcap seal which in Lohse is formed by the skirt of the overcap engaging a washer or gasket which rests upon the upper surface of the container cap. The court emphasized that in Lohse "(t)here are no seals above the threads and below the sprayer head." 220 F.Supp., at 419.

The Mellon patent (Fig. 5), however, discloses the idea of effecting a seal above the threads of the overcap. Mellon's device, likewise a shipper-sprayer, differs from Scoggin's in that its overcap screws directly on the container, and a gasket, rather than a rib, is used to effect the seal.

Finally, Livingstone (Fig. 6) shows a seal above the threads accomplished without the use of a gasket or washer. Although Livingstone's arrangement was designed to cover and protect pouring spouts, his sealing feature is strikingly similar to Scoggin's. Livingstone uses a tongue and groove technique in which the tongue, located on the upper surface of the collar, fits into a groove on the inside of the overcap. Scoggin employed the rib and shoulder seal in the identical position and with less efficiency because the Livingstone technique is inherently a more stable structure, forming an interlock that withstands distortion of the overcap when subjected to rough handling. Indeed, Cook Chemical has now incorporated the Livingstone closure into its own shipper-sprayers as had Calmar in its SS–40.

THE INVALIDITY OF THE PATENT.

Let us first return to the fundamental disagreement between the parties. Cook Chemical, as we noted at the outset, urges that the invention must be viewed as the overall combination, or-putting it in the language of the statute-that we must consider the subject matter sought to be patented taken as a whole. With this position, taken in the abstract, there is, of course, no quibble. But the history of the prosecution of the Scoggin application in the Patent Office reveals a substantial divergence in respondent's present position.

As originally submitted, the Scoggin application contained 15 claims which in very broad terms claimed the entire combination of spray pump and overcap. No mention of, or claim for, the sealing features was made. All 15 claims were rejected by the Examiner because (1) the applicant was vague and indefinite as to what the invention was, and (2) the claims were met by Lohse. Scoggin canceled these claims and submitted new ones. Upon a further series of rejections and new submissions, the Patent Office Examiner, after an office interview, at last relented. It is crystal clear that after the first rejection, Scoggin relied entirely upon the sealing arrangement as the exclusive patentable difference in his combination. It is likewise clear that it was on that feature that the

Examiner allowed the claims. In fact, in a letter accompanying the final submission of claims, Scoggin, through his attorney, stated that "agreement was reached between the Honorable Examiner and applicant's attorney relative to limitations which must be in the claims in order to define novelty over the previously applied disclosure of Lohse when considered in view of the newly cited patents of Mellon and Darley, Jr." (Italics added.)

Moreover, those limitations were specifically spelled out as (1) the use of a rib seal and (2) an overcap whose lower edge did not contact the container cap. Mellon was distinguished, as was the Darley patent, infra, n. 18, on the basis that although it disclosed a hold-down cap with a seal located above the threads, it did not disclose a rib seal disposed in such position as to cause the lower peripheral edge of the overcap "to be maintained out of contacting relationship with (the container) cap * * * when * * * (the overcap) was screwed (on) tightly * * *." Scoggin maintained that the "obvious modification" of Lohse in view of Mellon would be merely to place the Lohse gasket above the threads with the lower edge of the overcap remaining in tight contact with the container cap or neck of the container itself. In other words, the Scoggin invention was limited to the use of a rib-rather than a washer or gasket-and the existence of a slight space between the overcap and the container cap.

It is, of course, well settled that an invention is construed not only in the light of the claims, but also with reference to the file wrapper or prosecution history in the Patent Office. *Hogg v. Emerson*, 11 How. 587, 13 L.Ed. 824 (1850); *Crawford v. Heysinger*, 123 U.S. 589, 8 S.Ct. 399, 31 L.Ed. 269 (1887). Claims as allowed must be read and interpreted with reference to rejected ones and to the state of the prior art; and claims that have been narrowed in order to obtain the issuance of a patent by distinguishing the prior art cannot be sustained to cover that which was previously by limitation eliminated from the patent. *Powers-Kennedy Contracting Corp. v. Concrete Mixing & Conveying Co.*, 282 U.S. 175, 185–186, 51 S.Ct. 95, 99, 75 L.Ed. 278 (1930); *Schriber-Schroth Co. v. Cleveland Trust Co.*, 311 U.S. 211, 220–221, 312 U.S. 654, 61 S.Ct. 235, 239–240, 85 L.Ed. 132 (1940).

Here, the patentee obtained his patent only by accepting the limitations imposed by the Examiner. The claims were carefully drafted to reflect these limitations and Cook Chemical is not now free to assert a broader view of Scoggin's invention. The subject matter as a whole reduces, then, to the distinguishing features clearly incorporated into the claims. We now turn to those features.

As to the space between the skirt of the overcap and the container cap, the District Court found: "Certainly without a space so described, there could be no inner seal within the cap, but such a space is not new or novel, but it is necessary to the formation of the seal within the hold-down cap." To me this language is descriptive of an element of the patent but not a part of the invention. It is too simple, really, to require much discussion. In this device the hold-down cap was intended to perform two functions-to hold down the sprayer head and to form a solid tight seal between the shoulder and the collar below. In assembling the element it is necessary to provide this space in order to form the seal. 220 F.Supp. at 420.

The court correctly viewed the significance of that feature. We are at a loss to explain the Examiner's allowance on the basis of such a distinction. Scoggin was able to convince the Examiner that Mellon's cap contacted the bottle neck while his did not. Although the drawings included in the Mellon application show that the cap might touch the neck of the bottle when fully screwed down, there is nothing-absolutely nothing-which indicates that the cap was designed at any time to engage the bottle neck. It is palpably evident that Mellon embodies a seal formed by a gasket compressed between the cap and the bottle neck. It follows that the cap in Mellon will not seal if it does not bear down on the gasket and this would be impractical, if not impossible, under the construction urged by Scoggin before the Examiner. Moreover, the space so strongly asserted by Cook Chemical appears quite plainly on the Livingstone device, a reference not cited by the Examiner.

The substitution of a rib built into a collar likewise presents no patentable difference above the prior art. It was fully disclosed and dedicated to the public in the Livingstone patent. Cook Chemical argues, however, that Livingstone is not in the pertinent prior art because it relates to liquid containers having pouring spouts rather than pump sprayers. Apart from the fact that respondent made no such objection to similar references cited by the Examiner, so restricted a view of the applicable prior art is not justified. The problems confronting Scoggin and the insecticide industry were not insecticide problems; they were mechanical closure problems. Closure devices in such a closely related art as pouring spouts for liquid containers are at the very least pertinent references. See, II Walker on Patents § 260 (Deller ed. 1937).

Cook Chemical insists, however, that the development of a workable shipper-sprayer eluded Calmar, who had long and unsuccessfully sought to solve the problem. And, further, that the long-felt need in the industry for a device such as Scoggin's together with its wide commercial success supports its patentability. These legal inferences or subtests do focus attention on economic and motivational rather than technical issues and are, therefore, more susceptible of judicial treatment than are the highly technical facts often present in patent litigation. See Judge Learned Hand in *Reiner v. I. Leon Co.*, 285 F.2d 501, 504 (2d Cir.1960). See also Note, *Subtests of "Nonobviousness": A Nontechnical Approach to Patent Validity*, 112 U.Pa.L.Rev. 1169 (1964). Such inquiries may lend a helping hand to the judiciary which, as Mr. Justice Frankfurter observed, is most ill-fitted to discharge the technological duties cast upon it by patent legislation. *Marconi Wireless Telegraph Co. of America v. United States*, 320 U.S. 1, 60, 63 S.Ct. 1393, 87 L.Ed. 1731 (1943). They may also serve to "guard against slipping into use of hindsight," *Monroe Auto Equipment Co. v. Heckethorn Mfg. & Supply Co.*, 332 F.2d 406, 412

(1964), and to resist the temptation to read into the prior art the teachings of the invention in issue.

However, these factors do not, in the circumstances of this case, tip the scales of patentability. The Scoggin invention, as limited by the Patent Office and accepted by Scoggin, rests upon exceedingly small and quite non-technical mechanical differences in a device which was old in the art. At the latest, those differences were rendered apparent in 1953 by the appearance of the Livingstone patent, and unsuccessful attempts to reach a solution to the problems confronting Scoggin made before that time became wholly irrelevant. It is also irrelevant that no one apparently chose to avail himself of knowledge stored in the Patent Office and readily available by the simple expedient of conducting a patent search-a prudent and nowadays common preliminary to well organized research. *Mast, Foos & Co. v. Stover Mfg. Co.*, 177 U.S. 485, 20 S.Ct. 708, 44 L.Ed. 856 (1900). To us, the limited claims of the Scoggin patent are clearly evident from the prior art as it stood at the time of the invention.

We conclude that the claims in issue in the Scoggin patent must fall as not meeting the test of § 103, since the differences between them and the pertinent prior art would have been obvious to a person reasonably skilled in that art.

UNITED STATES v. ADAMS

United States Supreme Court, 1966.
383 U.S. 39, 148 U.S.P.Q. 479.

MR. JUSTICE CLARK delivered the opinion of the Court.

This is a companion case to Graham v. John Deere Co., 383 U.S. 1, 86 S.Ct. 684, decided this day along with *Calmar, Inc. v. Cook Chemical Co.* and *Colgate-Palmolive Co. v. Cook Chemical Co.* The United States seeks review of a judgment of the Court of Claims, holding valid and infringed a patent on a wet battery issued to Adams. This suit under 28 U.S.C. § 1498 (1964 ed.) was brought by Adams and others holding an interest in the patent against the Government charging both infringement and breach of an implied contract to pay compensation for the use of the invention. The Government challenged the validity of the patent, denied that it had been infringed or that any contract for its use had ever existed. The Trial Commissioner held that the patent was valid and infringed in part but that no contract, express or implied, had been established. The Court of Claims adopted these findings, initially reaching only the patent questions, 330 F.2d 622, 165 Ct.Cl. 576, but subsequently, on respondents' motion to amend the judgment, deciding the contract claims as well. 330 F.2d, at 634, 165 Ct.Cl., at 598. The United States sought certiorari on the patent validity issue only. We granted the writ, along with the others, in order to settle the important issues of patentability presented by the four cases. 380 U.S. 949, 85 S.Ct. 1090, 13 L.Ed.2d 968. We affirm.

II.

THE PATENT IN ISSUE AND ITS BACKGROUND.

The patent under consideration, U.S. No. 2,322,210, was issued in 1943 upon an application filed in December 1941 by Adams. It relates to a nonrechargeable, as opposed to a storage, electrical battery. Stated simply, the battery comprises two electrodes-one made of magnesium, the other of cuprous chloride-which are placed in a container. The electrolyte, or battery fluid, used may be either plain or salt water.

The specifications of the patent state that the object of the invention is to provide constant voltage and current without the use of acids, conventionally employed in storage batteries, and without the generation of dangerous fumes. Another object is "to provide a battery which is relatively light in weight with respect to capacity" and which "may be manufactured and distributed to the trade in a dry condition and rendered serviceable by merely filling the container with water." Following the specifications, which also set out a specific embodiment of the invention, there appear 11 claims. Of these, principal reliance has been placed upon Claims 1 and 10, which read: "1. A battery comprising a liquid container, a magnesium electropositive electrode inside the container and having an exterior terminal, a fused cuprous chloride electronegative electrode, and a terminal connected with said electronegative electrode." "10. In a battery, the combination of a magnesium electropositive electrode, and an electronegative electrode comprising cuprous chloride fused with a carbon catalytic agent."

For several years prior to filing his application for the patent, Adams had worked in his home experimenting on the development of a wet battery. He found that when cuprous chloride and magnesium were used as electrodes in an electrolyte of either plain water or salt water an improved battery resulted.

The Adams invention was the first practical, water-activated, constant potential battery which could be fabricated and stored indefinitely without any fluid in its cells. It was activated within 30 minutes merely by adding water. Once activated, the battery continued to deliver electricity at a voltage which remained essentially constant regardless of the rate at which current was withdrawn. Furthermore, its capacity for generating current was exceptionally large in comparison to its size and weight. The battery was also quite efficient in that substantially its full capacity could be obtained over a wide range of currents. One disadvantage, however, was that once activated the battery could not be shut off; the chemical reactions in the battery continued even though current was not withdrawn. Nevertheless, these chemical reactions were highly exothermic, liberating large quantities of heat during operation. As a result, the battery performed with little effect on its voltage or current in very low temperatures. Relatively high temperatures would not damage the battery. Consequently, the battery was operable from 65 below zero Fahrenheit to 200 Fahrenheit.

Less than a month after filing for his patent, Adams brought his discovery to the attention of the Army and Navy. Arrangements were quickly made for demonstrations before the experts of the United States Army Signal Corps. The Signal Corps scientists who observed the demonstrations and who conducted further tests themselves did not believe the battery was workable. Almost a year later, in December 1942, Dr. George Vinal, an eminent government expert with the National Bureau of Standards, still expressed doubts. He felt that Adams was making "unusually large claims" for "high watt hour output per unit weight," and he found "far from convincing" the graphical data submitted by the inventor showing the battery's constant voltage and capacity characteristics. He recommended, "Until the inventor can present more convincing data about the performance of his (battery) cell, I see no reason to consider it further."

However, in November 1943, at the height of World War II, the Signal Corps concluded that the battery was feasible. The Government thereafter entered into contracts with various battery companies for its procurement. The battery was found adaptable to many uses. Indeed, by 1956 it was noted that "(t)here can be no doubt that the addition of water activated batteries to the family of power sources has brought about developments which would otherwise have been technically or economically impractical." See TENTH ANNUAL BATTERY RESEARCH AND DEVELOPMENT CONFERENCE, SIGNAL CORPS ENGINEERING LABORATORIES, FORT MONMOUTH, N.J., p. 25 (1956). Also, see Finding No. 24, 330 F.2d, at 632, 165 Ct.Cl., at 592.

Surprisingly, the Government did not notify Adams of its changed views nor of the use to which it was putting his device, despite his repeated requests. In 1955, upon examination of a battery produced for the Government by the Burgess Company, he first learned of the Government's action. His request for compensation was denied in 1960, resulting in this suit.

III.

THE PRIOR ART.

The basic idea of chemical generation of electricity is, of course, quite old. Batteries trace back to the epic discovery by the Italian scientist Volta in 1795, who found that when two dissimilar metals are placed in an electrically conductive fluid an electromotive force is set up and electricity generated. Essentially, the basic elements of a chemical battery are a pair of electrodes of different electrochemical properties and an electrolyte which is either a liquid (in "wet" batteries) or a moist paste of various substances (in the so-called "drycell" batteries). Various materials which may be employed as electrodes, various electrolyte possibilities and many combinations of these elements have been the object of considerable experiment for almost 175 years. See generally, Vinal, Primary Batteries (New York 1950).

At trial, the Government introduced in evidence 24 patents and treatises as representing the art as it stood in 1938, the time of the Adams invention. Here, however, the Government has relied primarily upon only six of these references which we may summarize as follows.

The Niaudet treatise describes the Marie Davy cell invented in 1860 and De La Rue's variations on it. The battery comprises a zinc anode and a silver chloride cathode. Although it seems to have been capable of working in an electrolyte of pure water, Niaudet says the battery was of "little interest" until De La Rue used a solution of ammonium chloride as an electrolyte. Niaudet also states that "(t)he capital advantage of this battery, as in all where zinc with sal ammoniac (ammonium chloride solution) is used, consists in the absence of any local or internal action as long as the electric circuit is open; in other words, this battery does not work upon itself." Hayes likewise discloses the De La Rue zinc-silver chloride cell, but with certain mechanical differences designed to restrict the battery from continuing to act upon itself.

The Wood patent is relied upon by the Government as teaching the substitution of magnesium, as in the Adams patent, for zinc. Wood's patent, issued in 1928, states: "It would seem that a relatively high voltage primary cell would be obtained by using * * * magnesium as the * * * (positive) electrode and I am aware that attempts have been made to develop such a cell. As far as I am aware, however, these have all been unsuccessful, and it has been generally accepted that magnesium could not be commercially utilized as a primary cell electrode." Wood recognized that the difficulty with magnesium electrodes is their susceptibility to chemical corrosion by the action of acid or ammonium chloride electrolytes. Wood's solution to this problem was to use a "NEUTRAL ELECTROLYTE CONTAINING A STRONG soluble oxidizing agent adapted to reduce the rate of corrosion of the magnesium electrode on open circuit." There is no indication of its use with cuprous chloride, nor was there any indication that a magnesium battery could be water-activated.

The Codd treatise is also cited as authority for the substitution of magnesium. However, Codd simply lists magnesium in an electromotive series table, a tabulation of electrochemical substances in descending order of their relative electropositivity. He also refers to magnesium in an example designed to show that various substances are more electropositive than others, but the discussion involves a cell containing an acid which would destroy magnesium within minutes. In short, Codd indicates, by inference, only that magnesium is a theoretically desirable electrode by virtue of its highly electropositive character. He does not teach that magneisum could be combined in a water-activated battery or that a battery using magnesium would have the properties of the Adams device. Nor does he suggest, as the Government indicates, that cuprous chloride could be substituted for silver chloride. He merely refers to the cuprous ion-a generic term which includes an infinite number of copper compounds-and in no way suggests that cuprous chloride could be employed in a battery.

The Government then cites the Wensky patent which was issued in Great Britain in 1891. The patent relates to the use of cuprous chloride as a depolarizing agent. The specifications of his patent disclose a battery comprising zinc and copper electrodes, the cuprous chloride being added as a salt in an electrolyte solution containing zinc chloride as well. While Wensky recognized that cuprous chloride could be used in a constant-current cell, there is no indication that he taught a water-activated system or that magnesium could be incorporated in his battery.

Finally, the Skrivanoff patent depended upon by the Government relates to a battery designed to give intermittent, as opposed to continuous, service. While the patent claims magnesium as an electrode, it specifies that the electrolyte to be used in conjunction with it must be a solution of "alcoline, chloro-chromate, or a permanganate strengthened with sulphuric acid." The cathode was a copper or carbon electrode faced with a paste of "phosphoric acid, amorphous phosphorous, metallic copper in spangles, and cuprous chloride." This paste is to be mixed with hot sulfuric acid before applying to the electrode. The Government's expert testified in trial that he had no information as to whether the cathode, as placed in the battery, would, after having been mixed with the other chemicals prescribed, actually contain cuprous chloride. Furthermore, respondents' expert testified, without contradiction, that he had attempted to assemble a battery made in accordance with Skrivanoff's teachings, but was met first with a fire when he sought to make the cathode, and then with an explosion when he attempted to assemble the complete battery.

IV.

The Validity of the Patent.

The Government challenges the validity of the Adams patent on grounds of lack of novelty under 35 U.S.C. § 102(a) (1964 ed.) as well as obviousness under 35 U.S.C. § 103 (1964 ed.) As we have seen in *Graham v. John Deere Co.*, 383 U.S. 1, 86 S.Ct. 684, novelty and nonobviousness-as well as utility-are separate tests of patentability and all must be satisfied in a valid patent.

The Government concludes that wet batteries comprising a zinc anode and silver chloride cathode are old in the art; and that the prior art shows that magnesium may be substituted for zinc and cuprous chloride for silver chloride. Hence, it argues that the "combination of magnesium and cuprous chloride in the Adams battery was not patentable because it represented either no change or an insignificant change as compared the prior battery designs." And, despite "the fact that, wholly unexpectedly, the battery showed certain valuable operating advantages over other batteries (these advantages) would certainly not justify a patent on the essentially old formula."

There are several basic errors in the Government's position. First, the fact that the Adams battery is water-activated sets his device apart from the prior art. It is true that Claims 1 and 10, supra, do not mention a water electrolyte, but, as we have noted, a stated object of the invention was to provide a battery rendered serviceable by the mere addition of water. While the claims of a patent limit the invention, and specifications cannot be utilized to expand the patent monopoly, it is fundamental that claims are to be construed in the light of the specifications and both are to be read with a view to ascertaining the invention. Taken together with the stated object of disclosing a water-activated cell, the lack of reference to any electrolyte in Claims 1 and 10 indicates that water alone could be used. Furthermore, of the 11 claims in issue, three of the narrower ones include references to specific electrolyte solutions comprising water and certain salts. The obvious implication from the absence of any mention of an electrolyte-a necessary element in any battery-in the other eight claims reinforces this conclusion. It is evident that respondents' present reliance upon this feature was not the afterthought of an astute patent trial lawyer. In his first contact with the Government less than a month after the patent application was filed, Adams pointed out that "no acids, alkalines or any other liquid other than plain water is used in this cell. Water does not have to be distilled. * * *" Letter to Charles F. Kettering (January 7, 1942), R., pp. 415, 416. Also see his letter to the Department of Commerce (March 28, 1942), R., p. 422. The findings, approved and adopted by the Court of Claims, also fully support this conclusion.

Nor is *Sinclair & Carroll Co. v. Interchemical Corp.*, 325 U.S. 327, 65 S.Ct. 1143, 89 L.Ed. 1644 (1945), apposite here. There the patentee had developed a rapidly drying printing ink. All that was needed to produce such an ink was a solvent which evaporated quickly upon heating. Knowing that the boiling point of a solvent is an indication of its rate of evaporation, the patentee merely made selections from a list of solvents and their boiling points. This was no more than "selecting the last piece to put into the last opening in a jig-saw puzzle." 325 U.S., at 335, 65 S.Ct. at 1147. Indeed, the Government's reliance upon Sinclair & Carroll points up the fallacy of the underlying premise of its case. The solvent in Sinclair & Carroll had no functional relation to the printing ink involved. It served only as an inert carrier. The choice of solvent was dictated by known, required properties. Here, however, the Adams battery is shown to embrace elements having an interdependent functional relationship. It begs the question, and overlooks the holding of the Commissioner and the Court of Claims, to state merely that magnesium and cuprous chloride were individually known battery components. If such a combination is novel, the issue is whether bringing them together as taught by Adams was obvious in the light of the prior art.

We believe that the Court of Claims was correct in concluding that the Adams battery is novel. Skrivanoff disclosed the use of magnesium in an electrolyte completely different from that used in Adams. As we have mentioned, it is even open to doubt whether cuprous chloride was a functional element in Skrivanoff. In view of the unchallenged testimony that the Skrivanoff formulation was both dangerous and inoperable, it seems anomalous to suggest that it is an anticipation of Adams. An inoperable invention or one which fails to achieve its intended result does not negative novelty. *Smith v. Snow*, 294 U.S. 1, 17, 55 S.Ct. 279, 285, 79 L.Ed. 721 (1935). That in 1880 Skrivanoff may have been able to convince a foreign patent examiner to issue a patent on his device has little significance in the light of the foregoing.

Nor is the Government's contention that the electrodes of Adams were mere substitutions of pre-existing battery designs supported by the prior art. If the use of magnesium for zinc and cuprous chloride for silver chloride were merely equivalent substitutions, it would follow that the resulting device-Adams'-would have equivalent operating characteristics. But it does not. The court below found, and the Government apparently admits, that the Adams battery "wholly unexpectedly" has shown "certain valuable operating advantages over other batteries" while those from which it is claimed to have been copied were long ago discarded. Moreover, most of the batteries relied upon by the Government were of a completely different type designed to give intermittent power and characterized by an absence of internal action when not in use. Some provided current at voltages which declined fairly proportionately with time. Others were so-called standard cells which, though producing a constant voltage, were of use principally for calibration or measurement purposes. Such cells cannot be used as sources of power. For these reasons we find no equivalency.

We conclude the Adams battery was also nonobvious. As we have seen, the operating characteristics of the Adams battery have been shown to have been unexpected and to have far surpassed then-existing wet batteries. Despite the fact that each of the elements of the Adams battery was well known in the prior art, to combine them as did Adams required that a person reasonably skilled in the prior art must ignore that (1) batteries which continued to operate on an open circuit and which heated in normal use were not practical; and (2) water-activated batteries were successful only when combined with electrolytes detrimental to the use of magnesium. These long-accepted factors, when taken together, would, we believe, deter any investigation into such a combination as is used by Adams. This is not to say that one who merely finds new uses for old inventions by shutting his eyes to their prior disadvantages thereby discovers a patentable innovation. We do say, however, that known disadvantages in old devices which would naturally discourage the search for new inventions may be taken into account in determining obviousness.

Nor are these the only factors bearing on the question of obviousness. We have seen that at the time Adams perfected his invention noted experts expressed disbelief in it. Several of the same experts subsequently recognized the significance of the Adams invention, some even patenting improvements on the same system. Fischbach et al., U.S. Patent No. 2,636,060 (1953). Furthermore, in a crowded art replete with a century and a half of advancement, the Patent Office found not one reference to cite against the Adams application. Against the subsequently issued improvement patents to Fischbach, supra, and to Chubb, U.S. Reissue

Patent No. 23,883 (1954), it found but three references prior to Adams-none of which are relied upon by the Government.

We conclude that the Adams patent is valid. The judgment of the Court of Claims is affirmed.

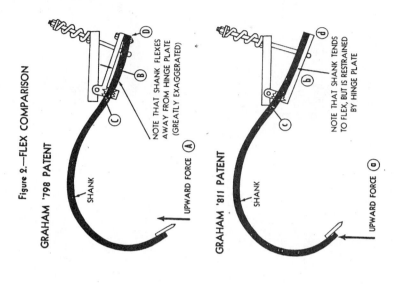

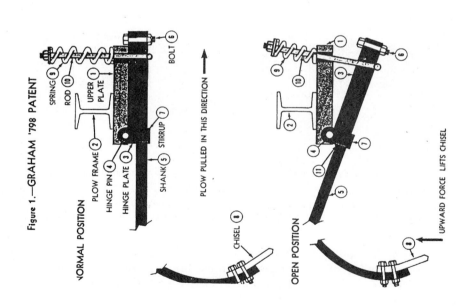

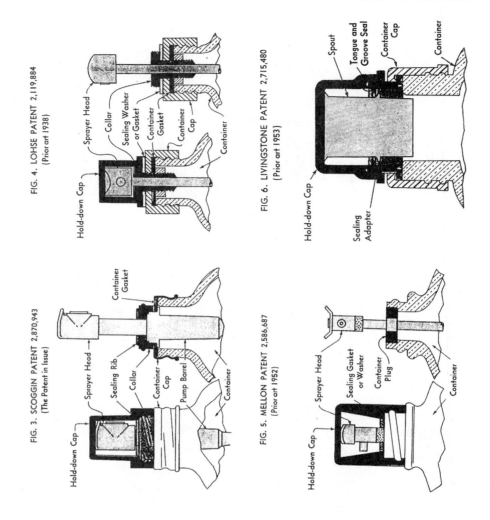

FIG. 4. LOHSE PATENT 2,119,884 (Prior art 1938)

FIG. 6. LIVINGSTONE PATENT 2,715,480 (Prior art 1953)

FIG. 3. SCOGGIN PATENT 2,870,943 (The Patent in Issue)

FIG. 5. MELLON PATENT 2,586,687 (Prior art 1952)

Notes

1. **Patent Invalidity.** The Federal Circuit has cast disapproval upon the terminology employed by the Supreme Court in the penultimate sentence of its *Adams* decision. In *Fromson v. Advance Offset Plate, Inc.*, 755 F.2d 1549, 1555 n. 1, 225 U.S.P.Q. 26 (Fed.Cir.1985), the Federal Circuit noted:

> Courts should not declare patents valid. There is never a need or occasion for such a declaration. Patents are born valid and remain so until proven otherwise. In a proper case, courts should find that "the party challenging validity failed to carry its burden under § 282." Where that burden is carried, courts should declare the patent invalid.

2. **Questions of Law and Fact.** The *Graham* court indicated that nonobviousness presents a mixed question of fact and law: although the ultimate conclusion of validity is a legal question, the underlying inquires are factual in nature. *See also, e.g., Minnesota Mining & Manufacturing Co.*

v. Johnson & Johnson Orthopaedics, Inc., 976 F.2d 1559, 24 U.S.P.Q.2d 1321 (Fed.Cir.1992); *In re Vaeck*, 947 F.2d 488, 20 U.S.P.Q.2d 1438 (Fed.Cir. 1991). How does the categorization of nonobviousness as law or fact impact the role of jury involvement in this decision? How about the standard of review before the Federal Circuit?

3. Post-*Graham* Developments at the Supreme Court. Two Supreme Court cases following the Trilogy, *Anderson's–Black Rock, Inc. v. Pavement Salvage Co.*, 396 U.S. 57 (1969) and *Sakraida v. Ag Pro, Inc.*, 425 U.S. 273 (1976), have attracted considerably less citation than their predecessors. The latter decision involved a patent describing a specially constructed dairy barn. By employing water which was stored in tanks or pools and flushed over sloped floors, the invention readily removed waste from the barn. Justice Brennan concluded, 425 U.S. at 282:

> We cannot agree that the combination of these old elements to produce an abrupt release of water directly on the barn floor from storage tanks or pools can properly be characterized as synergistic, that is, "result[ing] in an effect greater than the sum of the several effects taken separately." *Anderson's–Black Rock v. Pavement Co.*, 396 U.S. 57, 61 (1969). Rather, this patent simply arranges old elements with each performing the same function it had been known to perform, although perhaps producing a more striking result than in previous combinations. Such combinations are not patentable under standards appropriate for a combination patent. *Great A & P Tea Co. v. Supermarket, Corp., supra; Anderson's–Black Rock v. Pavement Co., supra.*

This language, and particularly the reference to the *A & P* case, were taken as a disappointing resurrection of the synergism requirement.

In its early decisions, the Federal Circuit essentially repudiated the holdings of *Anderson's–Black Rock* and *Sakraida*. *See, e.g., Chore–Time Equip., Inc. v. Cumberland Corp.*, 713 F.2d 774, 781, 218 U.S.P.Q. 673 (Fed.Cir.1983) ("A requirement that an invention reflect 'synergism' or achieve a 'synergistic result,' before it may be held patentable appears nowhere in the statute, 35 U.S.C.... References to synergism as a patentability requirement are, therefore, unnecessary and confusing."); *Medtronic, Inc. v. Cardiac Pacemakers, Inc.*, 721 F.2d 1563, 1566, 220 U.S.P.Q. 97 (Fed.Cir.1983) ("There is neither a statutory distinction between 'combination patents' and some other, never defined type of patent, nor a reason to treat the conditions for patentability differently with respect to 'combination patents.' "). Why hasn't a disgruntled litigant filed a writ of certiorari to the Supreme Court, urging that the Federal Circuit has ignored the Court's most recent precedent on the nonobviousness requirement?

What is the great flaw of the "synergism" test? Does it gauge the invention with hindsight? With knowledge of the invention, doesn't the synergism test attempt to decide if the inventive result was "greater than the sum of its parts" or "unexpected" or "exciting" or some other subjective measurement of the "gee-whiz" factor of invention? Doesn't invention often look easy in retrospect? How does the *Graham v. John Deere* application of the 1952 Act avoid this hindsight?

4. The Level of Skill in the Art. Determination of the appropriate level of skill in the art often proves a difficult inquiry. In *Environmental*

Designs, Ltd. v. Union Oil Co., 713 F.2d 693, 696, 218 U.S.P.Q. 865, 868 (Fed.Cir.1983), the court provided the following list of factors to be considered in determining the level of ordinary skill in the art:

    (1) the educational level of the inventor;

    (2) type of problems encountered in the art;

    (3) prior art solutions to those problems;

    (4) rapidity with which inventions are made;

    (5) sophistication of the technology;

    (6) educational level of active workers in the field.

Litigation experience shows that the accused infringer will seek to prove a high level of skill in the art; the patent holder, a low level of skill in the art. Why? Perhaps the ultimate example of this trend is demonstrated by the opinion of the European Patent Office Board of Appeal in T 60/89 (OJ 1992, 268), which rejected the argument that the person of skill in the art should be considered a Nobel Prize recipient. The Board concluded that:

> It is the opinion of the Board that the skilled person in the field of genetic engineering in 1978 is not to be defined as a Nobel Prize laureate, even if a number of scientists working in this field at that time were actually awarded the Nobel Prize. Rather, it is understood that the skilled person was to be seen as a graduate scientist or a team of scientists of that skill, working in laboratories which developed from molecular genetics to genetic engineering techniques at that time.

    5. How the Invention Was Made. The first sentence of § 103(a) indicates that "patentability shall not be negatived by the manner in which the invention was made." This language was meant to place on a level footing inventions inspired by a "flash of genius" with those created through the plodding path of exhaustive research and development. Thus, the patent statute offers its awards to accidental or lucky inventors, even though such incentives had nothing to do with the development of the invention. Why should patents be awarded to those technologists who were not inspired to invent by the patent system itself? Ironically, then, did pre-Trilogy courts have the matter precisely backwards? For an argument that the nonobviousness requirement stands as a proxy for such inquiries, see Edmund Kitch, *Graham v. John Deere Co.: New Standards for Patents*, 1966 Sup. Ct. Rev. 293, a portion of which is reprinted later in this chapter.

    6. Further Reading. For reflections by Justice Clark's law clerk on the circumstances leading to The Trilogy, see Charles D. Reed, *Some Reflections on* Graham v. John Deere Co., *in* Nonobviousness-The Ultimate Condition of Patentability 2:301 (John F. Witherspoon ed. 1978). A transcript of the oral argument in *United States v. Adams* is set forth as an Appendix to that text. A fine historical analysis of the requirement of inventive step in the English-speaking world is John Bochnovic, The Inventive Step (1982) (IIC Studies Vol. 5).

§ 7.2[b]   The Suggestion to Combine

    The introduction to this chapter discussed that section 103 requires a comparison of the prior art with the invention "as a whole." Section

103 forbids an analysis that chops the invention into its component parts and simply finds a prior art analog for each separate feature of the new combination. With this limitation, patent examiners and courts must have some way of showing that the invention as a whole would have been obvious to one of skill in the art at the time of invention. What then suffices to show that one of skill could have easily combined the various prior art references to obtain the new combination? Case law has answered this question. To render an invention obvious under section 103, an examiner or court may acquire evidence that a skilled artisan, confronted with the same problems as the inventor and with no knowledge of the claimed invention, would select the elements from the cited prior art references and combine them in the manner claimed. In practical terms, the examiner or court must show some suggestion or motivation, before the invention itself, to make the combination. This suggestion to combine test prevents an obviousness methodology that picks and chooses among individual parts of assorted prior art references as a mosaic to recreate a facsimile of the claimed invention. Thus, because of the suggestion to combine test, a patent examiner or judge cannot simply use the claimed invention as a blueprint to piece together elements in the prior art to render the invention obvious.

IN RE ROUFFET

United States Court of Appeals, Federal Circuit 1998.
149 F.3d 1350, 47 U.S.P.Q.2d 1453.

Before PLAGER, CIRCUIT JUDGE, ARCHER, SENIOR CIRCUIT JUDGE, RADER, CIRCUIT JUDGE.

RADER, CIRCUIT JUDGE.

Denis Rouffet, Yannick Tanguy, and Frederic Bethault (collectively, Rouffet) submitted application 07/888,791 (the application) on May 27, 1992. The Board of Patent Appeals and Interferences (the Board) affirmed final rejection of the application as obvious under 35 U.S.C. § 103(a). Because the Board reversibly erred in identifying a motivation to combine the references, this court reverses.

I.

Satellites in a geosynchronous or geostationary orbit remain over the same point on the Earth's surface. Their constant position above the Earth's surface facilitates communications. These satellites project a number of beams to the Earth. Each beam transmits to its area of coverage, or footprint, on the Earth's surface. In order to provide complete coverage, adjacent footprints overlap slightly and therefore must use different frequencies to avoid interference. However, two or more non-overlapping footprints can use the same set of frequencies in order to use efficiently the limited radio spectrum. Figure 1 from the application shows the coverage of a portion of the Earth's surface provided by multiple cone shaped beams:

FIG. 1

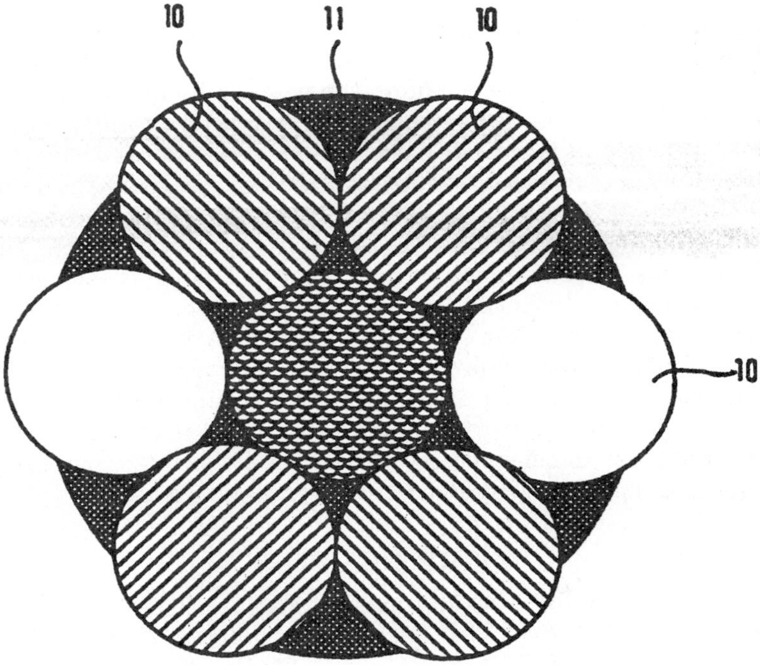

Frequency reuse techniques, however, have a limited ability to compensate for congestion in geostationary orbits. To alleviate the orbit congestion problem, new telecommunications systems use a network of satellites in low Earth orbit. When viewed from a fixed point on the Earth's surface, such satellites do not remain stationary but move overhead. A satellite's motion as it transmits a plurality of cone-shaped beams creates a new problem. The satellite's movement causes a receiver on the Earth's surface to move from the footprint of one beam into a second beam transmitted by the same satellite. Eventually, the satellite's motion causes the receiver to move from the footprint of a beam transmitted by one satellite into the footprint of a beam transmitted by a second satellite. Each switch from one footprint to another creates a "handover" event analogous to that which occurs when a traditional cellular phone travels from one cell to another. Handovers are undesirable because they can cause interruptions in signal transmission and reception.

Rouffet's application discloses technology to reduce the number of handovers between beams transmitted by the same satellite. In particular, Rouffet eliminates handovers caused solely by the satellite's motion. To accomplish this goal, Rouffet changes the shape of the beam transmitted by the satellite's antenna. Rouffet's satellites transmit fan-shaped beams. A fan beam has an elliptical footprint. Rouffet aligns the long axis of his beams parallel to the direction of the satellite's motion across the Earth's surface. By elongating the beam's footprint in the direction of satellite travel, Rouffet's invention ensures that a fixed point on the Earth's surface likely will remain within a single footprint until it is necessary to switch to another satellite. Because Rouffet's invention does not address handovers caused by the motion of the receiver across the Earth's surface, his arrangement reduces, but does not eliminate, handovers. Figure 3 from the application shows the footprints 12 from six beams aligned in the direction of satellite motion 15:

FIG. 3

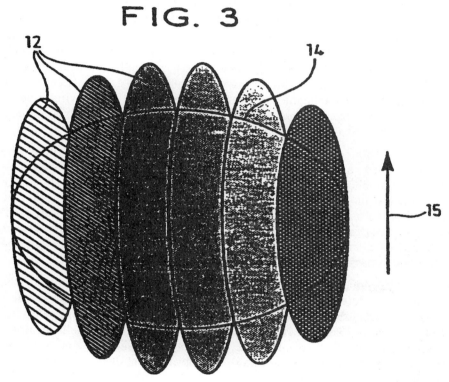

The application contains ten claims that stand or fall as a group. Claim 1 is representative:

> A low orbit satellite communications system for mobile terminals, wherein the communications antenna system of each satellite provides isoflux coverage made up of a plurality of fan beams that are elongate in the travel direction of the satellite.

The examiner initially rejected Rouffet's claims as unpatentable over U.S. Pat. No. 5,199,672 (King) in view of U.S. Pat. No. 4,872,015 (Rosen) and a conference report entitled "A Novel Non–Geostationary Satellite Communications System," Conference Record, International Conference on Communications, 1981 (Ruddy). On appeal to the Board, the examiner added an alternative ground for rejection, holding that the claims were obvious over U.S. Pat. No. 5,394,561 (Freeburg) in view of U.S. Pat. No. 5,170,485 (Levine).

On April 16, 1997, the Board issued its decision. Because Rouffet had specified that the claims would stand or fall as a group based on the patentability of claim 1, the Board limited its opinion to that claim. The Board unanimously determined that the examiner had properly rejected claim 1 as obvious over King in view of Rosen and Ruddy. The Board, on a split vote, also affirmed the rejection over Freeburg in view of Levine.

II

To reject claims in an application under section 103, an examiner must show an unrebutted prima facie case of obviousness. In the absence of a proper prima facie case of obviousness, an applicant who complies with the other statutory requirements is entitled to a patent. On appeal to the Board, an applicant can overcome a rejection by showing insufficient evidence of prima facie obviousness or by rebutting the prima facie case with evidence of secondary indicia of nonobviousness.

While this court reviews the Board's determination in light of the entire record, an applicant may specifically challenge an obviousness rejection by showing that the Board reached an incorrect conclusion of obviousness or that the Board based its obviousness determination on incorrect factual predicates. The factual predicates underlying an obviousness determination include the scope and content of the prior art, the differences between the prior art and the claimed invention, and the level of ordinary skill in the art.

The secondary considerations are also essential components of the obviousness determination. This objective evidence of nonobviousness includes copying, long felt but unsolved need, failure of others, commercial success, unexpected results created by the claimed invention, unexpected properties of the claimed invention, licenses showing industry respect for the invention, see and skepticism of skilled artisans before the invention, see *Graham v. John Deere Co.*, 383 U.S. 1, 17–18 (1966). The Board must consider all of the applicant's evidence.

When a rejection depends on a combination of prior art references, there must be some teaching, suggestion, or motivation to combine the references. See *In re Geiger*, 815 F.2d 686, 688 (Fed.Cir.1987). Although the suggestion to combine references may flow from the nature of the problem, see *Pro-Mold & Tool Co. v. Great Lakes Plastics, Inc.*, 75 F.3d 1568, 1573 (Fed.Cir.1996), the suggestion more often comes from the teachings of the pertinent references, see *In re Sernaker*, 702 F.2d 989, 994 (Fed.Cir.1983), or from the ordinary knowledge of those skilled in the art that certain references are of special importance in a particular field. Therefore, "[w]hen determining the patentability of a claimed invention which combines two known elements, 'the question is whether there is something in the prior art as a whole to suggest the desirability, and thus the obviousness, of making the combination.' "See *In re Beattie*, 974 F.2d 1309, 1311–12 (Fed.Cir.1992).

III

The parties agree that the five references asserted by the examiner are in the same field of endeavor as the invention. The parties also agree that the pertinent level of skill in the art—design of satellite communications systems—is high. On appeal, Rouffet asserts that the examiner and the Board erred by improperly combining references to render the claimed invention obvious.

THE COMBINATION OF KING, ROSEN, AND RUDDY

The Board first affirmed the rejection of Rouffet's claims over a combination of King, Rosen, and Ruddy. King discloses a system for launching a plurality of satellites into low Earth orbits from a single launch vehicle. Rosen teaches a geostationary satellite that uses a plurality of fan beams with their long axes oriented in an east-west direction to communicate with mobile and fixed terminals on the Earth.

The final, and most important, reference in this combination is Ruddy. Ruddy describes a television broadcast system that uses a series of satellites to retransmit signals sent from a ground station over a wide area. Rather than using a geostationary orbit, Ruddy teaches the use of a series of satellites in Molniya orbits. A satellite in a Molniya orbit always follows the same path through the sky when viewed from a fixed point on the ground. Viewed from the Earth, the orbital path includes a narrow, elliptical apogee loop. In order to transmit to these moving satellites from a ground station, Ruddy uses a fan beam with a long axis aligned with the long axis of the orbit's apogee loop. This alignment places the entire apogee loop within the footprint of the beam and eliminates the need for the ground station's antenna to track the satellite's motion around the apogee loop. Ruddy further teaches orbit parameters and spacing of multiple satellites to ensure that a satellite is always in the loop to receive and rebroadcast signals from the Earth station.

King and Rosen together teach the use of a network of satellites in low Earth orbit. Thus, Ruddy becomes the piece of the prior art mosaic that shows, in the reading of the Board, the use of "a plurality of fan beams that are elongate in the travel direction of the satellite." Ruddy, however, is different from the claimed invention in several respects. Specifically, the application claims the projection of multiple elliptical fan-shaped footprints from the satellite to the ground. See Claim 1, supra, see also Application at 6, lines 9–11 ("In addition, in this system, the geometrical shape of the beams 12 is changed: instead of being circular they are now elongate ellipses."). The application's written description further teaches that the invention's fan-shaped satellite beams will minimize handovers. See id. at lines 11–16 ("This considerably increases call durations between handovers.").

In contrast, Ruddy teaches that a ground station may use a single fan-shaped beam to transmit to a satellite in a unique Molniya orbit. The ground station transmits a beam into which a series of satellites in Molniya orbits will successively enter. At least two differences are evident: the application teaches projection of multiple beams from a satellite to the Earth, while Ruddy teaches projection of a single beam from the Earth to satellites. Moreover to the extent Ruddy contains a teaching about handovers, its teachings focus on use of the unique Molniya orbit to ensure that a satellite always falls within the beam transmitted by the ground station.

These differences suggest some difficulty in showing a prima facie case of obviousness. The Board, however, specifically found that artisans of ordinary skill in this field of art would know to shift the frame of reference from a ground station following a satellite to a satellite transmitting to the ground. According proper deference to the Board's finding of a lofty skill level for ordinary artisans in this field, this court discerns no clear error in the Board's conclusion that these differences would not preclude a finding of obviousness. While Ruddy does not expressly teach alignment of the fan beam with the apparent direction of the satellite's motion, this court perceives no clear error in the Board's determination that Ruddy would suggest such an alignment to one of skill in this art. Therefore, the Board did not err in finding that the combination of King, Rosen, and Ruddy contains all of the elements claimed in Rouffet's application.

However, the Board reversibly erred in determining that one of skill in the art would have been motivated to combine these references in a manner that rendered the claimed invention obvious. Indeed, the Board did not identify any motivation to choose these references for combination. Ruddy does not specifically address handover minimization. To the extent that Ruddy at all addresses handovers due to satellite motion, it addresses this subject through the selection of orbital parameters. Ruddy does not teach the choice of a particular shape and alignment of the beam projected by the satellite. Thus Ruddy addresses the handover problem with an orbit selection, not a beam shape. The Board provides no reasons that one of ordinary skill in this art, seeking to minimize handovers due to satellite motion, would combine Ruddy with Rosen and King in a manner that would render the claimed invention obvious.

Obviousness is determined from the vantage point of a hypothetical person having ordinary skill in the art to which the patent pertains. See 35 U.S.C. § 103(a). This legal construct is akin to the "reasonable person" used as a reference in negligence determinations. The legal construct also presumes that all prior art references in the field of the invention are available to this hypothetical skilled artisan.

As this court has stated, "virtually all [inventions] are combinations of old elements." *Environmental Designs, Ltd. v. Union Oil Co.*, 713 F.2d 693, 698, (Fed.Cir.1983). Therefore an examiner may often find every element of a claimed invention in the prior art. If identification of each claimed element in the prior art were sufficient to negate patentability, very few patents would ever issue. Furthermore, rejecting patents solely by finding prior art corollaries for the claimed elements would permit an examiner to use the claimed invention itself as a blueprint for piecing together elements in the prior art to defeat the patentability of the claimed invention. Such an approach would be "an illogical and inappropriate process by which to determine patentability." *Sensonics, Inc. v. Aerosonic Corp.*, 81 F.3d 1566, 1570, 38 U.S.P.Q.2d 1551, 1554 (Fed.Cir. 1996).

To prevent the use of hindsight based on the invention to defeat patentability of the invention, this court requires the examiner to show a motivation to combine the references that create the case of obviousness. In other words, the examiner must show reasons that the skilled artisan, confronted with the same problems as the inventor and with no knowledge of the claimed invention, would select the elements from the cited prior art references for combination in the manner claimed.

This court has identified three possible sources for a motivation to combine references: the nature of the problem to be solved, the teachings of the prior art, and the knowledge of persons of ordinary skill in the art. In this case, the Board relied upon none of these. Rather, just as it relied on the high level of skill in the art to overcome the differences between the claimed invention and the selected elements in the references, it relied upon the high level of skill in the art to provide the necessary motivation. The Board did not, however, explain what specific understanding or technological principle within the knowledge of one of ordinary skill in the art would have suggested the combination. Instead, the Board merely invoked the high level of skill in the field of art. If such a rote invocation could suffice to supply a motivation to combine, the more sophisticated scientific fields would rarely, if ever, experience a patentable technical advance. Instead, in complex scientific fields, the Board could routinely identify the prior art elements in an application, invoke the lofty level of skill, and rest its case for rejection. To counter this potential weakness in the obviousness construct, the suggestion to combine requirement stands as a critical safeguard against hindsight analysis and rote application of the legal test for obviousness.

Explanation of Motivation Required.

Because the Board did not explain the specific understanding or principle within the knowledge of a skilled artisan that would motivate one with no knowledge of Rouffet's invention to make the combination, this court infers that the examiner selected these references with the assistance of hindsight. This court forbids the use of hindsight in the selection of references that comprise the case of obviousness. Lacking a motivation to combine references, the Board did not show a proper prima facie case of obviousness. This court reverses the rejection over the combination of King, Rosen, and Ruddy.

Fatal

THE COMBINATION OF FREEBURG AND LEVINE

Freeburg teaches a cellular radiotelephone system based on a constellation of low Earth orbit satellites that use conical beams to transmit

Tactic - to attack a patent as obvious- use hindsight and find the references needed then show motivation as in commercial used

from the satellite to both fixed and mobile Earth stations. Levine teaches an Earth-based cellular radio system that uses fan beams broadcast from antenna towers. Levine's elliptical footprints are aligned with the road grid. To increase the capacity of traditional ground-based systems through frequency reuse techniques, Levine teaches the use of antennas that broadcast signals with smaller footprints than the prior art system. Thus, Levine actually increases the number of overlap regions between cells and, hence, the number of potential handovers. Figure 1 of the Levine patent illustrates its alignment of beam footprints:

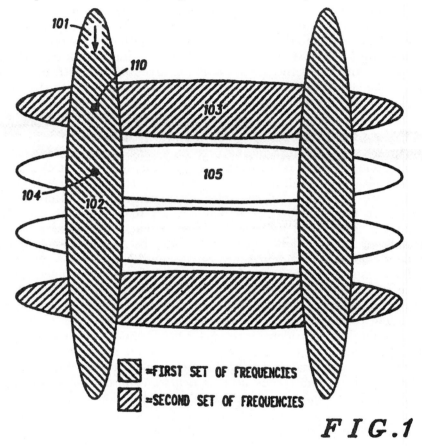

FIG.1

As a mobile unit (e.g., a driver using a car phone) moves though a succession of overlapping zones, Levine uses selection algorithms to determine which of the cells is aligned with the travel direction of the mobile unit. These algorithms then select this cell for use while continually monitoring intersecting cells in the event that the mobile unit changes direction.

Once again, this court notes significant differences between the teachings of the application and the Levine–Freeburg combination. The critical Levine reference again involves a beam from an Earth station without any reference to the "travel direction of [a] satellite." Moreover, Levine actually multiplies the number of potential handovers and then uses software to sort out the necessary handovers from the unnecessary. However, the Board explains the reasons that one possessing the lofty skills characteristic of this field would know to account for the differences between the claimed invention and the prior art combination. This court discerns no clear error in that reliance on the considerable skills in this field.

This court does, however, discern reversible error in the Board's identification of a motivation to combine Levine and Freeburg. In determining that one of skill in the art would have had motivation to combine Levine and Freeburg, the Board noted that "[t]he level of skill in the art is very high." As noted before, this observation alone cannot supply the required suggestion to combine these references. The Board posits that the high level of skill in the art overcomes the absence of any actual suggestion that one could select part of the teachings of Levine for combination with the satellite system disclosed by Freeburg.

As noted above, the suggestion to combine requirement is a safeguard against the use of hindsight combinations to negate patentability. While the skill level is a component of the inquiry for a suggestion to combine, a lofty level of skill alone does not suffice to supply a motivation to combine. Otherwise a high level of ordinary skill in an art field would almost always preclude patentable inventions. As this court has often noted, invention itself is the process of combining prior art in a nonobvious manner. Therefore, even when the level of skill in the art is high, the Board must identify specifically the principle, known to one of ordinary skill, that suggests the claimed combination. In other words, the Board must explain the reasons one of ordinary skill in the art would have been motivated to select the references and to combine them to render the claimed invention obvious.

The Board's naked invocation of skill in the art to supply a suggestion to combine the references cited in this case is therefore clearly erroneous. Absent any proper motivation to combine part of Levine's teachings with Freeburg's satellite system, the rejection of Rouffet's claim over these references was improper and is reversed.

Notes

1. Suggestion to Combine—Law or Fact? This question is not as simple as it may seem. On the one hand, as a subset of the legal obviousness test, the suggestion inquiry might appear to be a factual inquiry, like identifying the scope and content of the prior art. Moreover, to the extent that the suggestion test requires identifying references within the prior art that suggest combination, this function would again take on attributes of fact finding.

On the other hand, the determination of a suggestion to combine is practically synonymous with the obviousness determination itself. *Rouffet* states well the test for a suggestion to combine: "In other words, the examiner must show reasons that the skilled artisan, confronted with the same problems as the inventor and with no knowledge of the claimed invention, would select the elements from the cited prior art references for combination in the manner claimed." How is this different from obviousness? Stated otherwise, how is it possible to categorize the suggestion to combine test as a factual subset of the obviousness test when every finding of a suggestion to combine will also constitute a conclusion of obviousness?

Despite these interesting questions, the Federal Circuit has recently decided:

> The dispute here focuses on the combinability of the prior art. When an obviousness determination is based on multiple prior art references, there must be a showing of some "teaching, suggestion, or reason" to combine the references. Whether motivation to combine the references was shown we hold a question of fact.

Winner Int'l Royalty Corp. v. Wang, 202 F.3d 1340, 1348, 53 U.S.P.Q.2d 1580, 1586 (Fed.Cir.2000). The Federal Circuit does not really reason to this conclusion, but just states it. Do you agree?

2. Federal Circuit to PTO Board: Report Suggestion Precise-LEE, AccurateLEE, and CompleteLEE. In *In re Lee*, the Federal Circuit, speaking through Judge Pauline Newman, admonished the PTO Board sternly. The Board of Patent Appeals and Interferences rejected all claims of an application that claimed a method of automatically displaying functions of a video display device. The method instructed users to select and adjust functions in order to facilitate their responses. The Board rejected based on two references: Nortrup, a television monitor with adjustments to facilitate viewing, and a handbook for the video game Thunderchopper that taught adjustments to facilitate playing the game. The Board then opined: "The conclusion of obviousness may be made from common knowledge and common sense of a person of ordinary skill in the art without any specific hint or suggestion in a particular reference." Apparently the Board considered this claimed invention so easy to derive that common sense was sufficient to invoke an obviousness result. The Federal Circuit sharply rebuked this reasoning:

> For judicial review to be meaningfully achieved within these strictures, the agency tribunal must present a full and reasoned explanation of its decision. The agency tribunal must set forth its findings and the grounds thereof, as supported by the agency record, and explain its application of the law to the found facts.... With respect to Lee's application, neither the examiner nor the Board adequately supported the selection and combination of the Nortrup and Thunderchopper references ... This factual question of motivation is material to patentability, and could not be resolved on subjective belief and unknown authority.

In re Lee, 277 F.3d 1338, 1343–44, 61 U.S.P.Q.2d 1430, 1432–34 (Fed.Cir. 2002). *Lee* is one of the early obviousness opinions decided under the "strictures" of *Dickinson v. Zurko*, 527 U.S. 150 (1999), wherein the Supreme Court ordered the Federal Circuit to give more deference to PTO expertise. Is *Lee* a backlash against *Zurko*? Is the Federal Circuit putting some preconditions on its deference, namely a "full and reasoned explanation"?

What are the implications of *Lee* for administration at the Board? Over the years, the Board has experienced backlogs in its challenging workload. If the Board's Administrative Patent Judges must write "full and reasoned explanations" of every decision, will the Board fall still farther behind and delay further the issuance of patents? Moreover the Federal Circuit issues many of its opinions in brief, conclusory, nonprecedential form. Is the Federal Circuit holding the Board to a standard it does not meet itself?

3.   Obvious to Try. An invention may employ known principles, but of course nearly every invention employs known principles. Thus, as repeatedly stated, mere recitation of prior art or known principles does not render an invention obvious. The Federal Circuit and its predecessor have criticized incomplete obviousness analyses for stopping at the "obvious to try" stage.

The problem with an "obvious to try" approach is that a superficial similarity between the claimed invention and the prior art may lead to the casual conclusion that because of the close similarity it would be "obvious to try" that which the applicant has done. As may be learned from one of the cases denouncing the "obvious to try" approach, *In re Fine*, 837 F.2d 1071, 1075, 5 U.S.P.Q.2d 1596 (Fed.Cir.1988), the correct standard for obviousness requires a prospective suggestion in the prior art to combine teachings of references, and not the use of hindsight:

> Obviousness is tested by "what the combined teachings of the references would have suggested to those of ordinary skill in the art." *In re Keller*, 642 F.2d 413, 425, 208 U.S.P.Q. 871, 881 (CCPA 1981). But it "cannot be established by combining the teachings of the prior art to produce the claimed invention, absent some teaching or suggestion supporting the combination." *ACS Hosp. Sys.*, 732 F.2d at 1577, 221 U.S.P.Q. at 933. And "teachings of references can be combined only if there is some suggestion or incentive to do so." *Id.* Here, the prior art contains none.
>
> Instead, the Examiner relies on hindsight in reaching his obviousness determination. But this court has said, "To imbue one of ordinary skill in the art with knowledge of the invention in suit, when no prior art reference or references of record convey or suggest that knowledge, is to fall victim to the insidious effect of a hindsight syndrome wherein that which only the inventor taught is used against its teacher." *W.L. Gore*, 721 F.2d at 1553, 220 U.S.P.Q. at 312–13. It is essential that "the decisionmaker forget what he or she has been taught at trial about the claimed invention and cast the mind back to the time the invention was made * * * to occupy the mind of one skilled in the art who is presented only with the references, and who is normally guided by the then-accepted wisdom in the art." *Id.* One cannot use hindsight reconstruction to pick and choose among isolated disclosures in the prior art to deprecate the claimed invention.

Thus, the fundamental flaw of an "obvious to try" analysis is that it overlooks the requirement of some suggestion in the prior art to make the combination that results in obviousness. As the Federal Circuit makes clear, it is incorrect to "pick and choose among individual parts of assorted prior

art references 'as a mosaic to recreate a facsimile of the claimed invention.' "
Akzo N.V. v. U.S. Intern. Trade Comm., 808 F.2d 1471, 1481, 1 U.S.P.Q.2d
1241 (Fed.Cir.1986). Without some suggestion to combine, reconstructing
the teachings of the prior art would be improper "hindsight." *Id.* In sum, it
is improper to use the inventor's patent as an instruction book on how to
reconstruct the prior art. *Panduit Corp. v. Dennison Mfg. Co.*, 810 F.2d 1561,
1 U.S.P.Q.2d 1593 (Fed.Cir.1987). To combine references properly, one
challenging a patent or application must find some teaching, suggestion, or
inference to combine in the prior art or show that knowledge generally
accessible to one of ordinary skill in the art would have led to the combination.

In *In re O'Farrell*, 853 F.2d 894, 903, 7 U.S.P.Q.2d 1673, 1681 (Fed.Cir.
1988),the court considered an "obvious to try" rejection:

> The admonition that "obvious to try" is not the standard under § 103
> has been directed mainly at two kinds of error. In some cases, what
> would have been "obvious to try" would have been to vary all parame-
> ters or try each of numerous possible choices until one possibly arrived
> at a successful result, where the prior art gave either no indication of
> which parameters were critical or no direction as to which of many
> possible choices is likely to be successful. In others, what was "obvious
> to try" was to explore a new technology or general approach that
> seemed to be a promising field of experimentation, where the prior art
> gave only general guidance as to the particular form of the claimed
> invention or how to achieve it. Neither of these situations applies here.

> Obviousness does not require absolute predictability of success.
> Indeed, for many inventions that seem quite obvious, there is no
> absolute predictability of success until the invention is reduced to
> practice. There is always at least a possibility of unexpected results, that
> would then provide an objective basis for showing that the invention,
> although apparently obvious, was in law nonobvious. For obviousness
> under § 103, all that is required is a reasonable expectation of success.

The following citations supply some other instances where courts have
criticized this basis for rejection going back more than thirty years. See *In re
Tomlinson*, 363 F.2d 928, 53 C.C.P.A. 1421, 150 U.S.P.Q. 623 (1966) ("[a]s
we have said many times, obvious to try is not the standard of 35 USC
103."); *In re Antonie*, 559 F.2d 618, 620, 195 U.S.P.Q. 6, 8 (CCPA 1977)
("[d]isregard for the unobviousness of the results of 'obvious to try' experiments disregards the 'invention as a whole' concept of § 103 * * * ."); *In re
Goodwin*, 576 F.2d 375, 377, 198 U.S.P.Q. 1, 3 (CCPA 1978) (quoting
Tomlinson and Antonie); *Jones v. Hardy*, 727 F.2d 1524, 1530, 220 U.S.P.Q.
1021, 1026 (Fed.Cir.1984) ("obvious to try" improper in determining obviousness), cited in *Hybritech Inc. v. Monoclonal Antibodies*, 802 F.2d 1367,
1380, 231 U.S.P.Q. 81 (Fed.Cir.1986) (Rich, J.); *Uniroyal, Inc. v. Rudkin–
Wiley Corp.*, 837 F.2d 1044, 1053, 5 U.S.P.Q.2d 1434 (Fed.Cir.1988) (Archer,
J.) ("the often rejected obvious-to-try standard * * * ").

§ 7.2[c] The Objective Tests

Although jurists and patent examiners cannot literally go back in
time to perform experiments and acquire the experience of persons of

ordinary skill in the art, they can look to actual occurrences for insights into the question of nonobviousness. In the *Graham v. Deere* case, the Supreme Court made direct reference to these objective indicia or "secondary considerations" of nonobviousness: "Such secondary considerations as commercial success, long felt but unsolved needs, failure of others, etc., might be utilized to give light to the circumstances surrounding the origins of the subject matter sought to be patented. As indicia of obviousness or nonobviousness, these inquiries may have relevancy." 383 U.S. at 17–18. The Federal Circuit has struck the "may" from the last sentence of the Supreme Court's advice. These objective indicia are no longer merely "secondary," but are essential to the obviousness inquiry. Indeed a new invention is often better measured in the marketplace than in the courtroom.

There is one catch, however, to use of objective indicia of nonobviousness. The applicant or patentee must show a nexus between the claimed invention and the objective evidence. In the case of commercial success, for instance, the applicant or patentee must show that the success is the result of the innovative claims, not merely the result of effective marketing strategies or general popularity of like products in the prior art.

HYBRITECH INC. v. MONOCLONAL ANTIBODIES, INC.

United States Court of Appeals, Federal Circuit, 1986.
802 F.2d 1367, 231 U.S.P.Q. 81.

Before RICH, DAVIS and SMITH, CIRCUIT JUDGES.

RICH, CIRCUIT JUDGE.

This appeal is from the August 28, 1985, decision of the United States District Court for the Northern District of California, 623 F.Supp. 1344, 227 U.S.P.Q. 215, in favor of defendant Monoclonal Antibodies, Inc. (Monoclonal) holding that all 29 claims of plaintiff's patent No. 4,376,110 entitled "Immunometric Assays Using Monoclonal Antibodies" ('110 patent), issued to Dr. Gary S. David and Howard E. Greene and assigned to Hybritech Incorporated (Hybritech), are invalid as anticipated under 35 U.S.C. § 102(g), for obviousness under § 103, and under § 112 first and second paragraphs. We reverse and remand.

BACKGROUND

Vertebrates defend themselves against invasion by microorganisms by producing antibodies, proteins which can complex with the invading microorganisms and target them for destruction or removal. In fact, any foreign molecule of sufficient size can act as a stimulus for antibody production. Such foreign molecules, or antigens, bear particular sites or epitopes that represent antibody recognition sites. B cell lymphocytes, the cells that actually produce antibodies, recognize and respond to an epitope on an antigen by reproducing or cloning themselves and then producing antibodies specific to that epitope. Even if the antigen is highly purified, the lymphocytes will produce antibodies specific to different epitopes on the antigen and so produce antibodies with different specificities. Furthermore, because the body is exposed to many different antigens, the blood of a vertebrate will contain antibodies to many different antigenic substances.

Scientists and clinicians have long employed the ability of antibodies to recognize and complex with antigens as a tool to identify or label particular cells or molecules and to separate them from a mixture. Their source of antibodies has been primarily the serum separated from the blood of a vertebrate immunized or exposed to the antigen. Serum, however, contains a mixture of antibodies directed to numerous antigens and to any number of epitopes on a particular antigen. Because such a mixture of antibodies arises from many different clones of lymphocytes, it is called "polyclonal."

Recent technological advances have made it possible to isolate and cultivate a single clone of lymphocytes to obtain a virtually unlimited supply of antibodies specific to one particular epitope. These antibodies, known as "monoclonal antibodies" because they arise from a single clone of lymphocytes, are produced by a relatively new technology known as the hybridoma. Hybridomas are produced by fusing a particular cancer cell, the myeloma cell, with spleen cells from a mouse that has been injected or immunized with the antigen. These fusions are isolated by transferring them to a growth fluid that kills off the unfused cancer cells, the unfused spleen cells dying off by themselves. The fused hybrid spleen and myeloma cells, called hybridomas, produce antibodies to the antigen initially injected into the mouse. The growth fluid containing the hybridomas is then diluted and put into individual test tubes or wells so that there is only one hybridoma per tube or well. Each hybridoma then reproduces itself and these identical hybridomas each produce identical monoclonal antibodies having the same affinity and specificity. In this way, a virtually unlimited supply of identical antibodies is created, directed to only one epitope on an antigen rather than, as with polyclonal antibodies, to many different epitopes on many different antigens.

In addition to the specificity of antibodies to particular epitopes discussed above, antibodies also have a characteristic "sensitivity," the ability to detect and react to antigens. Sensitivity is expressed in terms of "affinity:" the greater an antibody's ability to bind with a particular antigen, the greater the antibody's affinity. The strength of that antibody-antigen bond is in part dependent upon the antibody's "affinity constant," expressed in liters per mole, for the antigen.

Immunoassays, the subject matter of the '110 patent, are diagnostic methods for determining the presence or amount of antigen in body fluids such as blood or urine by employing the ability of an antibody to recognize and bind to an antigen. Generally, the extent to which the antibody binds to the antigen to be quantitated is an indication of the amount of antigen present in the fluid. Labelling the antibody or, in some cases, the antigen, with either a radioactive substance, I 125, or an enzyme makes possible the detection of the antibody-antigen complex. In an extreme case, where the fluid sample contains a very low level of the antigen, binding might not occur unless the antibodies selected or "screened" for the procedure are highly sensitive.

In the case of a "competitive" immunoassay, a labelled antigen reagent is bound to a limited and known quantity of antibody reagent. After that reaction reaches equilibrium, the antigen to be detected is added to the mixture and competes with the labelled antigen for the limited number of antibody binding sites. The amount of labelled antigen reagent displaced, if any, in this second reaction indicates the quantity of the antigen to be detected present in the fluid sample. All of the antigen attached to the antibody will be labelled antigen if there is no antigen in the test fluid sample. The advantage of this method is that only a small amount of antibody is needed, its drawback, generally, that the system must reach equilibrium, and thus produces results slowly.

In the case of a "sandwich" assay, otherwise known as an immuno-metric assay, the latter being a term coined by Dr. Lawton Miles in 1971, a quantity of unlabelled antibody reagent is bound to a solid support surface such as the inside wall of a test tube containing a complex of the fluid sample containing the antigen to be detected and a labelled antibody reagent. The result is an insoluble three part complex referred to as a sandwich having antibody bread and antigen filling. This figure is illustrative of the sandwich concept:

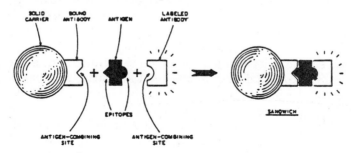

The advantage of the sandwich assay is that it is fast and simple, its drawback that enormous quantities of antibodies are needed.

HYBRITECH

Hybritech, started in 1978 and joined thereafter by coinventors Green and Dr. David, has, since 1979, been in the business of developing diagnostic kits employing monoclonal antibodies that detect numerous antigens and thus a broad range of conditions such as pregnancy, cancer, growth hormone deficiency, or hepatitis. Examples of antigens include influenza viruses, immunoglobulin E (IgE) which indicates allergic reaction, human chorionic gonadotropin (HCG) which indicates pregnancy, and prostatic acid phosphatase (PAP) which indicates prostate cancer, to name a few. Dr. Adams, a business-experienced scientist, joined the company in May 1980 as head of research and development. The '110 patent, application for which was filed August 4, 1980, issued March 8, 1983, with claims defining a variety of sandwich assays using monoclonal antibodies. Claim 19, apparently the broadest of the twenty-nine in the patent, is directed generally to a sandwich assay and reads:

19. In an immunometric assay to determine the presence or concentration of an antigenic substance in a sample of a fluid comprising forming a ternary complex of a first labelled antibody, said antigenic substance, and a second antibody said second antibody being bound to a solid carrier insoluble in said fluid wherein the presence of the antigenic substance in the samples is determined by measuring either the amount of labelled antibody bound to the solid carrier or the amount of unreacted labelled antibody, the improvement comprising employing monoclonal antibodies having an affinity for the antigenic substance of at least about 108 liters/mole for each of said labelled antibody and said antibody bound to a solid carrier.

Claim 1, directed particularly to a reverse sandwich assay, explained infra, reads:

1. A process for the determination of the presence of [sic, or] concentration of an antigenic substance in a fluid comprising the steps: (a) contacting a sample of the fluid with a measured amount of a soluble first monoclonal antibody to the antigenic substance in order to form a soluble complex of the antibody and antigenic substance present in said sample, said first monoclonal antibody being labelled; (b) contacting the soluble complex with a second monoclonal antibody to the antigenic substance, said second monoclonal antibody being bound to a solid carrier, said solid carrier being insoluble in said fluid, in order to form an insoluble complex of said first monoclonal antibody, said antigenic substance and said second monoclonal antibody bound to said solid carrier; (c) separating said solid carrier from the fluid sample and unreacted labelled antibody; (d) measuring either the amount of labelled antibody associated with the solid carrier or the amount of unreacted labelled antibody; and (e) relating the amount of labelled antibody measured with the amount of labelled antibody measured for a control sample prepared in accordance with steps (a)-(d), said control sample being known to be free of said antigenic substance, to determine the presence of antigenic substance in said fluid sample, or relating the amount of labelled antibody measured with the amount of labelled antibody measured for samples containing known amounts of antigenic substance prepared in accordance with steps (a)-(d) to determine the concentration of antigenic substance in said fluid sample, the first and second monoclonal antibodies having an affinity for the antigenic substance of at least about 108 liters/mole.

A. The References

Kohler and Milstein's Nobel Prize–Winning Work: Producing Monoclonal Antibodies In Vitro For the First Time

In early immunoassay work, polyclonal antibodies produced in vivo (in the body) in mice were used to bind with the antigen to be detected in the body fluid sample. Mice were immunized by injection with antigen so that the lymphocytes in their bodies produced antibodies that attacked the injected antigen. Those polyclonal antibodies were withdrawn from the animal's blood and used in immunoassays. The major problem was that when the mice's immune systems changed or the mice died, the antibodies changed or died too; supply was limited and uncertain.

As the examiner was aware, Kohler and Milstein developed a technique not only for producing antibodies in vitro, independent of a living body, thus eliminating dependence on a particular animal, but for in vitro production of monoclonal antibodies by hybridomas, discussed in the Background section, supra.

Given that sandwich assays require enormous amounts of antibodies, companies like appellant and appellee, which utilize monoclonal antibodies for sandwich assays, would not be in business were it not for the work of Kohler and Milstein.

The Cuello Article and the Jeong, Piasio, and Schurr Patents Considered by the Examiner

Cuello, dated July 1979, states that it describes the usefulness of monoclonal antibodies in the characterization and localization of neurotransmitters such as Substance P, a peptide clearly associated with the transmission of primary sensory information in the spinal cord. The article discloses producing monoclonal antibodies from hybrid myelomas (hybridomas), their use in conventional radioimmunoassay techniques, and the benefits from doing so which flow from the ability to derive permanent cell lines capable of continuous production of highly specific antibodies.

The district court found that the examiner twice rejected all of the claims of the '110 patent based on Cuello alone or in combination with the Jeong, Piasio, and Schurr references which disclose various sandwich assays using polyclonal antibodies. The court also found that the examiner allowed the claims after they were amended to include the 108 affinity limitation and after Richard Bartholomew, a Hybritech employee, submitted an affidavit alleging the advantages of using monoclonal rather than polyclonal antibodies in sandwich assays.

Apparently based on the testimony of Monoclonal's expert witness Judith Blakemore, a named inventor of the Jeong patent, manager of antibody programs at Bio–Rad Laboratories from 1975 to 1982, and currently manager of monoclonal antibody therapeutics at Cetus Corporation, a Hybritech competitor in immunoassay diagnostics, the district court stated that the "reasons for allowance were not well-founded because (1) the alleged advantages were expected as naturally flowing from the well-known natural characteristics of monoclonal antibodies ...; (2) ... were not significant ...; or (3) were at best minor," although they were "argued to the examiner as if they were" important.

These were Monoclonal's words from its pretrial submission adopted by the court.

The References That "Predicted" the Use of Monoclonal Antibodies in Immunoassays

The district court stated, again in Monoclonal's words, that "it is of the utmost importance" that the advantages of monoclonal antibodies were "predicted by a number of authorities," eight to be exact, not important enough to list here, after the Kohler and Milstein discovery and after monoclonal antibodies became available.

at the time of invention

IV. OBVIOUSNESS, 35 U.S.C. § 103

A section 103 obviousness determination-whether the claimed invention *now* would have been (not "would be" as the court repeatedly stated because Monoclonal's pretrial papers used that improper language) obvious at the time the invention was made is reviewed free of the clearly erroneous standard although the underlying factual inquiries-scope and content of the prior art, level of ordinary skill in the art, and differences between the prior art and the claimed invention-integral parts of the subjective determination involved in § 103, are reviewed under that standard. Objective evidence such as commercial success, failure of others, long-felt need, and unexpected results must be considered before a conclusion on obviousness is reached and is not merely "icing on the cake," as the district court stated at trial.

The Eight Articles "Predicting" Widespread Use of Monoclonal Antibodies

First, the latest four of the eight articles that the court stated were of the "utmost importance" because they "predicted" that the breakthrough in production of monoclonal antibodies by Kohler and Milstein would lead to widespread use of monoclonal antibodies in immunoassays are neither 102(a)/103 nor 102(b)/103 prior art because they are dated between late 1979 and March 6, 1980, well after the date of conception and within one year of the filing date of the '110 patent.

The earliest four of the eight articles, on the other hand, although clearly prior art, discuss production of monoclonal antibodies-admittedly old after Kohler and Milstein showed how to produce them-but none discloses sandwich assays. At most, these articles are invitations to try monoclonal antibodies in immunoassays but do not suggest how that end might be accomplished. To the extent the district court relied upon these references to establish that it would have been obvious to try monoclonal antibodies of 10 8 liters/mole affinity in a sandwich immunoassay that detects the presence of or quantitates antigen, the court was in error.

The Kohler and Milstein Work, the Cuello Article and the Jeong, Piasio, and Schurr Patents Considered by the Examiner

The district court's finding that Kohler and Milstein developed a method for producing monoclonal antibodies in vitro is correct, but that finding proves no more; although it made possible all later work in that it paved the way for a supply of monoclonal antibodies, it indisputably does not suggest using monoclonal antibodies in a sandwich assay in accordance with the invention claimed in the '110 patent.

The Cuello reference discloses monoclonal antibodies but not in a sandwich assay. The competitive assay in Cuello, moreover, uses only one monoclonal antibody and thus in no way suggests the claimed invention wherein a ternary complex of two monoclonal antibodies and an antigen form a sandwich. Furthermore, the court did not explain how this art, by itself or in combination with any of the other art, suggests the claimed subject matter and thus why that combination would have been obvious. We are of the opinion that it does not.

The district court correctly found that the use of polyclonal antibodies in sandwich assays was well known. The Jeong patent discloses the use of polyclonal antibodies in a simultaneous sandwich assay, with no suggestion that monoclonal antibodies be so used. It is prior art by virtue of § 102(e), application for the patent having been filed September 5, 1978, its effective date as a reference. The Piasio patent, disclosing a reverse sandwich assay using polyclonal antibodies, and Schurrs, disclosing a forward sandwich assay using the same, both § 102(a) prior art, are likewise devoid of any suggestion that monoclonal antibodies can be used in a similar fashion.

Objective Evidence of Nonobviousness

In one part of its opinion the court found that "the commercial success of the kits may well be attributed to the business expertise and acumen of the plaintiff's personnel, together with its capital base and marketing abilities" (emphasis ours) and later that "[w]here commercial success is based on the sudden availability of starting materials, in this instance the availability of monoclonal antibodies as a result of the Kohler and Milstein discovery, business acumen, marketing ability, and capital sources, no causal relationship is proven." (Citation omitted.)

i.   Commercial Success: Hybritech's Diagnostic Kits Grabbed a Substantial Market Share

The undisputed evidence is that Hybritech's diagnostic kits had a substantial market impact. The first diagnostic kit sales occurring in mid–1981, sales increased seven million dollars in just over one year, from $6.9 million in 1983 to an estimated $14.5 million in 1984; sales in 1980 were nonexistent. Competing with products from industry giants such as Abbott Labs, Hoffman LaRoche, Becton–Dickinson, and Baxter–Travenol, Hybritech's HCG kit became the market leader with roughly twenty-five percent of the market at the expense of market shares of the other companies. Its PAP kit ranks second only to a product sold by Dupont's New England Nuclear, surpassing products from Baxter–Travenol, Abbott, and others. Hybritech's other kits, indisputably embodying the invention claimed in the '110 patent, obtained similar substantial market positions.

Although the district court did not provide its insights into why commercial success was due to business acumen and not to the merits of the claimed invention, Monoclonal urges in support that it was due to Hybritech's spending disproportionate sums on marketing, 25–30% of income. The undisputed evidence was that expenditures of mature companies in this field are between 17 and 32%. Furthermore, the record shows that advertising makes those in the industry-hospitals, doctors, and clinical laboratories-aware of the diagnostic kits but does not make these potential users buy them; the products have to work, and there is no evidence that that is not the case here or that the success was not due to the merits of the claimed sandwich assays-clearly contrary to the district court's finding.

The trial court's finding that the "sudden availability of monoclonals" was the reason for the commercial success of Hybritech's diagnostic kits (Finding 11) is unsupported by the record and clearly erroneous. Monoclonal admits that monoclonal antibodies were available in the United States in 1978, and the evidence clearly reflects that. Thus, at least three years passed between the time monoclonal antibodies were available in adequate supply and the time Hybritech began selling its kits. Especially in the fast-moving biotechnology field, as the evidence shows, that is anything but sudden availability.

ii. Unexpected Advantages

Hybritech points to the testimony of three witnesses skilled in the diagnostic field who state that, based on tests done in their laboratories as a result of real-world comparisons in the normal course of research, the diagnostic kits that embody the '110 invention unexpectedly solved longstanding problems. Dr. Hussa, the head of a large referral laboratory and a world-wide consultant, testified that until Hybritech introduced its kits, he and others were very skeptical and had almost exclusively used competitive assays with a radioactive tracer (RIAs). In relation to an HCG Hybritech kit, he testified that he had first thought that the Hybritech HCG kit would not give accurate results for low antigen concentrations because that condition is indicated in the Hybritech kit by a low radioactivity reading, a reading difficult to differentiate from control samples containing no antigen. He also stated that in the past, RIA kits falsely detected HCG in nonpregnant women, a condition which would indicate cancer and surgery. He stated that when he employed the Hybritech HCG kit in such instances it demonstrated, correctly and absent any difficulty interpreting the data, that no HCG was present.

Dr. Blethen, an M.D. holding a Ph.D. in biochemistry, testified that she did not think that the Hybritech HGH kit, for detecting growth hormone in children, would offer any advantage, but she determined that it detected HGH deficiencies in children where conventional RIAs failed to do so. She also stated that the kit does not give false positive readings as do conventional RIA kits, an opinion shared by Dr. Hussa. A third witness, Dr. Herschman, who holds a master's degree in chemistry, testified that he spent years working on the development of an assay that would determine the presence of TSH (thyroid stimulating hormone) with greater sensitivity. He succeeded but discovered that the Hybritech TSH kit had the same sensitivity, the test being performed in four hours rather than the three days his kit required.

Having considered the evidence of nonobviousness required by § 103 and Graham, supra, we hold, as a matter of law, that the claimed subject matter of the '110 patent would not have been obvious to one of ordinary skill in the art at the time the invention was made and therefore reverse the court's judgment to the contrary. The large number of references, as a whole, relied upon by the district court to show obviousness, about twenty in number, skirt all around but do not as a whole suggest the claimed invention, which they must, to overcome the presumed validity, as a whole. Focusing on the obviousness of substitutions and differences instead of on the invention as a whole, as the district court did in frequently describing the claimed invention as the mere substitution of monoclonal for polyclonal antibodies in a sandwich assay, was a legally improper way to simplify the difficult determination of obviousness.

With respect to the objective indicia of nonobviousness, while there is evidence that marketing and financing played a role in the success of Hybritech's kits, as they do with any product, it is clear to us on the entire record that the commercial success here was due to the merits of the claimed invention. It cannot be argued on this record that Hybritech's success would have been as great and as prolonged as admittedly it has been if that success were not due to the merits of the invention. The evidence is that these kits compete successfully with numerous others for the trust of persons who have to make fast, accurate, and safe diagnoses. This is not the kind of merchandise that can be sold by advertising hyperbole.

Notes

1. **Commentary on the Objective Tests.** Edmund Kitch, Graham v. John Deere Co.: *New Standards for Patents*, 1966 SUPREME COURT REV. 293 (reprinted in 49 J. PAT. OFF. SOC'Y 237, 282–85), criticized the objective tests of nonobviousness as follows:

> But how is commercial success relevant to non-obviousness? The argument for commercial success is set out in a law review note cited with apparent approval by the [Supreme] Court in [the *Cook Chemical* cases]:
>
> > The possibility of market success attendant upon the solution of an existing problem may induce innovators to attempt a solution. If in fact a product attains a high degree of commercial success, there is a basis for inferring that such attempts have been made and failed. Thus the rationale is similar to that of longfelt demand and is for the same reasons a legitimate test of invention.
>
> [*Subtests of "Nonobviousness": A Nontechnical Approach to Patent Validity*, 112 U. PA. L. REV. 1169, 1175 (1964).] This argument involves four inferences. First, that the commercial success is due to the innovation. Second, that if an improvement has in fact become commercially suc-

cessful, it is likely that this potential commercial success was perceived before its development. Third, the potential commercial success having been perceived, it is likely that efforts were made to develop the improvement. Fourth, the efforts having been made by men of skill in the art, they failed because the patentee was the first to reduce his development to practice. Since men of skill in the art tried but failed, the improvement is clearly non-obvious.

Each inference is weak. The commercial success might not be due to the innovation but rather, as petitioners in *Cook* argued, to "sales promotion ability, manufacturing technique, ready access to markets, consumer appeal design factors, and advertising budget." But given the commercial success of the innovation, why is it likely that the commercial potential was perceived in advance? And why is it likely that because the commercial potential was perceived, men of skill began to work on the problems of that innovation as opposed to other potential improvements? And if men of skill start to work on the improvement, why does the fact that the patentee was first to perfect the improvement mean that others failed? Perhaps they were only a little slower. This seems a fragile thread on which to hang a conclusion of non-obviousness, particularly in a case where the patentee shows only commercial success but does not show that the commercial potential was perceived or that attempts actually were made but failed. How, then, does commercial success constitute a helping hand? The Court said that "there legal inferences or subtests do focus attention on economic and motivational rather than technical issues and are, therefore, more susceptible of judicial treatment than are the highly technical facts often present in patent litigation." Perhaps commercial success is a familiar distraction for judges confused by the facts.

It is not difficult to see why lawyers for patent owners are eager to introduce evidence of commercial success. By introducing evidence of commercial success the lawyer is telling the judge that his client's patent is very valuable and that if the judge holds the patent invalid he is destroying expectations of great value.... Since it is unlikely that patents that are not commercially successful will be brought to litigation, this amounts to a suggestion that borderline cases be decided in favor of patentees. In fact, if one is willing to infer from the litigation itself that the patent is valuable because it is worth litigating, and that since it is valuable it must be commercially successful, one ends up with the rule that all patents that are litigated should be held valid.

If commercial success is a relevant "economic issue," then one can argue that it should be a factor weighing against patentability in borderline cases. Commercially successful patents are the ones that truly impose a monopoly tax on the market, and therefore courts should be even more cautious in holding them valid. Furthermore, it is in the area of innovations that quickly meet consumer acceptance that the innovator has the best chance of recovering his special costs without a patent monopoly. The chances of doing this in any particular case depend, of course, on the good-will advantages of being the first and the speed with which potential competitors can enter. But the more quickly a substantial market can be developed and its profit returns enjoyed, the greater (as a general rule) would seem to be the advantages accruing to the innovator who enters the market first. He will not need extensive market development that will alert potential competitors before the profits begin. Thus, in the area of commercially successful improvement quickly recognized by the market, a patent is less likely to be necessary to evoke the improvement. The argument assumes, of course, that the commercial potential is perceived in advance by the innovator so that it can affect his decision to develop the innovation. This is not necessarily so, but the same assumption is made by the traditional argument for commercial success as a factor favoring a finding of invention. At the very least, these two arguments should cancel each other and leave commercial success with no role to play in a non-obviousness inquiry.

For quite the opposite view, see Jochen Pagenberg, *The Evaluation of "Inventive Step" in the European Patent System–More Objective Standards Needed*, 9 Int'l Rev. Indus. Prop. & Copyright L. 1, 121 (1978), urging that secondary considerations are more reliable indicia of nonobviousness and should hold a dominant position in inventive step determinations.

2. Copying. Copying, particularly when the accused infringer did not copy any other prior art, can be strong evidence of nonobviousness. *Specialty Composites v. Cabot Corp.*, 845 F.2d 981, 6 U.S.P.Q.2d 1601 (Fed.Cir.1988). Copying, too, must be given weight according to its context. Copying is not persuasive, for instance, when the accused product is not identical to the claimed invention and the accused infringer vigorously denies infringement. *Pentec Inc. v. Graphic Controls Corp.*, 776 F.2d 309, 227 U.S.P.Q. 766 (Fed.Cir.1985). Copying is a high form of flattery but could also occur because the copyist is confident that the invention is not patentable.

3. Prior Failures. Prior failures by other inventors has been called "virtually irrefutable" evidence of nonobviousness. *Panduit Corp. v. Dennison Mfg. Co.*, 774 F.2d 1082, 227 U.S.P.Q. 337 (Fed.Cir.1985), *vacated on other grounds*, 475 U.S. 809 (1986). However, once again, prior failures are not viewed uncritically. Evidence of prior failure is not persuasive if the person who failed had only scant knowledge of the prior art or, more important, was not motivated to succeed due to satisfaction with the status quo. *In re Sneed*, 710 F.2d 1544, 218 U.S.P.Q. 385 (Fed.Cir.1983). Moreover evidence of other failures very rarely relates to exactly the same problem that the invention solved. Therefore, the use of this evidence must assure that the failures sought the answer to the same problem.

4. Licenses. Evidence of extensive licensing may be persuasive of industry respect for the invention-strong evidence of nonobviousness. On the other hand, a long period of no infringement may show that the licenses are in fact motivated by a desire to avoid litigation, rather than by respect for the strength of the invention. *Pentec Inc. v. Graphic Controls Corp.*, 776 F.2d 309, 227 U.S.P.Q. 766 (Fed.Cir.1985); *EWP Corp. v. Reliance Universal Inc.*, 755 F.2d 898, 225 U.S.P.Q. 20 (Fed.Cir.1985). Moreover in a healthy market, many licenses are part of a larger cross-licensing arrangement that undermines the nexus between a particular license in a large package and the claimed features it licenses.

5. Long–Felt Need. The nature of the problem is certainly relevant to the obviousness inquiry. *Northern Telecom Inc. v. Datapoint Corp.*, 908 F.2d

931, 15 U.S.P.Q.2d 1321 (Fed.Cir.1990). Moreover, an invention need not solve some long-standing problem, but can instead create a new want or need and still be nonobvious. *Leinoff v. Louis Milona & Sons*, 726 F.2d 734, 220 U.S.P.Q. 845 (Fed.Cir.1984). On the other hand, the nexus requirement will place a burden on the applicant or patentee to show that the felt need correlates with the problem solved by the invention.

6. Unexpected Results. Does this sound like a recycled version of the "synergism" test? Remember that the "synergism" test *required* some superior or unexpected result to qualify for patent protection. In this case, this objective criterion acknowledges the common sense observation that surprise and commendation by experts at the time of learning of the invention buttresses a case for nonobviousness. *Specialty Composites v. Cabot Corp.*, 845 F.2d 981, 6 U.S.P.Q.2d 1601 (Fed.Cir.1988); *Burlington Indus. Inc. v. Quigg*, 822 F.2d 1581, 3 U.S.P.Q.2d 1436 (Fed.Cir.1987). On the other hand, this evidence can suffer from the hindsight problem. This evidence necessarily appears after the invention has changed expectations. Because expectations are by nature subjective, another danger is that litigation itself can alter the nature and intensity of expectations.

7. Skepticism. The skepticism of an expert, expressed before the inventor proved it wrong, bolsters the case for nonobviousness. *In re O'Farrell*, 853 F.2d 894, 7 U.S.P.Q.2d 1673 (Fed.Cir.1988). Because this evidence arises before the invention, it has particular persuasiveness. Sadly it is also among the rarest forms of objective evidence of nonobviousness. Skilled artisans rarely pronounce categorical judgments of doom on a technology that later revises all thinking in the field.

8. Commercial Success: Whose? Courts have sometimes counted the sales of infringers, as well as those of the patentee, in order to determine whether an invention enjoyed commercial success. "Commercial success of an invention is measured by the sales of the infringers as well as the sales of [the patentee]." *Syntex (U.S.A.) Inc. v. Paragon Optical Inc.*, 7 U.S.P.Q.2d 1001 (D.Ariz.1987). As noted in one dissent: "Now, as a matter of common sense, the way one proves commercial success of a patented invention is, first, to demonstrate the success of the patentee or one or more licensees. Second, once an infringer is sued and proved to be an infringer, its sales are appropriately proved and added to the others." *Truswal Sys. Corp. v. Hydro-Air Eng'g, Inc.*, 813 F.2d 1207, 2 U.S.P.Q.2d 1034 (Fed.Cir.1987) (Rich, J., dissenting). What difficulties does this approach create for discovery and the presentation of evidence during an infringement trial, particularly where the accused infringer contends that the claimed invention would have been obvious?

Depending on market factors, upon which no two economists agree, this evidence can be relevant to nonobviousness. Because easy to acquire, however; this type of evidence appears often in nonobviousness cases.

9. Independent development. Evidence of contemporaneous independent invention is objective evidence that may not benefit the applicant or patentee. If actually contemporaneous and not based on derivation from the purported inventor, this type of evidence may show that others could easily achieve the same invention. *See, Monarch Knitting Mach. Corp. v. Sulzer Morat GmbH*, 139 F.3d 877, 45 U.S.P.Q.2d 1977 (Fed.Cir.1998).

10. The Prima Facie Case of Nonobviousness. Patent Office procedures places considerable emphasis on a so-called "prima facie case" of nonobviousness. In *In re Oetiker*, 977 F.2d 1443, 24 U.S.P.Q.2d 1443 (Fed.Cir.1992), the Federal Circuit noted:

> The prima facie case is a procedural tool of patent examination, allocating the burdens of going forward as between examiner and applicant. The term "prima facie case" refers only to the initial examination step. As discussed in *In re Piasecki*, 745 F.2d 1468, 1472, 223 U.S.P.Q. 785, 788 (Fed.Cir.1984), the examiner bears the initial burden, on review of the prior art or on any other ground, of presenting a *prima facie* case of unpatentability. If that burden is met, the burden of coming forward with evidence or argument shifts to the applicant. After evidence or argument is submitted by the applicant in response, patentability is determined on the totality of the record, by a preponderance of evidence with due consideration to persuasiveness of argument.

> If examination at the initial stage does not produce a prima facie case of unpatentability, then without more the applicant is entitled to grant of the patent.

> In reviewing the examiner's decision on appeal, the Board must necessarily weigh all of the evidence and argument. An observation by the Board that the examiner made a prima facie case is not improper, as long as the ultimate determination of patentability is made on the entire record.

In practice this *prima facie* practice often means that the examiner will enter an initial rejection based on a comparison of the claimed invention with the prior art. At that stage of the prosecution process, the applicant is not likely to have submitted any objective evidence of nonobviousness. Upon receipt of the rejection, the burden shifts to the applicant to rebut the prima facie case of obviousness. At that point, the applicant my supply objective evidence along with the rest of its case for nonobviousness.

11. Prima Facie Obviousness in Biotech. How would you reconcile *Hybritech* and *O'Farrell* (the case that equated obviousness with a "reasonable expectation of success," as discussed previously)? In his thoughtful study of patent law and biotechnology, scholar-practitioner Kenneth Burchfield concludes that the Federal Circuit has presented three chief requirements for a prima facie obviousness rejection of particular pertinence to biotechnology:

> 1. The prior art must disclose or suggest the modification in the prior art process that is required for the invention, without reference to the applicant's specification.

> 2. The reference must convey to one skilled in the art that there is a reasonable expectation of success if the modification is made.

> 3. The reference must provide detailed enabling methodology for practicing the claimed invention.

KENNETH J. BURCHFIEL, BIOTECHNOLOGY AND THE FEDERAL CIRCUIT 107 (1995). Consider how these criteria hold up in view of *Hybritech* and *O'Farrell*, as well as the Federal Circuit's *Deuel* decision, reprinted later in this chapter.

§ 7.2[d]   Comparative Standards of Inventive Step

WINDSURFING INTERNATIONAL INC. v. TABUR MARINE (GREAT BRITAIN) LTD.

The Court Of Appeal, 1984.
[1985]   R.P.C. 59.

Before: Lord Justice Oliver Lord Justice O'Connor and Lord Justice Slade

This was an appeal by Windsurfing International Inc. from an order made by Whitford J. in the Patents Court on 7 April 1982 dismissing their action against Tabur Marine (Great Britain) Ltd. for infringement of the plaintiffs' patent No. 1258317 and ordering upon the defendants' counterclaim that the patent be revoked.

OLIVER LJ.

The patent in suit ("the Schweitzer patent") relates to the basic equipment employed in what has, in the past few years, become increasingly popular international sport, that of windsurfing, but, on the face of it, it covers also a very much wider field, namely that of wind-propelled vehicles generally. The plaintiffs, as their name suggests, are an American corporation and the patent in suit results from a convention application with a priority date of 27 March 1968. [The specification identifies] two problems, first that the effect of providing a sail on a normally sail-free vehicle such as a surfboard is to "denature" the vehicle and convert it substantially into a sailboat and secondly that, when a sail is fitted to a vehicle which does not have high roll stability, there is a danger of its being overturned by sudden or excessive winds:

A need therefore exists for safely providing wind-propulsion means for a vehicle not normally so equipped but which means preserves the original ride and control characteristics of the vehicle.

The consistory clause, which is reproduced in claim 1 of the claims, is in these terms:

In accordance with the present invention there is provided a wind-propelled vehicle comprising body means, an unstayed spar connected to said body means through a joint which will provide universal-type movement of the spar in the absence of support thereof by a user of the vehicle, a sail attached along one edge thereof to the spar, and a pair of arcuate booms, first ends of the booms being connected together and laterally connected on said spar, second ends of the booms being connected together and having means thereon connected to the sail such that said sail is held taut between the booms.

The specification goes on to expand upon the method of connection of the spar to the body by means of a universal joint to describe the purpose of the arcuate booms and to explain the method of operation of the invention.

What is illustrated is what we have been told is a conventional surfboard of the type known as a "Californian surfboard" (10) fitted with a leeboard, and having mounted on its upper surface immediately above the leeboard and approximately in the centre of the surfboard a block carrying a universal joint to which is attached a spar (12). Attached to the spar by its leading edge is a triangular sail (14) which is held taut by two arcuate booms (16 and 18) connected together at each end and connected at their forward ends to the spar.

What renders the combination novel is simply a particular feature of the spar, namely that it is not stayed but is free to move under the direct manual control of the user. That is the feature which distinguishes the apparatus from other conventional sailing apparatus and which meets the two problems postulated in the specification, namely that of "denaturing" the body on which the sail is mounted and that of overturning in high winds.

That is the essential teaching of the specification. Its attractiveness and utility as a means of transport may not be immediately apparent, at any rate to those lacking a high degree of tolerance to immersion in cold water. The evidence established, however, that sailboarding started to become a very popular aquatic sport during the mid–1970s although its popularity in the United Kingdom lagged behind that which it acquired in warmer climates. The climatic obstacles, however, were to a large extent overcome by the advent of the wet-suit and the establishment of sailboarding schools with land simulators and a successful advertising campaign have ensured that sailboarding is now established as an increasingly popular sport in this country and have resulted in a considerable commercial success for the plaintiffs and their licensees.

The defendants having dealt in this country in sailboard equipment incorporating the features described in claim 1 of the specification, the plaintiffs commenced infringement proceedings. Predictably, the response was a defence and counterclaim contesting the validity of the patent on various grounds, the material ones for present purposes being that the alleged invention so far as claimed in each and every claim was not new or was obvious, in support of which the defendants relied upon prior publication, prior use and prior common general knowledge.

The learned judge upheld the defendants' objections on the ground of obviousness, having regard to the prior publication referred to below.

It will be convenient to deal first with obviousness based upon prior publication. The document relied upon by the defendants here was an article by a Mr. Darby entitled "Sailboarding: Exciting New Water Sport" which had first appeared in an American publication, Popular Science Monthly, and which was reproduced in the United Kingdom in October 1966 in a publication entitled Practical Hydrofoils produced by the Amateur Yacht Research Society and circulated to its members who numbered some 600. That article described a sailboard with an unstayed sail attached to a spar held by the user and inserted into a hollow socket in a mast step mounted on the sailboard. The mast step was slotted immediately in front of the spar socket to carry a daggerboard. The basic concept, i.e. the use of an unstayed sail which is used to steer the vehicle and which can be jettisoned in case of trouble, is the same concept as that in the patent in suit. The principal differences are that the sail shown in the publication is a square sail actuated by the user standing on the lee side of it with his back to the spar, and that, instead of the spar being attached to the vehicle by a moveable joint, free movement is achieved by a socket from which the spar can be removed, the suggestion being that the sail should be attached to the sailboard by a lanyard to prevent their drifting apart when the sail is jettisoned.

The first of these two differences is, Mr. Pumfrey submits, crucial. The sail shown in the photographs and drawings is a square sail which is attached by its ends longitudinally to an 11' 6'' spar and laterally to an 8' 4'' yard, the spar and yard each being tapered at the tips so as to form a bow or arc holding the sail taut. What Darby teaches, he suggests, is essentially confined to a vessel propelled by a sail of this configuration, i.e. a square-rigged vessel, and he refers, in particular, to the manoeuvres which are figuratively described in the article (being manoeuvres appropriate to a square-rigged vessel) and to the following two passages. On page 73 of the publication it is said:

> "Learning to handle a sailboard is quite a change ... because you have no rudder and must steer with the sail. You also have to learn to handle what is really a square-rigged ship rather than a fore-and-aft Marconi rig like that on small sailboats you have known."

It should be mentioned that "Marconi rig" is an alternative description of the triangular sail described in the patent in suit, more commonly known as a Bermuda rig.

The other passage to which Mr. Pumfrey draws attention is the narrative on page 74, under the illustration of the basic sailing position, which reads:

> "sailing positions are similar to those for any sailboat, but this one is a square-rigger, so the wind pushes it. You steer by pivoting the mast in its socket, tilting sail".

The article goes on to describe how to build the sail and board, with diagrammatical illustrations, and concludes with a statement that a limited number of completed sailboards and kits can be obtained from the author.

As regards the second difference noted above, the learned judge observed:

> "The mast merely rests in position in the step, but is is free to move in any direction. The article does however suggest a more complex swivel step for advanced riders. That is a suggestion which we find in an illustration of the Darby sailboard at ... page 75 of the article. Exactly what is intended is not known but the words used, to my mind at least, plainly suggest some sort of universal joint."

The learned judge then postulated the question (which he answered in the negative):

"could there be any inventive step in substituting in a Darby board a fore-and-aft rig for a kite sail or a square rig sail, for if anyone decided to take this step it is I think on the face of it apparent, and indeed was confirmed in evidence by Mr. McAlpine–Downie, that you would need a pair of arcuate booms rather than one boom as you would be contemplating operating with the wind working on either side of the sail".

The learned judge concluded:

"In my judgment, a substitution of this kind must be obvious. It was a step which, on their evidence, certainly occurred to Mr. McAlpine-Downie and Professor Bradfield. I do, however, have this very much in mind, that they were individuals who could be described as highly skilled."

The plaintiffs challenge this conclusion. In the notice of appeal it is simply said that the judge's finding was contrary to the weight of the evidence but Mr. Pumfrey's submission to this court was rather more sophisticated than might appear from that rather bald challenge. What Mr. Pumfrey submits is that the learned judge went wrong in law in that he started from a false assumption that he must consider Darby as a starting point from which improvements required to be made and that he then applied to that assumption evidence which was in fact directed to answering a question which, as a matter of law, did not arise.

The witnesses on this aspect of the matter were four in number. The plaintiffs called two extremely highly qualified experts, Mr. McAlpine–Downie and Professor Bradfield, the former being an extremely experienced and successful designer of sailing craft, although without formal qualifications, and the latter a very highly qualified marine engineer and an expert on advanced wind-powered water-craft. Evidence was given for the defendants by Mr. I.M. Nicholson, a naval architect and a partner in a very old established firm of yacht designers and surveyors, and by Mr. R.M. Ellison, formerly an officer in the Merchant Navy and an experienced amateur yachtsman.

It is Mr. Pumfrey's submission that the learned judge reached the conclusion that he did quite simply by asking himself the wrong question. He accepts that, to anyone skilled in the art and contemplating the field of the patent in suit in 1968, Darby's article would be a relevant document, but, when considering the patent in suit in the context of whether or not it was inventive, he submits that it cannot be assumed that such a person would take Darby as his starting point and set about seeing whether he could make any improvements to it. The instant case is not one of which it can be said that there was an existing problem for which the sailing-boat or leisure industries had been searching for a solution, and Mr. Pumfrey submits that the burden lies on the defendants to show that Darby was a concept which a skilled man would have recognised as calling for development. Far from this being the case, he suggests, the evidence—and, in particular, that of Mr. McAlpine–Downie and Professor Bradfield—pointed in the opposite direction.

This submission discloses a fundamental difference between the appellants and the respondents as regards the approach of the court to published information claimed to render an alleged invention obvious and it calls for some analysis of a number of authorities in which the question has fallen to be considered.

In summary, Mr. Pumfrey's submission is that in 1966 nobody would have considered Darby as more than a beach novelty (which was the reaction of Mr. McAlpine–Downie and Professor Bradfield) and that; therefore, nobody would in fact have been interested in doing anything more than, perhaps, building it and playing with it. Thus, the argument proceeds, there would not have been any reason for developing Darby and hence no development, even of a routine nature, would have been obvious or even have occurred to the skilled man, who would merely have dismissed Darby as a not very practical toy. It is from this foundation that he goes on to submit that the learned judge asked himself the wrong question and wrongly accepted as evidence of what was obvious the evidence of witnesses as to how Darby might have been improved, for, in suggesting improvements to or embellishments upon that which called for no improvement or embellishment, they were doing so in response to an invitation to treat Darby as a springboard to further development and invention and were in fact suggesting inventive steps.

We have not felt able to accept Mr. Pumfrey's submissions. There are, we think, four steps which require to be taken in answering the jury question. The first is to identify the inventive concept embodied in the patent in suit. Thereafter, the court has to assume the mantle of the normally skilled but unimaginative addressee in the art at the priority date and to impute to him what was, at that date, common general knowledge in the art in question. The third step is to identify what, if any, differences exist between the matter cited as being "known or used" and the alleged invention. Finally, the court has to ask itself whether, viewed without any knowledge of the alleged invention, those differences constitute steps which would have been obvious to the skilled man or whether they require any degree of invention. As regards the first step, we respectfully agree with the learned judge that the inventive concept of the patent is the free-sail concept. It is that which constitutes the essential difference between the patent in suit and other conventional vehicles propelled by sail. Going back, then, to the priority date, anyone familiar with sailing and sailing craft would then have known, as part of his general knowledge, the difference between square sail and Bermuda rigs and the disadvantages as regards manoeuvrability presented by the former. He would also have been familiar with twin booms arcuate in shape known as "wishbone" booms which, though not in wide use in the 1960s, were well known to anyone interested in constructing light craft. Darby's article was addressed initially to the knowledgeable handyman for whom the American journal Popular Science Monthly (in which it first appeared) was designed and, so far as the publication in this country was concerned, was directed to members of a society dedicated to amateur research into yachts. It in fact disclosed, and disclosed to persons knowledgeable in the art, the self-same inventive step claimed by the patent in suit, the only difference of any substance being the use of the kite rig held by the crossed spar and boom instead of a Bermuda rig with a wishbone boom. We agree, of course, that one must not assume that the skilled man, casting his experienced eye over Darby, would at once be fired with the knowledge that here was something which had a great commercial future which he must bend every effort to develop and improve, but he must at least be assumed to appreciate and understand the free-sail concept taught by Darby and to consider, in the light of his knowledge and experience, whether it will work and how it will work. In the light of the evidence, it seems to us inescapable that anyone skilled in the art and contemplating Darby's article in 1966 would immediately recognise, as the witnesses did, that the kite rig suggested for this very simple and elementary device would suffer from the disadvantages that it would perform poorly upwind and would require to be manipulated from the lee side of the sail. It does not, in our judgment, require the attribution to the skilled addressee of any inventive faculty to say that, if he applied his mind to it at all, it would be immediately obvious to him that these disadvantages would disappear if the rig were changed to Bermuda, a change which, as would also be obvious to him, required the sail to be stretched by means of a wishbone boom. It may well be that nobody in the United Kingdom at that time would have considered that there was a commercial future in this interesting beach novelty, but that is not as we conceive the question which has to be answered. One has, in our judgment, to postulate a person who comes to Darby knowing of the advantages of a Bermuda rig over a square rig and who is at least sufficiently interested to read the article and consider how the vehicle described would work on the water. All the evidence suggests that such a person would immediately see, by application of his own general knowledge, the adoption of a Bermuda rig as an obvious way of improving the performance of the Darby vehicle.

We do not find an answer to this in the two forensic questions which Mr. Pumfrey poses, namely, why, if it was obvious that a fore-and-aft rig would perform better, did Darby himself (who clearly knew about such rigs) not suggest it and why, so far as the evidence shows, did no development of Darby take place in the United States? As to the former, there was, so far as we are aware, no evidence as to Mr. Darby's qualifications or experience, but in any event the answer is, we think, to be found in Mr. Nicolson's evidence that, in his view, Darby was merely directing himself to constructing the simplest possible design both as regards hull and rig. As to the latter, there was no evidence either way as to whether or not Darby was taken up or developed in the United States. No doubt, if the defendants had produced evidence that Darby's article excited great interest in the United States and that the kite rig was immediately replaced with a Bermuda rig, that would have reinforced their arguments on obviousness, but we do not think that it can be right to treat the lack of such evidence as detracting from the argument and as leading to the necessary conclusion that there was no interest and no development.

We are, therefore, unable to accept Mr. Pumfrey's criticism that the learned judge was wrong in saying that what happened in the United States was of no significance. Nor do we think that he can be legitimately criticised for his approach to the evidence. He had, as appears from his judgment, well in mind that he had, in Mr. McAlpine–Downie and Professor Bradfield, witnesses who were very highly qualified. It does not appear to us that the questions which they were asked involved the application to Darby of any inventive faculty. In our judgment, the learned judge did not make any wrong assumption. He asked himself the right questions and gave the right answers.

Notes

1. The Problem–Solution Approach. The European Patent Office uses a "problem-solution" approach, which descends from the mandate of European Patent Convention Rule 27(1)(c) that European applications "disclose the invention, as claimed, in such terms that the technical problem (even if not expressly stated as such) and its solution can be understood.... "The Guidelines for Examination in the European Patent Office, Part C at 50 (Dec. 1994), offer the following description:

> In the problem and solution approach there are three main stages:
>
> 1. determining the closest prior art,
>
> 2. establishing the technical problem to be solved, and
>
> 3. determining whether or not the claimed invention, starting from the closest prior art and the technical problem, would have been obvious to the skilled person.

This test is designed to lead to an objective assessment of inventive step which allows no room for consideration of the features of the claimed invention itself. To some extent, however, European practice may simply shift the difficulty from defining the standard of invention to framing the appropriate technical problem that the invention is supposed to solve. Moreover, what if the inventive step is realizing or identifying the problem?

The Technical Board of Appeal considered this problem in *Etching Process*, T 229/85 3.3.1, [1987] Offic. J. Eur. Pat. Off. 237, which involved a claimed process for etching metal surfaces useful in the production of printed circuits. Metals such as copper can be etched using solutions containing, for example, sulphuric acid and hydrogen peroxide. A practical difficulty in employing this etching solution is that metal ions released during the etching process catalyze the decomposition of hydrogen peroxide. The prior art, including a United States patent, added a negative catalyst to the solution in order to inhibit the undesired decomposition of hydrogen peroxide. The claimed process tried a new approach: it added hydrogen peroxide to the etching solution directly before the etching was to occur, and only in such small amounts that would, as a practical matter, be entirely consumed during the etching process. The Examining Division rejected the claim as lacking inventive step, but the Board disagreed, stating:

The disputed decision states that because of the problem set the solution proposed in the application would have been obvious by simply reasoning to a person skilled in the art having knowledge of [the United States patent]. The problem is seen as to prevent the decomposition of hydrogen peroxide without using negative catalysts (stabilisers). This definition of the problem, possibly influenced by the information contained in the present application ..., inadmissibly incorporates part of the solution offered by the invention. The idea of doing away with stabilisers is an essential part of the teaching of the invention as reflected in the solution given above and ultimately consisting in regulating the amount of hydrogen peroxide added to the solution and its timing. However, the technical problem addressed by an invention must be so formulated as not to contain pointers to the solution, since including part of a solution offered by an invention in the statement of the problem must, when the state of the art is assessed in terms of that problem, necessarily result in an ex post facto view being taken of inventive activity. For this reason alone the decision of the Examining Division cannot stand.

The Board preferred a statement of the problem as "to devise an etching process ... involving as low a consumption of hydrogen peroxide as possible and which permits the spent etching solution to be regenerated without difficulty...." Which version of the "problem" do you prefer? For further discussion, see George S.A. Szabo, *The Problem and Solution Approach in the European Patent Office*, 26 INT'L REV. INDUS. PROP. & COPYRIGHT L. 457 (1995).

2. Inventive Step in Japan. Another leading patent-granting state, Japan, sets forth its inventive step requirement in section 29(2) of the Japanese Patent Law. That statute provides:

Where an invention could easily have been made, prior to the filing of a patent application, by a person having ordinary skill in the art to which the invention pertains ... a patent shall not be granted for such an invention....

The Japanese Examination Guidelines provide that "a person having ordinary skill in the art" is a hypothetical person:

who has the common general knowledge in the art to which the invention pertains at the time of filing of an application, and has ability to use ordinary technical means for research and development;

who has ability to exercise ordinary creative ability in selecting materials and changing designs; and

who is able to comprehend as his own knowledge all technical matters in the state of the art in the field to which an invention pertains at the time of filing of a patent application.

In addition, a person skilled in the art is deemed to be able to comprehend as his own knowledge all technical matters in the field of technology relevant to a problem to be solved by an invention.

Is the standard of "easily made" the same as "would have been obvious"? See David J. Abraham, *Shinpo-Sei: Japanese Invention Step Meets U.S. Non–Obviousness*, 77 J. PAT. & TRADEMARK OFF. SOC'Y 528 (1995). The Guidelines go on to indicate that "a person skilled in the art could have been able to easily arrive at a claimed invention by exercising ordinary creativity" on the basis of the prior art.

3. Development of Inventive Step Abroad. A mandatory feature of contemporary patent systems, the origin of the inventive step requirement has been traced to the U.S. Supreme Court opinion in *Hotchkiss v. Greenwood. See* Friedrich–Karl Beier, *The Inventive Step in Its Historical Development*, 17 INT'L REV. INDUS. PROP. & COPYRIGHT L. 301 (1986). Development of this requirement in Germany took some unusual turns in that civil law regime. Although the first patent statute for the unified German Empire, the 1877 Act, did not include a requirement of technical advance or inventive step, by the turn of the century the Imperial Patent Office began imposing patentability requirements extending past novelty. *Id.* Observers of the British system follow the modern requirement of inventive step to at least as early as Lord Herschell's opinion for the House of Lords in *Vickers v. Sidell*, 7 R.P.C. 292 (1890), which intoned a standard of obviousness and, prophetically, counseled against the use of hindsight when judging inventions. France was quite a latecomer in requiring inventive step: the French Patent Law of 1844 stated only the requirements of novelty and industrial application, a situation that was not changed until the Patent Law of January 2, 1968. *See* Joanna Schmidt–Szalewski, *Nonobviousness as a Requirement of Patentability in French Law*, 23 INT'L REV. INDUS. PROP. & COPYRIGHT L. 725 (1992).

4. Closing Thoughts on Nonobviousness. Following the decision in *Molnlycke AB v. Procter & Gamble Ltd.*, [1990] R.P.C. 498, a lengthy trial resulted in the finding of patent infringement. The Court of Appeal affirmed this judgment on December 21, 1993. In its opinion, the Court of Appeal offered some interesting comments on obviousness that are worthy of considerable study.

> Secondary evidence of this type has its place and the importance, or weight, to be attached to it will vary from case to case. However, such evidence must be kept firmly in its place. It must not be permitted, by reason of its volume and complexity, to obscure the fact that it is no more than an aid in assessing the primary evidence.

> We had cited to us authorities extending back over 100 years in which various evidential considerations are discussed in relation to what were the common law or statutory precursors of the present statutory definition. It appears that the word "obvious" was first used in this connection by Lord Herschell in 1889 in *American Braided Wire v. Thompson* 6 RPC 518 at 528. As Lord Herschell pointed out in *Siddell v. Vickers & Sons Ltd* 15 App Cas 496, and adapting his language to the new statutory definition, obviousness connotes something which would at once occur to a person skilled in the art who was desirous of accomplishing the end, or, in Lopes LJ's much quoted phrase, "it must not be the obvious or natural suggestion of what was previously known": see *Savage v. Harris* 13 RPC 364, 370.

> There are many reported decisions by courts which have had to distinguish between an invention and mere workshop improvement where the evidentiary considerations are discussed and forensic tools developed. The cases cited to us included *Savage v. Harris, Samuel*

Parkes v. Cocker Bros (1929) 46 RPC 241, *Non Drip v. Strangers* 60 RPC 135 (long felt want), *Olin Mathieson v. Biorex* [1970] RPC 157, [1970] FSR 361, (for the use of the "Simkins List") and *Technograph v. Mills & Rockley* [1972] RPC 346 at 355, [1971] FSR 188, *Lucas v. Gaedor* [1978] RPC 297 (the guidance of contemporaneous events). In *Savage v. Harris*, Lopes LJ sounded a salutary warning:

> Cases, so far as regards the law, are most useful, but when they are applied to particular facts, they, as a rule, are of little service. Each case depends upon its own particular facts and the facts of almost every case differ.

> Citing previous decisions on a question of fact is not a useful, nor is it a proper, exercise.

§ 7.3 OBVIOUSNESS IN CHEMISTRY AND BIOTECHNOLOGY

With characteristic conclusiveness, the Federal Circuit noted: "[T]he requirement of unobviousness in the case of chemical inventions is the same as for other types of inventions." *In re Johnson*, 747 F.2d 1456, 1460, 223 U.S.P.Q. 1260, 1263 (Fed.Cir.1984). To the contrary, obviousness as applied to the landscape of chemical technologies has presented a distinct set of issues for the patent law. The search for a coherent nonobviousness doctrine in biotechnology has also proven elusive, as demonstrated by the enactment of § 103(b), a complex standard of nonobviousness for certain biotechnologies. An introduction to the considerable body of precedent concerning obviousness in chemistry and biotechnology follows.

§ 7.3[a] Composition Claims

Patenting in the chemical and biotechnology areas focuses first and foremost on claiming "new entities", shorter new molecules constituting "new chemical entities" and the longer chains from recombinant biotechnology. Unlike mechanical patenting where the "thing" to be patented can be accurately pictured in three dimensions through a plurality of drawings, the chemical entity is rarely if ever pictured as a three dimensional structure that in the end gives rise to its properties. Rather, chemists use a two-dimensional representation-the structural formula-to *identify* the structure.

For literally six decades in the patenting of chemical entities, the bar focused so intensely upon the "label," the structural formula, that for the patent profession the label became the reality. Thus, like a tic-tac-toe game of "X" and "O" marks on a two-dimensional surface, the battleground for patenting chemical entities was a determination whether the *label* for a claimed compound was or was not "obvious" from the *label* for a prior art compound. If the labels were very close, then the claimed compound was "structurally obvious". This conclusion closed the book on patenting the compound, per se. Instead, if the claimed compound possessed an unexpected property vis-a-vis the prior art compound, the inventor was encouraged to claim a method of use of the compound (as opposed to a claim to the compound *per se*.)

Numerous cases over a period of more than sixty years established a basis for denial of a claim to new chemical entity based upon "structural obviousness," dating back to at least *Bender v. Hoffmann*, 1898 C.D. 262, and sustained through *In re Henze*, 181 F.2d 196, 85 U.S.P.Q. 261 (CCPA 1950), and *In re Hass*, 141 F.2d 122, 60 U.S.P.Q. 544 (CCPA 1944). The primary thread throughout this line of cases was whether a certain change from an old compound was sufficiently removed so that it could not be considered "structurally obvious": This was the starting and end point of the investigation. *See generally* Harold C. Wegner, *Prima Facie Obviousness of Chemical Compounds*, 6 AM. PAT. L. ASS'N Q.J. 271 (1978).

Although the CCPA had earlier suggested in dictum that applicants could overcome a prima facie case of obviousness through a showing regarding the compound's properties, the court had not squarely applied these concepts until its seminal decision in *In re Papesch*.

IN RE PAPESCH

United States Court of Customs and Patent Appeals, 1963.
315 F.2d 381, 137 U.S.P.Q. 43.

The applicant claimed a family of compounds including representative compound 2,4,6–triethylpyrazolo(4,3–d)–4,5,6,7–tetrahydropyrimidine–5,7–dione (ethyl = CH_3-CH_2-), that was admittedly "structurally obvious" in light of a compound dislcosed by Robbins, 2,4,6–trimethylpyrazolo(4,3–d)–4,5,6,7–tetrahydropyrimidine–5,7–dione (methyl = CH_3-). The applicant stated in his specification that "[t]he tri[ethyl] compound[] ... ha[s] been found to possess unexpectedly potent anti-inflammatory activity in contrast to the [prior art] trimethyl compound." A researcher's affidavit reported comparative tests of the Robins et al. trimethyl compound and the applicant's triethyl compound which show that the latter is an active anti-inflammatory agent while the prior art compound is completely inactive for that utility.

WORLEY, CHIEF JUDGE and RICH, MARTIN, ARTHUR M. SMITH and ALMOND, ASSOCIATE JUDGES.

RICH, ASSOCIATE JUDGE.

[C]omparing the specific compound of claim 2 with the prior art, the compounds differ only in that where [Papesch] has three ethyl groups the [Robbins] prior art has three methyl groups, a total difference of three-CH_2 groups.

The claims are rejected only on the ground that they are [obvious] over a single reference which discloses ... a lower homolog of the claimed compounds ... and proof has been given showing that the compound of claim 2 ... possesses an advantageous pharmacological property shown not to be possessed by the prior art compound.

From the standpoint of patent law, a compound and all of its properties are inseparable; they are one and the same thing. The graphic formulae, the chemical nomenclature, the systems of classification and study such as the concepts of homology, isomerism, etc., are mere symbols by which compounds can be identified, classified, and compared. But a formula is not a compound and while it may serve in a claim to identify what is being patented, as the metes and bounds of a deed identify a plot of land, the thing that is patented is not the formula but the compound identified by it. And the patentability of the thing does not depend on the similarity of its formula to that of another compound but of the similarity of the former compound to the latter. There is no basis in law for ignoring any property in making such a comparison. An assumed similarity based on a comparison of formulae must give way to evidence that the assumption is erroneous.

The argument has been made that patentability is here being asserted only on the basis of one property, the anti-inflammatory activity, and that the compounds claimed and the compound of the prior art presumably have many properties in common. Presumably they do, but presumption is all we have here. The same is true of all of the compounds of the above cases which were held patentable over compounds of the prior art, many of which must have had more in common by way of properties than the compounds here because the relationships, structurally, were even closer than here.

As to the examiner's view that in a case such as this the applicant should claim his invention as a process utilizing the newly discovered property, the board appears to have ignored it, properly we think. It is contrary to practically all of the above decisions wherein no fault was found with granting product claims. Such claims have well-recognized advantages to those in the business of making and selling compounds, in contrast to process-of-use claims, because competitors in the sale of compounds are not generally users.

As should be apparent from the foregoing, we regard the board's opinion and decision as contrary to well established law. We see no reason to change that law. The decision is therefore reversed.

WORLEY, CHIEF JUDGE, concurred in the result.

* * *

Notes

1. *Papesch* at the Federal Circuit: An early Federal Circuit case confirmed the role of *Papesch* and displayed its continued doctrinal development. In *In re Lalu*, 747 F.2d 703, 223 U.S.P.Q. 1257 (Fed.Cir.1984), Judge Baldwin overturned the Board's finding of *prima facie* obviousness:

> Ultimately our analysis of the obviousness or nonobviousness of appellants' claimed compounds requires inquiry as to whether there is anything in the Oesterling reference which would suggest the expected properties of the claimed compounds or whether Oesterling discloses any utility for the intermediate sulfonyl chlorides which would support an expectation that the claimed compounds would have similar properties.

There is no disclosure that the Oesterling compounds would have any properties in common with those of appellants' compounds, as those properties of the former relate to the use of the compounds for base neutralization, catalysis, metal cleaning, and fuel. The mere fact that Oesterling's sulfonyl chlorides can be used as intermediates in the production of the corresponding sulfonic acids does not provide adequate motivation for one of ordinary skill in the art to stop the Oesterling synthesis and investigate the intermediate sulfonyl chlorides with an expectation of arriving at appellants' claimed sulfonyl halides for use as corrosion inhibiting agents, surface active agents, or leveling agents.

2. Balancing New and Old Uses. In the next case the full court took up the question of chemical obviousness where the closest prior art compounds had the same essential structure as the compounds claimed by the applicant, but the existence of an important property of both the prior art compounds and the claimed compounds was discovered by the applicant.

IN RE DILLON

United States Court of Appeals, Federal Circuit,
1990.919 F.2d 688, 16 U.S.P.Q.2d 1897.
cert. denied, 500 U.S. 904 (1991).

The applicant claimed compositions containing tetra-orthoesters useful as fuel additives to reduce soot emissions. The tetra-orthoesters were "structurally obvious" from tri-orthoesters that were also disclosed in the prior art as fuel additives, but in order to obtain a different benefit: dewatering. The PTO Board affirmed the examiner's rejection,, holding that there was a "reasonable expectation" that the tri-and tetra-orthoesther fuel compositions would have similar properties, based on "close structural and chemical similarity" between them and the fact that both the applicant and the prior art noted their use as fuel additives. According to the Board, the applicant could have traversed the obviousness rejection by showing an unexpected advantage or superiority of her claimed tetra-orthoesters as compared with the tri-orthoesthers, but had not done so.

A three-judge panel of the Federal Circuit reversed the rejection, stating that "a prima facie case of obviousness is not deemed made unless both (1) the new compound or composition is structurally similar to the reference compound or composition and (2) there is some suggestion or expectation in the prior art that the new compound or composition will have the same or a similar utility as that discovered by the applicant." In re Dillon, 892 F.2d 1554, 1560, 13 U.S.P.Q.2d 1337, 1341 (Fed.Cir.1989) (withdrawn panel opinion). From a petition for hearing en banc, this proceeding followed.

NIES, CHIEF JUDGE, RICH, CIRCUIT JUDGE, COWEN, SENIOR CIRCUIT JUDGE, MARKEY (who sat as chief judge during argument) PAULINE NEWMAN, ARCHER, MAYER, MICHEL, PLAGER, LOURIE, CLEVENGER, and RADER, CIRCUIT JUDGES.

LOURIE, CIRCUIT JUDGE.

THE ISSUE

The issue before this court is whether the Board erred in rejecting as obvious under 35 U.S.C. § 103 claims to Dillon's new compositions and to the new method of reducing particulate emissions, when the additives in the new compositions are structurally similar to additives in known compositions, having a different use, but the new method of reducing particulate emissions is neither taught nor suggested by the prior art.

The Board found that the claims to compositions of a hydrocarbon fuel and a tetra-orthoester were *prima facie* obvious over Sweeney '417 and '267 in view of Elliott and Howk. We agree. Appellant argues that none of these references discloses or suggests the new use which she has discovered. That is, of course, true, but the composition claims are not limited to this new use; *i.e.*, they are not physically or structurally distinguishable over the prior art compositions except with respect to the orthoester component. We believe that the PTO has established, through its combination of references, that there is a sufficiently close relationship between the tri-orthoesters and tetra-orthoesters (see the cited Elliott and Howk references) in the fuel oil art to create an expectation that hydrocarbon fuel compositions containing the tetra-esters would have similar properties, including water scavenging, to like compositions containing the tri-esters, and to provide the motivation to make such new compositions. Howk teaches use of both tri-and tetra-orthoesters in a similar type of chemical reaction. Elliott teaches their equivalence for a particular practical use.

Our case law well establishes that such a fact situation gives rise to a *prima facie* case of obviousness.

This court, in reconsidering this case *in banc*, reaffirms that structural similarity between claimed and prior art subject matter, proved by combining references or otherwise, where the prior art gives reason or motivation to make the claimed compositions, creates a *prima facie* case of obviousness, and that the burden (and opportunity) then falls on an applicant to rebut that *prima facie* case. Such rebuttal or argument can consist of a comparison of test data showing that the claimed compositions possess unexpectedly improved properties or properties that the prior art does not have (*In re Albrecht*, 514 F.2d 1389, 1396, 185 U.S.P.Q. 585, 590 (CCPA 1975); *Murch*, 464 F.2d at 1056, 175 U.S.P.Q. at 92), that the prior art is so deficient that there is no motivation to make what might otherwise appear to be obvious changes (*Albrecht*, 514 F.2d at 1396, 185 U.S.P.Q. at 590; *In re Stemniski*, 444 F.2d 581, 170 U.S.P.Q. 343 (CCPA 1971); *In re Ruschig*, 343 F.2d 965, 145 U.S.P.Q. 274 (CCPA 1965)), or any other argument or presentation of evidence that is pertinent. There is no question that all evidence of the properties of the claimed compositions and the prior art must be considered in determining the ultimate question of patentability, but it is also clear that the discovery that a claimed composition possesses a property not disclosed for the prior art subject matter, does not by itself defeat a *prima facie* case. *Shetty*, 566 F.2d at 86, 195 U.S.P.Q. at 756. Each situation must be considered on its own facts, but it is not necessary in order to establish a *prima facie* case of obviousness that both a structural similarity between a claimed and prior art compound (or a key component of a composition) be shown and that there be a suggestion in or expectation from *the prior art* that the claimed compound or composition will have the same or a similar utility *as one newly discovered by applicant.* To the extent that [*In re Wright*, 848 F.2d 1216, 6 U.S.P.Q.2d 1959 (Fed.Cir.1988)] suggests or holds to the contrary, it is hereby overruled. In particular, the statement that a *prima facie* obviousness rejection is not supported if no reference shows or suggests the newly-discovered properties and results of a claimed structure is not the law.

Under the facts ... we have concluded that a *prima facie* case has been established. The art provided the motivation to make the claimed compositions in the expectation that they would have similar properties. Appellant had the opportunity to rebut the *prima facie* case. She did not present any showing of data to the effect that her compositions had properties not possessed by the prior art compositions or that they possessed them to an unexpectedly greater degree. She attempted to refute the significance of the teachings of the prior art references. She did not succeed and we do not believe the PTO was in error in its decision.

While [the prior art] Sweeney [reference] does not suggest appellant's use, her composition claims are not limited to that use; the claims merely recite compositions analogous to those in the Sweeney patents, and appellant has made no showing overcoming the *prima facie* presumption of similar properties for those analogous compositions. The mention in the appealed claims that the amount of orthoester must be sufficient to reduce particulate emissions is not a distinguishing limitation of the claims, unless that amount is different from the prior art and critical to the use of the claimed composition. *See In re Reni*, 419 F.2d 922, 925, 164 U.S.P.Q. 245, 247 (CCPA 1970). That is not the case here. The amount of ester recited in the dependent claims can be from 0.05–49%, a very broad range; a preferred range is .05–9%, compared with a percentage in Sweeney '417 approximately equimolar to the amounts of water in the fuel which the ester is intended to remove (.01–5%).

Appellant urges that the Board erred in not considering the unexpected results produced by her invention and in not considering the claimed invention as a whole. The Board found, on the other hand, that no showing was made of unexpected results for the claimed compositions compared with the compositions of Sweeney. We agree. Clearly, in determining patentability the Board was obligated to consider all the evidence of the properties of the claimed invention as a whole, compared with those of the prior art. However, after the PTO made a showing that the prior art compositions suggested the claimed compositions, the burden was on the applicant to overcome the presumption of obviousness that was created, and that was not done. For example, she produced no evidence that her compositions possessed properties not possessed by the prior art compositions. Nor did she show that the prior art compositions and use were so lacking in significance that there was no motivation for others to make obvious variants. There was no attempt to argue the relative importance of the claimed compositions compared with the prior art.

[T]he cases [cited in the dissent] establish that if an examiner considers that he has found prior art close enough to the claimed invention to give one skilled in the relevant chemical art the motivation to make close relatives (homologs, analogs, isomers, etc.) of the prior art compound(s), then there arises what has been called a presumption of obviousness or a *prima facie* case of obviousness. *In re Henze*, 181 F.2d 196, 85 U.S.P.Q. 261 (CCPA 1950); *In re Hass*, 141 F.2d 122, 127, 130, 60 U.S.P.Q. 544, 548, 552 (CCPA 1944). The burden then shifts to the applicant, who then can present arguments and/or data to show that what appears to be obvious, is not in fact that, when the invention is looked at as a whole. *In re Papesch*, 315 F.2d 381, 137 U.S.P.Q. 43 (CCPA 1963). The cases of *Hass* and *Henze* established the rule that, unless an applicant showed that the prior art compound lacked the property or advantage asserted for the claimed compound, the presumption of unpatentability was not overcome.

Exactly what facts constituted a *prima facie* case varied from case to case, but it was not the law that, where an applicant asserted that an invention possessed properties not known to be possessed by the prior art, no *prima facie* case was established unless the reference also showed the novel activity. There are cases, cited in the dissent, in which a *prima facie* case was not established based on lack of structural similarity. Some of the cited cases also contained language suggesting that the fact that the claimed and the prior art compounds possessed the same activity were added factors in the establishment of the *prima facie* case. Those cases did not say, however, as the dissent asserts, that, in the absence of the similarity of activities, there would have been no *prima facie* case.

Stemniski ... overruled *[In re] Henze*[, 181 F.2d 196, 85 U.S.P.Q. 261 (CCPA 1950),] and *In re Riden*, 318 F.2d 761, 138 U.S.P.Q. 112 (CCPA 1963) (a case similar to *Henze*), "to the extent that [they] are inconsistent with the views expressed herein." 444 F.2d at 587, 170 U.S.P.Q. at 348. The views that were expressed therein were that:

> [w]here the prior art reference neither discloses nor suggests a utility for certain described compounds, why should it be said that a reference makes obvious to one of ordinary skill in the art an isomer, homolog or analog or related structure, when that mythical, but intensely practical, person knows of no "practical" reason to make the reference compounds, much less any structurally related compounds?

Id. at 586, 170 U.S.P.Q. at 347. Thus, *Stemniski*, rather than destroying the established practice of rejecting closely-related compounds as *prima facie* obvious, qualified it by holding that a presumption is not created when the reference compound is so lacking in any utility that there is no motivation to make close relatives.

Properties ... *are* relevant to the creation of a *prima facie* case in the sense of affecting the motivation of a researcher to make compounds closely related to or suggested by a prior art compound, but it is not required, as stated in the dissent, that the prior art disclose or suggest the properties newly-discovered by an applicant in order for there to be a *prima facie* case of obviousness.

The dissent cites the seminal case of *Papesch*, suggesting that it rejected the principle that we now "adopt," thereby implying that we are weakening *Papesch*. We are doing nothing of the sort. *Papesch* indeed stated that a compound and all of its properties are inseparable and must be considered in the determination of obviousness. We heartily agree and intend not to retreat from *Papesch* one inch. *Papesch*, however, did not deal with the requirements for establishing a *prima facie* case, but whether the examiner had to consider the properties of an invention at all, when there was a presumption of obviousness. 315 F.2d at 391, 137 U.S.P.Q. at 51. The reference disclosed a lower homolog of the claimed compounds, so it was clear that impliedly a *prima facie* case existed; the question was whether, under those circumstances, the biological data were admissible at all. The court ruled that they were, *id.* at 391, 137 U.S.P.Q. at 51, and we agree with that result. The dissent quotes the brief passage at the end of the *Papesch* opinion to the effect that the prior art must "at least to a degree" disclose the applicant's desired property, *id.* at 392, 137 U.S.P.Q. at 52, but this brief mention was not central to the decision in that case and did not refer to the requirements of a *prima facie* case. *Papesch* is irrelevant to the question of the requirements for a *prima facie* case, which is the question we have here.

The dissent mentions positions advanced by the Commissioner, including the *In re Mod*, 408 F.2d 1055, 161 U.S.P.Q. 281 (CCPA 1969), and *In re De Montmollin*, 344 F.2d 976, 145 U.S.P.Q. 416 (CCPA 1965) decisions. [W]e note that neither *Mod* nor *De Montmollin* dealt with the requirements of a *prima facie* case. They concerned the question whether the existence of a new property for claimed compounds in addition to a property common to both the claimed and related prior art compounds rendered the claimed compounds unobvious. We are not faced with that question today.

Other cases, e.g., *In re Gyurik*, 596 F.2d 1012, 1018, 201 U.S.P.Q. 552, 557–58 (CCPA 1979) ("[n]o common-properties presumption rises from the mere occurrence of a claimed compound at an intermediate point in a conventional reaction yielding a specifically named prior art compound"), have qualified the original rule of the Hass–Henze cases, but it is clear that they have not enunciated a rule that, in order to make a *prima facie* case of obviousness, the examiner must show that the prior art suggests a new property discovered by applicant. In not accepting that principle today, as urged in the dissent, we are therefore not retreating from the recent trend of case law development or changing the law.

Another example of the lack of direct pertinence of a case quoted in the dissent is *May*, which the dissent cites as an example of the consistent line of decisions to the effect that "both structure and properties must be suggested in the prior art before a *prima facie* case of obviousness was deemed made." This case does not state that both structure and properties "must" be suggested. The claimed and prior art compositions were both disclosed as having analgesic activity; it was conceded that a *prima facie* case was made out, but the court concluded that applicants had rebutted the presumed expectation that structurally similar compounds have similar properties with a showing of an actual unexpected difference of properties between the claimed compound and the prior art. 574 F.2d at 1095, 197 U.S.P.Q. at 611. The applicant in that case thus made a showing that Dillon did not make in this case.

Properties must be considered in the overall evaluation of obviousness, and the lack of any disclosure of useful properties for a prior art compound may indicate a lack of motivation to make related compounds, thereby precluding a *prima facie* case, but it is not correct that similarity of structure and a suggestion of *the activity of an applicant's compounds* in the prior art are necessary before a *prima facie* case is established.

Notes

1. Methods of Making. Consider the situation of a "structurally obvious" variation where the prior art discloses a use for the prior art compound, but no operative method to make a claimed variation. Hence, because the prior art supplies no operative method known or obvious to a worker skilled in the art to make the claimed compound, this situation would compel a conclusion of nonobviousness. See, *In re Hoeksema*, 399 F.2d 269, 158 U.S.P.Q. 596 (CCPA 1968) (N-methyl "homolog" of known amine established by affidavit as requiring inventive synthesis); see also *In re Grose*, 592 F.2d 1161, 201 U.S.P.Q. 57 (CCPA 1979) ("the absence of a known or obvious process for making the claimed compounds overcomes a presumption that the compounds are obvious".). Should the patentability of a product be predicated on the nonobviousness of the process of making the product? If not, why not? *See* 2 MARTIN J. ADELMAN, PATENT LAW PERSPECTIVES, § 2.6[10] at notes 93 and 94 (2d ed. 1991) for a general discussion of the applicability of this rule to certain biotechnology inventions.

2. New Uses. If a chemist invents a new chemical compound that is prima facie obvious (due to a prior art compound that teaches use of a closely related compound), should this inventor be able to overcome the obviousness problem by arguing that he discovered a new use for his compound that is far more important than the one known in the art? What if the closely related prior art compound, in fact, has the same newly discovered property? Why can't the inventor overcome the obviousness objection based on the newly discovered use? Is it proper to use unknown properties of prior art compounds to reject a claim of overcoming a prima facie obviousness rejection? Consider the following controversial analysis while thinking about these questions:

In discussing patent policy concerning product claims for chemical compositions, it is helpful to begin by remembering that there are two kinds of claims known to patent law, a claim to a physical entity (e.g., product, apparatus) and a claim to a physical activity (e.g., method, process, use). If available, an applicant, if required to make a choice, normally would want a patent on the product for which he has discovered a use rather than on a method of use because of ease of enforcement and because the product patent will cover additional uses discovered by others. In other words a product claim is easier to enforce and of greater scope. Still, the law does not require an election since both types of claims may be obtained based on the same invention, provided that the invention is one that justifies the grant of a product claim. Thus, patent law informed by policy must set standards for deciding when the discovery of a use should entitle the inventor to both a use and a product claim.

One who discovers a use for a chemical composition may not have made it for the first time. Arguably, one who discovers the first practical use for a known composition should have a good claim to a patent covering it. The public, before the inventor came along, lacked a use for it and arguably should reward the discoverer of that use with control over the composition. Yet, the law is clear that one who discovers this first use, but is not the first to create it, may not receive a product patent covering the existing product. This principle is rooted in the idea that one cannot patent what is already in existence, but it creates no barrier to a patent on a product that is structurally obvious. Such a product would be expected to have the same utility, but it is not in existence since it neither exists physically nor is it described in an enabling publication. Thus there is no legal bar to granting a patent on such a composition. The inventor has both brought the composition into existence and discovered a utility for it. Of course, the actual making of the composition may have been the routine application of well-known chemical principles, but since it did not formally exist, the question of granting a product claim to it can and should be decided based on patent policy. Here there is general agreement that granting a product patent to one who both formally brings the invention into existence and discovers a practical use for it, is sound policy for it provides considerable encouragement for the act of bringing forth and discovering a practical use of a product. This added incentive counterbalances the discouragement to third-party discovery of other uses.

The same reasoning supports permitting the discoverer of a new use for a new composition to patent that composition so long as the use discovered is, on balance, more important than the use known to the art. This would provide an added incentive to those seeking to discover new properties and at the same time, protect the public from having to pay for the known uses unless the new discovery is sufficiently important on balance to justify that imposition. The discoverer of that use should not lose his patent merely because his discover is so broad that it embraces compositions existing in the prior art. Thus, sound public policy would have permitted Dillon, if she had chosen to do so, to overcome the *prima facie* case against her by showing that her discovery of soot reduction was far more important, both technically and commercially, that the known dewatering use.

2 MARTIN J. ADELMAN, PATENT LAW PERSPECTIVES, § 2.6[7.–3–2] at n.132 (2d ed. 1996).

§ 7.3[b]   Chemical Obviousness in the setting of Hatch–Waxman

In 1984, Congress enacted the Hatch–Waxman Act to regulate the interplay between generic drug companies and research-based drug companies when a patented drug nears the end of its term. The Drug Price Competition and Patent Term Restoration Act, the Hatch–Waxman Act, amended the Federal Food, Drug, and Cosmetic Act, 21 U.S.C. §§ 301–397 (1994), to permit filing of an ANDA (abbreviated new drug application) to expedite FDA approval of a generic version of a drug previously approved by the FDA. See, e.g., *Bayer AG v. Elan Pharm. Research Corp.*, 212 F.3d 1241, 1244, 54 U.S.P.Q.2d 1711, 1712 (Fed.Cir. 2000). Generic drug companies need to perform tests on their products to satisfy Food and Drug Administration standards. In *Roche Prods. Inc. v. Bolar Pharm. Co.*, 733 F.2d 858, 221 U.S.P.Q. 937 (Fed.Cir.1984), the Federal Circuit ruled that the so-called experimental use exception did not allow generic companies to begin to make or use the patented drugs to perform pre-marketing tests while the drugs remained under patent. The Hatch–Waxman Act, as part of a larger compromise that gave research drug companies an extension of patent terms on drugs delayed in reaching the market by FDA standards, permitted generic drug companies to begin testing under some circumstances. The Hatch–Waxman Act also created procedures for challenging patent validity in the context of accelerating production of generic drugs for the marketplace. The Hatch–Waxman Act has taken on great significance for the pharmaceutical industry.

YAMANOUCHI PHARMACEUTICAL CO., LTD. v. DANBURY PHARMACAL, INC.

United States Court of Appeals, Federal Circuit, 2000.
231 F.3d 1339, 56 U.S.P.Q.2d 1641.

Before NEWMAN, RADER, and GAJARZA, CIRCUIT JUDGES.

RADER, CIRCUIT JUDGE.

On a motion for judgment as a matter of law (JMOL), the United States District Court for the Southern District of New York upheld the validity of claim 4 of U.S. Patent No. 4,283,408 (the '408 patent) in favor of Yamanouchi Pharmaceutical Co., Ltd. and Merck & Co., Inc. (collectively, Yamanouchi). Because the district court correctly upheld the validity of the '408 patent, this court affirms.

I.

The '408 patent, issued to Yamanouchi on August 11, 1981, relates to inhibitors of gastric acid secretion. Claim 4 of the '408 patent, the only claim at issue, claims famotidine for treating heartburn and ulcers. Famotidine belongs to a class of compounds known as histamine sub2 antagonists (H sub2 antagonists), which inhibit production of stomach acid. As Figure 1 illustrates, the general chemical structure of H sub2 antagonists includes a "substituted heterocycle" group, a "alkyl containing" chain (called a "bridge"), and a "polar tail," connected in that order:

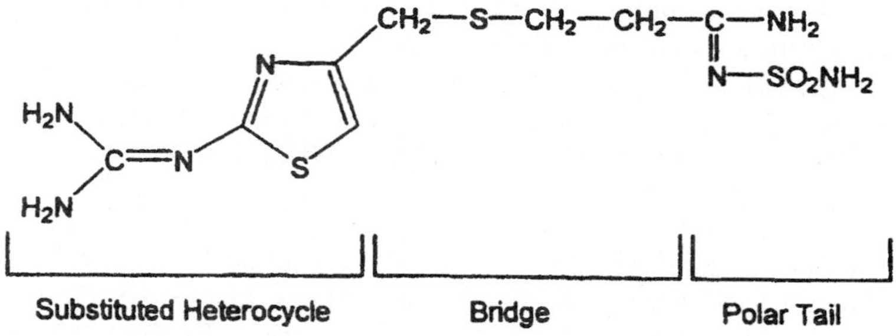

$$CH_2-S-CH_2-CH_2-\underset{\underset{N-SO_2NH_2}{\|}}{C}-NH_2$$

$$\underset{H_2N}{\overset{H_2N}{\diagdown}}C=N$$

| Substituted Heterocycle | Bridge | Polar Tail |

Figure 1 – Famotidine

During the 1960s and 70s, drug manufacturers searched for H sub2 antagonists with improved pharmacological properties, including low toxicity, high activity, and lack of side effects. Research revealed hundreds of thousands of potential compounds. Indeed, pharmaceutical companies synthesized more than 11,000 H sub2 antagonist compounds. Very rarely, however, were these compounds pharmacologically suitable H sub2 antagonists. Notable failures include tiotidine, which caused cancer in rats; burimamide, which was ineffective for oral dosing; metiamide, which caused white blood cell loss; lupitidine, which caused precancerous lesions in rats; and oxmetidine, which caused hepatitis.

Of the 11,000 candidates for suitable compounds, fewer than fifty showed enough promise to warrant human clinical trials. Ultimately, the FDA approved only four for consumer use: cimetidine (approved in 1977, sold as TAGAMET ®), ranitidine (approved in 1983, sold as ZANTA ®), famotidine (approved in 1986, sold as PEPCID ®), and nizatidine (approved in 1988, sold as AXID ®). Famotidine, the claimed compound at issue, has been extremely successful. In 1996, for example, prescription sales of famotidine in the United States alone reached over 690 million dollars.

Danbury is a subsidiary of Schein, which produces and markets generic drugs. In January 1997, Danbury filed an Abbreviated New Drug Application (ANDA) with the Food and Drug Administration (FDA) seeking approval to market generic famotidine. Under the ANDA procedure, an applicant seeks FDA approval to market a generic drug. Under the Hatch–Waxman Act, an ANDA filer must certify one of the following four statements concerning the previously approved drug: it is not patented (paragraph I certification), its patent has expired (paragraph II certification), its patent soon will expire on a specified date (paragraph III certification), or its patent "is invalid or will not be infringed by the manufacture, use, or sale of the new drug" covered by the ANDA (paragraph IV certification). To obtain approval of an ANDA, the FDCA requires only that the generic drug is the "bioequivalent" of the previously approved drug.

In Danbury's ANDA for famotidine, Danbury made a paragraph IV certification that claim 4 of the '408 patent is invalid. As the statute requires, Danbury, on March 26, 1997, sent Yamanouchi a Patent Certification Notice Letter. This certification letter informed Yamanouchi of Danbury's paragraph IV ANDA filing. Accompanying the certification letter were affidavits from Drs. Bernard Loev and John K. Siepler supporting Danbury's invalidity certification. The Notice Letter contained, as the statute requires, an analysis of the prior art and the reasons for the asserted invalidity.

Within forty-five days of receiving the certification letter, Yamanouchi filed suit against Danbury alleging infringement of the '408 patent. The parties agreed to a bench trial. After Danbury presented its last witness on obviousness, Yamanouchi moved for JMOL under Fed. R.Civ.P. 52(c). With that motion, Yamanouchi argued that Danbury had not shown by clear and convincing evidence that claim 4 of the '408 patent would have been obvious at the time of invention. The district court granted Yamanouchi's JMOL motion. Specifically, the district court found that Danbury had not shown any motivation to combine selected portions of various prior art compounds to create the specific compound famotidine and to obtain its extraordinary properties. The district court characterized Danbury's case for obviousness as largely hindsight, speculation, and argument without an adequate foundation. Based on those findings, the district court determined that Danbury willfully infringed the '408 patent.

II.

Obviousness rests on several critical factual underpinnings: (1) the scope and content of the prior art, (2) the differences between the prior art and the claimed invention, (3) the level of skill in the art, and (4) the objective indicia of nonobviousness. *Graham v. John Deere Co.*, 383 U.S. 1, 17(1966). For a chemical compound, a prima facie case of obviousness requires "structural similarity between claimed and prior art subject matter ... where the prior art gives reason or motivation to make the claimed compositions." *In re Dillon*, 919 F.2d 688, 692 (Fed.Cir.1990) (en banc). "[A] reasonable expectation of success, not absolute predictability" supports a conclusion of obviousness. *In re Longi*, 759 F.2d 887, 896 (Fed.Cir.1985).

As noted earlier, the district court discerned that Danbury had not proven any motivation to combine prior art references to produce the claimed invention. This court has recently reemphasized the importance of the motion to combine. *In re Rouffet*, 149 F.3d 1350, 1357–58 (Fed.Cir.1998).

At the heart of this validity dispute is whether one of skill in this art would have found motivation to combine pieces from one compound in a prior art patent with a piece of another compound in the second prior art patent through a series of manipulations. According to Danbury, one of skill in the art would have considered it obvious to select the example 44 compound from Yamanouchi's U.S. Patent No. 4,252,819 (the '819 patent) and tiotidine from the '378 patent to use as leads for making famotidine. These compounds, respectively, are three and eleven times more active than cimetidine—the benchmark compound at the time of invention (Figure 2). After selecting these two lead compounds, Danbury continues, it would have been obvious to combine the polar tail from example 44 (Figure 3) with the substituted heterocycle from tiotidine (Figure 4), thus creating the intermediate compound (Figure 5). Thereafter, to create famotidine, Danbury argues that it would have been obvious to perform a bioisosteric substitution of the carbamoyl ($CONH_2$) group in the intermediate compound with a sulfamoyl group (SO_2NH_2).

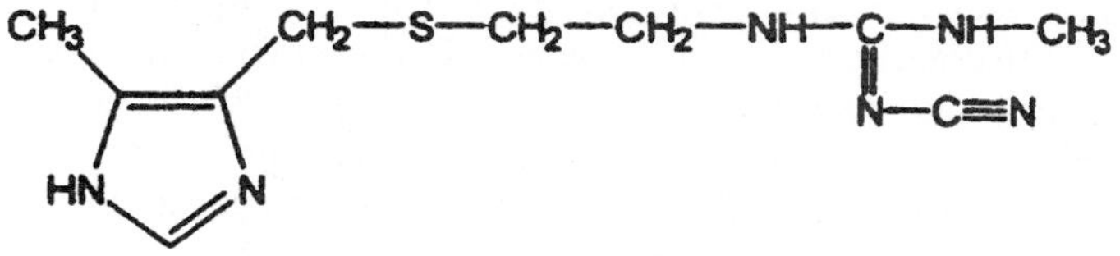

Figure 2 – Cimetidine

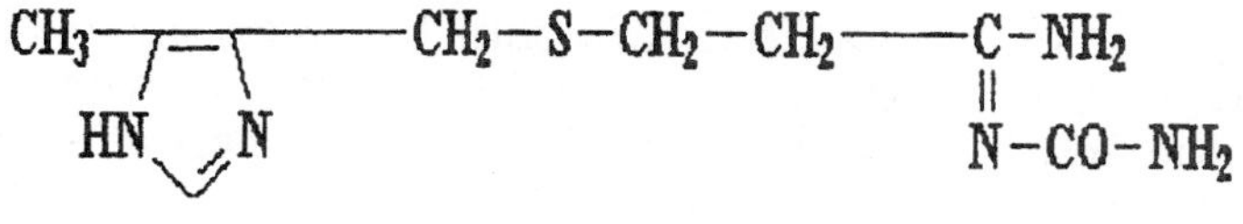

Figure 3 – Example 44

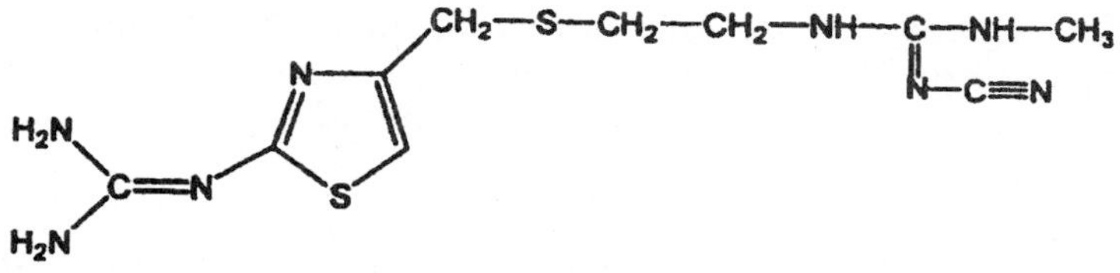

Figure 4 – Tiotidine

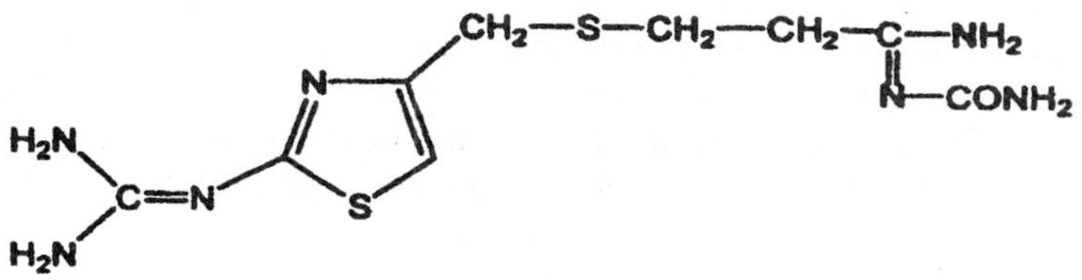

Figure 5 – Intermediate Compound

The district court correctly rejected Danbury's argument. Specifically, Danbury did not show sufficient motivation for one of ordinary skill in the art at the time of invention to take any one of the following steps, let alone the entire complex combination: (1) selecting example 44 as a lead compound, (2) combining the polar tail from example 44 with the substituted heterocycle from tiotidine, and (3) substituting the carbamoyl (CONH sub2) group in the intermediate compound with a sulfamoyl group (SO sub2 NH sub2) to create famotidine.

At the outset, Danbury did not show the required motivation for selecting example 44 as a lead compound. Danbury's assertion of motivation rests on the fact that example 44 is three times more active than cimetidine. That activity alone, however, is not sufficient motivation. As the trial court noted, other prior art references disclosed compounds with H sub2 antagonist activity up to ten times higher than cimetidine. If activity alone was the sole motivation, other more active compounds would have been the obvious choices, not example 44.

Danbury also does not show the motivation to combine the polar tail of example 44 with the substituted heterocycle of tiotidine, then to substitute the carbamoyl with a sulfamoyl. To show such motivation, Danbury argues only that an ordinary medicinal chemist would have reasonably expected the resulting compound to exhibit the baseline level of H sub2 antagonist activity. The baseline level of activity is a mere 1/165 th the activity of cimetidine. This level of motivation does not show a "reasonable expectation of success." *In re Longi*, 759 F.2d at 897. The success of discovering famotidine was not discovering one of the tens of thousands of compounds that exhibit baseline H sub2 antagonist activity. Rather, the success was finding a compound that had high activity, few side effects, and lacked toxicity. As Danbury's expert testified, the ordinary medicinal chemist would not have expected famotidine to have the "most desirable combination of pharmacological properties" that it possesses.

Furthermore, the prior art offers no suggestion to pursue the particular order of manipulating parts of the compounds. Danbury's proposed obvious course of invention requires a very specific series of steps. Any deviation in the order of combination would have taught away from famotidine. If, for instance, the sulfamoyl group were substituted for the carbamoyl group on example 44 without attaching the substituted heterocycle from tiotidine, the evidence showed that the resulting compound would have 1/100 times the activity of cimetidine. Famotidine, on the other hand, has 40 times the activity of cimetidine. Danbury offered no evidence suggesting what might have led an ordinary artisan in this field to follow the precise steps that produced a remarkable invention.

Danbury falls far short of satisfying its burden of showing a prima facie case for structural obviousness by clear and convincing evidence. Instead, as the district court aptly concluded, this case "has all the earmarks of somebody looking at this from hindsight." Because Danbury did not show even a prima facie case for obviousness, this court has considered, but need not separately address, the strong objective evidence of non-obviousness.

Accordingly, this court agrees with the district court's finding that Danbury was fully heard within the meaning of Rule 52(c). This court therefore affirms the district court's grant of JMOL, sustaining the validity of claim 4 of the '408 patent.

Notes

1. Cursory Treatment of Objective Criteria. Although the Federal Circuit, in dicta, gives great emphasis to objective criteria, few cases examine objective criteria in detail. *Cf. Ecolochem, Inc. v. Southern Calif. Edison*, 227 F.3d 1361, 56 U.S.P.Q.2d 1065 (Fed.Cir.2000). Does this case suggest the reason that objective criteria receive less attention than their purported importance would suggest (namely, the prima facie case usually disposes of obviousness without extensive analysis of objective criteria)?

2. The Starting Point in Obviousness Analyses. In this case, the Federal Circuit determined that it was not obvious to select Example 44 as the starting point to make famotidine. Compare this analysis with the English court in *Windsurfing,* which determined that it would have been obvious to start with the Darby article and make revisions to arrive at the claimed sailboard.

§ 7.3[c]   Obviousness for Biotechnology

As already discussed, chemical arts are already a novel art field that receives somewhat novel treatment in U.S. obviousness case law. The doctrine of obviousness has placed great emphasis on structure for chemical inventions. As a matter of science, chemistry's emphasis on structure does not have the same significance for genetic engineering in the biotechnology field. Unlike chemistry with over a hundred elements and countless isotopes bonded in infinite ways, genetic engineering uses only four building blocks (the nucleotide bases, Adenine, Guanine, Cytocine, and Thymine)—always linked in two pairs. In some ways, this aspect of biotechnology more resembles computer technology—1s and 0s constantly repeating to carry a code—than chemistry. In other words, biotechnology often features code breaking skills more often than chemical structure skills. Libraries of past codes (cDNA sequences) and known cloning methods (which design a probe that will bind or hybridize with the desired cDNA sequence) are the tools of biotechnology. Chemistry's emphasis on structure, therefore, may have limitations in its application to biotechnology just as it would have limitations in application to computer technology where the "structure" of a computer program can morph from hardware structure to software code with the touch of a button.

With this cursory introduction to differences between chemistry and biotechnology, the Federal Circuit's application of chemical standards for obviousness to biotechnological inventions takes on some context.

IN RE DEUEL

United States Court of Appeals, Federal Circuit, 1995.
51 F.3d 1552, 34 U.S.P.Q.2d 1210.

Before ARCHER, CHIEF JUDGE, NIES and LOURIE, CIRCUIT JUDGES.

LOURIE, CIRCUIT JUDGE.

Thomas F. Deuel, Yue–Sheng Li, Ned R. Siegel, and Peter G. Milner (collectively "Deuel") appeal from the November 30, 1993 decision of the U.S. Patent and Trademark Office Board of Patent Appeals and Interferences affirming the examiner's final rejection of claims 4–7 of application

Serial No. 07/542,232, entitled "Heparin–Binding Growth Factor," as unpatentable on the ground of obviousness under 35 U.S.C. § 103 (1988). Because the Board erred in concluding that Deuel's claims 5 and 7 directed to specific cDNA molecules would have been obvious in light of the applied references, and no other basis exists in the record to support the rejection with respect to claims 4 and 6 generically covering all possible DNA molecules coding for the disclosed proteins, we reverse.

BACKGROUND

The claimed invention relates to isolated and purified DNA and cDNA molecules encoding heparin-binding growth factors ("HBGFs"). HBGFs are proteins that stimulate mitogenic activity (cell division) and thus facilitate the repair or replacement of damaged or diseased tissue. DNA (deoxyribonucleic acid) is a generic term which encompasses an enormous number of complex macromolecules made up of nucleotide units. DNAs consist of four different nucleotides containing the nitrogenous bases adenine, guanine, cytosine, and thymine. A sequential grouping of three such nucleotides (a "codon") codes for one amino acid. A DNA's sequence of codons thus determines the sequence of amino acids assembled during protein synthesis. Since there are 64 possible codons, but only 20 natural amino acids, most amino acids are coded for by more than one codon. This is referred to as the "redundancy" or "degeneracy" of the genetic code.

DNA functions as a blueprint of an organism's genetic information. It is the major component of genes, which are located on chromosomes in the cell nucleus. Only a small part of chromosomal DNA encodes functional proteins. Messenger ribonucleic acid ("mRNA") is a similar molecule that is made or transcribed from DNA as part of the process of protein synthesis. Complementary DNA ("cDNA") is a complementary copy ("clone") of mRNA, made in the laboratory by reverse transcription of mRNA. Like mRNA, cDNA contains only the protein-encoding regions of DNA. Thus, once a cDNA's nucleotide sequence is known, the amino acid sequence of the protein for which it codes may be predicted using the genetic code relationship between codons and amino acids. The reverse is not true, however, due to the degeneracy of the code. Many other DNAs may code for a particular protein. The functional relationships between DNA, mRNA, cDNA, and a protein may conveniently be expressed as follows:

$$\begin{array}{ccccc}
\text{genomic} & & & & \\
\text{DNA} & \longrightarrow & \text{mRNA} & \longrightarrow & \text{protein} \\
& & \updownarrow & & \uparrow \\
& & \text{cDNA} & & \text{other DNAs}
\end{array}$$

Collections ("libraries") of DNA and cDNA molecules derived from various species may be constructed in the laboratory or obtained from commercial sources. Complementary DNA libraries contain a mixture of cDNA clones reverse-transcribed from the mRNAs found in a specific tissue source. Complementary DNA libraries are tissue-specific because proteins and their corresponding mRNAs are only made ("expressed") in specific tissues, depending upon the protein. Genomic DNA ("gDNA") libraries, by contrast, theoretically contain all of a species' chromosomal DNA. The molecules present in cDNA and DNA libraries may be of unknown function and chemical structure, and the proteins which they encode may be unknown. However, one may attempt to retrieve molecules of interest from cDNA or gDNA libraries by screening such libraries with a gene probe, which is a synthetic radiolabelled nucleic acid sequence designed to bond ("hybridize") with a target complementary base sequence. Such "gene cloning" techniques thus exploit the fact that the bases in DNA always hybridize in complementary pairs: adenine bonds with thymine and guanine bonds with cytosine. A gene probe for potentially isolating DNA or cDNA encoding a protein may be designed once the protein's amino acid sequence, or a portion thereof, is known.

As disclosed in Deuel's patent application, Deuel isolated and purified HBGF from bovine uterine tissue, found that it exhibited mitogenic activity, and determined the first 25 amino acids of the protein's N-terminal sequence. Deuel then isolated a cDNA molecule encoding bovine uterine HBGF by screening a bovine uterine cDNA library with an oligonucleotide probe designed using the experimentally determined N-terminal sequence of the HBGF. Deuel purified and sequenced the cDNA molecule, which was found to consist of a sequence of 1196 nucleotide base pairs. From the cDNA's nucleotide sequence, Deuel then predicted the complete amino acid sequence of bovine uterine HBGF disclosed in Deuel's application.

Deuel also isolated a cDNA molecule encoding human placental HBGF by screening a human placental cDNA library using the isolated bovine uterine cDNA clone as a probe. Deuel purified and sequenced the human placental cDNA clone, which was found to consist of a sequence of 961 nucleotide base pairs. From the nucleotide sequence of the cDNA molecule encoding human placental HBGF, Deuel predicted the complete amino acid sequence of human placental HBGF disclosed in Deuel's application. The predicted human placental and bovine uterine HBGFs each have 168 amino acids and calculated molecular weights of 18.9 kD. Of the 168 amino acids present in the two HBGFs discovered by Deuel, 163 are identical. Deuel's application does not describe the chemical structure of, or state how to isolate and purify, any DNA or cDNA molecule except the disclosed human placental and bovine uterine cDNAs, which are the subject of claims 5 and 7.

Claims 4–7 on appeal are all independent claims and read, in relevant part, as follows:

4. A purified and isolated DNA sequence consisting of a sequence encoding human heparin binding growth factor of 168 amino acids having the following amino acid sequence: Met Gln Ala ... [remainder of 168 amino acid sequence].

5. The purified and isolated cDNA of human heparin-binding growth factor having the following nucleotide sequence: GTCAAAGGCA ... [remainder of 961 nucleotide sequence].

6. A purified and isolated DNA sequence consisting of a sequence encoding bovine heparin binding growth factor of 168 amino acids having the following amino acid sequence: Met Gln Thr ... [remainder of 168 amino acid sequence].

7. The purified and isolated cDNA of bovine heparin-binding growth factor having the following nucleotide sequence: GAGTGGA-GAG ... [remainder of 1196 nucleotide sequence].

Claims 4 and 6 generically encompass all isolated/purified DNA sequences (natural and synthetic) encoding human and bovine HBGFs, despite the fact that Deuel's application does not describe the chemical structure of, or tell how to obtain, any DNA or cDNA except the two disclosed cDNA molecules. Because of the redundancy of the genetic code, claims 4 and 6 each encompass an enormous number of DNA molecules, including the isolated/purified chromosomal DNAs encoding the human and bovine proteins. Claims 5 and 7, on the other hand, are directed to the specifically disclosed cDNA molecules encoding human and bovine HBGFs, respectively.

During prosecution, the examiner rejected claims 4–7 under 35 U.S.C. § 103 as unpatentable over the combined teachings of Bohlen and Maniatis. The Bohlen reference discloses a group of protein growth factors designated as heparin-binding brain mitogens ("HBBMs") useful in treating burns and promoting the formation, maintenance, and repair of tissue, particularly neural tissue. Bohlen isolated three such HBBMs from human and bovine brain tissue. These proteins have respective molecular weights of 15 kD, 16 kD, and 18 kD. Bohlen determined the first 19 amino acids of the proteins' N-terminal sequences, which were found to be identical for human and bovine HBBMs. Bohlen teaches that HBBMs are brain-specific, and suggests that the proteins may be homologous between species. The reference provides no teachings concerning DNA or cDNA coding for HBBMs.

Maniatis describes a method of isolating DNAs or cDNAs by screening a DNA or cDNA library with a gene probe. The reference outlines a general technique for cloning a gene; it does not describe how to isolate a particular DNA or cDNA molecule. Maniatis does not discuss certain steps necessary to isolate a target cDNA, e.g., selecting a tissue-specific cDNA library containing a target cDNA and designing an oligonucleotide probe that will hybridize with the target cDNA.

The examiner asserted that, given Bohlen's disclosure of a heparin-binding protein and its N-terminal sequence and Maniatis's gene cloning method, it would have been prima facie obvious to one of ordinary skill in the art at the time of the invention to clone a gene for HBGF. According to the examiner, Bohlen's published N-terminal sequence would have motivated a person of ordinary skill in the art to clone such a gene because cloning the gene would allow recombinant production of HBGF, a useful protein. The examiner reasoned that a person of ordinary skill in the art could have designed a gene probe based on Bohlen's disclosed N-terminal sequence, then screened a DNA library in accordance with Maniatis's gene cloning method to isolate a gene encoding an HBGF. The examiner did not distinguish between claims 4 and 6 generically directed to all DNA sequences encoding human and bovine HBGFs and claims 5 and 7 reciting particular cDNAs.

In reply, Deuel argued, inter alia, that Bohlen teaches away from the claimed cDNA molecules because Bohlen suggests that HBBMs are brain-specific and, thus, a person of ordinary skill in the art would not have tried to isolate corresponding cDNA clones from human placental and bovine uterine cDNA libraries. The examiner made the rejection final, however, asserting that

> [t]he starting materials are not relevant in this case, because it was well known in the art at the time the invention was made that proteins, especially the general class of heparin binding proteins, are highly homologous between species and tissue type. It would have been entirely obvious to attempt to isolate a known protein from different tissue types and even different species.

No prior art was cited to support the proposition that it would have been obvious to screen human placental and bovine uterine cDNA libraries for the claimed cDNA clones. Presumably, the examiner was relying on Bohlen's suggestion that HBBMs may be homologous between species, although the examiner did not explain how homology between species suggests homology between tissue types.

The Board affirmed the examiner's final rejection. In its opening remarks, the Board noted that it is "constantly advised by the patent examiners, who are highly skilled in this art, that cloning procedures are routine in the art." According to the Board, "the examiners urge that when the sequence of a protein is placed into the public domain, the gene is also placed into the public domain because of the routine nature of cloning techniques." Addressing the rejection at issue, the Board determined that Bohlen's disclosure of the existence and isolation of HBBM, a functional protein, would also advise a person of ordinary skill in the art that a gene exists encoding HBBM. The Board found that a person of ordinary skill in the art would have been motivated to isolate such a gene because the protein has useful mitogenic properties, and isolating the gene for HBBM would permit large quantities of the protein to be produced for study and possible commercial use. Like the examiner, the Board asserted, without explanation, that HBBMs are the same as HBGFs and that the genes encoding these proteins are identical. The Board concluded that "the Bohlen reference would have suggested to those of ordinary skill in this art that they should make the gene, and the Maniatis reference would have taught a technique for 'making' the gene with a reasonable expectation of success." Responding to Deuel's argument that the claimed cDNA clones were isolated from human placental and bovine uterine cDNA libraries, whereas the combined teachings of Bohlen and Maniatis would only have suggested screening a brain tissue cDNA library, the Board stated that "the claims before us are directed to the product and not the method of isolation. Appellants have not shown that the claimed DNA was not present in and could not have been readily isolated from the brain tissue utilized by Bohlen." Deuel now appeals.

DISCUSSION

On appeal, Deuel challenges the Board's determination that the applied references establish a prima facie case of obviousness. In response, the PTO maintains that the claimed invention would have been prima facie obvious over the combined teachings of Bohlen and Maniatis. Thus, the appeal raises the important question whether the combination of a prior art reference teaching a method of gene cloning, together with a reference disclosing a partial amino acid sequence of a protein, may render DNA and cDNA molecules encoding the protein prima facie obvious under § 103.

Deuel argues that the PTO failed to follow the proper legal standard in determining that the claimed cDNA molecules would have been prima facie obvious despite the lack of structurally similar compounds in the prior art. Deuel argues that the PTO has not cited a reference teaching cDNA molecules, but instead has improperly rejected the claims based on the alleged obviousness of a method of making the molecules. We agree.

Because Deuel claims new chemical entities in structural terms, a prima facie case of unpatentability requires that the teachings of the prior art suggest the claimed compounds to a person of ordinary skill in the art. Normally a prima facie case of obviousness is based upon structural similarity, i.e., an established structural relationship between a prior art compound and the claimed compound. Structural relationships may provide the requisite motivation or suggestion to modify known compounds to obtain new compounds. For example, a prior art compound may suggest its homologs because homologs often have similar properties and therefore chemists of ordinary skill would ordinarily contemplate making them to try to obtain compounds with improved properties. Similarly, a known compound may suggest its analogs or isomers, either geometric isomers (cis v. trans) or position isomers (e.g., ortho v. para).

In all of these cases, however, the prior art teaches a specific, structurally-definable compound and the question becomes whether the prior art would have suggested making the specific molecular modifications necessary to achieve the claimed invention.

Here, the prior art does not disclose any relevant cDNA molecules, let alone close relatives of the specific, structurally-defined cDNA molecules of claims 5 and 7 that might render them obvious. Maniatis suggests an allegedly obvious process for trying to isolate cDNA molecules, but that, as we will indicate below, does not fill the gap regarding the subject matter of claims 5 and 7. Further, while the general idea of the claimed molecules, their function, and their general chemical nature may have been obvious from Bohlen's teachings, and the knowledge that some gene existed may have been clear, the precise cDNA molecules of claims 5 and 7 would not have been obvious over the Bohlen reference because Bohlen teaches proteins, not the claimed or closely related cDNA molecules. The redundancy of the genetic code precluded contemplation of or focus on the specific cDNA molecules of claims 5 and 7. Thus, one could not have conceived the subject matter of claims 5 and 7 based on the teachings in the cited prior art because, until the claimed molecules were actually isolated and purified, it would have been highly unlikely for one of ordinary skill in the art to contemplate what was ultimately obtained. What cannot be contemplated or conceived cannot be obvious.

The PTO's theory that one might have been motivated to try to do what Deuel in fact accomplished amounts to speculation and an impermissible hindsight reconstruction of the claimed invention. It also ignores the fact that claims 5 and 7 are limited to specific compounds, and any motivation that existed was a general one, to try to obtain a gene that was yet undefined and may have constituted many forms. A general motivation to search for some gene that exists does not necessarily make obvious a specifically-defined gene that is subsequently obtained as a result of that search. More is needed and it is not found here.

The genetic code relationship between proteins and nucleic acids does not overcome the deficiencies of the cited references. A prior art disclosure of the amino acid sequence of a protein does not necessarily render particular DNA molecules encoding the protein obvious because the redundancy of the genetic code permits one to hypothesize an enormous number of DNA sequences coding for the protein. No particular one of these DNAs can be obvious unless there is something in the prior art to lead to the particular DNA and indicate that it should be prepared. We recently held in *In re Baird*, 16 F.3d 380, 29 U.S.P.Q.2d 1550 (Fed.Cir.1994), that a broad genus does not necessarily render obvious each compound within its scope. Similarly, knowledge of a protein does not give one a conception of a particular DNA encoding it. Thus, a fortiori, Bohlen's disclosure of the N-terminal portion of a protein, which the PTO urges is the same as HBGF, would not have suggested the particular cDNA molecules defined by claims 5 and 7. This is so even though one skilled in the art knew that some DNA, albeit not in purified and isolated form, did exist. The compounds of claims 5 and 7 are specific compounds not suggested by the prior art. A different result might pertain, however, if there were prior art, e.g., a protein of sufficiently small size and simplicity, so that lacking redundancy, each possible DNA would be obvious over the protein. See *In re Petering*, 301

F.2d 676 (CCPA 1962) (prior art reference disclosing limited genus of 20 compounds rendered every species within the genus unpatentable). That is not the case here.

The PTO's focus on known methods for potentially isolating the claimed DNA molecules is also misplaced because the claims at issue define compounds, not methods. See *In re Bell*, 991 F.2d 781, 785, 26 U.S.P.Q.2d 1529, 1532 (Fed.Cir.1993). In *Bell*, the PTO asserted a rejection based upon the combination of a primary reference disclosing a protein (and its complete amino acid sequence) with a secondary reference describing a general method of gene cloning. We reversed the rejection, holding in part that "[t]he PTO's focus on Bell's method is misplaced. Bell does not claim a method. Bell claims compositions, and the issue is the obviousness of the claimed compositions, not of the method by which they are made." Id.

We today reaffirm the principle, stated in Bell, that the existence of a general method of isolating cDNA or DNA molecules is essentially irrelevant to the question whether the specific molecules themselves would have been obvious, in the absence of other prior art that suggests the claimed DNAs. A prior art disclosure of a process reciting a particular compound or obvious variant thereof as a product of the process is, of course, another matter, raising issues of anticipation under 35 U.S.C. § 102 as well as obviousness under § 103. Moreover, where there is prior art that suggests a claimed compound, the existence, or lack thereof, of an enabling process for making that compound is surely a factor in any patentability determination. See *In re Brown*, 329 F.2d 1006, 141 U.S.P.Q. 245 (CCPA 1964) (reversing rejection for lack of an enabling method of making the claimed compound). There must, however, still be prior art that suggests the claimed compound in order for a prima facie case of obviousness to be made out; as we have already indicated, that prior art was lacking here with respect to claims 5 and 7. Thus, even if, as the examiner stated, the existence of general cloning techniques, coupled with knowledge of a protein's structure, might have provided motivation to prepare a cDNA or made it obvious to prepare a cDNA, that does not necessarily make obvious a particular claimed cDNA. "Obvious to try" has long been held not to constitute obviousness. *In re O'Farrell*, 853 F.2d 894, 903, 7 U.S.P.Q.2d 1673, 1680–81 (Fed.Cir.1988). A general incentive does not make obvious a particular result, nor does the existence of techniques by which those efforts can be carried out. Thus, Maniatis's teachings, even in combination with Bohlen, fail to suggest the claimed invention.

The PTO argues that a compound may be defined by its process of preparation and therefore that a conceived process for making or isolating it provides a definition for it and can render it obvious. It cites *Amgen, Inc. v. Chugai Pharmaceutical Co.*, 927 F.2d 1200, 18 U.S.P.Q.2d 1016 (Fed.Cir.), *cert. denied*, 502 U.S. 856, 112 S.Ct. 169, 116 L.Ed.2d 132 (1991), for that proposition. We disagree. The fact that one can conceive a general process in advance for preparing an undefined compound does not mean that a claimed specific compound was precisely envisioned and therefore obvious. A substance may indeed be defined by its process of preparation. That occurs, however, when it has already been prepared by that process and one therefore knows that the result of that process is the stated compound. The process is part of the definition of the compound. But that is not possible in advance, especially when the hypothetical process is only a general one. Thus, a conceived method of preparing some undefined DNA does not define it with the precision necessary to render it obvious over the protein it encodes. We did not state otherwise in *Amgen*. See *Amgen*, 927 F.2d at 1206–09, 18 U.S.P.Q.2d at 1021–23 (isolated/purified human gene held nonobvious; no conception of gene without envisioning its precise identity despite conception of general process of preparation).

We conclude that, because the applied references do not teach or suggest the claimed cDNA molecules, the final rejection of claims 5 and 7 must be reversed. See also *Bell*, 991 F.2d at 784–85, 26 U.S.P.Q.2d at 1531–32 (human DNA sequences encoding IGF proteins nonobvious over asserted combination of references showing gene cloning method and complete amino acid sequences of IGFs).

Claims 4 and 6 are of a different scope than claims 5 and 7. As is conceded by Deuel, they generically encompass all DNA sequences encoding human and bovine HBGFs. Written in such a result-oriented form, claims 4 and 6 are thus tantamount to the general idea of all genes encoding the protein, all solutions to the problem. Such an idea might have been obvious from the complete amino acid sequence of the protein, coupled with knowledge of the genetic code, because this information may have enabled a person of ordinary skill in the art to envision the idea of, and, perhaps with the aid of a computer, even identify all members of the claimed genus. The Bohlen reference, however, only discloses a partial amino acid sequence, and thus it appears that, based on the above analysis, the claimed genus would not have been obvious over this prior art disclosure. We will therefore also reverse the final rejection of claims 4 and 6 because neither the Board nor the patent examiner articulated any separate reasons for holding these claims unpatentable apart from the grounds discussed above.

The Board's decision affirming the final rejection of claims 4–7 is reversed.

REVERSED.

Notes

1. What is the Obviousness Standard After *Deuel*? What exactly did the inventor Deuel contribute to the art that supported the grant of a patent? Would you agree with the proposition that the Federal Circuit in *Deuel* eliminated the need to consider § 103 where the claim is directed to a gene coding for a protein? If so, is there any public policy that you would assert supports this elimination of the obviousness requirement? In view of the redundancy of the genetic code, is a patent on the actual gene used in nature of any practical value?

Did *Deuel* overlook a prior and better test for obviousness in a biotech setting, namely *In re O'Farrell*, 853 F.2d 894, 7 U.S.P.Q.2d 1673 (Fed.Cir. 1988). In *O'Farrell*, Judge Rich stated: "[A]ll that is required [for obviousness] is a reasonable expectation of success." 853 F.2d at 903–04, 7 U.S.P.Q.2d at 1681. The *O'Farrell* court then acknowledged the processes that produce biotechnological inventions rather than deeming them "irrelevant" as in *Deuel*. On what basis can the Federal Circuit deem "a general method of isolating cDNA or DNA molecules ... essentially irrelevant to the question of whether the specific molecules themselves would have been obvious?" What would a biotechnologist use other than the methods and tools of biotechnology to obtain the claimed molecules? In any event, the *Deuel* rule is unique to the United States.

2. More About Product Claims Supported by a Nonobvious Method. In Note 1 after *In re Dillon*, a question is raised regarding the appropriateness of basing the patentability of chemical compounds on their method of manufacture. Assume you agree that *In re Hoeksema* was wrongly decided, does it follow that one should not be able to argue that a gene is nonobvious based on the fact that the method for discovering it was itself nonobvious. For an argument that genes are a special case see 2 MARTIN J. ADELMAN, PATENT LAW PERSPECTIVES, § 2.6[7.–2] at n.183 (2d ed. 1993) where the author states:

> The essential differences between discovering genes and discovering obviously desirable products arises because ordinarily one must practice the unobvious process to make the obviously desirable product. Take, for example, a claim to a purified protein made by an unobvious purification process. To make more of the protein, this process must be used. However, once one isolates a gene by an unobvious method, the gene can be used and cloned without limit without infringing a claim to the process of isolating the gene. Therefore, to give meaningful protection to this unobvious discovery product protection is required.

3. ESTs and Deuel. Can you craft an argument that § 103 precludes the patenting of ESTs that admittedly are produced by obvious methods? If not, and if we assume they are useful, is there any patent law doctrine that would preclude their patenting?

Nonobviousness Exercise

Your client has is concerned over the possibility that a competitor may assert United States Patent No. 5,291,976 against it. The '976 patent describes an improved wheeled suitcase and luggage support structure which includes:

(1) a rectangular frame with two horizontal and two vertical members;

(2) wheels on the lower horizontal members;

(3) a pull-up handle connected to the rectangular frame; and

(4) a wedging member, preferably frustroconical in shape, frictionally received in a bore which keeps the pull-up handle in a fully extended position.

According to the '976 patent, the suitcase can be attached to the rectangular frame either permanently, by rivets or other means, or temporarily, through use of an elastic cord or similar mechanism. The '976 patent indicates that the claimed design provides several advantages, including one-handed operation of the handle, no lost space in the suitcase due to the placement of the wheels and handle on the frame, and ease of manufacture. Claim 1 of the '976 patent provides:

1. A suitcase comprising: a luggage member, and a support structure attached to the luggage member, the support structure comprising a first horizontal member having two wheels thereon to facilitate towing on the ground, a second horizontal member, two tubular members coupling the first and second horizontal members, thereby forming a rectangular frame; a shaft in extensible slidable engagement in each of said tubular members, the shafts being connected by a first handle, the shafts being extensible between a collapsed portion in the tubular members and a fully extended portion to enable towing of the luggage member on the wheels, at least one of the shafts including a wedging member slidable within the respective tubular member which is received frictionally in a first bore provided at an end of the respective tubular member adjacent the second horizontal member to maintain the shafts in a fully extended position.

Figure 1 of the '976 patent shows a perspective view of the suitcase; Figure 2 illustrates the wedging and tubular members.

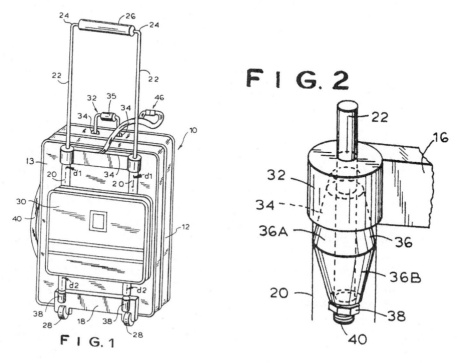

A prior art search has revealed three other U.S. patents, all of which serve as prior art to the '976 patent. None of these references was before the examiner during the prosecution of the '976 patent. The first, U.S. Patent No. 5,024,455, is entitled "Luggage Cart" and was filed by Schrecongost. The Schrecongost patent covers an external rectangular frame with two horizontal structures, two vertical members, wheels attached to an axle on the base of the frame, and a telescopically extendable U-shaped handle. The locking mechanism for the handle uses spring-loaded detents to encourage either of two pairs of notches in the U-shaped handle to hold the handle in either the extended or the collapsed position. Luggage may be attached permanently or temporarily to the frame via brackets. Figure 3 shows a front perspective view from the Schrecongost patent.

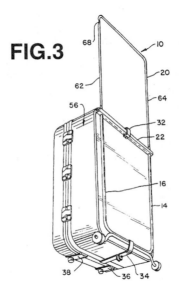

FIG.3

U.S. Patent No. 4,995,487, claiming a "Wheeled Suitcase and Luggage Support," lists one Plath as the inventor. The Plath patent describes a suitcase with built-in wheels and a retractable, friction-locking handle. Plath's locking mechanism differs somewhat from that of the '976 patent, however. When the handle has reached its maximum extension, offset guide means wedge the lower end segment of the handle road against its sleeve and brushing means, binding the handle frictionally in position. To retract the handle, the user must apply downward pressure to the gripping means to overcome the friction force of the rod against the inner through-bore of the brushing means and sleeve. Users may operate the locking mechanism with one hand. Figure 4 depicts a rear perspective view from the Plath patent; Figure 5 shows a partial elevational view of the suitcase showing the handle assembly in extended position.

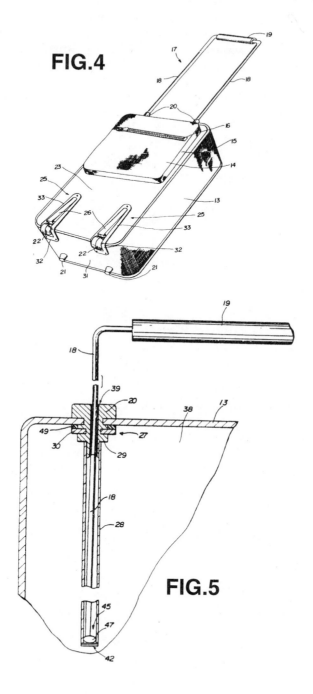

FIG.4

FIG.5

U.S. Patent No. 3,998,476 describes a "Portable Luggage Carrier with Telescoping Handle" invented by Kazmark. Kazmark discusses the use of a cart which is intended to be attached externally to a piece of luggage. The cart includes telescopically related tubes connected by a gripping handle. The tubes may be locked into their fully extended position by the use of a pair of locking mechanisms, which consist of spring-loaded button-shaped elements which are forced through a matching hole when the tubes are extended. The cart also includes wheels attached to an axle at the base of the cart. Figure 6 illustrates a perspective view from the Kazmark patent.

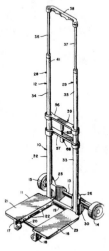

FIG.6

How would you advise your client regarding the validity of the '976 patent?

Chapter Eight

PRIOR ART FOR
NONOBVIOUSNESS

Conveniently for the student who has just considered novelty, discussion of whether a particular prior art reference is eligible to destroy the nonobviousness of a claimed invention is also framed within the categories set forth in § 102. Thus, the question courts have posed is whether technology described within, say, § 102(b), applies not only to a novelty analysis but also towards nonobviousness under § 103(a). Even more pleasantly, the case law has developed a general answer: with one significant qualification, art that applies to the novelty determination also applies for nonobviousness. So, it is often possible to take the same group of references relevant for novelty, and by combining them or looking past the contents of a single reference, undertake the nonobviousness inquiry. As will be seen, however, some controversy remains over the application of § 102(f) art to § 103.

Although this issue is now more settled for the dominant prior art categories, study of the contours of the prior art for § 103(a) remains interesting for some additional reasons. First, the cases have carved out a few narrowly defined exceptions where art that applies for novelty purposes does not apply for nonobviousness. Second, as an historical matter, the United States patent system has not always embraced each of the § 102 categories in the context of nonobviousness. The case law instead includes crucial points of departure that map the policy debate regarding the proper "scope and content of the prior art" of § 103(a). Finally, patent systems abroad have not always made the same choices as the United States when resolving issues pertaining to inventive step. An understanding of these differences is both worthwhile as a practical matter and an acknowledgment of the difficulties future harmonization efforts must face.

The significant qualification noted above relates to the additional requirement that a reference spring from a so-called "analogous" art in order to be considered pertinent for nonobviousness. Thus, the availability of a technology under § 102 is a necessary, but not sufficient condition for it to apply to an analysis under § 103(a). The technology must also issue from a technical discipline that is relevant to the claimed invention. The determination of whether an art is analogous to that of the claimed invention, and therefore a potential source of prior art for purposes of nonobviousness, is taken up in § 8.2 of this Chapter.

§ 8.1 SECTION 103 ART IN TERMS OF § 102

§ 8.1[a] Section 102(a) Art

U.S. patent law has never questioned the principle that technology developed prior to the invention date may be used as a reference for determining obviousness. The next decision provides one significant exception, however, which must be read with a careful eye towards Rule 131 practice.

IN RE STRYKER

Court of Customs and Patent Appeals, 1971.
435 F.2d 1340, 168 U.S.P.Q. 372.

Before RICH, ALMOND, BALDWIN, LANE, ASSOCIATE JUDGES, and NEWMAN, JUDGE, sitting by designation.

LANE, JUDGE, delivered the opinion of the court.

This appeal is from the decision of the Patent Office Board of Appeals, which affirmed the rejection of both claims in appellant's application serial No. 272,449, filed April 11, 1963, for an improved process for producing polypropylene. We reverse.

The invention is defined, and also adequately described for our purposes, by claim 1:

> The process of removing propylene diluent from a suspension consisting essentially of from about 50%–60% by weight polypropylene in liquid propylene obtained directly from a propylene polymerization reactor under the autogenous pressure of the reactor which consists essentially in feeding the said suspension from the reactor to a recovery zone of the cyclone type maintained at substantially atmospheric pressure, whereby propylene diluent is flashed from the solid particles of polypropylene, leaving on said particles not in excess of about 2% by weight propylene, and recovering the thus treated polypropylene.

The claims were rejected as obvious over Harban, who discloses separation of polypropylene from propylene by flashing of monomer from polymer in a cyclone-type flash zone. The Harban mixture is disclosed as containing 35% solids by weight, and the patent indicates that the separation achieved is nearly perfect, but does not state a specific percentage of separation.

Appellant contends that he discovered that, unexpectedly, the use of a suspension containing 50–60% by weight polymer permitted direct discharge of the suspension into a flashing zone maintained at atmospheric pressure, and resulted in a residual monomer level of 2% or less. We have considered appellant's arguments on this point, but we agree with the Patent Office that appellant's polymer concentration does not produce any unexpected results and does not render the claimed process unobvious over Harban.

We turn now to appellant's alternative contention, i.e., even if the claimed processes are obvious over Harban, Harban is removed as a reference by the antedating affidavit submitted on appellant's behalf by a representative of the assignee of the application. The board considered the affidavit deficient in that, while it alleged conception and reduction to practice of the claimed process, including the weight percentage limitations, before the Harban filing date, there was no corroborating evidence showing those weight percentage limitations. The board stated:

> The claimed invention must be shown in the affidavit, i.e., the alleged essence of the invention of flashing a suspension containing about 50%–60% by weight polypropylene in liquid propylene to obtain a polymer containing not in excess of about 2% by weight propylene must at least be demonstrated therein. *In re Tanczyn*, 347 F.2d 830, 146 U.S.P.Q. 298 (CCPA 1965).

We think the board erred in applying *Tanczyn* to the facts of this case. In *Tanczyn* we limited to a certain extent the language we used in *In re Stempel*, 44 CCPA 820, 241 F.2d 755, 113 U.S.P.Q. 77 (1957), wherein we had stated that "all the applicant can be required to show is priority with respect to so much of the claimed invention as the reference happens to show." It will be recalled that in *Tanczyn* the appellant sought to remove a reference by an affidavit which showed prior possession by the appellant of subject matter on which the claims did not read but which corresponded to the subject matter disclosed in the reference sought to be removed. We found the affidavit insufficient to remove the reference, but we held the claims to be unobvious over the reference. In other words, the subject matter shown in the reference and the affidavit was so different from the claimed invention that the claims were unobvious and patentable over the reference. In the case before us the differences between the claimed invention and the reference disclosure are so small as to render the claims obvious over the reference. The features which the board found inadequately corroborated by appellant's evidence are the very features considered insufficient to patentably distinguish over the Harban reference. To hold that Harban is not removed by the showing here presented would lead to an anomalous result, i.e., if appellant broadened his claims by deleting the weight limitations, so as to read literally on Harban, Harban would not be available as a reference against such broadened claims because appellant's antedating affidavit would be satisfactory in every respect.[3] It cannot be the law that the same affidavit is insufficient to remove the

---

3. We recognize that, had appellant presented broader claims, the Patent Office might have found other, earlier art on which to reject them.

same reference applied against the slightly narrower claims presented here.

For the foregoing reasons, the board's rejection of the claims as unpatentable over Harban, under 35 U.S.C. § 103, is reversed.

Notes

1. The *Stryker* Holding. Reflection upon the significance of the *Stryker* holding may prove difficult in light of its succinct discussion. Consider that Stryker claimed an invention narrower than that of the issued Harban patent. Both the Patent Office and the court agreed the Harban patent would render Stryker's invention obvious if that patent constituted a valid prior art reference. Therefore, Stryker had to bypass Harban in order to obtain a patent, and attempted to due so by filing a Rule 131 affidavit. Stryker's affidavit contained everything disclosed in the Harban reference but *not* the narrowing feature. The Patent Office found the affidavit inadequate because it did not show prior completion of the entire invention.

The court allowed Stryker's affidavit to remove the earlier filed Harban patent as a reference even though Stryker could not corroborate all of the features of the claimed invention. This unusual step was taken because the unconfirmed differences between the Stryker application and the Harban patent would have been obvious to a person skilled in the art. Thus, no *patentable* difference existed between Stryker and Harban. Therefore, a reference described by § 102(a)—in this case, Harban's patent—does not constitute prior art under § 103 if the applicant possessed an obvious variation of the reference prior to the third party. This rule should be taken as a limited exception to the general applicability of § 102(a) prior art to the obviousness inquiry. For further elaboration of the *Stryker* rule, see the PTO MANUAL OF PATENT EXAMINING PROCEDURE § 715.02.

2. Stryker's Application. Why didn't Stryker simply claim the broader invention of Harban and the obvious, narrowing feature as well? Further, what is the value of the patent issued to Harban following the issuance of this decision? Is more information needed to answer this latter question? Why should two patents be allowed to issue that are obvious variations of one another?

§ 8.1[b]   Prior Art Under Sections 102(b) and 102(d)

IN RE FOSTER

Court of Customs and Patent Appeals, 1965.
343 F.2d 980, 145 U.S.P.Q. 166.

Before WORLEY, CHIEF JUDGE, and RICH, MARTIN, SMITH and ALMOND, JUDGES.

ALMOND, JUDGE.

This is an appeal from the decision of the Board of Appeals affirming the rejection of the claims in appellant's patent application.

Because of the importance of the question to the law of patents, we have deemed it desirable to reconsider what is the statutory basis of this "unpatentable over" or obviousness type of rejection, such as we have here and had before us in [*In re Palmquist*, 319 F.2d 547, 51 CCPA 839, 138 U.S.P.Q. 234 (CCPA 1963),] under the circumstance that the reference or references have effective dates more than one year prior to the filing date of the applicant. More specifically, we have reconsidered the result again urged on us here, as allegedly authorized by section 103, that a reference having a date more than a year prior to the filing date may be disposed of by showing an invention date prior to the reference date, contrary to the express provision in Patent Office Rule 131.

[Section 102(b)] presents a sort of statute of limitations, formerly two years, now one year, within which an inventor, even though he has made a patentable invention, must act on penalty of loss of his right to patent. What starts the period running is clearly the availability of the invention to the public through the categories of disclosure enumerated in 102(b), which include "a printed publication" anywhere describing the invention. There appears to be no dispute about the operation of this statute in "complete anticipation" situations but the contention seems to be that 102(b) has no applicability where the invention is not completely disclosed in a single patent or publication, that is to say where the rejection involves the addition to the disclosure of the reference of the ordinary skill of the art or the disclosure of another reference which indicates what those of ordinary skill in the art are presumed to know, and to have known for more than a year before the application was filed. Upon a complete reexamination of this matter, we are convinced that the contention is contrary to the policy consideration which motivated the enactment by Congress of a statutory bar. On logic and principle we think this contention is unsound, and we also believe it is contrary to the patent law as it has actually existed since at least 1898.

First, as to principle, since the purpose of the statute has always been to require filing of the application within the prescribed period after the time the public came into possession of the invention, we cannot see that it makes any difference how it came into such possession, whether by a public use, a sale, a single patent or publication, or by combinations of one or more of the foregoing. In considering this principle we assume, of course, that by these means the invention has become obvious to that segment of the "public" having ordinary skill in the art. Once this has happened, the purpose of the law is to give the inventor only a year within which to file and this would seem to be liberal treatment. Whenever an applicant undertakes, under Rule 131, to swear back of a reference having an effective date more than a year before his filing date, he is automatically conceding that he made his invention more than a year before he filed. If the reference contains enough disclosure to make his invention obvious, the principle of the statute would seem to require denial of a patent to him. The same is true where a combination of two publications or patents makes the invention obvious and they both have dates more than a year before the filing date.

As to dealing with the express language of 102(b), for example, "described in a printed publication," technically, we see no reason to so read the words of the statute as to preclude the use of more than one reference; nor do we find in the context anything to show that "a printed publication" cannot include two or more printed publications. We do not have two publications here, but we did in *Palmquist*, and it is a common situation.

As to what the law has been, more particularly what it was prior to 1953, when the new patent act and its section 103 became effective, there is a paucity of direct precedents on the precise problem. We think there is a reason for this. Under the old law (R.S. § 4886, where 102(b) finds its origin) patents were refused or invalidated on references dated more than a year before the filing date because the invention was anticipated or, if they were not, then because there was no "invention," the latter rejection being based either on (a) a single nonanticipatory reference plus the skill of the art or (b) on a plurality of references. There was no need to seek out the precise statutory basis because it was R.S. § 4886 in any event, read in the light of the Supreme Court's interpretation of the law that there must always be "invention." This issue was determined on the disclosures of the references relied on and if they had dates more than one year before the filing date, it was assumed they could be relied on to establish a "statutory bar." There was an express prohibition in Rule 131 and in its predecessor Rule 75 against antedating a reference having a date more than a year prior to the filing date and there was no basis on which to contest it. The accepted state of law is exemplified by the following sentences in McCRADY's PATENT OFFICE PRACTICE, 4th ed. (1959), Sec. 127, p. 176:

> "Prior art specified by 35 USC 102, which has an effective date more than one year prior to the effective filing date of an application, constitutes a bar under the language of that statute. Until 1940 the period was two years."

> "Procedurally, the significance of the statutory bar lies in the fact that it cannot be antedated by evidence of applicant's earlier invention, as by affidavits under Rule 131, or by evidence presented in an infringement suit."

Our decision in *Palmquist* appears to have been the first to hold otherwise.

It would seem that the practical operation of the prior law was that references having effective dates more than a year before applicant's filing date were always considered to be effective as references, regardless of the applicant's date of invention, and that rejections were then predicated thereon for "lack of invention" without making the distinction which we now seem to see as implicit in sections 102 and 103, "anticipation" or no novelty situations under 102 and "obviousness" situations under 103. But on further reflection, we now feel bound to point out that of equal importance is the question of loss of right predicated on a one-year time-bar which, it seems clear to us, has never been limited to "anticipation" situations, involving only a single reference, but has included as well "no invention" (now "obviousness") situations. It follows that where the time-bar is involved, the actual date of invention becomes irrelevant and that it is not in accordance with either the letter or the principle of the law, or its past interpretation over a very long period, to permit an applicant to dispose of a reference having a date more than one year prior to his filing date by proving his actual date of invention.

Such a result was permitted by our decision in *Palmquist* and to the extent that it permitted a reference, having a publication date more than one year prior to the United States filing date to which the applicant was entitled, to be disposed of by proof of a date of invention earlier than the date of the reference, that decision is hereby overruled.

Notes

1. Extending the Impact of § 102(b). As a stepdaughter of the first-to-invent regime, § 102(b) works to spur inventors to file patent applications. If an inventor places a technology within the public domain, or observes that his invention is publicly available, then he is charged with a prompt application to preserve his patent rights. Why should this purpose impact § 103(a) art at all? Should inventors be charged with making their own nonobviousness determinations when deciding whether to apply for patent rights or not? Does this case support the view that § 102(b)'s primary function is to remedy a defect in the first-to-invent system by creating certain prior art that does not depend on when the patented invention was made?

2. § 102(d) and Nonobviousness. Prior art under § 102(d) rarely impacts the nonobviousness determination under § 103(a). International circumstances already result in infrequent resort to § 102(d); additionally, circumstances where an inventor files a United States application sufficiently different from an earlier foreign application to raise obviousness questions would be relatively rare. *See* Gerald Sobel, *Prior Art and Obviousness*, 47 J. PAT. OFF. SOC'Y 79, 84 (1965). However, the policy underpinnings of the § 102(b)—the encouragement of prompt filing—also largely inform § 102(d). Does *Foster*'s treatment of § 102(b) therefore allow any inferences to be drawn about the prior art effect of § 102(d) for obviousness determinations? Compare the dicta in the CCPA decision in *In re Bass, infra*, with the view of the Patent Office in *Ex parte Appeal No. 242–47*, 196 U.S.P.Q. 828 (Pat. & Tr. Bd.App.1976), as well as the Federal Circuit's opinion in *OddzOn* reprinted below.

§ 8.1[c] Prior Art Under Sections 102(e) and (g)

HAZELTINE RESEARCH, INC. v. BRENNER

United States Supreme Court, 1965.
382 U.S. 252.

MR. JUSTICE BLACK delivered the opinion of the Court.

The sole question presented here is whether an application for patent pending in the Patent Office at the time a second application is filed constitutes part of the "prior art" as that term is used in 35 U.S.C.

§ 103 (1964 ed.), which reads in part: "A patent may not be obtained * * * if the differences between the subject matter sought to be patented and the prior art are such that the subject matter as a whole would have been obvious at the time the invention was made to a person having ordinary skill in the art * * *."

The question arose in this way. On December 23, 1957, petitioner Robert Regis filed an application for a patent on a new and useful improvement on a microwave switch. On June 24, 1959, the Patent Examiner denied Regis' application on the ground that the invention was not one which was new or unobvious in light of the prior art and thus did not meet the standards set forth in § 103. The Examiner said that the invention was unpatentable because of the joint effect of the disclosures made by patents previously issued, one to Carlson (No. 2,491,644) and one to Wallace (No. 2,822,526). The Carlson patent had been issued on December 20, 1949, over eight years prior to Regis' application, and that patent is admittedly a part of the prior art insofar as Regis' invention is concerned. The Wallace patent, however, was pending in the Patent Office when the Regis application was filed. The Wallace application had been pending since March 24, 1954, nearly three years and nine months before Regis filed his application and the Wallace patent was issued on February 4, 1958, 43 days after Regis filed his application.

After the Patent Examiner refused to issue the patent, Regis appealed to the Patent Office Board of Appeals on the ground that the Wallace patent could not be properly considered a part of the prior art because it had been a "co-pending patent" and its disclosures were secret and not known to the public. The Board of Appeals rejected this argument and affirmed the decision of the Patent Examiner. Regis and Hazeltine, which had an interest as assignee, then instituted the present action in the District Court pursuant to 35 U.S.C. § 145 (1964 ed.) to compel the Commissioner to issue the patent. The District Court agreed with the Patent Office that the co-pending Wallace application was a part of the prior art and directed that the complaint be dismissed. 226 F.Supp. 459. On appeal the Court of Appeals affirmed *per curiam*. 119 U.S.App.D.C. 261, 340 F.2d 786. We granted certiorari to decide the question of whether a co-pending application is included in the prior art, as that term is used in 35 U.S.C. § 103.

Petitioners' primary contention is that the term "prior art," as used in § 103, really means only art previously publicly known. In support of this position they refer to a statement in the legislative history which indicates that prior art means "what was known before as described in section 102." They contend that the use of the word "known" indicates that Congress intended prior art to include only inventions or discoveries which were already publicly known at the time an invention was made.

If petitioners are correct in their interpretation of "prior art," then the Wallace invention, which was not publicly known at the time the Regis application was filed, would not be prior art with regard to Regis' invention. This is true because at the time Regis filed his application the Wallace invention, although pending in the Patent Office, had never been made public and the Patent Office was forbidden by statute from disclosing to the public, except in special circumstances, anything contained in the application.

The Commissioner, relying chiefly on *Alexander Milburn Co. v. Davis–Bournonville Co.*, 270 U.S. 390, 46 S.Ct. 324, 70 L.Ed. 651, contends that when a patent is issued, the disclosures contained in the patent become a part of the prior art as of the time the application was filed, not, as petitioners contend, at the time the patent is issued. In that case a patent was held invalid because, at the time it was applied for, there was already pending an application which completely and adequately described the invention. In holding that the issuance of a patent based on the first application barred the valid issuance of a patent based on the second application. Mr. Justice Holmes, speaking for the Court, said, "The delays of the patent office ought not to cut down the effect of what has been done. * * * (The first applicant) had taken steps that would make it public as soon as the Patent Office did its work, although, of course, amendments might be required of him before the end could be reached. We see no reason in the words or policy of the law for allowing (the second applicant) to profit by the delay * * *."

In its revision of the patent laws in 1952, Congress showed its approval of the holding in *Milburn* by adopting 35 U.S.C. § 102(e) which provides that a person shall be entitled to a patent unless "(e) the invention was described in a patent granted on an application for patent by another filed in the United States before the invention thereof by the application for patent." Petitioners suggest, however, that the question in this case is not answered by mere reference to § 102(e), because in *Milburn*, which gave rise to that section, the co-pending applications described the same identical invention. But here the Regis invention is not precisely the same as that contained in the Wallace patent, but is only made obvious by the Wallace patent in light of the Carlson patent. We agree with the Commissioner that this distinction is without significance here. While we think petitioners' argument with regard to § 102(e) is interesting, it provides no reason to depart from the plain holding and reasoning in the *Milburn* case. The basic reasoning upon which the Court decided the *Milburn* case applies equally well here. When Wallace filed his application, he had done what he could to add his disclosures to the prior art. The rest was up to the Patent Office. Had the Patent Office acted faster, had it issued Wallace's patent two months earlier, there would have been no question here. As Justice Holmes said in *Milburn*, "The delays of the patent office ought not to cut down the effect of what has been done."

To adopt the result contended for by petitioners would create an area where patents are awarded for unpatentable advances in the art. We see no reason to read into § 103 a restricted definition of "prior art" which would lower standards of patentability to such an extent that there might exist two patents where the Congress has plainly directed that there should be only one.

Affirmed.

Notes

1. **Secret Prior Art II.** If one already has an aversion to secret prior art, then its extension from novelty to nonobviousness considerations must be truly offensive. But for both considerations, surely the Patent Office needs a ready source of the state of the art. The patent law may also be less than sympathetic towards allowing as prior art applications which disclose, but do not claim, the invention. After all, such a technology is already within the grasp of the patent system. Is it reasonable to assume—as the patent law apparently does—that if an invention were of particular value, it would have been claimed in the earlier application?

2. **Comparative Approaches.** The holding of *Hazeltine Research* squarely conflicts with Articles 54(3) and 56 of the European Patent Convention and Article 29bis of the Japanese patent statute. Both statutes indicate that "secret" potentially novelty destroying technology, applicable as it is to novelty determinations, cannot be employed to reject an application for nonobviousness. Does the "now you see it, now you don't" applicability of this technology make any sense? Or is the impact of secret prior art so undesirable that any limitation upon its impact should be welcomed? Does the fact that the European and Japanese Patent Offices publish patent applications after 18 months affect your conclusions? What about the effects of self-collision and improvement patents under the EPO?

3. ***In re Bass* and § 103(c).** The Court of Customs and Patent Appeals extended the reasoning of *Hazeltine Research* to § 102(g) in its decision *In re Bass*, 474 F.2d 1276, 177 U.S.P.Q. 178 (CCPA 1973). There, co-inventors Bass, Jenkins and Horvat had applied for a patent on an air control system for carding machines. Their effective filing date was October 11, 1965. The PTO rejected their claims on the ground of nonobviousness, and following an appeal the CCPA affirmed. Among the references cited were two patents: a patent granted to Bass and Horvat, which had matured from an application filed on August 23, 1965; and a patent issued to Jenkins, based on an October 13, 1964, application.

The correspondence of inventor surnames between the application and the prior art patents was not a coincidence. In fact, the PTO and CCPA cited the earlier work of Bass, Jenkins and Horvat against them. They did so following the traditional patent law principle that each new combination of joint inventors constitutes a distinct inventive entity. This principle holds even where these combinations share individual inventors. For example, the joint inventors Bass, Jenkins and Horvat were considered a different inventive entity than the team of Bass and Horvat. Each group of natural persons essentially acquires its own legal identity; they, as a whole, constitute "the inventor" of that technology.

In re Bass demonstrated that the setting of contemporary technology development may lead to harsh results when corporations file patent applications. Where one corporation employs numerous experts to engage in collaborative research and development efforts, the shifting composition of inventive teams can result in rather strained holdings of nonobviousness. Ordinarily, the patent statute establishes that an inventor's own prior inventive efforts may not anticipate a subsequent patent application. For example, in § 102(g), the invention must be made by "another" to serve as prior art. But since legally distinct inventors result from different inventive entities, an anticipation rejection is possible even if only a slight change in personnel occurs. In a particularly fertile and interactive corporate research department, inventors could find themselves unable to obtain patents due to "in-house" rejections for obviousness based upon efforts by their peers, and even in part by themselves!

Congress enacted § 103(c) to solve the problem highlighted in *In re Bass*. As amended in 1999, this provision read:

> Subject matter developed by another person, which qualifies as prior art only under subsection (e), (f) or (g) of section 102 of this title, shall not preclude patentability under this section where the subject matter and the claimed invention were, at the time the invention was made, owned by the same person or subject to an obligation of assignment to the same person.

The workings of § 103(c) can prove elusive, but an example should lend some clarity to its provisions. Suppose that two inventors, Ryu and Yuko, each work for the Yoshida Corporation. As part of their employment contracts, Ryu and Yuko have agreed to assign inventions that they develop to the Yoshida Corporation. Ryu conceives of a new ultrasonic diagnosing apparatus on December 15, 2000. He immediately informs Yuko about his idea. Working diligently in his laboratory, Ryu reduces the invention to practice on January 31, 2001. The Yoshida Corporation files a patent application on Ryu's behalf on March 1, 2001. The Ryu patent issues on October 23, 2002.

On March 17, 2001, Yuko realizes that she can improve upon Ryu's ultrasonic diagnosing apparatus. Because of her workload, she does not start on the project until April 7, 2001. Without further consulting Ryu, she ultimately completes her ultrasonic diagnosing apparatus on May 20, 2001. Although Yuko's invention represents an improvement over Ryu's ultrasonic diagnosing apparatus, it would have been obvious in light of the Ryu apparatus. The Yoshida Corporation files a patent application on behalf of Yuko on October 1, 2001.

Under these facts, the Ryu patent cannot serve as prior art against Yuko. The statutory bars of § 102(b) and (d) are not triggered here. There is also no indication that Ryu's invention was "known or used by others" within the meaning of § 102(a), given the judicial requirement of a public knowledge or use. If § 103(c) were not available, the Ryu patent would constitute prior art under § 102(e) because Yuko's invention date occurred after the Ryu application was filed. Absent § 103(c), the Ryu patent would also serve as prior art under § 102(f) because Yuko derived a obvious variation of her invention from Ryu. Further, without § 103(c) Ryu's work would be available under § 102(g), Ryu both conceived and reduced his invention to practice prior to Yuko's conception date. However, because § 103(c) exempts § 102(e), (f) and (g) art from the nonobviousness inquiry where the inventions were subject to an common obligation of assignment, the Yoshida Corporation may obtain patents on both the Ryu and Yuko inventions.

Section 103(c) is a narrowly worded provision. If a reference is otherwise available as prior art, such as under § 102(a) or (b), then it remains pertinent to § 103(a). Also recall that § 103(c) solely concerns nonobviousness. It does not affect the availability of prior art for purposes of anticipation.

In a time of shrinking R & D budgets at major corporations, many corporate entities are entering into joint research agreements. Thus, a major petroleum refining company might contract with a major automobile company to study fuel efficiency. Under the joint research agreement, the corporations save research funds by exchanging information and pooling resources. The agreement might assign any chemical fuel enhancements to the refining company and any mechanical engine enhancements to the automobile company. Do you foresee any difficulties for this hypothetical joint research agreement under the 1984 Act? How would you redraft the agreement to avoid problems?

§ 8.1[d]   § 102(f) Art

ODDZON PRODUCTS, INC. v. JUST TOYS, INC.

United States Court of Appeals, Federal Circuit, 1997.
122 F.3d 1396, 43 U.S.P.Q.2d 1641.

Before MICHEL, LOURIE, and RADER, CIRCUIT JUDGES.

LOURIE, CIRCUIT JUDGE.

OddzOn Products, Inc. appeals from the decision of the United States District Court for the Northern District of California granting summary judgment in favor of defendants Just Toys, Inc., Lisco, Inc., and Spalding & Evenflo Companies, Inc. (collectively "Just Toys") on OddzOn's claims of design patent infringement, trade dress infringement, and state-law unfair competition.

OddzOn is a toy and sporting goods company that sells the popular "Vortex" tossing ball, a foam football-shaped ball with a tail and fin structure. The Vortex ball is OddzOn's commercial embodiment of its design patent, U.S. Patent D 346,001, which issued on April 12, 1994. Figure 1 of the patent is shown below:

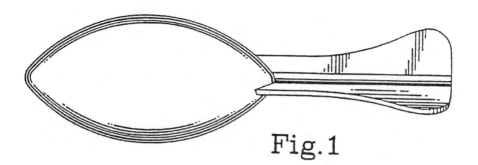

Fig.1

Just Toys, Inc., another toy and sporting goods company, sells a competing line of "Ultra Pass" balls. Two versions of the allegedly infringing Ultra Pass balls are shown below:

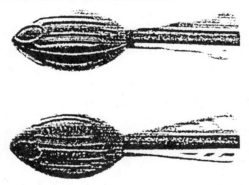

OddzOn sued Just Toys for design patent infringement, trade dress infringement, and state-law unfair competition, asserting that the Ultra Pass line of tossing balls was likely to be confused with OddzOn's Vortex ball, and that the Ultra Pass packaging was likely to be confused with the Vortex packaging. Just Toys denied infringement and asserted that the patent was invalid. On cross-motions for summary judgment, the district court held that the patent was not shown to be invalid and was not infringed. The court also held that Just Toys did not infringe OddzOn's trade dress.

The district court determined that two confidential designs that had been disclosed to the inventor qualified as subject matter encompassed within the meaning of 35 U.S.C. § 102(f) (1994) and concluded that these designs could be combined with other prior art designs for purposes of a challenge to the validity of the patent under 35 U.S.C. § 103 (1994). Nonetheless, the district court held that the patented design would not have been obvious in light of the prior art, including the two confidential designs. * * *

DISCUSSION

A. *The Prior Art Status of § 102(f) Subject Matter*

The district court ruled that two confidential ball designs (the "disclosures") which "inspired" the inventor of the ODDZON design were prior art for purposes of determining obviousness under § 103. The district court noted that this court had recently declined to rule definitively on the relationship between § 102(f) and § 103, *see Lamb–Weston, Inc. v. McCain Foods, Ltd.*, 78 F.3d 540, 544, 37 U.S.P.Q.2d 1856, 1858–59 (Fed.Cir.1996), but relied on the fact that the United States Patent and Trademark Office (PTO) interprets prior art under § 103 as including disclosures encompassed within § 102(f). ODDZON challenges the court's determination that subject matter encompassed within § 102(f) is prior art for purposes of an obviousness inquiry under § 103. ODD-ZON asserts that because these disclosures are not known to the public, they do not possess the usual hallmark of prior art, which is that they provide actual or constructive public knowledge. ODDZON argues that while the two disclosures constitute patent-defeating subject matter under 35 U.S.C. § 102(f), they cannot be combined with "real" prior art to defeat patentability under a combination of § 102(f) and § 103.

The prior art status under § 103 of subject matter derived by an applicant for patent within the meaning of § 102(f) has never expressly been decided by this court. We now take the opportunity to settle the persistent question whether § 102(f) is a prior art provision for purposes of § 103. As will be discussed, although there is a basis to suggest that § 102(f) should not be considered as a prior art provision, we hold that a fair reading of § 103, as amended in 1984, leads to the conclusion that § 102(f) is a prior art provision for purposes of § 103.

Section 102(f) provides that a person shall be entitled to a patent unless "he did not himself invent the subject matter sought to be patented." This is a derivation provision, which provides that one may not obtain a patent on that which is obtained from someone else whose possession of the subject matter is inherently "prior." It does not pertain only to public knowledge, but also applies to private communications between the inventor and another which may never become public. Subsections (a), (b), (e), and (g), on the other hand, are clearly prior art provisions. They relate to knowledge manifested by acts that are essentially public. Subsections (a) and (b) relate to public knowledge or use, or prior patents and printed publications; subsection (e) relates to prior filed applications for patents of others which have become public by grant; and subsection (g) relates to prior inventions of others that are either public or will likely become public in the sense that they have not been abandoned, suppressed, or concealed. Subsections (c) and (d) are loss-of-right provisions. Section 102(c) precludes the obtaining of a patent by inventors who have abandoned their invention. Section 102(d) causes an inventor to lose the right to a patent by delaying the filing of a patent application too long after having filed a corresponding patent application in a foreign country. Subsections (c) and (d) are therefore not prior art provisions.

In *In re Bass*, 59 C.C.P.A. 1342, 474 F.2d 1276, 1290, 177 U.S.P.Q. 178, 189 (CCPA 1973), the principal opinion of the Court of Customs and Patent Appeals held that a prior invention of another that was not abandoned, suppressed, or concealed (102(g) prior art) could be combined with other prior art to support rejection of a claim for obviousness under § 103. The principal opinion noted that the provisions of § 102 deal with two types of issues, those of novelty and loss-of-right. It explained: "Three of [the subsections,] (a), (e), and (g), deal with events prior to applicant's invention date and the other, (b), with events more than one year prior to the U.S. application date. These are the 'prior art' subsections." Id. The principal opinion added, in dictum (§ 102(f) not being at issue), that "[o]f course, (c), (d), and (f) have no relation to § 103 and no relevancy to what is 'prior art' under § 103." Id. There is substantial logic to that conclusion. After all, the other prior art provisions all relate to subject matter that is, or eventually becomes, public. Even the "secret prior art" of § 102(e) is ultimately public in the form of an issued patent before it attains prior art status.

Thus, the patent laws have not generally recognized as prior art that which is not accessible to the public. It has been a basic principle of patent law, subject to minor exceptions, that prior art is:

> technology already available to the public. It is available, in legal theory at least, when it is described in the world's accessible literature, including patents, or has been publicly known or in . . . public use or on sale "in this country." That is the real meaning of "prior art" in legal theory—it is knowledge that is available, including what would be obvious from it, at a given time, to a person of ordinary skill in the art.

Kimberly–Clark Corp. v. Johnson & Johnson, 745 F.2d 1437, 1453, 223 U.S.P.Q. 603, 614 (Fed.Cir.1984) (citations omitted).

Moreover, as between an earlier inventor who has not given the public the benefit of the invention, e.g., because the invention has been abandoned without public disclosure, suppressed, or concealed, and a subsequent inventor who obtains a patent, the policy of the law is for the subsequent inventor to prevail. *See W.L. Gore & Assocs., Inc. v. Garlock, Inc.*, 721 F.2d 1540, 1550, 220 U.S.P.Q. 303, 310 (Fed.Cir.1983) ("Early public disclosure is a linchpin of the patent system. As between a prior inventor [who does not disclose] and a later inventor who promptly files a patent application . . . , the law favors the latter."). Likewise, when the possessor of secret art (art that has been abandoned, suppressed, or concealed) that predates the critical date is faced with a later-filed patent, the later-filed patent should not be invalidated in the face of this "prior" art, which has not been made available to the public. Thus, prior, but non-public, inventors yield to later inventors who utilize the patent system.

However, a change occurred in the law after Bass was decided. At the time Bass was decided, § 103 read as follows:

> A patent may not be obtained though the invention is not identically disclosed or described as set forth in section 102 of this title, if the differences between the subject matter sought to be patented and the prior art are such that the subject matter as a whole would have been obvious at the time the invention was made to a person having ordinary skill in the art to which said subject matter pertains. Patentability shall not be negatived by the manner in which the invention was made.

35 U.S.C. § 103. The prior art being referred to in that provision arguably included only public prior art defined in subsections 102(a), (b), (e), and (g).

In 1984, Congress amended § 103, adding the following paragraph:

> Subject matter developed by another person, which qualifies as prior art only under subsection [e], (f) or (g) of section 102 of this title, shall not preclude patentability under this section where the subject matter and the claimed invention were, at the time the invention was made, owned by the same person or subject to an obligation of assignment to the same person.

35 U.S.C. § 103 (now § 103(c)). It is historically very clear that this provision was intended to avoid the invalidation of patents under § 103 on the basis of the work of fellow employees engaged in team research. *See Section-by-Section Analysis: Patent Law Amendments Act of 1984*, 130 Cong. Rec. 28069, 28071 (Oct. 1, 1984), reprinted in 1984 U.S.C.C.A.N. 5827, 5833 (stating that the amendment, which encourages communication among members of research teams, was a response to *Bass* and *In re Clemens*, 622 F.2d 1029, 206 U.S.P.Q. 289 (CCPA 1980), in which "an earlier invention which is not public may be treated under Section 102(g), and possibly under 102(f), as prior art"). There was no clearly apparent purpose in Congress's inclusion of § 102(f) in the amendment other than an attempt to ameliorate the problems of patenting the results of team research. However, the language appears in the statute; it was enacted by Congress. We must give effect to it.

The statutory language provides a clear statement that subject matter that qualifies as prior art under subsection (f) or (g) cannot be combined with other prior art to render a claimed invention obvious and hence unpatentable when the relevant prior art is commonly owned with the claimed invention at the time the invention was made. While the statute does not expressly state in so many words that § 102(f) creates a type of prior art for purposes of § 103, nonetheless that conclusion is inescapable; the language that states that § 102(f) subject matter is not prior art under limited circumstances clearly implies that it is prior art otherwise. That is what Congress wrote into law in 1984 and that is the way we must read the statute.

This result is not illogical. It means that an invention, A', that is obvious in view of subject matter A, derived from another, is also unpatentable. The obvious invention, A', may not be unpatentable to the inventor of A, and it may not be unpatentable to a third party who did not receive the disclosure of A, but it is unpatentable to the party who did receive the disclosure.

The PTO's regulations also adopt this interpretation of the statute. 37 C.F.R. § 1.106(d) (1996) ("Subject matter which is developed by another person which qualifies as prior art only under 35 U.S.C. § 102(f) or (g) may be used as prior art under 35 U.S.C. § 103."). Although the PTO's interpretation of this statute is not conclusive, we agree with the district court that it is a reasonable interpretation of the statute.

It is sometimes more important that a close question be settled one way or another than which way it is settled. We settle the issue here (subject of course to any later intervention by Congress or review by the Supreme Court), and do so in a manner that best comports with the voice of Congress. Thus, while there is a basis for an opposite conclusion, principally based on the fact that § 102(f) does not refer to public activity, as do the other provisions that clearly define prior art, nonetheless we cannot escape the import of the 1984 amendment. We therefore hold that subject matter derived from another not only is itself unpatentable to the party who derived it under § 102(f), but, when combined with other prior art, may make a resulting obvious invention unpatentable to that party under a combination of §§ 102(f) and 103. Accordingly, the district court did not err by considering the two design disclosures known to the inventor to be prior art under the combination of §§ 102(f) and 103.

Accordingly, the district court's judgment is affirmed.

Notes

1. § **102(f) Art and Nonobviousness.** Do you agree with the following comments regarding § 102(f) as prior art?

[C]onsider an applicant, X, who travels to Canada and observes a process in public use having steps ABCD when the prior art in the United States, under Section 102, is ABC. X then adds the step of E to the process and files for and obtains a patent on ABCDE. ABCDE is patentable over ABC, but not over ABCD, which in turn is not patentable over ABC.[1] Therefore, because X is a joint inventor with the Canadian inventor who developed ABCD, the filing of the application listing X as the sole inventor violated Section 116. Hence, [the result in *OddzOn* may be incorrect] so long as ABCD is not patentable over ABC and the Canadian inventor is treated as a joint inventor.

But what if the developer of ABCD was keeping its invention in confidence and X violated that confidence? So long as the law still

---

1. If ABCD is patentable over ABC, then arguably X has not contributed to- wards a patentable invention at all.

treated X as a joint inventor, the same result should be reached. However, if the law pertaining to joint inventors would not treat X as a joint inventor because of his violation of the confidential relationship, then [the conclusion reached in *OddzOn* seems the most desirable result]. X would be able to patent ABCDE even though his contribution was not itself patentable. In essence this practice would import into American patent law the theory of the patent of importation adopted in England in *Edgeberry v. Stephens* and legislatively abolished by the Patents Act 1977.

1 MARTIN J. ADELMAN, PATENT LAW PERSPECTIVES, § 2.3[8.–6] at n1 (2d ed. 1996).

2. Draft Legislation. An analysis of the legislative history of the contemporary United States Patent Act reveals a predecessor version of the draft which ultimately matured into § 103. This statute read, in part, as follows:

> A patent may not be obtained though the invention is not identically disclosed or described *in the prior art* set forth in section 102 of this title, if the differences between the subject matter sought to be patented and *that* prior art [are] such that the subject matter as a whole would have been obvious at the time the invention was made to a person having ordinary skill in the art to which said subject matter pertains.

Hearings before the Subcommittee No. 3 of the House Committee on the Judiciary on H.R. 3760, 82d Cong. 1st Sess. 6 (1951) (emphasis added). Is this language, with its more explicit definition of prior art, preferable to the ultimately enacted version? Would it have changed the result of any of the decisions considered here?

§ 8.2 ANALOGOUS ARTS

Simply because a technology is available under § 102 is not enough to render it applicable to the nonobviousness determination. The technology must also issue from an "analogous art"—a technical area judged sufficiently germane to that of the claimed invention. Thus, although a person of skill in a given technical area is presumed to have access to all of the technical knowledge comprising the state of the art, this knowledge can only be employed within the constraints of the abilities and expertise of practitioners within that field. The next decision considers the standard of pertinence for prior art in the obviousness equation.

IN RE CLAY

United States Court of Appeals, Federal Circuit, 1992.
966 F.2d 656, 23 U.S.P.Q.2d 1058.

Before PLAGER, LOURIE, and CLEVENGER, CIRCUIT JUDGES.

LOURIE, CIRCUIT JUDGE.

Carl D. Clay appeals the decision of the United States Patent and Trademark Office, Board of Patent Appeals and Interferences, Appeal No. 90–2262, affirming the rejection of claims 1–11 and 13 as being unpatentable under 35 U.S.C. § 103. These are all the remaining claims in application Serial No. 245,083, filed April 28, 1987, entitled "Storage of a Refined Liquid Hydrocarbon Product." We reverse.

BACKGROUND

Fig. 1

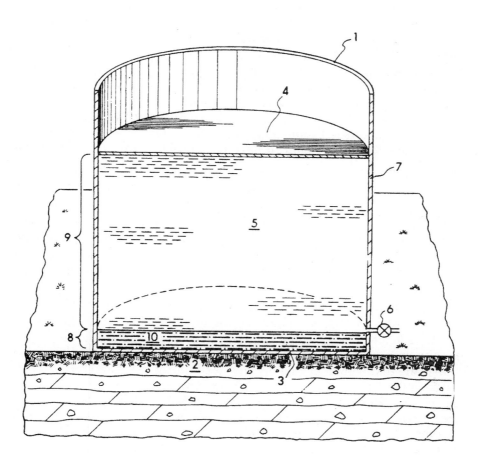

Clay's invention, assigned to Marathon Oil Company, is a process for storing refined liquid hydrocarbon product in a storage tank having a dead volume between the tank bottom and its outlet port. The process involves preparing a gelation solution which gels after it is placed in the tank's dead volume; the gel can easily be removed by adding to the tank a gel-degrading agent such as hydrogen peroxide.

Two prior art references were applied against the claims on appeal. They were U.S. Patent 4,664,294 (Hetherington), which discloses an apparatus for displacing dead space liquid using impervious bladders, or large bags, formed with flexible membranes; and U.S. Patent 4,683,949 (Sydansk), also assigned to Clay's assignee, Marathon Oil Company, which discloses a process for reducing the permeability of hydrocarbon-bearing formations and thus improving oil production, using a gel similar to that in Clay's invention.

The Board agreed with the examiner that, although neither reference alone describes Clay's invention, Hetherington and Sydansk combined support a conclusion of obviousness. It held that one skilled in the art would glean from Hetherington that Clay's invention "was appreciated in the prior art and solutions to that problem generally involved filling the dead space with something."

The Board also held that Sydansk would have provided one skilled in the art with information that a gelation system would have been impervious to hydrocarbons once the system gelled. The Board combined the references, finding that the "cavities" filled by Sydansk are sufficiently similar to the "volume or void space" being filled by Hetherington for one of ordinary skill to have recognized the applicability of the gel to Hetherington.

DISCUSSION

The issue presented in this appeal is whether the Board's conclusion was correct that Clay's invention would have been obvious from the combined teachings of Hetherington and Sydansk. Although this conclusion is one of law, such determinations are made against a background of several factual inquiries, one of which is the scope and content of the prior art.

A prerequisite to making this finding is determining what is "prior art," in order to consider whether "the differences between the subject matter sought to be patented and the prior art are such that the subject matter as a whole would have been obvious at the time the invention was made to a person having ordinary skill in the art." 35 U.S.C. § 103. Although § 103 does not, by its terms, define the "art to which [the] subject matter [sought to be patented] pertains," this determination is frequently couched in terms of whether the art is analogous or not, i.e., whether the art is "too remote to be treated as prior art." *In re Sovish*, 769 F.2d 738, 741, 226 U.S.P.Q. 771, 773 (Fed.Cir.1985).

Clay argues that the claims at issue were improperly rejected over Hetherington and Sydansk, because Sydansk is nonanalogous art. Whether a reference in the prior art is "analogous" is a fact question. Thus, we review the Board's decision on this point under the clearly erroneous standard.

Two criteria have evolved for determining whether prior art is analogous: (1) whether the art is from the same field of endeavor, regardless of the problem addressed, and (2) if the reference is not within the field of the inventor's endeavor, whether the reference still is reasonably pertinent to the particular problem with which the inventor is involved.

The Board found Sydansk to be within the field of Clay's endeavor because, as the Examiner stated, "one of ordinary skill in the art would certainly glean from [Sydansk] that the rigid gel as taught therein would have a number of applications within the manipulation of the storage and processing of hydrocarbon liquids ... [and that] the gel as taught in Sydansk would be expected to function in a similar manner as the bladders in the Hetherington patent." These findings are clearly erroneous.

The PTO argues that Sydansk and Clay's inventions are part of a common endeavor—"maximizing withdrawal of petroleum stored in petroleum reservoirs." However, Sydansk cannot be considered to be within Clay's field of endeavor merely because both relate to the petroleum industry. Sydansk teaches the use of a gel in unconfined and irregular volumes within generally underground natural oil-bearing formations to channel flow in a desired direction; Clay teaches the introduction of gel to the confined dead volume of a man-made storage tank. The Sydansk process operates in extreme conditions, with petroleum formation temperatures as high as 115 degrees C and at significant well bore pressures; Clay's process apparently operates at ambient temperature and atmospheric pressure. Clay's field of endeavor is the storage of refined liquid hydrocarbons. The field of endeavor of Sydansk's invention, on the other hand, is the extraction of crude petroleum. The Board clearly erred in considering Sydansk to be within the same field of endeavor as Clay's.

Even though the art disclosed in Sydansk is not within Clay's field of endeavor, the reference may still properly be combined with Hetherington if it is reasonably pertinent to the problem Clay attempts to solve. A reference is reasonably pertinent if, even though it may be in a different field from that of the inventor's endeavor, it is one which, because of the matter with which it deals, logically would have commended itself to an inventor's attention in considering his problem. Thus, the purposes of both the invention and the prior art are important in determining whether the reference is reasonably pertinent to the problem the invention attempts to solve. If a reference disclosure has the same purpose as the claimed invention, the reference relates to the same problem, and that fact supports use of that reference in an obviousness rejection. An inventor may well have been motivated to consider the reference when making his invention. If it is directed to a different purpose, the inventor would accordingly have had less motivation or occasion to consider it.

Sydansk's gel treatment of underground formations functions to fill anomalies so as to improve flow profiles and sweep efficiencies of injection and production fluids through a formation, while Clay's gel functions to displace liquid product from the dead volume of a storage tank. Sydansk is concerned with plugging formation anomalies so that fluid is subsequently diverted by the gel into the formation matrix, thereby forcing bypassed oil contained in the matrix toward a production well. Sydansk is faced with the problem of recovering oil from rock, i.e., from a matrix which is porous, permeable sedimentary rock of a subterranean formation where water has channeled through formation anomalies and bypassed oil present in the matrix. Such a problem is not reasonably pertinent to the particular problem with which Clay was involved—preventing loss of stored product to tank dead volume while preventing contamination of such product. Moreover, the subterranean formation of Sydansk is not structurally similar to, does not operate under the same temperature and pressure as, and does not function like Clay's storage tanks. *See In re Ellis*, 476 F.2d 1370, 1372, 177 U.S.P.Q. 526, 527 (CCPA 1973) ("the similarities and differences in structure and function of the invention disclosed in the references ... carry far greater weight [in determining analogy]").

A person having ordinary skill in the art would not reasonably have expected to solve the problem of dead volume in tanks for storing refined petroleum by considering a reference dealing with plugging underground formation anomalies. The Board's finding to the contrary is clearly erroneous. Since Sydansk is non-analogous art, the rejection over Hetherington in view of Sydansk cannot be sustained.

Notes

1. **Pertinent Prior Art.** Why need the patent law go to these lengths to distinguish analogous technical fields from nonpertinent prior art? Recall that novelty determination has no test of relevance; novelty-defeating technology can come from a technical fields very distant from that of the claimed invention. Why should nonobviousness differ from novelty in this respect?

2. **The Patent Office Classification Scheme.** The United States Patent and Trademark Office maintains a patent classification system to assist examiners in their searches of the prior art. Should this regime carry weight in determining whether prior art is analogous or not to the claimed invention? Most courts lend the PTO system some credence in this determination, but do not make it conclusive. As noted in *In re Mlot–Fijalkowski*, 676 F.2d 666, 213 U.S.P.Q. 713 (CCPA 1982): "Such evidence is inherently weak ... because considerations in forming a classification system differ from those relating to a person of ordinary skill seeking solution for a particular problem."

3. **Analogous Simple Mechanical Arts.** The breadth of knowledge embraced within the simple mechanical arts often leads to surprising results in patent cases. In *Sage Products Inc. v. Devon Industries Inc.*, 880 F.Supp. 718, 35 U.S.P.Q.2d 1321 (C.D.Cal.1994), the court held that a 1891 patent on a "simple and secure street letter-box" formed analogous art to a disposal container for hazardous medical waste. According to the court, the patent on the letter-box "was concerned with a container which could receive deposits, yet prevent persons from reaching inside," exactly the task to which the disposal container was directed. Another decision, *In re Paulsen*, 30 F.3d 1475, 31 U.S.P.Q.2d 1671 (Fed.Cir.1994), held that references "directed to hinges and latches as used in a desktop telephone directory, a piano lid, a kitchen cabinet, a washing machine cabinet, a wooden furniture cabinet, or a two-part housing for storing stereo cassettes" were analogous art to a claim for a portable computer. The court reasoned:

The problems encountered by the inventors of the [patented portable computer] were problems that were not unique to portable computers. They concerned how to connect and secure the computer's display housing to the computer while meeting certain size constraints and functional requirements. The prior art cited by the examiner discloses various means of connecting a cover (or lid) to a device so that the cover is free to swing radially along the connection axis, as well as means of securing the cover in an open or closed position. We agree with the Board that given the nature of the problem confronted by the inventors, one of ordinary skill in the art "would have consulted the mechanical arts for housings, hinges, latches, springs, etc." Thus, the cited references are "reasonably pertinent" and we therefore conclude that the Board's findings that the references are analogous was not clearly erroneous.

Does the application of such diverse and venerable art strike you as fair? What other approaches could the patent law adopt?

4. Comparative Approaches. Numerous decisions from the Boards of Appeal of the European Patent Office establish that, for purposes of a determination of "inventive step," the person of ordinary skill in the art will refer to the state of the art in neighboring fields as well as to general technical knowledge. That the determination of whether a field borders upon the subject matter of the invention is often a fine one is demonstrated by "Pencil Sharpener/Moebius," European Patent Office, Technical Board of Appeal 3.2.1, [1986] Off. J. Eur. Pat. Off. 50, where the Board reasoned that:

5.3 ... The Examining Division arrived at its conclusion because it was of the opinion that a person skilled in the art wishing to improve the sharpener according to the German application (Auslegeschrift) 1 003 093 could also be expected to take into account also the field of securing mechanisms for savings-box slots. Such securing mechanisms represented a neighbouring field because both pencil sharpeners and savings boxes belonged to the "broader field of the closing of containers." The Board is unable to share this view.

5.3.1 While it is indeed perfectly reasonable to expect a person skilled in the art if need be, i.e., in the absence of useful suggestions in the relevant field as to how a given problem might be solved, to look for suitable parallels in neighboring fields, the question of what is a neighbouring field is one of fact and the solution depends, in the opinion of the Board, on whether the fields are so closely related that the person skilled in the art seeking a solution to a given problem would take into account developments in the neighbouring field. It is furthermore quite reasonable to expect a skilled person to refer to the state of the art in the general field of technology in which the same problem or problems similar to those in the special field of the application extensively arise and of which a person skilled in the art must be expected to be aware.

5.3.2 In the present case, even adopting the same premise as the Examining Division that the person skilled in the art by abstracting the problem would eventually, in his search for suggestions as to how he might solve the problem underlying the application, turn to the broader, that is to say general field of container closing, while he would then have entered what the Examining Division considers to be the generic field, he would not have reached the field of securing mechanisms for savings-box slots. In view of the technological differences between the two fields—storage of coins in a container as opposed to sharpening of pencils with provision for collection of shavings—there is no reason why it should occur to a skilled person to refer to his specific area—which the Examining Division considers to be part of the same broader field—to see how similar problems are solved there. . . .

5.3.4   The field of such securing mechanisms is therefore not one of the neighbouring fields to which a skilled person concerned with the development of pencil sharpeners would also refer, should the need arise, in search of appropriate solutions to his problem.

Another example of this approach is provided by an application describing a carpet with fiber-optic cables woven into its pile. When exposed to a light source, the carpet produced decorative effects. The Examining Division rejected the application based upon a United States patent describing a wig which also featured fiber-optic cables, but the Mechanical Board of Appeal 3.2.3 reversed based upon the problems solved by the products and the demands made upon the products during use. T 767/89 (Apr. 16, 1991). Do you agree with the Board's distinction, or would you consider it instead mere hairsplitting?

IN RE WINSLOW

United States Court of Customs and Patent Appeals, 1966.
365 F.2d 1017, 151 U.S.P.Q. 48.

RICH, JUDGE, delivered the opinion of the court:

Appellant presents the usual argument that hindsight reconstruction has been employed by the examiner and the board. We disagree with that position. We think the proper way to apply the 103 obviousness test to a case like this is to first picture the inventor as working in his shop with the prior art references—which he is presumed to know—hanging on the walls around him. One then notes that what applicant Winslow built here he admits is basically a Gerbe bag holder having air-blast bag opening to which he has added two bag retaining pins. If there were any bag holding problem in the Gerbe machine when plastic bags were used, their flaps being gripped only by spring pressure between the top and bottom plates, Winslow would have said to himself, "Now what can I do to hold them more securely?" Looking around the walls, he would see Hellman's envelopes with holes in their flaps hung on a rod. He would then say to himself, "Ha. I can punch holes in my bags and put a little rod (pin) through the holes. That will hold them. After filling the bags, I'll pull them off the pins as does Hellman. Scoring the flap should make tearing easier."

Thus does appellant make his claimed invention merely by applying knowledge clearly present in the prior art. Section 103 requires us to presume full knowledge by the inventor of the prior art in the field of his endeavor. We see no "hindsight reconstruction" here, but only selection and application by the examiner of very pertinent art. That is his duty.

The decision of the board is affirmed.

SMITH, JUDGE (dissenting).

To say that a pin cooperating with aligning holes in a bag flap extension is the obvious answer to eliminating the drawbacks in Gerbe, is, I think, an unwarranted simplification which results only from hindsight reasoning. A comparison of the respective devices clearly indicates the differences between appellant's device and those of Hellman and Gerbe.

The problem as I see it is that the simplicity of appellant's device has obscured the unobvious merits of appellant's improvement over prior art devices. It is apparent ... that appellant's device clearly distinguishes itself from the prior art apparatus. All he has is a spring board, a clamping plate with pins, and an air funnel. The appealed claims to this structure are direct and uncomplicated. Appellant does not have a complicated structure from which he may create limitations for his claims in an effort to distinguish over prior art devices. Rather, his claims distinguish over the prior art by the absence of complicated structure; his claimed invention is simplicity itself in the art of opening and filling thermoplastic bags.

I would reverse the decision of the board.

Notes

1. A Compelling Image. The image of the inventor working in his laboratory with all the pertinent prior art hanging on the walls around him illustrates well the notion that an inventor is presumed to know analogous prior art. Can you detect, however, any danger in the image?

2. An Important Lesson. Following the issuance of *Winslow*, its image became very popular in trial court opinions. *See, e.g., Decca Ltd. v. United States,* 420 F.2d 1010, 1023, 164 U.S.P.Q. 348, 359 (Ct.Cl.1970). These courts often did not perceive the limitations of the image. The image cannot convey, for instance, that the analogous prior art references that the inventor is presumed to know would be randomly intermixed on his wall with voluminous amounts of non-analogous references and maybe even references that taught away from his solution. To visualize the inventor with only the closest analogous arts hanging in front of his eyes would be another form of prohibited hindsight—a hindsight editing of the most applicable references out of the vast array of inapplicable or misleading references by using the invention as the editing standard.

Years later, Judge Rich recognized the danger of his *Winslow* image and made a correction:

> The solicitor, on the other hand, relies on *In re Winslow,* for the proposition that a combination of feature shown by references is legally obvious is it would have been obvious to "the inventor ... working in his shop with the prior art references—which he is presumed to know—

hanging on the wall around him," [cite deleted], a statement made by the writer and limited by reference to "a case like this," which limitation it is desired to emphasize. As we have often remarked, *language* from an opinion should not be divorced from the facts of the case in which the language was used.

In *Winslow* we said that the principal secondary reference was "in the very same art" as appellant's invention and characterized all the references as "very pertinent art." The language relied on by the solicitor, quoted above, therefore, does not apply in cases where the very point in issue is whether one of ordinary skill In the art would have *selected*, without the advantage of hindsight and knowledge of the applicant's disclosure, the particular references which the examiner applied. As we also said in *Winslow*, "Section 103 requires us to presume full knowledge by the inventor of the *prior* art *in the field of his endeavor*" (emphasis, except of "prior," added), but it does not require us to presume full knowledge of the inventor of prior art *outside* the field of his endeavor, i.e., of "non-analogous" art. In that respect, it only requires us to presume that the inventor would have that ability to select and utilize knowledge from other arts reasonably pertinent to his particular problem which would be expected of a man of ordinary skill in the art to which the subject matter pertains.

In re Antle, 444 F.2d 1168, 170 U.S.P.Q. 285, 287–88 (CCPA 1971).

Prior Art for Nonobviousness Exercises

1. Since 1990, Whetstone and Blackstone have both worked for the Research and Development Division of the Sentinel Electronics Company of Arkham, Massachusetts. On December 15, 2000, Whetstone conceives of a new ultrasonic diagnosing apparatus. He immediately informs Blackstone about his idea for apparatus. Whetstone then works diligently in his laboratory until January 31, 2001, at which time he reduces the invention to practice. The Sentinel Electronics Company files a patent application on behalf of Whetstone on August 1, 2001.

On December 17, 2000, Blackstone realizes that she can improve upon Whetstone's ultrasonic diagnosing apparatus. Because of her workload, she does not start on the project until January 7, 2001. Without further consulting Whetstone, she ultimately completes her ultrasonic diagnosing apparatus on January 20, 2001. Although Blackstone's invention represents an improvement over Whetstone's, it would have been obvious in light of the Whetstone apparatus. The Sentinel Electronics Company files a patent application on behalf of Blackstone on October 1, 2001.

May a patent examiner properly cite the Whetstone invention as prior art against Blackstone's application?

2. Thales is an independent inventor living in Syracuse, New York. Thales files a patent application on April 1, 1999, on an invention that he conceived on February 28, 1997, and reduced to practice with due diligence on August 8, 1998. The patent examiner rejected all of the claims of the application under section 103 in light of two prior art references, Heraclitus and McTaggert. Heraclitus is a Greek patent which issued on January 5, 1998, and is based upon a Greek application filed on March 18, 1997.

McTaggert is a United States patent which issued on September 20, 1999, and is based upon a United States application filed on February 5, 1997. The examiner stated that it would have been obvious to modify the structure disclosed and claimed by Heraclitus as suggested by McTaggert.

Are Heraclitus and McTaggert valid prior art against Thales? What is the best way to respond to the patent examiner's rejection?

3. On October 25, 2000, inventors Disraeli and Pitt filed in the United States Patent and Trademark Office a patent application claiming an expandable watch strap. The examiner rejected the claims in the application as being obvious under the combination of § 102(e) and § 103 over a patent granted on April 1, 2001, to coinventors Disraeli and Gladstone who disclosed, but did not claim, the watch strap. Disraeli and Gladstone filed their patent application on December 25, 1998. At the time their respective inventions were made, Disraeli, Pitt and Gladstone were each obligated to assign their inventions to their common employer, the Veil Watch Company. *Can this rejection be avoided?*

Chapter Nine

THE PATENT SPECIFICATION: OBJECTIVE DISCLOSURE

Analogized to the contract law, the Patent Act permits the formation of binding agreements between inventors and the public. Under these agreements, inventors receive exclusive rights in exchange for full disclosure of their inventions. To ensure that the public gets its share of the bargain, the Patent Act includes provisions to ensure adequate disclosure of inventions. The U.S. patent statute sets forth these provisions at § 112 ¶ 1:

> The specification shall contain a written description of the invention, and of the manner and process of making and using it, in such full, clear, concise, and exact terms as to enable any person skilled in the art to which it pertains, or with which it is most nearly connected, to make and use the same, and shall set forth the best mode contemplated by the inventor of carrying out his invention.

This important section requires both that the applicant disclose "how to make" and "how to use" the claimed invention. Section 112 ¶ 1 further requires disclosure of the "best mode contemplated by the inventor," a unique aspect of United States law taken up in Chapter 10.

The central doctrine to ensure adequate disclosure—the "how to make and use" requirements—is referred to as "enablement." Enablement is potentially at issue for every claim in every patent. As the essential bargain for the exclusive right of the patent, the patentee must teach the public to make and use the invention. In other words, the patent instrument itself must "enable" other skilled artisans to practice the disclosed technology. The first U.S. patent statute, the Patent Act of 1790, expressed this policy as follows:

> [W]hich specification shall be so particular as * * * to enable a workman or other person skilled in the art of manufacture, whereof it is a branch, or wherewith it may be the nearest connected, to make, construct or use the same, to the end that the public may have the full benefit thereof, after the expiration of the patent term....

438

Enablement accomplishes more in the Patent Act than just requiring adequate disclosure of inventive details. As already noted, patent claims stake the outer boundaries of the right to exclude. Those claims, however, often use abstract and indeterminate terms to define the extent of those boundaries. Without a clear test to tie the claim disclosure to the extent of the inventor's contribution to the useful arts, those claims could expand to encompass more than the inventor actually invented. The enablement requirement serves to delimit the boundaries of patent protection by ensuring that the scope of a patent claim accords with the extent of the inventor's technical contribution.

Section 112 ¶ 1 also refers to a "written description," a reference upon which the case law has constructed a separate doctrine. The so-called "written description" doctrine ordinarily operates to police priority when inventors amend their disclosures. The Patent Act allows inventors to amend their applications during the application process and after their original filing date. When an applicant adds new claims or new subject matter to existing claims after the original filing date, the "written description" test requires that the original specification support the new matter. The written description requirement thus ensures that inventors may not improperly amend their patents by including subsequent technical advances in a previously filed application.

§ 9.1 ENABLEMENT—HOW TO MAKE

The "how to make" requirement of 35 U.S.C.A. § 112, ¶ 1, provides that "[t]he specification shall contain * * * the manner and process of making * * * [the invention], in such full, clear, concise, and exact terms as to enable any person skilled in the art to which it pertains, or with which it is most nearly connected, to make * * * the [invention]." The specification ideally provides a cookbook recipe showing a person of skill in the art "how to make" the invention. Starting with the state of technology in the prior art, enablement requires the specification to teach how to make the claimed invention.

GOULD v. HELLWARTH

United States Court of Customs and Patent Appeals, 1973.
472 F.2d 1383, 176 U.S.P.Q. 515.

Before MARKEY, CHIEF JUDGE, and RICH, ALMOND, BALDWIN, and LANE, ASSOCIATE JUDGES.

LANE, JUDGE.

This appeal is from the decision of the Board of Patent Interferences awarding Hellwarth, the junior party, priority of invention as to two counts to a so_called "Q-switched" or "Giant Pulse" laser. Hellwarth is involved on his application serial No. 128,458 filed August 1, 1961. The appellant, Gould, is involved on his application serial No. 804,540 filed April 6, 1959. The determinative issue is whether the disclosure of the Gould application was adequate to enable a person skilled in the art to make an operable device (35 U.S.C. 112). We agree with the board that it was not and affirm its decision.

The Subject Matter

The laser is a device which provides light amplification by stimulated emission of radiation. Amplification of electronic radiation by stimulated emission of radiation was first attained by devices operating in the microwave frequency range and known by the acronym "maser." The laser, also known as an "optical maser," resulted subsequently when such amplification was achieved at light or optical frequencies. The basic requirement of a maser or laser is a working medium, usually a gas or a solid, containing atoms or molecules having one or more sets of energy levels. Unlike the condition at equilibrium, where lower energy states of a material are more heavily populated than the higher energy states, material constituting a laser working medium must have a higher energy level populated by a significantly greater number of atoms or molecules than a lower level. A medium in such nonequilibrium condition is said to have an "inverted population" or "negative temperature." The medium may be excited or "pumped" to provide the inverted population by means of a source of electromagnetic energy, such as a strong light of suitable wavelength. Laser activity results from the medium in a state of population inversion emitting wave energy of a frequency corresponding to the separation of the inverted pair of energy levels.

The two counts define an "optical maser" comprising basic laser elements—a laser material, means for pumping the material to a condition of stimulated emission, and reflecting means defining a radiation path in the material for repeatedly reflecting the stimulated emission energy radiated by the material between the reflecting means. Additionally, they call for the combination with those elements of means intermediate the reflecting means in the path of the radiated energy for altering the amount of stimulated energy reflected by the reflecting means. The altering means permits impeding the reflections to prevent emissions from the laser for certain periods to allow build-up of the amount of population inversion so that "giant pulses" of greatly enhanced energy concentration are emitted when the impediment is removed. The name "Q-switched" is applied to the modified laser because the altering means controls or varies the electrical quality or "Q" of the "cavity" in which the working material is confined.

Count 3 is representative of the involved counts and reads as follows:

3. Apparatus for controlling the stimulated emission energy output of an optical maser comprising an optical maser material, means for pumping said material to a condition of stimulated emission, means for abstracting energy from said maser, reflecting means defining a radiation path including said maser material for repeatedly reflecting the stimulated emission energy radiated by said material between said reflecting means, [and] means in the path of

said radiated energy for altering the amount of stimulated energy reflected between said reflecting means.

THE PROCEEDINGS BELOW

Hellwarth asserted no date of invention prior to Gould's filing date. No priority evidence was submitted by either party and both parties rely on their filing dates. On motion by Hellwarth, final hearing was set to consider the sufficiency of the Gould application, and Hellwarth was granted permission to take testimony of Dr. Bela Lengyel on that question. Appellant took testimony of Dr. Arnold Bloom, Dr. Grant Fowles and Paul Rabinowitz in rebuttal. Lengyel had worked at Hughes Aircraft when the first operable laser was built there by Dr. Theodore H. Maiman in 1960. Lengyel was chairman of a college physics department at the time of testifying and had done extensive writing in the laser field. Bloom and Grant did extensive work in the laser field beginning in 1961 and 1962, respectively. Rabinowitz was employed by TRG, Inc. on laser projects which began in 1959. As the board recognized, all four witnesses were highly qualified in the laser field at the time they testified.

The Gould application includes a lengthy disclosure directed to obtaining laser action. It also suggests certain uses and refinements for an operable laser, including means for Q-switching such a laser. It is not questioned that the disclosure of the Q-switching feature would be adequate if the application adequately disclosed an operable laser in which the feature could be incorporated. Rather, appellee charged, and the board agreed, that the disclosure was insufficient as of its filing date to enable a person skilled in the art to make an operable laser.

Lengyel's testimony was summarized by the board as follows (with reference to the record omitted):

> The testimony of Lengyel is to the effect that as of 1959 the Gould disclosure did not have sufficient information for one skilled in the art to construct an operative laser of any kind and noted that the Schawlow–Townes paper included most of the information that was available but an operable laser was not made until 1960 by Maiman. According to Lengyel, in order to construct an operable laser one skilled in quantum electronics would have to know the physical parameters of the material, e.g., its temperature or temperature range; if gas filled, the pressure and approximate size or some relationship between the possible dimensions of the device. The minimum radiation necessary for its excitation if optically excited should be known. If excited by discharge, then the condition of operation of that discharge should be known. The basic properties of the cavity such as reflectivity and curvature of the mirrors should be known. The relation between the various parameters would have to be known quite precisely in order to obtain an operable laser.

Lengyel in his testimony reviewed the Gould disclosure and pointed out that although details are disclosed with respect to various lasers, the application does not disclose a complete set of operating parameters for any laser.

The board reviewed the testimony of appellant's witnesses at length, noting particularly that Bloom and Fowles expressed the opinion that the Gould application gave sufficient information as of 1959 to build a laser. However, it stated:

> The testimony of all the witnesses is fairly consistent in recognizing that the Gould application does disclose various working mediums, dimensions and theories but there is no information which is complete enough for one skilled in the art to build an operative laser particularly at a time when one "skilled in the art of lasers" was virtually non-existent.

The board also stated:

> The testimony of the witnesses has been helpful to the extent of indicating what knowledge is necessary to construct an operative laser. However, this knowledge, as evidenced by documents entered in evidence and submitted under Rule 282, is the summation of the work of many men spending considerable time experimenting. For the witnesses or any other men skilled in the art to state with certainty what they would have done with the Gould disclosure, coupled with whatever prior knowledge was available in 1959, even with an intense desire for success, is pure speculation.

In reaching the ultimate conclusion that "Gould had inadequate disclosure as of 1959 to build an operative laser," the board stated:

> The Gould specification has much disclosure but much work had to be done subsequent to the filing of the application before an operative laser was made. The patent statutes do not contemplate grant of patents for such a disclosure, which is merely a fertile field for experimentation.

OPINION

Appellant emphasizes that the counts are not drawn to a laser per se but to a laser modified by means for permitting Q-switched or pulsed operation. He also argues that Hellwarth derived the laser per se on which he imposes Q-switching from the ruby laser successfully operated by his then co-worker at Hughes Aircraft Company, Maiman, before the Hellwarth application was filed. It is apparent, however, that such circumstances are common, if not usual, with respect to improvement inventions like that involved here, and they have no bearing on the outcome. As in any priority dispute, Gould can prevail only if his application meets the requirements set out in the first paragraph of 35 U.S.C. 112. The application must include a disclosure of the invention "in such terms as to enable any person skilled in the art to which it pertains, or with which it is most nearly connected, to make and use the same."

As recognized by Gould in his application, the problem faced by one seeking to make an operable laser in 1959 was that of successfully applying the principle of amplification by stimulated emission of radiation, which had been successfully applied to microwaves in the maser, to optical or light radiation. Cavities or resonators used to confine the working medium in masers, which characteristically had dimensions in the order of one wavelength, e.g. 1–100 centimeters, could not be used in light amplification because of the comparatively short wavelength of light. As Gould points out in his brief:

> Masers operate at microwave frequencies so that their wavelengths differ by a factor of a thousand or more from those of lasers and thus make the maser microwave resonator technology inadaptable to lasers.

While all the difficulties faced in making an operable laser need not be enumerated, it is clear from events that followed that the transition from microwave to light wavelengths proved no easy task.

Dr. Townes, in cooperation with Dr. A. Schawlow of Bell Laboratories, suggested the possibility of making the extension from masers to light wavelengths in a paper published in 1958. Gould, who had been a graduate student at Columbia University where Townes taught, had begun a literature search in the field. He gained employment with TRG and prepared for it a proposal for research work to build a laser, based largely on the same material as his application. That proposal resulted in a contract with Advanced Research Projects Agency, a Government agency, for research and development work in the amount of nearly one million dollars. The resulting project was assigned a secret security classification. Gould continued to work for TRG but was excluded from the project for inability to obtain security clearance. TRG spent the nearly one million dollar sum in the year following Gould's filling date (May 1959 to May 1960) is attempting to build a laser, but its efforts resulted in failure.

In the meantime, other scientists were also seeking to produce a laser. Maiman achieved the first operable laser in a pink ruby medium in April of 1960. Appellee, a co-worker of Maiman at Hughes Aircraft, disclosed the Q-switched laser in conjunction with such a ruby laser in his application here. After Maiman's success, his ruby laser was promptly duplicated in other laboratories. Soon thereafter laser activity was achieved in other media by other experimenters. As an example, Javan, Bennett and Herriott of Bell Laboratories announced success with a helium-cesium laser at the end of 1960. Gould and others at TRG arrived at an optically pumped helium-cesium laser in 1961 or 1962.

This brief history of the attainment of the final operating lasers gives firm support to the board's conclusion that the Gould application was insufficient to teach a person skilled in the art how to make a laser. Whether the "person skilled in the art" is viewed in terms of the laser art, even though an operable laser had not yet been made, or with regard to the art to which the laser "is most nearly connected" (35 U.S.C. 112) is not material. The board, as well as the witnesses, considered the case in light of what would be taught to a highly trained person knowledgeable in the fields of microwave masers, spectroscopy, atomic physics and aware of published proposals for making a laser, and we do the same.

The testimony of appellant's witnesses was generally in agreement with Lengyel's view that the application does not disclose a complete set of parameters for a laser as well as his observations as to what knowledge was necessary to produce an operable laser. Opinions of Bloom and Fowles contrary to the board on the ultimate question of whether the Gould disclosure was adequate to enable a person skilled in the art to make an operable laser are incompatible with their testimony as well as that of Lengyel and the other evidence.

In arguing that he does disclose the parameters necessary for a particular laser, appellant states that "[p]erhaps the best example of a complete description of a specific embodiment in the Gould application" is a portion which suggests use of "a gaseous atmosphere comprising a mixture of sodium and mercury" as the working medium. However, both Lengyel, in 1967, and Bloom, in 1968, testified that no sodium-mercury laser had been known to operate. In view of the widespread efforts to obtain laser action in different media, which the record shows followed Maiman's initial success in 1960, no basis is seen for accepting this alleged "complete description" as teaching how to make an operable laser.

Appellant also refers to TRG's having constructed an operable helium-cesium laser "after the restrictions on Gould were relaxed enough to permit him to make significant contributions to the development." However, it is plain from the application and the testimony that neither physical dimensions nor particular operating conditions for such a laser are given in the Gould application. Also it was not until between January and April of 1962 that TRG's optically pumped helium-cesium laser was operated. By that time, the state of the art had been advanced by the successful operation of the ruby laser by Maiman and the helium-cesium laser by Javan and his associates. Additionally, a nearly confocal arrangement of mirrors, based on a proposal made by Bell Laboratories in 1961 and not on the Gould disclosure, was used. These circumstances are inconsistent with any claim that the Gould application adequately disclosed how to make an operable helium-cesium laser.

Nor does a claim by appellant that his application "discloses the ruby laser" find any factual support. The application merely lists ruby as a possible alternative medium with the suggestion that it be a single crystal. Information as to the type, size or orientation of the crystal and exactly how it is to be excited is not given. While ruby, in certain forms, was a known maser material, reports of TRG work made of record show that its workers considered it as a laser material in early 1960 but rejected it. Maiman made extensive investigation before finding that a particular ruby material, a pink ruby, would provide an operative laser under particular conditions.

We conclude that the Gould application involved herein does not provide an enabling disclosure of how to make the subject matter of the counts. The decision of the board awarding priority of invention to Hellwarth is accordingly affirmed.

Notes

1. Gould and the Laser Patent. Assume that once workers in the field learn how to make a laser, the disclosure in the '540 application would enable them to construct a Q-switched laser. How then could it be fair to hold that the claims of the '540 application were invalid because they were not enabled by that disclosure?

Gordon Gould's 1959 patent application spawned an impressive amount of litigation, of which the above case is merely one example. This case should not convey the incorrect impression that Gould lost all rights to obtain a patent on a laser. Creative patent attorneys later drafted claims to an optical amplifier based on Gould's original specification. In cases such as *Gould v. Control Laser Corp.*, 866 F.2d 1391 (Fed.Cir.1989), a jury held that laser devices infringed these claims. As a result, Gould later collected considerable royalties from the application.

2. The Specification as a Production Document. It is difficult to state concisely the precise level of detail required for a patent specification to satisfy the enablement requirement. The Federal Circuit in *Christianson v. Colt Industries Operating Corp.*, 822 F.2d 1544, 3 U.S.P.Q.2d 1241 (Fed.Cir. 1987) addressed this problem:

> Patents are not production documents, and nothing in the patent law requires that a patentee must disclose data on how to mass-produce the invented product.... [T]he law has never required that a patentee who elects to manufacture its claimed invention must disclose in its patents the dimensions, tolerances, drawings and other parameters of mass production not necessary to enable one skilled in the art to practice (as distinguished from mass-produce) the invention. Nor it is an objective of the patent system to supply, free of charge, production data and production drawings to competing manufacturers.

3. The Germ of an Idea. In *Genentech, Inc. v. Novo Nordisk*, 108 F.3d 1361, 42 U.S.P.Q.2d 1001 (Fed.Cir.1997), the court struck down a patent directed towards a method for producing a protein of hGH amino acids including the step of cleaving a conjugate protein to produce the desired protein, part of a process commonly called "cleavable fusion expression." The defendant, Novo, urged that the patent did not provide an enabling disclosure with a mere statement of the possibility of cleavable fusion expression, along with disclosure of the DNA sequence encoding hGH, a single enzyme for cleaving undisclosed conjugate proteins, and a statement of that enzyme's cleavage sites as being potential amino acid extensions conjugated to hGH. The patentee, Genentech, instead argued that those skilled in the art of recombinant protein expression and purification at the time of filing, July 5, 1979, would have been able to use cleavable fusion expression to produce hGH without undue experimentation. The Federal Circuit concluded:

There is no dispute that the portion of the specification chiefly relied upon by Genentech and by the district court, does not describe in any detail whatsoever how to make hGH using cleavable fusion expression. For example, no reaction conditions for the steps needed to produce hGH are provided; no description of any specific cleavable conjugate protein appears. The relevant portion of the specification merely describes three (or perhaps four) applications for which cleavable fusion expression is generally well-suited and then names an enzyme that might be used as a cleavage agent (trypsin), along with sites at which it cleaves ("arg-arg or lys-lys, etc."). Thus, the specification does not describe a specific material to be cleaved or any reaction conditions under which cleavable fusion expression would work....

Genentech's arguments, focused almost exclusively on the level of skill in the art, ignore the essence of the enablement requirement. Patent protection is granted in return for an enabling disclosure of an invention, not for vague intimations of general ideas that may or may not be workable. Tossing out the mere germ of an idea does not constitute enabling disclosure. While every aspect of a generic claim certainly need not have been carried out by an inventor, or exemplified in the specification, reasonable detail must be provided in order to enable members of the public to understand and carry out the invention. That requirement has not been met in this specification with respect to the cleavable fusion expression of hGH.

... However, when there is no disclosure of any specific starting material or of any of the conditions under which a process can be carried out, undue experimentation is required; there is a failure to meet the enablement requirement that cannot be rectified by asserting that all the disclosure related to the process is within the skill of the art. It is the specification, not the knowledge of one skilled in the art, that must supply the novel aspects of an invention in order to constitute adequate enablement.

What is the border between a "mere germ of an idea" and an enabled invention? This opinion at least gives some parameters for biotechnology— starting materials, conditions for a process, and disclosure of the process itself. Further discussion of the enablement requirement in the context of biotechnology follows later in this Chapter.

4. Enabling Edison? An old Supreme Court case presented an interesting historical setting for the enablement doctrine. Sawyer and Mann sued the Edison Electric Light Company for infringement of a patent claiming "[a]n incandescing conductor for an electric lamp, of carbonized fibrous or textile material...." Edison had independently discovered that a particular strain of bamboo, when carbonized, served best as a filament. The Supreme Court invalidated the Sawyer and Mann patent with the following reasoning:

Is the complainant entitled to a monopoly of all fibrous and textile materials for incandescent conductors? If the patentees had discovered in fibrous and textile substances a quality common to them all, or to them generally, as distinguishing them from other materials, such as minerals, etc., and such quality or characteristic adapted them peculiarly to incandescent conductors, such claim might not be too broad....

Instead of confining themselves to carbonized paper, as they might properly have done, and in fact did in their third claim, they made a broad claim for every fibrous or textile material, when in fact an examination of over 6,000 vegetable growths showed that none of them possessed the peculiar qualities that fitted them for that purpose. Was everybody, then, precluded by this broad claim from making further investigation? We think not.

* * *

The question really is whether the imperfectly successful experiments of Sawyer and Mann, with carbonized paper and wood carbon, conceding all that is claimed for them, authorize them to put under tribute the results of the brilliant discoveries made by others.

* * *

If the description be so vague and uncertain that no one can tell, except by independent experiments, how to construct the patented device, the patent is void.

Consolidated Elec. Light Co. v. McKeesport, 159 U.S. 465 (1895). The Supreme Court was apparently impressed with "the brilliant discoveries made by [Edison]" in competition with Sawyer and Man. This case illustrates a further purpose of enablement—delimiting the bounds of an invention to leave adequate room for further improvements. Thus, enablement draws the line between initial inventions and patentable improvements. Does the Supreme Court suggest how Sawyer and Man might have enabled their broad claims? Due to Sawyer's and Man's failure to enable the scope of their claims, is the Supreme Court justified in invalidating the patent? How does this result promote invention and innovation?

5. The Deposit Requirement. The advent of biotechnology placed new strains upon the enablement requirement. Some inventions cannot be enabled by a written explanation. The way to enable such inventions is to provide a sample. Major patent offices therefore adopted a procedure whereby inventors of novel microorganisms could fulfill statutory enablement requirements by depositing a sample of the organism in a facility open to the public. *E.g., Bäckerhefe* ("Baker's Yeast"), 1975 GRUR 430 (German Federal Supreme Court); *American Cyanamid Co. (Dann's) Patent*, [1971] RPC 425, [1970] FSR 443 (House of Lords); *In re Lundak*, 773 F.2d 1216, 227 U.S.P.Q. 90 (Fed.Cir.1985); *see also* Aiji Watanabe, *The Current Status and Problems in the Deposit of Patented Mircoorganisms in Japan*, in 4 IIP Bulletin 32 (1995). The inventor of a novel microorganism subsequently faced two significant problems when attempting to obtain patent protection in many different countries. First, with needless expense and repetition, the inventor had to deposit a sample of an organism in each country where patent protection was sought. Second, the inventor had to ensure that each depository would maintain a policy of public access for the duration of the patent.

The Budapest Treaty on the International Recognition of Deposits of Microorganisms for the Purposes of Patent Protection addressed these problems with duplicative deposit requirements. The Budapest Treaty establishes an international certification process for depository organizations that store, catalog and maintain samples of microorganisms. Treaty signatories have agreed that use of any single International Depository Authority (IDA) will fulfill the deposit requirement of their patent law. Thus, a deposit in one repository will operate as a deposit in each nation. The treaty is largely a procedural one, however; it does not address the extent of the disclosure requirements established by individual national patent laws.

Does the deposit concept have application outside the field of biotechnology? It bears similarity to the former requirement of United States patent law that applicants submit a model or exhibit along with their applications. Now, the U.S. Patent and Trademark Office only very rarely requires models along with applications, usually where the applicant claims a perpetual motion machine or apparatus of that nature. *See* 35 U.S.C. § 114; *Manual of Patent Examining Procedure* § 608.03. For discussion and sketches of the old U.S. Patent Office Model Room, as well as an enjoyable depiction of life in the Patent Office from its founding to the mid-twentieth century, see KENNETH W. DOBYNS, THE PATENT OFFICE PONY: A HISTORY OF THE EARLY PATENT OFFICE (1994).

6.   Enablement and Repetition. Suppose the successful implementation of an invention as disclosed depends on chance and is to some extent unrepeatable. A biotechnology application might involve a microbiological process involving mutations, where success in replicating the invention may not be certainly and reliably achieved. In contrast, an application in the electrical arts might concern the production of magnetic cores, where the limitations of current manufacturing techniques will render some portion of them inoperable. Are there any differences between these circumstances that should influence the decision whether or not to consider the disclosure enabling.

7.   Enablement and Scientific Truths. What if the inventor is unaware or actually misinformed about the scientific principles that form the basis of the technical advance? Consider Niels Anton Christiansen's patent on the O-ring, U.S. Patent No. 2,180,795 (1939), "which ranks with the safety pin, paper clip, and zipper on the short list of humankind's simplest, most useful, most ubiquitous, and most elegant inventions." George Wise, *Inventors and Corporations in the Maturing Electrical Industry, 1890–1940*, in INVENTIVE MINDS: CREATIVITY IN TECHNOLOGY 291 (Robert J. Weber & David N. Perkins, eds. 1992). The term "O-ring" describes a hard rubber donut in a square-sided groove with length greater than, and width slightly less than, the ring's cross-section diameter. The O-ring most commonly serves as a piston seal in devices ranging from fountain pens to hydraulic presses, allowing pistons to slide readily without blocking fluid flow. In 1986, design flaws concerning O-rings on the space shuttle *Challenger* focused national interest upon this common technology.

An examination of Christiansen's '795 patent indicates that the inventor did not possess an accurate knowledge of why a rubber ring arranged in this way did not suffer the wear and leaking of its predecessors. The patent's specification asserted that the O-ring was "continuously kneaded or worked to enhance its life," much as if the rubber donut were a sort of muscle continuously being flexed. Later experimentation revealed that the rubber ring in fact undergoes a brief rolling motion during usage, allowing the piston's hydraulic fluid to lubricate the ring. This lubrication increases the ring's life and reduces wear.

If later scientific advances reveal that earlier understandings regarding the operation of a particular invention were incorrect, should the patent be invalidated as nonenabling? *See Diamond Rubber Co. v. Consolidated Rubber Tire Co.*, 220 U.S. 428, 435–36 (1911).

8. Comparative Note. The patent laws of the United States, Europe and Japan are substantially harmonized on the point of how-to-make enablement. Article 83 of the European Patent Convention provides that: "The European patent application must disclose the invention in a manner sufficiently clear and complete for it to be carried out by a person skilled in the art."

In Japan, section 36(4) notes that: "The detailed explanation of the invention . . . shall state the purpose, constitution and effect of the invention in such a manner that it may be easily carried out by a person having ordinary skill in the art to which the invention pertains." The Tokyo High Court has recognized that the specification need not "disclose also the matters known at the technical level contemporary to the filing date (or priority date) and self-evident to those skilled in the art. Such matters could be understood to those skilled in the art who read the specification, without explicit explanation." (gyo-ke) No. 199/1975 (the "sodium aluminate" case); *see* Tetsu Tanabe & Harold C. Wegner, Japanese Patent Practice 120 (1986).

Despite the similarity of these requirements, most patent professionals familiar with foreign patent instruments will acknowledge that they tend to be quite shorter than those in the United States. This trend is explained in Tetsu Tanabe & Harold C. Wegner, Japanese Patent Law § 420 (1979):

> In Japan, the domestic applicant tends toward the drafting of a relatively brief disclosure of the invention. This is not due necessarily to any motive to "hide" aspects of how to make and use the invention, but is more from the standpoint that making a detailed, technically beautiful description of the invention takes *time*. In a first-to-file system, an applicant who painstakingly drafts his application only to find that his competitor has raced to the Patent Office with a completed application a day earlier, is hardly rewarded for such noble efforts of disclosure (if such are his motives). He has lost the race to the steps of the Patent Office and his beautiful application will be rejected.

ATLAS POWDER CO. v. E.I. DU PONT DE NEMOURS & CO.

United States Court of Appeals, Federal Circuit, 1984.
750 F.2d 1569, 224 U.S.P.Q. 409.

Before Markey, Chief Judge, and Baldwin and Miller, Circuit Judges.

Baldwin, Circuit Judge.

This is an appeal by E.I. du Pont De Nemours & Co. and its customer Alamo Explosives Co., Inc. (collectively, "Du Pont"). The appeal is from a final judgment of the United States District Court for the Northern District of Texas holding product claims 1–5, 7, 12–14, and 16–17 of U.S. Patent No. 3,447,978 ('978 patent), issued to Harold Bluhm on June 3, 1969 and assigned to the Atlas Powder Co. ("Atlas"), not invalid under 35 U.S.C. §§ 102, 103, and 112, not fraudulently procured, and infringed. We affirm.

BACKGROUND

Briefly, the '978 patent relates to blasting agents, i.e., chemical mixtures that are relatively insensitive to normal modes of detonation but can be made to detonate with a high strength explosive primer. By the mid–1960's, blasting agents consisted of two major types: "ANFO" and "water-containing".

An "ANFO" blasting agent comprised a mixture of particulate ammonium nitrate, usually in the form of small round aggregates known as "prills", and fuel oil (e.g., diesel fuel). They were widely used in mining and construction because of their low cost, ease of handling, and ability to be mixed at the blast site rather than prepackaged at the plant. However, to work properly they could be used only in "dry" holes (without water) because water desensitized the mixture, rendering it nondetonable.

A "water-containing" blasting agent, which was water resistant, generally comprised a slurry of particulate ammonium nitrate (or other oxidizing salt), a solid or liquid fuel, at least 5 percent water, and, as a sensitizer to increase explosive power, either a high explosive such as TNT or a chemical such as nitric acid. Often, a gelling agent was added, particularly in the chemical sensitized slurries, to prevent the separation of sensitizers from slurry by forming a gel (a colloid in which the disperse phase has combined with the continuous phase to produce a viscous, jelly-like product). The use of sensitizers in water-containing blasting agents made preparation and handling more difficult and dangerous and, hence, more costly.

Before the '978 invention, Atlas manufactured a gelled slurry blasting agent called Aquanite, based on U.S. Patent No. 3,164,503, issued to Gehrig and assigned to Atlas. Aquanite used as a sensitizer nitric acid, which was highly caustic to skin and clothing and tended to separate out of the product even in the presence of a gelling agent, thereby reducing the product's stability and shelf life. Also, Aquanite was "hypergolic", i.e., it ignited wood, coal and various chemicals upon contact, which was suspected of causing the blasting agent to detonate prematurely.

THE INVENTION

In 1965, Atlas assigned Harold Bluhm to investigate stabilizing its Aquanite gel. Bluhm experimented with various "emulsions" that did not contain nitric acid or a gelling agent. (An emulsion is a stable mixture of two immiscible liquids; a "water-in-oil" emulsion has a continuous oil and discontinuous aqueous phase; an "oil-in-water" emulsion is the reverse.) In early 1966, Bluhm formulated an intimately mixed water-in-oil, water resistant emulsion blasting agent. The product was sensitized with entrapped air rather than high explosives or chemicals and is the subject matter of the claims at issue. Representative is Claim 1:

1.   An emulsion blasting agent consisting essentially of:

an aqueous solution of ammonium nitrate forming a discontinuous emulsion phase;

a carbonaceous fuel forming a continuous emulsion phase;

an occluded gas dispersed within said emulsion and comprising at least 4% by volume, thereof at 70 degrees F. and atmospheric pressure;

and a water-in-oil type emulsifying agent;

said carbonaceous fuel having a consistency such that said occluded gas is held in said emulsion at a temperature of 70 degrees F.

Claim 1 is the only independent claim in suit. The other, dependent claims describe various ingredients, such as microspheres for the occluded gas, additional fuels (e.g., aluminum), specific ranges of ingredients, and various properties of the blasting agent.

Du Pont's Activities

Du Pont sold a gelled slurry blasting agent until the latter part of the 1970's. In 1976, Du Pont formed a team to study the feasibility of an emulsion blasting agent. The team succeeded in making a water-in-oil emulsion blasting agent which Du Pont began making and selling in August 1978. Atlas sued for infringement in December 1979.

The District Court Proceedings

A non-jury trial was held between January 28 and February 2, 1982. The district court [held] that ... the claims were not invalid for the patent's failure to comply with the "best mode", enablement, and "overclaiming" requirements of 35 U.S.C. § 112.... On appeal, Du Pont contests those holdings, except for the one on best mode.

Issue

Whether the district court erred in holding the patent claims at issue not invalid because of nonenablement.

OPINION

ENABLEMENT

The district court rejected Du Pont's arguments of "overly broad", "overclaiming", and "non-enablement", and its argument that the broad scope of the claims is not supported by the limited disclosure present. In essence, those arguments are one: the '978 disclosure does not enable one of ordinary skill in the art to make and use the claimed invention, and hence, the claimed invention is invalid under 35 U.S.C. § 112, ¶ 1.

To be enabling under § 112, a patent must contain a description that enables one skilled in the art to make and use the claimed invention. *Raytheon Co. v. Roper Corp.*, 724 F.2d at 960, 220 U.S.P.Q. at 599. That some experimentation is necessary does not preclude enablement; the amount of experimentation, however, must not be unduly extensive. Determining enablement is a question of law.

Du Pont argues that the patent disclosure lists numerous salts, fuels, and emulsifiers that could form thousands of emulsions but there is no commensurate teaching as to which combination would work. The disclosure, according to Du Pont, is nothing more than "a list of candidate ingredients" from which one skilled in the art would have to select and experiment unduly to find an operable emulsion.

The district court held it would have been impossible for Bluhm to list all operable emulsions and exclude the inoperable ones. Further, it found such list unnecessary, because one skilled in the art would know how to select a salt and fuel and then apply "Bancroft's Rule" to determine the proper emulsifier. Bancroft's Rule was found by the district court to be a "basic principle of emulsion chemistry," and Du Pont has not shown that finding to be clearly erroneous.

We agree with the district court's conclusion on enablement. Even if some of the claimed combinations were inoperative, the claims are not necessarily invalid. "It is not a function of the claims to specifically exclude ... possible inoperative substances...." *In re Dinh–Nguyen*, 492 F.2d 856, 858–59, 181 U.S.P.Q. 46, 48 (CCPA 1974). Of course, if the number of inoperative combinations becomes significant, and in effect forces one of ordinary skill in the art to experiment unduly in order to practice the claimed invention, the claims might indeed be invalid. That, however, has not been shown to be the case here.

Du Pont contends that, because the '978 examples are "merely prophetic", they do not aid one skilled in the art in making the invention.[1] Because they are prophetic, argues Du Pont, there can be no guarantee that the examples would actually work.

Use of prophetic examples, however, does not automatically make a patent non-enabling. The burden is on one challenging validity to show by clear and convincing evidence that the prophetic examples together with other parts of the specification are not enabling. Du Pont did not meet that burden here. To the contrary, the district court found that the "prophetic" examples of the specification were based on actual experiments that were slightly modified in the patent to reflect what the

---

1. The PTO Manual of Patent Examining Procedure (MPEP) § 608.01(p)(D) (5th ed. 1983), states: Simulated or predicted test results and prophetical examples (paper examples) are permitted in patent applications. Working examples correspond to work actually performed and may describe tests which have actually been conducted and results that were achieved. Paper examples describe the manner and process of making an embodiment of the invention which has not actually been conducted. Paper examples should not be represented as work actually done. Paper examples should not be described using the past tense.

inventor believed to be optimum, and hence, they would be helpful in enabling someone to make the invention.

Du Pont argues that of some 300 experiments performed by Atlas before the filing of the '978 patent application, Atlas' records indicated that 40 percent failed "for some reason or another". The district court agreed that Atlas' records showed 40 percent "failed", but found that Atlas' listing of an experiment as a "failure" or "unsatisfactory" was misleading. Experiments were designated "failures", the district court found, in essence because they were not optimal under all conditions, but such optimality is not required for a valid patent. The district court also found that one skilled in the art would know how to modify slightly many of those "failures" to form a better emulsion. Du Pont has not persuaded us that the district court was clearly erroneous in those findings.

Du Pont asserts that Atlas was able to produce suitable emulsions with only two emulsifiers, "Atmos 300" and "Span 80", and therefore, the disclosure should be construed to read upon only those two emulsifiers. However, Du Pont did not prove that the other disclosed emulsifiers were inoperable. The district court credited testimony by Atlas' expert, Dr. Fowkes, to the effect that he had successfully formed a number of detonable emulsions using a variety of emulsifiers specified in the '978 patent. Further, the district court found that one skilled in the art would know which emulsifiers would work in a given system. Indeed, the district court found that Du Pont's own researchers had little difficulty in making satisfactory emulsions with the emulsifying agents, salts, and fuels listed in the '978 patent. Those findings have not been shown to be clearly erroneous.

In sum, we conclude that Du Pont has failed to show that the district court erred in determining enablement.

Notes

1. **Prophetic Examples.** Does this case suggest to patent practitioners that it is OK to guess, so long as the guess turns out to be right?

2. **Inoperative Embodiments.** If the patent law is directed towards applied technology, why does it allow patents to describe, and even claim, embodiments that are inoperative? Should the burden fall on the applicant to claim a working invention or members of the public who must attempt to piece together the invention for themselves? How many inoperative combinations should suffice to render the patent invalid for lack of enablement?

3. **Enablement and Claim Scope.** In modern patent law, the enablement doctrine also operates to delimit the appropriate scope of patent claims. Specifically, enablement links the protection afforded by the claims to the extent of the inventor's contribution to the useful arts. The following decision explores this aspect of the enablement doctrine.

IN RE WRIGHT

United States Court of Appeals, Federal Circuit, 1993.
999 F.2d 1557, 27 U.S.P.Q.2d 1510.

Before RICH, NEWMAN, and RADER, CIRCUIT JUDGES.

RICH, J.

Dr. Stephen E. Wright appeals from the January 16, 1992 decision of the Board of Patent Appeals and Interferences (Board) of the United States Patent and Trademark Office (PTO) sustaining the Examiner's rejection of claims 1–23, 15–42, and 45–48 of application Serial No. 06/914,620 under 35 USC Section 112, first paragraph, as unsupported by an enabling disclosure. We affirm.

I. BACKGROUND

A. *The Invention*

The claims on appeal are directed to processes for producing live, non-pathogenic vaccines against pathogenic RNA viruses (claims 1–10, 22–37, 40, 45, and 46), vaccines produced by these processes (claims 11, 12, 15–21, 38, and 39), and methods of using certain of these claimed vaccines to protect living organisms against RNA viruses (claims 41 and 42). Wright's specification provides a general description of these processes, vaccines, and methods of use, but only a single working example.

In this example, Wright describes the production of a recombinant vaccine which confers immunity in chickens against the RNA tumor virus known as Prague Avian Sarcoma Virus (PrASV), a member of the Rous Associated Virus (RAV) family. To produce this vaccine, Wright first identified the antigenic gene region of the genome of PrASV as being in the envelope A (env A) gene region of this virus, and then isolated and cloned a large quantity of this antigenic gene region. Following cloning, Wright introduced by transfection the cloned env A genes into C/O cells, a particular chicken embryo cell line. The C/O cells were then infected with the endogenous, non-oncogenic, O-type Rous Associated Virus (RAV–O) and incubated. Genetic recombination and viral replication occurred during incubation, resulting in an impure vaccine containing particles of the recombinant virus referred to as RAV–O Acn, or RAV_O–A. Wright then purified this vaccine to obtain a vaccine containing only genetic recombinant RAV–Acn virus particles. The Examiner ultimately allowed claims 13, 14, 43, and 44, which are specific to the particular process and vaccine disclosed in this example.

Wright seeks allowance, however, of claims which would provide, in varying degrees, a much broader scope of protection than the allowed claims. For example, independent process claim 1 reads:

A process for producing a live non-pathogenic vaccine for a pathogenic RNA virus, comprising the steps of identifying the antigenic and pathogenic gene regions of said virus; performing gene alteration to produce a genome which codes for the antigenicity of the virus, but does not have its pathogenicity; and obtaining an expression of the gene.

Dependent claims 2–10, 22–35, and 40 recite additional limitations to this process. Independent claims 36 and 45 and claims 37 and 46 dependent therefrom, respectively, are also directed to processes for producing vaccines.

Independent product claim 11 reads:

A live, non-pathogenic vaccine for a pathogenic RNA virus, comprising an immunologically effective amount of a viral antigenic, genomic expression having an antigenic determinant region of the RNA virus, but no pathogenic properties.

Dependent claims 15–21 recite additional limitations to this vaccine. Independent claims 38 and 47 and claims 39 and 48 dependent therefrom, respectively, are also directed to vaccines.

Dependent claims 41 and 42 recite methods of protecting living organisms against RNA viruses, which comprise introducing into a host an immunologically effective amount of the vaccine of claims 11 and 38, respectively.

B.   The Rejection

The Examiner took the position in her Examiner's Answer that the claims presently on appeal are not supported by an enabling disclosure because one of ordinary skill in the art would have had to engage in undue experimentation in February of 1983 (the effective filing date of Wright's application) to practice the subject matter of these claims, given their breadth, the unpredictability in the art, and the limited guidance Wright provides in his application. The Examiner noted that many of Wright's claims read on vaccines against all pathogenic RNA viruses, even though RNA viruses are a very diverse and genetically complex group of viruses which include, among others, acquired immunodeficiency syndrome (AIDS) viruses, leukemia viruses, and sarcoma viruses. The Examiner argued that Wright's single working example merely evidenced that Wright had obtained successfully a particular recombinant virus vaccine, and that this single success did not provide "sufficient likelihood" that other recombinant RNA viruses could be constructed without undue experimentation, or if they were constructed, that they would be useful in the design of like viral vaccines. The Examiner noted the inability of the scientific community to develop an efficacious AIDS virus vaccine for humans despite devoting a considerable amount of time and money to do so.

The Examiner further argued that, even though retroviruses as a class may exhibit similar gene order and possess envelope proteins, this alone does not support a general conclusion that all RNA virus envelope proteins will confer protection against the corresponding virus. The Examiner asserted that this held true even among avian RNA tumor viruses. At page 11 of her Answer, the Examiner stated that "one envelope gene's immunogenicity cannot be extrapolated to another envelope gene. The efficacy of each should be ascertained individually."

To support the foregoing, the Examiner relied upon an article by Thomas J. Matthews et al., Prospects for Development of a Vaccine Against HIV, in Human Retroviruses, Cancer, and AIDS: Approaches to Prevention and Therapy 313–25 (1988). This article indicates that AIDS retroviruses, which represent only a subset of all RNA viruses, were known even as late as 1988 to show great genetic diversity, including divergent virus envelopes. It further indicates that, although AIDS retroviruses elicited strong immune responses in goats and chimps in 1988, the resulting antibodies did not prevent retrovirus infectivity. Moreover, this article also recognizes at page 321 that, as of 1988, animal models for HIV infection and disease were likely to be imperfect, and therefore testing of primary vaccine candidates in man was necessary to determine safety, immunogenicity and efficacy.

Finally, the Examiner also argued that, irrespective of immunogenicity and vaccine considerations, the methods of identification, isolation, cloning, and recombination which Wright describes in his application in only a very general manner were not so developed in 1983 as to enable, without undue experimentation, the design and production of recombinant virus vaccines against any and all RNA viruses. The Examiner also asserted that the considerable amount of time and effort that it took Wright to construct the particular avian recombinant virus described in his single working example and to establish its efficacy as a vaccinating agent illustrates the amount of undue experimentation that would have been required in February of 1983 to practice Wright's invention, especially given that the efficacy of the developed virus could not be extrapolated with any certainty to other recombinant viruses at that time.

C. The Board Decision

In its January 16, 1992 decision, the Board held that the Examiner did not err in questioning the enablement of the physiological activity required by the appealed claims, given the breadth of these claims and the fact that a vaccine must by definition provoke an immunoprotective response upon administration. The Board further held that the record did not support Wright's arguments that this single working example enables some of his dependent claims which are closer in scope to the allowed claims than to independent claims 1 and 11. The Board found that, even if Wright was correct in stating that it was generally known that an "immune response" is assured by use of an antigenic envelope protein, the record did not establish that such an "immune response" would have been an immunoprotective one, or moreover, that one skilled in this art would have expected such a result in February of 1983. The Board relied upon the Matthews et al. article as evidencing that "the mere use of an envelope protein gene in the present invention is not seen to necessarily result in the obtention of successful vaccines throughout the scope of even these more limited claims."

II. Discussion

In the present case, the PTO set forth a reasonable basis for finding that the scope of the appealed claims is not enabled by the general description and the single working example in the specification. Consequently, the burden shifted to Wright to present persuasive arguments, supported by suitable proofs where necessary, that the appealed claims are truly enabled. Wright failed to meet this burden.

Both the Examiner and the Board correctly pointed out that Wright's appealed claims are directed to vaccines, and methods of making and using these vaccines, which must by definition trigger an immunoprotective response in the host vaccinated; mere antigenic response is not enough. Both also correctly pointed out that Wright attempts to claim in many of the appealed claims any and all live, non_pathogenic vaccines, and processes for making such vaccines, which elicit immunoprotective activity in any animal toward any RNA virus. In addition, both properly stressed that many of the appealed claims encompass vaccines against AIDS viruses and that, because of the high degree of genetic, antigenic variations in such viruses, no one has yet, years after his invention, developed a generally successful AIDS virus vaccine.

The Matthews et al. article, published approximately 5 years after the effective filing date of Wright's application, adequately supports the Examiner's and the Board's position that, in February of 1983, the physiological activity of RNA viruses was sufficiently unpredictable that Wright's success in developing his specific avian recombinant virus vaccine would not have led one of ordinary skill in the art to believe reasonably that all living organisms could be immunized against infection by any pathogenic RNA virus by inoculating them with a live virus containing the antigenic code but not the pathogenic code of the RNA virus. The general description and the single example in Wright's specification, directed to a uniquely tailored in vitro method of producing in chicken C/O cells a vaccine against the PrASV avian tumor virus containing live RAV–Acn virus particles, did nothing more in February of 1983 than invite experimentation to determine whether other vaccines having in vivo immunoprotective activity could be constructed for other RNA viruses.

Wright argues that he has constructed successfully an env C recombinant vaccine according to the present invention and that certain recombinant AIDS virus vaccines carrying SIV (simian immunodeficiency virus) and HIV (human immunodeficiency virus) envelope genes have been produced which confer protective immunity in the animal models where they have been tested, and that these developments illustrate that the art is not so unpredictable as to require undue experimentation. However, all of these developments occurred after the effective filing date of Wright's application and are of no significance regarding what one skilled in the art believed as of that date. Furthermore, the fact that a few vaccines have been developed since the filing of Wright's application certainly does not by itself rebut the PTO's assertions regarding undue experimentation. Moreover, whether a few AIDS virus vaccines have been developed which confer immunity in some animal models is not the issue. The Examiner made reference to the difficulty that the scientific community is having in developing generally successful AIDS virus vaccines merely to illustrate that the art is not even today as predictable as Wright has suggested that it was back in 1983.

Wright also argues that several affidavits of record, namely, an October 22, 1984 declaration by Wright, an October 23, 1984 affidavit by O'Neill, and October 28, 1988 affidavits by Bennett and Burnett, successfully rebut the Board's and the Examiner's assertions regarding undue experimentation. However, Wright did not set forth in his brief to the Board any specific arguments regarding these affidavits, as required by 37 CFR 1.192(a), and therefore we are not required to address the arguments that Wright presents in this appeal regarding these affidavits.

Nevertheless, we note that each of these affidavits fails in its purpose because each merely contains unsupported conclusory statements as to the ultimate legal question. Furthermore, Burnett and Bennett do not even indicate in their affidavits that they actually reviewed the specification of Wright's application. In addition, although Wright states in his declaration that the individual steps making up his claimed process were "well within the skill of the art" at the time that he filed his application and makes reference to a list of publications that he contends supports this conclusory statement, a list which Wright also makes reference to in his arguments to this court, Wright fails to point out with any particularity in this declaration, or in his arguments to this court, how the listed documents evidence that a skilled artisan in February of 1983 would have been able to carry out, without undue experimentation, the identification, isolation, cloning, recombination, and efficacy testing steps required to practice the full scope of the appealed claims.

Wright further argues that, even if those claims which provide a broad scope of protection are not enabled, this is not the case as to those claims restricted to vaccines against avian tumor viruses. Wright maintains that there is no doubt that it was known in 1983 that the technique of producing a live vaccine proven effective for one particular strain of avian RNA viruses would be effective as to other strains of avian RNA viruses. Wright argues that the scientific literature supports the position that the art was predictable at least with respect to avian RNA viruses, because gene function and order are similar among all avian RNA viruses.

We are not persuaded. Wright has failed to establish by evidence or arguments that, in February of 1983, a skilled scientist would have believed reasonably that Wright's success with a particular strain of an avian RNA virus could be extrapolated with a reasonable expectation of success to other avian RNA viruses. Indeed, Wright has failed to point out with any particularity the scientific literature existing in February of

1983 that supports his position. Furthermore, Wright's May 17, 1989 declaration indicates that Wright himself believed during the relevant time period that in vivo testing was necessary to determine the efficacy of vaccines. In this declaration, Wright stated in pertinent part:

> Preparation of a patent application following conception of the invention awaited such time as there was a reasonable expectation that the results of innoculation [sic] would be successful. This became apparent only by reason of survival of the chickens that had been innoculated [sic].

Wright now argues that all he meant by the foregoing was that in vivo efficacy testing was necessary for the first avian RNA viruses vaccine that he developed in order to prove his hypothesis. Wright asserts that, once his hypothesis had been proven, a skilled artisan would have expected that similar in vivo results could be obtained for vaccines developed for other avian retroviruses. However, a paper that Wright co_authored with David Bennett, titled "Avian Retroviral Recombinant Expressing Foreign Envelope Delays Tumor Formation of ASV–A–Induced Sarcoma," which was attached to a declaration by Wright dated November 19, 1985, suggests that, even as late as 1985, the genetic diversity existing among chickens alone required efficacy testing even among the members of this narrow group.

Accordingly, we see no error in the Board's finding that one skilled in the art would not have believed as early as February of 1983 that the success of Wright's one example could be extrapolated with a reasonable expectation of success to all avian RNA viruses.

Notes

1. The Wright Result? How much patent protection do you believe Wright should have obtained based upon his single working example? If Wright was first to discover this method, why should he not have a right to exclude anyone who made a vaccine using as an antigen the antigenic section of that virus' genes? Or should his alternative argument, that he could obtain the right to exclude others from avian RNA viruses, have been accepted? Similarly, in regard to the *Enzo* case, *infra* at note 3, what protection should Masayori Inouye have received for the idea of antisense and its successful application to three genes in E. Coli?

2. Striking a Balance. Balancing the scope of patent protection and the extent of the inventor's contribution is a difficult task. If courts strictly limit the scope of patent protection to the specific examples disclosed in the specification, competitors could readily circumvent the patent through minor changes in design. But if the protection is advanced too liberally, then the patentee could obtain a windfall that strangles future technical advance. The Supreme Court's wariness of the latter was demonstrated when it encountered Samuel Morse's telegraphy patent. The final claim of that patent provided:

> Eighth. I do not propose to limit myself to the specific machinery, or parts of machinery, described in the foregoing specifications and claims; the essence of my invention being the use of the motive power of the

electric or falvanic current, which I call electro-magnetism, however developed, for making or printing intelligible characters, letters, or signs, at any distances, being a new application of that power, of which I claim to be the first inventor or discoverer.

See O'Reilly v. Morse, 56 U.S. (15 How.) 62, 86 (1854). The Court held the claim invalid:

> Indeed, if the eighth claim of the patentee can be maintained, there was no necessity for any specification, further than to say that he had discovered that, by using the motive power of electro-magnetism, he could print intelligible characters at any distance. We presume it will be admitted on all hands, that no patent could have issued on such a specification. Yet this claim can derive no aid from the specification filed. It is outside of it, and the patentee claims beyond it.

This rejection would today be cast in terms of enablement: Morse had simply claimed far more than he had invented. A more recent decision *In re Cook,* 439 F.2d 730, 169 U.S.P.Q. 298 (CCPA 1971), covers much the same ground.

   3. Making Sense of Antisense. In *Enzo Biochem, Inc., v. Calgene, Inc,* 188 F.3d 1362, 52 U.S.P.Q.2d 1129 (Fed.Cir.1999), the Federal Circuit considered a claim that essentially covered the use of antisense technology in all types of cells—based on a disclosure that taught how to use antitsense technology with respect to three genes in one organism (*E. coli*). As explained by Judge Lourie:

> Antisense technology aims to control the expression of a particular gene by blocking the translation of the mRNA produced by the transcription of that gene. Translation is blocked by incorporation of a specially designed DNA construct into the cell of interest; this construct contains part or all of the nucleotide sequence of the gene to be blocked, except that the sequence is inverted relative to its natural conformation.... The antisense DNA constructs typically resemble their native counterparts in that the inverted gene sequence is preceded by a promoter sequence ... and followed by a termination sequence.... The inverted gene sequence is transcribed by an RNA polymerase as if it were the gene sequence in its proper orientation, thereby generating an RNA strand which is complementary to, and thereby able to bind to, the mRNA transcript of the native gene. This RNA strand is known as messenger interfering complementary RNA ("micRNA"), because when it binds the native mRNA, that mRNA cannot be translated. Consequently, the protein for which that gene codes can no longer be produced, and gene expression is thereby blocked.

188 F.3d at 1366–67, 52 U.S.P.Q.2d at 1132–33. After concluding the Antisense technology is very unpredictable, the court remarked:

> The district court found that the amount of direction presented and the number of working examples provided in the specifications were "very narrow," despite the wide breadth of the claims at issue, the unpredictability of antisense technology, and the high quantity of experimentation necessary to practice antisense in cells outside of *E. coli....* Outside of the three genes regulated in *E. coli,* virtually no guidance, direction, or working examples were provided for practicing the invention in euka-

ryotes, or even any prokaryote other than *E. coli*. In addressing a similar case involving limited disclosure, we observed that:

> It is well settled that patent applicants are not required to disclose every species encompassed by their claims, even in an unpredictable art. However, there must be sufficient disclosure, either through illustrative examples or terminology, to teach those of ordinary skill how to make and use the invention as broadly as it is claimed.

Here, however, the teachings set forth in the specifications provide no more than a "plan" or "invitation" for those of skill in the art to experiment practicing antisense in eukaryotic cells; they do not provide sufficient guidance or specificity as to how to execute that plan....

Tossing out the mere germ of an idea does not constitute enabling disclosure. While every aspect of a generic claim certainly need not have been carried out by an inventor, or exemplified in the specification, reasonable detail must be provided in order to enable members of the public to understand and carry out the invention.

188 F.2d at 1374, 215 U.S.P.Q.2d at 1138.

4. Magic "Wands" for Enablement. In the *Enzo Biochem* case in the previous footnote, as in many other enablement cases, the Federal Circuit applied six factors to determine whether a disclosure requires "undue experimentation" to enable the invention. The Federal adopted these factors that originally appeared in decisions of the Board of Patent Appeals and Interferences at the PTO:

> Factors to be considered in determining whether a disclosure would require undue experimentation have been summarized by the board. They include (1) the quantity of experimentation necessary, (2) the amount of direction or guidance presented, (3) the presence or absence of working examples, (4) the nature of the invention, (5) the state of the prior art, (6) the relative skill of those in the art, (7) the predictability or unpredictability of the art, and (8) the breadth of the claims.

In re Wands, 858 F.2d 731 (1988). A review of the *Enzo Biochem* case in the prior footnote shows these factors at work. Do these factors still leave open the question of how much experimentation is "undue?"

5. Further Reading. Robert P. Merges & Richard R. Nelson, *On the Complex Economics of Patent Scope*, 90 COL. L. REV. 839 (1990), provides several examples and a thoughtful discussion of the relationship between disclosure, claim scope and innovation. In this regard see also *Biogen Inc. v. Medeva PLC*, [1997] R.P.C. 1[H.L.] and *Genentech Inc. v. Novo Nordisk A/S.*, 108 F.3d 1361, 42 U.S.P.Q.2d 1001 (Fed.Cir.1997). Both cases address technology that resulted from biotechnology research carried out in the late 1970s. For a analysis and comparison of these cases *see* 2 MARTIN J. ADELMAN, PATENT LAW PERSPECTIVES, § 2.9[2.–2–1] at n215 (2d ed. 1997).

6. The Rapamycin Debate Between Sir Hugh Laddie and Lord Justice Aldous. An extraordinary debate has taken place between Sir Hugh Laddie, the Chief Judge of the Patents Court in London, and Lord Justice Aldous, an experienced patent judge who spent many years on the Patents Court and who presently is the sole jurist with patent experience on the English Court of Appeal. The debate concerned the appropriate scope of a patent covering an important advance by Professor Calne. Professor Calne discovered that rapamycin, an old and rarely used antibiotic, was an effective immuno-suppressant particularly useful in kidney transplantation. The key to the debate was whether claims to chemicals with rapamycin-like properties were enabled by the disclosure of rapamycin itself. Essentially Professor Calne asserted that he was entitled to a patent covering rapamycin itself, as well as derivatives that similarly inhibit organ rejection. He prevailed before Sir Hugh Laddie, but lost on appeal. Unfortunately for students of patent law, the parties settled before the House of Lords could resolve this dispute.

AMERICAN HOME PRODUCTS CORP. v. NOVARTIS PHARMACEUTICALS U.K. LTD.

In the Patents Court.
[2000] R.P.C. 547.

Before: LADDIE J.

Is the scope of protection restricted to rapamycin alone?

I do not think that there was much dispute between the parties and I find as a fact that on reading the patent a skilled addressee would have understood the following as a result of the content of the patent and common knowledge in the art in the late 1980s:

(a) At that time it was very likely that the immunosuppressive effect discovered by Professor Calne, like the biological activity in other known large molecules, was dependent on the shape of the rapamycin molecule or a part of it.

(b) The immune response is a multi-stage process, details of which were not then (and even now are not) known. It was likely that rapamycin acted in the second half of the process but where precisely and how was not known and would be likely to take a long time to find out.

(c) The mechanism by which rapamycin worked was not known. That is to say, it was not known what part or parts of the molecule gave it its efficacy nor was the shape or location of the receptor sites in the molecules to which it attached itself known.

(d) There was a strong probability that other molecules derived from rapamycin would exhibit similar conformation in those areas which made rapamycin efficacious and would also exhibit similar immunosuppressant activity. Put the other way round, it was most unlikely that rapamycin was the only molecule of similar shape which exhibited such efficacy although it was not possible to be certain that this was so. As a corollary it was unlikely that Professor Calne had happened to hit upon the only molecule within the large number of molecules with similar composition and shape which happened to work.

(e) Similarly, it was unlikely that Professor Calne had struck upon the most efficacious molecule.

(f) Whether any particular molecule derived from rapamycin would work at all was impossible to predict with certainty.

(g) The number of possible derivatives of rapamycin is vast. It is almost certain that many of them would not exhibit immunosuppressant activity: just as it would not be possible to predict with certainty which derivatives have immunosuppressant activity, it would not be possible to predict how many would have such activity.

(h) It was likely, but not known, that the important part or parts of the shape of the rapamycin molecule was or were to be found on the macrolide ring.

(i) It was at the time possible to make changes to rapamycin which would be expected to produce little or no change to the shape of the macrolide ring and others which would be expected to produce large changes to the shape of that ring.

(j) Those derivatives of rapamycin which were most likely to work were those which involved small changes to the side chain rather than changes to the macrolide ring.

(k) A skilled addressee team would be able to make up a list of possible derivatives with those most likely to exhibit immunosuppressant activity at the top and those least likely to work at the bottom. Finding derivatives which work would involve a systematic and progressive iterative process in which different derivatives were made by modifying different parts of the rapamycin molecule. That process would not be rapid or guaranteed of success.

(*l*) Even if a rapamycin derivative were produced which had immunosuppressant activities, it would be impossible to be certain that it did not exhibit unpredictable defects, such as toxicity, low rates of absorption and so on which would render it unsuitable for clinical use. Discovering whether such defects exist would involve testing, some of it *in vivo*, and would take a long time.

As I say, I think that most of these propositions are common ground. However there was a difference of emphasis between the experts. In large part this was due to the fact that the defendants' experts' evidence was directed to whether it was possible to be *certain* that anything other than rapamycin would work whereas the claimants' experts' evidence was directed to whether molecules other than rapamycin were *likely* to work. However, even in relation to the likelihood of there being other molecules which would work, there was a difference of emphasis. Professor Bycroft was an optimist. He said, for example, that the hydroxyl functional groups at the C40 and C28 position of the rapamycin molecule would have stood out as the obvious candidates to derivatise. He also said that in 1989 he would have considered it highly likely that the change at C40 which produced SDZ RAD would not prejudice the immunosuppressant activity of rapamycin. By contrast

Professor Caldwell, called for the defendants, was much more pessimistic.

In the end, I do not think that much turns on the differences between these two witnesses. Whether one is optimistic or gloom laden, the same iterative process would have to be undertaken. Some derivatives would have been more promising than others. As the iterative process proceeded, further refinement would be possible. Nevertheless, having listened to the witnesses in the box and considered their written evidence, I accept Professor Bycroft's assessment as being the one which a relevant skilled addressee would have had at the time. I think that the addressee would have felt that other workable derivatives were very likely to exist and that it was quite likely that some would be even better than rapamycin itself. Finding them would inevitably take time and money, but he would be reasonably confident of success.

* * *

In practice it was inevitable that the discovery of the activity of rapamycin would lead workers in the art to look for similar molecules derived from rapamycin which would have a better profile of properties. That is inherent in the evidence of Professor Acheson, another of the defendants' expert witnesses. He said:

> "I have been informed by Novartis that the aim of the SDZ RAD program within Novartis was to develop new and improved rapamycin derivatives. Such a project was clearly justifiable. There is no reason why a natural product, such as rapamycin, should be the best drug for treating a particular medical condition. There are known examples of synthetic derivatives, developed from a natural product, which show improved or advantageous functions and properties over the natural product itself. The production and screening of potentially useful derivatives is a huge task but vital. Because there is no sure way of predicting which derivatives of complex biological molecules, if any, will possess new and improved properties, it is, however, a high risk venture."

* * *

Insufficiency

Mr. Carr's submissions on sufficiency are summarised by him in a number of short propositions. First, he says that the claim covers a class the scope of which is impossible to determine. Further the patent does not identify even one derivative which falls within the class. Second, in order to discover derivatives which are within the scope of the claim, the skilled man would need to embark on what is on any view, a prolonged research programme. This imposes an undue burden upon the public. . . . With this in mind I can turn to the principles which Mr. Carr advances.

The claim of the patent in suit covers a class the scope of which is impossible to determine

This is clearly true in the sense that no-one in 1989 was able to set down on a piece of paper with certainty what other derivatives work. There is no reason to believe that the position is any different today. Further, even among the experts, predicting which derivatives are most likely to work will produce different lists of candidate molecules. Sometimes this type of claim has been referred to disparagingly as a "free beer" claim. It covers all the molecules that work but leaves it uncertain as to which ones do and how many of them there are. If this amounts to insufficiency, there are two possible courses open to a patentee. First he could limit his patent to the particular molecule or molecules which he has shown will work. That, of course, is what Mr. Carr says is the correct course. As a practical matter here Professor Calne would have to be content with rapamycin alone. As Mr. Carr reminded me on a number of occasions, to prove efficacy each molecule would need to be subjected to a series of tests extending over a period of three to six months. No inventor could expect to try a wide range of molecules at the outset, so he would be left with the one or two he had looked at when he applied for his patent. For reasons I have already given, if that is what the inventor is forced to do, then patent protection becomes more or less valueless. This would not just undermine Professor Calne's patent. The effect would be felt far and wide. As Professor Acheson said, there is no sure way of predicting which derivatives of complex biological molecules, if any, will possess new and improved properties. This is true not just in relation to immunosuppressants but throughout therapeutic science and was confirmed by Dr Sedrani. It is consistent with all the evidence given in this action. There is no way of predicting *with certainty* what biological activity will be possessed by an untried molecule.

The alternative would be to take a calculated gamble and put down a class of similar molecules which the inventor predicts will work. If the inventor is lucky, his gamble will pay off, most or all of the members of the class will work and he will obtain valid protection. To reduce the risks, he may feel obliged to limit his predictions. If so, the large number of potential candidate molecules just outside his class will remain free for others to use. Of course, if his gamble does not pay off, he will lose his patent. The advantage of this approach is that it would mean that the patent will contain claims with neatly defined boundaries. But this is appearance of certainty is an illusion. It could be said that this type of claim is, if anything, worse than that which we are considering here. A claim which covers numerous molecules, most of which have never been tried, is more misleading in that it may be construed as promising success for all members of the class when it is impossible to make any such promise.

* * *

The patent does not identify even one derivative
which falls within the class

This is a forensic point which emphasises the extreme facts in this case. But it should not alter the principles which apply. No one has suggested that, in the time available to Professor Calne before he had to apply for patent protection so as to obtain early priority and to avoid being beaten by a possible competitor, he could have found and tested anything other than rapamycin. This is not because of difficulty in the sense of obscurity and the need for inventiveness in doing what was needed to find other molecules that worked, but because this area of technology is concerned with therapeutic agents for human use. The requirements of safety and minimal use of animal subjects forces the worker to embark on a prolonged, step by step process. That is a fact of life in this area of technology. The fact that only one molecule has been tried says nothing about sufficiency.

There has never been a requirement that all embodiments within the scope of a patent should have been tested. Sufficiency requires the monopoly to match the contribution. The fact that here, as in most if not all other pharmaceutical cases, there is no way of predicting with accuracy which derivative molecules will possess new and improved properties does not mean that a monopoly which covers all rapamycin derivatives which work extends beyond Professor Calne's contribution. On the contrary, although his discovery of the effectiveness of rapamycin was, no doubt, empirical, once that discovery had been made, it made available to the art the opening through which a new class of immuno-suppressants could be found. The discovery of other molecules which achieve the same or better results is no longer empirical. The addressee of the patent can work in a logical and predictable way from the one molecule disclosed in the patent to the similar molecules which are derived from it. Unlike the examples given in *Biogen*, this patent is not attempting to cover all new immunosuppressants. It is directed only to those molecules which can be reached as a result of rapamycin having shown the way. As the Technical Board of Appeal said in *Genentech I/Polypeptide Expression*, and as quoted by Lord Hoffmann at p. 48 of *Biogen*:

> "Unless variants of components are also embraced in the claims, which are, now or later on, equally suitable to achieve the same effect in a manner which could not have been envisaged without the invention, the protection provided by the patent would be ineffectual."

It follows that I do not think there is anything wrong in principle in the patent in suit covering not only the use of rapamycin but also derivatives from it which work in the same way. The patent teaches the essential discovery which discloses the derivatives as likely candidates even though it does not itself identify a single derivative which is shown to work. The cover matches what Professor Calne has made available to the public by his invention. Furthermore, there is no logical reason why Mr.

Carr's complaint should be limited to cases, such as this, where no derivatives are exemplified. If there are, say, potentially hundreds of workable derivatives, why should exemplifying one, two or three of them make the patent sufficient? Even if the patent exemplifies that small number, the same iterative process of formulation and testing would need to be conducted on all other derivatives of interest.

The patent imposes a prolonged research programme on its addressee

Mr Carr says that finding other derivatives which work would involve a prolonged research programme. No doubt he could add that to find all the derivatives that work would involve a nearly infinite programme. His point is supported by the evidence given on behalf of his clients. I have already referred above to Professor Acheson's evidence that to find a number of worthwhile derivatives would be a "huge task" and a "high risk venture". Once again, this is an area in which there is not a lot which separates the evidence given by the parties. Testing rapamycin itself, including the *in vitro* and *in vivo* tests was a lengthy and, no doubt, costly process. Doing the same thing for a number of derivatives would be commensurately longer and more costly. Depending on how many technicians were put on the task and how many derivatives were to be synthesised and tested, would determine whether it would take merely many months or years and, as I have said, trying to find all the working derivatives would be, as a practical matter, of vast duration and cost. Mr Carr says that this must make the patent insufficient. In support of this he relied on a number of well known cases.

* * *

In all these cases the underlying theme is that the patentee must not impose an undue burden on the man in the art. What is undue must depend upon the art in question. There is nothing to suggest that the iterative working through of likely candidates, as Dr Sedrani did, is anything other than the standard and expected work which would be involved in selecting out good candidates for any pharmaceutical activity. No inventiveness is involved. No one would have had any difficulty in setting up a workable programme for selecting out some useful derivatives. The fact that the programme would have taken time and money is not an indication either of obscurity in the teaching of the patent or that invention was needed to carry out the programme. It is only a reflection of the fact that the normal mundane iterative steps in this art are slow and expensive. The point was made particularly clearly by document "X3", which was used by Mr Carr during his cross-examination of Professor Bycroft. It is annexed to this judgment. It sets out an outline of standard toxicology tests which would have to be carried out on any molecule which is considered for medicinal use. They are the sort of tests which have to be conducted on rapamycin itself before it could be used. As the Professor pointed out, these tests are only conducted once the molecule has passed through sufficient tests to show that it is an effective immunosuppressant. Therefore X3 illustrates one part of what is required in this art to ensure safety of products. For example the last group of tests are referred to as "chronic toxicology and carcinogenicity studies". They last up to two years. Furthermore these tests are the ones which have to be conducted before any testing in humans would be contemplated. It will be appreciated that any regime which includes this type of testing inevitably imposes costs and delay. However that does not mean that, from a technical point of view, the work is other than mundane and run of the mill. It is in this context that Professor Acheson's evidence has to be understood. It is no doubt true that a full blown programme of systematically working through promising derivatives will be large and expensive. Since it cannot be predicted with certainty that it will produce a derivative which passes all the tests, including clinical tests on humans, to yield a viable commercial product, it is a risk.

No doubt it would be possible to run the same argument in relation to most other pharmaceutical patents. Furthermore, even if Professor Calne had been lucky and sufficiently funded enough to have a large team of technicians working with him so that he had been able to put into his patent application not only the good news about rapamycin but also the same good news about one or two derivatives, Mr Carr's argument would have applied with exactly the same force to all the other derivatives which had not been tried by the Professor and his team. In addition Mr Carr's argument would apply with equal force whether the scope of the patent is as I have held it to be here, namely applying to rapamycin and working derivatives, or had been limited to an arbitrary list of identified derivatives. In each case the same process of synthesis and testing would be needed. It would follow that the only safe course in this field would be to limit one's patents to those molecules you have tried and tested. Again, that would make patents in relation to pharmaceuticals more or less valueless. As a practical matter it is likely that *full* testing even of one molecule such as rapamycin itself is not possible before a patent is applied for.

I have come to the conclusion that the amount of work involved in finding useful derivatives of rapamycin does not impose an undue burden on those working in the field and this argument of insufficiency fails.

AMERICAN HOME PRODUCTS CORP. v. NOVARTIS PHARMACEUTICALS U.K. LTD.

In the Court of Appeal.
[2001] R.P.C. 8.

Before: Lord Justice Simon Brown, Lord Justice Aldous, Lord Justice Sedley

Aldous, LJ.

* * *

Insufficiency

* * *

The judge held that the number of possible derivatives was vast and whether any particular molecule derived from rapamycin would work at all was impossible to predict with certainty. Many derivatives would not exhibit immunosuppressant activity. Those which involved small changes to the side chain would be the most likely to work. Thus the skilled person could make up a list of possibles, with those believed to be the most likely at the top of the list. Even so, finding appropriate derivatives, if they existed, would involve a systematic and iterative process. Further, when a derivative which had appropriate activity had been identified, it would be impossible to be certain that it did not exhibit unpredictable defects. To discover whether it did would require further tests which would take a long time.

The very uncertainty and unpredictability found by the judge meant that the skilled person was being required to carry out research. The duty upon the patentee is to provide a description which enables the skilled person to perform the invention, in this case across the breadth of the claim; not to supply a starting point for a research programme. If the claim includes derivatives of rapamycin, an enabling description of such derivatives is needed so that the products of the claim can be ascertained.

The judge concluded in paragraph 65 of his judgment that the "amount of work involved in finding useful derivatives of rapamycin does not impose an undue burden on those working in the field and this argument of insufficiency fails". However the specification has to be sufficient to enable the invention to be performed. There is a difference between research to find out which derivatives work and the application of the teaching in the specification with appropriate skill and tenacity. In this case the specification tells the skilled man where to start but, upon the construction of claim 1 sought by the patentees, it leaves him to ascertain by research what will work. Once it is appreciated that a claim which encompasses derivatives has to be sufficient across its breadth, the extent of the research task becomes apparent. The number of derivatives is vast and the task of ascertaining which will satisfy the functional part of the claim will also be vast and correspondingly burdensome.

The judge appears to have been influenced by his view as to the needs of a patentee, such as Professor Sir Roy Calne, who has discovered a second medical use of one molecule, to obtain a monopoly covering more than the particular molecule in a case where the skilled person would realise that some derivatives were likely to work. . . .

For my part I do not agree that a patent limited to the second use of rapamycin is virtually valueless. The patent protects the second medical use and the long and expensive work that has been carried out to obtain regulatory approval. Thus a person who wishes to market a derivative has to make the derivative and then carry out the long and expensive work needed to get it on the market. Without the patent, other manufacturers could use the work of the patentees. In any case, I do not believe that the patent system should be used to enable a person to monopolise more than that which he has described in sufficient detail to amount to an enabling disclosure. If it was, it would in this case stifle research to find a derivative of rapamycin which was a substantially better immunosuppressant than rapamycin itself.

* * *

SEDLEY L.J.:

I agree.

SIMON BROWN L.J.:

I also agree.

Notes

1. Which decision should the House support? Appeals from the English Court of Appeal go to the Appellate Committee of the House of Lords. Would you, were you a Law Lord, reverse or affirm? Would your decision set a precedent for the scope of pharmaceutical patents generally? For practice try your hand at writing the decision for the House of Lords. In it assume U.S. decisions are persuasive, but not binding authority.

2. Regardless of how you answer the question above, is the Novartis compound patentable to it? Setting aside the question of whether the rapamycin-like compound developed by Novartis infringes, would you as a patent examiner reject a claim by Novartis to its compound as anticipated or obvious in view of the Calne patent discussed above? Would your answer depend on whether the Calne patent contained directions for trying to determine which rapamycin-like compounds would work?

§ 9.2 "WRITTEN DESCRIPTION"—PROSCRIPTION ON NEW MATTER

The written description requirement is a substitute for a different statutory provision. In 35 U.S.C.A. § 132, the Patent Act states: "No amendment shall introduce new matter into the disclosure of the invention." Thus, the Patent Act forbids any new claim, claim amendment, or addition to the specification after the filing date from introducing new matter into the disclosure. This requirement prevents an applicant from continually updating his application or adding new inventive ideas that actually came after the original filing date. Thus, this new matter prohibition polices the priority dates of inventive ideas. Thus, to amend a claim or add a new claim without encountering the new matter proscription, an applicant must show that the original application disclosed or contained the subject matter included in the amendment. In other words, any claims amended after the filing date or new claims filed after the filing date must contain the same invention as the original disclosure. The new claims or amendment cannot contain new matter.

In the United States, case law changed the legal basis for a new matter rejection to a written description rejection under 35 U.S.C.A.

§ 112. *In re Rasmussen*, 650 F.2d 1212, 211 U.S.P.Q. 323 (CCPA 1981). Written description, however, performs the same priority policing function. Therefore, although the written description requirement ordinarily serves a different purpose than enablement, the next case demonstrates that distinguishing the two doctrines and their statutory bases may prove more elusive. Moreover, as later cases will show, changing the legal basis of the new matter rejection in the United States has opened the door to unusual applications of the written description requirement.

VAS–CATH INC. v. MAHURKAR

United States Court of Appeals, Federal Circuit, 1991.
935 F.2d 1555, 19 U.S.P.Q.2d 1111.

Before RICH, MICHEL and PLAGER, CIRCUIT JUDGES.

RICH, CIRCUIT JUDGE.

Sakharam D. Mahurkar and Quinton Instruments Company (collectively Mahurkar) appeal from the partial final judgment of the United States District Court for the Northern District of Illinois, Easterbrook, J., sitting by designation. Granting partial summary judgment to Vas–Cath Incorporated and its licensee Gambro, Inc. (collectively Vas–Cath), the district court declared Mahurkar's two United States utility patents Nos. 4,568,329 ('329 patent) and 4,692,141 ('141 patent), titled "Double Lumen Catheter," invalid as anticipated under 35 U.S.C. § 102(b). In reaching its decision, the district court concluded that none of the twenty-one claims of the two utility patents was entitled, under 35 U.S.C. § 120, to the benefit of the filing date of Mahurkar's earlier-filed United States design patent application Serial No. 356,081 ('081 design application), which comprised the same drawings as the utility patents, because the design application did not provide a "written description of the invention" as required by 35 U.S.C. § 112, first paragraph. We reverse the grant of summary judgment with respect to all claims.

BACKGROUND

Sakharam Mahurkar filed the '081 design application, also titled "Double Lumen Catheter," on March 8, 1982. The application was abandoned on November 30, 1984. Figures 1–6 of the '081 design application are reproduced below.

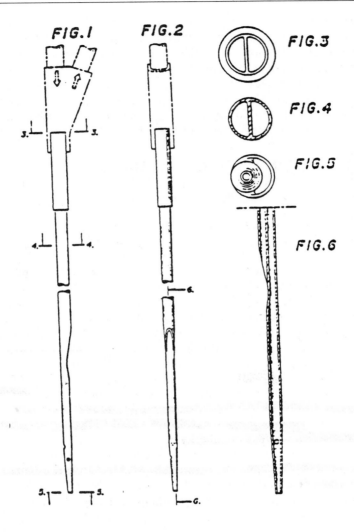

As shown, Mahurkar's catheter comprises a pair of tubes (lumens) designed to allow blood to be removed from an artery, processed in an apparatus that removes impurities, and returned close to the place of removal. Prior art catheters utilized concentric circular lumens, while Mahurkar's employs joined semi-circular tubes that come to a single tapered tip. Advantageously, the puncture area of Mahurkar's semicircular catheter is 42% less than that of a coaxial catheter carrying the same quantity of blood, and its conical tip yields low rates of injury to the blood. The prior art coaxial catheters are now obsolete; Mahurkar's catheters appear to represent more than half of the world's sales.

After filing the '081 design application, Mahurkar also filed a Canadian Industrial Design application comprising the same drawings plus additional textual description. On August 9, 1982, Canadian Industrial Design 50,089 (Canadian '089) issued on that application.

More than one year later, on October 1, 1984, Mahurkar filed the first of two utility patent applications that would give rise to the patents now on appeal. Notably, both utility applications included the same drawings as the '081 design application. Serial No. 656,601 ('601 utility application) claimed the benefit of the filing date of the '081 design application, having been denominated a "continuation" thereof. In an Office Action mailed June 6, 1985, the Patent and Trademark Office (PTO) examiner noted that "the prior application is a design application," but did not dispute that the '601 application was entitled to its filing date. On January 29, 1986, Mahurkar filed Serial No. 823,592 ('592 utility application), again claiming the benefit of the filing date of the '081 design application (the '592 utility application was denominated a continuation of the '601 utility application). In an office action mailed April 1, 1987, the examiner stated that the '592 utility application was "considered to be fully supported by applicant's parent application SN 356,081 filed March 8, 1982 [the '081 design application]." The '601 and '592 utility applications issued in 1986 and 1987, respectively, as the '329 and '141 patents, the subjects of this appeal.

[Representative of the contested claims is claim 7 of the '329 patent, which provided:

7. A double lumen catheter having an elongated tube with a proximal first cylindrical portion enclosing first and second lumens separated by an internal divider, the proximal end of said elongated tube connecting to two separate connecting tubes communicating with the respective first and second lumens for the injection and removal of fluid, the first lumen extending from the proximal end of said elongated tube to a first opening at the distal end of said elongated tube, and the second lumen extending from the proximal end of said elongated tube to a second opening at approximately the distal end of said first cylindrical portion, wherein the improvement comprises:

said elongated tube having at its distal end a smooth conical tapered tip that smoothly merges with a second cylindrical portion of said elongated tube,

and said second cylindrical portion enclosing the first lumen from the conical tapered tip to approximately the location of said second opening, said second cylindrical portion having a diameter substantially greater than one_half but substantially less than a full diameter of said first cylindrical portion,

said divider in said first cylindrical portion being planar,

the lumens being "D" shaped in cross_section in said first cylindrical portion,

the elongated tube being provided with a plurality of holes in the region of the conical tapered tip, and

said first cylindrical portion of the elongated tube smoothly merging with said second cylindrical portion of the elongated tube.]

Vas–Cath sued Mahurkar in June 1988, seeking a declaratory judgment that the catheters it manufactured did not infringe Mahurkar's '329 and '141 utility patents. Vas–Cath's complaint alleged, inter alia, that the '329 and '141 patents were both invalid as anticipated under 35 U.S.C. § 102(b) by Canadian '089. Vas–Cath's anticipation theory was premised on the argument that the '329 and '141 patents were not entitled under 35 U.S.C. § 120 to the filing date of the '081 design application because its drawings did not provide an adequate "written description" of the claimed invention as required by 35 U.S.C. § 112, first paragraph.

Mahurkar counterclaimed, alleging infringement. Both parties moved for summary judgment on certain issues, including validity. For purposes of the summary judgment motion, Mahurkar conceded that, if he could not antedate it, Canadian '089 would represent an enabling and thus [anticipating § 102(b)] reference against the claims of his '329 and '141 utility patents. Vas–Cath conceded that the '081 design drawings enabled one skilled in the art to practice the claimed invention within the meaning of 35 U.S.C. § 112, first paragraph. Thus, the question before the district court was whether the disclosure of the '081 design application, namely, the drawings without more, adequately *Issue* meets the "written description" requirement also contained in § 112, first paragraph, so as to entitle Mahurkar to the benefit of the 1982 filing date of the '081 design application for his two utility patents and thereby antedates Canadian '089.

Concluding that the drawings do not do so, and that therefore the utility patents are anticipated by Canadian '089, the district court held the '329 and '141 patents wholly invalid under 35 U.S.C. § 102(b). . . . This appeal followed.

DISCUSSION

The issue before us is whether the district court erred in concluding, on summary judgment, that the disclosure of the '081 design application does not provide a § 112, first paragraph "written description" adequate to support each of the claims of the '329 and '141 patents. If the court so erred as to any of the 21 claims at issue, the admittedly anticipatory disclosure of Canadian '089 will have been antedated (and the basis for the court's grant of summary judgment nullified) as to those claims.

THE "WRITTEN DESCRIPTION" REQUIREMENT OF § 112

Application of the "written description" requirement . . . is central to resolution of this appeal. The district court, having reviewed this court's decisions on the subject, remarked that "[u]nfortunately, it is not so easy to tell what the law of the Federal Circuit is." Perhaps that is so, and, therefore, before proceeding to the merits, we review the case law development of the "written description" requirement with a view to improving the situation.

The cases indicate that the "written description" requirement most often comes into play where claims not presented in the application when filed are presented thereafter. Alternatively, patent applicants often seek the benefit of the filing date of an earlier-filed foreign or United States application under 35 U.S.C. § 119 or 35 U.S.C. § 120, respectively, for claims of a later-filed application. The question raised by these situations is most often phrased as whether the application provides "adequate support" for the claim(s) at issue; it has also been analyzed in terms of "new matter" under 35 U.S.C. § 132. The "written description" question similarly arises in the interference context, where the issue is whether the specification of one party to the interference can support the claim(s) corresponding to the count(s) at issue, i.e., whether that party "can make the claim" corresponding to the interference count.

To the uninitiated, it may seem anomalous that the first paragraph of 35 U.S.C. § 112 has been interpreted as requiring a separate "description of the invention," when the invention is, necessarily, the subject matter defined in the claims under consideration. One may wonder what purpose a separate "written description" requirement serves, when the second paragraph of § 112 expressly requires that the applicant conclude his specification "with one or more claims particularly pointing out and distinctly claiming the subject matter which the applicant regards as his invention."

One explanation is historical: the "written description" requirement was a part of the patent statutes at a time before claims were required. A case in point is *Evans v. Eaton*, 20 U.S. (7 Wheat.) 356, 5 L.Ed. 472 (1822), in which the Supreme Court affirmed the circuit court's decision that the plaintiff's patent was "deficient," and that the plaintiff could not recover for infringement thereunder. The patent laws then in effect, namely the Patent Act of 1793, did not require claims, but did require, in its 3d section, that the patent applicant "deliver a written description of his invention, and of the manner of using, or process of compounding, the same, in such full, clear and exact terms, as to distinguish the same from all things before known, and to enable any person skilled in the art or science of which it is a branch, or with which it is most nearly connected, to make, compound and use the same...." In view of this language, the Court concluded that the specification of a patent had two objects, the first of which was "to enable artisans to make and use [the invention]...." The second object of the specification was to put the public in possession of what the party claims as his own invention, so as to ascertain if he claims anything that is in common use, or is already known, and to guard against prejudice or injury from the use of an invention which the party may otherwise innocently suppose not to be patented. It is, therefore, for the purpose of warning an innocent purchaser, or other person using a machine, of his infringement of the patent; and at the same time, of taking from the inventor the means of practising upon the credulity or the fears of other persons, by pretending that his invention is more than what it really is, or different from its ostensible objects, that the patentee is required to distinguish his invention in his specification. *Id.* at 434.

A second, policy-based rationale for the inclusion in § 112 of both the first paragraph "written description" and the second paragraph "definiteness" requirements was set forth in *Rengo Co. v. Molins Mach. Co.*, 657 F.2d 535, 551, 211 U.S.P.Q. 303, 321 (3d Cir.), *cert. denied*, 454 U.S. 1055 (1981): [T]here is a subtle relationship between the policies underlying the description and definiteness requirements, as the two standards, while complementary, approach a similar problem from different directions. Adequate description of the invention guards against the inventor's overreaching by insisting that he recount his invention in such detail that his future claims can be determined to be encompassed within his original creation. The definiteness requirement shapes the future conduct of persons other than the inventor, by insisting that they receive notice of the scope of the patented device.

With respect to the first paragraph of § 112 the severability of its "written description" provision from its enablement ("make and use") provision was recognized by this court's predecessor, the Court of Customs and Patent Appeals, as early as *In re Ruschig*, 379 F.2d 990, 154 U.S.P.Q. 118 (CCPA 1967). Although the appellants in that case had presumed that the rejection appealed from was based on the enablement requirement of § 112, the court disagreed:

> [The question is not whether [one skilled in the art] would be so enabled but whether the specification discloses the compound to him, specifically, as something appellants actually invented.... If [the rejection is] based on section 112, it is on the requirement thereof that "The specification shall contain a written description of the invention * * *."

The issue, as the court saw it, was one of fact: "Does the specification convey clearly to those skilled in the art, to whom it is addressed, in any way, the information that appellants invented that specific compound [claimed]?"

In a 1971 case again involving chemical subject matter, the court expressly stated that "it is possible for a specification to enable the practice of an invention as broadly as it is claimed, and still not describe that invention." *In re DiLeone*, 436 F.2d 1404, 1405, 168 U.S.P.Q. 592, 593 (CCPA 1971). As an example, the court posited the situation "where the specification discusses only compound A and contains no broadening language of any kind. This might very well enable one skilled in the art to make and use compounds B and C; yet the class consisting of A, B and C has not been described."

Since its inception, the Court of Appeals for the Federal Circuit has frequently addressed the "written description" requirement of § 112. A fairly uniform standard for determining compliance with the "written description" requirement has been maintained throughout: "Although [the applicant] does not have to describe exactly the subject matter claimed, ... the description must clearly allow persons of ordinary skill in the art to recognize that [he or she] invented what is claimed." *In re Gosteli*, 872 F.2d 1008, 1012, 10 U.S.P.Q.2d 1614, 1618 (Fed.Cir.1989) (citations omitted). "[T]he test for sufficiency of support in a parent application is whether the disclosure of the application relied upon 'reasonably conveys to the artisan that the inventor had possession at that time of the later claimed subject matter.' "*Ralston Purina Co. v. Far–Mar–Co, Inc.*, 772 F.2d 1570, 1575, 227 U.S.P.Q. 177, 179 (Fed.Cir. 1985). Our cases also provide that compliance with the "written description" requirement of § 112 is a question of fact, to be reviewed under the clearly erroneous standard.

The purpose of the "written description" requirement is broader than to merely explain how to "make and use"; the applicant must also convey with reasonable clarity to those skilled in the art that, as of the filing date sought, he or she was in possession of the invention. The invention is, for purposes of the "written description" inquiry, whatever is now claimed.

The District Court's Analysis

We agree with the district court's conclusion that drawings alone may be sufficient to provide the "written description of the invention" required by § 112, first paragraph.

Whether the drawings are those of a design application or a utility application is not determinative, although in most cases the latter are much more detailed. In the instant case, however, the design drawings are substantially identical to the utility application drawings.

Although we join with the district court in concluding that drawings may suffice to satisfy the "written description" requirement of § 112, we can not agree with the legal standard that the court imposed for "written description" compliance, nor with the court's conclusion that no genuine issues of material fact were in dispute.

With respect to the former, the district court stated that although the '081 design drawings in question "allowed practice" [i.e., enabled], they did not necessarily show what the invention is, when "the invention" could be a subset or a superset of the features shown. Is the invention the semi_circular lumens? The conical tip? The ratio at which the tip tapers? The shape, size, and placement of the inlets and outlets? You can measure all of these things from the diagrams in serial '081 and so can practice the device, but you cannot tell, because serial '081 does not say, what combination of these things is "the invention", and what range of variation is allowed without exceeding the scope of the claims. To show one example of an invention, even a working model, is not to describe what is novel or important.

We find the district court's concern with "what the invention is" misplaced, and its requirement that the '081 drawings "describe what is novel or important" legal error. There is "no legally recognizable or protected 'essential' element, 'gist' or 'heart' of the invention in a combination patent." *Aro Mfg. Co. v. Convertible Top Replacement Co.*,

365 U.S. 336, 345, 81 S.Ct. 599, 604, 5 L.Ed.2d 592 (1961). "The invention" is defined by the claims on appeal. The instant claims do not recite only a pair of semi-circular lumens, or a conical tip, or a ratio at which the tip tapers, or the shape, size, and placement of the inlets and outlets; they claim a double lumen catheter having a combination of those features. That combination invention is what the '081 drawings show. As the district court itself recognized, "what Mahurkar eventually patented is exactly what the pictures in serial '081 show."

We find the "range of variation" question, much emphasized by the parties, more troublesome. The district court stated that "although Mahurkar's patents use the same diagrams, [the claims] contain limitations that did not follow ineluctably [i.e., inevitably] from the diagrams." As an example, the court stated (presumably with respect to independent claims 1 and 7 of the '329 patent) that the utility patents claim a return lumen that is "substantially greater than one-half but substantially less than a full diameter" after it makes the transition from semi-circular to circular cross-section, and the drawings of serial '081 fall in this range. But until the utility application was filed, nothing established that they had to—for that matter that the utility patent would claim anything other than the precise ratio in the diagrams. . . .". Mahurkar argues that one of ordinary skill in this art, looking at the '081 drawings, would be able to derive the claimed range.

The declaration of Dr. Stephen Ash, submitted by Mahurkar, is directed to these concerns. Dr. Ash, a physician specializing in nephrology (the study of the kidney and its diseases) and chairman of a corporation that develops and manufactures biomedical devices including catheters, explains why one of skill in the art of catheter design and manufacture, studying the drawings of the '081 application in early 1982, would have understood from them that the return lumen must have a diameter within the range recited by independent claims 1 and 7 of the '329 patent. Dr. Ash explains in detail that a return (longer) lumen of diameter less than half that of the two lumens combined would produce too great a pressure increase, while a return lumen of diameter equal or larger than that of the two lumens combined would result in too great a pressure drop. "Ordinary experience with the flow of blood in catheters would lead directly away from any such arrangement," Ash states.

Although the district court found this reasoning "logical," it noted that later patents issued to Mahurkar disclose diameter ratios closer to 1.0 (U.S.Patent No. 4,584,968) and exactly 0.5 (U.S.Des.Patent No. 272,651). If these other ratios were desirable, the district court queried, "how does serial '081 necessarily exclude the[m]?"

The district court erred in taking Mahurkar's other patents into account. Mahurkar's later patenting of inventions involving different range limitations is irrelevant to the issue at hand. Application sufficiency under § 112, first paragraph, must be judged as of the filing date.

The court further erred in applying a legal standard that essentially required the drawings of the '081 design application to necessarily exclude all diameters other than those within the claimed range. We question whether any drawing could ever do so. At least with respect to independent claims 1 and 7 of the '329 patent and claims depending therefrom, the proper test is whether the drawings conveyed with reasonable clarity to those of ordinary skill that Mahurkar had in fact invented the catheter recited in those claims, having (among several other limitations) a return lumen diameter substantially less than 1.0 but substantially greater than 0.5 times the diameter of the combined lumens. Consideration of what the drawings conveyed to persons of ordinary skill is essential.

CONCLUSION

The district court's grant of summary judgment, holding all claims of the '329 and '141 patents invalid under 35 U.S.C. § 102(b), is hereby reversed as to all claims, and the case remanded for further proceedings consistent herewith.

REVERSED and REMANDED.

Notes

1. Description by Design? Was the district court so far off in its analysis of the effect of the design patent application? This original design application showed just one embodiment of the invention that was later claimed in the utility patent application. The inventor essentially argued that the other claimed embodiments were readily apparent from the design patent application drawings. But doesn't the fact that the inventor filed a design patent application rather than a utility application suggest that he believed he had only developed a new design, and that the other embodiments were developed later? The inventor had previously testified that he was an independent researcher at the time he developed the double lumen catheter. He further testified the he filed the design patent application because it was significantly less expensive to prosecute than a utility patent application. Should this make a difference?

2. On Remand. Judge Easterbrook concluded on remand that, in light of the Federal Circuit's opinion in Vas–Cath:

> I must decide whether such a person would understand the drawings of the design application as showing that Mahurkar was in possession, when he filed the design application, of the features claimed in the utility application. The answer to that question must be "yes." The drawings accompanying the design and utility applications are identical (except for the addition of arrows and numbers to the utility drawings). The utility application simply lays out the details of what the design drawings show—to be precise, the utility claims narrate what features of the drawings are important, without adding anything. I find that Mahurkar was in possession of the whole invention when he filed the design applications, and the drawings in the design application would have enabled a person of ordinary skill in the art to draft the written claims that appeared in the design application.

In re Mahurkar Patent Litigation, 831 F.Supp. 1354, 28 U.S.P.Q.2d 1801 (N.D.Ill.1993), aff'd, 71 F.3d 1573, 37 U.S.P.Q.2d 1138 (Fed.Cir.1995). A third Federal Circuit opinion addressing the double lumen catheter patent may be found in *Mahurkar v. C.R. Bard, Inc.,* 79 F.3d 1572, 38 U.S.P.Q.2d 1288 (Fed.Cir.1996).

3. **The Amendment of Patent Claims.** Why should the patent law allow applicants to amend patent claims at all? Don't third parties have an interest in learning the extent of the protected technology as soon as possible? Or is the ultimate scope of protection best determined after a comprehensive examination by expert patent office examiners, rather than preliminarily by the applicant? See Rudolf Krasser, Possibilities of Amendment of Patent Claims During the Examination Procedure, 23 INT'L REV. INDUS. PROP. & COPYRIGHT L. 467 (1992).

4. **The Future of the Written Description Rejection.** Although the United States once set its patent term as seventeen years from the issuance date, it now grants a patent term of twenty years from the filing date. Do you believe this shift will result in any changes in the frequency with which the written description requirement is the subject of litigation?

5. **Written Description and Genus/Species Problems.** Courts and the Patent Office sometimes confront thorny written description issues when considering cases involving initial genus and subsequent species claims. To what extent should the initial disclosure of a broad genus allow the applicant to claim subsequently a narrow species? Although various tribunals addressing this issue have vacillated in their responses to this issue, see *In re Smith,* 458 F.2d 1389, 173 U.S.P.Q. 679 (CCPA 1972), the current answer was well stated in *Ex parte Westphal,* 26 U.S.P.Q.2d 1858 (Bd. Pat. App. & Int'f):

> It has specifically been held that the disclosure of a genus and a species of a subgenus within that genus is not sufficient description of the subgenus to comply with the description requirement ... unless there are specific facts which lead to a determination that a subgenus is implicitly described.

6. **A Thought on Specification vs. Claims.** From *In re Dossel,* 115 F.3d 942, 42 U.S.P.Q.2d 1881 (Fed.Cir.1997):

> Modern usage does not always conform to that statutory structure. For example, when discussing the process of claim construction, it is not uncommon for the process to be described as requiring an examination of the claims, the specification, and the prosecution history, treating them as distinct entities.... The emphasis in today's law on the centrality of claims has made this a natural enough construct, and the same point might be made, in the terms of the statute, by saying: "To ascertain the meaning of claims, we consider three sources: the claims, the written description, and the prosecution history."

> To make the point even clearer, and without changing the terms of the statute, it might be written in the following manner:

> § 112 Specification

> (1) Written description. The specification shall contain a written description ... as to enable any person skilled in the art ...

(2) Claims. The written description shall be followed by one or more claims.

(a) A claim shall particularly point out and distinctly claim the subject matter

. . . .

(b) A claim may be written in independent or dependent form. . . .

(c) A claim in dependent form shall contain. . . .

(d) A claim in multiple dependent form shall contain. . . .

(e) An element in a claim for a combination may be expressed as a means or step for performing a specified function . . .

7. Comparative Note. The European Patent Convention indicates at Article 123(2) that: "A European patent application or a European patent may not be amended in such a way that it contains subject matter which extends beyond the content of the application as filed." The Japanese patent statute includes a similar standard. In Chapter 14 a decision of the Enlarged Board of Appeal of the European Patent Office (same invention) discusses the European standard in the context of determining the law on priority claiming.

§ 9.3 "WRITTEN DESCRIPTION"—PROSCRIPTION APPLIED TO CLAIMS WITHOUT PRIORITY ISSUES

In a remarkable decision with little, if any, apparent support in the statute or case law or in the statutory or case law of any other country, the Federal Circuit held in the case that follows that the specification did not adequately describe originally filed subject matter. This quixotic rule is unique to American patent law. While the case involved several issues, the focus for students is whether an originally filed claim in the application that led to U.S. Patent 4,652,525 ('525) is invalid for failure to satisfy the written description requirement.

REGENTS OF THE UNIVERSITY OF CALIFORNIA v. ELI LILLY & CO.

United States Court of Appeals, Federal Circuit, 1997.
119 F.3d 1559, 43 U.S.P.Q.2d 1398.

Before NEWMAN, LOURIE, and BRYSON, Circuit JUDGES.

LOURIE, CIRCUIT JUDGE.

* * *

The patents in suit relate to recombinant DNA technology and, more specifically, to recombinant plasmids and microorganisms that producehuman insulin, a protein involved in the regulation of sugar metabolism. A person unable to produce insulin is afflicted with diabetes. Prior to the development of recombinant techniques for the production of human insulin, diabetic patients were treated with injections of animal insulin, which often caused allergic reactions. Human insulin produced by recombinant methods is less likely to produce such reactions. It consists of two separate amino acid chains, a 21–amino acid A chain and a 30–amino acid B chain, which are linked only by disulfide bonds. Healthy people produce insulin in vivo via the terminal enzymatic cleavage of preproinsulin (PPI) to yield proinsulin (PI), a single amino acid chain consisting of the A and B chains, linked by a sequence of additional amino acids that positions the A and B chains so that the disulfide bonds are readily formed. The PI is then further cleaved to liberate the linking sequence and yield insulin.

The '525 patent, the application for which was filed in May 1977, was based upon the determination of the PI and PPI cDNA sequences found in rats. Claim 1 of that patent reads as follows: "A recombinant plasmid replicable in procaryotic host containing within its nucleotide sequence a subsequence having the structure of the reverse transcript of an mRNA of a vertebrate, which mRNA encodes insulin." Claim 2 relates to a recombinant procaryotic microorganism containing vertebrate insulin-encoding cDNA. Claims 4 and 5 depend from claim 2, and are limited, respectively, to mammalian and human insulin cDNA. Claim 6 depends from claim 1 and requires that the plasmid contain "at least one genetic determinant of the plasmid col E1." Claim 7 depends from claim 2 and requires that the microorganism be of a particular strain.

* * *

The district court ruled that all of the claims of the '525 patent that UC asserted against Lilly, viz., claims 1, 2, and 4–7, are invalid under § 112, ¶ 1, because the specification, although it provided an adequate written description of rat cDNA, did not provide an adequate written description of the cDNA required by the asserted claims. 39 USPQ2d at 1239–41.

Whether a specification complies with the written description requirement of § 112, ¶ 1, is a question of fact, which we review for clear error on appeal from a bench trial. *Vas-Cath Inc. v. Mahurkar*, 935 F.2d 1555, 1563, 19 USPQ2d 1111, 1116 (Fed.Cir.1991); *Ralston Purina Co. v. Far–Mar–Co, Inc.*, 772 F.2d 1570, 1575, 227 USPQ 177, 179 (Fed.Cir. 1985). To fulfill the written description requirement, a patent specification must describe an invention and do so in sufficient detail that one skilled in the art can clearly conclude that "the inventor invented the claimed invention." *Lockwood v. American Airlines, Inc.*, 107 F.3d 1565, 1572, 41 USPQ2d 1961, 1966 (1997); *In re Gosteli*, 872 F.2d 1008, 1012, 10 USPQ2d 1614, 1618 (Fed.Cir.1989) ("[T]he description must clearly allow persons of ordinary skill in the art to recognize that [the inventor] invented what is claimed."). Thus, an applicant complies with the written description requirement "by describing the invention, with all its claimed limitations, not that which makes it obvious," and by using "such descriptive means as words, structures, figures, diagrams, formulas, etc., that set forth the claimed invention." *Lockwood*, 107 F.3d at 1572, 41 USPQ2d at 1966.

An adequate written description of a DNA, such as the cDNA of the recombinant plasmids and microorganisms of the '525 patent, "requires a precise definition, such as by structure, formula, chemical name, or physical properties," not a mere wish or plan for obtaining the claimed chemical invention. *Fiers v. Revel*, 984 F.2d 1164, 1171, 25 USPQ2d 1601, 1606 (Fed.Cir.1993). Accordingly, "an adequate written description of a DNA requires more than a mere statement that it is part of the invention and reference to a potential method for isolating it; what is required is a description of the DNA itself." Id. at 1170, 25 USPQ2d at 1606.

We first consider claim 5, which is specific to a microorganism containing a human insulin cDNA. UC argues that the district court clearly erred in finding that claim 5 is invalid under § 112, ¶ 1. Specifically, UC argues that a constructive or prophetic example in the '525 specification describes in sufficient detail how to prepare the claimed organism. Lilly responds that the district court properly applied the written description requirement, as this court applied it in *Fiers*, 984 F.2d at 1170–71, 25 USPQ2d at 1605–06, and thus did not clearly err in finding that the cDNA encoding human insulin required by claim 5 is not adequately described in the '525 patent.

Claim 5 is directed to a recombinant procaryotic microorganism modified so that it contains "a nucleotide sequence having the structure of the reverse transcript of an mRNA of a [human], which mRNA encodes insulin." Thus, the definition of the claimed microorganism is one that requires human insulin-encoding cDNA. The patent describes a method of obtaining this cDNA by means of a constructive example, Example 6. This example, however, provides only a general method for obtaining the human cDNA (it incorporates by reference the method used to obtain the rat cDNA) along with the amino acid sequences of human insulin A and B chains. Whether or not it provides an enabling disclosure, it does not provide a written description of the cDNA encoding human insulin, which is necessary to provide a written description of the subject matter of claim 5. The name cDNA is not itself a written description of that DNA; it conveys no distinguishing information concerning its identity. While the example provides a process for obtaining human insulin-encoding cDNA, there is no further information in the patent pertaining to that cDNA's relevant structural or physical characteristics; in other words, it thus does not describe human insulin cDNA. Describing a method of preparing a cDNA or even describing the protein that the cDNA encodes, as the example does, does not necessarily describe the cDNA itself. No sequence information indicating which nucleotides constitute human cDNA appears in the patent, as appears for rat cDNA in Example 5 of the patent. Accordingly, the specification does not provide a written description of the invention of claim 5.

As indicated, Example 6 provides the amino acid sequence of the human insulin A and B chains, but that disclosure also fails to describe the cDNA. Recently, we held that a description which renders obvious a claimed invention is not sufficient to satisfy the written description requirement of that invention. *Lockwood*, 107 F.3d at 1572, 41 USPQ2d at 1966. We had previously held that a claim to a specific DNA is not made obvious by mere knowledge of a desired protein sequence and methods for generating the DNA that encodes that protein. *See, e.g., In re Deuel*, 51 F.3d 1552, 1558, 34 USPQ2d 1210, 1215 (1995) ("A prior art disclosure of the amino acid sequence of a protein does not necessarily render particular DNA molecules encoding the protein obvious because the redundancy of the genetic code permits one to hypothesize an enormous number of DNA sequences coding for the protein."); *In re Bell*, 991 F.2d 781, 785, 26 USPQ2d 1529, 1532 (Fed.Cir.1993). Thus, a fortiori, a description that does not render a claimed invention obvious does not sufficiently describe that invention for purposes of § 112, ¶ 1. Because the '525 specification provides only a general method of producing human insulin cDNA and a description of the human insulin A and B chain amino acid sequences that cDNA encodes, it does not provide a written description of human insulin cDNA. Accordingly, the district court did not err in concluding that claim 5 is invalid for failure to provide an adequate written description.

UC also argues that the district court erred in holding claims 1 and 2, which generically recite cDNA encoding vertebrate insulin, and claim 4, which is directed generically to cDNA encoding mammalian insulin, invalid. Dependent claims 6 and 7 similarly recite cDNA encoding vertebrate insulin. In support of this argument, UC cites the disclosure of a species (the rat insulin-encoding cDNA) within the scope of those generic claims. UC argues, citing *In re Angstadt*, 537 F.2d 498, 190 USPQ 214 (Cust. & Pat.App.1976) and *Utter v. Hiraga*, 845 F.2d 993, 6 USPQ2d 1709 (Fed.Cir.1988), that because the '525 specification meets the requirements of § 112, ¶ 1, for a species within both of these genera, the specification necessarily also describes these genera. Lilly responds that the district court did not clearly err in finding that cDNA encoding mammalian and vertebrate insulin were not adequately described in the '525 patent, because description of one species of a genus is not necessarily a description of the genus.

We agree with Lilly that the claims are invalid. Contrary to UC's argument, a description of rat insulin cDNA is not a description of the broad classes of vertebrate or mammalian insulin cDNA. A written description of an invention involving a chemical genus, like a description of a chemical species, "requires a precise definition, such as by structure, formula, [or] chemical name," of the claimed subject matter sufficient to distinguish it from other materials. *Fiers*, 984 F.2d at 1171, 25 USPQ2d at 1606; *In re Smythe*, 480 F.2d 1376, 1383, 178 USPQ 279, 284–85 (Cust. & Pat.App.1973) ("In other cases, particularly but not necessarily, chemical cases, where there is unpredictability in performance of certain species or subcombinations other than those specifically enumerated, one skilled in the art may be found not to have been placed in possession of a genus . . . .").

The cases UC cites in support of its argument do not lead to the result it seeks. These cases do not compel the conclusion that a description of a species always constitutes a description of a genus of which it is a part. These cases only establish that every species in a genus need not be described in order that a genus meet the written description requirement. *See Utter*, 845 F.2d at 998–99, 6 USPQ2d at 1714 ("A specification may, within the meaning of § 112 ¶ 1, contain a written description of a broadly claimed invention without describing all species that claim encompasses.") (affirming board's finding that an application that "describes in detail the geometry and components that make its internal pivot embodiment work" also sufficiently describes an interference count that is "silent as to the location of the pivot"). In addition, Angstadt is an enablement case and Utter involves machinery of limited scope bearing no relation to the complex biochemical claims before us.

In claims involving chemical materials, generic formulae usually indicate with specificity what the generic claims encompass. One skilled in the art can distinguish such a formula from others and can identify many of the species that the claims encompass. Accordingly, such a formula is normally an adequate description of the claimed genus. In claims to genetic material, however, a generic statement such as "vertebrate insulin cDNA" or "mammalian insulin cDNA," without more, is not an adequate written description of the genus because it does not distinguish the claimed genus from others, except by function. It does not specifically define any of the genes that fall within its definition. It does not define any structural features commonly possessed by members of the genus that distinguish them from others. One skilled in the art therefore cannot, as one can do with a fully described genus, visualize or recognize the identity of the members of the genus. A definition by function, as we have previously indicated, does not suffice to define the genus because it is only an indication of what the gene does, rather than what it is. *See Fiers*, 984 F.2d at 1169–71, 25 USPQ2d at 1605–06 (discussing *Amgen*). It is only a definition of a useful result rather than a definition of what achieves that result. Many such genes may achieve that result. The description requirement of the patent statute requires a description of an invention, not an indication of a result that one might achieve if one made that invention. *See In re Wilder*, 736 F.2d 1516, 1521, 222 USPQ 369, 372–73 (Fed.Cir.1984) (affirming rejection because the specification does "little more than outlin[e] goals appellants hope the claimed invention achieves and the problems the invention will hopefully ameliorate."). Accordingly, naming a type of material generally known to exist, in the absence of knowledge as to what that material consists of, is not a description of that material.

Thus, as we have previously held, a cDNA is not defined or described by the mere name "cDNA," even if accompanied by the name of the protein that it encodes, but requires a kind of specificity usually achieved by means of the recitation of the sequence of nucleotides that make up the cDNA. *See Fiers*, 984 F.2d at 1171, 25 USPQ2d at 1606. A description of a genus of cDNAs may be achieved by means of a recitation of a representative number of cDNAs, defined by nucleotide sequence, falling within the scope of the genus or of a recitation of structural features common to the members of the genus, which features constitute a substantial portion of the genus. This is analogous to enablement of a genus under § 112, ¶ 1, by showing the enablement of a representative number of species within the genus. *See Angstadt*, 537 F.2d at 502–03, 190 USPQ at 218 (deciding that applicants "are not required to disclose every species encompassed by their claims even in an unpredictable art" and that the disclosure of forty working examples sufficiently described subject matter of claims directed to a generic process); *In re Robins*, 429 F.2d 452, 456–57, 166 USPQ 552, 555 (Cust. & Pat.App.1970) ("Mention of representative compounds encompassed by generic claim language clearly is not required by § 112 or any other provision of the statute. But, where no explicit description of a generic invention is to be found in the specification . . . mention of representative compounds may provide an implicit description upon which to base generic claim language."); *Cf. Gosteli*, 872 F.2d at 1012, 10 USPQ2d at 1618 (determining that the disclosure of two chemical compounds within a subgenus did not describe that subgenus); *In re Grimme*, 274 F.2d 949, 952, 124 USPQ 499, 501 (Cust. & Pat.App.1960) ("[I]t has been consistently held that the naming of one member of such a group is not, in itself, a proper basis for a claim to the entire group. However, it may not be necessary to enumerate a plurality of species if a genus is sufficiently identified in an application by 'other appropriate language.'") (citations omitted). We will not speculate in what other ways a broad genus of genetic material may be properly described, but it is clear to us, as it was to the district court, that the claimed genera of vertebrate and mammal cDNA are not described by the general language of the '525 patent's written description supported only by the specific nucleotide sequence of rat insulin.

Accordingly, we reject UC's argument that the district court clearly erred in finding claims 1, 2, 4, 6, and 7 invalid for failure to provide an adequate written description. Because we affirm the district court's ruling that all of the claims of the '525 patent asserted against Lilly are invalid, we need not consider whether Lilly infringed those claims. *See B.F. Goodrich Co. v. Aircraft Braking Sys. Corp.*, 72 F.3d 1577, 1583, 37 USPQ2d 1314, 1319 (Fed.Cir.1996).

Notes

1. Assume Enablement. If the specification taught how to obtain cDNA coding for human insulin without undue experimentation, why did the Federal Circuit determine that the inventor must actually derive the human insulin and then obtain and disclose its nucleotide-by-nucleotide sequence? Do you believe that actually characterizing the cDNA should be a requirement of patentability assuming all other requirements of the law are met?

2. *Lilly* Description and *In re Deuel*. Both the description doctrine set out in *Lilly* and the obviousness test for biotechnological inventions set forth in *Deuel* are unique to U.S. patent law. Of course, obviousness carries the role of preventing the public from bearing the costs of a patent for technological advances that produce only negligible gain in valuable scientific knowledge. *Deuel* left almost no obviousness bar to miniscule advances in biotech inventions. Does *Lilly* (wittingly or unwittingly) try to use the description doctrine to fill the gap left by *Deuel*? Can a description doctrine perform that function? Does this description doctrine render invalid technology worthy of patentability for lack of a technical disclosure and also admit technology that an operative obviousness test might exclude?

3. Does Chemical Structure Properly Describe the Inventive Features of Genetic Engineering? *Lilly*, with its emphasis on disclosure of a structure, formula or chemical name, uses chemical structure as the legal analogue to evaluate inventions in the field of genetic engineering. The chemical arts are already a novel art field which receives somewhat novel treatment in the case law of patents. As a matter of science, does chemistry's emphasis on structure properly reflect the inventive feature of many .genetic engineering inventions? Consider again some of the differences between chemical arts and the art of genetic engineering. Unlike chemistry with over a hundred elements and countless isotopes bonded in infinite ways, genetic engineering uses only a few nucleic acids as building blocks and for DNA the nucleic acids are used in pairs. Would it be proper to say that genetic engineering more resembles computer technology—1s and 0s constantly repeating to carry a code—than chemistry? In other words, genetic engineering features code breaking skills more than chemical structure skills. Indeed libraries of past codes (cDNA sequences) and known cloning methods (which design a probe that will bind or hybridize with the desired cDNA sequence) are everyday tools. In sum, chemical compounds are synthesized; proteins created through the methods of genetic engineering are analyzed. While the structure of a chemical compound depends on the electrical and physical relationship of those elements to each other, the structure of a protein created by genetic engineering is the result of a sequence code expressed in nucleic acids. In short, is chemical structure the proper standard to evaluate full description of a genetic engineering invention when that art does not appear to be a structure-based art?

4. Debate at the Federal Circuit. In the case that follows four judges of the Federal Circuit voted to consider *Lilly en banc* (and another indicated publicly his willingness to reconsider *Lilly* when another case arises). While the court's opinion is itself interesting, the most informative opinions are the dissent of Judge Rader joined by Judges Gajarsa and Linn to the denial of a hearing *en banc* and Judge Lourie's considered response joined in by Judge Newman.

ENZO BIOCHEM, INC. v. GEN–PROBE INC.

United States Court of Appeals for the Federal Circuit, 2002.
296 F.3d 1316, 63 U.S.P.Q.2d 1609.

RADER, CIRCUIT JUDGE, with whom GAJARSA and LINN, CIRCUIT JUDGES, join, dissenting from the court's decision not to hear the case *en banc*.

Because the greater mistake in this case is misapplication of this court's written description case law, this opinion devotes only a few paragraphs to the statutory interpretation question. The United States' brief as *amicus curiae* in support of rehearing *en banc* states concisely this Enzo opinion's disregard for the statute:

A straightforward reading of the text of section 112 suggests that the test for an adequate written description is whether it provides enough written information for others to make and use the invention. The statute provides that the "specification shall contain a written description of the invention ... in such full, clear, concise, and exact terms as to enable any person skilled in the art ... to make and use the same." 35 U.S.C. § 112 ¶ 1. Thus, an adequate written description assures that others can "make and use" the invention.

If it is possible to characterize disregard of statutory text as a secondary mistake, this case fits that classification. The more important problem is disregard for the case law that originated the written description requirement and applied it for over thirty years.

ORIGIN AND HISTORY OF THE WRITTEN DESCRIPTION REQUIREMENT

The words "written description" first appeared in the Patent Act of 1793. At that time, of course, patents did not require claims but only a written description sufficient "to distinguish [the invention] from all other things before known or used." In *Evans v. Eaton*, 20 U.S. 356 (1822), the Supreme Court construed the description language to require applicants to enable their inventions and to provide the notice function of claims:

> [After enablement,] [t]he other object of the specification is to put the public in possession of what the party claims as his own invention, so as to ascertain if he claims any thing that is in common use, or is already known ...

Id. at 433. In later enactments, this notice function was assigned to claims, leaving enablement as the only purpose of the "written description" language. As noted in the United States' brief, the modern descendant of the 1793 phrase still requires only a written description "in such ... terms as to enable [the invention]." 35 U.S.C. § 112. In *J.E.M. AG Supply*, the Supreme Court acknowledged only enablement as the disclosure quid pro quo of the Patent Act: "In addition [to novelty, utility, and nonobviousness], to obtain a utility patent, a breeder must describe the plant with sufficient specificity to enable others to 'make and use' the invention after the patent term expires." *J.E.M. AG Supply, Inc. v. Pioneer Hi–Bred Int'l, Inc.*, 122 S.Ct. 593, 604 (2001). Reading the statute, the Supreme Court correctly found no general disclosure requirement in title 35 other than enablement.

Before 1967, this court's predecessor, the United States Court of Customs and Patent Appeals also did not differentiate written description from enablement. In 1966, that predecessor court wrote in detail about section 112, paragraph 1, and found only two requirements— enablement (the A requirement under Judge Rich's terminology) and best mode (the B requirement). *In re Gay*, 309 F.2d 769, 772, 135 USPQ 311, 315 (CCPA, 1962).

In 1967, the Court of Customs and Patent Appeals first separated a new written description (WD) requirement from the enablement requirement of § 112. The reason for this new judge-made doctrine needs some explanation. Every patent system must have some provision to prevent applicants from using the amendment process to update their disclosures (claims or specifications) during their pendency before the patent office. Otherwise applicants could add new matter to their disclosures and date them back to their original filing date, thus defeating an accurate accounting of the priority of invention. Priority–always a vital issue in patent prosecution procedures—often determines entitlement to an invention. Before 1967, the United States Patent Office and the Court of Customs and Patent Appeals used a "new matter" rejection to ensure that applicants did not update their disclosures after the original filing date of the application. This "new matter" rejection had a statutory basis: "No amendment shall introduce new matter into the disclosure of the invention." 35 U.S.C. § 132.

In 1967, in *In re Ruschig*, 379 F.2d 990, 154 USPQ 118 (CCPA 1967), this court's predecessor created for the first time a new WD doctrine to enforce priority. In the context of a new claim added "[a]bout a year after the present application was filed," the *Ruschig* court sought to determine "whether [the new] claim 13 is supported by the disclosure of appellants' application." Id. at 991. Rather than use § 132, however, *Ruschig* assigned the role of policing priority to § 112. As a technical matter, the Court of Customs and Patent Appeals distinguished between adding new matter to the specification and adding new matter to the claims. Under PTO practice, new matter in the claims would draw a § 132 *rejection* of the claims; new matter in the specification would draw a § 132 *objection* to the addition. The *Ruschig* court, for the first time, decided to treat the objection alone as a § 132 matter. To deal with new matter in the claims, the court calved a new WD doctrine out of the § 112 enablement requirement. As long as the new WD doctrine applied according to its original purpose as an identical twin of the § 132 new matter doctrine, these technical distinctions were of little practical consequence.

In any event, the WD doctrine, at its inception had a very clear function preventing new matter from creeping into claim amendments. Judge Rich, the author of *Ruschig,* often reiterated the purpose of WD. For instance in the case of *In re Wertheim*, 541 F .2d 257, 191 USPQ 90 (CCPA 1976), the Court of Customs and Patent Appeals confronted a priority issue:

The dispositive issue under this heading is whether appellants' parent and Swiss applications comply with 35 U.S.C. § 112, first paragraph, including the description requirement, as to the subject matter of these claims. If they do, these claims are entitled to the filing dates of the *parent* application. . . . [A] right of foreign *priority* in appellants'

Swiss application will antedate Pfluger 1966 and remove it as prior art against the claims.

Id. at 261 (emphasis added). In resolving this question, Judge Rich stated again the purpose of WD: "The function of the description requirement is to ensure that the inventor had possession, as of the filing date of the application relied on, of the specific subject matter *later* claimed by him." *Id.* at 262 (emphasis added). In sum, WD was a new matter doctrine, a priority policeman.

Returning to the history of WD, after 1967, the PTO continued to use new matter rejections under § 132, but also embraced the coterminous written description analysis. Thus, for many years, the PTO rejected priority errors in claims under both § 132 and § 112.

In 1981, the Court of Customs and Patent Appeals noted that the two rejections were interchangeable: "This court, ha[s] said that a rejection of an amended claim under § 132 is *equivalent* to a rejection under § 112, first paragraph." *In re Rasmussen*, 650 F.2d 1212, 1214, 211 USPQ 323, 325 (CCPA, 1981) (emphasis added). To avoid confusion between new matter rejections and objections, the court chose to eliminate the § 132/ § 112 rejections and to use § 112 for new matter rejections (claims): "The proper basis for rejection of a claim amended to recite elements thought to be without support in the original disclosure, therefore, is § 112, first paragraph, not § 132." Id. The purpose of the doctrine did not change. As the sentence above states explicitly, the § 112 doctrine, like its corollary § 132, policed priority, nothing more. At no time did either the CCPA or the Federal Circuit purport to apply the equivalent new matter/written description rejections to original claims or other claims without priority problems. *See, e.g., In re Koller*, 613 F.2d 819, 823, 204 USPQ 702, 706 (CCPA 1980) ("[O]riginal claims constitute their own description."). WD, the equivalent of the statutory new matter doctrine, simply has no application to claims without priority problems.

The Federal Circuit continued to follow this binding precedent. See, e.g., *Vas–Cath*, 935 F.2d at 1560 ("The question raised by these situations is most often phrased as whether the application provides 'adequate support' for the claim(s) at issue; it has also been analyzed in terms of 'new matter' under 35 U.S.C. § 132."); *In re Wright*, 866 F.2d 422, 424, 9 USPQ2d 1649, 1651 (Fed.Cir.1989) ("When the scope of a claim has been changed by amendment in such a way as to justify an assertion that it is directed to a *different invention* than was the original claim, it is proper to inquire whether the newly claimed subject matter was *described* in the patent application when filed as the invention of the applicant. That is the essence of the so-called 'description requirement' of § 112, first paragraph.") (emphases added); *In re Kaslow*, 707 F.2d 1366, 217 USPQ 1089 (Fed.Cir.1983). In fact, this Circuit's test for written description required assessment of the specification to check "later claimed subject matter." Id. at 1375 ("The test for determining compliance with the written description requirement is whether the disclosure of the application as originally filed reasonably conveys to the artisan that the inventor had possession at that time of the *later* claimed subject matter, *rather than the presence or absence of literal support in the specification for the claim language.*") (emphasis added). In fact, this standard emphasizes that WD does not examine the specification for "literal support" of the claim language unless priority is in question. In any event, this Circuit did not apply WD to claims without priority problems because the doctrine had no purpose beyond policing priority.

THE DEVIATION FROM THIRTY YEARS OF PRECEDENT

In 1997, for the first time, this court purported to apply WD as a general disclosure doctrine in place of enablement, rather than as a priority doctrine. *Regents of the Univ. of Cal. v. Eli Lilly and Co.*, 119 F.3d 1559, 43 USPQ2d 1398 (Fed.Cir.1997). In *Lilly*, this court found that the '525 patent specification does not provide a WD of human insulin cDNA despite the disclosure of a general method of producing human insulin cDNA and a description of the human insulin A and B chain amino acid sequences that cDNA encodes. 119 F.3d at 1567. In the words of the court, "a description that does not render a claimed invention obvious does not sufficiently describe that invention for purposes of § 112, ¶ 1." Id. At another point, the court stated: "An adequate written description of a DNA ... 'requires a precise definition, such as by structure, formula, chemical name, or physical properties.... ' " Id. at 1566. In sum, the *Lilly* opinion does not test a later claim amendment against the specification for priority, but asserts a new free-standing disclosure requirement in place of the statutory standard of enablement. Based on the absence of a nucleotide-by-nucleotide recitation in the specification of the human insulin cDNA, the court determined that the applicant had not adequately described the invention. For the first time, this court purported to apply WD without any priority question. *But see, Kaslow*, 707 F.2d at 1375 ("rather than the presence or absence of literal support in the specification for the claim language."). Even accepting that WD can be isolated as a separate requirement from enablement in § 112, ¶ 1, the words "written description" hardly prescribe a standard that requires nucleotide-by-nucleotide disclosure.

Under the correct written description test, one of skill in the art would have recognized that the '525 patent in *Lilly* had no new matter or priority problems. In terms of the statutory test for adequacy of disclosure, the patent disclosure undoubtedly warranted rejection for lack of enablement. Under the *Wands* test for enablement, 858 F.2d 731, 8 USPQ2d 1400 (Fed.Cir.1988), the inventor certainly did not show one of skill in the art how to make human insulin cDNA.[2] Moreover the

---

2. U.S. Pat. No. 4,652,525, the patent at issue in *Lilly,* was filed in 1983, but claimed priority to a parent filed in 1977. In 1977, biotechnology was still in its infancy. In fact, the Maxam and Gilbert method of sequencing DNA was just published in 1977. Cloning in that era was, at a minimum, unpredictable and would have re- quired vast amounts of experimentation to accomplish. Therefore, the patent's prophetic disclosure of human insulin cDNA hardly enabled its production as claimed. Instead of pursuing this obvious avenue of rejection, the Federal Circuit reached out beyond the statute and the case law to create a new general disclosure test.

patent claimed vertebrate insulin cDNA—a category ranging from fish to humans—again claims whose scope far exceeds the patent's enabling disclosures. In fact, the patent disclosure only revealed that the in ventor had enabled cloning of rat insulin. Instead of invalidating under the statutory test for adequacy of disclosure, i.e., enablement, the *Lilly* court purported to create a new doctrine for adequacy of disclosure that it labeled incorrectly "written description." As noted, from its creation through thirty years of application, WD had never been a free-standing substitute for enablement.

Although it should not be necessary, a brief defense of the statutory standard for adequate disclosure shows the flaws of the new form of WD. Enablement already requires inventors to disclose how to make (repro-duce, replicate, manufacture) and how to use the invention (by definition rendering it a "useful art"). Therefore, because the competitor can make the invention, it can then acquire the DNA sequence or any other characteristic whenever it desires. Meantime the competitor can use, exploit, commercialize (outside the patent term) or improve upon and design around (within the patent term) as much of the invention as it cares to make. In other words, the statutory standard for sufficiency of disclosure serves masterfully the values of the patent system.

* * *

WHY DOES THIS MATTER?

As both *Lilly* and this case show, the aberrant form of WD requires far more specific disclosure than enablement. Because the Lilly applica-tion of § 112, ¶ 1 requires a far more demanding disclosure, defendants will have no need to invoke enablement, but will proceed directly to the more demanding *Lilly* § 112, ¶ 1 requirements. Thus, the new breed of WD evident in *Lilly* and this case threatens to further disrupt the patent system by replacing enablement the statutory test for adequate disclo-sure. *See*, Rai, Arti, "*Intellectual Property Rights in Biotechnology: Addressing New Technology*" 34 Wake Forest L.Rev. 827, 834–35 (Fall, 1999) ("Thus in [*Lilly*] . . . the CAFC broke new ground by applying the written description requirement not only to later-filed claims but also to claims filed in the original patent. . . . T]he *Lilly* court used the written description requirement as a type of elevated enablement require-ment."); Mueller, Janice M., "*The Evolving Application of the Written Description Requirement to Biotechnological Inventions*" 13 Berkeley Tech. L.J. 615, 617 (Spring 1998) ("The Lilly decision establishes uniquely rigorous rules for the description of biotechnological subject matter that significantly contort written description doctrine away from its historic origins and policy grounding. The *Lilly* court elevate[s] written description to an effective 'super enablement' standard. . . . ").

Replacement of enablement doctrines with an ill-defined general disclosure doctrine of WD imperils the integrity of the patent system. Enablement, arguably the most important patent doctrine after obvious-ness, has many important applications. Beyond mere adequacy of disclosure, it serves as the line of demarcation between the visionary theorist (adds nothing to the useful arts) and the visionary pioneer (contributes to the useful arts), *see, e.g., Gould v. Hellwarth*, 472 F.2d 1383, 176 USPQ 515 (CCPA 1973), and also serves to limit claim scope thus demarking the boundary between pioneer inventions and patentable improvements, *see, e.g., In re Wright*, 999 F.2d 1557 (Fed.Cir.1993). The WD possession test cannot perform these functions.

* * *

For biotech inventions, according to the *Lilly* standard, § 112, ¶ 1 requires a precise listing of the DNA sequence nucleotide-by-nucleotide. Enablement, on the other hand, requires that the specification show one of skill in the art how to acquire that sequence on their own. As a test for biotech claims without priority issues, WD may well jeopardize a sizeable percentage of claims filed before the Lilly departure in 1997. These patents had no notice of a change in the statutory standard for disclosure. Moreover the *Lilly/Enzo* rule prejudices university or small inventors who do not have the expensive and time-consuming resources to process every new biotechnological invention to extract its nucleotide sequence.

* * *

Saving the obvious for last, *Lilly* really cannot depart from decades of established case law on § 112, ¶ 1. . . . *Lilly* is a panel case and cannot override the statute that makes enablement the general disclosure doctrine and the vast body of case law limiting WD to its original purpose.

[This dissent then includes an appendix with every written description case of the Federal Circuit or the CCPA from 1967 to the present showing that each of them, with the exception of *Lilly* applied the written description test only to police priority.]

LOURIE, CIRCUIT JUDGE, with whom NEWMAN, CIRCUIT JUDGE, joins, concurring in the court's decision not to hear the case *en banc*.

The dissenters believe that the written description requirement is simply a requirement for enablement. With all due respect, that is incorrect. The complete statutory provision is as follows:

> *The specification shall contain a written description of the invention*, and of the manner and process of making and using it, in such full, clear, concise, and exact terms as to enable any person skilled in the art to which it pertains or with which it is most nearly connected, to make and use the same, and shall set forth the best mode contemplated by the inventor of carrying out his invention.

35 U.S.C. § 112, ¶ 1 (1994) (emphasis added). I read the statute so as to give effect to its language. The statute states that the invention must be described. That is basic patent law, the *quid pro quo* for the grant of a patent. Judge Rader notes that historically the written description requirement served a purpose when claims were not re-

quired. While that may be correct, when the statute began requiring claims, it was not amended to delete the requirement; note the comma between the description requirement and the enablement provision, and the "and" that follows the comma. Judge Rich, whom Judge Rader cites, was in fact one of the earliest interpreters of the statute as having separate enablement and written description requirements. *In re Ruschig*, 379 F.2d 990, 995–996, 154 USPQ 118, 123 (C.C.P.A.1967); *Vas–Cath Inc. v. Mahurkar*, 935 F.2d 1555, 1563, 19 USPQ2d 1111, 1117 (Fed.Cir.1991).

* * *

It is said that applying the written description requirement outside of the priority context was novel until several years ago. Maybe so, maybe not; certainly such a holding was not precluded by statute or precedent. New interpretations of old statutes in light of new fact situations occur all the time. I believe these issues have arisen in recent years for the same reason that more doctrine of equivalents issues are in the courts, viz., because perceptions that patents are stronger tempt patent owners to try to assert their patents beyond the original intentions of the inventors and their attorney. That is why the issues are being raised and that is why we have to decide them. Claims are now being asserted to cover what was not reasonably described in the patent.

Moreover, the dissenters would limit the requirement, to the extent that they credit the written description portion of the statute as being a separate requirement at all, to priority issues. The statute does not say "a written description of the invention for purposes of policing priority." While it has arisen primarily in cases involving priority issues, Congress has not so limited the statute, and we have failed to so limit it as well. As for the lack of earlier cases on this issue, it regularly happens in adjudication that issues do not arise until counsel raise them, and, when that occurs, courts are then required to decide them. Even now, a written description issue should not arise unless a patentee seeks to have his claims interpreted to include subject matter that he has not adequately disclosed in his patent. Although it is true that the written description requirement has been applied rigorously in some recent cases, I do not believe that any of those cases were decided wrongly. * * * Interpretation of written description as this court has done furthers the goal of the law to have claims commensurate in scope with what has been disclosed to the public.

I believe that the dissenters miss the point in seeing this case as involving an original claim or in *ipsis verbis* issue. There is no question that an original claim is part of the specification. That was the question answered in the affirmative by *In re Gardner*, 480 F.2d 879, 178 USPQ 149 (C.C.P.A.1973), in which the CCPA found compliance with the written description requirement over the objection of the PTO Commissioner, who argued that an original claim should not be considered part of the written description unless the specification was amended to contain the subject matter of the original claim. However, the question here is whether the disclosure, as an original claim, or in the specification, adequately describes the invention. It is incorrect that the mere appearance of vague claim language in an original claim or as part of the specification necessarily satisfies the written description requirement or shows possession of a generic invention.

* * *

Moreover, even if written description is related to and overlaps with "new matter," so what? One can fail to meet the requirements of the statute in more than one manner, and in any event the case cited as equating those two requirements in fact distinguishes § § 112 and 132 as concerning: (1) claims not supported by the disclosure; and (2) the prohibition of new matter to the disclosure, respectively. *In re Rasmussen*, 650 F.2d 1212, 1214–15, 211 USPQ 323, 326 (C.C.P.A.1981). *Rasmussen* states that "[t]he proper basis for rejection of a claim amended to recite elements thought to be without support in the original disclosure, therefore, is § 112, first paragraph, not § 132." Id.

In addition, we do not "elevate 'possession' to the posture of a statutory test of patentability." Rather, the opinion refines the "possession" test for circumstances such as these in which the inventors showed possession of a species of the invention by reference to a deposit, but may not have described what else within the scope of the claims they had possession of. While "possession" is a relevant factor in determining whether an invention is described, it is only a criterion for satisfying the statutory written description requirement. Showing possession is not necessarily equivalent to providing a written description.

* * *

Still, in terms of the more practical aspects of complying with the statute, meeting the description requirement is the first task in drafting a patent application. Enabling one of skill in the art to make and use the invention is a separate requirement. To interpret the written description requirement only as an enablement provision is to let the tail wag the dog. Perhaps there is little difference in electrical and mechanical inventions between describing an invention and enabling one to make and use it, but that is not true of chemical and chemical-like inventions.

* * *

In sum, we have evolved a consistent body of law over a number of years, based on the statute and basic principles of patent law. I see no reason to hear this case *en banc* and rewrite the statute.

Notes

1. Harmonization. As noted, no other country has a *Lilly* doctrine. If you were the chief negotiator for the United States with the charge to obtain a treaty that preserves all essential features of United States patent law, would you insist that all countries adopt the *Lilly* doctrine?

2. Petition for *certiorari* in *Enzo*. If you are hired as patent counsel for Enzo and you ultimately lost in the Federal Circuit because of the application of the *Lilly* doctrine, what arguments would you put in your petition for certiorari?

Objective Disclosure Exercise

Rameau is an inventor and licensed United States patent agent. Late in the evening on December 31, 1997, he conceives of the idea of an improved champagne corkscrew. He subsequently prepares a sales brochure with a detailed and complete description of the new corkscrew for distribution at the wine festival at a regional wine festival held in Napa, California, on September 10, 1998.

Two days before the festival, Rameau considers whether he should file a patent application on the corkscrew. Although 35 U.S.C. § 102(b) provides him with a one-year grace period in the United States, he recalls that most foreign patent systems are absolute novelty regimes. Distribution of the sales brochures could thus be fatal to Rameau's potential patent rights elsewhere. Rameau hastily drafts an application that evening and files it at the United States Patent and Trademark Office the next day, on September 9, 1998.

At the festival, Rameau distributes over 1500 brochures to prospective customers. A few days later, Rameau reviews his patent application and realizes that he did not describe grasping arms which seize the champagne stopper, a key feature of the invention that the sales brochure detailed. Rameau very much doubts that skilled workers in the field could make or use his invention without this additional information.

How may Rameau modify his patent specification in order to meet § 112, first paragraph? Does Rameau possess any other options in order to fulfill the requirements of § 112, first paragraph?

Chapter Ten

THE PATENT SPECIFICATION: BEST MODE

In addition to setting out the wholly objective requirements, section 112 further provides that the specification "shall set forth the best mode contemplated by the inventor of carrying out his invention." This provision requires disclosure in the patent specification of any specific instrumentalities or techniques that the inventor recognized at the time of filing as the best way of carrying out the invention. Thus, beyond enabling one of skill in the art to make and use the claimed invention, the specification must also disclose the inventor's trade secrets for practicing the invention.

As with the materials discussed in Chapter 6, *Novelty: Prior Invention*, the best mode requirement is unique to the United States. Other patent systems generally do not oblige an inventor to describe the best mode. In particular, European and Japanese representatives have pushed for the abolition of this requirement within the United States as well.

CHEMCAST CORP. v. ARCO INDUSTRIES CORP.

United States Court of Appeals, Federal Circuit, 1990.
913 F.2d 923, 16 U.S.P.Q.2d 1033.

Before ARCHER and MAYER, CIRCUIT JUDGES, and GEORGE, DISTRICT JUDGE.

MAYER, CIRCUIT JUDGE.

Chemcast Corporation appeals the judgment of the United States District Court for the Eastern District of Michigan that Claim 6 of United States Patent No. 4,081,879 ('879 patent), the only claim in suit, is invalid because of the inventor's failure to disclose the best mode as required by 35 U.S.C. § 112. See 12 U.S.P.Q.2d 2005 (1989). We affirm.

BACKGROUND

The '879 patent claims a sealing member in the form of a grommet or plug button that is designed to seal an opening in, for example, a sheet metal panel. Claim 6, the only claim in suit, depends from Claim 1.

1.   A grommet for sealing an opening in a panel, said grommet comprising an annular base portion having a continuous circumferential and axial extending sealing band surface, an annular locking portion having a continuous circumferential and axial extending ridge portion approximately the same diameter as said sealing band surface, said sealing band surface constituting an axial extending continuation of said ridge portion, said locking portion and said base portion being in contact with each other and integrally bonded together, said base portion comprising an elastomeric material and said locking portion being more rigid than said base portion, whereby when the grommet is installed in a panel opening, the locking portion is inserted through the opening to a position on the opposite side of the panel from the base portion locking the grommet in place, and said sealing band surface forms a complete seal continuously around the entire inner periphery of the panel opening.

6.   The grommet as defined in claim 1 wherein the material forming said base portion has a durometer hardness reading of less than 60 Shore A and the material forming said locking portion has a durometer hardness reading of more than 70 Shore A.

The grommet of Claim 6 is referred to as a dual durometer grommet because it may be composed either of two materials that differ in hardness or of a single material that varies in hardness. In either case, the different hardnesses can be, and for a sufficiently large hardness differential must be, measured with different durometers: Shore A for the softer base portion and Shore D for the harder locking portion. The harder locking portion of the grommet is the focus of this case.

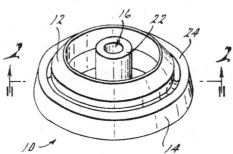

Chemcast and its competitor Arco Industries Corporation are both engaged in the manufacture and sale of sealing members such as grommets, gaskets, and plug buttons. Both sell their products primarily to the automobile industry. Ex–Arco employee Phillip L. Rubright founded Chemcast in 1973 and subsequently conceived of and designed specifically for Oldsmobile, a Chemcast customer, the dual durometer '879 grommet. He filed a patent application together with an assignment of invention to Chemcast in January of 1976; the '879 patent issued in April of 1978.

Chemcast subsequently sued Arco for infringement of Claim 6 of the '879 patent. Arco counterclaimed that the patent was invalid on several grounds, including Rubright's failure to comply with 35 U.S.C. § 112.

[The district court invalidated the patent for failure to satisfy the best mode requirement.] According to the court, the principal shortcomings of the disclosure were its failure to specify (1) the particular type, (2) the hardness, and (3) the supplier and trade name, of the material used to make the locking portion of the grommet. Therefore, it held that the application as filed failed adequately to disclose the best mode of practicing the invention contemplated by Rubright. Chemcast appeals.

Discussion

A.

The first paragraph of 35 U.S.C. § 112 (1982) provides: "The specification [A] shall contain a written description of the invention, and of the manner and process of making and using it, in such full, clear, concise, and exact terms as to enable any person skilled in the art to which it pertains, or with which it is most nearly connected, to make and use the same, and [B] shall set forth the best mode contemplated by the inventor of carrying out his invention." We long ago drew and often have focused upon the critical distinction between requirement [A], "enablement," and requirement [B], "best mode." The essence of portion [A] is that a specification shall disclose an invention in such a manner as will enable one skilled in the art to make and utilize it. Separate and distinct from portion [A] is portion [B], the essence of which requires an inventor to disclose the best mode contemplated by him, as of the time he executes the application, of carrying out his invention. Manifestly, the sole purpose of this latter requirement is to restrain inventors from applying for patents while at the same time concealing from the public preferred embodiments of their inventions which they have in fact conceived.

The best mode inquiry focuses on the inventor's state of mind as of the time he filed his application—a subjective, factual question. But this focus is not exclusive. Our statements that "there is no objective standard by which to judge the adequacy of a best mode disclosure," and that "only evidence of concealment (accidental or intentional) is to be considered," *In re Sherwood*, 613 F.2d 809, 816, 204 U.S.P.Q. 537, 544 (CCPA 1980), quoted in *DeGeorge v. Bernier*, 768 F.2d 1318, 1324, 226 U.S.P.Q. 758, 763 (Fed.Cir.1985), assumed that both the level of skill in the art and the scope of the claimed invention were additional, objective metes and bounds of a best mode disclosure.

Of necessity, the disclosure required by section 112 is directed to those skilled in the art. Therefore, one must consider the level of skill in the relevant art in determining whether a specification discloses the best mode. We have consistently recognized that whether a best mode disclosure is adequate, that is, whether the inventor concealed a better mode of practicing his invention than he disclosed, is a function of not only what the inventor knew but also how one skilled in the art would have understood his disclosure.

The other objective limitation on the extent of the disclosure required to comply with the best mode requirement is, of course, the scope of the claimed invention. "It is concealment of the best mode of practicing the claimed invention that section 112 ¶ 1 is designed to prohibit." *Randomex Inc. v. Scopus Corp.*, 849 F.2d at 585, 588, 7 U.S.P.Q.2d at 1050, 1053 (Fed.Cir.1988); see *Christianson v. Colt Indus. Oper. Corp.*, 870 F.2d 1292, 1301, 10 U.S.P.Q.2d 1352, 1359 (7th Cir.1989) ("Again, the focus of the best mode requirement, as it was with the enablement requirement, is on the claimed invention. Thus, before determining whether there is evidence of concealment, the scope of the invention must be delimited."). Thus, in *Randomex*, the inventor's deliberate concealment of his cleaning fluid formula did not violate the best mode requirement because his "invention neither added nor claimed to add anything to the prior art respecting cleaning fluid." 849 F.2d at 590, 7 U.S.P.Q.2d at 1054. Similarly, in *Christianson*, the inventor's failure to disclose information that would have enabled the claimed rifle parts to be interchangeable with all M–16 rifle parts did not invalidate his patents because "the best mode for making and using and carrying out the claimed inventions [did] not entail or involve either the M–16 rifle or interchangeability." 870 F.2d at 1302, 10 U.S.P.Q.2d at 1360. Finally, in *DeGeorge* we reversed a finding that an inventor's nondisclosure of unclaimed circuitry with which his claimed circuitry interfaced violated the best mode requirement: "Because the properly construed count does not include a word processor, failure to meet the best mode requirement here should not arise from an absence of information on the word processor."

In short, a proper best mode analysis has two components. The first is whether, at the time the inventor filed his patent application, he knew of a mode of practicing his claimed invention that he considered to be better than any other. This part of the inquiry is wholly subjective, and resolves whether the inventor must disclose any facts in addition to those sufficient for enablement. If the inventor in fact contemplated such a preferred mode, the second part of the analysis compares what he knew with what he disclosed—is the disclosure adequate to enable one skilled in the art to practice the best mode or, in other words, has the inventor "concealed" his preferred mode from the "public"? Assessing the adequacy of the disclosure, as opposed to its necessity, is largely an objective inquiry that depends upon the scope of the claimed invention and the level of skill in the art.

Notwithstanding the mixed nature of the best mode inquiry, and perhaps because of our routine focus on its subjective portion, we have consistently treated the question as a whole as factual. "Compliance with the best mode requirement, because it depends on the applicant's state of mind, is a question of fact subject to the clearly erroneous standard of review." [*Spectra–Physics, Inc. v. Coherent, Inc.*, 827 F.2d

1524, 1535, 3 U.S.P.Q.2d 1737, 1745 (Fed.Cir.1987).] We adhere to that standard here, and review the district court's best mode determination accordingly.

B.

Chemcast alleges that the trial court erred in its best mode analysis by failing to focus, as required, on the claimed invention and on whether *Issue* the inventor, Rubright, concealed a better mode than he disclosed. Neither allegation has any merit.

Chemcast first argues that, because the '879 patent does not claim any specific material for making the locking portion of the grommet, Rubright's failure to disclose the particular material that he thought worked the best does not violate the best mode requirement. This argument confuses best mode and enablement. A patent applicant <u>must</u> disclose the best mode of carrying out his claimed invention, not merely a mode of making and using what is claimed. A specification can be enabling yet fail to disclose an applicant's contemplated best mode. See *Spectra-Physics*, 827 F.2d at 1537, 3 U.S.P.Q.2d at 1746. Indeed, most of the cases in which we have said that the best mode requirement was violated addressed situations where an inventor failed to disclose non-claimed elements that were nevertheless necessary to practice the best mode of carrying out the claimed invention. See, e.g., *Spectra-Physics*, 827 F.2d at 1536, 3 U.S.P.Q.2d at 1745 (failure to disclose specific braze cycle constituting preferred means of attachment violated best mode even though no particular attachment means claimed).

Moreover, Chemcast is mistaken in its claim interpretation. While the critical limitation of Claim 6 is a hardness differential of 10 points on the Shore A scale between the grommet base and locking portions, and not a particular material type, some material meeting both this limitation and that of Claim 1, that "said base portion compris[e] an elastomeric material and said locking portion be[ ] more rigid than said base portion," is claimed. That the claim is broad is no reason to excuse noncompliance with the best mode requirement. Here, the information the applicant is accused of concealing is not merely necessary to practice the claimed invention, as in *Dana* fluoride surface treatment was "necessary to satisfactory performance" of the claimed valve stem seal; it also describes the preferred embodiment of a claimed element, as in *Spectra–Physics* the undisclosed braze cycle was the preferred "means for attaching" and "securing" claimed in the patents at issue.

Chemcast's second argument is equally misplaced. The court devoted no fewer than 13 factual findings to what the inventor Rubright knew as of the filing date of the '879 application. Those findings focus, as did the parties, on the type, hardness, and supplier of the material used to make the locking portion of the grommet. The court found that Rubright selected the material for the locking portion, a rigid polyvinyl chloride (PVC) plastisol composition; knew that the preferred hardness of this material was 75 + /−5 Shore D; and purchased all of the grommet material under the trade name R–4467 from Reynosol Corporation

(Reynosol), which had spent 750 man-hours developing the compound specifically for Chemcast. Furthermore, the court found that at the time the '879 application was filed, the only embodiment of the claimed invention known to Rubright was a grommet composed of R–4467, a rigid PVC plastisol composition with a locking portion hardness of 75 + /−5 Shore D. Id. at 2006.

In light of what Rubright knew, the specification, as issued, was manifestly deficient. It disclosed the following: The annular locking portion [ ] of the sealing member [ ] is preferably comprised of a rigid castable material, such as a castable resinous material, either a thermoplastic or thermosetting resin, or any mixtures thereof, for example, polyurethane or polyvinyl chloride. The [locking] portion [ ] also should be made of a material that is sufficiently hard and rigid so that it cannot be radially compressed, such as when it is inserted in the opening [ ] in the panel [ ]. Materials having a durometer hardness reading of 70 Shore A or harder are suitable in this regard. Col. 4, ll.53–63. The material hardness (75 Shore D) and supplier/trade name (Reynosol compound R–4467) are not explicitly disclosed here or anywhere else in the specification.

Nor, in light of the level of skill in the art, are they implicitly disclosed. Given the specification, one skilled in the art simply could not divine Rubright's preferred material hardness. The court found that "the specification of the open-ended range of materials of '70 Shore A or harder' conceals the best mode 75 Shore D material in part because materials of Shore A and Shore D hardnesses are recognized as different types of materials with different classes of physical properties." As for the specific supplier and trade name designation of the preferred material, the court found that disclosing a list of generic potential materials was "not an adequate disclosure of the best mode PVC Re[y]nosol Compound R–4467."

We agree. That "at least eight other PVC composition suppliers [ ] could have formulated satisfactory materials for the dual durometer grommet," 5 U.S.P.Q.2d at 1235, does not, as Chemcast urges, excuse Rubright's concealment of his preferred material, and the only one of which he was aware. Again Chemcast confuses enablement and best mode. The question is not whether those skilled in the art could make or use the '879 grommet without knowledge of Reynosol compound R–4467; it is whether they could practice Rubright's contemplated best mode which, the court found, included specifically the Reynosol compound. Rubright knew that Reynosol had developed R–4467 specifically for Chemcast and had expended several months and many hundred man-hours in doing so. Because Chemcast used only R–4467, because certain characteristics of the grommet material were claimed elements of the '879 invention, and because Rubright himself did not know the formula, composition, or method of manufacture of R–4467, section 112 obligated Rubright to disclose the specific supplier and trade name of his preferred material.

Other facts Chemcast points to as obviating the need for Rubright's disclosure of "Reynosol R–4467" are simply irrelevant. That Reynosol considered the formulation of R–4467 a trade secret and that it offered the compound only to Chemcast, id., do not bear on the state of Rubright's knowledge or the quality of his disclosure. First, it is undisputed that Rubright did not know either the precise formulation or method of manufacture of R–4467; he knew only that it was a rigid PVC plastisol composition denominated "R–4467" by Reynosol. Whatever the scope of Reynosol's asserted trade secret, to the extent it includes information known by Rubright that he considered part of his preferred mode, section 112 requires that he divulge it. Second, whether and to whom Reynosol chooses to sell its products cannot control the extent to which Rubright must disclose his best mode. Were this the law, inventors like Rubright could readily circumvent the best mode requirement by concluding sole-user agreements with the suppliers of their preferred materials.

Nor does the fact that Rubright developed his preferred mode with the requirements of a particular customer in mind excuse its concealment; compliance with section 112 does not turn on why or for whom an inventor develops his invention. An inventor need not disclose manufacturing data or the requirements of a particular customer if that information is not part of the best mode of practicing the claimed invention, see *Christianson*, 870 F.2d at 1302, 10 U.S.P.Q.2d at 1360 (citing *Christianson*, 822 F.2d at 1563, 3 U.S.P.Q.2d at 1255), but the converse also is true. Whether characterizable as "manufacturing data," "customer requirements," or even "trade secrets," information necessary to practice the best mode simply must be disclosed.

Given the specification and the level of skill or understanding in the art, skilled practitioners could neither have known what Rubright's contemplated best mode was nor have carried it out. Indeed, on these facts, they would not even have known where to look. This is not a case, like Randomex, where the inventor indiscriminately disclosed his preferred mode along with other possible modes. See 849 F.2d at 589, 7 U.S.P.Q.2d at 1054. Rubright did not disclose his preferred mode at all. His preferred material hardness, 75 Shore D, is three hardness scales removed from the 70 Shore A hardness mentioned in the specification. Neither his preferred source, Reynosol Compound R–4467, nor any other is disclosed.

In this situation and on these facts, where the inventor has failed to disclose the only mode he ever contemplated of carrying out his invention, the best mode requirement is violated.

Accordingly, the judgment of the district court is affirmed. .

Notes

1. Best Mode Policy. The best mode requirement appears to be based on the idea that the public is entitled to have access to the patentee's best mode from the patent instrument itself. Isn't it better to ask whether the public needs access to the best mode at all? Consider a hypothetical where an inventor contemporaneously submits an article to a leading technical publication including the best mode and files a patent application without this information. By the time the application matures into an issued patent, the published article has been in the public domain for several years. In this situation, does it make any sense to strike down the patent for failure to disclose the best mode?

2. Burying the Best Mode. In *Randomex Inc. v. Scopus Corp.*, 849 F.2d 585, 7 U.S.P.Q.2d 1050 (Fed.Cir.1988), the court considered the possibility of "burying" the best mode by concealing it among a large number of less favored alternatives. Here, the majority opinion held that the patentee did not violate § 112 through the "indiscriminate disclosure in this instance of the preferred cleaning fluid along with one other possible cleaning fluid...." Judge Mayer dissented:

> [The inventor]only named [the preferred embodiment] as one among many possible solutions, and then only by its trade name, not generically. He did not disclose which of the suggested modes was the "best mode contemplated by him" for practicing the invention. His disclosure does not satisfy section 112 because he buried his best mode in a list of less satisfactory ones.

849 F.2d at 592, 7 U.S.P.Q.2d at 1056. Note that although some drafters explicitly identify one embodiment as the best mode, no statute or rule mandates how the patent instrument should set forth the best mode. In fact Judge Bissell, who wrote for the court in *Randomex* gave an example of best mode disclosure:

> For example, if one should invent a new and improved internal combustion engine, the best mode requirement would require a patentee to divulge the fuel on which it would run best. The patentee, however, would not be required to disclose the formula for refining gasoline or any other petroleum product. Every requirement is met if the patentee truthfully stated that the engine ran smoothly and powerfully on Brand X super-premium lead free "or equal."

849 F.2d at 590 n. *, 7 U.S.P.Q.2d at 1055 n. *. Is Judge Bissel correct that a claim to an engine requires disclosure of a preferred fuel? The inventor did not invent a fuel, why would a fuel be a best mode? This question gets more coverage in the next case in this chapter.

3. Burying the Best Mode II. One of the more unusual fact patterns in Federal Circuit history involved burying (literally) the best mode. *See Shearing v. Iolab Corp.*, 975 F.2d 1541, 24 U.S.P.Q.2d 1133 (Fed.Cir.1992). Dr. Shearing acquired a process patent, U.S. Patent No. 4,159,546, for an improved method of implanting an artificial optic lens into the posterior chamber of the eye. Before Dr. Shearing's innovation, physicians would implant a J-loop artificial lens in front of the iris, a process that often tore delicate eye tissue. Dr. Shearing sued Iolab for infringement. Iolab countered that a Dr. Simcoe had practiced the method before Dr. Shearing and that Dr. Shearing did not disclose his best mode, namely compressing both loops on the artificial lens to fit it past the small opening in the pupil. To resolve the issue, the patentee actually exhumed the body of one of Dr. Simcoe's patients. Upon exhumation of the body, an examination showed Dr. Simcoe had not implanted a J-loop artificial lens at all. The Federal Circuit also sustained the jury's conclusion that Dr. Shearing had not concealed a best mode:

> The jury also heard testimony refuting any concealment by Dr. Shearing of superior loop compression. In addition to the language about "directing" the second strand, at least two references in the '546 specification suggest superior loop compression:
>
> > Thus, since full compression of at least one of the strands during implantation is essential according to the procedure described herein. . . .
>
> U.S. Patent No. 4,159,546, col. 5, lines 18–20. This statement suggests compression of more than just one strand or loop. The specification also states:
>
> > directing said second strand against the ciliary body opposite said first strand. . . .

Id. at col. 6, lines 8–9. This statement would also teach one skilled in the art to compress both strands.

975 F.2d at 1545–46, 24 U.S.P.Q.2d at 1137. In addition to teaching the rewards of full discovery, this case teaches that the best mode need only be disclosed in terms sufficient to inform one of skill in the practice of the invention.

4. Best Mode Abroad. The best mode requirement appears to be a unique one to common law systems. Section 4 of the now-superseded British Patent Act of 1949 mandated that applicants "shall disclose the best method of performing the invention which is known to the applicant and for which he is entitled to claim protection." An earlier Canadian statute tracked the "best mode" language of the United States statute more closely; as explained in IMMANUEL GOLDSMITH, PATENTS OF INVENTION § 177 (1981), the Canadian patent law required that the inventor "put the public in possession of the invention in as full and ample a manner as he himself possesses it and give to them the opportunity of deriving benefits therefrom equal to the benefits accruing to him." However, these and other jurisdictions have since abrogated requirements that parallel the United States "best mode" requirement.

Although foreign patent systems do not impose a best mode requirement, foreign applicants often include this information in their applications as well. In no small part they do so because they contemplate the possibility of filing an application in the United States under the Paris Convention. Because the applicant may not augment her initial disclosure when later filing in the United States, but must fulfill disclosure requirements such as best mode, inclusion of the best mode is often prudent. Similarly, the following passage, directed towards Japanese law, explains why American applicants seldom delete the best mode from their foreign applications that are based on a United States priority date.

> The United States patent law requires under the first paragraph of 35 U.S.C.A. § 112 that the inventor set forth the "best mode contemplated" for carrying out the invention as of the filing date. This is *recommended* by the Japanese Patent Office, but it is not a basis for a ground of rejection of the application or of invalidity of the patent.

It would seem unwarranted to *delete* the best mode known to the applicant from the American text serving as the draft for the Japanese application. Presumably, the best mode will be published in the form of an American patent, and it would be naive to presume that Japanese industry is not aware of the American patent literature.

Assume that the best mode of the American text is taken out of the Japanese case, and that eventually a copier of the best mode is sued for infringement in a District Court in Japan. If the wording of the claims and the specification make the generic coverage unclear, it is possible that the judge may well ... leav[e] the best mode outside the scope of protection.

TETSU TANABE & HAROLD C. WEGNER, JAPANESE PATENT LAW § 422 (1979).

5.   "The inventor" Means "The Inventor." In *Glaxo Inc. v. Novopharm Ltd.*, 52 F.3d 1043, 34 U.S.P.Q.2d 1565 (Fed.Cir.1995), the Federal Circuit confronted the question of who is the inventor for purposes of best mode enforcement. In a case involving the anti-ulcer medication Zantac ®, Glaxo's patent counsel learned that Glaxo had a secret process that made the invention easier to put into pharmaceutical compositions. In sum, Glaxo's attorney and others within the corporation knew of a best mode. The inventor, Dr. Crookes, did not know that Glaxo had developed the best mode. The Federal Circuit determined that only the inventor's knowledge is relevant to the best mode inquiry:

> The statutory language could not be clearer. The best mode of carrying out an invention, indeed if there is one, to be disclosed is that "contemplated by the inventor." ... There is simply no evidence in the record before us that the inventor of the '431 patent knew of and concealed the azeotroping process when his application was filed.

52 F.3d at 1049, 32 U.S.P.Q.2d at 1569. Even though Glaxo apparently screened Crookes from any knowledge of the best mode, the Federal Circuit refused to invalidate the patent. Judge Mayer dissented:

> With this case, the court blesses corporate shell games resulting from organizational gerrymandering and willful ignorance by which one can secure the monopoly of a patent while hiding the best mode of practicing the invention the law expects to be made public in return for its protection.

52 F.3d at 1053, 32 U.S.P.Q.2d at 1571. As the director of a corporate research and development department, what advice would you give to the inventors in your division after *Glaxo*? Why do you think the Federal Circuit takes such a literal approach to enforcing the best mode requirement? The next case again offers some hints about an answer.

6.   *Chemcast* recast: In *Chemcast*, Judge Mayer opined that "most of the cases in which we have said that the best mode requirement was violated addressed situations where the inventor failed to disclose non-claimed elements that were nevertheless necessary to practice the best mode." *Chemcast*, 913 F.2d at 927, 16 U.S.P.Q.2d at 1037. This statement seems to defy the standard rule that the best mode requirement only extends to claimed elements of the invention. This statement prompted an explanation in Judge Rader's concurrence in *Bayer*, the next case in this chapter:

Despite its language about "non-claimed elements," the *Chemcast* claim recited a "locking portion . . . more rigid than said base portion." *Id.* at 925. Thus, the best mode violation in that case—a grommet of specified rigidity—was within the scope of the claims. *Chemcast* 's comment about "non-claimed elements" was purely dicta. Contrary to the *Chemcast* dicta, an undisclosed feature only becomes a "best mode" candidate—by statutory definition—if it arises within the scope of the claimed invention.

    In *Chemcast*, the inventor's specification disclosed a grommet of "rigid castable resinous material . . . for example, polyurethane or polyvinyl chloride . . . [with] a durometer hardness reading of 70 Shore A or harder." Chemcast, 913 F.2d at 929. No doubt the inventor thought that this disclosure was sufficient. After all, the inventor disclosed a preferred embodiment. Moreover, Chemcast Corporation's actual product, R-4467, was indeed PVC with a hardness reading above Shore A 70—consistent with that disclosure.

    The Federal Circuit, however, perceived concealment—the second prong of the best mode requirement. This court noted that R–4467 had a material hardness of 75 on the Shore D scale—"three hardness scales removed from the 70 Shore A hardness mentioned in the specification." *Id.* at 930. This circuit further stressed that the inventors had "expended several months and many hundred man-hours" developing R 4467. *Id.* at 929. Chemcast is a concealment case, indeed an enthusiastic application of the concealment standard. In its zeal to reach the concealment issue, the Federal Circuit stretched its purported definition of best modes to encompass "unclaimed features," but that certainly does not override prior binding case law.

Bayer v. Schein Pharm., 301 F.3d 1306 at n. 6, 2002 WL 1830197 at n. 6 (Fed.Cir.2002)(Rader J., concurring). The best mode requirement has two prongs—"contemplation" and "concealment." Although a violation requires satisfaction of both prongs, can a strong case of "concealment" strengthen a weak case of "contemplation"?

BAYER AG v. SCHEIN PHARMACEUTICALS, INC.

United States Court of Appeals, Federal Circuit, 2002.
301 F.3d 1306.

Before CLEVENGER,RADER and DYK, CIRCUIT JUDGES.

CLEVENGER, CIRCUIT JUDGE.

    In these four consolidated patent infringement suits, Bayer AG and Bayer Corporation (collectively, "Bayer") sued Schein Pharmaceutical, Inc., Danbury Pharmacal, Inc., Reddy–Cheminor, Inc., Mylan Pharmaceuticals, Inc., and Mylan Laboratories Inc. (collectively, "Schein") for infringement of U.S. Patent No. 4,670,444 and Reexamination Certificate B1 4,670,444 (collectively, the " '444 patent"), directed towards a class of chemical compounds that includes the broad-spectrum antibiotic ciprofloxacin, better known as Cipro. Schein raised an affirmative defense of invalidity under 35 U.S.C. § 102(d). On cross-motions for summary judgment, the district court held that the '444 patent was entitled to the filing date of its U.S. parent, Application No. 292,560 (the " '560 application") and thus was not invalid under section 102(d), and therefore the court granted Bayer's motion for summary judgment on validity. *Bayer AG v. Schein Pharm., Inc.*, 129 F.Supp.2d 705, 725 (D.N.J.2001).

On appeal, Schein argues that the '444 patent cannot claim the benefit of the parent application because the parent is invalid for failure to satisfy the best mode requirement of 35 U.S.C. § 112. Because we find that the '444 patent is entitled to the filing date of the '560 application under 35 U.S.C. § 120, we affirm.

I

BACKGROUND

Ciprofloxacin is a relatively simple heterocyclic organic compound developed by Bayer in the 1980s and shown in the figure below, where R^a is hydrogen.

During the 1970s a group of scientists at Bayer experimented with a group of similar antibiotics, and they discovered that substitution of a cyclopropyl group at the 1–position, i.e., on the nitrogen of the heterocycle ring, greatly increased the potency of the resulting antibiotic. In the fall of 1980, Dr. Klaus Grohe, one of the Bayer scientists, attended a conference at which a Japanese firm disclosed the structure of norfloxacin, a broad-spectrum antibiotic that it had developed. The structure of norfloxacin is identical to that depicted in the figure above for ciprofloxacin, except that norfloxacin has an ethyl rather than a cyclopropyl group on the ring nitrogen. From his earlier research, Dr. Grohe knew that substituting a cyclopropyl group for the ethyl group of norfloxacin would increase antibiotic activity, and he hastened home from the conference determined to make such a compound.

Although Dr. Grohe succeeded in making numerous compounds similar in structure to ciprofloxacin, his standard synthetic methodology failed when he attempted to make ciprofloxacin. The problematic part of the synthesis was the construction of the starting bicyclic, 6–fluoroquinolinic acid ("6–FQA"). Dr. Grohe's standard method of making the starting bicyclics used a "cycloaracylation" reaction that he had previously developed and had disclosed in a published patent application. However, in the case of ciprofloxacin, Dr. Grohe could not make the starting material he needed for the cycloaracyclation reaction. Therefore, he enlisted the help of one of his colleagues at Bayer, Dr. Klauke, who successfully synthesized the precursor 2,4–dichloro–5–fluorobenzoyl chloride, the so-called "Klauke compound," necessary to make 6–FQA via cycloaracyclation. While Dr. Grohe concededly had difficulty making the Klauke compound without assistance, it is undisputed that a person of skill in the art could readily obtain the Klauke compound by using commercially-available starting materials and known synthetic methods retrieved through a routine search of the chemical literature.

Using the Klauke compound, Dr. Grohe performed the cycloaracylation reaction to obtain 6–FQA, which he then converted to ciprofloxacin. The overall reaction sequence Dr. Grohe used to make ciprofloxacin can be regarded as containing three primary steps: (1) synthesis of the Klauke compound; (2) synthesis of 6–FQA via cycloaracyclation of the Klauke compound; and (3) addition of piperazine to 6–FQA to synthesize ciprofloxacin.

Bayer ultimately obtained patents on both the Klauke compound, U.S. Patent No. 4,439,620, and 6–FQA, U.S. Patent No. 4,620,007. It also, of course, sought and obtained a patent on the target compound itself, ciprofloxacin: the '444 patent.

[At this point, the opinion sets for the facts invoking § 102 (d). Bayer filed its first CIPRO application in Chile on August 12, 1981. The next day, August 13, 1981, it filed the '560 application in the United States. The defendants in this case filed Abbreviated New Drug Applications ("ANDAs") with the Food and Drug Administration (FDA) under 21 U.S.C. § 355(j) seeking approval to market generic versions of ciprofloxacin. Bayer sued under 35 U.S.C. § 271(e)(2), alleging that filing the ANDAs infringed the '444 patent. Schein conceded infringement but argued that the '444 patent is invalid based on the filing and issuance of the Chilean, South African, Spanish and Argentinean patents, because under 35 U.S.C. § 102(d) those foreign patents are prior art that would invalidate the '444 patent. Bayer countered that the '444 patent is entitled to the filing date of its German application, October 29, 1981. Schein argued that Bayer cannot rely on the '560 application because, in its view, that application does not disclose Dr. Grohe's best mode of making ciprofloxacin as required by section 112.]

The district court granted Bayer's motion for summary judgment, holding that the '560 application satisfies the best mode requirement. *Id.* at 724. After setting forth the two-pronged test for whether a disclosure satisfies the best mode requirement, the court proceeded to analyze the first prong, i.e., whether Dr. Grohe subjectively possessed a preferred mode of practicing his invention. *Id.* at 719. As to the first prong, the court focused on whether Dr. Grohe preferred a particular method of synthesizing the starting material 6–FQA, and determined that "the undisputed testimony ... indicates that Dr. Grohe did not have a preference . . . for the Klauke compound or any other particular compound for use as a starting material in the synthesis of 6–FQA." However, the court determined that Dr. Grohe did have a preference for using the general class of compounds that includes the Klauke compound, because such compounds would allow him to make 6–FQA via cycloaracylation. The court then turned to whether the '560 application adequately disclosed Dr. Grohe's preference. In answering this question, the court noted that the scope of the claims limits the extent of the required disclosure, and held that because Dr. Grohe's preference pertained to unclaimed subject matter, "the best mode requirement does not compel disclosure of the unclaimed method and the unclaimed starting material beyond enablement." *Id.* at 721.

[In analyzing § 102 (d), the Federal Circuit determined that "Bayer may defeat the 102(d) bar only if the '560 application fulfills the disclosure requirements of section 112."]

Schein argues here, as it did before the district court, that the '560 application does not comply with section 112 because it does not set forth the best mode contemplated by Dr. Grohe for making ciprofloxacin. Specifically, the '560 application does not disclose the synthesis of the Klauke compound or the use of the cycloaracylation reaction to make 6 FQA. Concededly, both 6–FQA and the Klauke compound are synthetic intermediates not claimed in the '444 patent. However, Schein asserts that 6–FQA and its synthesis via cycloaracylation of the Klauke compound are novel, and that disclosure of Dr. Grohe's preferred method of making 6–FQA is therefore necessary to adequately describe the best mode of practicing the invention—ciprofloxacin—claimed in the '444 patent. *See Eli Lilly & Co. v. Barr Labs., Inc.,* 251 F.3d 955, 964(Fed.Cir.2001). It is undisputed that the disclosure in the '560 application is sufficient to enable one of skill in the art to obtain 6–FQA, even though the compound is otherwise novel and unobvious. Schein claims that the disclosure is insufficient, arguing that for best mode purposes the specification must provide the actual synthetic route that Dr. Grohe preferred to make 6–FQA.

For the reasons given below, we conclude that the '560 application complies with section 112 and therefore may be relied upon by Bayer to defeat Schein's section 102(d) invalidity defense.

A.

The first paragraph of 35 U.S.C. § 112 provides:

The specification shall contain a written description of the invention, and of the manner and process of making and using it, in such full, clear, concise, and exact terms as to enable any person skilled in the art to which it pertains, or with which it is most nearly connected, to make and use the same, and shall set forth the best mode contemplated by the inventor of carrying out his invention.

As we have observed on numerous occasions, section 112 contains both an enablement requirement and a best mode requirement. See *Chem-*

cast, 913 F.2d at 926, 8 USPQ2d at 1035; *Spectra-Physics, Inc. v. Coherent, Inc.*, 827 F.2d 1524, 1532, 3 USPQ2d 1737, 1742 (Fed.Cir. 1987). The enablement requirement ensures that "that a specification shall disclose an invention in such a manner as will enable one skilled in the art to make and utilize it." *In re Gay*, 309 F.2d at 772, 135 USPQ at 315. Because an enabling disclosure by definition turns upon the objective understanding of a skilled artisan, the enablement requirement can be met by reference to the knowledge of one of ordinary skill in the relevant art.

The best mode requirement is "separate and distinct" from enablement and "requires an inventor to disclose the best mode contemplated by him, as of the time he executes the application, of carrying out the invention." *In re Gay*, 309 F.2d at 772. Unlike enablement, the existence of a best mode is a purely subjective matter depending upon what the inventor actually believed at the time the application was filed. Because of the subjective nature of the best mode inquiry, the best mode disclosure requirement—unlike enablement—cannot be met by mute reference to the knowledge of one of skill in the art. The reason is pragmatic. It is unreasonable if not impossible to require the ordinary artisan to peer into the inventor's mind to discover his or her idiosyncratic preferences as of the filing date. Rather, because the existence of a best mode of carrying out the invention is by definition known only to the inventor, section 112 demands actual disclosure regardless of whether, as an abstract matter, practicing that mode would be within the knowledge of one of ordinary skill in the art.

But while the best mode requirement cannot be met solely by reference to the knowledge of one of skill in the art, neither does it demand disclosure of every preference an inventor possesses as of the filing date. As is always the case, the text of the statute provides the proper boundaries of the disclosure requirement. Section 112 only demands disclosure of "the best mode contemplated by the inventor of carrying out his invention." 35 U.S.C. § 112 (1994). Thus, only preferred ways of "carrying out [the] invention" need be disclosed. As we recently noted in *Teleflex, Inc. v. Ficosa North America Corp.*, No. 01–1372, slip op. at 24, (Fed. Cir. June 21, 2002), we stated in *Wahl Instruments, Inc. v. Acvious, Inc.*, 950 F.2d 1575, 1579, 21 USPQ2d 1123, 1126 (Fed.Cir. 1991), that "the term 'mode' and the phrase 'carrying out the invention' are not definable with precision." Nonetheless, before *Wahl* we had referred to the best mode "for making and using" the claimed invention, *Christianson v. Colt. Indus. Operating Corp.*, 822 F.2d 1544, 1563, 3 USPQ2d 1241, 1255 (Fed.Cir.1987), thus suggesting that the statute is susceptible of interpretation.

Our cases examining the scope of the best mode requirement demonstrate that the best mode disclosure requirement only refers to the invention defined by the claims. The earliest statement on this matter was given by our predecessor court in *In re Brebner*, 455 F.2d 1402 (CCPA 1972). In that case, the court reversed a Patent Office Board of Appeals decision sustaining a rejection, on best mode grounds, of a patent application claiming a blend of two polymers, polyethylene and an ethylene-methacrylic acid copolymer. The Board sustained the rejection because the application did not disclose a method of making the two polymers—the starting materials—that comprised the claimed blend. The court reversed because "[a]ppropriate inquiries into the best mode requirement should pertain to the contemplated mode of carrying out the invention, which in this case is the blend and not the starting materials." *Id.* at 1404. Similarly, in *DeGeorge v. Bernier*, we reversed the Board of Patent Interference's finding that the inventor failed the best mode requirement by not disclosing the preferred species of an unclaimed word processor. 768 F.2d 1318, 1325 (Fed.Cir.1985). *DeGeorge* is a significant case in our best mode jurisprudence. In that case, we explained that "[b]ecause the properly-construed count does not include a word processor, failure to meet the best mode requirement here should not arise from an absence of information on the word processor." *Id.* The word processor bore no relationship whatsoever to the claim, and therefore fell wholly outside the best mode requirement. In *Zygo Corp. v. Wyko Corp.*, we rejected a best mode challenge based on a failure to disclose a particular commercial embodiment that enclosed the invention in a box. 79 F.3d 1563, 1567 (Fed.Cir.1996). We declared emphatically that "in keeping with the statutory mandate, our precedent is clear that the parameters of a section 112 inquiry are set by the CLAIMS." *Id.* Thus, "[b]ecause the claims simply do not require packaging of any sort, the failure to disclose the enclosure is not a violation of section 112." *Id.*

In accordance with the focus on the claimed subject matter, we have long held that compliance with the best mode requirement requires disclosing the inventor's preferred embodiment of the claimed invention. See, e.g., *Dana Corp. v. IPC Ltd. P'ship*, 860 F.2d 415, 418 (Fed.Cir. 1988) ("The purpose of the best mode requirement is to ensure that the public, in exchange for the rights given the inventor under the patent laws, obtains from the inventor a full disclosure of the preferred embodiment of the invention."). This result is hardly surprising, for if an inventor has developed a preferred way of practicing the invention, he typically will state that preference in his description of the preferred embodiment. Furthermore, fulfillment of the requirement via disclosure of the preferred embodiment comports with the purpose of the best mode requirement. As our predecessor court held in *In re Gay*, "[m]anifestly, the sole purpose of [the best mode] requirement is to restrain inventors from applying for patents while at the same time concealing from the public preferred embodiments of their inventions which they have in fact conceived." *Id.*

Notwithstanding that the best mode requirement keys only on carrying out the claimed invention, "we have found violations of the best mode requirement for failure to disclose subject matter not strictly within the bounds of the claims.... " *Teleflex*, slip op. at 26. In the history of this court and our predecessor courts, we have held claims invalid for failure to satisfy the best mode requirement on only seven occasions. As we will see, these cases involved either failure to disclose a preferred embodiment, or else failure to disclose a preference that materially affected making or using the invention.

In *Spectra–Physics*, which concerned patents on a laser and a method of constructing a laser, the inventor preferred to use a TiCuSil active metal brazing process to attach a copper cup to the inside wall of a ceramic tube structure. 827 F.2d at 1530. Although the specification disclosed the inventor's preference for using TiCuSil as a brazing material, it did not disclose any of the parameters for performing the six-stage brazing cycle that the inventor had developed for using the TiCuSil brazing material to attach the cup to the tube. *Id.* at 1536–37. The patents in suit each stressed the importance of brazing to produce the bond between the copper cups and the ceramic tube, explaining in detail why less than ideal bonding will adversely affect the efficiency and reliability of the claimed lasers. *Id.* at 1529. We affirmed the district court's finding that "[t]he six-stage braze cycle employed by Coherent [the inventor], and developed by it, are [sic, is] necessary to the enjoyment of the invention taught by the patents in suit ... and are [sic] not sufficiently disclosed. "*Id.* at 1537. Thus, failure to disclose the actual method of brazing preferred by the inventor rendered the patent claims invalid for "fail[ure] to disclose the best mode contemplated by the inventors for practicing their ... inventions." *Id.*

Dana involved a patent on a valve stem seal for use in an internal combustion engine. 860 F.2d at 416. The seal included a "portion of elastomeric material positioned atop said valve guide.... " *Id.* The inventor conducted a series of tests comparing the effectiveness of various seal designs; each design was tested with and without a 60–second fluoride surface treatment. *Id.* at 418. The inventor concluded that the fluoride surface treatment was "necessary to satisfactory performance of [the] seal," id., because without the treatment, the seal leaked. In other words, the undisclosed fluoride surface treatment had a material effect on the properties of the claimed invention. But although the inventor "believed that the best way of carrying out his invention included fluoride treating the surface of the valve seals," *id.* at 419–20, the specification never "disclose[d] that a fluoride treatment must or even should be applied to the surface of the patented seals" as preferred by the inventor, *id.* at 420. Thus, we held the patent invalid for failure to disclose the best mode of carrying out the invention.

In *Northern Telecom, Inc. v. Datapoint Corp.*, 908 F.2d 931, 940 (Fed.Cir.1990), the defendant raised a best mode challenge to claims directed towards capturing data on ordinary magnetic tape cassettes. The inventor preferred audio cassettes "of its own design and specifications and ... these were different from standard audio tapes in their yield strength and magnetic characteristics." *Id.* Of all the brands on the market as of the filing date, only a single brand of commercially-available audiotape met the inventor's specifications. We held that failure to disclose either the one conforming brand, or, alternatively, the inventor's specifications for its preferred tape violated the best mode requirement. In effect, the inventor had developed a preferred embodiment of his invention that used a very specific type of audiotape, and failure to disclose that preferred embodiment rendered the claims invalid.

Like *Northern Telecom*, *Chemcast* involved an inventor's failure to disclose his preferred embodiment of the claimed invention, a grommet made of a material of a distinct hardness. *Chemcast*, 913 F.2d at 928. The inventor preferred a particular material to make the locking portion of the grommet, but failed to disclose this fact in the specification. *Id.* at 929. We found the patent's disclosure "manifestly deficient." *Id.* We noted that "[g]iven the specification and the level of skill or understanding in the art, skilled practitioners could neither have known what [the inventor's] contemplated best mode was nor have carried it out. Indeed, on these facts, they would not even have known where to look." *Id.* at 930. Because this amounted to concealment of the inventor's preferred embodiment, we affirmed the judgment of the district court invalidating the claim to the grommet for failure to disclose the inventor's best mode.

In *United States Gypsum Co.*, 74 F.3d at 1213–14, we confronted yet another example of failure to disclose the inventor's preferred embodiment of a discrete claim limitation—an embodiment preferred because the inventor believed it improved the efficacy of his invention. The claims recited a joint compound that contained, inter alia, "expanded perlite which has been treated with a silicone compound to render it water-insensitive." *Id.* at 1211 n. 5. During the course of his investigations, the inventor discovered that a particular perlite, Sil–42, offered numerous advantages in his invention. It obviated the need for screening before use, "eliminated the coarse look of other lightweight fillers, resisted breakdown under vacuum treatment, and yielded a joint compound that was lightweight, easy to sand, and exhibited good non-cracking and adhesion properties." *Id.* at 1211. We rejected the argument that the preference related merely to commercial considerations and thus need not be disclosed as part of the best mode, noting that "[i]n short, [the inventor] believed that Sil–42 perlite was essential to improving the invention; the material was not selected as a matter of commercial expediency." *Id.* at 1213. Failure to disclose the Sil–42 perlite was, therefore, fatal to the validity of the patent.

In *Great Northern Corp. v. Henry Molded Products, Inc.*, 94 F.3d 1569, 1571, 39 USPQ2d 1997, 1999 (Fed.Cir.1996), we found a best mode violation due to a failure to disclose preferred diamond indentations that were placed on a roll stacker made of papier-mache. The diamond indentations were crucial to producing a usable version of the invention because without diamonds the stacker simply collapsed under the weight of the rolls it was supposed to hold. Id. at 1572. Thus, we rejected the patentee's argument that the diamonds were merely a production detail unrelated to the "quality or nature of the invention." Id. On the contrary, because the diamonds materially affected the properties of the claimed invention, they had to be disclosed to comply with the best mode requirement. Because the specification did not disclose the diamonds, we held the claims invalid for failure to disclose the best mode of carrying out the invention.

Finally, *Nobelpharma AB v. Implant Innovations, Inc.*, 141 F.3d 1059 (Fed.Cir.1998), presents a paradigm example of failure to disclose the inventor's preferred mode of making the invention. The patent claimed "an element intended for implantation into bone tissue" and recited that the element contain micropits. Id. at 1062. "For whatever reason," the patentee introduced testimony from the inventor that:

> (1) "there were some minor details that were not included [in the patent] and which proved to be quite important," (2) other skilled artisans would have to be "lucky" to obtain a piece of suitable micropitted implant "by cutting a piece of titanium at a speed less than twenty meters per minute," the cutting speed disclosed in the patent, and (3) "any of the small detailed recipes that I discussed but did not specify" in the patent "can cause you to fail to get micropitting even though you were cutting the metal at less than twenty meters per minute."

Id. at 1065. We noted that production of the implant depended critically on "a variety of undisclosed machining parameters," and the evidence showed that the inventor knew and preferred these parameters before the filing date. "Thus, the evidence at trial leads to only one reasonable conclusion: [the inventor] possessed a preferred method of making the claimed invention and failed to disclose it sufficiently to enable those skilled in the art to practice that method." *Id.* at 1065. The inventor's undisclosed preferences related to manufacture of the claimed implant, and were critical to production of a functional implant, i.e., one that would work correctly. *Id.* The undisclosed preference thus materially affected the properties of the claimed invention. Hence, we held the patent invalid for failure to disclose the best mode of carrying out the invention.

Thus, we have held a patent invalid for failure to satisfy the best mode requirement in two situations. First, we have invalidated patents when they do not adequately disclose a preferred embodiment of the invention. This is what occurred in *Northern Telecom*, *Chemcast*, and *United States Gypsum Co.* Consequently, if an inventor fails to disclose the preferred embodiment of the invention, the best mode requirement is not satisfied.

Second, we have invalidated patents when the patentee failed to disclose aspects of making or using the claimed invention and the undisclosed matter materially affected the properties of the claimed invention. In *Spectra–Physics* and *Nobelpharma*, the inventors failed to disclose subjective preferences that related to making the inventions, and the undisclosed information materially affected the properties of the claimed invention. In *Dana* and *Great Northern*, the inventors failed to disclose subjective preferences that related to the use of the claimed inventions, and the undisclosed information materially affected the properties of the claimed inventions.

As noted above, *DeGeorge* is one of the key cases for understanding the best mode requirement. *DeGeorge* stands for the proposition that the best mode requirement is strictly limited to disclosures that concern preferences for carrying out the claimed invention. In DeGeorge, the interference dealt with a count drawn to certain electrical circuitry designed to obtain automatic indentation of a block of text. The claimed circuitry was designed for use in word processors. The Board of Patent Interferences drew the count to include a word processor with which the claimed circuitry would be used. Absent disclosure of any such word processor, the Board found a best mode violation. We reversed that decision, for the simple reason that the Board had misinterpreted the count. Properly drawn, the count did not claim a word processor. No allegation was made that the choice of any particular word processor would have any effect whatsoever on carrying out the claimed invention, which was the claimed circuitry. In short, a particular word processor had no effect on carrying out the claimed invention.

The instances in which we have held that an inventor failed to disclose the best mode of carrying out his invention are consistent with *DeGeorge*. Each instance in which best mode violations have been found in our precedent deal with the invention itself, and in each of those cases the failure to disclose a preference for carrying out the claimed invention directly impacted the invention itself. In short, we have held that the best mode of making or using the invention need be disclosed if it materially affects the properties of the claimed invention itself.

We now turn to whether Dr. Grohe possessed a best mode of carrying out the invention, and if so, whether the '560 application fails to adequately disclose it.

B

The general contours of our test for compliance with the best mode requirement are well known: Compliance with best mode is a question of fact composed of two subsidiary factual inquiries. "First, the factfinder must determine whether, at the time of filing the application, the inventor possessed a best mode for practicing the invention." *Eli Lilly*, 251 F.3d at 963. The first prong, we have explained, is highly subjective and focuses on the inventor's state of mind as of the date of filing the application. Id.; see also *N. Telecom Ltd. v. Samsung Elec. Co.*, 215 F.3d 1281, 1286 (Fed.Cir.2000). Second, if the inventor subjectively considered one mode to be preferred over all others, then "[t]he second inquiry is whether the inventor's disclosure is adequate to enable one of ordinary skill in the art to practice the best mode of the invention. This inquiry is objective and depends upon the scope of the claimed invention and the level of skill in the relevant art." *N. Telecom*, 215 F.3d at 1286.

As in enablement, the "invention" referred to in the best mode requirement is the invention defined by the claims. See, e.g., *United States Gypsum Co.*, 74 F.3d at 1212, 37 USPQ2d at 1390 (The first prong of the best mode inquiry requires a "determin[ation] whether, at the time the patent application was filed, the inventor had a best mode of practicing the claimed invention "(emphasis added)). Because the scope of the invention obviously impacts what it means to carry out the invention, in *Northern Telecom*, 215 F.3d at 1286–87, we held that the first step in a best mode inquiry, before application of the familiar two-part best mode test, must be to define the invention by construing the claims. Definition of the invention "is a legal exercise, wherein the ordinary principles of claim construction apply." *Id.* Defining the invention by analyzing the claim language is a crucial predicate to the factual portions of the best mode inquiry because it ensures that the finder of fact looks only for preferences pertaining to carrying out the claimed invention.

Once the invention has been defined by examining the claims, the finder of fact—be it the court or a jury—can proceed to determine whether the inventor subjectively possessed a best mode of practicing the claimed invention, and if so whether the specification adequately discloses that mode.

With the proper legal test for compliance with the best mode requirement in hand, we turn to its specific application to the undisputed facts of this case. Under *Northern Telecom* we first must determine the identity of the invention recited in the claims of the '444 patent at issue: claims 1–2, 5, 11–12, 16, 18–21, 25, 27, 29–32, 34, and 36–39. The claims are directed towards compositions of matter that either comprise or consist solely of the target antibiotic compound—in this case, ciprofloxacin. Importantly, the claims do not recite 6–FQA or any other starting bicyclic. The invention, therefore, consists of the final antibiotic product and not the starting materials.

The existence of a subjective preference is not disputed. First, of the various possible synthetic routes to ciprofloxacin, it is undisputed that Dr. Grohe preferred to make his invention by manipulating 6–FQA by reacting it with piperazine. The patent disclosed this reaction, and it disclosed the structure of the intermediate 6–FQA. Schein does not dispute that Dr. Grohe's preferences regarding the reaction of 6–FQA with piperazine were adequately disclosed.

Second, the district court found, and Bayer does not dispute, "that Dr. Grohe had a preference prior to August 13, 1981 for a starting material comprised of benzoyl halide with leaving groups in the 2–and 4–positions and a fluorine atom in the 5–position [i.e., a class of starting materials including the Klauke compound] so that he could create 6–FQA through the cycloaracyclation method." *Bayer AG*, 129 F.Supp.2d at 720. It is also undisputed that the '560 application does not disclose either the Klauke compound or its use in making 6–FQA through cycloaracyclation.

Schein feels that failure to disclose Dr. Grohe's preferred route to 6–FQA is a fatal flaw. We disagree. As we discussed above, not every preference constitutes a best mode of carrying out the invention. Preferences that are reflected in a preferred embodiment or that relate to making or using the invention and have a material effect on the properties of the claimed invention must be disclosed. Schein concedes that Dr. Grohe's preferred way of making the 6–FQA intermediate has no material effect on the properties of the claimed ciprofloxacin end product. Thus, this case is clearly distinguishable from the four cases in which this court has found a best mode violation where an undisclosed preference clearly had a material affect on the properties of the claimed invention.

For the reasons given above, Schein has failed to show that the '560 application did not disclose the best mode contemplated by Dr. Grohe of carrying out his invention, ciprofloxacin. Therefore we affirm the district court's judgment that the '444 is not invalid under section 102(d).

AFFIRMED.

RADER, CIRCUIT JUDGE, concurring.

Because the alleged best mode in this case was an intermediate, not the claimed invention, the district court correctly concluded that the best mode requirement "does not compel disclosure of the unclaimed method." Bayer AG, 129 F.Supp.2d at 721. On this basis, I would affirm. I write to underscore the district court's correct application of the statutory test for best modes. The alleged best mode in this case does not fall within the scope of the claims. Therefore, this case simply does not require creation of a new test for best modes.

I.

Title 35 requires disclosure of "the best mode contemplated by the inventor of carrying out his invention." 35 U.S.C. § 112 (1994). The most important words in this phrase are "his invention." These words invoke the claims. Based on this direct statutory language, the bulk of this court's precedent states that the disclosure necessary to satisfy the best mode requirement depends on the scope of the claimed invention. Teleflex, slip op. at 22–29; Eli Lilly, 251 F.3d at 963 ("[T]he extent of information that an inventor must disclose depends on the scope of the claimed invention.").

One of these precedents deserves special emphasis as the earliest Federal Circuit case to address the rule for identifying a best mode. DeGeorge was very clear that the Board erred by defining the claim too broadly and identifying an alleged best mode beyond the proper claim scope:

> The board found no best mode in the DeGeorge applications. The board's analysis, however, was influenced by its erroneous claim construction.... Because the properly construed count does not include a word processor, failure to meet the best mode requirement here should not arise from an absence of information on the word processor.

DeGeorge, 768 F.2d at 1325. Thus, this court's earliest precedent explains that the claimed invention sets the bounds of the best mode inquiry. The *DeGeorge* court certainly did not inquire about a material effect on properties of the invention.

Moreover this emphasis on the claimed invention did not begin with the Federal Circuit. Indeed this court's predecessor followed the same standard:

> The claimed invention is a blend of uniformly random ethylene-methacrylic acid copolymer and polyethylene.... Appropriate inquiries into the best mode requirement should pertain to the contemplated mode of carrying out the invention, which in this case is the blend and not the starting materials.

In re Brebner, 455 F.2d at 1404. The Court of Customs and Patent Appeals limited the scope of "appropriate" best mode inquiries to the scope of the claims. Indeed the present case is very similar to *Brebner*. In *Brebner*, the claims did not recite the starting materials; here, the claims do not recite an intermediate. In both cases, "appropriate inquiries" into the best mode need not exceed the scope of the claims.

II.

With the "scope of the claimed invention" rule governing the identification of best modes, this court should have halted its analysis when the district court correctly applied that rule. Up to the point of acknowledging the claimed invention, this Bayer opinion reflects well the bulk of this court's best mode jurisprudence. Then, inexplicably and without support in the statute or case law, this Bayer opinion widens its best mode net to capture the properties of the claimed invention and further sweeps in any material effect or impact on those properties.

A closer look at the policy and rationale for the best mode requirement discloses the disturbing implications of extending the best mode requirement beyond the reach of the claims. In most instances, the best mode requirement is self-enforcing. If an inventor does not disclose a critical trade secret within the best mode requirement, that nondisclosure puts the value of the entire patented invention at risk—a risk beyond the requirements of § 112. Competitors in the same technology can, and invariably will, discover the undisclosed trade secret and claim it in a separate patent application. When that application ripens into a patent, the competitor will have a blocking patent that could compromise much of the value of the original patent. Therefore, an informed patent applicant will never withhold a genuine best mode. Informed patent applicants will always either disclose the best mode in the original patent's specification (often as a dependent claim) or, if the trade secret is not part of the claimed invention (as in this case), file a separate patent application on the separate innovation (also as in this case). Because informed patent applicants know to avoid best mode problems, this § 112 requirement is invariably little more than a trap for the uninformed applicant—usually a university or independent inventor without corporate legal resources. Because the best mode requirement is a trap for the unwary, the Federal Circuit has wisely followed the statutory "scope of the claimed invention" rule to confine the reach of this snare.

When extended beyond the scope of the claimed invention, the best mode requirement becomes as insidious and destructive as a hidden landmine. One of the cases emphasized by this opinion, *Dana*, 860 F.2d 415, illustrates those disturbing implications. In *Dana*, the inventor claimed a seal apparatus, not any method at all, let alone a method of treating elastomeric material to ensure its longevity. Having invented a unique seal apparatus, the inventor could not have guessed that the best mode would reach out to encompass a process to increase the useful life of one component of the invention a process that was already well known in the prior art to boot. *Dana*, 860 F.2d at 419. Nonetheless, this court invalidated the patent because the undisclosed method affected the life of the elastomeric material and thus the satisfactory performance of the seal.

At the outset, the *Dana* relationship test could sponsor a potentially boundless inquiry into any undisclosed method or property that could affect the satisfactory performance of the invention. Patent law in general is not concerned with the performance of an invention, let alone its satisfactory performance. *Hildreth v. Mastoras*, 257 U.S. 27, 34 (1921) ("The machine patented may be imperfect in its operation; but if it embodies the generic principle and works ... it is enough."). Notwithstanding this bedrock principle of patent law, *Dana* would inexplicably make satisfactory performance the critical identifier for best modes.

Sadly this Bayer opinion incorporates *Dana* within its "material effects" test: "In *Dana*, ... the inventors failed to disclose subjective preferences that related to the use of the claimed inventions, and the undisclosed information materially affected the properties of the claimed inventions." Apparently this opinion, like *Dana*, would include all uses and properties of the invention within the best mode.

Indeed if the rule for identifying a best mode expands to capture potentially innumerable unclaimed "uses" and "properties," as in *Dana*, the best mode requirement becomes a minefield for wary and unwary alike. At the outset, one might question the need for a new test. The Federal Circuit has identified best modes for twenty years without a material effect or properties test. Moreover, the Federal Circuit already has a claimed invention rule based on the language of § 112.

In expanding the best mode test to accommodate *Dana*, this new *Bayer* test unfortunately creates new conflicts with many cases in which this court found no best mode. Thus this new material effect test contravenes much of the calculus the Federal Circuit has employed in best mode cases.... [At this point, the concurrence analyzes the facts of *Teleflex*, 299 F.3d at 1332, *Brebner*, *Eli Lilly*, and *N. Telecom* and concludes that the "material effects" test would produce different results, and thus conflicts with binding case law.]

In sum, a review of the totality of this Circuit's best mode cases, as opposed to a few cases that found a violation, shows that this court does not use an "effect on properties" test to identify best modes, but instead uses a scope of the claimed invention test. Thus, to my eyes, this opinion fails in its effort to erect a new test that is, in any event, beyond the facts of this case.

III.

As I mentioned at the outset, this district court did its job well. It determined that the scope of the claimed invention did not include any intermediates. Because the defendants could not identify any alleged best mode within the scope of the claimed invention, the trial judge disposed of the best mode allegation as outside the statutory reference to the "invention." In fact, as this court's opinion notes, the inventor fully disclosed the intermediate, but not in this patent's specification. Instead the inventor disclosed the intermediate in a separate patent application. The proposed best mode in this case was so far removed from the scope of the claimed invention that it was itself a separate invention.

Thus, the district court got it exactly right. It applied Federal Circuit law and deserves commendation. Instead, this court purports to use this easy case to erect a new best mode test. Fortunately, both this court's failure to find a best mode in this case and the wealth of prior case law render this Bayer case mostly dicta. Otherwise, the next district judge encountering a best mode case would have to ask several imponderable questions: What is the Federal Circuit rule for the reach of the best mode rule? Even under this case, what is the test to identify a best mode—scope of the claimed invention, necessary relationship to performance of the claimed invention, or material effect on the properties of the claimed invention? What is a "property?" What is a "material effect?" How "material" is "material?" The district court correctly decided this easy best mode case. This court certainly did not need to plant any new traps in the best mode minefield.

Notes

1. Claiming Implications of the Best Mode Rule: Both opinions seem to agree that the claims are relevant to the scope of the best mode rule. The majority opinion purports to extend the rule even further. Consider the implications of the rule that the best mode requirement extends only to the claimed invention. Consider a hypothetical: You invent a new cap for an oil filter. If you draft your claims to cover only the cap, you need only to disclose trade secrets about making and using that cap itself. If you draft your claims broader to encompass the filter/cap combination, then you would have to disclose trade secrets about the filter mechanism as well as the cap technology. What would you ask an inventor before undertaking claim drafting in order to avoid best mode problems?

2. Do You Believe That an Inventor Will Always Choose Patenting Over Secrecy? Judge Rader in his concurring opinion argues that an inventor will not conceal a trade secret needed to practice his invention owing to the risk that another will discover and patent that secret. Do you agree with this assertion? Is it necessary to accept this proposition to support his conclusion?

3. Best Mode and Continuing Applications. In *Transco Products Inc. v. Performance Contracting, Inc.*, 38 F.3d 551, 32 U.S.P.Q.2d 1077 (Fed.Cir.1994), Judge Rich concluded that so-called continuing applications, considered here at Chapter 12, need not be updated with the inventor's most recent best mode. One commentator noted the countervailing policies as follows:

> If there is a strong policy reason for the best mode requirement, and there is not, then if one sought the special benefits of the continuation procedure, one of the costs of that benefit might fairly be an updated disclosure. After all, other patent systems do not given an applicant the right to continue prosecution simply through the mechanism of paying a fee in return for the right to file a continuation application. Hence, it would not be unreasonable to assert that in addition to paying an additional fee, an applicant may file a continuation application, but to do so requires that he update his best mode disclosure.

3 MARTIN J. ADELMAN, PATENT LAW PERSPECTIVES § 2.9 [2.4–1] (1996).

4. Comparison with Inequitable Conduct. Contrast an applicant's failure to disclose the best mode with inequitable conduct, a topic this casebook takes up at Chapter 12. Is failure to include the best mode something of a "lesser included offense" relevant to inequitable conduct? Do you observe a significant difference between the penalties/invalidity as compared with unenforceability for violation of these standards? Keep in mind that the best mode requirement applies to each claim individually while inequitable conduct as to one claim invalidates all claims in the patent.

5. The Advisory Commission Report. Consider the following paragraphs from the 1992 Advisory Commission on Patent Law Reform.

> The Commission recommends elimination of the best mode requirement. First, the best mode requirement is not necessary to ensure "full and fair" disclosures of patented inventions. The objective requirement of enablement ensures that the public is put in possession of at least one operable embodiment of a patented invention....

> Second, aside from the positive requirement for adequate disclosure imposed by the enablement requirement, there are substantive deterrents to concealment of useful or material information in patent documents. Active concealment by a patent applicant of a material element of his invention renders the entire patent unenforceable, through the inequitable conduct doctrine. Concealment of non-material information, but "significant" embodiments of a patented invention places a "concealment-oriented" patent applicant at risk from later innovators who discover and then patent the significantly superior improvement....

> Third, the best mode requirement does not effectively compel higher quality disclosures. This is due to the substantive and non-mandatory nature of the requirement. The best mode requirement does not require disclosure of an objectively superior method; it only requires disclosure of what the applicant perceives to be the best mode at the time the patent application was filed.... If, at the time the patent application

was filed, the applicant does not view one mode as being superior to others, there is no best mode to disclose. Thus, the requirement will have not direct effect on compelling a higher quality disclosure.

Fourth, in rapidly evolving technologies, such as biotechnology or computer-program related inventions, the "best mode" of an invention at the time the patent application is filed may differ dramatically, and is likely to be inferior to the "best mode" at the time the patent is granted. . . .

Finally, the best mode requirement as we know it has been an element of the U.S. patent system only since the 1952 Patent Act. . . . Thus, the best mode requirement is not the long-standing and integral element of the patent system some perceive it to be.

THE ADVISORY COMMISSION ON PATENT LAW REFORM, A REPORT TO THE SECRETARY OF COMMERCE 102–03 (1992). At least one defender of the best mode requirement found these comments misplaced. Jerry R. Selinger, *In Defense of "Best Mode": Preserving the Benefit of the Bargain for the Public*, 43 CATHOLIC U. L. REV. 1071, 1104–05 (1994), traces the best mode requirement to the earliest U.S. patent statutes and offers the following counterarguments to the Advisory Commission:

Best mode serves two purposes that complement enablement: (1) to ensure the public receives not merely a disclosure of the invention, but the best way contemplated by the inventor of carrying out the invention; and (2) to allow the public to compete fairly with the patentee after the patent expires. Clearly, if the statutory best mode obligation is repealed, the public will no longer receive the benefit of the additional disclosure compelled by best mode. There are several cases in which patentees have satisfied the enabling obligation, while still concealing relevant information. Even with the present statutory best mode disclosure requirement, applicants sometimes withhold important technical details to which the public is entitled. Inventors realistically will not disclose more than they are absolutely required to divulge. Without a best mode obligation, enablement will establish both the upper and lower boundaries of disclosure. The Advisory Commission's reasons for eliminating best mode and the supposed benefits to be derived therefrom must be weighed against the definable, if not quantifiable, loss of information that the public will suffer. . . .

Seeking to justify its premise, the Advisory Commission suggests that "there are substantive deterrents to concealment of useful or material information in patent documents." One such deterrent is said to be the doctrine of inequitable conduct. Inequitable conduct relates to how the inventor and patent counsel conduct themselves during negotiations with the Patent Office, normally after the application has been filed. A finding of inequitable conduct requires a misrepresentation that is material to the examination process. While a material misrepresentation is an essential element of inequitable conduct, the essence of non-compliance with best mode is concealment rather than overt misrepresentation. Inequitable conduct would not inhibit an inventor from disclosing a second-best mode. Consequently, reliance on inequitable conduct has not-and will not-protect the important public policies embodied in the best mode requirement.

Enablement also differs from best mode in that compliance with enablement inherently does not compel disclosure of the best mode. For an enablement analysis, a court makes an objective determination as to whether a hypothetical person skilled in the art could practice the invention. A factfinder need not consider whether the inventor intended to deceive or mislead, so long as the patent specification is enabling. Invalidity for failure to provide an enabling disclosure is not an effective alternative either.

In your estimation, who has the better arguments?

Best Mode Exercises

1. Priam conceives of a new cleaning solution useful for cleaning plate heat exchangers. On January 19, 2003, he reduces the solution to practice. The next day, Priam shares his technical concepts with his colleague, Laertes, who conducts further experimentation. Laertes discovers that the solution achieves optimal performance when heated to above 50EC, and so informs Priam. On June 1, 2003, Priam files a patent application claiming a method for cleaning plate heat exchanges using that solution. Priam does not disclose any details concerning the cleaning solution temperature discovered by Laertes. *Did Priam comply with the best mode requirement?*

2. Lombard conceives of a new method of forming polymer microspheres on October 1, 1998. The method calls for the formation of a reaction mixture including a porogen. Lombard immediately contacts her patent attorney, Picard, who files a patent application claiming the method on March 21, 1999. On November 11, 2000, Picard receives a Final Rejection from the United States Patent and Trademark Office. Picard decides that the filing of a continuation application under 35 U.S.C. § 120 would be wise. When Picard calls Lombard to advise her of this option, she explains that she learned on August 2, 1999, that the method works best when the porogen is toluene. *Must Picard include this information in the continuation application?*

3. Takanohana is an inventor resident in Japan. On September 1, 1999, he conceives of, and on November 1, 1999, he reduces to practice, a new amplifier circuit. He immediately files an application at the Japanese Patent Office describing and claiming the circuit. Consistent with the patent laws of Japan, he does not disclose a particular implementation of his circuit that he believes will yield the best results. However, in truth Takanohana's favored implementation is somewhat less effective than a "working example" that his Japanese application describes in considerable detail.

On October 22, 2000, Takanohana files an exact translation of his application in the United States Patent and Trademark Office, along with a proper claim to priority under § 119 to his Japanese application. The application matures into an issued United States patent on March 11, 2002. *Does the United States patent issued to Takanohana comply with the best mode requirement?*

Chapter Eleven

CLAIMS

The essence of the patent right is the right to exclude others from making, using, selling, or offering to sell the claimed invention. The claims define the bounds of that right to exclude. Accordingly, the claims are the most significant part of the entire patent instrument. As such, they are the principal focus of the dialogue the patent drafter will have with an inventor, of the entire prosecution process, and ultimately of any licensing activity or infringement suit to enforce patent rights.

Claims are, without doubt, the most difficult legal instrument to draft. Claims are both legal and technical instruments. As legal instruments, they must precisely define entitlements for worldwide markets and industries. As technical documents, they must inform other scientists and skilled artisans of the technical advance. In performing these two functions, claims must accurately reflect and distinguish all prior art–a retrospective challenge. Claims must also envision prospectively the direction of subsequent research to ensure improvements within the scope of the invention cannot evade the property rights. Finally, of course, the claims must capture the entirety of the inventive advance.

The starting point for patent claims is the statute, 35 U.S.C.A. § 112, that sets forth formal and substantive requirements for drafting and interpreting claims. With the paragraphs numbered for convenience, § 112 provides:

§ 112. Specification

* * *

[¶ 2] The specification shall conclude with one or more claims particularly pointing out and distinctly claiming the subject matter which the applicant regards as his invention.

[¶ 3] A claim may be written in independent or, if the nature of the case admits, in dependent or multiple dependent form.

[¶ 4] Subject to the following paragraph, a claim in dependent form shall contain a reference to a claim previously set forth and then specify a further limitation of the subject matter claimed. A claim in dependent form shall be construed to incorporate by reference all the limitations of the claim to which it refers.

[¶ 5] A claim in multiple dependent form shall contain a reference, in the alternative only, to more than one claim previously set forth and then specify a further limitation of the subject matter claimed. A multiple dependent claim shall not serve as a basis for any other multiple dependent claim. A multiple dependent claim shall be construed to incorporate by reference all the limitations of the particular claim in relation to which it is being considered.

[¶ 6] An element in a claim for a combination may be expressed as a means or step for performing a specified function without the recital of structure, material, or acts in support thereof, and such claim shall be construed to cover the corresponding structure, material, or acts described in the specification and equivalents thereof.

The core provision, paragraph 2, instructs patent drafters to set forth distinctly the bounds of the invention. Patent claims must give a clear indication to others of the limits of the property right. The remaining paragraphs address specific claim formats: paragraphs 3–5 govern so-called "dependent" claims, while the sixth paragraph of § 112 provides for "means-plus-function" claims.

This introduction to the nature of claims and a couple notable claim formats is just that—an introduction. Proper drafting and prosecution of claims is a legal and technical skill worthy of a lifetime of study. That study would necessarily embrace much more than the statutory requirements. United States patent claiming practice is largely driven by Patent Office policies, past judicial treatment of claim terms and formats, and well-established traditions of the patent bar. This Chapter will introduce some of the directives of the Patent Act as well as the significant extra-statutory law that governs the art of claim drafting. Perhaps the best service of this chapter is to caution future practitioners that claim drafting requires considerable experience and skill.

§ 11.1 UNITED STATES PERIPHERAL CLAIMING TECHNIQUE

EX PARTE FRESSOLA

U.S. Patent and Trademark Office Board of Patent
Appeals and Interferences, 1993.
27 U.S.P.Q.2d 1608.

Before SEROTA, CHAIRMAN, LOVEL, MCCANDLISH, HAIRSTON, and CARDILLO, EXAMINERS-IN-CHIEF.

SEROTA, CHAIRMAN.

This is an appeal from the examiner's final rejection of claim 42. The disclosed invention is described by appellant as follows:

The invention includes a method and system of producing stereographic images of celestial objects which use distance information to offset one of two images produced on a display device. A digital computer under program control is used in combination with a user input device, such as keyboard, and a display device, such as a computer monitor and/or a printer.

Claim 42 reads:

42. A system for the display of stereographic three-dimensional images of celestial objects as disclosed in the specification and drawings herein.

The appealed claim 42 stands rejected under 35 U.S.C. Section 112 ¶ 2 as failing to particularly point out and distinctly claim the subject matter which applicant regards as his invention. We affirm.

OPINION

35 U.S.C. Section 112 ¶ 2

The claims measure the scope of the protected patent right and "must comply accurately and precisely with the statutory requirements." *United Carbon Co. v. Binney & Smith Co.*, 317 U.S. 228, 232, 55 U.S.P.Q. 381, 383–84 (1942). Claims in utility applications[1] that define the invention entirely by reference to the specification and/or drawings, so-called "omnibus" or "formal" claims, while perhaps once accepted in American patent practice, are properly rejected under Section 112 ¶ 2 as failing to particularly point out and distinctly claim the invention.

The written description and the claims are separate statutory requirements. Modern claim practice requires that the claims stand alone to define the invention. Incorporation into the claims by express reference to the specification and/or drawings is not permitted except in very limited circumstances.

Early claim forms were significantly different in style and content from modern claims. *See Pennwalt Corporation v. Durand–Wayland, Inc.*, 833 F.2d 931, 957–59, 4 U.S.P.Q.2d 1737, 1758–1760 (Fed.Cir.1987), *cert. denied*, 485 U.S. 961 (1988) (NEWMAN, J., commentary) (evolution of claim form); DELLER, Sections 1–11. The original method of claiming in this country was based on the central definition where the claims named the broad features of the invention (often just an enumeration of the elements and the reference characters of the drawings) together with a phrase such as "substantially as set forth." These claims were construed to "incorporate by reference the description in the specification and equivalents thereof." *Pennwalt*, 833 F.2d at 959, 4 U.S.P.Q.2d at 1759. During this early period, "[t]he drawings and description were the main thing, the claims merely an adjunct thereto." DELLER, Section 4.

---

1. This analysis is limited to claims in utility applications. Plant patent claims are defined "in formal terms to the plant shown and described." 35 U.S.C. Section 162. Claims in design patents are recited in formal terms to the ornamental design "as shown" or, where there is a properly included special description of the design, the ornamental design "as shown and described." MPEP Section 1503.01.

Beginning with the Patent Act of 1870, the claims took on more importance. As described in DELLER, Section 7:

> They became much more self-sufficient in that they gave the cooperative relationship of the elements enumerated, instead of a mere catalog of elements followed by some such phrase as "constructed and adapted to operate substantially as set forth."

The method of claiming shifted from the central definition to the peripheral definition. As described in DELLER, Section 5:

> Central definition involves the drafting of a narrow claim setting forth a typical embodiment coupled with broad interpretation by the courts to include all equivalent constructions. Peripheral definition involves marking out the periphery or boundary of the area covered by the claim and holding as infringements only such constructions as lie within that area.

The conversion from the central definition to the peripheral definition was due to the more rigorous requirements for the claim to stand alone to define the invention and the refusal of the courts to expand the scope of the claims beyond their literal terms. Modern claim interpretation is based on the peripheral system where the scope of the claim is not expanded. *See Wilson Sporting Goods Co. v. David Geoffrey & Assoc.*, 904 F.2d 677, 684, 14 U.S.P.Q.2d 1942, 1948 (Fed.Cir.), *cert. denied*, 111 S.Ct. 537 (1990) (doctrine of equivalents does not expand claims, it only expands right to exclude to "equivalents"). Modern claim interpretation requires that the claims particularly point out and distinctly claim the invention without reading in limitations from the specification

Phrases in claims referring back to the description and drawing such as "substantially as described" or "as herein shown and described" were once customary in claims in the days of the central definition. Deller, Section 25. Expressions referring back to the disclosure are sometimes referred to by patent authors as "backfiring" expressions. The "substantially as described" expressions were generally used as an addendum to the elements of the claim. Insofar as we have been able to determine, claims consisting entirely of a reference to the specification and/or drawings were held to be indefinite very early in the period of transition toward increased definiteness in claiming. As stated in *Ex parte Rice*, 1874 Dec. Comm'r Pat. 44, 45 (Comm'r Pat. 1874):

> In this case the applicant puts in but a single claim, reading as following:
>
> *As a new article of manufacture, mats made of corn-husks, substantially in the manner described.*

The examiner ought to have objected to this claim, for the reason that it does not properly comply with the requirements of section 26 of the patent act, which, after setting forth what shall be the character of a specification, says, "and he shall particularly point out and distinctly claim the part, improvement, or combination which he claims as his invention or discovery." The mere reference to the body of the specification by the terms "substantially in the manner described" is not "particularly" pointing out and "distinctly" claiming the alleged invention, and therefore does not comply with the requirements of the statute.

In *National Tube Co. v. Mark*, 216 F. 507, 515–22 (6th Cir.1914), the court reviewed the authorities and held that phrases such as "substantially as described" should be given no interpretative importance. To the extent that such phrases require the claim to be read in light of the specification, they add nothing to the claim. The court in *National Tube* did not review any cases where the claim was entirely a reference to the specification, probably because it, like us, was unable to find any. The *National Tube* case marks the beginning of the end of the use of expressions referring back to the specification and drawings. *See* Jessup, *The Doctrine of Equivalents*, 54 J. PAT. OFF. SOC'Y 248 (1972). The Patent Office has consistently refused to afford weight to "substantially as described" and similar expressions....

ANALYSIS AND DECISION

We agree with the examiner's conclusion that claim 42 is indefinite and fails to particularly point out and distinctly claim what applicant regards as his invention as required by Section 112 ¶ 2. First, claim 42 does not comply with the requirement of Section 112 ¶ 2 that the claims particularly point out and distinctly describe the invention because it relies entirely on incorporation by reference of the specification and drawings. The written description and the claims are separate statutory requirements. As stated long ago in *Ex parte Holt*, 1884 Dec. Comm'r Pat. 43, 62–63 (Comm'r Pat. 1884):

> The aim, end, and purpose of the specification, under the present statute, is to describe the invention sought to be covered by the patent, and the manner of making, constructing, and using the same. The aim, the end, the purpose of the claim is to point out particularly and distinctly define the invention to be secured to the individual. The claim is the measure of the patent, and the day has passed when the courts will search the specification for information which it is the very office of the claim to impart.

A claim which refers to the specification defeats the purpose of a claim. The limited exceptions which permit incorporation by reference do not apply because the system can be described in words without reference to the specification and drawings....

Second, the history of phrases which incorporate by reference to the specification and/or drawings shows the difficulty and inconsistency in interpreting such phrases, which have no fixed legal meaning. Claim 42 is indefinite because it is impossible to determine how much of the disclosure is incorporated by reference into claim 42, or to what extent claim 42 would be interpreted to cover equivalents. The phrase "as disclosed in the specification and drawings herein" in claim 42 is interpreted to read on the whole or any part of the disclosure.

Third, assuming, arguendo, that incorporation by reference were a permissible mode of claiming, claim 42 is indefinite because the specification and drawings to which it refers do not particularly point out and distinctly define what invention is intended to be circumscribed by claim 42. Instead of succinctly enumerating the elements and limitations which constitute the boundary of the invention, claim 42 requires that the limitations be gleaned from an analysis of 19 figures of drawings and 147 pages of specification, including 28 pages of description of the background prior art and the method, 45 pages of program listing in Table 1, 73 pages of data in Table 2, and additional disclosed commercial Turbo Graphix (Registered) procedures. As has been held by our former reviewing court in the case of *In re Clemens*, 622 F.2d 1029, 206 U.S.P.Q. 289 (CCPA 1980), the specification in order to comply with the requirements of the first paragraph of 35 U.S.C. 112, frequently includes matter which is not the invention of the applicant. The description includes large quantities of extraneous matter such as example images, descriptions of prior art, alternative features (inverse display, marking arrow, stereo versus non-stereo display, etc.), which obscures the system claim boundaries; it does not particularly point out and distinctly claim the invention. The fact that the specification is directed primarily at the method for displaying, while claim 42 is for a system, further contributes to making claim 42 indefinite. The specification is also indefinite because of the following statements in the specification:

> Although described in part by a computer program written in Turbo Pascal (Registered) for use on an IBM PC (Registered) or compatible personal computer, it is apparent that the concepts described can be readily adapted to other computer languages and computer systems.

Appellant apparently wants to protect the underlying process steps of the program source code in Table 1 as performed by the computer, not the source code itself which does not run on the computer. However, instead of reciting the steps performed by the program in terms of English language descriptions, the specification requires extraction of the steps embedded in the program code written in Pascal programming language; this does not particularly point out or distinctly claim the invention. The following statement at the end of the specification also renders the scope of claim 42 indefinite (page 29):

> [S]ince changes may be made in carrying out the methodology of the invention, including the computer program or other instructions used, it is intended that all matter contained in the above description or shown in the accompanying drawings shall be interpreted as illustrative, and not in a limiting sense.

In view of this statement, it is impossible to tell what parts of the specification are and are not intended to be limiting, or what modifications would fall within the scope of claim 42.

We turn now to appellant's arguments. It is argued:

Because Congress has placed no limitations on how an applicant claims his invention, applicant respectfully argues that claim 42, a so-called "omnibus" claim, specifically references the specification and, therefore, particularly points out and distinctly claims the subject matter which the applicant regards as his invention.

Aside from the formal single sentence claim requirement, there are few restrictions on how an invention must be claimed as long as the claim satisfies Section 112 ¶ 2. However, the omnibus claim does not satisfy Section 112 § 2 because the claim does not itself define the invention, but relies on external material.

It is argued that claim 42 is, in effect, a "picture claim" which is limited to the exact structure of the invention as shown in specification and figures:

> [A] claim which merely recites the specification and the drawings is most limited in scope and protects only the device shown and described.

This is only appellant's interpretation of claim 42. Claim 42 can be interpreted to incorporate all or only part of the disclosure. In addition, it is not certain that claim 42 is limited to the exact description in the specification and drawings in view of the statements made at page 29 of the specification discussed, supra. It is argued that claim 42 provides the requisite notice to the public of what will infringe:

> [T]he rejected claim 42 is quite clear and would be understandable to one of ordinary skill in the art as such person would simply examine the specification and the corresponding figures and would know exactly what the invention is. In fact, a person of ordinary skill in the art would be provided with more specific notice because if his product was not specifically described and shown in the specification and the figures, he would be sure that he was not infringing the patent.

As discussed, supra, we do not agree that the specification and drawings, assuming they could be incorporated by reference into claim 42, particularly point out and distinctly claim the invention. The claims define the boundary of the invention. The metes and bounds of what the Appellant regards as his invention must be clearly set forth in order that the public at a time after the patent is granted may evaluate what is infringed, and what would be dominated by or within the patented claims.

Appellant notes that omnibus-style claims are accepted in the United Kingdom and that the United Kingdom's patent law regarding claim requirements is substantially similar to Section 112 ¶ 2. The only issue is United States law. We decline to speculate on the reasons why foreign countries allow or require omnibus-style claims.

CONCLUSION

The rejection of claim 42 for failing to particularly point out and distinctly claim the invention under 35 U.S.C. Section 112 ¶ 2 is affirmed.

AFFIRMED.

Notes

1. **Claims and the Specification.** Although the United States patent system rejects omnibus claims in utility patents, one should not take this ruling as denying any interplay between a patent's claims and the remainder of its specification. In fact, courts interpret claims in light of the specification. *Markman v. Westview Instruments, Inc.*, 52 F.3d 967 (Fed.Cir.1995), *aff'd*, 517 U.S. 370 (1996). Further, in instances where the drafter invokes § 112 ¶ 6, the statute directs that the structure in the specification (corresponding to the claimed function) will govern the literal meaning of the functional element. *See* § 11.2[c], *infra*. Chapter 15, *Infringement*, considers further the relationship between claims and the remainder of the specification.

2. **The One–Sentence Rule.** The United States Patent and Trademark Office additionally mandates that a patent claim be composed as a single English sentence. This rule was challenged in *Fressola v. Manbeck*, 36 U.S.P.Q.2d 1211 (D.D.C.1995), on the basis of the Administrative Procedure Act. The court replied:

> The Plaintiff here contends that the one-sentence requirement bears no reasonable relationship to the language of and policies behind 35 U.S.C. Section 112. As noted above, this statute requires patent applications to conclude with "one or more claims particularly pointing out and distinctly claiming the subject matter which the applicant regards as his invention."

> The Plaintiff first argues that no reasonable relationship links the one-sentence rule to the statutory requirement that the claim "particularly point[ ] out" and "distinctly claim [ ]" the invention. Id. The Court, however, discerns no tension between this statutory language and the application of the one-sentence rule. Although this portion of the statute undoubtedly seeks to protect the inventor and the public from the uncertainty that would arise from unclear claims, the record in this case supports the Defendant's expert judgment that the one-sentence rule has no impact on the clarity of claims and has fostered the efficient processing of several million patent applications. Through simple changes in punctuation, an applicant could transform any multiple-sentence claim into a single-sentence claim. Indeed, the Court believes the one-sentence rule may even advance these statutory goals by encouraging claims that are generally more succinct than multiple-sentence claims of the same scope.

> The Plaintiff also argues that, because the one-sentence rule limits the manner in which an applicant can claim his discovery, it does not reasonably relate to the statute's dictate that the claim describe "the subject matter which the applicant regards as his invention." Once again, the Court finds that the one-sentence rule does not conflict with this portion of the statute. While the statutory language may give the applicant ultimate control over the substance of his claim, it does not appear to speak to matters of pure form, such as the number of sentences allowed per claim; in other words, since an applicant can (as

described above) make exactly the same claim in one sentence as he could in multiple sentences, the uniform format prescribed by the one-sentence rule does not interfere with his ability to claim whatever he "regards as his invention."

3. The Art of Claim Drafting. Claims drafting is, without doubt, the most difficult form of technical writing, requiring considerable analytic and research skills, as well as scientific and technical competence. Claims must reduce sophisticated technical concepts to a single sentence, and yet present an accurate description of the invention. They must also reflect a keen awareness of the technical field in which the invention lies. Often only a few carefully chosen words of limitation mark a patentable distinction between the claimed invention and prior technical knowledge.

Claims drafters also operate within the true "multiple claim" system long in effect in the United States. Each patent may have multiple claims. Moreover a patentee may assert each and every claim of a patent, either alone or in combination, against an accused infringer. Each claim is important. The result of this system is that claims drafters typically craft a series of claims in each application, forming a "reverse pyramid" of successively narrower claims. The first claim of the patent is very broad and abstract. The narrowest claim usually describes a product the inventor would actually consider putting into commercial practice. Intermediate claims are set to varying levels of abstraction, each taking a place on the spectrum of technologies surrounding the narrowly focused commercial embodiment of the invention.

Why? Because the patentee wishes to enforce the narrowest possible claim against an accused infringer; the narrower the claim, the greater the likelihood that such a claim will withstand a defense of invalidity. As the number of limitations in a claim rises, the likelihood that prior art will render that claim anticipated (35 U.S.C.A. § 102) or obvious (35 U.S.C.A.§ 103) falls. Importantly, experienced claim drafters recognize that pertinent prior art may well emerge after patent issuance. Thus, they must foresee the possibility of new prior art references arising when the claims are tested in court. Also, the narrower the claim, the greater the difficulty an accused infringer will have in making an attack based upon enablement (35 U.S.C.A. § 112).

On the other hand, the patentee also wants the broadest claim possible in order to have the possibility of reaching as many competitors as possible. Therefore a skillful claims drafter seeks to write the broadest claim the PTO will allow to acquire enforceable protection in each patent instrument.

§ 11.2 PATENT CLAIM FORMAT

Although patent applicants enjoy relatively free hands in setting forth the substance of a claim, years of Patent Office interpretation and judicial precedent have resulted in relatively standardized claim formatting. The United States Patent and Trademark Office requires a three-part claim: the preamble, the transition phrase, and the body. As assisted by the courts, the Patent and Trademark Office has also developed rules regarding the meaning and effect of each of these portions of a claim.

Further, a discrete number of well-known claim formats have arisen over decades of patent practice. Most claims that patent practitioners will read or draft fall into the categories of apparatus, article of manufacture, composition of matter, or method claims. In other words, claims to the categories of statutory subject matter set forth in § 101. But in addition, some specialized claim formats, with particularized meanings in the art, have emerged to accommodate the demands of technical subject matter. This section further explores four of these: product-by-process, functional, Jepson, and Markush claim styles.

§ 11.2[a]   Elemental Claim Structure

§ 11.2[a][1]   The Preamble

A claim begins with the object of the sentence, e.g., "*A method of making coffee....*" The preamble generally states the general use or purpose of the invention. It thus helps to show the broad area of technology to which the invention belongs and may help the PTO assign the invention to an examining group.

A primary question in patent enforcement that arises again and again is whether the preamble recitation serves to limit the scope of the claims. The rule for this question is not easy to state. Depending on its importance to give meaning to the claim, the introduction ("preamble") may or may not constitute a limitation on the scope of the claim. In somewhat colloquial (and admittedly illogical) terms, when it matters, the preamble will serve as a limitation on the claimed subject matter. Stated more elegantly, a preamble has the import that the claim as a whole assigns to it. *Bell Comm. Research v. Vitalink Comm. Corp.*, 55 F.3d 615 (Fed.Cir.1995). Of course, the colloquial overstatement of the rule at least serves to warn claim drafters to anticipate that unnecessary verbiage in the preamble can reduce the scope of patent coverage. A recent Federal Circuit case explores the factors determining when a preamble limits and the implications of that limitation.

CATALINA MARKETING INTERNATIONAL v. COOLSAVINGS.COM, INC.

United States Court of Appeals, Federal Circuit, 2002.
289 F.3d 801, 62 U.S.P.Q.2d 1781.

Before MAYER, CHIEF JUDGE, and RADER, and PROST, CIRCUIT JUDGES.

RADER, CIRCUIT JUDGE.

On summary judgment, the United States District Court for the Northern District of Illinois held that Coolsavings.com, Inc. (Coolsavings) did not infringe, either literally or by equivalents, the claims of Catalina Marketing International, Inc.'s (Catalina's) U.S. Patent No. 4,674,041 (the '041 patent). Because the district court erroneously relied on non-limiting language in the preamble of Claim 1, this court affirms-in-part, reverses-in-part, vacates-in-part, and remands.

I.

The '041 patent, filed on September 15, 1983, claims a selection and distribution system for discount coupons. In a preferred embodiment, the system dispenses coupons to consumers at remote, kiosk-like terminals connected to a central host computer system. When a consumer activates the terminal in a retail outlet, the terminal displays available coupons on the screen. The consumer selects a coupon and a printer connected to the terminal prints it. The terminal selectively communicates with the central computer system to acquire coupon information for display. When the number of dispensed coupons for a certain product reaches a limit specified by a coupon provider, the central computer system stops providing that particular coupon. Figure 3a depicts the terminal:

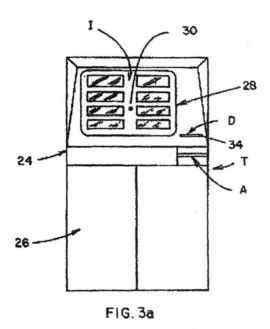

FIG. 3a

There are two independent claims at issue, namely Claims 1 and 25. [Claim 1] reads as follows:

1. A system for controlling the selection and dispensing of product coupons at a plurality of remote terminals *located at predesignated sites such as consumer stores* wherein each terminal comprises:

activation means for activating such terminal for consumer transactions;

display means operatively connected with said activation means for displaying a plurality of coupons available for selection;

selection means operatively connected with said display means provided to permit selection of a desired displayed coupon by the consumer;

print means operatively connected with said selection means for printing and dispensing the coupon selected by the consumer; and

control means operatively connected with said display means for monitoring each consumer transaction and for controlling said display means to prevent the display of coupons having exceeded prescribed coupon limits.

'041 patent, col. 30, ll. 46–65 (emphasis added).

[Claim 25 is very similar to claim 1. In claim 25, however, the preamble was shortened slightly and an additional limitation was added after the "comprises" transition phrase. As a result, claim 25 recites (with emphasis added):

25. A system for controlling the selection and dispensing of product coupons at a plurality of remote terminals *located at predesignated sites such as consumer stores*, comprising:

a plurality of free standing coupon display terminals *located at predesignated sites such as consumer stores*, each of said terminals being adapted for

bidirectional data communication with a host central processing unit; each of said terminals comprising

activation means . . . ;

display means . . . ;

selection means. . . .]

During prosecution of the '041 patent, the examiner rejected all of the original claims as obvious in light of U.S. Patent No. 4,449,186 (the Kelley patent), which disclosed a terminal system for dispensing airline tickets. The examiner concluded that the only difference between the applicants' claimed invention and the Kelley patent was the location of the coupon terminal. In response, the applicants provided a general overview of the invention and amended the structural limitations of Claim 1 to distinguish the Kelley patent. The examiner again rejected all of the pending claims.

Responsive to the second rejection, the applicants again amended Claim 1 and submitted several declarations to bolster their assertion of nonobviousness. The applicants did not amend the claim language relating to the location of the terminals. Although stating that their invention involved terminals "located in stores" for the dispensing of coupons "on-site," the applicants also did not argue that the location of the terminals in stores distinguished the invention from the Kelley patent.

Coolsavings uses a web-based coupon system to monitor and control the distribution of coupons from its www.coolsavings.com website. After registering with the coolsavings.com website and providing demographic data, users can browse the website for available coupons. Users then select and print coupons for in-store redemption. Additionally, in some cases, users may access a coupon provider's website for on-line redemption of a coupon offer for on-line products. A centralized computer system stores coupon and user data. Users may access the Coolsavings system from any Internet-accessible computer by simply logging onto the coolsavings.com website. Coolsavings received U.S. Patent No. 5,761,648 (the '648 patent) for its web-based coupon system. Catalina's '041 patent was cited during prosecution of the '648 patent.

Catalina sued Coolsavings, alleging that Coolsavings' web-based coupon system infringed the '041 patent. The district court construed the claim language "located at predesignated sites such as consumer stores," and held that Coolsavings did not infringe, either literally or by equivalents, the construed language. After determining that Coolsavings did not infringe under the doctrine of equivalents, the district court then alternatively held that prosecution history estoppel barred Catalina from seeking equivalents on the location of the terminals.

On appeal, Catalina argues that the disputed language, which appears only in the preamble of Claim 1, is not a limitation because it merely states an intended use for the claimed system. Alternatively, Catalina contends that the district court misconstrued the "located at predesignated sites such as consumer stores" claim language. In addition, Catalina asserts that prosecution history estoppel does not bar equivalents when the applicants did not amend the disputed language or argue patentability based on that language.

II.

The district court's claim construction focused solely on the phrase "located at predesignated sites such as consumer stores." This phrase appears in the preamble of Claim 1, and in both the preamble and body of Claim 25. The district court construed this disputed phrase without discussion as to whether the phrase, which appears only in the preamble of Claim 1, was indeed a limitation of Claim 1.

Whether to treat a preamble as a limitation is a determination "resolved only on review of the entire[ ] ... patent to gain an understanding of what the inventors actually invented and intended to encompass by the claim." *Corning Glass Works v. Sumitomo Electric U.S.A., Inc.*, 868 F.2d 1251, 1257 (Fed.Cir.1989). In general, a preamble limits the invention if it recites essential structure or steps, or if it is "necessary to give life, meaning, and vitality" to the claim. *Pitney Bowes*, 182 F.3d at 1305. Conversely, a preamble is not limiting "where a patentee defines a structurally complete invention in the claim body and uses the preamble only to state a purpose or intended use for the invention." *Rowe v. Dror*, 112 F.3d 473, 478(Fed.Cir.1997).

No litmus test defines when a preamble limits claim scope. *Corning Glass*, 868 F.2d at 1257. Some guideposts, however, have emerged from various cases discussing the preamble's effect on claim scope. For example, this court has held that Jepson claiming generally indicates intent to use the preamble to define the claimed invention, thereby limiting claim scope. *Rowe*, 112 F.3d at 479. Additionally, dependence on a particular disputed preamble phrase for antecedent basis may limit claim scope because it indicates a reliance on both the preamble and claim body to define the claimed invention. *Bell Communications Research, Inc. v. Vitalink Communications Corp.*, 55 F.3d 615, 620 (Fed.Cir.1995) ("[W]hen the claim drafter chooses to use both the preamble and the body to define the subject matter of the claimed invention, the invention so defined, and not some other, is the one the patent protects."). Likewise, when the preamble is essential to understand limitations or terms in the claim body, the preamble limits claim scope. *Pitney Bowes*, 182 F.3d at 1306.

Further, when reciting additional structure or steps underscored as important by the specification, the preamble may operate as a claim limitation. *Corning Glass*, 868 F.2d at 1257. Moreover, clear reliance on the preamble during prosecution to distinguish the claimed invention from the prior art transforms the preamble into a claim limitation because such reliance indicates use of the preamble to define, in part, the claimed invention. Without such reliance, however, a preamble generally is not limiting when the claim body describes a structurally complete invention such that deletion of the preamble phrase does not affect the structure or steps of the claimed invention. Thus, preamble language merely extolling benefits or features of the claimed invention does not limit the claim scope without clear reliance on those benefits or features as patentably significant. Moreover, preambles describing the use of an invention generally do not limit the claims because the patentability of apparatus or composition claims depends on the claimed structure, not on the use or purpose of that structure. *In re Gardiner*, 36 C.C.P.A. 748, 171 F.2d 313, 315–16, 80 USPQ 99, 101 (1948) ("It is trite to state that the patentability of apparatus claims must be shown in the structure claimed and not merely upon a use, function, or result thereof."). Indeed, "[t]he inventor of a machine is entitled to the benefit of all the uses to which it can be put, no matter whether he had conceived the idea of the use or not." *Roberts v. Ryer*, 91 U.S. 150, 157, 23 L.Ed. 267 (1875). More specifically, this means that a patent grants the right to exclude others from making, using, selling, offering to sale, or importing the claimed apparatus or composition for any use of that apparatus or composition, whether or not the patentee envisioned such use. *See* 35 U.S.C. § 271 (1994). Again, statements of intended use or asserted benefits in the preamble may, in rare instances, limit apparatus claims, but only if the applicant clearly and unmistakably relied on those uses or benefits to distinguish prior art. Likewise, this principle does not mean that apparatus claims necessarily prevent a subsequent inventor from obtaining a patent on a new method of using the apparatus where that new method is useful and nonobvious.

Perhaps a hypothetical best illustrates these principles: Inventor A invents a shoe polish for shining shoes (which, for the sake of example, is novel, useful, and nonobvious). Inventor A receives a patent having composition claims for shoe polish. Indeed, the preamble of these hypothetical claims recites "a composition for polishing shoes." Clearly, Inventor B could not later secure a patent with composition claims on the same composition because it would not be novel. Likewise, Inventor B could not secure claims on the method of using the composition for shining shoes because the use is not a "new use" of the composition but, rather, the same use—shining shoes.

Suppose Inventor B discovers that the polish also repels water when rubbed onto shoes. Inventor B could not likely claim a method of using the polish to repel water on shoes because repelling water is inherent in the normal use of the polish to shine shoes. In other words, Inventor B has not invented a "new" use by rubbing polish on shoes to repel water. Upon discovering, however, that the polish composition grows hair when rubbed on bare human skin, Inventor B can likely obtain method claims directed to the new use of the composition to grow hair. *See* 35 U.S.C. § 101 (1994) ("Whoever invents or discovers any new and useful process . . . may obtain a patent therefor."); 35 U.S.C. § 100(b) (1994) ("The term 'process' means process, art or method, and includes a new use of a known process, machine, manufacture, composition of matter, or material."). Hence, while Inventor B may obtain a blocking patent on the use of Inventor A's composition to grow hair, this method patent does not bestow on Inventor B any right with respect to the patented composition. Even though Inventor A's claim recites "a composition for polishing shoes," Inventor B cannot invoke this use limitation to limit Inventor A's composition claim because that preamble phrase states a use or purpose of the composition and does not impose a limit on Inventor A's claim.

In this case, the claims, specification, and prosecution history of the '041 patent demonstrate that the preamble phrase "located at predesignated sites such as consumer stores" is not a limitation of Claim 1. The applicant did not rely on this phrase to define its invention nor is the phrase essential to understand limitations or terms in the claim body. Although the specification refers to terminals located at points of sale, and even once states that terminals may be placed in retail stores, the specification, in its entirety, does not make the location of the terminals an additional structure for the claimed terminals.

The applicants also did not rely on the preamble phrase to distinguish over the Kelly patent. Rather, the examiner expressly rejected the claims on the basis that the location of the terminals in stores was not patentably significant. In response, the applicants amended structural limitations in the claim body to distinguish the Kelly patent. Thus, while the applicants stated during prosecution that their invention involved terminals "located in stores" for the dispensing of coupons "on-site," such statements, without more, do not indicate a clear reliance on the preamble to distinguish the prior art, especially where the examiner's initial rejection considered terminal location insignificant for patentability.

Moreover, deletion of the disputed phrase from the preamble of Claim 1 does not affect the structural definition or operation of the terminal itself. The claim body defines a structurally complete invention. The location of the terminals in stores merely gives an intended use for the claimed terminals. As already noted, the applicants did not rely on this intended use to distinguish their invention over the prior art.

In this case, the disputed preamble language does not limit Claim 1—an apparatus claim. To hold otherwise would effectively impose a method limitation on an apparatus claim without justification. Accordingly, this court holds that the district court erroneously treated the preamble as a limitation of Claim 1.

While the phrase "located at predesignated sites such as consumer stores" appears only in the preamble of Claim 1, this language appears in both the preamble and body of Claim 25." Hence, the applicants specifically included this language in the claim not once, but twice. By virtue of its inclusion in the body of Claim 25, this phrase limits Claim 25. [The Circuit then proceeded to analyze the trial court's claim construction and determined that the claim requires location of terminals at "predesignated" locations. In the words of the Circuit, "Claim 25 requires that the physical position of the terminal be designated before placement of the terminal at a point of sale location. For Coolsavings to be liable for literal infringement Coolsavings' accused system must designate the physical position of the terminals before location of the terminals at a point of sale. Coolsavings' system, however, does not designate (or even recognize) the physical position of computers connecting to its website; thus, Coolsavings' system does not literally satisfy this limitation of Claim 25."]

Because the district court erroneously relied on non-limiting language in the preamble of Claim 1, this court vacates the district court's judgment of non-infringement of Claim 1, both literally and by equivalents, to give the district court the opportunity to construe the limitations of Claim 1. [B]ecause the accused system does not infringe literally Claim 25, as properly construed, this court affirms the holding of no literal infringement of Claim 25. This court vacates and remands the holding of no infringement of Claim 25 by equivalents because the trial court should have an opportunity to develop and assess the record under the proper claim construction.

Notes

1. **Unique Kind of Preamble.** One of the special claim formats discussed later this chapter, the Jepson claim, intentionally employs the preamble as a tool to recite important structural claim limitations. Thus, in a Jepson claim, the preamble is impliedly admitted to be prior art unless it reflects the inventor's own work. In any event, Jepson claims invoke a special rule for preambles.

2. "Dot.com" Cases. Besides explicating the rules for construing a preamble as a claim limitation, this case is also one of the early "dot.com" cases before the Federal Circuit. Does this case give an indication about the Federal Circuit's approach to the application of old technology in a new setting, namely the Internet?

§ 11.2[a][2]   The Transition

The transition phrase falls between the preamble and various defining elements in the body of the claim. This phrase performs the essential legal function of signaling that the claim is "open" or "closed" to additional elements. In practice, the drafter must choose from one of three phrases: "comprising," "consisting of," or "essentially consisting of." This choice has significant substantive effect, for these words determine that the claim is open to structures containing *at least* the recited elements (open or hybrid terminology) or is limited to structures with only those elements (closed terminology). Note that the words "the steps of" appear after the transition when the claim is directed towards a method.

The Open Transition ("comprising"): The use of the term "comprising" captures any product or process that contains each and every element described in the body of the claim. The presence of additional elements in an accused (allegedly infringing) product or process does not affect at all the coverage of the claims. The claimed invention encompasses the recited elements and may embrace more. Thus, if a claim recites elements "A" and "B", a device with "A", "B" *and others* is an infringement. *Mannesmann Demag Corp. v. Engineered Metal Products Co., Inc.*, 793 F.2d 1279, 230 U.S.P.Q. 45 (Fed.Cir.1986). Open terminology—the broadest and most preferred transition phrase—captures elements *in addition to* the enumerated elements. For example, consider the claim:

A composition of matter which *comprises*:

    (i) element A;

    (ii) element B; and

    (iii) element C.

The term "comprises" makes the claim "open" to the inclusion of additional ingredients. This open claim includes any composition with *at least* elements A+B+C. Thus, the claim encompasses a product or process with elements A+B+C or A+B+C+"X".

The closed transition ("consisting of"): In contrast, a claim with the transition phrase "consisting of" is "closed" to additional ingredients. Infringement can occur only when the accused technology has exactly the same elements recited in the claim—no more, no less. Consider the same claim hypothetical with the new transition phrase:

A composition of matter *consisting of*:

    (i) element A;

    (ii) element B; and

(iii) element C.

In this hypothetical, identical except for the transition phrase, sale of a composition with ingredients A+B+C+"X" is *outside* the literal scope of the claim. Infringement of this claim under the doctrine of equivalents is another matter.

Why would anyone want to employ such a limiting transitional phrase? Often, the nature of an invention lies in the elimination of certain components or process steps. "Closed" claim language allows an inventor to claim an existing technology or patented invention (minus the deleted feature or step) without running into the prior art. As one can imagine, however, claim drafters do not favor this transition because a potential infringer can easily avoid literal infringement by the mere addition of a superfluous element.

The Hybrid Transition ("Consisting Essentially of"): The open and closed transitions have legal implications parallel to the ordinary meaning of those phrases. The hybrid phrase, "consisting essentially of * * * ," is unique to patent law and usage. This term of art, however, dates back to the nineteenth century, with a well-developed practice to support its application. This hybrid phrase renders the claim "open" to include additional elements that do not materially affect the basic and novel characteristics of the claimed combination. Consider again the hypothetical, this time with the hybrid transition:

A composition of matter *consisting essentially of*:

(i) element A;

(ii) element B; and

(iii) element C.

If element "X" would *not* materially change the composition, then A+B+C+"X" *is* within the scope of this "consisting essentially of" claim. If "X" would materially change the properties versus A+B+C alone, then A+B+C+"X" is *not* within the scope of the claim. In appropriate situations, this form of transition can be very powerful. *See U.S. Steel Corp. v. Phillips Petroleum Co.*, 865 F.2d 1247, 9 U.S.P.Q.2d 1461 (Fed.Cir.1989) ("Normally solid polypropylene *consisting essentially of* recurring propylene units, having a substantial crystalline polypropylene content."). The "consisting essentially of" language is thus a hybrid. Claim drafters prefer it to the extremely restrictive closed phrase "consisting of."

§ 11.2[a][3] The Body

The body of the claim recites the elements of the invention, as well as their interaction with each other either structurally or functionally. Claims ordinarily devote one clause to each of the primary elements of the invention. These clauses may be given a reference label, such as "(a)," "(b)," "(c)," to allow readers to parse its language more readily. The drafter should also indicate how that element interacts with the others to form an operative technology, employing such language as "attached to," "operated by," or "positioned above."

As this chapter repeatedly stresses, drafting claims requires knowledge that some words carry meanings affected by years of judicial gloss. Just a few of such terms are "integral," *see Advanced Cardiovascular Systems, Inc. v. Scimed Life Systems, Inc.*, 887 F.2d 1070, 12 U.S.P.Q.2d 1539 (Fed.Cir.1989); "extrinsic," *see Nobell, Inc. v. Sharper Image Corp.*, 950 F.2d 732, 22 U.S.P.Q.2d 1873 (Fed.Cir.1991); "approximately," *see Borg–Warner Corp. v. Paragon Gear Works, Inc.*, 355 F.2d 400, 148 U.S.P.Q. 1 (1st Cir.1965); "horizontal," *see In re Gordon*, 221 U.S.P.Q. 1125 (Fed.Cir.1984); and "solid," *see Standard Oil Co. v. Montedison S.p.A.*, 206 U.S.P.Q. 676 (D.Del.1980). *See generally* IRWIN M. AISENBERG, ATTORNEY'S DICTIONARY OF PATENT CLAIMS (1997).

Elements of an invention are ordinarily introduced with an indefinite article, such as "a" or "an," as well as terms such as "one," "several," or "a plurality of." Reference to elements recited earlier in the claim usually requires a signaling term, such as the definite article "the" or the term "said." If a drafter places a "the" or a "said" before an element appearing for the first time in the claim, then the patent examiner may reject the claim for lack of an "antecedent basis." The following claim from U.S. Patent No. 5,632,254 employs the signaling articles correctly:

> 1.　A combustion enhancement device, comprising:
>
> > a housing which defines an interior chamber;
> >
> > at least one magnet disposed within said interior chamber; and
> >
> > a far infrared ray generating composition comprising SiO_2, Al_2O_3, CaO, MnO, TiO_2, and Ag or Au disposed within said interior chamber.

This claim also illustrates a peculiarity of patent law: the reluctance to claim an empty space, such as a chamber, hollow, hole, or gap, directly. Instead, drafters usually define such spaces in terms of the structures that form them. "This 'rule' may seem to make little sense, but it is another founded in antiquity like the single sentence rule. Perhaps someone thought that a hole, etc. is nothing-and that people should not claim nothing." ROBERT C. FABER, LANDIS ON MECHANICS OF PATENT CLAIM DRAFTING § 26 (4th ed. 1996).

Section 112, paragraphs 3–5 allow the use of so-called "dependent" patent claims. The statute mandates that dependent claims must recite an earlier claim and provide additional limitations. For example, following independent claim 1, dependent claim 2 might provide: "A waffle iron as recited in claim 1, further comprising...." Such claims include all of the limitations of the independent claim as well as the new limitations recited in claim 2. Patent law also permits multiple dependent claims, such as a claim which recites "A waffle iron as recited in claims 1 or 2, further comprising...." The statute instructs readers to "incorporate by reference all the limitations of the particular claim in relation to which it is being considered."

Patent applicants have attempted to interlink their trademark and patent protection by using trademarks or trade names within a patent claim. One early case rejected a claim reciting the term "Formica" because the manufacturer could change the nature of its flooring product at any time. *See Ex parte Bolton*, 42 U.S.P.Q. 40 (Pat. Off. Bd. App. 1938). Should the uncertain duration of trademark protection also influence this result? Suppose the specification first describes the nature of the product subject to the trademark before employing the trademark in a claim? *See Ex parte Canter*, 70 U.S.P.Q. 372 (Pat. Off. Bd. App. 1946); *see generally* Butler, *Rules Defining the Use of Trade Terms in Patent Applications*, 51 J. Pat. Off. Soc'y 339 (1969). The European Patent Office also disfavors the use of trademarks in claims "unless their use is unavoidable." Guidelines for Examination in the European Patent Office, Part C, Chapter III, Paragraph 4.5b (Dec. 1994).

U.S. cases routinely state that patent applicants may coin their own terms to define their invention. As stated in the vernacular of patent law, "a patentee is free to be his or her own lexicographer...." *Hormone Research Foundation, Inc. v. Genentech, Inc.*, 904 F.2d 1558, 1563, 15 U.S.P.Q.2d 1039, 1043 (Fed.Cir.1990). However, an applicant cannot use mis-descriptive terms nor banal terms like "gadget" or "widget."

§ 11.2[b] Product-by-Process Claims

In some circumstances a new product cannot be defined other than by the process of making it. In other instances inventors claim a new product by its structure and also add another backup claim defining the product by the process for making it. In either instance, the product-by-process claim specifies a product defined only by several process steps. Nonetheless the standard rule is that a product claim covers that product regardless of how it is made. Thus, although a product-by-process claim sets forth only one way of making the product, it might be construed to cover all ways of making that same product. In fact, a Federal Circuit panel concluded in 1991:

> In determining patentability we construe the product as not limited by the process stated in the claims. Since claims must be construed the same way for validity and for infringement, the correct reading of product-by-process claims is that they are not limited to product prepared by the process set forth in the claims.

Scripps Clinic & Research Fdn. v. Genentech, Inc., 927 F.2d 1565, 1583, 18 U.S.P.Q.2d 1001, 1016 (Fed.Cir.1991). In *Scripps Clinic*, the product was Factor VIII C, a coagulant or clotting agent. Factor VIII C was not a new product: "Before the invention..., scientists had succeeded in concentrating Factor VIII C in plasma. This concentrate had been used to replace transfusions of whole blood in the treatment of hemophilia. The process was expensive...." *Id.* at 1568. Scripps Clinic thus patented a process that separated Factor VIII C from the other complex materials in blood. This process involved straining plasma through a column packed with agarose beads. Scripps Clinic obtained both product claims and product-by-process claims. Scripps Clinic then sued Genentech, which cheaply and efficiently made pure Factor VIIIC with a recombinant DNA process. During trial, one of the primary issues was the purity of Factor VIII C produced by the Scripps' process, namely were the Scripps Clinic and Genentech products synonymous. Genentech also challenged the Scripps Clinic patents on grounds of enablement, best mode, anticipation, inequitable conduct, and infringement. In a well-reasoned opinion citing the Supreme Court cases mentioned in the *Atlantic Thermoplastics* case (which follows this note), the district court granted Genentech summary judgment of noninfringement of the product-by-process claims. Without addressing the Supreme Court precedent, the panel in *Scripps Clinic* made the statement quoted above. Less than a year later, another panel of the Federal Circuit confronted a case that directly presented the question of the coverage for product-by-process claims.

ATLANTIC THERMOPLASTICS
CO. INC. v. FAYTEX CORP.

United States Court of Appeals, Federal Circuit, 1992.
970 F.2d 834, 23 U.S.P.Q.2d 1481.

Before ARCHER, MICHEL, and RADER, CIRCUIT JUDGES.

RADER, J.

Atlantic Thermoplastics owns U.S. Patent No. 4,674,204 ('204 patent) entitled "Shock Absorbing Innersole and Method of Preparing Same." Atlantic sued Faytex Corporation for infringing the '204 patented process with innersoles manufactured by two separate processes. After a bench trial, the United States District Court for the District of Massachusetts held that Faytex infringed the '204 patent by selling innersoles manufactured by Surge, Inc. The court held, however, that Faytex did not infringe the '204 patent by selling innersoles manufactured by Sorbothane, Inc.

BACKGROUND

The '204 patent contains both process claims and product-by-process claims for a shock absorbing shoe innersole. The innersole is formed in a mold having a contoured heel and arch section. Two different materials combine to make the innersole: an elastomeric material in the heel section, and a polyurethane foam. The elastomeric heel insert enhances shock absorption. The polyurethane foam forms around the heel insert and supplies the rest of the innersole.

Claim 1 of the '204 patent defines the process:

In a method of manufacturing a shock-absorbing, molded innersole for insertion in footwear, which method comprises:

(a) introducing an expandable, polyurethane into a mold; and

(b) recovering from the mold an innersole which comprises a contoured heel and arch section composed of a substantially open-celled polyurethane foam material, the improvement which comprises:

(i) placing an elastomeric insert material into the mold, the insert material having greater shock-absorbing properties and being less resilient than the molded, open-celled polyurethane foam material, and the insert material having sufficient surface tack to remain in the placed position in the mold on the introduction of the expandable polyurethane material so as to permit the expandable polyurethane material to expand about the insert material without displacement of the insert material; and

(ii) recovering a molded innersole with the insert material having a tacky surface forming a part of the exposed bottom surface of the recovered innersole.

Faytex distributes half-sole innersoles, or heel cups, with an elastomeric heel insert. Two different manufacturers-Surge Products and Sorbothane-make Faytex's innersoles. The Surge process for making innersoles differs from the Sorbothane process. Surge first manually places a solid elastomeric insert into the heel section of the innersole mold. Surge then injects polyurethane around the solid heel insert to form the innersole. Sorbothane, on the other hand, first injects a liquid elastomeric precursor into the mold, which solidifies to form the heel insert. While the heel insert is solidifying, Sorbothane injects polyurethane into the same mold to form the rest of the innersole.

The parties agree that the Surge process infringes the '204 patent. The district court concluded that the Sorbothane process did not infringe the '204 patent. The district court read the claims to require placement of a solid elastomeric insert into the mold. This reading leaves injection of liquid elastomers outside the scope of the claims. Atlantic contests this construction.

Because Faytex does not manufacture the innersoles, Atlantic cannot charge Faytex with infringement of the process claims. However, claim 24 of the '204 patent states: "The molded innersole produced by the method of claim 1." Atlantic argues that Faytex, by distributing products allegedly made by the claimed process, is liable as an infringer. Faytex cross-appeals from the award of lost profit damages for the sale of surge and Sorbothane innersoles. Faytex also appeals the district court's determination that the '204 patent is not invalid under the on-sale bar of 35 U.S.C. Section 102(b).

DISCUSSION

Atlantic argues that *Scripps Clinic & Research Foundation v. Genentech, Inc.*, 927 F.2d 1565 (Fed.Cir.1991) demands reversal of the noninfringement finding, even under the district court's present interpretation of the claims. In Scripps Clinic, this court stated:

> [T]he correct reading of product-by-process claims is that they are not limited to product prepared by the process set forth in the claims.

Atlantic states that the Sorbothane process results in innersoles which are indistinguishable from innersoles made by the Surge process and claimed in the '204 patent. Therefore, according to Atlantic, the Sorbothane innersoles—though made by a different non-infringing process—also infringe. In sum, Atlantic urges this court to ignore the process claim language in its product-by-process claim.

A. Supreme Court History

To construe and apply the product-by-process claim of the '204 patent, this court must examine the history of products claimed with process terms. [*From footnote:* This court in *Scripps Clinic* ruled without reference to the Supreme Court's previous cases involving product claims with process limitations. In the absence of responsive briefing of the issues by the *Scripps Clinic* parties, this court noted that it was reviewing an "undeveloped record," and devoted one paragraph to resolving the jurisdictional issue and one paragraph to the merits. *Scripps Clinic & Research Foundation v. Genentech, Inc.,* 927 F.2d 1565, 1583–84, 18 U.S.P.Q.2d 1001, 1015 (Fed.Cir.1991). A decision that fails to consider Supreme Court precedent does not control if the court determines that the prior panel would have reached a different conclusion if it had considered controlling precedent. See *Tucker v. Phyfer,* 819 F.2d 1030, 1035 n. 7 (11th Cir.1987). For the reasons set forth below, we necessarily so conclude.] This inquiry begins with several century-old Supreme Court cases.

In *Smith v. Goodyear Dental Vulcanite Co.,* 93 U.S. 486, 493 (1877), the Supreme Court construed a patent claiming a "plate of hard rubber, or vulcanite, or its equivalent, for holding artificial teeth, or teeth and gums, substantially as described." This claim was not drafted in contemporary product-by-process terms, but instead incorporated the specification. The specification, in turn, described a process for embedding teeth in soft vulcanite which later hardened to hold the artificial teeth firmly in place. The Supreme Court stated that the product could not be separated from the process by which it was made:

> The invention, then, is a product or manufacture made in a defined manner. It is not a product alone separated from the process by which it is created.... The process detailed is thereby made as much a part of the invention as are the materials of which the product is composed.

Smith, 93 U.S. at 493. The Supreme Court concluded that both the process and the product of that process were patentable.

A few years later, the same patent was again before the Supreme Court, this time in an infringement context. *Goodyear Dental Vulcanite Co. v. Davis,* 102 U.S. 222 (1880). A district court had held that a celluloid plate for artificial teeth with its differing process did not infringe the patent. The Supreme Court first quoted from its Smith opinion to clarify that the patent claimed both product and process. On that basis, the Supreme Court concluded:

> Hence, to constitute an infringement of the patent, both the material of which the dental plate is made, or its equivalent, and the process of constructing the plate, or a process equivalent thereto, must be employed.

Id. at 224. After noting that "the [celluloid] process is wholly unlike that employed in making hard rubber or vulcanite plates," id. at 229, the Court affirmed the district court's noninfringement decree. The Court also reasoned that the product of that process, a celluloid plate, is not "substantially the same as one made of hard rubber." Id.

In *Cochrane v. Badische Anilin & Soda Fabrik*, 111 U.S. 293 (1884) (BASF), the Supreme Court considered an infringement case. BASF involved alizarine, a dye. BASF obtained Reissue Patent No. 4,321 covering the product, artificial alizarine, as produced by a bromine reaction process. The claim stated:

> Artificial alizarine, produced from anthracine or its derivatives by either of the methods herein described, or by any other method which will produce a like result.

Id. at 296. The Supreme Court noted, "No. 4,321 furnishes no test by which to identify the product it covers, except that such product is to be the result of the process it describes." *Id.* at 305.

Cochrane, the accused infringer, sold artificial alizarine made by a sulfuric acid reaction process. BASF sued Cochrane for infringing the 4,321 patent. The district court determined that Cochrane's product made by a sulfuric process infringed the 4,321 patent. The circuit agreed. Before the Supreme Court, BASF contended that Cochrane infringed because it made artificial alizarine "from anthracine or its derivatives by some method." Id. at 309. BASF argued that Cochrane made artificial alizarine; therefore, the process did not matter. Id. at 310. The Supreme Court disagreed.

Instead, the Supreme Court enunciated a rule for products claimed with process limitations:

> Every patent for a product or composition of matter must identify it so that it can be recognized aside from the description of the process for making it, or else nothing can be held to infringe the patent which is not made by that process.

Id. at 310. Based on this standard, the Supreme Court held the claim of the 4,321 patent not infringed because the defendants had used a different process.

After stating this rule for claim construction, the Supreme Court offered an alternative "view of the case." *BASF*, 111 U.S. at 311. BASF's artificial alizarine was an "old article." *Id.* In the words of the Supreme

Court, "While a new process for producing it was patentable, the product itself could not be patented, even though it was a product made artificially for the first time." *Id.; see also The Wood Paper Patent,* 90 U.S. 566, 596 (1874). In other words, a patent applicant could not obtain exclusive rights to a product in the prior art by adding a process limitation to the product claim. A new process, although eligible for a process patent, could not capture exclusive rights to a product already in the prior art. Therefore, BASF could have claimed a new process for making artificial alizarine, but it had no rights to claim the product.

Thus, in *BASF,* the Supreme Court addressed both infringement and validity (in terms of patentability) of product claims containing process limitations. In judging infringement, the Court treated the process terms as limitations on the patentee's exclusive rights. In assessing validity in terms of patentability, the Court forbade an applicant from claiming an old product by merely adding a new process. The infringement rule focused on the process as a limitation; the other rule focused on the product with less regard for the process limits. A decision from the Patent Office, for instance, cited BASF twice-once for an infringement rule and once for a patentability rule. *Ex parte Fesenmeier,* 1922 C.D. 18, 302 Off. Gaz. Pat. Office 199 (1922).

In *General Electric v. Wabash Appliance,* 304 U.S. 364 [37 U.S.P.Q. 466] (1938), the Supreme Court considered a product claim for a filament in incandescent lamps. Under R.S. 4888 (the forerunner of the current 35 U.S.C. Section 112 (1988)), the Supreme Court determined that the claim did not adequately describe the invention. *General Elec.,* 304 U.S. at 368. In reviewing the claim, the Court considered whether the process described in the specification made the claim more definite. In that context, the Court stated:

> Although in some instances a claim may validly describe a new product with some reference to the method of production, a patentee who does not distinguish his product from what is old except by reference, express or constructive, to the process by which he produced it, cannot secure a monopoly on the product by whatever means produced.

General Elec., 304 U.S. at 373 (footnote omitted). At that point, the Court quoted from *BASF:* "nothing can be held to infringe the patent which is not made by that process." *Id.* at 373–74.

Thus, the Supreme Court stated in a line of cases that the infringement inquiry for product claims with process limitations focuses on whether the accused product was made by the claimed process or its equivalent. Commentators have generally read this line of cases to mean that, in infringement proceedings, the process in a product-by-process claim serves as a limitation. In his treatise, Donald Chisum states:

> A "product-by-process" claim is one in which the product is defined at least in part in terms of the method or process by which it is made. Most decisions hold that such a claim is infringed only by a product made through a substantially identical process. . . .

2 D. CHISUM, PATENTS § 8.05 (1991) (footnotes omitted). Lipscomb's Walker on Patents states:

> A claim to a product by a specific process is not infringed by the same product made by a different process.

3 E. LIPSCOMB III, LIPSCOMB'S WALKER ON PATENTS § 11:19 (3d ed. 1985). Finally, one treatise concludes:

> There is considerable case authority supporting th[e] position [that product-by-process claims cover only products made by the process specified in the claim] including a nineteenth century Supreme Court decision. [This precedent represents] a hundred years of prior law. . . .

2 MARTIN J. ADELMAN ET AL., PATENT LAW PERSPECTIVES § 2.6 [10] (2d ed. 1991). These commentators discerned a rule treating process terms as limitations on product-by-process claims in infringement actions.

B.   PTO and Court of Customs and Patent Appeals (CCPA)

The CCPA consistently stated the general rule that an applicant must claim an article of manufacture by its structural characteristics, not by reference to its manufacturing process. For instance, the court stated:

> This court has repeatedly held that a claim for an article capable of such definition must define the article by its structure and not by the process of making it.

Thus, the Patent and Trademark Office's Manual of Patent Examining Procedure (MPEP) still refers to product-by-process claims as "peculiar" in comparison to products "claimed in the conventional fashion." MPEP 706.03(e) (5th ed. 1983, rev. 1989). Recognizing this rule, the CCPA contrasted product-by-process claims with "true product claims." *In re Hughes*, 496 F.2d 1216, 1219 (CCPA 1974).

For years, the PTO, with the approval of the CCPA, limited the [product-by-process claiming] exception to those instances where the applicant could describe an invention in no way other than in terms of its manufacturing process. The CCPA also recognized further reasons for the product-by-process exception:

> [T]he right to a patent on an invention is not to be denied because of the limitations of the English language. . . . [T]he limitations of known technology concerning the subject matter sought to be patented should not arbitrarily defeat the right to a patent on an invention.

Bridgeford, 357 F.2d at 682. Thus, where applicants could not adequately describe their inventions in terms of structural characteristics, whether due to language lagging behind innovations or existing technology lagging behind in the ability to determine those characteristics, the court permitted product-by-process claiming. As noted, however, this claim format remained an exception to the general rule.

As product-by-process claiming became more common, the CCPA moved toward accepting product-by-process without a showing of necessity. In 1969, the court reversed a Board of Appeal's decision holding a product-by-process claim improper because the applicant could claim the invention without relying on the process. *In re Pilkington*, 411 F.2d 1345 (CCPA 1969). The court instead determined that the applicant had adequately described the invention in accordance with the requirements of section 112. Id. Thus, the court shifted the emphasis away from the necessity for product-by-process claiming and toward determining whether the claim adequately defines the invention.

In *Hughes*, the CCPA permitted product-by-process claims even though the applicant could describe the invention in structural terms. The court regarded "true product claims" as broader in scope than product-by-process claims–a distinction which acknowledges the process as limiting the scope of the claim. Therefore, an applicant could claim a product in product-by-process terms as a hedge against the possibility that those broader product claims might be invalidated. Id. The court, however, continued to regard product-by-process claims as an exception to the general rule. *Id.* at 1218.

The overall effect of these cases made the product-by-process exception more available to applicants. The CCPA began to handle an increasing number of cases where applicants sought exclusive rights to an old or obvious product claimed by reference to a new process for its manufacture. The court uniformly followed the Supreme Court's rule. An applicant could obtain a process patent for a new, useful, and nonobvious process, but could not claim rights to a product already in the prior art by merely adding a process limitation.

As the PTO confronted more product-by-process claims, it encountered a daunting administrative task. In weighing patentability, the PTO lacked facilities to replicate processes and compare the resultant product with prior art. The CCPA recognized this difficulty:

As a practical matter, the Patent Office is not equipped to manufacture products by the myriad of processes put before it and then obtain prior art products and make physical comparisons therewith. *Brown*, 459 F.2d at 535. The PTO's administrative difficulty presented another reason that the CCPA continued to regard product-by-process claims as exceptions to the general rule. *Hughes*, 496 F.2d at 1218.

The CCPA, even in reviewing only for patentability, treated the claimed process as a limitation. In *Hughes*, for instance, the court clarified that the process defines and limits the scope of the claim. *Hughes*, 496 F.2d at 1218–19 (product claim was of a broader scope than product-by-process claims). In fact, if the process limitations of a product-by-process claim did not adequately define the invention, an applicant would fail to satisfy section 112. In other words, the process is a defining limit. In *Moeller*, the court stated:

We think the rule is well established that where one has produced an article in which invention rests over prior art articles, and where it is not possible to define the characteristics which make it inventive except by referring to the process by which the article is made, he is permitted to so claim his article, but is limited in his protection to articles produced by his method referred to in the claims.

117 F.2d at 568.

In sum, the PTO and the CCPA acknowledged product-by-process claims as an exception to the general rule requiring claims to define products in terms of structural characteristics. This exception, however, permitted an applicant to claim a product in process terms, not to acquire exclusive rights to a product already in the prior art. Though using only process terms, a product-by-process applicant sought rights to a product, not a process. Therefore, the applicant had to show that no prior art product anticipated or rendered obvious the product defined in process terms.

The PTO and the CCPA did not reason that the process was not a defining limit of the product. To the contrary, the process was the only way to define and limit-in sum, to claim-the product. *Hughes*, 496 F.2d at 1218. Thus, in both patentability actions before the CCPA and infringement actions before the Supreme Court or the regional circuits, the courts regarded the process language in product-by-process claims as limiting the claim. Indeed by definition in most cases, the product could not be claimed in any other terms.

This court, in its initial consideration of a product-by-process claim for patentability, acknowledged that process claim limitations define the product:

> Product-by-process claims are not specifically discussed in the patent statute. The practice and governing law have developed in response to the need to enable an applicant to claim an otherwise patentable product that resists definition by other than the process by which it is made. For this reason, even though product-by-process claims are limited by and defined by the process, determination of patentability is based on the product itself.

In re Thorpe, 777 F.2d 695, 697, 227 U.S.P.Q. 964, 966 (Fed.Cir.1985).

The entire history of product-by-process claims suggests a ready explanation for the apparent difference of view about treatment of those claims during ex parte administrative proceedings and during litigation. This court already distinguishes treatment of claims for patentability before the PTO from treatment of claims for validity before the courts. This court permits the PTO to give claims their broadest reasonable meaning when determining patentability. During litigation determining validity or infringement, however, this approach is inapplicable. Rather the courts must consult the specification, prosecution history, prior art, and other claims to determine the proper construction of the claim language. Thus, accommodating the demands of the administrative process and recognizing the capabilities of the trial courts, this court treats claims differently for patentability as opposed to validity and infringement. The PTO's treatment of product-by-process claims as a product claim for patentability is consistent with policies giving claims their broadest reasonable interpretation. The same rule, however, does not apply in validity and infringement litigation. In any event, claims mean the same for infringement and validity.

Moreover, accepting Atlantic's invitation to ignore the process limitations in the '204 patent's product-by-process claims would require this court to disregard several other mainstay patent doctrines. For instance, Atlantic in effect invites this court to discount the significance of excluding claim limitations from infringement analysis. See, e.g., *Continental Paper Bag Co. v. Eastern Paper Bag Co.*, 210 U.S. 405, 419 (1908) ("[T]he claims measure the invention."). This court has repeatedly stated that infringement requires the presence of every claim limitation or its equivalent. An accused infringer can avoid infringement by showing that the accused device lacks even a single claim limitation. Thus, ignoring the claim limits of a product-by-process claim would clash directly with basic patent principles enunciated by the Supreme Court and this court.

In so holding, this court acknowledges that it has in effect recognized another reason to regard product-by-process claims as exceptional. This court recognizes that product-by-process claims will receive different treatment for administrative patentability determinations than for judicial infringement determinations. This difference originated with the Supreme Court's BASF rules-a difference this court endorsed as recently as 1985.

This court, therefore, rejects Atlantic's invitation to ignore the process limitations in its product-by-process claims. This court's infringement rules do not require reversal of the district court's non-infringement finding regarding the Sorbothane process. Neither does this court disturb the PTO's present practice for assessing patentability of product-by-process claims. * * *

VACATED–IN–PART, AFFIRMED–IN–PART, AND REMANDED

Notes

1. The Impact of *Atlantic Thermoplastics*. The classic rule for product-by-process claiming only allowed this claim form if the applicant could not otherwise describe the invention. Using contemporary technology to discern the nature of an invention, applicants can describe almost any invention in terms of its structure or characteristics. The classic justification for product-by-process techniques has practically disappeared. Nonetheless patent drafters often include product-by-process claims as backup claims behind product claims. What advice would you give inventors about this practice in light of *Scripps Clinic* and *Atlantic Thermoplastics*? If you were defending an obscure chemical patent that could not be defined structurally at all but only by its process, how would you present an argument to evade the *Atlantic Thermoplastics* holding? In the *Scripps Clinic* case, the Federal Circuit remanded the case to the District Court. If on remand the trial court found that Genentech produced a far more pure product far more cheaply under its process, what would you argue as counsel for Genentech to avoid infringement of the Scripps patent?

2. District Court Reaction. In *Tropix, Inc. v. Lumigen*, 825 F.Supp. 7, 27 U.S.P.Q.2d 1475 (D.Mass.1993), the court was squarely faced with the choice between the two lines of Federal Circuit precedent regarding product-by-process claims. There, the asserted patent included product-by-process claims covering a process for producing purified chemiluminescent, water-soluble 1,2–dioxetane derivatives. The defendant manufactured identical derivatives by a different process. The plaintiff claimed that its product-by-process claims covered the product, no matter how produced, relying on *Scripps Clinic*, while the defendant cited *Atlantic Thermoplastics Co.* for the proposition that a product-by-process patent covers only products produced via the claimed process. Noting that "the judges of the Federal Circuit Court are in open disagreement on the point," the court concluded:

> If it should be determined as a matter of fact that the purified substance is a totally novel product, then the choice between Scripps and Atlantic becomes crucial. There is much to be said as a matter of policy for Judge Newman's distinction between a process which produces a totally new substance and a novel process applied to a product which exists in the prior art, particularly in the present age of rampant biotechnology. I do not find any authority for this proposition before Scripps, however. The cases establishing the proposition that the claims are limited to the process originate from the period where product-by-process patents were allowed when the product could not be defined or distinguished from the prior art except by reference to the process. Judge Newman's assertion that there must be symmetry between the position taken by the Patent Office and the position taken by the courts in determining infringement does not appear to be supported by any authority, given the different functions of each institution. Even if symmetry were desirable, it would seem that the practice of the Patent Office should conform to the substantive rule of the courts rather than the other way around. It would appear to me, even in the confused state of the record, that a majority of the judges of the Federal Circuit would rule that Atlantic states the controlling law, and I so rule in this case.

825 F. Supp. at 10, 27 U.S.P.Q.2d at 1478. *But see Trustees of Columbia University v. Roche Diagnostics GmbH*, 126 F.Supp.2d 16, 57 U.S.P.Q.2d 1825 (D.Mass.2000).

3. Approaches Across the Atlantic (and Pacific). European patent law recognizes "product-by-process" claims. As noted in the Guidelines for Examination in the European Patent Office, Part C, Chapter III, Paragraph 4.7b:

> Claims for products defined in terms of processes of manufacture are admissible only if the products as such fulfill the requirements for patentability, i.e. inter alia that they are new and inventive. A product is not rendered novel merely by the fact that it is produced by means of a new process (see T 150/82, OJ 7/1984, 309). A claim defining a product

in terms of a process is to be construed as a claim to the product as such and the claim should preferably take the form "Product X obtainable by process Y," or any wording equivalent thereto, rather than "Product X obtained by Process Y."

In *Kirin–Amgeu Inc. v. Transkaryotic Therapies, Inc.,* 2002 WL 1654964, the English Court adopted the approach of the *Thermoplastics* panel.

The Japanese Examination Guidelines provide for more limited use of product-by-process claims and are ambivalent about the effect of their use,

EXAMINATION GUIDELINES FOR PATENT AND UTILITY MODEL IN JAPAN, PART I at 5–6 (AIPPI 1994).

    4. Judicial Dilemma. The *Atlantic Thermoplastics* case went before the full court pursuant to a petition suggesting *en banc* review. The court declined to reconsider the case *en banc*, but Judge Rich wrote a colorful opinion dissenting from the denial of *en banc*. Judge Rich felt that the *Scripps Clinic* decision should bind the *Atlantic* panel: "This is not only insulting to the *Scripps* panel (Chief Judge Markey, Judge Newman and a visiting judge), it is mutiny. It is heresy. It is illegal." Do you think the *Atlantic* panel gave an adequate justification for departing from the *Scripps Clinic* statement? By confronting the conflict with *Scripps Clinic* directly, the *Atlantic* panel introduced some uncertainty into the law because subsequent cases must choose which rule to apply. On the other hand, would the *Atlantic* panel have created any less uncertainty by taking the standard judicial course of acknowledging the *Scripps Clinic* case and then distinguishing it and in effect creating an exception to the prior case?

§ 11.2[c]   **Functional Claiming**

    Title 35 specifically authorizes inventors to claim an element in a new combination in functional terms. In fact, the section in The Patent Act that permits functional claiming is the only provision that expressly authorizes a particular claim format. 35 U.S.C. § 112, ¶ 6 permits an inventor to claim an invention as a means for performing a function, commonly known as a means-plus-function claim. The United States alone amongst the world's patent systems gives special treatment to functional claims. The history of functional claiming begins long before § 112 became part of title 35 in 1952. One of the earliest and most famous patent cases in the United States involved a functional claim. In *O'Reilly v. Morse,* 56 U.S. (15 How.) 62 (1854), the famous inventor of the telegraph, Samuel Morse, claimed "use of [electricity] ... for marking or printing intelligible characters." With this language, Morse really sought approval of a claim containing a single means clause. A single means claim is now clearly forbidden under § 112 which requires "that the enabling disclosure of the specification be commensurate in scope with the claim." *In re Hyatt,* 708 F.2d 712 (Fed.Cir.1983) (citing *O'Reil-*

ly, 56 U.S. at 112). The Supreme Court rejected Morse's claim because its breadth encompassed far more than the telegraph machine Morse had in fact invented. *See, O'Reilly*, 56 U.S. at 112.

After the famous *O'Reilly* case, however, functional claims began to appear in combination claims, as distinguished from Morse's single means claim. In fact, functional claim elements perform an important "function" in claim drafting. In a sentence, this claim form permits a drafter to list a multitude of the ways to perform a claimed function. To understand the importance of this convenience, consider a claim for an invention that for the first time attaches a flash mechanism to a camera. To simplify this hypothetical, the claim would recite a camera and a flash device. Then the claim must recite the relationship between the camera and the flash device. Of course, the flash is fastened to the camera. At this point the problem arises. How does the drafter claim the myriad ways of fastening—rivets, bolts, screws, glue, and so forth? The novelty of this invention is not the way of fastening, but the combination of a camera and an attached flash mechanism. Thus, the claim drafter wants to find a convenient way to claim all known ways of fastening that will facilitate the invention. A functional claim will accomplish that classic purpose with just a few words: "means for fastening." On their face, those words appear to capture all known ways of fastening.

In any event, in 1946, the Supreme Court again dealt with the breadth of functional claiming. At that time, the Supreme Court prohibited use of functional claims at the exact point of novelty in a combination claim. *See Halliburton Oil Well Cementing Co. v. Walker* 329 U.S. 1, 9 (1946) ("The language of the claim thus describes this most crucial element in the 'new' combination in terms of what it will do rather than in terms of its own physical characteristics.... We have held that a claim with such a description of a product is invalid.... "). The Supreme Court foresaw that functional language could embrace every conceivable way of performing a function, thus claiming more than the inventor had invented or claiming subject matter already available to the public. To prevent "the broadness, ambiguity, and overhanging threat of the functional claim," *Halliburton*, 329 U.S. at 9, the Supreme Court prohibited this particular functional claim. Read carefully, *Halliburton* does not create a problem for functional claiming, only for functional claiming at the exact point of novelty in a claim. In terms of our earlier hypothetical, if the camera and flash combination was old and the only new feature in the invention was a new connector (perhaps a plastic snap attachment which allows removal and reattachment), then a claim that recited broadly a "means for fastening" would not distinguish the novel new connector from all old fasteners. In this context, *Halliburton* makes intuitive sense and does not endanger the classic purpose of functional claiming.

Nonetheless, a few years later, as part of a major restructuring of patent law, the United States Congress undertook to protect functional claiming in the wake of the *Halliburton* case. Acknowledging the utility of the functional format to embrace conveniently a wide variety of ways to perform an element of a combination, Congress authorized means-plus-function claims by adding § 112, ¶ 6 to title 35. The 1952 Act did not ignore the problem of breadth in functional language. In the words of the Federal Circuit: "The second clause of [§ 112, ¶ 6], however, places a limiting condition on an applicant's use of means-plus-function language. [Otherwise a] claim limitation described as a means for performing a function, if read literally, could encompass any conceivable means for performing the function." *Valmont*, 983 F.2d at 1042. This second clause confines the breadth of protection otherwise permitted by the first clause. *See id.* It requires the applicant to describe in the patent specification the various structures that the inventor expects to perform the specified function. The statute then expressly confines coverage of the functional claim language to "the corresponding structure, material, or acts described in the specification and equivalents thereof."

Since enactment, § 112, ¶ 6 has been one of the most frequently litigated sections of the Patent Act. For many years, whether this statutory provision applied to the U.S. Patent and Trademark Office had also been the subject of competing views–with the PTO on one side of the argument and the Federal Circuit on the other. The following Federal Circuit opinion effectively ended that controversy.

IN RE DONALDSON CO.

United States Court of Appeals, Federal Circuit, 1994.
16 F.3d 1189, 29 U.S.P.Q.2d 1845.

Before NIES, CHIEF JUDGE, and RICH, NEWMAN, ARCHER, MAYER, MICHEL, PLAGER, LOURIE, CLEVENGER, RADER, and SCHALL, CIRCUIT JUDGES.

RICH, CIRCUIT JUDGE.

The Donaldson Company (Donaldson) appeals from the January 30, 1991 decision of the Board of Patent Appeals and Interferences (Board) of the United States Patent and Trademark Office (PTO), reaffirmed on reconsideration on April 17, 1991, sustaining the Examiner's rejection of claim 1 of reexamination application Serial No. 90/001,776 (Schuler application) under 35 U.S.C. § 103. We reverse.

I. BACKGROUND

A. *The Invention*

The present invention relates to industrial air-filtering devices often referred to as "dust collectors." Fig. 2 of the Schuler application is reproduced on the following page.

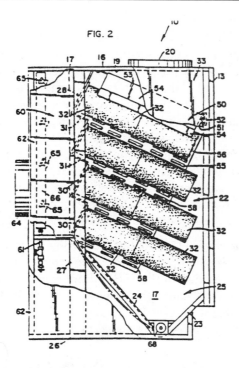

FIG. 2

In operation, dust-laden air enters dirty-air chamber (22) through air inlet (20) at the top, passes through filters (32), and then exits through clean-air outlet (64) at the left. During this process, dust is collected on the outside of the filters. To periodically dislodge accumulated dust from the filters, the Schuler collector includes valve and nozzle assemblies (65), which direct jets of compressed air into the hollow interior of each filter. In doing so, the normal direction of air flow is reversed, thus dislodging a substantial portion of the dust accumulated on the outside of each filter. The dislodged dust then falls through the dirty-air chamber and accumulates at the bottom of the chamber in hopper (25), where it is removed by auger screw (68).

One problem with conventional collectors is that the dust accumulated in the hopper tends to harden or cake, thus interfering with the free movement of the accumulated dust downward to the auger screw. To overcome this problem, the Schuler collector takes advantage of the fact that every pulse of air from the nozzles causes the pressure within the dirty-air chamber to increase momentarily. At least one wall of the hopper of the Schuler collector (24) is made from a flexible material which in essence transforms the hopper into a diaphragm-like structure which expands outward in response to the temporary pressure increases. This movement breaks up any dust that may have hardened or caked onto the hopper. This flexible-wall, diaphragm-like structure also provides the additional advantages of deadening the sounds of the cleaning pulses and expanding the volume of the dirty-air chamber, thus allowing the air pulses to act more vigorously on the filters.

Claim 1, the only claim on appeal, reads, with insertion of reference numerals in brackets, as follows:

An air filter assembly [10] for filtering air laden with particulate matter, said assembly [10] comprising:

a housing having a clean air chamber [60] and a filtering chamber [22], said housing having an upper wall [16], a closed bottom [26], and a plurality of side walls [17, 62] depending from said upper wall [16];

a clean air outlet [64] from said clean air chamber [60] in one of said side walls [62];

a dirty air inlet [20] to said filtering chamber [22] positioned in a wall [16] of said housing in a location generally above said clean air outlet [64];

means [28] separating said clean air chamber [60] from said filtering chamber [22] including means mounting a plurality of spaced-apart filter elements [32] within said filtering chamber [22], with each of said elements [32] being in fluid communication with said air outlet [64];

pulse-jet cleaning means [65], intermediate said outlet [64] and said filter elements [32], for cleaning each of said filter elements [32];

and a lowermost portion [25] in said filtering chamber [22] arranged and constructed for the collection of particulate matter, said portion [25] having means [24], responsive to pressure increases in said chamber [22] caused by said cleaning means [65], for moving particulate matter in a downward direction to a bottommost point [68] in said portion [25] for subsequent transfer to a location exterior to said assembly [10].

B. The Board Decision

In its initial January 30, 1991 decision, the Board relied solely upon the dust collector disclosed in U.S. Patent No. 3,421,295 (Swift patent) to affirm the Examiner's rejection of claim 1. The Board did not find the secondary references relied upon by the Examiner necessary to sustain the rejection. Swift's dust collector, illustrated on the following page by Fig. 2 of the Swift patent, uses pulses of compressed, high-energy gas to counteract normal filter flow. These pulses of compressed gas dislodge particulate matter from spaced-apart filter elements (14), and the dislodged particulate matter moves towards the bottom of the hopper (16).

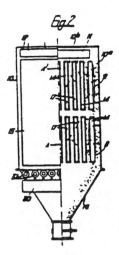

[T]he Board noted Donaldson's arguments that Swift fails to disclose the use in its dust collector of a flexible surface which flexes in response to the gas pulses therein, but stated that: while such a flexible sloping surface is a recited feature of the apparatus of claims 2, 3, and 5, this is not the case as to the apparatus of claim 1. Thus, [Donaldson's] argument is of no moment to claim 1. Moreover, we are convinced that hopper 16 of the gas filtering apparatus of Swift is "responsive" to pressure increases in the apparatus caused by the jet-cleaning means whereby filtered particulate matter is caused to move in a downward direction. Thus, we agree with the examiner that there is no apparent distinction between the "lowermost portion" of the apparatus recited in claim 1 and the corresponding portion of the apparatus of Swift.

Thus, the Board did not interpret the "means, responsive to pressure increases in said chamber caused by said cleaning means, for moving particulate matter in a downward direction" language recited in the last paragraph of claim 1 as limited to the flexible wall, diaphragm-like structure disclosed in Schuler's specification, and equivalents thereof. Indeed, the Board specifically stated at page 2 of its decision on reconsideration mailed April 17, 1991: It is axiomatic that particular features or limitations appearing in the specification are not to be read into the claims of an application. [citations omitted] Thus, contrary to [Donaldson's] argument, a flexible sloping surface is not a feature of the air filtering apparatus of claim 1 which distinguishes it over the air filtering apparatus of Swift.

C. Donaldson's Assertions

For purposes of this appeal, Donaldson effectively concedes that Swift teaches or suggests each and every element of the apparatus recited in Schuler's claim 1 except for the "means, responsive to pressure increases in said chamber caused by said cleaning means, for moving particulate matter in a downward direction" recited in the last segment of claim 1. As to this limitation, Donaldson argues that the Board erred in holding that Swift teaches or suggests such a means as it is described in Schuler's specification. Donaldson further argues that the Board's error in this regard is the result of a fundamental legal error by the Board, namely the Board's failure to obey the statutory mandate of 35 U.S.C. § 112, paragraph six, in construing this claim.

II. DISCUSSION

35 U.S.C. § 112, Paragraph Six

The plain and unambiguous meaning of paragraph six is that one construing means-plus-function language in a claim must look to the specification and interpret that language in light of the corresponding structure, material, or acts described therein, and equivalents thereof, to the extent that the specification provides such disclosure. Paragraph six does not state or even suggest that the PTO is exempt from this mandate, and there is no legislative history indicating that Congress intended that the PTO should be. Thus, this court must accept the plain and precise language of paragraph six. *See Diamond v. Chakrabarty*, 447 U.S. 303, 308, 100 S.Ct. 2204, 2207, 65 L.Ed.2d 144 (1980) ("courts 'should not read into the patent laws limitations and conditions which the legislature has not expressed' "). Accordingly, because no distinction is made in paragraph six between prosecution in the PTO and enforcement in the courts, or between validity and infringement, we hold that paragraph six applies regardless of the context in which the interpretation of means-plus-function language arises, i.e., whether as part of a patentability determination in the PTO or as part of a validity or infringement determination in a court. To the extent that *In re Lundberg*, 244 F.2d 543, 113 U.S.P.Q. 530 (CCPA 1957), *In re Arbeit*, 206 F.2d 947, 99 U.S.P.Q. 123 (CCPA 1953), or any other precedent of this court suggests or holds to the contrary, it is expressly overruled.

The Commissioner argues that his interpretation is entitled to deference in view of what the Commissioner alleges is the PTO's sweeping and long-standing practice of not applying paragraph six during examination. We disagree. The fact that the PTO may have failed to adhere to a statutory mandate over an extended period of time does not justify its continuing to do so. In addition, paragraph six facially covers every situation involving the interpretation of means-plus-function language, and the Commissioner's attempts to create an ambiguity in paragraph six where none exists are to no avail. The fact that paragraph six does not specifically state that it applies during prosecution in the PTO does not mean that paragraph six is ambiguous in this respect. Quite the contrary, we interpret the fact that paragraph six fails to distinguish between prosecution in the PTO and enforcement in the courts as indicating that Congress did not intend to create any such distinction.

In addition, section 112 as a whole relates to requirements for the specification and claims without regard to whether a patent or patent application is involved. Moreover, section 112 is found in Chapter 11 of Title 35, titled "Application for Patent," which supports our holding that section 112, paragraph six, governs the interpretation of "means" clauses in a claim for a combination when being examined in pending applications.

The Commissioner argues that Congress enacted paragraph six to codify the "reverse doctrine of equivalents" for means-plus-function claim language, a claim interpretation tool which finds application only in the litigation context, wherefore Congress must have intended paragraph six to apply only in the context of post-issuance infringement and validity actions. We see no merit in this imaginative reasoning, and no support for it has been cited. The record is clear on why paragraph six was enacted. In *Halliburton Oil Well Cementing Co. v. Walker*, 329 U.S. 1, 67 S.Ct. 6, 91 L.Ed. 3 (1946), the Supreme Court held that means-plus-function language could not be employed at the exact point of novelty in a combination claim. Congress enacted paragraph six, originally paragraph three, to statutorily overrule that holding. *See In re Fuetterer*, 319 F.2d 259, 264 n. 11, 138 U.S.P.Q. 217, 222 n. 11 (CCPA 1963) (noting that it was Congress's intent to restore the law regarding broad functional language in combination claims to its state prior to *Halliburton*). The fact that the question of how to treat means-plus-function language came to Congress's attention through the context of infringement litigation does not suggest that Congress did not intend paragraph six to apply to all interpretations of means-plus-function claim language. Furthermore, there is no legislative history suggesting that Congress's purpose in enacting paragraph six was to codify the reverse doctrine of equivalents, and thus there is no reason to believe that Congress intended to limit the application of paragraph six to post-issuance claim interpretation.

Contrary to suggestions by the Commissioner, our holding does not conflict with the principle that claims are to be given their "broadest reasonable interpretation" during prosecution. *See, e.g., In re Prater*, 415 F.2d 1393, 1404–05, 162 U.S.P.Q. 541, 550–51 (CCPA 1969). Generally speaking, this claim interpretation principle remains intact. Rather, our holding in this case merely sets a limit on how broadly the PTO may construe means-plus-function language under the rubric of "reasonable interpretation." Per our holding, the "broadest reasonable interpretation" that an examiner may give means-plus-function language is that statutorily mandated in paragraph six. Accordingly, the PTO may not disregard the structure disclosed in the specification corresponding to such language when rendering a patentability determination.

Our holding similarly does not conflict with the second paragraph of section 112. Indeed, we agree with the general principle espoused in *In re Lundberg*, 244 F.2d at 547–48, 113 U.S.P.Q. at 534 (CCPA 1979), that the sixth paragraph of section 112 does not exempt an applicant from the requirements of the first two paragraphs of that section. Although paragraph six statutorily provides that one may use means-plus-function language in a claim, one is still subject to the requirement that a claim "particularly point out and distinctly claim" the invention. Therefore, if one employs means-plus-function language in a claim, one must set forth in the specification an adequate disclosure showing what is meant by that language. If an applicant fails to set forth an adequate disclosure, the applicant has in effect failed to particularly point out and distinctly claim the invention as required by the second paragraph of section 112.

Also contrary to suggestions by the Commissioner, our holding does not conflict with the general claim construction principle that limitations found only in the specification of a patent or patent application should not be imported or read into a claim. *See In re Priest*, 582 F.2d 33, 37, 199 U.S.P.Q. 11, 15 (CCPA 1978). The Commissioner confuses impermissibly imputing limitations from the specification into a claim with properly referring to the specification to determine the meaning of a particular word or phrase recited in a claim. *See E.I. du Pont de Nemours & Co. v. Phillips Petroleum Co.*, 849 F.2d 1430, 1433, 7 U.S.P.Q.2d 1129, 1131 (Fed.Cir.1988) (discusses importance of distinguishing between the two). What we are dealing with in this case is the construction of a limitation already in the claim in the form of a means-plus-function clause and a statutory mandate on how that clause must be construed.

Application of Paragraph Six to Claims

For the foregoing reasons, the PTO was required by statute to look to Schuler's specification and construe the "means" language recited in the last segment of claim 1 as limited to the corresponding structure disclosed in the specification and equivalents thereof. The particular means language of claim 1 at issue reads:

> means, responsive to pressure increases in said chamber caused by said cleaning means, for moving particulate matter in a downward direction to a bottommost point in said [lowermost] portion for subsequent transfer to a location exterior to said assembly.

A review of the [Schuler specification] leads to the inescapable conclusion that Schuler's specification defines the "means, responsive to pressure increases in said chamber . . . , for moving particulate matter in a downward direction" language recited in claim 1 as a flexible-wall, diaphragm-like structure, such that the hopper is made up of at least one flexible wall which expands outward upon pressure increases, thus causing caked-on dust to break loose from the wall of the hopper and fall towards the auger screw due to gravity.

D.   Swift

The Swift collector does not teach or suggest the flexible-wall, diaphragm-like structure claimed by Schuler. Indeed, there is no teaching or suggestion in Swift that the hopper walls therein be anything but rigid and non-responsive to any pressure increases within the collector. Consequently, it would not have been obvious to one of ordinary skill in the art to modify Swift to obtain Schuler's flexible-wall, diaphragm-like structure. In this regard, we note that the Board itself specifically held at page 6 of its initial decision that the examiner had failed to establish a prima facie case of obviousness as to claims 2, 3, and 5, because Swift and the other references relied upon by the examiner fail to disclose or render obvious the feature of the lowermost portion of the claimed apparatus comprising the flexible sloping surface which flexes in response to increases in pressure in the apparatus caused by the pulse-jet cleaning means whereby filtered particulate matter is moved in a downward direction.

Notwithstanding this explicit holding by the Board that Swift fails to teach or suggest the flexible-wall, diaphragm-like structure that Schuler discloses in his specification as corresponding to the "means" language recited in the last segment of claim 1, the Commissioner nevertheless argues that the examiner found, and the Board allegedly implicitly agreed, that Swift's hopper walls respond to jet-cleaning pressure increases by vibrating, and that Donaldson has failed to establish that this allegedly responsive structure is not an "equivalent" to Schuler's disclosed flexible-wall, diaphragm-like structure. The Commissioner further contends that the slanted hopper walls in Swift's collector satisfy the "means, responsive to pressure" language of claim 1.

Nevertheless, as explained previously, section 112, paragraph six, requires us and the PTO to construe the "means, responsive to pressure" language recited in claim 1 as limited to a flexible-wall, diaphragm-like structure as disclosed in Schuler's specification, or an "equivalent" thereof. In this regard, the Commissioner has failed to establish the existence in conventional hopper structures like Swift's of any inherent vibrations resulting from pulse-jet cleaning sufficient to loosen hardened dust that gathers on hopper walls. Thus, because the Commissioner's unsupported assertion that Swift's hopper walls would vibrate in response to pressure increases caused by pulse-jet cleaning is mere speculation unsupported by any rational basis for believing it might be true, the burden clearly did not shift to Schuler to establish non-equivalence. Furthermore, the Commissioner has failed to persuade us that such vibration, even if it did occur, should be viewed as making Swift's hopper structure an "equivalent" of Schuler's flexible-wall, diaphragm-like structure.

As to the Commissioner's arguments regarding Swift's slanted hopper walls, we note that neither the examiner nor the Board ever asserted that these slanted walls by themselves represent an "equivalent" of Schuler's flexible-wall, diaphragm-like structure. In addition, the Commissioner has failed to set forth any reasonable explanation as to how Swift's walls are "responsive to pressure increases."

CONCLUSION

For the foregoing reasons, we hold, as a matter of law, that Swift does not render the structure defined by claim 1 obvious under 35 U.S.C. § 103, and therefore we reverse the decision of the Board. On the record before us, we see no reason to remand this case for further findings as to "equivalents" as suggested by the Commissioner.

REVERSED.

Notes

1. Criticizing *Donaldson*. In *Donaldson*, the court discussed the CCPA opinion *In re Lundberg*. In that 1957 case, Judge Rich joined the court's decision holding that § 112 ¶ 6 does not apply to validity issues. What happened between 1957 and 1994 to change Judge Rich's mind regarding what Congress intended in 1952? For an argument that *Donaldson* was wrongly decided, *see* 3 MARTIN J. ADELMAN, PATENT LAW PERSPECTIVES, § 2.9[5] at n.58 (2d ed. 1994).

2. Functional Claim Language in Japan. Prior to 1996 amendments to the Japanese patent statute, the Japanese patent system took a strict view of functional claim language. Courts often restricted coverage of such claims to the specific technical examples provided in the specification. While the earlier statute provided that the claims must set forth the features indispensable for the constitution of the invention, Article 36, Paragraph 5 now provides: "The applicant has to state, claim by claim, all the features which he considers necessary for identifying the invention for which a patent is sought."

3. Functional Claim Language in Europe. The Guidelines for Examination issued by the President of the EPO allow for functional instead of structural claim limitations. The Technical Board of Appeal in *Synergistic herbicides/Ciba Geigy*, T68/85, held that functional definitions may be used if the invention cannot be defined structurally without restricting the scope of the invention. For a general review of the law regarding functional claims in the EPO see GERALD PATERSON, THE EUROPEAN PATENT SYSTEM 160–63 (1992). For a history of the treatment of functional claims in England see Peter Ford, *Functional Claims*, 16 INT'L REV. INDUS. PROP. & COPYRIGHT L. 335 (1985).

4. *Donaldson*: a Rarity. For all of its importance, *Donaldson* presents a very rare instance where a case involving § 112, ¶ 6 comes to the Federal Circuit from the PTO. Why would such cases be very rare? In any event, as illustrated by the next case, most functional claim cases arise in infringement suits and often feature issues involving structural equivalents (a form of literal infringement based on the statutory language of sec. 112) and the doctrine of equivalents.

AL–SITE CORP. v. VSI INTERNATIONAL, INC.

United States Court of Appeals, Federal Circuit, 1999.
174 F.3d 1308, 50 U.S.P.Q.2d 1161.

Before MAYER, CHIEF JUDGE, RICH and RADER, CIRCUIT JUDGES.

RADER, CIRCUIT JUDGE.

I.

Magnivision and VSI both sell non-prescription eyeglasses. Magnivision is the assignee of U.S. Patent Nos. 4,976,532 (the '532 patent),

5,144,345 (the '345 patent), 5,260,726 (the '726 patent), and 5,521,911 (the '911 patent). These patents claim technology for displaying eyeglasses on racks. The claimed inventions allow consumers to try on eyeglasses and return them to the rack without removing them from their display hangers.

The jury determined that one of VSI's products (the Version 1 hanger tag) literally infringed the '532 patent. The jury also determined that a second VSI product (the Version 2 hanger tag) did not literally infringe the '345, '726, and '911 patents, but did infringe those patents under the doctrine of equivalents.

II.

Literal Infringement of the '532 patent

The jury determined that the Version 1 hanger tag literally infringes claims 8, 9, 14, 15, and 17 of the '532 patent. Claim 8, the independent claim from which the other infringed claims depend, claims the combination of a pair of eyeglasses and a hanger means for removably mounting the eyeglasses on a cantilevered support. The claim itself gives some structural definition of the hanger means as "including a body having aperture means adapted" for suspending the hanger and eyeglasses on the cantilevered support. Additionally, the hanger means includes an extension projecting from the bottom edge portion of the hanger body. This extension encircles the nose bridge of the eyeglasses. The claim specifies that "fastening means in engagement with said extension" hold the extension in a closed loop. Figure 1 from the '532 patent illustrates these claimed features:

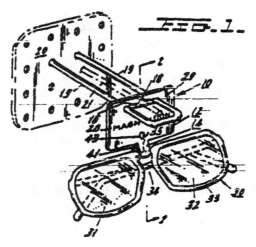

The district court determined that the "fastening means" was a means-plus-function element subject to the interpretation requirements of 35 U.S.C. § 112, ¶ 6 (1994). Consistent with that determination, the trial court instructed the jury that "the fastening means ... is either a rivet or a button and hole arrangement as shown in the '532 patent or the structural equivalents thereof." Neither party challenges this part of the district court's claim construction.

On appeal, VSI contends that its Version 1 hanger tag does not infringe because it does not include the "fastening means" required by claim 8. VSI's Version 1 hanger tag is a one-piece paper sticker having two large portions connected by a narrow extension. The entire back of the tag, including the extension, is coated with an adhesive. Backing paper covers the adhesive to prevent undesired adhesion. In use, a merchant removes the backing paper from the large portions of the tag. The extension (still covered with backing paper) then wraps around the nose bridge of the glasses. This wrapping glues the large portions together. In use, therefore, glue secures the two large portions of the tag to each other, leaving the narrow extension of the tag wrapped around the bridge of the eyeglasses.

The adhesive used by VSI is not identical to the fastening structure (namely, a rivet or button) described in the '532 patent. The jury, however, applying the rules of § 112, ¶ 6, determined that the VSI adhesive was equivalent to the structure disclosed in the specification. Accordingly, the jury returned a verdict of literal infringement of the '532 patent. VSI argues that substantial evidence does not support the jury's finding of literal infringement.

VSI first challenges the jury determination that adhesive is structurally equivalent to the mechanical fasteners disclosed in the specification of the '532 patent. Magnivision's technical expert, Mr. Anders, testified that, for one of ordinary skill in the art, it would be an insubstantial change "to substitute a rivet for a staple or for glue or for any other method that's standard in the [point of purchase] industry to maintain this loop as a closed loop." *See Chiuminatta Concrete Concepts, Inc. v. Cardinal Indus., Inc.*, 145 F.3d 1303, 1309 (Fed.Cir.1998) ("The proper test [for determining equivalence under § 112, ¶ 6] is whether the differences between the structure in the accused device and any disclosed in the specification are insubstantial. . . . The question of known interchangeability is . . . an important factor in determining equivalence [under § 112, ¶ 6]."). Mr. Anders further testified that the use of glue "in between the two layers of the body . . . is an insubstantial change from the other structure . . . which was one of a rivet. People in point of purchase displays use glue or rivets or staples to accomplish the same function." *But see Chiuminatta*, 145 F.3d at 1309 ("Almost by definition, two structures that perform the same function may be substituted for one another. The question of known interchangeability is not whether both structures serve the same function, but whether it was known that one structure was an equivalent of another."). Mr. Anders additionally testified that "equivalent fastening means could be a rivet, glue or staple or some such similar [structure]." This testimony constitutes sufficient evidence to sustain the jury's verdict that persons of ordinary skill in the art consider glue an equivalent structure to those disclosed in the specification for maintaining a closed loop.

As a fallback position, VSI argues that, even if the glue is an equivalent of the rivet or button, Magnivision presented no evidence that the glue was "in engagement" with the extension as claim 8 requires. On cross examination, Mr. Anders identified the middle section of the Version 1 hanger tag as the "extension" element. Mr. Anders also identified the glue as the "fastening means" element. Because VSI leaves the backing paper on its extension (presumably to prevent the tag from adhering to the eyeglasses), VSI argues that its extension does not engage the fastening means as required by the claims of the '532 patent.

VSI's argument is unpersuasive. The claims of the '532 patent only require that the fastening means be "in engagement with" the extension. As noted above, VSI coats the extension of its Version 1 hanger tag with glue—the fastening means identified by Mr. Anders. Furthermore, Mr. Anders' testimony explains that the extension and the glued portions are one integral piece. The jury could have interpreted his testimony to mean that the extension includes more than the narrow, middle portion of the Version 1 tag. Under this interpretation, the extension would also directly engage the glue fastening means. Alternatively, the jury could have determined that the extension is only the narrow portion of the Version 1 tag, but that the fastening means includes one of the two portions of the tag body in addition to the glue. Under any of these reasonable views of the accused product, the extension of the Version 1 hanger tag is in engagement with the glue fastening means as required by the claims.

As the finder of fact, the jury receives deference for its function of weighing witness demeanor, credibility, and meaning. *See Anderson v. City of Bessemer City, North Carolina*, 470 U.S. 564, 575 (1985) (factfinder entitled to deference on credibility determinations). Substantial evidence therefore supports the jury's verdict that VSI's Version 1 hanger tag literally infringes the '532 patent.

INFRINGEMENT OF THE '345, '726, AND '911 PATENTS

The jury determined that VSI's Version 2 hanger tag and display rack did not literally infringe claims 1 and 2 of the '345 patent; claims 1 and 2 of the '726 patent; or claims 1, 2, and 3 of the '911 patent. The jury nevertheless found infringement of each of these claims under the doctrine of equivalents. Magnivision argues that the district court misconstrued these claims, and that, under the proper claim construction, VSI's products literally infringe these claims as a matter of law. VSI, on the other hand, embraces the district court's claim construction and argues that prosecution history estoppel precludes a finding of infringement under the doctrine of equivalents.

Claim 1 of the '345 patent and claim 1 of the '726 patent are similar. Both claim "[t]he combination of an eyeglass display member and an eyeglass hanger member." In each of these claims, this combination includes a "display member" with "cantilever support means" and "an eyeglass hanger member for mounting a pair of eyeglasses." Both claims further define the structure of the eyeglass hanger member. Claim 1 of the '345 patent describes the eyeglass hanger member as "made from flat sheet material," and having an "opening means formed ... below [its] upper edge." According to claim 1 of the '726 patent, the eyeglass hanger member has "an attaching portion attachable to a portion of said frame of said pair of eyeglasses to enable the temples of the frame [to be opened and closed]." Similarly, claim 2 of the '726 patent encompasses a "method of displaying eyeglass/hanger combinations ... the eyeglass hangers having an attaching portion attached to a portion of the frame of an associated pair of eyeglasses."

Claims 1, 2, and 3 of the '911 patent encompass a "combination of an eyeglass display member and an eyeglass contacting member." The '911 patent further describes the structure of the "eyeglass contacting member" as "having an encircling portion adapted to encircle a part of said frame of said pair of eyeglasses."

The district court construed the "eyeglass hanger member" element of the '345 patent as a means-plus-function claim element subject to § 112, ¶ 6. Accordingly, the district court instructed the jury that "[t]he 'eyeglass hanger member for mounting a pair of eyeglasses' [in claim 1 of the '345 patent] is the body of the hanger disclosed in the '345 patent and its drawings and the structural equivalents thereof." The district court similarly interpreted the "eyeglass hanger member" element of the '726 patent. The district court instructed the jury that "[t]he 'eyeglass hanger member for mounting a pair of eyeglasses' [in claim 1 of the '726 patent] is the hanger disclosed in the '726 patent and its drawings as having a body, an aperture, and an attaching portion and the structural equivalents thereof."

With respect to the '911 patent, the district court concluded that the "eyeglass contacting member" was a means-plus-function element. The district court therefore instructed the jury that the "eyeglass contacting member" is "the hanger disclosed in the '911 patent and its drawings having a body and an aperture and an 'encircling portion,' and the structural equivalents thereof."

This court reviews the district court's claim interpretation without deference. See *Cybor Corp. v. FAS Technologies, Inc.*, 138 F.3d 1448, 1454–56 (Fed.Cir.1998) (en banc). This court has delineated several rules for claim drafters to invoke the strictures of 35 U.S.C. § 112, ¶ 6. Specifically, if the word "means" appears in a claim element in combination with a function, it is presumed to be a means-plus-function element to which § 112, ¶ 6 applies. See *Sage Prods., Inc. v. Devon Indus., Inc.*, 126 F.3d 1420, 1427 (Fed.Cir.1997). Nevertheless, according to its express terms, § 112, ¶ 6 governs only claim elements that do not recite sufficient structural limitations. See 35 U.S.C. § 112, ¶ 6. Therefore, the presumption that § 112, ¶ 6 applies is overcome if the claim itself recites sufficient structure or material for performing the claimed function. See *Sage*, 126 F.3d at 1427–28 ("[W]here a claim recites a function, but then goes on to elaborate sufficient structure, material, or acts within the claim itself to perform entirely the recited function, the claim is not in means-plus-function format.'').

Although use of the phrase "means for" (or "step for") is not the only way to invoke § 112, ¶ 6, that terminology typically invokes § 112, ¶ 6 while other formulations generally do not. See *Greenberg*, 91 F.3d at 1583–84. Therefore, when an element of a claim does not use the term "means," treatment as a means-plus-function claim element is generally not appropriate. See *Mas–Hamilton Group v. LaGard, Inc.*, 156 F.3d 1206, 1213–15 (Fed.Cir.1998). However, when it is apparent that the element invokes purely functional terms, without the additional recital of specific structure or material for performing that function, the claim element may be a means-plus-function element despite the lack of express means-plus-function language. See, e.g., *Cole*, 102 F.3d at 531 ("[M]erely because an element does not include the word 'means' does not automatically prevent that element from being construed as a means-plus-function element."); *Mas-Hamilton*, 156 F.3d at 1213–15 (interpreting "lever moving element" and "movable link member" under § 112, ¶ 6).

Under this established analytical framework, the "eyeglass hanger member" elements in the claims of both the '345 and the '726 patents do not invoke § 112, ¶ 6. In the first place, these elements are not in traditional means-plus-function format. The word "means" does not appear within these elements. Moreover, although these claim elements include a function, namely, "mounting a pair of eyeglasses," the claims themselves contain sufficient structural limitations for performing those functions. As noted above, claim 1 of the '345 patent describes the eyeglass hanger member as "made from flat sheet material" with an "opening means formed ... below [its] upper edge." This structure removes this claim from the purview of § 112, ¶ 6. Similarly, according to claim 1 of the '726 patent, the eyeglass hanger member has "an attaching portion attachable to a portion of said frame of said pair of eyeglasses to enable the temples of the frame [to be opened and closed]." This structure also precludes treatment as a means-plus-function claim element. The district court therefore improperly restricted the "eyeglass hanger member" in these claims to the structural embodiments in the specification and their equivalents.

The district court also erred in interpreting the "attaching portion attachable to a portion of said frame of said pair of eyeglasses" element of claim 1 of the '726 patent as a means-plus-function element. It instructed the jury that the "attachable portion" is "a mechanically fastened loop that goes around the nose bridge of the glasses as disclosed in the specification, or the structural equivalent thereof." Because this claim element is also not in traditional means-plus-function form and supplies structural, not functional, terms, the trial court erred by applying § 112, ¶ 6 to this claim element. This error caused the district court to incorporate unduly restrictive structural limitations into the claim.

For reasons similar to those discussed above with respect to the claim elements of the '345 and the '726 patents, the "eyeglass contacting member" element of the '911 patent claims is also not a means-plus-function element. Again, this claim element is not in traditional means-plus-function form. Furthermore, the claim itself recites sufficient structure for performing the recited function. Specifically, claim 1 of the '911 patent describes the "eyeglass contacting member" as "having an encircling portion adapted to encircle a part of said frame of said pair of eyeglasses to enable the temples of the frame to be selectively [opened and closed]." Similarly, claim 3 of the '911 patent describes the "eyeglass contacting member" as "having an attaching portion attachable to a portion of said frame of said eyeglasses." Therefore, the district court erred by applying § 112, ¶ 6 to these claim elements.

Magnivision also complains that the district court erred in its construction of the language "means for securing a portion of said frame of said eyeglasses to said hanger member" in claim 1 of the '345 patent. With respect to this element, the district court instructed the jury that "[t]he 'means for securing' limitation is a mechanically fastened loop that goes around the nose bridge of the glasses ... or an equivalent thereof." The district court went on, however, to instruct the jury that "[t]he means for securing can be formed from a separate extension or integral extension and includes either the rivet fastener or the button and hole fastener." Magnivision argues that the district court should have included the phrase "or equivalents thereof" after "button and hole fastener" in its instruction to the jury. Absent this and the other claimed errors in the district court's interpretation of claim 1 of the '345 patent, Magnivision argues that the jury would have found literal infringement rather than infringement under the doctrine of equivalents.

The "means for securing" claim element is in conventional means-plus-function format without specific recital of structure and therefore invokes § 112, ¶ 6. The jury's finding of infringement of claim 1 of the '345 patent under the doctrine of equivalents indicates that the jury found every element of the claim literally or equivalently present in the accused device. The question before this court, therefore, is whether the jury's finding that the accused structure was equivalent to the "means for securing" element under the doctrine of equivalents, also indicates that it is equivalent structure under § 112, ¶ 6.

This court has on several occasions explicated the distinctions between the term "equivalents" found in § 112, ¶ 6 and the doctrine of equivalents. See, e.g., *Valmont Indus., Inc. v. Reinke Mfg. Co.*, 983 F.2d 1039, 1042–44 (Fed.Cir.1993); *Chiuminatta*, 145 F.3d at 1310; *Dawn Equipment Co. v. Kentucky Farms Inc.*, 140 F.3d 1009, 1018–23 (Fed.Cir. 1998) (Plager, J., additional views) (Newman, J., additional views) (Michel, J., additional views). Indeed, the Supreme Court recently acknowledged distinctions between equivalents as used in § 112, ¶ 6 and the doctrine of equivalents. See *Warner–Jenkinson Co. v. Hilton Davis Chem. Co.*, 520 U.S. 17, 27 (1997) ("[Equivalents under § 112, ¶ 6] is an application of the doctrine of equivalents in a restrictive role, narrowing the application of broad literal claim elements. [Section 112, ¶ 6] was enacted as a targeted cure to a specific problem.... The added provision, however, is silent on the doctrine of equivalents as applied where there is no literal infringement.")

Section 112, ¶ 6 recites a mandatory procedure for interpreting the meaning of a means-or step-plus-function claim element. These claim limitations "shall be construed to cover the corresponding structure, material, or acts described in the specification and equivalents thereof." 35 U.S.C. § 112, ¶ 6. Thus, § 112, ¶ 6 procedures restrict a functional claim element's "broad literal language ... to those means that are 'equivalent' to the actual means shown in the patent specification." *Warner–Jenkinson*, 117 S.Ct. at 1048. Section 112, ¶ 6 restricts the scope of a functional claim limitation as part of a literal infringement analysis. See *Pennwalt Corp. v. Durand–Wayland, Inc.*, 833 F.2d 931, 934 (Fed. Cir.1987). Thus, an equivalent under § 112, ¶ 6 informs the claim meaning for a literal infringement analysis. The doctrine of equivalents, on the other hand, extends enforcement of claim terms beyond their literal reach in the event "there is 'equivalence' between the elements of the accused product or process and the claimed elements of the patented invention." *Warner–Jenkinson*, 117 S.Ct. at 1045.

One important difference between § 112, ¶ 6 and the doctrine of equivalents involves the timing of the separate analyses for an "insubstantial change." As this court has recently clarified, a structural equivalent under § 112 must have been available at the time of the issuance of the claim. See *Chiuminatta*, 145 F.3d at 1310. An equivalent structure or act under § 112 cannot embrace technology developed after the issuance of the patent because the literal meaning of a claim is fixed upon its issuance. An "after arising equivalent" infringes, if at all, under the doctrine of equivalents. See *Warner–Jenkinson*, 117 S.Ct. at 1052; *Hughes Aircraft Co. v. U.S.*, 140 F.3d 1470, 1475 (Fed.Cir.1998). Thus, the temporal difference between patent issuance and infringement distinguish an equivalent under § 112 from an equivalent under the doctrine of equivalents. In other words, an equivalent structure or act under § 112 for literal infringement must have been available at the time of patent issuance while an equivalent under the doctrine of equivalents may arise after patent issuance and before the time of infringement. An "after-arising" technology could thus infringe under the doctrine of equivalents without infringing literally as a § 112, ¶ 6 equivalent.[2] Furthermore, under § 112, ¶ 6, the accused device must

2. These principles, as explained in *Chiuminatta Concrete Concepts,* 145 F.3d 1303, (Fed.Cir.1998), suggest that title 35 will not produce an "equivalent of an equivalent" by applying both § 112, ¶ 6 and the doctrine of equivalents to the structure of a given claim element. A proposed equivalent must have arisen at a definite period in time, i.e., either before or after patent issuance. If before, a § 112, ¶ 6 structural equivalents analysis applies and any analysis for equivalent structure under the doctrine of equivalents collapses into the § 112, ¶ 6 analysis. If after, a non-textual infringement analysis proceeds under the doctrine of equivalents. Patent policy supports application of the doctrine of equivalents to a claim element expressed in

perform the identical function as recited in the claim element while the doctrine of equivalents may be satisfied when the function performed by the accused device is only substantially the same.

Although § 112, ¶ 6 and the doctrine of equivalents are different in purpose and administration, "a finding of a lack of literal infringement for lack of equivalent structure under a means-plus-function limitation may preclude a finding of equivalence under the doctrine of equivalents." *Chiuminatta*, 145 F.3d at 1311. Both equivalence analyses, after all, apply "similar analyses of insubstantiality of the differences." *Id.* This confluence occurs because infringement requires, either literally or under the doctrine of equivalents, that the accused product or process incorporate each limitation of the claimed invention. See *Warner–Jenkinson*, 117 S.Ct. at 1049; *Pennwalt*, 833 F.2d at 935. Therefore, if an accused product or process performs the identical function and yet avoids literal infringement for lack of a § 112, ¶ 6 structural equivalent, it may well fail to infringe the same functional element under the doctrine of equivalents. See *Chiuminatta*, 145 F.3d at 1311. This same reasoning may be applied in reverse in certain circumstances. Where, as here, there is identity of function and no after-arising technology, a means-plus-function claim element that is found to be infringed only under the doctrine of equivalents due to a jury instruction failing to instruct on § 112, ¶ 6 structural equivalents is also literally present in the accused device.

VSI's Version 2 hanger tag has a central body and two arms, with one arm extending from each side of the body. Each arm has a hole near the end for receipt of an eyeglasses temple. The body also has an aperture through which a cantilever rod can be placed so the hanger tag can be hung from a display rack. VSI's Version 2 hanger tag is the subject of U.S. Patent No. 5,141,104 (the '104 patent). Figure 4 of the '104 patent illustrates these features.

FIG. 4

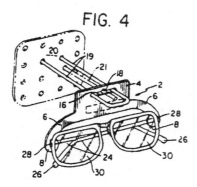

means-plus-function form in the case of "after-arising" technology because a patent draftsman has no way to anticipate and account for later developed substitutes for a claim element. Therefore, the doctrine of equivalents appropriately allows marginally broader coverage than § 112, ¶ 6.

As noted above, the doctrine of equivalents and structural equivalents under § 112, ¶ 6, though different in purpose and administration, can at times render the same result. In this case, the jury found infringement under the doctrine of equivalents. This finding presupposes that the jury found an equivalent for each element of the claimed invention, including the "means for securing." The holes in the arms of VSI's Version 2 hanger tag secure a portion of the eyeglasses frame (the temples) to the hanger member and therefore perform the identical function of the claim element in question. The jury was instructed that the "means for securing" disclosed in the '345 patent "is a mechanically fastened loop that . . . can be formed from a separate extension or integral extension and includes either the rivet fastener or the button and hole fastener." Based on this instruction, the jury found that the holes in the arms of the Version 2 hanger tag were equivalent to the mechanically fastened loop of the '345 patent under the doctrine of equivalents.

The parties do not dispute that the holes in the arms of the accused device perform a function identical to the extension of the patented device. Furthermore, the holes do not constitute an after-arising technology. Because the functions are identical and the holes are not an after-arising technology, the jury's finding of infringement under the doctrine of equivalents indicates that the jury found insubstantial structural differences between the holes in the arms of the Version 2 hanger tag and the loop of the '345 patent claim element. That finding is also sufficient to support the inference that the jury considered these to be structural equivalents under § 112, ¶ 6. For these reasons, any perceived error in the district court's jury instruction regarding the "means for securing" is, at most, harmless.

In sum, the district court erred by interpreting several of the claim elements in the '345, '726 and '911 patents as means-plus-function elements subject to § 112, ¶ 6. Because, properly construed, these claims do not call for interpretation under § 112, ¶ 6, the district court's reading unnecessarily limited their scope. This court has cautioned against incorporating unwarranted functional or structural limitations from the specification into the claims. *See Transmatic, Inc. v. Gulton Indus., Inc.*, 53 F.3d 1270, 1277 (Fed.Cir.1995). Despite the district court's unwarranted restriction of the claims, the jury found infringement under the doctrine of equivalents. Although a reasonable dispute as to the application of the correctly interpreted claims to the accused structure prevents a determination of literal infringement as a matter of law, because the jury found infringement under the trial court's more restricted reading of the claims, this court need not remand for an infringement determination according to this court's broader claim interpretation. Proceeding claim element by claim element, the jury has already found infringement. This court's correction of the claim scope does not disturb that determination.

Notes

1. **The Hypothetical Returns to Haunt.** Every patent teacher in the decades since the 1952 Act has probably taught the implications of

§ 112, ¶ 6 with the hypothetical "a fastening means." This case serves as warning to both teachers and students. Sometimes the banal examples of today form the crux of the ghastly litigation of tomorrow. Does this case follow the usual advice of the hypothetical? The "fastening means" described in the specification included only mechanical fasteners (rivets and buttons) yet the jury found that this means included a chemical fastener. How does the Federal Circuit reason that the jury was within its rights to include chemical fasteners within a term limited to mechanical fasteners?

2. When *Does "After Arising"* Technology Arise? The Federal Circuit takes considerable care to explain differences between the doctrine of equivalents and structural equivalents. Perhaps the most significant difference is the application to "after arising" technology. "[B]ecause the literal meaning of a claim is fixed upon its issuance," the Federal Circuit reasons, structural equivalents cannot embrace technology developed after patent issuance but only technology "insubstantially different" from technology described in the specification to perform the claimed function.

Technology arising after patent issuance infringes, if at all, under the doctrine of equivalents. Is patent issuance the proper place to draw this line? Because the meaning of words are fixed in claim at the filing date, *In re Hogan,* 559 F.2d 595 (CCPA 1977), would patent filing be a better cut-off date? Does it make any difference whether technology created between patent filing and patent issuance is analyzed for infringement under the doctrine of equivalents or under the structural equivalents principles? When considering this question, recall that the patent law looks backward when considering validity, but gazes forward when assessing infringement.

3. Step-plus-function. § 112, ¶ 6 expressly permits step-plus-function claims for processes. The Federal Circuit has only rarely addressed the legal requirements of such claims, however. In the case of *Seal-Flex, Inc. v. Athletic Track and Court Construction,* 172 F.3d 836, 50 U.S.P.Q.2d 1225 (Fed.Cir.1999), the claims included step-plus-function language. The appellate court declined to enunciate requirements for step-plus-function claims, but a concurrence by Judge Rader discussed the claim format at length. Judge Rader's concurrence stressed that "[t]he statute's format and language suggest a strong correlation between means and step-plus-function claim elements in both their identification and interpretation." Step-plus-function claims, however, present an additional problem, namely "[t]he difficulty of distinguishing acts from functions in step-plus-function claim elements." The concurrence offered some guidance on this question:

> This difficulty places a significant burden on the claim drafter to choose language with a definite and clear meaning. To invoke a presumption of § 112, ¶ 6 application, a claim drafter must use language that expressly signals the recitation of a function as distinguished from an act.
>
> As used in § 112, ¶ 6, "step" is the generic term for "acts" in the same sense that "means" is the generic term for "structure" and "material." The word "step," however, may introduce either an act or a function depending on context within the claim. Therefore, use of the word "step," by itself, does not invoke a presumption that § 112, ¶ 6 applies. For example, method claim elements may begin with the phrase

"steps of" without invoking application of § 112, ¶ 6. The phrase "steps of" colloquially signals the introduction of specific acts, rather than functions, and should therefore not presumptively invoke application of § 112, ¶ 6.

Unlike "of," the preposition "for" colloquially signals the recitation of a function. Accordingly, the phrase "step for" generally introduces functional claim language falling under § 112, ¶ 6. Thus, the phrase "step for" in a method claim raises a presumption that § 112, ¶ 6 applies. This presumption gives legal effect to the commonly understood meanings of "of"—introducing specific materials, structure or acts—and "for"——introducing a function.

The semantic distinction between the words "step of" and "step for" seems quite small. Is Judge Rader's guidance for § 112, ¶ 6 loading that distinction with too much significance? The PTO has recently drafted guidelines for functional claiming. The PTO guidelines follow at least some of the reasoning of the concurrence by stating that use of the term "step for" invokes a presumption that the claim drafter intended § 112, ¶ 6 coverage. In any event, the Federal Circuit in *Masco Corp. v. United States*, 303 F.3d 1316 (Fed.Cir.2002), followed Judge Rader's methodology in deciding whether certain claim limitations were step-plus-function limitations.

4. Recognizing a Functional Claim. As this case demonstrates, a means-plus-function claim invokes a very different method for interpretation. Claim language, however, can mix functional and structural elements and complicate the task of recognizing when to use § 112, ¶ 6. Although this case addresses the subject, a few more Federal Circuit cases might supply further guidance about classifying claim language as functional or structural. In interpreting a claim to a new conveyor belt technology, Chief Judge Nies wrote for the court:

> The recitation of some structure in a means plus function element does not preclude the applicability of section 112 (6). For example, in this case, the structural description in the joining means clause merely serves to further specify the function of that means. The recited structure tells only what the means-for-joining *does,* not what it *is* structurally.

Laitram Corp. v. Rexnord, Inc., 939 F.2d 1533, 1536, 19 U.S.P.Q.2d 1367, 1369 (Fed.Cir.1991). In another case, the Federal Circuit interpreted a claim to a liner for the bed of a pickup truck with ridges to lock a load in place:

> In determining whether to apply the statutory procedures of section 112, paragraph 6, the use of the word "means" triggers a presumption that the inventor used this term advisedly to invoke the statutory mandates for means-plus-function clauses.

* * *

> The claim language, however, does not link the term "means" to a function ... Without an identified function, the term "means" in this claim cannot invoke 35 U.S.C. section 112 (6). Without a "means" sufficiently connected to a recited function, the presumption in use of the word "means" does not operate. In any case, the structural limits of

the claim language limit its scope. Thus, this court construes this claim without reference to section 112, paragraph 6.

York Products Inc. v. Central Tractor Farm & Family Center, 99 F.3d 1568, 40 U.S.P.Q.2d 1619, 1623–24 (Fed.Cir.1996). *See also Greenberg v. Ethicon Endo–Surgery, Inc.*, 91 F.3d 1580, 1584, 39 U.S.P.Q.2d 1783, 1787 (Fed.Cir. 1996) ("[T]he use of the term 'means' has come to be so closely associated with 'means-plus-function' claiming that it is fair to say that the use of the term 'means' (particularly as used in the phrase 'means for') generally invokes section 112 (6) . . .").

The presumption discussed in *York* and *Greenberg*, however, seems to have additional limits. In a later case, the Federal Circuit construed a claim involving disposable diapers with sides that easily tear open to facilitate removal of the soiled brief. The claim term in question read: "perforation means extending from the leg band means to the waist band means through the outer impermeable layer means for tearing the outer impermeable layer means for removing the training brief in the case of an accident by the user...." The district court determined on summary judgment that a "perforation means" is merely a "perforation" and that the bonded tearable side seams on the accused briefs were not perforations. The Federal Circuit, declining to apply § 112 ¶ 6, agreed:

> The drafter of claim 1 in the '239 patent was clearly enamored of the word "means": six of seven elements in that claim include the word "means," which occurs in the claim fourteen times. We find, however, no reason to construe any of the claim language in claim 1 as reciting means-plus-function elements within the meaning of § 112, ¶ 6. For example, the "perforation means ... for tearing" element of Cole's claim fails to satisfy the statute because it describes the structure supporting the tearing function (i.e., perforations). The claim describes not only the structure that supports the tearing function, but also its location (extending from the leg band to the waist band) and extent (extending through the impermeable layer). An element with such a detailed recitation of its structure, as opposed to its function, cannot meet the requirements of the statute.

Cole v. Kimberly–Clark Corp., 102 F.3d 524, 531, 41 U.S.P.Q.2d 1001, 1006 (Fed.Cir.1996). A dissent in this case, relying on *Laitram* and *York*, noted: "the word 'perforation' [does not] provide enough structure to negate the import of the very next word–'means.'"102 F.3d at 533, 41 U.S.P.Q.2d at 1008. Is *Cole* consistent with *Laitram* and *York*?

Don't answer the last question too quickly. In *Laitram*, the Federal Circuit clarified that the claimed structure in that case operated primarily "to further specify the function," 939 F.2d at 1536, not to define a recognizable structure. The claimed structure informed the court of what the means "does, not what it is structurally." *Id*. Moreover the Federal Circuit did not say that the presence of structure in a claim is irrelevant to use of section 112 (6). Instead it said "some structure" would not preclude application of section 112 (6). *Id*. at 1536. In *Cole*, the court expressly noted the "detailed recitation" of structure. Moreover, can *Cole* be read to mean that definite and complete structure in the claim can overcome the presumption alluded to in *York*? In any event, *Cole* seems to raise the inevitable question, how much structure removes a claim with the word "means" from § 112 ¶ 6 treatment? How much structure is too much? What guidance would you give claim drafters about means-plus-function claiming? As a matter of policy, is the patent system better served by a rule that invariably requires structure in the specification whenever an inventor uses the words "means for"?

§ 11.2[d]   Jepson Claims

A "Jepson claim" defines an invention in two parts: a preamble which recites the admitted prior art, followed by an "improvement" clause which recites what the applicant regards as his invention. The consequences of use of this claim format are significant. The next opinion, among the last issued by the Court of Customs and Patent Appeals before formation of the Federal Circuit, examines the implications of Jepson claims.

IN RE FOUT

United States Court of Customs and Patent Appeals, 1982.
675 F.2d 297, 213 U.S.P.Q. 532.

Before MARKEY, CHIEF JUDGE, and RICH, BALDWIN, MILLER, and NIES, ASSOCIATE JUDGES.

MILLER, JUDGE.

This is an appeal from the decision of the Patent and Trademark Office ("PTO") Board of Appeals ("board") holding claims 1–20 in appellants' application obvious under 35 USC 103. We affirm.

BACKGROUND

The Invention

Appellants claim an improvement over the process of Pagliaro et al. ("Pagliaro") which was the subject of our decision in *In re Pagliaro* 657 F.2d 1219, 210 U.S.P.Q. 888 (CCPA 1981). The Pagliaro process is a method for producing a decaffeinated vegetable material such as coffee or tea. A fatty material is used to extract caffeine from the vegetable material. The caffeine-laden fatty material is separated from the vegetable material and may be regenerated by contacting it with water, which reduces its caffeine content. The resultant aqueous solution may then be treated to recover caffeine. The Pagliaro process, minus the regeneration step, is set forth in the preamble of appellants' Jepson-format claims. Appellants describe and claim their invention as an improvement over the Pagliaro process which comprises regenerating the fatty material by evaporative distillation instead of aqueous extraction. Claim 1 is representative:

> *In a process* for producing a decaffeinated vegetable material suitable for consumption in beverage form wherein caffeine-containing vegetable material is extracted with a volume of recirculating liquid, water-immiscible edible fatty material in a decaffeination

zone for a period of time sufficient to transfer caffeine from said vegetable material into said fatty material, and wherein the caffeine-laden fatty material resultant from extraction is separated from said vegetable material and is conveyed to a regeneration zone for removal of caffeine prior to recirculation to said decaffeination zone, *the improvement which comprises* subjecting the caffeine-laden fatty material in said zone to regenerative vaporization conditions such as to vaporize caffeine from said fatty material and further to vaporize from said fatty material any fatty material degradation products present therein. [Emphasis added.]

Dependent claims 2–6, 8–10, 12–14, 19, and 20 contain various limitations that specify fatty material, vegetable material, time, and temperature and that the caffeine be evaporated from a thin film of fatty material. Claims 7, 11, 15, and 16 specify that a carrier gas be passed over the fatty material to increase the rate of removal of caffeine. Claims 17 and 18 specify the moisture content of the coffee beans.

The References

Waterman et al. ("Waterman"), U.S. patent No. 2,129,596, teaches suspending solid material in vegetable oil, then subjecting the material to evaporative distillation. Evaporative distillation is accomplished by heating the oil-solid mixture in a vacuum. The mixture may be in the form of a film. The reference states: "Solid alkaloids usually regarded as non-volatile, such as caffeine may be recovered in pure form under the present invention, avoiding the usual more tedious physical and chemical processes. Fine ground tea or coffee is suspended in oil and transmitted through the still, the alkaloids distilling over and being condensed."

Barch, U.S. patent No. 2,817,588, teaches a decaffeination process in which caffeine is removed from a solvent by evaporating the solvent, which is then recirculated.

The Rejection

The examiner maintained that because the preamble of the claims is in Jepson format, it sets forth "that which is known." Claims 1–6, 8–10, 12–14, 19, and 20 were rejected on the preamble in view of Barch and Waterman.

The Board's Decision

The board affirmed the examiner's rejections and adopted his reasoning as its own. As to whether the preamble portion of the claims was available as prior art, the board stated:

The essence of appellants' position appears to be that the process steps set forth in the preamble portion of claim 1 may not in any way be used as prior art against the presently claimed subject matter, since such steps were not patented or described in a printed publication in this or a foreign country, nor were they publicly known or practiced in this country, more than one year prior to the effective filing date of this application. Appellants' contentions are without merit.

It is well established that the use of Jepson format is, in effect, an admission by appellants that the process steps recited in the preamble are known in the art, leaving for consideration whether the recitation following the improvement clause imparts patentability to the claims. Moreover, appellants readily acknowledge that they did not invent the process of decaffeinating a vegetable material with an edible fatty material, which process is summarized in the preamble of claim 1, note page 2, last three lines of the Reply Brief. In view of the foregoing admission, the steps set forth in the preamble of claim 1 may be considered prior art for any purpose, including as evidence of obviousness under 35 USC § 103. Appellants have conceded what is to be considered as prior art in determining the obviousness of their improvement.

Issues

The issues presented are: (1) whether the Pagliaro invention, set forth in the preamble, constitutes "prior art" under 35 USC 103, and (2) if so, whether the subject matter claimed would have been obvious to a person of ordinary skill in the art at the time the invention was made in view of that prior art and the references of record.

OPINION

1. The Pagliaro Invention

The Solicitor contends that appellants' use of the Jepson format preamble in claim 1 constitutes an admission that the Pagliaro process described in the preamble is prior art to them. Appellants do not dispute that the Pagliaro process was prior to their invention and that they had knowledge of it before making their invention. That process is what was before us in the 1981 Pagliaro case, supra, and appellants specifically refer to the applications describing it in the application now before us. They then describe the presently claimed invention as "an improved means for regenerating used fatty material employed in the decaffeination of vegetable materials." That improved means is then stated to be "removing the caffeine by vaporization." In other words, they have invented an improvement on the last step of the Pagliaro process, the removal from the fatty material of the caffeine, and, coincidentally, any degradation products which may be present. Appellants' brief concedes:

The board's opinion stated (correctly, we emphasize), "appellants readily acknowledge that they did not invent the process of decaffeinating a vegetable material with an edible fatty material, which process is summarized in the preamble of claim 1."

What appellants argue is that the above concession is not an admission that said decaffeination process is "legally available as prior art against the claims," and that the PTO's position is in conflict with the decision of this court in *In re Ehrreich*, 590 F.2d 902, 200 U.S.P.Q. 504 (CCPA 1979). Thus, the first issue is raised.

The way appellants state the issue is: "The preamble of appellants' own claims cannot properly be used as a reference against them." However, more is involved than the claim preamble. Claims must always be read in the light of the specification. Here, the specification makes plain what appellants did and did not invent, as we have noted above, and the claims, taken as a whole, are entirely consistent therewith. Appellants in their brief concede what they did not invent, leaving only the question of law—whether we can use the Pagliaro invention described in the preamble as "prior art" under section 103.

This court has recognized that section 102 is not the only source of section 103 prior art. Valid prior art may be created by the admissions of the parties. Nor is it disputed that certain art may be prior art to one inventive entity, but not to the public in general.

We hold that appellants' admission that they had actual knowledge of the prior Pagliaro invention described in the preamble constitutes an admission that it is prior art to them. The Pagliaro process was appellants' acknowledged point of departure, and the implied admission that the Jepson format preamble of claim 1 describes prior art has not been overcome. It is not unfair or contrary to the policy of the patent system that appellants' invention be judged on obviousness against their actual contribution to the art.

2. *Obviousness*

[The court held that in view of the cited references, the claimed invention would have been obvious to one of ordinary skill in the art.]

The decision of the board is affirmed.

Notes

1. Rebutting the Presumption. An early case from the United States Court of Appeals for the Federal Circuit, *Reading & Bates Construction Co. v. Baker Energy Resources Corp.*, 748 F.2d 645, 223 U.S.P.Q. 1168, 1172 (Fed.Cir.1984), held that the presumption of prior art status of preamble recitations may be rebutted. In a case involving the preamble's recitation of the inventor's prior invention, the court noted that no statutory basis existed for treating the preamble's recitation as prior art. "[W]here an inventor continues to improve upon his own work product, his foundational work product should not, without a statutory basis, be treated as prior art solely because he admits knowledge of *his own work*." *Fout* was distinguished because, in that case, "the Pagliaro process, claimed in a co-pending application by a different inventive entity, was prior art to their invention and that they had knowledge of it before making their invention."

2. Patent Examiners and Jepson Claims. Jepson claims are highly favored by many Examiners for the obvious reason that their job is greatly simplified by the instant admission of prior art status for everything in the claim but the "improvement" clause. Consider the two following claims to the same invention, where the inventor has a combination of elements A, B and C, and his "main" feature resides in new species C':

    1.   The combination of elements A, B and C'.

    2.   In the combination of elements A, B and C, the improvement which comprises use of C' as the element C.

In the first claim, the Examiner must show that the combination of A, B and C' is obvious in light of prior art. This entails a prior art search on each of the three elements and a showing of motivation to combine them. With a Jepson claim, however, the Examiner starts the "given" that the combination $A + B + C$ is old, admittedly so by the use of Jepson terminology. Then the only task remaining is to show that the use of C' is obvious in place of C generally.

Contemporary patent drafters generally consider the Jepson claim to be a very poor form of claim draftsmanship because the form itself constitutes an *admission* that everything in the preamble is prior art. Nonetheless, their use in the patents involved in such cases as *Warner–Jenkinson*, reprinted here in Chapter 15, is a tribute to their enduring character.

§ 11.2[e] Markush Groups

"Markush" claims are common only in chemical practice. A proper Markush claim is a generic claim which defines a family of compounds by showing the common structural nucleus for all members of that family, with the variable substituent being defined by an "R" (or other letter) to represent the various alternatives. Traditionally, a Markush group is proper when it applies to products with at least one common utility. When defining a family of chemical compounds with Markush terminology, clarity within a claim often requires a vast amount of verbiage that stretches the length of the claim into an indigestible chunk. Thus, an applicant can present a generic claim that runs for pages, rather than recognizing that the critical novelty of the entire group of generic compounds is one particular shared feature. Students should also bear in mind that a document that discloses a large Markush group may later serve as prior art against a sub-genus or even one compound that a later inventor is claiming is a selection invention raising the question of when a genus invention should anticipate or render obvious a compound within the genus.

The term "Markush" has become internationally accepted as describing this sort of claim. The GUIDELINES FOR EXAMINATION IN THE EUROPEAN PATENT OFFICE, Part C, Chapter II, Paragraph 7.4a (Dec. 1994) provide:

> Where a single claim defines (chemical or non-chemical) alternatives, i.e., a so-called "Markush grouping", unity of invention should be considered to be present when the alternatives are of a similar nature.

When the Markush grouping is for alternatives of chemical compounds, they should be regarded as being of a similar nature where:

(i) all alternatives have a common property or activity, and

(ii) a common structure is present, i.e., a significant structural element is shared by all of the alternatives, or all alternatives belong to a recognized class of chemical compounds in the art to which the invention pertains.

The Japanese Patent Office employs a similar standard. EXAMINATION GUIDELINES FOR PATENT AND UTILITY MODEL IN JAPAN, Part I at 4 (AIPPI 1994).

Those with a bent for history should know that the Markush group is an invention of nineteenth century German dyestuff chemists who would use the "R" ("Rest") or "X" letter to tabulate a series of compounds where the only variable was in the particular *Rest* or group. German *Patentanwälte* borrowed this terminology for German patents which, when translated and filed in the United States, entered American practice. Controversy arose when, decades later, the hapless Mr. Markush had to petition to have the practice continued in *Ex parte Markush*, 1925 C.D. 126. Examples of Markush patents are U.S. patents 623,638 (1899), 599,425 (1898), and 603,659 (1898), discussed in Harold C. Wegner, *The Right to Generic Chemical Coverage*, 6 AM. INTEL. PROP. L. ASS'N. Q. J. 257, 262–63 (1978).

§ 11.3 CLAIM DEFINITENESS

Because of the importance of claims, the second paragraph of § 112 requires the patent instrument to close with claims "particularly pointing out and distinctly claiming the subject matter which the applicant regards as his invention." "Distinctly" means that the claim must give a clear definition of the scope of the invention when construed in light of the entire patent document. This requirement ensures that patentees have staked well-marked boundaries around their technological property rights. These boundaries, in turn, provide competitors notice of which technologies are proprietary and which are available for exploitation. Thus, this requirement sets a standard for claim adequacy.

§ 11.3[a]   Claim Definiteness

ORTHOKINETICS, INC. v. SAFETY TRAVEL CHAIRS, INC.

United States Court of Appeals, Federal Circuit, 1986.
806 F.2d 1565, 1 U.S.P.Q.2d 1081.

JUDGES: MARKEY, CHIEF JUDGE, NEWMAN, CIRCUIT JUDGE, and SWYGERT, SENIOR CIRCUIT JUDGE.

MARKEY, CHIEF JUDGE.

Orthokinetics, Inc. (Orthokinetics) appeals from orders granting a judgment notwithstanding the verdict (JNOV) holding that claims 1–5 of its U.S. Patent Re. 30,867 ('867 patent) are invalid under 35 U.S.C. § 112. We reverse and remand with instructions to reinstate the jury verdicts.

BACKGROUND

I.   The Claimed Inventions

Orthokinetics manufactures products for invalids and handicapped individuals, including pediatric wheelchairs. It is the assignee of the '586 patent issued to Raymond A. Kazik (Kazik) on June 11, 1974, entitled "Orthopedic Chair With Scoliosis Pads" and of the '867 patent reissued to Edward J. Gaffney (Gaffney) on February 16, 1982, entitled "Travel Chair".

The '867 reissue patent discloses a collapsible pediatric wheelchair which facilitates the placing of wheelchair-bound persons, particularly children, in and out of an automobile. Orthokinetics asserted infringement of claims 1 through 5 by Safety. Claim 1 reads:

> 1.   In a wheel chair having a seat portion, a front leg portion, and a rear wheel assembly, the improvement wherein said front leg portion is so dimensioned as to be insertable through the space between the doorframe of an automobile and one of the seats thereof whereby said front leg is placed in support relation to the automobile and will support the seat portion from the automobile in the course of subsequent movement of the wheel chair into the automobile, and the retractor means for assisting the attendant in retracting said rear wheel assembly upwardly independently of any change in the position of the front leg portion with respect to the seat portion while the front leg portion is supported on the automobile and to a position which clears the space beneath the rear end of the chair and permits the chair seat portion and retracted rear wheel assembly to be swung over and set upon said automobile seat.

II.   Procedural History

Orthokinetics introduced the Travel Chair to the market in November of 1973. In 1978, Safety Travel Chairs, Inc. (STC) began to sell similar chairs manufactured by Entron, Inc. (Entron).

OPINION

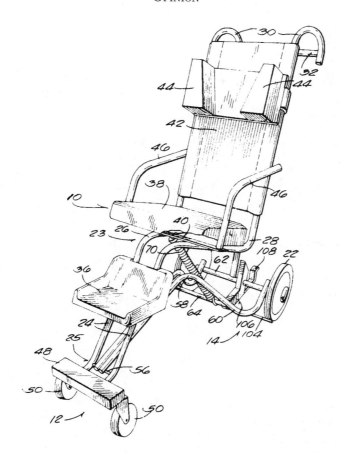

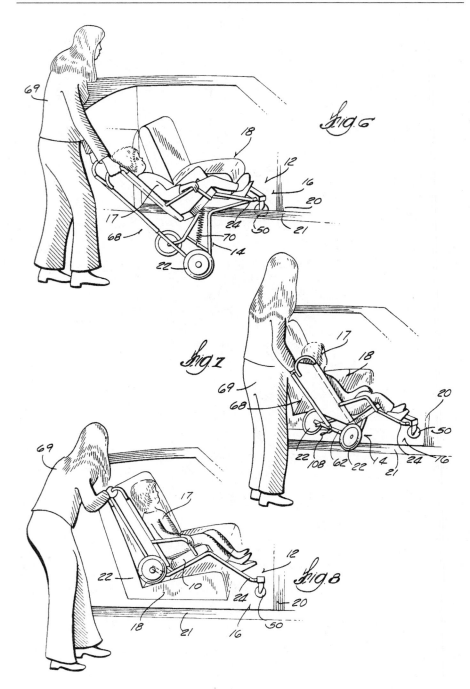

The jury found (question No. 51) that Safety failed to prove by clear and convincing evidence that the '867 patent was invalid because of claim language that does not particularly point out and distinctly claim the invention. 35 U.S.C. § 112, 2d ¶. The district court determined otherwise and granted Safety's motion for JNOV.

Claim 1, from which the rest of the claims depend, contains the limitation: "wherein said front leg portion is so dimensioned as to be insertable through the space between the doorframe of an automobile and one of the seats thereof."

Noting the testimony of Orthokinetics' expert, Mr. Hobbs, who said the dimensions of the front legs depend upon the automobile the chair is designed to suit, the district court stated:

> In response to this testimony, which clearly and convincingly establishes that claim 1 of the patent does not describe the invention in "full, clear, concise and exact terms," Orthokinetics points only to the conclusory statements of Hobbs, Gaffney and expert witness William McCoy, Jr., that the patent is, in fact definite. These conclusory statements are not an adequate basis for the jury to reject Safety's defense. The undisputed, specific testimony of Gaffney and Hobbs demonstrates that an individual desiring to build a noninfringing travel chair cannot tell whether that chair violates the ['867] patent until he constructs a model and tests the model on vehicles ranging from a Honda Civic to a Lincoln Continental to a Checker cab. Without those cars, "so dimensioned" is without meaning.

The foregoing statement employs two measures impermissible in law: (1) it requires that claim 1 "describe" the invention, which is the role of the disclosure portion of the specification, not the role of the claims; and (2) it applied the "full, clear, concise, and exact" requirement of the first paragraph of § 112 to the claim, when that paragraph applies only to the disclosure portion of the specification, not to the claims. The district court spoke, inappropriately, of indefiniteness of the "patent," and did not review the claim for indefiniteness under the second paragraph of § 112.

A decision on whether a claim is invalid under § 112, 2d para., requires a determination of whether those skilled in the art would understand what is claimed when the claim is read in light of the specification.

It is undisputed that the claims require that one desiring to build and use a travel chair must measure the space between the selected automobile's doorframe and its seat and then dimension the front legs of the travel chair so they will fit in that particular space in that particular automobile. Orthokinetics' witnesses, who were skilled in the art, testified that such a task is evident from the specification and that one of ordinary skill in the art would easily have been able to determine the appropriate dimensions. The jury had the right to credit that testimony and no reason exists for the district court to have simply discounted that testimony as "conclusory".

The claims were intended to cover the use of the invention with various types of automobiles. That a particular chair on which the claims read may fit within some automobiles and not others is of no moment. The phrase "so dimensioned" is as accurate as the subject matter permits, automobiles being of various sizes. As long as those of ordinary skill in the art realized that the dimensions could be easily obtained, § 112, 2d ¶ requires nothing more. The patent law does not require that all possible lengths corresponding to the spaces in hundreds of different automobiles be listed in the patent, let alone that they be listed in the claims.

Compliance with the second paragraph of § 112 is generally a question of law. On the record before us, we observe no failure of compliance with the statute, and thus no basis on § 112 grounds for disturbing the jury's verdict. The district court's grant of Safety's motion for JNOV for claim indefiniteness was in error and must be reversed.

Notes

1. Definiteness Established by the Subject Matter. "The degree of precision necessary for adequate claims is a function of the nature of the subject matter." *Miles Laboratories, Inc. v. Shandon Inc.*, 997 F.2d 870, 875 (Fed.Cir.1993). If a skilled artisan would find the claim language sufficiently distinct to understand its meaning, then even claim limitations such as "close proximity" will be considered "as precise as the subject matter permits." *Rosemount, Inc. v. Beckman Instruments, Inc.*, 727 F.2d 1540, 1547, 221 U.S.P.Q. 1, 7 (Fed.Cir.1984).

2. Weasel Words. Perplexing issues of definiteness often arise when patent claims employ words of degree, such as "about," "approximately," "close to," "substantially equal," or "closely approximate." The Federal Circuit has noted that these terms "are ubiquitous in patent claims. Such usages, when serving reasonably to describe the claimed subject matter to those of skill in the field of the invention, and to distinguish the claimed subject matter from the prior art, have been accepted in patent examination and upheld by the courts." *Andrew Corp. v. Gabriel Electronics*, 847 F.2d 819, 6 U.S.P.Q.2d 2010 (Fed.Cir.1988). According to *Seattle Box Co. v. Industrial Crating & Packing Inc.*, 731 F.2d 818, 221 U.S.P.Q. 568 (Fed.Cir. 1984), "[w]hen a word of degree is used the district court must determine whether the patent's specification provides some standard for measuring that degree. The trial court must decide, that is, whether one of ordinary skill in the art would understand what is claimed when the claim is read in light of the specification."

Although it is fair to say that the Federal Circuit has been fairly accepting of the use of such words of approximation, in some cases the court has held that such terms violate § 112 ¶ 2. In *Amgen, Inc. v. Chugai Pharmaceutical Co.*, 927 F.2d 1200, 18 U.S.P.Q.2d 1016 (Fed.Cir.1991), the court considered U.S. Patent 4,677,195, entitled "Method for the Purification of Erythropoietin and Erythropoietin Compositions." The patent claims both homogeneous EPO and compositions thereof and a method for purifying human EPO using reverse phase high performance liquid chromatography. Claim 4 of the '195 patent provided:

4. Homogeneous erythropoietin characterized by a molecular weight of about 34,000 daltons on SDS PAGE, movement as a single peak on reverse phase high performance liquid chromatography and a specific activity of at least about 160,000 IU per absorbance unit at 280 nanometers.

The district court had earlier held that "bioassays provide an imprecise form of measurement with a range of error" and that use of the term "about" 160,000 IU/AU, coupled with the range of error already inherent in the specific activity limitation, served neither to distinguish the invention over the close prior art (which described preparations of 120,000 IU/AU), nor to permit one to know what specific activity values below 160,000 might constitute infringement. On appeal, the Federal Circuit affirmed the holding of the district court that the specific activity limitation of "at least about 160,000" was indefinite, reasoning:

> The court found the "addition of the word 'about' seems to constitute an effort to recapture ... a mean activity somewhere between 120,000, which the patent examiner found was anticipated by the prior art, and [the] 160,000 IU/AU" claims which were previously allowed. Because "the term 'about' 160,000 gives no hint as to which mean value between the Miyake et al. value of 128,620 and the mean specific activity level of 160,000 constitutes infringement," the court held the "at least about" claims to be invalid for indefiniteness. This holding was further supported by the fact that nothing in the specification, prosecution history, or prior art provides any indication as to what range of specific activity is covered by the term "about," and by the fact that no expert testified as to a definite meaning for the term in the context of the prior art. In his testimony, Fritsch tried to define "about" 160,000, but he could only say that while "somewhere between 155[,000] might fit within that number," he had not "given a lot of direct considerations to that...."

The court hastened to add that: "In arriving at this conclusion, we caution that our holding that the term "about" renders indefinite [claim 4] should not be understood as ruling out any and all uses of this term in patent claims. It may be acceptable in appropriate fact situations, e.g., W.L. Gore & Assocs., Inc. v. Garlock, Inc., 721 F.2d 1540, 1557, 220 U.S.P.Q. 303, 316 (Fed.Cir.1983) ("use of 'stretching ... at a rate exceeding about 10% per second' in the claims is not indefinite"), even though it is not here."

3. Whereby Clauses. A discussion earlier in this Chapter discussed the effect of the preamble upon the scope of a patent claim. Similarly perplexing is the drafter's use of "whereby" clauses, an example of which may be found in claim 1 of the United States Patent No. 4,081,879, set forth in the *Chemcast* case. 913 F.2d 923 (Fed.Cir.1990). Although the use of a "whereby" or similar clauses may appear as an admirable attempt to further delimit the claimed invention in keeping with § 112 ¶ 2, the extent to which such clauses actually limit the scope of the claimed invention often presents difficult issues. In *Texas Instruments Inc. v. United States International Trade Commission*, 988 F.2d 1165, 26 U.S.P.Q.2d 1018 (Fed.Cir.1993), the court considered claims directed towards a process for encapsulating electronic components in plastic through a process called transfer molding. The court discussed the asserted claims and effect of "whereby" clauses as follows:

> Claim 12 concludes with a clause that states "whereby the fluid will not directly engage the device and electrical connection means at high velocity, and the conductors will be secured against appreciable displacement by the fluid." Claims 14 and 17 conclude with the clause "to preclude direct high velocity engagement between the fluid and the device and the electrical connections thereto." The Commission determined that the "whereby" clause in claim 12 and the "to preclude" clauses in claims 14 and 17 only express the necessary results of what is recited in the claims. For this reason, the Commission gave them no weight in its infringement analysis.

> Respondents assert that the "whereby/to preclude" clauses of these claims establish specific further limitations to the claims relating to the velocity of the fluid inside the mold and the manner of securing the conductors which must be met in the respondents' opposite-side gating processes in order for those processes to infringe the claims of the '027 patent. We disagree. A "whereby" clause that merely states the result of the limitations in the claim adds nothing to the patentability or substance of the claim. Israel v. Cresswell, 166 F.2d 153, 156, 35 C.C.P.A. 890, 76 U.S.P.Q. 594, 597 (1948). The "whereby/to preclude" clauses of claims 12, 14 and 17 merely describe the result of arranging the components of the claims in the manner recited in the claims: the fluid does not directly engage the device and the electrical connection means because the gate through which the fluid enters is remote from them; the conductors are secured against appreciable displacement by the fluid because they are clamped in notches by the upper and lower halves of the mold die. Therefore, the Commission correctly determined that the "whereby/to preclude" clauses do not contain any limitations not inherent to the process found in claims 12, 14 and 17.

The use of whereby clauses is somewhat more popular in the Commonwealth, although many applications of domestic origin also employ such clauses. Why would a drafter wish to employ a "whereby" clause in lieu of: (1) putting the language in the preamble; (2) employing a means-plus-function claim under § 112 ¶ 6; or (3) not including a particular result in the patent claim at all?

4. Claiming Requirements Abroad. Article 84 of the European Patent Convention mandates that claims "shall define the matter for which protection is sought. They shall be clear and concise and be supported by the specification." Section 35(5) of the Japanese patent statute requires that the claims contain "all matters which an applicant for a patent considers necessary in defining an invention for which a patent is sought." Section 35(6) of the Japanese statute goes on to mandate that the claims must be clear, concise and directed towards an invention that is described in the specification.

5. Claiming Criticized. To some, claim drafting is a rigid, formalistic art that erects considerable barriers against the accurate description of technological inventions. Formalized drafting conventions, such as the single sentence rule; the limited number of claim formats; and the evolution of settled meanings of claim terms such as "integral" or "grooved" as a result of decades of judicial and administrative interpretation, render claim drafting a needlessly complex undertaking. *See* John R. Thomas, *The Question Concerning Patent Law and Pioneer Inventions*, 10 HIGH TECH. L. J. 35, 53–55 (1995). Would you propose any changes to the current scheme of patent claiming? Alternatively, what other means of establishing boundaries to an applicant's technological properties could be established?

6. Further Reading. Additional sources on the significant body of law that surrounds patent claims include ROBERT C. FABER, LANDIS ON MECHANICS OF PATENT CLAIM DRAFTING (4th ed. 1999); ANTHONY W. DELLER, PATENT CLAIMS (2d ed. 1971); EMERSON STRINGHAM, PATENT CLAIM DRAFTING (2d ed. 1952); and RISDALE ELLIS, PATENT CLAIMS (1949).

Claim Drafting Exercises

Note

The PTO Registration Examination. The United States Patent and Trademark Office requires individuals to pass a Registration Examination for Patent Practitioners in order to practice before the PTO in patent matters. Although one need not be admitted to a state bar to sit for the Registration Examination, the PTO requires individuals to have obtained certain technical or scientific credentials. You can find the latest information on the "patent bar" examination at www.uspto.gov.

Exercise One. Your desktop is constantly cluttered with computer equipment, papers and other office supplies. Because you often like to drink a beverage while working at your desk, you frequently place a can of soda on what is often the only free space available, your computer mouse pad. In this way, you avoid leaving water marks on your desktop. But you have found this solution less than satisfactory: condensation from the can often leaves water on the mouse pad, damaging your mouse, and the cord that connects the mouse to the computer sometimes knocks the can over.

One day, you arrive at a solution. By attaching a coaster to the mouse pad made of foam material, you find that the soda can is always readily within your grasp. Because the lower surface of the mouse pad has a high coefficient of friction, the attached coaster is far more stable than a free-standing coaster. The upper surface of the mouse pad has a relatively low coefficient of friction, allowing ready movement of the mouse. Because the coaster is so effective at preventing spills and capturing condensation, you decide to seek patent protection on your invention.

You perform a search of the prior art and discover that an earlier patent, granted to one Lee, described the concept of a child's table mat including a beverage holder. Lee's table mat is constructed of a hard plastic material, however. Further, Lee does not describe the use of a computer mouse, nor does it disclose the use of different coefficients of friction on the different surfaces of the mat.

You also decide to expand upon your invention by attaching a pencil holder to the mouse pad as well. The pencil holder consists simply of a base with four sockets. It is fashioned from a material of sturdier construction than the foam mouse pad. Each socket is sized such that inserted pencils are snugly held.

Draft three claims to the mouse pad with beverage holder. Claim 1 should be directed towards the combination of mouse pad and coaster. Claim 2 should depend from claim 1 and include the concept of differing frictional surfaces. Claim 3 should depend from claim 2 and add the pencil holder feature. When drafting the claims, attempt to use the most broad and general language that you can to describe the features of the invention, yet distinguish over the Lee reference.

Exercise Two. The invention illustrated and described below is directed towards a three ring loose-leaf album. Figure 1 shows an end view with the album in the closed position. Figure 2 depicts a view of the exterior surface of the album in the open position.

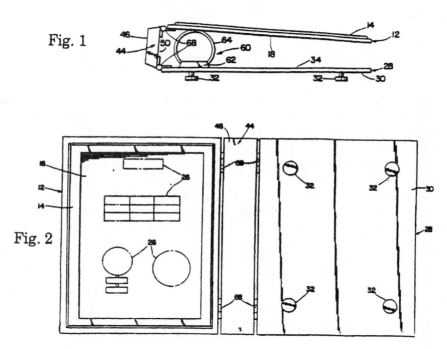

The album includes top 12 and bottom 38 covers; spine 44; exterior surfaces 14, 30 and 46; interior surfaces 18, 34, and 50; a ring assembly 60 including base 62 and three rings 64 equally spaced along the base; feet 32; four hinges 68; recessed exterior surface portion 16; and indicia 26.

One feature of the invention is a recessed portion 16 in the exterior surface 14 of the top cover 12 wherein personalized indicia 26 are positioned. An important feature of the invention is the presence of a hardened polymer resin which has been poured into the recess to bond the indicia in place. The hardened polymer resin is clear to permit the indicia to be visible. Another feature is the four projecting feet 32 on the back cover. Although not specifically illustrated, the feet may be decorative, e.g., ball and claw, as in the instance when the top and bottom covers and the spine are made of wood. Whether or not the feet or decorative, they permit the album to be displayed in a fashion similar to furniture.

Another important feature of the invention is the arrangement of hinges 68 so that there is a minimal external exposure of the hinges and so as not to detract from the decorative aspects of the album when cover 12 and 28 are in a closed position as shown in Figure 1. When opened, the top cover exposes a three ring loose-leaf assembly of a base 62 and three rings 64, equally spaced along the base.

Draft a single claim to a three ring loose-leaf album as described above and shown in Figures 1 and 2. Your claim must include and interrelate at least the following elements: the hardened polymer resin; top and bottom covers 12 and 28; spine 44; hinges 68; interior surfaces 18, 34 and 50; base 62 and rings 64; feet 32; exterior surfaces 14, 30, and 46; recess 16; and indicia 26.

Chapter Twelve

PROSECUTION

Prosecution refers to the administrative process for acquisition of a patent. Easily the largest portion of work performed by patent practitioners, it is also the task assigned to most entry-level patent lawyers. Even those engaged exclusively in patent litigation need to be thoroughly apprised of the events at the U.S. Patent and Trademark Office that led to the grant of any patent in suit. Attorneys not engaged in patent law may also find themselves more frequently approached by inventors seeking a patent than by patent proprietors who wish to enforce their intellectual property rights. For all these reasons, some review of patent prosecution itself should accompany even the most basic review of the patent law.

A topic conveniently taken up alongside prosecution is that of inventorship. As we have seen, prior art under § 102 must be the work of someone other than the inventor. The identification of the appropriate individuals as inventors is thus a significant preliminary step in the acquisition of patent rights in the United States. Although the patent statute demonstrates a liberal approach towards the naming of inventors in a given application, it is insistent that they ultimately be correctly named. These issues are taken up in § 12.2 of this Chapter.

The remaining two sections of this Chapter consider the law relating to applicant abuses of the patent acquisition system. The first of these abuses is inequitable conduct, defined as failure to disclose material information, or submission of false material information, to the PTO with an intent to deceive. Because the prosecution process is *ex parte*, the PTO relies to a great extent upon applicant observance of a duty of candor. Patent law recognizes, however, that applicants may be tempted not to disclose information that might jeopardize the patentability of an application. Thus, inequitable conduct—the intentional refusal to disclose material prior art—brings a severe penalty: courts will refuse to enforce the issued patent.

A second applicant abuse of the patent acquisition process relates to double patenting. The patent system envisions the issuance of only a single patent per invention. Otherwise, a patentee might extend the statutory period of exclusivity by filing a series of related patent applications directed towards the same invention. The need for this doctrine in light of the statutory definition of prior art, as well as the thorny problem of obviousness-type double patenting, are considered at the close of the Chapter.

§ 12.1 OVERVIEW OF PATENT PROSECUTION

§ 12.1[a] Prosecution in the United States

As befits one of the more venerable governmental agencies in the United States, the PTO has established an elaborate administrative practice. This casebook can present only an overview of this specialized field of law. Further details on patent prosecution may be found in two primary sources: The Rules of Practice in Patent Cases, housed in Title 37 of the Code of Federal Regulations, and the MANUAL OF PATENT EXAMINING PROCEDURE (MPEP). The latter, an imposing volume relied upon by examiners and members of the patent bar alike, provides detailed rules and regulations on which the public can rely. The MPEP is promulgated by the PTO and therefore does not bind the courts. *See, e.g., In re Recreative Technologies*, 83 F.3d 1394, 38 U.S.P.Q.2d 1776 (Fed.Cir.1996).

A threshold issue concerning patent prosecution is the identity of the individual preparing and pursuing the application. Although any inventor is free to prosecute his own application, the vast majority choose to seek the assistance of a professional representative. Patent acquisition thus ordinarily begins with a discussion between a patent attorney and the inventor, from which the attorney obtains a full description of the invention. Usually, the attorney will arrange for a search of the prior art to determine whether an existing patent or printed publication bears upon the novelty or nonobviousness of the disclosed invention. With this prior art in hand, the attorney can assist the inventor or his assignee in determining whether a patent application should be filed or not. If the decision is made to go forward, the patent attorney then initiates patent prosecution with the filing of a patent application to the Commissioner of the United States Patent and Trademark Office. 35 U.S.C.A. § 111 offers the applicant two choices: nonprovisional applications under § 111(a), or provisional applications under § 111(b).

Provisional applications present simplified requirements in comparison with nonprovisional applications. Most noticeably, the provisional application need not include patent claims. The PTO does not examine these applications and will consider the applicant to have abandoned them after 12 months. Their primary importance lies in the entitlement of nonprovisional applications to the benefit of the filing date of earlier provisional applications to the same invention. In a sense, then, an applicant may subsequently perfect a provisional application by later filing an nonprovisional application without loss of the earlier filing date.

Importantly, the pendency of a provisional application does not subtract from the twenty-year term of any subsequent nonprovisional application that matures into an issued patent.

In contrast, nonprovisional applications filed under § 111(a) will be examined as quickly as an examiner is able to turn to the task. 35 U.S.C. § 131 authorizes the Commissioner to order the examination of an ordinary application by providing simply:

Examination of Application

> The Commissioner shall cause an examination to be made of the application and the alleged new invention; and if on such examination it appears that the applicant is entitled to a patent under the law, the Commissioner shall issue a patent therefor.

When the PTO receives an applicant's filing, it designates the application with a filing date and serial number. After determining that the filed papers comprise a complete patent application, it then forwards the application to the appropriate Examining Group. The application is then assigned to an examiner, who ordinarily considers applications in the order of their filing date. The examiner first considers whether the application conforms with the PTO's formal requirements. Rejection of an application can result at this early stage from an incomprehensible English translation, poorly executed drawings, and other defects.

The examiner next conducts a search of the prior art. In addition to art disclosed by the applicant, the examiner will then search domestic and foreign patents as well as various printed publications. To assist examiners in this regard, the PTO maintains a library of patents from around the world along with various technical journals and texts.

Following the search, the examiner then turns to examination of the application. This task entails ensuring that the application satisfies the disclosure requirements and warrants a patent in light of the prior art. 35 U.S.C.A. § 132 then provides:

Notice of Rejection; Reexamination

> Whenever, on examination, any claim for a patent is rejected, or any objection or requirement made, the Commissioner shall notify the applicant thereof, stating the reasons for such rejection, or objection or requirement, together with such information and references as may be useful in judging of the propriety of continuing the prosecution of his application; and if after receiving such notice, the applicant persists in his claim for a patent, with or without amendment, the application shall be reexamined. No amendment shall introduce new matter into the disclosure of the invention.

The examiner's notification is denominated an Office Action. The Office Action identifies each claim, indicates whether it has been rejected or allowed, and offers the examiner's reasoning. The Office Action also provides a period for response by the applicant.

If a rejection has resulted, the attorney will usually respond by either asserting that the rejection was improper or by amending the claims. Under the first option, the attorney offers substantive arguments that the rejection was improper. PTO nomenclature designates these arguments a "traverse." Alternatively, the attorney will amend the claims, typically augmenting the claim language in order to overcome a rejection founded on the prior art or lack of claim definiteness.

If still unconvinced, the examiner will issue a second Office Action titled a "Final Rejection." The applicant ordinarily has three options: abandon the application, file a so-called "continuing application," or seek review of the examiner's actions by filing a petition to the Commissioner or appeal to the Board of Patent Appeals and Interferences. This chapter discusses the latter two options. Of course, the examiner may agree that the amended or explained application deserves a patent and issue a "notice of allowance." Then, upon payment of an issuance fee, the applicant receives a patent. The PTO then publishes the patent's abstract and broadest claim, along with a selected drawing, in its Official Gazette. At that point, the public has access to the patent itself, its "prosecution history" or "file wrapper," comprising the entire record of the administrative process that produced the patent.

§ 12.1[b]   Continuing Application Practice

In addition to ordinary and provisional applications, other sorts of patent applications may arise during the course of the patent prosecution process. An excerpt from the following decision explains this possibility.

TRANSCO PRODUCTS INC. v. PERFORMANCE CONTRACTING, INC.

United States Court of Appeals, Federal Circuit, 1994.
38 F.3d 551, 32 U.S.P.Q.2d 1077.

An applicant may file a continuation, divisional, or continuation-in-part (CIP) application of a prior application, all of which the PTO characterizes as "continuing" applications. See MPEP § 201.11. In general, a continuing application is one filed during the pendency of another application which contains at least part of the disclosure of the other application and names at least one inventor in common with that application.

"Continuation" and "divisional" applications are alike in that they are both continuing applications based on the same disclosure as an earlier application. They differ, however, in what they claim. A "continuation" application claims the same invention claimed in an earlier application, although there may be some variation in the scope of the subject matter claimed. See MPEP § 201.07. A "divisional" application, on the other hand, is one carved out of an earlier application which disclosed and claimed more than one independent invention, the result being that the divisional application claims only one or more, but not all, of the independent inventions of the earlier application. *See* MPEP § 201.06. A "CIP" application is a continuing application containing a portion or all of the disclosure of an earlier application together with added matter not present in that earlier application. *See* MPEP § 201.08. The term "parent" is often used to refer to the immediately preceding application upon which a continuing application claims priority; the term "original" is used to refer to the first application in a chain of continuing applications. *See* MPEP §§ 201.04, 201.04(a).

The PTO has noted that the expressions "continuation," "divisional," and "continuation-in-part" are merely terms used for administrative convenience. *See* MPEP § 201.11.

Section 120 appeared in the statutes for the first time in the Patent Act of 1952. Prior to 1952, continuing application practice was a creature of patent office practice and case law, and section 120 merely codified the procedural rights of an applicant with respect to this practice. Before section 120 was enacted, the Supreme Court noted that a continuing application and the application on which it is based are considered part of the same transaction constituting one continuous application. The legislative history of section 120 does not indicate any congressional intent to alter the Supreme Court's interpretation of continuing application practice.

Notes

As discussed in *Transco*, the statutory basis for continuation applications is provided in § 120, which reads:

Benefit of Earlier Filing Date in the United States

> An application for patent for an invention disclosed in the manner provided by the first paragraph of section 112 of this title in an application previously filed in the United States, or as provided by section 363 of this title, which is filed by an inventor or inventors named in the previously filed application shall have the same effect, as to such invention, as though filed on the date of the prior application, if filed before the patenting or abandonment of or termination of proceedings on the first application or on an application similarly entitled to the benefit of the filing date of the first application and if it contains or is amended to contain a specific reference to the earlier application.

The parallel between this provision and § 119, discussed here in Chapter 14, should be apparent. Both parts of the Patent Act allow applicants to obtain the effect of an earlier filing date of another application. While § 119 relates to international application priority, § 120 concerns domestic application priority. Continuation applications are based upon a parent application and, compared to that application, contain no additional disclosure. The continuation application's claims are directed to the same invention as the parent, although the scope of the claims may change as the prosecution process continues.

Continuation application practice exists out of the recognition that the path to a Final Rejection can be a short one. The filing of an ordinary application usually purchases the applicant a scant two Official Actions by the examiner. Agreement often cannot be reached by this point, however, leaving the applicant with only the alternatives of abandonment of patent protection or the filing of an appeal. By instead filing a continuation application and paying the appropriate fee, an applicant essentially purchases an additional period of prosecution. This time allows additional further dialogue between the applicant and examiner, with the goal of more accurate and proper claiming of a previously disclosed invention without the necessity of an appeal.

The Patent Act provides for divisional applications at § 121, which reads in part:

Divisional Applications

If two or more independent and distinct inventions are claimed in one application, the Commissioner may require the application to be restricted to one of the inventions. If the other invention is made the subject of a divisional application which complies with the requirements of section 120 of this title it shall be entitled to the benefit of the filing date of the original application.

The restriction requirement serves several distinct purposes. Easily the most important is the maintenance of the integrity of the Patent and Trademark Office's fee structure. Otherwise, applicants would be sorely tempted to cut their prosecution costs by claiming several different inventions in one application. The PTO also desires to limit the size of a particular patent instrument and to ensure that examiners may confine their search and examination efforts to a particular technological art.

The remaining sort of continuing applications is the so-called "continuation-in-part" or CIP. Such applications rely to some extent upon the disclosure of a parent application. However, they also contain so-called "new matter" not disclosed in the earlier application. Continuation-in-part applications thus have two or more effective filing dates. Claims in the continuation-in-part application that were present in the parent application, or were first included in the continuation-in-part application but are supported entirely by the parent application's disclosure, are entitled to the filing date of the parent application. Otherwise, they must rely upon the later filing date of the continuation-in-part application.

§ 12.1[c]   U.S. Patent Appeal and Petition Practice

An impasse between examiner and applicant results in either a petition to the Commissioner or an appeal to the Board of Patent Appeals and Interferences, 35 U.S.C.A. § 134. As explained in *In re Searles*, 422 F.2d 431, 435, 164 U.S.P.Q. 623, 626 (CCPA 1970):

Decisions of the examiner directly relating to the rejection of claims are subject to appeal. These questions generally deal with the merits of the invention, involving factual determinations and the legal conclusions drawn therefrom regarding the application disclosure, the claims and the prior art. The examiner's rulings dealing with procedural matters, such as whether an affidavit or amendment is untimely, and formal requirements, such as whether a new application title will be required, are reviewable upon petition.

Prior to 1984, the PTO housed both a Board of Appeals and Board of Interferences; these entities were merged in order to streamline interference proceedings and minimize jurisdictional disputes. The Board consists of a number of experienced examiners, currently titled "Administrative Patent Judges," who ordinarily sit in panels of three. *See* 35 U.S.C.A. § 6. The Board is required to provide opinions sufficiently thorough to satisfy Rule 52(a) of the Federal Rules of Civil Procedure. *See Gechter v. Davidson*, 116 F.3d 1454, 43 U.S.P.Q.2d 1030 (Fed.Cir. 1997). The Federal Circuit clarified the relationship between the Board and the Commissioner as follows:

> Even though Board members serve an essential function, they are but examiner-employees of the PTO, and the ultimate authority regarding the granting of patents lies with the Commissioner. For example, if the Board rejects an application, the Commissioner can control the PTO's position in any appeal through the Solicitor of the PTO; the Board cannot demand that the Solicitor attempt to sustain the Board's position. Conversely, if the Board approves an application, the Commissioner has the option of refusing to sign a patent; an action which would be subject to a mandamus action by the applicant. The Commissioner has an obligation to refuse to grant a patent if he believes that doing so would be contrary to law. The foregoing evidences that the Board is merely the highest level of the Examining Corps, and like all other members of the Examining Corps, the Board operates subject to the Commissioner's overall ultimate authority and responsibility.

In re Alappat, 33 F.3d 1526, 1535, 31 U.S.P.Q.2d 1545, 1550 (Fed.Cir. 1994) (*in banc*).

An unsuccessful petitioner may seek judicial review through a number of mechanisms, including the Administrative Procedure Act, 5 U.S.C.A. §§ 701–706; the All Writs Act, 28 U.S.C.A. § 1651; or a civil action against the Commissioner under 28 U.S.C.A. § 1338(a). Such actions may be brought in any United States district court, with the Federal Circuit as the court of second instance. The choice of fora from an adverse decision of the Board is more limited: the applicant must bring a civil action against the Commissioner in the United States District Court for the District of Columbia, 35 U.S.C.A. § 145, or file an appeal at the Court of Appeals for the Federal Circuit, 35 U.S.C.A. § 141. The primary advantage of the former route is that the applicant may submit new evidence into the record, an option unavailable at the Federal Circuit. Appeals from suits lodged in the D.C. District Court under § 145 go to the Federal Circuit as well.

§ 12.1[d] Publication of Pending Applications

The U.S. PTO traditionally maintained pending patent applications in confidence. Patents were published only on the date that they issued.

However, the American Inventors Protection Act changed this long-standing principle, to some degree aligning U.S. practice with global norms. One of the titles of the American Inventors Protection Act, the Domestic Publication of Foreign Filed Patent Applications Act of 1999, now requires the PTO Director to publish certain pending patent applications promptly after the expiration of 18 months from the earliest filing date to which they are entitled. Significantly, not all applications will be published prior to their issuance. If an applicant certifies that the invention disclosed in the U.S. application will not be the subject of a patent application in another country that requires publication of applications 18 months after filing, then the PTO will not publish the application. *See* 35 U.S.C. § 122(b).

Some background into international and comparative patent law will assist understanding of this provision. First, as will be discussed further in Chapter 14, there is no global patent system. Patent rights must be applied for and secured in each jurisdiction. In a world where technology knows no borders and international trade increasingly dominates, patent protection in a single country is often insufficient to protect inventors.

In recognition of these realities, the United States has long been a signatory of the Paris Convention for the Protection of Industrial Property. This treaty attempts to ease the burdens of maintaining patent rights in many jurisdictions. Among the chief provisions of the Paris Convention is the so-called priority right. The priority right allows patent applicants to benefit from an earlier filing date in a foreign country. So long as an inventor files abroad within one year of his first filing and complies with certain formalities, his subsequent foreign filings will be treated as if they were made as of the date of his initial filing.

A second important background principle is that foreign patent offices ordinarily publish patent applications 18 months after their first effective filing date. As an example, suppose that an inventor filed an application at the U.S. PTO on June 1, 1996. Suppose further that the inventor sought patent rights in Germany, which is also a signatory to the Paris Convention. If the inventor files a German patent application by June 1, 1997, his application will be treated as having been filed on the U.S. filing date of June 1, 1996. The German Patent Office will publish the German application on December 1, 1997, 18 months after the first effective filing date to which the inventor is entitled.

In contrast to overseas regimes, the U.S. patent system for many years maintained all applications in secrecy. This regime advantaged patent applicants because it allowed them to understand the scope of any allowed claims before disclosing an invention. Thus, applicants retained the final option to issue the allowed claims or to abandon the application and retain their invention as a trade secret.

However, this secrecy regime has been perceived as imposing costs as well. Others might well engage in repetitive research efforts during the pendency of patent applications, unaware that an earlier inventor had already staked a claim to that technology. Without publication of applications, inventors could also commence litigation on the very day a patent issues, without any degree of notice to the rest of the technological community.

The Domestic Publication of Foreign Filed Patent Applications Act of 1999 attempts to strike a middle ground. U.S. patent applications will be published 18 months from the date of filing, except where the inventor represents that he will not seek patent protection abroad. In effect, the Act calls for the publication of applications domestically only when their foreign counterparts would be published prior to grant anyway. To discourage applicants from delaying their claims of foreign priority under the Paris Convention, the Act allows the PTO Director to consider the failure of the applicant to file a timely claim for priority as a waiver of such claim.

Sometimes inventors seek more robust patent protection in some countries than in others. This step may be taken for business reasons or due to differences in the patent or competition laws in varying jurisdictions. The Domestic Publication of Foreign Filed Patent Applications Act therefore contains a provision allowing applicants to "submit a redacted copy of the application filed in the Patent and Trademark Office eliminating any part or description of the invention in such application that is not also contained in any of the corresponding application filed in a foreign country." As a result, if an applicant seeks broader patent protection in the United States than in other countries, only the more limited version of the application will be published here.

This Act also creates so-called provisional rights that may attach to published patent applications. Provisional rights are equivalent to a reasonable royalty, the amount that the patentee would have charged an infringer had the two parties entered into a licensing arrangement at the time the infringement began. Persons who employ the invention as claimed in the published patent application are potentially liable for this amount. Provisional rights are subject to several qualifications. They are only effective at such time as the patent issues, apply only when the infringer had actual notice of the published patent application and the claims of the published application are "substantially identical" to those of the issued patent.

An example may clarify the workings of provisional rights. Suppose that an inventor files a U.S. patent application on February 1, 2003. Assuming the inventor does not file the appropriate certification, the PTO will publish the application 18 months later, on August 1, 2004. Suppose further that this application results in an issued patent that the PTO formally grants on June 1, 2005. Under these facts, the inventor may file a patent infringement suit on or after June 1, 2005. Assuming the statutory requirements are fulfilled, the inventor may claim provisional rights equivalent to a reasonable royalty from August 1, 2004, the date the application was published, through June 1, 2005, the date the patent was granted. Infringing acts that occur after June 1, 2005, will be subject to the full range of remedies under the Patent Act of 1952, including an injunction and damages based upon the lost profits of the patentee.

§ 12.1[e]   Patent Term

Once the Patent and Trademark Office issues a patent, that patent enjoys an effective term established by the statute. The publication of the book finds United States patent law in a transition period regarding patent term. Formerly, patents extended for 17 years from the date the patent issued. *See generally* C. Michael White, *Why a Seventeen Year Patent*, 38 J. PAT. OFF. SOC'Y 839 (1956). As a result of the Uruguay Round Agreements Act (URAA), however, patents endure for 20 years from the date that the patent application was filed. As noted in *Merck & Co. v. Kessler*, 80 F.3d 1543, 38 U.S.P.Q.2d 1347 (Fed.Cir.1996):

> The purpose of the URAA was not to extend patent terms, although it has that effect in some cases, but to harmonize the term provision of United States patent law with that of our leading trading partners which grant a patent term of 20 years from the date of filing of the patent application. Prior to June 8, 1995, U.S. patents had an expiration date under 35 U.S.C. § 154 measured as 17 years from the date the patent issued, except where terminal disclaimers were filed. Amended section 154(a) now reads:

> > Subject to the payment of fees under this title, such grant shall be for a term beginning on the date on which the patent issues and ending 20 years from the date on which the application for the patent was filed in the United States or, if the application contains a specific reference to an earlier filed application or applications under section 120, 121, or 365(c) of this title, from the date on which the earliest such application was filed.

35 U.S.C. § 154(a)(2) (1994).

> For certain patents which were issued and for pending applications which were filed prior to June 8, 1995, a transitional provision preserves a guaranteed 17–year term, if it is longer than 20 years from filing, by the following provision:

> > The term of a patent that is in force on or that results from an application filed before the date that is 6 months after the date of the enactment of the Uruguay Round Agreements Act shall be the greater of the 20–year term as provided in subsection (1), or 17 years from grant, subject to any terminal disclaimers.

Id. at § 154(c)(1). Patents in the section 154(c)(1) category thus are entitled to keep or to enjoy the 17–year term from issuance of the patent or a 20–year from filing term, whichever is longer.

Although the distinction between the two regimes may not appear to loom particularly large, significant consequences flow from United States adoption of a twenty-year patent term measured from the filing date. Prior to June 8, 1995, the filing of continuing applications did not affect the length of the effective patent term. Once the patent issued, it obtained a seventeen-year term. Currently, the term of a patent is measured as twenty years from the earliest filing date. The new term scheme puts an end to so-called "submarine" patents that plagued particular industries in the United States. Submarine patents emerged from a series of concealed continuation applications, sometimes filed thirty or more years earlier, to "torpedo" industries that had developed in ignorance of the pending applications.

Several significant qualifications exist to the twenty-year rule. First, under § 154(b), patentees may obtain term extensions of up to five years due to delays caused by the declaration of an interference, the imposition of secrecy order, or the successful pursuit of an appeal to the Board of Patent Appeals and Interferences or federal court. Second, the term of a patent may also be extended under § 156, a provision of the Hatch–Waxman Act. This complex statute authorizes increased patent terms on inventions that have been subject to a lengthy pre-market approval process under the Federal Food, Drug and Cosmetic Act.

Third, enjoyment of the full patent term is subject to the payment of maintenance fees. Currently, a patent expires after four, eight, or twelve years if maintenance fees are not timely paid on each occasion. As of October 1, 2001, the amounts due are $880 by the fourth year, $2,020 by the eighth year, and $3,100 by the twelfth year. As only about thirty-three percent of the patents issued in the United States are maintained beyond their eleventh year, maintenance fees effectively dedicate a great deal of patented technology into the public domain.

Finally, the Patent Term Guarantee Act of 1999 provides certain deadlines that, if not met by the PTO, result in an automatic extension of the term of individual patents. The most significant of these deadlines appear to be fourteen months for a First Office Action and four months for a subsequent Office Action. As well, the prosecution of an original patent application must be complete within three years of the actual U.S. filing date, with exceptions granted for continuing applications and appeals. The Director is charged with calculating any patent term extensions that might result from missed PTO deadlines.

Patent term has been of considerable interest to economists, who have long pondered what the optimal patent duration should be. Because different industries are marked by varying environments of technological growth, some scholars have concluded that patent term should be adjusted on an industry-by-industry basis. A good introduction to the economic literature may be found in W. NORDHAUS, INVENTION, GROWTH AND ECONOMIC WELFARE (1969), and F.M. Scherer, *Nordhaus's Theory of Optimal Patent Life: A Geometric Reinterpretation*, 62 AM. ECON. REV. 422 (1972).

§ 12.1[f]   Patent Prosecution Abroad

In addition to understanding the basics of domestic prosecution procedures, patent attorneys are well advised to possess some grasp of the practice of other national and regional patent offices. Inventors increasingly seek protection outside the United States and often request that domestic patent counsel coordinate these efforts. Although United States practitioners ordinarily engage knowledgeable overseas associates as part of this effort, some sense of the differences among the world's patent offices will allow more efficient interaction with colleagues abroad as well as more competent client representation. Because approximately 80% of the world's patents currently in force issued from either the U.S. PTO, European Patent Office or Japanese Patent Office, *see* European Patent Office, et al., Trilateral Statistical Report (1993), this chapter focuses primarily on these three offices.

Unlike many other patent offices, the U.S. system allows for essentially unlimited prosecution—at least until twenty years passes from the filing date, when no patent rights could possibly accrue from the application. Most other patent systems are not so generous: if an impasse is reached, the proper route is to begin an appeal of the examiner's final decision, not to attempt to reinitiate dialogue by paying an additional fee and filing a continuation application.

A notable aspect of patent practice in other nations, particularly in Japan and Germany, is that the actual prior art search and examination is automatically deferred following submission of an application. Rather than examine every submitted application, certain patent offices instead merely publish the application. Applicants, and sometimes third parties, seeking an actual examination must submit additional requests for a search and then an examination. Such requests must occur within a specified time, and be accompanied by the appropriate fee. Deferred examination systems may be justified in that they allow applicants to further postpone their decision to pursue patent coverage or not, but they often are adopted in order to increase patent office revenues and reduce agency backlogs. Note that the PTO does allow examination to be deferred for short periods in cases of "good and sufficient cause"; for example, where the applicant lacks funds to continue the prosecution. *See* 37 C.F.R. § 1.103.

The United States remains unique in its mandate that the actual inventor or inventors file the patent application, rather than the assignee of the inventor. The result in the United States is that most applications are filed by the inventors' assignees—usually their employer—in the name of the inventors. Foreign patent offices avoid this complexity by allowing assignee filing. Although the U.S. rule may appear strictly procedural, it sometimes leads to unusual substantive consequences, particularly with respect to the best mode requirement. *See* Chapter 10. It also renders the filing of applications more burdensome, with minimal perceived benefits towards upholding the individual rights of inventors. The 1992 Advisory Commission Report recommended that the United

States adopt assignee filing along with certain procedural obligations designed to safeguard the interests of inventor-assignors. *See* THE ADVISORY COMMISSION ON PATENT LAW REFORM, A REPORT TO THE SECRETARY OF COMMERCE 179–81 (1992).

§ 12.2 INVENTORSHIP

Section 102(f) requires that the patentee be the actual inventor of the patented technology. In keeping with this substantive law, the Patent Act and judicial opinions have consistently required that patents and applications identify the true inventors of the technology set forth. *See* 35 U.S.C.A. § 111; *Kennedy v. Hazelton*, 128 U.S. 667 (1888). The following opinion not only introduces inventorship concepts, it also illustrates their extraordinary significance.

ETHICON, INC. v. UNITED STATES SURGICAL CORP.

United States Court of Appeals, Federal Circuit, 1998.
135 F.3d 1456, 45 U.S.P.Q.2d 1545.

Before NEWMAN, Circuit Judge, SKELTON, Senior Circuit Judge, AND Rader, Circuit Judge.

RADER, Circuit Judge.

In this patent infringement action, Dr. InBae Yoon (Yoon) and his exclusive licensee, Ethicon, Inc. (Ethicon), appeal from the judgment of the United States District Court for the District of Connecticut. In 1989, Yoon and Ethicon sued United States Surgical Corporation (U.S. Surgical) for infringement of U.S. Patent No. 4,535,773 (the '773 patent). In 1993, the parties stipulated to the intervention of Mr. Young Jae Choi (Choi) as defendant-intervenor. Choi claimed to be an omitted co-inventor of the '773 patent and to have granted U.S. Surgical a retroactive license under that patent. On U.S. Surgical's motion to correct inventorship of the '773 patent under 35 U.S.C. § 256, the district court ruled that Choi was an omitted co-inventor of two claims, and subsequently granted U.S. Surgical's motion to dismiss the infringement complaint. Because the district court's determination of co-inventorship was correct, and because Choi is a joint owner of the '773 patent who has not consented to suit against U.S. Surgical, this court affirms.

I. BACKGROUND

The '773 patent relates to trocars, an essential tool for endoscopic surgery. A trocar is a surgical instrument which makes small incisions in the wall of a body cavity, often the abdomen, to admit endoscopic instruments. Trocars include a shaft within an outer sleeve. One end of the shaft has a sharp blade. At the outset of surgery, the surgeon uses the blade to puncture the wall and extend the trocar into the cavity. The surgeon then removes the shaft, leaving the hollow outer sleeve, through which the surgeon may insert tiny cameras and surgical instruments for the operation.

Conventional trocars, however, pose a risk of damage to internal organs or structures. As the trocar blade punctures the cavity wall, the sudden loss of resistance can cause the blade to lunge forward and injure an internal organ. The '773 patent claims a trocar that alleviates this danger. In one embodiment, the invention equips the trocar with a blunt, spring-loaded rod. As the trocar pierces the cavity wall, the rod automatically springs forward to precede the blade and shield against injury. A second embodiment has a retractable trocar blade that springs back into a protective sheath when it passes through the cavity wall. The patent also teaches the use of an electronic sensor in the end of the blade to signal the surgeon at the moment of puncture.

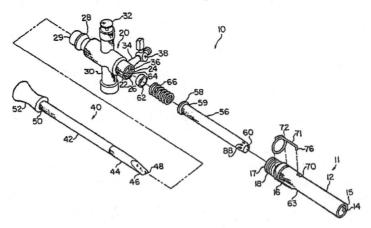

Yoon is a medical doctor and inventor of numerous patented devices for endoscopic surgery. In the late 1970s, Yoon began to conceive of a safety device to prevent accidental injury during trocar incisions. Yoon also conceived of a device to alert the surgeon when the incision was complete. In 1980, Yoon met Choi, an electronics technician, who had some college training in physics, chemistry, and electrical engineering, but no college degree. Choi had worked in the research and development of electronic devices. After Choi had demonstrated to Yoon some of the devices he had developed, Yoon asked Choi to work with him on several projects, including one for safety trocars. Choi was not paid for his work.

In 1982, after collaborating for approximately eighteen months, their relationship ended. Choi believed that Yoon found his work unsatisfactory and unlikely to produce any marketable product. For these reasons, Choi withdrew from cooperation with Yoon.

In the same year, however, Yoon filed an application for a patent disclosing various embodiments of a safety trocar. Without informing Choi, Yoon named himself as the sole inventor. In 1985, the Patent and Trademark Office issued the '773 patent to Yoon, with fifty-five claims. Yoon thereafter granted an exclusive license under this patent to Ethicon. Yoon did not inform Choi of the patent application or issuance.

In 1989, Ethicon filed suit against U.S. Surgical for infringement of claims 34 and 50 of the '773 patent. In 1992, while this suit was still pending, U.S. Surgical became aware of Choi, and contacted him regarding his involvement in Yoon's safety trocar project. When Choi confirmed his role in the safety trocar project, U.S. Surgical obtained from Choi a "retroactive license" to practice "Choi's trocar related inventions." Under the license, Choi agreed to assist U.S. Surgical in any suit regarding the '773 patent. For its part, U.S. Surgical agreed to pay Choi contingent on its ultimate ability to continue to practice and market the invention. With the license in hand, U.S. Surgical moved to correct inventorship of the '773 patent under 35 U.S.C. § 256, claiming that Choi was a co-inventor of claims 23, 33, 46, and 47. Following an extensive hearing, the district court granted U.S. Surgical's motion, finding that Choi had contributed to the subject matter of claims 33 and 47.

U.S. Surgical next moved for dismissal of the infringement suit, arguing that Choi, as a joint owner of the patent, had granted it a valid license under the patent. By its terms, the license purported to grant rights to use the patent extending retroactively back to its issuance. The district court granted U.S. Surgical's motion and dismissed the suit.

Ethicon appeals the district court's finding of co-inventorship and its dismissal of the complaint. Specifically, Ethicon contends that (1) Choi supplied insufficient corroboration for his testimony of co-invention; (2) Choi presented insufficient evidence to show co-invention of claims 33 and 47 clearly and convincingly; [and] (4) the terms of the license agreement limit it to only that part of the invention to which Choi contributed, not the entire patent.

II. Co-Inventorship

Patent issuance creates a presumption that the named inventors are the true and only inventors. *See Hess v. Advanced Cardiovascular Sys., Inc.,* 106 F.3d 976, 980, 41 USPQ2d 1782, 1785–86 (Fed.Cir.), *cert. denied,* 520 U.S. 1277, 117 S.Ct. 2459, 138 L.Ed.2d 216 (1997). Inventorship is a question of law, which this court reviews without deference. *See Sewall v. Walters,* 21 F.3d 411, 415, 30 USPQ2d 1356, 1358 (Fed.Cir. 1994). However, this court reviews the underlying findings of fact which uphold a district court's inventorship determination for clear error.

A patented invention may be the work of two or more joint inventors. *See* 35 U.S.C. § 116 (1994). Because "[c]onception is the touchstone of inventorship," each joint inventor must generally contribute to the conception of the invention. *Burroughs Wellcome Co. v. Barr Lab., Inc.,* 40 F.3d 1223, 1227–28, 32 USPQ2d 1915, 1919 (Fed.Cir.1994). "Conception is the 'formation in the mind of the inventor, of a definite and permanent idea of the complete and operative invention, as it is hereafter to be applied in practice.' " *Hybritech, Inc. v. Monoclonal Antibodies, Inc.,* 802 F.2d 1367, 1376, 231 USPQ 81, 87 (Fed.Cir.1986) (quoting 1 *Robinson on Patents* 532 (1890)). An idea is sufficiently "definite and permanent" when "only ordinary skill would be necessary to reduce the invention to practice, without extensive research or experimentation." *Burroughs Wellcome,* 40 F.3d at 1228.

The conceived invention must include every feature of the subject matter claimed in the patent. Nevertheless, for the conception of a joint invention, each of the joint inventors need not "make the same type or amount of contribution" to the invention. 35 U.S.C. § 116. Rather, each needs to perform only a part of the task which produces the invention. On the other hand, one does not qualify as a joint inventor by merely assisting the actual inventor after conception of the claimed invention. One who simply provides the inventor with well-known principles or explains the state of the art without ever having "a firm and definite idea" of the claimed combination as a whole does not qualify as a joint inventor. *See Hess,* 106 F.3d at 981 (citing *O'Reilly v. Morse,* 56 U.S. (15 How.) 62, 111, 14 L.Ed. 601 (1853)). Moreover, depending on the scope of a patent's claims, one of ordinary skill in the art who simply reduced the inventor's idea to practice is not necessarily a joint inventor, even if the specification discloses that embodiment to satisfy the best mode requirement.

Furthermore, a co-inventor need not make a contribution to every claim of a patent. *See* 35 U.S.C. § 116. A contribution to one claim is enough. Thus, the critical question for joint conception is who conceived, as that term is used in the patent law, the subject matter of the claims at issue.

35 U.S.C. § 256 provides that a co-inventor omitted from an issued patent may be added to the patent by a court "before which such matter is called in question." To show co-inventorship, however, the alleged co-inventor or co-inventors must prove their contribution to the conception of the claims by clear and convincing evidence. However, "an inventor's testimony respecting the facts surrounding a claim of derivation or priority of invention cannot, standing alone, rise to the level of clear and convincing proof." *Price v. Symsek,* 988 F.2d 1187, 1194, 26 USPQ2d 1031, 1036 (Fed.Cir.1993). The rule is the same for an alleged co-inventor's testimony. Thus, an alleged co-inventor must supply evidence to corroborate his testimony. Whether the inventor's testimony has been sufficiently corroborated is evaluated under a "rule of reason" analysis. Under this analysis, "[a]n evaluation of *all* pertinent evidence must be made so that a sound determination of the credibility of the [alleged] inventor's story may be reached."

Corroborating evidence may take many forms. Often contemporaneous documents prepared by a putative inventor serve to corroborate an inventor's testimony. Circumstantial evidence about the inventive process may also corroborate. Additionally, oral testimony of someone other than the alleged inventor may corroborate.

A. *Claim 33*

The district court determined that Choi contributed to the conception of the subject matter of claim 33. Claim 33 (with emphasis to highlight relevant elements) reads:

A surgical instrument for providing communication through an anatomical organ structure, comprising:

means having an abutment member and *shaft longitudinally accommodatable within an outer sleeve,* longitudinal movement of said shaft inside said sleeve being limited by contact of said abutment member with said sleeve, said shaft having a distal end with a distal blade surface tapering into a sharp distal point, *said distal blade surface being perforated along one side by an aperture,* for puncturing an anatomical organ structure when subjected to force along the longitudinal axis of said shaft;

means having a blunt distal bearing surface, slidably extending through said aperture, for reciprocating through said aperture while said abutment member is in stationary contact with said sleeve;

means positionable between said puncturing means and said reciprocating means for biasing a distal section of said reciprocating means to protrude beyond said aperture and permitting said distal section of said reciprocating means to recede into said aperture when said bearing surface is subject to force along its axis . . . ; and

means connectible to the proximal end of said puncturing means *for* responding to longitudinal movement of said reciprocating means relative to said puncturing means and *creating a sensible signal* having one state upon recision of said distal section of said reciprocating means into said aperture and another state upon protrusion of said distal section of said reciprocating means from said aperture.

To determine whether Choi made a contribution to the conception of the subject matter of claim 33, this court must determine what Choi's contribution was and then whether that contribution's role appears in the claimed invention. If Choi in fact contributed to the invention defined by claim 33, he is a joint inventor of that claim.

Figures 18 and 19 of the '773 patent illustrate an embodiment of claim 33. These figures show a trocar blade with an aperture through which a blunt rod can extend. When the trocar blade penetrates the inner wall of a cavity, a spring releases the rod, which juts out past the end of the trocar blade and prevents the blade from cutting further. The embodiment also includes a structure that gives the surgeon aural and visual signals when the blade nears penetration.

The district court found that Yoon conceived of the use of a blunt probe. However, the court found that Choi conceived of and thereby contributed two features contained in the embodiment shown in figures 18 and 19: first, Choi conceived of locating the blunt probe in the trocar shaftand allowing it to pass through an aperture in the blade surface; second, Choi conceived of the "means . . . for . . . creating a sensible signal."

If Choi did indeed conceive of "locating the blunt probe in the shaft and allowing it to pass through an aperture in the blade surface," he contributed to the subject matter of claim 33. Claim 33 requires that the "distal blade surface" be "perforated along one side by an aperture" and requires the "shaft" to be "longitudinally accommodatable within [the] outer sleeve." Properly construed, claim 33 includes the elements that Choi contributed to the invention according to the district court's findings.

In making this finding, the district court relied extensively on Choi's testimony. Choi testified that the idea of extending the blunt probe through an aperture in the trocar blade itself was his idea. To corroborate this testimony, Choi produced a series of sketches he created while working with Yoon. One sketch shows a probe inside the shaft of a trocar blade, extending through an opening in the side of the end of the blade.

To rebut Choi's showing, Yoon presented a drawing dated July 1973, which disclosed elements of claim 33. The district court determined, however, that Dr. Yoon had altered this drawing. In fact, according to the district court, it had originally depicted a device from an entirely different patent. Due to its suspicious origins, the trial court rejected it as unreliable.

The court also discounted Yoon's testimony for lack of credibility. Indeed the record supports the trial court's conclusion that Yoon altered and backdated documents to make it appear that he had independently invented trocars, shields, and electronics. Moreover, Yoon's trial testimony clashed with his earlier deposition testimony. For instance, before learning of Choi's role in the case, Yoon falsely testified at his deposition that (1) he had worked with Choi as early as 1975 and (2) the sketches at issue in this case had been drawn completely by him. However, the two did not meet until 1980, and when later questioned about authorship of the documents, Yoon replied, "If I said [that] at that time, then maybe I was confused." The district court justifiably discounted Yoon's testimony.

In sum, after full consideration of the relevant evidence, the district court determined that Choi conceived part of the invention recited in claim 33. This court detects no cause to reverse this determination.

B. Claim 47

The district court also determined that Choi contributed to the conception of the subject matter of claim 47. Claim 47 (with emphasis to highlight relevant elements) reads:

> A surgical instrument for providing communication through an anatomical organ structure, comprising:
>
> means having an elongate shaft exhibiting a longitudinal axis and terminating in a sharp, distal end, for puncturing the cavity wall of an anatomical organ structure;
>
> means borne by said puncturing means distal end for converting counterforce exerted by said cavity wall against said distal end into transmissible energy;

means connected to said converting means for conveying said transmissible energy toward the proximal end of said puncturing means;

means having an interior bore coaxially aligned with the longitudinal axis of said shaft for receiving said puncturing means proximal end;

means for biasing said puncturing means proximal end to withdraw into said interior bore;

means interposed between said puncturing means proximal end and said interior bore assuming a normally protruding position for detaining said puncturing means proximal end extended from said interior cavity in opposition to said biasing means.

To determine whether Choi made a contribution to the conception of the subject matter of claim 47, this court must determine what Choi's contribution was and then construe the claim language to determine if Choi's contribution found its way into the defined invention.

Figures 34, 35, and 36 illustrate the invention in claim 47. In these embodiments, a cocked spring pulls the trocar back into a protective sheath as soon as the blade has punctured the inner wall. Release of the detaining means triggers the retracting spring action. The two detaining means disclosed in the specification are (1) a detent extending radially outward from the trocar through a hole in the sheath and (2) a rod extending horizontally from the proximal end of the trocar that butts against an off-center, but slidable, bar with a hole in its center. In the case of the detent detaining means, when a sensor detects that the trocar blade has pierced the wall of a cavity, the plunger of a solenoid pushes the detent out of the hole in the sheath. In the case of the rod detaining means, the solenoid plunger positions the bar so that the hole in its center aligns with the rod.

The district court concluded that Yoon generally invented the retractable trocar, but that Choi invented both of the detaining means disclosed in the specification. In addition to oral testimony of the parties, the district court cited Choi's sketches, one of which clearly shows the rod detaining means. However, the sketch in which the district court would find the detent detaining means appears to work differently than the embodiment described in the '773 patent. Instead of a detent that extends radially outward through a hole in the sheath, the sketch illustrates the use of the solenoid plunger itself as a detent, extending radially *inward* through a hole in the sheath. Thus, the record does not show that Choi contributed to the detent detaining means. Therefore, this court affirms the district court's finding that Choi contributed the rod detaining means, but determines that the trial court clearly erred in finding that Choi contributed the detent detaining means.

In this instance, however, claim 47 recites a "means . . . for [detaining]." The use of the word "means" gives rise to "a presumption that the inventor used the term advisedly to invoke the statutory mandates for means-plus-function clauses." *York Prods., Inc. v. Central Tractor*

Farm & Family Ctr., 99 F.3d 1568, 1574, 40 USPQ2d 1619, 1623 (Fed.Cir.1996). Although the presumption is not conclusive, the means language here invokes the interpretation regimens of section 112, paragraph 6. Thus applying section 112, paragraph 6 to interpret this claim, the language adopted the two structures in the specification to define the means for detaining.

Choi showed contribution to one of these alternative structures. The contributor of any disclosed means of a means-plus-function claim element is a joint inventor as to that claim, unless one asserting sole inventorship can show that the contribution of that means was simply a reduction to practice of the sole inventor's broader concept. Although the district court found that Yoon first conceived of a retractable trocar generally, Yoon did not show that Choi's contribution was simply a reduction to practice of the broader concept of using any detaining means commensurate with the scope of claim 47. Thus, Choi showed entitlement to the status of co-inventor for this claim as well.

C. Corroboration

As corroboration for his testimony of co-invention, Choi proffers sketches of his work. These sketches were in Yoon's possession since their creation. The parties do not dispute, however, that Choi in fact created the sketches. Instead, Yoon contends that he first disclosed the invention to Choi, who then made the sketches to illustrate what he learned from Yoon. Absent sufficient corroboration, inventorship would turn solely on a credibility contest between Yoon and Choi. The district court, however, found sufficient corroboration.

Taken together, the alleged co-inventor's testimony and the corroborating evidence must show inventorship "by clear and convincing evidence." This requirement is not to be taken lightly. Under the "rule of reason" standard for corroborating evidence, the trial court must consider corroborating evidence in context, make necessary credibility determinations, and assign appropriate probative weight to the evidence to determine whether clear and convincing evidence supports a claim of co-inventorship.

In this case, Choi's sketches show the invention. The parties agree that Choi made the sketches. The contest involves whether Choi conceived of the material in the sketches or merely drew what Yoon conceived. The district count noted many circumstantial factors further corroborating Choi's conception claim: (1) Yoon's need for a person with expertise in electronics; (2) Choi's background in electronics, (3) Yoon's proposal that he and Choi should work together to develop new products, including safety trocars, (4) their informal business relationship, (5) the length of time they worked together, (6) the absence of any pay to Choi for his work, (7) the similarity between Choi's sketches and the patent figures, and (8) the letter in which Choi stated that he could no longer be a "member" of Yoon's business. Additionally, U.S. Surgical introduced expert testimony that some of the sketches dealt with sophisticated concepts that only an electrical engineer or technician would understand.

Consequently, the district court found that Choi was presenting ideas to Yoon as the sketches were drawn, rather than the other way around.

On appeal, this court declines to reweigh the evidence. Instead, this court determines that the record shows that corroboration evidence in this case satisfies the "rule of reason." Thus, this court must only further assess whether the district court's factual conclusions, given the clear and convincing evidence standard, were clearly erroneous. Here, given the sketches, Choi's testimony, and the established circumstances, in contrast with Yoon's testimony, expressly found to lack credibility by the trial court, this court discerns no clear error.

In reaching this determination, this court has also considered alleged inconsistencies in Choi's testimony. In August 1992, U.S. Surgical's counsel first sent Choi a copy of the '773 patent. Choi circled figures and claims describing that which he claimed to have contributed. Choi circled some claims that he does not now assert to have had a role in inventing. He also did not circle claims he now claims to have co-invented. However, the district court could have reasonably found that a layman, untrained in the language of the patent law, may reasonably err in interpreting claim language. Moreover, Choi might well have confused the legal distinction between conception (which justifies a finding of inventorship) and reduction to practice (which does not). In any event, this court affirms the district court's holding that Choi was a co-inventor of claims 33 and 47.

IV. Scope of the Choi–U.S. Surgical License

Questions of patent ownership are distinct from questions of inventorship. In accordance with this principle, this court has nonetheless noted that "an invention presumptively belongs to its creator."

Indeed, in the context of joint inventorship, each co-inventor presumptively owns a *pro rata* undivided interest in the entire patent, no matter what their respective contributions. Several provisions of the Patent Act combine to dictate this rule. 35 U.S.C. § 116, as amended in 1984, states that a joint inventor need not make a contribution "to the subject matter of every claim of the patent." In amending section 116 as to joint inventorship, Congress did not make corresponding modifications as to joint ownership. For example, section 261 continues to provide that "patents shall have the attributes of personal property." This provision suggests that property rights, including ownership, attach to patents as a whole, not individual claims. Moreover, section 262 continues to speak of "joint owners of a patent," not joint owners of a claim. Thus, a joint inventor as to even one claim enjoys a presumption of ownership in the entire patent.

This rule presents the prospect that a co-inventor of only one claim might gain entitlement to ownership of a patent with dozens of claims. As noted, the Patent Act accounts for that occurrence: "Inventors *may* apply for a patent jointly even though ... each did not make a contribution to the subject matter of every claim." 35 U.S.C. § 116 (emphasis added). Thus, where inventors choose to cooperate in the inventive process, their joint inventions may become joint property without some express agreement to the contrary. In this case, Yoon must now effectively share with Choi ownership of all the claims, even those which he invented by himself. Thus, Choi had the power to license rights in the entire patent. [After reviewing the terms of the license between Choi and U.S. Surgical, the majority concluded that Choi had indeed licensed to U.S. Surgical all of his rights as a joint owner.]

Because Choi did not consent to an infringement suit against U.S. Surgical and indeed can no longer consent due to his grant of an exclusive license with its accompanying "right to sue," Ethicon's complaint lacks the participation of a co-owner of the patent. Accordingly, this court must order dismissal of this suit.

VI. Conclusion

Accordingly, the judgment of the United States District Court for the District of Connecticut is affirmed.

Pauline Newman, Circuit Judge, dissenting.

I respectfully dissent, for whether or not Mr. Choi made an inventive contribution to two of the fifty-five claims of the '773 patent, he is not a joint owner of the other fifty-three claims of the patent. Neither the law of joint invention nor the law of property so requires, and indeed these laws mandate otherwise.

A. The Law of Joint Invention

The purpose of the amendment of § 116 was to remedy the increasing technical problems arising in team research, for which existing law, deemed to require simultaneous conception as well as shared contribution by each named inventor to every claim, was producing pitfalls for patentees, to no public purpose. As stated in its legislative history, the amendment to 35 U.S.C. § 116 "recognizes the realities of modern team research." 130 Cong. Rec. 28,069–71 (1984) (statement of Rep. Kastenmeier).

Before 1984 precedent did not permit naming as an inventor a person who did not share in the conception of the invention and who did not contribute to all of the claims of the patent. If different persons made an inventive contribution to various parts of an invention or to different claims of a patent, the legalistic problems that arose were not readily soluble, even by the complex, expensive, and often confusing expedient of filing separate patent applications on separate claims.

The progress of technology exacerbated the inventorship problems. Patents were invalidated simply because all of the named inventors did not contribute to all the claims; and patents were also invalidated when there were contributors to some of the claims who were not named. Indeed, at the time the '773 patent application was filed in 1982, most practitioners believed that a separate application was required if it was desired to present, for example, the two claims that contain Mr. Choi's contribution.

As team research increased with the growth of technology-based industry, so did the dilemma, for the rules of joint inventorship were not readily adaptable to the development of complex inventions. It became apparent that legislative remedy was needed. The amendment of 35 U.S.C. § 116 provided a simple solution to a complex problem:

> § 116 [second sentence]. Inventors may apply for a patent jointly even though (1) they did not physically work together or at the same time, (2) each did not make the same type or amount of contribution, or (3) each did not make a contribution to the subject matter of every claim of the patent.

Pub.L. 98–622, § 104, 98 Stat. 3384, Nov. 8, 1984. The amendment identified the three major pitfalls that had arisen, and removed them.

This amendment did not also deal with the laws of patent ownership, and did not automatically convey ownership of the entire patent to everyone who could now be named as an inventor, whatever the contribution. The amendment simply permitted persons to be named on the patent document, whether as minor contributors to a subordinate embodiment, or full partners in the creation and development of the invention. The ownership relationships among the persons who, under § 116, could now be recognized as contributors to the invention, is irrelevant to the purpose of the amendment of § 116, and to its consequences. Section 116 has nothing to do with patent ownership.

B. The Law of Joint Ownership

The pre–1984 rule of joint ownership of joint inventions can be readily understood in its historical context, for a legally cognizable "joint invention" required mutuality of interaction and a real partnership in the creation and development of the invention. On this foundation, a "joint inventor" was also, justly and legally, an equal owner of the idea and of any patent thereon.

The law of patent ownership has its roots in the common law of property—although a patent has its own peculiar character, for it deals with intangibles. Certain incidents of patent ownership have been created or clarified by statute, *see* 35 U.S.C. § 262, yet the common law provided the basic rules, as manifested in the concepts of tenancy in common and undivided interests that courts have drawn upon in patent ownership disputes.

The jurisprudence governing property interests is generally a matter of state law. Even when the property is the creation of federal statute, private rights are usually defined by state laws of property. This has long been recognized with respect to patent ownership and transfers. It is equally established that inventorship and patent ownership are separate issues.

Most of the disputes concerning patent ownership that reached the Supreme Court dealt not with joint invention, but assignments and other transfers. The oft-cited case of *Waterman v. Mackenzie,* 138 U.S. 252, 11 S.Ct. 334, 34 L.Ed. 923 (1891) dealt with a dispute among the inventor's spouse and various assignees concerning ownership of the fountain pen patent, not inventorship. Occasionally an issue of ownership of patent property arose based on whether the claimant actually shared fully in the creation of the invention. In such cases, as cited *supra,* the decision on "joint invention" also decided the issue of ownership, for a person who had fully shared in the creation of the invention was deemed to be a joint owner of the entire patent property. On this premise each joint inventor was deemed to occupy the entirety of the patented subject matter, on a legal theory of tenancy in common. *See* 7 Richard R. Powell, *Powell on Real Property* ¶ 602[5] (1997) ("undivided fractional shares held by tenants in common are usually equal and are presumed equal unless circumstances indicate otherwise"). As patent property became viewed more precisely as personal property, *see* 35 U.S.C. § 261, the concept of tenancy in common was adjusted to that of an undivided interest, although with no substantial change in legal rights.

After the major change that the 1984 amendment to § 116 made in "joint invention," by authorizing the naming of any contributor to any claim of a patent, the legal premise that each named person had made a full and equal contribution to the entire patented invention became obsolete. It is not an implementation of the common law of property, or its statutory embodiments, to treat all persons, however minor their contribution, as full owners of the entire property as a matter of law. The law had never given a contributor to a minor portion of an invention a full share in the originator's patent.

By amending § 116 in order to remove an antiquated pitfall whereby patents were being unjustly invalidated, the legislators surely did not intend to create another inequity. Apparently no one foresaw that judges might routinely transfer pre–1984 ownership concepts into the changed inventorship law. I have come upon no discussion of this anomaly in various scholarly articles on the amended § 116.

In the case at bar, the district court recognized that Dr. Yoon originated the fundamental concept and the major aspects of its implementation. The court, however, construed the law as requiring that since Mr. Choi was named as a "joint inventor" (in accordance with the retroactivity legislated for the amendment to § 116) he automatically owned an undivided interest in the entire patent, and had the unencumbered and unfettered right to alienate an interest in the entire patent. Thus Mr. Choi, who would not pass the pre–1984 test of joint inventor, was nonetheless awarded full property rights in the entire invention and patent, as if he had been a true joint inventor of all the claims.

The panel majority, confirming this error, holds that Mr. Choi's contribution to two claims means and requires that Yoon "must now effectively share with Choi ownership of all the claims, even those which he invented by himself." That is incorrect. As I have discussed, the law of shared ownership was founded on shared invention, a situation that admittedly does not here prevail. Whether or not Mr. Choi is now properly named under § 116 because of his contribution to two claims, he is not a joint owner and he does not have the right to grant a license under all fifty-five claims. No theory of the law of property supports such a distortion of ownership rights. Thus I must, respectfully, dissent from the decision of the panel majority.

Notes

1. Legal Aspects of Inventorship. As demonstrated by *Ethicon v. U.S. Surgical*, the combination of the liberality of § 116 and the importance of the inventive entity under § 102 can lead to some sophisticated legal strategizing as to which claims to place within a particular patent application. Consider, for example, two inventors, Avo and Bolivar, who have assigned rights to their inventions to their common employer, Xino Ltd. Suppose that Avo files an application directed towards a technology of which he is the sole inventor. Later, Avo and Bolivar jointly develop an obvious variant on Avo's earlier claimed technology and file a patent application with both as named inventors. Still later, Avo's application matures into an issued patent.

Under these circumstances, the patent examiner could properly reject Avo and Bolivar's joint application in light of Avo's prior application, due to the combination of § 102(e) and § 103(a). Xino Ltd. might respond by eliminating all of Bolivar's technical contributions from the claims of the subsequent application. *See* 37 C.F.R. § 1.48(b). With Avo as the sole inventor in both applications, his earlier application no longer comprises a valid § 102(e) reference as it was not filed "by another"—that is, by a different inventive entity. Note that double patenting concerns might arise in such a scenario, however, as described later in this Chapter.

2. Inventorship and the Patent Instrument. Despite the significant consequences that attach to the inventive entity, at present the U.S. patent instrument simply lists all the inventors corresponding to its set of claims. Do you believe that patentees should be required to name the appropriate inventors on a claim-by-claim basis?

3. Practical Aspects of Inventorship. As inventors named in a patent often receive benefits ranging from financial rewards from their employers to recognition from the technical community, intracorporate disputes over inventorship are not uncommon. Patent attorneys must often demonstrate persistence and tact in order to ensure that the appropriate individuals are named in a given patent. They should also be aware of corporate technical disclosure forms and other documents that label a person as the "inventor"; such determinations are often made without awareness of the strictures of the Patent Act.

4. Joint Ownership. *Ethicon v. U.S. Surgical* explains that joint inventors ordinarily become joint owners of any patents resulting from their efforts. Although § 262 invites joint owners to contract their way around the statute, the grant of a patent often acts to turn technological partners into business competitors. Do you find this policy a wise one?

Patent law apparently reflects such a strong desire to encourage the commercial development of patented inventions that the courts are willing to enforce mercenary attitudes among patent co-owners. On the other hand, one can readily imagine the sorts of transaction costs that the patent law bluntly sweeps away by allowing any joint owner to exploit or license a patented technology. Does society favor commercial development of inventions so greatly such that other policies, such as equity among joint owners, should play no role whatsoever? Do you see a difference between personal working and licensing of a patented technology that the United States joint ownership rule would do well to recognize? Robert P. Merges & Lawrence A. Locke, *Co-Ownership of Patents: A Comparative and Economic View*, 72 J. PAT. & TRADEMARK OFF. SOC'Y 586 (1990), offers further economic, historical and comparative perspectives on patent co-ownership.

5. Muddy Waters. One court noted the conceptual complexities surrounding joint inventorship:

> The exact parameters of joint inventorship are quite difficult to define. It is one of the muddiest concepts in the muddy metaphysics of the patent law. On the one hand, it is reasonably clear that a person who has merely followed instructions of another in performing experiments is not a co-inventor of the object to which those experiments are directed. To claim inventorship is to claim at least some role in the final conception of that which is sought to be patented. Perhaps one need not be able to point to a specific component as one's sole idea, but one must be able to say that without his contribution to the final conception, it would have been less—less efficient, less simple, less economical, less something of benefit.

Mueller Brass Co. v. Reading Indus., 352 F.Supp. 1357, 1372, 176 U.S.P.Q. 361, 372 (E.D.Pa.1972), *aff'd*, 487 F.2d 1395 (3d Cir.1973). If you would tend to agree, consider the following case, where the Federal Circuit may have forgotten that one who suggests using a prior art element in a patented combination is doing more than simply acting as a technical library.

HESS v. ADVANCED CARDIOVASCULAR SYSTEMS, INC.

United States Court of Appeals, Federal Circuit, 1997.
106 F.3d 976, 41 U.S.P.Q.2d 1782.

Before NEWMAN, CIRCUIT JUDGE, FRIEDMAN, SENIOR CIRCUIT JUDGE, and MICHEL, CIRCUIT JUDGE.

FRIEDMAN, SENIOR CIRCUIT JUDGE.

This appeal challenges the decision of the United States District Court for the Northern District of California that the materials and suggestions the appellant Robert L. Hess provided to the listed inventors of a patent did not make him a co-inventor of the patented device. We affirm.

I.

A. United States Patent No. 4,323,071 (the '071 patent), which listed Drs. John B. Simpson and Edward W. Robert as the inventors, covers a balloon angioplasty catheter that is inserted into a patient's artery which has a partial blockage, or stenosis. The balloon, fitted to the catheter, is inflated by forcing a radiographic fluid into it under pressure; the resulting expansion of the balloon eliminates or reduces the blockage of the artery.

While developing the catheter, Drs. Simpson and Robert were post-doctoral Cardiology Fellows at Stanford University Medical Center. A Swiss physician, Dr. Gruntzig, had pioneered the development of balloon angioplasty. After hearing Dr. Gruntzig speak at a cardiology conference at Stanford in March 1977 and later meeting him, Dr. Simpson spent time with Dr. Gruntzig in Europe, observing him perform balloon angioplasty procedures.

Upon returning to the United States Dr. Simpson discovered that Gruntzig catheters, made only in Switzerland, were in short supply. Drs. Simpson and Robert then decided to construct their own catheter. They had not examined the Gruntzig catheter in detail, but knew it had a balloon mounted on a shaft.

In attempting to find a material from which a balloon could be made, the doctors first experimented with a plastic called polyvinylchloride, which was ineffective, and next tried Teflon tubing, which produced unsatisfactory balloons. One of their Stanford colleagues (Bill Sanders) then referred them to the appellant Mr. Hess, an engineer at Raychem Corporation. At that time Mr. Hess was a technical liaison between Raychem's domestic and foreign operations; prior to that he had headed a business development group. Sanders made the suggestion because Raychem was one of the largest manufacturers of heat shrinkable materials and "might have some material" with which they could work.

The doctors told Mr. Hess, who had no previous experience with angioplasty, about the Gruntzig catheter. They stated they "wanted to ... build a catheter ... that incorporated a balloon on the end of a shaft." They explained what they were attempting to do, the problems they had encountered in finding a suitable material for the balloon, and that they were looking for a new material. They stated that the materials they had tried did not enable them properly to control balloon expansion.

Mr. Hess suggested that the doctors try Raychem's heat shrinkable irradiated modified polyolefin tubing and demonstrated how such a material could be used to form a balloon by heating the tubing above its crystalline melting point, applying pressure, and then cooling the material. Mr. Hess also suggested the use of an adhesive-free seal to attach the balloon to the catheter. He described how one end of the tubing could be shrunk fit onto the central shaft of the catheter without the use of any potentially-toxic adhesive chemicals. Mr. Hess stated that "the basic principles which I taught them"—involving heating the tubing "above its crystalline melting point, expanding it while it remains heated using internal pressure and then cooling it in its expanded state while your [sic] maintaining the pressure"—were "in various published textbooks and the like" and "was a generally known process to a number of companies."

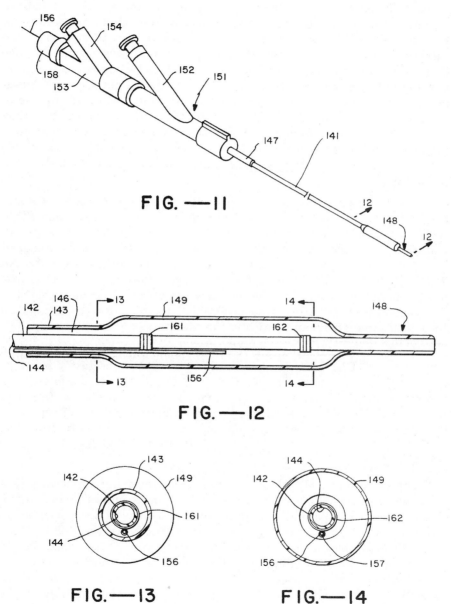

FIG. —11

FIG. —12

FIG.—13   FIG.—14

Mr. Hess provided "multiple samples of . . . tubing," with which the doctors "experimented." At that meeting and in further discussions with the doctors, Mr. Hess also suggested "approaches to construction of the catheter" using the Raychem tubing. Using that tubing, Drs. Simpson and Robert then developed and built their catheter. They had "difficulty . . . developing the . . . catheter" and spent "hours and days trying to configure this system to make it work," including "experimentation . . . with the tubing" Mr. Hess "gave" them. The two doctors worked on the catheter "virtually every day [for] four or five hours or more." The doctors finally developed the balloon using a technique called free-blowing, a technique which Mr. Hess admittedly did not suggest. Pursuant to Mr. Hess's suggestion, the doctors attempted to avoid the use of adhesives and shrink fit the balloon to the catheter shaft, but they encountered leakage problems. Without Mr. Hess's assistance and after further experimentation, the doctors ultimately developed an acceptable adhesive-free seal. Mr. Hess did not participate in the day-to-day experimentation.

The doctors applied for a patent on their catheter in April, 1978 and the '071 patent issued with twenty-one claims (the "original claims") in April, 1982. The two inventors organized the appellee company Advanced Cardiovascular Systems, Inc. (ACS), to which they assigned the '071 patent, and began manufacturing and selling the catheter. An ACS officer stated that the "catheter gained widespread success in the marketplace, and sales of the product grew rapidly," and that the Simpson–Robert catheter "was profitable" to ACS. Raychem supplied ACS with tubing for manufacturing the catheters.

B. In 1987, ACS sued SciMed Life Systems, Inc. (SciMed) in the United States District Court for the District of Minnesota for infringement of the '071 patent. The district court granted SciMed's motion for summary judgment of non-infringement, based on its interpretation of the claims. This court, however, vacated and remanded, rejecting the district court's claim interpretation. *Advanced Cardiovascular Sys., Inc. v. Scimed Life Sys., Inc.*, 887 F.2d 1070, 12 U.S.P.Q.2D (BNA) 1539 (Fed.Cir.1989).

The question of Mr. Hess's alleged co-inventorship apparently first arose when in its answer SciMed asserted, as one ground for challenging the validity of the patent, that there was a "failure of the patentees to join Hess as a co-patentee." In a declaration Mr. Hess executed in 1988, which SciMed filed in the patent infringement case, he described the aid he had given to Drs. Simpson and Robert in connection with the development of their catheter. In a 1990 affidavit, he repeated those statements and asserted that he "made substantive contributions to the subject matter disclosed" in the '071 patent and "should be named as a co-inventor thereof."

In September, 1987, ACS requested reexamination of certain claims in the '071 patent. In May 1990, the Patent and Trademark Office issued a reexamination certificate, which upheld the original claims and added claims 22–52 (the "reexamination claims").

In the summer of 1990, Mr. Hess intervened in the ACS–SciMed suit to file a cross-complaint against ACS seeking a declaration that he was a joint inventor of the catheter the '071 patent covered and seeking correction of the patent to reflect his status. The district court dismissed Mr. Hess's cross-complaint for failing to state a claim on which relief could be granted because the complaint was barred by laches. This court vacated the dismissal and remanded, holding that there were disputed issues of material fact with respect to laches that precluded dismissal. *Advanced Cardiovascular Sys., Inc. v. SciMed Life Sys., Inc.*, 988 F.2d 1157, 26 U.S.P.Q.2D (BNA) 1038 (Fed.Cir.1993).

While that appeal was pending, Mr. Hess filed suit in United States District Court for the Northern District of California against ACS, alleging that he was a co-inventor of the catheter the reexamination claims covered.

On the eve of trial ACS and SciMed settled their infringement suit. The Minnesota District Court then transferred to the Northern District of California Court the remaining portion of the case, which was Mr. Hess's cross-complaint asserting his co-inventorship of the catheter the '071 patent covers. The California District Court consolidated the two cases.

The California District Court granted summary judgment that Mr. Hess's claim of co-inventorship of the catheter the original claims covered was barred by laches, and set for trial the co-ownership issue with respect to the reexamination claims.

After a bench trial, the district court held that the evidence did not establish Mr. Hess's claim of co-inventorship of the catheter the reexamination claims covered. Ruling from the bench, the court determined that Mr. Hess was required to prove co-inventorship by clear and convincing evidence. The court stated:

> All that Mr. Hess needs to establish is that he conceived some important element or some important claim that is claimed in the patent....
>
> . . .
>
> . . . I don't think it's necessary for Mr. Hess to conceive of every feature of the catheter, but that he have some conceptual role in at least an important or a necessary element, or important and necessary claim.

The court noted:

> Inventors can obtain the services and ideas and product of others without losing their exclusive right to ownership....
>
> . . .
>
> So merely that Mr. Hess was consulted, Mr. Hess made some contribution, doesn't in and of itself rise to the level of conception

particularly if he's doing nothing more than explaining to the inventors what the then state of the art was and supplying a product to them for use in their invention.

The court found that

the information provided by Mr. Hess really didn't rise to the level of conception; that most, if not all, of his discussion with them were [sic] telling them what was available in the marketplace by way of product, and telling them how the product worked, and they, that is, Simpson and Robert, were the ones who used the product or used the—yes, used the product provided in their work.

. . .

When they were meeting with Mr. Hess, I think what Mr. Hess was doing was showing them available product, telling them its properties, telling them how it could be used, and how it might be used.

. . . Raychem became a supplier of product to Simpson and Robert, really all of which really leaves [sic] me to the conclusion that Mr. Hess' role was really as a representative of Raychem who is making available to a customer or potential customer the product that Raychem has, and its property uses and adaptation to what the inventors here wanted to do.

. . .

It's [sic] also clear from the record that Mr. Hess didn't know anything about angioplasty or medical catheters until discussion with Dr. Robert and Dr. Simpson.

Finally, the court stated:

I do wish to state for the record that on a factual basis after having heard the evidence in the case, I'm also concluding that the evidence did not establish coinventorship of the original claims in the '071 patent and not just the reissue claims for that patent.

II.

The patent laws provide that whoever "invents" patentable subject matter is entitled to a patent thereon, 35 U.S.C. § 101 (1994), and that when an "invention" is "made by two or more persons jointly, they shall apply for [a] patent jointly." 35 U.S.C. § 116 (1994). The statute also deals with the situation where an inventor is not named in the application or the issued patent. 35 U.S.C. §§ 116, 256 (1994). Section 256 provides that if "through [inadvertent] error an inventor is not named in an issued patent . . . the Commissioner [of Patents] may . . . issue a certificate correcting such error," and that "the court . . . may order correction of the patent . . . and the Commissioner shall issue a certificate accordingly."

Mr. Hess concedes that the district court "articulated the appropriate test for inventorship." The district court's standard was whether Mr.

Hess "conceived some important element or some important claim that is claimed in the patent," and whether he had "some conceptual role in at least an important or a necessary element, or important and necessary claim." Mr. Hess argues, however, that the court "completely misapplied" that standard "in finding that Hess's contributions were not inventive." This argument, however, is in reality only a reformulation of the contention that the district court's findings upon which the court based its conclusion that Mr. Hess had not established co-inventorship, are clearly erroneous.

We have carefully reviewed the evidence in the record. Although there is some conflict on the question of co-inventorship, the district court's findings that Mr. Hess was not a co-inventor of the catheter claimed in the '071 patent are not clearly erroneous.

When Drs. Simpson and Robert first met with Mr. Hess, he was totally unfamiliar with angioplasty catheterization and the problems it involved. They explained to him what they were trying to do, and what difficulties they encountered. He recommended a Raychem product that he believed would be suitable for making a balloon, showed them how a balloon could be formed by heating both ends of the tube (a procedure they did not use in making their patented catheter) and made other suggestions for making the catheter, using the Raychem tubing. Although the doctors followed and utilized some of Mr. Hess's suggestions in their extensive further research, testing and construction of their catheter, the district court justifiably concluded on this record that it was they, and not Mr. Hess, who actually conceived and made the patented invention and that Mr. Hess's contributions to the inventions did not constitute the conception necessary to establish co-inventorship.

More than 140 years ago the Supreme Court, in holding that Samuel Morse's discussions with scientists in connection with his invention of the telegraph did not alter his status of the sole inventor of that device, stated: No invention can possibly be made, consisting of a combination of different elements . . . without a thorough knowledge of the properties of each of them, and the mode in which they operate on each other. And it can make no difference, in this respect, whether [the inventor] derives his information from books, or from conversation with men skilled in the science. If it were otherwise, no patent, in which a combination of different elements is used, could ever be obtained. *O'Reilly v. Morse*, 56 U.S. 62, 111, 14 L. Ed. 601 (1853).

Similarly, in *Shatterproof Glass*, this court stated that an inventor "may use the services, ideas, and aid of others in the process of perfecting his invention without losing his right to a patent." *Shatterproof Glass Corp. v. Libbey–Owens Ford Co.*, 758 F.2d 613, 624, 225 U.S.P.Q. (BNA) 634, 641 (Fed.Cir.1985).

Here the district court found that in his consultations with Drs. Simpson and Robert, Mr. Hess was "doing nothing more than explaining to the inventors what the then state of the art was and supplying a product to them for use in their invention"; that "most, if not all, of his discussion with them were [sic] telling them what was available in the marketplace by way of product, and telling them how the product worked"; and that "what Mr. Hess was doing was showing them available product, telling them its properties, telling them how it could be used, and how it might be used." The principles Mr. Hess explained to them were well known and found in textbooks. Mr. Hess did no more than a skilled salesman would do in explaining how his employer's product could be used to meet a customer's requirements. The extensive research and development work that produced the catheter was done by Drs. Simpson and Robert. Our review of the record satisfies us that those findings are not clearly erroneous, and that they support the district court's conclusion that whatever contribution Mr. Hess made to Drs. Simpson and Robert did not constitute conception and therefore did not make Mr. Hess a co-inventor of the catheter claimed in the '071 patent.

Mr. Hess relies on snippets of the doctors' testimony in which, he asserts, the doctors conceded that Mr. Hess was responsible for significant portions of the invention the '071 patent disclosed. Those statements, however, cannot bear the weight Mr. Hess gives them. In the context of the entire record, they do not refute the factual sufficiency of the evidence supporting the district court's decision.

The judgment of the district court that Mr. Hess has not established his claim to co-inventorship of the catheter disclosed in the '071 patent is

AFFIRMED.

Notes

1. So What If What Hess Told Simpson and Robert Was Prior Art Material? In *Hess*, the Federal Circuit heavily relied upon the fact that the contributions of Hess were already known to the art. Suppose, however, that the contribution of Hess was an important part of the whole combination? Indeed, the use of heat shrinkable materials may well have been the basis for the nonobviousness of the patented combination. In the case of mechanical inventions such as catheter, how often will any co-inventor contribute subject matter that does not lie within the prior art?

2. Comparative Approaches. Although foreign patent systems are no less concerned with identifying the appropriate individuals to which credit as an inventor is due than is the U.S. regime, the first-to-file priority framework and more streamlined prior art definitions ordinarily found overseas often result in less emphasis upon inventorship as a recurring theme of patent acquisition and enforcement. In addition, most patent regimes allow assignees to file patent applications in their own name, rather than that of the inventor, as discussed below. An example of this lesser weight is demonstrated by Section 7(1) of the German patent statute, which provides:

> In order not to delay substantive examination of the patent application by determining the identity of the inventor, the applicant shall, for the purpose of proceedings before the Patent Office, be deemed to be entitled to request grant of the patent.

Under German law, inventorship may be readily corrected with the consent of the displaced individual. German Patent Law § 63. Alternatively, an individual may bring an action in district court claiming at least partial title to the patent. German Patent Law § 8. This suit must be instituted within two years following grant of the patent. Otherwise, the displaced inventor's only recourse is to bring a so-called nullity action, German Patent Law § 22, which if successful will result in patent invalidity, rather than transfer to the proper inventors. German nullity actions are briefly described in this casebook in Chapter 13.

§ 12.3 INEQUITABLE CONDUCT

Patent acquisition procedures are conducted *ex parte*. A consequence of this administrative setting is that the usual advantages of an adversarial system are unavailable. In addition, the Patent and Trademark Office does not operate laboratories, perform product testing, or verify submitted data attesting to commercial success through independent market research. The result is that the patent system relies to a great extent upon applicant observance of a duty of truthfulness towards the PTO. Experience teaches, however, that applicant obligations of candor may be tempered by the great incentive they possess not to disclose information that might deleteriously impact their prospective patent rights. Thus the concept of inequitable conduct: the intentional failure to disclose material information brings about the unenforceability of the resulting patent. The following materials explore the applicant's disclosure duties during prosecution and the consequences of their breach.

§ 12.3[a] The Duty of Disclosure

An applicant's duty of disclosure is governed by an important provision set forth by the Patent and Trademark Office at 37 C.F.R. § 1.56. As amended in 1992, Rule 56 provides:

CODE OF FEDERAL REGULATIONS TITLE 37, CHAPTER I, SUBCHAPTER A

§ 1.56 Duty to disclose information material to patentability.

(a) A patent by its very nature is affected with a public interest. The public interest is best served, and the most effective patent examination occurs when, at the time an application is being examined, the Office is aware of and evaluates the teachings of all information material to patentability. Each individual associated with the filing and prosecution of a patent application has a duty of candor and good faith in dealing with the Office, which includes a duty to disclose to the Office all information known to that individual to be material to patentability as defined in this section. The duty to disclose information exists with respect to each pending claim until the claim is canceled or withdrawn from consideration, or the application becomes abandoned. Information material to the patentability of a claim that is canceled or withdrawn from consideration need not be submitted if the information is not material to the patentability of any claim remaining under consideration in the application. There is no duty to submit information which is not material to the patentability of any existing claim. The duty to disclose all information known to be material to patentability is deemed to be satisfied if all information known to be material to patentability of any claim issued in a patent was cited by the Office or submitted to the Office in the manner prescribed by §§ 1.97(b)–(d) and 1.98. However, no patent will be granted on an application in connection with which fraud on the Office was practiced or attempted or the duty of disclosure was violated through bad faith or intentional misconduct. The Office encourages applicants to carefully examine:

(1) prior art cited in search reports of a foreign patent office in a counterpart application, and

(2) the closest information over which individuals associated with the filing or prosecution of a patent application believe any pending claim patentably defines, to make sure that any material information contained therein is disclosed to the Office.

(b) Under this section, information is material to patentability when it is not cumulative to information already of record or being made of record in the application, and

(1) It establishes, by itself or in combination with other information, a prima facie case of unpatentability of a claim; or

(2) It refutes, or is inconsistent with, a position the applicant takes in:

(i) Opposing an argument of unpatentability relied on by the Office, or

(ii) Asserting an argument of patentability.

A prima facie case of unpatentability is established when the information compels a conclusion that a claim is unpatentable under the preponderance of evidence, burden-of-proof standard, giving each term in the claim its broadest reasonable construction consistent with the specification, and before any consideration is given to evidence which may be submitted in an attempt to establish a contrary conclusion of patentability.

(c) Individuals associated with the filing or prosecution of a patent application within the meaning of this section are:

(1) Each inventor named in the application;

(2) Each attorney or agent who prepares or prosecutes the application; and

(3) Every other person who is substantively involved in the preparation or prosecution of the application and who is associated with the inventor, with the assignee or with anyone to whom there is an obligation to assign the application.

(d) Individuals other than the attorney, agent or inventor may comply with this section by disclosing information to the attorney, agent, or inventor.

The Federal Circuit has not yet offered definitive guidance about the impact of the changes to Rule 56 upon its own jurisprudence. In *Molins PLC v. Textron Inc.*, 48 F.3d 1172 n. 8, 33 U.S.P.Q.2d 1823 n. 8 (Fed.Cir.1995), the court noted:

> The duty to disclose information material to patentability has been codified in 37 C.F.R. § 1.56 (Rule 56), which was promulgated pursuant to 35 U.S.C. §§ 6 and 131. From 1977 to 1992, Rule 56 defined information as "material" when "there is a substantial likelihood that a reasonable examiner would consider it important in deciding whether to allow the application to issue as a patent." We have adopted this standard as the threshold standard of materiality. *See LaBounty Mfg., Inc. v. United States Int'l Trade Comm'n*, 958 F.2d 1066, 1074, 22 U.S.P.Q.2d 1025, 1031 (Fed.Cir.1992). In 1992, the PTO changed Rule 56 to provide that information is material to patentability when it is not cumulative to information already of record or being made of record in the application, and (1) It establishes, by itself or in combination with other information, a prima facie case of unpatentability of a claim; or (2) It refutes, or is inconsistent with, a position the applicant takes in: (i) Opposing an argument of unpatentability relied on by the Office, or (ii) Asserting an argument of patentability. 37 C.F.R. § 1.56 (1992). "[A]dministrative rules will not be construed to have retroactive effect unless their language requires this result." *Bowen v. Georgetown Univ. Hosp.*, 488 U.S. 204, 208, 109 S.Ct. 468, 471, 102 L.Ed.2d 493 (1988); see also 57 FED.REG. 2021 (Jan. 17, 1992) (PTO notice of final rulemaking stating that new Rule 56 will be applicable to all applicants and reexamination proceedings pending or filed after March 16, 1992). We thus make no comment regarding the meaning of new Rule 56.

Many cases continue to be guided by the predecessor to the current Rule 56, with its standard of whether "there is a substantial likelihood that a reasonable examiner would consider it important in deciding whether to allow the application to issue as a patent." However, there is no reason to believe that the Federal Circuit will not apply the new standard to conduct occurring after March 16, 1992.

§ 12.3[b] Intent

KINGSDOWN MEDICAL CONSULTANTS, LTD. v. HOLLISTER INC.

United States Court of Appeals, Federal Circuit, 1988.
863 F.2d 867, 9 U.S.P.Q.2d 1384.

Before MARKEY, CHIEF JUDGE, SMITH and ARCHER, CIRCUIT JUDGES.

MARKEY, CHIEF JUDGE.

Kingsdown Medical Consultants, Ltd. and E.R. Squibb & Sons, Inc., (Kingsdown) appeal from a judgment of the United States District Court for the Northern District of Illinois, No. 84 C 6113, holding U.S. Patent No. 4,460,363 ('363) unenforceable because of inequitable conduct before the United States Patent and Trademark Office (PTO). We reverse and remand.

BACKGROUND

Kingsdown sued Hollister Incorporated (Hollister) for infringement of claims 2, 4, 5, 9, 10, 12, 13, 14, 16, 17, 18, 27, 28, and 29 of Kingsdown's '363 patent. The district court held the patent unenforceable because of Kingsdown's conduct in respect of claim 9 and reached no other issue.

The invention claimed in the '363 patent is a two-piece ostomy appliance for use by patients with openings in their abdominal walls for release of waste.

The two pieces of the appliance are a pad and a detachable pouch. The pad is secured to the patient's body encircling the abdominal wall opening. Matching coupling rings are attached to the pad and to the pouch. When engaged, the rings provide a water tight seal. Disengaging the rings allows for removal of the pouch.

A. The Prosecution History

Kingsdown filed its original patent application in February 1978. The '363 patent issued July 17, 1984. The intervening period of more than six-and-a-half years saw a complex prosecution, involving the submission, rejection, amendment, re-numbering, etc., of 118 claims, a continuation application, an appeal, a petition to make special, and citation and discussion of 44 references.

After a series of office actions and amendments, Kingsdown submitted claim 50. With our emphasis on the language of interest here, claim 50 read:

> A coupling for an ostomy appliance comprising a pad or dressing having a generally circular aperture for passage of the stoma, said *pad or dressing aperture encircled by a coupling member* and an ostomy bag also having a generally circular aperture for passage of the stoma, *said bag aperture encircled by a second coupling member*, one of said coupling members being two opposed walls of closed looped annular channel form and the other coupling member of closed loop form having a rib or projection dimensioned to be gripped between the mutually (sic) opposed channel walls when said coupling members are connected, said rib or projection having a thin resilient deflectable seal strip extending therefrom, which, when said rib or projection is disposed between said walls, springs away therefrom to sealingly engage one of said walls, and in which each coupling member is formed of resilient synthetic plastics material.

The examiner found that claim 50 contained allowable subject matter, but rejected the claim for indefiniteness under 35 U.S.C. § 112, second paragraph, objecting to "encircled", because the coupling ring could not, in the examiner's view, "encircle" the aperture in the pad, the ring and aperture not being "coplanar." The examiner had not in earlier actions objected to "encircled" to describe similar relationships in other claims. Nor had the examiner found the identical "encircled" language indefinite in original claims 1 and 6 which were combined to form claim 50.

To render claim 50 definite, and thereby overcome the § 112 rejection, Kingsdown amended the claim. With our emphasis on the changed language, amended claim 50 read:

> A coupling for an ostomy appliance comprising a pad or dressing having *a body contacting surface and an outer surface with* a generally circular aperture for passage of the stoma *extending through* said pad or dressing, a coupling member *extending outwardly from said outer pad or dressing surface and encircling the intersection of said aperture and said outer pad or dressing surface,* and an ostomy bag also having a generally circular aperture *in one bag wall* for passage of the stoma *with* a second coupling member *affixed to said bag wall around the periphery of said bag wall aperture and extending outwardly from said bag wall,* one of said coupling members being two opposed walls of closed looped *annular* channel form and the other coupling member of closed loop form having a rib or projection dimensioned to be gripped between the mutually opposed channel walls when said coupling members are connected, said rib or projection having a thin resilient deflectable seal strip extending therefrom, which, when said rib or projection is disposed between said walls, springs away therefrom to sealingly engage one of said walls, and in which each coupling member is formed of resilient synthetic plastic material.

To avoid the § 112 rejection, Kingsdown had thus added the pad's ~PHE ?~ two surfaces, replaced "aperture encircled", first occurrence, with "encircling the intersection of said aperture and said outer pad or dressing surface", and deleted "encircled", second occurrence. In an advisory action, the examiner said the changes in claim language overcame the § 112 rejection and that amended claim 50 would be allowable.

While Kingsdown's appeal of other rejected claims was pending, Kingsdown's patent attorney saw a two-piece ostomy appliance manufactured by Hollister. Kingsdown engaged an outside counsel to file a continuation application and withdrew the appeal.

Thirty-four claims were filed with the continuation application, including new and never-before-examined claims and 22 claims indicated as corresponding to claims allowed in the parent application. In prosecuting the continuation, a total of 44 references, including 14 new references, were cited and 29 claims were substituted for the 34 earlier filed, making a total of 63 claims presented. Kingsdown submitted a two-column list, one column containing the claim numbers of 22 previously allowed claims, the other column containing the claim numbers of the 21 claims in the continuation application that corresponded to those previously allowed claims. That list indicated, incorrectly, that claim 43 in the continuation application corresponded to allowed claim 50 in the parent application. Claim 43 actually corresponded to the unamended claim 50 that had been rejected for indefiniteness under § 112. Claim 43 was renumbered as the present claim 9 in the '363 patent.

There was another claim 43. It was in the parent application and was combined with claim 55 of the parent application to form claim 61 in the continuation. Claim 55 contained the language of amended claim 50 relating to "encircled." It was allowed as submitted and was not involved in any discussion of indefiniteness. Claim 61 became claim 27 of the patent. Claim 27 reads as follows:

> An ostomy appliance comprising a pad or dressing having a body contacting surface and an outer surface with an aperture for passage of the stoma extending through said pad or dressing, *a coupling member extending outwardly from said pad or dressing and encircling the intersection of said aperture and the outer surface of said pad or dressing* and an ostomy bag also having an aperture in one bag wall for passage of the stoma with a second coupling member affixed to said bag wall around the periphery of said bag wall aperture and extending outwardly from said bag wall, said bag coupling member being two opposed walls of closed loop channel form and said pad or dressing coupling member being a closed loop form having a rib or projection dimensioned to be gripped between the opposed channel walls when said coupling members are connected, and a thin resilient seal strip extending at an angle radially inward from an inner surface of said rib or projection which engages the outer surface of said inner channel wall and wherein said rib or projection has a peripheral bead extending therefrom in a direction opposite said deflectable seal strip and said outer channel wall has a complementary bead on its inner surface, each of said two beads having an annular surface inclined to the common axis of said coupling members when connected, the arrangement being such that said two annular surfaces are in face-to-face contact when said two members are in their mutually coupled positions. (emphasis provided)

B. *The District Court*

Having examined the prosecution history, the district court found that the examiner could have relied on the representation that claim 43 corresponded to allowable claim 50 and rejected Kingsdown's suggestion that the examiner must have made an independent examination of claim 43, because: (1) in the Notice of Allowance, the examiner said the claims were allowed "in view of applicant's communication of 2 July 83"; (2) there was no evidence that the examiner had compared the language of amended claim 50 with that of claim 43; and (3) the examiner could justifiably rely on the representation because of an applicant's duty of candor.

The district court stated that the narrower language of amended claim 50 gave Hollister a possible defense, i.e., that Hollister's coupling member does not encircle the intersection of the aperture and the pad surface because it has an intervening "floating flange" member. The court inferred motive to deceive the PTO because Kingsdown's patent attorney viewed the Hollister appliance after he had amended claim 50 and before the continuation application was filed. The court expressly declined to make any finding on whether the accused device would or would not infringe any claims, but stated that Kingsdown's patent attorney must have perceived that Hollister would have a defense against infringement of the amended version of claim 50 that it would not have against the unamended version.

ISSUE

Whether the district court's finding of intent to deceive was clearly erroneous, rendering its determination that inequitable conduct occurred an abuse of discretion.

OPINION

We confront a case of first impression, in which inequitable conduct has been held to reside in an incorrect inclusion in a continuation application of a claim that contained allowable subject matter, but had been rejected as indefinite in the parent application.

Inequitable conduct resides in failure to disclose material information, or submission of false material information, with an intent to deceive, and those two elements, materiality and intent, must be proven by clear and convincing evidence. *J.P. Stevens & Co., Inc. v. Lex Tex Ltd., Inc.*, 747 F.2d 1553, 1559, 223 U.S.P.Q. 1089, 1092 (Fed.Cir.1984), *cert. denied*, 474 U.S. 822, 106 S.Ct. 73, 88 L.Ed.2d 60 (1985). The findings on materiality and intent are subject to the clearly erroneous standard of Rule 52(a) FED.R.CIV.P. and are not to be disturbed unless this court has a definite and firm conviction that a mistake has been committed.

Inequit. Conduct

"To be guilty of inequitable conduct, one must have intended to act inequitably." *FMC Corp. v. Manitowoc Co., Inc.*, 835 F.2d 1411, 1415, 5 U.S.P.Q.2d 1112, 1115 (Fed.Cir.1987). Kingsdown's attorney testified that he was not aware of the error until Hollister mentioned it in March 1987, and the experts for both parties testified that they saw no evidence of deceptive intent. As above indicated, the district court's finding of Kingsdown's intent to mislead is based on the alternative grounds of: (a) gross negligence; and (b) acts indicating an intent to deceive. Neither ground, however, supports a finding of intent in this case.

Intent

a. Negligence

The district court inferred intent based on what it perceived to be Kingsdown's gross negligence. Whether the intent element of inequitable conduct is present cannot always be inferred from a pattern of conduct that may be described as gross negligence. That conduct must be sufficient to require a finding of deceitful intent in the light of all the circumstances. We are not convinced that deceitful intent was present in Kingsdown's negligent filing of its continuation application or, in fact, that its conduct even rises to a level that would warrant the description "gross negligence."

It is well to be reminded of what actually occurred in this case—a ministerial act involving two claims, which, because both claims contained allowable subject matter, did not result in the patenting of anything anticipated or rendered obvious by anything in the prior art and thus took nothing from the public domain. In preparing and filing the continuation application, a newly-hired counsel for Kingsdown had two versions of "claim 50" in the parent application, an unamended rejected version and an amended allowed version. As is common, counsel renumbered and transferred into the continuation all (here, 22) claims "previously allowed". In filing its claim 43, it copied the "wrong", i.e., the rejected, version of claim 50. That error led to the incorrect listing of claim 43 as corresponding to allowed claim 50 and to incorporation of claim 43 as claim 9 in the patent. In approving the continuation for filing, Kingsdown's regular attorney did not, as the district court said, "catch" the mistake.

In view of the relative ease with which others also overlooked the differences in the claims, Kingsdown's failure to notice that claim 43 did not correspond to the amended and allowed version of claim 50 is insufficient to warrant a finding of an intent to deceive the PTO. Undisputed facts indicating that relative ease are: (1) the similarity in language of the two claims; (2) the use of the same claim number, 50, for the amended and unamended claims; (3) the multiplicity of claims involved in the prosecution of both applications; (4) the examiner's failure to reject claims using "encircled" in the parent application's first and second office actions, making its presence in claim 43 something less than a glaring error; (5) the two-year interval between the rejection/amendment of claim 50 and the filing of the continuation; (6) failure of the examiner to reject claim 43 under § 112 or to notice the differences between claim 43 and amended claim 50 during what must be presumed, absent contrary evidence, to have been an examination of the continuation; and (7) the failure of Hollister to notice the lack of correspondence between claim 43 and the amended version of claim 50 during three years of discovery and until after it had carefully and critically reviewed the file history 10 to 15 times with an eye toward litigation. That Kingsdown did not notice its mistake during more than one opportunity of doing so, does not in this case, and in view of Hollister's frequent and focused opportunities, establish that Kingsdown intended to deceive the PTO.

We do not, of course, condone inattention to the duty of care owed by one preparing and filing a continuation application. Kingsdown's counsel may have been careless, but it was clearly erroneous to base a finding of intent to deceive on that fact alone.

Thus the first basis for the district court's finding of deceitful intent (what it viewed as "gross negligence") cannot stand.

b. *Acts*

The district court also based its finding of deceitful intent on the separate and alternative inferences it drew from Kingsdown's acts in viewing the Hollister device, in desiring to obtain a patent that would "cover" that device, and in failing to disclaim or reissue after Hollister charged it with inequitable conduct. The district court limited its analysis here to claim 9 and amended claim 50.

It should be made clear at the outset of the present discussion that there is nothing improper, illegal or inequitable in filing a patent application for the purpose of obtaining a right to exclude a known competitor's product from the market; nor is it in any manner improper to amend or insert claims intended to cover a competitor's product the applicant's attorney has learned about during the prosecution of a patent application. Any such amendment or insertion must comply with all statutes and regulations, of course, but, if it does, its genesis in the marketplace is simply irrelevant and cannot of itself evidence deceitful intent.

The district court appears to have dealt with claim 9 in isolation because of Hollister's correct statement that when inequitable conduct occurs in relation to one claim the entire patent is unenforceable. *J.P. Stevens*, 747 F.2d at 1561, 223 U.S.P.Q. at 1093. But Hollister leapfrogs from that correct proposition to one that is incorrect, i.e., that courts may not look outside the involved claim in determining, in the first place, whether inequitable conduct did in fact occur at all. Claims are not born, and do not live, in isolation. Each is related to other claims, to the specification and drawings, to the prior art, to an attorney's remarks, to co-pending and continuing applications, and often, as here, to earlier or later versions of itself in light of amendments made to it. The district court accepted Hollister's argument that Kingsdown included claim 43 (unamended claim 50) in its continuing application because its chances of proving infringement of claim 43 were greater than would have been its chances of proving infringement of amended claim 50, in view of Hollister's "floating flange" argument against infringement of the latter. Neither the court nor Hollister tells us how Kingsdown could have known in July 1982 what Hollister's defense would be years later, when suit was filed.

Faced with Hollister's assertion that an experienced patent attorney would knowingly and intentionally transfer into a continuing application a claim earlier rejected for indefiniteness, without rearguing that the claim was not indefinite, the district court stated that "how an experienced patent attorney could allow such conduct to take place" gave it "the greatest difficulty." A knowing failure to disclose and knowingly false statements are always difficult to understand. However, a transfer of numerous claims en masse from a parent to a continuing application, as the district court stated, is a ministerial act. As such, it is more vulnerable to errors which by definition result from inattention, and is less likely to result from the scienter involved in the more egregious acts of omission and commission that have been seen as reflecting the deceitful intent element of inequitable conduct in our cases.

Because there has been no decision on whether any of claims 2, 4, 5, and 27 are infringed by Hollister's product, or on whether Kingsdown could have reasonably believed they are, it cannot at this stage be said that Kingsdown needed claim 9 to properly bring suit for infringement. If it did not, the district court's implication of sinister motivation and the court's inference of deceptive intent from Kingsdown's acts would collapse.

The district court, in finding intent, made a passing reference to Kingsdown's continuation of its suit after Hollister charged inequitable conduct. Hollister vigorously argues before us that Kingsdown's continuing its suit while failing to disclaim or reissue is proof of bad faith. A failure to disclaim or reissue in 1987, however, would not establish that Kingsdown acted in bad faith when it filed its continuation application in 1982. Moreover, a suggestion that patentees should abandon their suits, or disclaim or reissue, in response to every charge of inequitable conduct raised by an alleged infringer would be nothing short of ridiculous. The right of patentees to resist such charges must not be chilled to extinction by fear that a failure to disclaim or reissue will be used against them as evidence that their original intent was deceitful. Nor is there in the record any basis for expecting that any such disclaimer or reissue would cause Hollister to drop its inequitable conduct defense or refrain from reliance on such remedial action as support for that defense. Kingsdown's belief in its innocence meant that a court test of the inequitable conduct charge was inevitable and appropriate. A requirement for disclaimer or reissue to avoid adverse inferences would merely encourage the present proliferation of inequitable conduct charges.

We are forced to the definite and firm conviction that a mistake has been committed, amounting to an abuse of discretion. The district court's finding of deceitful intent was clearly erroneous.

RESOLUTION OF CONFLICTING PRECEDENT[16]

"Gross Negligence" and The Intent Element of Inequitable Conduct

Some of our opinions have suggested that a finding of gross negligence compels a finding of an intent to deceive. *In re Jerabek*, 789 F.2d 886, 891, 229 U.S.P.Q. 530, 533 (Fed.Cir.1986); *Driscoll v. Cebalo*, 731 F.2d 878, 885, 221 U.S.P.Q. 745, 751 (Fed.Cir.1984). Others have indicated that gross negligence alone does not mandate a finding of intent to deceive. *FMC Corp. v. Manitowoc Co.*, 835 F.2d 1411, 1415 n. 9, 5 U.S.P.Q.2d 1112, 1116 n. 9 (Fed.Cir.1987).

16. Because precedent may not be changed by a panel, *South Corp. v. United States*, 690 F.2d 1368, 1370 n. 2 (Fed.Cir. 1982) (*in banc*), this section has been considered and decided by an in banc court.

"Gross negligence" has been used as a label for various patterns of conduct. It is definable, however, only in terms of a particular act or acts viewed in light of all the circumstances. We adopt the view that a finding that particular conduct amounts to "gross negligence" does not of itself justify an inference of intent to deceive; the involved conduct, viewed in light of all the evidence, including evidence indicative of good faith, must indicate sufficient culpability to require a finding of intent to deceive. *See Norton v. Curtiss*, 433 F.2d 779, 167 U.S.P.Q. 532 (CCPA 1970).

Holding

Nature of Question

Some of our opinions have indicated that whether inequitable conduct occurred is a question of law. *In re Jerabek*, 789 F.2d at 890, 229 U.S.P.Q. at 532–33 (Fed.Cir.1986). In *Gardco Mfg. Inc. v. Herst Lighting Co.*, 820 F.2d 1209, 1212, 2 U.S.P.Q.2d 2015, 2018 (Fed.Cir.1987) (citing *Precision Instrument Mfg. Co. v. Automotive Maintenance Mach. Co.*, 324 U.S. 806, 65 S.Ct. 993, 89 L.Ed. 1381 (1945)), the court indicated that the inequitable conduct question is equitable in nature. We adopt the latter view, i.e., that the ultimate question of whether inequitable conduct occurred is equitable in nature.

Standard of Review

As an equitable issue, inequitable conduct is committed to the discretion of the trial court and is reviewed by this court under an abuse of discretion standard. We, accordingly, will not simply substitute our judgment for that of the trial court in relation to inequitable conduct.

Effect of Inequitable Conduct

When a court has finally determined that inequitable conduct occurred in relation to one or more claims during prosecution of the patent application, the entire patent is rendered unenforceable. We, in banc, reaffirm that rule as set forth in *J.P. Stevens & Co. v. Lex Tex Ltd.*, 747 F.2d 1553, 1561, 223 U.S.P.Q. 1089, 1093–94 (Fed.Cir.1984), *cert. denied*, 474 U.S. 822, 106 S.Ct. 73, 88 L.Ed.2d 60 (1985).

CONCLUSION

Having determined that the district court's finding of intent is clearly erroneous, the panel reverses the judgment based on a conclusion of inequitable conduct before the PTO and remands the case for such further proceedings as the district court may deem appropriate.

REVERSED AND REMANDED.

Notes

1. Inequitable Conduct at the PTO. The Commissioner of the Patent Office announced in 1988 that the "Office will no longer investigate and reject original or reissue applications under 37 C.F.R. § 1.56 and to the extent 37 C.F.R. § 1.56 now requires the Office to do so, it is hereby waived." Noting that *Kingsdown* required a high level of proof of applicant intent to mislead the examiner, the Commissioner reasoned that the Office was not well-equipped to make such a determination. The PTO does continue to consider inequitable conduct in a few contexts, notably interference proceedings where one party asserts inequitable conduct, and in disciplinary proceedings against a patent practitioner for violation of ethical standards. Inequitable conduct has therefore become almost exclusively a matter for the judicial forum with its ability to issue subpoenas, hear live testimony and provide for cross-examination.

What do you think of the PTO's current policy? Note that at least one Federal Circuit decision, *Paragon Podiatry Lab., Inc. v. KLM Labs., Inc.*, 984 F.2d 1182, 25 U.S.P.Q.2d 1561 (Fed.Cir.1993), affirmed a finding of intent to mislead the office based upon a motion for summary judgment, without the use of live testimony. Consider also the small number of issued patents that are actually subject to litigation. Why should inequitable conduct be relevant only for such a meager subset of patents?

2. Limited to Claimed Subject Matter? The Federal Circuit clarified that inequitable conduct applies to the entire prosecution process, not merely that part of the process which produces the final claims:

> Appellant argues that Finch, who drafted claims which the PTO rejected, alone intended to mislead. Therefore, according to appellant, because inequitable conduct pertains only to rejected claims, the trial court may enforce the '301 patent's claims. This court disagrees.

* * *

> The duty of candor extends throughout the patent's entire prosecution history. In determining inequitable conduct, a trial court may look beyond the final claims to their antecedents. "Claims are not born, and do not live, in isolation.... [cite deleted] Therefore, a breach of the duty of candor early in the prosecution may render unenforceable all claims which eventually issue from the same or a related application."

Fox Indus. v. Structural Preservation Sys., 922 F.2d 801, 803–04, 17 U.S.P.Q.2d 1579 (Fed.Cir.1990). In this case, the intentionally withheld prior art was Douglas Fox's own sales brochure which issued in 1971, more than one year before the patent application. Fox had given the brochure to his patent attorney, Finch, who used it to draft the 1973 application. Whose intent gave rise to the inequitable conduct? Is this case a sufficient warning for prospective patent attorneys?

3. Truth or Consequences. The effect of misconduct before the PTO may reach further than noted in *Kingsdown*. As indicated by Judge Nies in her concurring opinion in *Argus Chemical Corp. v. Fibre Glass–Evercoat Co.*, 812 F.2d 1381, 1387, 1 U.S.P.Q.2d 1971, 1975–76 (Fed.Cir.1987):

> On the merits it may be helpful to add my view that, in sum, our cases reflect three standards for judging the misconduct by a patentee dependent upon the extent of relief which opposing litigant seeks: (1) misconduct which makes a patent unenforceable (which we have termed "inequitable conduct"); (2) misconduct which is sufficient to make a case "exceptional" under 35 U.S.C.A. § 285 so as to warrant, in the discretion of the trial judge, an award of attorney fees, and (3) misconduct which rises to the level of common law fraud and which will support an antitrust claim. As a litigant moves from a purely defensive

position, to a recoupment request, to an affirmative claim for damages, it is reasonable to impose more stringent requirements.

The leading case on the third point, *Walker Process Equipment, Inc. v. Food Machinery & Chemical Corp.*, 382 U.S. 172, 147 U.S.P.Q. 404 (1965), held that the maintenance and enforcement of a patent acquired by fraud may serve as the basis for an antitrust violation. There, the district court had earlier held that the defendant committed fraud by failing to disclose a public use that would have barred the patent under § 102(b).

§ 12.3[c]   Materiality

MOLINS PLC v. TEXTRON, INC.

United States Court of Appeals, Federal Circuit, 1995.
48 F.3d 1172, 33 U.S.P.Q.2d 1823.

LOURIE, CIRCUIT JUDGE.

Molins PLC and John Coventry Smith, Jr. appeal from a judgment of the United States District Court for the District of Delaware holding U.S. Patents 4,369,563 and 4,621,410 unenforceable due to inequitable conduct.

BACKGROUND

Molins is a United Kingdom limited liability corporation, having its principal office at Milton Keynes, England. Between 1963 and 1973, Molins operated a machine tool division for the design, manufacture, and sale of machine tools used in the high speed machining of light alloys.

In 1965, Molins' Research Director, Dr. David Williamson, developed a method for improving batch machining involving a plurality of machine tools arranged to accommodate the manual transport of pallet-mounted workpieces to and from the machine tools (the "batch process"). Molins filed a British patent application for the batch process in the fall of 1965 and filed counterpart applications in a number of countries, including the United States.

In 1966, Williamson invented a fully automated machining system that allows several related families of parts to be machined simultaneously (the "system 24"). Molins filed patent applications for the system 24 in the United Kingdom, the United States, and in other countries during 1966–67. In 1967, the U.S. batch process application was combined with the U.S. system 24 application in a continuation-in-part. The '563 patent later matured from a continuation-in-part of the combined U.S. application. Before the patent issued in January of 1983, however, the batch process claims were cancelled and only claims drawn to the system 24 apparatus issued. The '410 patent issued from a divisional application and is directed to the system 24 method of machining.

The '563 patent discloses a system of complementary, numerically-controlled machine tools. Materials to be machined, or "workpieces," are subjected to selected machining operations on selected machine tools in a selected order by the delivery of common form pallets loaded with the workpieces. Transporters deliver pallets between the machine tools, a storage rack, and work stations where the workpieces are automatically delivered in bins from a bin store and are loaded on the pallets. Tool magazines are delivered between a rack and the machine tools by a transporter. A computer controls transport and machining operations, and receives signals from monitors indicating the location of pallets, tool magazines, and bins.

Dennis Whitson began working for Molins in 1967 as one of several British chartered patent agents working in Molins' in-house patent department. He managed Molins' patent department from 1974 through 1981 and was responsible for the prosecution of all of Molins' patent applications directed to the batch process and system 24 inventions. When Whitson retired in 1981, Ivan Hirsh, employed by Molins since 1968, assumed the responsibilities as manager of Molins' patent department. After becoming manager, Hirsh assumed responsibility for prosecuting the applications relating to the patents in suit and for conducting the litigation involving Molins' patents.

Smith served as the primary United States counsel to Molins, representing Molins at the United States Patent and Trademark Office ("PTO") from 1966 through the relevant time period in this case. Beginning in 1967, Smith prosecuted the patent applications leading to the issuance of the '563 and '410 patents.

Between the fall of 1967 and April 1968, while the relevant U.S. patent applications were pending, Molins' patent department, and specifically Whitson, became aware of prior art referred to here as the "Wagenseil reference." Upon evaluating the Wagenseil reference, Whitson concluded that it fully anticipated the "batch process" claims that Molins initially filed in the United Kingdom and in many other countries including the United States. Accordingly, in 1968 and 1969, Whitson abandoned all the foreign patent applications to the batch process. However, Whitson decided not to abandon the pending U.S. application because it contained both batch process and system 24 claims.

Prosecution of the U.S. and foreign system 24 applications continued. Wagenseil was cited to and by several foreign patent offices, but was not cited by Molins to the PTO. In 1975, Whitson told Smith that there were oppositions to the German system 24 patent application, but he did not inform Smith of the art cited in Germany, which included the Wagenseil reference. Eventually, Molins abandoned all foreign system 24 applications. In the United States, the '563 patent issued in January of 1983, after Molins prevailed in an interference with two other parties.

Later in 1983, Hirsh reviewed the files of the foreign system 24 applications, all of which had been abandoned in the late 1970s. Hirsh found the references that had been cited in the foreign patent prosecution, but not the PTO, including the Wagenseil reference. Hirsh also found Whitson's correspondence relating to the references and to their citation to and by foreign patent offices. Hirsh then informed Smith of the foreign citations. Together, they consulted with outside counsel and, on September 21, 1984, although the '563 patent had already issued, filed a lengthy prior art statement under 37 C.F.R. § 1.501 (Rule 501) on behalf of Molins, listing the Wagenseil reference together with all other prior art references that had been cited during the foreign prosecution.

In October of 1984, Cross & Trecker, Incorporated, the parent corporation of defendant Kearney & Trecker Corporation, filed a request for reexamination of the '563 patent in view of several IBM references. Cross & Trecker filed a Form PTO–1449 listing Wagenseil, which was initialed by the examiner as having been considered in June of 1985. During the reexamination, Molins referred the examiner to the Rule 501 prior art statement previously filed in the '563 patent file. The examiner indicated that, in order to make the prior art of record, Molins was required to submit English language translations of the foreign language references. Accordingly, Molins filed the translations and a brief statement of the relevance of the cited art. The examiner initialed each reference Molins had listed, indicating that he had considered it. The examiner's final office action in the reexamination stated that he had considered all of the cited references. No claims were rejected based on Wagenseil during the reexamination. Re–Examination Certificate B1 4,369,563 was issued on May 13, 1986.

Late in 1986, Molins and Smith filed suit against Textron, Incorporated, Kearney & Trecker, and Avco Corporation (collectively "Textron"), alleging infringement of the '563 and '410 patents.

On November 24, 1992, the court held that both patents were unenforceable due to inequitable conduct.

DISCUSSION

Inequitable Conduct

Applicants for patents are required to prosecute patent applications in the PTO with candor, good faith, and honesty. A breach of this duty constitutes inequitable conduct.

Inequitable conduct includes affirmative misrepresentation of a material fact, failure to disclose material information, or submission of false material information, coupled with an intent to deceive. One who alleges inequitable conduct arising from a failure to disclose prior art must offer clear and convincing proof of the materiality of the prior art, knowledge chargeable to the applicant of that prior art and of its materiality, and the applicant's failure to disclose the prior art, coupled with an intent to mislead the PTO.

The withholding of information must meet thresholds of both materiality and intent. Once threshold findings of materiality and intent are established, the court must weigh them to determine whether the equities warrant a conclusion that inequitable conduct occurred. In light of all the circumstances, an equitable judgment must be made concerning whether the applicant's conduct is so culpable that the patent should not be enforced.

The ultimate determination of inequitable conduct is committed to the trial judge's discretion and is reviewed by this court under an abuse of discretion standard. To overturn such a determination, the appellant must establish that the ruling is based on clearly erroneous findings of fact or on a misapplication or misinterpretation of applicable law, or evidences a clear error of judgment on the part of the district court. Id. Findings of materiality and intent are subject to the clearly erroneous standard of Federal Rule of Civil Procedure 52(a) and will not be disturbed on appeal unless this court has a definite and firm conviction that a mistake has been committed.

Whitson's Nondisclosure of Wagenseil During Original Prosecution

Calling this case "the exceptional case among exceptional cases," the district court concluded that Whitson, Molins' in-house patent agent, had engaged in inequitable conduct in the procurement of the '563 patent because he failed to disclose Wagenseil to the PTO, even though he knew it was highly material. The court stated that "[a]lthough [Textron has] not produced direct evidence of Whitson's intent to deceive, i.e. there are no 'smoking memos' implicating bad faith on the part of Whitson, the overwhelming circumstantial evidence presented in this case leaves little doubt that Whitson intentionally concealed the Wagenseil reference from the U.S. PTO knowing that it was highly material to the U.S. applications."

Although Molins concedes that Wagenseil is highly material to the batch process invention, Molins asserts that the court erred in finding that Wagenseil was material to the '563 patent claims, which relate only to the system 24 invention. Molins points out that, although Wagenseil was cited to and considered by the examiner during reexamination of the '563 patent and during examination of the divisional '410 patent, Wagenseil was not relied upon by the examiner to reject pending claims. According to Molins, Wagenseil was ipso facto not material.

Information is "material" when there is a substantial likelihood that a reasonable examiner would have considered the information important in deciding whether to allow the application to issue as a patent. If the information allegedly withheld is not as pertinent as that considered by the examiner, or is merely cumulative to that considered by the examiner, such information is not material.

We have held that the result of a PTO proceeding that assesses patentability in light of information not originally disclosed can be of strong probative value in determining whether the undisclosed information was material. However, the standard to be applied in determining whether a reference is "material" is not whether the particular examiner of the application at issue considered the reference to be important; rather, it is that of a "reasonable examiner." *Western Electric Co. v. Piezo Tech., Inc.*, 860 F.2d 428, 433, 8 U.S.P.Q.2d 1853, 1857 (Fed.Cir.

1988). Nor is a reference immaterial simply because the claims are eventually deemed by an examiner to be patentable thereover. Thus, the fact that the examiner did not rely on Wagenseil to reject the claims under reexamination or the '410 method claims is not conclusive concerning whether the reference was material.

The court found that Wagenseil was material because, among other things, it showed a storage and retrieval system in combination with a transfer system, a combination for which the examiner had relied upon two, separate references to reject the '563 patent application claims. Moreover, the court found that Wagenseil disclosed relevant features beyond that shown in the prior art; in particular, Wagenseil disclosed a capability for workpieces to recirculate into a machining system and for workpieces to bypass certain machine tools within the system. None of the other prior art systems taught the "recirculate" and "bypass" features taught by Wagenseil.

The court further based its finding of materiality on extensive evidence showing that Whitson indicated during foreign prosecution that Wagenseil was the most relevant prior art to the corresponding foreign system 24 applications of which he was aware. Also, the evidence showed that patent examiners in several foreign countries considered Wagenseil material to the system 24 claims and that Whitson had amended and distinguished system 24 claims in foreign patent offices over Wagenseil. In this regard, the court was mindful of the risk in relying on foreign patent prosecution in light of differences in disclosure requirements, claim practice, form of application, and standard of patentability. On the evidence presented, even that independent of the admissions in the foreign prosecution, we cannot say that the court clearly erred in finding that a reasonable examiner would have considered Wagenseil important in deciding the patentability of the pending system 24 claims in the U.S. application.

Molins next argues that the court erred in finding that Whitson possessed the requisite intent to deceive the PTO.

The court based its finding of intent on the following evidence. Whitson, a seasoned patent practitioner, who was aware of the duty to disclose material information to the PTO, knew of a highly material reference but did not cite it, or any other reference, to the PTO during the entire 13 years in which he was involved in prosecuting the U.S. patent applications that led to the '563 patent. During the time the applications were pending, Whitson represented to foreign patent offices that Wagenseil was the closest prior art. Whitson was on several occasions reminded of Wagenseil's materiality through its prominence in the prosecution of several foreign counterpart applications with which Whitson was intimately involved. The court rejected Molins' argument that Whitson had acted in good faith and simply overlooked Wagenseil, since he or his associates had focused on that reference several times during more than ten years of foreign prosecution and never cited Wagenseil during 13 years of prosecution. Under these circumstances, we cannot say that the court improperly inferred that Whitson made a deliberate decision to withhold a known, material reference. Failure to cite to the PTO a material reference cited elsewhere in the world justifies a strong inference that the withholding was intentional.

Issues of inequitable conduct are most difficult both for trial courts and reviewing appellate courts. One who has engaged in inequitable conduct has inflicted damage on the patent examining system, obtaining a statutory period of exclusivity by improper means, and on the public, which must face an unlawfully-granted patent. Loss of one's patent and damage to reputation are justified penalties for such conduct. On the other hand, unjustified accusations of inequitable conduct are offensive and unprofessional. They have been called a "plague" on the patent system. *See Burlington Indus., Inc. v. Dayco Corp.*, 849 F.2d 1418, 1422, 7 U.S.P.Q.2d 1158, 1161 (Fed.Cir.1988) ("[T]he habit of charging inequitable conduct in almost every major patent case has become an absolute plague."). Unjustified accusations may deprive patentees of their earned property rights and impugn fellow professionals. They should be condemned.

Separating one from the other is a difficult task assigned to trial courts, who have the opportunity to find facts, hear witnesses, and judge credibility. Were we to have been in the trial court's shoes in this case, we do not know how we would have come out. We are, however, "only" the reviewing court, obligated to determine whether the court misapplied the law, made clearly erroneous findings of fact, or abused its discretion. We do not believe it committed any of these errors with regard to Whitson's failure to cite Wagenseil.

We are mindful of the complexities of conducting a worldwide patent prosecution in a crowded art, attempting to represent one's client or company properly, and yet fulfill one's duty to various patent offices. Things can "fall through the floorboards" and not arise from an intent to deceive. We recognize that Wagenseil and other references from the foreign prosecution were cited eventually to the PTO and that the examiner initialed them and passed the reexamination application to issue thereafter. However, the references were not cited when they should have been. There were findings that Wagenseil was known to be material, and the trial court heard testimony and judged matters of credibility concerning intent. Those who are not "up front" with the PTO run the risk that, years later, a fact-finder might conclude that they intended to deceive. That is what appears to have happened here and we must affirm the trial court with respect to Whitson's behavior.

Molins has not persuaded us that the trial court, which conducted a thorough and careful analysis of the case, clearly erred in determining that Whitson knew of a material reference and that he intentionally withheld it from the PTO. We therefore conclude that the court did not make clear errors of fact and did not abuse its discretion in determining that Whitson's nondisclosure of Wagenseil amounted to inequitable conduct. Having determined that inequitable conduct occurred in the procurement of the '563 patent, all claims of that patent are accordingly unenforceable.

The court also concluded that the inequitable conduct in the prosecution of the '563 patent extended to the '410 patent, since that patent "relied on the '563 patent." This determination has not been challenged by appellants. Thus, the '410 patent is unenforceable as well.

Notes

1. **Mulling Over _Molins_.** Do you agree with the following comment?

> The suggestion that the court did not know how it would have decided the issue had it engaged in a _de novo_ review is astonishing. The documentary evidence proved beyond a doubt that, at least, Whitson knew of the high degree of pertinency of Wagenseil. There was no evidence whatsoever that Wagenseil was merely overlooked. Perhaps, this strange remark of the court was simply designed to emphasize that it understood that it was not its job to substitute its opinion for that of the trial court.

5 Martin J. Adelman, Patent Law Perspectives, § 17.2[2] at n.341 (2d ed. 1995). On the other hand, what other steps should Molins management have taken to "do the right thing" upon their rediscovery of the Wagenseil reference? Isn't the US PTO examiner's own evaluation of the Wagenseil reference entitled to at least as much deference as that made by Whitson?

2. **Purging Inequitable Conduct.** In _Rohm & Haas Co. v. Crystal Chemical Co._, 722 F.2d 1556, 220 U.S.P.Q. 289 (Fed.Cir.1983), the court set forth three requirements for purging inequitable conduct:

> The first requirement to be met by an applicant, aware of misrepresentation in the prosecution of his application and desiring to overcome it, is that he expressly advised the PTO of its existence, stating specifically wherein it resides. The second requirement is that, if the misrepresentation is of one or more facts, the PTO be advised what the actual facts are, the applicant making it clear that further examination in light thereof may be required if any PTO action has been based on the misrepresentation. Finally, on the basis of the new and factually accurate record, the applicant must establish patentability of the claimed subject matter.... It does not suffice that one knowing of misrepresentation in an application or in its prosecution merely supplies the examiner with accurate facts without calling to his attention to the untrue or misleading assertions sought to be overcome, leaving him to formulate his own conclusions.

As to whether inequitable conduct can be purged in a reissue proceeding, considered in Chapter 13, see _Hewlett-Packard Co. v. Bausch & Lomb, Inc._, 882 F.2d 1556, 1563 n. 7, 11 U.S.P.Q.2d 1750, 1756 (Fed.Cir.1989).

3. **Immunized by Examiner's Independent Discovery?** In a portion of this opinion edited out of this book, Judge Lourie discussed the effect of nondisclosure of prior art references which the examiner later discovered on his own:

"When a reference was before the examiner whether through the examiner's search or the applicant's disclosure, it cannot be deemed to have been withheld from the examiner." *Scripps*, 927 F.2d at 1582, 18 U.S.P.Q.2d at 1015; *Orthopedic Equipment Co. v. All Orthopedic Appliances, Inc.*, 707 F.2d 1376, 217 U.S.P.Q. 1281, 1286 (Fed.Cir.1983).

Molins, 48 F.3d at 1185, 33 U.S.P.Q.2d at 1832. In a spirited dissent, also not reported in this book, Judge Nies took issue with the above statement:

Not only is the statement relied on [from *Scripps*] overly broad dicta [footnote deleted], it conflicts with an earlier decision of this court. [Prior to our decision in *Scripps*, this court found inequitable conduct based on a failure to disclose art that eventually was independently discovered by the Examiner and made of record. *A. B. Dick Co. v. Burroughs Corp.*, 798 F.2d 1392, 230 U.S.P.Q. 849 (Fed.Cir.1986).... Thus, prior to *Scripps*, this court concluded that a reference not disclosed to the Examiner but which is later discovered by the Examiner *can* be deemed to be withheld from the PTO, on facts similar in nature to those of the present case.]

Molins, 48 F.3d at 1189–90, 33 U.S.P.Q.2d at 1836. Is this an instance where one panel at the Federal Circuit declined to follow a prior ruling on the same issue? Although the rule in *Newell Cos., Inc. v. Kenney Mfg. Co.*, 864 F.2d 757, 765, 9 U.S.P.Q.2d 1417 (Fed.Cir.1988), obligates a panel to follow an earlier ruling, what is the remedy when a panel does not follow the *Newell* rule? In any event, after *Molins*, the Federal Circuit remains unclear on whether an examiner's independent discovery of undisclosed prior art immunizes the applicant.

Which of these inconsistent positions should the Federal Circuit adopt? Consider whether you agree with the following:

The law of "inequitable conduct" is designed to discourage certain forms of behavior. The success or failure of that behavior should be irrelevant. It is similar to the situation where one shoots someone in the head with the intent to kill. But, the intended victim has a metal plate in his head due to an old war injury which deflects the bullet harmlessly. Why should the existence of the metal plate effect the decision to punish or not to punish?

8 Martin J. Adelman, Patent Law Perspectives, § 17.2[1] at n.57 (2d ed. 1996).

4. Cumulative References. Suppose the applicant fails to disclose a reference that merely duplicates the teachings of cited references, but is nonetheless quite relevant to the claimed invention. Should such a reference be considered material? In *Halliburton Co. v. Schlumberger Technology Corp.*, 925 F.2d 1435, 17 U.S.P.Q.2d 1834 (Fed.Cir.1991), the court observed that "a patentee has no obligation to disclose an otherwise material reference if the reference is cumulative or less material than those already before the examiner." The Federal Circuit overturned the district court's holding of inequitable conduct based on the conclusion that references discovered by the examiner were more pertinent to the claimed invention than those that were not cited. Do you agree that examiner competence should provide a windfall to an otherwise unscrupulous patentee?

Another Federal Circuit opinion dealt with the problem of cumulative affidavits. In *Refac Int'l, Ltd. v. Lotus Development Corp.*, 81 F.3d 1576, 38 U.S.P.Q.2d 1665 (Fed.Cir.1996), the court affirmed the holding that the asserted patent was invalid for inequitable conduct. The inventors there had submitted several affidavits attesting to the sufficiency of the patent's disclosure. One of the affidavits did not mention that the affiant had worked for the inventors' company and had helped develop the commercial embodiment of the patented software process. On appeal, the patentee argued that because the tainted affidavit was merely cumulative to others that had been submitted, it was not material as a matter of law. Acknowledging the holding in *Halliburton Co. v. Schlumberger Technology Corp.*, the court nonetheless rejected the patentee's argument:

> We decline to place submitted cumulative affidavits in the same status as unsubmitted cumulative prior art. While it is not necessary to cite cumulative prior art because it adds nothing to what is already of record (although it may be prudent to do so), one cannot excuse the submission of a misleading affidavit on the ground that it was only cumulative. Affidavits are inherently material, even if only cumulative. The affirmative act of submitting an affidavit must be construed as being intended to be relied upon. It is not comparable to omitting an unnecessary act.

5. "Plague!" The Federal Circuit opined in 1988: "[T]he habit of charging inequitable conduct in almost every major patent case has become an absolute plague." *Burlington Indus. v. Dayco Corp.*, 849 F.2d 1418, 1422, 7 U.S.P.Q.2d 1158, 1161 (Fed.Cir.1988). Assuming that the Federal Circuit is correct about abuse of this defense, why is it overused? What advantages does a litigant get from charging inequitable conduct? If the Federal Circuit in 1988 actually considered inequitable conduct an overused "plague," what changes might you expect in the law of inequitable conduct? Have those changes occurred?

6. Inequitable Conduct Overseas. To the surprise of many United States practitioners, inequitable conduct is generally unavailable as an infringement defense abroad. At least three reasons support this result. First, many countries allow individuals to bring a so-called "nullity action" against an issued patent throughout the life of the patent. *See Chapter 13.* This proceeding is typically brought before a specialized patent tribunal; given this expertise and the focus of the proceeding upon patent validity issues, the time and expense of such proceedings are far less than that of a United States patent infringement trial. Second, most countries follow the so-called "English rule" and routinely award attorney fees to the victorious litigant. Inventors and their assignees who knowingly fail to disclose pertinent prior art may find themselves bearing the entire expenses of a nullity action. Finally, no other nation has yet adopted American-style discovery, so the likelihood that an applicant's inequitable conduct might even be found out is far less than in the United States.

7. Questioning Inequitable Conduct. John F. Lynch, *An Argument for Eliminating the Defense of Patent Unenforceability Based on Inequitable Conduct*, 16 AM. INTELL. PROP. L. ASS'N Q.J. 7 (1988), offers some interesting commentary upon the inequitable conduct doctrine:

The strategic and technical advantages that the inequitable conduct defense offers the accused infringer make it almost too attractive to ignore. In addition to the potential effect on the outcome of the litigation, injecting the inequitable conduct issue into patent litigation wreaks havoc in the patentee's camp. The inequitable conduct defense places the patentee on the defensive, subjects the motives and conduct of the patentee's personnel to intense scrutiny, and provides an avenue for discovery of attorney-client and work product documents. * * *

The author offers the following proposal in light of these perceived difficulties:

The defense of unenforceability because of inequitable conduct in the Patent and Trademark Office (PTO) should not be available in private patent litigation to render unenforceable a patent that is otherwise valid. Under this proposal, parties opposing a patent would have available only defenses of invalidity, noninfringement and purgeable unenforceability resulting from patent misuse. Thus, if no "but for" materiality existed, an inequitable conduct defense would be unavailing. Of course, a party opposing a patent who was successful in establishing invalidity and inequitable conduct might be awarded attorney fees, or might base an unfair competition action or an antitrust claim upon that inequitable conduct under existing authority.

It should be emphasized that we are focusing upon patents which are wholly and completely valid. Not one change in one claim would be necessary to sustain the validity of the patents that this argument seeks to preserve. The societal benefit which is derived from refusing to enforce a patent that is wholly and completely valid because of some supposed "wrong" that occurred during the obtaining of the patent is remote, and perhaps illusory. If there should exist any right to challenge the enforceability of a patent based only upon conduct occurring in the United States Patent and Trademark Office, that right should be one reserved to the government as sovereign in a district court action initiated expressly for that purpose.

What do you make of these observations? What other mechanisms might the United States patent system effectively employ to encourage candor during prosecution?

§ 12.4 DOUBLE PATENTING

Recall that 35 U.S.C.A. § 101 provides, with emphasis added, that:

Whoever invents or discovers any new and useful process, machine, manufacture, or composition of matter, or any new and useful improvement thereof, may obtain *a patent* therefor, subject to the conditions and requirements of this title.

The Patent Office and the courts have interpreted this language to require the issuance of only a single patent per invention. When an inventor files duplicative applications directed towards the same invention, the examiner should issue a double patenting rejection. If the examiner fails to do so, then double patenting may serve as a validity defense during infringement litigation. One policy rationale for this rejection is straightforward: otherwise, the inventor might extend the statutory period of exclusivity by filing a series of related patent applications covering the same invention.

You may be surprised to learn that no other statutory mechanism operates to achieve this effect. However, your knowledge of 35 U.S.C.A. § 102 should reinforce the need for a double patenting doctrine. Recall that many activities must be performed *by another* to be patent-defeating under § 102, including the secret prior art established by § 102(e). Only the statutory bars of § 102(b) may be the result of the inventor's own work and still deny a patent to the applicant. Thus, in the absence of other activities that disclose the invention to the public, an inventor could extend the statutory protection period through a simple policy: file an application no later than one year after an earlier, related application has matured into a patent.

Suppose that the applications do not disclose the identical invention, but instead obvious variations of each other? In such cases the patent will also be struck down under so-called "obviousness-type double patenting," a doctrine with the same policy foundation but altogether less sure statutory moorings. In contrast to a double patenting rejection based on multiple claims to the same invention, judges and patent examiners may employ prior art references in combination with the claims of the earlier application or issued patent to determine whether the invention claimed in the later application or patent is obvious to those of skill in the art.

IN RE VOGEL

United States Court of Customs and Patent Appeals, 1970.
422 F.2d 438, 164 U.S.P.Q. 619.

Before RICH, ACTING CHIEF JUDGE, ALMOND, BALDWIN, LANE, JUDGES, and MATTHEWS, SENIOR JUDGE, United States District Court for the District of Columbia, sitting by designation.

LANE, JUDGE.

This appeal is from the decision of the Patent Office Board of Appeals affirming the rejection of all claims (7, 10 and 11) in appellants' patent application serial No. 338,158, filed January 16, 1964, for "Process of Preparing Packaged Meat Products for Prolonged Storage."

The ground of rejection for each claim is double patenting, based upon the claims of appellants' U.S. patent 3,124,462, issued March 10, 1964, in view of a reference patent of Ellies, Re. 24,992, reissued May 30, 1961. No terminal disclaimer has been filed.

THE APPEALED CLAIMS

Claims 7 and 10 are directed to a process of packaging meat generally. Claim 10 is illustrative:

10.　A method for prolonging the storage life of packaged meat products comprising the steps of: removing meat from a freshly slaughtered carcass at substantially the body bleeding temperature thereof under ambient temperature conditions; comminuting the meat during an exposure period following slaughter while the meat is at a temperature between said bleeding and ambient temperatures; sealing the comminuted meat within a flexible packaging material having an oxygen permeability ranging from 0.01 X 10–(10) to 0.1 X 10–(10) cc.mm/sec/cm(2) /cm Hg at 30 degrees C during said exposure period and before the meat has declined in temperature to the ambient temperature; and rapidly reducing the temperature of the packaged meat to a storage temperature below the ambient temperature immediately following said packaging of the meat.

The invention is based on appellants' discovery that spoilage and discoloration of meat are markedly accelerated if the meat is allowed to reach ambient temperature before packaging.

Claim 11 is directed to a similar process specifically limited to beef.

Prior Art

The only reference of record is Ellies. Ellies teaches the use of meat-packaging material having the oxygen permeability range recited in the claims.

The Patent

Appellants' patent, which is not prior art, claims a method of processing pork. Claim 1 of the patent is illustrative.

> 1. A method of preparing pork products, comprising the steps of: bonding a freshly slaughtered carcass while still hot into trimmings; grinding desired carcass trimmings while still warm and fluent; mixing the ground trimmings while fluent and above approximately 80 degrees F., mixing to be complete not more than approximately 3 1/2 hours after the carcass has been bled and stuffing the warm and fluent mixed trimmings into air impermeable casings.

The Board

The board characterized the rejection as follows:

> The sole ground of rejection is that claims 7, 10 and 11 are unpatentable over appellants' copending patented claims in Vogel et al., in view of Ellies. This is a double-patenting type rejection, whose statutory basis is 35 U.S.C. 101. . . .

Thus the board viewed this case as involving "same invention" type double patenting. The board then discussed the differences between the appealed claims and the patent claims and found that the former did not define a "patentable advance" over the latter. It is thus clear that the board was not at all dealing with "same invention" type double patenting but with the "obvious variation" type. The board found that the appealed claims merely extended the pork process to beef, and that this was not a "patentable advance." Such language states only a conclusion, since patentability is the very issue to be determined. The board gave the following analysis to support its conclusion:

> We agree with the Examiner's reasons for holding the application of the claimed method to beef to be an unpatentable adaptation. In addition, the definition of "sausage" in Webster's 3rd New International Dictionary of 1963, on page 2019 is pertinent:
>
> > "sausage—a highly seasoned finely divided meat that is usually a mixture (as of beef or pork) * * *"

The examiner's reasons as stated in his answer were that the process steps are essentially the same, and the choice of beef rather than pork "is of no patentable significance since this would appear to be a judicious choice of available meat products, well within the ordinary skill of the art, and particularly so, in the absence of any unusual or unobvious result."

The board's use of the dictionary meaning of "sausage," as above quoted, is apparently intended to show that beef and pork are equivalents. Whatever may be their equivalency in other contexts, the dictionary definition of "sausage" does not show that beef and pork are equivalents in the sense of the invention now claimed. Appellants contend that the examiner and the board used the disclosure of the patent as a basis for concluding obviousness. To the effect that consideration of the patent disclosure is improper in testing for obvious-type double patenting, appellants cite *In re Baird*, 348 F.2d 974, 52 CCPA 1747 (1965).

OPINION

The proceedings below in this case indicate the advisability of a restatement of the law of double patenting as enunciated by this court.

The first question in the analysis is: Is the same invention being claimed twice? 35 U.S.C. § 101 prevents two patents from issuing on the same invention. As we have said many times, "invention" here means what is defined by the claims, whether new or old, obvious or unobvious; it must not be used in the ancient sense of "patentable invention," or hopeless confusion will ensue. By "same invention" we mean identical subject matter. Thus the invention defined by a claim reciting "halogen" is not the same as that defined by a claim reciting "chlorine," because the former is broader than the latter. On the other hand, claims may be differently worded and still define the same invention. Thus a claim reciting a length of "thirty-six inches" defines the same invention as a claim reciting a length of "three feet," if all other limitations are identical. In determining the meaning of a word in a claim, the specification may be examined. It must be borne in mind, however, especially in non-chemical cases, that the words in a claim are generally not limited in their meaning by what is shown in the disclosure. Occasionally the disclosure will serve as a dictionary for terms appearing in the claims, and in such instances the disclosure may be used in interpreting the coverage of the claim. *In re* Baird, supra. A good test, and probably the only objective test, for "same invention," is whether one of the claims could be literally infringed without literally infringing the other. If it could be, the claims do not define identically the same invention. This is essentially the test applied in *In re Eckel*, 393 F.2d 848, 55 CCPA 1068 (1968). There the court rejected the idea of "colorable variation" as a comparison category and stated that inventions were either the same, or obvious variations, or unobvious variations. The court's holding in Eckel was that same invention means identically same invention.

If it is determined that the same invention is being claimed twice, 35 U.S.C. § 101 forbids the grant of the second patent, regardless of the presence or absence of a terminal disclaimer. If the same invention is not being claimed twice, a second question must be asked.

The second analysis question is: Does any claim in the application define merely an obvious variation of an invention disclosed and claimed in the patent? In considering the question, the patent disclosure may not be used as prior art. This does not mean that the disclosure may not be used at all. As pointed out above, in certain instances it may be used as a dictionary to learn the meaning of terms in a claim. It may also be used as required to answer the second analysis question above. We recognize that it is most difficult, if not meaningless, to try to say what is or is not an obvious variation of a claim. A claim is a group of words defining only the boundary of the patent monopoly. It may not describe any physical thing and indeed may encompass physical things not yet dreamed of. How can it be obvious or not obvious to modify a legal boundary? The disclosure, however, sets forth at least one tangible embodiment within the claim, and it is less difficult and more meaningful to judge whether that thing has been modified in an obvious manner. It must be noted that this use of the disclosure is not in contravention of the cases forbidding its use as prior art, nor is it applying the patent as a reference under 35 U.S.C. § 103, since only the disclosure of the invention claimed in the patent may be examined.

If the answer to the second question is no, there is no double patenting involved and no terminal disclaimer need be filed. If the answer is yes, a terminal disclaimer is required to prevent undue timewise extension of monopoly.

We now apply this analysis to the case before us.

The first question is: Is the same invention being claimed twice? The answer is no. The patent claims are limited to pork. Appealed claims 7 and 10 are limited to meat, which is not the same thing. Claims 7 and 10 could be infringed by many processes which would not infringe any of the patent claims. Claim 11 is limited to beef. Beef is not the same thing as pork.

We move to the second question: Does any appealed claim define merely an obvious variation of an invention disclosed and claimed in the patent? We must analyze the claims separately.

As to claim 11 the answer is no. This claim defines a process to be performed with beef. We must now determine how much of the patent disclosure pertains to the invention claimed in the patent, which is a process to be performed with pork, to which all the patent claims are limited. The specification begins with certain broad assertions about meat sausages. These assertions do not support the patent claims. The patent claims recite "pork" and "pork" does not read on "meat." To consider these broad assertions would be using the patent as prior art, which it is not. The specification then states how the process is to be carried out with pork. This portion of the specification supports the patent claims and may be considered. It describes in tabular form the time and temperature limits associated with the pork process. Appealed claim 11, reciting beef, does not read on the pork process disclosed and claimed in the patent. Further, we conclude that claim 11 does not define merely an obvious variation of the pork process. The specific time and temperature considerations with respect to pork might not be applicable to beef. There is nothing in the record to indicate that the spoliation characteristics of the two meats are similar. Accordingly, claim 11 does not present any kind of double patenting situation.

Appealed claim 10, supra, will now be considered. It recites a process to be performed with "meat." "Meat" reads literally on pork. The only limitation appearing in claim 10 which is not disclosed in the available portion of the patent disclosure is the permeability range of the packaging material; but this is merely an obvious variation as shown by Ellies. The answer to the second analysis question, therefore, is yes, and the claim is not allowable in the absence of a terminal disclaimer. The correctness of this conclusion is demonstrated by observing that claim 10, by reciting "meat," includes pork. Its allowance for a full term would therefore extend the time of monopoly as to the pork process. It is further noted that viewing the inventions in reverse order, i.e. as though the broader claims issued first, does not reveal that the narrower (pork) process is in any way unobvious over the broader (meat) invention disclosed and claimed in the instant application. The same considerations and result apply to claim 7.

The decision of the board is affirmed as to claims 7 and 10 and reversed as to claim 11.

Notes

1. Double Patenting at the Patent Office. Suppose a patent examiner encounters two pending applications by the same inventive entity claiming the same invention. Because the examiner is as yet unsure whether these application will mature into patents, what result should follow? In such cases, the Patent and Trademark Office ordinarily issues a provisional rejection on the duplicative application. When all other prosecution issues are resolved with respect to the application, the examiner will allow the initial application to issue as a patent. At that time, the provisional rejection of any conflicting claims in subsequent applications is then converted into an actual double patenting rejection. *See* MANUAL FOR PATENT EXAMINING PROCEDURE § 804.n.

2. Difficulties in Application. The test for double patenting is whether the claims of the two patents cover the same thing. *See Carman Indus. Inc. v. Wahl*, 724 F.2d 932, 940, 220 U.S.P.Q. 481 (Fed.Cir.1983). This test requires a very difficult exercise: the comparison of one set of claims to another. (Other patent doctrines compare claim language to accused devices or known prior art.) Because a claim does not describe any particular thing but only attempts to set an outer boundary of patent protection, interpreting a single set of claims can be one of the most challenging enterprises in the law. *See In re Vogel.* Yet double patenting requires interpretation of two sets of malleable words and then a comparison of the two interpretations. To the difficulties of that task, add the complexities of an obviousness determination for obviousness-type double patenting. Recognizing the mounting difficulties of this doctrine, the Federal Circuit adopts the CCPA method in *Vogel*, namely compare one claim with a disclosed tangible embodiment that falls within the scope of the other claim. *See In re Braat*, 937 F.2d 589, 592 (Fed.Cir.1991)("We note at the outset the difficulty which arises in all obviousness-type double patenting cases of determining when a claim is or is not an obvious variation of another *claim*."). At the same time it condones this method, the Federal Circuit insists that the patent disclosure must not be used as prior art. Are you convinced? Can you see why the Federal Circuit imposes a heavy burden of proof on one seeking to prove this defense?

3. Terminal Disclaimers. The reader of *Vogel* obtains the fortunately rare privilege of learning about the making of both law and sausages. Beyond this, the court notes the possibility of a terminal disclaimer to prevent the unauthorized extension of the statutory patent term. 35 U.S.C.A. § 253 provides one tool for overcoming obviousness-style double patenting rejections by stating:

> Whenever, without any deceptive intention, a claim of a patent is invalid the remaining claims shall not thereby be rendered invalid. A patentee, whether of the whole or any sectional interest therein, may, on payment of the fee required by law, make disclaimer of any complete claim, stating therein the extent of his interest in such patent. Such disclaimer shall be in writing and recorded in the Patent and Trademark Office; and it shall thereafter be considered as part of the original patent to the extent of the interest possessed by the disclaimant and by those claiming under him.

> In like manner any patentee or applicant may disclaim or dedicate to the public the entire term, or any terminal part of the term, of the patent granted or to be granted.

By arranging for the expiration dates of all related patents to arise at the same time, the patentee overcomes the concerns of extended patent protection for a single invention. The terminal disclaimer technique allows inventors to file applications claiming obvious variants on a single inventive idea, in order to create prior art against other applicants and to obtain a tight fit for potential infringements. The usual price the applicant pays, however, is a reduction in patent term. Thus, patent applicants ordinarily dispute obviousness-type double patenting rejections by arguing that the rejected claims would not have been rendered obvious in light of the earlier application or patent, along with any other relevant prior art. Can you think of other ways to circumvent such a rejection?

Patents which issue with terminal disclaimers may be subject to abuse. Suppose that the owner of several closely related patents—all but one valid due to the filing of terminal disclaimers—sells one patent each to different, unrelated entities. Wouldn't this situation potentially subject an accused infringer to multiple infringement suits based on patents to the same invention? Such concerns led the Patent and Trademark Office to promulgate the following rule, now embodied at 37 C.F.R. § 1.321(c):

> A terminal disclaimer, when filed to obviate a double patenting rejection in a patent application ... must:

> Include a provision that any patent granted on that application ... shall be enforceable only for and during such period that said patent is commonly owned with the application or patent which formed the basis for the rejection.

This requirement was judicially approved in *In re Van Ornum*, 686 F.2d 937, 214 U.S.P.Q. 761 (CCPA 1982).

4. The *Vogel* Trailer. Given its liberal view of double patenting, *Vogel* encourages applicants to adopt a policy of maintaining continuation applications at the PTO even where they have already obtained an issued patent on a particular disclosure. This so-called "continuation policy" allows applicants to monitor competitors and adjust claims in the continuation application without regard to the strictures of the reissue statute. In particular, applicants may avoid the two-year limitations period for a broadening reissue through this technique. Reissue and other post-grant procedures are discussed here at Chapter 13. In honor of the case that firmly opened up this possibility, the later-issued patent is sometimes termed a "*Vogel* trailer."

A leading patent jurist, Judge Avern Cohn of the Eastern District of Michigan, considered the propriety of a "*Vogel* trailer" patent in *Bott v. Four Star Corp.*, 675 F.Supp. 1069, 3 U.S.P.Q.2d 1652 (E.D.Mich.1987), *aff'd mem.*, 856 F.2d 202 (Fed.Cir.1988). There, the accused infringer, Four Star, asserted the defense of equitable estoppel in light of the continuation policy of Bott, the patentee. The court responded:

> Whatever the importance to the proper operation of the patent system of the public being able to determine the limits of the protection granted to a patentee by denying a patentee the right to cancel broad claims and then reassert them in a continuing chain, as argued by Four Star, the public policy is not for me to decide at this time.... The question faced by Four Star in its design-around effort was not the limits of protection afforded Bott by his issued patents but whether Bott was in a position to obtain a patent [with broadened claims]. He was. Four Star ignored this possibility even though there were "footprints in the sand." Robinson Crusoe knew of Friday's presence even though he could not see him; Four Star should have known of the likelihood of the [*Vogel* trailer] even though it was not aware of [Bott's continuation application].

675 F. Supp. at 1078, 3 U.S.P.Q.2d at 1659. Would you have decided differently? *Cf. Symbol Technologies, Inc. v. Lemelson Medical, Education & Research Foundation,* 277 F.3d 1361, 61 U.S.P.Q.2d 1515 (Fed.Cir.2002).

ELI LILLY AND COMPANY v. BARR LABORATORIES, INC.

United States Court of Appeals, Federal Circuit, 2001.
251 F.3d 955, 58 U.S.P.Q.2d 1865.

GAJARSA, CIRCUIT JUDGE.

On the petition for rehearing or rehearing *en banc,* the court accepted the petition for rehearing *en banc.* Acting *en banc,* the court vacated the panel's original opinion entered on August 9, 2000, which is reported at 222 F.3d 973, 55 USPQ2d 1609 (Fed.Cir.2000). The *en banc* court reassigned the opinion to the panel for a specific revision of the double patenting section.... The panel's original judgment, which reversed the district court's determination that claim 7 of U.S. Patent No. 4,626,549 ("the '549 patent") is not invalid for double patenting, is reaffirmed, but on a different legal basis.

In December 1995, Barr Laboratories, Inc. ("Barr") filed an Abbreviated New Drug Application ("ANDA") under the Hatch Waxman Act, *see* 21 U.S.C. § 355(j)(2)(A)(vii)(IV) (1994), seeking approval from the Food and Drug Administration ("FDA") to market fluoxetine hydrochloride as an antidepressant. Fluoxetine hydrochloride is the active ingredient in Eli Lilly and Company's ("Lilly's") antidepressant drug Prozac. Lilly, on April 10, 1996, pursuant to 35 U.S.C. § 271(e)(2)(A) (1994), brought an infringement action in the United States District Court for the Southern District of Indiana, alleging that Barr's ANDA application infringed claim 5 of U.S. Patent No. 4,314,081 ("the '081 patent") and claim 7 the '549 patent. Lilly subsequently brought infringement actions against Geneva Pharmaceuticals, Inc., Apotex, Inc., and Bernard C. Sherman, all of whom had also filed ANDA applications with the FDA, and the actions were consolidated.

Barr and the other defendants (collectively "Barr") argued, *inter alia,* that ... claim 7 of the '549 patent is invalid for double patenting. On cross-motions for summary judgment, the district court held in favor of Lilly.... Barr appeals the district court's summary judgment rulings.... Because we hold that ... claim 7 of the '549 patent is invalid for obviousness-type double patenting, we affirm-in-part and reverse-in-part.

I.   BACKGROUND

The present appeal concerns the validity of claim 5 of the '081 patent, which covers the pharmaceutical compound fluoxetine hydrochloride—the active ingredient in Lilly's antidepressant drug Prozac—and claim 7 of the '549 patent, which covers the administration of fluoxetine hydrochloride to inhibit serotonin uptake in an animal's brain neurons.

On January 10, 1974, Lilly filed application Serial No. 432,379 ("the '379 application") containing claims for a class of compounds, therapeutic methods of using those compounds, and pharmaceutical compositions comprising those compounds. The '379 application named Bryan B. Molloy ("Molloy") and Klaus K. Schmiegel as inventors. After its filing, the '379 application engendered a progeny of divisional applications, continuation applications, and patents that rivals the Hapsburg legacy. When the last patent stemming from the '379 application issued in December 1986, the application had spawned four divisional applications, three continuation applications, and six patents. During that twelve-year period, Lilly obtained six patents relating to fluoxetine hydrochloride—the '081 and '549 patents, as well as U.S. Patent Nos. 4,018,895 ("the '895 patent"), 4,194,009 ("the '009 patent"), 4,590,213 ("the '213 patent"), and 4,329,356 ("the '356 patent"). The '213 and '356 patents did not stem from the '379 application, and during the course of this litigation, Lilly disclaimed those patents.

The '009 patent, which expired in April 1994, claimed a class of pharmaceutical compounds, including fluoxetine hydrochloride, for administration in pyschotropically effective amounts. The '895, '213, and '356 patents related to methods for treating particular ailments by administering a pharmaceutical compound within a class of compounds that includes fluoxetine hydrochloride. Specifically, the '895 patent, which expired in April 1994, concerned the treatment of humans suffering from depression; the '213 patent concerned the treatment of humans suffering from anxiety; and the '356 patent concerned the treatment of animals suffering from hypertension.

In December 1995, pursuant to a Paragraph IV certification under the Hatch Waxman Act, *see* 21 U.S.C. § 355(j)(2)(A)(vii)(IV), Barr filed an ANDA application seeking FDA approval to market fluoxetine hydrochloride as an antidepressant. Lilly responded by bringing an action in district court under 35 U.S.C. § 271(e)(2)(A), asserting that Barr's ANDA application infringed claim 7 of the '549 patent and claim 5 of the '081 patent.

At the district court, Barr argued that ... claim 7 of the '549 patent is invalid for obviousness-type double patenting.... Barr advanced three independent arguments, contending that claim 7 of the '549 patent is invalid in light of (1) the '356 and '213 patents, (2) the '895 and '009 patents, and (3) the '081 patent.

On cross motions for summary judgment, the district court held in favor of Lilly, concluding that claim 5 of the '081 patent and claim 7 of the '549 patent do not violate the best mode requirement and that claim 7 is not invalid for double patenting under any of Barr's theories. The district court recognized that Barr contended that claim 7 of the '549 patent is invalid for double patenting over, *inter alia,* the '213 patent because it merely sets forth the "scientific explanation" for the subject matter of that and other Lilly patents. Yet, the district court determined that Barr failed to provide any authoritative, reliable scientific opinion to establish that claim 7 of the '549 patent constitutes merely the scientific explanation of what was already claimed in the patents that came before it, including the '213 patent.

This appeal followed.

THE CLAIMS AT ISSUE

A. Claim 5 of the '081 patent

Stemming directly from the '379 application, the '081 patent issued on February 2, 1982. Claim 5 of the '081 patent, which depends from claim 1, covers the compound N-methyl 3–(p-trifluoromethylphenoxy)–3–phenylpropylamine hydrochloride-commonly referred to as fluoxetine hydrochloride-and pharmaceutically—acceptable acid addition salts thereof formed with non-toxic acids. Claim 1, in turn, provides as follows:

A compound of the formula

wherein each R' is independently H or CH sub3 and R is m-or p-chlorophenyl, o-, m-, or p-methoxyphenyl, phenyl, o-or m-fluorophenyl, o-or p-tolyl, 2,4–difluorophenyl or p-trifluoromethylphenyl and acid addition salts formed with pharmaceutically-acceptable acids.

B. Claim 7 of the '549 patent

On March 31, 1986, Lilly filed continuation-in-part application Serial No. 846,448, claiming the benefit of the 1974 filing date of the '379 application under 35 U.S.C. § 120. On December 2, 1986, the application matured into the '549 patent. Claim 7 of the '549 patent, which depends on claim 4, relates to blocking the uptake of the monoamine serotonin in an animal's brain neurons through administration of the compound N methyl–3–(p-trifluoromethylphenoxy)–3–phenylpropylamine hydrochloride—commonly referred to as fluoxetine hydrochloride. Claim 4 provides as follows:

A method of blocking the uptake of monoamines by brain neurons in animals comprising administering to said animal a monoamine blocking amount of a compound of the formula wherein each R' is independently hydrogen or methyl; wherein R is naphthyl or

wherein R" and R'' are halo, trifluoromethyl, C sub1-C sub4 alkyl, C sub1-C sub3 alkyloxy or C sub3-C sub4 alkenyl; and wherein n and m are 0, 1 or 2; and acid addition salts thereof formed with pharmaceutically-acceptable acids.

E. Double Patenting: The '213 patent

On May 20, 1986, the '213 patent issued from an application filed on April 8, 1983. Claim 1 of the '213 patent provides:

A method for treating anxiety in a human subject in need of such treatment which comprises the administration to such human an effective amount of fluoxetine or norfluoxetine or pharmaceutically acceptable salts thereof.

III. DOUBLE PATENTING

Through a statutorily prescribed term, Congress limits the duration of a patentee's right to exclude others from practicing a claimed invention. 35 U.S.C. § 154(a)(2) (1994). The judicially-created doctrine of obviousness-type double patenting cements that legislative limitation by prohibiting a party from obtaining an extension of the right to exclude through claims in a later patent that are not patentably distinct from claims in a commonly owned earlier patent. *In re Longi*, 759 F.2d 887, 892, 225 USPQ 645, 648 (Fed.Cir.1985) (explaining that, even though no explicit statutory basis exists for obviousness-type double patenting, the doctrine is necessary to prevent a patent term extension through claims in a second patent that are not patentably distinct from those in the first patent). As one of our predecessor courts explained, "[t]he fundamental reason for the rule [of obviousness-type double patenting] is to prevent unjustified timewise extension of the right to exclude granted by a patent no matter how the extension is brought about." *In re Van Ornum,* 686 F.2d 937, 943–44, 214 USPQ 761, 766 (CCPA 1982).

Generally, an obviousness-type double patenting analysis entails two steps. First, as a matter of law, a court construes the claim in the earlier patent and the claim in the later patent and determines the differences. the later patent and determines the differences. *Georgia-Pacific Corp. v. United States Gypsum Co.,* 195 F.3d 1322, 1326, 52 USPQ2d 1590, 1593 (Fed.Cir.1999). Second, the court determines whether the differences in subject matter between the two claims render the claims patentably distinct. Id. at 1327, 52 USPQ2d at 1595. A later claim that is not patentably distinct from an earlier claim in a commonly owned patent is invalid for obvious-type double patenting. *In re Berg,* 140 F.3d 1428, 1431, 46 USPQ2d 1226, 1229 (Fed.Cir.1998). A later patent claim is not patentably distinct from an earlier patent claim if the later claim is obvious over, or anticipated by, the earlier claim.

On appeal, we limit our inquiry to an analysis of whether claim 7 of the '549 patent is invalid for obvious-type double patenting over claim 1 of the '213 patent.[7] In accordance with the two-prong obviousness-type double patenting test demarcated in *Georgia–Pacific,* we first construe the claims at issue and determine the differences in subject matter between these two claims. The relevant portion of claim 1 of the '213 patent is directed to a method for treating anxiety in a human by administering an effective amount of fluoxetine or a pharmaceutically-acceptable salt thereof. '213 patent, col. 2, ll. 34–39. Claim 7 of the '549 patent covers a method of blocking the uptake of serotonin by brain neurons in animals by administering the compound fluoxetine hydrochloride. '549 patent, col. 20, ll. 7–9.

A person of ordinary skill in the art would have recognized that fluoxetine hydrochloride is a pharmaceutically-acceptable salt of fluoxetine. In fact, hydrochloride salts are the most common pharmaceutically acceptable salts of basic drugs, and hence are obvious compounds. *See, e.g., The Merck Index of Chemicals and Drugs* (Paul G. Stecher et al. eds., 7th ed. 1960) (listing multiple hydrochloride salts of drugs).

Therefore, the only difference between claim 1 of the '213 patent and claim 7 of the '549 patent is that the former addresses a method of

---

7. A two-way double patenting test does not apply in this case. The two-way test is only appropriate in the unusual circumstance where, *inter alia,* the United States Patent and Trademark Office ("PTO") is "*solely* responsible for the delay in causing the second-filed application to issue prior to the first." (emphasis added). *In re Berg,* 140 F.3d at 1437, 46 USPQ2d at 1233 (Fed.Cir. 1998); *see also In re Goodman,* 11 F.3d 1046, 1053, 29 USPQ2d 2010, 2016 (Fed. Cir.1993) (holding that PTO actions did not dictate the rate of prosecution when Goodman accepted early issuance of species claims and filed a continuation application to prosecute genus claims). Such circum-

stances are not present in this case, because the PTO was not solely responsible for the delay. Indeed, the '549 patent issued in December 1986, approximately eight months after a continuation-in-part was filed, which stemmed from a continuation application, which in turn stemmed from a divisional of the original '379 application that was filed in January 1974. Further, an expert hired on behalf of Lilly in the matters of PTO and corporate intellectual property practice, in discussing claim 7 of the '549 patent, stated: "[I]t is true that the claim could have been presented earlier...." This statement indicates that the delay was not solely caused by the PTO.

treating anxiety in humans with fluoxetine hydrochloride while the latter claims a method of using fluoxetine hydrochloride to block serotonin uptake in animals. Having recognized the difference between the claims at issue, we must decide whether this difference renders the claims patentably distinct.

Serotonin uptake inhibition is a natural biological activity that occurs when fluoxetine hydrochloride is administered to an animal, such as a human, for any purpose, including the treatment of anxiety. That is, serotonin uptake inhibition is an inherent property of fluoxetine hydrochloride upon its administration. Barr has offered a panoply of evidence to support the recognition of this inherent biological function of fluoxetine hydrochloride.

In Lilly's March 24, 1998 10–K filing with the Securities and Exchange Commission, Lilly pointed out that serotonin uptake inhibition is the "process by which Prozac works." The title of a 1995 article published by Lilly also indicates that Prozac is a serotonin uptake inhibitor: *Minireview Prozac (Fluoxetine, Lilly 110140), The First Selective Serotonin Uptake Inhibitor and Antidepressant Drug: Twenty Years Since Its First Publication.* David T. Wong, Frank P. Bymaster, & Eric A. Engleman, at 1 (1995). The summary of this article "describe[s] the evolutionary process involved in the discovery of the selective 5–HT [serotonin] uptake inhibitor, fluoxetine.... " The first full sentence of the article states: "Fluoxetine (Prozac) first appeared in scientific literature as Lilly 110140 (the hydrochloride form), a selective serotonin uptake inhibitor, in the August 15, 1974 issue of *Life Sciences.*" *Id.* The article continues: "After twenty-plus years of extensive investigations, inhibition of serotonin uptake remains the major mechanism of action for fluoxetine.... " *Id.* Several tables in the article specifically demarcate amounts of serotonin uptake inhibition resulting from fluoxetine administration. *Id.* at 7, 10–12, 14, 18. The article even illustrates chemical structures of several serotonin uptake inhibitors, one of which is fluoxetine. *Id.* at 9. The article concludes by stating that despite "intensive investigation," including over 5500 research papers on the subject, fluoxetine "is still regarded as a selective [serotonin] uptake inhibitor."

During a deposition, Lilly's expert, Alan Frazer, divulged that "[t]here is no doubt in my mind" that fluoxetine hydrochloride inhibits serotonin reuptake in "the vast majority" of people that ingest fluoxetine hydrochloride. Frazer also stated that he had "no doubt" that inhibition reuptake in brain neurons is the expected consequence of administering fluoxetine hydrochloide. Frazer further acknowledged in a sworn statement that: "Clearly, there are [sic] a wealth of data demonstrating that the uptake of serotonin is inhibited in most humans when fluoxetine is administered." Another one of Lilly's experts, Louis Lemberger, stated in the course of a deposition: "If you give fluoxetine hydrochloride to a human being you are going to inhibit serotonin uptake.... " Yet another Lilly expert, Irwin Slater, also agreed that ingesting fluoxetine hydrochloride will result in the inhibition of serotonin uptake in brain neurons.

Likewise, Barr's expert, Fridolin Sulser, stated in an affidavit that "[t]he pharmalogical effect of administering fluoxetine hydrochloride is to inhibit serotonin reuptake in brain neurons." He also recognized that "it is literally impossible to treat someone for anxiety ... with fluoxetine hydrochloride without at the same time inhibiting serotonin reuptake." In an expert report, Dr. Sulser again reiterated that "the primary pharmalogical effect of fluoxetine is the inhibition of serotonin reuptake in brain neurons." He further reiterated that administering fluoxetine hydrochloride "will inherently and inevitably block the reuptake of serotonin...." He provided a wealth of support for these opinions. Another Barr expert, Robert Roth, also stated that "[t]he biological activity of claim 7 of the '549 patent[ ] inherently and inevitably occurs whenever someone practices ... the '213 ... patent[ ]." He continued, stating that "there is no doubt" that "administration of fluoxetine hydrochloride inherently and inevitably blocks the reuptake of serotonin...." Dr. Roth provided a plethora of support for his opinion.

Lilly has not proffered any significant evidence rebutting Barr's ample foundation for the proposition that administration of fluoxetine hydrochloride naturally and inherently inhibits the uptake of serotonin.

A reference is anticipatory if it discloses every limitation of the claimed invention either explicitly or inherently. A reference includes an inherent characteristic if that characteristic is the "natural result" flowing from the reference's explicitly explicated limitations. In this case, it is clear from all of the evidence proffered by Barr that the natural result flowing from administration of fluoxetine hydrochloride is inhibition of serotonin uptake. Therefore, the limitation of claim 7 of the '549 patent directed to blocking serotonin uptake by use of fluoxetine hydrochloride is an inherent characteristic of the administration of fluoxetine hydrochloride for any purpose, including the treatment of anxiety.

A patentable distinction does not lie where a later claim is anticipated by an earlier one. That is, a later patent claim that fails to provide novel invention over an earlier claim is not patentably distinct from the earlier claim. Salient aspects of the case at issue are factually similar to *Burroughs Wellcome Co. v. Barr Labs., Inc.*, 40 F.3d 1223, 32 USPQ2d 1915 (Fed.Cir.1994). That case involved several patents directed to the use of 3'-azidothymidine ("AZT") to treat individuals infected with the human immunodeficiency virus ("HIV") or individuals who had acquired immunodeficiency syndrome ("AIDS"), and involved United States Patent No. 4,818,750 ("the '750 patent"), which covered a method of using AZT to increase the T-lymphocyte count of persons infected with HIV. *Burroughs Wellcome,* 40 F.3d at 1225, 32 USPQ2d at 1916–17. While never directly addressed by the majority, in his partial dissent, Judge Lourie articulated that the '750 patent should have been invalidated for double patenting because the method claimed in the '750 patent "is an inherent, inevitable result of the practice of the other method patents claiming treatment of HIV or AIDS." *Id.* at 1233, 32 USPQ2d at 1924 (Lourie, J., dissenting-in-part). He stated that because the method claimed in the '750 patent was inherent in the use of AZT to treat HIV and AIDS patients, it lacked novelty. *Id.* He continued, suggesting that allowing a common owner to receive both a patent claiming the physical act of treating individuals that have HIV or AIDS and a patent covering the result that such treatment accomplishes makes "no sense." *Id.* at 1234, 32 USPQ2d at 1924. "It amounts to deciding that treating a person in pain with aspirin is one invention and invoking the pain relieving mechanism by means of that treatment is another." *Id.*

Similarly, in the case at bar, claim 7 of the '549 patent simply describes the process by which fluoxetine hydrochloride physically acts on individuals who receive the drug. That is, fluoxetine hydrochloride inherently blocks serotonin uptake upon administration. Therefore, no patentable distinction rests between administering fluoxetine hydrochloride for treatment of anxiety and inhibition of serotonin uptake by administration of fluoxetine hydrochloride.

The only other difference between claim 1 of the '213 patent and claim 7 of the '549 patent is that the former is directed to humans while the latter is directed to animals. Humans are a species of the animal genus. Our case law firmly establishes that a later genus claim limitation is anticipated by, and therefore not patentably distinct from, an earlier species claim.

A motion for summary judgment shall be granted "if the pleadings, depositions, answers to interrogatories, and admissions on file, together with affidavits, if any, show that there is no genuine issue as to any material fact, and that the moving party is entitled to judgment as a matter of law." Fed.R.Civ.P. 56(c). In this case, Barr moved for summary judgment that claim 7 of the '549 patent was invalid for double patenting over, *inter alia*, claim 1 of the '213 patent. Barr has presented an abundance of evidence indicating that the natural result of fluoxetine hydrochloride is the inhibition of serotonin uptake. Lilly has not proffered sufficient evidence in response to this evidence. Therefore, there remains no genuine issue of fact as to this issue. That is, there is not sufficient evidence on which a jury could base a finding that fluoxetine hydrochloride does not inhibit the uptake of serotonin. Accordingly, the district court erred by indicating that Barr failed to establish that inhibition of serotonin uptake merely describes a biological result of fluoxetine hydrochloride administration for the treatment of anxiety. Further, there is no issue of fact as to whether a human is a species of the animal genus or whether fluoxetine hydrochloride is a pharmaceutically-acceptable salt of fluoxetine. Consequently, the double patenting issue in this case is solely a matter of law.

We have compared the differences between the claims at issue as a whole and conclude that they are not patentably distinct. Therefore, we reverse the district court's denial of the portion of Barr's motion for summary judgment contending that claim 7 of the '549 patent is invalid for obviousness-type double patenting over claim 1 of the '213 patent. Consequently, the portion of Barr's motion for summary judgment pertaining to double patenting is granted. The district court's grant of Lilly's motion for summary judgment pertaining to double patenting is reversed.

IV. CONCLUSION

Because we hold that . . . claim 7 of the '549 patent . . . is invalid for obviousness-type double patenting in view of claim 1 of the '213 patent, we affirm-in-part and reverse-in-part.

The court considered a request for an *en banc* hearing of the order issued on May 30, 2001.

PAULINE NEWMAN, CIRCUIT JUDGE, dissenting from the refusal to reconsider the case en banc.

The Federal Circuit, sitting *en banc,* vacated the panel's prior opinion issued on August 9, 2000 and returned the case to the panel for further consideration. The panel now again holds claim 7 of the '549 (Molloy) patent invalid for double patenting, but this time it bases that determination on a different patent, the '213 patent (Stark). The panel now grants summary judgment invalidating claim 7 of the '549 patent for double patenting with the Stark patent. However, this shift has led the panel into factual and legal areas that were not developed at trial, and into misapplication and misstatement of the law of double patenting. I must, respectfully, dissent.

Obviousness-Type Double Patenting

The judge made law of obviousness-type double patenting was developed to cover the situation where patents are not citable as a reference against each other and therefore can not be examined for compliance with the rule that only one patent is available per invention. Double patenting thus is applied when neither patent is prior art against the other, usually because they have a common priority date. As the court explained in *In re Boylan,* 55 C.C.P.A. 1041, 392 F.2d 1017, 1018 n. 1, 157 USPQ 370, 371 n. 1 (CCPA 1968), "it must always be carefully observed that the appellant's patent is not 'prior art' under either section 102 or section 103 of the 1952 Patent Act."

These fundamental requirements for application of the law of double patenting are not met by the '549 and Stark patents. The Stark patent was filed nine years after the effective filing date of the '549 patent; there is no formal relationship between them; the '549 disclosure was a cited reference against Stark; and they have different inventorships. The panel ignores these routine criteria and the effect they have on a double patenting analysis. Whatever effect the '549 and Stark patents may have on each other, it is not "double patenting."

The district court had rejected Barr's double patenting arguments after summary judgment proceedings, ruling that:

Barr's primary contention is that claim 7 of the '549 patent is invalid for double patenting because it merely sets forth the "scientific explanation" for the subject matter of certain of Lilly's other patents. Barr's summary judgment briefing on this issue is a confusing amalgamation of broad patent law principles that are not clearly applicable to the issues before the Court. In fact, the only case law cited in support of its theory is a dissenting opinion, never adopted thereafter by any court as best we could determine. Even disregarding any limitation on the application of this legal theory to the issues at hand, we observe that Barr's briefs focus extensively on the formulation and restatement of its legal theory to the exclusion of any evidence sufficient to explain or support it. Most notably, Barr has failed to provide any authoritative, reliable scientific opinion to establish that claim 7 of the '549 patent constitutes merely the later scientific explanation of what has already been claimed in the patents that came before.

On presumably the same record, the panel now grants summary judgment and *sua sponte* finds double patenting between claim 7 of the '549 patent and claim 1 of the Stark patent. The '549 disclosure, in the form of three issued divisional patents, was prior art cited against the Stark patent. Patentability of the Stark claims over this prior art was successfully argued in the PTO. The panel reaches the anomalous conclusion that the earlier filed '549 patent (effective filing date January 10, 1974) is invalid for obviousness-type double patenting with the Stark patent that was filed nine years later (April 8, 1983). Such a result is not available under the laws of 35 U.S.C. § 102 and § 103; neither can it be achieved under the rubric of double patenting.

The claims are:

Claim 7 of the '549 Molloy patent:

> The method of claim 4 [blocking the uptake of monoamines by brain neurons in animals] comprising administering to said animal a monoamine blocking amount of N methyl 3–p-trifluoromethylphenoxy–3—phenylproplyamine [fluoxetine] or a pharmaceutically-acceptable acid addition salt thereof.

Claim 1 of the '213 Stark patent:

> A method for treating anxiety in a human subject in need of such treatment which comprises the administration to said human of an effective amount of fluoxetine or norfluoxetine or pharmaceutically-acceptable salts thereof.

The panel holds that the later-discovered and later-filed anxiety-treatment use of fluoxetine invalidates the patent on the earlier discovery of monoamine (serotonin) blocking use because the earlier discovery is "inherent" in the later one. That is not a correct statement of either the law of double patenting or the law of inherency. The 1974 invention can not be invalidated based on what was filed and claimed in the 1983 application, even on the panel's incorrect view of the law of inherency as applied to biological inventions.

The district court remarked on the absence of reliable evidence as well as legal precedent to support Barr's proffered theories. The panel, however, finds that "Barr has offered a panoply of evidence to support the recognition of this inherent biological function." I take note that the panel cites only references dated after the '549 application was filed. These references are not prior art to the '549 claims. Later discoveries and scientific advances may well elucidate the earlier ones, but that does not retrospectively erase the patentability of the earlier work.

The complex factual issues that have been raised in the record, in connection with the relationship between serotonin uptake and the various pharmaceutical uses of fluoxetine, can not be resolved in favor of Barr and adversely to Lilly on the summary judgment record, for the material facts have been placed squarely at issue. Indeed, the scientific evidence in the record weighs heavily against the panel's findings.

It is highly relevant that the Stark application was examined in light of prior art that included the '549 Molloy disclosure. While Barr cites cases that established rules with respect to the subsequent patentability of a genus when a species is known, this has no relevance to the question at bar. Further, these rules relate to whether a subsequent invention is patentable, not a prior one. Here, however, it is the first-filed (Molloy) invention that the panel invalidates in view of the later-filed Stark invention. Although the Stark patent issued seven months before the '549 patent, the panel incorrectly holds that the later-filed but earlier-issued Stark claim renders obvious the '549 claim of nine years earlier priority. Neither *In re Berg,* 140 F.3d 1428, 46 USPQ2d 1226 (Fed.Cir.1998), relied on by the panel, nor any other case, supports such an inverted holding.

When two patents issue with claims that are not patentably distinct, the principle served by the judge made law of double patenting is that because patent protection started with the first patent to issue, it should not extend to the expiration of the second patent to issue. Thus the law of double patenting does not consider the patents as prior art; the law simply requires elimination of the extension of exclusivity by truncating the term of the second patent to issue, to coincide with the term of the first patent to issue.

When the second patent to issue is (as here) the first patent that was filed, an anomaly may arise when there is a valid charge of obviousness-type double patenting. I repeat, that charge is not here available because the first patent that was filed was in fact a reference against the second patent. The panel, ignoring this immutable fact, undertakes an obviousness-type double patenting analysis. When two patents are appropriately considered for obviousness-type double patenting, an anomaly arises, for example, when the claims of patent B are "obvious" in light of the claims of patent A, but the claims of patent A are not obvious in light of the claims of patent B. An illustration is shown in *In re Berg,* where one patent was directed to a species, and the other to a genus that included the species. A genus is usually not patentable over a species, but a species may, depending on the facts, be patentable over the genus. Judge made law has developed a special and simple test for double patenting in such a situation: the requirement of "cross-reading." By applying the rules of cross-reading, double patenting will not lie, for cases in which the first patent to issue is the second patent that was filed, unless the claims cross read; that is, unless the claims of each patent would have been obvious in view of the claims of the other patent. This simple expedient avoids the analytical trap into which the panel fell.

The panel has reached the truly anomalous result of holding invalid for obviousness, on a theory of obviousness-type double patenting, an invention that was made and applied for nine years before the asserted "prior art" was filed.

The panel states that *In re Berg* requires that unless the PTO is solely and exclusively responsible for all delays in issuing the first-filed patent, the patentee can not rely on the fact of its earlier filing. That is not the *Berg* holding. In *Berg* the same inventors filed, on the same day, patent applications whose claims stood in the relationship of genus and species of the same method for preparing an abrasive particle suitable for use in an abrasive composition. When the species application was about to issue, the examiner rejected the genus application on the grounds of obviousness-type double patenting. Berg argued that each application should be evaluated as to whether it represented a patentable advance over the other, a two-way test of cross-reading applied in particular circumstances. This court stated that the purpose of the two-way test, as it had been developed in our precedent, was "to prevent rejections for obviousness-type double patenting when the applicants filed first for a basic invention and later for an improvement, but, through no fault of the applicants, the PTO decided the applications in reverse order of filing, rejecting the basic application although it would have been allowed if the applications had been decided in the order of their filing." The Federal Circuit then held that Berg was not entitled to the benefits of the two-way test because he could have included all of the claims in a single application. Neither the facts of *Berg* nor the law as developed therein applies to the patents here under consideration.

The panel also holds that because Lilly disclaimed the Stark patent before trial, this bars Lilly from disclaiming that portion of the '549 patent that would have extended beyond the Stark patent's original life. No precedent so holds, and I discern no basis for such a new rule. A terminal disclaimer is a standard response to a charge of double patenting; this remedy need not be withheld, at least in the absence of fraud or bad faith. To deny a patentee the opportunity of simplifying the issues or improving its litigation position is an unnecessary if not a punitive action, unwarranted on this record.

The New Rules of Patentability of Biological Inventions

The panel states that "the natural result of fluoxetine hydrochloride is the inhibition of serotonin uptake," and holds that a discovery of a new and unobvious biological property is unpatentable because it is inherent in the chemical compound. As authority the panel cites a dissenting opinion in *Burroughs Wellcome Co. v. Barr Labs., Inc.,* 40 F.3d 1223, 1233, 32 USPQ2d 1915, 1924 (Fed.Cir.1994) (Lourie, J. dissenting in part), the dissent suggesting that a patent to a method which "is an inherent, inevitable result of the practice" of another method patent constitutes same-invention double patenting. Thus the panel holds the '549 claim to serotonin inhibition to be invalid as the natural and inherent result of the Stark treatment for relief of anxiety. However, every biological property is a natural and inherent result of the chemical structure from which it arises, whether or not it has been discovered. To negate the patentability of a discovery of biological activity because it is "the natural result" of the chemical compound can have powerful consequences for the patentability of biological inventions. The narrow facts of *Burroughs Wellcome* and the dissenting view therein do not warrant the new rule now adopted.

The panel also states that "there is not sufficient evidence on which a jury could base a finding that fluoxetine hydrochloride does not inhibit the uptake of serotonin." Indeed, it is far from clear what could be proved, as well as what must be proved, on the panel's theory of double patenting, for the many scientific articles cited in the record show the complexity of the mechanism of action of fluoxetine. However, the panel's ruling that Lilly would have to prove that serotonin inhibition does not occur on treatment with fluoxetine, in order to avoid double patenting invalidity of its claim for serotonin inhibition on treatment with fluoxetine, will surely add confusion and uncertainty to patent practice.

In this period of unprecedented development of patent-supported biological advance, the nation needs a stable and comprehensible patent law, lest this court falter in its leading role in implementing the law's fundamental purposes.

Notes

1. What's So Silly About *Eli Lilly*? The *Eli Lilly v. Barr* ruling attracted considerable attention in the media, principally because it resulted in early introduction of generic versions of Prozac®. The significance of *Eli Lilly v. Barr* extends beyond one drug, however. The decision appears to stand for the proposition that the same entity cannot separately patent both a biological property and a chemical structure that exhibits that property. If called upon to advise a pharmaceutical company, what prosecution strategies would you encourage in order to avoid the impact of *Eli Lilly v. Barr*? By the way, would the outcome have been the same in this case had the '549 and '213 patents been owned by different enterprises?

2. Why is *Eli Lilly* a Double Patenting Case? As Judge Newman notes in dissent, the PTO had previously reached a favorable patentability decision when considering Lilly's later-filed improvement invention over its patent describing the basic invention. Why, then, should the Federal Circuit have employed a double patenting analysis in the first instance?

3. One-way or Two-way Street. In *Vogel*, after determining that "same invention" double patenting does not apply, the CCPA stated the obviousness prong of double patenting as follows: "Does any claim in the application define merely an obvious variation of an invention disclosed and claimed in the patent?" 422 F.2d at 441. "If the answer to [that] question is no," the court continues, "there is no double patenting involved and no terminal disclaimer need be filed." But, "[I]f the answer is yes, a terminal disclaimer is required to prevent timewise extension. . . . "*Id.* at 442. Thus *Vogel* seems to envision a one-way street with comparison only of the application to the prior patent for assessment of obviousness. Several cases apply this same one-way street analysis. *See General Foods Corp. v. Studiengesellschaft Kohle mbH*, 972 F.2d 1272, 1280, 23 U.S.P.Q.2d 1839 (Fed.Cir.1992); *Quad Environmental Technologies v. Union Sanitary District*, 946, F.2d 870, 873, 20 U.S.P.Q.2d 1392 (Fed.Cir.1991); *In re Longi*, 759 F.2d 887, 892, 225 U.S.P.Q. 645 (Fed. Cir.1985).

As discussed in *Eli Lilly*, other cases suggest that obviousness-type double patenting requires a two-way analysis–comparison of the application with the "prior art" patent and comparison of the patent with the potentially "prior art" application because delays at the PTO may have caused a patent to issue ahead of a prior-filed application. *In re Braat*, for instance, states:

> The crux of this appeal comes down to whether the Board erred in applying a "one-way" patentability determination instead of a "two-way" determination.
>
> * * * *
>
> [T]he Board erred in sustaining the double patenting rejection without making such a "two-way" determination.
>
> * * * *
>
> The rationale behind this proposition is that an applicant (or applicants), who files applications for basic and improvement patents should not be penalized by the rate of progress of the applications through the PTO, a matter over which the applicant does not have complete control.

937 F.2d 589, 593–94, 19 U.S.P.Q.2d 1289, 1292 (Fed.Cir.1991). A subsequent Federal Circuit case, however, seems to limit *In re Braat* to the facts of that case:

> In *In re Braat*, 937 F.2d 589, 593 (Fed.Cir.1991), this court required in certain circumstances, an additional inquiry to support the double patenting obviousness rejection. Under these circumstances, a double patenting obviousness rejection will only be sustained if the application claims are not patentably distinct from the prior patent claims, and the prior patent claims are also not patentably distinct from the application claims. This "two-way" analysis is necessary because a later-filed im-

provement patent may issue before an earlier-filed basic invention. *Id.*; see *Stanley*, 214 F.2d 151.

In *Braat*, the later-filed application contained claims to a patentable combination that included a subcombination which was the subject of an independent prior application. Although the later-filed application became a patent first, this court did not reduce the term of the earlier-filed, but later-issued, patent. This court did not require a terminal disclaimer because Braat's application was held up not by the applicant, but by "the rate of progress of the application through the PTO, over which the applicant does not have complete control." *Braat*, 937 F.2d at 593. *Cf., Stanley*, 214 F.2d 151 (holding that the broad genus of an earlier-filed application was patentable even though a patent issued for a species of that genus).

This case requires no "two-way" analysis. Although application claims 12 and 13 form the genus containing the species of patent claim 3, PTO actions did not dictate the rate of prosecution. Rather, appellant chose to file a continuation and seek early issuance of the narrow species claims. The appellant also chose to forego an immediate appeal to this court on its broader claims when it filed a continuation application. Moreover, appellant argues that a terminal disclaimer is unwarranted.

* * * *

We also affirm the rejection of claims 10–13 for double patenting.

In re Goodman, 11 F.3d 1046, 1053, 29 U.S.P.Q.2d 2010, 2016 (Fed.Cir. 1993). Is this a conflict within Federal Circuit case law or do the cases adequately define when a "two-way" analysis for obviousness-type double patenting is necessary? Should the law require a two-way analysis only when the patent owner has a strong equitable argument for obtaining the benefit of that rule?

4. One Way to Approach Two–Way. Do you agree with the following approach to double patenting directed to two or more patents derived from the same disclosure under the pre–1995 law?

The same inventor obvious type double patenting doctrine is best understood by dividing the cases into two categories. The first is where the disclosure of the second application is different from that found in the patent, but where there are claims in the application that are obvious in view of the claims of the patent. Then where the application has an effective filing date that is after the effective filing date of the patent, and is based on an invention that is later in time than that of the patent, the application claims are rejectable under the court created doctrine of same inventor obvious type double patenting. This scenario had led the courts to state that the doctrine of same inventor obvious type double patenting is tested by requiring that all claims of a later issued patent must be nonobvious over claims of an earlier issued patent to the same inventor. This doctrine comes from the need for a first inventor system to prevent an inventor from patenting a succession of inventions that are obvious over what he has already patented, thus extending his patent monopoly for more than seventeen years. This is less of a problem for modern first-to-file systems because the patent with the earliest effective filing date becomes prior art eighteen months after its effective filing date. Thus, in such systems an inventor has only an eighteen month window to file on obvious developments.

The basic American rule governing same inventor obvious type double patenting leads to a potential injustice if the inventor's first patent issues on a later filed application. Plainly, the doctrine of double patenting would prevent the basic application from issuing as a patent without the filing of a terminal disclaimer even when the second filed application—which issued as a patent—is patentable over the claims of the first filed application. Where there is no effort to manipulate the system, it is fair to exempt the first application from being rejected over the last to have filed, but first to have issued patent. Courts have accomplished this by imposing the requirement of a "two way" analysis.

The second fact pattern is where the second application is a continuation of the first to issue application. Assume for the moment that the applications disclose a genus and three species. Assume further that one of the species, s1, is patentable over the genus and each of the other two species. Does the doctrine of double patenting preclude the inventor from obtaining two separate patents, for example, one covering the genus and the two obvious species and the other on s1? If the application covering s1 issues first, then the second patent is subject to a double patenting rejection under the standard same inventor obvious type double patenting doctrine. The only way to save the second application is to require a "two way" analysis. There is no policy reason why a court should impose a "two way" analysis under these circumstances. A continuation application is simply part of the original application in the PTO, and it should not lead to a separate and independent patent. However, what if the application with the genus claim issues first? Then the double patenting question is whether the genus claim is found to include s1. In essence, what is meant when courts rule that a second application by the inventor must be patentable over the claims of the issued patent in order to avoid a double patenting rejection? The proper analysis is to consider the claim to cover all of the technology in the disclosure that is related to the claim. Basically, the question is the same as that asked when the term "patented" is interpreted in Sections 102 (a) and (b). After all, a claim is not designed to disclose an invention, but rather to define its metes and bounds. Thus, the genus claim would embrace s1 and the applicant should be required to file a terminal disclaimer in order to obtain a separate patent on s1.

2 Martin J. Adelman, Patent Law Perspectives, § 2.8[1] at n.54 (2d ed. 1995).

Prosecution Exercises

1. Norton, Shottky and Thevenin each work for the Consolidated Technology Corporation. Norton, a technical manager, directs research engineer Shottky to develop an improved snowboard boot. Shottky studies the various products available on the market and conceives of the concept of a removable stiffening stay housed in a pocket on the upper portion of the boot. He then instructs Thevenin, a laboratory technician, to construct such a boot with a stiffening stay. Thevenin constructed the boot following Shottky's instructions and ran standardized tests that demonstrated its

improved quality. Norton subsequently directs that a patent application be filed relating to an adjustably stiffenable boot for use with snowboarding. *Which individuals should be named as inventors?*

2. Rosenberg filed a nonprovisional utility patent application on May 3, 1994, in the United States claiming an apparatus and method for cryogenically cleaning surfaces. Rosenberg also filed an application in Belgium on April 2, 1995, directed to the identical apparatus and method. The Belgian application was patented and published on May 1, 1996.

As of July 8, 1998, Rosenberg had abandoned the application he had filed on May 3, 1994. Previously, on July 2, 1997, Rosenberg filed a continuation of the original application, making specific reference to the original application. The continuation matured into a patent claiming only the method of cryogenically cleaning surfaces on February 14, 1998. On February 10, 1998, Rosenberg filed a third application, claiming the apparatus, which specifically referred to and was properly labeled a division of the application filed July 2, 1997. However, this third application did not mention the original application Rosenberg had filed May 3, 1994.

The Examiner rejects the claims of the third application as being anticipated by the Belgian patent. *Is the Examiner's rejection proper? What steps might Rosenberg take to overcome the rejection?*

3. Landau obtained a patent containing one claim to a pencil sharpener on January 19, 2000. On November 17, 1999, Landau had on file a second application containing two claims. Claim 1 is drawn to a pencil sharpener having the same scope as the pencil sharpener covered by the Landau patent, but uses somewhat different descriptive language. Claim 2 is drawn to a pencil sharpener with a support bracket. In view of the Landau patent and another reference, a prior art article written by Mowery, the subject matter of claim 2 would have been obvious.

During prosecution of the second application, the Examiner rejects claims 1 and 2 on the ground of double patenting. In response to the rejection, Landau's patent attorney files an appropriate terminal disclaimer and argues that the double patenting rejection should be withdrawn. The Examiner nonetheless makes the rejection final. *Did the Examiner act appropriately?*

4. Lattimore, while an employee of the ABC Company, filed a first application in the PTO on August 17, 2001, and assigned it to ABC. On December 15, 2001, she left the ABC Company and started work at the XYZ Company. On June 19, 2002, as part of her duties at XYZ Company, Lattimore devised an improvement over the invention claimed in the first application. A second application was filed in the PTO and assigned to the XYZ Company. The XYZ Company subsequently receives an Office Action in which the claims of the second application have been rejected over the claims of the first on the ground of obviousness-type double patenting. As representative of the XYZ Company, you have copies of both of Lattimore's applications and do not believe that the improvement would have been obvious. *What steps should you take in response to the Office Action?*

5. Anthony and Carter are employed by the Retro Bowling Company. Working together, they developed a vacuum vice for holding bowling balls

during drilling operations. Anthony and Carter turned over their laboratory notebooks describing their invention to their supervisor, Dalzell. Dalzell thoroughly reviewed the invention and later instructed Schenkel, a patent attorney, to prepare a patent application directed towards a vice.

On September 1, 2002, Schenkel filed the application at the PTO naming Anthony and Carter as the inventors. On December 1, 2002, Dalzell discovered some sales literature that was published by a competitor on January 10, 1990, and brought these documents to the attention of Schenkel. Dalzell and Schenkel agreed that the sales literature would plainly anticipate some of the claims in the pending patent application. *Under Rule 56, which individuals are obliged to bring the sales literature to the attention of the PTO?*

Chapter Thirteen

POST–GRANT PROCEDURES

The Patent and Trademark Office's involvement in the U.S. patent system does not necessarily end when it formally grants a patent. The law has long recognized the numerous possibilities for mistakes, ranging from insignificant typesetting errors to substantive flaws that render the patent invalid or unenforceable, to creep into the patent instrument. The patent statute thus provides the PTO with several different mechanisms for correcting the inevitable. The magnitude of the mistake largely determines which procedure will be employed.

The least onerous and most frequently used of these procedures is a *certificate of correction*, as set forth at 35 U.S.C.A. §§ 254 and 255. A certificate of correction is ordinarily used to address minor typographical errors and may be obtained by filing a simple petition. Mistakes incurred through the fault of the PTO may be corrected free of charge; otherwise, the petitioner must submit a fee along with proof that the error occurred in good faith. Use of a certificate of correction is ordinarily uncontroversial and will not be further reviewed here.

A second, more significant correction technique comprises the *reissue* proceeding, governed by 35 U.S.C.A. §§ 251 and 252. Reissue allows applicants to correct more significant errors affecting the validity and enforceability of an issued patent. It presents the most versatile possibility for correction and is often used to prepare a patent for enforcement litigation. This Chapter considers reissue proceedings at § 13.1, along with a potential consequence of a reissued patent, so-called *intervening rights*, in § 13.2.

The third sort of correction mechanism, *reexamination*, is more limited than a reissue. As codified at 35 U.S.C.A. § 302–307, the statutory reexamination proceeding allows applicants or third parties to request that the PTO reconsider the validity of a patent. The most recent changes in the patent law occurred on November 2, 2002, when President Bush signed into law patent reexamination reforms that are considered at § 13.2, *Reexamination*. More and more, the patent community is moving toward acceptance of the global norm of the European and

Japanese patent systems that provide for an administrative revocation of patents. As traditionally structured, reexamination proceedings were largely *ex parte* in nature. The American Inventors Protection Act of 1999 added a new form of reexamination, termed *inter partes* reexamination, that provides a more significant role for the party challenging the patent. Reexamination is considered here at § 13.2.

Last, § 13.3 of this Chapter considers additional post-grant possibilities at foreign patent offices. Not only is knowledge of these options abroad helpful in its own right, it also provides a useful comparative model against which the effectiveness of the regime of U.S. post-grant proceedings may be judged.

§ 13.1 REISSUE

When is the reissue proceeding available to an applicant? The next decision discusses this point, with reference to the reissue "oath." As set forth in 37 C.F.R. § 1.175(a), the reissue oath, or declaration filed by the patentee, must provide in part that:

> (1) The applicant believes the original patent to be wholly or partly inoperative or invalid by reason of a defective specification or drawing, or by reason of the patentee claiming more or less than the patentee had the right to claim in the patent, stating at least one error being relied upon as the basis for reissue; and

> (2) All errors being corrected in the reissue application up to the time of filing of the oath or declaration under this paragraph arose without any deceptive intention on the part of the applicant.

HEWLETT–PACKARD CO. v. BAUSCH & LOMB INC.

United States Court of Appeals, Federal Circuit, 1989.
882 F.2d 1556, 11 U.S.P.Q.2d 1750.

Before NIES and BISSELL, CIRCUIT JUDGES, and BALDWIN, SENIOR CIRCUIT JUDGE.

NIES, CIRCUIT JUDGE.

Bausch and Lomb Incorporated (B & L) appeals from a final judgment, in favor of Hewlett–Packard Company (HP), entered by the United States District Court for the Northern District of California in a patent infringement suit. Hewlett–Packard Co. v. Bausch & Lomb Inc., 692 F.Supp. 1118 (N.D.Cal.1988). The judgment is based on the district court's holdings that B & L's United States Patent No. Re. 31,684 ('684) is unenforceable and partially invalid. We affirm-in-part, vacate-in-part, and remand.

The court held claims 10–12, which were added during reissue, invalid because B & L filed blatantly inaccurate affidavits to support reissue. Absent the affidavits, the court held, B & L failed to comply with the requirements of the oath specified in 35 U.S.C. § 251 (1982) and 37 C.F.R. § 1.175 (1988).

We affirm the court's holding that claims 10–12, but not claims 1–9, are invalid because the reissue application was defective. We vacate that part of the judgment [concerning inequitable conduct] and remand for reconsideration.

I

Issues

Is a failure to include narrower or dependent claims in a patent sufficient in itself to establish error warranting reissue under 35 U.S.C. § 251?

II

Background

John Yeiser invented an "X–Y Plotter," described in United States Patent No. 3,761,950 ('950), in which chart paper moves under a marking pen. Yeiser's patent issued in 1973 with nine claims. Following a series of assignments, the Milton Roy Company (MRC) acquired the '950 patent. The invention claimed in that patent was commercialized only briefly. MRC had been out of the plotter business for some time when, in late 1980 or early 1981, HP introduced its first moving-paper X–Y plotter, with great success.

B & L, a competitor of HP, discovered the '950 patent during an investigation of HP's patent protection on its plotter. In 1982, B & L bought the '950 patent from MRC for $30,000, admittedly for the purpose of gaining leverage in negotiations—hoping to obtain a cross license from HP—and possible litigation. The record indicates that B & L was concerned, however, that claim 1, which arguably covers HP's plotter and is the only independent claim asserted, was overly broad. To obtain narrower claims which would incorporate details of the HP plotter specifically, B & L filed a reissue application containing three new claims, 10–12. The original nine claims of the '950 patent were included in the reissue application without substantive change.

The PTO rejected the application, inter alia, on the grounds that B & L failed to specify either an error warranting reissue or how the error occurred. B & L successfully overcame the PTO rejections by supplementing the initial declaration with two affidavits signed by the patent agent, Lawrence Fleming, who had prosecuted the original patent. The facts surrounding those affidavits and the effect they had on the reissue will be discussed below in detail in connection with addressing the issues of the validity and enforceability of the '684 patent, which are the central issues of this appeal.

With issuance of the '684 patent imminent, B & L charged HP with infringement. HP countered with a petition for reexamination of claims 1, 2, and 10–12 over certain prior art. The PTO found that HP's petition raised a substantial new question of patentability, but ultimately upheld the validity of all claims. HP then filed a declaratory judgment action in October 1984, asserting invalidity of all claims of the '684 patent under

35 U.S.C. §§ 102, 103, 112, and 251 (1982), and later added an allegation of unenforceability for inequitable conduct in B & L's prosecution of the reissue application. B & L counterclaimed, charging HP with infringement of claims 1 and 2, which were original claims, and claims 10–12 added by reissue.

On a summary judgment motion, the district court held claims 10–12, but not claims 1–9, invalid. More specifically, the court found that the oath (declaration) in the application for reissue was defective. B & L contends that, as a matter of law, the oath was not defective. On the other hand, HP urges that, because the oath was defective, the district court should have held original claims 1–9 also invalid.

III

FACTS CONCERNING THE REISSUE AFFIDAVITS

The facts surrounding the two Fleming affidavits submitted by B & L to support the reissue application are central to the issues of validity and enforceability. Accordingly, those facts must be set forth in detail.

Upon acquisition of the '950 patent, B & L immediately began steps to secure its reissue. The matter was handled by Bernard Bogdon, B & L's in-house counsel, and William Hyer, outside patent counsel. Hyer delegated the task to an associate of his firm, Jonathan Jobe. It was Jobe's first experience with drafting a reissue application.

Working from the '950 patent file and the specifics Hyer gave him on the HP plotter, Jobe drafted the reissue application, adding three dependent claims to Claim 1 to cover specific features of the HP plotter. Jobe drafted the declaration, later signed by B & L's vice president, George More, to state that the '950 patent was "partly or wholly inoperative ... by reason of the patentee claiming less than he had a right to claim in that he had a right to claim [his invention] more specifically," and that the omission of the dependent claims was caused "because of oversight and without deceptive intent on the part of said John O. Yeiser or his attorney." No one had at that time consulted with Lawrence Fleming, the patent agent (by then retired) who had prosecuted the '950 patent.

Although he signed the declaration, More knew nothing about the alleged "error," either personally or based on others' investigations. Indeed, he was told that he was better off not asking any questions. Jobe testified that he included the reference to an "oversight" because "it is required by the statute" and because he could not "imagine any deceptive reason for not including those claims."

Filed in due course, the reissue application was rejected on the ground:

> The declaration is insufficient because it does not specify an error. The addition of narrower claims, by itself, is not an error. Note that there is no allegation that base claim 1 is inoperative or invalid. Why are claims of narrower scope necessary? The declara-

tion is further insufficient because it does not specify how the error arose or occurred. The statement that the alleged errors occurred or arose because of oversight on the part of the inventor or his attorney does not specify in detail how and why such an oversight occurred. A declaration from the original attorney may be in order.

Following the examiner's rejection, Jobe made his first contact with Fleming, by telephone, informing him generally of the nature of the reissue application and of the PTO rejection and asking how Fleming's alleged "oversight" occurred. In essence, per the district court, Jobe asked Fleming how he could have made the "tremendous blunder" of omitting claims specifically encompassing features of the pinch roller assembly. Hewlett–Packard, 692 F.Supp. at 1140, 8 U.S.P.Q.2d at 1198. Fleming attempted to justify his action with the explanation, later confirmed by letter, that he was unable to get much information from Yeiser.

Jobe then prepared an affidavit for Fleming, which was submitted to the PTO. Essentially, Fleming averred that he had only limited contacts and ability to communicate with the inventor; that no one at the company where Fleming was employed, or its predecessor, provided any substantive help or guidance during prosecution of the patent application; that Yeiser sent him a single, brief memorandum to guide him on what to claim; and that claims which further define and distinguish the invention from the prior art could have been drafted and allowed had further communications and guidance been received. Although Fleming had made references to his "old file" in discussing matters with Jobe, Jobe never asked for documentation or otherwise sought confirmation of Fleming's averments.

The PTO maintained its rejection of B & L's reissue application despite the first Fleming affidavit, reiterating the same grounds as in its initial rejection. Specifically, the PTO found that the More declaration and the Fleming affidavit failed to specify an error or how, when, and why the alleged error arose. Particularly addressing Fleming's affidavit, the examiner stated:

> The Fleming affidavit states that the contacts and ability to communicate with the inventor by the agent who prepared the application were significantly limited. It is acceptable on this point. It is not acceptable however as to how and by whom the scope of the subject matter claimed was determined and why.

At this point, house counsel Howard Robbins took over prosecution of the reissue. After speaking with Fleming, Robbins drafted the second Fleming affidavit. In that affidavit, Fleming averred that he had been given a "crude model of the invention" to review on only one occasion for about two hours; that the scope of the claims was determined solely by him based on this brief disclosure; that he had no discussions with Yeiser concerning the scope of the claims; and that Yeiser had sold his plotter business and was not focusing on such matters. Robbins' accompanying argument to the PTO reiterated these "facts" and that Fleming's action was "without full cognizance of what was significant in view of the art." The PTO reconsidered the original declaration, together with the two Fleming affidavits, and found them sufficient under 37 C.F.R. § 1.175. Accordingly, the PTO allowed claims 1–12 in reissue patent '684.

V

VALIDITY

A. Reissue Claims 10–12 Are Invalid

Even before specific provisions were included in the patent statute for correcting defective patents, Chief Justice Marshall, in *Grant v. Raymond*, 31 U.S. (6 Pet.) 218, 244, 8 L.Ed. 376 (1832), articulated the principle that a defective patent was an inadequate exchange for the patentee's disclosure of an invention and that a new patent should be issued, in appropriate circumstances, which secures to the patentee the benefits which the law intended. The circumstances under which reissue is permissible are now set forth in 35 U.S.C. § 251, which provides in pertinent part:

> Whenever any patent is, through error without any deceptive intention, deemed wholly or partly inoperative or invalid, by reason of a defective specification or drawing, or by reason of the patentee claiming more or less than he had a right to claim in the patent, the Commissioner shall, on the surrender of such patent and the payment of the fee required by law, reissue the patent for the invention disclosed in the original patent, and in accordance with a new and amended application, for the unexpired part of the term of the original patent. No new matter shall be introduced into the application for reissue.

B & L argues that an "error" is present, within the meaning of section 251, if it can be discerned from the patent specification, claims, and prosecution history that the patentee could have included a narrower claim, unless there is evidence that such "omission" was intentional. The omission of narrower claims 10–12, per B & L, also falls within the statutory language that the patentee claimed "less than he had a right to claim."

The district court found that the facts in the Fleming affidavits were essential to reissue and that without those facts, which turned out to be "grossly inaccurate," there was no error warranting reissue. Conversely, B & L asserts that More's original declaration established "reissuable error" and that the Fleming affidavits were both unnecessary and wrong only in immaterial details. Our precedent rejects B & L's simplistic interpretation of the reissue statute with respect to what constitutes error under section 251.

As explained in *In re Wilder*, 736 F.2d 1516, 222 U.S.P.Q. 369 (Fed.Cir.1984), *cert. denied*, 469 U.S. 1209, 105 S.Ct. 1173, 84 L.Ed.2d 323 (1985):

There are two distinct statutory requirements that a reissue oath or declaration must satisfy. First, it must state that the patent is defective or partly inoperative or invalid because of defects in the specification or drawing, or because the patentee has claimed more or less than he is entitled to. Second, the applicant must allege that the defective, inoperative, or invalid patent arose through error without deceptive intent.

In sum, the statutorily required "error" of section 251 has two parts: (1) error in the patent, and (2) error in conduct.

On the first part, the precedent of this court is that the expression "less than he had a right to claim" generally refers to the scope of a claim. Thus, that provision covers the situation where the claims in the patent are narrower than the prior art would have required the patentee to claim and the patentee seeks broader claims. Conversely, the alternative that the patentee claimed "more ... than he had a right to claim" comes into play where a claim is too broad in scope in view of the prior art or the specification and the patentee seeks narrower claims.

In this case, B & L averred that the inventor claimed "less" than he had a right to claim, which ordinarily would mean that B & L sought broader claims by reissue. But B & L did not seek broader claims; instead, B & L sought to add several dependent claims in hopes that it could assert the patent should independent claim 1 be held invalid. Otherwise, the dependent claims add nothing to the patent's protection against infringements. Any device that infringes new claims 10–12 ipso facto infringes carry-over claim 1, which B & L maintains is valid. Thus, in fact, B & L is not asserting that the claims in the '684 patent are inoperative (i.e., ineffective to protect the invention) by reason of the patentee claiming either too much or too little in scope, but because he included, in a sense, too few claims.

Although neither "more" nor "less" in the sense of scope of the claims, the practice of allowing reissue for the purpose of including narrower claims as a hedge against the possible invalidation of a broad claim has been tacitly approved, at least in dicta, in our precedent. For purposes of this case, we will assume that that practice is in accordance with the remedial purpose of the statute, although B & L clearly did not allege an "error" in the patent which meets the literal language of the statute. We need not decide here whether omission of narrow claims which more specifically cover a broadly claimed invention meets the first prong of the requirement for error, that is, error in the patent, because B & L clearly did not establish the second prong, namely, inadvertent error in conduct. Contrary to B & L's position, a reissue applicant does not make a prima facie case of error in conduct merely by submitting a sworn statement which parrots the statutory language.

The language of the current statute, "error without deceptive intent," replaced, but did not substantively change, the language of the prior statute, section 4916 of the Revised Statutes, 35 U.S.C. § 64 (1946), "error ... by inadvertence, accident, or mistake, and without fraudulent or deceptive intent." The term "error" encompasses "inadvertence, accident or mistake," and those words were eliminated as redundant. As explained in *Ball Corp. v. United States,* 729 F.2d 1429, 1435 & n. 9, 221 U.S.P.Q. 289, 294 & n. 9 (Fed.Cir.1984):

> The 1952 revision of the patent laws made no substantive change in the definition of error under section 251.... "Error" is interpreted in the same manner as under section 64 of the old law, i.e., accident, inadvertence, or mistake.

The statutory provision has been implemented and expanded by the PTO regulations of 37 C.F.R. § 1.175.

B & L asserts the theory that, whenever it is apparent that narrower claims could have been obtained, error warranting reissue exists. Under B & L's theory, the dual error inquiry collapses into one because the omission of additional narrow claims not only makes the patent "defective," but also gives rise to an inference of "oversight". Were that theory correct, it is difficult to conceive of any extant patent for which a right of reissue would not exist, a view which this court has unequivocably and repeatedly rejected. For example, as explained in *In re Weiler,* 790 F.2d 1576, 229 U.S.P.Q. 673 (Fed.Cir.1986), reissue is not intended to give the patentee simply a second chance to prosecute the patent application:

> The reissue statute was not enacted as a panacea for all patent prosecution problems, nor as a grant to the patentee of a second opportunity to prosecute de novo his original application.

Id. at 1582, 229 U.S.P.Q. at 677. *Weiler* further advises:

> [T]he grant of reissues [is not required] on anything and everything mentioned in a disclosure.... [Section] 251 does not authorize a patentee to re-present his application. Insight resulting from hindsight on the part of new counsel does not, in every case, establish error.

Id. at 1583 n. 4, 229 U.S.P.Q. at 677–78 n. 4.

B & L seeks to avoid the admonitions of Weiler with an argument, in effect, that an error in conduct must be presumed, absent affirmative evidence that the defect in the patent which is asserted in the reissue application was intentional. For this premise, B & L relies on language in Ball stating that reissue was there appropriate because "there is no evidence that the [patentee] intentionally omitted or abandoned the claimed subject matter". 729 F.2d at 1435–36, 221 U.S.P.Q. at 294. In Ball, that analysis was apropos; it is not germane here. The patentee in Ball was seeking broader claims and an abandonment inquiry was necessary under the facts presented. B & L does not suggest circumstances which would constitute abandonment of the subject matter of the dependent claims while not, at the same time, abandoning the subject matter of the independent claim. Thus, B & L's proposed restriction on reissue where narrower claims are sought is, in truth, no restriction at all.

Returning to the district court's holdings, we discern no legal error in its conclusion that the original More declaration in itself was inadequate to establish error and that the supplemental Fleming affidavits were necessary. The Fleming affidavits were critical to provide the required explanation of what his error was and how and why it occurred.

The evidence of record establishes beyond doubt that Fleming's affidavits, in explaining why narrow claims were not included, were factually untrue. We need not repeat those errors, which are set out above and are substantially undisputed. B & L argues that the misstatements were innocent and should be ignored. Assuming that they were due only to Fleming's faulty memory, the misstatements are not thereby corrected to provide a valid assertion of error. Accordingly, the district court properly held that the factual inaccuracy of the affidavits eliminated the basis for reissue and rendered the '684 patent invalid, albeit only as to claims 10–12.

B.   "Carry–Over" Claims 1–9 Remain Valid

Only claims 10–12 were added by B & L during prosecution of the reissue application. Aside from correction of a typographical error in claim 3, the original claims 1–9 of the '950 patent remained identical. HP contends that the effect of the court's holding that B & L failed to submit a valid reissue application is to render the '684 patent invalid in its entirety, that is, all claims must be held invalid. The district court noted that there was some illogic in invalidating the reissue patent and, at the same time, upholding the carry-over claims therein. The carry-over claims cannot be asserted based on the original patent, because the patent owner must surrender the original patent upon reissuance. 35 U.S.C. § 252 (1982). Logically, it would follow that B & L has no claims to enforce. Indeed, some precedent exists to support invalidation of all claims when the reissue declaration is found wanting. We agree with the district court, however, that such a result is neither compelled by the patent statute nor by the circumstances here.

There is no disagreement with the long-standing proposition that invalidation of a new claim (added during reissue) on prior art does not invalidate the other claims. Nor could there be any disagreement, for the patent statute provides: "Whenever, without any deceptive intention, a claim of a patent is invalid the remaining claims shall not thereby be rendered invalid." 35 U.S.C. § 253 (1982). That proposition offers little guidance, however, because the invalidity resulting from a defective reissue application may be viewed as affecting the entire patent and not merely any particular claim.

We find support for upholding carry-over claims in *Gage v. Herring*, 107 U.S. 640, 27 L.Ed. 601 (1883). There, the Supreme Court expressed its view that the inadequacy of the ground for reissuing a patent did not "impair the validity of the original claim which is repeated and separately stated in the reissued patent." *Gage* is especially on point because the invalidity of the reissue claim did not turn on prior art but on the negation of a right to reissue. The patentee repeated one claim from his original patent and attempted to add a second claim by reissue, arguing that the original claim was "too much restricted." The Supreme Court held the added claim invalid because that claim was one the patentee "did not make, or suggest the possibility of, in the original patent." Nevertheless, the Court upheld the validity of the original claim.

We see no reason to reach a contrary result under the circumstances here. Accordingly, we affirm the district court's ruling that the lack of error warranting reissue invalidates only new claims 10–12, and not original claims 1–9.

Notes

1. Can the Decision not to Include Narrower Claims in a Patent Ever Be Deceptive? Do you agree with the following comment respecting *Hewlett–Packard*?

In the United States, in contrast to some foreign systems, the PTO does not examine narrower claims once it allows a broad claim or set of claim. The fees and legal expenses for such claims, at least when written in dependent form, are small and it is probably malpractice not to put a reasonable set into an application. Thus the court went astray when it disregarded the remedial nature of the reissue statute in *Hewlett-Packard*. The patent law uses dependent claims to cope with the principle that limitations from the specification cannot be read into claims to save them from invalidity. Bausch & Lomb was merely dealing with a possible future problem in its reissue application, a problem that could only be the result of error rather than any strategic calculation during the prosecution of the original patent.

Further, the court's decision is not consistent with the fundamental philosophy of reissue law. Essentially the only reason for placing limits on what can be corrected during reissue is because if actions taken or omissions made during the prosecution of the original patent are correctable there is less incentive for the original applicant to get it right in the first place. Thus, the best approach to reissue law would carefully balance these two considerations, how far to permit remedial action with the inevitable lessening of pressure to get it correct in the first place, in deciding "error without any deceptive intention" questions.

6 MARTIN J. ADELMAN, PATENT LAW PERSPECTIVES, § 10.2[2] at n.38 (2d ed. 1990).

2. Erroneous Policy? Given the uncertainties surrounding the sorts of mistakes that suffice to file a reissue application, should the concept of "error" as a requirement for reissue simply be abolished? The 1992 Advisory Commission thought so. It stated:

The statutory requirement of an "error" unduly limits the basis for reissue and generates a great deal of uncertainty. The courts have been inconsistent in their interpretation of "error" as it appears in 35 U.S.C.A. § 251. *Compare, e.g., In re Byers*, 230 F.2d 451, 454 (CCPA 1956), *with In re Wesseler*, 367 F.2d 838, 839 (CCPA 1966), *and with In re Wadlinger*, 496 F.2d 1200, 1207 (CCPA 1974). What mistakes constitute error for purposes of reissue are also subject to differing opinions. *Compare In re Wilder*, 736 F.2d 1516, 1519 (Fed.Cir.1984), *and In re*

Richman, 424 F.2d 1388, 1391–92 (CCPA 1970), *with Hewlett–Packard, supra, and In re Weiler*, 790 F.2d 1576, 1582–83 (Fed.Cir.1986). The public's need for certainty is not helped by the uncertain limits on the right to a reissue. There is no public policy reason for limiting reissue to "errors" except in the case of deceptive intent. Absent the latter, and subject to time limits on broader claims, a patentee should be entitled to obtain by reissue any valid claim to which he or she would have been entitled during the original prosecution.

THE ADVISORY COMMISSION ON PATENT LAW REFORM, A REPORT TO THE SECRETARY OF COMMERCE 129 (1992).

3. Effect of Reissue Application. When the Patent Office accepts a reissue application, it essentially starts prosecution *ab initio*. The PTO requests that reissue applicants include the originally issued patent instrument (the so-called "ribboned copy") along with the other paperwork. This requirement is in keeping with the statute's mandate that the patentee surrender the original patent in order to obtain a reissued patent. Although a patentee may ultimately abandon a reissue proceeding and receive her patent back, she should be reluctant to do so: the cloud this abandoned application would cast upon the abandoned application will be duly noted by courts and competitors.

The usual sequence of Office Actions and responses applies, and applicants may also file continuation and divisional applications as necessary. *See In re Graff*, 111 F.3d 874, 42 U.S.P.Q.2d 1471 (Fed.Cir.1997). Note that continuation-in-part applications are not allowed during reissue proceedings: this step would involve the introduction of new matter, which is prohibited by § 251, first paragraph. The second paragraph of § 251 also allows several patents to issue from a single reissue application.

Reissue proceedings are open to the public. To this end, the Patent and Trademark Office Official Gazette announces the filing of reissue applications each week. PTO regulations then mandate that the reissue proceeding not commence for at least two months, in order to allow third parties to submit evidence and arguments relating to the patentability of the reissue application.

Reissue proceedings therefore expose the patentee to some risk. Although he may have carefully calculated the steps he needs to take to move through the reissue proceeding, these plans may be thrown off by interested parties. Competitors and licensors in particular may vigorously contest the reissue of the patent by submitting additional prior art or arguments against patentability. If the patent reissues, however, the patentee has likely strengthened his patent for use in licensing negotiations or during litigation.

4. Broadening Reissues. When a patentee seeks to expand the scope of its claims, thereby increasing the technologies that constitute an infringement, she is said to have applied for a "broadening reissue." The fourth paragraph of § 251 sets forth a two-year statute of limitations for seeking a reissue that enlarges the scope of the claims. Meeting this deadline has proved a somewhat subtle affair, as suggested by two cases, *In re Doll*, 419 F.2d 925, 164 U.S.P.Q. 218 (CCPA 1970), and *In re Graff*, 111 F.3d 874, 42 U.S.P.Q.2d 1471 (Fed.Cir.1997).

In *Doll*, the patentee filed a reissue application containing broadened claims within the two-year statutory period. The claims were further broadened during the course of prosecution after the two-year period had expired, prompting a rejection by the examiner under the § 251, fourth paragraph. The Court of Customs and Patent Appeals reversed in a tersely drafting opinion, holding that the reissue oath was proper.

Graff involved an applicant who filed a reissue application approximately twenty-two months after the issuance date. The initial reissue application was solely directed towards an erroneous drawing and contained no changes to the claims whatsoever. During the course of prosecution and following the expiration of the two-year period, however, Griff introduced broadened claims. The examiner rejected these claims as untimely under § 251, fourth paragraph. On appeal, the Federal Circuit affirmed. The court characterized the holding in *Doll* as recognizing that "the public was placed on notice of the patentee's intention to enlarge the claims by the filing of a broadening reissue application within the two year statutory period." According to the Federal Circuit, because the public lacked notice that Graff sought a broadening reissue within the statutory period, any enlarged claims were properly rejected.

5. The Recapture Rule. Along with the two-year statute of limitations, the courts have developed another significant restriction on broadening reissues. The recapture rule prevents a patentee from acquiring through reissue claims of the same or broader scope that those canceled from the original application. *See Ball Corp. v. United States*, 729 F.2d 1429, 221 USPQ 289 (Fed.Cir.1984). This doctrine typically arises when an examiner rejected the original application based upon the prior art. If the patentee opted to narrow its claims to avoid a prior art reference, then he cannot use the reissue proceeding to recapture the abandoned subject matter.

The Federal Circuit opinion in *Mentor Corp. v. Coloplast, Inc.*, 998 F.2d 992 (Fed.Cir.1993), demonstrates the recapture rule. Mentor had obtained a patent claiming a condom catheter that transferred an adhesive from its outer to its inner surfaces upon unrolling. A review of the prosecution history indicated that Mentor had inserted this limitation into the claims following the examiner's prior art rejection. Mentor later learned of Coloplast's competing product, a catheter with adhesive applied directly to its inner surface. Aware that its patent claims did not read directly on the Coloplast product, Mentor initiated a reissue proceeding at the PTO. After Mentor submitted detailed evidence of commercial success, the examiner reissued the patent. Notably absent from the reissued claims were limitations calling for adhesive transfer.

Mentor then sued Coloplast for infringement of both the original and reissue patents. Coloplast denied infringement of the original patent claims because its catheters did not transfer adhesive from the outer to the inner surface. Coloplast admitted infringement of the reissue patent but asserted that Mentor had improperly invoked the reissue statute by recapturing what it had deliberately surrendered during the original prosecution in response to a prior art rejection. The jury disagreed, and the trial judge denied Coloplast's motion for judgment as a matter of law after the adverse verdict.

On appeal, the Federal Circuit reversed. The court concluded that Mentor could not use the reissue proceeding to modify its deliberate actions during the original prosecution. Because Mentor had deliberately added claim language requiring adhesive transfer following the examiner's prior art rejection, the court reasoned, Mentor should not be allowed to recapture that subject matter by deleting these claim limitations during reissue. In so doing, the court justified the recapture rule both upon the requirement of error as well as concerns for the reliance interests of third parties. The Federal Circuit did not consider Mentor's deliberate decision to narrow its claims, instead of filing a continuation application or appealing to the Board, to be the sort of error comprehended by the reissue statute. Additionally, the court sympathized with a hypothetical third party that might have reviewed the prosecution history and made commercial decisions based upon Mentor's express surrender of claimed subject matter.

6. Uncorrectable Errors. Some errors in a patent are simply too grave to be corrected through the use of a reissue proceeding. These include a specification that does not fulfill the requirements of § 112; when the applicant has engaged in inequitable conduct during the original prosecution; and when the invention has been entirely anticipated under § 102. What other options does the patentee possess in such instances?

7. Intervening Rights. Congress recognized that third parties may have made commercial decisions based upon the precise wording of the claims of an issued patent. If that patent is later reissued with different claims, this reliance interest could be frustrated. In order to protect individuals who may have relied upon the scope of the claims of the original patent, the second paragraph of section 251 provides for so-called intervening rights. There are two sorts of intervening rights: absolute and equitable.

Absolute intervening rights are set forth in the first sentence of the second paragraph of section 251. According to that provision, no reissued patent shall prevent one from employing a "specific thing" covered by the reissue patent, so long as that individual made use of that thing prior to the grant of the reissue. Absolute intervening rights are limited to the sale or continued use of individual machines, manufactures or products covered by the reissue patent. There is one significant exception: if the infringed claim of the reissue patent was also within the original patent, then no absolute intervening right arises.

The second sentence of the second paragraph of section 251 provides for equitable intervening rights. This statute allows a court to authorize the continued practice of an invention claimed in a reissue patent "to the extent and under such terms as the court deems equitable for the protection of investments made or business commenced before the grant of the reissue." To qualify for equitable intervening rights, an infringer must have made at least substantial preparations to practice the patented invention. As with the absolute intervening right, equitable intervening rights apply only when a valid, infringed claim appears solely in the reissue patent.

That intervening rights may apply to broadening reissues should be apparent. Less intuitive is that intervening rights may also arise when the claims are narrowed during reissue. However, even prior to a narrowing reissue, a defendant may have believed the original, broader claims to be invalid. Such grounds as anticipation, nonobviousness, indefiniteness or lack of an enabling disclosure may apply to the claims of the original patents but not to those that were reissued. The better view is that intervening rights may apply during any reissue, not just a broadening one.

A paucity of case law considers either sort of intervening right. This absence is likely due to artful reissue practice on behalf of patentees. Wise to the wording of the reissue statute, most patentees transfer as many claims from the original patent to the reissued patent as possible without amendment. Of course, if the defendant infringes a claim that appears in both the original and reissued patents, then no intervening rights are possible.

§ 13.2 REEXAMINATION

Reexamination proceedings were introduced into the U.S. patent law in 1980. The American Inventors Protection Act of 1999 renamed the traditional sort of reexamination as an *"ex parte* reexamination" and also introduced the possibility of an *"inter partes* reexamination." The principal purpose of either sort of reexamination is to provide third parties with an avenue for resolving validity disputes more quickly and less expensively than litigation.

The following decision concerns an *ex parte* reexamination. Under this procedure, any individual, including the patentee, a licensee, and even the Commissioner of the United States Patent and Trademark Office himself may cite a patent or printed publication to the PTO and request that a reexamination occur. If the PTO determines that this art raises "a substantial new question of patentability," 35 U.S.C.A. § 303(a), then it will essentially reinitiate examination of the patent, ordinarily opening with a rejection of some of the patent's claims over the prior art.

As you read the following case, keep in mind that a law enacted on November 2, 2002 liberalizes the use of prior art in any reexamination that had been previously cited or considered by the examiner. A note following the case discusses this further. The 2002 law also—but for *inter partes* reexamination only—grants third party requesters an opportunity to participate in appeals to the Board of Patent Appeals and Interferences and to the Federal Circuit. Thus, if the patentee has been successful in gaining a determination confirming the patentability of any claim, then the third party in an *inter partes* reexamination proceeding has the right to initiate an appeal to both the Board and to the Federal Circuit.

IN RE RECREATIVE TECHNOLOGIES CORP.

United States Court of Appeals, Federal Circuit, 1996.
83 F.3d 1394, 38 U.S.P.Q.2d 1776.

Before ARCHER, CHIEF JUDGE, and RICH and NEWMAN, CIRCUIT JUDGES.

PAULINE NEWMAN, CIRCUIT JUDGE.

Recreative Technologies Corp. ("Recreative") appeals the decision of the Patent and Trademark Office ("PTO") Board of Patent Appeals and

Interferences holding claims 1, 2, and 4 of United States Patent No. 4,912,800 ("the '800 patent"), upon reexamination, to be unpatentable. We conclude that the Board exceeded the statutory authorization that governs reexamination. We reverse the decision of the Board, and remand for further proceedings consistent with this opinion.

BACKGROUND

The '800 patent is directed to a cleaning device for use by golfers. The device is structured to be secured to a golf bag for use to clean items such as golf clubs, balls, and shoes. The cleaning device is comprised of several elements including a water absorbent towel body, a brush member secured to the towel body and a mounting means to releasably mount the towel body/brush to a golf bag. After Recreative sued Preferred Response Marketing ("Preferred") for infringement, Preferred requested reexamination of the '800 patent, citing as new references five patents and three publications, and stating that these new references raised a substantial new question of patentability. The PTO granted the request for reexamination.

On reexamination the examiner rejected claims 1, 2, 4–7, and 17 as unpatentable on the ground of obviousness, 35 U.S.C. § 103, in view of a reference to Ota. The examiner did not reject any claim on any of the eight new references cited by Preferred, and did not cite any reference other than Ota. The examiner confirmed original claims 13–16 and 18–20 and held patentable original claims 3 and 8–12. The Ota reference had been cited in the original examination on the same ground, obviousness, and the claims had been held patentable over Ota.

Recreative appealed the reexamination rejection to the Board. The Board reversed the examiner's rejection of claims 1, 2, 4–7, and 17, holding that the claims were not obvious in view of Ota. However, the Board sua sponte rejected claims 1, 2, and 4 based on the same Ota reference, but now under 35 U.S.C. § 102, for lack of novelty. This appeal followed.

DISCUSSION

The Reexamination Statute

Recreative states that the PTO had no authority to reject the claims, on reexamination, on the same ground on which the application was examined and the claims allowed during the original prosecution. Recreative states that the reexamination statute limits reexamination to "a substantial new question of patentability," and does not authorize repetition of a rejection on the same grounds that had been resolved in favor of the applicant during the original examination. 35 U.S.C. § 303 requires the examiner to determine whether a "substantial new question of patentability" is raised by the reexamination request. Only if a new question of patentability is raised, can the patent be reexamined.

Recreative states that the examiner merely repeated the same rejection for obviousness, based on the same Ota reference, as during the initial examination. Recreative states that it had successfully traversed the rejection based on the Ota reference in the initial examination, and that the reexamination statute was written to limit reexamination to new questions.

The Commissioner argues that "[o]nce initiated, the scope of reexamination includes reexamination of the patent in view of any pertinent patents and printed publications," new or old. The Commissioner thus contends that the repeat examination on the same ground was proper practice. However, the reexamination statute was designed to exclude repeat examination on grounds that had already been successfully traversed. Thus, the statute, on its face, does not accommodate the Commissioner's position.

The statute authorizes reexamination only when there is a substantial new question of patentability. A second examination, on the identical ground that had been previously raised and overcome, is barred. Thus, once it becomes apparent that there is no new question of patentability, it is improper to conduct reexamination on an old question that had been finally resolved during the initial examination. The Commissioner's argument that a different interpretation should prevail, and that the PTO has authority to reach a different result on reexamination on the identical ground, has led us to review the considerations that underlay the statute at the time of enactment.

Legislative History of Public Law 96–517

The reexamination statute was an important part of a larger effort to revive the United States' competitive vitality by restoring confidence in the validity of patents issued by the PTO. *Patlex Corp. v. Mossinghoff*, 758 F.2d 594, 601, 225 U.S.P.Q. 243, 248, *aff'd on reh'g* 771 F.2d 480, 226 U.S.P.Q. 985 (Fed.Cir.1985). Congressman Robert Kastenmeier described the reexamination proposal as "an effort to reverse the current decline in U.S. productivity by strengthening the patent and copyright systems to improve investor confidence in new technology." 126 Cong. Rec. 29,895 (1980).

The proponents of reexamination anticipated three principal benefits. First, reexamination based on references that were not previously included in the patentability examination could resolve validity disputes more quickly and less expensively than litigation. Second, courts would benefit from the expertise of the PTO for prior art that was not previously of record. Third, reexamination would strengthen confidence in patents whose validity was clouded because pertinent prior art had not previously been considered by the PTO. *Patlex*, 758 F.2d at 602, 225 U.S.P.Q. at 248–49. These benefits are achieved by authorizing the PTO to correct errors in the prior examination:

> The reexamination statute's purpose is to correct errors made by the government, to remedy defective governmental (not private) action, and if need be to remove patents that never should have been granted.... A defectively examined and therefore erroneously

granted patent must yield to the reasonable Congressional purpose of facilitating the correction of governmental mistakes.

Patlex, 758 F.2d at 604, 225 U.S.P.Q. at 250.

However, Congress recognized that this broad purpose must be balanced against the potential for abuse, whereby unwarranted reexaminations can harass the patentee and waste the patent life. The legislative record and the record of the interested public reflect a serious concern that reexamination not create new opportunities for abusive tactics and burdensome procedures. Thus reexamination as enacted was carefully limited to new prior art, that is, "new information about pre-existing technology which may have escaped review at the time of the initial examination of the patent application." H.R.Rep. No. 96–1307, 96th Cong., 2d Sess. 3 (1980), *reprinted in* 1980 U.S.C.C.A.N. 6460, 6462. No grounds of reexamination were to be permitted other than based on new prior art and sections 102 and 103. As explained in the legislative history, matters that were decided in the original examination would be barred from reexamination:

> This "substantial new question" requirement would protect patentees from having to respond to, or participate in unjustified reexaminations. Further, it would act to bar reconsideration of any argument already decided by the Office, whether during the original examination or an earlier reexamination.

Id. at 7, reprinted in 1980 U.S.C.C.A.N. at 6466.

Thus the statute guarded against simply repeating the prior examination on the same issues and arguments. Commissioner Diamond explained the importance of this safeguard:

> [The proposed statute] carefully protects patent owners from reexamination proceedings brought for harassment or spite. The possibility of harassing patent holders is a classic criticism of some foreign reexamination systems and we made sure it would not happen here.

Industrial Innovation & Patent & Copyright Law Amendments: Hearings on H.R. 6933, 6934, 3806 & 214 Before the Subcomm. on Courts, Civil Liberties and the Administration of Justice of the House Comm. on the Judiciary, 96th Cong., 2d Sess. 594 (1980) (statement of Sidney Diamond, Cmr. of Patents & Trademarks).

In this case, the Commissioner points out that the MANUAL OF PATENT EXAMINING PROCEDURE authorizes the procedure that was followed. Section 2258 of the M.P.E.P. states that

> [O]nce initiated, the scope of reexamination includes reexamination of the patent in view of any pertinent patents or printed publications, including issues previously addressed by the Office.

Thus the Commissioner argues that it is within the examiner's authority to apply the old ground of rejection on the Ota reference, as the only ground of rejection. We can not agree. This is the very action against which the statute protects. The Commissioner's argument that reexamination, once begun, can be limited to grounds previously raised and finally decided, can not be accommodated by the statute, and is directly contravened by the legislative history. Although Congress may entrust the administrative agency with administration of a statute, the agency can not depart from the statutory purpose.

> [The courts] must reject administrative constructions of the statute, whether reached by adjudication or by rulemaking, that are inconsistent with the statutory mandate or that frustrate the policy that Congress sought to implement.

Patlex, 771 F.2d at 487, 226 U.S.P.Q. at 989 (quoting *Federal Election Commission v. Democratic Senatorial Campaign Committee*, 454 U.S. 27, 31–32, 102 S.Ct. 38, 41–42, 70 L.Ed.2d 23 (1981)).

We take note that § 2258 of the M.P.E.P. was not among the original reexamination rules that were adopted to implement the reexamination statute. See revision 7 to the 4th edition, July 1981. The current text of § 2258 appeared in subsequent editions of the M.P.E.P. We do not know its genesis, yet it plainly exceeds the statutory authorization. It is also in apparent conflict with other procedural instructions in the Manual. Compare M.P.E.P. § 2216, which states that requests for reexamination should point out how the questions of patentability newly raised are substantially different from those raised in the original prosecution. Also compare M.P.E.P. § 2242, which includes the following:

> If the prior art patents and printed publications raise a substantial new question of patentability of at least one claim of the patent, then a substantial new question of patentability is present, unless it is clear to the examiner that the same question of patentability has already been decided (1) [by a court] . . . (2) by the Office either in the original examination, the examination of a reissue patent, or an earlier concluded reexamination.

M.P.E.P. § 2242, which bars review of a question that "has already been decided," does not readily harmonize with M.P.E.P. § 2258, which permits reexamination of "issues previously addressed." Thus although the M.P.E.P. usefully implements the patent statute, when a section of the M.P.E.P. is inconsistent with the statute it must yield to the legislative purpose.

The statutory instruction that a new question of patentability must be raised is explicit in 35 U.S.C. § 303. Reexamination is barred for questions of patentability that were decided in the original examination. That power can not be acquired by internal rule of procedure or practice. The policy balance reflected in the reexamination statute's provisions can not be unilaterally realigned by the agency. To the extent that M.P.E.P. § 2258 enlarges the statutory authorization, it is void. See *Patlex*, 771 F.2d at 487 (regulation promulgated under statutory authority not valid if not reasonably related to the purposes of the enabling legislation).

The Ota Reference

The question of patentability in view of the Ota reference was decided in the original examination, and thus it can not be a substantial new question. The Commissioner argues that the examiner failed to appreciate the Ota reference during the first examination, citing *Standard Havens Products, Inc. v. Gencor Industries, Inc.*, 897 F.2d 511, 13 U.S.P.Q.2d 2029 (Fed.Cir.1990). In *Standard Havens* the Commissioner ordered reexamination in view of a reference that had not been cited in the original examination, the Commissioner observing that it was uncertain whether the reference had been considered. Id. at 514, 897 F.2d 511, 13 U.S.P.Q.2d at 2031. Ota, however, had been cited. It was the subject of extensive prosecution during the original examination, and the rejection had been overcome.

On the reexamination appeal to the Board, the Board had reversed the examiner's reexamination rejection under § 103, stating that obviousness had not been shown. The Board then spontaneously rejected claims 1, 2, and 4 for lack of novelty, again based on Ota. Recreative points out that "anticipation is the epitome of obviousness," and that the original examiner necessarily considered novelty when examining the claims for obviousness. We need not reach this aspect, for this procedure by the Board can not overcome the fact that reexamination should not have been granted or should have been dismissed at the examination stage when no new grounds of rejection were raised.

It can not have been the statutory intent that a patentee would not know whether there was a new ground of rejection, as required for reexamination, until the reexamination was completed on the old ground, was appealed to the Board, and was decided by the Board not on the old ground but on a possibly new ground that was not previously part of the reexamination. Thus even on the Commissioner's argument that a rejection on the same reference but styled as lack of novelty instead of obviousness is a "new ground"—an interesting question that we do not reach—the requirement of § 303 was not met. It would eviscerate the statutory safeguard to permit the Board to cure an improper reexamination with the creation of a new issue at the appellate stage of the reexamination proceeding.

In sum, the argument based on Ota did not present a new question of patentability. Recreative is correct that the reexamination should have been terminated when no other ground of rejection was raised.

REVERSED AND REMANDED.

Notes

1. When is a "Substantial New Question of Patentability" Substantially New? In *In re Portola Packaging, Inc.*, 110 F.3d 786, 42 U.S.P.Q.2d 1295 (Fed.Cir.1997), the Federal Circuit reversed a rejection after a reexamination because the examiner rejected on the basis of art considered in the initial granting of the patent. The invention was a flexible bottle neck and cap combination. In the initial examination, the examiner rejected some claims as anticipated by the Hunter patent and other claims as obvious in light of the Faulstich patent and two other references. After amendments, a few remaining claims issued.

About ten years later, a reexamination commenced. The examiner rejected all claims in light of a new reference, the Von Hagel patent. The inventor, Portola responded to the Von Hagel art by cancelling some claims and combining others. These claims the examiner rejected as obvious in light of Hunter and Faulstich. Upon appeal to the Federal Circuit, the question was only whether Hunter and Faulstich—previously considered in the first examination—could serve as the basis of rejecting the new reexamination claims. The Federal Circuit announced that even though the initial examination did not combine Hunter and Faulstich, this new combination was not a "new ground" of rejection because both references were before the examiner in the first examination. 110 F.3d at 790, 42 U.S.P.Q.2d at 1299. In the words of Judge Lourie:

> Whether the earlier examination was correct or not, reexamination of the same claims in light of the same references does not create a substantial new question of patentability, which is the statutory criterion for reexamination.

Id. Were the reexamination claims in fact "the same claims" as in the initial patent? After all Portola amended these claims during reexamination to evade Von Hagel. The Federal Circuit answered that question:

> That the claims were amended by Portola does not mean that a new examination of the amended claims involved substantial new issues of patentability. It is clear that the scope of a patent claim may not be enlarged by amendment during reexamination.

Id. Even if the scope of claims remains the same, does a new formulation of claim terms with the same scope raise new issues of patentability?

More importantly, how does the result and reasoning in *Portola* square with the language of the reexamination statute? 35 U.S.C.A. § 303 gives the Commissioner authority to commence a reexamination whenever "a substantial new question of patentability . . . is raised." Where does the statute limit reexaminations to new prior art? A substantial new question of patentability (as determined by the Commissioner) certainly seems broader than simply new prior art.

Additionally, note that the Portola reexamination seemingly was properly triggered by new prior art. Once properly underway, § 305 commands that reexamination should proceed "according to the procedures established for initial examination." Standard examination procedures would plainly permit the rejection of the new reexamination claims. Did the Federal Circuit import an erroneous "new prior art" requirement into "procedures established for initial examination"?

2. Overturned by Legislation! *In re Recreative Technologies* and *In re Portola Packaging, Inc.* might have restricted the effectiveness of reexamination, but they were set aside by a new law. *Portola* had erected the rule that a reexamination could not be based upon a prior art patent that was cited or considered in the regular examination of the application leading up to the grant of a patent. This was true–per *Portola Packaging*—even where it was evident that the examiner had not understood the relevance of the prior art. The November 2, 2002 law, however, adds a new, final sentence to 35 USC § 303(a) for *ex parte* reexamination (with a comparable change for *inter partes* reexamination). The new sentence of the law creates a partial definition what constitutes a "substantial new question of patentability:" "The existence of a substantial new question of patentability is not precluded by the fact that a patent or printed publication was previously cited by or to the Office or considered by the Office." The new law made the same change for *inter partes* reexamination as well.

3. The Preliminary Statement. *Ex parte* reexamination actually may have a short-lived *inter partes* initial phase. If the *ex parte* reexamination requestor is other than the patentee, the patentee is initially allowed to file a preliminary statement "including any amendment to his patent and new claim or claims he may wish to propose, for consideration in the reexamination." 35 U.S.C.A. § 304. If the patentee submits such a statement, the requestor "may file and have considered in the reexamination a reply to any statement filed by the patent owner." *Id.* Because patentees are ordinarily loath to allow the input of an opponent of a patent before the PTO, however, they usually observe silence at this early stage, foregoing any opportunity of the *ex parte* reexamination requestor to provide further objections to the claims of the patent.

4. Constitutional Challenges. The *ex parte* reexamination statute survived an attack based upon the due process clause of the Fifth Amendment as well as the jury trial guarantee of the Seventh Amendment. In *Patlex Corp. v. Mossinghoff*, 758 F.2d 594, 225 U.S.P.Q. 243 (Fed.Cir.), *modified*, 771 F.2d 480, 226 U.S.P.Q. 985 (Fed.Cir.1985), the court reasoned that because the reexamination statute qualified as a curative statute, designed to correct defects in an administrative system, the usual disfavor cast upon retroactive legislation under due process analysis did not apply. The court noted this purpose again, as well as the existence of the reissue proceeding, in holding that the Seventh Amendment was also not offended.

5. Citation of Prior Art. In lieu of provoking a reexamination, individuals may simply cite patents or printed publications to the Patent and Trademark Office under 35 U.S.C.A. § 301. If accompanied by a written explanation of the relevance of the cited prior art to the patent, this submission will be included in the patent's official record. Section 301 allows competitors to place prior art on the record, ensuring that it will be considered if a reexamination is declared. Of course, particularly pertinent prior art will undoubtedly hamper the patentee's enforcement or licensing efforts, and may even encourage another party to file a reexamination itself.

6. Reexamination at the Request of the Commissioner. Section 303(a) allows the Commissioner of the United States Patent and Trademark Office to undertake reexamination on his own initiative. This relatively rare step typically occurs where the issuance of a frivolous or plainly invalid patent results in public outcry against the PTO. One example of a Commissioner-requested reexamination took place with regard to U.S. Patent No. 5,241,671, relating to a multimedia search system. The '671 patent issued on August 31, 1993, and featured broad claims which covered numerous applications of CD–ROM multimedia technology. The patentee, Compton's NewMedia Encyclopedia, quickly announced a royalty and licensing fee structure under the patent at an industry trade show. Pressured by complaints from multimedia developers which otherwise failed to seek reexamination themselves, the Commissioner requested reexamination on December 17, 1993. The PTO ultimately canceled all claims of the '671 patent. For further discussion of the Compton's multimedia patent, along with a critical view of the Commissioner's action, see Terri Suzette Hughes, Comment, *Patent Reexamination and the PTO: Compton's Patent Invalidated at the Commissioner's Request*, 14 J. Marshall J. Computer & Info. L.J. 379 (1996).

7. *Inter Partes* **Reexamination.** As traditionally structured, the *ex parte* reexamination statute encountered criticism. As the title *"ex parte* reexamination" suggests, the role of the reexamination requestor is very limited in these proceedings. Only the patentee may participate in the dialogue with the examiner, and only the patentee may appeal the matter to the Board or to the courts if the PTO reaches an unsatisfactory conclusion. Many third parties did not believe the limited role provided for them offered a viable alternative to validity challenges in court. As a result, the ability of *ex parte* reexamination to provide an expert forum as a faster, less expensive alternative to litigation of patent validity was compromised. Data supported these observations, for far fewer *ex parte* reexaminations were requested than had been originally anticipated. *See* Mark D. Janis, *Rethinking Reexamination: Toward a Viable Administrative Revocation System for U.S. Patent Law*, 11 Harv. J. L. & Tech. 1 (1997).

The Optional Inter Partes Reexamination Procedure Act of 1999 responded to these concerns by providing third party requesters with an additional option. *See* 35 U.S.C. §§ 311–318. They may employ the traditional reexamination system, which has been renamed an *ex parte* reexamination. Or, they may opt for a considerable degree of participation in the newly minted *inter partes* reexamination. Under this legislation, third party requesters may opt to submit written comments to accompany patentee responses to the PTO. The requester may also appeal PTO determinations that a reexamined patent is not invalid to the Board and the courts. To discourage abuse of *inter partes* reexamination proceedings, the statute provides that third party participants are estopped from raising issues that they raised or could have raised during reexamination during subsequent litigation. Unsuccessful challengers are also *not* allowed to appeal to the Federal Circuit. *Inter partes* reexaminations also present more costly fees, in particular a $8,800 request filing fee as of October 1, 2001.

Up through an amendment of the *inter partes* reexamination law on November 2, 2002, there had been virtually no use at all of *inter partes* reexamination. The PTO had received a mere handful of requests for *inter partes* reexamination. The new 2002 law, however, permits third parties a right of appeal an *inter partes* reexamination to the Board of Patent Appeals and Interferences and all the way to the Federal Circuit. This advantage for third parties is unique to the *inter partes* reexamination proceeding and not shared by the *ex parte* reexamination requester.

8. **Reexamination vs. Reissue Review.** The difference between a reexamination and a reissue may appear elusive, but the following points should illuminate the distinctions between the two post-grant proceedings:

- A request for reexamination may be filed by "any person," while a reissue must be filed with the approval of the patentee.

- A request for reexamination need not point out "error" without deceptive intent, while a reissue application must do so. Thus, the patentee may use reexamination to add narrower claims to the patent without having to file affidavits explaining why they were not included in the original patent.

- A reexamination is directed towards prior art patents and printed publications, while a reissue is directed towards any issue that may be considered in an original application. Where the patentee amends matter in the patent, however, ancillary issues concerning compliance with § 112 and other statutes may arise in a reexamination as well.

- A reexamination cannot be employed to broaden the patent's claims. An applicant may employ a reissue to provide broadened claims if the reissue application is filed within two years from the date of the patent grant, and may also choose to abandon the reissue and the return of its original patent from the PTO. A reexamination cannot be abandoned once initiated by the PTO.

- Claims may be copied from a reissue application in order to place the application into an interference. Reexaminations do not give rise to interferences.

§ 13.3   OVERVIEW OF POST–GRANT PROCEDURES ABROAD

Foreign post-grant procedures are of two sorts: opposition proceedings, held at the Patent Office, and nullity proceedings, adjudicated by a specialized Patent Court. The European Patent Convention allows third parties to file an opposition at the European Patent Office during the first nine months of the patent's term; this period is supposedly long enough to allow competitors to evaluate the patent, but does not excessively limit the patent owner's rights. Although previously the European Patent Office had allowed patent proprietors to bring oppositions against their own patents—a useful tool for amending the patent on a continental basis, without resorting to multiple proceedings at various national patent offices—the Enlarged Board of Appeal has now abrogated this practice. The possible bases of an opposition are limited: patent-eligible subject matter, lack of novelty or inventive step, and inadequate disclosure. *See* European Patent Convention Art. 52–57.

An opposition is a full-featured *inter partes* proceeding held at the European Patent Office. Parties may offer evidence as well as the testimony of experts and the inventors. Where multiple parties have filed oppositions, the European Patent notifies each opponent; this step effectively allows opponents to coordinate their attacks on the patent. Additionally, entities accused of infringement may join an ongoing opposition even though the nine-month deadline has passed.

Oppositions in both Europe and Japan have tapered off in the past few years. Japanese oppositions today are at a rate of roughly two percent. The Japanese government is now considering legislation that would abolish the opposition system and merge that practice into a trial for invalidation–a procedure that has existed in parallel with the opposition system throughout modern Japanese patent law. The Japanese trial for invalidity has been greatly strengthened, with the typical procedure often being completed in less than fifteen months. A Japanese invalidity trial goes on appeal to the Tokyo High Court as well.

Depending on the particular legal system, nullity proceedings are conducted in either the Patent Office, the general courts, or a specialized patent court. For example, the German Federal Patent Court ordinarily adjudicates these disputes employing panels of five judges, of which three possess technical backgrounds and the remaining two legal qualifications. Nullity proceedings may be brought at any time during the life of the patent, in large part for the same grounds as an opposition. They may result in the total or partial cancellation of any of the patent's claims. Note that within Europe, nullity proceedings are purely a national matter, with no parallel in the European Patent Convention.

Post–Grant Procedure Exercises

1. The '777 patent contains one independent and two dependent claims. The owner of the '777 patent, Johnson, files a reissue application fourteen months following the patent's issue date. As requested, the PTO reissues claim 1 as in the original patent, but broadens the scope of claims 2 and 3. Later, Johnson sues Boswell for patent infringement. Boswell admits infringement of all claims of the reissued patent and that the claims are valid. May Boswell successfully raise the defense of intervening rights?

2. The '888 patent relates to an exhaust hood assembly useful for placement above a stove or other cooking apparatus. It issued to MacDaniel on January 5, 2001, with a single claim defining elements A, B, and C. Element B consisted of "a fan with five blades." On July 1, 2003, MacDaniel filed a reissue application, again with a single claim. That claim comprised elements A, B, C, D and E, where element B consisted of "a fan with a plurality of blades." Did MacDaniel file a proper reissue application?

3. Which of the following may *not* be corrected via reissue?

(A) One of the actual inventors is not named on the patent.

(B) Foreign priority was not claimed under § 119.

(C) The applicant failed to disclose an extremely pertinent prior art reference of which he had knowledge.

(D) The applicant knew, but did not disclose, a particular mode that was determined only after the time of filing to be the superior method of practicing the invention; he did disclose what he in good faith considered to be the best mode.

4. On January 4, 1998, Lestrade, a registered patent attorney, filed in the United States Patent Office a patent application on behalf of inventor Moriarity. The application is directed towards an O-ring seal

useful with various chemical processing techniques. The patent ultimate-ly issued on December 13, 1999.

On April 1, 1999, Moriarity begins selling O-rings that were fully disclosed in his application. On September 4, 2000, Moriarity realized that his patent does not claim the precise elements that comprise the O-ring he is actually selling. Moriarity tells Lestrade, "I would like to file a reissue application to seek broadened claims to cover the O-rings I have been selling. However, I'm worried about an on-sale bar under section 102(b). What is the last possible date on which I can file—or should have filed—a reissue application?"

What is the last possible date that a broadening reissue may be filed with respect to the Moriarity patent?

5.   A United States patent issued to Nimmer on September 1, 1997. The Nimmer patent describes and claims a coffee grinding machine. Nimmer's chief competitor, Goldstein, wishes to file a third party re-quest for reexamination. He is aware of the following possibilities for filing the request:

(A) Goldstein's own patent application filed on August 12, 1995. The application disclosed, but did not claim, the identical coffee grinding machine in Nimmer's patent. However, Goldstein ultimate-ly abandoned the application on May 1, 1997, and no patent ever arose out of that application.

(B) Evidence that Nimmer sold the claimed invention to the Brown & Denicola Company of Boston, Massachusetts, on January 5, 1996.

(C) Evidence that a third party, the Litman Coffee Company, publicly used the same coffee grinder in Ann Arbor, Michigan, from March through June, 1996.

(D) A British patent, issued to Dworkin, which describes and claims the invention. The British patent issued on November 6, 1991, based upon an application filed in the United Kingdom on January 28, 1990.

May Goldstein file a request for reexamination with any chance of success? On what ground, if any?

Chapter Fourteen

INTERNATIONAL PROSECUTION

To be effective in an increasingly global economy, inventors often must secure patent rights within many different jurisdictions. So in addition to prosecuting patent applications before their own national or regional patent office, patent attorneys are often called upon to coordinate patent acquisition efforts before many different administrative agencies overseas. Despite the existence of international agreements like the Paris Convention, the Patent Cooperation Treaty, and the TRIPS Agreement, this effort frequently requires attorneys to address multiple substantive patent laws, granting procedures and languages. Further, the coordinating attorney must ensure that prosecution efforts in one country do not imperil patentability elsewhere, for example, by invoking one of the several statutory bars under § 102.

The foundational patent law treaty, the Paris Convention, takes some steps to ease this onerous task. As noted in Chapter 1, the Paris Convention, in essence, allows an applicant to obtain a priority date by filing an initial application, typically in the inventor's home country. The applicant may then file a patent application in any country bound by the Convention within twelve months and maintain the earlier priority date. This basic scheme includes some significant details, which require a more thorough examination of Article 4 of the Paris Convention and its implementing provision, § 119 of the United States Patent Act.

§ 14.1 THE PARIS CONVENTION

PARIS CONVENTION FOR THE PROTECTION OF INDUSTRIAL PROPERTY

July 14, 1967.
21 U.S.T. 1583, T.I.A.S. 6295, 828 U.N.T.S. 305.

ARTICLE 4, SECTION A

1. Any person who has duly filed an application for a patent, or for the registration of a utility model, or of an industrial design, or of a trademark, in one of the countries of the Union, or his successor in title,

shall enjoy, for the purpose of filing in the other countries, a right of priority during the periods hereinafter fixed.

2. Any filing that is equivalent to a regular national filing under the domestic legislation of any country of the Union or under bilateral or multilateral treaties concluded between countries of the Union shall be recognized as giving rise to the right of priority.

3. By a regular national filing is meant any filing that is adequate to establish the date on which the application was filed in the country concerned, whatever may be the subsequent fate of the application.

ARTICLE 4, SECTION B

Consequently, any subsequent filing in any of the other countries of the Union before the expiration of the periods referred to above shall not be invalidated by reason of any acts accomplished in the interval, in particular, another filing, the publication or exploitation of the invention, the putting on sales of copies of the design, or the use of the mark, and such acts cannot give rise to any third-party right or any right of personal possession. Rights acquired by third parties before the date of the first application that serves as the basis for the right of priority are reserved in accordance with the domestic legislation of each country of the Union.

ARTICLE 4, SECTION C

(1) The periods of priority referred to above shall be twelve months for patents and utility models, and six months for industrial designs and trademarks.

(2) These periods shall start from the date of filing of the first application; the day of filing shall not be included in the period....

ARTICLE 4, SECTION H

Priority may not be refused on the ground that certain elements of the invention for which priority is claimed do not appear among the claims formulated in the application in the country of origin, provided that the application documents as a whole specifically disclose such elements.

Notes

1. **The Significance of the Paris Convention.** The Paris Convention is the starting point for a consideration of any intellectual property rights in virtually every part of the world. The original Paris treaty from 1883 has been revised several times and today stands in the form of its 1967 Stockholm Revision. Intermediate revisions were completed in Brussels (1900), Washington, D.C. (1911), The Hague (1925), London (1934) and Lisbon (1958). While this casebook focuses upon patents, the treaty is equally important for trademarks and designs. For more information on the Paris Convention, *see* Friedrich–Karl Beier, *One Hundred Years of International Cooperation—The Role of the Paris Convention in the Past, Present and Future*, 15 INT'L REV. INDUS. PROP. & COPYRIGHT L. 1 (1984).

The most fundamental, practical right under Paris is the offensive priority right: By filing in the United States (or in any union country), the clock stands still for one year. Article 4, Section B thus creates a bar against actions leading to patent invalidity based on activities that occurred after the filing in the first union state, but before the filing in any second union state within that one-year period. Thus for this purpose only, one can talk about dating the application in the second union state back to the original union state filing. Of course, the applicant must make a timely claim for priority and meet other formalities. For example, some signatory states require that a priority claim be made simultaneously with the filing of the second application, while others require the filing of a ribboned, certified copy of the priority filing document along with the national application.

2. Implementation of Article 4 of the Paris Convention in § 119(a). Section 119(a) lays out the following requirements for ensuring a claim to priority based upon a foreign application.

Both applications must be filed by the same applicant, legal representative or assigns.

Both applications must be for the same invention.

The foreign application must be for a patent. As with § 102, consider the meaning of the term "patent" in light of different schemes.

The first filing must be in an appropriate foreign country. The recognition of the right of priority is not limited to Paris Convention signatories, but to those foreign countries "which afford similar privileges in the case of applications filed in the United States or to citizens of the United States." Note that, in particular, Article 2 of the TRIPS Agreement requires that WTO members comply with Articles 1–12 and 19 of the Paris Convention. The United States is also a party to the scantly invoked Inter–American Convention on Inventions, Patents, Designs, and Industrial Models, 38 Stat. 1811 (1910), which provides for a comparable priority right to that of the Paris Convention.

The United States application must be filed within twelve months of the foreign filing.

A one-year grace period must be respected. Section 119(a) closes with the admonition that "no patent shall be granted on any application for patent for an invention which had been patented or described in a printed publication in any country more than one year before the date of the actual filing of the application in this country, or which had been in public use or on sale in this country more than one year prior to such filing." Is this statute consistent with the Paris Convention? Can you create a fact pattern where this restatement of § 102(b) invalidates a patent that was based on a Paris Convention filing?

3. Importance of the Filing Date. The Paris Convention is concerned only with the initial filing date, without regard to whether that filing actually matures into a granted patent. Thus, the application could be rejected over the prior art or abandoned, yet the filing would remain valid for preserving the right of priority in subsequent filings abroad. However, suppose an inventor files an application claiming a pharmaceutical compound in a country where such inventions are not patent-eligible. Should such an application give rise to a priority right as well?

4. Notice of Priority Filing. The applicant must declare he is relying upon the priority right for it to be effective under Article 4, Section D of the Paris Convention, under § 119(b). This provision also allows each national patent system to set "the latest date on which such declaration must be made." In particular, the Japanese system has imposed strict requirements. TETSU TANABE & HAROLD WEGNER, JAPANESE PATENT PRACTICE 133 (1986). In the United States, failure to claim the benefit of the priority right may be corrected through a reissue proceeding, considered in this casebook at Chapter 13.

5. Patent Office Priority Practice. The U.S. Patent and Trademark Office instructs examiners to make use of claimed priority applications during patent acquisition proceedings only as need requires. "The only times during *ex parte* prosecution that the examiner considers the merits of an applicant's claim or priority is when a reference is found with an effective date of the foreign filing and the date of filing and the United States and when an interference situation is under consideration." MANUAL OF PATENT EXAMINING PROCEDURE § 201.15 (8th ed. 2001). Priority is determined on a claim-by-claim basis, so some claims of a single patent may be entitled to priority from an earlier application, and others may not. Further, an applicant may rely upon two or more foreign applications and may be entitled to the filing date of one of them with regard to certain claims, and to another application with regard to other claims.

6. Resetting the Clock. Article 4(C)(4) permits an applicant to reset his priority date by effectively cancelling the first application:

> A subsequent application * * * in the same country * * * shall be considered as the first application [for purposes of starting the priority year] if, at the time of filing the subsequent application, the said previous application has been withdrawn, abandoned, or refused, without having been laid open to public inspection and without leaving any rights outstanding, and if it has not yet served as a basis for claiming a right of priority. The previous application may not thereafter serve as a basis for claiming a right of priority.

The one-year period of priority does not apply for design patents, which has only a six month period.

7. Provisional Applications. Could an inventor file a provisional application in the United States, as provided in § 111(b) and considered here at Chapter 12, and then claim a right of priority based upon the application when filing abroad? If so, is the filing of a provisional application always the first union application? Alternatively, could an inventor who filed first overseas subsequently file a provisional application in the United States, claiming the priority right? *See* 35 U.S.C.A. § 111(b)(7).

8. Supremacy of Paris over other Treaties. The PCT, EPC and any other treaties are "sub-treaties" under Paris. They are specifically tolerated through Article 19 of the Paris Convention, which allows signatories to"reserve the right to make separately between themselves special agreements for the protection of industrial property, in so far as these agreements do not contravene the provisions of this Convention."

The recent Trade Related Aspects of Intellectual Property of the World Trade Organization (WTO) is now in force for developed countries and is to be fully implemented even in developing countries by 2005. The TRIPS Agreement sets minimum standards that are complementary to Paris.

9. Disclosure Requirements. Under Paris Convention Article 4H, the invention claimed in subsequent Convention applications must be one in which "the [priority] application documents as a whole specifically discloses [the claimed] elements." The following opinion explores this requirement in further detail.

IN RE GOSTELI

United States Court of Appeals, Federal Circuit, 1989.
872 F.2d 1008, 10 U.S.P.Q.2d 1614.

Before BISSELL and ARCHER, CIRCUIT JUDGES, and RE, CHIEF JUDGE.

BISSELL, CIRCUIT JUDGE.

DECISION

The decision of the United States Patent and Trademark Office (PTO) Board of Patent Appeals and Interferences (Board), affirming the examiner's final rejection of claims 48–51 in the patent application, Serial No. 423,348, of Jacques Gosteli, Ivan Ernest and Robert B. Woodward [hereinafter Gosteli or Applicants], under 35 U.S.C. § 102(e) (1982), is affirmed.

BACKGROUND

Gosteli's patent application discloses bicyclic thia-aza compounds containing a beta-lactam ring unsubstituted in the beta-position and having antibiotic properties. The claimed compounds are chemical intermediates used in the preparation of antibiotics known as 2–penems. Claims 48 and 49 are Markush-type genus claims, and dependent claims 50 and 51 are subgenus claims, each consisting of 21 specific chemical species. The examiner rejected claims 48–51 under section 102(e) as being anticipated by United States Patent No. 4,155,912 (Menard). Menard discloses, but does not claim, a first species that is within the scope of claims 48 and 50, and a second species, that is within the scope of claims 49 and 51.

Attempting to antedate Menard, Gosteli claimed the benefit, under 35 U.S.C. § 119 (1982), of their Luxembourg patent application's foreign priority date. The disclosure of the Luxembourg application is not as complete as that of Gosteli's United States application. The Luxembourg application discloses a subgenus of the genus claimed in the United States application and specifically describes the two chemical species disclosed by Menard. Menard's effective date is December 14, 1977, seven months after the May 9, 1977, filing date of Gosteli's Luxembourg application, but five months before Gosteli's May 4, 1978, United States filing date. Thus, Menard is not an effective reference under section 102(e) if Applicants are entitled to their Luxembourg priority date.

The Board denied Gosteli the benefit of their Luxembourg priority date reasoning that:

> [Gosteli's] problem in attempting to antedate the Menard reference is that their Luxembourg priority application does not disclose the "same invention" in a manner that complies with the first paragraph of 35 USC 112 as is claimed in the claims on appeal (48–51). In other words claims 48–51 contain considerable subject matter which is not specifically disclosed in the Luxembourg application.... Since [Gosteli's] Luxembourg application does not provide a written description of the entire subject matter set forth in the appealed claims 48–51, as required by the first paragraph of 35 USC 112, we have concluded that claims 48–51 have an effective filing date as of the May 4, 1978 filing date of [Gosteli's] grandparent application Serial No. 902,639, and not as of the Luxembourg filing date. Accordingly, [Applicants have] not antedated the Menard reference.

Alternatively, Gosteli attempted to swear behind Menard by using declarations submitted under 37 C.F.R. § 1.131 (1988) (Rule 131). The Board rejected the use of Rule 131, because "the declaration does not ... contain 'facts showing a completion of the invention in this country before the filing date of' Menard." Gosteli appeals from the Board's decision.

ISSUES

1. Whether claims 48–51 are entitled, under section 119, to the benefit of a foreign priority date.

2. Whether Rule 131 allows Gosteli to swear behind the two chemical species disclosed in Menard by establishing a constructive reduction to practice in this country based on Gosteli's foreign priority date of those two species.

3. Whether Gosteli's Luxembourg priority application provides a written description sufficient to support the entire subject matter of claims 48–51, as required by 35 U.S.C. § 112, ¶ 1 (1982).

OPINION

I. Section 119

Claims 48–51 of Gosteli's application stand rejected under section 102(e) as anticipated by Menard. The two chemical species disclosed by Gosteli's Luxembourg priority application are disclosed by Menard and also fall within the scope of the claims on appeal. Section 102(e) bars the issuance of a patent if its generic claims are anticipated by prior art disclosing individual chemical species. *See, e.g., In re Slayter,* 276 F.2d 408, 411, 125 USPQ 345, 347 (CCPA 1960) (stating that species anticipate a generic claim). The parties agree that Menard is an effective anticipatory prior art reference unless Applicants are entitled to their Luxembourg priority date.

Generally, an applicant may antedate prior art by relying on the benefit of a previously filed foreign application to establish an effective date earlier than that of the reference. See 35 U.S.C. § 119; *In re Wertheim*, 541 F.2d 257, 261, 191 USPQ 90, 95–96 (CCPA 1976); Rollins, *35 USC 119–Description and Enablement Requirements*, 67 J.Pat.Off. Soc'y 386, 386 (1985). Under section 119, the claims set forth in a United States application are entitled to the benefit of a foreign priority date if the corresponding foreign application supports the claims in the manner required by section 112, ¶ 1. *Wertheim*, 541 F.2d at 261–62, 191 USPQ at 95–96; *Kawai v. Metlesics*, 480 F.2d 880, 887–89, 178 USPQ 158, 164–65 (CCPA 1973).

Gosteli contends that their rights under section 119 are determined by focusing on (1) what is the subject matter disclosed in the Luxembourg priority application, and (2) whether that subject matter removes Menard. We disagree with Gosteli's reading of section 119. The statute provides, in pertinent part: An application for patent for an invention filed in this country by any person who has ... previously regularly filed an application for a patent for the same invention in a foreign country ... shall have the same effect as the same application would have if filed in this country on the date on which the application for patent for the same invention was first filed in such foreign country.... 35 U.S.C. § 119. The reference to the "invention" in section 119 clearly refers to what the claims define, not what is disclosed in the foreign application. Cf. *In re Scheiber*, 587 F.2d 59, 61, 199 USPQ 782, 784 (CCPA 1978) (stating that "invention" as used in 35 U.S.C. § 120 (Supp. IV 1986), refers to what is claimed). Section 119 provides that a foreign application "shall have the same effect" as if it had been filed in the United States. 35 U.S.C. § 119. Accordingly, if the effective filing date of what is claimed in a United States application is at issue, to preserve symmetry of treatment between sections 120 and 119, the foreign priority application must be examined to ascertain if it supports, within the meaning of section 112, ¶ 1, what is claimed in the United States application. Compare *Kawai*, 480 F.2d at 886, 178 USPQ at 162–63 (construing the section 112, ¶ 1 requirements of section 119) with *Scheiber*, 587 F.2d at 62, 199 USPQ at 784–85 (construing the section 112, ¶ 1 requirements of section 120).

At oral argument, the government conceded that if Gosteli claims the species disclosed in the Luxembourg application they would be entitled to the foreign priority date with regard to those claims. Thus, Menard would be ineffective as a reference against those claimed species, or any other claim properly supported by the Luxembourg disclosure as required by section 112, ¶ 1. We conclude, therefore, that claims 48–51 are entitled to the benefit of their foreign priority date under section 119 only if the foreign priority application properly supports them as required by section 112, ¶ 1. An application relying on the benefit of an earlier filing date in the United States would receive the same treatment under 35 U.S.C. § 120. See *Kawai*, 480 F.2d at 886, 178 USPQ at 163.

II. *Rule 131*

As an alternative position, Gosteli contends that they can swear behind Menard, under Rule 131, by establishing a constructive reduction to practice in this country based on their foreign priority date of the two species disclosed by Menard. They reason that the use of a foreign priority date to establish the reduction to practice component for a Rule 131(b) showing is authorized by *In re Mulder*, 716 F.2d 1542, 1544–46, 219 USPQ 189, 192–94 (Fed.Cir.1983), and therefore, showing priority with respect only to as much of the invention as Menard discloses is needed. Gosteli cites the rationale in *In re Stempel*, 241 F.2d 755, 760, 113 USPQ 77, 81 (CCPA 1957), in support of their reasoning. We disagree.

Rule 131 requirements are quite specific. To antedate a prior art reference, the applicant submits an oath or declaration alleging acts that establish a completion of the invention in this country before the effective date of the prior art. 37 C.F.R. § 1.131(a).

The requirements and operation of section 119 differ from those of Rule 131. Rule 131 provides a mechanism for removing specific prior art references, whereas section 119 is concerned only with an applicant's effective filing date. Because section 119, unlike Rule 131, operates independently of the prior art, it is appropriate that the showing required under section 119 differs from that required under Rule 131.

This case is distinguishable from *Mulder*. Gosteli's declarations make no mention of acts in this country. Gosteli relies on their Luxembourg application for a constructive reduction to practice date for the two chemical species at issue. That reliance is misplaced. *Mulder* is not purely a section 119 case. In *Mulder*, the conception date was based on activity in the United States, a date earlier than the prior art. Mulder was permitted to establish a constructive reduction to practice date based on his foreign filing. However, the constructive reduction to practice date was after the prior art. Rule 131 permitted Mulder to swear behind the reference, from the constructive reduction to practice date back to his conception date. The use of a foreign filing date in such circumstances is not inconsistent with our decisions. In *Mulder*, there was no dispute about compliance with the section 112 requirements subsumed in section 119. See *Mulder*, 716 F.2d at 1543, 219 USPQ at 191 (stating that "[t]here is no question that applicants complied with all the formalities required by § 119 and related PTO rules").

Gosteli does not point to any activity inside the United States. Furthermore, Gosteli would not need activity in this country if section 119 gave them the benefit of an effective foreign filing date prior to Menard. Under these circumstances, Rule 131 is irrelevant. Thus, we affirm the Board; Gosteli cannot use the Rule 131 declarations filed to swear behind Menard.

III. Written Description Requirement

The Board found that Gosteli's Luxembourg application did not provide a sufficient written description of the entire subject matter of claims 48–51, as required by the first paragraph of section 112, and, accordingly, section 119 was not effective to antedate Menard. Although Gosteli does not have to describe exactly the subject matter claimed, *In re Lukach*, 442 F.2d 967, 969, 169 USPQ 795, 796 (CCPA 1971), the description must clearly allow persons of ordinary skill in the art to recognize that Gosteli invented what is claimed. *Wertheim*, 541 F.2d at 262, 191 USPQ at 96. We review this factual inquiry under the clearly erroneous standard. See id.

"[T]he PTO has the initial burden of presenting evidence or reasons why persons skilled in the art would not recognize in the disclosure a description of the invention defined by the claims." Id. at 263, 191 USPQ at 97. In this case, the PTO has met that burden by pointing out a number of differences between what is disclosed in the Luxembourg priority application and what is claimed in Gosteli's United States application. Gosteli does not dispute that additional subject matter is present in the United States application. Accordingly, the Board's findings are not clearly erroneous.

The Board's decision is

AFFIRMED.

Notes

1. The Impact of *Gosteli*. After filing a Paris convention application, inventors will often make further advances in the claimed technology. The inventors want to include those advances in their later-filed applications at the end of the Paris Convention year. These later advances, however, are not supported by earlier-filed applications from which the inventor hopes to obtain priority. The Federal Circuit's insistence that Gosteli's priority document literally describe the expanded chemical genus, or Markush group, recited in claims 48–51 suggests a strict stance towards these circumstances. Although *Gosteli* involved a chemical technology, its holding might reach other sorts of inventions as well. Consider, for example, a priority document that contains a specific pH, temperature, or voltage, followed by a later United States filing that claims a range of such characteristics.

2. Responding to *Gosteli*. In light of *Gosteli*, applicants should be certain to include some claims in a later-filed application which correspond precisely to the disclosure in the priority document. This step will allow at least some patent protection and allow the patent instrument itself to indicate the priority document, a step the United States Patent and Trademark Office takes even where only one claim is entitled to priority. Note that if the later-filed United States patent has issued and the applicant becomes aware of an intervening reference, the applicant may be able to take advantage of reissue proceedings in order to obtain claims that match the disclosure of the priority document. For other strategies on complying with *Gosteli*, see Donald G. Daus, *Paris Convention Priority*, 77 J. Pat. & Trademark Off. Soc'y 138, 149 (1995).

3. Impact of Changes to § 104. The Federal Circuit handed down *Gosteli* prior to United States adherence to the TRIPS Agreement. Among other things, the TRIPS Agreement caused the United States to amend 35 U.S.C.A. § 104, thereby allowing individuals to submit evidence of inventive activity that took place abroad. Does this change in the statute weaken Judge Bissel's reasoning in Part III of her opinion? You may wish to review *In re Stryker*, reprinted here in Chapter Eight, as you answer this question.

4. Comparative Approaches. An Enlarged Board of Appeal of The European Patent Office faced a similar fact pattern to that of *Gosteli* and cited *Gosteli* with approval in *Priority Interval*, Case No. G03/93, [1994] E.P.O.R. 521. As with the Federal Circuit in *Gosteli*, the *Priority Interval* Board held that intermediate prior art that taught no more than the priority document was prior art, because the priority document did not teach the same invention claimed in the patent application. The *Priority Interval* ruling led to the critical question of whether there is any play whatsoever in the definition of the same invention. An Enlarged Board of Appeal said "no" when it handed down the following landmark decision.

SAME INVENTION

Enlarged Board of Appeal, 2001.
[2002]   E.P.O.R. 17, G02/98.

MESSERLI, MOSER, ANDRIES, DAVIES, SAISSET, TESCHEMACHER, TURRINI.

On July 29, 1998, the President of the EPO, making use of his power under Article 112 (1) (b) EPC, referred the following point of law to the Enlarged Board of Appeal:

(1a) Does the requirement of the "same invention" in Article 87 (1) EPC mean that the extent of the right to priority derivable from a priority application for a later application is determined by, and at the same time limited to, what is at least implicitly disclosed in the priority application?

(1b) Or can a lesser degree of correspondence between the priority application and the subject-matter claimed in the later application be sufficient in this respect and still justify a right to priority?

(2) If question (1b) is answered in the affirmative, what are the criteria to be applied in assessing whether the claim in the later application is in respect of the same invention as is in the priority application?

(3) In particular, where features not disclosed, even implicitly, in the priority application have been added in the relevant claim of the later application, or where features defined in broader terms in the priority application have been more specifically or more narrowly defined in the later application, can a right to priority nevertheless be derived from the priority application and, if so, what are the criteria which must be met to justify the priority in such cases?

* * *

In order to answer question (1a) of the referral as to whether the concept of "the same invention" referred to in Article 87 (1) EPC means that the extent of the right of priority derivable from a priority application for a later application is determined by, and at the same time limited to, what is at least implicitly disclosed in the priority application, it has to be examined in the first place whether a narrow or strict interpretation of this concept, equating it with the concept of "the same subject-matter" referred to in Article 87 (4) EPC, is consistent with the relevant provisions of both the Paris Convention and the EPC. Such a narrow or strict interpretation gives rise to the requirement that the subject-matter of a claim defining the invention in the European patent application, i.e. the specific combination of features present in the claim, must at least implicitly be disclosed in the application whose priority is claimed.

* * *

Pursuant to Article 4H of the Paris Convention, priority may not be refused on the ground that certain elements of the invention for which priority is claimed do not appear among the claims formulated in the application whose priority is claimed, provided that the application as a whole specifically discloses such elements. It follows that priority for a claim, i.e. an "element of the invention" within the meaning of Article 4H of the Paris Convention, is to be acknowledged, if the subject-matter of the claim is specifically disclosed be it explicitly or implicitly in the application documents relating to the disclosure, in particular, in the form of a claim or in the form of an embodiment or example specified in the description of the application whose priority is claimed, and that priority for the claim can be refused, if there is no such disclosure.

* * *

Article 4F of the Paris Convention, first paragraph, provides, *inter alia*, that priority may not be refused on the ground that an application claiming one or more priorities contains one or more elements that were not included in the application or applications whose priority is claimed, provided that there is unity of invention within the meaning of the law of the country. From the second paragraph of this provision it follows that, with respect to these elements, the filing of the subsequent application shall give rise to a right of priority under ordinary conditions. These elements would then be contained in the application whose priority is claimed in respect of a further application. Since, according to Article 4H of the Paris Convention, an invention for which priority is claimed need not be defined in a claim of the application whose priority is claimed, an "element" within the meaning of Article 4F of the Paris Convention represents subject-matter specifically disclosed be it explicitly or implicitly in the application documents relating to the disclosure, in particular, in the form of a claim or in the form of an embodiment or example specified in the description of the application claiming one or more priorities. This is in line with the purpose of Article 4F of the Paris Convention. The possibility of claiming multiple priorities was introduced into the Paris Convention in order to avoid improvements of the original invention having to be prosecuted in applications for patents of addition. This makes it clear that "element" was not understood as a feature but as an embodiment (Actes de la Confrence de Washington de 1911, Bern 1911, pp. 45 et seq.).

Furthermore, since priority for a claim can be refused under Article 4H of the Paris Convention , if the subject-matter of the claim is not disclosed in the application whose priority is claimed, unity of invention as required under Article 4F of the Paris Convention, first paragraph, must exist between two or more inventions disclosed in the application claiming one or more priorities, and not, as submitted in some statements by third parties pursuant to Article 11b of the Rules of Procedure of the Enlarged Board of Appeal, between an invention disclosed in the application claiming one or more priorities and an invention disclosed in an application whose priority is claimed.

In fact, a narrow or strict interpretation of the concept of "the same invention" referred to in Article 87 (1) EPC, equating it with the concept of "the same subject-matter" referred to in Article 87 (4) EPC, is perfectly consistent with Articles 4F and 4H of the Paris Convention, which are provisions representing substantive law. Furthermore, the requirement of "the same subject-matter" does not contravene Article 4A (1) of the Paris Convention although this provision makes no mention of the subject-matter of the subsequent application. It is, however, generally held that the subsequent filing must concern the same subject-matter as the first filing on which the right of priority is based (cf. Wieczorek, *Die Unionsprioritt im Patentrecht*, Koeln, Berlin, Bonn, Muenchen, 1975, p. 149). This follows from the very aim and object of the right of priority: the protection from novelty-destroying disclosures during a period of 12 months from the date of filing of the first application is necessary only in case of the filing of a subsequent application relating to the same invention. Finally, such a narrow or strict interpretation is also consistent with Article 4C (4) of the Paris Convention, which provides that a subsequent application concerning the same subject as a previous first application shall be considered the first application if, at the time of filing the subsequent application, the previous first application satisfies certain requirements; there is no reason why in this particular situation the concept of "the same invention" should be interpreted differently.

* * *

Pursuant to Article 88 (4) EPC, priority may be granted, even if certain elements of the invention for which priority is claimed do not appear among the claims formulated in the previous application, provided the documents of the previous application as a whole specifically disclose such elements. Article 88 (3) EPC provides that, if one or more priorities are claimed in respect of a European patent application, the right of priority shall cover only those elements of the European patent application which are included in the application or applications whose priority is claimed. Since, pursuant to Article 84 EPC, the claims of the European patent application define the matter for which protection is sought and hence determine the matter for which priority may be claimed, the term "elements of the invention", referred to in Article 88 (4) EPC, and the term "elements of the European patent application", referred to in Article 88 (3) EPC, are to be considered synonymous. Both an "element of the invention" and an "element of the European patent application" actually constitute subject-matter as defined in a claim of the European patent application.

* * *

It seems therefore that a narrow or strict interpretation of the concept of "the same invention" referred to in Article 87 (1) EPC, equating it with the concept of "the same subject-matter" referred to in Article 87 (4) EPC, is perfectly consistent with paragraphs 2 to 4 of Article 88 EPC. Such a narrow or strict interpretation is also consistent with Article 87 (4) EPC, which corresponds to Article 4C (4) of the Paris Convention and which provides that a subsequent application for the same subject-matter as a previous first application shall be considered the first application for the purposes of determining priority, provided that, at the date of filing the subsequent application, the previous first application satisfies certain requirements; there is no reason why in this particular situation the concept of "the same invention" should be interpreted differently.

* * *

In order to assess whether a claim in a later European patent application is in respect of the same invention as the priority application pursuant to Article 87 (1) EPC, a distinction is made in Decision T73/88, and in a statement by third parties pursuant to Article 11b of the Rules of Procedure of the Enlarged Board of Appeal, between technical features which are related to the function and effect of the invention and technical features which are not. This approach is problematic because there are no suitable and clear, objective criteria for making such a distinction; it could thus give rise to arbitrariness. In fact, the features of a claim defining the invention in the form $A + B + C$ do not represent a mere aggregation, but are normally inherently connected with each other. Therefore, if the above-mentioned distinction is to be made, the answer to the question whether the claimed invention remains the same, if one of these features is modified or deleted, or if a further feature D is added, depends very much on the actual assessment of the facts and circumstances of the case by each individual deciding body. Different deciding bodies may thus arrive at different results when assessing these facts and circumstances. Furthermore, as pointed out in the referral of the President of the EPO, it has to be borne in mind that the assessment by these different deciding bodies of whether or not certain technical features are related to the function and effect of the claimed invention may completely change in the course of proceedings. This is the case, in particular, if new prior art is to be considered, with the possible consequence that the validity of a hitherto acknowledged right of priority could be put in jeopardy. Such dependence would, however, be at variance with the requirement of legal certainty.

If the invention claimed in a later European patent application constitutes a so-called selection invention—i.e. typically, the choice of individual entities from larger groups or of sub-ranges from broader ranges of numerical values—in respect of the subject-matter disclosed in a first application whose priority is claimed, the criteria applied by the EPO with a view to assessing novelty of selection inventions over the prior art must also be considered carefully when assessing whether the claim in the European patent application is in respect of the same invention as the priority application within the meaning of Article 87 (1) EPC. Otherwise, patent protection for selection inventions, in particular in the field of chemistry, could be seriously prejudiced if these criteria were not thoroughly complied with when assessing priority claims in respect of selection inventions. Hence such priority claims should not be acknowledged if the selection inventions in question are considered "novel" according to these criteria.

From the analysis under point 8 above, it follows that an extensive or broad interpretation of the concept of "the same invention" referred to in Article 87 (1) EPC, making a distinction between technical features which are related to the function and effect of the invention and technical features which are not, with the possible consequence that a claimed invention is considered to remain the same even though a feature is modified or deleted, or a further feature is added, is inappropriate and prejudicial to a proper exercise of priority rights. Rather, according to that analysis, a narrow or strict interpretation of the concept of "the same invention", equating it to the concept of "the same subject-matter" referred to in Article 87 (4) EPC, is necessary to ensure a proper exercise of priority rights in full conformity, inter alia, with the principles of equal treatment of the applicant and third parties and legal certainty and with the requirement of consistency with regard to the assessment of novelty and inventive step. Such an interpretation is solidly supported by the provisions of the Paris Convention and the provisions of the EPC, and is perfectly in keeping with Opinion G03/93. It means that priority of a previous application in respect of a claim in a European patent application in accordance with Article 88 EPC is to be acknowledged only if the person skilled in the art can derive the subject-matter of the claim directly and unambiguously, using common general knowledge, from the previous application as a whole.

CONCLUSION

For these reasons the point of law referred to the Enlarged Board of Appeal by the President of the EPO is answered as follows:

The requirement for claiming priority of "the same invention", referred to in Article 87 (1) EPC, means that priority of a previous application in respect of a claim in a European patent application in accordance with Article 88 EPC is to be acknowledged only if the skilled person can derive the subject-matter of the claim directly and unambiguously, using common general knowledge, from the previous application as a whole.

Note

Provisional Applications and the Paris Convention. The law applied in *Same Invention* would be applicable to the use of a provisional application as the basis for a priority claim in the EPO. Would the law be the same in the USPTO for a priority claim based on a provisional application? See New Railhead Manufacturing, L.L.C. v. Vermeer Manufacturing Co., 298 F.3d 1290, 63 U.S.P.Q.2d 1843 (Fed.Cir.2002). Do you agree with the strict approach to a priority claim followed in both *Same Invention* and *New Railhead*?

§ 14.2   THE DEFENSIVE, PATENT–DEFEATING RIGHT

§ 14.2[a]   International Norms

Many interpret the "third-party right" language of Paris Convention Article 4B as providing a patent-defeating right to the patentee as to whatever is claimed in his patent, retroactive to his priority date. Commentators sometimes refer to this entitlement as the "senior right." Most patent systems will reject an applicant's claim in an application filed after another individual's priority date. Consider the following sequence of applications, each claiming the identical invention:

	Files	Files	
Inventor A ---Country X -------------------Country Z--------------------- >
Jan. 24, 1957	Jan. 23, 1958

	Files	Files	
Inventor B --------------------Country Y--------------------Country Z----- >
July 31, 1957	July 25, 1958

Under these circumstances, the officials of the Country Z Patent Office will reject Inventor B's application due to the priority of the Country X application of Inventor A.

Under this view of the Paris Convention only a "prior claim" approach would be required. This would give a patent owner a patent-defeating right retroactive to the priority date for what is claimed in the patent. The Swiss continue to employ this narrow minimum scope definition of the patent-defeating right.

Most other countries go further and provide a broader patent-defeating right. They employ a "whole contents" patent-defeating effect that covers everything disclosed in the priority document that is carried forward into the patent application. Furthermore, the patent-defeating effect exists not when the patent issues, but at the publication date of 18 months after the priority date. For a general discussion of these issues, see Richard Wieczorek, *Convention Application as Patent–Defeating Rights*, 6 INT'L REV. INDUS. PROP. & COPYRIGHT L. 135 (1975).

§ 14.2[b] The United States *Hilmer* Rule

Exceptionally, the United States law does not provide for any patent-defeating effect based on a Paris Convention filing. This rule was established in the infamous *Hilmer* opinions set forth below. As set forth in these decisions, the facts are as in the diagram above, with A as Habicht, B as Hilmer, Country X as Switzerland, Country Y as Germany and Country Z as the United States.

IN RE HILMER

United States Court of Customs and Patent Appeals, 1966.
359 F.2d 859, 149 U.S.P.Q. 480.

Before WORLEY, CHIEF JUDGE, and RICH, MARTIN, SMITH and ALMOND, JUDGES.

RICH JUDGE.

The sole issue is whether a majority of the Patent Office Board of Appeals erred in overturning a consistent administrative practice and interpretation of the law of nearly forty years standing by giving a United States patent effect as prior art as of a foreign filing date to which the patentee of the reference was entitled under 35 U.S.C. 119.

Because it held that a U.S. patent, cited as a prior art reference under 35 U.S.C. 102(e) and 103, is effective as of its foreign "convention" filing date, relying on 35 U.S.C. 119, the board affirmed the rejection of claims 10, 16, and 17 of application serial No. 750,887, filed July 25, 1958, for certain sulfonyl ureas.

This opinion develops the issue, considers the precedents, and explains why, on the basis of legislative history, we hold that section 119 does not modify the express provision of section 102(e) that a reference patent is effective as of the date the application for it was "filed in the United States."

The two "references" relied on are:

Habicht 2,962,530 Nov. 29, 1960 (filed in the United States January 23, 1958, found to be entitled to priority as of the date of filing in Switzerland on January 24, 1957)

Wagner et al. 2,975,212 March 14, 1961 (filed in the United States May 1, 1957)

The rejection here is the aftermath of an interference (No. 90,218) between appellants and Habicht, a priority dispute in which Habicht was the winning party on a single count. He won because appellants conceded priority of the invention of the count to him. The earliest date asserted by appellants for their invention is their German filing date, July 31, 1957, which, we note, is a few months later than Habicht's priority date of January 24, 1957.

After termination of the interference and the return of this application to the examiner for further ex parte prosecution, the examiner rejected the appealed claims on Habicht, as a primary reference, in view of Wagner et al., as a secondary reference, holding the claimed compounds to be "unpatentable over the primary reference in view of the secondary reference which renders them obvious to one of ordinary skill in the art."

Appellants appealed to the board contending, inter alia, that "The Habicht disclosure cannot be utilized as anticipatory art." They said, "The rejection has utilized * * * the disclosure of the winning party as a basis for the rejection. The appellants insist that this is contrary to the patent statutes." Explaining this they said:

> * * * the appellants' German application was filed subsequent to the Swiss filing date (of Habicht) *but prior to the U.S. filing date of the Habicht application.* The appellants now maintain that the Habicht disclosure cannot be utilized as anticipatory in view of 35 U.S.C. 119 which is entitled "Benefit of Earlier Filing Date in Foreign Countries: Right of Priority." This section defines the rights of foreign applicants and more specifically defines those rights with respect to dates to which they are entitled if this same privilege is awarded to citizens of the United States. There is no question (but) that Section 119 only deals with "right of priority." The section does not provide for the use of a U.S. patent as an anticipatory reference as of its foreign filing date. This interpretation of Section 119 is also set forth in the Manual of Patent Examining Procedure (Section 715.01). The Manual refers to *Viviani v. Taylor v. Herzog*, 72 USPQ 448, wherein Commissioner Coe clarified the question of priority rights with respect to foreign and domestic filing.

Appellants further pointed out that:

> "The interference only decided the priority of the interference issue (i.e. the count); there was no decision made nor was there any attempt to decide who was the inventor of the disclosure. The appellants readily admit the priority of Habicht as to the interference issue, but there is no admission as far as the remaining subject matter is concerned."

The board, one member dissenting with an opinion, affirmed the rejection.

The board's statement of the issue is that "the reference patent is found to be entitled to the date of a prior foreign application under 35 USC 119 * * *." To some degree this loads the question. There is in it an implicit assumption that if the patent is "entitled to the date of a prior foreign application," it is *entitled* to it, and that is that. But one must examine closely into what is meant by the word "entitled." In essence, that is the problem in this appeal and we wish to point to it at the outset to dispel any mistaken assumptions. A patent may be "entitled" to a foreign filing date for some purposes and not for others, just as a patent may be "used" in two ways. A patent owner uses his patent as a legal right to exclude others, granted to him under 35 U.S.C. 154. Others, wholly unrelated to the patentee, use a patent, not as a legal right, but simply as evidence of prior invention or prior art, i.e., as a "reference." This is not an exercise of the patent right. This is how the Patent Office is "using" the Habicht patent. These are totally different things, governed by different law, founded on different theories, and developed through different histories.

We have seen that 35 U.S.C. 119 is involved with respect to the so-called "priority date" of the Habicht reference patent. The other statutory provision involved in this case, applicable to both of the references, is 35 U.S.C. 102(e). Section 102 has been aptly described (Meyer article, infra) as containing "patent defeating provisions." They fall into two classes, events prior to an applicant's date of invention and events prior to filing his U.S. application, related respectively to the requirement of novelty and to provisions for loss of right through delay in filing after certain events have made the invention public. Subsection (e) is one of the novelty provisions, one of the "conditions for patentability," and if the facts of an applicant's case bring him within it, his right to a patent is defeated.

Thus, though both references here were patents copending with appellants' application, issuing after it was filed, 102(e) makes then available as of their U.S. filing dates which are earlier than appellants' U.S. filing date. However, since 102(e) refers to the applicant's date of invention, not to his filing date, he is entitled to an opportunity to establish his date of invention to show that his invention possessed statutory novelty when he made it. In this case appellants did this by showing that they filed a German application earlier than the U.S. filing dates of the references, specified in 102(e), and that they were entitled to its date for "priority" under section 119. This right is not in question. The board ruled:

> Appellants have overcome the U.S. filing date of Habicht by claiming the benefit under 35 USC 119 of an application filed in Germany on July 31, 1957. The specification of this German application has been examined and is found to contain a full disclosure of the subject matter of the claims, and the U.S. filing date of Habicht is considered overcome.

We can now summarize the issue and simultaneously state the board's decision. Continuing the above quotation, the board said:

> The Examiner insists, however, that the effective date of the Habicht patent is January 24, 1957, the date of an application filed in Switzerland which is claimed by Habicht under 35 USC 119. Appellants have not overcome this earlier date of Habicht. The issue is hence presented of whether the foreign priority date of a United States patent can be used as the effective filing date of the patent when it is used as a reference. (And this is the second statement of the issue by the board.) Our conclusion is that the priority date governs * * *.

This is the decision alleged to be in error. We think it was error.

OPINION

The board's construction is based on the idea that the language of [§ 119] is plain, that it means what it says, and that what it says is that the application filed abroad is to have the same effect as though it were filed here—for all purposes. We can reverse the statement to say that the actual U.S. application is to have the same effect as though it were filed in the U.S. on the day when the foreign application was filed, the whole thing being a question of effective date. We take it either way because it makes no difference here.

Before getting into history, we note first that there is in the very words of the statute a refutation of this literalism. It says "shall have the same effect" and it then says "but" for several situations it shall not have the same effect, namely, it does not enjoy the foreign date with respect to any of the patent-defeating provisions based on publication or patenting anywhere in the world or public use or being on sale in this country more than one year before the date of actual filing in this country.

As to the other statute involved, we point out that the words of section 102(e), which the board "simply" reads together with section 119, also seem plain. Perhaps they mean precisely what they say in specifying, as an express patent-defeating provision, an application by another describing the invention but only as of the date it is "filed in the United States."

The great logical flaw we see in the board's reasoning is in its premise (or is it an a priori conclusion?) that "these two provisions must be read together." Doing so, it says 119 in effect destroys the plain meaning of 102(e) but the board will not indulge the reverse construction in which the plain words of 102(e) limit the apparent meaning of 119. We see no reason for reading these two provisions together and the board has stated none. We believe, with the dissenting board member, that 119 and 102(e) deal with unrelated concepts and further that the historical origins of the two sections show neither was intended to affect the other, wherefore they should not be read together in violation of the most basic rule of statutory construction, the "master rule," of carrying out the legislative intent. Additionally, we have a long and consistent administrative practice in applying an interpretation contrary to the new view of the board, confirmed by legislation ratification in 1952. We will consider these matters separately.

Section 119

We shall now take up the history and purpose of section 119. The board opinion devotes the equivalent of four pages in the printed record to a scholarly and detailed review of the history of section 119 with all of which we agree, except for the interwoven conclusions as to its meaning as it bears on the effective date of a U.S. patent used as a reference.

The board shows that the predecessor statute (R.S. 4887), containing the words "shall have the same force and effect," was enacted March

3, 1903 (32 Stat. 1225). Theodore Roosevelt signed it into law. The bill was drafted and proposed by a Commission created by Act of Congress in 1898 (30 Stat. 431) to study the effect of the Convention of Paris for the Protection of Industrial Property of 20th March 1883, which was under revision at Brussels even as the Commission deliberated, the revision being adopted at Brussels on 14th December 1900. (It was last revised at Lisbon on 31st October 1958.) The Commission made a report November 27, 1900, printed in 1902, entitled "Report of the Commissioners Appointed to Revise the Laws Relating to Patents, Trademarks, and Trade Names, with Reference to Existing Conventions and Treaties," which is fairly descriptive of its purpose. The section entitled "The Revision of the Patent Law," which we have read, extends from page 6 to page 39. It begins by saying (p. 6):

We have found it desirable in considering the question of revision of the patent law to first consider what changes in the law are needed to give full force and effect to the treaty obligations which the United States has undertaken touching the protection of inventions made by the subjects or citizens of certain foreign countries.

Under the heading "Priority Under the Convention," it says (p. 12):

The second provision of the Convention to be noticed, and one which may be of very great advantage to those of our citizens who desire to secure patents in foreign countries for their inventions, is that contained in article 4, and relates to the so called "delay of priority," or "period of priority."

It then explained that in most countries no valid patent can be obtained if *before the application is filed*, the invention has been described in a printed publication, either in the country of application or even, as in the case of France and six other countries, in any country; that the same was true as to public use of the invention; and that the convention gives applicants in member countries a period (then 7 months, soon extended to 12) in which they can file applications in other countries after the filing in their own country and obtain valid patents notwithstanding publication or use in the interval and before the filing of the foreign application. This, it explained, is the "delay of priority." In plain English, it was the right of an applicant to have the foreign application treated at law as prior to the intervening publication or public use, though in fact it was not, by giving a right to that applicant to delay filing in the foreign country, instead of filing simultaneously with the home application, yet have it treated as though filed on the date of the home application. This is what today we call simply "Convention priority," or just "priority." The foreign filing date is the "convention date" or the "priority date."

This priority right was a protection to one who was trying to obtain patents in foreign countries, the protection being against patent-defeating provisions of national laws based on events intervening between the time of filing at home and filing abroad. Under the heading "Recapitulation of Advantages Secured by the Convention," the Commission said, so far as relevant here (pp. 14–15):

> The advantages to our citizens in the matter of patents directly afforded by the convention may be thus recapitulated.
>
> First. The enjoyment in foreign countries of equal rights with subjects or citizens of those countries.
>
> Second. The "delay of priority" of seven months within which to file applications abroad after filing in this country.
>
> Third. The privilege of introducing articles embodying the invention manufactured in this country into foreign countries to a certain extent without thereby causing the forfeiture of the patents taken out there.

Note the emphasis repeatedly placed in the Commission Report on advantages to United States citizens. It was felt we should do what was necessary to comply with the reciprocity provisions to enjoy the benefits of the convention for our own citizens. It was also believed that by reason of Opinions of Attorneys General, Vol. 19, 273, "the International Convention, in so far as the agreements therein contained are not in accordance with the present laws of the United States, is without force and effect; that it is not self-executing, but requires legislation to render it effective * * * and * * * it is our opinion that such legislation should be adopted * * *." (Report p. 19.)

Specific to the question here, the Commission Report says (p. 24):

> We are, therefore, of the opinion that an amendment to the law should be made, providing that the foreign application shall have, in case an application is filed in this country by the applicant abroad within the specified period, the same effect as if filed here on the day it was filed abroad.

The board thinks this "shows the intention of the Commissioners" to create "a status of (an application) having been filed in the U.S. for all purposes * * *." In the contest of this case, that means for the purpose of using a U.S. patent, obtained with a claim of priority, as a prior art patent to defeat the right of a third party to a patent on subject matter which does not patentably distinguish from anything that happens to be disclosed in such patent—or at least from anything disclosed "relevant to the (there) claimed invention," depending on which recent board opinion one looks at. We have read every word of the Commission Report looking for any suggestion of such a concept and have found none. All the board found was the above quotation. We deem it wholly inadequate as a basis for finding an intent to create a "status" for an application—to say nothing of the patent granted thereon—"for all purposes." There are other factors to consider which negative any such legislative intent.

There is another sentence in the Commission Report we should consider on page 26. It called attention to the fact that in most foreign countries the patent is granted to the first to apply and said:

The Convention has created an exception to the rule and made an application in any State of the Union for the Protection of Industrial Property of the same effect as an application in the country where an application is subsequently made within the time specified as a period of priority.

This couples very nicely with the wording of the first recommendation for a change in U.S. laws on page 27 where it was said:

First. The application for a patent filed within seven months of the filing of an application for a patent for the same invention in any foreign country which is a party to the International Convention should be given the same force as regards the question of priority that it would have if filed on the date on which the foreign application was filed.

The Commission, page 36, recommended proposed legislation, which is, in substance, the amendment to R.S. 4887 which was passed and is, with no change in substance, what we have today in section 119. The proposed bill in the Commission Report was entitled "A BILL to give effect to treaty stipulations relating to letters patent for inventions." The Act passed was entitled "An Act To effectuate the provisions of the additional act of the international convention for the protection of industrial property." Throughout, the same phrase has always appeared, "shall have the same force and effect," until it was simplified in the 1952 codification to "shall have the same effect." This change was mere modernization in legislative drafting. The Revisers Note to the section says: "The first paragraph is the same as the present law with changes in language." The Federico Commentary on the 1952 Act, 35 U.S.C.A., says (p. 29):

This so-called right of priority was provided for in the second paragraph of R.S. 4887 which is the basis for the first paragraph of section 119 of this title. * * * (he here states the 4 conditions for obtaining the right) * * * The new statute made no changes in these conditions of the corresponding part of the old statute except to revise the language slightly * * *.

We need not guess what Congress has since believed to be the meaning of the disputed words in section 119, for it has spoken clearly. World wars interfere with normal commerce in industrial property. The one-year period of priority being too short for people in "enemy" countries, we had after World War I a Nolan Act (41 Stat. 1313, Mar. 3, 1921) and after World War II a Boykin Act. Foreign countries had reciprocal acts. One purpose was to extend the period of priority. House Report No. 1498, January 28, 1946, by Mr. Boykin, accompanied H.R. 5223 which became Public Law 690 of the 79th Cong., 2d Sess., Aug. 8, 1946, 60 Stat. 940. Section 1 of the bill, the report says, was to extend "the so-called period of priority," which then existed under R.S. 4887. On p. 3 the report says:

In this connection, it may be observed that the portion of the statute which provides that the filing of a foreign application—shall have the same force and effect as the same application would have if filed in this country on the date on which the application for patent for the same invention, discovery, or design was first filed in such foreign country—is intended to mean "shall have the same force and effect," etc., insofar as applicant's right to a patent is concerned. This statutory provision has no bearing upon the right of another party to a patent except in the case of an interference where the two parties are claiming the same patentable invention. U.S.Code Congressional Service 1946, p. 1493.

We emphasize none of those words because we wish to emphasize them all. We cannot readily imagine a clearer, more definitive statement as to the legislature's own view of the words "same effect," which now appear in section 119. This statement flatly contradicts the board's views. The board does not mention it. * * *

For the foregoing reasons, we are clearly of the opinion that section 119 is not to be read as anything more than it was originally intended to be by its drafters, the Commission appointed under the 1898 Act of Congress, namely, a revision of our statutes to provide for a right of priority in conformity with the International Convention, for the benefit of United States citizens, by creating the necessary reciprocity with foreign members of the then Paris Union.

The board has mentioned that it was not limited in its terms to that treaty, which is true, so that it also functions relative to other treaties and reciprocal laws. We are unable to deduce from this any intent to affect the date as of which U.S. reference patents are effective. Nor can we do so by reason of another "deviation" from the Convention the board finds in section 4887 (now 119) as to the protection of third parties.

Section 102(e)

We have quoted this section above and pointed out that it is a patent-defeating section, by contrast with section 119 which gives affirmative "priority" rights to applicants notwithstanding it is drafted in terms of "An application." The priority right is to save the applicant (or his application if one prefers to say it that way) from patent-defeating provisions such as 102(e); and of course it has the same effect in guarding the validity of the patent when issued.

Section 102(e), on the other hand, is one of the provisions which defeats applicants and invalidates patents and is closely related in fact and in history to the requirement of section 102(a) which prohibits a patent if

> (a) the invention was known or used by others in this country, or patented or described in a printed publication in this or a foreign country, before the invention thereof by the applicant for patent, * * *.

In fact, section 102(e) springs straight from 102(a)'s predecessor, R.S. 4886, by decision of the United States Supreme Court in 1926. It was pure case law until 1952 when, having become firmly established, that law was codified by incorporating it in the statute.

We will not undertake to trace the ancestry of 102(e) back of its immediate parentage but clearly it had ancestors or it would never have come to the Supreme Court. We will regard its actual birth as the case of *Alexander Milburn Co. v. Davis–Bournonville* Co., 270 U.S. 390, 46 S.Ct. 324, 70 L.Ed. 651 (March 8, 1926), which we shall call *Milburn*....

We need not go into the reasoning of the *Milburn* case, which has its weaknesses, because all that matters is the rule of law it established: That a complete description of an invention in a U.S. patent application, filed before the date of invention of another, if it matures into a patent, may be used to show that that other was not the first inventor. This was a patent-defeating, judge-made rule and now is section 102(e). The rule has been expanded somewhat subsequent to 1926 so that the reference patent may be used as of its U.S. filing date as a general prior art reference, as shown by *In re Harry*, 333 F.2d 920, 51 CCPA 1541 (1964), and the December 8, 1965 Supreme Court decision in *Hazeltine Research, Inc. v. Brenner*, 382 U.S. 252, 86 S.Ct. 335, 15 L.Ed.2d 304.

What has always been pointed out in attacks on the *Milburn* rule, or in attempts to limit it, is that it uses, as prior knowledge, information which was secret at the time as of which it is used—the contents of U.S. patent applications which are preserved in secrecy, generally speaking, 35 U.S.C. 122. This is true, and we think there is some validity to the argument that that which is secret should be in a different category from knowledge which is public. Nevertheless we have the rule. However, we are not disposed to extend that rule, which applies to the date of filing applications in the United States, the actual filing date when the disclosure is on deposit in the U.S. Patent Office and on its way, in due course, to publication in an issued patent.

The board's new view, as expressed in this case and in the Zemla and Rapala decisions, the latter sustained in Lilly, has the practical potential effect of pushing back the date of the unpublished, secret disclosures, which ultimately have effect as prior art references in the form of U.S. patents, by the full one-year priority period of section 119. We think the *Milburn* rule, as codified in section 102(e), goes far enough in that direction. We see no valid reason to go further, certainly no compelling reason.

We have seen that section 119 originated in 1903 and that its purpose was to grant protective priority rights so that the United States might be a participating member in the International Convention by giving reciprocal priority rights to foreign applicants with respect to the obtaining of patents. We have also seen that section 102(e) was the codification of a court-developed patent-defeating rule based on a statutory requirement that an applicant's invention must not have been previously known by others in this country. We see no such relation between these two rules of law as requires them to be read together and it is our view that section 119 should not be so read with 102(e) as to modify the express limitation of the latter to applications "filed in the United States."

Section 104

It seems clear to us that the prohibitions of 104, the limitations in sections 102(a) and 102(g) to "in this country," and the specifying in 102(e) of an application filed "in the United States" clearly demonstrates a policy in our patent statutes to the effect that knowledge and acts in a foreign country are not to defeat the rights of applicants for patents, except as applicants may become involved in priority disputes. We think it follows that section 119 must be interpreted as giving only a positive right or benefit to an applicant who has first filed abroad to protect him against possible intervening patent-defeating events in obtaining a patent. Heretofore it has always been so interpreted with the minor exceptions, of little value as precedents, hereinafter discussed. So construed, it has no effect on the effective date of a U.S. patent as a reference under section 102(e).

Section 120

At oral argument the Patent Office Solicitor argued by "analogy" from 35 U.S.C. 120 (a section which he said gives one U.S. application the benefit of an earlier U.S. application under specified circumstances for all purposes) that section 119 should similarly give to a patent, used as a reference under section 102(e), effect as of an earlier foreign filing date.

* * * One aspect of it is that sections 119 and 120 contain the "same phrase," namely "shall have the same effect."

We find no substance in this argument because: (1) as above pointed out, out statute law makes a clear distinction between acts abroad and acts here except for patents and printed publications. Section 120, following policy in sections 102(a), (e) and (g) and 104, contains the limitation to applications "filed in the United States," excluding foreign applications from its scope. (2) Use of the same expression is mere happenstance and no reason to transfer the meaning and effect of section 120 as to U.S. filing dates to section 119 with respect to foreign filing dates. Section 120 was not drafted until 49 years after the predecessor of section 119 was in the statute.

* * * The decision of the board is reversed and the case is remanded for further proceedings consistent herewith.

Reversed and remanded.

IN RE HILMER (HILMER II)

United States Court of Customs and Patent Appeals, 1970.
424 F.2d 1108, 165 U.S.P.Q. 255.

Before RICH, ACTING CHIEF JUDGE, ALMOND, BALDWIN, and LANE, JUDGES, and MATTHEWS, SENIOR JUDGE, United States District Court for the District of Columbia, sitting by designation.

RICH, ACTING CHIEF JUDGE.

This is a sequel to our opinion in *In re Hilmer* (herein "*Hilmer I*"), familiarity with which is assumed.

In *Hilmer I*, under the heading "Reason for Remand," we pointed out that as to claims 10 and 16 there was a rejection with which the board had not dealt and remanded the case for clarification of the board's position "on the rejection of claims 10 and 16 as 'unpatentable over' the interference count in view of Wagner et al."

In *Hilmer I*, the question we decided was whether the Habicht patent was effective as a prior art reference under 35 U.S.C. § 102(e) as of the Swiss filing date. We held that it was not and that it was "prior art" under 102(e) only as of the U.S. filing date, which date Hilmer could overcome by being entitled to rely on the filing date of his German application to show his date of invention. This disposed of a rejection predicated on the disclosure of the Habicht patent, as a primary reference, coupled with a secondary prior art patent to Wagner et al., No. 2,975,212, issued March 14, 1961, filed May 1, 1957 (herein "Wagner").

The board's conclusion was that the subject matter of claim 1, the compound claimed, is prior art against Hilmer. As to the basis on which it can be considered to be, or treated as, prior art, the board divided. Two members stated that the statutory basis is 35 U.S.C. § 102(g) combined with § 119 and read in the light of § 104. The third member declined to accept this, concurred only in the result, and said, "I see no reason to go beyond the concession of priority filed by Hilmer et al. * * *." Since his view was not determinative of the appeal, we consider that what we have before us for review is only the correctness of the reasoning of the majority.

Note must be taken of the fact that the rejection here is under 103 for obviousness wherefore it is clear that the subject matter of the appealed claims is different from the subject matter of Habicht's claim 1, allegedly, however, only in an obvious way by reason of the further disclosures of Wagner. Were the appealed claims to the same subject matter, it seems clear that Hilmer, because he conceded priority to Habicht, would not be entitled to them and Hilmer appears to have admitted as much throughout this appeal. But, it is contended, the situation is different when the claims on appeal are to different subject matter. We confess to some difficulty in determining just what appellants' view is but it seems to come down to this: Appellants are entitled to the benefit of their German filing date and this antedates Habicht's U.S. filing date, which is the earliest date as of which Habicht's claim 1 invention can be "prior art." The words appellants use, referring to Habicht's U.S. filing date, are, "the only possible date that can be considered for anticipation purposes." Appellants appear to use the term "anticipation" in the broad sense to mean "prior."

We turn now to the reasoning by which the board majority arrived at the conclusion that the compound of Habicht claim 1 is in the prior art—i.e., ahead of Hilmer's German filing date—and usable with the

Wagner patent to support a section 103 obviousness rejection. We note at the outset that the board majority in no way relied on what occurred in the interference, on the concession of priority, or on any estoppel growing out of the interference.

Before examining the board majority's statutory theory, we will recall the fact that in Hilmer I we dealt with another statutory theory that by combining § 102(e) and § 119 a U.S. patent had an effective date as a prior art reference for all it discloses as of its foreign convention filing date. We reversed that holding and remanded. We now are presented with another theory that by combining § 102(g) with § 119 at least the claimed subject matter of a U.S. patent is prior art as of the convention filing date. The crux of the matter lies in § 102(g), which we must have before us. * * *

The board majority's rationalization begins thus:

> Section 102(g) of the statute refers to the prior invention of another as a basis for refusing a patent. Inasmuch as the subject matter of the claim of the Habicht patent is patented to another, it must be recognized as an invention of another, and being the invention of another, some date of invention must be ascribed to it. When nothing else is available, the date of filing the application (in the United States) is by law taken as the date of invention since the invention obviously must have been made on or before the day the application for a patent for it was filed.

But this much, assuming its correctness, would not sustain the rejection because appellants are entitled to a date of invention which is earlier than the day the Habicht application was filed in the United States, the date obviously referred to in the above quotation. To sustain the rejection it was necessary for the board to accord an earlier date to Habicht's invention, the only such date available being the date Habicht filed his application in Switzerland. This, however, is not in compliance with the provision of 102(g) that the invention be "made" (or at the very least be) "in this country." The board majority attempted to vault this hurdle as follows:

> While Section 102(g) refers to the prior invention as made "in this country", this limitation is removed as to application filing date by Section 119 of the statute which provides that an application for a patent for an invention shall have the same effect as though filed in this country on the date a prior application was filed in a foreign country, under the conditions prescribed. That this is the effect of Section 119 is also evident from Section 104.... The Habicht invention is ... entitled to the filing date of the application in Switzerland as its date of invention in this country. Hence, we conclude on the basis of Section 102(g) and Section 119 that the claimed subject matter of the Habicht patent is available for use against the present application (as patent-defeating prior art) as of the date of the application filed in Switzerland.

We disagree with this line of reasoning.

In *Hilmer I* we explained at length why we could not accept similar reasoning about § 119 which was there alleged to remove or qualify the limitation in § 102(e) to the date when an application was filed "in the United States." For the same reasons we hold, contrary to the ipse dixit of the board, that § 119 does not remove the limitation of § 102(g) found in the phrase "in this country."

We disagree with the board that such an effect "is also evident from Section 104." Section 104 merely states that, except as provided by § 119, an applicant or patentee may not establish a date of invention "by reference to knowledge or use thereof, or other activity" in a foreign country. Thus § 119 and § 104 relate, respectively, only to what an applicant or patentee may and may not do to protect himself against patent-defeating events occurring between his invention date and his U.S. filing date. Moreover, we discussed § 104 and § 102(a), (e), and (g) in *Hilmer I* and there showed that they indicate an intention on the part of Congress that knowledge and acts in a foreign country are not to defeat the rights of an applicant for a patent, except as the applicant may become involved in a priority dispute with another applicant entitled to § 119 benefits. The present appeal does not involve a priority dispute. * * *

As we understand the meaning of the term "priority," it refers either (a) to the issue which exists in the interference proceedings, namely, which of two or more rival inventors attempting to patent the same invention shall be deemed prior or first in law and entitled to the patent or (b) preservation of an effective filing date during a period such as the "convention" year as against acts which would otherwise bar the grant of a patent, for the protection of an applicant against loss of right to a patent. Nothing we have seen tends to indicate that this matter of "priority" has ever been intended to modify the long-standing provisions of our statutes as to what shall be deemed "prior art" under § 103.

Since we disagree with the board's interpretation of the statute, we disagree with its conclusion that the Habicht claim 1 subject matter is "prior art" as of any date earlier than Habicht's U.S. filing date (if it is "prior art" at all). Appellants have an earlier effective date. The rejection, on the board majority's theory, is therefore reversed. Habicht's claim 1 compound being removed as "prior art," it is unnecessary to reach the second question posed by the board, whether the subject matter of claim 1 can be used in combination with the other reference, Wagner.

The decision of the board affirming the rejection of claims 10 and 16 is reversed.

Notes

1. The Effect of *Hilmer*. Does the *Hilmer* rule result in more granted United States patents or fewer? Do strong policy reasons support the granting of more than one valid patent towards inventions that are not patentably distinct?

2.   Criticizing *Hilmer*. "It is one thing to say that *Hilmer I* violates the Paris Convention or is unfair. It is yet another thing to criticize *Hilmer I* as violating existing U.S. law. It is quite conceivable that *Hilmer I* is a correct interpretation of statutory law, even if in violation of the Paris Convention." Harold C. Wegner, Patent Harmonization § 1042 (1993). Do you agree? Hostility to the *Hilmer* rule outside of the United States remains high, and harmonization treaty attempts have often included discussion over statutory abrogation of the *Hilmer* rule. But given that Hilmer, himself a foreign inventor, obtained the right to a patent here, how valid are such complaints? Further, if Habicht had sought patent protection on the invention ultimately sought by Hilmer, why did he merely disclose, rather than claim that "inventive concept"?

3.   Bypassing *Hilmer*. One way to avoid the *Hilmer* holdings is to file an application in the United States as quickly as possible after the foreign filing. A ready means of doing this is by filing a provisional patent application under § 111(b), given its diminished formal requirements as compared to an ordinary application. See Chapter 12 of this casebook for more details. An impediment against this approach may be a particular national patent system's requirement for a foreign patent filing license, analogous to § 181 of the United States Patent Act. Another way is to file a PCT application and then have it published in English. For more information on this method see the PCT materials, *infra*.

4.   Combinations with 102(g). In *Hilmer II*, the PTO tried to combine section 119 with section 102(g) to make Habicht disqualifying prior art. The CCPA rejected this combination because section 119 is a defensive priority-preserver, not an offensive patent-defeater. The Federal Circuit also rejected another effort to combine section 102(g) with section 102(e). In *Sun Studs Inc. v. ATA Equipment Leasing, Inc.*, 872 F.2d 978, 10 U.S.P.Q.2d 1338 (Fed.Cir.1989), an accused infringer argued that the patent was invalid because of a patent issued to Mouat. Mouat, however, had filed for patent protection after the date of conception of Mason, the patentee. The infringer argued that Mouat had actually conceived before Mason's conception and therefore, under 102(g), Mouat invalidated Mason. To show the invalidation, the infringer introduced the disclosure from the Mouat patent. Judge Newman clarified that this form of prior art falls under 102 (e) alone, not 102 (g). Thus the Mouat patent was only effective as of its filing date:

> Both sides appear to have confused interference practice under section 102(g) with prior art status under 102(e). The Mouat reference, as the district court held, does not describe or claim the identical invention to Mason. It is not prior art under section 102(g), but under 102(e).... Under 35 U.S.C. section 102(e), the entire disclosure of Mouat's specification is effective as a reference, but only as of Mouat's filing date.

872 F.2d at 983–84, 10 USPQ2d at 1343.

5.   Further Reading. The *Hilmer* rule finds a defender in Kate H. Murashige, *The* Hilmer *Doctrine, Self–Collision, Novelty and the Definition of Prior Art*, 26 J. Marshall L. Rev. 549 (1993). Kevin L. Leffel, Comment, Hilmer *Doctrine and Patent System Harmonization: What Does A Foreign*

Inventor Have At Stake?, 26 Akron L. Rev. 355 (1992) describes the origin of the *Hilmer* doctrine and proposes legislative reforms.

IN RE DECKLER

United States Court of Appeals, Federal Circuit, 1992.
977 F.2d 1449, 24 U.S.P.Q.2d 1448.

Before Nies, Chief Judge, Friedman, Senior Circuit Judge, and Mayer, Circuit Judge.

Friedman, Senior Circuit Judge.

The sole issue in this appeal from the Board of Patent Appeals and Interferences (Board), is whether the Board correctly ruled that the losing party in an interference proceeding was not entitled to a patent covering claims that that party admits are patentably indistinguishable from the claim involved in the interference. We affirm.

I

The appellant Deckler seeks a patent for an improved seed planter. In an interference proceeding under the "old" rules between Deckler and Grataloup, involving a claim the examiner had suggested to Deckler, the Board awarded priority of invention to Grataloup. The Board determined that although Deckler was first to reduce the invention to practice, he suppressed the invention until after Grataloup's priority date obtained by filing a foreign patent application. Grataloup subsequently was issued a patent on his invention, Claim 11 of which corresponds to the interference count.

Deckler's application was returned to ex parte prosecution. The examiner rejected all remaining claims, giving numerous grounds for rejection. In Deckler's appeal of claims 1–9, the Board reversed all but one of the rejections. The Board affirmed the examiner's rejection of claims 1 through 3 and 7 on the ground that the decision in the interference precluded Deckler from allowance of those claims, because they define the same invention as the interference count.

In his opening brief, Deckler challenged both the Board's conclusion that "the subject matter of claims 1 through 3 and claim 7 are not patentably distinct from the subject matter of the lost count," and the rejection based on estoppel by judgment. In his reply brief and at oral argument, however, Deckler withdrew the first contention, thereby in effect conceding that the claims on appeal are not patentably distinct from the interference count. The sole issue on appeal therefore is the propriety of the rejection of his claims based on the preclusive effect of the interference judgment.

II

A. 1. In rejecting Deckler's claims, the examiner relied on the Board's decision in *Ex parte Tytgat*, 225 USPQ 907 (Bd.Pat.App.Int. 1985). In that case, Tytgat, like Deckler here, lost in an interference proceeding in which priority was awarded to the other party based on a foreign application filing date, and his application was returned to ex parte prosecution. The examiner rejected all remaining claims "on the ground of judicial doctrine and/or interference estoppel." *Id.* at 908.

An augmented Board panel upheld the rejection. It first concluded that the subject matter of Tytgat's claims on appeal was "not patentably distinct" from the subject matter of the interference counts on which he lost. *Id.* at 910. The Board stated that "if a patent containing [Tytgat's] claims on appeal is issued to Tytgat, those claims and at least [four] claims . . . of [the interfering patent] would define a single inventive concept (i.e., would not be patentably distinct)." *Id.* The Board then explained its rationale for relying on the judgment in the interference and "general principles of res judicata and collateral estoppel" to reject Tytgat's claims: We think it most unlikely that Congress could have intended for two patents to be issued to different parties for a single inventive concept. Thus, we think it unlikely that Congress could have intended for a patent to be issued to Tytgat under the circumstances present here. *Id.* at 911.

The rejection avoided the undesirable result that "if the judgment involving the 'lost' counts of the . . . interference cannot be used to reject the claims on appeal, a second interference will have to be declared between those claims and the claims of the [interfering] patent." *Id.* The second interference would involve a priority dispute over the same patentable subject matter to which the winning party was awarded priority in the first interference. The Board concluded that such a result would be unfair to the winning party in the original interference, and would be inconsistent with the general principle of res judicata that a judgment should settle finally all issues that were decided or should have been decided.

2. In the present case, as in Tytgat, the Board relied on the judgment in the interference to reject claims patentably indistinct from the lost count. The Board concluded that if the judgment involving the "lost" count of the interference can not be used to reject claims 1 through 3 and 7 which are not patentably distinct from the lost count, a second interference will have to be declared between those claims and the claims of Grataloup. Furthermore, this interference would be declared with respect to subject matter identical to the subject matter of the count in the original Deckler/Grataloup interference. Deckler acknowledged at oral argument that the count in a second interference between Deckler and Grataloup involving Deckler's claims 1–3 and 7 would be the same as the count in the first interference.

3. The judgment in the interference in this case awarded Grataloup priority of invention over Deckler—a result Deckler does not challenge—and resulted in the issuance of a patent to Grataloup that included the claim corresponding to the interference count. Since Deckler has in effect conceded that the subject claims in his application are patentably indistinguishable from his claim corresponding to the inter-

ference count, the Board properly concluded that the interference judgment barred Deckler from obtaining a patent containing those claims. As the Court of Customs and Patent Appeals pointed out in *Aelony v. Arni,* 547 F.2d 566, 570, 192 USPQ 486, 490 (CCPA 1977), "[s]ections 102, 103, and 135 of 35 U.S.C. clearly contemplate—where different inventive entities are concerned—that only one patent should issue for inventions which are either identical to or not patentably distinct from each other." The court also noted that the patent statute intends that "only one patent should issue for one inventive concept."

The Board's decision that the interference judgment bars Deckler from obtaining a patent for claims that are patentably indistinguishable from the claim on which Deckler lost the interference constituted a permissible application of settled principles of res judicata and collateral estoppel. Under those principles, a judgment in an action precludes relitigation of claims or issues that were or could have been raised in that proceeding. Similarly, this court has applied interference estoppel to bar the assertion of claims for inventions that are patentably indistinct from those in an interference that the applicant had lost.

The interference judgment conclusively determined that, as between Deckler and Grataloup, Grataloup was entitled to claim the patentable subject matter defined in the interference count. It is therefore proper, and consistent with the policies of finality and repose embodied in the doctrines of res judicata and collateral estoppel, to use that judgment as a basis for rejection of claims to the same patentable invention.

The Board correctly noted the unfortunate consequences that would follow if the interference judgment were not given that preclusive effect. There would be a second interference between Deckler's claims "and the claims of Grataloup. Furthermore, this interference would be declared with respect to subject matter identical to the subject matter of the count in the original Deckler/Grataloup interference." The Board should not be required to conduct such an unfair and cumbersome process unless the governing statutes, regulations or judicial decisions compel it. We discern nothing in them that so requires.

4.   Deckler argues that because 35 U.S.C. § 135(a) states that the Commissioner "may" declare an interference, it does not follow that a second interference would necessarily ensue. The Commissioner, however, has stated that such an interference would be declared, and we have no reason to reject that conclusion. Since both Deckler and Grataloup would have claims defining the same patentable subject matter, only an interference could determine priority of invention with respect to them.

B.   Deckler contends that three decisions of our predecessor court, the Court of Customs and Patent Appeals, the decisions of which bind us, *South Corp. v. United States,* 690 F.2d 1368, 1369–71, 215 USPQ 657, 657–58 (1982) (*in banc*), require a contrary conclusion. Although the factual situations out of which those cases developed are similar to the situation in the present case, the grounds of decision in those cases were quite different from those of the Board in the present case. Those cases do not control this case, and we decline to extend their reasoning to require rejection of the Board's rationale in the present case.

The first case was *In re Hilmer*, 359 F.2d 859, 149 USPQ 480 (CCPA 1966). Habicht was awarded priority over Hilmer in an interference, based on Habicht's foreign filing date, which was earlier than Hilmer's United States filing date. The Board then upheld the examiner's subsequent rejection of Hilmer's remaining claims as obvious under 35 U.S.C. § 103. The Board relied primarily on the Habicht disclosures, which it held 35 U.S.C. § 119 made prior art because of Habicht's earlier foreign filing date.

The Court of Customs and Patent Appeals reversed. Noting that the Board had concluded that "the foreign priority date of a U.S. patent is its effective date as a reference," the court held that "section 119 does not modify the express provision of section 102(e) that a reference patent is effective as of the date the application for it was 'filed in the United States.'" The court remanded the case for the Board to clarify its position on two other claims in the application, the validity of which the Board did not decide.

The second case grew out of the remand, in which the Board rejected as obvious Hilmer's two other claims, on the ground that the subject matter of claim 1 of Habicht's patent was prior art under 35 U.S.C. §§ 102(g), 119, and 104 as of Habicht's foreign filing date. The Court of Customs and Patent Appeals again reversed. *In re Hilmer*, 424 F.2d 1108, 165 USPQ 255 (CCPA 1970). Noting that "the rejection here is under § 103 for obviousness," the court held that the subject matter of Habicht's claim was prior art under section 102(g), if at all, as of Habicht's U.S. filing date, and could not in fact be prior art with respect to Hilmer because Hilmer's U.S. filing date preceded Habicht's.

In the third case, *In re McKellin*, 529 F.2d 1324, 188 USPQ 428 (CCPA 1976), the "sole issue" before the court was "whether claims may be rejected under 35 U.S.C. § 103 on the ground that a losing party to an interference is not entitled to claims which are asserted to be obvious variations of the invention defined in the counts, when section 102(g) and interference estoppel are not applicable."

McKellin had lost an interference in which the winning party prevailed solely on the basis of a foreign priority date. The Board rejected McKellin's remaining claims under section 103 as unpatentable in view of the counts of the interference or in view of the disclosure of the interfering patent. The court reversed, holding that because the interference was decided solely on the basis of the winning party's right to the benefit of an earlier foreign filing date, there was no "statutory basis for finding that either the subject matter of the lost counts or the disclosure of the [interfering] patent is prior art, in the sense of 35 U.S.C. § 103, to [McKellin]." In so holding, the court also rejected the Commissioner's theory that the count was statutory prior art under 35 U.S.C. § 135(a) for purposes of section 103.

In a concurring opinion, Judge Rich, the author of the two prior *Hilmer* opinions, "emphasize[d] that there clearly is no rejection before us other than a § 103 obviousness rejection."

The issue in each of those cases was the validity of an obviousness rejection based upon the Board's holdings, on various grounds in the different cases, that under the governing statute the foreign filing date could not be used to make the patent prior art for obviousness purposes.

In the present case, in contrast, there was no obviousness rejection. The Board's sole ground of rejection was that under principles of res judicata and collateral estoppel, Deckler was not entitled to claims that were patentably indistinguishable from the claim on which he lost the interference. Indeed, in this case, the Board, citing McKellin, reversed the examiner's "rejections based on obviousness where Grataloup is used in a rejection under § 103, inasmuch as the lost count is not a bar to appellant's claims and Grataloup is not prior art with respect to appellant."

Unlike the situation in those three cases, here the Board did not use the interference count as prior art in making an obviousness determination, but based its decision on a wholly different theory. We decline to extend those decisions to the different issue in this case.

The decision of the Board is

AFFIRMED

Notes

1.   The Rationale of *Deckler*. Do you find the court's distinction of the *Hilmer* cases, along with *McKellin*, persuasive? How could 35 U.S.C.A. § 135, the statutory basis for interferences, serve as ground for the *rejection* of an application? What are the merits of an estoppel holding that also lacks a statutory grounding? Is this a case about two magic words: "interference estoppel"?

2.   *Deckler* versus *Hilmer*. Is *Deckler* the panacea awaited by those opposed to the *Hilmer* rule, or is its holding limited to those rare situations where the losing interference party admits that the claims are not patentably distinct from the lost count? Commentators have squared off on this issue in the context to the maintenance of the "in this country" mandate of 35 U.S.C.A. § 102(g) despite the requirement of Article 17(1) of the TRIPS Agreement that "patents shall be available and patent rights enjoyable without discrimination as to the place of invention.... " Some observers have seen *Deckler* as essentially overruling *Hilmer*:

> An amendment to § 102(g) is not necessary to preclude two patents from issuing to different parties on patentably indistinct inventions. The doctrine of interference estoppel has been applied in similar circumstances to avoid this clearly undesirable result. *In re Deckler....*

Charles E. Van Horn, *Effects of GATT and NAFTA on PTO Practice*, 77 J. PAT. & TRADEMARK OFF. SOC'Y 231, 234 (1995). Others are far more skeptical:

> [W]ithout an adverse judgment properly statutorily grounded [in an amended § 102(g)], what is there to estop? Interference estoppel is an

estoppel to deny that an adverse party to the interference established a prior invention in this country ... with respect to certain claims. The claims subject to the estoppel are any claims that a party could have placed in issue in the interference, but neglected to contest (e.g., by the filing of an appropriate "preliminary motion"). But if no prior invention in this country is put into evidence, what estoppel can exist? No basis for judgment must emphatically mean no basis for estoppel.

Robert A. Armitage, *The Foreign–Based Inventor's Unprecedented Opportunities Under the URAA* 6–93 (21st Annual Intellectual Property Law Workshop 1995). This debate is reviewed in Harold C. Wegner, *TRIPS Boomerang—Obligations for Domestic Reform*, 29 VAND. J. TRANSNAT'L L. 535 (1996); *see also* Thomas L. Irving & Stacy D. Lewis, *Proving A Date of Invention and Infringement After GATT/TRIPS*, 22 AM. INTELLECTUAL PROP. L. ASS'N Q.J. 309 (1994).

3.   Two Related Statutes. When considering § 119, you should note two other similar statutory provisions. Section 120 is analogous to § 119, but applies purely in the domestic context. It allows applicants to form a series of so-called "continuing applications," thereby extending the period of prosecution—and opportunity to obtain an issued patent from an examiner—all entitled to the filing date of the original application. Continuing applications are discussed here in Chapter 12. Section 365(a) allows applicants to obtain priority as under § 119, but within the context of the PCT.

4.   Avoid *Hilmer* by Publishing your PCT Application in English. The Patent Cooperation Treaty is discussed in detail *infra*. In the American Inventors Protection Act of 1999, § 102(e) was amended to read in part as follows:

(e) the invention was described in—

(1) an application for patent, published pursuant to section 122(b), by another filed in the United States before the invention by the applicant for patent, except that an international application filed under the treaty defined in section 351(a) shall have the effect under this subsection of a national application published under section 122(b) only if the international application designating the United States was published under Article 21(2)(a) of such treaty in the English language....

Why do you think that a PCT application published in English has prior art effect as of its filing date, while a published Japanese language PCT application would have prior art effectiveness only as of its actual publication date?

§ 14.3   COMPLEMENTARY INTERNATIONAL AGREEMENTS

§ 14.3[a]   The Patent Cooperation Treaty

Open to any Paris Convention signatory, the PCT complements that treaty by providing for the filing of a patent application than can have an effect in many countries. Within the one-year Paris Convention deadline for foreign filing, one may file a PCT application in his home country patent office that *designates* the states for which protection is desired. This step serves as an alternative to filing in numerous foreign patent offices, deferring the huge costs of foreign filings that often include expensive translations.

The PCT application is processed in the home patent office that operates as a PCT "Receiving Office". The application is automatically published eighteen months from the priority date. Officials from a PCT office also conduct a prior art search. Within nineteen months from priority date, an optional fee may be paid with a request for an international preliminary examination.

An international preliminary examination is a most abbreviated affair, creating a non-binding opinion on the patentability of the invention. Within thirty months from the priority date, the patent applicant must convert the PCT application into a series of parallel foreign applications as part of the "national stage." Failure to convert to the national stage constitutes a forfeiture of the patent application for such states.

The PCT filing is important today as a time and cost shifting mechanism. Global rights can be put on hold, at the Paris Convention deadline, for a moderate fee of several thousand dollars—putting off the several tens of thousands of dollars in fees that will be required thirty months from the priority date when the "national stage" is to be entered. Often, the money for the PCT application can be raised simply through giving a right to negotiate or an option on foreign rights. The patent applicant then has a precious, additional eighteen months until the thirty month national stage deadline to evaluate the invention and raise funding for the large foreign filing costs that will kick in at the thirty month national stage deadline. Or, the application can be abandoned in good conscience when no takers appear after a diligent effort.

§ 14.3[b]   The European Patent Convention

Under the European Patent Convention, applicants file a single European application instead of in some or all of the member states of the treaty. After conclusion of this single prosecution, a single opposition period occurs for the granted European patent. Thereafter, the European rights are split into a country-by-country situation of patent validity and claim interpretation, with rights being enforced and defended individually.

§ 14.4   A MULTINATIONAL TECHNOLOGY PROTECTION PRIMER

A common mistake is to think of "the patent" as a discrete document, once considered and then forgotten. For each country, the technologist should contemplate at least three separate levels of patent filings: the priority application designed to obtain the earliest filing date; the perfected application, and subsequent improvement applications. The priority application is generally filed only in the United States, but provides a basis for claiming priority worldwide. The perfected applications are filed at 12 months under the Paris Convention, with the existence of improvement applications dependent upon subsequent emergence of the technology.

§ 14.4[a]   Early Filing for Worldwide Priority

As soon as possible, a United States patent application should be filed, even if this document is not perfect. Even an imperfect document may provide some level of protection. Failure to file "immediately" may create fatal forfeiture of positive rights and may lead to a failure to bar third parties, both here and abroad. In practice, the international community sponsors a "race to *any* Patent Office" system for protection of technology.

Consider the situation where two, independent inventors have come up with the same Widget, one in LaJolla, California, and one in Nagoya, Japan. Worldwide rights go to the winner of the race to the first patent office. Under the Paris Convention, patent applicants generally have one year in which to convert their domestic patent rights into international rights under the laws of most foreign countries. The most important aspect of the Paris Convention is thus to delay entry into foreign country patent systems for up to one year. The foreign patent application that is filed within one year of the first filing in any convention country is effectively dated back to the first filing date.

The U.S. national seeking a patent in Japan, Europe or any other Paris Convention country is able to treat his U.S. patent application simultaneously as a "foreign" case during the first 12 months of the patent. By filing "today", the applicant is also able to block foreign patents to the same invention to any third party who is yet to file his patent application. Consider the LaJolla manufacturer who files in the United States on January 14, 1997. If, for example, the Nagoya competitor files his Japanese patent application on January 15, 1997, and his LaJolla competitor files his Japanese application on January 14, 1998, the LaJolla competitor has a full, patent-defeating effect against the Nagoya competitor, because under the Paris Convention his Japanese case is dated back to his United States filing date.

§ 14.4[b]   Worldwide Text at 12 Months

Every important application must be carefully reviewed within 12 months of first filing to determine expansion of the scope of the case. At the 12th month anniversary, the "worldwide" text is prepared for all foreign countries. This stage often presents the final occasion on which the application can be readily augmented.

The applicant should primarily consider whether or not to include any subsequent developments in the foreign application. Consideration should also be made of later-filed domestic applications towards improvement technologies. If a second-filed patent application concerns closely related subject matter, it may be combined with the first case for the purpose of foreign filings. Even if only a single patent application on file, attention should be focused upon the direction the company's research and business planning are leading. Has a new area of technology become the focus of attention in the past twelve months? If so, perhaps the direction of the claims should be broadened to better protect that new area.

U.S. applicants should also be aware of the need for foreign filing licenses. Just a few years ago, when a worldwide text was to be updated with new information, applicants first needed to obtain a foreign filing license from the PTO, 35 U.S.C.A. § 184, unless the applicant planned to employ the PCT exclusively for the foreign filings. 1988 amendments to the patent statute liberalized foreign filing license requirements, however. Currently, once a "general nature" foreign filing license has been provided—typically indicated on the blue official filing receipt letter that is mailed a few weeks after the original U.S. filing date—changes may be made to the specification that do not change the "general nature" of the invention.

§ 14.4[c] Practical Use of the PCT

In years past, the applicant wishing to preserve his foreign rights was faced with more than ten different substantive laws for the most important countries of Europe plus Japan, and needed to file in each of these countries to maintain his important foreign rights. Today, thanks to the EPC and PCT, all that is necessary at the 12th month is the refiling of the U.S. application as a PCT application at the U.S. PTO.

In the PCT application itself, the applicant must request that the application be searched at either the U.S. PTO or by the European Patent Office at its Hague branch. Applicants often prefer to nominate the Hague for this search. The original U.S. search for the priority application will ordinarily have been conducted by a monolingual Examiner at Crystal City, Virginia; the Hague search will be conducted by a likely more experienced and certainly multilingual search examiner. Whether or not the Hague search is better, it will complement the search results at Crystal City to give a more complete picture of the state of art.

The PCT application is published automatically in Geneva by the WIPO, at a time keyed to 18 months from the priority date. This publication comprises neither an advantage or disadvantage, as the same publication would have occurred in various national patent granting authorities around the world at the same time, had a non-PCT route been taken. At 18 months or shortly thereafter, the search results are published, giving the applicant and the public a better idea of the scope of coverage that the applicant may obtain.

Applicants may then obtain an international examination under the PCT at the European Patent Office, thanks to a nearly universal implementation of "Chapter II" for the PCT member states. This election may be made only (a) if the European (Hague) search was nominated in the original PCT filing; and (b) not later than 19 months from the effective filing date. If the applicant decides to forego the Chapter II election of an International Preliminary Examination, or if the 19 month deadline has been passed without the necessary "demand" for such examination, then the deadline for entering the national stage expires at 20 months from the priority date. The same formalities otherwise required at 30 months from the priority date are due at 20 months. Where a "demand" has been filed, no special deadline occurs at 20 months.

The international examination generally takes place between the 22nd and 28th months. If favorable, it is essentially binding on the European Examiner during the later prosecution of the regular European case; if unfavorable, it is advisory only, and in fact helpful by giving the applicant an early clue as to how he may need to amend the case to obtain allowance, or what comparative tests he may need to conduct in order to demonstrate patentability in the later national stage.

Only a minority of patent applicants now use Chapter II and its international preliminary examination. Prior to 2002, a main reason to use Chapter II was to purchase a delay of thirty months before entry into the national stage, when huge expenses for global patent protection start to mount. In 2002, the national stage was set at 30 months *with or without* a Chapter II international preliminary examination.

Only at 30 months from the priority date does the "national stage" occur. At this point, the local patent granting authorities take over on a country-by-country or, for Europe, regional basis. Whereas prior to PCT it was necessary to nominate patent attorneys and agents in each of the territories at 12 months, now with PCT the deadline is pushed back to 30 months. For a typical filing in ten or so countries, perhaps several tens of thousands of dollars in expenses will have been deferred to this 30th month. Up until this 30th month, licensees can be found or the case dropped, or otherwise financed.

§ 14.4[d] Declining Priorities and Deferring Deadlines

Effective July 1, 1992, applicants may defer deadlines by *prospectively* waiving priority claims. Up until either the 19th month "demand" or the 30th month "national stage" deadline, the patent application may *waive* one or more Paris Convention priorities in his PCT application. Normally, the PCT application is filed at or nearly at the 12th month from the priority date, which means that a waiver of the priority will add up to one full year for taking otherwise expensive actions.

Consider the following situation. In just a few weeks, an applicant faces a 30th month "national stage" deadline with likely government fees, translations and foreign agent costs on the order of anywhere from $5,000 to $25,000 or more, depending upon the number of countries where protection is to be maintained, the length of the application (for translation costs) and the fees of the individual foreign patent agents. But, the patent applicant simply cannot find the necessary fees to cover such foreign filing by the 30th month, and the applicant is reasonably sure that no third party publication or other patent-defeating event has occurred in the 12 months between the priority filing and the actual PCT application filing.

In this example, the PCT applicant may decide that the risk of loss of rights due to an unknown publication or other event in the Paris Convention year is reasonably low versus the great expense of the fees to enter the national stage. In this case, the applicant files a paper with the appropriate Patent Office *waiving* his priority claim, which then resets the deadline for entering the national stage until the 30th month from the *actual* PCT application filing date, i.e., some 42 months from the original priority date.

Forfeiture of a priority right is a very dangerous point because once forfeited, an intervening publication may well be fatal. There may be situations where the forfeiture is warranted. For example, the applicant may have included features in the PCT application itself, above and beyond the priority document, which serve as the basis for the patent. Or, the priority application may have only a very narrow scope that is not basis for a broad claim that is in any event highly desirable or necessary; here, again, forfeiture of the priority right is not as important.

In some cases, enough funding may exist to cover certain European as well as a Japanese filing, but funds are lacking to cover filings through additional countries. Here, the applicant may wish to maintain the European and Japanese rights without waiver of priority, while forfeiting the other designations for secondary countries.

§ 14.4[e]   Salvaging Foreign Rights With Lost Priorities

In some cases, the applicant may lose her original priority year. Situations may arise where financial considerations, or lack of appreciation of the importance of an invention at the time, may cause an applicant to miss the 12–month deadline. If the invention has been published, then this ordinarily creates a fatal bar to European and Japanese rights, as noted here in Chapter 4. The failure to meet the Paris Convention deadline will be fatal only if a third party has filed a patent application in the interval, or if the invention has been published. If the only patent filing was in the United States, and the patent has not yet been issued, it is entirely possible that there has so far been no publication of the invention anywhere in the world.

If the American company finds itself with a sudden expression of interest by an overseas potential licensee in an invention not filed abroad and where the Paris Convention year has expired, the easiest way to "freeze" the situation is to file a PCT application. Today's date can be the filing date for all PCT states, so that negotiations can commence immediately with the overseas potential licensee. The filing of a PCT application designating every possible foreign country creates an actual filing date for the designated countries as of that particular date. The applicant need not incur the time delay of translations and filings in each foreign country. Furthermore, this PCT case is without any priority, and provides a full 18 months of continued secrecy of the invention until publication from the date of actual filing.

For example, consider the normal convention filing at 12 months, which has an automatic publication at 18 months keyed from the priority date. If, instead, the PCT application is filed non-convention at 13 months, the publication will be a further 18 months later as there is no priority right, i.e., a total of 31 months from the earliest filing date. The total cost of the PCT filing will be less than $2,000, the filing can be virtually "instantly" (a copy in PCT format of the U.S. case), and in the coming 18 months the applicant can determine whether to maintain the case.

§ 14.4[f]   Country Selection for Foreign Patent Protection

Selection of countries in which patent protection should be sought need not be made immediately, due to the one year grace period of the Paris Convention. The selection should not wait until the end of the Paris Convention year; at least two months should be allowed for preparation and filing the application in the various foreign countries. If the PCT is to be *exclusively* used for the foreign filings, then this lead time can be further shortened. Several factors should be considered in country selection:

(1) Does the particular country include a market for that technology, even if there is no manufacturing in that country?

(2) Does sufficient manufacturing capability exist to produce the particular product, perhaps only for export to third countries?

(3) May a foreign patentee enter that particular country with meaningful rights, including exclusivity for the life of the patent and freedom to expatriate profits?

These factors should be considered on a case-by-case basis. For example, Austria may not normally considered a first level country for protection. But, if the invention relates to snow ski bindings, Austria may be a first level country; if the invention relates to underwater diving equipment, Austria might not be considered. The third factor eliminates otherwise important markets for many inventions, including India, certain other Asian and African countries, as well as most of South America.

Europe. Filings may take place in the several European states with or without a parallel EPC filing. If parallel filings occur, a patent is granted relatively promptly from the national authorities of several key countries. If the EPC ultimately grants a parallel European patent, then the corresponding (already granted) national patent is terminated in nearly all EPC countries.

Some technologists may find that filing only on a national basis is preferable, as various problems arise with use of the EPC. A major factor is the costs of a European patent. In addition. there are many procedural problems. Obtaining protection for an originally defined, but unclaimed subgeneric invention often requires the filing of an expensive divisional application. Oppositions may also serve as a serious problem, particularly in terms of the delay in the final outcome of the patent. For the roughly seven percent or so of patents that are granted with an opposition, only one-third of all patents survive without amendment. Another third are maintained in amended form and a final third are lost altogether.

As a result, many entities forego filing under the European Patent Convention and instead consider old-fashioned national filings under the Paris Convention for the core five technology markets of the European Union—Germany, France, the United Kingdom, Italy and the Netherlands. Although the Netherlands is the smallest of these markets, the leadership role taken by the courts of the Netherlands in adjudicating pan-European patent disputes renders Dutch patents increasingly valuable, as discussed in this casebook in Chapter 18. Spain may also be added to this so-called "Eurocore" strategy. Note that the Patent Cooperation Treaty is also unavailable under this approach, as national patents cannot be obtained for either France or Italy based upon a PCT application.

The core filing approach can be used to virtually guarantee four national patents in short order in each of these countries but Germany. However, in Germany, all significant costs may be deferred for up to seven years when an examination request must be lodged. Rapidly granted patents will then be the rule for registration or simplified examinations that result in patents for the United Kingdom, France, Italy and the Netherlands. None of these four countries has an opposition system of any kind. In Germany, the lower volume of work that has resulted due to the parallel European route means that when an invention is on the verge of commercialization, a quick examination can then be had (followed by an opposition proceeding).

At the turn of the century, the European Union countries are essentially regarded as a single territory for patent purposes. This effect is due less to overall market integration than to the fact that the European Court of Justice has interpreted the Treaty of Rome to provide the free circulation of goods within the EU. As a result, if a patentee or his licensee sells his product in any member state, then the goods may be freely circulated within the EU.

Two factors accompany the "free circulation" principle to block an effective intra-European exclusive position amongst several licensees. First, does a significant price differential for the product exist amongst several European states; and second, are transportation costs concerning product shipment between the states minimal? If the answers to these two questions are affirmative, then no exclusive sales position is likely possible in Europe between the customers of different licensees. The case of pharmaceuticals provides the most notorious example. Where, for example, the Dutch price is much higher than the socialized British price, and transportation costs are negligible, parallel imports of the patented drug are a likely possibility.

If a competitor produces goods outside the Common Market, then importation of these goods into the EU comprises a violation of national patents. Thus, a Japanese licensee is not free to sell products in Germany in violation of the German patent; no "exhaustion" of the patent for sales outside the territory occurs. A similar result applies for Japan if the purchaser of goods outside Japan understands that he is restricted from reselling in Japan; if goods are sold outside Japan without restriction, then an implied license allows the purchaser to sell in Japan.

Japan. Outside of the United States, Japan represents the most important country for patent filing. Its population is considerably larger than any single European country and is quite affluent. Additionally, Japanese companies often adopt an aggressive patent filing strategy that yields plural patents to protect a company's products, even though the Japanese company may be dominated by a foreigner's pioneer patent. To provide leverage for a cross-license in the United States and Europe in the event that one of these patents will dominate the United States company's product, it is useful to have as strong a patent position in Japan as possible as a basis for negotiations.

Japanese patents may be obtained under the Paris Convention either through a regular Paris Convention filing at the 12th month, or through the PCT. In either case, applicants may find that they prefer to defer examination.

China and Korea. China and Korea have become very popular designations for foreign protection, particularly by Japanese patent applicants. Indeed, while the United States is the Number Two country for protection by Japanese nationals, in some industries China has become Number Three–ahead of even European countries.

The Americas. Traditionally, patent protection in the United States has dominated the "Americas" market so that an United States patent would largely block a third party competitor, but today Canadian patents are quite important because some technologies manufacture high-tech products in Canada. Outside of the pharmaceutical market, others often possess little incentive to launch a competing product that could be sold only outside the United States. Today, however, Canadian patents have become quite attractive in the United States. They are easy to obtain, relatively inexpensive and require no translation. Further, Brazil in 1996 greatly improved its patent system. As the single largest economic power in Latin America and now with a strengthened patent system, Brazil bears consideration by global technologists.

Other Countries. Those unfamiliar with the patenting process often fear waiving protection in a whole host of countries. All PCT states may be designated for a blanket fee that will cover not only the top ten PCT countries—Canada, China, France, Germany, Italy, Japan, Netherlands, Spain, United Kingdom and the United States—but also more than seventy other countries. While blanket designations are often used, exceedingly few cases arise where all the countries reach the "national stage". Why, then, would one ever choose to blanket designate? Because no fee accrues for blanket designation (beyond the minimum number of country designations), and thus there is no harm in doing so. In the meantime, if a business interest develops in a particular market, conceivably the national stage could be entered to perfect patent protection and provide a licensing basis for rights in that country.

International Priority Exercises

1.   Okimoto files a patent application at the Japanese Patent Office on March 12, 2000. Its specification describes a toothbrush with bristles fabricated from a novel artificial fiber which supposedly is particularly effective at removing plaque. The specification also describes a specially-shaped handle which is easy to grip. The sole claim of the patent claims the artificial fiber for use as a toothbrush bristle material.

Is Okimoto able to obtain priority in the United States based upon the Japanese application in the following circumstances? Unless otherwise noted, all subsequent applications are precise translations of the Japanese original.

> a.   Okimoto files a United States application on March 12, 2001.

> b.   Okimoto notifies the Japanese Patent Office that he will abandon his application on April 2, 2000. He then files a United States application on January 25, 2001.

> c.   Okimoto files a German application on September 1, 2000. He then files a United States application on May 1, 2001.

> d.   Okimoto files a United States application on December 1, 2000, with a single claim directed to a particular shape of a toothbrush handle.

2.   Although a very low number of actual patent application filings occur in most developing countries, statistics provided by the World Intellectual Property Organization (WIPO) show very high numbers of PCT designations for such nations. Explain the discrepancy.

3.   Ideally, the Acme Widget Company wants patent protection for its new and improved Widget "everywhere"—throughout Europe, Asia, Africa and the Americas. Total sales percentages that are expected would be: U.S.A. (50%); Canada (7%); France (7%); Germany (12%); Italy (7%); Japan (2%), and U.K. (8%); with twenty-five other countries accounting for most of the remaining sales. However, Acme provides budgetary limitations on foreign filing such that you must select only three countries beyond the United States for foreign filing. Absent any further information and assuming, for purposes of this problem, a rough equality of government costs and effectiveness of the several patent systems, which countries do you select, and how do you explain your choice to Acme?

4.   Would your answer to Question 3 differ if it were assumed that third party competitors would have access to excellent manufacturing and marketing facilities in Japan but in no other foreign country, and

any manufacturer would supply the Canadian market only from the United States?

5.   You are considering buying stock in a publicly traded corporation, Consolidated Technology Inc., and are reviewing company literature. You note that a Consolidated prospectus indicates that it filed 1000 United States patent applications in 1999, and that it ultimately sought corresponding protection in Japan for the technologies disclosed in 400 of these applications. However, your independent review of Japanese Patent Office published patent applications indicates that Consolidated only filed 250 applications in Japan based upon its 1999 United States filings. How can you explain this discrepancy?

Chapter Fifteen

INFRINGEMENT

With few words, the patent statute addresses infringement at section 271:

> Except as otherwise provided in this title, whoever without authority makes, uses, offers to sell, or sells any patented invention, within the United States or imports into the United States any patented invention during the term of the patent therefor, infringes the patent.

This modest provision carries much of the weight of the Patent Act. For instance, § 271(a) twice uses the term "patented invention"—a deceptively simple phrase. The words "patented invention" determine the scope of the infringement inquiry. If the accused infringer appropriated the patented invention without authority, he has infringed and must "face the music." Before any determination of infringement or remedies, however, § 271(a) demands a definition of the "patented invention." As the preceding chapters have shown, the one task in patent law that may rival the difficulty of drafting claims is discerning what these claims mean. The following magisterial dicta serve as a fine prelude to this thorny issue.

AUTOGIRO CO. OF AMERICA v. UNITED STATES
United States Court of Claims, 1967.
384 F.2d 391, 155 U.S.P.Q. 697.

I

* * *

The claims of the patent provide the concise formal definition of the invention. They are the numbered paragraphs which "particularly (point) out and distinctly (claim) the subject matter which the applicant regards as his invention." 35 U.S.C. § 112. It is to these wordings that one must look to determine whether there has been infringement. Courts can neither broaden nor narrow the claims to give the patentee something different than what he has set forth. No matter how great the temptations of fairness or policy making, courts do not rework claims. They only interpret them. Although courts are confined by the language of the claims, they are not, however, confined to the language of the claims in interpreting their meaning.

Courts occasionally have confined themselves to the language of the claims. When claims have been found clear and unambiguous, courts have not gone beyond them to determine their content. Courts have also held that the fact that claims are free from ambiguity is no reason for limiting the material which may be inspected for the purpose of better understanding the meaning of claims.

We find both approaches to be hypothetical. Claims cannot be clear and unambiguous on their face. A comparison must exist. The lucidity of a claim is determined in light of what ideas it is trying to convey. Only by knowing the idea, can one decide how much shadow encumbers the reality.

The very nature of words would make a clear and unambiguous claim a rare occurrence. Writing on statutory interpretation, Justice Frankfurter commented on the inexactitude of words:

> They are symbols of meaning. But unlike mathematical symbols, the phrasing of a document, especially a complicated enactment, seldom attains more than approximate precision. If individual words are inexact symbols, with shifting variables, their configuration can hardly achieve invariant meaning or assured definiteness.

Frankfurter, *Some Reflections on the Reading of Statutes*, 47 Col.L.Rev. 527, 528 (1947). *See, also, A Re–Evaluation of the Use of Legislative History in the Federal Courts*, 52 Col.L.Rev. 125 (1952).

The inability of words to achieve precision is none the less extant with patent claims than it is with statutes. The problem is likely more acute with claims. Statutes by definition are the reduction of ideas to print. Since the ability to verbalize is crucial in statutory enactment, legislators develop a facility with words not equally developed in inventors. An invention exists most importantly as a tangible structure or a series of drawings. A verbal portrayal is usually an afterthought written to satisfy the requirements of patent law. This conversion of machine to words allows for unintended idea gaps which cannot be satisfactorily filled. Often the invention is novel and words do not exist to describe it. The dictionary does not always keep abreast of the inventor. It cannot. Things are not made for the sake of words, but words for things. To overcome this lag, patent law allows the inventor to be his own lexicographer.

Allowing the patentee verbal license only augments the difficulty of understanding the claims. The sanction of new words or hybrids from old ones not only leaves one unsure what a rose is, but also unsure whether a rose is a rose. Thus we find that a claim cannot be interpreted without going beyond the claim itself. No matter how clear a claim appears to be, lurking in the background are documents that may completely disrupt initial views on its meaning.

The necessity for a sensible and systematic approach to claim interpretation is axiomatic. The Alice-in-Wonderland view that something means whatever one chooses it to mean makes for enjoyable reading, but bad law. Claims are best construed in connection with the other parts of the patent instrument and with the circumstances surrounding the inception of the patent application. In utilizing all the patent documents, one should not sacrifice the value of these references by the 'unimaginative adherence to well-worn professional phrases.' Frankfurter, *supra*, at 529. Patent law is replete with major canons of construction of minor value which have seldom provided useful guidance in the unraveling of complex claims. Instead, these canons have only added confusion to the problem of claim interpretation.

II

In deriving the meaning of a claim, we inspect all useful documents and reach what Justice Holmes called the "felt meaning" of the claim. In seeking this goal, we make use of three parts of the patent: the specification, the drawings, and the file wrapper.

Specification.—Section 112 of the 1952 Patent Act requires the specification to describe the manner and process of making and using the patent so that any person skilled in the patent's art may utilize it. In serving its statutory purpose, the specification aids in ascertaining the scope and meaning of the language employed in the claims inasmuch as words must be used in the same way in both the claims and the specification. The use of the specification as a concordance for the claim is accepted by almost every court, and is a basic concept of patent law. Most courts have simply stated that the specification is to be used to explain the claims; others have stated the proposition in different terms, but with the same effect.

Drawings.—The patent may contain drawings. In those instances where a visual representation can flesh out words, drawings may be used in the same manner and with the same limitations as the specification.

File wrapper.—The file wrapper contains the entire record of the proceedings in the Patent Office from the first application papers to the issued patent. Since all express representations of the patent applicant made to induce a patent grant are in the file wrapper, this material provides an accurate charting of the patent's pre-issuance history. One use of the file wrapper is file wrapper estoppel, which is the application of familiar estoppel principles to Patent Office prosecution and patent infringement litigation. The patent applicant must convince the patent examiner that his invention meets the statutory requirements; otherwise, a patent will not be issued. When the application is rejected, the applicant will insert limitations and restrictions for the purpose of inducing the Patent Office to grant his patent. When the patent is issued, the patentee cannot disclaim these alterations and seek an interpretation that would ignore them. He cannot construe the claims narrowly before the Patent Office and later broadly before the courts. File wrapper estoppel serves two functions in claim interpretation; the applicant's statements not only define terms, but also set the barriers within which the claim's meaning must be kept. These results arise when the file wrapper discloses either what the claim covers or what it does not cover.

The file wrapper also has a broader and more general use. This is its utilization, like the specification and drawings, to determine the scope of claims. For example, the prior art cited in the file wrapper is used in this manner. In file wrapper estoppel, it is not the prior art that provides the guidelines, but the applicant's acquiescence with regard to the prior art. In its broader use as source material, the prior art cited in the file wrapper gives clues as to what the claims do not cover.

Notes

1. The Hermeneutics of *Autogiro*. This wandering dicta from the Court of Claims remains among the leading attempts to set forth broadly applicable norms of that fundamental task of the patent bar, claim interpretation. Because the patent law first and foremost transforms technology into text, patent lawyers share much in common with practitioners of the disciplines of linguistic philosophy, philology, hermeneutics, and, more recently, the "law and literature" movement. Yet few jurists turn to the teaching of these authorities, perhaps with good reason; why should one read patent claims differently from, say, a historical narrative or a work of fiction? What holistic comments can you offer about these technological aphorisms, such as the grammar, internal consistency, physical embodiment, or intent of the drafter regarding a particular claim? Should any of these factors even bear relevance to the ontological task of the reader? As you will see in the pages that follow, the search for a serviceable lodestar of patent claim interpretation has been an elusive one.

2. Interpretation vs. Construction. As seen in the *Markman* opinion which follows, most courts and commentators employ the terms "interpretation" and "construction" interchangeably to refer to the process of understanding the meaning of a patent claim. However, at one point, the United States Patent and Trademark Office contended that a substantive difference existed between these terms. More specifically, according to the PTO, courts were the only entities which "construed" claims, while the PTO performed the task of "interpretation." The PTO pointed to language in opinions such as *Burlington Industries v. Quigg*, 822 F.2d 1581, 1583, 3 U.S.P.Q.2d 1436, 1438 (Fed.Cir.1987), which provided that "[i]ssues of judicial claim construction such as arise after patent issuance, for example during infringement litigation, have no place in prosecution of pending claims before the PTO...." Should the use of the term "construed" in § 112 ¶ 6 influence this decision? How about the holding in *In re Donaldson*, reprinted here in Chapter 11?

The Federal Circuit has recognized one significant difference that does arise between claim interpretation at the PTO versus claim interpretation during infringement litigation. As stated in *In re Zletz,* 893 F.2d 319, 13 U.S.P.Q.2d 1320 (Fed.Cir.1989):

> The Board erred in its interpretation of claims 13 and 14, the error apparently flowing from the Board's choice of inapplicable legal premise. The Board applied the mode of claim interpretation that is used by the courts in litigation, when interpreting the claims of issued patents in connection with determinations of infringement or validity. *See, e.g., Tandon Corp. v. United States Int'l Trade Comm'n,* 831 F.2d 1017, 1021, 4 U.S.P.Q.2d 1283, 1286 (Fed.Cir.1987) (meaning of claims of issued patent interpreted in light of specification, prosecution history, prior art, and other claims). That is not the mode of claim interpretation that is applicable during prosecution of a pending application before the PTO.
>
> During patent examination the pending claims must be interpreted as broadly as their terms reasonably allow. When the applicant states the meaning that the claim terms are intended to have, the claims are examined with that meaning, in order to achieve a complete exploration of the applicant's invention and its relation to the prior art. The reason is simply that during patent prosecution when claims can be amended, ambiguities should be recognized, scope and breadth of language explored, and clarification imposed. An essential purpose of patent examination is to fashion claims that are precise, clear, correct, and unambiguous. Only in this way can uncertainties of claim scope be removed, as much as possible, during the administrative process.

893 F.2d at 321–22, 13 U.S.P.Q.2d at 1321–22.

3. Copyright Contrast. Note that unlike copyright law, patent law does not require that infringers copy the protected subject matter. A competitor who independently creates the claimed invention is still an infringer. Why do you think the protection offered by a patent is so much stronger? Is this simply a matter for legal historians, or does such a telling difference exist between patentable inventions and works of authorship that justifies the dissimilarities between these intellectual property schemes?

In considering this question, imagine what you would advise corporate engineers who are working on a new technology. Would you instruct them not to read anything for fear that anything they learn from reading will lead to liability? Would you demand clean-room conditions? *See* Martin J. Adelman, *Property Rights Theory and Patent–Antitrust: The Role of Compulsory Licensing,* 52 N.Y.U. L. Rev. 977, 983–84 (1977).

4. Trademark Contrast. The essential test of trademark infringement stands markedly close to one of the chief aims of trademark law itself: prevention of consumer confusion. As will be seen throughout this chapter, patent infringement law has not achieved this transparency. How could standards of patent infringement law be better tuned towards the constitutionally mandated aspiration of promoting the useful arts? For some suggestions, see James Boyle, Shamans, Software and Spleens 172 (1996) ("Patents should be voidable at the instance of any party who can prove that an adequate return would have been provided merely by being first to market, with the state paying the legal fees for successful suits."); Robert P. Merges & Richard R. Nelson, *On the Complex Economics of Patent Scope,* 90 Col. L.

REV. 839 (1990) (advocating use of the reverse doctrine of equivalents and other mechanisms governing claim breadth in order to optimize the promotion of technological development).

5. Patent Infringement and Intent. Similarly, a defendant's intent is irrelevant to the outcome of an infringement inquiry. Even an individual who has never previously known of the asserted patent or even of the entire patent system may be found to be an infringer. Infringement analyses thus have a *quasi in rem* flavor; they are entirely based upon a comparison of the patent's claim to a physical technology. Note, however, that an infringer's intent may be relevant to indirect infringement, discussed later in this Chapter; as well as when a remedy is fashioned, as considered in Chapter 17. Further, some judges would bring an equitable flavor into infringement inquiries under the Doctrine of Equivalents, which could introduce intent elements there as well.

6. Infringing Acts. Before 1996, § 271(a) and its predecessor statutes defined as infringements only the acts of making, using or selling the patented invention. Domestic legislation implementing the TRIPS Agreement augmented this definition by including the acts of making "offers to sell" and introducing "imports into the United States" as well. Under § 271(i), an offer to sell only infringes where the sale will occur before expiration of the patent.

§ 15.1 LITERAL INFRINGEMENT

Before the Federal Circuit, jury trials in patent cases were somewhat rare. No doubt the difficulty of defending the patent against validity challenges contributed to that rarity. Nonetheless the advent of the Federal Circuit invigorated the practice of patent law and the frequency of jury trials. More jury trials also prompted serious questions about a lay jury's ability to comprehend and resolve complex scientific and legal issues. Claim interpretation, of course, was particularly difficult for juries. At length, the Federal Circuit resolved to settle *en banc* the question of whether claim interpretation is an issue within the ambit of the Seventh Amendment. This *en banc* opinion became perhaps the most important patent opinion of the 1990s because it defines the modern approach to claim interpretation.

MARKMAN v. WESTVIEW INSTRUMENTS, INC.

United States Court of Appeals, Federal Circuit,
1995.52 F.3d 967, 34 U.S.P.Q.2d 1321.
aff'd, 517 U.S. 370, 38 U.S.P.Q.2d 1461 (1996).

Opinion for the Court filed by CHIEF JUDGE ARCHER, in which CIRCUIT JUDGES RICH, NIES, MICHEL, PLAGER, LOURIE, CLEVENGER, and SCHALL join. Concurring opinions filed by CIRCUIT JUDGES MAYER, and RADER. Dissenting opinion filed by CIRCUIT JUDGE NEWMAN.

ARCHER, CHIEF JUDGE.

* * *

I.

A. In the dry-cleaning industry, articles of clothing typically are taken in from customers, recorded in some form, and then sorted according to criteria such as type of clothing and type of cleaning required. During the sorting process, articles of clothing belonging to one customer may be combined together, and also may be combined with similar clothing belonging to other customers, in order to make the cleaning process more efficient and less costly. After the articles of clothing are sorted, they may be cleaned in the same establishment or transported to another establishment for cleaning. During the cleaning process, the articles of clothing move through different locations in the establishment. After cleaning, of course, the articles of clothing must be unsorted and returned to the respective customers.

Markman is the inventor named in and the owner of United States Reissue Patent No. 33,054 (the '054 patent), titled "Inventory Control and Reporting System for Drycleaning Stores." Markman's original patent No. 4,550,246 was reissued and the reissue is the patent in suit. Positek is a licensee under the patent in the dry-cleaning business.

The '054 patent is directed to an inventory-control system that assertedly solves inventory-related problems prevalent in the dry-cleaning business. As the '054 patent specification discusses, articles of clothing can be lost in the sorting and cleaning process, and it has been found in the dry-cleaning business that even a small percentage-loss of articles of clothing will generate great consumer dissatisfaction. Also, attendant personnel might send clothing through the cleaning process but pocket the proceeds of the transactions and destroy or fail to do the appropriate paperwork, thereby servicing the customers adequately but stealing from the business. In such circumstances it is difficult for the business owner to locate the loss of profits and to deter such activities.

The invention of the '054 patent is described in detail in the specification which states that the inventory control system is "capable of monitoring and reporting upon the status, location and throughput of inventory in an establishment," and that by using the invention of the '054 patent, "the progress of articles through the laundry and drycleaning system can be completely monitored." In this way, the business owner can "reconcile[ ] [the inventory] at any point in the sequence" of sorting, cleaning, and unsorting clothing, and can "detect and localize spurious additions to inventory as well as spurious deletions therefrom."

[A]s customers bring in their articles of clothing for cleaning, the articles are accumulated by an attendant.... A data processor stores and processes the data entered by the attendant, associating sequential customers and transactions with a unique indicium such as a number. The processor is connected to a printer that generates a written record of the stored information associated with the particular customers and transactions. No transaction can proceed without generating a written record, thereby ensuring that each transaction is accounted for.

The patent specification specifies that the written record is to have different portions. For example, the written record includes a customer ticket or receipt, a management ticket copy, and a plurality of article tags. The article tags are to be attached to individual articles or groups of articles in inventory.

Optical detector devices are then used to read the bar code indicia, and they may be located at various points in the cleaning process, including at least at the customer service station. The articles are logged through a particular station by scanning the tags containing the bar codes with the detector. The bar codes are used to call up information associated with the customer or transaction, and used to generate reports containing information such as the location of articles within the system, the number of articles located at a particular point in the system, etc. The overall result is that additions to and deletions from inventory can be located-wherever an optical detector appears-and can be associated with particular customers and articles of clothing. In this way the inventory can be fully reconciled.

In claim 1, the only independent claim involved in this appeal, Markman claims his invention to be:

1.   The inventory control and reporting system, comprising:

a data input device for manual operation by an attendant, the input device having switch means operable to encode information relating to sequential transactions, each of the transactions having articles associated therewith, said information including transaction identity and descriptions of each of said articles associated with the transactions;

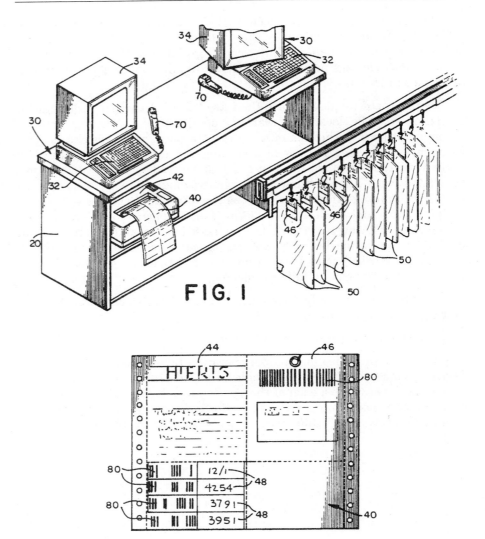

FIG. 1

FIG. 2

a data processor including memory operable to record said information and means to maintain an inventory total, said data processor having means to associate sequential transactions with unique sequential indicia and to generate at least one report of said total and said transactions, the unique sequential indicia and the descriptions of articles in the sequential transactions being reconcilable against one another;

a dot matrix printer operable under control of the data processor to generate a written record of the indicia associated with sequential transactions, the written record including optically-detectable bar codes having a series of contrasting spaced bands, the bar codes being printed only in coincidence with each said transaction and at least part of the written record bearing a portion to be attached to said articles; and,

at least one optical scanner connected to the data processor and operable to detect said bar codes on all articles passing a predetermined station,

whereby said system can detect and localize spurious additions to inventory as well as spurious deletions therefrom.

In dependent claim 10, Markman specifies that in the invention of claim 1, the input device is an alpha-numeric keyboard wherein single keys may be used to enter attributes of items being entered.

B. Markman sued Westview and Althon for infringement of claims 1, 10, and 14 of the '054 patent. Westview makes and sells specialty electronic devices, including the system accused of being an infringement of the '054 patent. Althon owns and operates two dry-cleaning sites and uses Westview's device in one of its shops.

The accused Westview device consists of two separate pieces of equipment, which Westview calls the DATAMARK and the DATASCAN. The DATAMARK is a stationary unit comprising a keyboard, electronic display, processor, and printer. When a customer brings articles of clothing in for cleaning, an attendant enters on a keypad information about the customer, articles to be cleaned, and charges for the cleaning. The DATAMARK then prints a bar-coded ticket or invoice listing the information about the customer, the clothes to be cleaned, and the charges for the cleaning. The DATAMARK retains permanently in memory only the invoice number, date, and cash total. The DATAMARK is thus used to print bar-coded tickets for the articles and to retain an invoice list.

The DATASCAN is a portable unit comprising a microprocessor and an optical detector for reading bar-coded tickets or invoices at any location in the dry-cleaning establishment. To use the DATASCAN, first the invoice list is transferred from the DATAMARK to the DATASCAN. Then, the DATASCAN is carried about to read the bar-codes on tickets or invoices in the establishment. As it does this, it can report any discrepancy between the particular invoice read (or not read) and the invoice list. In this way the DATASCAN identifies extra or missing invoices.

* * *

"To ascertain the meaning of claims, we consider three sources: The claims, the specification, and the prosecution history." *Unique Concepts, Inc. v. Brown*, 939 F.2d 1558, 1561 (Fed.Cir.1991); *accord Autogiro Co. of Am. v. United States*, 384 F.2d 391, 396–98, 181 Ct.Cl. 55, 155 U.S.P.Q. 697, 701–03 (1967). "Expert testimony, including evidence of how those skilled in the art would interpret the claims, may also be used." *Fonar Corp. v. Johnson & Johnson*, 821 F.2d 627, 631 (Fed.Cir.1987). In construing the claims in this case, all these sources, as well as extrinsic evidence in the form of Westview's sales literature, were included in the record of the trial court proceedings.

Claims must be read in view of the specification, of which they are a part. *Autogiro*, 384 F.2d at 397, 155 U.S.P.Q. at 702. The specification contains a written description of the invention that must enable one of ordinary skill in the art to make and use the invention. For claim construction purposes, the description may act as a sort of dictionary, which explains the invention and may define terms used in the claims. *See In re Vogel*, 422 F.2d 438, 441, 164 U.S.P.Q. 619, 621 (CCPA 1970) ("Occasionally the disclosure will serve as a dictionary for terms appearing in the claims, and in such instances the disclosure may be used in interpreting the coverage of the claim."). As we have often stated, a patentee is free to be his own lexicographer. *Autogiro*, 384 F.2d at 397, 155 U.S.P.Q. at 702. The caveat is that any special definition given to a word must be clearly defined in the specification. *Intellicall, Inc. v. Phonometrics, Inc.*, 952 F.2d 1384, 1388, 21 U.S.P.Q.2d 1383, 1386 (Fed.Cir.1992). The written description part of the specification itself does not delimit the right to exclude. That is the function and purpose of claims.

To construe claim language, the court should also consider the patent's prosecution history, if it is in evidence. *Graham v. John Deere Co.*, 383 U.S. 1, 33, 86 S.Ct. 684, 701, 15 L.Ed.2d 545, 148 U.S.P.Q. 459, 473 (1966). This "undisputed public record" of proceedings in the Patent and Trademark Office is of primary significance in understanding the claims. *See Autogiro*, 384 F.2d at 397, 155 U.S.P.Q. at 702 (the "file wrapper" is "part [ ] of the patent"). The court has broad power to look as a matter of law to the prosecution history of the patent in order to ascertain the true meaning of language used in the patent claims.

Although the prosecution history can and should be used to understand the language used in the claims, it too cannot "enlarge, diminish, or vary" the limitations in the claims.

Extrinsic evidence consists of all evidence external to the patent and prosecution history, including expert and inventor testimony, dictionaries, and learned treatises. This evidence may be helpful to explain scientific principles, the meaning of technical terms, and terms of art that appear in the patent and prosecution history. Extrinsic evidence may demonstrate the state of the prior art at the time of the invention. It is useful "to show what was then old, to distinguish what was new, and to aid the court in the construction of the patent." *Brown v. Piper*, 91 U.S. 37, 41, 23 L.Ed. 200 (1875).

The court may, in its discretion, receive extrinsic evidence in order "to aid the court in coming to a correct conclusion" as to the "true meaning of the language employed" in the patent. *Seymour v. Osborne*, 78 U.S. (11 Wall.) 516, 546, 20 L.Ed. 33 (1871) (reviewing a decree in equity).

* * *

Through this process of construing claims by, among other things, using certain extrinsic evidence that the court finds helpful and rejecting other evidence as unhelpful, and resolving disputes en route to pronouncing the meaning of claim language as a matter of law based on the patent documents themselves, the court is not crediting certain evidence over other evidence or making factual evidentiary findings. Rather, the court is looking to the extrinsic evidence to assist in its construction of the written document, a task it is required to perform. The district court's claim construction, enlightened by such extrinsic evidence as may be helpful, is still based upon the patent and prosecution history. It is therefore still construction, and is a matter of law subject to de novo review.

B. Applying this analysis of claim construction, we conclude that (1) the trial court did not abuse its discretion when it admitted the extrinsic evidence offered by Markman—Markman's testimony and the testimony of Markman's "patent expert"—on the issue of claim construction, and that (2) the trial court properly rejected this extrinsic evidence to the extent it contradicted the court's construction of the claims based on the specification and prosecution history. Although in this case the trial court might have granted Westview's motion for directed verdict and should have instructed the jury as to the meaning of the claims (including the disputed term "inventory"), its failure to do so was rendered harmless by the court's subsequent response to Westview's post-trial motion.

We agree with the trial court that the term "inventory" refers, at least in part, to articles of clothing, contrary to Markman's contention that "inventory" may be limited to just cash or inventory receipts. As the district court noted, the claim phrase "detect and localize spurious additions to inventory as well as spurious deletions therefrom" does not make sense using Markman's definition of "inventory." Dollars or invoice totals are not "localized" since dollars do not travel through the cleaning process and the location of invoices is irrelevant. Location is relevant to clothing, since it moves through and sometimes without the establishment, where it can be lost, stolen, or damaged. Also, "spurious" additions and deletions logically relate to clothing because "dollars" would not be spuriously added to a dry-cleaner's inventory. Thus, the language of the claim itself suggests the conclusion that the dry-cleaner's "inventory" includes clothing.

The patent specification confirms this. The specification is pervasive in using the term "inventory" to consist of "articles of clothing." Rather than set forth each instance, we refer the reader to a few examples:

This invention relates to inventory control devices capable of monitoring and reporting upon the status, location and throughput of inventory in an establishment. [Col. 1, lines 12–17.]

The best inventory control and management reporting information systems has [sic] the ability to determine and report the current location of any given article in inventory. [Col. 5, lines 14–17.]

Every transaction is recorded, including identification of the articles placed in inventory. [Col. 5, lines 8–10.]

[I]ncoming articles to be placed in inventory are accumulated over a counter.... [Col. 6, lines 7–8.]

[A]rticles to be cleaned are associated with a unique bar code indicia for later automatic or semiautomatic optical scanning and data input, whereby the progress of articles through the laundry and drycleaning systems can be completely monitored. [Col. 2, lines 53–57.]

The prosecution history is also in accord. During prosecution of the original patent application in this case, Markman amended claim 1 in order to overcome an obviousness rejection by adding limitations reciting among other things "whereby said system can detect and localize spurious additions to inventory as well as spurious deletions therefrom." Markman argued in his remarks to the examiner that unlike the usual system in which apparatus generates non-unique indicia (e.g., Stewart's price indicia) and/or indicia that is [sic] not produced concurrently with the commencement of a transaction (e.g., pre-printed tags), applicant's system is operable to keep a running reconcilable inventory total by adding input articles and subtracting output articles, and also protects against the possibility of undocumented or spuriously-documented articles entering the system.

Markman also referred the examiner to "features present" in claim 1, explaining:

Means are also provided for reconciling the very same unique and concurrently-generated indicia at later points during processing whereby the entry or exit of inventory articles in irregular ways can be localized.

It is evident from Markman's explanation of the claims to the examiner that he used "inventory" in the patent and the examiner understood "inventory" to consist of "articles of clothing." The prosecution history thus confirms the meaning of "inventory" as including "articles of clothing."

Markman argues that the extrinsic evidence of record provides substantial evidence in support of the jury's and his claim construction. Markman testified as an inventor of the patent in suit and as one of ordinary skill in the art (or, perhaps more accurately, one of "extraordinary" skill in the art) that "inventory" did not need to include articles of clothing. Markman's "patent expert" testified likewise, when giving his opinion on the proper construction of the claims. Finally, Markman argues that the testimony of Westview's president and some of its sales literature also support such claim construction. We do not find Markman's arguments persuasive.

First, the testimony of Markman and his patent attorney on the proper construction of the claims is entitled to no deference. For example, they both testified as to how the patent should be construed based on the text of the patent. This testimony about construction, however, amounts to no more than legal opinion-it is precisely the process of construction that the court must undertake. Thus, as to these types of opinions, the court has complete discretion to adopt the expert legal opinion as its own, to find guidance from it, or to ignore it entirely, or even to exclude it.

Second, the extrinsic evidence of record cannot be relied on to change the meaning of the claims. In this case, as fully discussed above, the patent and prosecution history make clear that "inventory" in claim 1 includes in its meaning "articles of clothing."

Notes

1. **Supreme Court Review.** The Supreme Court later affirmed the Federal Circuit's e*n banc* opinion in *Markman.* The Supreme Court opinion appears in Chapter 18. In its affirming opinion, the Supreme Court stated:

> We have also spoken of the line as one between issues of fact and law. [citations deleted] But the sounder course, when available, is to classify a mongrel practice (like construing a term of art following receipt of evidence) by using the historical method, much as we do in characterizing the suits and the actions within which they arise.

* * *

> We said in *Miller v. Fenton,* 474 U.S. 104, 114 (1985), that when an issue "falls somewhere between a pristine legal standard and a simple historical fact, the fact/law distinction at times has turned on a determination that, as a matter of the sound administration of justice, one judicial actor is better positioned than another to decide the issue in question." So it turns out here, for judges, not juries, are the better suited to find the acquired meaning of terms.

* * *

> We accordingly think there is sufficient reason to treat construction of terms of art like many other responsibilities we cede to a judge in the normal course of trial, notwithstanding its evidentiary underpinnings.

517 U.S. 370, 378, 389–90 (1996). Apparently the Supreme Court did not adopt the Federal Circuit's reasoning that claim interpretation is a question of law, calling it instead a "mongrel" mixture of law and fact. Instead the Supreme Court made a practical determination that judges will handle claim construction better than juries. What are the implications of the Supreme Court's language?

2. **Practical Implications: Statistical Inquiry.** In *Markman,* the Federal Circuit set out to improve patent law administration by removing uncertainties (chiefly, jury results) from trials. The chief benefit was the prospect of trial courts supplying a claim interpretation early in the process before expensive trials. With a claim interpretation in hand, parties could calculate the economic factors and reach early settlements. To achieve these benefits, the Federal Circuit worked the magic by declaring claim interpretation a question of law exclusively for the judge. A trial was not necessary to get an early claim interpretation. An early claim interpretation, in turn,

promised to clarify the parties' legal positions and promote early settlements. Making claim interpretation a pure question of law, however, had a side effect that threatened many of *Markman's* benefits. As a question of law, the Federal Circuit reviewed claim interpretation without deference. If the Federal Circuit overturns a high percentage of district court claim interpretations, then parties will discount the trial court's interpretation pending the final word from the appellate court. The trial court's interpretation would provide little early certainty, but only open the bidding. Indeed trial strategies themselves might concentrate on ways to set up an effective appeal. In any event, to get a certain claim interpretation, parties may have to go beyond the trial court's *Markman* hearing, beyond the entirety of discovery, beyond the entire trial on the merits, beyond post-trial motions, beyond appellate briefing and argument-indeed beyond almost every step in federal litigation.

These prospects led to considerable statistical debate over the Federal Circuit's rate of reversing trial courts. Two studies in 2001 fueled the debate. *See* Christian Chu, *Empirical Analysis of the Federal Circuit's Claim Construction Trends*, 16 BERK TECH. L. J. 1075 (2001)(giving a reversal rate of 44%); Kimberly Moore, *Are District Court Judges Equipped to Resolve Patent Cases?*, 15 HARV. J.L. TECH. 1 (2001) (giving a reversal rate of 33%). The discrepancy between the Moore and Chu findings derives from two factors. The two studies cover slightly different time frames. More important, Moore includes within her population of cases the non-controversial matters resolved by Rule 36 summary affirmance at the Federal Circuit. When Chu factored into his statistical base the summary affirmances, he found a reversal rate of 36.6%.

Another interesting subject for empirical study might be the rise in the number of summary judgment dispositions in patent cases. If indeed, as most patent lawyers would affirm, the number of summary judgment dispositions has risen markedly after *Markman*, then the decision is producing more certainty at an early stage, even with the uncertainties on appeal in close cases. Has *Markman* shifted the locus of most patent decisions to the very end of the federal judicial process, at which point, of course, every outcome is certain anyway? What about the savings and benefits of early settlements or early disposition via summary judgment? How can the Federal Circuit address these practical considerations?

3. Terminology. Even though courts and commentators commonly refer to "patent infringement," infringement analyses are actually based upon a particular claim of a patent. A claim is also said to "read on" an accused product or process in the event of literal infringement occurs. *Baxter Health-care Cory. v. Spectramed, Inc.,* 49F.3d1575–, 34 U. & P.Q.2d 1120 (Fed.Cir. 1995).

4. Additions & Omissions. To literally infringe, an accused product or process must include each and every limitation of a claim. Therefore, the *omission* of any limitation is fatal to literal infringement. As noted in *Lantech, Inc. v. Keip Machine Co.*, 32 F.3d 542, 31 U.S.P.Q.2d 1666 (Fed.Cir. 1994), "[f]or literal infringement, each limitation of the claim must be met by the accused device exactly, any deviation from the claim precluding a finding of infringement." The *addition* of elements beyond those recited in a claim, however, has different implications. Additions beyond the claimed elements have different effects on literal infringement depending on the particular transition phrase in the claim. Transition phrases receive attention in Chapter 11.

5. The Patentee's Commercial Embodiment. Section 271 (a) states clearly that the infringement inquiry compares the accused product or process to the "patented invention," or in other words, to the claims. Thus, the patentee's commercial products are not relevant to the infringement inquiry. The Federal Circuit has made this point clear: "As we have repeatedly said, it is error for a court to compare in its infringement analysis the accused product or process with the patentee's commercial embodiment or other version of the product or process; the only proper comparison is with the claims of the patent." *Zenith Labs. v. Bristol–Myers Squibb Co.,* 19 F.3d 1418, 30 U.S.P.Q.2d 1285 (Fed.Cir.1994).

6. Extrinsic Evidence and Claim Interpretation. In the late 1990's, the United States patent bar demonstrated a keen awareness of the following statement from *Vitronics Corp. v. Conceptronic, Inc.,* 90 F.3d 1576, 39 U.S.P.Q.2d 1573 (Fed.Cir.1996):

> Extrinsic evidence is that evidence which is external to the patent and file history, such as expert testimony, dictionaries, and technical treatises and articles. [Although technical treatises and dictionaries fall within the category of extrinsic evidence, as they do not form a part of an integrated patent document, they are worthy of special note. Judges are free to consult such resources at any time in order to better understand the underlying technology and may also rely on dictionary definitions when construing claim terms, so long as the dictionary definition does not contradict any definition found in or ascertained by a reading of the patent documents.]

> However, as we have recently re-emphasized, extrinsic evidence in general, and expert testimony in particular, may be used only to help the court come to the proper understanding of the claims; it may not be used to vary or contradict the claim language. Nor may it contradict the import of other parts of the specification. Indeed, where the patent documents are unambiguous, expert testimony regarding the meaning of a claim is entitled to no weight. "Any other rule would be unfair to competitors who must be able to rely on the patent documents themselves, without consideration of expert opinion that then does not even exist, in ascertaining the scope of a patentee's right to exclude." Nor may the inventor's subjective intent as to claim scope, when unexpressed in the patent documents, have any effect. Such testimony cannot guide the court to a proper interpretation when the patent documents themselves do so clearly.

90 F.3d at 1584–85, 39 U.S.P.Q.2d at 1578–79. This passage caused concern amongst trial judges and in the patent bar because it appeared to discredit experts as a source of technical information essential to understanding and interpreting the claims. In *Pitney Bowes, Inc. v. Hewlett–Packard Co.,* 182 F.3d 1298, 51 U.S.P.Q.2d 1161 (Fed.Cir.1999), the Federal Circuit elaborated on *Vitronics*:

> In *Vitronics Corp. v. Conceptronic, Inc.,* . . . , we explained that "[e]x-trinsic evidence is that evidence which is external to the patent and file

history, such as expert testimony, inventor testimony, dictionaries, and technical treatises and articles." Despite the district court's statements to the contrary, *Vitronics* does not prohibit courts from examining extrinsic evidence, even when the patent document is itself clear.... Moreover, *Vitronics* does not set forth any rules regarding the admissibility of expert testimony into evidence. Certainly, there are no prohibitions in *Vitronics* on courts hearing evidence from experts. Rather, *Vitronics* merely warned courts not to *rely* on extrinsic evidence in claim construction to contradict the meaning of claims discernible from thoughtful examination of the claims, the written description, and the prosecution history—the intrinsic evidence. *See id.,* 90 F.3d at 1583; *see also Bell & Howell Document Management Prods. Co. v. Altek Sys.,* 132 F.3d 701, 706 (Fed.Cir.1997) ("Use of expert testimony to explain an invention may be useful. But *reliance* on extrinsic evidence to interpret claims is proper only when the claim language remains genuinely ambiguous after consideration of the intrinsic evidence....").

182 F.3d at 1308. An unusual two-judge concurrence in the *Pitney Bowes* cases gave additional reasons to credit reliable expert testimony in the court's claim construction process:

> *Vitronics* offers good counsel when it urges trial judges to focus on the patent document—notably the claims themselves—to ascertain the scope of patent coverage. This appellate court, however, should refrain from dictating a claim interpretation process that excludes reliable expert testimony. The process of claim construction at the trial court level will often benefit from expert testimony which may (1) supply a proper technological context to understand the claims (words often have meaning only in context), (2) explain the meaning of claim terms as understood by one of skill in the art (the ultimate standard for claim meaning, see *Markman v. Westview Instruments Inc.,* 52 F.3d 967, 986 (1996)), and (3) help the trial court understand the patent process itself (complex prosecution histories—not to mention specifications—are not familiar to most trial courts).

182 F.3d at 1314. Underlying the surface of these commentaries is a concern over "battles of the experts." Those "battles" indeed can mislead and confuse juries. Are the considerations in favor of protecting the trial process against "hired guns" as prominent when district judges construe claims on their own?

7. Claim Interpretation after *Markman*. With the jury no longer part of the claim construction process, judges sought clarification on the legal standards for construing claims. After years of experience, claim construction still resembles statutory construction. In both cases, a variety of factors often influence the process. No single method or theory of construction seems to capture all the nuances of the complex enterprise. The following cases merely exemplify the vast jurisprudence of claim construction.

CCS FITNESS, INC. v. BRUNSWICK CORP.

United States Court of Appeals, Federal Circuit, 2002
288 F.3d 1359, 62 U.S.P.Q.2d 1658.

Before MAYER, CHIEF JUDGE, MICHEL and LOURIE, CIRCUIT JUDGES.

MICHEL, CIRCUIT JUDGE.

* * *

I

This case involves a stationary exercise device more commonly known as an elliptical trainer. As shown by the preferred embodiment pictured in CCS Fitness' patents, elliptical trainers comprise a vertical frame attached to a base structure at a right angle, with the base structure resting on the floor. A user approaches this machine from the rear, where he mounts two footpads, each of which lies at the end of a "foot member," a structure that extends and attaches to the vertical frame.

The foot members also intersect with "reciprocating members" (432, below), longitudinal structures that run "substantially parallel" to the floor, with one end of that structure attached to a shaft and crank system located at the vertical-frame end of the machine. The other end of a "member" has "rollers" or wheels attached to it so that the members can "reciprocate" or move back and forth on the floor as the user pushes up and down (or "climbs") on the machine's footpads. As the user does so, the front end of the member rotates around the crankshaft, thereby causing the reciprocating member to rotate in a circular motion before gradually changing into a linear motion. The elliptical trainer generally allows a user to engage in high-intensity cardiovascular exercise without putting undue stress on the user's knees.

FIG.5

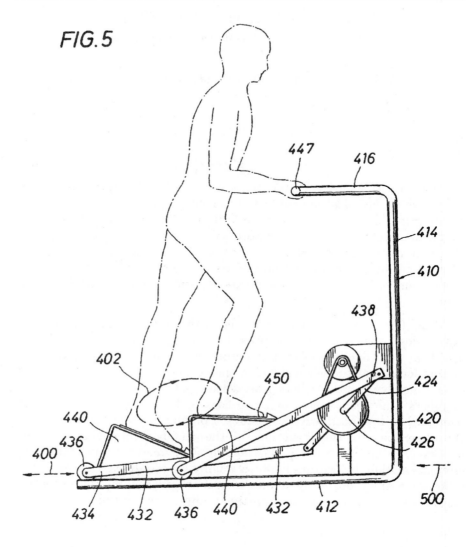

CCS Fitness owns by assignment the three combination patents that claim this stationary exercise device: U.S. Patent Nos. 5,924,962 ('962 patent); 5,938,567 ('567 patent); and 5,683,333 ('333 patent). Claim 9 from the '962 patent and claim 1 of the '567 patent are representative:

> 9. An apparatus for exercising comprising: a frame having a base portion adapted to be supported by a floor; first and second *reciprocating members,* each reciprocating member having a first and a second end, a portion of said first and second reciprocating members being adapted for substantially linear motion; . . . .

> 1. An apparatus for exercising comprising: a frame having a base portion adapted to be supported by a floor; first and second *reciprocating members,* each reciprocating member having a rear support and a front end; . . . .

U.S. Patent No. 5,924,962, col. 8, lines 17–24, 42–49; U.S. Patent No. 5,938,567, col. 6, lines 56–62, col. 7, lines 29–32 (emphases added). Besides the description set forth above, nothing in the claim language of the three patents describes the shape of the reciprocating members or whether it consists of a single-component structure only, as opposed to a structure consisting of multiple components.

In addition, nothing in the respective patents' abstract, summary of invention or detailed description sets forth the shape or makeup of these structures. The drawings for the patents' preferred embodiments depict the reciprocating members as a single-component, straight-bar structure. The prosecution history, meanwhile, discusses only the "angle" taken by a "foot platform relative to a reciprocating member" and the members' wheels and attachment to the crankshaft.

In April 1998, CCS Fitness sued Brunswick Corporation and its division Life Fitness (collectively referred to as "Life Fitness"), alleging that two of Life Fitness' elliptical exercisers literally infringed claims 9, 10 and 12 of the '962 patent, claims 1—5 of the '567 patent and further infringed, under the doctrine of equivalents, claims 1—6 of the '333 patent. The parties do not dispute that, in lieu of "reciprocating members," Life Fitness' accused machines use "pedal levers," structures that curve upward as they approach the frame end of the machine. The "pedal levers" also use multiple components to attach to and rotate around a crankshaft, not a single component.

Both parties moved for summary judgment, with CCS Fitness arguing that the reciprocating members contained in each of the claims at issue comprised more than simply a single-component, straight bar— they also included the curved, multi-component structure used in the accused devices. The parties agreed that "reciprocating" referred to the "back and forth" movement of the "member"; but the district court disagreed with CCS Fitness' proposed construction of "member," reasoning that the claim language never alluded to the reciprocating members as having multiple parts. Further, said the district court, the "illustrations in the three patents-in-suit show a reciprocating member ... made of one contiguous piece of hard material, with no connections or joints."

As to the shape of the reciprocating members, the court noted that nothing in the claims, specifications or prosecution history indicates what shape these structures had to take; but again, it reasoned that the "figures [of the claimed invention] illustrate a straight bar." Citing *Bocciarelli v. Huffman*, 43 C.C.P.A. 873, 232 F.2d 647, 652 (1956), the district court maintained that if CCS Fitness wanted to claim a device whose reciprocating member included a curved, multi-component structure, its patents should have included an illustration that showed these embodiments. To shore up this analysis, the district court then substituted the language "single straight bars that move back and forth" in lieu of the claims' use of "reciprocating members," concluding that its interpretation was "logical" when read in that light. Accordingly, because the accused devices used a curved reciprocating member that consisted of multiple components, the district court concluded that it did not literally infringe CCS Fitness' '962 or '567 patents as a matter of law, thereby entitling Life Fitness to summary judgment.

* * *

CCS Fitness appeals, arguing again that the ordinary meaning of the term "reciprocating member"—whether defined by an ordinary or a technical dictionary—covers a curved structure consisting of one or more components. In support of this argument, CCS Fitness directs our attention to what it calls the "Alternative A" and "Alternative B" set of components used by the accused devices. Life Fitness counters that (among other things) the specification and the drawings can limit the scope of the claimed reciprocating members, since "member" is a vague term whose scope requires clarification from the specification and drawings. To support this argument, Life Fitness points to an affidavit from an expert who avers that "member" has no customary meaning to one of ordinary skill, thereby necessitating resort to the specification. The record, however, also contains an affidavit from the inventor who asserts that "member" has a broad, ordinary meaning in the relevant art.

II

* * *

Generally speaking, we indulge a "heavy presumption" that a claim term carries its ordinary and customary meaning. *Johnson Worldwide*, 175 F.3d at 989; *accord Gart*, 254 F.3d at 1341; Kegel, 127 F.3d at 1427. "[I]f an apparatus claim recites a general structure without limiting that structure to a specific subset of structures, we will generally construe the term to cover all known types of that structure" that the patent disclosure supports. *Renishaw*, 158 F.3d at 1250. Sensibly enough, our precedents show that dictionary definitions may establish a claim term's ordinary meaning. *Rexnord Corp. v. Laitram Corp.*, 274 F.3d 1336, 1344 (Fed.Cir.2001) (using Random House Unabridged Dictionary to define the ordinary meaning of "portion" as encompassing both a one-piece and a two-piece structure); *Renishaw*, 158 F.3d at 1250 (noting that the meaning of a claim term may come from a "relevant dictionary" so long as the definition does not fly "in the face of the patent disclosure"); *Kegel*, 127 F.3d at 1427 (using Webster's Third New International Dictionary to define the claim term "assembly"); *Vitronics Corp. v. Conceptronic, Inc.*, 90 F.3d 1576, 1584 n. 6, (Fed.Cir.1996).

An accused infringer may overcome this "heavy presumption" and narrow a claim term's ordinary meaning, but he cannot do so simply by pointing to the preferred embodiment or other structures or steps disclosed in the specification or prosecution history. *Johnson Worldwide*, 175 F.3d at 989–90, 992; *Burke*, 183 F.3d at 1340. Indeed, contrary to the district court's analysis here, our case law makes clear that a patentee need not "describe in the specification every conceivable and possible future embodiment of his invention." *Rexnord*, 274 F.3d at 1344 (citations omitted).

Rather, as shown by our precedents, a court may constrict the ordinary meaning of a claim term in at least one of four ways. First, the claim term will not receive its ordinary meaning if the patentee acted as his own lexicographer and clearly set forth a definition of the disputed claim term in either the specification or prosecution history. *E.g., Johnson Worldwide*, 175 F.3d at 990; *Rexnord*, 274 F.3d at 1342. Second, a claim term will not carry its ordinary meaning if the intrinsic evidence shows that the patentee distinguished that term from prior art on the basis of a particular embodiment, expressly disclaimed subject matter, or described a particular embodiment as important to the invention. *E.g., Spectrum Int'l*, 164 F.3d at 1378 (narrowing a claim term's ordinary meaning based on statements in intrinsic evidence that distinguished claimed invention from prior art); *SciMed Life Sys., Inc. v. Adv. Cardiovascular Sys., Inc.*, 242 F.3d 1337, 1343–44 (Fed.Cir.2001) (limiting claim term based in part on statements in the specification indicating that "all embodiments" of the claimed invention used a particular structure); *Toro Co. v. White Consol. Indus., Inc.*, 199 F.3d 1295, 1301 (Fed.Cir.1999) (limiting claim term based in part on statements in the specification describing a particular structure as "important to the invention").

Third, and most relevant to this case, a claim term also will not have its ordinary meaning if the term "chosen by the patentee so deprive[s] the claim of clarity" as to require resort to the other intrinsic evidence for a definite meaning. *E.g., Johnson Worldwide*, 175 F.3d at 990; *Gart*, 254 F.3d at 1341. Last, as a matter of statutory authority, a claim term will cover nothing more than the corresponding structure or step disclosed in the specification, as well as equivalents thereto, if the patentee phrased the claim in step-or means-plus-function format. 35 U.S.C. § 112 ¶ 6; *Watts v. XL Sys., Inc.*, 232 F.3d 877, 880–81 (Fed.Cir.2000) (construing § 112 ¶ 6).

1

Applying these principles, we hold that the claim term "reciprocating member," as used in the asserted patents, encompasses the multi-component, curved structure used by the accused exercise machines. The parties agreed before the district court that "reciprocating" simply means to move back and forth, and we accept that definition on appeal. More important, "member," as defined by common and technical dictionaries, refers to a "structural unit such as a ... beam or tie, or a combination of these," *see* McGraw-Hill Dictionary of Scientific and Technical Terms 1237 (5th ed.1994), or to a "distinct part of a whole," *see* American Heritage Dictionary 849 (3d ed.1996). Based on these definitions, we agree with CCS Fitness that the term "member" denotes a beam-like structure that is "a single unit in a larger whole." It is not limited to a straight-bar structure comprising a single component only.

In addition, Life Fitness has not shown that anything in the specification or prosecution history overcomes the "heavy presumption" that "member" carries its ordinary meaning. The specification never requires a certain number of components or certain shape; nor does it limit the "member" in either regard. Contrary to the district court's analysis, moreover, the specifications did not need to include a drawing of a multi-component, curved member for the claimed invention to cover that particular embodiment. The drawings merely illustrated a particular embodiment of the claimed member and the specifications did not clearly assign a unique definition to "member," distinguish "member" based on the prior art, disclaim subject matter or describe a single-component, straight-bar "member" as important to the invention.

Nor does the prosecution history contain any clear statements that would narrow the ordinary meaning of the claimed "member." Indeed, Life Fitness itself characterizes the statements in the prosecution history as posing a mere "inconsistency" with the ordinary meaning of "member," not as assertions that, e.g., clearly disclaimed subject matter. In any event, having reviewed the statements identified by Life Fitness, we see nothing that bears on the shape or the number of components comprised by the term "member." We see only a terse mention of the "angle" that a "foot platform" takes "relative to a reciprocating member" and the members' wheels and attachment to the crankshaft.

Life Fitness also relies on expert testimony, but this testimony does not establish the assertion that "member" lacks clear meaning. First, we can resolve the ordinary meaning of the claimed "member" by resort to the intrinsic evidence and dictionary definitions only. Thus, we do not need to examine expert testimony. Even doing so, however, we do not view this expert testimony as particularly helpful, since the inventor himself, presumably also an artisan of ordinary skill in the art, offered testimony that essentially contradicts the expert's assertion that "member" lacks an ordinary meaning. In other words, the battle between Life Fitness' expert testimony and CCS Fitness' inventor testimony is inconclusive. Unsurprisingly, the district court's infringement analysis did not rely on the testimony of either the expert witness or the inventor in reaching its claims construction conclusions. Neither do we.

SciMed Life Systems does not compel a different conclusion. *See* 242 F.3d at 1342–44. In that case, we determined that the claim term "lumen," as used in three patents covering a type of catheter, meant a "coaxial lumen" only. The specification distinguished the claimed invention from the prior art based on that art's use of "dual lumens" and pointed out the advantages of coaxial lumens. It also described "the present invention" as using a coaxial lumen, and it stated that "all embodiments of the present invention" use coaxial lumens. We therefore determined that a catheter employing coaxial lumens was the invention. Id. at 1345, 242 F.3d 1337.

Here, on the other hand, nothing in the specifications distinguishes the claimed "member" from prior art based on its shape or number of components. And the specifications do not even imply that "all embodiments" of the claimed exercise machine must use a single-component, straight-bar member or else tout the advantages of using that particular structure. In short, Life Fitness cannot use the intrinsic evidence's silence to narrow the ordinary meaning of an unambiguous claim term. *See, e.g., Johnson Worldwide*, 175 F.3d at 992 ("[M]ere inferences drawn from the description of an embodiment of the invention cannot serve to limit claim terms."); *Kegel*, 127 F.3d at 1427 ("Without an express intent to impart a novel meaning to a claim term, the term takes on its ordinary meaning."); *see also Wang Labs.*, 197 F.3d at 1384 (limiting term "frame" to the character-based system in the specification when (among other things) the prosecution history distinguished the claimed invention from prior art based on that system).

In *Toro Company*, also relied on by Life Fitness, we limited a claim term—"said cover including means for increasing pressure"—to the structure shown in the patent's specifications and drawings. 199 F.3d at 1300–01. We did so because dictionary definitions of "cover" and "including" did not "shed dispositive light" on the scope of that claim limitation, *id.* at 1300, 199 F.3d 1295, and the specification described the particular structure at issue, a ring physically attached to the cover, as "important to the invention." *Id.* at 1301, 199 F.3d 1295. But this precedent does not rescue Life Fitness' argument, for unlike the intrinsic evidence in *Toro*, nothing in the intrinsic evidence here describes a single-component, straight-bar "member" as important to the invention. *See id.; see also Watts*, 232 F.3d at 882–83 (limiting claim term "sealingly connected" to the "misaligned taper angles" disclosed in the specification when the claim term was "not clear on its face" and the prosecution history showed that the patentee had distinguished the claimed invention from prior art based on the "misaligned taper angles"); *Ethicon Endo–Surgery, Inc. v. U.S. Surgical Corp.*, 93 F.3d 1572, 1579, 1581 (Fed.Cir.1996) (limiting term "pusher assembly" to the structures stated in the claims themselves and shown in the drawings when the claim term itself did not define the makeup of the "assembly" and the specification provided only "minimal guidance" about the term's scope).

CATALINA MARKETING INT'L, INC.
v. COOLSAVINGS.COM, INC.

United States Court of Appeals, Federal Circuit.
289 F.3d 801, 62 U.S.P.Q.2d 1781.

This case appears in Chapter 11 to illustrate the interpretation of a claim's preamble.

INTERACTIVE GIFT EXP. INC.
v. COMPUSERVE, INC.

United States Court of Appeals, Federal Circuit, 2001.
256 F.3d 1323, 59 U.S.P.Q.2d 1401.

Before SCHALL, CIRCUIT JUDGE, PLAGER, SENIOR CIRCUIT JUDGE, and LINN, CIRCUIT JUDGE.

LINN, CIRCUIT JUDGE.

Interactive Gift Express, Inc. ("IGE"), now known as E–Data, Corp., seeks review of a judgment of noninfringement of U.S. Patent No. 4,528,643 ("Freeny patent") entered by the United States District Court for the Southern District of New York on March 12, 1999. Because the district court erred as a matter of law in the construction of each of the five claim terms giving rise to IGE's noninfringement stipulation, we vacate and remand.

BACKGROUND

A. The Freeny Patent

The Freeny patent is directed to a system for reproducing information in material objects at point of sale locations. Prior to the invention disclosed in the Freeny patent, information disseminated to consumers in material objects, such as tape recordings, books, and records, was recorded onto the material objects at a central manufacturing facility, and the material objects were then shipped to remote retail locations for sale. These systems required centralized manufacturing facilities for reproducing the information in the material objects and extended distribution networks for distributing the material objects, once made, to various point of sale locations for sale to consumers. The manufacturing facilities and distribution networks represented substantial costs ultimately borne by consumers.

In such prior art systems, manufacturers had to estimate consumer demand for each new information-specific product and had to manufacture and ship quantities of material objects sufficient to meet the estimated demand at each retail location. Retailers had to make similar estimates to determine how many material objects for each information-specific product to order and keep in inventory. A low estimate of consumer demand resulted in unsatisfied customers and lost sales. On the other hand, high estimates left some material objects unsold, resulting in unrecouped costs.

To overcome these and other related problems, the Freeny patent provides a system for the distributed manufacture and sale of material objects at multiple locations directly serving consumers. The system includes a central control station, referred to in the Freeny patent as an "information control machine" or "ICM," and a plurality of remotely located manufacturing stations referred to as "information manufacturing machines" or "IMMs." At each IMM, a consumer selects the desired information and initiates a communication from the IMM to the ICM to gain authorization for copying of the selected information onto a desired type of material object. The consumer then waits for the IMM to receive the authorization, after which the selected information is copied by the IMM onto a blank material object. The invention can be used with a wide variety of information and material objects, such as music on cassettes and text on paper. Irrespective of the type of information and material object, the invention requires the purchase of the material object by the consumer, and the material object must contain information that was copied onto it at the point of sale location.

Claim 1 of the Freeny patent is representative of the method claims at issue and defines the invention as follows:

1. A method for reproducing information in material objects utilizing information manufacturing machines located at point of sale locations, comprising the steps of:

> providing from a source remotely located with respect to the information manufacturing machine the information to be reproduced to the information manufacturing machine, each information being uniquely identified by a catalog code;

> providing a request reproduction code including a catalog code uniquely identifying the information to be reproduced to the information manufacturing machine requesting to reproduce certain information identified by the catalog code in a material object;

> providing an authorization code at the information manufacturing machine authorizing the reproduction of the information identified by the catalog code included in the request reproduction code; and

> receiving the request reproduction code and the authorization code at the information manufacturing machine and reproducing in a material object the information identified by the catalog code included in the request reproduction code in response to the authorization code authorizing such reproduction.

Freeny patent, col. 28, ll. 22–47.

B.　The Accused Activities

The defendants are computer software and publishing companies and one retail bookstore. Plaintiff contends that the computer software and publishing companies infringe the Freeny patent by selling software or documents "online," that is, over the Internet and the World Wide Web. Plaintiff maintains that the retail bookstore infringes the Freeny patent by selling books that include a CD–ROM containing encrypted computer applications, access to which is not possible until the consumer retrieves a password. Plaintiff, through the construction it proffered in its Revised Claim Construction Report of November 12, 1996, has effectively conceded that none of the defendants are direct infringers.

With the one exception of the retail bookstore defendant, all of the accused systems distribute information directly to consumers' personal computers without using an intermediate retail location, the consumer instead dealing directly with a web-site over the Internet. Information is distributed and downloaded onto a consumer's own internal hard disk or other storage device without the purchase of any material object such as a floppy disk or CD–ROM. In the case of the CD–ROMs sold to consumers by the retail bookstore defendant, if a consumer is interested in one or more of the encrypted programs contained on the CD–ROM, a password must first be requested. The password enables the consumer to decrypt the desired program and copy it for later use. As with the other accused systems, the CD–ROM product avoids the need for a consumer to purchase a material object, such as a floppy disk or a CD–ROM, because the decrypted data is copied directly onto the consumer's own storage device.

C. Proceedings Below

The district court limited discovery to claim construction matters and ordered IGE to file a binding claim construction report. There are five disputed claim limitations. IGE's binding report dealt with four of them: "point of sale location" (referred to in the report as "point of sale"); "material object"; "information manufacturing machine"; and "authorization code." The fifth is termed the "real-time transactions" limitation, arising out of an alleged requirement that certain steps of claim 1 be performed in order, and requiring that the information be provided to and stored at the IMM before the consumer requests it.

DISCUSSION

In construing claims, the analytical focus must begin and remain centered on the language of the claims themselves, for it is that language that the patentee chose to use to "particularly point[ ] out and distinctly claim[ ] the subject matter which the patentee regards as his invention." 35 U.S.C. § 112, ¶ 2.

"It is well-settled that, in interpreting an asserted claim, the court should look first to the intrinsic evidence of record, i.e., the patent itself, including the claims, the specification and, if in evidence, the prosecution history. Such intrinsic evidence is the most significant source of the legally operative meaning of disputed claim language." *Vitronics Corp. v. Conceptronic, Inc.*, 90 F.3d 1576, 1582 (Fed.Cir.1996). All intrinsic evidence is not equal however. *See id. Pitney Bowes, Inc. v. Hewlett–Packard Co.*, 182 F.3d 1298, 1305 (Fed.Cir.1999) ("The starting point for any claim construction must be the claims themselves"). Then we look to the rest of the intrinsic evidence, beginning with the specification and concluding with the prosecution history, if in evidence. *See Vitronics*, 90 F.3d at 1582, (delineating this order).

If the claim language is clear on its face, then our consideration of the rest of the intrinsic evidence is restricted to determining if a deviation from the clear language of the claims is specified. A deviation may be necessary if "a patentee [has chosen] to be his own lexicographer and use terms in a manner other than their ordinary meaning." *Vitronics*, 90 F.3d at 1582. A deviation may also be necessary if a patentee has "relinquished [a] potential claim construction in an amendment to the claim or in an argument to overcome or distinguish a reference." *Elkay Mfg. Co. v. Ebco Mfg. Co.*, 192 F.3d 973, 979 (Fed.Cir.1999). If however the claim language is not clear on its face, then our consideration of the rest of the intrinsic evidence is directed to resolving, if possible, the lack of clarity.

Resort to the specification is particularly important in this case because IGE has conceded that the claim limitations in dispute include technical terms that are defined in the specification. However, in looking to the specification to construe claim terms, care must be taken to avoid reading "limitations appearing in the specification . . . into [the] claims." *Intervet Am., Inc. v. Kee–Vet Lab., Inc.*, 887 F.2d 1050, 1053 (Fed.Cir. 1989). "We recognize that there is sometimes a fine line between reading a claim in light of the specification, and reading a limitation into the claim from the specification." *Comark Communications, Inc. v. Harris Corp.*, 156 F.3d 1182, 1186 (Fed.Cir.1998). In locating this "fine line" it is useful to remember that we look "to the specification to ascertain the meaning of the claim term as it is used by the inventor in the context of the entirety of his invention," and not merely to limit a claim term. *Id.* at 1187.

If the meaning of the claim limitations is apparent from the totality of the intrinsic evidence, then the claim has been construed. If however a claim limitation is still not clear, we may look to extrinsic evidence to help resolve the lack of clarity. Relying on extrinsic evidence to construe a claim is "proper only when the claim language remains genuinely ambiguous after consideration of the intrinsic evidence." *Bell & Howell Document Mgmt. Prods. Co. v. Altek Sys.*, 132 F.3d 701, 706 (Fed.Cir. 1997). "Such instances will rarely, if ever, occur." *Vitronics*, 90 F.3d at 1585.

Extrinsic evidence may always be consulted, however, to assist in understanding the underlying technology. See *Pitney Bowes*, 182 F.3d at 1312. But extrinsic evidence may never be used "for the purpose of varying or contradicting the terms in the claims." *Markman*, 52 F.3d at 981.

Throughout the construction process, it is important to bear in mind that the viewing glass through which the claims are construed is that of a person skilled in the art. *See Intellicall, Inc. v. Phonometrics, Inc.*, 952 F.2d 1384, 1387 (Fed.Cir.1992).

Additionally, a party's claim construction position on appeal may be subject to waiver or judicial estoppel.

Although the district court provided a thorough and accurate description of the patent and of the relevant law, its claim construction impermissibly read limitations from the specification into each of the five disputed claim limitations. We treat each of these disputed claim limitations below, and then address the issues of waiver and judicial estoppel.

I. Point of Sale Location

The district court made several findings with regard to the construction of the expression "point of sale location." We address these findings below, agreeing with some and disagreeing with others.

In response to the district court's request for binding definitions of the disputed terms, described earlier, IGE identified the passage at column 5, lines 47–50 as defining a point of sale location. That passage states that a point of sale location is "a location where a consumer goes to purchase material objects embodying predetermined or preselected information." Freeny patent, col. 5, ll. 47–50. The district court held this definition to be correct, and we agree. Clear support is provided for this definition in the Freeny patent specification at column 5, lines 47–50.

The district court further held that, although point of sale locations are not restricted to retail locations, a home is not a point of sale location. IGE contends that the district court was wrong. IGE urges that a point of sale location is simply the location at which the consumer makes or effects a purchase. IGE argues that the concept of a home being a point of sale location is not new, citing home shopping networks, pay-per-view cable television, and home Internet shopping. IGE further argues that the specification defines a home as a point of sale location and discloses at least two embodiments in which the home is a point of sale location. The appellees respond that IGE's asserted definition before the district court precludes a home from being a point of sale location, and that any references in the specification to homes as point of sale locations cannot overcome this definition.

We agree with IGE's position that a home is not precluded from being a point of sale location. Looking first, as we must, to the claim language itself, we find nothing precluding a home from being a point of sale location. Except for requiring that an IMM be present, the independent claims are silent regarding the possible venues of a point of sale location.

Looking next to the specification, we acknowledge the great likelihood that a point of sale location will not be a home, given that: (1) IGE's asserted definition, with which we agree, requires that a consumer go to a point of sale location "to purchase material objects," Freeny patent, col. 5, ll. 48–49; and (2) the specification requires, and IGE does not dispute, that the IMM be located at the point of sale location, *see, e.g.,* Freeny patent, col. 5, ll. 32–33, col. 12, ll. 66–67. However, IGE's asserted definition, premised on the specification at column 5, lines 48 and 49, does not preclude a home from serving as a point of sale location, and the specification further describes a vending machine embodiment that could be utilized in a home. *See* Freeny patent, cols. 26–27. This intrinsic evidence unambiguously allows a home to serve as a point of sale location. Therefore, it is unnecessary to address IGE's arguments alleging that the prosecution history additionally supports our conclusion.

Given the lack of ambiguity in the intrinsic evidence, it would be improper to address any of the parties' arguments relating to extrinsic evidence, such as other examples of point of sale locations and standard references.

The district court also held that a point of sale location must have blank material objects "available for sale to consumers." IGE argues that this limitation is not recited in the claim or required by the specification and has improperly been read into the claim from a particular embodiment. Notably, the appellees do not argue in defense of this limitation. We agree with IGE that a point of sale location need not have any blank material objects separately for sale.

Looking again to the claims, nothing in the claim language itself requires that blanks be for sale. The claims require only that information be reproduced in a material object. *See, e.g.*, Freeny patent, col. 28, ll. 22–23 (preamble to claim 1) and 44–45 (step four of claim 1); *id.* at col. 36, ll. 45–46 (preamble to claim 37) and ll. 62–63 (single element of claim 37). Looking next to the specification, we note that nothing in IGE's asserted definition, derived from the Freeny patent at column 5, lines 47–50, requires that blanks be for sale. That definition refers exclusively to the purchase of non-blank material objects, that is, to "material objects embodying . . . information."

The district court based its conclusion that blanks must be for sale on the passage at column 13, lines 25–44. However, that passage does not state that the blanks are sold to the customers as blanks, but only that the retailer is reimbursed for the cost of blanks on which information is reproduced. *See* Freeny patent, col. 13, ll. 25–44. The district court, therefore, misconstrued the specific embodiment in that passage. Further, there is no support in the rest of the specification for this requirement; all of the embodiments are directed at providing material objects with information on them and not at selling blank material objects. *See, e.g., id.* at col. 13, ll. 1–13 (reproducing information on an 8 track or cassette tape); *id.* at col. 22, l. 62—col. 23, l. 6 (describing various material objects in which information can be reproduced); *id.* at cols. 26–27 (describing the reproduction of information in the vending machine embodiment). Indeed, the opening sentence of the background section of the Freeny patent states that "[t]he present invention relates generally to a system for reproducing information in a material object." Freeny patent, col. 1, ll. 7–8 (emphasis added).

Accordingly, we construe a point of sale location to be a location where a consumer goes to purchase material objects embodying predetermined or preselected information. This construction permits a home to be a point of sale location. A point of sale location need not have more than one blank material object and it need not have any material objects separately for sale as blanks.

* * * * *

[At this point, Judge Linn's analysis construed the other disputed claim terms with extensive reference to the patent specification.]

WAIVER

The doctrine of waiver is limited in its application. As it relates to claim construction, the doctrine has been applied to preclude a party from adopting a new claim construction position on appeal. *See Sage*, 126 F.3d at 1426 (effectively applying waiver by precluding Sage's claim construction of "elongated slot" and "container body" because, differing from the claim construction urged at trial, they were not preserved for appeal). In each of the above-cited cases, the claim construction proffered on appeal was considered to be "new" because it changed the scope of the claim construction. The doctrine has not been invoked, however, to prevent a party from clarifying or defending the original scope of its claim construction, or from supporting its existing claim construction position with new citations to the specification.

This distinction does not compromise the basic requirement, embodied in the doctrine of waiver, that the parties develop their positions at trial. That basic requirement is reflected in *Finnigan Corp. v. International Trade Commission*, 180 F.3d 1354 (Fed.Cir.1999), where this court stated that "a party's argument should not be a moving target." *Id.* at 1363, 51 USPQ2d at 1007. This court explained that statement as follows:

> The argument at the trial and appellate level should be consistent, thereby ensuring a clear presentation of the issue to be resolved, an adequate opportunity for response and evidentiary development by the opposing party, and a record reviewable by the appellate court that is properly crystallized around and responsive to the asserted argument.

Id. at 1363 (citing *Sage*).

The concerns expressed above in *Finnigan* and *Sage* would certainly preclude a party from changing its claim construction, that is, the scope of its claim construction, on appeal. However, those concerns would not necessarily preclude a party from proffering additional or new supporting arguments, based on evidence of record, for its claim construction.

Applying the doctrine of waiver to the present case, IGE is precluded from proffering a claim construction on appeal that changes the scope of any of the claim construction positions that it advanced in its binding report. IGE is not barred, however, from proffering additional arguments from the specification in support of its existing claim construction.

We hold that the district court erred in at least one aspect of its construction of each of the five claim limitations upon which the judgment of noninfringement was based. Accordingly, we vacate and remand for further proceedings consistent with the claim construction provided in this opinion.

Notes

1. **The Role of the Specification in Claim Construction.** In *Markman*, the Federal Circuit reiterated the standard doctrine that "[c]laims must be read in view of the specification, of which they are part." *Markman* also repeated the standard caution that "[t]he written description part of the specification does not delimit the right to exclude. That is the purpose and function of the claims." Stated in more conventional terms, this last caution translates to a prohibition against importing limitations from the specification into the claims. The distinction between "reading claim terms in light of the specification" and the prohibited practice of "importing limitations from the specification into the claims," *see, SRI Intern'l v.*

Matsushita Elec. Corp., 775 F.2d 1107 (Fed.Cir.1985), is not easy to draw. Can you articulate a neutral standard for distinguishing the permitted from the prohibited uses of the specification?

2. The Meaning of "A." In a Federal Circuit case featuring a meningitis vaccine, the inventor discovered that linking a protein along the polysaccharide chain of the vaccine enhances the immune response. The claim specified linking a protein to "*a terminal portion* of the polysaccharide." The accused vaccine linked a protein to both terminal ends of the polysaccharide, not just to one terminal end. The Federal Circuit determined that the accused vaccine did not infringe because the linkage was limited to a terminal portion:

> While it is generally accepted in patent parlance that "a" can mean one or more, *see*, ROBERT C. FABER, LANDIS ON MECHANICS OF PATENT CLAIM DRAFTING 531 (3d ed. 1990) ("In a claim, the indefinite article A or AN connotes 'one or more'.") there is no indication in the specification that the inventors here intended it to have other than its normal singular meaning.

North American Vaccine v. American Cyanamid Co., 7 F.3d 1571, 1575–76, 28 U.S.P.Q.2d 1333, 1336 (Fed.Cir.1993). This single sentence is astounding in its inconsistency. It acknowledges the general rule that "a" means "one or more," but then abandons the rule because the specification did not contain anything against a singular reading. The rule was already against a singular reading. If the court majority is correct that "a" or "an" in claim drafting parlance means "one or more," then would an inventor need to include anything in a specification to invoke this normal patent usage? The basic rule, of course, is that inventors need only address the meaning of terms in their specification if they vary from the accepted meaning of those terms. *See, e.g., Intellicall Inc. v. Phonometrics, Inc.*, 952 F.2d 1384, 1388, 21 U.S.P.Q.2d 1383 (Fed.Cir.1992). The court majority seemed to rely on the absence of any specification language varying from the normal patent usage of the word "a." This reliance on what the specification did not say to vary from a normal construction rule may be a high point for the role of the specification in claim construction. By the way, even if the accused vaccine did attach a protein at both terminal ends or multiple terminal ends, why doesn't the claim language still read on the accused composition?

In any event the Federal Circuit now says that "a" means "one or more." By the year 2000 the Federal Circuit had become accustomed to interpreting "a." In *KCJ Corp. v. Kinetic Concepts, Inc.*, 223 F.3d 1351, 55 U.S.P.Q.2d 1835 the Federal Circuit said: "This court has encountered "a" or "an" in patent claims on several occasions. This court has uniformly applied the general rule for indefinite articles.... Moreover, standing alone, a disclosure of a preferred or exemplary embodiment encompassing a singular element does not disclaim a plural embodiment. [A]lthough the specifications may well indicate that certain embodiments are preferred, particular embodiments appearing in a specification will not be read into the claims when the claim language is broader than such embodiments." *Electro Med. Sys., S.A. v. Cooper Life Sciences, Inc.*, 34 F.3d 1048, 1054, 32 U.S.P.Q.2d 1017, 1021 (Fed.Cir.1994). Thus, as the rule dictates, when the claim language or context calls for further inquiry, this court consults the written description for a clear intent to limit the invention to a singular embodiment. Does this formulation state a neutral principal for specification use?

3. Another Claim Interpretation Rule (Perhaps Not a Tool). In the *North American Vaccine* case above, 7 F.3d at 1577, the Federal Circuit also relied on the doctrine of claim differentiation, a claim interpretation aid for patents having multiple claims of different scope. This rule builds on the familiar axiom that each claim defines a separate invention. Therefore, according to the claim differentiation rule, the terms of a broad claim must be kept distinct from narrower claims. *See, e.g., SRI International v. Matsushita Elec. Corp.,* 775 F.2d 1107, 227 U.S.P.Q. 577 (Fed.Cir.1985); *D.M.I., Inc. v. Deere & Co.,* 755 F.2d 1570, 225 U.S.P.Q. 236 (Fed.Cir.1985). Thus, where claims use different words, the claim differentiation doctrine assumes that those different words describe a separate invention. For a moment, test this assumption against your experience with patents. Do claim drafters actually use different language to describe different inventions or do they use different claim forms and terms to describe the exact same invention? If each patent is supposed to cover only a single invention, do multiple claims in the same patent cover different inventions? Indeed the Federal Circuit has acknowledged that two claims that read differently can cover the same subject matter. *Tandon Corp. v. United States ITC,* 831 F.2d 1017, 4 U.S.P.Q.2d 1283 (Fed.Cir.1987). On this point, Judge Archer stated:

> The doctrine of claim differentiation ... although well-established in our cases, cannot overshadow the express and contrary intentions of the patent draftsman. It is not unusual that separate claims may define the invention using different terminology, especially where (as here) independent claims are involved.

Hormone Research Foundation v. Genentech, Inc., 904 F.2d 1558, 1567 n. 15, 15 U.S.P.Q.2d 1039 (Fed.Cir.1990). Where does this discussion leave claim differentiation? Perhaps it is safe to say that no neutral standard delineates when the doctrine should operate and when it should not. A more cynical observation might suggest that claim differentiation is rarely, if ever, the essential element of a claim interpretation. Instead, the doctrine is usually "thrown in" when it supports an advocate's or the court's preferred claim interpretation and ignored when it does not. Stated more kindly, "[c]laim differentiation is a guide, not a rigid rule." *Laitram Corp. v. Rexnord, Inc.,* 939 F.2d 1533, 1538, 19 U.S.P.Q.2d 1367 (Fed.Cir.1991) (quoting *Autogiro Co. of Am. v. U.S.,* 384 F.2d 391, 404 (Ct.Cl.1967)). Thus the safer course may be to avoid reliance on the claim differentiation doctrine alone.

§ 15.2 THE DOCTRINE OF EQUIVALENTS OR NON–TEXTUAL INFRINGEMENT

In a statement of law that holds up remarkably well in the United States, the House of Lords provided in *C. Van der Lely N.V. v. Bamfords Ltd.,* [1963] RPC 61 (H.L. 1962) that:

> Copying an invention by taking its "pith and marrow" without textual infringement of the patent is an old and familiar abuse which the law has never been powerless to prevent. It may be that

in doing so there is some illogicality, but our law has always preferred good sense to strict logic. The illogicality arises in this way. On the one hand the patentee is tied strictly to the invention which he claims and the mode of effecting an improvement which he says is his invention. Logically it would seem to follow that if another person is ingenious enough to effect that improvement by a slightly different method he will not infringe. But it has long been recognised that there "may be an essence or substance of the invention underlying the mere accident of form; and that invention, like every other invention, may be pirated by a theft in a disguised or mutilated form, and it will be in every case a question of fact whether the alleged piracy is the same in substance and effect, or is a substantially new or different combination." (Per James, L.J., in *Clark v. Adie* (1873) L.R. 10 Ch. 667.)

Every modern non-textual infringement case traces its roots to the following United States Supreme Court decision. A case over fifty years old would hardly seem to warrant consideration in light of the Supreme Court's more recent pronouncements in 1997 and 2002. Nonetheless, the Supreme Court itself invoked its fifty-year-old case as a foundation for its newer explanations. As the Federal Circuit explains in *Johnson & Johnston*, another case in this section, this case features a unique fact situation. Specifically, one of the Jones patent's claims literally described the accused product. That claim, however, had been invalidated for describing one or two inoperative embodiments (a now-antiquated doctrine). Despite the unique facts, the language of this opinion reappears repeatedly even five decades later.

GRAVER TANK v. LINDE AIR PRODUCTS CO.

United States Supreme Court, 1950.
339 U.S. 605, 85 U.S.P.Q. 328.

MR. JUSTICE JACKSON delivered the opinion of the Court.

* * *

In determining whether an accused device or composition infringes a valid patent, resort must be had in the first instance to the words of the claim. If accused matter falls clearly within the claim, infringement is made out and that is the end of it.

But courts have also recognized that to permit imitation of a patented invention which does not copy every literal detail would be to convert the protection of the patent grant into a hollow and useless thing. Such a limitation would leave room for—indeed encourage—the unscrupulous copyist to make unimportant and insubstantial changes and substitutions in the patent which, though adding nothing, would be enough to take the copied matter outside the claim, and hence outside the reach of law. One who seeks to pirate an invention, like one who seeks to pirate a copyrighted book or play, may be expected to introduce minor variations to conceal and shelter the piracy. Outright and forthright duplication is a dull and very rare type of infringement. To prohibit no other would place the inventor at the mercy of verbalism and would be subordinating substance to form. It would deprive him of the benefit of his invention and would foster concealment rather than disclosure of inventions, which is one of the primary purposes of the patent system.

The doctrine of equivalents evolved in response to this experience. The essence of the doctrine is that one may not practice a fraud on a patent. Originating almost a century ago in the case of *Winans v. Denmead*, 15 How. 330, 14 L.Ed. 717, it has been consistently applied by this Court and the lower federal courts, and continues today ready and available for utilization when the proper circumstances for its application arise. "To temper unsparing logic and prevent an infringer from stealing the benefit of the invention" a patentee may invoke this doctrine to proceed against the producer of a device "if it performs substantially the same function in substantially the same way to obtain the same result." *Sanitary Refrigerator Co. v. Winters*, 280 U.S. 30, 42, 50 S.Ct. 9, 13, 74 L.Ed. 147. The theory on which it is founded is that "if two devices do the same work in substantially the same way, and accomplish substantially the same result, they are the same, even though they differ in name, form or shape." *Union Paper–Bag Machine Co. v. Murphy*, 97 U.S. 120, 125, 24 L.Ed. 935. The doctrine operates not only in favor of the patentee of a pioneer or primary invention, but also for the patentee of a secondary invention consisting of a combination of old ingredients which produce new and useful results, *Imhaeuser v. Buerk*, 101 U.S. 647, 655, 25 L.Ed. 945, although the area of equivalence may vary under the circumstances. The wholesome realism of this doctrine is not always applied in favor of a patentee but is sometimes used against him. Thus, where a device is so far changed in principle from a patented article that it performs the same or a similar function in a substantially different way, but nevertheless falls within the literal words of the claim, the doctrine of equivalents may be used to restrict the claim and defeat the patentee's action for infringement. *Westinghouse v. Boyden Power–Brake Co.*, 170 U.S. 537, 568, 18 S.Ct. 707, 722, 42 L.Ed. 1136. In its early development, the doctrine was usually applied in cases involving devices where there was equivalence in mechanical components. Subsequently, however, the same principles were also applied to compositions, where there was equivalence between chemical ingredients. Today the doctrine is applied to mechanical or chemical equivalents in compositions or devices. See discussions and cases collected in 3 WALKER ON PATENTS (Deller's ed. 1937) §§ 489–492; ELLIS, PATENT CLAIMS (1949) §§ 59–60.

What constitutes equivalency must be determined against the context of the patent, the prior art, and the particular circumstances of the case. Equivalence, in the patent law, is not the prisoner of a formula and is not an absolute to be considered in a vacuum. It does not require complete identity for every purpose and in every respect. In determining equivalents, things equal to the same thing may not be equal to each other and, by the same token, things for most purposes different may sometimes be equivalents. Consideration must be given to the purpose for which an ingredient is used in a patent, the qualities it has when combined with the other ingredients, and the function which it is intended to perform. An important factor is whether persons reasonably skilled in the art would have known of the interchangeability of an ingredient not contained in the patent with one that was.

A finding of equivalence is a determination of fact. Proof can be made in any form: through testimony of experts or others versed in the technology; by documents, including texts and treatises; and, of course, by the disclosures of the prior art. Like any other issue of fact, final determination requires a balancing of credibility, persuasiveness and weight of evidence. It is to be decided by the trial court and that court's decision, under general principles of appellate review, should not be disturbed unless clearly erroneous. Particularly is this so in a field where so much depends upon familiarity with specific scientific problems and principles not usually contained in the general storehouse of knowledge and experience.

In the case before us, we have two electric welding compositions or fluxes: the patented composition, Unionmelt Grade 20, and the accused composition, Lincolnweld 660. The patent under which Unionmelt is made claims essentially a combination of alkaline earth metal silicate and calcium fluoride; Unionmelt actually contains, however, silicates of calcium and magnesium, two alkaline earth metal silicates. Lincolnweld's composition is similar to Unionmelt's, except that it substitutes silicates of calcium and manganese—the latter not an alkaline earth metal—for silicates of calcium and magnesium. In all other respects, the two compositions are alike. The mechanical methods in which these compositions are employed are similar. They are identical in operation and produce the same kind and quality of weld.

The question which thus emerges is whether the substitution of the manganese which is not an alkaline earth metal for the magnesium which is, under the circumstances of this case, and in view of the technology and the prior art, is a change of such substance as to make the doctrine of equivalents inapplicable; or conversely, whether under the circumstances the change was so insubstantial that the trial court's invocation of the doctrine of equivalents was justified.

Without attempting to be all-inclusive, we note the following evidence in the record: Chemists familiar with the two fluxes testified that manganese and magnesium were similar in many of their reactions. There is testimony by a metallurgist that alkaline earth metals are often found in manganese ores in their natural state and that they serve the same purpose in the fluxes; and a chemist testified that "in the sense of the patent" manganese could be included as an alkaline earth metal. Much of this testimony was corroborated by reference to recognized texts on inorganic chemistry. Particularly important, in addition, were the disclosures of the prior art, also contained in the record. The Miller patent, No. 1,754,566, which preceded the patent in suit, taught the use of manganese silicate in welding fluxes. Manganese was similarly disclosed in the Armor patent, No. 1,467,825, which also described a welding composition. And the record contains no evidence of any kind to show that Lincolnweld was developed as the result of independent research or experiments.

* * *

The trial judge found on the evidence before him that the Lincolnweld flux and the composition of the patent in suit are substantially identical in operation and in result. He found also that Lincolnweld is in all respects equivalent to Unionmelt for welding purposes. And he concluded that "for all practical purposes, manganese silicate can be efficiently and effectively substituted for calcium and magnesium silicates as the major constituent of the welding composition." These conclusions are adequately supported by the record; certainly they are not clearly erroneous.

It is difficult to conceive of a case more appropriate for application of the doctrine of equivalents. The disclosures of the prior art made clear that manganese silicate was a useful ingredient in welding compositions. Specialists familiar with the problems of welding compositions understood that manganese was equivalent to and could be substituted for magnesium in the composition of the patented flux and their observations were confirmed by the literature of chemistry. Without some explanation or indication that Lincolnweld was developed by independent research, the trial court could properly infer that the accused flux is the result of imitation rather than experimentation or invention. Though infringement was not literal, the changes which avoid literal infringement are colorable only. We conclude that the trial court's judgment of infringement respecting the four flux claims was proper, and we adhere to our prior decision on this aspect of the case.

Affirmed.

MR. JUSTICE MINTON took no part in the consideration or decision of this case.

MR. JUSTICE BLACK, with whom MR. JUSTICE DOUGLAS concurs, dissenting.

I heartily agree with the Court that "fraud" is bad, "piracy" is evil, and "stealing" is reprehensible. But in this case, where petitioners are not charged with any such malevolence, these lofty principles do not justify the Court's sterilization of the Acts of Congress.

* * *

MR. JUSTICE DOUGLAS, dissenting.

* * *

[The dissents fail to discuss the implications of the fact that the claims in the patent covered the accused flux. In addition, while mentioning the possibility of reissue, there is no discussion of a comparison between a narrowing reissue and the use of the Doctrine of Equivalents.]

Notes

1. Criticizing *Graver Tank*. Is *Graver Tank* right as a matter of chemistry? One commentator notes that "[m]anganese and magnesium are both metals and start with an 'm' and have at least three syllables, but otherwise are so different structurally that they are in different categories on the periodic table of elements." Harold C. Wegner, *Equitable Equivalents: Weighing the Equities to Determine Patent Infringement in Biotechnology and Other Emerging Technologies*, 18 RUTGERS COMPUTER AND TECH. L.J. 1, 28–29 n.100 (1992).

2. Should the Doctrine of Equivalents Be Available as a Vehicle for Correcting Applicant Errors? In Martin J. Adelman & Gary L. Francione, *The Doctrine of Equivalents in Patent Law: Questions that Pennwalt Did Not Answer*, 137 U. PA. L. REV. 673 (1989) the authors argue that the most frequent use of the doctrine of equivalents in cases decided by the Federal Circuit is to correct errors made by applicants. Further, they argue that *Graver Tank* was unusual in that it was not a case where the use of the doctrine of equivalents was used to correct error. The PTO had passed on the patentability of the accused flux and the public had been notified that the accused flux was within the scope of the patent as issued by the PTO.

As an alternative to the fact pattern of *Graver Tank*, which is essentially unique to the case law, the doctrine of equivalents can be explored more effectively using the following more typical hypothetical cases:

> Hypothetical one assumes that the patent disclosed only the four alkaline earth metal silicates which, at the time of filing, were the only ones known to be effective. The PTO then issues the patent with only the alkaline earth silicates claims, drafted precisely in the same way as the claims held not valid by the Supreme Court. Later, someone discovers a flux made from manganese silicate functioned almost exactly as the one using magnesium silicate. Arguably, the discovery of the functioning of manganese silicate may even be patentable over the teachings of the patent-in-suit. Under the facts of this hypothetical, the patent specification would not support a claim that would literally cover a flux using manganese silicate. Hence the failure to obtain such a claim could not be because of a mistake. While cases of this type where a court applied the doctrine of equivalents are not common, a modern example is *Atlas Powder Co. v. E.I. du Pont De Nemours & Co.*, 750 F.2d 1569, 224 U.S.P.Q. 409 (Fed.Cir.1984).

> Hypothetical two assumes that once one skilled in the art proved the efficacy of magnesium silicate, he would know that manganese silicate would be effective as well. The patent specification would therefore support a claim that incorporated manganese silicate, whether or not the chemical was specifically mentioned as a substitute for magnesium silicate. Under such circumstances, the failure to claim manganese silicate could well be a mistake. A claim that did incorporate manganese silicate, however, would be broader than one limited to alkaline earth silicates. This form of the hypothetical covers a large number of cases applying the doctrine of equivalents.

3 MARTIN J. ADELMAN, PATENT LAW PERSPECTIVES, § 3.4[1] at n.66 (2d ed. 1989).

The Federal Circuit had occasion to muse on this theme in *Sage Products, Inc. v. Devon Industries, Inc.*, 126 F.3d 1420, 44 U.S.P.Q.2d 1103 (Fed.Cir.1997). There, the patentee Sage accused a competitor of infringing a narrowly drafted claim with a number of structural limitations. Writing for the court, Judge Rader rejected the attempt to apply the doctrine of equivalents to correct a claiming error:

> The claim at issue defines a relatively simple structural device. A skilled patent drafter would foresee the limiting potential of [a narrowly drawn structural] limitation. No subtlety of language or complexity of the technology, nor any subsequent change in the state of the art, such as later-developed technology, obfuscated the significance of this limitation at the time of its incorporation into the claim. If Sage desired broad patent protection . . . , it could have sought claims with fewer structural encumbrances. . . . However, as between the patentee who had a clear opportunity to negotiate broader claims but did not do so, and the public at large, it is the patentee who must bear the cost of its failure to seek protection for this foreseeable alteration of its claimed structure.

> This court recognizes that such reasoning places a premium on forethought in patent drafting. Indeed this premium may lead to higher costs of patent prosecution. However, the alternative rule—allowing broad play for the doctrine of equivalents to encompass foreseeable variations, not just of a claim element, but of a patent claim—also leads to higher costs. Society at large would bear these latter costs in the form of virtual foreclosure of competitive activity within the penumbra of each issued patent claim.

126 F.3d at 1425, 44 U.S.P.Q.2d at 1107–08.

3. Further Reading. Paul M. Janicke, *Heat of Passion: What Really Happened in* Graver Tank, 24 AM. INTELL. PROP. L. ASS'N Q.J. 1 (1996), presents a detailed historical account of the circumstances leading to the Supreme Court's opinion in *Graver Tank*.

WARNER–JENKINSON COMPANY v. HILTON DAVIS CHEMICAL CO.

United States Supreme Court, 1997.
520 U.S. 17, 41 U.S.P.Q.2d 1865.

THOMAS, J., delivered the opinion for unanimous Court. GINSBURG, J., filed a concurring opinion, in which KENNEDY, J., joined.

JUSTICE THOMAS delivered the opinion of the Court.

Nearly 50 years ago, this Court in *Graver Tank & Mfg. Co. v. Linde Air Products Co.*, 339 U.S. 605 (1950), set out the modern contours of what is known in patent law as the "doctrine of equivalents." Under this doctrine, a product or process that does not literally infringe upon the express terms of a patent claim may nonetheless be found to infringe if there is "equivalence" between the elements of the accused product or process and the claimed elements of the patented invention. Id., at 609. Petitioner, which was found to have infringed upon respondent's patent under the doctrine of equivalents, invites us to speak the death of that doctrine. We decline that invitation. The significant disagreement within the Court of Appeals for the Federal Circuit concerning the application of Graver Tank suggests, however, that the doctrine is not free from confusion. We therefore will endeavor to clarify the proper scope of the doctrine.

I

The essential facts of this case are few. Petitioner Warner–Jenkinson Co. and respondent Hilton Davis Chemical Co. manufacture dyes. Impurities in those dyes must be removed. Hilton Davis holds United States Patent No. 4,560,746 ('746 patent), which discloses an improved purification process involving "ultrafiltration." The '746 process filters impure dye through a porous membrane at certain pressures and pH levels, resulting in a high purity dye product.

The '746 patent issued in 1985. As relevant to this case, the patent claims as its invention an improvement in the ultrafiltration process as follows:

> "In a process for the purification of a dye ... the improvement which comprises: subjecting an aqueous solution ... to ultrafiltration through a membrane having a nominal pore diameter of 5–15 Angstroms under a hydrostatic pressure of approximately 200 to 400 p.s.i.g., at a pH from approximately 6.0 to 9.0, to thereby cause separation of said impurities from said dye...."

The inventors added the phrase "at a pH from approximately 6.0 to 9.0" during patent prosecution. At a minimum, this phrase was added to distinguish a previous patent (the "Booth" patent) that disclosed an ultrafiltration process operating at a pH above 9.0. The parties disagree as to why the low-end pH limit of 6.0 was included as part of the claim.[1]

In 1986, Warner–Jenkinson developed an ultrafiltration process that operated with membrane pore diameters assumed to be 5–15 Angstroms, at pressures of 200 to nearly 500 p.s.i.g., and at a pH of 5.0. Warner–Jenkinson did not learn of the '746 patent until after it had begun commercial use of its ultrafiltration process. Hilton Davis eventually learned of Warner–Jenkinson's use of ultrafiltration and, in 1991, sued Warner–Jenkinson for patent infringement.

As trial approached, Hilton Davis conceded that there was no literal infringement, and relied solely on the doctrine of equivalents. Over Warner–Jenkinson's objection that the doctrine of equivalents was an equitable doctrine to be applied by the court, the issue of equivalence was included among those sent to the jury. The jury found that the '746 patent was not invalid and that Warner–Jenkinson infringed upon the patent under the doctrine of equivalents. The jury also found, however,

---

1. Petitioner contends that the lower limit was added because below a pH of 6.0 the patented process created "foaming" problems in the plant and because the process was not shown to work below that pH level. Brief for Petitioner 4, n. 5, 37, n. 28. Respondent counters that the process was successfully tested to pH levels as low as 2.2 with no effect on the process because of foaming, but offers no particular explanation as to why the lower level of 6.0 pH was selected. Brief for Respondent 34, n. 34.

that Warner–Jenkinson had not intentionally infringed, and therefore awarded only 20% of the damages sought by Hilton Davis. The District Court denied Warner–Jenkinson's post-trial motions, and entered a permanent injunction prohibiting Warner–Jenkinson from practicing ultrafiltration below 500 p.s.i.g. and below 9.01 pH. A fractured *en banc* Court of Appeals for the Federal Circuit affirmed. 62 F. 3d 1512 (C.A.Fed.1995).

The majority below held that the doctrine of equivalents continues to exist and that its touchstone is whether substantial differences exist between the accused process and the patented process. The court also held that the question of equivalence is for the jury to decide and that the jury in this case had substantial evidence from which it could conclude that the Warner–Jenkinson process was not substantially different from the ultrafiltration process disclosed in the '746 patent.

There were three separate dissents, commanding a total of 5 of 12 judges. Four of the five dissenting judges viewed the doctrine of equivalents as allowing an improper expansion of claim scope, contrary to this Court's numerous holdings that it is the claim that defines the invention and gives notice to the public of the limits of the patent monopoly. The fifth dissenter, the late Judge Nies, was able to reconcile the prohibition against enlarging the scope of claims and the doctrine of equivalents by applying the doctrine to each element of a claim, rather than to the accused product or process "overall." As she explained it, "[t]he 'scope' is not enlarged if courts do not go beyond the substitution of equivalent elements." All of the dissenters, however, would have found that a much narrowed doctrine of equivalents may be applied in whole or in part by the court.

We granted certiorari and now reverse and remand.

II

In Graver Tank we considered the application of the doctrine of equivalents to an accused chemical composition for use in welding that differed from the patented welding material by the substitution of one chemical element. The substituted element did not fall within the literal terms of the patent claim, but the Court nonetheless found that the "question which thus emerges is whether the substitution [of one element for the other] . . . is a change of such substance as to make the doctrine of equivalents inapplicable; or conversely, whether under the circumstances the change was so insubstantial that the trial court's invocation of the doctrine of equivalents was justified." The Court also described some of the considerations that go into applying the doctrine of equivalents:

> "What constitutes equivalency must be determined against the context of the patent, the prior art, and the particular circumstances of the case. Equivalence, in the patent law, is not the prisoner of a formula and is not an absolute to be considered in a vacuum. It does not require complete identity for every purpose and in every respect.

In determining equivalents, things equal to the same thing may not be equal to each other and, by the same token, things for most purposes different may sometimes be equivalents. Consideration must be given to the purpose for which an ingredient is used in a patent, the qualities it has when combined with the other ingredients, and the function which it is intended to perform. An important factor is whether persons reasonably skilled in the art would have known of the interchangeability of an ingredient not contained in the patent with one that was."

Considering those factors, the Court viewed the difference between the chemical element claimed in the patent and the substitute element to be "colorable only," and concluded that the trial court's judgment of infringement under the doctrine of equivalents was proper.

A

Petitioner's primary argument in this Court is that the doctrine of equivalents, as set out in Graver Tank in 1950, did not survive the 1952 revision of the Patent Act, 35 U.S.C. § 100 et seq., because it is inconsistent with several aspects of that Act. In particular, petitioner argues: (1) the doctrine of equivalents is inconsistent with the statutory requirement that a patentee specifically "claim" the invention covered by a patent, 35 U.S.C. § 112; (2) the doctrine circumvents the patent reissue process-designed to correct mistakes in drafting or the like-and avoids the express limitations on that process, 35 U.S.C. §§ 251–252; (3) the doctrine is inconsistent with the primacy of the Patent and Trademark Office (PTO) in setting the scope of a patent through the patent prosecution process; and (4) the doctrine was implicitly rejected as a general matter by Congress' specific and limited inclusion of the doctrine in one section regarding "means" claiming, 35 U.S.C. § 112, ¶ 6. All but one of these arguments were made in Graver Tank in the context of the 1870 Patent Act, and failed to command a majority.

The 1952 Patent Act is not materially different from the 1870 Act with regard to claiming, reissue, and the role of the PTO. *Compare, e.g.,* 35 U.S.C. § 112 ("The specification shall conclude with one or more claims particularly pointing out and distinctly claiming the subject matter which the applicant regards as his invention") *with* The Consolidated Patent Act of 1870, ch. 230, § 26, 16 Stat. 198, 201 (the applicant "shall particularly point out and distinctly claim the part, improvement, or combination which he claims as his invention or discovery"). Such minor differences as exist between those provisions in the 1870 and the 1952 Acts have no bearing on the result reached in Graver Tank, and thus provide no basis for our overruling it. In the context of infringement, we have already held that pre–1952 precedent survived the passage of the 1952 Act. *See Aro Mfg. Co. v. Convertible Top Replacement Co.,* 365 U.S. 336, 342 (1961) (new section defining infringement "left intact the entire body of case law on direct infringement"). We see no reason to reach a different result here.[2]

Petitioner's fourth argument for an implied congressional negation of the doctrine of equivalents turns on the reference to "equivalents" in the "means" claiming provision of the 1952 Act. Section 112, ¶ 6, a provision not contained in the 1870 Act, states:

> "An element in a claim for a combination may be expressed as a means or step for performing a specified function without the recital of structure, material, or acts in support thereof, and such claim shall be construed to cover the corresponding structure, material, or acts described in the specification and equivalents thereof."

Thus, under this new provision, an applicant can describe an element of his invention by the result accomplished or the function served, rather than describing the item or element to be used (e.g., "a means of connecting Part A to Part B," rather than "a two-penny nail"). Congress enacted § 112, ¶ 6 in response to *Halliburton Oil Well Cementing Co. v. Walker*, which rejected claims that "do not describe the invention but use 'conveniently functional language at the exact point of novelty,'" 329 U.S. 1, 8 (1946) (citation omitted). *See In re Donaldson Co.*, 16 F. 3d 1189, 1194 (C.A.Fed.1994) (Congress enacted predecessor of § 112, ¶ 6 in response to *Halliburton*). Section 112, ¶ 6 now expressly allows so-called "means" claims, with the proviso that application of the broad literal language of such claims must be limited to only those means that are "equivalent" to the actual means shown in the patent specification. This is an application of the doctrine of equivalents in a restrictive role, narrowing the application of broad literal claim elements. We recognized this type of role for the doctrine of equivalents in *Graver Tank* itself. The added provision, however, is silent on the doctrine of equivalents as applied where there is no literal infringement.

Because § 112, ¶ 6 was enacted as a targeted cure to a specific problem, and because the reference in that provision to "equivalents" appears to be no more than a prophylactic against potential side effects of that cure, such limited congressional action should not be overread for negative implications. Congress in 1952 could easily have responded to *Graver Tank* as it did to the *Halliburton* decision. But it did not. Absent something more compelling than the dubious negative inference offered by petitioner, the lengthy history of the doctrine of equivalents strongly supports adherence to our refusal in *Graver Tank* to find that the Patent Act conflicts with that doctrine. Congress can legislate the doctrine of equivalents out of existence any time it chooses. The various policy

---

2. Petitioner argues that the evolution in patent practice from "central" claiming (describing the core principles of the invention) to "peripheral" claiming (describing the outer boundaries of the invention) requires that we treat Graver Tank as an aberration and abandon the doctrine of equivalents. Brief for Petitioner 43–45. We disagree. The suggested change in claiming practice predates *Graver Tank*, is not of statutory origin, and seems merely to reflect narrower inventions in more crowded arts. Also, judicial recognition of so-called "pioneer" patents suggests that the abandonment of "central" claiming may be overstated. That a claim describing a limited improvement in a crowded field will have a limited range of permissible equivalents does not negate the availability of the doctrine vel non.

arguments now made by both sides are thus best addressed to Congress, not this Court.

B

We do, however, share the concern of the dissenters below that the doctrine of equivalents, as it has come to be applied since *Graver Tank*, has taken on a life of its own, unbounded by the patent claims. There can be no denying that the doctrine of equivalents, when applied broadly, conflicts with the definitional and public-notice functions of the statutory claiming requirement. Judge Nies identified one means of avoiding this conflict:

> "[A] distinction can be drawn that is not too esoteric between substitution of an equivalent for a component in an invention and enlarging the metes and bounds of the invention beyond what is claimed."
>
> . . .
>
> "Where a claim to an invention is expressed as a combination of elements, as here, 'equivalents' in the sobriquet 'Doctrine of Equivalents' refers to the equivalency of an element or part of the invention with one that is substituted in the accused product or process."
>
> . . .
>
> "This view that the accused device or process must be more than 'equivalent' overall reconciles the Supreme Court's position on infringement by equivalents with its concurrent statements that 'the courts have no right to enlarge a patent beyond the scope of its claims as allowed by the Patent Office.' [Citations omitted.] The 'scope' is not enlarged if courts do not go beyond the substitution of equivalent elements."

We concur with this apt reconciliation of our two lines of precedent. Each element contained in a patent claim is deemed material to defining the scope of the patented invention, and thus the doctrine of equivalents must be applied to individual elements of the claim, not to the invention as a whole. It is important to ensure that the application of the doctrine, even as to an individual element, is not allowed such broad play as to effectively eliminate that element in its entirety. So long as the doctrine of equivalents does not encroach beyond the limits just described, or beyond related limits to be discussed infra, we are confident that the doctrine will not vitiate the central functions of the patent claims themselves.

III

Understandably reluctant to assume this Court would overrule Graver Tank, petitioner has offered alternative arguments in favor of a more restricted doctrine of equivalents than it feels was applied in this case. We address each in turn.

A

Petitioner first argues that *Graver Tank* never purported to supersede a well-established limit on non-literal infringement, known variously as "prosecution history estoppel" and "file wrapper estoppel." According to petitioner, any surrender of subject matter during patent prosecution, regardless of the reason for such surrender, precludes recapturing any part of that subject matter, even if it is equivalent to the matter expressly claimed. Because, during patent prosecution, respondent limited the pH element of its claim to pH levels between 6.0 and 9.0, petitioner would have those limits form bright lines beyond which no equivalents may be claimed. Any inquiry into the reasons for a surrender, petitioner claims, would undermine the public's right to clear notice of the scope of the patent as embodied in the patent file.

We can readily agree with petitioner that *Graver Tank* did not dispose of prosecution history estoppel as a legal limitation on the doctrine of equivalents. But petitioner reaches too far in arguing that the reason for an amendment during patent prosecution is irrelevant to any subsequent estoppel. In each of our cases cited by petitioner and by the dissent below, prosecution history estoppel was tied to amendments made to avoid the prior art, or otherwise to address a specific concern-such as obviousness-that arguably would have rendered the claimed subject matter unpatentable. Thus, in *Exhibit Supply Co. v. Ace Patents Corp.*, Chief Justice Stone distinguished inclusion of a limiting phrase in an original patent claim from the "very different" situation in which "the applicant, in order to meet objections in the Patent Office, based on references to the prior art, adopted the phrase as a substitute for the broader one" previously used. 315 U.S. 126, 136 (1942). Similarly, in *Keystone Driller Co. v. Northwest Engineering Corp.*, 294 U.S. 42 (1935), estoppel was applied where the initial claims were "rejected on the prior art," and where the allegedly infringing equivalent element was outside of the revised claims and within the prior art that formed the basis for the rejection of the earlier claims.

It is telling that in each case this Court probed the reasoning behind the Patent Office's insistence upon a change in the claims. In each instance, a change was demanded because the claim as otherwise written was viewed as not describing a patentable invention at all-typically because what it described was encompassed within the prior art. But, as the United States informs us, there are a variety of other reasons why the PTO may request a change in claim language. And if the PTO has been requesting changes in claim language without the intent to limit equivalents or, indeed, with the expectation that language it required would in many cases allow for a range of equivalents, we should be extremely reluctant to upset the basic assumptions of the PTO without substantial reason for doing so. Our prior cases have consistently applied prosecution history estoppel only where claims have been amended for a limited set of reasons, and we see no substantial cause for requiring a more rigid rule invoking an estoppel regardless of the reasons for a change.[3]

In this case, the patent examiner objected to the patent claim due to a perceived overlap with the Booth patent, which revealed an ultrafiltration process operating at a pH above 9.0. In response to this objection, the phrase "at a pH from approximately 6.0 to 9.0" was added to the claim. While it is undisputed that the upper limit of 9.0 was added in order to distinguish the Booth patent, the reason for adding the lower limit of 6.0 is unclear. The lower limit certainly did not serve to distinguish the Booth patent, which said nothing about pH levels below 6.0. Thus, while a lower limit of 6.0, by its mere inclusion, became a material element of the claim, that did not necessarily preclude the application of the doctrine of equivalents as to that element. *See Hubbell v. United States*, 179 U.S. 77, 82 (1900) ("'[A]ll [specified elements] must be regarded as material,'" though it remains an open "question whether an omitted part is supplied by an equivalent device or instrumentality" (citation omitted)). Where the reason for the change was not related to avoiding the prior art, the change may introduce a new element, but it does not necessarily preclude infringement by equivalents of that element.[4]

We are left with the problem, however, of what to do in a case like the one at bar, where the record seems not to reveal the reason for including the lower pH limit of 6.0. In our view, holding that certain reasons for a claim amendment may avoid the application of prosecution history estoppel is not tantamount to holding that the absence of a reason for an amendment may similarly avoid such an estoppel. Mindful that claims do indeed serve both a definitional and a notice function, we think the better rule is to place the burden on the patent-holder to establish the reason for an amendment required during patent prosecution. The court then would decide whether that reason is sufficient to overcome prosecution history estoppel as a bar to application of the doctrine of equivalents to the element added by that amendment. Where no explanation is established, however, the court should presume that the PTO had a substantial reason related to patentability for including the limiting element added by amendment. In those circumstances, prosecution history estoppel would bar the application of the doctrine

3. That petitioner's rule might provide a brighter line for determining whether a patentee is estopped under certain circumstances is not a sufficient reason for adopting such a rule. This is especially true where, as here, the PTO may have relied upon a flexible rule of estoppel when deciding whether to ask for a change in the first place. To change so substantially the rules of the game now could very well subvert the various balances the PTO sought to strike when issuing the numerous patents which have not yet expired and which would be affected by our decision.

4. We do not suggest that, where a change is made to overcome an objection based on the prior art, a court is free to review the correctness of that objection when deciding whether to apply prosecution history estoppel. As petitioner rightly notes, such concerns are properly addressed on direct appeal from the denial of a patent, and will not be revisited in an infringement action. *Smith v. Magic City Kennel Club, Inc., supra*, at 789–790. What is permissible for a court to explore is the reason (right or wrong) for the objection and the manner in which the amendment addressed and avoided the objection.

equivalents as to that element. The presumption we have described, one subject to rebuttal if an appropriate reason for a required amendment is established, gives proper deference to the role of claims in defining an invention and providing public notice, and to the primacy of the PTO in ensuring that the claims allowed cover only subject matter that is properly patentable in a proffered patent application. Applied in this fashion, prosecution history estoppel places reasonable limits on the doctrine of equivalents, and further insulates the doctrine from any feared conflict with the Patent Act.

Because respondent has not proffered in this Court a reason for the addition of a lower pH limit, it is impossible to tell whether the reason for that addition could properly avoid an estoppel. Whether a reason in fact exists, but simply was not adequately developed, we cannot say. On remand, the Federal Circuit can consider whether reasons for that portion of the amendment were offered or not and whether further opportunity to establish such reasons would be proper.

B

Petitioner next argues that even if *Graver Tank* remains good law, the case held only that the absence of substantial differences was a necessary element for infringement under the doctrine of equivalents, not that it was sufficient for such a result. Relying on *Graver Tank*'s references to the problem of an "unscrupulous copyist" and "piracy," 339 U. S., at 607, petitioner would require judicial exploration of the equities of a case before allowing application of the doctrine of equivalents. To be sure, *Graver Tank* refers to the prevention of copying and piracy when describing the benefits of the doctrine of equivalents. That the doctrine produces such benefits, however, does not mean that its application is limited only to cases where those particular benefits are obtained.

Elsewhere in *Graver Tank* the doctrine is described in more neutral terms. And the history of the doctrine as relied upon by *Graver Tank* reflects a basis for the doctrine not so limited as petitioner would have it. In *Winans v. Denmead*, 15 How. 330, 343 (1854), we described the doctrine of equivalents as growing out of a legally implied term in each patent claim that "the claim extends to the thing patented, however its form or proportions may be varied." Under that view, application of the doctrine of equivalents involves determining whether a particular accused product or process infringes upon the patent claim, where the claim takes the form—half express, half implied—of "X and its equivalents."

Machine Co. v. Murphy, 97 U.S. 120, 125 (1878), on which *Graver Tank* also relied, offers a similarly intent-neutral view of the doctrine of equivalents:

"[T]he substantial equivalent of a thing, in the sense of the patent law, is the same as the thing itself; so that if two devices do the same work in substantially the same way, and accomplish substantially the same result, they are the same, even though they differ in name, form, or shape.''

If the essential predicate of the doctrine of equivalents is the notion of identity between a patented invention and its equivalent, there is no basis for treating an infringing equivalent any differently than a device that infringes the express terms of the patent. Application of the doctrine of equivalents, therefore, is akin to determining literal infringement, and neither requires proof of intent.

LOGIC

Petitioner also points to *Graver Tank*'s seeming reliance on the absence of independent experimentation by the alleged infringer as supporting an equitable defense to the doctrine of equivalents. The Federal Circuit explained this factor by suggesting that an alleged infringer's behavior, be it copying, designing around a patent, or independent experimentation, indirectly reflects the substantiality of the differences between the patented invention and the accused device or process. According to the Federal Circuit, a person aiming to copy or aiming to avoid a patent is imagined to be at least marginally skilled at copying or avoidance, and thus intentional copying raises an inference—rebuttable by proof of independent development—of having only insubstantial differences, and intentionally designing around a patent claim raises an inference of substantial differences. This explanation leaves much to be desired. At a minimum, one wonders how ever to distinguish between the intentional copyist making minor changes to lower the risk of legal action, and the incremental innovator designing around the claims, yet seeking to capture as much as is permissible of the patented advance.

Intent irrelevant

But another explanation is available that does not require a divergence from generally objective principles of patent infringement. In both instances in *Graver Tank* where we referred to independent research or experiments, we were discussing the known interchangeability between the chemical compound claimed in the patent and the compound substituted by the alleged infringer. The need for independent experimentation thus could reflect knowledge—or lack thereof—of interchangeability possessed by one presumably skilled in the art. The known interchangeability of substitutes for an element of a patent is one of the express objective factors noted by *Graver Tank* as bearing upon whether the accused device is substantially the same as the patented invention. Independent experimentation by the alleged infringer would not always reflect upon the objective question whether a person skilled in the art would have known of the interchangeability between two elements, but in many cases it would likely be probative of such knowledge.

DOE – no intent required

Although *Graver Tank* certainly leaves room for petitioner's suggested inclusion of intent-based elements in the doctrine of equivalents, we do not read it as requiring them. The better view, and the one consistent with *Graver Tank* 's predecessors and the objective approach to infringement, is that intent plays no role in the application of the doctrine of equivalents.

C

Finally, petitioner proposes that in order to minimize conflict with the notice function of patent claims, the doctrine of equivalents should be limited to equivalents that are disclosed within the patent itself. A milder version of this argument, which found favor with the dissenters below, is that the doctrine should be limited to equivalents that were known at the time the patent was issued, and should not extend to after-arising equivalents.

As we have noted, with regard to the objective nature of the doctrine, a skilled practitioner's knowledge of the interchangeability between claimed and accused elements is not relevant for its own sake, but rather for what it tells the fact-finder about the similarities or differences between those elements. Much as the perspective of the hypothetical "reasonable person" gives content to concepts such as "negligent" behavior, the perspective of a skilled practitioner provides content to, and limits on, the concept of "equivalence." Insofar as the question under the doctrine of equivalents is whether an accused element is equivalent to a claimed element, the proper time for evaluating equivalency-and thus knowledge of interchangeability between elements-is at the time of infringement, not at the time the patent was issued. And rejecting the milder version of petitioner's argument necessarily rejects the more severe proposition that equivalents must not only be known, but must also be actually disclosed in the patent in order for such equivalents to infringe upon the patent.

IV

The various opinions below, respondents, and amici devote considerable attention to whether application of the doctrine of equivalents is a task for the judge or for the jury. However, despite petitioner's argument below that the doctrine should be applied by the judge, in this Court petitioner makes only passing reference to this issue. *See* Brief for Petitioner 22, n. 15 ("If this Court were to hold in *Markman v. Westview Instruments, Inc.*, No. 95–26 (argued Jan. 8, 1996), that judges rather than juries are to construe patent claims, so as to provide a uniform definition of the scope of the legally protected monopoly, it would seem at cross-purposes to say that juries may nonetheless expand the claims by resort to a broad notion of 'equivalents' "); Reply Brief for Petitioner 20 (whether judge or jury should apply the doctrine of equivalents depends on how the Court views the nature of the inquiry under the doctrine of equivalents).

Petitioner's comments go more to the alleged inconsistency between the doctrine of equivalents and the claiming requirement than to the role of the jury in applying the doctrine as properly understood. Because resolution of whether, or how much of, the application of the doctrine of equivalents can be resolved by the court is not necessary for us to answer the question presented, we decline to take it up. The Federal Circuit held that it was for the jury to decide whether the accused process was equivalent to the claimed process. There was ample support in our prior cases for that holding. *See, e.g., Machine Co. v. Murphy*, 97 U. S., at 125 ("in determining the question of infringement, the court or jury, as the case may be, . . . are to look at the machines or their several devices or elements in the light of what they do, or what office or function they perform, and how they perform it, and to find that one thing is substantially the same as another, if it performs substantially the same function in substantially the same way to obtain the same result"); *Winans v. Denmead*, 15 How., at 344 ("[It] is a question for the jury" whether the accused device was "the same in kind, and effected by the employment of [the patentee's] mode of operation in substance"). Nothing in our recent *Markman* decision necessitates a different result than that reached by the Federal Circuit. Indeed, *Markman* cites with considerable favor, when discussing the role of judge and jury, the seminal *Winans* decision. *Markman v. Westview Instruments, Inc.*, 517 U.S. 370, 384–85 (1996). Whether, if the issue were squarely presented to us, we would reach a different conclusion than did the Federal Circuit is not a question we need decide today.

V

All that remains is to address the debate regarding the linguistic framework under which "equivalence" is determined. Both the parties and the Federal Circuit spend considerable time arguing whether the so-called "triple identity" test-focusing on the function served by a particular claim element, the way that element serves that function, and the result thus obtained by that element-is a suitable method for determining equivalence, or whether an "insubstantial differences" approach is better. There seems to be substantial agreement that, while the triple identity test may be suitable for analyzing mechanical devices, it often provides a poor framework for analyzing other products or processes. On the other hand, the insubstantial differences test offers little additional guidance as to what might render any given difference "insubstantial."

In our view, the particular linguistic framework used is less important than whether the test is probative of the essential inquiry: Does the

8. With regard to the concern over unreviewability due to black-box jury verdicts, we offer only guidance, not a specific mandate. Where the evidence is such that no reasonable jury could determine two elements to be equivalent, district courts are obliged to grant partial or complete summary judgment. *See* Fed. Rule Civ. Proc. 56; *Celotex Corp. v. Catrett*, 477 U.S. 317, 322–323 (1986). If there has been a reluctance to do so by some courts due to unfamiliarity with the subject matter, we are confident that the Federal Circuit can remedy the problem. Of course, the various legal limitations on the application of the doctrine of equivalents are to be determined by the court, either on a pretrial motion for partial summary judgment or on a motion for judgment as a matter of law at the close of the evidence and after the jury verdict. Fed. Rule Civ. Proc. 56; Fed. Rule Civ. Proc. 50. Thus, under the particular facts of a case, if prosecution history estoppel would apply or if a theory of equivalence would entirely vitiate a particular claim element, partial or complete judgment should be rendered by the court, as there would be no further material issue for the jury to resolve. Finally, in cases that reach the jury, a special verdict and/or interrogatories on each claim element could be very useful in facilitating review, uniformity, and possibly postverdict judgments as a matter of law. *See* Fed. Rule Civ. Proc. 49; Fed. Rule Civ. Proc. 50. We leave it to the Federal Circuit how best to implement procedural improvements to promote certainty, consistency, and reviewability to this area of the law.

accused product or process contain elements identical or equivalent to each claimed element of the patented invention? Different linguistic frameworks may be more suitable to different cases, depending on their particular facts. A focus on individual elements and a special vigilance against allowing the concept of equivalence to eliminate completely any such elements should reduce considerably the imprecision of whatever language is used. An analysis of the role played by each element in the context of the specific patent claim will thus inform the inquiry as to whether a substitute element matches the function, way, and result of the claimed element, or whether the substitute element plays a role substantially different from the claimed element. With these limiting principles as a backdrop, we see no purpose in going further and micromanaging the Federal Circuit's particular word-choice for analyzing equivalence. We expect that the Federal Circuit will refine the formulation of the test for equivalence in the orderly course of case-by-case determinations, and we leave such refinement to that court's sound judgment in this area of its special expertise.

VI

Today we adhere to the doctrine of equivalents. The determination of equivalence should be applied as an objective inquiry on an element-by-element basis. Prosecution history estoppel continues to be available as a defense to infringement, but if the patent-holder demonstrates that an amendment required during prosecution had a purpose unrelated to patentability, a court must consider that purpose in order to decide whether an estoppel is precluded. Where the patent-holder is unable to establish such a purpose, a court should presume that the purpose behind the required amendment is such that prosecution history estoppel would apply. Because the Court of Appeals for the Federal Circuit did not consider all of the requirements as described by us today, particularly as related to prosecution history estoppel and the preservation of some meaning for each element in a claim, we reverse and remand for further proceedings consistent with this opinion.

It is so ordered.

JUSTICE GINSBURG, with whom JUSTICE KENNEDY joins, concurring.

I join the opinion of the Court and write separately to add a cautionary note on the rebuttable presumption the Court announces regarding prosecution history estoppel. I address in particular the application of the presumption in this case and others in which patent prosecution has already been completed. The new presumption, if applied woodenly, might in some instances unfairly discount the expectations of a patentee who had no notice at the time of patent prosecution that such a presumption would apply. Such a patentee would have had little incentive to insist that the reasons for all modifications be memorialized in the file wrapper as they were made. Years after the fact, the patentee may find it difficult to establish an evidentiary basis that would overcome the new presumption. The Court's opinion is sensitive to this problem, noting that "the PTO may have relied upon a flexible rule of estoppel when deciding whether to ask for a change" during patent prosecution. Ante, at 13, n. 6.

Because respondent has not presented to this Court any explanation for the addition of the lower pH limit, I concur in the decision to remand the matter to the Federal Circuit. On remand, that court can deter mine-bearing in mind the prior absence of clear rules of the game-whether suitable reasons for including the lower pH limit were earlier offered or, if not, whether they can now be established.

Notes

1. **Return to the Federal Circuit.** On remand, the Federal Circuit restated its holding that a pH of 5.0 was equivalent to the claimed pH of "approximately 6.0" under the circumstances of the case, reasoning:

> We have reconsidered the pH equivalence issue in light of the Supreme Court's guidance and hold that there is substantial record evidence to support the jury's verdict of equivalence. The '746 patent claim recites a pH range "from approximately 6.0 to 9.0." Warner–Jenkinson performed the process using a pH of 5.0. Although there is nothing in the written description part of the specification to indicate that the invention extends beyond the specific range given in the claim, there is substantial record evidence to prove that one of ordinary skill in the art would know that performing ultrafiltration at a pH of 5.0 will allow the membrane to perform substantially the same function in substantially the same way to reach substantially the same result as performing ultrafiltration at 6.0. In this regard, Dr. Cook, one of the inventors, testified that the process would work to separate the dye from the impurities at pH values as low as 2.0 (albeit with foaming). More-over, Warner–Jenkinson's expert testified that the Hilton Davis process would operate at a pH of 5.0. The jury's finding that the accused process with a pH of 5.0 is equivalent to the claimed process with a lower limit of approximately 6.0 does not therefore vitiate the claim limitation. Accordingly, assuming prosecution history estoppel does not preclude such a finding, we reaffirm our prior decision that a pH of 5.0 is equivalent to a pH of "approximately 6.0" in the context of the claimed process.

Hilton Davis Chem. Co. v. Warner–Jenkinson Co., 114 F.3d 1161, 1164, 43 U.S.P.Q.2d 1152, 1154–55 (Fed.Cir.1997).

In doing this, the Federal Circuit also provided the Supreme Court with a chemistry tutorial. In its first footnote in *Warner–Jenkinson,* the Supreme Court had noted: "Although measurement of pH is on a logarithmic scale, with each whole number difference representing a ten-fold difference in acidity, the practical significance of any such difference will often depend on the context." Apparently impressed by a ten-fold difference *in acidity,* the Supreme Court asked the Federal Circuit to consider whether application of the doctrine of equivalents to permit a ten-fold difference did not allow "such broad play as to effectively eliminate that element in its entirety." 520 U.S. at 29. In a footnote, the Federal Circuit supplied its tutorial to explain its summary disposition: "We observe, however, that the pH number is derived from hydrogen ion concentration, and a one unit change in pH states a ten-fold difference in hydrogen ion concentration, rather than literally indicating a ten-fold difference in 'acidity.' " The Circuit also noted that the record showed that the process would work at pH values as low as 2.0.

Perhaps this footnote was the Federal Circuit's subtle way of noting that it had not overlooked the question of preserving the meaning of each claim element at all in its original opinion. To the contrary, the Circuit seems to say, it had in fact considered and summarily dismissed that issue on a correct understanding of the facts of the case. The Supreme Court, in reliance on a Federal Circuit dissent, had perhaps stated too much when it remanded "[b]ecause the Federal Circuit did not consider all of the requirements as described by us today . . ." 520 U.S. at 41.

The Federal Circuit further remanded the case to the district court on the issue of prosecution history estoppel, leaving "the district court to conduct an inquiry to ascertain whether Hilton Davis can rebut the presumption by showing the reason for the amendment of the claim to place a lower pH limit of approximately 6.0 on the ultrafiltration process and whether that reason is sufficient to overcome the estoppel bar to the application of the doctrine of equivalents." 114 F.3d at 1163, 43 U.S.P.Q.2d at 1154.

2. The *Dolly* Doctrine and Tension in Application of Equivalents. *Warner–Jenkinson* sought to strictly limit application of the doctrine of equivalents. A developing line of Federal Circuit cases implements that direction. In *Dolly, Inc. v. Spalding & Evenflo Cos. Inc.,* 16 F.3d 394, 29 U.S.P.Q.2d 1767 (Fed.Cir.1994), the Federal Circuit linked the doctrine closely to the nature of the claim. In that case, the claim recited a portable, adjustable child's play-chair with a stable, rigid frame to which the assembler adds a seat panel and a back panel. The accused device lacked a stable, rigid frame. Instead the seat and back of the accused device fit together to form a rigid frame. Judge Rader noted that the doctrine of equivalents "cannot embrace a structure that is specifically excluded from the scope of the claims. A stable rigid frame assembled from the seat and back panels is not the equivalent of a separate stable rigid frame which the claim language specifically [requires]." 16 F.3d at 400, 29 U.S.P.Q.2d at 1771. Many cases have since followed *Dolly*, but some of them have not recognized the limits on application of the *Dolly* rule. The isolated quote from *Dolly* suggests that the doctrine does not apply whenever the claim "specifically excludes" the theory of equivalents. Read out of the context of the case, this exception would swallow the entire doctrine of equivalents because infringement under the doctrine presupposes that the infringing device falls outside the claims. Read in context, *Dolly* shows that the court read the express language of the child safety chair claim to include a negation of certain coverage. In the context of the familiar *Warner–Jenkinson* facts, the *Dolly* claim included language like: "a pH range of about 6–9, *but not 5.*" The claim language thus "specifically excluded" coverage that the patentee later tried to capture by equivalents. The patentee could not claim that 5 was an equivalent of the 6–9 range because other parts of the claim had "specifically excluded" coverage of 5.

The classic case misapplying the *Dolly* principle is *Athletic Alternatives, Inc. v. Prince Manufacturing, Inc.,* 73 F.3d 1573, 37 U.S.P.Q.2d 1365 (Fed.Cir.1996). This case quoted the "specifically excluded" principle beyond the restraints of the *Dolly* claim. In the context of the *Warner–Jenkinson* facts again, the *Athletic Alternatives* tennis racket claim included the language: "a pH range of about 6–9." When the patentee tried to claim that 5 was an equivalent, the court said that the claimed range of 6–9 "specifically excluded" 5. Under this reasoning of course, anything not expressly covered by the claims is excluded from claims. Absent some unstated limiting principle, this reasoning of *Athletic Alternatives* obliterates the doctrine of equivalents. Moreover this reasoning really amounts to a factual finding on appeal that 5 is not the equivalent of 6.

This juxtaposition presents the challenge: How does a district court decide whether claim language is clear enough to specifically negate coverage under the doctrine of equivalents in some cases and not in others? The differences between *Dolly*'s express negation and *Athletic Alternatives*'s implicit negation is clear in those cases, but less clear in others. Where is the border between impermissible vitiation of claim terms and permissible equivalents?

In sum, *Dolly* stands for the principle that claim language itself may expressly and ambiguously negate a theory of equivalents. It does not suggest that anything not covered by the claims is "specifically excluded" from the DOE. This latter *Athletic Alternatives* notion of implied negotiation eliminates (without saying so) the entire doctrine of equivalents, a result the Supreme Court rejected in *Warner–Jenkinson*. In sum, is the *Dolly* doctrine an application of the Court's admonition that "[i]t is important to ensure that the application of the doctrine, even as to an individual element, is not allowed such broad play as to effectively eliminate that element in its entirety."?

3. Can 47.8% be the equivalent of a majority? *Moore U.S.A., Inc. v. Standard Register Co.*, 229 F.3d 1091, 56 U.S.P.Q. 2d 1225 (Fed.Cir.2000), featured a patent claiming a mailer-type business form. The patent's claims called for longitudinal strips of adhesive that extended "the majority" of the lengths of the form. The accused product featured adhesive strips running 47.8% of the form's length. The Federal Circuit upheld the district court's *summary judgment* of noninfringement, concluding that "it would defy logic to conclude that a minority—the very antithesis of a majority—could be insubstantially different from a claim limitation requiring a majority, and no reasonable juror could find otherwise." 229 F.3d at 1106, 56 U.S.P.Q.2d at 1236. Besides demonstrating the current tenor of equivalency law at the Federal Circuit, *Moore* again invokes the implicit negation principle to find an effective elimination of a claimed element. Is there any number less than 50.1% that could be an equivalent under this approach?

4. Elemental Equivalents. Did *WJ* present a good opportunity for the Supreme Court to discuss the all elements rule? Was this a case about an absent claim limitation or simply one that was not literally met? This casebook further considers the All Elements Rule in the next section. Additionally, why didn't the patentee employ the limitation "at a pH from approximately 6 to 9," rather than referring to 6.0 and 9.0? What does the addition of a significant digit mean to you? *See Air Products and Chemicals, Inc. v. Chas. S. Tanner Co.*, 219 U.S.P.Q. 223, 246 (D.S.C.1983) (positing distinction between claimed term "1" vis-a-vis "1.0").

5. Federal Circuit Supervisory Authority. Compare footnote 8 of the Supreme Court's opinion with the statement from *Petersen Manufacturing Co. v. Central Purchasing, Inc.,* 740 F.2d 1541, 222 U.S.P.Q. 562 (Fed.Cir.1984) that: "Unlike other Circuit Courts of Appeal, (see e.g., *Cord v. Smith,* 338 F.2d 516, 526 (9th Cir.1964)), we have no direct supervisory authority over district courts. *C.P.C. v. Nosco Plastics, Inc.,* 719 F.2d 400 (Fed.Cir.1983)." Absent an *en banc* change to this line of precedent, how will the Federal Circuit be able to implement the Supreme Court's advice in footnote 8?

§ 15.3 Limitations on the Doctrine of Equivalents

As noted in the decisions previously presented here, three legal tenets restrain the reach of non-textual infringement. The first of these is the "all elements" rule: the requirement that the doctrine of equivalents can only apply to an accused product or process that contains each limitation of a claim, either literally or equivalently. Non-textual infringement, unlike obviousness or other patent doctrines, is not oriented to a patent claim as a whole, but instead applies element-by-element within a claim. In *Warner–Jenkinson,* the Supreme Court endorsed this rule: "It is important to ensure that the application of the doctrine, even as to an individual element, is not allowed such broad play as to effectively eliminate that element in its entirety." Another limitation on non-textual infringement is prosecution history estoppel, a doctrine that precludes recapture under the doctrine of equivalents of subject matter surrendered during the patent application process. The third restraint on the doctrine of equivalents springs from the scope of the prior art for an invention. Sound patent policy dictates that patentees should not be able to extend their exclusive rights to cover technologies that prior art would have rendered unpatentable. The following cases explore these limitations and suggest as well that a fourth limitation may be emerging in the case law.

§ 15.3[a] The "All Elements" Rule

The Supreme Court embraced the "all elements" rule in its *Warner–Jenkinson* opinion. Of course, the Federal Circuit had articulated and applied this rule for years before *WJ.* In 1987, the Federal Circuit, sitting *en banc,* defined this limitation on the doctrine of equivalents. *Pennwalt Corp. v. Durand–Wayland, Inc.,* 833 F.2d 931, 4 U.S.P.Q.2d 1737 (Fed.Cir.1987). In the *Pennwalt* case, the patent bore the title "Sorter for Fruit and the Like." The claims of this '628 patent included several means-plus-function elements, including a "position indicating means" to show the position of the fruit along the conveyor belt sorter. The patent specification disclosed a network of hardware registers to perform this claimed function. Thus, the claimed sorter registered the location of the fruit at each station (color, weight, size, etc.) along the conveyor. Pennwalt sued Durand–Wayland for infringement, but was unsuccessful at trial. The accused device employed a data structure in software to record information about fruit moving along its conveyor. According to the district court, the accused device lacked a position indicating means that could show the location of the fruit at any given time along the conveyor belt. The Federal Circuit, citing its own earlier opinions, affirmed:

> [I]n applying the doctrine of equivalents, each limitation must be viewed in the context of the entire claim.... "It is ... well settled that each element of a claim is material and essential, and that in order for a court to find infringement, the plaintiff must show the presence of every element or its substantial equivalent in the accused device." *Lemelson v. United States*, 752 F.2d 1538, 1551, 224 USPQ 526, 533 (Fed.Cir.1985).

Pennwalt, 833 F.2d at 935. *Pennwalt* played a central role in nearly every doctrine of equivalents case and became a centerpiece of *Warner–Jenkinson*, as already noted. Incidentally, the Federal Circuit did answer the obvious question about simply programming the accused software information system to record position: "Theoretically, a microprocessor could be programmed to perform those functions. However, the district court found that the microprocessor in the accused devices was not so programmed." *Id*. Another Federal Circuit case reflects the contours of the *Pennwalt* limitation.

CORNING GLASS WORKS v. SUMITOMO ELECTRIC USA, INC.

United States Court of Appeals, Federal Circuit, 1989.
868 F.2d 1251, 9 U.S.P.Q.2d 1962.

Before RICH, NIES and BISSELL, CIRCUIT JUDGES.

NIES, CIRCUIT JUDGE.

Sumitomo Electric U.S.A., Inc.... appeal[s] from the judgment of the United States District Court for the Southern District of New York holding Sumitomo liable for infringement of claims 1 and 2 of United States Patent No. 3,659,915 ('915) and claim 1 of United States Patent No. 3,884,550 ('550), all directed to the structure of optical waveguide fibers. On appeal, Sumitomo challenges the validity of both patents and the finding of infringement of the '915 patent by one of its accused products. We affirm the judgment in all respects.

I

BACKGROUND

A.   General Technology

The inventions involved in this case relate to optical waveguide fibers of the type now widely used for telecommunications, such as long-distance telephone transmissions. Such fibers were developed as a medium for guiding the coherent light of a laser a distance suitable for optical communications.

It had long been known that light could be guided through a transparent medium that was surrounded by another medium having a lower refractive index (RI). A glass fiber surrounded by air, for example, will function as a conduit for light waves, because air has a lower RI than glass. To prevent scratches, imperfections, or foreign materials on the fiber surface from scattering light away from the fiber, glass fibers were cladded with a glass layer having a lower RI. Before 1970, however, these glass-clad, glass-core fibers, referred to generally as "fiber optics," were capable of transmitting light of practical intensity only for very short distances due to high attenuation of the glass fibers then available. While suitable for illumination or for imaging systems, as in endoscopic probes, they could not be used for optical communications.

Another impediment to the use of conventional fiber optics for optical communications was the need that the fiber limit the transmitted light to preselected rays or "modes." In contrast, conventional fibers were designed to pass the maximum amount of incident light. The relatively large core diameter of conventional fibers permitted modes of light to enter the core over a fairly wide range of angles which, provided they entered at less than the critical angle, would be propagated along the fiber. Upon entering a fiber core, the light modes travel to the cladding and then back into the core, thus "bouncing" back and forth in a zig-zag path along the length of the fiber. The shallower the angle at which the modes enter the core, the less they will "bounce" and the sooner they will reach the receiving end of the fiber. When the number of modes are restricted, intelligibility of the information transmitted increases. The optimum restriction is achieved when only a single mode is transmitted, and by limiting the core diameter, that purpose is accomplished.

By the mid–1960's, worldwide efforts were ongoing to develop long-distance lightwave transmission capability. In particular, the British Post Office sought an optical waveguide with an attenuation of 20 db/km, the approximate transmission efficiency of the copper wire commonly used in telephone communications.

B.   The '915 Invention

Corning's work on optical waveguides began in 1966, when it was contacted by the British Post Office. Drs. Robert D. Maurer and Peter C. Schultz, working at Corning, developed the world's first 20 db/km optical waveguide fiber by early 1970. That achievement was due, in part, to the development of a fiber with a pure fused silica cladding and a fused silica core containing approximately three percent by weight of titania as the dopant in the core. It was also due to the careful selection of the core diameter and the RI differential between the core and the cladding.

Bell Laboratories confirmed the attenuation measurements of Corning's fibers and considered Corning's achievement an important breakthrough, making long-distance optical telecommunications possible. Dr. Maurer first publicly reported the achievement of a 20 db/km optical waveguide fiber at the Conference on Trunk Telecommunications by Guided Waves held in London, England. That announcement created enormous interest and was the subject of many articles in both technical and general publications. The inventors' advancement in technology won them accolades from various societies and institutes, for which they were presented with many prestigious awards and honors.

In addition, the invention of the '915 patent has achieved impressive commercial success on a worldwide basis. The district court determined that "[t]he 915 patent clearly covers a basic, pioneering invention." 671 F.Supp. at 1377, 5 U.S.P.Q.2d at 1551.

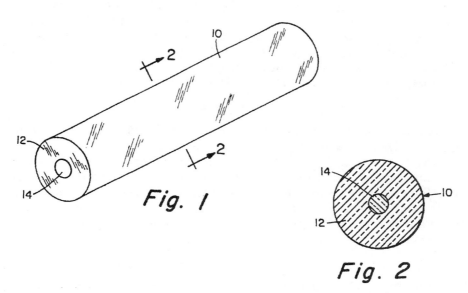

Fig. 1

Fig. 2

The '915 patent discloses a fused silica optical waveguide fiber capable of limiting the transmitted light to preselected modes for use in optical communication systems. Specifically, such a fiber is disclosed as having a doped fused silica core and a fused silica cladding (doping optional), wherein the RI of the core is greater than that of the cladding. Prior to the filing date of the application for the '915 patent, the inventors had experimented with dopants which increased the RI of fused silica, e.g. titania, and the '915 specification mentions only such positive dopant materials. At the time the application was filed, the inventors did not know of specific dopants that would decrease the RI of fused silica, although it had been known in the art since 1954 that the introduction of fluorine decreases the RI of certain multicomponent glasses.

[Claim 1 of the '915 patent provides:

An optical waveguide comprising

(a) a cladding layer formed of a material selected from the group consisting of pure fused silica and fused silica to which a dopant material on at least an elemental basis has been added, and

(b) a core formed of fused silica to which a dopant material on at least an elemental basis has been added to a degree in excess of that of the cladding layer so that the index of refraction thereof is of a value greater than the index of refraction of said cladding layer, said core being formed of at least 85 percent by weight of fused silica and an effective amount up to 15 percent by weight of said dopant material.]

C.   The '550 Invention

Corning's titania-doped fibers required heat treatment to reduce attenuation to an acceptable level. An undesirable result of that treatment was a lowering of the mechanical strength of the fibers. Consequently, Corning sought to develop a low attenuation fiber which did not require heat treatment. In 1972, Drs. Maurer and Schultz found a solution in doping a fused silica core with germania, which also had the advantage of transmitting more light than using titania.

D.   The '454 Invention

Corning recognized that when optical waveguide fibers were produced by flame hydrolysis, they contained hydroxyl ions. The residual hydroxyl ions absorbed light at certain wavelengths used in optical communications and, if they remained, would increase the attenuation of the fiber at those wavelengths. Working at Corning, Dr. Robert D. DeLuca invented a process to overcome this inherent problem by introducing a chlorine-containing drying atmosphere into the furnace during the "consolidation" phase.

E.   District Court

Corning is the assignee of the three patents at issue. SEI and its subsidiaries, SERT and SEUSA, are engaged in the manufacture and sale of optical waveguide fibers. This appeal involves two suits which were consolidated: an action by SERT seeking a declaration of invalidity and noninfringement of Corning's '915 and '454 patents with a counterclaim by Corning alleging SERT's infringement of those patents, and a suit by Corning against SEUSA and SEI asserting infringement of the '915, '550, and '454 patents.

The trial court held, inter alia, that claims 1 and 2 of the '915 patent and claim 1 of the '550 patent were not invalid and were infringed by Sumitomo. It found no infringement of the '454 patent. These rulings are the subject of this appeal . . . :

II

INFRINGEMENT OF CLAIMS 1 AND 2 OF '915 PATENT

The infringement issue on appeal involves only Sumitomo's S–3 fibers which were found to infringe under the doctrine of equivalents. * * * The district court found that th[e] test for infringement was met, stating:

> Although fiber S–3 is not within the literal language of either claim 1 or 2 of the '915 patent, it performs substantially the same function in substantially the same way to obtain the same result as

the optical waveguide fiber described in those claims of the '915 patent.

Corning Glass Works v. Sumitomo Elec. U.S.A., Inc., 671 F.Supp. 1369, 1387, 5 U.S.P.Q.2d 1545, 1559 (S.D.N.Y.1987).

In the instant case, there is no dispute that the accused S–3 fiber performs substantially the same overall function to obtain the same overall result as the claimed invention. The question then is whether it does so in "substantially the same way." As stated in *Perkin–Elmer Corp. v. Westinghouse Electric Corp.*:

> Perkin–Elmer's repeated assertions that the claimed and accused devices perform substantially the same function and achieve substantially the same end result are not helpful. That circumstance is commonplace when the devices are sold in competition. That a claimed invention and an accused device may perform substantially the same function and may achieve the same result will not make the latter an infringement under the doctrine of equivalents where it performs the function and achieves the result in a substantially different way. *Graver Tank & Mfg. Co. v. Linde Air Products Co.*, 339 U.S. 605, 608, 70 S.Ct. 854, 856, 94 L.Ed. 1097, 85 U.S.P.Q. 328, 330 (1950).

822 F.2d 1528, 1531 n. 6, 3 U.S.P.Q.2d 1321, 1323–24 n. 6 (Fed.Cir. 1987).

The accused S–3 fibers are optical waveguides as defined in the claims at issue in that the fibers have the differential in RI between core and cladding and the structural dimensions necessary for the preselection of particular modes of light waves. Thus, these limitations of claim 1 which, as above indicated, are required by the preamble are met in the accused S–3 fibers. Also, there is no dispute over a literal reading of paragraph (a) on these fibers. Corning concedes, however, that all of the limitations of paragraph (b) do not literally read on the accused fibers. Although each claim limitation may not literally be found in the accused structure, the "substantially the same way" prong of the Graver Tank test is met if an equivalent of a recited limitation has been substituted in the accused device.

Applying these principles, the district court found that the accused S–3 fibers infringed the '915 claims. In so ruling, the district court recognized that the claim limitation calling for addition of a dopant to the core was not literally met in the accused S–3 fibers. 671 F.Supp. at 1387, 5 U.S.P.Q.2d at 1559. Nevertheless, the court found that the substitution of "fluorine ... dopant which negatively alters the index of refraction of fused silica[ ] in the cladding" equivalently met the limitation requiring the addition to the core of "a dopant which positively alters the index of refraction of fused silica." *Id.* at 1386–87, 5 U.S.P.Q.2d 1559.

Sumitomo alleges clear error in the court's finding of equivalency. Per Sumitomo, nothing was substituted in the core of the S–3 fiber for a dopant which performed the function of increasing the core's refractive index, and, therefore, "an element" required by the claim, namely, a doped core, is entirely missing. Sumitomo asserts, that where an element of a claim is entirely missing, there is no infringement. The premise on which Sumitomo relies, known as the "All Elements" rule, *see* 4 D. CHISUM, PATENTS § 18.03[4] (1986), correctly states the law of this circuit adopted *in banc* in *Pennwalt. See Pennwalt Corp.*, 833 F.2d at 935, 4 U.S.P.Q.2d at 1739–40 (infringement requires that each element of a claim or its substantial equivalent be found in the accused device). However, we do not agree that an "element" of the claim is entirely "missing" from the S–3 fibers.

Sumitomo's analysis illustrates the confusion sometimes encountered because of misunderstanding or misleading uses of the term "element" in discussing claims. "Element" may be used to mean a single limitation, but it has also been used to mean a series of limitations which, taken together, make up a component of the claimed invention. In the All Elements rule, "element" is used in the sense of a limitation of a claim. *See Julien v. Zeringue*, 864 F.2d 1569, 1571 (Fed.Cir.1989) ("If a claim limitation or its substantial equivalent is not present, there can be no infringement."). Sumitomo's analysis is faulty in that it would require equivalency in components, that is, the substitution of something in the core for the absent dopant. However, the determination of equivalency is not subject to such a rigid formula. An equivalent must be found for every limitation of the claim somewhere in an accused device, but not necessarily in a corresponding component, although that is generally the case.

Corning urges that the question of equivalency here is a narrow one: Is the substitution of a negative dopant in the cladding equivalent to a positive dopant in the core? When the limitations of paragraph (b) are analyzed individually, the accused S–3 fibers literally meet the limitation that the fiber be composed of a core of fused silica as well as the limitation that "the index of refraction [of the core] is of a value greater than the index of refraction of said cladding layer." The question of equivalency then does center on the part of the claim following the word "core," namely, "to which a dopant material ... has been added to a degree in excess of that of the cladding layer." If those limiting words are met equivalently, no "element," i.e., limitation, of the claim is missing.

This court has not set out in its precedent a definitive formula for determining equivalency between a required limitation or combination of limitations and what has been allegedly substituted therefor in the accused device. Nor do we propose to adopt one here. We note that the district court resolved the question by comparison of the function/way/result of the substitution with the function/way/result of the limitation in the context of the invention; that is, the court made a subsidiary analysis comparable to the overall function/way/result analysis mandated for determining infringement of the claim under the doctrine of equivalents. In particular, after explaining how the negative dopant of the S–3 fiber worked, it found:

> [t]he use of fluorine as a [negative] dopant in the cladding thus performs substantially the same function in substantially the same way as the use of a [positive] dopant in the core to produce the same result of creating the refractive index differential between the core and cladding of the fiber which is necessary for the fiber to function as an optical waveguide.

671 F.Supp. at 1387, 5 U.S.P.Q.2d at 1559.

The district court's "function/way/result" equivalency analysis with respect to a claim limitation appears to be a helpful way to approach the problem and entirely in accord with the analysis actually made in *Graver Tank*, 339 U.S. at 609–10, 70 S.Ct. at 856–57. Support for this approach is found in our precedent. As one of our predecessor courts stated:

> It is fundamental patent law that infringement is not avoided by substituting for an element in a claimed device another element which is its full equivalent, i.e., does substantially the same thing in substantially the same way to get substantially the same result. Equivalency is a question of fact and must be resolved in each instance by analyzing the function of the elements or parts concerned.

Tektronix, Inc. v. United States, 445 F.2d 323, 329, 170 U.S.P.Q. 100 [Ct.Cl. 1971]. Although not stated exactly as above, this court has made that type of analysis repeatedly in determining whether a substitution was, in the context of the entire claim, an equivalent of a limitation. In Atlas Powder, for example, the court used the following similar language to assess the equivalency of the substituted ingredient:

> Where, as here, the accused product avoids literal infringement by changing one ingredient of a claimed composition, it is appropriate for a court to consider in assessing equivalence whether the changed ingredient has the same purpose, quality, and function as the claimed ingredient.

[750 F.2d 1569, 1579–80, 224 U.S.P.Q. 409, 416 (Fed.Cir.1984).]

Finally, Sumitomo asserts that because the prior art, namely, United States Patent No. 3,320,114 (the Litton patent) teaches that a differential in the RI can be achieved between core and cladding in a fiber optic by negative doping of the cladding, Corning cannot assert equivalency between positive dopant in the core and negative dopant in the cladding. To do so, per Sumitomo, would "expan[d] the claim to encompass what was already in the public domain, i.e., a fiber with a pure undoped core." Contrary to Sumitomo's argument, the substitution of an ingredient known to be an equivalent to that required by the claim presents a classic example for a finding of infringement under the doctrine of equivalents. *Graver Tank*, 339 U.S. at 609, 70 S.Ct. at 856 (important factor [in determining equivalency] is whether persons reasonably skilled in the art would have known of the interchangeability).

Nothing is taken from the "public domain" when the issue of equivalency is directed to a limitation only, in contrast to the entirety of the claimed invention. This is such a case. The Litton patent teaches nothing about optical waveguides. Thus, the finding of equivalency in the substitution of a negative dopant in the cladding takes nothing from the "public domain."

In sum, we are unpersuaded of error either in the district court's understanding of the law; in its finding that adding negative dopant to the cladding is equivalent to adding positive dopant to the core in the context of the claimed invention; or in its finding that the S–3 fiber is an infringement of the inventions of claims 1 and 2 of the '915 patent.

AFFIRMED.

Notes

1.   *Pennwalt* and Claim Drafting. Should the scope of patent protection for a claim depend upon how a claim drafter has chosen to organize a description of an invention? Consider the following simplified claims:

> 1.   A fork comprising a cylindrical handle; and four tines attached to said handle.

> 2.   A fork comprising a cylindrical handle; a first tine attached to said handle; a second tine attached to said handle; a third tine attached to said handle; and a fourth tine attached to said handle.

These claims appear to provide the same scope of protection in terms of literal infringement. Yet, suppose a competitor markets a fork with three tines. Can you imagine any differences between the outcome of an equivalents analysis for these two claims under the all elements rule? How then could the *Pennwalt* claims be redrafted to capture the accused infringement?

2.   *Corning Glass* and Claim Drafting. Does the observation that the all elements rule renders concise claim drafting advisable hold true following *Corning Glass*? What about the statement in *Corning Glass* that: " 'Element' may be used to mean a single limitation, but it has also been used to mean a series of limitations which, taken together, make up a component of the claimed invention"? Consider a process that performs four steps. Steps A, B, and C consist of novel and nonobviousness technology, while step D is one that is well known to the art. Would the patentee be better off claiming $A+B+C$ or $A+B+C+D$?

Before you answer too quickly, consider an accused process that performs $A'+B'+C'+D$. In the accused process, step A' presents substantial differences from A, step B' presents substantial differences from B, and step C' presents substantial differences from C. However, when the three steps are considered as a whole, the differences between $A+B+C$ and $A'+B'+C'$ are insubstantial. Step D is common to both processes. Wouldn't the addition of step D in a claim take the patentee away from the holistic approach rejected in *Pennwalt* and allow application of the rule of *Corning Glass*? If these two cases do not necessarily teach that streamlined claims are preferable, what do they tell us about claim drafting?

3. *Corning Glass*, **Past and Future.** However important the all-elements rule might appear to be, as a practical matter, it stands for nothing more than the principle that a claim for a combination invention cannot be infringed by a sub-combination. This became abundantly clear from the original panel decision in *Festo Corp. v. Shoketsu Kinzoku Kogyo Kabushiki Co. Ltd.*, 172 F.3d 1361, 50 U.S.P.Q.2d 1385 (Fed.Cir.1999). On that point, the panel decision survived both the Federal Circuit *en banc* and the Supreme Court. The vacated *Festo* panel opinion explained that *Warner-Jenkinson* teaches that it is appropriate to inquire into the "role" of the pair of sealing rings, and to compare that role with the role of the substituted two-way sealing ring.... (considering the role of each element in the context of the claim). Applying this principle, the court observed that the pair of sealing rings, as stated in the claim, effect a fluid-tight seal with the cylinder. The accused SMC devices preserve this role in the two-way sealing ring. The accused device fully performed the claimed function with the two-way sealing ring. Thus, the court reasoned: "The claimed pair of sealing rings has not been eliminated in its entirety, but has been substituted with a single two-way sealing ring that fully preserves the function stated in the claim. We therefore again affirm the district court's ruling that the all-elements rule is met by the sealing ring structure in the SMC devices, and that consideration of equivalency *vel non* of this limitation is not barred." *Id.* Thus, as always, the important question is the application of the Court's admonition that "[i]t is important to ensure that the application of the doctrine, even as to an individual element, is not allowed such broad play as to effectively eliminate that element in its entirety."

§ 15.3[b] Prosecution History Estoppel

Prosecution history estoppel is a very useful doctrine for a defendant because it enables an accused infringer to win on summary judgment. A defendant may prevail by simply introducing the prosecution history. The Supreme Court invoked this doctrine in *Warner–Jenkinson*. At one point in its discussion, the Supreme Court explained: "Where no explanation is established [explaining the reason for a narrowing amendment], however, the court should presume that the PTO had a substantial reason related to patentability for including the limiting element added by amendment. In those circumstances, prosecution history estoppel would bar the application of the doctrine of equivalents as to that element." This reference to a "bar" on non-textual infringement caused a split in the Federal Circuit that was resolved by *en banc* action. When the Federal Circuit's *en banc* ruling prompted many requests, including that of the Solicitor General of the United States, for further review, the Supreme Court agreed to revisit prosecution history estoppel and non-textual infringement.

FESTO CORP. v. SHOKETSU KINZOKU
KOGYO KABUSHIKI CO., LTD.

United States Supreme Court, 2002.
122 S.Ct. 1831, 62 U.S.P.Q.2d 1705.

MR. JUSTICE KENNEDY delivered the opinion of the Court.

This case requires us to address once again the relation between two patent law concepts, the doctrine of equivalents and the rule of prosecution history estoppel. The Court considered the same concepts in *Warner-Jenkinson Co. v. Hilton Davis Chemical Co.*, 520 U.S. 17, 117 S.Ct. 1040, 137 L.Ed.2d 146 (1997), and reaffirmed that a patent protects its holder against efforts of copyists to evade liability for infringement by making only insubstantial changes to a patented invention. At the same time, we appreciated that by extending protection beyond the literal terms in a patent the doctrine of equivalents can create substantial uncertainty about where the patent monopoly ends. *Id.*, at 29, 117 S.Ct. 1040. If the range of equivalents is unclear, competitors may be unable to determine what is a permitted alternative to a patented invention and what is an infringing equivalent.

To reduce the uncertainty, *Warner–Jenkinson* acknowledged that competitors may rely on the prosecution history, the public record of the patent proceedings. In some cases the Patent and Trademark Office (PTO) may have rejected an earlier version of the patent application on the ground that a claim does not meet a statutory requirement for patentability. 35 U.S.C. § 132 (1994 ed., Supp. V). When the patentee responds to the rejection by narrowing his claims, this prosecution history estops him from later arguing that the subject matter covered by the original, broader claim was nothing more than an equivalent. Competitors may rely on the estoppel to ensure that their own devices will not be found to infringe by equivalence.

In the decision now under review the Court of Appeals for the Federal Circuit held that by narrowing a claim to obtain a patent, the patentee surrenders all equivalents to the amended claim element. Petitioner asserts this holding departs from past precedent in two respects. First, it applies estoppel to every amendment made to satisfy the requirements of the Patent Act and not just to amendments made to avoid pre-emption by an earlier invention, *i.e.*, the prior art. Second, it holds that when estoppel arises, it bars suit against every equivalent to the amended claim element. The Court of Appeals acknowledged that this holding departed from its own cases, which applied a flexible bar when considering what claims of equivalence were estopped by the prosecution history. Petitioner argues that by replacing the flexible bar with a complete bar the Court of Appeals cast doubt on many existing patents that were amended during the application process when the law, as it then stood, did not apply so rigorous a standard.

We granted certiorari to consider these questions.

I

Petitioner Festo Corporation owns two patents for an improved magnetic rodless cylinder, a piston-driven device that relies on magnets to move objects in a conveying system. The device has many industrial uses and has been employed in machinery as diverse as sewing equipment and the Thunder Mountain ride at Disney World. Although the precise details of the cylinder's operation are not essential here, the prosecution history must be considered.

Petitioner's patent applications, as often occurs, were amended during the prosecution proceedings. The application for the first patent, the Stoll Patent (U.S. Patent No. 4,354,125), was amended after the patent examiner rejected the initial application because the exact method of operation was unclear and some claims were made in an impermissible way. (They were multiply dependent.) 35 U.S.C. § 112 (1994 ed.). The inventor, Dr. Stoll, submitted a new application designed to meet the examiner's objections and also added certain references to prior art. 37 CFR § 1.56 (2000). The second patent, the Carroll Patent (U.S. Patent No. 3,779,401), was also amended during a reexamination proceeding. The prior art references were added to this amended application as well. Both amended patents added a new limitation—that the inventions contain a pair of sealing rings, each having a lip on one side, which would prevent impurities from getting on the piston assembly. The amended Stoll Patent added the further limitation that the outer shell of the device, the sleeve, be made of a magnetizable material.

After Festo began selling its rodless cylinder, respondents (whom we refer to as SMC) entered the market with a device similar, but not identical, to the ones disclosed by Festo's patents. SMC's cylinder, rather than using two one-way sealing rings, employs a single sealing ring with a two-way lip. Furthermore, SMC's sleeve is made of a nonmagnetizable alloy. SMC's device does not fall within the literal claims of either patent, but petitioner contends that it is so similar that it infringes under the doctrine of equivalents.

SMC contends that Festo is estopped from making this argument because of the prosecution history of its patents. The sealing rings and the magnetized alloy in the Festo product were both disclosed for the first time in the amended applications. In SMC's view, these amendments narrowed the earlier applications, surrendering alternatives that are the very points of difference in the competing devices—the sealing rings and the type of alloy used to make the sleeve. As Festo narrowed its claims in these ways in order to obtain the patents, says SMC, Festo is now estopped from saying that these features are immaterial and that SMC's device is an equivalent of its own.

The United States District Court for the District of Massachusetts disagreed. It held that Festo's amendments were not made to avoid prior art, and therefore the amendments were not the kind that give rise to estoppel. A panel of the Court of Appeals for the Federal Circuit affirmed. 72 F.3d 857 (1995). We granted certiorari, vacated, and remanded in light of our intervening decision in *Warner–Jenkinson v. Hilton Davis Chemical Co.,* 520 U.S. 17, 117 S.Ct. 1040, 137 L.Ed.2d 146 (1997). After a decision by the original panel on remand, 172 F.3d 1361 (1999), the Court of Appeals ordered rehearing en banc to address questions that had divided its judges since our decision in *Warner–Jenkinson,* 187 F.3d 1381 (1999).

The en banc court reversed, holding that prosecution history estoppel barred Festo from asserting that the accused device infringed its patents under the doctrine of equivalents. 234 F.3d 558 (2000). The court held, with only one judge dissenting, that estoppel arises from any amendment that narrows a claim to comply with the Patent Act, not only from amendments made to avoid prior art. *Id.,* at 566. More controversial in the Court of Appeals was its further holding: When estoppel applies, it stands as a complete bar against any claim of equivalence for the element that was amended. *Id.,* at 574–575. The court acknowledged that its own prior case law did not go so far. Previous decisions had held that prosecution history estoppel constituted a flexible bar, foreclosing some, but not all, claims of equivalence, depending on the purpose of the amendment and the alterations in the text. The court concluded, however, that its precedents applying the flexible-bar rule should be overruled because this case-by-case approach has proved unworkable. In the court's view a complete-bar rule, under which estoppel bars all claims of equivalence to the narrowed element, would promote certainty in the determination of infringement cases.

Four judges dissented from the decision to adopt a complete bar. *Id.,* at 562. In four separate opinions, the dissenters argued that the majority's decision to overrule precedent was contrary to *Warner–Jenkinson* and would unsettle the expectations of many existing patentees. Judge Michel, in his dissent, described in detail how the complete bar required the Court of Appeals to disregard 8 older decisions of this Court, as well as more than 50 of its own cases. 234 F.3d, at 601–616.

We granted certiorari. 533 U.S. 915, 121 S.Ct. 2519, 150 L.Ed.2d 692 (2001).

II

The patent laws "promote the Progress of Science and useful Arts" by rewarding innovation with a temporary monopoly. U.S. Const., Art. I, § 8, cl. 8. The monopoly is a property right; and like any property right, its boundaries should be clear. This clarity is essential to promote progress, because it enables efficient investment in innovation. A patent holder should know what he owns, and the public should know what he does not. For this reason, the patent laws require inventors to describe their work in "full, clear, concise, and exact terms," 35 U.S.C. § 112, as part of the delicate balance the law attempts to maintain between inventors, who rely on the promise of the law to bring the invention forth, and the public, which should be encouraged to pursue innovations, creations, and new ideas beyond the inventor's exclusive rights. *Bonito*

Boats, Inc. v. Thunder Craft Boats, Inc., 489 U.S. 141, 150, 109 S.Ct. 971, 103 L.Ed.2d 118 (1989).

Unfortunately, the nature of language makes it impossible to capture the essence of a thing in a patent application. The inventor who chooses to patent an invention and disclose it to the public, rather than exploit it in secret, bears the risk that others will devote their efforts toward exploiting the limits of the patent's language:

> "An invention exists most importantly as a tangible structure or a series of drawings. A verbal portrayal is usually an afterthought written to satisfy the requirements of patent law. This conversion of machine to words allows for unintended idea gaps which cannot be satisfactorily filled. Often the invention is novel and words do not exist to describe it. The dictionary does not always keep abreast of the inventor. It cannot. Things are not made for the sake of words, but words for things." *Autogiro Co. of America v. United States,* 181 Ct.Cl. 55, 384 F.2d 391, 397 (1967).

The language in the patent claims may not capture every nuance of the invention or describe with complete precision the range of its novelty. If patents were always interpreted by their literal terms, their value would be greatly diminished. Unimportant and insubstantial substitutes for certain elements could defeat the patent, and its value to inventors could be destroyed by simple acts of copying. For this reason, the clearest rule of patent interpretation, literalism, may conserve judicial resources but is not necessarily the most efficient rule. The scope of a patent is not limited to its literal terms but instead embraces all equivalents to the claims described. *See Winans v. Denmead,* 56 U.S. (15 How.) 330, 347, 14 L.Ed. 717 (1854).

It is true that the doctrine of equivalents renders the scope of patents less certain. It may be difficult to determine what is, or is not, an equivalent to a particular element of an invention. If competitors cannot be certain about a patent's extent, they may be deterred from engaging in legitimate manufactures outside its limits, or they may invest by mistake in competing products that the patent secures. In addition the uncertainty may lead to wasteful litigation between competitors, suits that a rule of literalism might avoid. These concerns with the doctrine of equivalents, however, are not new. Each time the Court has considered the doctrine, it has acknowledged this uncertainty as the price of ensuring the appropriate incentives for innovation, and it has affirmed the doctrine over dissents that urged a more certain rule. When the Court in *Winans v. Denmead, supra,* first adopted what has become the doctrine of equivalents, it stated that "[t]he exclusive right to the thing patented is not secured, if the public are at liberty to make substantial copies of it, varying its form or proportions." *Id.,* at 343. The dissent argued that the Court had sacrificed the objective of "[f]ul[l]ness, clearness, exactness, preciseness, and particularity, in the description of the invention." *Id.,* at 347 (opinion of Campbell, J.).

The debate continued in *Graver Tank & Mfg. Co. v. Linde Air Products Co.*, 339 U.S. 605, 70 S.Ct. 854, 94 L.Ed. 1097 (1950), where the Court reaffirmed the doctrine. *Graver Tank* held that patent claims must protect the inventor not only from those who produce devices falling within the literal claims of the patent but also from copyists who "make unimportant and insubstantial changes and substitutions in the patent which, though adding nothing, would be enough to take the copied matter outside the claim, and hence outside the reach of law." *Id.*, at 607, 70 S.Ct. 854. Justice Black, in dissent, objected that under the doctrine of equivalents a competitor "cannot rely on what the language of a patent claims. He must be able, at the peril of heavy infringement damages, to forecast how far a court relatively unversed in a particular technological field will expand the claim's language. . . . " *Id.*, at 617, 70 S.Ct. 854.

Most recently, in *Warner–Jenkinson*, the Court reaffirmed that equivalents remain a firmly entrenched part of the settled rights protected by the patent. A unanimous opinion concluded that if the doctrine is to be discarded, it is Congress and not the Court that should do so:

> "[T]he lengthy history of the doctrine of equivalents strongly supports adherence to our refusal in *Graver Tank* to find that the Patent Act conflicts with that doctrine. Congress can legislate the doctrine of equivalents out of existence any time it chooses. The various policy arguments now made by both sides are thus best addressed to Congress, not this Court." 520 U.S., at 28, 117 S.Ct. 1040.

III

Prosecution history estoppel requires that the claims of a patent be interpreted in light of the proceedings in the PTO during the application process. Estoppel is a "rule of patent construction" that ensures that claims are interpreted by reference to those "that have been cancelled or rejected." *Schriber–Schroth Co. v. Cleveland Trust Co.*, 311 U.S. 211, 220–221, 61 S.Ct. 235, 85 L.Ed. 132 (1940). The doctrine of equivalents allows the patentee to claim those insubstantial alterations that were not captured in drafting the original patent claim but which could be created through trivial changes. When, however, the patentee originally claimed the subject matter alleged to infringe but then narrowed the claim in response to a rejection, he may not argue that the surrendered territory comprised unforeseen subject matter that should be deemed equivalent to the literal claims of the issued patent. On the contrary, "[b]y the amendment [the patentee] recognized and emphasized the difference between the two phrases[,] . . . and [t]he difference which [the patentee] thus disclaimed must be regarded as material." *Exhibit Supply Co. v. Ace Patents Corp.*, 315 U.S. 126, 136–137, 62 S.Ct. 513, 86 L.Ed. 736 (1942).

A rejection indicates that the patent examiner does not believe the original claim could be patented. While the patentee has the right to appeal, his decision to forgo an appeal and submit an amended claim is taken as a concession that the invention as patented does not reach as far as the original claim. *See Goodyear Dental Vulcanite Co. v. Davis,* 102 U.S. 222, 228, 26 L.Ed. 149 (1880) ("In view of [the amendment] there can be no doubt of what [the patentee] understood he had patented, and that both he and the commissioner regarded the patent to be for a manufacture made exclusively of vulcanites by the detailed process"); *Wang Laboratories, Inc. v. Mitsubishi Electronics America, Inc.,* 103 F.3d 1571, 1577–1578 (C.A.Fed.1997) ("Prosecution history estoppel ... preclud[es] a patentee from regaining, through litigation, coverage of subject matter relinquished during prosecution of the application for the patent"). Were it otherwise, the inventor might avoid the PTO's gatekeeping role and seek to recapture in an infringement action the very subject matter surrendered as a condition of receiving the patent.

Prosecution history estoppel ensures that the doctrine of equivalents remains tied to its underlying purpose. Where the original application once embraced the purported equivalent but the patentee narrowed his claims to obtain the patent or to protect its validity, the patentee cannot assert that he lacked the words to describe the subject matter in question. The doctrine of equivalents is premised on language's inability to capture the essence of innovation, but a prior application describing the precise element at issue undercuts that premise. In that instance the prosecution history has established that the inventor turned his attention to the subject matter in question, knew the words for both the broader and narrower claim, and affirmatively chose the latter.

A

The first question in this case concerns the kinds of amendments that may give rise to estoppel. Petitioner argues that estoppel should arise when amendments are intended to narrow the subject matter of the patented invention, for instance, amendments to avoid prior art, but not when the amendments are made to comply with requirements concerning the form of the patent application. In *Warner–Jenkinson* we recognized that prosecution history estoppel does not arise in every instance when a patent application is amended. Our "prior cases have consistently applied prosecution history estoppel only where claims have been amended for a limited set of reasons," such as "to avoid the prior art, or otherwise to address a specific concern—such as obviousness—that arguably would have rendered the claimed subject matter unpatentable." 520 U.S., at 30–32, 117 S.Ct. 1040. While we made clear that estoppel applies to amendments made for a "substantial reason related to patentability," *id.,* at 33, 117 S.Ct. 1040, we did not purport to define that term or to catalog every reason that might raise an estoppel. Indeed, we stated that even if the amendment's purpose were unrelated to patentability, the court might consider whether it was the kind of reason that nonetheless might require resort to the estoppel doctrine. *Id.,* at 40–41, 117 S.Ct. 1040.

Petitioner is correct that estoppel has been discussed most often in the context of amendments made to avoid the prior art. See *Exhibit Supply Co., supra,* at 137, 62 S.Ct. 513; *Keystone Driller Co. v. Northwest*

Engineering Corp., 294 U.S. 42, 48, 55 S.Ct. 262, 79 L.Ed. 747 (1935). Amendment to accommodate prior art was the emphasis, too, of our decision in *Warner-Jenkinson, supra,* at 30, 117 S.Ct. 1040. It does not follow, however, that amendments for other purposes will not give rise to estoppel. Prosecution history may rebut the inference that a thing not described was indescribable. That rationale does not cease simply because the narrowing amendment, submitted to secure a patent, was for some purpose other than avoiding prior art.

We agree with the Court of Appeals that a narrowing amendment made to satisfy any requirement of the Patent Act may give rise to an estoppel. As that court explained, a number of statutory requirements must be satisfied before a patent can issue. The claimed subject matter must be useful, novel, and not obvious. 35 U.S.C. § § 101–103 (1994 ed. and Supp. V). In addition, the patent application must describe, enable, and set forth the best mode of carrying out the invention. § 112 (1994 ed.). These latter requirements must be satisfied before issuance of the patent, for exclusive patent rights are given in exchange for disclosing the invention to the public. See *Bonito Boats,* 489 U.S., at 150–151, 109 S.Ct. 971. What is claimed by the patent application must be the same as what is disclosed in the specification; otherwise the patent should not issue. The patent also should not issue if the other requirements of § 112 are not satisfied, and an applicant's failure to meet these requirements could lead to the issued patent being held invalid in later litigation.

Petitioner contends that amendments made to comply with § 112 concern the form of the application and not the subject matter of the invention. The PTO might require the applicant to clarify an ambiguous term, to improve the translation of a foreign word, or to rewrite a dependent claim as an independent one. In these cases, petitioner argues, the applicant has no intention of surrendering subject matter and should not be estopped from challenging equivalent devices. While this may be true in some cases, petitioner's argument conflates the patentee's reason for making the amendment with the impact the amendment has on the subject matter.

Estoppel arises when an amendment is made to secure the patent and the amendment narrows the patent's scope. If a § 112 amendment is truly cosmetic, then it would not narrow the patent's scope or raise an estoppel. On the other hand, if a § 112 amendment is necessary and narrows the patent's scope—even if only for the purpose of better description—estoppel may apply. A patentee who narrows a claim as a condition for obtaining a patent disavows his claim to the broader subject matter, whether the amendment was made to avoid the prior art or to comply with § 112. We must regard the patentee as having conceded an inability to claim the broader subject matter or at least as having abandoned his right to appeal a rejection. In either case estoppel may apply.

B

Petitioner concedes that the limitations at issue—the sealing rings and the composition of the sleeve—were made for reasons related to § 112, if not also to avoid the prior art. Our conclusion that prosecution history estoppel arises when a claim is narrowed to comply with § 112 gives rise to the second question presented: Does the estoppel bar the inventor from asserting infringement against any equivalent to the narrowed element or might some equivalents still infringe? The Court of Appeals held that prosecution history estoppel is a complete bar, and so the narrowed element must be limited to its strict literal terms. Based upon its experience the Court of Appeals decided that the flexible-bar rule is unworkable because it leads to excessive uncertainty and burdens legitimate innovation. For the reasons that follow, we disagree with the decision to adopt the complete bar.

Though prosecution history estoppel can bar challenges to a wide range of equivalents, its reach requires an examination of the subject matter surrendered by the narrowing amendment. The complete bar avoids this inquiry by establishing a *per se* rule; but that approach is inconsistent with the purpose of applying the estoppel in the first place— to hold the inventor to the representations made during the application process and to the inferences that may reasonably be drawn from the amendment. By amending the application, the inventor is deemed to concede that the patent does not extend as far as the original claim. It does not follow, however, that the amended claim becomes so perfect in its description that no one could devise an equivalent. After amendment, as before, language remains an imperfect fit for invention. The narrowing amendment may demonstrate what the claim is not; but it may still fail to capture precisely what the claim is. There is no reason why a narrowing amendment should be deemed to relinquish equivalents unforeseeable at the time of the amendment and beyond a fair interpretation of what was surrendered. Nor is there any call to foreclose claims of equivalence for aspects of the invention that have only a peripheral relation to the reason the amendment was submitted. The amendment does not show that the inventor suddenly had more foresight in the drafting of claims than an inventor whose application was granted without amendments having been submitted. It shows only that he was familiar with the broader text and with the difference between the two. As a result, there is no more reason for holding the patentee to the literal terms of an amended claim than there is for abolishing the doctrine of equivalents altogether and holding every patentee to the literal terms of the patent.

This view of prosecution history estoppel is consistent with our precedents and respectful of the real practice before the PTO. While this Court has not weighed the merits of the complete bar against the flexible bar in its prior cases, we have consistently applied the doctrine in a flexible way, not a rigid one. We have considered what equivalents were surrendered during the prosecution of the patent, rather than imposing a complete bar that resorts to the very literalism the equivalents rule is designed to overcome. *E.g., Goodyear Dental Vulcanite Co.*, 102 U.S., at 230, 26 L.Ed. 149; *Hurlbut v. Schillinger*, 130 U.S. 456, 465, 9 S.Ct. 584, 32 L.Ed. 1011 (1889).

The Court of Appeals ignored the guidance of *Warner-Jenkinson*, which instructed that courts must be cautious before adopting changes that disrupt the settled expectations of the inventing community. See 520 U.S., at 28, 117 S.Ct. 1040. In that case we made it clear that the doctrine of equivalents and the rule of prosecution history estoppel are settled law. The responsibility for changing them rests with Congress. *Ibid.* Fundamental alterations in these rules risk destroying the legitimate expectations of inventors in their property. The petitioner in *Warner-Jenkinson* requested another bright-line rule that would have provided more certainty in determining when estoppel applies but at the cost of disrupting the expectations of countless existing patent holders. We rejected that approach: "To change so substantially the rules of the game now could very well subvert the various balances the PTO sought to strike when issuing the numerous patents which have not yet expired and which would be affected by our decision." *Id.*, at 32, n. 6, 117 S.Ct. 1040; see also *id.*, at 41, 117 S.Ct. 1040 (GINSBURG, J., concurring) ("The new presumption, if applied woodenly, might in some instances unfairly discount the expectations of a patentee who had no notice at the time of patent prosecution that such a presumption would apply"). As *Warner-Jenkinson* recognized, patent prosecution occurs in the light of our case law. Inventors who amended their claims under the previous regime had no reason to believe they were conceding all equivalents. If they had known, they might have appealed the rejection instead. There is no justification for applying a new and more robust estoppel to those who relied on prior doctrine.

In *Warner–Jenkinson* we struck the appropriate balance by placing the burden on the patentee to show that an amendment was not for purposes of patentability:

> "Where no explanation is established, however, the court should presume that the patent application had a substantial reason related to patentability for including the limiting element added by amendment. In those circumstances, prosecution history estoppel would bar the application of the doctrine of equivalents as to that element." *Id.*, at 33, 117 S.Ct. 1040.

When the patentee is unable to explain the reason for amendment, estoppel not only applies but also "bar[s] the application of the doctrine of equivalents as to that element." *Ibid.* These words do not mandate a complete bar; they are limited to the circumstance where "no explanation is established." They do provide, however, that when the court is unable to determine the purpose underlying a narrowing amendment— and hence a rationale for limiting the estoppel to the surrender of particular equivalents—the court should presume that the patentee surrendered all subject matter between the broader and the narrower language.

Just as *Warner–Jenkinson* held that the patentee bears the burden of proving that an amendment was not made for a reason that would give rise to estoppel, we hold here that the patentee should bear the burden of showing that the amendment does not surrender the particular equivalent in question. This is the approach advocated by the United States, see Brief for United States as *Amicus Curiae* 22–28, and we regard it to be sound. The patentee, as the author of the claim language, may be expected to draft claims encompassing readily known equivalents. A patentee's decision to narrow his claims through amendment may be presumed to be a general disclaimer of the territory between the original claim and the amended claim. *Exhibit Supply,* 315 U.S., at 136–137, 62 S.Ct. 513 ("By the amendment [the patentee] recognized and emphasized the difference between the two phrases and proclaimed his abandonment of all that is embraced in that difference"). There are some cases, however, where the amendment cannot reasonably be viewed as surrendering a particular equivalent. The equivalent may have been unforeseeable at the time of the application; the rationale underlying the amendment may bear no more than a tangential relation to the equivalent in question; or there may be some other reason suggesting that the patentee could not reasonably be expected to have described the insubstantial substitute in question. In those cases the patentee can overcome the presumption that prosecution history estoppel bars a finding of equivalence.

This presumption is not, then, just the complete bar by another name. Rather, it reflects the fact that the interpretation of the patent must begin with its literal claims, and the prosecution history is relevant to construing those claims. When the patentee has chosen to narrow a claim, courts may presume the amended text was composed with awareness of this rule and that the territory surrendered is not an equivalent of the territory claimed. In those instances, however, the patentee still might rebut the presumption that estoppel bars a claim of equivalence. The patentee must show that at the time of the amendment one skilled in the art could not reasonably be expected to have drafted a claim that would have literally encompassed the alleged equivalent.

IV

On the record before us, we cannot say petitioner has rebutted the presumptions that estoppel applies and that the equivalents at issue have been surrendered. Petitioner concedes that the limitations at issue—the sealing rings and the composition of the sleeve—were made in response to a rejection for reasons under § 112, if not also because of the prior art references. As the amendments were made for a reason relating to patentability, the question is not whether estoppel applies but what territory the amendments surrendered. While estoppel does not effect a complete bar, the question remains whether petitioner can demonstrate that the narrowing amendments did not surrender the particular equivalents at issue. On these questions, respondents may well prevail, for the sealing rings and the composition of the sleeve both were noted expressly in the prosecution history. These matters, however, should be determined in the first instance by further proceedings in the Court of Appeals or the District Court.

The judgment of the Federal Circuit is vacated, and the case is remanded for further proceedings consistent with this opinion.

It is so ordered.

Notes

1. **Why the Special Treatment For Amended Claims?** How did the Court explain the special rule applicable to amended claim elements? Are you satisfied with the differential treatment of amended and unamended claim elements?

2. **Prosecution History Estoppel Without a Claim Amendment.** Often during prosecution a claim element is narrowed by arguments that narrow the meaning of a pending claim element so that the claim literally covers less than it would cover in the absence of the prosecution history. Indeed the Federal Circuit's *en banc* version of *Festo* explained: "Arguments made voluntarily during prosecution may give rise to prosecution history estoppel if they evidence a surrender of subject matter." 234 F. 3d at 569. In most instances, the Federal Circuit requires the explanations during prosecution to show a "clear and unmistakable surrender" of subject matter. *KCJ Corp. v. Kinetic Concepts, Inc.*, 223 F.3d 1351, 1359–60 (Fed.Cir.2000). Nothing in the Supreme Court opinion alters this established principle that prosecution history estoppel does not require an amendment. These principles complicate the acquisition of a patent considerably. An applicant must realize that amending claims relinquishes both literal scope and the doctrine of equivalents, but arguing to avoid amendment can have the same implications. What might an applicant do to avoid either amending or arguing against amendment?

3. **Is a Claim Element Treated As Amended if a Similar Element of a Broader Claim is Rejected as Unpatentable and Then Cancelled?** One proposed strategy for avoiding Festo is to write many claims that differ only slightly from each other and then instead of amending claim to obtain allowance simply cancel the broadest claims until the application contains only allowable claims. Such claims, themselves, would never have been amended. Will this avoidance scheme succeed?

4. **The *Festo* Rule.** Justice Kennedy explained that the Supreme Court's presumption in favor of estoppel is not "just the complete bar by another name." The Supreme Court apparently believes that its three exceptions to the presumption will operate to avoid a complete bar:

> There are some cases, however, where the amendment cannot reasonably be viewed as surrendering a particular equivalent. The equivalent may have been unforeseeable at the time of the application; the rationale underlying the amendment may bear no more than a tangential relation to the equivalent in question; or there may be some other reason suggesting that the patentee could not reasonably be expected to have described the insubstantial substitute in question.

Thus, the three exceptions are: (1) unforeseeable equivalents for which the applicant could not have fashioned literal claim coverage, (2) amendments with only tangential relations to the equivalent in question, and (3) some other reason frustrating accurate description in claims. Can you apply these exceptions to the *Festo* facts? Was a two-way seal unforeseeable? Were the amendments tangential to a two-way seal? Was a two-way seal beyond description? Are these separate exceptions really separate? If an applicant can foresee a particular equivalent, will that known technology likely be difficult to describe?

5.   Was the Supreme Court Case a Win for *Festo*? The *Festo* case was widely perceived to be the most important commercial case of the Court's 2002–03 term. The high-profile nature of the case was established by Festo's retention of Robert Bork to argue its case. However, it is difficult to see how Festo can ultimately prevail based upon the principles set forth in the Supreme Court opinion. Did Festo's appeal achieve anything more than correction of the obvious error pointed out in the following partial dissent in the Federal Circuit's *en banc* decision:

> A primary justification for the doctrine of equivalents is to accommodate after-arising technology. Without a doctrine of equivalents, any claim drafted in current technological terms could be easily circumvented after the advent of an advance in technology. A claim using the terms "anode" and "cathode" from tube technology would lack the "collectors" and "emitters" of transistor technology that emerged in 1948. Thus, without a doctrine of equivalents, infringers in 1949 would have unfettered license to appropriate all patented technology using the outdated terms "cathode" and "anode". Fortunately, the doctrine of equivalents accommodates that unforeseeable dilemma for claim drafters. Indeed, in *Warner–Jenkinson Co., Inc.*, the Supreme Court acknowledged the doctrine's role in accommodating after-arising technology.

> Unfortunately, by barring all application of the doctrine of equivalents for amended claims, this court does not account at all for the primary role of the doctrine. All patent protection for amended claims is lost when it comes to after-arising technology, while the doctrine of equivalents will continue to accommodate after-arising technology in unamended claims. For a reason far more important than disparate treatment of claims, however, this result defies logic. . . . By definition, applicants could not have surrendered something that did not even exist at the time of the claim amendment, namely after-arising technology. . . . [O]ne thing is beyond question: Because after-arising technology was not in existence during the patent application process, the applicant could not have known of it, let alone surrendered it. Nonetheless, the court would apply an estoppel where none exists and defeat the doctrine of equivalents.

234 F.3d at 558, 619–20, 56 U.S.P.Q.2d at 1913–14 (Rader, J., concurring-in-part, dissenting-in-part). This dissent posits that accommodation of after-arising technology is a primary purpose of the doctrine of equivalents. Apply the Supreme Court's three *Festo* exceptions to a case of after-arising technology, like the transistor example in this dissent. Would an after-arising equivalent be "unforeseeable," "tangential," "undescribable?" What do these exceptions cover beyond after-arising technology?

6. Will Unamended Claim Elements Be Treated Differently Under the Doctrine of Equivalents and, if so, How? Did *Festo* Make it More Difficult for Patentees With Unamended Claim Elements? This question, of course, has no definitive answer, but the following section of the Court's opinion provides some hints:

> By amending the application, the inventor is deemed to concede that the patent does not extend as far as the original claim. It does not follow, however, that the amended claim becomes so perfect in its description that no one could devise an equivalent. After amendment, as before, language remains an imperfect fit for invention. The narrowing amendment may demonstrate what the claim is not; but it may still fail to capture precisely what the claim is. There is no reason why a narrowing amendment should be deemed to relinquish equivalents unforeseeable at the time of the amendment and beyond a fair interpretation of what was surrendered. Nor is there any call to foreclose claims of equivalence for aspects of the invention that have only a peripheral relation to the reason the amendment was submitted. The amendment does not show that the inventor suddenly had more foresight in the drafting of claims than an inventor whose application was granted without amendments having been submitted. It shows only that he was familiar with the broader text and with the difference between the two. As a result, there is no more reason for holding the patentee to the literal terms of an amended claim than there is for abolishing the doctrine of equivalents altogether and holding every patentee to the literal terms of the patent.

122 S.Ct. at 1840–41. Before answering this question study the following case that was decided by the Federal Circuit *en banc* during the time the Supreme Court was drafting its version of *Festo*.

JOHNSON & JOHNSTON ASSOCIATES INC., v. R.E. SERVICE CO., INC.

United States Court of Appeals, Federal Circuit, 2002.
285 F.3d 1046, 62 U.S.P.Q.2d 1225.

Before MAYER, CHIEF JUDGE, NEWMAN, CIRCUIT JUDGE, ARCHER, SENIOR CIRCUIT JUDGE, MICHEL, LOURIE, CLEVENGER, RADER, SCHALL, BRYSON, GAJARSA, LINN, DYK AND PROST, CIRCUIT JUDGES.

PER CURIAM.

Johnson and Johnston Associates (Johnston) asserted United States Patent No. 5,153,050 (the '050 patent) against R.E. Service Co. and Mark Frater (collectively RES). A jury found that RES willfully infringed claims 1 and 2 of the patent under the doctrine of equivalents and awarded Johnston $1,138,764 in damages. Upon entry of judgment, the United States District Court for the Northern District of California further granted Johnston enhanced damages, attorney fees, and expenses. *Johnson & Johnston Assocs. v. R.E. Serv. Co.,* No. C97–04382 CRB, 1998 WL 908925 (N.D.Cal.1998). After a hearing before a three-judge panel on December 7, 1999, this court ordered *en banc* rehearing of the doctrine of equivalents issue, *Johnson & Johnston Assocs. v. R.E.*

Serv. Co., 238 F.3d 1347 (Fed.Cir.2001), which occurred on October 3, 2001. Because this court concludes that RES, as a matter of law, could not have infringed the '050 patent under the doctrine of equivalents, this court reverses the district court's judgment of infringement under the doctrine of equivalents, willfulness, damages, attorneys fees, and expenses.

I.

The '050 patent, which issued October 6, 1992, relates to the manufacture of printed circuit boards. Printed circuit boards are composed of extremely thin sheets of conductive copper foil joined to sheets of a dielectric (nonconductive) resin-impregnated material called "prepreg." The process for making multi-layered printed circuit boards stacks sheets of copper foil and prepreg in a press, heats them to melt the resin in the prepreg, and thereby bonds the layers.

In creating these circuit boards, workers manually handle the thin sheets of copper foil during the layering process. Without the invention claimed in the '050 patent, stacking by hand can damage or contaminate the fragile foil, causing discontinuities in the etched copper circuits. The '050 patent claims an assembly that prevents most damage during manual handling. The invention adheres the fragile copper foil to a stiffer substrate sheet of aluminum. With the aluminum substrate for protection, workers can handle the assembly without damaging the fragile copper foil. After the pressing and heating steps, workers can remove and even recycle the aluminum substrate. Figure 5 of the '050 patent shows the foil-substrate combination, with the foil layer peeled back at one corner for illustration:

Surface Ci is the protected inner surface of the copper foil; Ai is the inner surface of the aluminum substrate. A band of flexible adhesive 40 joins the substrate and the foil at the edges, creating a protected central zone CZ. The specification explains:

> Because the frail, thin copper foil C was adhesively secured to its aluminum substrate A, the [laminate] is stiffer and more readily handled resulting in far fewer spoils due to damaged copper foil. The use of the adhered substrate A, regardless of what material it is made of, makes the consumer's (manufacturer's) objective of using thinner and thinner foils and ultimately automating the procedure more realistic since the foil, by use of the invention, is no longer without the much needed physical support.

'050 patent, col. 8, ll. 21–30. The specification further describes the composition of the substrate sheet:

> While aluminum is currently the preferred material for the substrate, other metals, such as stainless steel or nickel alloys, may be used. In some instances . . . polypropelene [sic] can be used.

'050 patent, col. 5, ll. 5–8.

As noted, the jury found infringement of claims 1 and 2:

Claim 1. A component for use in manufacturing articles such as printed circuit boards comprising:

a laminate constructed of a sheet of copper foil which, in a finished printed circuit board, constitutes a functional element and a sheet of *aluminum* which constitutes a discardable element;

one surface of each of the copper sheet and the *aluminum* sheet being essentially uncontaminated and engageable with each other at an interface,

a band of flexible adhesive joining the uncontaminated surfaces of the sheets together at their borders and defining a substantially uncontaminated central zone inwardly of the edges of the sheets and unjoined at the interface.

'050 patent, Claim 1, col. 8, ll. 47–60 (emphasis supplied). Claim 2 defines a similar laminate having sheets of copper foil adhered to both sides of the aluminum sheet.

* * *

In 1997, RES began making new laminates for manufacture of printed circuit boards. The RES products, designated "SC2" and "SC3," joined copper foil to a sheet of steel as the substrate instead of a sheet of aluminum. Johnston filed a suit for infringement. *See Johnson & Johnston Assocs. v. R.E. Serv. Co. v.,* No. C–97–04382 CRB, slip op. at 2, 1998 WL 908925 (N.D.Cal. Dec.23, 1998). In this case, the district court granted RES's motion for summary judgment of no literal infringement. *Johnson & Johnston Assocs. v. R.E. Serv. Co.,* No. C–97–04382 CRB, slip op., 1998 WL 545010 (N.D.Cal. Aug.24, 1998). With respect to the doctrine of equivalents, RES argued, citing *Maxwell v. J. Baker, Inc.,* 86 F.3d 1098, 39 USPQ2d 1001 (Fed.Cir.1996), that the '050 specification, which disclosed a steel substrate but did not claim it, constituted a dedication of the steel substrate to the public. Johnston argued that the steel substrate was not dedicated to the public, citing *YBM Magnex, Inc. v. Int'l Trade Comm'n,* 145 F.3d 1317, 46 USPQ2d 1843 (Fed.Cir.1998). On cross-motions for summary judgment, the district court ruled that the '050 patent did not dedicate the steel substrate to the public, and set the question of infringement by equivalents for trial, along with the issues of damages and willful infringement. *Johnson & Johnston Assocs. v. R.E. Serv. Co.,* No. C–97–04382 CRB, slip op., 1998 WL 545010 (N.D.Cal. Aug.24, 1998).

The jury found RES liable for willful infringement under the doctrine of equivalents and awarded Johnston $1,138,764 in damages....

II.

On appeal, RES does not challenge the jury's factual finding of equivalency between the copper-steel and copper-aluminum laminates. Instead, citing *Maxwell,* RES argues that Johnston did not claim steel substrates, but limited its patent scope to aluminum substrates, thus dedicating to the public this unclaimed subject matter. On this ground,

RES challenges the district court's denial of its motion for summary judgment that RES's copper-steel laminates are not equivalent, as a matter of law, to the claimed copper-aluminum laminates. Johnston responds that the steel substrates are not dedicated to the public, citing *YBM Magnex.* In other words, the two parties dispute whether *Maxwell* or *YBM Magnex* applies in this case with regard to infringement under the doctrine of equivalents.

In *Maxwell,* the patent claimed a system for attaching together a mated pair of shoes. 86 F.3d at 1101–02. Maxwell claimed fastening tabs between the inner and outer soles of the attached shoes. Maxwell disclosed in the specification, but did not claim, fastening tabs that could be "stitched into a lining seam of the shoes." U.S. Patent No. 4,624,060, col. 2, l. 42. Based on the "well-established rule that 'subject matter disclosed but not claimed in a patent application is dedicated to the public,'" this court held that Baker could not, as a matter of law, infringe under the doctrine of equivalents by using the disclosed but unclaimed shoe attachment system. *Maxwell,* 86 F.3d at 1106 (quoting *Unique Concepts, Inc. v. Brown,* 939 F.2d 1558, 1562–63, 19 USPQ2d 1500, 1504 (Fed.Cir.1991)). This court stated further:

> By [Maxwell's failure] to claim these alternatives, the Patent and Trademark Office was deprived of the opportunity to consider whether these alternatives were patentable. A person of ordinary skill in the shoe industry, reading the specification and prosecution history, and interpreting the claims, would conclude that Maxwell, by failing to claim the alternate shoe attachment systems in which the tabs were attached to the inside shoe lining, dedicated the use of such systems to the public.

Maxwell, 86 F.3d at 1108.

In *YBM Magnex,* the patent claimed a permanent magnet alloy comprising certain elements, including "6,000 to 35,000 ppm oxygen." U.S. Patent No. 4,588,439 (the '439 patent), col. 3, l. 12. The accused infringer used similar magnet alloys with an oxygen content between 5,450 and 6,000 ppm (parts per million), which was allegedly disclosed but not claimed in the '439 patent. In *YBM Magnex,* this court stated that *Maxwell* did not create a new rule of law that doctrine of equivalents could never encompass subject matter disclosed in the specification but not claimed. 145 F.3d at 1321. Distinguishing *Maxwell,* this court noted:

> Maxwell avoided examination of the unclaimed alternative, which was distinct from the claimed alternative. In view of the distinctness of the two embodiments, both of which were fully described in the specification, the Federal Circuit denied Maxwell the opportunity to enforce the unclaimed embodiment as an equivalent of the one that was claimed.

Id. at 1320. In other words, this court in *YBM Magnex* purported to limit *Maxwell* to situations where a patent discloses an unclaimed alternative distinct from the claimed invention. Thus, this court must decide whether a patentee can apply the doctrine of equivalents to cover unclaimed subject matter disclosed in the specification.

III.

Both the Supreme Court and this court have adhered to the fundamental principle that claims define the scope of patent protection. *See, e.g., Aro Mfg. v. Convertible Top Replacement Co.,* 365 U.S. 336, 339 (1961) ("[T]he claims made in the patent are the sole measure of the grant.... "); *Cont'l Paper Bag Co. v. E. Paper Bag Co.,* 210 U.S. 405, 419 (1908) ("[T]he claims measure the invention."); *Atl. Thermoplastics Co. v. Faytex Corp.,* 974 F.2d 1299, 1300, 24 USPQ2d 1138, 1139–40 (Fed.Cir.1992) ("The claims alone define the patent right."). The claims thus give notice of the scope of patent protection. *See, e.g., Mahn v. Harwood,* 112 U.S. 354, 361 (1884) ("The public is notified and informed by the most solemn act on the part of the patentee, that his claim to invention is for such and such an element or combination, and for nothing more."). The claims give notice both to the examiner at the U.S. Patent and Trademark Office during prosecution, and to the public at large, including potential competitors, after the patent has issued.

Consistent with its scope definition and notice functions, the claim requirement presupposes that a patent applicant defines his invention in the claims, not in the specification. After all, the claims, not the specification, provide the measure of the patentee's right to exclude. *Milcor Steel Co. v. George A. Fuller Co.,* 316 U.S. 143, 146 (1942) ("Out of all the possible permutations of elements which can be made from the specifications, he reserves for himself only those contained in the claims."); *SRI Int'l,* 775 F.2d at 1121, n. 14 ("Specifications teach. Claims claim.").

Moreover, the law of infringement compares the accused product with the claims as construed by the court. Infringement, either literally or under the doctrine of equivalents, does not arise by comparing the accused product "with a preferred embodiment described in the specification, or with a commercialized embodiment of the patentee." *SRI Int'l,* 775 F.2d at 1121.

Even as early as the 1880s, the Supreme Court emphasized the predominant role of claims. For example, in *Miller v. Bridgeport Brass Co.,* a case addressing a reissue patent filed fifteen years after the original patent, the Supreme Court broadly stated: "[T]he claim of a specific device or combination, and an omission to claim other devices or combinations apparent on the face of the patent, are, in law, a dedication to the public of that which is not claimed." 104 U.S. 350, 352, 26 L.Ed. 783 (1881). Just a few years later, the Court repeated that sentiment in another reissue patent case: "[T]he claim actually made operates in law as a disclaimer of what is not claimed; and of all this the law charges the patentee with the fullest notice." *Mahn,* 112 U.S. at 361. The Court explained further:

Of course, what is not claimed is public property. The presumption is, and such is generally the fact, that what is not claimed was not invented by the patentee, but was known and used before he made his invention. But, whether so or not, his own act has made it public property if it was not so before. The patent itself, as soon as it is issued, is the evidence of this. The public has the undoubted right to use, and it is to be presumed does use, what is not specifically claimed in the patent.

Id. at 361.

The doctrine of equivalents extends the right to exclude beyond the literal scope of the claims. The Supreme Court first applied the modern doctrine of equivalents in *Graver Tank & Mfg. Co. v. Linde Air Prods. Co.* (*Graver II*). In that case, the Court explained: "equivalency must be determined against the context of the patent, the prior art, and the particular circumstances of the case." 339 U.S. 605, 609, 70 S.Ct. 854, 94 L.Ed. 1097 (1950). In *Graver I,* a predecessor case addressing the validity of the claims at issue, the Court held invalid composition claims 24 and 26 comprising "silicates" and "metallic silicates." *Graver Tank & Mfg. v. Linde Air Prods. Co.,* 336 U.S. 271, 276–77, 69 S.Ct. 535, 93 L.Ed. 672 (1949) (*Graver I*). Specifically, the Court found those claims too broad because they encompassed some inoperative silicates along with the nine operative metallic silicates in the specification. *Id.* at 276, 69 S.Ct. 535. The Court did not hold invalid narrower claims comprising "alkaline earth metals."

Thus, in the infringement action of *Graver II,* the Supreme Court addressed only the narrower claims comprising "alkaline earth metals." The alleged infringing compositions in *Graver II* are similar to the compositions of the narrower claims, except that they substitute silicate of manganese—a metallic silicate such as in the earlier invalidated claims—for silicates of "alkaline earth metals" (e.g., magnesium or calcium) claimed in the narrower claims. Because the Court determined that "under the circumstances the change was so insubstantial," and because the accused compositions "perform[ed] substantially the same function in substantially the same way to obtain the same result," the Court upheld the finding of infringement under the doctrine of equivalents. *Graver II,* 339 U.S. at 608–10, 70 S.Ct. 854 (quoting *Sanitary Refrigerator Co. v. Winters,* 280 U.S. 30, 42, 50 S.Ct. 9, 74 L.Ed. 147 (1929)). The Court's holding and the history of *Graver II* show that the patentee had not dedicated unclaimed subject matter to the public. In fact, the patentee had claimed the "equivalent" subject matter, even if the Court eventually held the relevant claims too broad.

In 1997, less than a year after this court decided *Maxwell,* the Supreme Court addressed the doctrine of equivalents again in *Warner–Jenkinson Co. v. Hilton Davis Chem. Co.,* 520 U.S. 17, 117 S.Ct. 1040, 137 L.Ed.2d 146. In that case, Warner–Jenkinson invited the Court "to speak the death" of the doctrine of equivalents. *Id.* at 21, 117 S.Ct. 1040. The Court declined that invitation. In *Warner-Jenkinson,* the patentee added the phrase "at a pH from approximately 6.0 to 9.0" to claim 1 during prosecution. *Id.* at 22, 117 S.Ct. 1040. The alleged infringer operated its ultrafiltration process at a pH of 5.0. *Id.* at 23, 117 S.Ct. 1040. The Supreme Court stated that "while a lower limit of [pH] 6.0, by its mere inclusion, became a material element of the claim, that did not necessarily preclude the application of the doctrine of equivalents as to that element." *Id.* at 32, 117 S.Ct. 1040 (emphasis omitted). On remand, the Supreme Court instructed this court to determine the patentee's reason, if any, for adding the lower pH limit of 6.0 during prosecution.

The patent at issue in *Warner–Jenkinson* did not disclose or suggest an ultrafiltration process where the pH of the reaction mixture was 5.0. *Hilton Davis Chem. Co. v. Warner–Jenkinson Co.*, 114 F.3d 1161, 1164 (Fed.Cir.1997). In fact, the specification practically repeated the claim language: "it is preferred to adjust the *pH to approximately 6.0 to 8.0* before passage through the ultrafiltration membrane." U.S. Patent No. 4,560,746, col. 7, ll. 59–61 (emphasis added). Thus, *Warner–Jenkinson* did not present an instance of the patentee dedicating subject matter to the public in its specification. In 1998, less than a year later, this court decided *YBM Magnex.*

V.

Ded. to public

As stated in *Maxwell,* when a patent drafter discloses but declines to claim subject matter, as in this case, this action dedicates that unclaimed subject matter to the public. Application of the doctrine of equivalents to recapture subject matter deliberately left unclaimed would "conflict with the primacy of the claims in defining the scope of the patentee's exclusive right." *Sage Prods. Inc. v. Devon Indus., Inc.*, 126 F.3d 1420, 1424, 44 USPQ2d 1103, 1107 (Fed.Cir.1997); *see also Conopco, Inc. v. May Dep't Stores Co.*, 46 F.3d 1556, 1562, 32 USPQ2d 1225, 1228 (Fed.Cir.1994) ("The doctrine of equivalents cannot be used to erase 'meaningful structural and functional limitations of the claim on which the public is entitled to rely in avoiding infringement.' "(internal citations omitted)); *Charles Greiner & Co. v. Mari–Med Mfg., Inc.*, 962 F.2d 1031, 1036 (Fed.Cir.1992) ("Most important, however, a court must, in applying the doctrine, avoid significant conflict with the fundamental principle that claims define the limits of patent protection.").

Moreover, a patentee cannot narrowly claim an invention to avoid prosecution scrutiny by the PTO, and then, after patent issuance, use the doctrine of equivalents to establish infringement because the specification discloses equivalents. "Such a result would merely encourage a patent applicant to present a broad disclosure in the specification of the application and file narrow claims, avoiding examination of broader claims that the applicant could have filed consistent with the specification." *Maxwell,* 86 F.3d at 1107 (citing *Genentech, Inc. v. Wellcome Found. Ltd.*, 29 F.3d 1555, 1564, 31 USPQ2d 1161, 1167 (Fed.Cir.1994)). By enforcing the *Maxwell* rule, the courts avoid the problem of extending the coverage of an exclusive right to encompass more than that properly examined by the PTO. *Keystone Bridge Co. v. Phoenix Iron Co.*, 95 U.S.

274, 278, 24 L.Ed. 344 (1877) ("[T]he courts have no right to enlarge a patent beyond the scope of its claim as allowed by the Patent Office, or the appellate tribunal to which contested applications are referred.").

IV.

In this case, Johnston's '050 patent specifically limited the claims to "a sheet of aluminum" and "the aluminum sheet." The specification of the '050 patent, however, reads: "While aluminum is currently the preferred material for the substrate, other metals, such as stainless steel or nickel alloys may be used." Col. 5, ll. 5–10. Having disclosed without claiming the steel substrates, Johnston cannot now invoke the doctrine of equivalents to extend its aluminum limitation to encompass steel. Thus, Johnston cannot assert the doctrine of equivalents to cover the disclosed but unclaimed steel substrate. To the extent that *YBM Magnex* conflicts with this holding, this *en banc* court now overrules that case.

A patentee who inadvertently fails to claim disclosed subject matter, however, is not left without remedy. Within two years from the grant of the original patent, a patentee may file a reissue application and attempt to enlarge the scope of the original claims to include the disclosed but previously unclaimed subject matter. 35 U.S.C. § 251 (2000). In addition, a patentee can file a separate application claiming the disclosed subject matter under 35 U.S.C. § 120 (2000) (allowing filing as a continuation application if filed before all applications in the chain issue). Notably, Johnston took advantage of the latter of the two options by filing two continuation applications that literally claim the relevant subject matter.

Conclusion

For the reasons stated above, the district court erred as a matter of law in concluding that RES infringed the '050 patent under the doctrine of equivalents by using a steel substrate. Consequently, this court reverses the district court's judgment of infringement under the doctrine of equivalents, the judgment of willful infringement, as well as the award of enhanced damages and attorney fees and expenses.

REVERSED.

RADER, CIRCUIT JUDGE, with whom MAYER, CHIEF JUDGE, joins, concurring.

While endorsing the results and reasoning of the court, I would offer an alternative reasoning. This alternative would also help reconcile the preeminent notice function of patent claims with the protective function of the doctrine of equivalents. This reconciling principle is simple: the doctrine of equivalents does not capture subject matter that the patent drafter reasonably could have foreseen during the application process and included in the claims. This principle enhances the notice function of claims by making them the sole definition of invention scope in all foreseeable circumstances. This principle also protects patentees against copyists who employ insubstantial variations to expropriate the claimed invention in some unforeseeable circumstances.

Few problems have vexed this court more than articulating discernible standards for non-textual infringement. On the one hand, the Supreme Court has recognized that the doctrine of equivalents provides essential protection for inventions: "[T]o permit imitation of a patented invention which does not copy every literal detail would be to convert the protection of the patent grant into a hollow and useless thing ... leav[ing] room for indeed encourag[ing] the unscrupulous copyist to make unimportant and insubstantial changes." *Graver Tank & Mfg. Co. v. Linde Air Prods. Co.,* 339 U.S. 605, 607, 70 S.Ct. 854, 94 L.Ed. 1097 (1950). The protective function of non-textual infringement, however, has a price. Recently, the Supreme Court acknowledged that a broad doctrine of equivalents can threaten the notice function of claims: "There can be no denying that the doctrine of equivalents, when applied broadly, conflicts with the definitional and public-notice functions of the statutory claiming requirement." *Warner-Jenkinson Co. v. Hilton Davis Chem. Co.,* 520 U.S. 17, 29, 117 S.Ct. 1040, 137 L.Ed.2d 146 (1997). These competing policies make it difficult to set a standard that protects the patentee against insubstantial changes while simultaneously providing the public with adequate notice of potentially infringing behavior.

In general, the Supreme Court and this court have attempted to deal with these competing principles by placing limits on non-textual infringement. Thus, in furtherance of the notice objective, *Pennwalt* and *Warner-Jenkinson* require an equivalent for each and every element of a claim (applying the doctrine of equivalents to the claim as a whole gives too much room to enforce the claim beyond its notifying limitations). *Pennwalt Corp. v. Durand–Wayland, Inc.,* 833 F.2d 931, 935, 4 USPQ2d 1737, 1740 (Fed.Cir.1987) (citing *Lemelson v. United States,* 752 F.2d 1538, 1551, 224 USPQ 526, 533 (Fed.Cir.1985)); *Warner-Jenkinson,* 520 U.S. at 40, 117 S.Ct. 1040. Similarly, to enhance notice, *Festo* and *Warner-Jenkinson* propose to bar patentees from expanding their claim to embrace subject matter surrendered during the patent acquisition process. *Festo Corp. v. Shoketsu Kinzoku Kogyo Kabushiki Co.,* 234 F.3d 558, 564–65, 56 USPQ2d 1865, 1868–70 (Fed.Cir.2000); *Warner-Jenkinson,* 520 U.S. at 34, 117 S.Ct. 1040. Finally, *Wilson Sporting Goods* prevents the doctrine of equivalents from expanding claim scope to embrace prior art. *Wilson Sporting Goods Co. v. David Geoffrey & Assocs.,* 904 F.2d 677, 683, 14 USPQ2d 1942, 1947–48 (Fed.Cir.1990).

Perhaps more than each of these other restraints on non-textual infringement, a foreseeability bar would concurrently serve both the predominant notice function of the claims and the protective function of the doctrine of equivalents. When one of ordinary skill in the relevant art would foresee coverage of an invention, a patent drafter has an obligation to claim those foreseeable limits. This rule enhances the notice function of claims by making them the sole definition of invention scope in all foreseeable circumstances. When the skilled artisan cannot have foreseen a variation that copyists employ to evade the literal text of the claims, the rule permits the patentee to attempt to prove that an "insubstantial variation" warrants a finding of non-textual infringement. In either event, the claims themselves and the prior art erect a foreseeability bar that circumscribes the protective function of non-textual infringement. Thus, foreseeability sets an objective standard for assessing when to apply the doctrine of equivalents.

A foreseeability bar thus places a premium on claim drafting and enhances the notice function of claims. To restate, if one of ordinary skill in the relevant art would reasonably anticipate ways to evade the literal claim language, the patent applicant has an obligation to cast its claims to provide notice of that coverage. In other words, the patentee has an obligation to draft claims that capture all reasonably foreseeable ways to practice the invention. The doctrine of equivalents would not rescue a claim drafter who does not provide such notice. Foreseeability thus places a premium on notice while reserving a limited role for the protective function of the doctrine of equivalents.

This court actually already has articulated this foreseeability principle in the context of the doctrine of equivalents. Six months after the Supreme Court decided *Warner-Jenkinson,* this court decided *Sage Prods., Inc. v. Devon Indus., Inc.,* 126 F.3d 1420, 44 USPQ2d 1103 (Fed.Cir.1997). In that case, this court found no infringement, either literally or under the doctrine of equivalents, of a patent on a disposal system for sharp medical instruments. *Id.* at 1421. When addressing the doctrine of equivalents issue, this court applied the foreseeability bar:

> The claim at issue defines a relatively simple structural device. *A skilled patent drafter would foresee the limiting potential of the "over said slot" limitation. No subtlety of language or complexity of the technology, nor any subsequent change in the state of the art, such as later-developed technology, obfuscated the significance of this limitation at the time of its incorporation into the claim.* If Sage desired broad patent protection for any container that performed a function similar to its claimed container, it could have sought claims with fewer structural encumbrances. Had Sage done so, then the Patent and Trademark Office (PTO) could have fulfilled its statutory role in helping to ensure that exclusive rights issue only to those who have, in fact, contributed something new, useful, and unobvious. Instead, Sage left the PTO with manifestly limited claims that it now seeks to expand through the doctrine of equivalents. However, *as between the patentee who had a clear opportunity to negotiate broader claims but did not do so, and the public at large, it is the patentee who must bear the cost of its failure to seek protection for this foreseeable alteration of its claimed structure.*

Id. at 1425 (emphasis added). The *Sage* court emphasized that a "skilled patent drafter would foresee the limiting potential of the 'over the slot' limitation." *Id.* Thus, the court barred application of the doctrine of equivalents "for this foreseeable alteration of [the] claimed structure." *Id.*

In *Sage,* this court also noted specifically some types of subject matter that may not be foreseeable during the application process subject matter arising from a "subsequent change in the state of the art, such as later-developed technology," *id.; see also Warner–Jenkinson,* 520 U.S. at 37, 117 S.Ct. 1040 (noting that the doctrine extends to after-arising technology); *Al Site Corp. v. VSI Int'l, Inc.,* 174 F.3d 1308, 1320, 50 USPQ2d 1161, 1168 (Fed.Cir.1999) ("An 'after-arising' technology could thus infringe under the doctrine of equivalents without infringing literally as a § 112, ¶ 6 equivalent."); *Pennwalt,* 833 F.2d at 938 ("[T]he facts here do not involve later-developed computer technology which should be deemed within the scope of the claims to avoid the pirating of an invention."), or subject matter cloaked by the "subtlety of language or complexity of the technology," 126 F.3d at 1425; *see also Mahn v. Harwood,* 112 U.S. 354, 361, 5 S.Ct. 174, 28 L.Ed. 665 (1884) ("If the specification is complicated and the claim is ambiguous or involved, the patentee may be entitled to greater indulgence; and of this the court can rightfully judge in each case.").

Sage is not the only case to acknowledge the value of a foreseeability limit on non-textual infringement. *Fin Control Sys. Pty, Ltd. v. OAM, Inc.,* 265 F.3d 1311, 1320–21, 60 USPQ2d 1203, 1209–10 (Fed.Cir.2001); *SciMed Life Sys., Inc. v. Advanced Cardiovascular Sys., Inc.,* 242 F.3d 1337, 1346–47, 58 USPQ2d 1059, 1066–67 (Fed.Cir.2001); *Zodiac Pool Care, Inc. v. Hoffinger Indus., Inc.,* 206 F.3d 1408, 1416, 54 USPQ2d 1141, 1147 (Fed.Cir.2000); *Moore U.S.A, Inc. v. Standard Register Co.,* 229 F.3d 1091, 1106, 56 USPQ2d 1225, 1235 (Fed.Cir.2000); *Antonious v. Spalding & Evenflo Cos.,* 44 F.Supp.2d 732, 738 (D.Md.1998), *aff'd in part, rev'd in part,* 217 F.3d 849 (Fed.Cir.1999); *Kinzenbaw v. Deere & Co.,* 741 F.2d 383, 389, 222 USPQ 929, 933 (Fed.Cir.1984). In one of those cases, *Kinzenbaw v. Deere & Co.,* this court concluded that the "doctrine of equivalents is designed to protect inventors from unscrupulous copyists . . . and *unanticipated equivalents.*" 741 F.2d at 389 (emphasis added). Referencing a case involving after-arising technology, the Federal Circuit did not require the patent applicant to claim "all future developments which enable the practice of [each limitation of] his invention in substantially the same way." *Id.* (quoting *Hughes Aircraft Co. v. United States,* 717 F.2d 1351, 1362, 219 USPQ 473, 481 (Fed.Cir. 1983) (a case involving after-arising technology, namely microprocessors installed on board a satellite)). In other words, the court acknowledged the role of foreseeability in enforcing the doctrine of equivalents. Nonetheless, prosecution history estoppel precluded the patentee's reliance on non-textual infringement. The court explained further that the variation from the claims was neither copied nor unforeseeable to the patentee at the time of filing. In reaching this result, the court suggested that if variation had been unforeseeable during the application process, the doctrine of equivalents would still have been available to the patentee. *Id.*

Finally, turning more specifically to the issue in this case, in *Maxwell v. J. Baker, Inc.,* 86 F.3d 1098, 39 USPQ2d 1001 (Fed.Cir.1996), this court again dealt with the doctrine of equivalents. This court found that "Maxwell limited her claims to fastening tabs attached between the inner and outer soles." *Id.* at 1108. This court underscored that one of ordinary skill in the shoe industry would have discerned from reading the patent that the drafter could have foreseen and claimed the alternative shoe attachment system, but declined to do so. *Id.* Thus, this court concluded that Maxwell had dedicated the alternative attachment system to the public. *Id.* While not expressly invoking foreseeability as in *Sage* and *Kinzenbaw,* this court relied on the perspective of one of skill in the art, thus suggesting that objective foreseeability adds weight to its foreclosure of equivalents.

In this case, Johnston's '050 patent claimed only a "sheet of aluminum" and "the aluminum sheet" twice specifying the aluminum limitation. The patent specification then expressly mentioned other potential substrate metals, including stainless steel. col. 5, ll. 5–10. Johnston's patent disclosure expressly admits that it foresaw other metals serving as substrates. Yet the patent did not claim anything beyond aluminum. Foreseeability bars Johnston from recapturing as an equivalent subject matter not claimed but disclosed. In *Sage* terms, "as between [Johnston] who had a clear opportunity to negotiate broader claims but did not do so, and the public at large, it is [Johnston] who must bear the cost of its failure to seek protection for this foreseeable alteration of its claimed structure." 126 F.3d at 1425.

Foreseeability relegates non-textual infringement to its appropriate exceptional place in patent policy. The doctrine of equivalents should not rescue claim drafters who fail to give accurate notice of an invention's scope in the claims. The Patent Act supplies a correction process for applicants who have claimed "more or less than [they] had a right to claim in the patent." 35 U.S.C. § § 251, 252 (2001). The doctrine of equivalents need not duplicate the statute's means of correcting claiming errors.

Implicit in the protective function of the doctrine of equivalents is the notion that the patentees could not have protected themselves with reasonable care and foresight. Enforcing this *Sage* principle more aggressively will help achieve a better balance between the notice function of claims and the protective function of non-textual infringement.

Notes

1.   Is There Language in *Festo* that Would Suggest the Supreme Court Should Reverse *Johnston*'s Dedication Doctrine? In the *Johnston* case, one of the claim limitations at issue recited "a sheet of aluminum." That limitation was not amended in the PTO, and yet it did not receive the benefit of equivalents. Therefore, if *Festo* decided that unamended claim elements cover whatever they literally describe and equivalents, then *Johnston* seems to conflict with *Festo*. Would you be willing to argue that the Court should reverse *Johnston*?

2.   Does *Johnston* Penalize Disclosure? Suppose that, contrary to the facts of *Johnston*, the '050 patent disclosed only an aluminum sheet. Further suppose that considerable evidence showed that skilled artisans were fully aware that a steel sheet could be substituted for an aluminum sheet. If an equivalent is foreseeable, but not claimed and not disclosed in the specification (and thus not dedicated to the public), why should that equivalent be treated differently from situations where the equivalent actually was disclosed in the specification? Has *Johnston* penalized disclosure? The *Johnston* court did not address this question. Can you justify *Johnston* if indeed foreseeable, unclaimed, and undisclosed technology is permitted equivalents coverage?

3. A Less Sanguine View of Foreseeability. In a concurring opinion in *Johnston*, Judge Lourie stated that "I am not convinced that introducing the concept of foreseeability is the answer to the equivalence dilemma." He further explained:

> I do not agree that the concept of foreseeability would simplify equivalence issues and make them more amenable to summary judgment. In fact, it would raise new factual issues. Determining what is foreseeable would often require expert testimony as to what one skilled in the art would have foreseen. How would a trial judge know whether to grant summary judgment other than to make factual findings? What is foreseeable is quite different from what is disclosed in the patent, as in our case here, which is readily determinable. Foreseeability is not solely a question of law.
>
> Moreover, the concept of foreseeability seems akin to obviousness. Assuming that the concepts are similar, and that foreseeability or obviousness precludes equivalence, would not a plaintiff asserting equivalence have to show that the accused device would not have been obvious, or foreseeable, in order to avoid a finding of nonequivalence? And would not a defendant have to assert that his device was obvious and hence ineligible for equivalence protection in order to escape liability for patent infringement? It seems counterintuitive for a patentee to have to assert that an accused device was nonobvious or for the accused to have to assert that it was obvious. A patentee seeking to establish equivalence wants to show that the accused is merely making a minor variation of his invention, an obvious one, not a nonobvious improvement. One accused of infringement wants to show that he has made an important advance, not that he is a copier, and that his device was obvious over the patented invention, or foreseeable.
>
> What about the case of a separately patented accused device, which is thus presumptively nonobvious? For such a device to be eligible for equivalence, the improvement therein would have to be found to be not foreseeable, which would seem to run counter to the frequent rubric that equivalence requires substantially the same function, way, and result, a test that is closer to obviousness, not nonobviousness. Should a manufacturer planning to market a product that is close to the claims of an issued patent have to forego a patent in order to be able to assert that its device would have been obvious, hence foreseeable, and thus not covered by equivalence? That is contrary to the patent policy that encourages an innovator to file for a patent and disclose his invention. Thus, foreseeability creates conflicts with conventional patent law ideas.

285 F.3d at 1046, 1063, 62 U.S.P.Q.2d at 1225, 1237. Of course, the Supreme Court opinion in *Festo*, issued shortly after the *Johnston* decision from the

en banc Federal Circuit, seems to make foreseeability part of the question under the doctrine of equivalents. Do you think Judge Lourie is correct that trial courts will need to hold "*Festo* hearings" to ascertain facts before applying non-textual infringement? Chapter 7 taught that obviousness often involves the combination of prior art references, viewed in light of the objective criteria of nonobviousness. Do you agree with Judge Lourie that obviousness might have some relationship to an infringement doctrine, namely foreseeability within the doctrine of equivalents?

4.   Burn the File Wrapper! Professor Thomas has been a vigorous opponent of the use of prosecution history as a tool of claim interpretation. He concludes that the patent bar ought to renew its focus upon the claims as ultimately granted, rather than on preparatory texts of uncertain relationship to the proprietary right ultimately granted. What do you make of the following points urged by Professor Thomas?

- Because patent applications may be held in secret by the PTO, and patentees not infrequently launch infringement actions on the day such a patent issues, notice is a poor justification for the use of prosecution histories in claim interpretation.

- Aware that a court may review each stage of their work product, PTO examiners tend to rely upon the prosecution history to define the patented invention, rather than requiring the applicant to spell out limitations within the claims themselves. Use of the prosecution history to interpret claims also disrupts the integrity of prosecution by encouraging formulaic applicant responses rather than more forthcoming, unhindered dialogue.

- To the extent that the patent community encourages the use of prosecution histories, it promotes a cyclical search for meaning that requires a transcoding from one text to another. Prosecution histories too much be interpreted, and resort to them increases our burdens rather than lessens them.

- An essential element of the traditional estoppel doctrine is reliance, a consideration that is wholly absent from prosecution history estoppel decisions. At a minimum, the courts should determine whether the accused infringer actually relied upon the prosecution history in its technical decision making, rather than turning to the file wrapper only after the patentee filed its infringement suit.

- Thanks to the *Wilson Sporting Goods* line of cases, considered in this casebook immediately below, the courts already possess techniques for accounting for the prior art in claim interpretation. The use of prosecution histories serves as an inferior proxy for this established, objective mechanism for restraining the scope of equivalency.

- If unforeseeability is the post-*Festo* gatekeeper to equivalency, then why look at the prosecution history at all? Nothing within the file wrapper could possibly illuminate what was unknown to the applicant.

See John R. Thomas, *On Preparatory Texts and Proprietary Technologies: The Place of Prosecution Histories in Patent Claim Interpretation*, 47 UCLA L. REV. 183 (1999).

§ 15.3[c] Prior Art Limitations

The third limitation on the doctrine of equivalents relates to the coverage of prior art. Obviously no system of patent law can permit an exclusive right to encompass a product or process already in the prior art. That principle may include as well subject matter that is obvious in light of the prior art. The case that follows adopts this approach. Later cases have adopted a more stringent standard.

WILSON SPORTING GOODS CO. v. DAVID GEOFFREY & ASSOCIATES

United States Court of Appeals, Federal Circuit, 1990.
904 F.2d 677, 14 U.S.P.Q.2d 1942.

Before MARKEY, CHIEF JUDGE, RICH, CIRCUIT JUDGE, and COWEN, SENIOR CIRCUIT JUDGE.

RICH, CIRCUIT JUDGE.

These appeals, consolidated by agreement, are from judgments of the United States District Court for the District of South Carolina in two actions brought by Wilson Sporting Goods Co. (Wilson) for infringement of United States Patent 4,560,168 ('168), entitled "Golf Ball." Trial was before a United States Magistrate by consent. In the first action, the magistrate entered judgment of liability against Dunlop Slazenger Corporation (Dunlop) upon jury verdicts of patent validity and willful infringement. In the second action, the magistrate entered summary judgment of liability against David Geoffrey & Associates (DGA) under the doctrine of collateral estoppel, holding that DGA had been effectively represented by Dunlop in the first action. We reverse in part and vacate in part each judgment.

BACKGROUND

A. The Proceedings

Wilson is a full-line sporting goods company and is one of about six major competitors in the golf ball business. Among its well-known balls are the ProStaff and Ultra. Dunlop is also a major player in the golf ball business. It competes head-to-head with Wilson by selling the Maxfli Tour Limited and Slazenger balls. It sells the Maxfli Tour Limited ball to numerous distributors, but sells the Slazenger ball only to DGA, which distributes the ball to U.S. customers

On August 2, 1988, Wilson separately sued Dunlop and DGA for patent infringement in the United States District Court for the District of South Carolina. Wilson accused Dunlop of infringing claims 1, 7, 15–16, and 19–22 of its '168 patent, and made a general accusation of infringement against DGA.

B. The Technology

For more than a century, golfers have been searching for a "longer" ball. As one of the parties put it, "distance sells." Inventors have experimented with numerous aspects of ball design over the years, but as United States Golf Association (U.S.G.A.) rules began to strictly control ball size, weight, and other parameters, inventors focused their efforts on the "dimples" in the ball's surface. According to one witness, new dimple designs provide the only real opportunity for increasing distance within the confines of U.S.G.A. rules.

Dimples create surface turbulence around a flying ball, lessening drag and increasing lift. In lay terms, they make the ball fly higher and farther. While this much is clear, "dimple science" is otherwise quite complicated and inexact: dimples can be numerous or few, and can vary as to shape, width, depth, location, and more.

Wilson's '168 patent claims a certain configuration of dimples on a golf ball cover. The shape and width of the dimples in the '168 patent is for the most part immaterial. What is critical is their location on the ball. The goal is to create a more symmetrical distribution of dimples.

Generally speaking, the dimples in the patent are arranged by dividing the cover of a spherical golf ball into 80 imaginary spherical triangles and then placing the dimples (typically several hundred) into strategic locations in the triangles. The triangles are constructed as follows. First, the ball is divided into an imaginary "icosahedron," as shown in Figure 1. An icosahedral golf ball is completely covered by 20 imaginary equilateral triangles, 5 of which cover each pole of the ball and ten of which surround its equator. Second, the midpoints of each of the sides of each of the 20 icosahedral triangles are located, as shown in Figure 2. Third, the midpoints are joined, thus subdividing each icosahedral triangle into four smaller triangles.

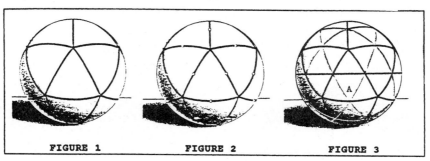

FIGURE 1   **FIGURE 2**   **FIGURE 3**

The resulting 80 imaginary triangles are shown in Figure 3. Critically important are the light lines which join the midpoints. As can be seen from Figure 3, they form the arcs of circles which pass completely around the widest part of the ball. There are six such circles, referred to in the patent as "great circles."

All of the claims of the '168 patent require this basic golf ball having eighty sub-triangles and six great circles. Particular claims require variations on the placement of dimples in the triangles, with one common theme?the dimples must be arranged on the surface of the ball so that no dimple intersects any great circle. Equivalently stated, the dimples must be arranged on the surface of the ball so that no dimple intersects the side of any central triangle. See Figure 4, below. When the dimples are arranged in this manner, the ball has six axes of symmetry, compared to prior balls which had only one axis of symmetry.

C. Patent and Trademark Office (PTO) Proceedings

Wilson employee Steven Aoyama filed his patent application on April 27, 1984. Twenty seven claims were presented. All were allowed on the first action without comment by the examiner. The patent issued on December 24, 1985, to Wilson as assignee of Aoyama.

Claim 1, the only independent claim, reads:

1.   A golf ball having a spherical surface with a plurality of dimples formed therein and six great circle paths which do not intersect any di[m]ples, the dimples being arranged by dividing the spherical surface into twenty spherical triangles corresponding to the faces of a regular icosahedron, each of the twenty triangles being sub-divided into four smaller triangles consisting of a central triangle and three apical triangles by connecting the midpoints [of the sides] of each of said twenty triangles along great circle paths, said dimples being arranged so that the dimples do not intersect the sides of any of the central triangles. [Bracketed insertions ours.]

The remaining 26 claims are dependent upon claim 1. They contain further limitations as to the number and location of dimples in the sub-triangles. Claim 7, for example, requires that all "central triangles [have] the same number of dimples." Other dependent claims locate dimples on the perimeter of the apical triangles, so that dimples are shared by adjacent apical triangles. See Figure 5.

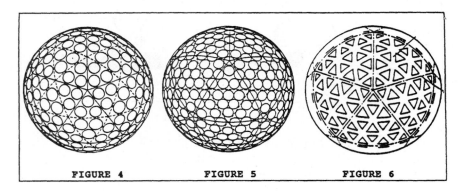

FIGURE 4   FIGURE 5   FIGURE 6

D. The Prior Art

The most pertinent prior art is a 1932 British patent to Pugh, which was cited by the examiner. Pugh teaches that a golf ball can be divided into any regular polyhedron, including an icosahedron. Pugh also discloses sub-dividing each of the twenty icosahedral triangles into smaller triangles. As an example, shown in Figure 6, Pugh divides each icosahedral triangle into sixteen sub-triangles, in contrast to the four sub-triangles required by the '168 patent. (The dimples in Pugh are triangular.) Nonetheless, Figure 6 (which is Figure 3 of the Pugh patent) makes clear that Pugh's sixteen sub-triangles are merely further divisions of four larger sub-triangles. Claim 3 of Pugh explains his invention:

> 3.   A method of distributing a pattern with substantial uniformity over the surface of a sphere, such as a golf ball, which consists in . . . form[ing] equilateral triangles in the case of the . . . icosahedron . . . , dividing the sides of the triangles so found into the same number of equal or substantially equal parts and finally joining corresponding points in each pair of sides of each triangle by a series of arcs of great circles, substantially as described.

The prior art also includes several patents to Uniroyal and a Uniroyal golf ball sold in the 1970's. The Uniroyal ball is an icosahedral ball having six great circles with 30 or more dimples intersecting the great circles by about 12?15 thousandths of an inch. We discuss it extensively below.

E.   The Accused Balls

There are four accused products, all of which the jury found to infringe. The following table summarizes the characteristics of each accused ball:

Ball	Dimples	Cover	Infringer
Maxfli Tour Limited MD	432	Surlyn	Dunlop
Maxfli Tour Limited HT	432	Balata	Dunlop
Slazenger Interlock 480 (S)	480	Surlyn	Dunlop & DGA
Slazenger Interlock 480 (B)	480	Balata	Dunlop & DGA

The accused balls (collectively "Dunlop's balls") have dimples which are arranged in an icosahedral pattern having six great circles, but the six great circles are not dimple-free as the claims literally require. The number of dimples which intersect great circles and the extent of their intersection were disputed by the parties, but the evidence most favorable to appellee Wilson can be summarized as follows (units of last two columns are 0.001'):

Ball	Dimples	Dimples Intersected	Dimple Radius	Extent of Intersection
MD	432	60	60-80	7.5
HT	432	60	60-80	8.7
Interlock (S)	480	60	60-80	4.0
Interlock (B)	480	60	60-80	4.0

OPINION

1. Dunlop's Argument

The only theory of liability presented to the jury by Wilson was infringement under the doctrine of equivalents. Dunlop's argument for reversal is straightforward. It contends that there is no principled difference between the balls which the jury found to infringe and the prior art Uniroyal ball; thus to allow the patent to reach Dunlop's balls under the doctrine of equivalents would improperly ensnare the prior art Uniroyal ball as well.   *Prior art incl. patent as equivalent*

2. Independent Claim 1

Infringement may be found under the doctrine of equivalents if an accused product "performs substantially the same overall function or work, in substantially the same way, to obtain substantially the same overall result as the claimed invention." *Pennwalt Corp. v. Durand–Wayland, Inc.*, 833 F.2d 931, 934, 4 U.S.P.Q.2d 1737, 1739 (Fed.Cir. 1987) (en banc), *cert. denied*, 485 U.S. 961, 108 S.Ct. 1226, 99 L.Ed.2d 426, 485 U.S. 1009, 108 S.Ct. 1474, 99 L.Ed.2d 703 (1988). Even if this test is met, however, there can be no infringement if the asserted scope of equivalency of what is literally claimed would encompass the prior art. *Id.; Senmed, Inc. v. Richard–Allan Medical Indus.*, 888 F.2d 815, 821, 12 U.S.P.Q.2d 1508, 1513 (Fed.Cir.1989). This issue—whether an asserted range of equivalents would cover what is already in the public domain—   *Issue* is one of law, which we review de novo, but we presume that the jury resolved underlying evidentiary conflicts in Wilson's favor, *see DMI, Inc. v. Deere & Co.*, 802 F.2d 421, 425, 231 U.S.P.Q. 276, 279 (Fed.Cir.1986).

This court on occasion has characterized claims as being "expanded" or "broadened" under the doctrine of equivalents. Precisely speaking, these characterizations are inaccurate. To say that the doctrine of equivalents extends or enlarges the claims is a contradiction in terms. The claims—*i.e.*, the scope of patent protection as defined by the claims—remain the same and application of the doctrine expands the right to exclude to "equivalents" of what is claimed. The doctrine of equivalents, by definition, involves going beyond any permissible interpretation of the claim language; *i.e.*, it involves determining whether the accused product is "equivalent" to what is described by the claim language.

right, not claim, expanded

This distinction raises an interesting question: If the doctrine of equivalents does not involve expanding the claims, why should the prior art be a limitation on the range of permissible equivalents? It is not because we construe claims narrowly if necessary to sustain their validity. As we have said, the doctrine of equivalents does not involve expansion of the claims. Nor is it because to hold otherwise would allow the patentee to preempt a product that was in the public domain prior to the invention. The accused products here, as in most infringement cases, were never "in the public domain." They were developed long after the invention and differ in several respects from the prior art.

[The answer is that a patentee should not be able to obtain, under the doctrine of equivalents, coverage which he could not lawfully have obtained from the PTO by literal claims.] The doctrine of equivalents exists to prevent a fraud on a patent, *Graver Tank & Mfg. Co. v. Linde Air Prods. Co.*, 339 U.S. 605, 608, 70 S.Ct. 854, 856, 94 L.Ed. 1097 (1950), not to give a patentee something which he could not lawfully have obtained from the PTO had he tried. Thus, since prior art always limits what an inventor could have claimed, it limits the range of permissible equivalents of a claim.

Whether prior art restricts the range of equivalents of what is literally claimed can be a difficult question to answer. To simplify analysis and bring the issue onto familiar turf, it may be helpful to conceptualize the limitation on the scope of equivalents by visualizing a hypothetical patent claim, sufficient in scope to literally cover the accused product. The pertinent question then becomes whether that hypothetical claim could have been allowed by the PTO over the prior art. If not, then it would be improper to permit the patentee to obtain that coverage in an infringement suit under the doctrine of equivalents. If the hypothetical claim could have been allowed, then prior art is not a bar to infringement under the doctrine of equivalents.

Viewing the issue in this manner allows use of traditional patentability rules and permits a more precise analysis than determining whether an accused product (which has no claim limitations on which to focus) would have been obvious in view of the prior art. Compare with *Ryco, Inc. v. Ag–Bag Corp.*, 857 F.2d 1418, 1426, 8 U.S.P.Q.2d 1323, 1330 (Fed.Cir.1988) (comparing accused product with prior art). In fact, the utility of this hypothetical broader claim may explain why "expanded claim" phraseology, which we now abandon, had crept into our jurisprudence. Finally, it reminds us that Wilson is seeking patent coverage beyond the limits considered by the PTO examiner.

In this context it is important to remember that the burden is on Wilson to prove that the range of equivalents which it seeks would not ensnare the prior art Uniroyal ball. The patent owner has always borne the burden of proving infringement, and there is no logical reason why that burden should shift to the accused infringer simply because infringement in this context might require an inquiry into the patentability of a hypothetical claim. Any other approach would ignore the realities of what happens in the PTO and violate established patent law. Leaving this burden on Wilson does not, of course, in any way undermine the presumed validity of Wilson's actual patent claims. In the present situation, Wilson's claims will remain valid whether or not Wilson persuades us that it is entitled to the range of equivalents sought here.

The specific question before us, then, is whether Wilson has proved that a hypothetical claim, similar to claim 1 but broad enough to literally cover Dunlop's balls, could have been patentable. As we have explained above, Dunlop's balls are icosahedral balls with six great circles, five of which are intersected by dimples. The balls contain 432 to 480 dimples, 60 of which intersect great circles in amounts from 4 to 9 thousandths of an inch. In order for a hypothetical claim to cover Dunlop's balls, its limitations must permit 60 dimples to intersect the great circles by at least 9 thousandths of an inch. Thus, the issue is whether a hypothetical claim directed to an icosahedral ball having six great circles intersected by 60 dimples in amounts up to 9 thousandths of an inch could have been patentable in view of the prior art Uniroyal ball.

On the Uniroyal ball, the extent to which the dimples intersect the great circles is from 12 to 15 thousandths of an inch. Stated as a percentage of dimple radius, the intersection permitted in the hypothetical claim is 13% or less, and the dimples on the Uniroyal ball intersect by 17% to 21%. The number of dimples which intersect the great circles is also similar for the hypothetical claim and the prior art Uniroyal ball. The pertinent hypothetical claim limitation reads on any ball having 60 or less intersecting dimples. This limitation reads on the prior art Uniroyal ball, which has 30 intersecting dimples. If viewed in relative terms, the hypothetical claim limitation reads on any ball which has less than 14% of its dimples intersecting great circles. Roughly 12% of the dimples on the Uniroyal ball intersect great circles.

We hold that these differences are so slight and relatively minor that the hypothetical claim—which permits twice as many intersecting dimples, but with slightly smaller intersections—viewed as a whole would have been obvious in view of the Uniroyal ball. As Dunlop puts it, there is simply "no principled difference" between the hypothetical claim and the prior art Uniroyal ball. Accordingly, Wilson's claim 1 cannot be given a range of equivalents broad enough to encompass the accused Dunlop balls.

3. Dependent Claims

Before separately analyzing the asserted dependent claims, we should first explain why we are bothering to do so. This court has stated: "It is axiomatic that dependent claims cannot be found infringed unless the claims from which they depend have been found to have been infringed." *Wahpeton Canvas Co., Inc. v. Frontier, Inc.*, 870 F.2d 1546, 1553 & n. 9, 10 U.S.P.Q.2d 1201, 1208 & n. 9 (Fed.Cir.1989). While this proposition is no doubt generally correct, it does not apply in the circumstances of this case.

Here, we have reversed the judgment of infringement of independent claim 1 solely because the asserted range of equivalents of the claim limitations would encompass the prior art Uniroyal ball. The dependent claims, of course, are narrower than claim 1; therefore, it does not automatically follow that the ranges of equivalents of these narrower claims would encompass the prior art, because of their added limitations.

Holding

We have considered each asserted dependent claim and conclude that none could be given a range of equivalents broad enough to encompass Dunlop's balls because that would extend Wilson's patent protection beyond hypothetical claims it could lawfully have obtained from the PTO.

[Judgment of infringement reversed.]

Notes

1. The Progeny of *Wilson Sporting Goods*. Immediately after the issuance of *Wilson Sporting Goods*, the trial practitioners within the patent bar widely criticized the opinion because it appeared to place on patentees the burden of both concocting, and proving the validity of, a hypothetical claim as part of their case in chief. *See* Henrik D. Parker, *Doctrine of Equivalents Analysis after Wilson Sporting Goods: The Hypothetical Claim Hydra*, 18 AM. INTELL. PROP. L. ASS'N Q. J. 262 (1990). Indeed, the Federal Circuit has stepped back somewhat from the *Wilson Sporting Goods*, as demonstrated by the following statement from *Key Manufacturing Group, Inc. v. Microdot, Inc.*, 925 F.2d 1444, 1449, 17 U.S.P.Q.2d 1806, 1810 (Fed.Cir.1991):

> The Microdot structure also does not infringe under the doctrine of equivalents. Rather Microdot's structure is described in the prior art, specifically in the Chaivre, Allmanna, and Erdmann patents.

> While not obligatory in every doctrine of equivalents determination, the hypothetical claim rationale of *Wilson Sporting Goods* helps define the limits imposed by prior art on the range of equivalents. The *Wilson* hypothetical claim analysis does not envision application of a full-blown patentability analysis to a hypothetical claim. *Wilson* simply acknowledges that prior art limits the coverage available under the doctrine of equivalents. A range of equivalents may not embrace inventions already disclosed by prior art.

> A hypothetical claim drawn to cover literally the Microdot nut would not be patentable over the prior art. The Chaivre, Allmanna, and Erdmann patents would make the Microdut nut obvious. Contrary to Key's assertion, no single prior art reference need include each element of the hypothetical claim. The question under *Wilson* is whether the hypothetical claim "could have been allowed by the PTO over the prior art." Because the Microdot nuts and, thus the hypothetical claim, are obvious in light of these three prior are references, the doctrine of equivalents does not reach the accused nuts.

See also International Visual Corp. v. Crown Metal Mfg. Co., 991 F.2d 768, 26 U.S.P.Q.2d 1588 (Fed.Cir.1993).

2. Is the Hypothetical Claim Approach Now Mandatory? However-
er, in *Streamfeeder, LLC v. Sure–Feed Systems, Inc.*, 175 F.3d 974, 50
U.S.P.Q.2d 1515 (Fed.Cir.1999), Streamfeeder's hypothetical claim may well
have been non-obvious because of the narrowing of certain limitations.
These narrowed limitations may have provided a basis for patentability. The
Federal Circuit appeared to concede that the Sure–Feed feeder may have
been patentable over the prior art. Therefore, the Federal Circuit did not
find the Sure–Feed device obvious over the prior art, but instead set out a
key restriction on the drafting of a hypothetical claim, i.e.that the limitations
can be expanded, but not narrowed so as to read on the disclosure and on
the accused product or process, but not on the prior art. Do you approve of
this hypothetical claim requirement over the simple rule that the alleged
infringing device cannot be obvious from the prior art? For a detailed
discussion of the added restrain put on the doctrine of equivalents by
Streamfeeder, see 3 Martin J. Adelman, Patent Law Perspectives, § 3.4[1]
n.373 (2d ed. 1999).

§ 15.4 THE REVERSE DOCTRINE OF EQUIVALENTS

In theory, the doctrine of equivalents need not always operate in
favor of the patentee. In some circumstances, it "may be used to restrict
the claim and defeat the patentee's action for infringement," in the
words of *Graver Tank*. The following excerpt describes the latest Federal
Circuit pronouncement on the reverse doctrine of equivalents. Its discussion follows a detailed review and a rejection of the practicing the prior
art defense. It simply says that if you are practicing the prior art you
should be able to easily show that any claims that cover the accused
product or process are invalid for obviousness or anticipation.

TATE ACCESS FLOORS, INC. v. INTERFACE ARCHITECTURAL RESOURCES, INC.

United States Court of Appeals, Federal Circuit, 2002.
279 F.3d 1357, 61 U.S.P.Q.2d 1647.

Before Gajarsa,, Circuit Judge, PLAGER, Senior Circuit Judge, and
DYK, Circuit Judge.

Gajarsa, Circuit Judge.

Interface argues that the existence of the reverse doctrine of equivalents proves that the literal infringement inquiry cannot end upon a
finding that a claim, as properly construed, reads on the accused device.
The reverse doctrine of equivalents, Interface contends, may result in a
finding of noninfringement even when the accused device possesses each
and every limitation of an asserted claim. Interface therefore urges this
court to adopt its "practicing the prior art" defense as a rebuttal similar
to its conception of the reverse doctrine of equivalents.

We reject this argument. The Supreme Court referred to the reverse
doctrine of equivalents in *Graver Tank & Manufacturing Co. v. Linde
Air Products Co.*, 339 U.S. 605, 608–609, 70 S.Ct. 854, 94 L.Ed. 1097, 85
USPQ 328, 330 (1950). It applies "where a device is so far changed in

principle from a patented article that it performs the same or a similar function in a substantially different way, but nevertheless falls within the literal words of the claim." *Id.* at 609, 339 U.S. 605, 70 S.Ct. 854, 94 L.Ed. 1097, 85 USPQ at 330. In such a case, the reverse doctrine of equivalents "may be used to restrict the claim and defeat the patentee's action for infringement." *Id.*

Not once has this court affirmed a decision finding noninfringement based on the reverse doctrine of equivalents. And with good reason: when Congress enacted 35 U.S.C. § 112, after the decision in Graver Tank, it imposed requirements for the written description, enablement, definiteness, and means-plus-function claims that are co-extensive with the broadest possible reach of the reverse doctrine of equivalents. *See In re Donaldson Co.*, 16 F.3d 1189, 1194 & n. 5, 29 USPQ2d 1845, 1849–50 & n. 5 (Fed.Cir.1994) (rejecting Commissioner's argument that by enacting § 112 Congress intended only to codify the reverse doctrine of equivalents and thereby to render the requirements applicable only in the litigation context, and therefore holding that the requirements of § 112, ¶ 6 apply to all interpretations of means-plus-function claim language, but noting that one result of enacting § 112 may have been to codify the reverse doctrine of equivalents); *cf. Hilton Davis Chem. Co. v. Warner–Jenkinson Co.*, 62 F.3d 1512, 1569, 35 USPQ2d 1641, 1688–89 (Fed.Cir.1995) (en banc) (Nies, J., dissenting) (noting that the reverse doctrine of equivalents was originally used by the courts to reduce the scope of broad "means" claims to "cover only what the inventor discloses and equivalents thereof"), *rev'd and remanded*, 520 U.S. 17, 117 S.Ct. 1040, 137 L.Ed.2d 146, 41 USPQ2d 1865 (1997).

Even were this court likely ever to affirm a defense to literal infringement based on the reverse doctrine of equivalents, the presence of one anachronistic exception, long mentioned but rarely applied, is hardly reason to create another. We therefore decline the invitation to adopt Interface's "practicing the prior art" defense on these grounds.

Notes

1. The Reverse Doctrine of Equivalents at the Federal Circuit. The Reverse Doctrine of Equivalents was discussed in an important early biotech patent case, *Scripps Clinic* as follows:

> The so-called "reverse doctrine of equivalents" is an equitable doctrine invoked in applying properly construed claims to an accused device. Just as the purpose of the "doctrine of equivalents" is to prevent "pirating" of the patentee's invention, *Graver Tank*, so the purpose of the "reverse" doctrine is to prevent unwarranted extension of the claims beyond a fair scope of the patentee's invention.

> The reverse doctrine of equivalents flows from the Supreme Court's statement in *Graver Tank* that an accused article may avoid infringement, even if it is within the literal words of the claim, if it is "so far changed in principle from a patented article that it performs the same or a similar function in a substantially different way." 339 U.S. at 608–09, 70 S.Ct. at 856, 85 U.S.P.Q. at 330. Application of the doctrine requires

that facts specific to the accused device be determined and weighed against the equitable scope of the claims, which in turn is determined in light of the specification, the prosecution history, and the prior art.

The record contained evidence of the properties of plasma-derived and recombinantly produced VIII:C, which was presented primarily by Scripps in connection with its proofs of infringement. There was deposition testimony that there were differences between VIII:C from plasma and VIII:C obtained by recombinant techniques; a Scripps' witness described the products as "apples and oranges", referring specifically to stability and formulations. The parties disputed, in connection with the summary judgment motions, the capabilities of the respective processes in terms of the purity and specific activities that were enabled for the respective products. The record on this point is extensive.

Genentech argues that its product is equitably seen as changed "in principle", particularly when viewed in the context of the prior art. Genentech asserts that the specific activities and purity that are obtainable by recombinant technology exceed those available by the Scripps process; an assertion disputed by Scripps, but which if found to be correct could provide—depending on the specific facts of similarities and differences—sufficient ground for invoking the reverse doctrine. These aspects were not discussed by the district court.

The principles of patent law must be applied in accordance with the statutory purpose, and the issues raised by new technologies require considered analysis. Genentech has raised questions of scientific and evidentiary fact that are material to the issue of infringement. Consideration of extrinsic evidence is required, and summary judgment is inappropriate. *See C.R. Bard, Inc. v. Advanced Cardiovascular Systems, Inc.,* 911 F.2d 670, 673, 15 U.S.P.Q.2d 1540, 1542 (Fed.Cir.1990).

The grant of summary judgment of infringement of claims 24, 25, 28, and 29 is reversed. The issue requires trial.

Scripps Clinic Research Found. v. Genentech, Inc., 927 F.2d 1565, 1581, 18 U.S.P.Q.2d 1001, 1014 (Fed.Cir.1991). If the products of Scripps Clinic's process and Genentech's process were so different as to require a trial, why was this a reverse doctrine of equivalents question rather than a noninfringement question? Also notable is the germinal case on the reverse doctrine, *Boyden Power–Brake Co. v. Westinghouse,* 170 U.S. 537 (1898).

2. The Reverse Doctrine of Equivalents and the Patentability of a Product Claim Based on its Method of Manufacture. The proper response to a charge that a claim is overinclusive is not to suggest that the reverse doctrine of equivalents can correct overinclusiveness. The proper response is to ask why the PTO allowed such a broad claim in the first place. If that question is asked about the Scripps invention, the answer is that the law may allow one who develops a nonobvious method for making a new product to obtain a patent on the product itself even though those skilled in the art knew what properties the product would possess, although they didn't know how to make it. For arguments concerning whether discovering a nonobvious method for making an obviously desirable product should justify a product rather than a product patent *see* 2 MARTIN J. ADELMAN, PATENT LAW PERSPECTIVES, § 2.6[10] at ns. 75, 76 (2d ed. 1991).

3. The Reverse Doctrine of Equivalents and § 112, ¶ 6. In *Johnston v. IVAC Corp.*, 885 F.2d 1574, 1580, 12 U.S.P.Q.2d 1382, 1386 (Fed.Cir. 1989), Chief Judge Nies provided an interesting analogy:

> Section 112 ¶ 6 does not, in any event, expand the scope of the claim. An element of a claim described as a means for performing a function, if read literally, would encompass any means for performing the function. But section 112 ¶ 6 operates to cut back on the types of means which could literally satisfy the claim language. On the other hand, the section has no effect on the function specified—it does not extend the element to equivalent functions. Properly understood section 112 ¶ 6 operates more like the reverse doctrine of equivalents than the doctrine of equivalents because it restricts the scope of the literal claim language.

4. The Reverse Doctrine and Accidental Anticipation. The reverse doctrine of equivalents provides some insight into the interplay between anticipation, nonobviousness and infringement. Recall the discussion in Chapter 6 of this casebook on the lack of anticipatory effect of accidental prior art uses. Also from that Chapter recall the "classic test of anticipation" that was somewhat modified in *Lewmar Marine*: "That which will infringe, if later, will anticipate." From these two doctrines, could you produce as a necessary corollary the reverse doctrine of equivalents?

5. Further Reading. Professors Robert Merges and Richard Nelson have asserted that the patent law should, in appropriate circumstances, pay careful attention to the maintenance of an environment where improvement technologies can be marketed free from the influence of a broad, pioneering patent. Under their proposal, courts should selectively curtail protection for patents on pioneering inventions so that other inventors would be able to develop noninfringing refinements more readily. Chief among the means courts would employ under this proposal is the Reverse Doctrine of Equivalents. For more details on this proposal and the role of the Reverse Doctrine of Equivalents, *see* Robert P. Merges & Richard R. Nelson, *On the Complex Economics of Patent Scope*, 90 COLUM. L. REV. 839 (1990).

§ 15.5 EXPERIMENTAL USE

The patent law purports to provide a *de minimis* exception to the definition of infringement provided in § 271. Its origin is commonly traced to *Whittemore v. Cutter*, 29 F.Cas. 1120, 1121 (C.C.Mass.1813) (No. 17,600), where Justice Story stated:

> [I]t could never have been the intention of the legislature to punish a man, who constructed such a machine merely for philosophical experiments, or for the purpose of ascertaining the sufficiency of the machine to produce its described effects.

Fifty years later, the law was "well-settled that an experiment with a patented article for the sole purpose of gratifying a philosophical taste, or curiosity, or for mere amusement is not an infringement of the rights of the patentee." *Poppenhusen v. Falke*, 19 F.Cas. 1048, 1049 (C.C.S.D.N.Y.1861) (No. 11,279). Cases in which the accused infringer can successfully plead an experimental use defense are relatively rare, however. *See* Note, *Experimental Use as Patent Infringement: The Impropriety of a Broad Exception*, 100 YALE L.J. 2169 (1991); Richard E. Bee, *Experimental Use as An Act of Patent Infringement*, 39 J. PAT. OFF. SOC'Y 357 (1957).

This aged and somewhat discredited doctrine took on new life with enactment of the Hatch–Waxman Act in 1984. This statute enacted a form of the old experimental use doctrine to govern the interface between patented and generic pharmaceuticals. Statutes and agency regulations frequently require medical products to undergo a time-consuming approval process prior to marketing. When a competitor becomes interested in marketing a product patented by another, it will often begin this testing process during the term of the patent so that its product may be promptly sold following expiration of the patent. An infringement suit was the inevitable result of these pressures, with the experimental use exemption to infringement at least theoretically implicated. The following decision traces the reaction of courts and Congress to this set of competing interests.

INTERMEDICS, INC. v. VENTRITEX, CO., INC.

United States District Court, N.D. California, 1991.775
F.Supp. 1269, 20 U.S.P.Q.2d 1422.
aff'd, 991 F.2d 808, 26 U.S.P.Q.2d 1524 (Fed.Cir.1993).

WAYNE D. BRAZIL, UNITED STATES MAGISTRATE JUDGE.

Defendants have moved this court for an order dismissing the complaint, or, in the alternative, for entry of summary judgment, on the ground that defendants are immunized from suit by 35 U.S.C. § 271(e)(1).

A. INTRODUCTION

§ 271(e)(1) exempts from claims of patent infringement otherwise infringing activity that is "solely for uses reasonably related" to obtaining FDA approval. Defendants' implantable defibrillator, the Cadence, is a Class III device which must be approved by the FDA before it can be commercially distributed.

Section 515(a) of the Food, Drug and Cosmetic Act (21 U.S.C. § 360e(a)) requires that an application for a pre-market approval (PMA) be filed and granted by the FDA for all Class III devices. To make the necessary showing of safety and efficacy, a manufacturer of a Class III device typically conducts a clinical investigation of the device, during the course of which the device is implanted in human subjects by investigators at various institutions. The investigators will then, on behalf of the manufacturer, monitor the patients and gather data, which in turn is submitted to the FDA as part of the PMA application.

In order to be able to conduct the clinical investigation, the manufacturer is required to apply for and obtain an investigational device exemption (IDE) from the FDA. Upon the FDA's approval of the IDE application, the manufacturer may proceed with the clinical investigation and eventually submit its application for a PMA. After receiving a PMA the manufacturer is authorized by the FDA to commercially distribute the device. Pursuant to an IDE granted by the FDA, defendants are currently engaged in clinical trials of the Cadence. The data gathered in these trials has been prepared for submission to the FDA.

Defendants argue that because the Cadence is currently involved in the clinical trials described above they are exempt from claims of patent infringement under § 271(e)(1). Plaintiff argues that defendants also have engaged in a variety of activities unrelated to obtaining FDA approval. According to plaintiff, these activities demonstrate that defendants' allegedly infringing use of the Cadence is not "solely for uses reasonably related" to FDA approval.

B. THE OPERATION OF § 271(E)(1)

1. *History and Purposes of § 271(e)(1)*

To reason reliably about the issues raised by these motions, we must recall the history and purposes of this statutory provision. Congress enacted § 271(e)(1) in 1984 in order to reverse the opinion of the United States Court of Appeals for the Federal Circuit in *Roche Products, Inc. v. Bolar Pharmaceutical Co.*, 733 F.2d 858 (Fed.Cir.1984). The *Roche* court had ruled that the experimental use exception was not broad enough to protect manufacturers of generic drugs while they were conducting the extensive field tests of their products that were necessary to generate the data that the FDA required before granting permission to market the drugs commercially. After the opinion in *Roche* issued, generic drug interests lobbied Congress vigorously for a statutory amendment that would grant such protection. In the legislative battles that ensued, it was clear that a principal purpose of the generic drug interests was to position themselves to be able to market their products on a massive commercial scale just as soon as the patent rights expired on the drugs which the generics incorporated.

We believe that when it responded positively to the lobbying of the generic drug manufacturers by enacting § 271(e)(1), Congress made a fully self-conscious choice between two directly competing interests: continuing full protection of the rights of patent holders, on the one hand, and, on the other, assuring access by the public to medically beneficial new products at truly competitive market prices (i.e., lower prices) immediately after the expiration of the terms of relevant patents. In essence, Congress elevated the health care interests of the public above the pecuniary interests of the patent holders.

In making this election, Congress reduced the scope of the rights of patent holders in two significant respects. First, it permitted potential competitors, during the life of the patent, to engage in acts that otherwise clearly would constitute acts of infringement, as long as those acts generated data the FDA would use in deciding whether to approve a product for the commercial marketplace. Since Congress knew that the

FDA sometimes required data based on considerable use of a product, Congress knew that creating this protection would deprive patent holders of sales that might well be significant, even though Congress apparently expected the patent holders in most instances to retain the lion's share of the relevant markets.

The second negative impact on the interests of patent holders that Congress effected through the adoption of § 271(e)(1) was arguably even more significant. Under the scenarios that would have obtained under *Roche*, a competitor could not have begun generating data for the FDA until after expiration of the patent. Because generating the data required by the FDA, and processing an application to market a new product through the FDA bureaucracy, predictably took considerable time, the practical effect of *Roche*, was to add several years of life to patents by making it impossible for competitors to be ready to enter the commercial marketplace in any significant measure for several years after the formal expiration of the patent holder's rights. Congress knew that enacting § 271(e)(1) would dramatically change this situation. We believe that in enacting this exemption Congress clearly decided that it wanted potential competitors to be able to ready themselves, fully, during the life of the patent, to enter the commercial marketplace in a large scale way as soon as the relevant patents expired. Only by permitting this preparation to enter the market meaningfully could Congress achieve its goal of assuring the public prompt access to new medical products at the lowest commercially feasible prices.

Understanding the hard choices that Congress made and the policy objectives it sought to achieve when it enacted § 271(e)(1) helps inform our interpretation and application of this exemption.

2. Interpreting § 271(e)(1) in Context of this Litigation

In relevant part, § 271(e)(1) declares that:

> It shall not be an act of infringement to make, use, or sell a patented invention ... solely for uses reasonably related to the development and submission of information under a Federal law which regulates the manufacture, use, or sale of drugs or veterinary biological products.

In *Eli Lilly and Co. v. Medtronic, Inc.*, 496 U.S. 661 (1990), the Supreme Court held that this statutory exemption is available not only to drug and veterinary products, but also to medical devices (like those in issue here) that cannot be marketed without FDA approval under § 515 of the Federal Food, Drug, and Cosmetic Act, 21 U.S.C. § 360e.

Through § 271(e)(1), Congress changed the status in law only of acts which, but for this exemption, would constitute acts of infringement. Thus the only kinds of acts to which this legislation applies are acts which would constitute acts of infringement. When trying to determine whether a party is protected by this exemption, the target of a court's inquiry is on those acts of manufacture, use, or sale of a patented invention that would constitute acts of infringement but for this exemption. It is these kinds of acts, only, that must be "solely for uses reasonably related" to generating data for submission to the FDA. It is these kinds of acts whose "uses" are in issue, and the exemption is lost only if the court concludes that acts of these kinds have been undertaken for "uses" that are outside those permitted under the statute.

Despite intimations to the contrary in some of plaintiff's earlier papers, the inquiry is not generally whether the allegedly infringing party has engaged in conduct that shows that it has purposes beyond generating and presenting data to the FDA. Congress obviously knew that companies that were trying to position themselves to enter the commercial market in a significant way immediately after a patent expired would engage in a range of business activities (like raising capital, establishing mechanisms for product distribution, etc.) for uses other than simply generating data for the FDA. Congress was concerned about those activities only to the extent that, but for § 271(e)(1), they would constitute acts of infringement. Thus, the exemption Congress provided is not lost simply as a result of a showing that the defendant has engaged in non-infringing acts whose "uses" fall outside those permitted by the statute.

Do activities that would not constitute infringements have any possible relevance to a court's determination of whether a party is protected by this statutory exemption? Plaintiff has argued that we should take a full look at a wide range of non-infringing acts by defendants in order to determine what the real purposes were of those activities by defendants that would constitute infringements but for § 271(e)(1). Plaintiff insists that the character of the non-infringing activities shows that defendants have engaged in the allegedly infringing acts of making, using, and selling its product not solely for purposes reasonably related to generating data for the FDA, but also, clearly, for independent commercial purposes.

[W]e feel considerable reluctance to endorse this line of reasoning. That reluctance is informed by several considerations. First, we feel that it is significant that when Congress chose the words in which to articulate the conditions under which the exemption would attach it did not use the word "purposes" at all, but, instead, settled on the word "uses." Given the obviousness of the alternative, we think that the selection by Congress of the word "uses" at this critical juncture in the exemption supports two related inferences: (1) that Congress intended the "test" for determining whether the exemption has been lost to be "objective" rather than "subjective" (focusing on conduct rather than motive or ultimate aim) and (2) that Congress wanted the courts, in applying this statute, to focus on conduct ("uses") that actually has occurred (as opposed to uses to which a party might put its product in the future) and that would constitute infringement but for the exemption.

Strong textual support for the view that Congress intended the test to be objective derives from the legislators' selection of the phrase "reasonably related" to modify the word "uses." "Reasonably related" is language that clearly has become associated with objective standards.

Our reluctance to conclude that Congress intended the courts, when construing this section of the statute, to ascribe much (or any) significance either to the indirect (ripple) effects of a defendant's otherwise infringing activities, or to inferences about "purposes" that might be drawn from focusing on collateral (i.e., non-infringing) conduct is reinforced by two factors. First, as we noted above, Congress clearly intended, by enacting this exemption, to create a legal environment in which the potential competitors of patent holders would be free, through non-infringing activities like raising capital, to position themselves to enter the market in a commercially significant way just as soon as the relevant patents expired. And at least with respect to products like those in issue here, products that are extremely sophisticated, that will carry a large price tag if they reach the retail stage, and that are very expensive to develop, potential competitors foreseeably must engage in considerable "business" development and promotion activity just to meet the FDA's requirements, let alone to be in a position to market their products meaningfully when the various legal barriers have been overcome. Collateral (i.e., non-infringing) activities undertaken by an entity that is trying to prepare itself to enter a competitive commercial marketplace and to survive there will virtually always be inspired, at least in substantial measure, by "business purposes," rather than simply by a desire to generate data for the FDA. Since virtually all collateral activities will have business purposes, to permit finders of fact to infer that infringing uses have business purposes from the fact that non-infringing uses have business purposes would be to invite wholesale loss of the exemption and, with that, frustration of Congress' objective in enacting it.

For all these reasons, Congress sensibly chose words in the exemption that would lead courts to focus not on "purposes" or motives, but on "uses," and not on collateral activities, but only on the kinds of conduct which, absent the exemption, would constitute infringement.

Thus, our inquiry is relatively straightforward. We focus only on those acts by Ventritex which would be deemed "infringing" but for § 271(e)(1) and in which Ventritex actually has engaged (as opposed to the acts in which the company might engage in the future). With respect to those actual acts, we do not ask what underlying motives might have inspired them or what indirect, ripple effects (e.g., long range consequential benefits) they might bring. Instead, we simply ask: are these actual uses "solely ... reasonably related to the development and submission of information" to the FDA. If so, the exemption protects Ventritex. But if there are any actual, non-de minimis uses that are not reasonably related to generating data for the FDA, the exemption will not protect Ventritex.

C. APPLICATION

After explaining (earlier in the pretrial period) our interpretation of the operation of § 271(e)(1) to the parties, the court ordered plaintiff to identify those activities of the defendants that plaintiff believes, but for operation of the statute, would constitute acts of infringement under § 271(a).

[The Plaintiff identified the following activities:]

1. Manufacture of several hundred Cadences;

2. Sales of the Cadence to hospitals in the U.S.;

3. Sales of the Cadence to international distributors; [and]

4. Testing of the Cadence (particularly certain testing done in Germany),

5. Demonstrations of the Cadence at "trade shows".

1. Manufacture of the Cadences. There are no disputed facts regarding the actual manufacture of the Cadence. In the setting we confront here, where it is undisputed that most of the Cadences have been used to generate data for the FDA, the fact of manufacture, by itself, does not deprive defendants of the statutory exemption. In the paragraphs that follow we consider each of the other alleged uses by defendants, determining, one at a time, whether a rational trier of fact could conclude that one or more was not reasonably related to securing FDA approval.

2. Sales of the Cadence to U.S. Hospitals. It is undisputed that every single Cadence sold to a U.S. hospital has been used only in clinical trials. Plaintiff has not offered any evidence that a single Cadence has been sold to a hospital for any use other than clinical testing of the device.

Plaintiff emphasizes, however, that Ventritex has continued to sell Cadences to clinical investigators even after submitting its application for pre-market approval (PMA) to the FDA. Plaintiff claims that the filing of this application establishes that Ventritex has accumulated enough data for the FDA to determine whether it will approve the Cadence for general commercial marketing. Thus, according to plaintiff, additional sales to clinical investigators are unnecessary and cannot be solely for uses reasonably related to obtaining FDA approval.

Plaintiff has not presented any evidence to contradict defendants' assertion that it is reasonable to continue to generate clinical data after submitting an initial PMA application. As we noted earlier, congress' decision to include the phrase "reasonably related" reflects an intention that a manufacturer not be denied the protections afforded by the statute simply because it turns out, after the fact, that some of the manufacturer's testing activities generated information which the FDA did not end up needing or relying on. Rather, the question is whether it would be objectively reasonable for a company in Ventritex's position to believe that continuing the clinical trials would, relatively directly, contribute to the generation of the kind of data relevant to the FDA's inquiry. We find that a reasonable trier of fact would be constrained to conclude that Ventritex's continuing sales of Cadences to clinical investigators were reasonably related to obtaining FDA approval.

3.   Sales of the Cadence to International Distributors. It is undisputed that defendants have sold Cadences, pursuant to distribution agreements, to individual distributors. Because some of these distribution agreements described "market share criteria" and encouraged the distributor to promote the Cadence, plaintiff argues that these sales are not solely for uses reasonably related to obtaining FDA approval.

Defendants have adduced competent evidence that the market share language was inadvertently included "boilerplate" language that has since been changed to clarify that there may be no general commercial sales (i.e., other than to a duly selected test site facility) or promotion of the Cadence until after FDA approval is obtained. Much more importantly, defendants' evidence establishes that these overseas distributors perform the limited function of clearing the devices through customs so that they may be delivered to the clinical sites overseas. Defendants submissions show that every Cadence sold to a distributor has been subsequently resold to an FDA approved clinical investigator.

Plaintiff has failed to present any evidence to suggest that these distributors functioned in any capacity other than as middle-persons between Ventritex and its foreign clinical investigators. Plaintiffs have not identified a single sale of a Cadence to a distributor that did not result in the immediate resale to a clinical investigator. Because there is no genuine dispute about the role which these distributors played, and because that role was directly related to the development of information to be submitted to the FDA, we find that a reasonable trier of fact could conclude only that Ventritex's use of these distributors was reasonably related to obtaining FDA approval.

4.   Testing of the Cadence in Germany. In addition to domestic testing of the Cadence, which indisputably is related to securing FDA approval, plaintiff contends that Ventritex decided to conduct clinical tests of the Cadence in Germany because Ventritex had formed a plan to commercially market the Cadence in Germany and believed that the German government would not permit such marketing unless the product had been tested clinically within Germany. This line of argument, however, appears to proceed from the incorrect assumption that the outcome of § 271(e)(1) analysis turns on a party's "purposes" or ultimate objectives, rather than its actual uses of the product in question. The focus of our inquiry at this point must be on evidence of actual uses. We ask, more specifically, whether plaintiff can point to evidence that would support an inference that Ventritex has in fact actually used the Cadence in Germany to secure permission from governmental authorities there to market the product commercially.

Having considered the evidence in the light most favorable to the plaintiff, we conclude, for reasons we explain below, that a reasonable trier of fact could only conclude that defendants testing activities in Germany were reasonably related to generating data for submission to the FDA.

It does not follow from the undisputed fact that it was not necessary to conduct clinical trials in Germany to obtain FDA approval that such trials were not reasonably related to obtaining FDA approval. The FDA permits the submission of foreign-generated clinical data so long as the procedures used in compiling the data comply with FDA requirements. Moreover, although foreign testing may be more expensive than domestic testing, it would be both reasonable and responsible for a manufacturer conducting clinical trials to utilize the most experienced and well respected investigators available, even if some of them practice overseas. Defendants have adduced uncontradicted evidence that the clinical investigator that they selected in Germany is one of the preeminent figures in the world in this field. A reasonable trier of fact could only conclude that it was reasonable for defendants to determine that Dr. Klein's clinical tests would contribute to the generation of the kind of data that the FDA would consider in deciding whether to grant pre-market approval.

More importantly, it is undisputed that every single defibrillator that was sold and sent to Germany was used for implantation by a clinical investigator and that all data generated in those clinical trials in fact has been submitted only to the FDA. Plaintiff has not presented any evidence that defendants have submitted test data to or in fact sought approval from any regulatory agency other than the FDA.

* * *

5. Demonstrations of the Cadence at scientific trade shows. Finally, plaintiff alleges that (1) defendants' demonstrated the Cadence at various scientific trade shows, (2) that these uses would constitute acts of infringement but for the exemption, and (3) that these uses of the Cadence were not reasonably related to obtaining FDA approval.

Plaintiff claims that defendants demonstrated the Cadence at various medical conferences, at least in part, to generate commercial interest in the device. Thus, plaintiff alleges that defendants have engaged in an actual, non-*de minimis,* use of the Cadence that is not reasonably related to obtaining FDA approval. Defendants, on the other hand, claim that they attended the trade shows and demonstrated the Cadence to identify potential clinical investigators and that that activity was clearly reasonably related to obtaining FDA approval.

A reasonable trier of fact would be compelled to conclude that at least some of Ventritex's demonstration activity was reasonably related to identifying potential clinical investigators and, therefore, to generating data for submission to the FDA. A manufacturer such as Ventritex relies on professional contacts within the medical community to locate investigators. (See, Fisher declaration at 2). It is undisputed that these conferences, which are attended by many of the doctors who are qualified to act as investigators, provide a prime opportunity for a manufacturer of a medical device to cultivate business contacts within the relevant medical community and to educate potential investigators about an investigational device like the Cadence. *Id.* Defendants' evidence shows that these conferences are, in fact, a principal means by which they identify potential clinical investigators. *Id.* Because the evidence is uncontradicted that the visibility achieved by attending these conferences and educating the medical community about the Cadence facilitates the process of locating qualified investigators, we find, as a matter of law, that it was reasonable for defendants to believe that demonstration of the Cadence at the trade shows would contribute, ultimately, to the generation of data for submission to the FDA.

Although plaintiff does not dispute that the demonstrations were, in part, reasonably related to obtaining FDA approval, plaintiff argues that defendants made an additional (perhaps secondary) use of the Cadence at these conferences that was not reasonably related to generating data for the FDA and, instead, was solely related to increasing market awareness of the Cadence.

In support of this contention plaintiff points to evidence that defendants (1) continued to demonstrate the Cadence, both domestically and in Germany, after defendants had all of the investigators they needed and (2) at least on some occasions during the trade shows, failed to prequalify individuals as potential investigators before demonstrating the Cadence to them.

Turning first to the "additional use" that consisted of continuing to demonstrate the Cadence after defendants allegedly had a sufficient list of potential investigators, we point out that the magnitude of this use is readily exaggerated. On the record presented to us, a reasonable trier of fact could not conclude that this use was large or significant. This follows because defendants have presented evidence that would compel the conclusion that it was reasonable, even after they had a long list of potential investigators, for them to continue to attempt to identify additional, highly qualified physicians who might serve as clinical investigators. Defendants have never been in a position where they could know with certainty that the FDA would not demand additional data from them. Given that indisputable fact, and the unforseeability of how much more data the FDA might want, and from what kinds of settings, it clearly was reasonable for Ventritex to seek to add highly qualified potential investigators to its lists. Since the trier of fact would be constrained to find that some of this particular "additional use" was reasonably related to securing FDA approval of the Cadence, it would not be reasonable, given the volume of such "extra" demonstration activity evidenced in the record before us, to conclude that whatever additional "unrelated" use remained was legally significant.

At this juncture we turn to consider the potential magnitude of the second of the allegedly unrelated uses: defendants' alleged failure to prequalify individuals as potential investigators before demonstrating the Cadence to them.

On the record presented to us, we find, as a matter of law, that Ventritex' failure to determine that all of the people to whom it demonstrated the Cadence at medical trade shows were qualified to serve as potential investigators does not significantly threaten the interests that the limiting provisions of § 271(e)(1) seek to protect and, therefore, must be deemed *de minimis.*

D. CONCLUSION RE DEFENDANTS' INVOCATION OF THE § 271(e)(1) DEFENSE

For the reasons set forth in detail above, we hold that there are genuine disputes as to none of the facts that are material to a determination that defendants are entitled to the protections of § 271(e)(1), and that defendants have shown that, as a matter of law, they are entitled to summary judgment on the basis of this statutory exemption to plaintiffs patent infringement claims (Counts I–VII). We therefore GRANT defendants' motion for summary judgment on these first seven counts and ORDER immediate entry of judgment thereon.

Notes

1. **Common Law Experimental Use**. Contrast the common law experimental use exception with the language of § 271(a) itself. In light of this statutory exclusivity, why should the patent law dally with an experimental use doctrine at all? Or should the statute instead provide that an infringer must intend to use the patented invention for a profit? Is the experimental use defense truly necessary? In answering that question, consider the sort of damages award the patentee might obtain if the infringer's use were truly experimental. *See Embrex, Inc. v. Service Engineering Corp.* 216 F.3d 1343, 55 U.S.P.Q.2d 1161 (Fed.Cir.2000) (Rader J., concurring) ("I write separately because, in my judgment, the Patent Act leaves no room for any de minimis or[common law] experimental use excuses for infringement. Because the Patent Act confers the right to preclude 'use,' not 'substantial use,' no room remains in the law for a de minimis excuse. Similarly, because intent is irrelevant to patent infringement, an experimental use excuse cannot survive. When infringement is proven either minimal or wholly non-commercial, the damage computation process provides full flexibility for courts to preclude large (or perhaps any) awards for minimal infringements.").

2. **Experimental Use and Research Technologies.** As certain contemporary technologies are increasingly of strong or even sole interest to research users, experimental use principles can loom quite large for an entire class of issued patents. A thoughtful discussion of this issue is found in Rebecca S. Eisenberg, *Patents and the Progress of Science: Exclusive Rights and Experimental Use*, 56 U. CHI. L. REV. 1017 (1989).

3. **Experimental Use and Pharmaceuticals Abroad.** Article 69(1) of the Japanese Patent Act provides that "[t]he effects of the patent right shall not extend to the working of the patent right for the purposes of experiment or research." On April 16, 1999 the Supreme Court of Japan in *Ono Pharmaceutical Co. Ltd. v. Kyoto Pharmaceutical Co. Ltd.* decided that activities designed to obtain marketing approval in order to begin commercial activities after the expiration of the patent are for experiment and research under Section 69(1). The court gave the following as its reasons:

(a) The patent system encourages creation of inventions by rewarding persons who disclose inventions to the public with an exclusive right for a limited time, and contributes to the development of industry by giving third parties opportunities to exploit the disclosed invention. One of the fundamental purposes of the patent system is to benefit society as a whole by allowing persons to freely exploit an invention once its patent term expires.

(b) The Drug Regulation Act requires, as a means of ensuring drug safety, approval from the Ministry of Health prior to manufacturing a new drug. The statute requires an applicant to conduct several types of clinical testing and attach resulting data to its application. With respect to a generic drug, the application requirements are the same as for a new drug in that an applicant must conduct the specified testing over a significant period of time. In conducting the testing, an applicant must produce and use a chemical compound or pharmaceutical product that falls within the technical scope of the patentee's patented invention. If the Court were to find that said testing is not an "experiment" under Article 69, Paragraph 1 of the Patent Act, thereby preventing an applicant from engaging in said production and use, third parties would not be able to freely exploit the invention for a significant time after the expiration of a patent. This result conflicts with the fundamental purpose of the patent system stated in the above paragraph.

(c) On the other hand, if a third party exploits the invention beyond the scope required to apply for approval under the Drug Regulation Act, and produces a patented generic drug or produces and uses a patented chemical compound with intent to assign them after the expiration of the patent, such exploitation constitutes an infringement and is not permissible. This interpretation guarantees patentees exclusive exploitation of their patented invention during the protection term. If, on the other hand, patentees are given the right to prevent third parties from engaging in said production and use of the patented invention for testing necessary to apply for manufacturing approval, this would result in a significant extension of the patent protection term. This result exceeds the benefit to patentees intended under the Patent Act.

Similarly, the European Community Patent Convention indicates that "acts done for experimental purposes relating to the subject-matter of the patented invention" are exempted from infringement. CPC Article 31. Although the CPC is not yet in force in Europe, the laws of many member states already reflect this principle. Jochen Pagenberg, *Clinical Tests ("Klinische Versuche"),* 28 INT'L REV. INDUS. PROP. & COPYRIGHT L. 103 (1997), presents an English translation and commentary regarding a controversial decision of the German Federal Supreme Court ("*Bundesgerichtshof*"). Another English translation is found at [1997] R.P.C. 623. Shortly thereafter came *Klinische Versuche II* from the same court, [1998] R.P.C. 423. These cases hold that one who seeks to discover new knowledge relating to the subject-matter of the patent is not infringing the patent even if the purpose for obtaining such knowledge is to obtain marketing approval. An extensive comparative study may be found in DAVID GILAT, EXPERIMENTAL USE AND PATENTS (1995) (Studies in Industrial Property and Copyright Law Vol. 16).

4. Do the Various Provisions Relating to Experimental Use for Pharmaceuticals Found For Example in the Patent Laws of the United States, Germany and Japan violate the TRIPS Agreement? The complexities of the TRIPS agreement as applied to experimental use provisions are manifest. For a detailed analysis see *WTO, Report of the Panel, Canada—Patent Protection of Pharmaceutical Products*, WT/DS114/R, 2000 WL 301021 (Mar. 17, 2000).

§ 15.6 INDIRECT INFRINGEMENT

The patent statute provides the patentee with two additional exclusive rights conveniently discussed together. 35 U.S.C.A. § 271(b) tersely provides for inducement of infringement as follows:

> Whoever actively induces infringement of a patent shall be liable as an infringer.

35 U.S.C.A. § 271(c) next sets forth the standard for "contributory infringement":

> Whoever offers to sell or sells within the United States or imports into the United States a component of a patented machine, manufacture, combination or composition, or a material or apparatus for use in practicing a patented process, constituting a material part of the invention, knowing the same to be especially made or especially adapted for use in an infringement of said patent, and not a staple article or commodity of commerce suitable for substantial noninfringing use, shall be liable as a contributory infringer.

These provisions, addressing two species of "indirect infringement," allow patentees to reach those entities whose acts facilitate a direct infringement by others. The next decision explores the elements of contributory infringement and inducement of infringement.

HEWLETT–PACKARD CO. v. BAUSCH & LOMB INC.

United States Court of Appeals, Federal Circuit, 1990.
909 F.2d 1464, 15 U.S.P.Q.2d 1525.

Before COWEN, SENIOR CIRCUIT JUDGE, and RICH and NEWMAN, CIRCUIT JUDGES.

RICH, J.

Bausch & Lomb Incorporated (B & L) appeals from the September 13, 1989 Judgment of the United States District Court for the Northern District of California, holding U.S. Pat. No. 4,384,298 (LaBarre) valid and infringed by B & L Hewlett–Packard Company (HP) cross-appeals from that portion of the Judgment holding that B & L had not actively induced infringement of the LaBarre patent subsequent to September of 1985. We affirm.

BACKGROUND

Two patents are discussed extensively throughout this opinion. The first is the patent in suit, LaBarre, which is assigned to HP. The second is U.S. Pat. No. Re 31,684 (Yeiser), which is assigned to B & L and which is the sole piece of prior art argued by B & L to invalidate the LaBarre patent. Both patents relate to X–Y plotters used to create a two-dimensional plot, such as a chart or a graph, on a sheet or paper. Such plotters can be broadly divided into two categories: one in which the paper is held stationary and a pen is attached to a gantry movable in one direction (the Y-direction) and a carriage movable in a second, orthogonal direction (the X-direction); and another in which the paper is moved in the Y-direction, while the pen is attached to a carriage movable in the X-direction. Both LaBarre and Yeiser relate to this second type of plotter, and both show that the movement of the paper in the Y-direction can be effectuated by one or more pairs of pinch rollers between which the paper is placed.

In order to draw accurate plots, it is critical in devices like those disclosed in Yeiser and LaBarre that the paper be moved back and forth without slippage between the paper and the pinch rollers. With this in mind, Yeiser teaches that at least one of the pinch wheels should have a surface with a high coefficient of friction formed "by knurling or by a layer of rubber or the like." LaBarre, on the other hand, teaches that an efficient way to effectively eliminate slippage between the rollers and the paper is to simply cover one of the pinch wheels with silicon carbide grit. The grit not only increases the friction between the pinch wheels and the paper, but also causes small indentations to be formed in the paper. These indentations repeatedly mate with the grit as the paper is moved back and forth in the Y-direction, thus further inhibiting slippage between the pinch wheels and the paper. Due to this mating effect between the grit and the indentations in the paper, HP urges that the LaBarre printer should be considered to be a "positive drive" plotter, wherein the paper is drawn along using "teeth" (i.e., the grit) which engage in "holes" (i.e., the indentations) in the paper, as opposed to a "friction drive" plotter, wherein the moving force on the paper is caused simply by the friction between the wheels and the paper.

B & L, through a division called Houston Instruments, began selling plotters having grit-covered pinch wheels ("grit wheel plotters") sometime in late 1982 or early 1983. However, in September of 1985, B & L entered into a "PURCHASE AGREEMENT" with Ametek, Inc. (Ametek) pursuant to which B & L sold the Houston Instruments division (including all "assets, properties, rights and business") to Ametek for a total purchase price of $43,000,000. Concurrent with execution of the PURCHASE AGREEMENT, B & L and Ametek also entered into an "AGREEMENT WITH RESPECT TO PATENTS," in which the parties agreed that, among other things, (1) B & L would grant Ametek a license under the Yeiser patent; (2) B & L would indemnify Ametek against liability for infringing the LaBarre patent up to a cap of $4.6 million; (3) B & L and Ametek would jointly work toward developing a plotter which would not infringe the LaBarre patent; and (4) Ametek would comply with a so-called "gag order;" (i.e., would not communicate with HP concerning the LaBarre patent).

HP brought the present suit against B & L in May of 1986, accusing B & L of direct infringement of the LaBarre patent for the time period prior to the sale of Houston Instruments to Ametek, and of active inducement of infringement under 35 U.S.C. § 271(b) for the period subsequent to the sale of Houston Instruments. As to the charge of direct infringement, B & L admitted infringement, but defended on the grounds that, among other things, the asserted claims of LaBarre were invalid for obviousness under 35 U.S.C. § 103 in view of the Yeiser patent. In particular, B & L argued that the knurled wheel taught by Yeiser would inherently create indentations which would mate with the rough surface of the knurled wheel, as required by the claims of LaBarre. As to the charge of inducing infringement, B & L denied that its activities surrounding the sale of Houston Instruments to Ametek in September of 1985 constituted active inducement of infringement.

The district court, in an extensive Findings of Fact, Conclusions of Law and Order Thereon, found claim 1 of LaBarre would not have been obvious in view of Yeiser and that B & L was liable for infringement prior to the sale of Houston Instruments in September of 1985. However, the district court further found that B & L did not actively induce infringement of the LaBarre patent by Ametek under 35 U.S.C. § 271(b), and so found no liability subsequent to the 1985 sale. These appeals followed.

OPINION

Active Inducement—35 U.S.C. § 271(b)

At the outset, we feel that it is necessary to make clear the distinction, often confused, between active inducement of infringement under § 271(b) and contributory infringement under § 271(c). Prior to the enactment of the Patent Act of 1952, there was no statute which defined what constituted infringement. However, infringement was judicially divided into two categories: "direct infringement," which was the unauthorized making, using or selling of the patented invention, and "contributory infringement," which was any other activity where, although not technically making, using or selling, the defendant displayed sufficient culpability to be held liable as an infringer. Such liability was under a theory of joint tortfeasance, wherein one who intentionally caused, or aided and abetted, the commission of a tort by another was jointly and severally liable with the primary tortfeasor.

The most common pre–1952 contributory infringement cases dealt with the situation where a seller would sell a component which was not itself technically covered by the claims of a product or process patent but which had no other use except with the claimed product or process. In such cases, although a plaintiff was required to show intent to cause infringement in order to established contributory infringement, many courts held that such intent could be presumed because the component had no substantial non-infringing use.

The legislative history of the Patent Act of 1952 indicates that no substantive change in the scope of what constituted "contributory infringement" was intended by the enactment of § 271. *See* S.Rep. No. 1979, 82d Cong., 2d Sess. 8, 28 (1952); *Aro Mfg. Co. v. Convertible Top Replacement Co.*, 377 U.S. 476, 485–86, [141 U.S.P.Q. 681] (1964) ("*Aro II*"). However, the single concept of "contributory infringement" was divided between §§ 271(b) and 271(c) into "active inducement" (a type of direct infringement) and "contributory infringement," respectively. Section 271(c) codified the prohibition against the common type of contributory infringement referred to above, and made clear that only proof of a defendant's knowledge, not intent, that his activity cause infringement was necessary to establish contributory infringement. [Although not clear on the face of the statute, subsequent case law held that § 271(c) required not only knowledge that the component was especially made or adapted for a particular use but also knowledge of the patent which proscribed that use. *See Aro II*, 377 U.S. at 488.] Section 271(b) codified the prohibition against all other types of activity which, prior to 1952, had constituted "contributory infringement."

That, however, leaves open the question of what level of knowledge or intent is required to find active inducement under § 271(b). On its face, § 271(b) is much broader than § 271(c) and certainly does not speak of any intent requirement to prove active inducement. However, in view of the very definition of "active inducement" in pre–1952 case law and the fact that § 271(b) was intended as merely a codification of pre–1952 law, we are of the opinion that proof of actual intent to cause the acts which constitute the infringement is a necessary prerequisite to finding active inducement. And it is proof of that intent which is missing in the present case.

Looking at the totality of events surrounding the sale of Houston Instruments, it is clear that B & L was merely interested in divesting itself of Houston Instruments at the highest possible price. B & L had no interest in what Ametek did with Houston Instruments and certainly did not care one way or the other whether Houston Instruments, under Ametek's ownership, continued to make grit wheel plotters. HP attempts to make much of the fact that part of the sale of Houston Instruments included the sale of specific plans for making grit wheel plotters as well as key personnel knowledgeable in this area. However, this is simply a result of the fact that Houston Instruments was sold "lock, stock and barrel" (i.e. with all "assets, properties, rights and business" included). B & L had no interest in nor control over what Ametek chose to do with the plans or the personnel. In this regard, it should also be kept in mind that grit wheel plotters constituted only a portion of Houston Instruments' sales. The PURCHASE AGREEMENT between B & L and Ametek indicates that Houston Instruments was also in the business of developing, manufacturing and selling analog and digital recorders, digitizers, computer-assisted drafting equipment, and other products.

We do not find any of the remaining details of the agreement between B & L and Ametek to be sufficiently probative of intent to induce infringement. The grant of a license from B & L to Ametek under the Yeiser patent is not probative of any intent to induce infringement. The license agreement between B & L and Ametek did not purport to give Ametek the right to make, use and sell X–Y plotters; it merely freed Ametek from whatever bar the Yeiser patent would have been to such activity. Both parties clearly knew, as evidenced by their discussion of the LaBarre patent in the AGREEMENT WITH RESPECT TO PATENTS, that other patents could still be a bar to making, using and selling X–Y plotters. The agreement between B & L and Ametek to work together to find a way to avoid infringement of the LaBarre patent establishes, if anything, an intent by B & L not to induce infringement by helping Ametek to develop a plotter which would not infringe.

The most troubling aspect of the agreement between B & L and Ametek is the indemnification clause. Cases have held that an indemnification agreement will generally not establish an intent to induce infringement, but that such intent can be inferred when the primary purpose is to overcome the deterrent effect that the patent laws have on would-be infringers. *See* Miller, *Some Views on the Law of Patent Infringement by Inducement*, 53 J.PAT.OFF. SOC'Y 86, 150–51 (1971), and the cases cited therein. While overcoming the deterrent of the patent laws might have been the ultimate effect of the indemnification agreement in the present case, we cannot say that that was its purpose. We are once again led back to our conclusion that what B & L really wanted out of this agreement was the sale of Houston Instruments at the greatest possible price. Therefore B & L agreed that, if Ametek should wish to continue the manufacture and sale of grit-wheel plotters, B & L would bear the risk of those plotters ultimately being found to infringe the LaBarre patent. The indemnification agreement certainly facilitated the sale of Houston Instruments at the particular price at which it was sold, but we cannot agree that B & L used it to induce infringement by Ametek.

CONCLUSION

The district court's decision holding the LaBarre patent valid and holding B & L not liable for the period subsequent to the sale of Houston Instruments is affirmed.

Notes

1. Distinguishing § 271(b) and § 271(c). Students who attempt to determine the distinction between § 271(b) and (c) by looking only at these two statutory paragraphs will find the exercise bewildering indeed. In fact, all conduct which falls under § 271(c) could also fall under § 271(b). Section 271(b) is drawn towards situations where the technology has multiple uses, only one of which infringes. Section 271(c) addresses situations where only a single substantial infringing use exists. Because mere promotion of technology could by itself constitute an inducement where the only substantial use of that technology infringes, all conduct falling under § 271(c) would also be addressed by § 271(b).

Why, then, does § 271 house these two paragraphs? A review of § 271(d) reveals the elusive answer: Congress had declared that conduct falling under § 271(c) does not constitute misuse of the patent. Chapter 19 of this Casebook further discusses § 271(d), and also includes the fine discussion of contributory infringement in the Supreme Court's 1980 *Dawson Chemical* opinion.

2. Intent and Indirect Infringement. What do you think of the standard that one need only intend "the acts which constitute the infringement" to be found liable under the theory of inducement of infringement? How often does one accidentally make, use, sell, offer to sell or import into the United States a technology? Doesn't this standard essentially amount to one of no intent at all? Moreover, is this intent standard consistent with the standard in the Supreme Court's *Aro* cases, referred to in the principal case and in note 5?

3. Dependent Infringement. The Federal Circuit sometimes groups the concepts of induced and contributory infringement under the rubric of "dependent infringement." *See Joy Technologies, Inc. v. Flakt, Inc.*, 6 F.3d 770, 28 U.S.P.Q.2d 1378 (Fed.Cir.1993).

4. Liability of Officers and Directors. Section 271(b) has also served as a font of personal liability for officers and directors of corporations under the traditional theory of "piercing the corporate veil." *See Orthokinetics, Inc. v. Safety Travel Chairs, Inc.*, 806 F.2d 1565, 1 U.S.P.Q.2d 1081 (Fed.Cir.1986). Thus, "[t]he tort of 'inducement' under 35 U.S.C.A. Section 271(b), when applied to invoke personal liability, is premised on a concept of tortfeasance whereby persons in authority and control may in appropriate circumstances be deemed liable for wrongdoing, when inducing direct infringement by another." *Sensonics Inc. v. Aerosonic Corp.*, 81 F.3d 1566, 38 U.S.P.Q.2d 1551 (Fed.Cir.1996). *Hoover Group Inc. v. Custom Metalcraft Inc.*, 84 F.3d 1408, 38 U.S.P.Q.2d 1860 (Fed.Cir.1996), discusses what these "appropriate circumstances" might be:

[A]cts of a corporate officer that are within the scope of the officer's responsibility are not always sufficient grounds for penetrating the corporate protection and imposing personal liability. The policy considerations that underlie the corporate structure yield to personal liability for corporate acts only in limited circumstances.

In general, a corporate officer is personally liable for his tortious acts, just as any individual may be liable for a civil wrong. This general rule "does not depend on the same grounds as 'piercing the corporate veil,' that is, inadequate capitalization, use of the corporate form for fraudulent purposes, or failure to comply with the formalities of corporate organization." *Crigler v. Salac*, 438 So.2d 1375, 1380 (Ala.1983). When personal wrongdoing is not supported by legitimate corporate activity, the courts have assigned personal liability for wrongful actions even when taken on behalf of the corporation. However, this liability has been qualified, in extensive jurisprudence, by the distinction between commercial torts committed in the course of the officer's employment, and negligent and other culpable wrongful acts.

Thus when a person in a control position causes the corporation to commit a civil wrong, imposition of personal liability requires consideration of the nature of the wrong, the culpability of the act, and whether the person acted in his/her personal interest or that of the corporation. *See* 3A WILLIAM MEADE FLETCHER, FLETCHER CYCLOPEDIA OF THE LAW OF PRIVATE CORPORATIONS §§ 1134–1166 (1994 Revised Volume) (XXIX "Liability of Officers and Directors to Third Persons for Torts"). The decisions have not always distinguished among the various legal premises, i.e. (1) justification for piercing the corporate veil based on such criteria as absence of corporate assets or use of the corporate form for illegal purposes; (2) corporate commitment of a commercial tort (such as interference with contract or business advantage, or patent infringement) caused by the officer acting as agent of the corporation; (3) actions similar to (2) but exacerbated by culpable intent or bad faith on the part of the officer; or (4) personal commitment of a fraudulent or grossly negligent act.

For example, corporate officers have been held personally liable when they participated in conversion, breach of fiduciary duty, fraud, and malicious prosecution; and have been held not to be personally liable for commercial torts such as interference with contractual relations if they were acting in the corporation's interest. The fact-dependency of such issues is apparent in decisions relating to patent infringement.

For an example of the latter point, compare *Sensonics*, affirming an award of officer liability under § 271(b), with *Hoover Group*, which reversed a similar judgment.

    5. The *Aro* Decisions and the Implied Right to Repair. A pair of Supreme Court cases resulting from the same patent litigation, *Aro Manufacturing Co. v. Convertible Top Replacement Co.*, 365 U.S. 336, 128 U.S.P.Q. 354 (1961) (*"Aro I"*) and *Aro Manufacturing Co. v. Convertible Top Replacement Co.*, 377 U.S. 476, 141 U.S.P.Q. 681 (1964) (*"Aro II"*), are the leading authorities on contributory infringement and the implied right to repair. This principle essentially holds that a purchaser of patented goods obtains an implied license to repair a patented good; thus, those who sell replacement parts to the patentee's customers cannot be held to have committed contributory infringement.

The patent at issue in the *Aro* cases was directed towards the combination of various mechanical parts and a cloth top. Certain car manufacturers employed the claimed invention, including General Motors, which took a license under the patent, and Ford Motor, which did not. When the patentee brought suit against a manufacturer of replacement cloth tops, the Supreme Court held that General Motors customers possessed the right to repair their cars by replacing the tops. Because no direct infringement had occurred, neither could the defendant be found a contributory infringer. However, because Ford Motor customers had no right to employ the claimed invention, the defendant was liable for contributory infringement with respect to those cars.

A more contemporary decision is set forth below.

JAZZ PHOTO CORP. v. UNITED STATES INT'L TRADE COMM.

United States Court of Appeals, Federal Circuit, 2001.
264 F.3d 1094, 59 U.S.P.Q.2d 1907.

Before NEWMAN, MICHEL, and GAJARSA, CIRCUIT JUDGES.

PAULINE NEWMAN, CIRCUIT JUDGE.

In an action brought under section 337 of the Tariff Act of 1930 as amended, 19 U.S.C. § 1337, Fuji Photo Film Co. charged twenty-seven respondents, including the appellants Jazz Photo Corporation, Dynatec International, Inc., and Opticolor, Inc., with infringement of fifteen patents owned by Fuji. The charge was based on the respondents' importation of used "single-use" cameras called "lens-fitted film packages" (LFFP's), which had been refurbished for reuse in various overseas facilities. Section 337 makes unlawful "[t]he importation into the United States ... of articles that ... infringe a valid and enforceable United States patent ... [or that] are made, produced, processed, ... under, or by means of, a process covered by the claims of a valid and enforceable United States patent." 19 U.S.C. § 1337(a)(1)(B). Eight respondents did not respond to the Commission's complaint, ten more failed to appear before the Commission, and one was dismissed. Eight respondents participated in the hearing, and three have taken this appeal.

The Commission determined that twenty-six respondents, including the appellants, had infringed all or most of the claims in suit of fourteen Fuji United States patents, and issued a General Exclusion Order and Order to Cease and Desist. *In the Matter of Certain Lens–Fitted Film Packages,* Inv. No. 337–TA–406 (Int'l Trade Comm'n June 28, 1999). This court stayed the Commission's orders during this appeal. *Dynatec Int'l, Inc. v. Int'l Trade Comm'n,* No. 99–1504 (Fed.Cir. Sept. 24, 1999) (unpublished).

The Commission's decision rests on its ruling that the refurbishment of the used cameras is prohibited "reconstruction," as opposed to permissible "repair." On review of the law and its application, we conclude that precedent does not support the Commission's application of the law to the facts that were found. We conclude that for used cameras whose first sale was in the United States with the patentee's authorization, and for which the respondents permitted verification of their representations that their activities were limited to the steps of (1) removing the cardboard cover, (2) cutting open the plastic casing, (3) inserting new film and a container to receive the film, (4) replacing the winding wheel for certain cameras, (5) replacing the battery for flash cameras, (6) resetting the counter, (7) resealing the outer case, and (8) adding a new cardboard cover, the totality of these procedures does not satisfy the standards required by precedent for prohibited reconstruction; precedent requires, as we shall discuss, that the described activities be deemed to be permissible repair.

For those cameras that meet the criteria outlined above, the Commission's ruling of patent infringement is reversed and the Commission's exclusion and cease and desist orders are vacated. For all other cameras, the Commission's orders are affirmed.

DISCUSSION

* * *

The Patented Inventions

The LFFP is a relatively simple camera, whose major elements are an outer plastic casing that holds a shutter, a shutter release button, a lens, a viewfinder, a film advance mechanism, a film counting display, and for some models a flash assembly and battery. The casing also contains a holder for a roll of film, and a container into which the exposed film is wound. At the factory a roll of film is loaded into the camera. The casing is then sealed by ultrasonic welding or light-tight latching, and a cardboard cover is applied to encase the camera.

LFFPs are intended by the patentee to be used only once. After the film is exposed the photo-processor removes the film container by breaking open a pre-weakened portion of the plastic casing which is accessed by removal of the cardboard cover. Discarded LFFPs, subsequently purchased and refurbished by the respondents, are the subject of this action.

The parts of an LFFP are illustrated in Figure 8 of the '087 patent:

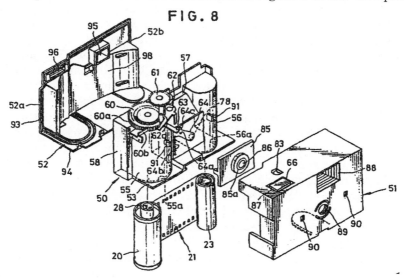

FIG. 8

Claim 1 of the '087 patent is representative of claims directed to the entire LFFP:

1. A lens-fitted photographic film package having an externally operable member for effecting an exposure, comprising:

a light-tight film casing which must be destroyed to open the same, having an opening through which said exposure is made when said externally operable member is operated;

an unexposed rolled film disposed on one side of said opening in said light-tight casing;

a removable light-tight film container having a film winding spool therein disposed on the opposite side of said opening in said light-tight casing from said rolled film, one end of said rolled film being attached to said film winding spool;

means for winding said rolled film into said light-tight film container and around said film winding spool;

and winding control means responsive to operation of said externally operable member for allowing said film winding spool to rotate so as to enable said rolled film to be advanced by only one frame after every exposure; said winding control means including: a sprocket wheel driven by movement of said rolled film;

and a frame counter driven by said sprocket wheel, said frame counter being provided with indications designating a series of frame numbers and means for disabling said winding control means responsive to said frame counter indicating there remains on said unexposed film no film frame capable of being exposed.

Other patents are directed to various components of the LFFP. The '857 patent is directed to a specific film winding mechanism. The '495 patent is directed to a mechanism whereby the film in the LFFP is advanced smoothly without being scratched or gouged, and which prevents the film roll from becoming loose. The '774 patent is directed to the film chambers and film path. The '364 patent claims the LFFP with a flash unit comprising a circuit board, a capacitor, a discharge (flash) tube, and a battery. The '111 patent is directed to the pushbutton that trips the shutter and has a protective structure that prevents the pushbutton from accidentally being depressed. The '200 patent is directed to the shutter mechanism, including the shutter mount, shutter opening, and shutter blade. The '288 patent claims an LFFP in which the winding wheel and film cassette are positively linked through a gear and shaft mechanism requiring the two to rotate relative to each other, avoiding the loss of usable film. The '685 patent is directed to an LFFP assembly that allows easier recycling of used plastic and metal, in which the plastic casing including the film path and film chambers is easily separable from the photo-taking unit containing metal parts including the shutter mechanism and the winding and stop mechanisms.

FIG. 1

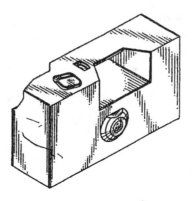

It is not disputed that the imported refurbished cameras contain all of the elements of all or most of the claims in suit.

The Accused Activities

The appellants import used LFFPs that have been refurbished by various overseas entities (called "remanufacturers" in the ITC proceeding). Some of the remanufacturers refused discovery entirely or in part, and some presented evidence that the ALJ found incomplete or not credible. The Commission explains: "Since so little was known about the accused infringing processes, the ALJ considered the common steps that each participating respondent admitted during the hearing were part of their processes." ITC Brief at 15–16. The ALJ summarized these common steps as follows:

removing the cardboard cover;

opening the LFFP body (usually by cutting at least one weld);

replacing the winding wheel or modifying the film cartridge to be inserted;

resetting the film counter;

replacing the battery in flash LFFPs;

winding new film out of a canister onto a spool or into a roll;

resealing the LFFP body using tape and/or glue;

applying a new cardboard cover.

Initial Determination at 108–109. The Commission held that these activities constitute prohibited reconstruction. In view of this holding, it was not material to the Commission's ruling that the full extent of various respondents' activities was not made known, for in all events the importation would be infringing and unlawful.

The appellants argue that they are not building new LFFPs, but simply replacing the film in used cameras. They argue that the LFFPs have a useful life longer than the single use proposed by Fuji, that the patent right has been exhausted as to these articles, and that the patentee can not restrict their right to refit the cameras with new film by the procedures necessary to insert the film and reset the mechanism. Unless these activities are deemed to be permissible, infringement of at least some of the patents in suit is conceded.

* * *

The Law of Permissible Repair and Prohibited Reconstruction

The distinction between permitted and prohibited activities, with respect to patented items after they have been placed in commerce by the patentee, has been distilled into the terms "repair" and "reconstruction." The purchaser of a patented article has the rights of any owner of personal property, including the right to use it, repair it, modify it, discard it, or resell it, subject only to overriding conditions of the sale. Thus patented articles when sold "become the private individual property of the purchasers, and are no longer specifically protected by the patent laws." *Mitchell v. Hawley,* 83 U.S. (16 Wall.) 544, 548, 21 L.Ed. 322 (1872). The fact that an article is patented gives the purchaser neither more nor less rights of use and disposition. However, the rights of ownership do not include the right to construct an essentially new article on the template of the original, for the right to make the article remains with the patentee.

While the ownership of a patented article does not include the right to make a substantially new article, it does include the right to preserve the useful life of the original article. It is readily apparent that there is a continuum between these concepts; precedent demonstrates that litigated cases rarely reside at the poles wherein "repair" is readily distinguished from "reconstruction." Thus the law has developed in the body of precedent, illustrating the policy underlying the law as it has been applied in diverse factual contexts. *Cf. Goodyear Shoe Mach. Co. v. Jackson,* 112 F. 146, 150 (1st Cir.1901) ("It is impracticable, as well as unwise, to attempt to lay down any rule on this subject, owing to the number and infinite variety of patented inventions.")

The principle of the distinction between permissible and prohibited activities was explained in *Wilson v. Simpson,* 50 U.S. (9 How.) 109, 13 L.Ed. 66 (1850), where the Court distinguished the right of a purchaser of a patented planing machine to replace the machine's cutting-knives when they became dull or broken, from the patentee's sole right to make or renew the entire machine. The Court observed that the knives had to be replaced every 60–90 days whereas the machines would last for several years, explaining, "what harm is done to the patentee in the use of his right of invention, when the repair and replacement of a partial injury are confined to the machine which the purchaser has bought?" *Id.* at 123.

This principle underlies the application of the law. It was elaborated by the Court in *Aro Manufacturing Co. v. Convertible Top Replacement Co.,* 365 U.S. 336, 81 S.Ct. 599, 5 L.Ed.2d 592 (1961), where the patented combination was a fabric convertible top and the associated metal support structure. The Court explained that replacement of the worn fabric top constituted permissible repair of the patented combination, and could not be controlled by the patentee. The Court restated the principles that govern the inquiry as applied to replacement of unpatented parts of a patented article:

The decisions of this Court require the conclusion that reconstruction of a patented entity, comprised of unpatented elements, is limited to such a true reconstruction of the entity as to "in fact make a new article," *United States v. Aluminum Co. of America,* [148 F.2d 416, 425 (2d Cir.1945)], after the entity, viewed as a whole, has become spent. In order to call the monopoly, conferred by the patent grant, into play for a second time, it must, indeed, be a second creation of the patented entity, as, for example, in *American Cotton–Tie Co. v. Simmons,* [106 U.S. 89, 1 S.Ct. 52 (1882)]. Mere replacement of individual unpatented parts, one at a time, whether of the same part repeatedly or different parts successively, is no more than the lawful right of the owner to repair his property. 365 U.S. at 346, 81 S.Ct. 599.

This right of repair, provided that the activity does not "in fact make a new article," accompanies the article to succeeding owners. In *Wilbur–Ellis Co. v. Kuther,* 377 U.S. 422, 84 S.Ct. 1561, 12 L.Ed.2d 419, 141 USPQ 703 (1964), the Court dealt with the refurbishing of patented fish-canning machines by a purchaser of used machines. The Court held that the fairly extensive refurbishment by the new owner, including modification and resizing of six separate parts of the machine, although more than customary repair of spent or broken components, was more like repair then reconstruction, for it extended the useful life of the original machine. *See id.* at 425, 141 USPQ at 704–05 ("Petitioners in adapting the old machines to a related use were doing more than repair in the customary sense; but what they did was kin to repair for it bore on the useful capacity of the old combination, on which the royalty had been paid.")

Precedent has classified as repair the disassembly and cleaning of patented articles accompanied by replacement of unpatented parts that had become worn or spent, in order to preserve the utility for which the article was originally intended. In *General Electric Co. v. United States,* 215 Ct.Cl. 636, 572 F.2d 745, 198 USPQ 65 (1978), the court held that the Navy's large scale "overhauling" of patented gun mounts, including disassembly into their component parts and replacement of parts that could not be repaired with parts from other gun mounts or new parts, was permissible repair of the original gun mounts. The court explained that the assembly-line method of reassembly, without regard to where each component had originated, was simply a matter of efficiency and economy, with the same effect as if each gun mount had been refurbished individually by disassembly and reassembly of its original components with replacement of a minor amount of worn elements. *Id.* at 780–86, 198 USPQ at 95–100.

Similarly, in *Dana Corp. v. American Precision Co.*, 827 F.2d 755, 3 USPQ2d 1852 (Fed.Cir.1987), the court held that the "rebuilding" of worn truck clutches, although done on a commercial scale, was permissible repair. The defendants in *Dana Corp.* acquired worn clutches that had been discarded by their original owners, disassembled them, cleaned and sorted the individual parts, replaced worn or defective parts with new or salvaged parts, and reassembled the clutches. Although the patentee stressed that some new parts were used and that the rebuilding was a large scale commercial operation, the activity was held to be repair. *Id.* at 759, 827 F.2d 755, 3 USPQ2d at 1855. The court also observed that in general the new parts were purchased from Dana, the original manufacturer of the patented clutches, and that repair of used clutches was contemplated by the patentee. The court rejected the argument that the complete disassembly and production-line reassembly of the clutches constituted a voluntary destruction followed by a "second creation of the patented entity," invoking the phrase of *Aro Manufacturing*, 365 U.S. at 346, 81 S.Ct. 599.

"Reconstruction," precedent shows, requires a more extensive rebuilding of the patented entity than is exemplified in *Aro Manufacturing*, *Wilbur–Ellis*, *General Electric*, and *Dana Corp. See also, e.g., Bottom Line Mgmt., Inc. v. Pan Man, Inc.*, 228 F.3d 1352, 56 USPQ2d 1316 (Fed.Cir.2000) (repair of cooking device by reapplying non-stick coating); *Hewlett–Packard Co. v. Repeat–O–Type Stencil Mfg. Corp.*, 123 F.3d 1445, 43 USPQ2d 1650 (Fed.Cir.1997) (modifying unused printer cartridges akin to repair); *Kendall Co. v. Progressive Med. Tech., Inc.*, 85 F.3d 1570, 38 USPQ2d 1917 (Fed.Cir.1996) (replacement of used pressure sleeve in medical device is repair); *Sage Prods., Inc. v. Devon Indus., Inc.*, 45 F.3d 1575, 33 USPQ2d 1765 (Fed.Cir.1995) (replacement of inner container for medical waste is repair); *FMC Corp. v. Up–Right, Inc.*, 21 F.3d 1073, 30 USPQ2d 1361 (Fed.Cir.1994) (replacing worn unpatented picking heads of harvester is repair); *Everpure, Inc. v. Cuno, Inc.*, 875 F.2d 300, 10 USPQ2d 1855 (Fed.Cir.1989) (replacement of entire cartridge containing spent filter is repair); *Porter v. Farmers Supply Serv., Inc.*, 790 F.2d 882, 229 USPQ 814 (Fed.Cir.1986) (replacement of disks in tomato harvester head is repair). In contrast, in *Sandvik Aktiebolag v. E.J. Co.*, 121 F.3d 669, 43 USPQ2d 1620 (Fed.Cir. 1997), reconstruction was held to apply when a patented drill bit was "recreated" by construction of an entirely new cutting tip after the existing cutting tip could no longer be resharpened and reused. The court explained that it was not dispositive that the cutting tip was the "novel feature" of the invention, but that prohibited reconstruction occurred because a "new article" was made after the patented article, "viewed as a whole, has become spent." *See also Lummus Indus., Inc. v. D.M. & E. Corp.*, 862 F.2d 267, 8 USPQ2d 1983 (Fed.Cir.1988) (jury verdict of reconstruction for cutter wheels that were material part of patented invention).

Underlying the repair/reconstruction dichotomy is the principle of exhaustion of the patent right. The unrestricted sale of a patented article, by or with the authority of the patentee, "exhausts" the patentee's right to control further sale and use of that article by enforcing the patent under which it was first sold. In *United States v. Masonite Corp.,* 316 U.S. 265, 278, 62 S.Ct. 1070, 86 L.Ed. 1461 (1942), the Court explained that exhaustion of the patent right depends on "whether or not there has been such a disposition of the article that it may fairly be said that the patentee has received his reward for the use of the article." *See, e.g., Intel Corp. v. ULSI Sys. Tech., Inc.,* 995 F.2d 1566, 1568, 27 USPQ2d 1136, 1138 (Fed.Cir.1993) ("The law is well settled that an authorized sale of a patented product places that product beyond the reach of the patent.") Thus when a patented device has been lawfully sold in the United States, subsequent purchasers inherit the same immunity under the doctrine of patent exhaustion. However, the prohibition that the product may not be the vehicle for a "second creation of the patented entity" continues to apply, for such re-creation exceeds the rights that accompanied the initial sale.

Fuji states that some of the imported LFFP cameras originated and were sold only overseas, but are included in the refurbished importations by some of the respondents. The record supports this statement, which does not appear to be disputed. United States patent rights are not exhausted by products of foreign provenance. To invoke the protection of the first sale doctrine, the authorized first sale must have occurred under the United States patent. *See Boesch v. Graff,* 133 U.S. 697, 701–703, 10 S.Ct. 378, 33 L.Ed. 787 (1890) (a lawful foreign purchase does not obviate the need for license from the United States patentee before importation into and sale in the United States). Our decision applies only to LFFPs for which the United States patent right has been exhausted by first sale in the United States. Imported LFFPs of solely foreign provenance are not immunized from infringement of United States patents by the nature of their refurbishment.

Application of the Law

In the Commission's Initial Determination the administrative judge, applying the four factors discussed in *Sandvik Aktiebolag,* 121 F.3d at 673, 43 USPQ2d at 1623, held that the remanufacturers had made a new LFFP after the useful life of the original LFFP had been spent. Thus, the ALJ ruled that the remanufacturers were engaged in prohibited reconstruction. The Commission adopted the ALJ's findings and conclusions that the remanufacturers were not simply repairing an article for which either the producer or the purchaser expected a longer useful life, pointing out that the purchaser discarded the camera after use. The Commission ruled that the respondents were not simply repairing the LFFP in order to achieve its intended life span, but created a new single use camera that would again be discarded by its purchaser after use.

Although the Commission's conclusion is supported by its reasoning and reflects concern for the public interest, for there was evidence of imperfections and failures of some refurbished cameras, precedent requires that these cameras be viewed as repaired, not reconstructed. In

Dana Corp., for example, the truck clutches had lived their intended lives as originally produced, yet the court ruled that the "rebuilding" of the used clutches was more akin to repair than to reconstruction. The activities of disassembly and rebuilding of the gun mounts of *General Electric* were similarly extensive, yet were deemed to be repair. *Aro Manufacturing* and the other Supreme Court decisions which underlie precedent require that infringing reconstruction be a "second creation" of the patented article. Although the Commission deemed this requirement met by the "remanufactured" LFFPs, precedent places the acts of inserting new film and film container, resetting the film counter, and resealing the broken case—the principal steps performed by the remanufacturers—as more akin to repair.

The Court has cautioned against reliance on any specific set of "factors" in distinguishing permissible from prohibited activities, stating in *Aro Manufacturing* that "While there is language in some lower court opinions indicating that 'repair' or 'reconstruction' depends on a number of factors, it is significant that each of the three cases of this Court, cited for that proposition, holds that a license to use a patented combination includes the right 'to preserve its fitness for use. . . .' " 365 U.S. at 345, 81 S.Ct. 599. Indeed, this criterion is the common thread in precedent, requiring consideration of the remaining useful capacity of the article, and the nature and role of the replaced parts in achieving that useful capacity. The appellants stress that all of the original components of the LFFP except the film and battery have a useful remaining life, and are reused. The appellants state that but for the exposed roll of film and its container, any portion of the case that was broken by the photo processor, and the winding wheel in certain cameras, the refurbished LFFP is substantially the original camera, for which the patent right has been exhausted.

The Commission placed weight on Fuji's intention that the LFFP not be reused. The '087 patent specification states that

> forming an opening in the film package makes it impossible to reuse the film package. Therefore, it will be impossible to refill a new film into the used film package in order to reclaim a film package for reuse.

'087 patent, col. 6, lines 14–18. However, the patentee's unilateral intent, without more, does not bar reuse of the patented article, or convert repair into reconstruction. *See Hewlett–Packard,* 123 F.3d at 1453, 43 USPQ2d at 1658 ("a seller's intent, unless embodied in an enforceable contract, does not create a limitation on the right of a purchaser to use, sell, or modify a patented product so long as a reconstruction of the patented combination is avoided").

Claim 7 of the '087 patent is representative of those claims that specifically recite the film container and unexposed film roll, elements that are replaced by the remanufacturers:

7. A lens-fitted photographic film package comprising:

a light-tight film casing which must be destroyed to open the same, having an opening through which an exposure is made;

a light-tight film container having a film winding spool therein disposed on one side of said opening in said light-tight film casing;

a rotatable spool disposed on the opposite side of said opening in said light-tight film casing from said light-tight film container;

one end of said spool being exposed outside said light-tight film casing;

a film roll of unexposed film of which one end is attached to said film winding spool in said light-tight film container and which is rolled around said rotatable spool.

The appellants state that the film and its removable container are commercial items, and that their replacement in a camera can not be deemed to be reconstruction. As discussed in *Aro Manufacturing,* the replacement of unpatented parts, having a shorter life than is available from the combination as a whole, is characteristic of repair, not reconstruction. On the totality of the circumstances, the changes made by the remanufacturers all relate to the replacement of the film, the LFFP otherwise remaining as originally sold.

Several of the Fuji patents in suit are directed to specific components of LFFPs, including the '495 (film path), '774 (film chambers and film path), '111 (pushbutton), '200 (shutter mechanism), '685 (recyclable LFFP body), and RE '168 (LFFP body) patents. For example, claim 1 of the '111 patent is directed to a LFFP having a pushbutton designed to avoid inadvertent activation during handling of the camera:

1. A lens-fitted photographic film unit containing a photographic film and being adapted to take photographs, comprising:

at least one plastic pushbutton formed integrally with a wall of said film unit, only a portion of said pushbutton being separated from said wall by a slit which surrounds most but not all of said pushbutton, said pushbutton being connected to said film unit by an integral bridge, said pushbutton being adapted to be depressed inwardly of the wall from an initial position and to move back outwardly to said initial position when released;

and a barrier formed on an outer surface of said wall surrounding said pushbutton only partially, said barrier projecting outwardly relative to an actuating surface of said pushbutton when said pushbutton is in said initial position, said barrier terminating in two ends disposed on opposite sides of said bridge.

The ruling of reconstruction as to these patents is incorrect, because the remanufacturing processes simply reuse the original components, such that there is no issue of replacing parts that were separately patented. If the claimed component is not replaced, but simply is reused, this component is neither repaired nor reconstructed.

* * *

Conclusion

The judgment of patent infringement is reversed with respect to LFFPs for which the patent right was exhausted by first sale in the United States, and that were permissibly repaired. Permissible repair is limited, as discussed herein, to the steps of removing the cardboard cover, cutting open the casing, inserting new film and film container, resetting the film counter, resealing the casing, and placing the device in a new cardboard cover. Included in permissible repair is replacement of the battery in flash cameras and the winding wheel in the cameras that so require. For these products the Commission's orders are vacated.

* * *

AFFIRMED IN PART, REVERSED IN PART, AND REMANDED; STAY LIFTED.

Note

1. Reconstruction at the Federal Circuit. The great majority of Federal Circuit cases addressing the distinction between repair and recontruction find that the defendant's activities constituted the former, and therefore were noninfringing. One of the few exceptions is *Sandvik Aktiebolag v. E.J. Co.*, 121 F.3d 669, 43 U.S.P.Q.2d 1620 (Fed.Cir.1997). That case involved Sandvik's patented drill and a drill repair service operated by E.J. E.J. claimed that by retipping Sandvik drills, it was merely repairing them. Sandvik instead asserted that these activities amounted to an infringing reconstruction. The court sided with Sandvik, reasoning:

> The drill tip was not manufactured to be a replaceable part, although it could be resharpened a number of times to extend its life. It was not intended or expected to have a life of temporary duration in comparison to the drill shank. And finally, the tip was not attached to the shank in a manner to be easily detachable. . . .

> Finally, there was no intent evidenced by the patentee that would support E.J.'s argument that replacement of tips was a repair. . . . The evidence shows that Sandvik never intended its drills to be retipped. It did not manufacture or sell replacement drill tips. It did not publish instructions on how to retip its patented drills or suggest that drills could or should be retipped. Sandvik was aware that the drill tip would need occasional resharpening and instructed its customer on how to resharpen the tip. There is, therefore, no objective evidence that Sandvik's drill tip was intended to be a replaceable part. Although the repair or recontrcuction issue does not turn on the intention of the patentee alone, the fact that no replacement drill tips have ever been made or sold by the patentee is consistent with the conclusion that replacement of the carbide tip is not a persmissible repair.

How would you harmonize the holdings of *Jazz Photo* with *Sandvik*?

2. A [T]axing Inquiry. The distinction between repair and reconstruction can be a vexing one. In this context one court was reminded of "the apocryphal axe, of which the owner brags: 'This is my great-grandfather's original axe, although the handle has been replaced five times, and the head twice.' " *FMC Corp. v. Up–Right, Inc.*, 816 F.Supp. 1455, 1464 n. 15 (N.D.Cal.1993), *aff'd*, 21 F.3d 1073 (Fed.Cir.1994). "So what does it take to 'make' a new axe?", Professor Mark Janis asks, concluding the courts would do better to focus on the implied license between patentee and purchaser, rather than on whether the original product is sufficiently "spent." *See* Mark D. Janis, *A Tale of the Apocryphal Axe: Repair, Reconstruction and the Implied License In Intellectual Property Law*, 58 Md. L. Rev. 423 (1999).

3. Exportation of Components under § 271(f). Prior to 1984 amendments to the Patent Act, the manufacture and exportation of the unassembled of components of a patented article was not considered an infringing act. Exemplifying this rule was *Deepsouth Packing Co. v. Laitram Corp.*, 406 U.S. 518, 173 U.S.P.Q. 769 (1972). Here, the defendant manufactured all the components of a patented shrimp peeler and shipped them in an unassembled state to clients abroad. The Supreme Court held that no infringement occurred because the defendant had not made or sold the combination of mechanical features that fulfilled the conditions of the asserted claims.

Congress reacted to the *Deepsouth* decision by enacting § 271(f). This provision was intended to prevent copiers from avoiding U.S. patents by supplying components of a patented product in this country so that the assembly of the components may be completed abroad. The clear parallel between § 271(f)(1) and § 271(b), as well as § 271(f)(2) and § 271(c), is discussed in *T.D. Williamson Inc. v. Laymon*, 723 F.Supp. 587, 13 U.S.P.Q.2d 1417 (N.D.Okla.1989), *aff'd*, 923 F.2d 871, 18 U.S.P.Q.2d 1575 (Fed.Cir.1990), *cert. dismissed*, 500 U.S. 901 (1991).

§ 15.7   PROCESS PATENTS

Among the more venerable principles of patent law was that an individual would not infringe a process patent by activities involving a product (even if made by the claimed process). *United States v. Studiengesellschaft Kohle m.b.H.*, 670 F.2d 1122, 212 U.S.P.Q. 889 (D.C.Cir. 1981). This principle suffered a serious blow with the passage of the Process Patent Amendments Act of 1988. The 1988 Act provided process patent owners with the right to exclude others from using or selling in the United States, or importing into the United States, products made by a claimed process. The provisions of the Process Patent Amendments Act were codified in part at 35 U.S.C. § 271(g), a statute subject to a thorough analysis in the following opinion.

ELI LILLY & CO. v. AMERICAN CYANAMID CO.

United States Court of Appeals, Federal Circuit, 1996.
82 F.3d 1568, 38 U.S.P.Q.2d 1705.

Before Clevenger, Rader, and Bryson, Circuit Judges.

Bryson, Circuit Judge.

The ongoing struggle between "pioneer" drug manufacturers and generic drug distributors has once more come before our court. Eli Lilly and Company (Lilly), the "pioneer" drug manufacturer in this case, has filed suit for patent infringement against the appellees, who are involved in various ways in the distribution of a particular generic drug. Lilly sought a preliminary injunction, arguing that the importation and sale of the generic drug in this country infringed Lilly's patent on a process for making a related compound. After a hearing, the United States District Court for the Southern District of Indiana denied Lilly's request for a preliminary injunction. The court found that Lilly had failed to show that it was likely to prevail on the merits of its infringement claim and had failed to show that it would suffer irreparable harm in the absence of preliminary injunctive relief. *Eli Lilly & Co. v. American Cyanamid Co.*, 896 F.Supp. 851, 36 U.S.P.Q.2d 1011 (S.D.Ind.1995). Because Lilly has failed to overcome the substantial hurdle faced by a party seeking to overturn the denial of a preliminary injunction, we affirm.

I

The pharmaceutical product at issue in this case is a broad-spectrum antibiotic known as "cefaclor." Cefaclor is a member of the class of cephalosporin antibiotics, all of which are based on the cephem nucleus. Although there are many different cephem compounds, only a few have utility as antibiotic drugs. Each of the known commercial methods for producing cefaclor requires the production of an intermediate cephem compound known as an enol. Once the desired enol cephem intermediate is obtained, it is then subjected to several processing steps in order to produce cefaclor.

A

Lilly developed cefaclor and patented it in 1975. Until recently, Lilly has been the exclusive manufacturer and distributor of cefaclor in this country. In addition to its product patent on cefaclor, Lilly obtained several patents covering different aspects of the manufacture of cefaclor, including processes for producing enol cephem intermediates. Many of those patents have now expired.

In 1995, Lilly purchased the patent at issue in this case, U.S. Patent No. 4,160,085 (the '085 patent). Claim 5 of that patent defines a method of producing enol cephem compounds, including what is called "compound 6," an enol cephem similar to the one Lilly uses in its process for manufacturing cefaclor. The '085 patent will expire on July 3, 1996.

Compound 6 differs from cefaclor in three respects. Although both compound 6 and cefaclor are based on the cephem nucleus, compound 6 has a hydroxy group at the 3–position on the cephem nucleus, a para-nitrobenzyl carboxylate ester at the 4–position, and a phenylacetyl group at the 7–position. Cefaclor has different groups at each of those positions: it has a chlorine atom at the 3–position, a free carboxyl group at the 4–position, and a phenylglycyl group at the 7–position. Each of those differences between compound 6 and cefaclor contributes to the effectiveness of cefaclor as an orally administered antibiotic drug. The free carboxyl group at the 4–position is believed important for antibacterial activity; the chlorine increases cefaclor's antibiotic potency; and the phenylglycyl group enables cefaclor to be effective when taken orally.

To produce cefaclor from compound 6 requires four distinct steps. First, the hydroxy group is removed from the 3–position and is replaced by a chlorine atom, which results in the creation of "compound 7." Second, compound 7 is subjected to a reaction that removes the phenylacetyl group at the 7–position, which results in the creation of "compound 8." Third, a phenylglycyl group is added at the 7–position, which results in the creation of "compound 9." Fourth, the para-nitrobenzyl carboxylate ester is removed from the 4–position, which results in the creation of cefaclor.

B

On April 27, 1995, defendants Zenith Laboratories, Inc., (Zenith) and American Cyanamid Company (Cyanamid) obtained permission from the Food and Drug Administration to distribute cefaclor in this country. Defendant Biocraft Laboratories, Inc., (Biocraft) had applied for FDA approval to manufacture and sell cefaclor in the United States but had not yet obtained that approval. All three have obtained large quantities of cefaclor that were manufactured in Italy by defendant Biochimica Opos, S.p.A. (Opos).

On the same day that Zenith and Cyanamid obtained FDA approval to sell cefaclor in this country, Lilly obtained the rights to the '085 patent and filed suit against Zenith, Cyanamid, Biocraft, and Opos. In its complaint, Lilly sought a declaration that the domestic defendants' importation of cefaclor manufactured by Opos infringed Lilly's rights under several patents, including the '085 patent. Lilly also requested a preliminary injunction, based on the alleged infringement of claim 5 of the '085 patent, to bar the defendants from importing or inducing the importation of cefaclor manufactured by Opos.

Based on the evidence presented at the hearing, the district court concluded that Lilly had shown that it was likely to prevail on the issue of the validity of the '085 patent. With respect to the infringement issue, however, the court held that Lilly had not met its burden of showing that it was likely to prevail.

The district court found that compound 6 and cefaclor differ significantly in their structure and properties, including their biological activity. Citing the Senate Report on the Process Patent Amendments Act, the district court found that, because the processing steps necessary to convert compound 6 to cefaclor " 'change the physical or chemical properties of the product in a manner which changes the basic utility of the product,' "896 F.Supp. at 857, 36 U.S.P.Q.2d at 1016 (citing S.Rep. No. 83, 100th Cong., 1st Sess. 50 (1987)), Lilly was not likely to succeed on its claim that the defendants infringed Lilly's rights under claim 5 of the '085 patent by importing and selling cefaclor.

The district court also found that Lilly had failed to prove that it would suffer irreparable harm in the absence of a preliminary injunction.

The presumption of irreparable harm that is available when a patentee makes a strong showing of likelihood of success on the merits was not available here, the court held, because of Lilly's failure to make such a showing on the issue of infringement. In addition, the court was not persuaded by Lilly's arguments that it faced irreparable economic injury if it were not granted immediate equitable relief. Under the circumstances of this case, the district court found that an award of money damages would be an adequate remedy in the event that Lilly ultimately proves that the importation of cefaclor made by the Opos process infringes the '085 patent. In light of Lilly's failure to establish either a likelihood of success on the merits or irreparable harm, the court found it unnecessary to articulate findings regarding the other factors bearing on the propriety of preliminary injunctive relief—the balance of the hardships and the effect of the court's action on the public interest.

II

The Process Patent Amendments Act of 1988 was enacted to close a perceived loophole in the statutory scheme for protecting owners of United States patents. Prior to the enactment of the 1988 statute, a patentee holding a process patent could sue for infringement if others used the process in this country, but had no cause of action if such persons used the patented process abroad to manufacture products, and then imported, used, or sold the products in this country. In that setting, the process patent owner's only legal recourse was to seek an exclusion order for such products from the International Trade Commission under section 337a of the Tariff Act of 1930, 19 U.S.C. § 1337a (1982). By enacting the Process Patent Amendments Act, the principal portion of which is codified as 35 U.S.C. § 271(g), Congress changed the law by making it an act of infringement to import into the United States, or to sell or use within the United States "a product which is made by a process patented in the United States . . . if the importation, sale, or use of the product occurs during the term of such process patent."

A concern raised during Congress's consideration of the process patent legislation was whether and to what extent the new legislation would affect products other than the direct and unaltered products of patented processes—that is, whether the new statute would apply when a product was produced abroad by a patented process but then modified or incorporated into other products before being imported into this country. Congress addressed that issue by providing that a product that is "made by" a patented process within the meaning of the statute "will . . . not be considered to be so made after—(1) it is materially changed by subsequent processes; or (2) it becomes a trivial and nonessential component of another product." 35 U.S.C. § 271(g).

That language, unfortunately, is not very precise. Whether the product of a patented process is a "trivial and nonessential component" of another product is necessarily a question of degree. Even less well defined is the question whether the product of a patented process has been "materially changed" before its importation into this country.

While applying that statutory language may be relatively easy in extreme cases, it is not at all easy in a closer case such as this one.

A

Lilly argues that the "materially changed" clause of section 271(g) must be construed in light of its underlying purpose, which is to protect the economic value of U.S. process patents to their owners. Prior to the enactment of the Process Patent Amendments Act, the value of a U.S. process patent could be undermined by a manufacturer who used the process abroad and then imported the product into this country. Because the purpose of the process patent legislation was to protect against such subversion of protected economic rights, Lilly argues that the statute should be read to apply to any such scheme that undercuts the commercial value of a U.S. process patent. In Lilly's view, the product of a patented process therefore should not be considered "materially changed" if the principal commercial use of that product lies in its conversion into the product that is the subject of the infringement charge. Because cefaclor is the only product of compound 6 that is sold in the United States market, Lilly argues, the change in compound 6 that results in cefaclor—no matter how significant as a matter of chemical properties or molecular structure—is not a "material change" for purposes of section 271(g).

Although we are not prepared to embrace Lilly's argument, we acknowledge that it has considerable appeal. Congress was concerned with the problem of the overseas use of patented processes followed by the importation of the products of those processes, and a grudging construction of the statute could significantly limit the statute's effectiveness in addressing the problem Congress targeted. That is especially true with respect to chemical products, as to which simple, routine reactions can often produce dramatic changes in the products' structure and properties.

Nonetheless, while the general purpose of the statute informs the construction of the language Congress chose, purpose cannot displace language, and we cannot stretch the term "materially changed" as far as Lilly's argument would require. The problem is that the language of the statute refers to changes in the product; the statute permits the importation of an item that is derived from a product made by a patented process as long as that product is "materially changed" in the course of its conversion into the imported item. The reference to a "changed" product is very hard to square with Lilly's proposed test, which turns on the quite different question of whether the use or sale of the imported item impairs the economic value of the process patent.

The facts of this case demonstrate how far Lilly's test strays from the statutory text. While Lilly notes that there are only four steps between compound 6 and cefaclor, and that all four steps involve relatively routine chemical reactions, Lilly does not suggest any limiting principle based on the structure of the intermediate product or the nature of the steps necessary to produce the imported product. Thus, even if there were ten complex chemical reactions that separated compound 6 from cefaclor, Lilly's test would characterize the two compounds as not "materially" different as long as the primary commercial use of compound 6 in this country was to produce cefaclor.

Besides not responding to the natural meaning of the term "changed," Lilly's construction of the "materially changed" clause would create a curious anomaly. Lilly's value-based construction of the clause turns in large measure on Lilly's contention that the only commercial use for compound 6 in this country is to produce cefaclor; that is, Lilly views compound 6 and cefaclor as essentially the same product because compound 6 has no commercial use in the U.S. market except to produce cefaclor. Under that approach, however, the question whether compound 6 was "materially changed" in the course of its conversion to cefaclor would depend on whether and to what extent other derivative products of compound 6 are marketed in this country. Thus, under Lilly's theory compound 6 would become materially different from cefaclor if and when compound 6 came to have other commercial uses in the United States, even though the respective structures and properties of the two compounds remained unchanged.

That is asking the statutory language to do too much work. We cannot accept the argument that the question whether one compound is "materially changed" in the course of its conversion into another depends on whether there are other products of the first compound that have economic value. We therefore do not adopt Lilly's proposed construction of section 271(g). We look instead to the substantiality of the change between the product of the patented process and the product that is being imported.

In the chemical context, a "material" change in a compound is most naturally viewed as a significant change in the compound's structure and properties. Without attempting to define with precision what classes of changes would be material and what would not, we share the district court's view that a change in chemical structure and properties as significant as the change between compound 6 and cefaclor cannot lightly be dismissed as immaterial. Although compound 6 and cefaclor share the basic cephem nucleus, which is the ultimate source of the antibiotic potential of all cephalosporins, the cephem nucleus is common to thousands of compounds, many of which have antibiotic activity, and many of which are dramatically different from others within the cephem family. Beyond the cephem nucleus that they have in common, compound 6 and cefaclor are different in four important structural respects, corresponding to the four discrete chemical steps between the two compounds. While the addition or removal of a protective group, standing alone, might not be sufficient to constitute a "material change" between two compounds (even though it could dramatically affect certain of their properties), the conversion process between compound 6 and cefaclor involves considerably more than the removal of a protective group. We therefore conclude that the statutory text of section 271(g) does not support Lilly's contention that it is likely to prevail on the merits of its infringement claim.

B

In aid of their differing approaches to the issue of statutory construction, both sides in this dispute seek support for their positions in the legislative history of the 1988 statute. As is often the case, there is something in the legislative history for each side. On Lilly's side, for example, are characterizations of the legislation as creating process patent protection that is "meaningful and not easily evaded," H.R.Rep. No. 60, 100th Cong., 1st Sess. 13 (1987), and as excluding products only if they "cease to have a reasonable nexus with the patented process," S.Rep. No. 83, 100th Cong., 1st Sess. 36 (1987). On the other side are directions for applying the statute to chemical intermediates—directions that suggest a narrower construction of the statute than Lilly proposes. On balance, while we do not find the legislative history dispositive, we conclude that it does not unequivocally favor Lilly's position and thus does not raise doubts about the district court's statutory analysis as applied to the facts of this case.

AFFIRMED.

RADER, CIRCUIT JUDGE, concurring.

Sadly this decision will create another massive loophole in the protection of patented processes. This decision will, in effect, deny protection to holders of process patents on intermediates as opposed to "final" products. This decision denies protection to a patented process anytime it is not the only way to make an intermediate, even if it is the most economically efficient way to produce the intermediate.

In view of the purpose of the statute, compound 6 and cefaclor are essentially the same product. Compound 6 has no commercial use in the U.S. market except to make cefaclor. The patented process is thus in use to make compound 6—a product only four simple, well-known steps from cefaclor. The record shows no other current commercial use of compound 6.

Rather than attempting to distill an elixir from this intoxicating witches brew of enactment history, this court should interpret "material change" consistent with the overriding purpose of the Act—to provide protection to process patent holders. With its eye firmly fixed on the purpose of the Act, this court would avoid eliminating processes for intermediates from the protections of the 1988 Act.

Notes

1. Domestic Application. Does § 271(g) apply to purely domestic situations? This issue has generated some extreme positions among the United States district courts. The decision in *Shamrock Technologies Inc. v. Precision Micron Powders Inc.*, 20 U.S.P.Q.2d 1797, 1798 (E.D.N.Y.1991) provided:

PMP contends that according to the legislative history of 35 U.S.C.A. § 271(g) (added to the Patent Act in 1988), section 271(g) was enacted to create a cause of action against manufacturers and importers of infringing goods but not against domestic sellers of infringing goods like PMP. The plain language of the statute, however, clearly states that whoever without authority sells within the United States a product made by a patented process shall be liable as an infringer.

However, in *Hughes Aircraft Co. v. National Semiconductor Corp.*, 857 F.Supp. 691 (N.D.Cal.1994), the court concluded:

General Motors' second argument raises a more fundamental and troubling problem: whether the imposition of liability on General Motors under the PPAA given the particular facts of this case would be consistent with the legislative history and purpose of that statute. According to the Report of the Senate Judiciary Committee, the primary purpose of the PPAA was "to modernize our patent laws" by providing "patent protection against the importation, and subsequent use or sale, of products made abroad ... using a process patented in the United States." S.Rep. No. 83, 100th Cong., 1st Sess., 29–30 (1987). The Committee later reiterates that the PPAA was intended to "protect against the entry into the U.S. marketplace of goods made abroad without authorization from [an] inventor who has a process patent in this country." Id. at 30. Finally, and most importantly to the case at bar, the Committee states that

The primary target of the U.S. process patent holder will naturally be the manufacturer, who is practicing the process and importing [sic] the resulting goods into the United States. If that manufacturer is subject to the jurisdiction of the U.S. courts then it would be the preferred defendant because of its direct knowledge of the process. Since the manufacturer may not be subject to jurisdiction, [the PPAA] also allows the patentholder to sue the persons receiving the goods in this country in the belief that they may be in the best position, apart from the manufacturer, to determine how the goods were made.

Id. at 39.

Based on its legislative history, it appears that the PPAA was designed to provide a remedy within the United States for United States process patent holders whose processes were being used in other countries to manufacture goods for importation into the United States. It does not appear to have been designed to provide a basis for holding a domestic, downstream seller of goods, such as General Motors, liable for infringement merely because it has incorporated an allegedly infringing good produced by a domestic, upstream manufacturer, such as Delco Electronics, into its finished product. Accordingly, General Motors is entitled to summary judgment on NSC and Fairchild's claim that it directly infringed the process patents under 35 U.S.C.A. § 271(g).

857 F. Supp. at 698–99.

2. Comparative Approaches. Article 34 of the TRIPS Agreement also provides for more liberal standards for demonstrating the infringement of process patents. To this end, Article 64(2) of the European Patent

Convention stipulates that "[i]f the subject-matter of the European patent is a process, the protection conferred by the patent shall extend to the products directly obtained by such process." The key word in this provision is "directly." European law on this subject is extensively discussed in a case from the English Court of Appeal, *Pioneer Electronics Capital Inc. v. Warner Music Manufacturing Europe GmbH,* [1997] R.P.C. 757. Section 104 of the Japanese Patent Act also establishes that "any identical product shall be presumed to have been manufactured by that process" in the event that a process patent is asserted.

3. Does 271(g) Cover a Product Discovered by Using a Patented Research Method Outside of the United States? One of the most important issues concerning the scope of patents on research tools is whether what is discovered is covered by § 271(g). For a good discussion of this important question see *Bayer AG v. Housey Pharmaceuticals, Inc.*, 169 F.Supp.2d 328, 61 U.S.P.Q.2d 1051 (D.Del.2001).

§ 15.8 INFRINGEMENT ANALYSES OVERSEAS

§ 15.8[a] Europe

In the growing body of nations which are signatories to the European Patent Convention, patents granted by individual national patent offices coexist with those with those granted by the European Patent Office. But, for the time being, a patent issued by the EPO is nothing more than the grant of a bundle of national patents. Once this so-called "European patent" springs into being, various national laws largely control its legal effect, and in particular its enforcement. This point is punctuated by EPC Article 64(3), which unequivocally states that "[a]ny infringement of a European patent shall be dealt with by national law."

On central points, the patent law of Europe is substantially harmonized. But infringement issues, and in particular points of claim interpretation, remain difficult ones for the various courts of Europe to reconcile. Historical approaches to claim interpretation have differed greatly among EPC signatories, with the two greatest patent powers, the United Kingdom and Germany, forming antipodes of narrow and broad claim interpretation, respectively. Anticipating this issue, the EPC drafters specifically addressed patent claim interpretation through the following provisions.

European Patent Convention Article 69(1)

The extent of protection conferred by a European patent or a European patent application shall be determined by the terms of the claims. Nevertheless, the description and drawings shall be used to interpret the claims.

Protocol on the Interpretation of Article 69

Article 69 should not be interpreted in the sense that the extent of protection conferred by a European patent is to be understood as that defined by the strict, literal meaning of the wording used in the claims, the description and drawings being employed only for the purpose of resolving an ambiguity found in the claims. Neither should it be interpreted in the sense that the claims serve only as a guideline and that the actual protection conferred may extent to what, from a consideration of the description and drawings by a person skilled in the art, the patentee has contemplated. On the contrary, it is to be interpreted as defining a position between these extremes which combines a fair protection for the patentee with a reasonable degree of certainty for third parties.

The Protocol to Article 69 was amended in November 2000, resulting in the addition of the following sentence:

For the purpose of determining the extent of protection conferred by a European patent, due account shall be taken of any element which is equivalent to an element specified in the claims.

Despite this supposedly pan-European approach to claim interpretation, national jurists continue to exhibit difficulty in shedding their pre-EPC approaches towards equivalents. Discrepancies between their conclusions regarding the same patent and accused technology have led to interesting comparative litigation studies, particularly in the notorious *Epilady* litigation. The following two opinions, the leading infringement decisions from Germany and the United Kingdom, suggest how such different results can be achieved.

§ 15.8[a][1] The Doctrine of Equivalents in Germany

FORMSTEIN

German Federal Supreme Court, 1986.
[1991] RPC 597.

OFFICIAL HEADNOTES

(a) Under section 14 of the Patent Law 1981, the extent of protection generally includes equivalents of the invention protected by the claims.

(b) The defence that the embodiment alleged to be equivalent would not be patentable in view of the prior art is admissible.

JUDGMENT

The plaintiff is the proprietor of German patent 2944622 filed on 5 November 1979 in respect of a molded curbstone. The grant was published on 19 August 1982. Claims 1 and 2 of the patent read as follows:

1. An integral or cross-sectionally multi-part molded curbstone with a longitudinal trough for drainage channels at a roadside, characterised in that it comprises at least one cross-channel branching off from the longitudinal trough and opening into the side of the curbstone facing away from the centre of the road.

2. A molded curbstone as claimed in claim 1, characterised in that the cross-channel has a slight inclination.

The defendant town built a road within its administrative area having a surface of compound paving stones at a cross-slope of 2%. As a lateral edging and abutting the compound paving stones, a horizontal row of curbstones was laid which ran alongside the road surface. These consisted of commercially available rounded curbstones raised six centimetres, which were laid with three-centimetre gaps between them to provide lateral drainage. Run-off water seeped into a gravel layer lying one centimetre below the actual level of the road surface.

The plaintiff believed this to be an infringement of the patent in suit and sued for an injunction, the rendering of an account and for the defendant's liability in damages to be established.

The defendant has denied infringement and set up a right of prior use.

The Landgericht found against the defendant. On appeal by the defendant, the Court of Appeal dismissed the action. The plaintiff's appeal to this court on points of law is allowed and the case is referred back to the Court of Appeal.

On the following grounds:

1. The patent in suit relates to an integral or cross-sectionally multi-part molded curbstone with a longitudinal trough for drainage channels for use at the roadside.

The specification of the patent begins with a description of a previously known integral or cross-sectionally multi-part molded curbstone with a longitudinal trough for drainage channels at the roadside for the support and definition of road surfaces at the same level. The disadvantage of this molded curbstone is alleged to be that all the rainwater falling on the road surface is drained off, so that the rainwater sewers have to be correspondingly large in size and any accumulated debris will be carried into the sewage system.

The specification then describes the technical problem underlying the invention as being the provision of a molded curbstone which, at the roadside, provides for safe and reliable drainage of rainwater falling on the road surface and which, in all weather conditions, will channel a proportion of the rainwater laterally into adjoining ground.

The specification describes the advantage of the invention as being that even large quantities of rainwater may thereby be drained from the road surface and that the debris it contains, which appears mainly at the onset of rain, is almost all drained laterally through the cross-channels.

In the light of the disadvantages of the prior art as described in the specification and of the advantages of the solution proposed, the Court of Appeal identified the technical problem as being to improve runoff at the side of the road, to have a beneficial effect on the ground-water level, to reduce the amount of debris in drain water entering the sewage system, and to make it possible to use smaller rainwater sewers.

Whether this fully defines the problem may presently be left undecided since the question of identical use of the invention is alone of relevance.

2. Claim 1 of the patent in suit proposes the following solution to this problem:

    a) an integral or cross-sectionally multi-part molded stone (for drainage channels at a roadside),

    b) having a longitudinal trough,

    c) and a cross-channel,

        aa) branching off from the longitudinal trough,

        bb) and opening into the side of the molded stone facing away from the centre of the road.

3. The Court of Appeal correctly based its determination of the scope of protection on section 14 of the Patent Law 1981 (formerly section 6a). This provision corresponds to Article 69 paragraph 1 of the European Patent Convention. Section 14 of the Patent Law 1981 is applicable to patent applications filed after 1 January 1978.

4. The appeal on points of law is unsuccessful in its assertion that the Court of Appeal failed to appreciate that the defendant made identical use of the patent in suit.

    a) The Court of Appeal commented on this as follows. In producing its roadside support the defendant did not use molded stones as described in the patent in suit, which differed from conventional stones in terms of their specific purpose, but used conventional stones in the form of cubes or bricks as well as conventional rounded curbstones. The alleged infringement was further held not to be a "cross-sectionally multi-part molded stone" because a cross-section taken from the area of the drainage gaps between the front ends of the rounded curbstones showed only the longitudinally arranged paving stones, the gravel hardcore, which was not part of the object of the patent in suit, and the road surface. The alleged infringement also exhibited no longitudinal trough. The patent in suit protects a molded stone with an integral longitudinal trough. In contrast, the longitudinal trough in the alleged infringement was located within the road. The longitudinal trough therefore had no cross-channel branching off from it, the base of which, according to claim 1 of the patent, had to be formed by the molded stone itself and not, as in the case of the alleged infringement, by the gravel hardcore.

    b) This reasoning of the Court of Appeal contains no legal error.

The Court of Appeal correctly assumed that, in the case of the molded stone according to claim 1 of the patent, the longitudinal trough and the cross-channel branching off from it are molded in the stone. This follows from the specification, from the examples of the embodiment of the invention as shown in the drawings and finally from the wording of claim 1 itself. [Diagrams in the patent] also show the longitudinal trough and cross-channel in multi-part molded stones. The specification states that each molded stone has a cross-channel and that the latter opens into the side of the molded stone. Claim 1 is also worded in this way.

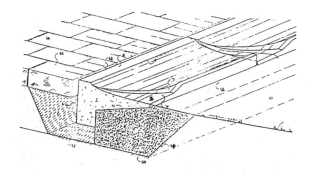

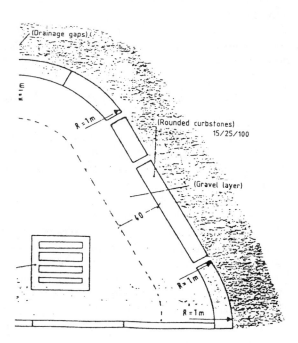

The longitudinal trough and the cross-channel in the alleged infringement are formed by the round curbstone, the row of paving stones and the adjacent road surface—but they are not integrated in the stone itself. This is accepted in the appeal.

5.   The appellant correctly argues however, that there has been a legally erroneous assessment of an equivalent use of the invention by the defendant.

a) The Court of Appeal proceeded upon the basis that an equivalent use of an invention presupposed that the alleged infringement solved the technical problem by means which were not identical with those protected by the patent, but coincided as to their technical function, i.e. they achieved essentially the same effect. The Court of Appeal further required that the alleged infringement must make full use of the principle of the solution protected by the patent. It rejected the equivalent use of what was described in the patent in suit because the alleged infringement was not based on the principle of the patented solution in spite of the fact that their purposes coincided. The principle was held to consist in an integral or cross-sectionally multi-part molded stone with integral troughs and channels to support and delineate the road surface at the same level. The defendant, in contrast, adopted a procedure for supporting roadsides with curbstones using features which were freely available from the prior art and by making use of commercially available stones: this fulfilled other purposes in addition to solving the drainage problem. The raised arrangement of curbstones was intended to prevent motorists driving over planted areas and to stop soil from the planted areas being washed away. An ordinary high curbstone could not be converted into a channelled molded stone as a result of the way in which it was laid. The defendant's embodiment was thus far removed from the proposal of the patent in suit.

b) These observations contain a legal error.

As explained above, the extent of protection of the patent in suit is to be determined under section 14 of the Patent Law 1981. In contrast to the legal situation obtaining until 1978, claims are now not merely the starting point but rather the standard basis for determining the extent of protection. Under section 14(2) of the Patent Law 1981, the scope of a claim has to be determined as a matter of construction, taking the description and the drawings into account. As may be seen from the Protocol on the Interpretation of Article 69 paragraph 1 of the European Patent Convention, which corresponds to section 14 of the Patent Law 1981, construction serves not merely to remove any ambiguities in the claims but also to define the technical concepts used therein and to clarify the meaning and scope of the invention described in them. In the explanatory note to the government draft of the present section 14 of the Patent Law (at that time section 6a), the Federal Government made reference to this Protocol, stating that the principles laid down in it should also be effective under German law (BT–Drucksache [Bundestag publication] 7/3712, page 30); only in this way was it possible to achieve the objective sought by the introduction of the new provision, namely a definition of the scope of patent protection in Europe which was as uniform as possible. This Law required that the principles of protection agreed upon by the contracting states of the European Patent Convention as set out in the Protocol on the Interpretation of Article 69, must be taken into account in determining the extent of protection afforded by German patents.

Under the Protocol on the Interpretation of Article 69, the extent of protection afforded by a patent does not merely include what follows from the precise wording of the claims. The way is therefore open to determine the extent of protection in a manner that goes beyond the wording of the claims so as to include modifications of the invention described in the claims. It is within the knowledge of the court that the extension of protection beyond the wording of the claims to equivalent forms of embodiment corresponds to the legal concept which the states participating in the European Patent Convention had in mind, even though significant differences of detail still exist, both as to the method of determining the factual extent of protection and as to the scope of the protection granted.

The extent of protection afforded by patents filed after 1 January 1978 is to be determined in terms of the use of the invention by equivalents, according to the meaning of the claims as ascertained by interpretation. The scope of the invention as recognised by a person skilled in the art is decisive in this context. What must be asked is: whether a person skilled in the art, has managed, on the basis of the invention protected by the claims, to solve the problem solved by the invention using methods which have the same effect, ie has achieved the desired result with other means which lead to the same result. Solutions which a person of normal skill in the art, on the basis of the invention described in the claims, and with the aid of his specialist knowledge, can discover to have the same effect will ordinarily be within the protection of the patent. The adequate remuneration of inventors requires this, as does the requirement for the legal certainty.

In the view of the Court of Appeal, the technical problem underlying the patent in suit, namely to channel rainwater into the area at the roadside, was also solved in the alleged infringement. In ascertaining the technical problem, the Court of Appeal referred exclusively to the information set out in the specification and perhaps because of this, gained an incomplete understanding of the technical problem actually solved by the invention. It is not merely a question of the words used in the specification but rather of what technical problem is actually (objectively) solved by the invention in a manner recognisable by a person skilled in the art (cf BGHZ [Decisions of the Federal High Court in Civil Cases] 78, 358, 364—Spinnturbine II). The patented curbstone could lead to a simplified approach to the construction of drainage channels at roadsides because the collection channel and cross-channel are already molded into the stone and do not have to be specially produced in situ.

Insofar as the Court of Appeal, when examining equivalents, compared the solution of the protected embodiment with that of the alleged infringement and ruled out infringement on the ground that in the alleged infringement the defendant had departed from the principle of the solution proposed in the patent, its judgment is legally in error. In determining the extent of protection of patents filed after 1 January 1978, the basic question is whether the person of normal skill in the art could, on the basis of his specialist knowledge, discover the methods used in the alleged infringement, which achieve the same effect from the claims, and using the specification and drawings—and not whether the "principle" is the same. Furthermore, the Court of Appeal has fallen into error in that it has limited the "principle" underlying the patent in suit to the direct realisation of the object of the invention (moulding of longitudinal trough and cross-channel).

Neither should the Court of Appeal have ruled out equivalent use of the patent on the ground that the object of the patent being a molded stone, the defendant had used a specific procedure merely to support roadsides. A claim relating to the structure of an article affords protection against any use of that product, without reference to the manner or means of its production. The defendant's roadside support may fall within the ambit of protection of the patent in its tangible embodiment even if the process used by the defendant to produce it differs from the method of production of the molded stone subject of the patent. It is therefore a question of whether the defendant has created an article with characteristics equivalent to those of the patent in suit by placing the cross-channel not in the stone, eg. on its outer edge, but directly to one side of it, so that in each case two stones produce the sides of a cross-channel.

Nor should the Court of Appeal have rejected equivalent use on the ground that while the patent in suit related to a molded stone for road surfaces at the same level as the road surface, the alleged infringement used an elevated curb. Claim 1 of the patent contains no limitation to a molded stone for the support of roadsides at the same level. The wording of the claim includes molded stones forming a curb. A narrow interpretation of the claim to molded stones laid at the same level, would amount to an inadmissible interpretation of the patent which is more limited than the wording of the claim. The specification makes reference to a channelled molded stone known from German Gebrauchsmuster No 7430185, which serves to define road surfaces at the same level. Elsewhere in the specification, the advantages of the molded stone subject of the patent when it is laid at the same level as that of the road are described. This does not however restrict the disclosure of the patent to molded stones laid at the same level as the road.

6.   The reasoning of the Court of Appeal that the defendant had used a prior art procedure and commercially available stones for the support of roadsides and the defendant's argument that the alleged infringement did not satisfy patentability requirements, does not at this stage of the proceedings justify the dismissal of the action.

a) In determining the extent of protection under section 14 of the Patent Law 1981, the defence that the alleged infringement which is claimed to be an equivalent is not a patentable invention in the light of the prior art is admissible. The defendant can therefore defend himself in an infringement action not only by showing that the alleged infringement is within the prior art but also by stating that in view of the latter, it does not constitute an invention.

The availability of this defence, for which the burden rests on the defendant, does not limit the reward due to the inventor for the disclosure of a patentable invention.

In infringement actions, the defendant may refer to the prior art as defined in section 3 paragraph 1 of the Patent Law 1981 and assert that the alleged infringement is derived from the prior art in a manner obvious to a person skilled in the art (section 4 sentence 1 of the Patent Law 1981). In this way, in the free non-inventive development of prior art, all knowledge is used which is decisive in assessing the patentability of the patent in suit and therefore for determining whether a reward is due to the inventor for the disclosure of his invention.

b) The Court of Appeal did not—understandably—examine this question. Since the facts require further judicial clarification, the decision should be reversed and the case referred back to the Court of Appeal for further consideration and decision.

7. a) In such further proceedings, the parties will have the opportunity to address the technical problem underlying the invention, and to comment on the defence that the product claimed is not an invention in the light of the prior art. If it should emerge that the problem disclosed in the specification is of minor importance in comparison to a further problem, then the question of equivalent effect might possibly have to be ruled out. If the Court of Appeal should come to the conclusion that the alleged infringement formed part of the prior art or that in view of that prior art there was no patentable invention, there can be no infringement.

If the review by the Court of Appeal shows that, on the basis of the prior art, inventive activity was necessary to discover the alleged infringement then infringement has of course occurred only if a person skilled in the art could deduce the alleged infringement as having the same effect, from the invention as claimed, and in addition, utilizing the description and drawings claimed (see point 5.b of the grounds of the decision).

The Court of Appeal will have to consider whether an expert should be appointed to examine the above issues.

b) If, as in the first proceedings, the defendant should then appeal on the ground of a right of prior use, the Court of Appeal will have to bear in mind that the acquisition of such a right presupposes ownership of the invention, and must be supported by use. This requires evidence of actions which have already been taken for the purpose of making practical use of the invention and which clearly demonstrate an intention of putting it to use as soon as possible.

c) In addition, the Court of Appeal will have to consider the following: the plaintiff has based its application for an injunction on the wording of claims 1 and 2 of the patent in suit. This is permissible only if the infringement falls within the literal wording of the claims. As the Court of Appeal has however determined without legal error that the defendant is not in fact making identical use of the patent in suit, it will therefore have to ensure (Section 139 paragraph 1 sentence 1 ZPO [Code of Civil Procedure]) that the injunctive relief granted will be in terms relating to the particular infringement complained of. This applies to both its technical characteristics and the way in which the alleged infringement is used.

d) In the event that the defendant has to pay damages and render an account, the Court of Appeal will further have to take into consideration the fact that the patent is dated 19 August 1982. It cannot be said that the defendant had failed in its duty of care in that it had not become aware of the existence of the patent on the very day of publication of the grant and of the fact that the alleged infringement in fact infringed the patent. As a rule, an examination period of up to four weeks from the date of publication of the grant may be appropriate; thus the question of liability arises only after the expiry of such a period of investigation.

Notes

1. **_Formstein_ and the Federal Circuit.** Does _Formstein_ espouse essentially the same test as _Wilson Sporting Goods_? How does this decision comport with the subsequent movement at the Federal Circuit to render nonobviousness a measure of substantial change in light of _Hilton Davis_?

2. **Earlier German Law on Equivalents.** Preceding _Formstein_ was a considerable body of German case law and academic commentary regarding the appropriate scope of protection for a patent claim. As summarized by C. Sijp, _Scope of Protection Afforded by a European Patent_, 10 INT'L REV. INDUS. PROP. & COPYRIGHT L. 433 (1979), the case law developed a _Dreiteilungslehre_, or Tripartite Doctrine for applying the subject matter of the invention to a particular accused technology. This test was heavily influenced by the jurisdictional split that continues to exist between German courts and the Patent Office, whereby German courts may reach only issues of infringement, and cannot pass on the validity of the claims before them. The Tripartite Doctrine included three levels of increasing broad scope of protection as follows:

1. **The Direct Subject of the Invention**, or "_Unmittelbarer Gegenstand der Erfindung_," analogous to literal infringement under U.S. law. A court would grant this level of protection where it believed the patent was anticipated by the prior art, leaving revocation of the patent to the Patent Office.

2. **The Subject Matter of the Invention**, or "_Gegenstand der Erfindung_," the wording employed by section 6 of the German Patent Act. Protection was extended here to so-called "evident equivalents," or "_glattes Äquivalent_," and is perhaps analogous to the scope of equivalents available to a means clause under § 112 ¶ 6 of the U.S. patent statute. Patents claiming novel inventions were extended this level of protection.

3. **The General Inventive Idea**, or "_Allgemeiner Erfindungsgedanke_". As articulated by Chief Justice Lindenmaier of the German

Supreme Court, *see* Fritz Lindenmaier, *Der Schutzumgan des Patents nach der Neueren Rechtsprechung*, 1944 GRUR 49, protection here was quite broad, reaching to cover "non-evident equivalents" or "*nicht-glattes Äquivalent.*" The scope of equivalency corresponded to a broader version of the U.S. Doctrine of Equivalents. According to "*Kautelen von Lindenmaier,*" or "Lindenmainer's Provisos," a patentee could obtain protection for his "general inventive idea" if it fulfilled three conditions:

(1) The general inventive idea must have been obvious to those skilled in the art at the time the patent application was filed.

(2) Determination of the general inventive idea must not itself require inventive effort.

(3) The general inventive idea must itself satisfy all patentability requirements.

German adoption of the European Patent Convention gave rise to the German Patent Act of 1981, which embodies Article 69 and the more streamlined theory of equivalency set forth in *Formstein. See generally* Jochen Pagenberg, *More Refined Rules of Claim Interpretation in Germany—Are They Necessary?*, 26 INT'L REV. INDUS. PROP. & COPYRIGHT L. 228 (1995); Jochen Pagenberg, *New Trends in Patent Claim Interpretation in Germany—Goodbye to the "General Inventive Idea,"* 19 INT'L REV. INDUS. PROP. & COPYRIGHT L. 788 (1988).

3. The 2000 Amendments. During the November 2000 European Patent Convention revision conference, proposals to (1) define the term "equivalents," (2) determine the point in time at which equivalency should be determined, and (3) introduce a doctrine of prosecution history estoppel were each abandoned. Does the failure of these proposals suggest distinctions between the doctrine of equivalents in the United States and abroad?

§ 15.8[a][2] The Doctrine of Equivalents in the United Kingdom

CATNIC COMPONENTS LTD. v. HILL AND SMITH LTD.

House of Lords.
[1981] FSR 60, [1982] RPC 183.

Lord Diplock: MY LORDS, This appeal concerns a claim by the appellants ("Catnic") for infringement of a simple but successful patent of which they are the registered proprietors for galvanised steel lintels for use in spanning the spaces above window and door openings in cavity walls built of bricks or similar constructional units. Since lintels are supported only at either end by the brick courses on which they rest and must themselves support the superimposed brick courses above the window or door space that they span, rigidity and strength are necessary characteristics. Heavy beams of timber or heavy-gauge metal girders possess these characteristics and had long been used for this purpose. In the patent in suit the necessary strength and rigidity was obtained by adopting a box-girder structure with consequent lightness, economy of material, and ease of handling.

The simplest way of explaining the invention is by reproducing figure 1 of the complete specification, which is of a vertical section through the lintel, showing the outer and inner courses of the cavity wall. The lintel can be made in two modules, a three-course module (as shown) where the height between the upper and lower horizontal plates is equivalent to three courses of bricks and mortar and a two-course module which the height is equivalent to two courses only.

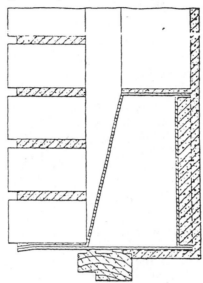

Of the claims in the specification it is only necessary for present purposes to reproduce the first.

"1. A lintel for use over apertures in cavity walls having an inner and outer skin comprising a first horizontal plate or part adapted to support a course or a plurality of superimposed units forming part of the inner skin and a second horizontal plate or part substantially parallel to the first and spaced therefrom in a downward vertical direction and adapted to span the cavity in the cavity wall and be supported at least at each end thereof upon courses forming parts of the outer and inner skins respectively of the cavity wall adjacent an aperture, and a first rigid inclined support member extending downwardly and forwardly from or near the front edge adjacent the cavity of the first horizontal plate or part at an intermediate position which lies between the front and rear edge of the second plate or part and adapted to extend across the cavity, and a second rigid support member extending vertically from or from near the rear edge of the first horizontal plate or part to join with the second plate or part adjacent its rear edge."

The complete specification was filed on the 29th December 1969 and published on 6th December 1972. Lintels manufactured in accordance with the patent quickly achieved considerable success upon the market.

At about the beginning of 1974 the respondents ("Hill and Smith") who are old established fabricators of galvanised steel products, and had for some time past been carrying out large contracts for the manufacture of crash-barriers for roads, foresaw a contraction of the demand for this particular product and decided to prepare to enter the market for builders' products and, in particular, for galvanised steel lintels. With this in view they examined trade brochures issued by various manufacturers of steel lintels, including one published by Catnic. They decided that the Catnic lintel was the best; they were unaware that it was the subject-matter of a patent; so they copied it and manufactured it.

Your Lordships are not concerned with the first type of galvanised steel lintel (referred to in the courts below as "DH2") which Hill and Smith manufactured in consequence of what they had seen in Catnic's brochure. It was the subject of a writ issued by Catnic in March 1975 claiming an injunction and damages for infringement of patent, and this was subsequently amended to add a claim for damages for breach of copyright in certain of Catnic's drawings. DH2 was held at the trial by Whitford J. to infringe the patent and there was no appeal against this part of his judgment. He also found that there had been no breach of copyright, and, although this finding was contested unsuccessfully by Catnic in the Court of Appeal, no appeal has been brought to your Lordships' House from their endorsement of the learned judge's finding. Service of that writ, however, alerted Hill and Smith's Managing Director, Mr. Hodgetts, to the danger of infringement of Catnic's patent by galvanised steel lintels of the type DH2 that they were then engaged in introducing on the market. Coincidently, one of their first customers had complained that the Hill and Smith lintels, (in which the lower horizontal plate did not extend rearward beyond the point at which the vertical back plate joined it) presented difficulties in plastering the soffit. Hill and Smith then produced a modified design (referred to in the courts below as "DH4") which became the subject of the second writ. It was substantially in the form sketched below.

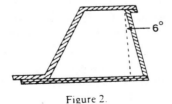

Figure 2.

Between this design and that described in Claim 1 of the patent the difference which is relied upon by Hill and Smith to save it from being an infringement, is that the back plate is not precisely vertical but is inclined at a slight angle to the vertical, viz 6 deg in the case of the three-course module and 8 deg in the case of the two course module. Referring to the circumstances in which this modification to the previous design took place, the learned judge said: "I am in no doubt that the consideration chiefly working on Mr. Hodgetts' mind was avoidance of infringement, although it did not meet [the customer's] complaint, and I accept that this was a further consideration operating in Mr. Hodgetts' mind". I apprehend, however, that your Lordships are concerned not so much with the motives for the alteration as with the effect of it. Did the substitution of a back plate that was slightly inclined to the true vertical for one that was precisely vertical change what the patentee by his specification had made an essential feature of the invention claimed having regard to the patentee's description of the back plate in Claim 1 as "extending vertically"?

The invention is a simple one; to understand what it does and how it works calls for no great technological or scientific expertise. It is designed for use by builders engaged in ordinary building operations; they constitute the readers to whom the specification is addressed. As any knowledgeable builder would know, indeed as would be known even by one of Lord Macaulay's schoolboys, who had reached the triangle of forces in his study of elementary mechanics, a slight inclination from the vertical of an upright support reduces its load bearing capacity proportionately to the cosine of the angle of such inclination. Where that angle is 6 deg as in the Hill and Smith three-course module DH4 the reduction is 0.6%, where it is 8 deg as in the two course module the reduction is still only 1.2%. From the point of view of function a reduction of this order in vertical support provided for the upper horizontal plate is negligible.

Whitford J. held that on the proper interpretation of the claim the modified design DH4 did not amount to what he described as an "infringement in terms", but he went on to hold it to be an infringement under the "pith and marrow doctrine".

The majority of the Court of Appeal (Buckley and Waller L.JJ.) disagreed with the learned judge on the application of the pith and marrow doctrine to the alleged infringement; the third member (Sir David Cairns) would have upheld his judgment. There was no discernible difference of opinion between the three members of the court as to the applicable law, which they derived principally from the speeches in this House in *Van Der Lely v. Bamfords* [1963] RPC.61 and *Rodi and Weinenberger A.G. v. Harry Showell Ltd.* [1969] RPC.367, [1968] FSR 100. Where they differed was as to the application of the law to the facts of the instant case. Buckley L.J. was of the opinion that although it was not in fact essential to the working of the invention that the back plate should be precisely vertical (i.e. at an angle of 90 deg exactly to the horizon) the patentee nevertheless by the language used in his specification had made such precision an essential feature of the monopoly he claimed. Waller L.J. regarded "vertical", and presumably also the adverb "vertically", as capable only of being used as a word of precision; and for him this was decisive against any claim for infringement by any lintel in which the back plate was not at an angle of 90 deg exactly to the horizon.Sir David Cairns expressed the view that DH4 was not "a textual infringement" of the patent, but held it to infringe the "pith and marrow" of Claim 1.

My Lords, in their closely reasoned written cases in this House and in the oral argument, both parties to this appeal have tended to treat "textual infringement" and infringement of the "pith and marrow" of an invention as if they were separate causes of action, the existence of the former to be determined as a matter of construction only and of the latter upon some broader principle of colourable evasion. There is, in my view, no such dichotomy; there is but a single cause of action and to treat it otherwise, particularly in cases like that which is the subject of the instant appeal, is liable to lead to confusion.

The expression "no textual infringement" has been borrowed from the speeches in this House in the hay-rake case, *Van Der Lely v. Bamfords*, [1963] RPC 61 where it was used by several of their Lordships as a convenient way of saying that the word "hindmost" as descriptive of rake wheels to be dismounted could not as a matter of linguistics mean "foremost"; but this did not exhaust the question of construction of the specification that was determinative of whether there had been an infringement of the claim or not. It left open the question whether patentee had made his reference to the "hindmost" (rather than any other wheels) as those to be dismounted, an essential feature of the monopoly that he claimed. It was on this question that there was a division of opinion in this House and in the Court of Appeal in the hay-rake case.

My Lords, a patent specification is a unilateral statement by the patentee, in words of his own choosing, addressed to those likely to have a practical interest in the subject matter of his invention (i.e. "skilled in the art"), by which he informs them what he claims to be the essential features of the new product or process for which the letters patent grant him a monopoly. It is those novel features only that he claims to be essential that constitute the so-called "pith and marrow" of the claim. A patent specification should be given a purposive construction rather than a purely literal one derived from applying to it the kind of meticulous verbal analysis in which lawyers are too often tempted by their training to indulge. The question in each case is: whether persons with practical knowledge and experience of the kind of work in which the invention was intended to be used, would understand that strict compliance with a particular descriptive word or phrase appearing in a claim was intended by the patentee to be an essential requirement of the invention so that any variant would fall outside the monopoly claimed, even though it could have no material effect upon the way the invention worked.

The question, of course, does not arise where the variant would in fact have a material effect upon the way the invention worked. Nor does it arise unless at the date of publication of the specification it would be obvious to the informed reader that this was so. Where it is not obvious, in the light of the then-existing knowledge, the reader is entitled to assume that the patentee thought at the time of the specification that he had good reason for limiting his monopoly so strictly and had intended to do so, even though subsequent work by him or others in the field of the invention might show the limitation to have been unnecessary. It is to be answered in the negative only when it would be apparent to any reader skilled in the art that a particular descriptive word or phrase used in a claim cannot have been intended by a patentee, who was also skilled in the art, to exclude minor variants which, to the knowledge of both him and the readers to whom the patent was addressed, could have no material effect upon the way in which the invention worked.

My Lords, upon analysis of the speeches in this House in *Van Der Lely v. Bamfords* [1963] RPC 61 the division of opinion between Lord Reid and the remainder of their Lordships appears to have been due to his thinking that it would be obvious to the informed reader that dismounting the "foremost" rather than the "hindmost" wheels was an immaterial variant, whereas the majority were not satisfied that this was even the fact, let alone that it was obviously so. In the bracelet case, *Rodi and Weinenberger A.G. v. Harry Showell Ltd.*, [1969] RPC 367, [1968] FSR 100 (ubi sup.) where this House was more evenly divided, the difference between the majority and the minority appears to have turned upon their respective views as to whether the particular variant alleged to be an infringement, had a material effect upon what were claimed to be the advantages obtained by the patented invention—as to which they differed. In the third of the trilogy of leading cases in this House upon this topic, the ampicillin case, *Beecham Group Ltd. v. Bristol Laboratories Ltd.*, [1977] FSR 215, the descriptive phrase was "an amino group in the alpha position". In the alleged infringing antibiotic, hetacillin, this amino group had been temporarily converted by a further chemical reaction into a molecular structure that was no longer an amino group; but the reaction was reversible and upon being put to use as an antibiotic, (which necessitated contact with water) it reverted to its original form as an amino group and in that form produced is prophylactic effects. This House unanimously held that this temporary masking of the amino group amounted to an immaterial variant. It would be obvious to anyone skilled in the specialised art of selecting and synthesising polymers for use as antibiotics that the essential feature of the invention was that when put to use for its intended purpose, the product should have an amino group in the alpha position; and that, accordingly, the patentee's reference to this feature of his claim cannot have been intended by him to exclude products in which the amino group in that position was temporarily displaced during a period before the product was put to any prophylactic use.

The essential features of the invention that is the subject of Claim 1 of the patent in suit in the instant appeal are much easier to understand than those of any of the three patents to which I have just referred; and this makes the question of its construction simpler. Put in a nutshell the question to be answered is: Would the specification make it obvious to a builder familiar with ordinary building operations that the description of a lintel in the form of a weight-bearing box girder of which the back plate was referred to as "extending vertically" from one of the two horizontal plates to join the other, could not have been intended to exclude lintels in which the back plate although not positioned at precisely 90 deg to both horizontal plates was close enough to 90 deg to make no material difference to the way the lintel worked when used in building operations? No plausible reason has been advanced why any rational patentee should want to place so narrow a limitation on his invention. On the contrary, to do so would render his monopoly for practical purposes worthless, since any imitator could avoid it and take all the benefit of the invention by the simple expedient of positioning the back plate a degree or two from the exact vertical.

It may be that when used by a geometer addressing himself to fellow geometers, such expressions descriptive of relative position as "horizontal", "parallel", "vertical" and "vertically" are to be understood as words of precision only; but when used in a description of a manufactured product intended to perform the practical function of a weight-bearing box girder in supporting courses of brickwork over window and door spaces in buildings, it seems to me that the expression "extending vertically" as descriptive of the position of what in use will be the upright member of a trapezoid-shaped box girder, is perfectly capable of meaning positioned near enough to the exact geometrical vertical to enable it in actual use to perform satisfactorily all the functions that it could perform if it were precisely vertical; and having regard to those considerations to which I have just referred that is the sense in which my opinion "extending vertically" would be understood by a builder familiar with ordinary building operation. Or, putting the same thing in another way, would be obvious to him that the patentee did not intend to make exact verticality in the positioning of the back-plate an essential feature of the invention claimed.

My Lords, if one analyses line by line the ways in which the various expressions are used in the specification, one can find pointers either way as to whether in particular lines various adjectives and adverbs descriptive of relative position are used in words of precision or not. Some of these are discussed in the judgments of the majority of the Court of Appeal who found the pointers in favour of precision stronger than those to the contrary, of which one example is the description of the two "horizontal" plates as being only "substantially parallel". For my part I find the result of such analysis inconclusive and of little weight as compared with the broad considerations to which I have referred and which are a consequence of giving, as I think one should, a purposive construction to the specification.

It follows that I have reached the same conclusion as the trial judge and Sir David Cairns, although not by the route of drawing a distinction between "textual infringement" and infringement of the "pith and marrow" of the invention. Accordingly I would allow the appeal.

Notes

1. The Level of Skill in the Art in *Catnic*. Does your experience comport with that of Lord Diplock that any knowledgeable builder would know that "a slight inclination from the vertical of an upright support reduces its load bearing capacity proportionately to the cosine of the angle of such inclination"?

2. Reformulating Diplock. A few years after the House decided *Catnic*, Sir Leonard Hoffmann (now Lord Hoffmann) reformulated its holding into three questions in *Improver Corp. v. Remington Consumer Products Ltd.*, 1990 F.S.R. 181 (Patents Ct.). *Improver Corp.* is one of a series of cases involving infringement of a European patent corresponding to U.S. Patent 4,524,772 ('772) covering a motorized depilatory known as the Epilady. It essentially uses a coiled spring attached at both ends to a motor. The motor drives one end of the spring clockwise and the other end counterclockwise and the rotating curved spring pulls out hair. The Epilady was a great commercial success. The accused device made by Remington and sold under the name Smooth and Silky is the subject of U.S. Patent No. 4,726,375 ('375). It essentially substitutes a plastic (rubber) tube with grooves for the spring. It was specifically designed to improve on the Epilady design. The independent claim of the European patent corresponding to the '772 reads:

> An electrically powered depilatory device comprising: a hand held portable housing (2); motor means (4, 4') disposed in said housing; and a helical spring (24) comprising a plurality of adjacent windings arranged to be driven by said motor means in rotational sliding motion relative to skin bearing hair to be removed, said helical spring (24) including an arcuate hair engaging portion arranged to define a convex side whereat the windings are spread apart and a concave side corresponding thereto whereat the windings are pressed together, the rotational motion of the helical spring (24) producing continuous motion of the windings from a spread apart orientation at the convex side to a pressed together orientation on the concave side and for the engagement and plucking of hair from the skin of the subject, whereby the surface velocities of the windings relative to the skin greatly exceed the surface velocity of the housing relative thereto.

The three *Improver* questions are as follows:

> (1) Does the variant have a material effect upon the way the invention works? If yes, the variant is outside the claim. If no—

> (2) Would this (i.e. that the variant had no material effect) have been obvious at the date of publication of the patent to a reader skilled in the art. If no, the variant is outside the claim. If yes—

> (3) Would the reader skilled in the art nevertheless have understood from the language of the claim that the patentee intended that strict compliance with the primary meaning was an essential requirement of the invention. If yes, the variant is outside the claim.

A key issue posed by the *Improver* reformulation of Catnic is the meaning of obviousness in question (2). Did this question simply ask whether the new combination was obvious over the old? If we assume that the '375 patent was valid, the answer would have to be "no." Alternatively did obviousness mean that what alleged to be an equivalent is treated as already known, then the question becomes would it have been obvious to substitute the after-arising equivalent as of the filing date. The *Improver* court explained that it was the latter:

> Mr Young interpreted this question to mean that the variant must be one which would have suggested itself to the skilled man as an obvious alternative to the thing denoted by the literal meaning. In this case, he said, the term "helical spring" did not suggest a rubber rod as an obvious alternative. On the contrary, it was an inventive step. He relied upon the evidence of Dr Laming who said that mention of a helical spring would not have made him think of a rubber rod and that the choice of the latter was innovative.

> I do not think that this is what Lord Diplock meant by the question and I think that Mr Young has been misled by Lord Diplock's use of the word "obvious" into thinking that he must have been intending to refer to the rule that an obvious improvement is not an inventive step. In my view the question supposes that the skilled man is told of both the invention and the variant and asked whether the variant would obviously work in the same way. An affirmative answer would not be inconsistent with the variant being an inventive step. For example, the choice of some material for the bendy rod which was a priori improbable (eg on account of its expense) but had been discovered to give some additional advantage (eg. painless extraction) might be a variant which obviously worked in the same way as the invention and yet be an inventive step. Nor would it matter that the material in question, being improbable, would not have suggested itself to the skilled man as an obvious alternative. Questions such as these may be relevant to the question of construction (Lord Diplock's third question) but not at this stage of the inquiry. Dr Laming and Dr Sharp, the eminent engineer called as an expert by the plaintiff, agreed that it would have been obvious to the skilled man that the attributes which enabled the helical spring to function in the way described in the specification were that it was capable of rotating, capable of transmitting torque along its length to resist the forces involved in plucking hairs, bendy (to form an arc) and slitty (to entrap hairs by the opening and closing effect of rotation). They also agreed that it would have been obvious that any rod which had these qualities in sufficient degree and did not have other defects such as overheating or falling to bits would in principle work in the same way and that the rubber rod plainly belonged to that class. On this evidence the second question must in my judgment be answered yes. I express no view on whether the rubber rod was also an inventive step.

> On the other hand, the evidence shows that although the rubber rod could be used in a device which would function in the way described in claim 1 of the patent in suit, it would work only in a limited number of embodiments. In particular, it could not be used in the loop formation described as the preferred embodiment.

Do you believe that the *Improver* court's use of an obvious test to be appropriate? Under this test what is the time for determining equivalency using the obviousness test? If it is the time of infringement, then is this reformulation consistent with purposive construction as originally explained by Lord Diplock?

Another key issue is whether question (3) is really an objective standard. Why for example would an inventor ever want to be limited to the literal words of the claim? In fact the *Improver* court used question (3) to find that the patent was not infringed. In this way that court decided the case differently than other courts on the same facts.

3. More on Epilady. *Improver* was one of a series of cases throughout Europe involve the European Epilady patent. While the patentee lost in the U.K. because of question (3), it won in other jurisdictions. primarily because their interpretation of Article 69 and its protocol do not include a question (3). The District Court of Düsseldorf granted a preliminary injunction, which was then vacated by the appeals court; later, however, the Regional Court of Düsseldorf found that Remington infringed on the merits. The Dutch courts issued a provisional injunction, which was vacated following an unfavorable result during European Patent Office opposition proceedings. Following the reversal of the opposition holding on appeal, the Dutch restored the injunction. The Commercial Court of Vienna readily held for Remington, while the patentee won a final decision on the merits in Milan. In the process of reaching these and other varying judgments, the courts often offered strong criticisms of the holdings of their brethren. A 1992 settlement between the litigants prevented any of these cases from reaching the highest courts of appeal.

4. The Community Patent Convention. The European patent community currently employs a few relatively modest solutions to divergent judicial approaches to equivalents. European advocates cite favorable opinions from courts of other EPC signatory nations, of course. Further, a Symposia of European Patent Judges convenes every two years to encourage discussion among jurists. A more effective approach has lie dormant for many years: the Community Patent Convention, a successor to the European Patent Convention which would create a single European patent effective for all of its signatories. The CPC would also establish a single, Federal Circuit-like Community Patent Court to hear appeals from designated national patent tribunals. Excessive cost, particularly with regard to translations into all the languages of the European states, has long been the chief complaint of those who have commented upon the CPC. As of 2002 there remains considerable pressure in Europe for the creation of a unitary patent system. Much of this activity is briefly reviewed in Kara M. Bonitatibus, *The Community Patent System Proposal And Patent Infringement Proceedings: an Eye Towards Greater Harmonization in European Intellectual Property Law*, 22 PACE L. REV. 201 (2001).

5. Further Reading. AMIRAM BENYAMINI, PATENT INFRINGEMENT IN THE EUROPEAN COMMUNITY (1993) presents a thorough and thoughtful comparative discussion of the law of patent infringement. Despite its modest title, this work also addresses United States and Commonwealth approaches at some length. More succinct reviews of *Catnic* and its progeny may be found in Paul Cole, *Purposive Construction under English Law*, 16 EUR. INTELL. PROP. REV. 455 (1994), and John Beton, *Are International Standards for Patent Claim Interpretation Possible?*, 16 EUR. INTELL. PROP. REV. 276 (1994).

§ 15.8[b]   The Doctrine of Equivalents in Japan

No country's patent system has received more criticism than that of Japan. *See, e.g., The Effect of the Japanese Patent System on American Business, Subcommittee on Foreign Commerce and Tourism, Senate Committee on Commerce, Science, and Transportation*, 100th Cong. (1988). Among the chief complaints is that the courts award patent claims with an extremely narrow scope, and that the Doctrine of Equivalents does not exist at all. All of this has changed in view of the following decision of the Japanese Supreme Court .

TSUBAKIMOTO SEIKO CO. LTD. v. THK K.K.

Supreme Court of Japan, 1998.
Case No. 1994 (*o*) 1083.

1.   The present case is a suit seeking damages for patent infringement. The Tokyo High Court found the following facts:

(1) The patent in suit is Japanese Patent No. 999139. The filing date of the patent is April 26, 1971. Its publication date is July 7, 1978 and its registration date is May 30, 1980. Its claim reads as follows:

An endlessly sliding ball spline shaft bearing comprising:

> an outer cylinder having torque transmitting load bearing ball-guiding grooves with a U-shaped cross-section and torque transmitting non-load bearing ball-guiding grooves with a U-shaped cross-section being slightly deeper than that of the load bearing ball-guiding grooves, the load bearing ball-guiding groove and the non-load bearing ball-guiding groove extending alternately in the axial direction within the cylindrical inner wall, the outer cylinder having an annular circumferentially directed groove at each end with the same depth as that of the deeper groove;

> a thin wall portion and a thick wall portion formed respectively in conformity with the torque transmitting load bearing ball-guiding groove and the torque transmitting non-load bearing ball-guiding groove formed in the axial direction within the inner wall of the outer cylinder;

> a joint portion between the thin wall portion and the thick wall portion having a through-hole;

> a retainer with an endless track groove for allowing balls to smoothly slide into the non-load ball-guiding groove formed in the thick wall portion; and

> a spline shaft provided with a plurality of ribs extending in the axial direction thereof, said ribs being shaped to conform with a plurality of recessed spaces formed by the balls incorporated between the retainer and said outer cylinder for engaging the spline shaft with the outer cylinder.

The accused product was manufactured and sold from January, 1983 to October, 1988 and has a step of about 50 microns in height between the non-load ball-guiding groove and the cylindrical portion. The Tokyo High Court found that it literally met all limitations except for the "outer cylinder" limitation and the "thin wall portion" limitation. As to the "outer cylinder" limitation it found there are elements such as "U-shaped cross-section" and "annular circumferentially directed grooves". Whereas, with respect to the accused product, the corresponding portions of these elements are "semi-circular cross-section" and "cylindrical portion", and hence differ from the claimed features.

With respect to the "thin wall portion limitation", the retainer is an integral structure providing the functions of guiding balls to move in endless circulation, retaining balls when the spline shaft is withdrawn, and forming a recessed portions for guiding the rib portions of the spline shaft. Whereas, the accused product has cooperative action of three members, i.e. the upper edge portions of the ribs formed between the load bearing ball-guiding grooves of the outer cylinder, a plate-like member and a return cap. Nevertheless the Tokyo High Court found that the accused product is substantially the same as that shown in the patent with respect to the solution for the technical problem, the basic technical idea, and the effects obtained. . . .

However, the decision of the Tokyo High Court cannot be affirmed for the following reasons:

In determining whether an accused product or method falls within the technical scope of a patented invention, the technical scope of the invention must be determined with respect to the claim (see Patent Law Section 70 (1). If there are elements that differ between the claim and the accused product, the accused product and the like cannot be said to fall within the technical scope of the patented invention. On the other hand, even if there are elements in the claim that differ from the corresponding product and the like, the corresponding product and the like may be equivalent and may appropriately be said to fall within the technical scope of the patented invention if the following conditions are satisfied: (1) the differing elements are not the essential elements in the patented invention; (2) even if the differing elements are interchanged by elements of the accused product and the like, the object of the patented invention can be achieved and the same effects can be obtained; (3) by interchanging as above, a person of ordinary skill in the art to which the invention pertains (hereinafter referred to as an artisan) could have easily arrived at the accused product and the like at the time of manufacture; (4) the accused product and the like are not the same as the known art at the time of application for patent or could not have been easily conceived by an artisan at the time of application for patent; and (5) there is not any special circumstances such that the accused product and the like are intentionally excluded from the scope of the claim during patent prosecution).

The above results from the fact that it is very difficult to describe claims to cover all possible infringing embodiments of the patented invention. If a competitor can escape from patent enforcement including injunction etc. by simply replacing some claimed elements with a material or technical means etc that are developed after the patent application, incentive for innovation is significantly reduced, which conflicts with the goal of patent system to contribute the industrial developments through the protection and encouragement of inventions. Further, such an interpretation of law to allow competitors to escape from the charge of infringement would be unfair to the sense of justice in the society and conflict with the concept of fairness. In considering these points, the substantial value of a patented invention extends to a structure which would have been readily conceived by a third party from the structure recited in the claim as being substantially identical to a patented invention. It is proper to assume that a third party must expect such extension of the patent protection. On the other hand, the technical scope of a patent cannot include an accused product which is part of the state of art as of the application time of the patented invention, or would have been readily conceived by one skilled from the state of art because no one could have obtained a patent on such accused product (Patent Law, Article 29). Additionally, under the rule of estoppel, a patentee is prevented from claiming a patent rights on an accused product which was intentionally removed by an applicant from the claim scope during the patent prosecution where the applicant admitted that the accused product does not fall within the technical scope of the patented invention or the applicant's behavior indicates such removal of the accused product from the claim scope.

[The Japanese Supreme Court ultimately remanded the matter for further determination of whether the accused product would have been obvious in view of the prior art.]

Notes

1. Which Elements are Essential? It is widely believed that the House of Lords in *Catnic* adopted purposive construction to avoid the necessity of determining whether an element was essential. Why do you think the Japanese Supreme Court adopted this requirement in 1998? Is an amended claim element by definition an essential element? If so, did the Japanese Supreme Court adopt the absolute bar rule adopted by the Federal Circuit in *Festo*.

2. Is the Obviousness Test of (3) the One Adopted by *Improver* Court? When thinking about this question remember that the Supreme Court specifically said that equivalency is judged as of the time of manufacture of the accused product.

3. In Addition to Adopting a Theory of Prosecution History Estoppel, does (5) include *Improver* question 3? *Improver* Question 3 relates to the teaching of the specification itself and asks whether it effectively disclaimed equivalents. If you were writing the law for a country such as Japan, would you adopt a doctrine of prosecution history estoppel; *Improver* question 3; or neither?

4. Further Reading. With regard to infringement law, TOSHIKO TAKENAKA, INTERPRETING PATENT CLAIMS: THE UNITED STATES, GERMANY AND JAPAN (1995) presents a painstakingly researched comparative analysis with particular strengths in Japanese law. Two earlier, more broadly focused texts are TETSU TANABE & HAROLD C. WEGNER, JAPANESE PATENT PRACTICE (1986), and TETSU TANABE & HAROLD C. WEGNER, JAPANESE PATENT LAW (1979).

Infringement Exercise

You are employed as a patent attorney in Alexandria, Virginia. On September 2, 2001, Mr. Vance Varnish, president of Varnish, Inc., comes to your office seeking advice. "Our primary client, Massive Motors, has just been sued for patent infringement!" he exclaims.

After Mr. Varnish has relaxed somewhat, he shows you a copy of United States Patent No. 9,999,999. The '999 patent was filed on June 15, 1996, issued on February 1, 1998, and has been assigned to the Primer Products Corporation. The patent bears the title "Method for Coating Metal," and has only a single claim, Claim 1. According to the patent specification, the disclosed method for coating metal results in a painted surface that is particularly long-lasting and corrosion resistant. Claim 1 of the '999 patent provides:

Claim 1. A method for coating a metal surface with paint, comprising the steps of:

spraying said metal surface with urea;

heating said metal surface to approximately 300E C;

spraying said metal surface with said paint; and

drying said metal surface.

Mr. Varnish explains that Varnish, Inc. sells painting supplies to various automobile manufacturers, primarily the Massive Motors Company. Varnish, Inc. works closely with Massive Motors in designing new paints, as well as ways to apply these paints to automobile surfaces. "This entire affair began on April 1, 2000," Mr. Varnish says. "That's when Primer Products Corporation sent our chief customer, Massive Motors, a letter." Mr. Varnish shows you the letter, which provides in part:

April 1, 2000

To the Massive Motors Company:

We are pleased to call to your attention United States Patent No. 9,999,999, directed towards a "Method for Coating Metal." We ask you to review your product line to ensure that you are not infringing claim 1 of the '999 patent. We will be in touch shortly to inquire as to the results of your infringement study.

Sincerely yours,

Paul Primer

President, Primer Products Corporation

"After reading the '999 patent, I asked a chemist to see if the results obtained by the patented process were as good as the patent stated," Mr. Varnish continues. "It was true—the experimental results he reached were far superior to our existing painting techniques! I decided that this kind of finishing was the wave of the future, but that Varnish, Inc. shouldn't risk infringing the '999 patent. After spending almost four months and about $500,000 in company funds, we came up with the following technique." Mr. Varnish then hands you a piece of paper which reads:

VARNISH INC.'S PROPRIETARY PAINTING PROCESS

Top Secret!

1. *Spray the metal surface with paint.*

2. *Spray the metal surface with melamine resin.*

3. *Heat the metal surface to 365E C.*

"Look, I'm a business person, not a chemist. But see how different our technique is!" Mr. Varnish exclaims. "Not only do we employ melamine resin, not urea, the order of the process steps is crucial. It's like making a piece of toast with strawberry jam. If you spread strawberry jam on a piece of bread before putting the bread in the toaster, you would burn the jam and not reach the desired result."

You then ask Mr. Varnish whether, once the metal surface has been heated, Massive Motors dries the metal surface or not. "Oh, Primer Products Corporation just wants to ensure that the paint is fully dry," Mr. Varnish explains. "But because the metal surface is quite hot at this point, we've learned that the paint dries in a matter of two or three minutes even without additional work. So Massive Motors doesn't bother to do anything after heating the surface—it just waits a few moments and then moves the part down the assembly line."

"Anyway, we had no further contact with Primer Products Corporation until yesterday, September 1, 2001," Mr. Varnish continues, "when Primer Products Corporation filed suit for patent infringement against Massive Motors. Not only am I worried about Massive Motors being found liable for patent infringement, I've heard that Varnish, Inc. could be sued itself. We sell the paint and the melamine resin to Massive Motors, which actually performs our method in its factory. While both the paint and melamine resin are available on the market generally, we sell these products in appropriate amounts for use in automobile assembly. With each sale, we also include a set of instructions on how to use these materials in accordance with our own coating method."

Promising you will call Mr. Varnish back tomorrow, you escort him to his automobile—a late-model Massive Motors brand, of course. Upon consulting a chemical encyclopedia, you are able to construct the following chart comparing melamine and urea:

Trait	Urea	Melamine
Formula	$H_2N\text{-}CO\text{-}NH_2$	$(N\acute{e}C\text{-}NH_2)_3$
Formula Weight	60.6	126.12
Appearance	Colorless crystalline solid	White solid
Melting Point	132.7° C	355° C
Specific Gravity	1.335	1.56

Confused and lacking technical knowledge in this area, you call a noted chemistry professor, Dr. Cheryl Shellac, and describe the patented and accused coating techniques. She explains: "Although urea and melamine seem fairly distinct, in fact the only practical way to make melamine is to synthesize it from urea. First, urea is thermally decomposed into a gas mixture of cyanic acid and NH_3; second, cyanic gas is thermally decomposed into a melamine-CO_2 vapor. This simple two-step endothermic reaction is extremely well-known to the art. Indeed, you can think of melamine as a straightforward derivative of urea."

Professor Shellac continues: "Melamine resins are well known to possess outstanding resistance to heat, water and various chemicals. However, until early 1995, it was extremely expensive to make these resins on a large scale. Advances in chemical processing technologies that occurred in late 1998 and early 1999 have made melamine resins quite cheap to synthesize. At that time, they became sufficiently inexpensive and practical enough to employ in everyday manufacturing."

Professor Shellac goes on to explain: "Regarding the order of the steps, all that the patented process does is mix the paint together with a reactant, urea, at a high temperature. The order in which the paint and reactant are applied to the metal surface is immaterial. So long as they both occupy the same heated metal surface at the same time, the melamine resin almost instantly polymerizes and the result is a superior, long-lasting coating."

You thank Professor Shellac and next conduct some research on an on-line database. You discover an article in an industry journal, *The Thinner Times*, written by a Primer Products Corporation researcher. The researcher describes how he invented the patented process after three years of painstaking research, at a total cost of nearly five million dollars.

As you are signing off the database, a courier arrives from Varnish, Inc., with a copy of the '999 patent's prosecution history in hand. You carefully examine the prosecution history. You note that the examiner offered a Notice of Allowance with regard to the '999 patent on his First Office Action. The only comment offered in the Reasons for Allowance was: "The claims patentably distinguish over the prior art."

Last, you order a prior art search. The searcher finds only one pertinent reference: an article written by one Ulrich Undercoat, published on November 1, 1995, in a trade journal entitled *The Pigment Pages*. Undercoat discloses a process for coating the surfaces of certain steel machine parts in order to increase their working life. According to Undercoat, superior results are obtained when the surface of the machine parts is heated to 380^E C; paint is subsequently applied to the heated surface; and the surface is then immediately sprayed with melamine resin.

How would you advise Mr. Varnish as to the prospects of Primer Products Corporation's possible charges of infringement against the Massive Motors Company and Varnish, Inc.?

Chapter Sixteen

ADDITIONAL DEFENSES

In addition to such doctrines as inequitable conduct and double patenting, reviewed here at Chapter 12, U.S. patent law includes a number of other defenses that may ultimately bar the patentee from relief in an infringement action. Chief among them are laches, estoppel, the implied license termed a "shop right," and the first inventor defense. These doctrines relate not to the validity of a patent but to its enforceability against another. If successfully invoked, they provide the defendant with a limited license to practice the patented technology.

The first two defenses considered here, laches and estoppel, are hardly unique to the patent law. However, the factual patterns that recur in patent infringement cases, as well as the patent statute itself, create particular nuances that are worthy of review. The remaining two defenses, shop rights and the first inventor defense, are likely less familiar and therefore deserving of a more thorough introduction.

The majority of contemporary inventors act within the context of their employment, a setting where a shop right may arise. In many of the world's patent systems, legislation provides employed inventors with rights to their inventions. The same result is said to hold in the United States through the common law, although the existence of a license or assignment may change this result and, in practice, ordinarily does. Such licenses or assignments may be express, which are typically a condition of employment for technology professionals, or implied, if the employee was hired to perform a specific function that would include inventing. Even where no express agreement exists between the employee and the employer and where the employee was not hired to invent, however, the employee's right may nonetheless be limited. An implied license, termed a "shop right," may arise in favor of the employer. The materials which follow provide more of the details.

The first inventor defense excuses infringements committed by an earlier inventor of a method of doing or conducting business that was later patented by another. Introduced into the patent law with the American Inventors Protection Act of 1999, and codified at 35 U.S.C.A.

§ 273, the first inventor defense is akin to more full-fledged "prior user rights" available in many foreign jurisdictions. Not yet the subject of a reported judicial opinion, the first inventor defense is taken up in a brief textual note below.

§ 16.1   LACHES AND ESTOPPEL

In its watershed *Auckerman* decision, the *in banc* Federal Circuit refined and in some aspects redefined the defenses of laches and estoppel in patent cases.

A.C. AUKERMAN CO. v. R.L. CHAIDES CONSTRUCTION CO.

United States Court of Appeals, Federal Circuit, 1992.
960 F.2d 1020, 22 U.S.P.Q.2d 1321.

Before NIES, CHIEF JUDGE, RICH, NEWMAN, ARCHER, MAYER, MICHEL, PLAGER, LOURIE, CLEVENGER, and RADER, CIRCUIT JUDGES.

NIES, CHIEF JUDGE.

This court reheard Appeal No. 90–1137 in banc to reconsider the principles of laches and equitable estoppel applicable in a patent infringement suit. A.C. Aukerman Co. sued R.L. Chaides Construction Co. in the United States District Court for the Northern District of California for infringement of Aukerman's patents, U.S. Patent Nos. 3,793,133 ('133) and 4,014,633 ('633). The district court held on summary judgment that Aukerman was barred under principles of laches and equitable estoppel from maintaining the suit and Aukerman appeals. We conclude that the correct standards, which we have clarified herein, were not applied in the district court's grant of summary judgment. Moreover, upon application of the correct law, genuine issues of material fact arise with respect to the issues of laches and equitable estoppel. Accordingly, we reverse the court's ruling on the motion for summary judgment and remand for proceedings consistent with this opinion.

I.

BACKGROUND

The following facts are not disputed. Aukerman is the assignee of the '133 and '633 patents, relating to, respectively, a method and device for forming concrete highway barriers capable of separating highway surfaces of different elevations. The device allows a contractor to slip-form an asymmetrical barrier as the mold is moved down the highway, i.e., to pour the barriers directly onto the highway without having to construct a mold. In settlement of litigation with Gomaco Corporation, a manufacturer of slip-forms which may be used to form regular or variable height barriers, Aukerman entered into an agreement in 1977 which made Gomaco a licensee under the patents and required Gomaco to notify Aukerman of all those who purchased Gomaco's adjustable slip-forms.

Upon notification that Chaides had purchased a slip-form from Gomaco, counsel for Aukerman advised Chaides by letter dated February 13, 1979, that use of the device raised "a question of infringement with respect to one or more of [Aukerman's patents-in-suit]," and offered Chaides a license. Follow-on letters were sent by Aukerman's counsel to Chaides on March 16 and April 12, 1979. Chaides replied by telephone on April 17, 1979 but was unable to speak with counsel for Aukerman. By letter of April 24, 1979, Aukerman's counsel advised Chaides that Aukerman was seeking to enforce its patents against all infringers and that, even though Chaides might be among the smaller contractors, it had the same need for a license as larger firms. He advised further that Aukerman would waive liability for past infringement and infringement under existing contracts if Chaides took a license by June 1, 1979. Chaides responded in late April with a note handwritten on Aukerman's last letter stating that he felt any responsibility was Gomaco's and that, if Aukerman wished to sue Chaides "for $200–$300 a year," Aukerman should do so. There was no further correspondence or contact between the parties for more than eight years. In the interim, Chaides increased its business of forming asymmetrical highway barrier walls. Sometime in the mid–80's, Chaides made a second adjustable mold for pouring step wall which Aukerman alleges is an infringement.

Apparently in 1987, one of Aukerman's licensees, Baumgartner, Inc., advised Aukerman that Chaides was a substantial competitor for pouring asymmetrical wall in California. This advice prompted Aukerman's new counsel to send a letter to Chaides on October 22, 1987, referencing the earlier correspondence, advising that litigation against another company had been resolved, and threatening litigation unless Chaides executed the licenses previously sent within two weeks. Another period of silence followed. On August 2, 1988, Aukerman's counsel again wrote Chaides explaining more fully Aukerman's licensing proposal. When no reply was received, on October 26, 1988, Aukerman filed suit charging Chaides with infringing its '133 and '633 patents.

The district court granted summary judgment in favor of Chaides, holding that the doctrines of laches and estoppel barred Aukerman's claims for relief.

II.

Summary

The court has taken this case in banc to clarify and apply principles of laches and equitable estoppel which have been raised as defenses in this patent infringement suit. In summary, for reasons to be more fully discussed, we hold with respect to laches:

1. Laches is cognizable under 35 U.S.C. § 282 (1988) as an equitable defense to a claim for patent infringement. 2. Where the defense of laches is established, the patentee's claim for damages prior to suit may be barred. 3. Two elements underlie the defense of laches: (a) the patentee's delay in bringing suit was unreasonable and inexcusable, and

(b) the alleged infringer suffered material prejudice attributable to the delay. The district court should consider these factors and all of the evidence and other circumstances to determine whether equity should intercede to bar pre-filing damages. 4. A presumption of laches arises where a patentee delays bringing suit for more than six years after the date the patentee knew or should have known of the alleged infringer's activity. 5. A presumption has the effect of shifting the burden of going forward with evidence, not the burden of persuasion.

With respect to equitable estoppel against a patent infringement claim, we hold that: 1. Equitable estoppel is cognizable under 35 U.S.C. § 282 as an equitable defense to a claim for patent infringement. 2. Where an alleged infringer establishes the defense of equitable estoppel, the patentee's claim may be entirely barred. 3. Three elements must be established to bar a patentee's suit by reason of equitable estoppel: a. The patentee, through misleading conduct, leads the alleged infringer to reasonably infer that the patentee does not intend to enforce its patent against the alleged infringer. "Conduct" may include specific statements, action, inaction, or silence where there was an obligation to speak. b. The alleged infringer relies on that conduct. c. Due to its reliance, the alleged infringer will be materially prejudiced if the patentee is allowed to proceed with its claim. 4. No presumption is applicable to the defense of equitable estoppel.

As equitable defenses, laches and equitable estoppel are matters committed to the sound discretion of the trial judge and the trial judge's decision is reviewed by this court under the abuse of discretion standard. We appreciate that the district court, in deciding the instant case, did not have the benefit of these statements of legal principles which differ in some respects from our precedent. We have no alternative, however, but to rule that, when these principles are applied to the record before us, the district court erred in granting summary judgment in favor of Chaides.

III.

LACHES

It is . . . well settled that, to invoke the laches defense, a defendant has the burden to prove two factors: 1. the plaintiff delayed filing suit for an unreasonable and inexcusable length of time from the time the plaintiff knew or reasonably should have known of its claim against the defendant, and 2. the delay operated to the prejudice or injury of the defendant.

The length of time which may be deemed unreasonable has no fixed boundaries but rather depends on the circumstances. The period of delay is measured from the time the plaintiff knew or reasonably should have known of the defendant's alleged infringing activities to the date of suit. However, the period does not begin prior to issuance of the patent.

Material prejudice to adverse parties resulting from the plaintiff's delay is essential to the laches defense. Such prejudice may be either economic or evidentiary. Evidentiary, or "defense" prejudice, may arise by reason of a defendant's inability to present a full and fair defense on the merits due to the loss of records, the death of a witness, or the unreliability of memories of long past events, thereby undermining the court's ability to judge the facts.

Economic prejudice may arise where a defendant and possibly others will suffer the loss of monetary investments or incur damages which likely would have been prevented by earlier suit. Such damages or monetary losses are not merely those attributable to a finding of liability for infringement. Economic prejudice would then arise in every suit. The courts must look for a change in the economic position of the alleged infringer during the period of delay. On the other hand, this does not mean that a patentee may intentionally lie silently in wait watching damages escalate, particularly where an infringer, if he had had notice, could have switched to a noninfringing product. Indeed, economic prejudice is not a simple concept but rather is likely to be a slippery issue to resolve.

A court must also consider and weigh any justification offered by the plaintiff for its delay. Excuses which have been recognized in some instances, and we do not mean this list to be exhaustive, include: other litigation; negotiations with the accused; possibly poverty and illness under limited circumstances; wartime conditions; extent of infringement; and dispute over ownership of the patent. The equities may or may not require that the plaintiff communicate its reasons for delay to the defendant.

A patentee may also defeat a laches defense if the infringer "has engaged in particularly egregious conduct which would change the equities significantly in plaintiff's favor." Conscious copying may be such a factor weighing against the defendant, whereas ignorance or a good faith belief in the merits of a defense may tilt matters in its favor.

In the simplest or purest form of laches, there need be no direct contact between the plaintiff and the defendant from the time the plaintiff becomes aware of its claim until the suit. In other instances, the plaintiff may make an objection to the defendant and then do nothing more for years. Where there has been contact or a relationship between the parties during the delay period which may give rise to an inference that the plaintiff has abandoned its claim against the defendant, the facts may lend themselves to analysis under principles of equitable estoppel, as well as laches. However, the two defenses are not the same. As we have indicated, laches focuses on the reasonableness of the plaintiff's delay in suit. As will become evident, equitable estoppel focuses on what the defendant has been led to reasonably believe from the plaintiff's conduct. Thus, for laches, the length of delay, the seriousness of prejudice, the reasonableness of excuses, and the defendant's conduct or culpability must be weighed to determine whether the patentee dealt unfairly with the alleged infringer by not promptly bringing suit. In sum, a district court must weigh all pertinent facts and equities in making a decision on the laches defense. [The court concluded that:] Upon the record before us, summary judgment of laches was improperly granted. The issue of laches must be tried.

EFFECT OF LACHES DEFENSE

The district court ruled that laches can bar relief in a patent suit only for infringement prior to suit. The general rule is that laches may bar partial or entire relief. A question was raised in the original panel opinion concerning this difference in the effect of a laches defense. Inasmuch as this case will be remanded, it is appropriate to address this issue for the guidance of the district court.

Probably no better statement of reasons for limiting a laches defense in patent cases to past acts can be found than in *George J. Meyer Mfg. v. Miller Mfg.*, 24 F.2d 505, 507 (7th Cir.1928):

> There are peculiar and special reasons why the holder of a patent should not be barred from enforcing his right under the patent because of his failure to promptly sue infringers. Frequently the position of the patentee (financial and otherwise) prevents the institution of suits. The patent litigation is often prolonged and expensive. Moreover from the very nature of the thing he cannot be fully cognizant of all infringements that occur throughout the length and breadth of this country. His information may be largely hearsay. Then, also, the validity of his patent and the infringement thereof may be, as here, disputed. These defenses present mixed questions of fact and law concerning which there is necessarily some doubt and uncertainty. In many cases, if not in most cases, the doubts are serious ones. For an infringer naturally avoids making [an exact] copy of the patent. In a doubtful case the commercial success of the patented art is at times determinative of the issue of validity. This factor cannot be shown save as time establishes it. Moreover, common experience proves that inventions which appear to be revolutionary are often not accepted by the public and never become a commercial success. A patentee is therefore justified in waiting to ascertain whether realizations equal expectations. We think, therefore, that there is justification in patent suits for withholding damages for infringements committed prior to the commencement of the suit when laches is established, notwithstanding injunctional relief be granted. But, when it can be shown that the holder of the patent in addition to being guilty of laches has, by his conduct, estopped himself from asserting his rights under the patent, all relief should be denied and the bill dismissed.

As an additional reason, we do not believe future relief should be barred as a result of the presumption afforded to a patent defendant in the usual laches situation.

Finally, the general rule had to be broadly stated to cover a single wrong as well as a series of continuing wrongful acts. All relief would generally be denied by a finding of laches if there is only a single wrong.

Relief from liability for past wrongs, but not future wrongs, is viewed as only a partial defense. No conflict between the rule stated in our precedent and the general rule necessarily exists.

In any event, we will continue to hold, as a matter of policy, that laches bars relief on a patentee's claim only with respect to damages accrued prior to suit. At least on the facts presented in this case, we have no reason to revisit this accepted principle.

IV.

EQUITABLE ESTOPPEL

A. *General Principles*

Equitable estoppel to assert a claim is another defense addressed to the sound discretion of the trial court. Where equitable estoppel is established, all relief on a claim may be barred. Like laches, equitable estoppel is not limited to a particular factual situation nor subject to resolution by simple or hard and fast rules. At most, courts have provided general guidelines based on fact patterns which have been litigated, albeit attempting to provide a unifying set of principles.

The following statement of the underlying factual elements of equitable estoppel which generally are deemed significant reflects a reasonable and fairly complete distillation from the case law:

> An [equitable] estoppel case ... has three important elements. [1] The actor, who usually must have knowledge of the true facts, communicates something in a misleading way, either by words, conduct or silence. [2] The other relies upon that communication. [3] And the other would be harmed materially if the actor is later permitted to assert any claim inconsistent with his earlier conduct.

[D.B. DOBBS, HANDBOOK ON THE LAW OF REMEDIES] § 2.3, at 42. In other authorities, elements [2] and [3] are frequently combined into a single "detrimental reliance" requirement. However, the statement of reliance and detriment as separate factors adds some clarity in this confusing area of the law.

Unlike laches, equitable estoppel does not require the passage of an unreasonable period of time in filing suit. However, the patent cases which have come before this court involving the issue of a patentee's inequitable delay in suing have almost invariably raised the defense not only of laches but also of equitable estoppel. In [*Jamesbury Corp. v. Litton Indus. Prods.*, 839 F.2d 1544, 5 U.S.P.Q.2d 1779 (Fed.Cir.1988),] which was such a case, we stated that equitable estoppel requires: (1) unreasonable and inexcusable delay in filing suit, (2) prejudice to the infringer, (3) affirmative conduct by the patentee inducing the belief that it abandoned its claims against the alleged infringer, [later defined to include silence] and (4) detrimental reliance by the infringer. This listing of factors followed earlier case law in our sister circuits.

The test set out in *Jamesbury* confusingly intertwines the elements of laches and equitable estoppel and is expressly overruled. Delay in filing suit may be evidence which influences the assessment of whether the patentee's conduct is misleading but it is not a requirement of equitable estoppel. Even where such delay is present, the concepts of equitable estoppel and laches are distinct from one another.

The first element of equitable estoppel concerns the statements or conduct of the patentee which must "communicate something in a misleading way." The "something" with which this case, as well as the vast majority of equitable estoppel cases in the patent field is concerned, is that the accused infringer will not be disturbed by the plaintiff patentee in the activities in which the former is currently engaged. The patentee's conduct must have supported an inference that the patentee did not intend to press an infringement claim against the alleged infringer. It is clear, thus, that for equitable estoppel the alleged infringer cannot be unaware—as is possible under laches—of the patentee and/or its patent. The alleged infringer also must know or reasonably be able to infer that the patentee has known of the former's activities for some time. In the most common situation, the patentee specifically objects to the activities currently asserted as infringement in the suit and then does not follow up for years. However, plaintiff's inaction must be combined with other facts respecting the relationship or contacts between the parties to give rise to the necessary inference that the claim against the defendant is abandoned.

The second element, reliance, is not a requirement of laches but is essential to equitable estoppel. The accused infringer must show that, in fact, it substantially relied on the misleading conduct of the patentee in connection with taking some action. Reliance is not the same as prejudice or harm, although frequently confused. An infringer can build a plant being entirely unaware of the patent. As a result of infringement, the infringer may be unable to use the facility. Although harmed, the infringer could not show reliance on the patentee's conduct. To show reliance, the infringer must have had a relationship or communication with the plaintiff which lulls the infringer into a sense of security in going ahead with building the plant.

Finally, the accused infringer must establish that it would be materially prejudiced if the patentee is now permitted to proceed. As with laches, the prejudice may be a change of economic position or loss of evidence.

Another significant difference from laches is that no presumption adheres to an equitable estoppel defense. Despite a six-year delay in suit being filed, a defendant must prove all of the factual elements of estoppel on which the discretionary power of the court rests. The reasons for this are two-fold. First, the presumed laches factors, that is, unreasonable and inexcusable delay and prejudice resulting therefrom are not elements of estoppel. Second, the relief granted in estoppel is broader than in laches. Because the whole suit may be barred, we conclude that the defendant should carry a burden to establish the defense based on proof, not a presumption.

Finally, the trial court must, even where the three elements of equitable estoppel are established, take into consideration any other evidence and facts respecting the equities of the parties in exercising its discretion and deciding whether to allow the defense of equitable estoppel to bar the suit.

B. Application of Equitable Estoppel Against Aukerman

While equitable estoppel may be determined on summary judgment, we conclude that the district court improvidently granted summary judgment in this case.

The district court concluded that Aukerman's conduct led Chaides to believe Aukerman had abandoned its claim, that Chaides had relied on Aukerman's conduct to its detriment, and that Chaides was not guilty of unclean hands which would bar Chaides from assertion of an equitable defense. We conclude that the elements supporting equitable estoppel were in genuine dispute, that the evidence was not perceived in the light most favorable to Aukerman, that inferences of fact were drawn against Aukerman and that the entire issue must, in any event, be tried in light of the principles adopted here.

The initial dispute is whether the patentee's conduct was misleading in that Chaides reasonably inferred from Aukerman's conduct that it would be unmolested in using Aukerman's invention. Chaides argued that this factor was shown by the last letter from Aukerman in 1979 setting a deadline for taking a license followed by nine plus years of silence. Aukerman argued that Chaides had to prove intentionally misleading silence. The district court properly rejected Aukerman's argument respecting the need to prove intent to mislead on the basis of Hottel. How one characterizes a patentee's silence is immaterial. Properly focused, the issue here is whether Aukerman's course of conduct reasonably gave rise to an inference in Chaides that Aukerman was not going to enforce the '133 and '633 patents against Chaides. Moreover, silence alone will not create an estoppel unless there was a clear duty to speak, or somehow the patentee's continued silence reenforces the defendant's inference from the plaintiff's known acquiescence that the defendant will be unmolested. Finally, on summary judgment, such inference must be the only possible inference from the evidence.

In view of the Aukerman/Chaides correspondence, Chaides was in a position to infer, following Chaides' reply stating any infringement problem was Gomaco's, that by remaining silent Aukerman abandoned its claim against Chaides. The length of the delay also favors drawing the inference because the longer the delay, the stronger the inference becomes. Aukerman argues that the delay is excused by reason of litigation against others, even though Chaides was not informed of the litigation. However, that argument is off the mark. A party must generally notify an accused infringer about other litigation for it to impact the defense of equitable estoppel. This "requirement" is a matter of logic. Other litigation can not logically enter into whether Chaides reasonably drew an inference that it would not be sued if such facts are not known to Chaides.

While the above factors favor the nonenforcement inference, Chaides' further statement that Aukerman would only recover $200–$300 a year could lead one in Chaides' position to infer that Aukerman did not sue because the amount in issue was de minimis, not that Aukerman was abandoning its claim against Chaides for all time regardless of quantum. At most Aukerman could merely have been waiving an infringement claim for $300.00 per year.

In view of the different inferences which could be drawn from the exchange of correspondence, it is clear that the court drew an unfavorable inference against Aukerman. That is impermissible on summary judgment.

We conclude that summary judgment, holding that Aukerman was equitably estopped from assertion of infringement against Chaides, was improperly granted and is reversed. The issue is remanded for trial.

Notes

1. *De Minimus* Infringement and Estoppel. Do you agree that Auckerman should not have been equitably estopped—at least for purposes of summary judgment—based on the response Chaides provided to Auckerman's assertion of patent infringement? This decision suggests that responses to an infringement charge should be carefully considered. If, as here, a competitor dissuades the patentee from suing based upon the minimal nature of its infringement, it may be left without an equitable estoppel defense if its use of the patented technology increases.

2. The Significance of *Aukerman*. The *Aukerman* decision was generally seen as weakening the effectiveness of the laches defense in patent litigation, particularly when employed in a summary judgment motion. As noted in the excerpt from the *Aukerman* opinion above, and as discussed in greater detail in a portion of the opinion not reprinted here, the presumption of laches only shifts the burden of going forward with this evidence, not the burden of persuasion. The accused infringer always maintains the burden or proof with regard to laches and estoppel—matters that may be more readily demonstrated or disproved by evidence within the possession of the patentee. Some observers believe that, in practice, patentees are too readily able to present reasons excusing their delay for filing suit. Further, in the event the trier of fact cannot decide whether the patentee's delay was reasonable or unreasonable, the patentee would still prevail. *See* Evan Finkel, *What Remains of the Laches and Estoppel Defenses After* Aukerman?, 9 Santa Clara Computer & High Tech. L.J. 1 (1993); Jerry R. Selinger, Aukerman *and Equitable Defenses: Evolution or Revolution?*, 1 Tex. Intell. Prop. L.J. 87 (1993); Russell D. Slifer, Comment, *En Banc Ruling Bursts More Than Bubbles in Patent Litigation:* A.C. Aukerman Co. v. R.L. Chaides Construction Co. *and Its Impact*, 13 N. Ill. U. L. Rev. 335 (1993).

Aukerman is thus of considerable importance in an era where patent litigation has become an increasingly lucrative endeavor. Patentees have demonstrated a renewed willingness to review their portfolios in order to consider whether any claims are being infringed. Sometimes this effort results in the "dusting off" of patents that are near expiration or have in fact expired, and infringement suits filed regarding infringements that began years before. If *Aukerman* indeed limits the availability of laches as a defense, then accused infringers possess a decreased opportunity to defend against such suits. Does this opinion present sound patent policy?

3. Other Letters. Beyond working an estoppel, patentee letters to suspected infringers invoke two other principal concerns. First, such a letter may serve as sufficient notice to allow the patentee to recover damages, as set forth in § 287. This text addresses the concepts of notice and marking in Chapter 17. Second, the letter may serve as the basis for a declaratory judgment action brought by the addressee against the patent owner. Declaratory judgment jurisdiction is briefly discussed here at Chapter 18.

§ 16.2 SHOP RIGHTS

McELMURRY v. ARKANSAS POWER & LIGHT CO.

United States Court of Appeals, Federal Circuit, 1993.
995 F.2d 1576, 27 U.S.P.Q.2d 1129.

Before NIES, CHIEF JUDGE, RICH, and MAYER, CIRCUIT JUDGES.

RICH, CIRCUIT JUDGE.

Max C. McElmurry and White River Technologies, Inc. (WRT) appeal the February 10, 1992 Judgment of the U.S. District Court for the Eastern District of Arkansas, Northern Division, granting a motion for summary judgment filed by Arkansas Power & Light Company (AP & L) and Entergy Corporation. The district court held that there were no relevant or material factual disputes precluding a finding that AP & L holds "shop rights" to certain subject matter claimed in U.S. Patent No. 4,527,714, titled "Pressure Responsive Hopper Level Detector System" (Bowman patent), and thus, as a matter of law, AP & L had not infringed any claim of the Bowman patent. For the reasons set forth below, we affirm.

A. BACKGROUND

AP & L hired Harold L. Bowman, the patentee, as a consultant on October 24, 1980, to assist in the installation, maintenance and operation of electrostatic precipitators at AP & L's White Bluff Steam Electric Station (White Bluff) located near Redfield, Arkansas. An electronic precipitator is a device which removes granular ash particles (fly ash) from the gasses emitted by coal-fired boilers used to generate steam. As fly ash is removed, it is collected in hoppers referred to as precipitator hoppers. Prior to April of 1982, the precipitator hoppers at White Bluff employed a level detector system using a nuclear power source (K-ray system) to detect the level of fly ash in the hoppers.

AP & L was not satisfied with the K-ray system. As a result, in the early part of 1982, Bowman discussed with a Mr. Richard L. Roberts, an AP & L employee, replacing the K-ray system with a new level detector, an initial design of which they drew on a napkin. In the proposed level detector, a vacuum gauge was connected to a pipe inserted and welded into the wall of a precipitator hopper. If the level of the fly ash collected in the hopper extended above the point where the pipe was inserted into the hopper, the vacuum gauge would no longer indicate that a vacuum existed, as it would if the level of the fly ash were below that point. Thus, by monitoring the vacuum gauge, one could determine whether the fly ash exceeded a certain level in the hopper.

AP & L considered the proposed level detector and, during a power outage in March of 1982, ordered its installation on one hopper at White Bluff for testing purposes. When it proved successful, AP & L ordered that the level detector be installed on a total of sixteen (16) precipitator hoppers at White Bluff. In each case, level detectors were installed both near the bottom and top of the hopper, thus allowing for the detection of the fly ash at two different levels in the hopper. When this system proved successful, AP & L ordered that the level detectors be installed on the remaining one hundred and twelve (112) precipitator hoppers at White Bluff. All costs associated with the installation and testing of the level detector on the one hundred and twenty eight (128) hoppers at White Bluff, including materials and working drawings, were paid by AP & L.

On October 24, 1982, Bowman moved from White Bluff to AP & L's Independence Steam Electric Station (ISES) located near Newark, Arkansas, to assist in the start-up, maintenance and operation of electronic precipitators at that facility. In November of 1982, Bowman formed White Rivers Technology, Inc. with McElmurry and a Mr. Johnny Mitchum, to market certain inventions on which Bowman held patents or was planning to seek patent protection. Bowman filed a patent application on the level detector on February 18, 1983, and the patent-in-suit issued on July 9, 1985. At some point prior to its issuance, Bowman assigned his patent rights to WRT.

While at ISES, Bowman assisted another AP & L engineer, a Mr. Will Morgan, in installing the level detector on precipitator hoppers at that facility. AP & L requested bids for the project and ultimately contracted with WRT to install the level detector on sixty four (64) of the hoppers at that location. An outside contractor other than WRT installed the level detector on the remaining sixty four (64) hoppers. AP & L did contract with WRT, however, to install certain electronic components of the level detectors installed by the outside contractor. The level detectors had been installed and were in operation on all one hundred and twenty eight (128) precipitator hoppers by the end of 1984, prior to the issuance of the Bowman patent. Bowman's contract with ISES ended, however, in October of 1983 before completion of the project. All costs associated with the installation and testing of the level detectors at ISES, including materials and working drawings, were paid by AP & L even though some of the work was contracted out.

In 1985, based upon the success of the level detector on the precipitator hoppers at White Bluff and ISES, another AP & L engineer, a Mr.

John Harvey, implemented a plan to install the level detector on fourteen (14) hydroveyer hoppers at ISES. Harvey informed Bowman of the plan to install the level detector on the hydroveyer hoppers, and Bowman indicated that he thought it was a good idea. Bowman also indicated that WRT would be interested in bidding on the project. AP & L ultimately awarded the contract, however, to another contractor because WRT was not the low bidder. In soliciting bids on the hydroveyer project, AP & L provided the contractors with specifications prepared by AP & L showing the work to be performed. The installation of the level detectors on the hydroveyer hoppers at ISES was completed in 1985, and all costs associated with their installation were paid by AP & L.

B.   District Court Litigation

On April 25, 1990, WRT brought suit against AP & L for patent infringement based on AP & L's solicitation of and contracting with a party other than WRT to install Bowman's patented level detector on the hydroveyer hoppers at ISES. The district court granted summary judgment in favor of AP & L on the basis that AP & L had acquired a "shop right" in the level detector claimed in the Bowman patent. AP & L argued and the court agreed that, as a matter of law, Bowman's development of the patented level detector at AP & L's facilities at AP & L's expense entitled AP & L, under the "shop rights" rule, to reproduce and use the level detector in its business. WRT then appealed to this court.

C.   Analysis

A "shop right" is generally accepted as being a right that is created at common law when the circumstances demand it, under principles of equity and fairness, entitling an employer to use without charge an invention patented by one or more of its employees without liability for infringement. However, as recognized by several commentators, the immense body of case law addressing the issue of "shop rights" suggests that not all courts agree as to the doctrinal basis for "shop rights," and, consequently, not all courts agree as to the particular et of circumstances necessary to create a "shop right."

For example, many courts characterize a "shop right" as being a type of implied license, and thus the focus is often on whether the employee engaged in any activities, e.g., developing the invention on the employer's time at the employer's expense, which demand a finding that he impliedly granted a license to his employer to use the invention. Other courts characterize a "shop right" as a form of equitable estoppel, and thus the focus is often on whether the employee's actions, e.g., consent or acquiescence to his employer's use of the invention, demand a finding that he is estopped from asserting a patent right against his employer. Neither characterization appears to be inherently better than the other, and the end result under either is often the same, given that the underlying analysis in each case is driven by principles of equity and fairness, and given that the courts often analyze a "shop right" as being a combination of the two even though they may characterize it in name as one or the other.

It is thus not surprising that many courts adopt neither characterization specifically, instead choosing to characterize a "shop right" more broadly as simply being a common law "right" that inures to an employer when the circumstances demand it under principles of equity and fairness. These courts often look to both the circumstances surrounding the development of the invention and the facts regarding the employee's activities respecting that invention, once developed, to determine whether it would be fair and equitable to allow an employee to preclude his employer from making use of that invention. This is essentially the analysis that most courts undertake regardless of how they characterize "shop rights."

In view of the foregoing, we believe that the proper methodology for determining whether an employer has acquired a "shop right" in a patented invention is to look to the totality of the circumstances on a case by case basis and determine whether the facts of a particular case demand, under principles of equity and fairness, a finding that a "shop right" exists. In such an analysis, one should look to such factors as the circumstances surrounding the development of the patented invention and the inventor's activities respecting that invention, once developed, to determine whether equity and fairness demand that the employer be allowed to use that invention in his business. A factually driven analysis such as this ensures that the principles of equity and fairness underlying the "shop rights" rule are considered. Because this is exactly the type of analysis that the district court used to reach its decision, we see no error in the district court's analysis justifying reversal.

To reach its decision, the district court looked to the discussion of "shop rights" set forth in the often-cited Dubilier case, in which the Court said:

> where a servant, during his hours of employment, working with his master's materials and appliances, conceives and perfects an invention for which he obtains a patent, he must accord his master a nonexclusive right to practice the invention. [citation omitted] This is an application of equitable principles. Since the servant uses his master's time, facilities and materials to attain a concrete result, the latter is in equity entitled to use that which embodies his own property and to duplicate it as often as he may find occasion to employ similar appliances in his business.

[*United States v. Dubilier Condenser Corp.*, 289 U.S. 178, 188–89 (1933).] The district court also accepted a discussion of "shop rights" set forth in one of WRT's briefs filed in the district court action as correctly summarizing several factors that may be considered in analyzing a "shop rights" case. At pages 9–10 of its opinion, the district court included the following excerpt from pages 6–8 of WRT's Memorandum Brief in Support of Response to Motion for Summary Judgment:

Because broad equitable principles are involved in determining whether shop rights in [an] invention arise, "[t]he full nature of the parties' relationship must be examined to determine whether a shop right exists." ROSENBERG, PATENT LAW FUNDAMENTALS, § 11.04, 11–20 (1991). The following factors have been considered: the contractual nature of the relationship between employer and employee, whether the employee consented to the employer's use of the invention, and whether the employee induced, acquiesced in, or assisted the employer in the use of the invention. . . . [footnote omitted]

An employer will have shop rights in an invention in situations where the employer has financed an employee's invention by providing wages, materials, tools and a work place. Other factors creating shop rights include an employee's consent, acquiescence, inducement, or assistance to the employer in using the invention without demanding compensation or other notice of restriction.

Applying Dubilier and the summary of the law set forth in WRT's own brief to the facts of this case, the district court properly found that AP & L had acquired a "shop right" in Bowman's patented level detector which entitled AP & L to duplicate the level detector for use in its business.

Bowman developed the patented level detector while working at AP & L and suggested it to AP & L as an alternative to the K-ray system. AP & L installed the level detector on one hundred and twenty eight (128) precipitator hoppers at White Bluff with Bowman's consent and participation. Bowman also consented to, and participated at least in part in, the installation of the level detector on one hundred and twenty eight (128) precipitator hoppers at ISES. In addition, the level detectors on half of the hoppers at ISES were installed by a contractor other than WRT, with Bowman's and WRT's knowledge and consent. All costs and expenses associated with the testing and implementation of the level detector on the hoppers at White Bluff and ISES were paid by AP & L.

Furthermore, Bowman never asserted that AP & L was precluded from using the level detector without his permission or that AP & L was required to compensate him for its use. Indeed, the record suggests that Bowman believed quite the opposite. As recognized by the district court:

Bowman admitted in a deposition that he believed all along that AP & L would have shop rights. His patent attorney had informed him of that possibility and he subsequently shared the attorney's opinion with his partners in WRT.

WRT argues that Bowman's consent or acquiescence after he had assigned his rights in the Bowman application to WRT is irrelevant. Even if this were true, Bowman's actions at White Bluff prior to this assignment justify the district court's finding that a "shop right" was created. Nevertheless, WRT, of which Bowman was a part owner during the relevant time period, acquiesced both to AP & L's continued use of the level detector at White Bluff and ISES and to the installation of the level detector by outside contractors at ISES. This lends further support to the district court's decision.

WRT also argues that, even if AP & L had acquired a "shop right" to use the patented level detector, AP & L somehow exceeded the scope of that right when it allegedly "carelessly and casually disseminated the design and specifications of the patented device to private contractors." WRT argues that, by putting information of this nature on the open market, AP & L rendered the patent "worthless" and robbed Bowman of the "fruit of his labor." We find these arguments unpersuasive for two reasons.

First, WRT has failed to explain how AP & L's mere dissemination of specifications of the patented level detector constituted patent infringement. Clearly, it did not. The owner of a patent right may exclude others from making, using or selling the subject matter of a claimed invention. AP & L's dissemination of information obviously does not fall into any of these categories. Even so, it is also unclear how disseminating specifications of the level detector after it was patented rendered the Bowman patent "worthless." The owner of the Bowman patent still retained the right to exclude all others than AP & L from practicing the claimed invention.

Second, we find no error in the district court's holding that AP & L's "shop right" entitled it to duplicate the level detector and to continue to use it in its business. Furthermore, AP & L's "shop right" was not limited to AP & L's use of level detectors that AP & L itself had manufactured and installed. Quite to the contrary, we find that AP & L's "shop right" entitled it to procure the level detector from outside contractors.

AFFIRMED.

Notes

1. **Comparative Approaches to Employed Inventors.** The *Arbeitnehmererfinderrecht,* or German Employed Inventor's Rights Law, provides far greater mandatory compensation for employed inventors than does the United States law. The German Act distinguishes between so-called "tied" and "free" inventions; the employer obtains rights in only the former, which must result from the employee's tasks or are based upon the activities of the employer. In the case of a tied invention, the inventor obtains the right to demand reasonable compensation from the employer. The Act forbids employees from waiving their rights to compensation by prior agreement with the employer. For a fine English-language discussion of the German law on employee inventions, see Dr. Matthias Brandi–Dohrn & Peter Chrocziel, *Federal Republic of Germany: Patent Law* § 2G, in WORLD INTELLECTUAL PROPERTY GUIDEBOOK: FEDERAL REPUBLIC OF GERMANY, AUSTRIA, SWITZERLAND (Dr. Bernd Rüster, ed., 1991).

2. **Reform for the Employed Inventor.** A considerable body of literature is critical of the current United States regime, under which employers almost universally obtain rights to their employees' inventions through contractual mechanisms. Proposed solutions include the creation of

a "reverse shop right" for the inventor; the establishment of government guidelines for determining compensation to the employed inventor, backed up by a Patent Office arbitration board; and the voiding of contractual provisions whereby the employee-inventor assigns his entire interest in any invention to the inventor, particularly where such clauses concern periods following the termination of the employment relationship. *See, e.g.,* Marc B. Hershovitz, Note, *Unhitching the Trailer Clause: The Rights of Inventive Employees and their Employers*, 3 J. INTELL. PROP. L. 187 (1995); Henrik D. Parker, Note, *Reform for Rights of Employed Inventors*, 57 S. CAL. L. REV. 603 (1984); William P. Hovell, Note, *Patent Ownership: An Employer's Rights to his Employee's Invention,* 58 NOTRE DAME L. REV. 863 (1983); Jay Dratler, Jr. *Incentives for People: The Forgotten Purpose of the Patent System*, 16 HARV. J. LEGIS. 129 (1979).

3. Other Implied Licenses. Recall from Chapter 15 that the United States patent law provides for other sorts of implied licenses beyond shop rights. Most commonly, this license arises when the patentee sells a patented good; in such circumstances the patentee is said to "exhaust" his right to future remuneration from the public.

§ 16.3 THE FIRST INVENTOR DEFENSE

One of the titles of the American Inventors Protection Act of 1999, the First Inventor Defense Act, created an infringement defense for an earlier inventor of a method of doing or conducting business that was later patented by another. *See* 35 U.S.C.A. § 273. The defendant must have reduced the infringing subject matter to practice one year before the effective filing date of the patent and made commercial use of that subject matter in the United States before the effective filing date.

The impetus for this provision lies in the rather complex relationship between the law of trade secrets and the patent system. As discussed in Chapter One of this casebook, trade secrecy protects individuals from misappropriation of valuable information that is useful in commerce. One reason an inventor might maintain the invention as a trade secret rather than seek patent protection is that the subject matter of the invention may not be regarded as patentable. Such inventions as customer lists or data compilations have traditionally been regarded as amenable to trade secret protection but not to patenting. Inventors might also maintain trade secret protection due to ignorance of the patent system or because they believe they can keep their invention secret longer than the period of exclusivity granted through the patent system.

It is important to note from the outset that the patent system has not favored trade secret holders. Well-established patent law establishes that an inventor who makes a secret, commercial use of an invention for more than one year prior to filing a patent application at the PTO forfeits his own right to a patent. *See W.L. Gore & Associates v. Garlock, Inc.*, 721 F.2d 1540, 220 U.S.P.Q. 303 (Fed.Cir.1983) (discussed in this casebook in Chapter Five). This policy is principally based upon the desire to maintain the integrity of the patent term. The Patent Act grants patents a term of twenty years commencing from the date a patent application is filed. 35 U.S.C. § 154(a)(2). If the trade secret holder could make commercial use of an invention for many years before choosing to file a patent application, he could disrupt this regime by delaying the expiration date of his patent.

On the other hand, settled patent law principles established that prior secret uses would not defeat the patents of later inventors. *See Gore v. Garlock, supra.* If an earlier inventor made secret commercial use of an invention, and another person independently invented the same technology later and obtained patent protection, then the trade secret holder could face liability for patent infringement. This policy was based upon the reasoning that issued, published patent instruments fully inform the public about the invention, while trade secrets do not. As between a subsequent inventor who patented the invention, and had disclosed the invention to the public, and an earlier trade secret holder who did not, the law favored the patent holder.

Legal developments in the late 1990's concerning methods of doing business focused attention upon the relationship between patents and trade secrets. Inventors of methods of doing business traditionally relied upon trade secret protection because such inventions had long been regarded as unpatentable subject matter. As a result, inventors of innovative business methods obtained legal advice not to file applications at the PTO. This advice was sound under the patent law as it then stood.

The 1998 Federal Circuit opinion in *State Street Bank & Trust Co. v. Signature Financial Group, Inc.*, 149 F.3d 1368, 47 U.S.P.Q.2d 1596 (Fed.Cir.1998) (discussed in this casebook in Chapter Two), altered this traditional principle. In the *State Street Bank* opinion, the Federal Circuit explained that no bar prevented the issuance of patents on methods of doing business. As a consequence, inventors in such sectors as finance, insurance and services have sought proprietary interests in their inventions through the patent system.

The change in this background principle was perceived as dealing a harsh blow to individuals that have invented business methods prior to the issuance of the *State Street Bank* opinion. Many of these inventors had maintained their innovative business methods as trade secrets for many years. As a result, they were unable belatedly to obtain patent protection on their business methods. As well, because trade secrets did not constitute prior art against the patent applications of others, a subsequent inventor would be able to obtain patent protection. Under these circumstances, a trade secret holder could find himself an adjudicated infringer of a patented business method that he actually invented first.

The First Inventor Defense Act reconciles these principles by providing an infringement defense for an earlier inventor of a method of doing business that was later patented by another. This infringement defense is subject to several qualifications. First, the defendant must have reduced the infringing subject matter to practice at least one year before the effective filing date of the patent application. Second, the defendant must have commercially used the infringing subject matter prior to the effective filing date of the patent. Finally, any reduction to practice or use must have been made in good faith, without derivation from the patentee or persons in privity with the patentee.

The first inventor defense has yet to be the subject of a reported judicial opinion. When such case arises, it will be interesting to learn the court's interpretation of the phrase "method of doing or conducting business," a term Congress opted not to define. Looking further forward, it would seem a rather straightforward matter to alter the first inventor defense to embrace a more expansive range of patentable subject matter. In this regard the first inventor defense could prove quite similar to those prevailing in other countries. These statutes are commonly referred to as creating "prior user rights." Unlike the more limited regime created by the First Inventor Defense Act, prior user rights abroad are not limited to methods of doing business. They instead apply to any sort of invention. Experience with the First Inventor Defense Act might suggest whether the Congress should consider a more full-fledged prior user rights regime, or maintain the current system as a limited cure of a specific problem.

Additional Defenses Exercise

Lawson, who was incarcerated in a Federal Correctional Institution, volunteered to work as an unskilled laborer in a special government manufacturing program. The program produced helmets for use by the military. The helmets were made in part of a synthetic fiber that was known by its trademark, Kevlar. Lawson quickly learned that Kevlar was an exceptionally difficult material to cut. His cutting device frequently failed during production, damaging the helmet he was attempting to manufacture. Other program workers shared his difficulties.

An experienced machinist, Lawson thought that he could develop an improved technique for cutting Kevlar. He took some scrap materials to his cell and worked on the invention during his free time. By November 15, 1990, he had developed an effective cutting device for use with Kevlar. Lawson demonstrated his device to prison guards on December 1, 1990. Impressed with the technology, program officials adopted Lawson's invention for general use on December 20, 1990. The device was enormously successful, allowing the program to double the number of manufactured helmets each year from 1990 through 1999.

Upon his release from the Federal Correctional Institution on January 10, 1991, Lawson immediately contacted a patent attorney. An application was filed on August 1, 1991, directed towards an improved Kevlar cutting device. The application ultimately matured into the '999 patent on February 10, 1992.

While reading an industry newsletter on October 1, 1992, Lawson noticed an advertisement placed by the HeadsUp Equipment Company.

The advertisement described a Kevlar cutting device which appeared to infringe the '999 patent. Lawson directed correspondence to the Heads-Up Equipment Company on October 5, 1992, which included the following language he had taken from a legal form book:

> I believe you are selling Kevlar cutting devices of a type covered by one or more of the claims of the '999 patent. I am willing to consider granting you a license under the patent on reasonable terms. If, however, you should continue your infringing activities without a license, I am prepared to take whatever action is necessary to enforce my patent rights.

> Please let me know promptly if you are interested in a license under the patent. I am docketing this matter for further attention two weeks from the date of this letter in the event I do not receive a satisfactory response from you.

Lawson received no response to his letter. Busy working on another invention, Lawson subsequently took no immediate action regarding the '999 patent. Lawson then filed suit against the United States government in the Court of Federal Claims on July 15, 1998, and against the HeadsUp Equipment Company in the District Court for the Eastern District of Virginia on July 22, 1998.

Address the following issues:

(1) Does the U.S. government possess a shop right in Lawson's patented invention?

(2) Is Lawson barred by laches or estoppel from pursuing his claims against either the United States government or the HeadsUp Equipment Company?

Chapter Seventeen

REMEDIES

Once a court has determined that a patent claim is not invalid and infringed, it must then shape the remedy due to the patentee. This effort primarily involves the following provisions of U.S. Code Title 35:

§ 283. Injunctive Relief.

The several courts having jurisdiction of cases under this title may grant injunctions in accordance with the principles of equity to prevent the violation of any right secured by patent, on such terms as the court deems reasonable.

§ 284. Damages.

Upon finding for the claimant the court shall award the claimant damages adequate to compensate for the infringement, but in no event less than a reasonable royalty for the use made of the invention by the infringer, together with interest and costs as fixed by the court.

A right to exclude, by definition, implies injunctive relief. In most instances, the most attractive remedy for a patent owner is an injunction to exclude infringers from making, using, and selling the invention.

In one sense, damages are an indication of the value of the invention. Beyond compensating a patent owner for infringement, however, damages theories also significantly influence substantive patent law. The availability and amount of damages informs an applicant's claiming techniques and even the administrative practices of the U.S. Patent and Trademark Office. Remedies also demark the borders between patent law and other, related regimes, particularly the law of antitrust and unfair competition. In short, the remedial aspects of U.S. patent law hold more significance than may be apparent at first blush, and are well worthy of careful study.

§ 17.1 INJUNCTIONS

Early in its history, the Federal Circuit noted the importance of injunctive relief to patent holders:

> The very nature of the patent right is the right to exclude others. Once the patentee's patents have been held to be valid and infringed, he should be entitled to the full enjoyment and protection of his patent rights. The infringer should not be allowed to continue his infringement in the face of such a holding. A court should not be reluctant to use its equity powers once a party has so clearly established his patent rights.

Smith Int'l, Inc. v. Hughes Tool Co., 718 F.2d 1573, 219 U.S.P.Q. 686 (Fed.Cir.1983). Indeed, more so than the monetary relief, injunctive relief is often the most valuable remedy for patentees. Above all, a patent owner may wish to protect its first mover advantage and its market share. Foreign patent systems, particularly those emanating from the civil law tradition, reflect this truth: injunctive relief often comprises the only practical infringement remedy available in certain jurisdictions. Injunctive relief is available at three stages of litigation: preliminary to adjudication, accompanying a final judgment, and subsequent to enforcement of the injunction via contempt proceedings.

§ 17.1[a] Preliminary Injunctions

Prior to the creation of the Federal Circuit, patentees often faced formidable obstacles in obtaining preliminary injunctive relief. The patent owner usually faced two insurmountable obstacles. First, the equitable nature of injunctive relief required showing a likelihood of success in proving both validity and infringement at trial. In the era of uncertainty in patentability standards, the likelihood of sustaining the patent's validity was a difficult burden at a preliminary stage. Another court's earlier judgment of patent validity was typically a requisite to obtaining a preliminary injunction. Beyond the likelihood of success, equity also required a court to find no adequate remedy at law before imposing a preliminary injunction. Typically an accused infringer could successfully assert that damages would supply an adequate remedy at law in the event of infringement. As the next decision demonstrates, however, the Federal Circuit considerably liberalized the standard for obtaining a preliminary injunction in a patent case.

H.H. ROBERTSON, CO. v. UNITED STEEL DECK, INC.

United States Court of Appeals, Federal Circuit, 1987.
820 F.2d 384, 2 U.S.P.Q.2d 1926.

Before NEWMAN and BISSELL, CIRCUIT JUDGES, and NEWMAN, SENIOR JUDGE.

PAULINE NEWMAN, CIRCUIT JUDGE.

United Steel Deck, Inc. (USD) and Nicholas J. Bouras, Inc., (Bouras) appeal the Order of Preliminary Injunction of the United States District

Court for the District of New Jersey in favor of the H.H. Robertson Company (Robertson). USD and Bouras were enjoined pendente lite from making, using, and selling certain structures which were found to infringe United States Patent No. 3,721,051 (the '051 or Fork patent). We affirm.

BACKGROUND

Robertson is the owner of the '051 patent, invention of Frank W. Fork, issued on March 20, 1973 and entitled "Bottomless Sub–Assembly for Producing an Underfloor Electrical Cable Trench". The invention is a concrete deck structure sub-assembly for distributing electrical wiring.

Robertson charged Bouras and its affiliated manufacturing company USD with infringement (inducing and contributory infringement) of claims 1, 2, 4, 6, 9, 13, and 14 of the Fork patent. In moving for preliminary injunction Robertson alleged that "there is a reasonable probability of eventual success on the patent infringement claim"; that "the Fork patent was held valid, infringed, contributorily infringed and enforceable by the United States District Court for the Northern District of Ohio in [*H.H. Robertson Co. v. Bargar Metal Fabricating Co.*, 225 U.S.P.Q. 1191 (N.D.Ohio 1984) ('*Bargar*')]; that the 'accused structures of USD and Bouras are the same or substantially the same as those held ... to infringe in *Bargar*'; that '[w]here, as here, the patent has been held valid and infringed, irreparable harm is presumed ... and the harm ... cannot be fully compensated by money damages'; and that the 'balance of equities heavily weighs in favor of Robertson.' "

The district court held a four-day hearing on the motion, during which witnesses including experts testified on the issues of patent validity and infringement. The legal and equitable issues were briefed and argued. The court concluded that Robertson had "established a basis for the relief it seeks," and granted the preliminary injunction.

ANALYSIS

The standards applied to the grant of a preliminary injunction are no more nor less stringent in patent cases than in other areas of the law. The court in Smith International discussed the so-called "more severe" rule that has at times weighed against the grant of preliminary injunctions in patent cases, stating: "The basis for the more severe rule appears to be both a distrust of and unfamiliarity with patent issues and a belief that the ex parte examination by the Patent and Trademark Office is inherently unreliable." [718 F.2d] at 1578, 219 U.S.P.Q. at 690. *See also Atlas Powder Co. v. Ireco Chemicals*, 773 F.2d 1230, 1233, 227 U.S.P.Q. 289, 292 (Fed.Cir.1985) ("burden upon the movant should be no different in a patent case than for other kinds of intellectual property"). The existing standards for relief pendente lite, fairly applied, can accommodate any special circumstances that may arise.

The grant or denial of a preliminary injunction is within the discretionary authority of the trial court. Appellate review is on the basis of whether the court "abused its discretion, committed an error of law, or seriously misjudged the evidence." *Smith International*, 718 F.2d at 1579, 219 U.S.P.Q. at 691.

The district court applied to Robertson's motion the Third Circuit standard:

> An applicant for a preliminary injunction against patent infringement must show:

> (1) a reasonable probability of eventual success in the litigation and (2) that the movant will be irreparably injured pendente lite if relief is not granted.... Moreover, while the burden rests upon the moving party to make these two requisite showings, the district court "should take into account, when they are relevant, (3) the possibility of harm to other interested persons from the grant or denial of the injunction, and (4) the public interest."

Test

This is substantially the same standard enunciated by this court. See, for example, *Roper Corp. v. Litton Systems, Inc.*, 757 F.2d 1266, 1270–73, 225 U.S.P.Q. 345, 347–50 (Fed.Cir.1985), and *Atlas Powder*, 773 F.2d at 1231?34, 227 U.S.P.Q. at 290–93.

PATENT VALIDITY

The first question before the district court was whether the movant Robertson had demonstrated a reasonable likelihood that USD and Bouras would fail to meet their burden at trial of proving, by clear and convincing evidence, that the Fork patent claims were invalid.

The burden of proving invalidity is with the party attacking validity. The evidence adduced in connection with a motion for preliminary relief must be considered in this light.

Robertson retained the burden of showing a reasonable likelihood that the attack on its patent's validity would fail. Indeed, the district court placed a greater burden on Robertson than was required, referring to our statement in *Atlas Powder*, 773 F.2d at 1233, 227 U.S.P.Q. at 292, that a patentee seeking a preliminary injunction must " 'clearly show[ ]' that his patent is valid".

This court's statement in Atlas Powder does not change the immutable allocation to the challenger of the burden of proving invalidity, but rather reflects the rule that the burden is always on the movant to demonstrate entitlement to preliminary relief. Such entitlement, however, is determined in the context of the presumptions and burdens that would inhere at trial on the merits. *See Anderson v. Liberty Lobby, Inc.*, 477 U.S. 242, 106 S.Ct. 2505, 2512, 91 L.Ed.2d 202 (1986), wherein the Court observed that in deciding a motion for summary judgment the trial court must be cognizant of "the substantive evidentiary standard of proof that would apply at the trial on the merits". A similar cognizance is appropriate to a motion for preliminary injunction.

Before the district court, USD and Bouras argued that all of the Fork patent claims at issue were invalid for obviousness in terms of 35

U.S.C. § 103, and that claim 2 was invalid in terms of 35 U.S.C. § 112. The asserted invalidity for obviousness was based on references that had been before the Ohio court in *Bargar*, including references that had been before the patent examiner during prosecution of the Fork patent application, and three references that were newly presented. The patent claims, the details of the references, and the evidence and argument offered by both sides, need not be here repeated.

The district court in its opinion referred to the detailed analysis by the Ohio court and to its decision that the accused infringers in that case had failed to establish the invalidity of the claims. The district court stated that the "finding of validity of the Fork '051 patent in *Bargar* is persuasive evidence of validity" with respect to the references before that court. The district court further held, upon reviewing the three additional references, that "considering them as part of the prior art does not render obvious the Fork bottomless trench invention." We discern no error in the court's conclusion that "the finding in *Bargar* and the evidence submitted in the present case lead to the conclusion that there is a reasonable probability that Robertson will ultimately succeed on the issue of obviousness".

The issue of validity of claim 2 under section 112 raised the question of whether the written description was enabling to one skilled in this art. Reviewing the evidence, including expert testimony, the district court held that "the patent requirements of § 112 are met". The court's determination that the disclosure had not been proven not to be enabling has not been shown to be in error.

Bouras accuses the district court of giving undue weight to the Ohio court's decision of validity and infringement against a different defendant. The district court stated that it "did not rely on *Bargar* as evidence of infringement" but only as evidence of validity with respect to the references actually considered by the Ohio court. There was no error in its so doing. Substantial weight may be given to a patent's litigation history in connection with a motion for relief *pendente lite*. Even the "severe rule" against the grant of preliminary injunctions in patent cases was tempered when a patent had been upheld in other forums or its validity had been acquiesced in by others. *See* 8 A.W. DELLER, DELLER'S WALKER ON PATENTS § 686, 416?22 (2d ed. 1973 & Supp.1985) and cases cited therein. A prior adjudication upholding patent validity after a fully litigated trial, including similar issues of fact and law, contributes strong support to the grant of a preliminary injunction.

The decision for our review is not a final judgment of patent validity. Rather, we ascertain whether the district court correctly concluded that Robertson had demonstrated a reasonable likelihood that it will prevail on this issue. On the record before us, the court's conclusion is based on factual findings that have not been shown to be clearly erroneous, it was not error to place weight on the Ohio district court's ruling on validity, and no error in law has been shown.

INFRINGEMENT

USD and Bouras argue that their current trench, the Blue Cross–Blue Shield design, is not "truly bottomless", and that the claims must be interpreted as a matter of law to exclude trenches that are only partially bottomless. To the district court USD and Bouras presented expert testimony in support of this position, countered by expert testimony on behalf of Robertson. The witnesses testified at length concerning the prosecution history and its impact on the interpretation and scope of the claims.

The district court's construction of the claims is explained in relation to its holding on infringement, the court stating that the "key portion of the trench remains bottomless, *i.e.*, the portions giving direct access to the cells." We are not persuaded of error in the district court's construction of the term "bottomless" to apply to the "key portion" of the trench, based on the evidence before it.

The accused structures, and the application thereto of the patent claims, were the subject of analysis and explanation by witnesses on both sides, aided by the physical exhibits. Our review shows thorough exposition of the opposing positions. The district court found that the accused subassemblies are "bottomless in that upper surface portions of the cellular units of the metal subfloor in the region between said opposite sides cooperate with the sub-assembly to create an underfloor electrical cable trench, confront the cover plate, and are exposed to view when the cover plate is removed." The court found that "the horizontal metal sections . . . and the horizontal metal strip . . . serve no function [and the] key portion of the trench remains bottomless."

In its factual application of the claims to the accused devices, the findings of the district court have not been shown to be clearly in error.

The grant of a preliminary injunction does not require that infringement be proved beyond all question, or that there be no evidence supporting the viewpoint of the accused infringer. The grant turns on the likelihood that Robertson will meet its burden at trial of proving infringement. We sustain the district court's conclusion that "there is a reasonable probability that Robertson will eventually establish that Bouras and USD induced infringement of the Fork '051 patent".

EQUITABLE CONSIDERATIONS

The movant for preliminary injunction must show not only a reasonable likelihood of success on the merits, but also the lack of adequate remedy at law or other irreparable harm.

In matters involving patent rights, irreparable harm has been presumed when a clear showing has been made of patent validity and infringement. This presumption derives in part from the finite term of the patent grant, for patent expiration is not suspended during litigation, and the passage of time can work irremediable harm. The opportunity to practice an invention during the notoriously lengthy course of patent litigation may itself tempt infringers.

The nature of the patent grant thus weighs against holding that monetary damages will always suffice to make the patentee whole, for the principal value of a patent is its statutory right to exclude. The presumption of irreparable harm in patent cases is analogous to that applicable to other forms of intellectual property.

The district court held that irreparable injury was presumed because Robertson had established a "strong likelihood of success in establishing validity and infringement." Such presumption of injury was not, however, irrebuttable. The parties gave scant attention in their appellate briefs to the issues of irreparable injury and the balance of harms. During oral argument, in response to an inquiry from the bench, USD and Bouras urged that money damages are an adequate remedy. In response, Robertson emphasized the few remaining years of patent life.

Even when irreparable injury is presumed and not rebutted, it is still necessary to consider the balance of hardships. The magnitude of the threatened injury to the patent owner is weighed, in the light of the strength of the showing of likelihood of success on the merits, against the injury to the accused infringer if the preliminary decision is in error. Results of other litigation involving the same patent may be taken into account, and the public interest is considered. No one element controls the result.

When the movant has shown the likelihood that the acts complained of are unlawful, the preliminary injunction "preserves the status quo if it prevents future trespasses but does not undertake to assess the pecuniary or other consequences of past trespasses." *Atlas Powder Co.*, 773 F.2d at 1232, 227 U.S.P.Q. at 291. The court in *Atlas Powder* thus distinguished between remedies for past infringement, where there is no possibility of other than monetary relief, and prospective infringement, "which may have market effects never fully compensable in money." The cautionary corollary is that a preliminary injunction improvidently granted may impart undeserved value to an unworthy patent.

Thus substantial deference is due the district court's equitable judgment. The district court in its opinion referred to the USD/Bouras portrayal of disruption, loss of business, and loss of jobs, and to Robertson's business needs and patent rights. Observing that "[t]his patent does not have many more years to run", the court held "the equities weigh heavily against the wrongdoer." The court stated that the "protection of patents furthers a strong public policy . . . advanced by granting preliminary injunctive relief when it appears that, absent such relief, patent rights will be flagrantly violated."

The grant of a preliminary injunction, if not based on legal error or a serious misjudgment of the evidence, is reviewable only to ascertain whether the grant was within a reasonable range of discretion. We have considered all of the arguments of the parties, and the record before us. The district court's conclusion reflects a reasonable consideration and balance of the pertinent factors, evaluated in accordance with the established jurisprudence, and does not exceed the court's discretionary authority.

AFFIRMED.

Notes

1. Trends at the Federal Circuit. Many Federal Circuit observers considered the court to be overly sympathetic to patent holders in its early years, with the more ready availability of preliminary injunctions as a leading point of commentary. Within the 1990's, the court's willingness to affirm the denial of a preliminary injunction, *see Rosemount, Inc. v. U.S. Int'l Trade Comm'n*, 910 F.2d 819, 15 U.S.P.Q.2d 1569 (Fed.Cir.1990), or even to vacate the district court's grant of preliminary relief, *see We Care, Inc. v. Ultra–Mark Int'l, Corp.*, 930 F.2d 1567, 18 U.S.P.Q.2d 1562 (Fed.Cir. 1991), appears to have increased somewhat. After that initial case law, the Federal Circuit seems to have settled on the concept "that a preliminary injunction is a drastic and extraordinary remedy ... not to be routinely granted." *Intel Corp. v. ULSI Sys. Tech., Inc.*, 995 F.2d 1566, 1568, 27 U.S.P.Q.2d 1136, 1138 (Fed.Cir.1993).

2. Irreparable Harm. Evidence of the more stern review preliminary injunctions receive at the Federal Circuit may be found in the court's analysis of irreparable harm. Early decisions such as *Smith International*, cited above, held that "where validity and continuing infringement have been clearly established, ... immediate irreparable harm is presumed." 718 F.2d at 1581, 219 U.S.P.Q. at 686. Although later decisions continue to recite this standard, *see Canon Computer Sys., Inc. v. Nu–Kote Int'l, Inc.*, 134 F.3d 1085, 45 U.S.P.Q.2d 1355 (Fed.Cir.1998), the Federal Circuit has indicated that this presumption is not irrefutable, as demonstrated by the following passage from *High Tech Medical Instrumentation Inc. v. New Image Industries Inc.*, 49 F.3d 1551, 33 U.S.P.Q.2d 2005 (Fed.Cir.1995).

> The district court based its finding of irreparable harm not on any affirmative showing of prospective harm to HTMI, but on a presumption of irreparable harm stemming from the strength of HTMI's showing on the merits. HTMI follows the same tack: it does not identify any specific injury it would suffer from the denial of a preliminary injunction, but instead relies entirely on the presumption of irreparable harm.

> Reasoning by analogy from decisions involving other forms of intellectual property, this court has held that a presumption of irreparable harm arises when a patentee makes a clear showing that a patent is valid and that it is infringed. The presumption of irreparable harm is unavailable here, however, because, as we have discussed, the record does not support HTMI's claim that it is likely to succeed in proving that the AcuCam infringes claim 24 of the '001 patent. Aside from the presumption, the district court pointed to no evidence that would support a finding of irreparable injury, and we find none.

> HTMI does not make or sell dental endoscopes and does not license their manufacture and sale under the '001 patent. Although a patentee's failure to practice an invention does not necessarily defeat the patentee's claim of irreparable harm, the lack of commercial activity by the patentee is a significant factor in the calculus ... [T]he evidence shows

that HTMI offered a license to New Image, so it is clear that HTMI is willing to forgo its patent rights for compensation. That evidence suggests that any injury suffered by HTMI would be compensable in damages assessed as part of the final judgment in the case.

49 F.3d at 1556–57, 33 U.S.P.Q.2d at 2009–10.

3. The Balance of Hardships. With respect to this preliminary injunction factor, an accused infringer's lone argument that the grant of a preliminary injunction would render it insolvent ordinarily falls on deaf ears. As the court noted in *Windsurfing Int'l, Inc. v. AMF Inc.*, 782 F.2d 995, 1003 n. 12, 228 U.S.P.Q. 562, 568 n. 12 (Fed.Cir.1986): "That sailboards are Downwind's primary product, and that an injunction might therefore put Downwind out of business, cannot justify denial of that injunction. One who elects to build a business on a product found to infringe cannot be heard to complain if an injunction against continuing infringement destroys the business so elected." For a softening of this statement under different factual circumstances, see *Standard Havens Products Inc. v. Gencor Industries Inc.*, 897 F.2d 511, 13 U.S.P.Q.2d 2029 (Fed.Cir.1990).

4. The Public Interest. Courts routinely note the strong public interest in protecting rights secured by valid patents en route to granting a preliminary injunction. That the accused infringer markets the contested technology at a lower cost has been held not to serve the public interest; "[w]ere that to be a justification for patent infringement, most injunctions would be denied because copiers universally price their products lower than innovators." *Payless Shoesource Inc. v. Reebok Int'l Ltd.*, 998 F.2d 985, 991, 27 U.S.P.Q.2d 1516, 1521 (Fed.Cir.1993). However, preliminary injunctions have been denied based on overriding social concerns, particularly where a public health concerns are implicated. *E.g., Hybritech Inc. v. Abbott Labs.*, 849 F.2d 1446, 7 U.S.P.Q.2d 1191 (Fed.Cir.1988).

5. The Federal Circuit argues with itself? The Federal Circuit has not always sent a clear message about denial of a preliminary injunction if less than all four factors favor the movant. *Matsushita Elec. Indus. Co. v. United States*, 823 F.2d 505 (Fed.Cir.1987), suggests that the movant's failure to meet just one of the elements of the preliminary injunction test is enough to deny the remedy:

> We hold the court's finding of irreparable injury was clearly erroneous, and that the preliminary injunction therefore must be reversed. We do not address the findings of the Court of International Trade on the other three elements.

Id. at 509. *Reebok Int'l Ltd. v. J. Baker, Inc.*, 32 F.3d 1552, 31 U.S.P.Q.2d 1781 (Fed.Cir.1994) agrees:

> Arguably, our cases suggest that a district court must always consider all four factors when deciding whether to issue a preliminary injunction. In such cases the district court did consider all four factors. . . .

> While a district court may consider all four factors before *granting* a preliminary injunction to determine whether the moving party has carried its burden of establishing each of the four, we specifically decline today to require a district court to articulate findings on the third and

fourth factors when the court *denies* a preliminary injunction because a party fails to establish *either* of the two critical factors.

32 F.3d at 1556, 31 U.S.P.Q.2d at 1784. On the other hand, *Smith Int'l, Inc. v. Hughes Tool Co.*, 718 F.2d 1573, 219 U.S.P.Q. 686 (Fed.Cir.1983), states categorically: "[I]n reaching its decision, the district court must consider ... [all four] factors and balance all of the elements. No one element will necessarily be dispositive of the case." 718 at 1579, 219 U.S.P.Q. at 691. Similarly *Chrysler Motors Corp. v. Auto Body Panels of Ohio, Inc.*, 908 F.2d 951, 15 U.S.P.Q.2d 1469 (Fed.Cir.1990) concurs:

> Under this rule, no one factor, taken individually, is necessarily dispositive. If a preliminary injunction is granted by the trial court, the weakness of the showing regarding one factor may be overborne by the strength of others. If the injunction is denied, the absence of an adequate showing with regard to any one factor may be sufficient, given the weight of lack of it assigned to the other factors, to justify the denial. And as a basic proposition, the matter lies largely in the sound discretion of the trial judge.

908 F.2d at 953, 15 U.S.P.Q. 2d at 1471. In light of this apparent split, what course do you take as a practitioner in a trial seeking a preliminary injunction?

6. Preliminary Measures Available Abroad. Legal regimes based overseas feature a variety of preliminary measures available to patent holders. Some, such as Italian precautionary measures and Austrian interim injunctions, are roughly analogous to United States preliminary injunctions. *See* Paul Traxler, *Interim Measures in Patent Infringement Proceedings Under Austrian Law*, 24 INT'L REV. INDUS. PROP. & COPYRIGHT L. 751 (1993); Massimo Scuffi, *European Patents and Interlocutory Injunctions for Acts of Patent Infringement Under Italian Law*, 22 INT'L REV. INDUS. PROP. & COPYRIGHT L. 1009 (1991). Also of note are various ex parte orders, including the British "Anton Piller" order and the French saisie-contrefaçon. Such orders do not aim to allow patentees to confiscate infringing technologies, but are in a sense are a form of discovery, allowing patentees to establish the origin and extent of the infringement. *See Anton Piller v. Manufacturing Processes*, [1976] R.P.C. 719; André Bertrand, *Seizures to Acquire Evidence Under French Patent Law*, 26 INT'L REV. INDUS. PROP. & COPYRIGHT L. 175 (1995).

The effectiveness of such proceedings varies considerably. In Japan, a patentee's application for a preliminary injunction is typically conducted as a separate proceeding from the primary lawsuit, although the same judges may be involved in both matters. Because the duration of the preliminary injunction suit may not be considerably shorter than that of the primary suit, experienced litigants often do not seek a preliminary injunction at all. In contrast, the most potent preliminary measure at the close of the Twentieth Century has proven to be the Dutch *kort geding*, or short proceeding, considered further in this text in Chapter 18. Often the period between initiation of the proceeding and a written opinion is a matter of weeks, sometimes resulting in an injunction which is effective throughout Europe. *See* Jan J. Brinkhof, *Between Speed and Thoroughness: The Dutch*

'Kort Geding' Procedure in Patent Cases, 18 EUR. INTELL. PROP. REV. 499 (1996).

§ 17.1[b] Permanent Injunctions

Courts routinely grant permanent injunctions upon entry of a final judgment of infringement. Indeed the Federal Circuit has noted that the Patent Act supplies injunctive relief to protect patentees against future infringement that may have market effects never fully compensable in monetary damages. *Reebok Int'l Ltd. v. J. Baker, Inc.*, 32 F.3d 1552, 31 U.S.P.Q.2d 1781 (Fed.Cir.1994). For instance, harm to business reputation caused by consumer confusion between an inferior infringing product and a patented invention is the type of injury often not fully compensable in damages. *Id.* Moreover, once adjudication has established infringement of a valid patent, courts routinely presume irreparable harm will occur with continued infringement. *Richardson v. Suzuki Motor Co.*, 868 F.2d 1226, 9 U.S.P.Q.2d 1913 (Fed.Cir.1989).

Nonetheless, as the text of § 283 indicates, a permanent injunction following a finding of infringement is not automatic, but lies within the discretion of the trial court. As a practical matter, a court only withholds this remedy in compelling circumstances, such as a threat to public health. *Id.* The most famous modern case is *City of Milwaukee v. Activated Sludge, Inc.*, 69 F.2d 577, 21 U.S.P.Q. 69 (7th Cir.1934), where the Seventh Circuit vacated a permanent injunction granted by the trial court because it believed that enjoining the infringing system of sewerage disposal would have caused the city of Milwaukee to dump its sewerage into Lake Michigan. The patentee was not using its patent. Therefore an injunction would have caused great harm to the public health and welfare without any substantial benefit to the patentee.

Occasionally litigation arises over the scope of a permanent injunction. *Joy Technologies, Inc. v. Flakt, Inc.*, 6 F.3d 770, 28 U.S.P.Q.2d 1378 (Fed.Cir.1993). Usually this litigation features contempt enforcement of a permanent injunction. Once a court has judged an accused technology to infringe and has issued an injunction, the infringer will often modify the adjudicated technology and reenter the market. The infringer will then assert that the modified technology does not fall within the scope of the injunction. In such circumstances, the patent holder will claim that the injunction has been violated and seek to enforce the injunction via contempt proceedings. Because the patentee could also bring a second infringement action, the Federal Circuit addressed the standard for contempt enforcement. In *KSM Fastening Systems, Inc. v. H.A. Jones Company, Inc.*, 776 F.2d 1522, 227 U.S.P.Q. 676 (Fed.Cir.1985), the Circuit rejected a standard under which a court could merely determine whether the differences between the adjudicated infringement and modified technology were less than "colorable:"

> In sum, the initial question to be answered in ruling on a motion for contempt is whether contempt proceedings are appropriate. That question is answered by the trial court's judging whether substantial disputed issues must be litigated. The second question, whether an

injunction against infringement has been violated, requires, at a minimum, a finding that the accused device is an infringement.

A concurring opinion by Judge Newman faulted the majority for easing "the way to enabling an adjudged infringer to oblige a court to retry any colorable modification the infringer can create, with fresh consideration of prior art and prosecution history, renewed claim interpretation, and the trappings of discovery and expert witnesses that accompany trial of those issues." The *KSM* decision is criticized in John E. Tsavaris II, Note, *Patent Contempt Proceedings After* KSM*: Has the Federal Circuit Infringed Patentees' Rights?*, 54 FORDHAM L. REV. 1005 (1986).

§ 17.2   DAMAGES

§ 17.2[a]   Basic Principles

PANDUIT CORP. v. STAHLIN BROS. FIBRE WORKS, INC.

United States Court of Appeals, Sixth Circuit, 1978.
575 F.2d 1152, 197 U.S.P.Q. 726.

Before PHILLIPS, CHIEF CIRCUIT JUDGE, CELEBREZZE, CIRCUIT JUDGE, and MARKEY, CHIEF JUDGE OF THE COURT OF CUSTOMS AND PATENT APPEALS.

MARKEY, CHIEF JUDGE.

Appeal from a judgment of the district court, adopting, with an unpublished opinion, the report of the special master awarding plaintiff, as damages for patent infringement, a reasonable royalty of 21/2%. We reverse and remand.

LITIGATION BACKGROUND

In 1964 plaintiff Panduit Corp. (Panduit) sued defendant Stahlin Bros. Fibre Works, Inc. (Stahlin) for infringement of Panduit's Walch patent No. 3,024,301, covering duct for wiring of electrical control systems. In 1969, the district court found claim 5 valid and infringed by the "Lok-slot" and "Web-slot" ducts made and sold by Stahlin, enjoined Stahlin from further infringement, and ordered an accounting. That judgment was affirmed on appeal.

Thereafter, the district court adjudged Stahlin in contempt of the court's injunction, because of Stahlin's making and selling the "Tear Drop" duct, a colorable imitation of the infringing "Lok-slot." That judgment was also affirmed on appeal.

In 1971, the district court appointed a master to determine Panduit's damages pursuant to 35 U.S.C. § 284, to take evidence, and render a report on the issues of treble damages, interest, costs, and attorney fees. The district court, in adopting in toto the master's report, considered the master's findings of fact not clearly erroneous, and stated that "the Master had correctly applied the law to the circumstances of this case." The report recommended $44,709.60 in damages, based on a royalty of 2½% of gross sales price, the percentage being calculated on Stahlin's testimony that its normal profit on all of its products was 4.04% and the concept that a "reasonable royalty" entailed some level of profit to the "licensee".

FACT BACKGROUND

The duct manufactured by Panduit was invented by its president, Jack Caveney. Panduit began to make and sell the duct in 1955, and Caveney applied for a patent in 1956. In an interference proceeding in the Patent Office, it was determined that Walch, an employee of General Electric, was the first inventor of the duct. A patent issued to General Electric, as Walch's assignee, on March 6, 1962. Panduit then acquired the Walch patent from General Electric and established a firm policy of exercising its right to that patent property, i.e., of the right to exclude others from making and selling the patented duct.

Stahlin began to manufacture and sell the "Lok-slot" and "Web-slot" ducts in 1957, and continued to do so after issuance of the Walch patent and its sale to Panduit in 1962. On January 1, 1963, Stahlin introduced a price cut of approximately 30% on its "Lok-slot" and "Web-slot" ducts.

Panduit seeks $808,003 as damages for lost profits on lost sales over the period March 6, 1962, the date of first infringement, to August 7, 1970, the effective date of the initial injunction; or, alternatively, a 35% reasonable royalty rate yielding $625,940. In addition, Panduit seeks $4,069,000 in profits lost on Panduit's own sales because of Stahlin's price cut.

ISSUE

The dispositive issue is whether the master's determination of a reasonable royalty was in error.

OPINION

The statute, 35 U.S.C. § 284, requires that the patent owner receive from the infringer "damages adequate to compensate for the infringement." In *Aro Mfg. Co. v. Convertible Top Replacement Co.*, 377 U.S. 476 at 507, 84 S.Ct. 1526, 1543, 12 L.Ed.2d 457, 141 U.S.P.Q. 681 at 694 (1964), the Supreme Court stated:

> But the present statutory rule is that only "damages" may be recovered. These have been defined by this Court as "compensation for the pecuniary loss he (the patentee) has suffered from the infringement, without regard to the question whether the defendant has gained or lost by his unlawful acts." *Coupe v. Royer*, 155 U.S. 565, 582, 15 S.Ct. 199, 39 L.Ed. 263. They have been said to constitute "the difference between his pecuniary condition after the infringement, and what his condition would have been if the infringement had not occurred." *Yale Lock Mfg. Co. v. Sargent*, 117 U.S. 536, 552, 6 S.Ct. 934, 29 L.Ed. 954. The question to be asked in

determining damages is "how much had the Patent Holder and Licensee suffered by the infringement. And that question (is) primarily: had the Infringer not infringed, what would Patent Holder– Licensee have made?"

Panduit argues that the district court erred (1) in denying Panduit its lost profits due to lost sales, or, in the alternative, a 35% reasonable royalty; and (2) in denying Panduit its lost profits from its own actual sales due to Stahlin's price cut.

Lost Profits Due to Lost Sales

To obtain as damages the profits on sales he would have made absent the infringement, i.e., the sales made by the infringer, a patent owner must prove: (1) demand for the patented product, (2) absence of acceptable noninfringing substitutes, (3) his manufacturing and marketing capability to exploit the demand, and (4) the amount of the profit he would have made. 3 R. White, Patent Litigation: Procedure and Tactics § 9.03(2).

It is not disputed that Panduit established elements (1) and (3). Regarding (2), the master found that: "The evidence clearly shows the existence of acceptable non-infringing substitute ducts which would have permitted the defendant to retain its customers." That finding, as discussed below, was in error. However, Panduit is not entitled to its lost profits on lost sales in this case because of its failure to establish element (4).

The district court upheld as not clearly erroneous the master's finding that "there was insufficient evidence from which a fair determination could be made as to the amount of profit plaintiff would have made on such sales."

Panduit's Achilles heel on element (4) is a lack of evidence on its fixed costs. Panduit alleges that its omission is overcome by other evidence. . . .

In the present case, Stahlin did dispute Panduit's accounting theory, presenting its own expert witnesses to contradict it. [T]he accuracy of the patent owner's accounting method is "a matter to be decided on the basis of testimony in the hearing before the Master." The master here found, on the basis of the evidence before him, and the district court agreed, that Panduit's accounting theory was deficient.

On the issue of Panduit's lost profits on lost sales, we affirm the district court.

Reasonable Royalty

When actual damages, e.g., lost profits, cannot be proved, the patent owner is entitled to a reasonable royalty. 35 U.S.C. § 284. A reasonable royalty is an amount "which a person, desiring to manufacture and sell a patented article, as a business proposition, would be willing to pay as a royalty and yet be able to make and sell the patented article, in the market, at a reasonable profit." *Goodyear Tire and Rubber Co. v. Overman Cushion Tire Co.*, 95 F.2d 978 at 984, 37 U.S.P.Q. 479 at 484 (6th Cir.1937).

The key element in setting a reasonable royalty after determination of validity and infringement is the necessity for return to the date when the infringement began. In the present case, that date is March 6, 1962. On that date, Panduit possessed the particular property right found to have been infringed by Stahlin. At that point Stahlin chose to continue the making and selling of the patented product.

As a result of Stahlin's election to infringe its property right, Panduit has suffered substantially. *See United States Frumentum Co. v. Lauhoff*, 216 F. 610 (6th Cir.1914). Though unable to prove the actual amount of lost profits or to establish a damage figure resulting from Stahlin's price cut, Panduit was clearly damaged by having been forced, against its will, to share sales of the patented product with Stahlin. Further, Panduit has been forced into thirteen years of expensive litigation, involving $400,000 in attorney fees, a trial, a contempt proceeding to enforce the court's injunction, a hearing on damages, and three appeals. For all this, the "damages adequate to compensate for the infringement," 35 U.S.C. § 284, have thus far been found to total $44,709.60.

Having elected to continue the manufacture and sale of the patented duct after the patent issued, and having elected to manufacture and sell a second infringing product in the face of the court's injunction, Stahlin was able to make infringing sales, as found by the master, totalling $1,788,384.

The setting of a reasonable royalty after infringement cannot be treated, as it was here, as the equivalent of ordinary royalty negotiations among truly "willing" patent owners and licensees. That view would constitute a pretense that the infringement never happened. It would also make an election to infringe a handy means for competitors to impose a "compulsory license" policy upon every patent owner.

Except for the limited risk that the patent owner, over years of litigation, might meet the heavy burden of proving the four elements required for recovery of lost profits, the infringer would have nothing to lose, and everything to gain if he could count on paying only the normal, routine royalty non-infringers might have paid. As said by this court in another context, the infringer would be in a "heads-I-win, tails-you-lose" position.

Determination of a "reasonable royalty" after infringement, like many devices in the law, rests on a legal fiction. Created in an effort to "compensate" when profits are not provable, the "reasonable royalty" device conjures a "willing" licensor and licensee, who like Ghosts of Christmas Past, are dimly seen as "negotiating" a "license." There is, of course, no actual willingness on either side, and no license to do anything, the infringer being normally enjoined, as is Stahlin, from further manufacture, use, or sale of the patented product.

In determining that a reasonable royalty rate here was 2 1/2%, the master found: (1) there were present in the market on the date of first infringement acceptable noninfringing substitutes and competing duct producers, (2) Panduit could not have maintained a high price differential in the face of competition from the substitute ducts, (3) on the hypothetical negotiation date, both Panduit and Stahlin would have been aware of the competitive state of the market, and of the probability of future price cuts, including Stahlin's. We disagree.

In the present case, the master's finding that Panduit had competitors was not erroneous, but the implication drawn therefrom was. At the time the patent issued, there were four competitors, but they were recognized as making and selling not substitutes but infringing ducts. Competition between those selling infringing ducts was admittedly fierce. Infringer Stahlin, however, cannot expect to pay a lesser royalty, as compensation for its infringement, on the ground that it was not the only infringer.

Illustrative of the absence of acceptable substitutes is Stahlin's inability to avoid infringement, even if it had ever wanted to. Having begun manufacture of the duct in 1957, Stahlin continued after the patent issued in 1962, after Panduit instituted its infringement suit in 1964, and after the district court's injunction in 1969.

At the time of the first injunction, virtually all of Stahlin's sales of electrical duct were of the infringing type. Stahlin's early-but-grudging recognition of the unique advantages of Panduit's patented duct was evidenced by an intra-company memo. Dated June 21, 1957, it was issued in the earliest stages of Stahlin's manufacture of the "Lok–Slot:"

> It seems that some of our customers have preferred a full-slotted channel; one that permits slipping the wire in place rather than threading the end through an opening. It's advantages are questionable but we always try to give our customers even more than they want. Thus, we have developed the Lok–Slot construction.

> . . . and Lok–Slot is the best design approach yet to this form of channel.

Proof of the absence of noninfringing substitutes:

> (I)nvolves some of the same evidence as that which was introduced in support of the validity of the patent. The patent owner who had proved a long-felt need for a particular invention has a lighter burden in establishing that his customers, as well as the infringer's customers, were in fact seeking to obtain the patented solution to such need or problem. The other side of the coin involves a strong showing by the infringer that although the patent may have embodied some trifling improvement which was patentable to a narrow extent, such improvement did not create any preference for the patented product rather than a noninfringing substitute. . . .

3 R. WHITE, § 9.03(2). The prior district and appellate court opinions leave no doubt that the patented product filled a waiting need and met

with commercial success due to its merits. Stahlin's own intra-company memo (PX 58), and its $1,788,384 sales of infringing ducts during the period when allegedly acceptable noninfringing substitutes are now said to have been available, leave no doubt that the patented improvement created a substantial customer preference. A product lacking the advantages of that patented can hardly be termed a substitute "acceptable" to the customer who wants those advantages. The post-hoc circumstance that Stahlin, when finally forced to obey the court's injunction, was successful in "switching" customers to a noninfringing product, does not destroy the advantage-recognition attributable to the patent over the prior 15 years. Those preferred advantages were recognized by Stahlin itself, by other infringers, by customers, by the district court, and by this court.

Hence, the 2 ½% royalty rate recommended by the master and adopted by the district court is clearly erroneous on its face, the master's recommendation having been based in large part on erroneous finding (1), that there were "acceptable" noninfringing substitutes during the relevant period.

Conclusion

Elements necessary to the determination of a reasonable royalty in the present case Panduit's actual profit margin in March 1962, and the customary profit allowed licensees in the electrical duct industry, were not determined by the master in his report and cannot be discerned from the record. They therefore must be determined on remand. On remand, the following factors must also be considered: (1) the lack of acceptable noninfringing substitutes, (2) Panduit's unvarying policy of not licensing the Walch patent, (3) the future business and attendant profit Panduit would expect to lose by licensing a competitor, and (4) that the infringed patent gave the entire marketable value to the infringed duct.

For the reasons stated, we reverse the district court's determination of a reasonable royalty, and remand the case for further proceedings consistent herewith.

Notes

1. **The Nonexclusive Standard.** Many Federal Circuit cases follow the four-part test of *Panduit*, which Professor Roberta Morris has conveniently summarized as the DAMP test. Although the court just as frequently states that the *Panduit* test is not the exclusive standard for proving lost profits, *see BIC Leisure*, reprinted below, it has been less forthcoming with other approved methodologies for doing so. The Federal Circuit has held that an award of lost profits may be based upon an inference of lost revenue is proper in markets where only two suppliers exist: the patentee and the adjudicated infringer. *See Kaufman Co. v. Lantech, Inc.*, 926 F.2d 1136, 17 U.S.P.Q.2d 1828 (Fed.Cir.1991); *Lam, Inc. v. Johns–Manville Corp.*, 718 F.2d 1056, 219 U.S.P.Q. 670 (Fed.Cir.1983).

2. **A True Coin Flip?** Is it true that an infringer has nothing to lose if it can count on paying a reasonable royalty? Has the Sixth Circuit forgotten

that an infringer might also be preliminarily enjoined, and almost certainly will be permanently enjoined, during the course of the infringement litigation? Unless the infringer can cheaply switch to a noninfringing alternative, then it would ordinarily be in far worse shape than if it had never started to infringe.

Consider also whether these statements from *Panduit* are sound patent policy. Society should encourage fair challenges to patents in order that courts may strike down invalid patents. To some degree, then, the law should support the socially useful activity some accused infringers will perform. Yet, because the *Panduit* methodology puts infringers in a worse position than they would have been had they paid royalties to the patentee, competitors are actually discouraged from challenging patents they may believe are invalid. For an alternative approach from the House of Lords, see *General Tire and Rubber Co. v. Firestone Tyre and Rubber Co. Ltd.*, [1975] 2 All E. R. 173.

3. Lost Profits vs. Reasonable Royalty. Patent holders typically seek lost profits damages under the *Panduit* test, otherwise hoping for a reasonable royalty as a lesser alternative. Does this relationship always hold? Can you construct a situation where the deal struck at a hypothetical negotiation would ultimately exceed the profits the patentee would have realized? Consider a market where demand is very elastic (a small price change produces a big shift in the quantity sold) and the infringer actually is more efficient and has a distinct cost advantage over the patentee's production. In that circumstance, the infringer can sell greater quantities, due to efficiencies, at a lower price. The patentee in that circumstance may actually profit more by taking a royalty.

4. Deterrence vs. Compensation as a Damages Model. *Panduit* follows a deterrence model for damages. The language of *Panduit* evinces a primary desire to punish infringement and protect property owners. The following opinion, the leading Federal Circuit opinion on monetary relief for patent infringement, shifts the emphasis for monetary recovery towards a compensation model.

RITE-HITE CORP. v. KELLEY CO.

United States Court of Appeals, Federal Circuit, 1995.
56 F.3d 1538, 35 U.S.P.Q.2d 1065,
cert. denied, 516 U.S. 867 (1995).

Before ARCHER, CHIEF JUDGE, RICH, CIRCUIT JUDGE, SMITH, SENIOR CIRCUIT JUDGE and NIES, NEWMAN, MAYER, MICHEL, PLAGER, LOURIE, CLEVENGER, RADER, and SCHALL, CIRCUIT JUDGES.

LOURIE, CIRCUIT JUDGE.

Kelley Company appeals from a decision of the United States District Court for the Eastern District of Wisconsin, awarding damages for the infringement of U.S. Patent 4,373,847, owned by Rite–Hite Corporation. *Rite–Hite Corp. v. Kelley Co.*, 774 F.Supp. 1514, 21 U.S.P.Q.2d 1801 (E.D.Wis.1991). The district court determined, inter alia, that Rite–Hite was entitled to lost profits for lost sales of its devices that were in direct competition with the infringing devices, but which themselves were not covered by the patent in suit. The appeal has been taken in banc to determine whether such damages are legally compensable under 35 U.S.C. § 284. We affirm in part, vacate in part, and remand.

Background

On March 22, 1983, Rite–Hite sued Kelley, alleging that Kelley's "Truk Stop" vehicle restraint infringed Rite–Hite's U.S. Patent 4,373,-847 ("the '847 patent"). The '847 patent, issued February 15, 1983, is directed to a device for securing a vehicle to a loading dock to prevent the vehicle from separating from the dock during loading or unloading. Any such separation would create a gap between the vehicle and dock and create a danger for a forklift operator.

Rite–Hite distributed all its products through its wholly-owned and operated sales organizations and through independent sales organizations (ISOs). During the period of infringement, the Rite–Hite sales organizations accounted for approximately 30 percent of the retail dollar sales of Rite–Hite products, and the ISOs accounted for the remaining 70 percent. Rite–Hite sued for its lost profits at the wholesale level and for the lost retail profits of its own sales organizations.

The district court bifurcated the liability and damage phases of the trial and, on March 5, 1986, held the '847 patent to be not invalid and to be infringed by the manufacture, use, and sale of Kelley's Truk Stop device. The court enjoined further infringement. The judgment of liability was affirmed by this court.

On remand, the damage issues were tried to the court. Rite–Hite sought damages calculated as lost profits for two types of vehicle restraints that it made and sold: the "Manual Dok–Lok" model 55 (MDL–55), which incorporated the invention covered by the '847 patent, and the "Automatic Dok–Lok" model 100 (ADL–100), which was not covered by the patent in suit. The ADL–100 was the first vehicle restraint Rite–Hite put on the market and it was covered by one or more patents other than the patent in suit. The Kelley Truk Stop restraint was designed to compete primarily with Rite–Hite's ADL—100. Both employed an electric motor and functioned automatically, and each sold for $1,000–$1,500 at the wholesale level, in contrast to the MDL–55, which sold for one-third to one-half the price of the motorized devices. Rite–Hite does not assert that Kelley's Truk Stop restraint infringed the patents covering the ADL–100.

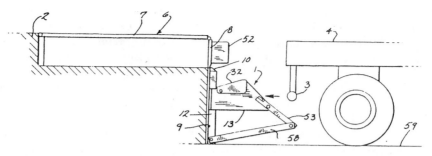

Of the 3,825 infringing Truk Stop devices sold by Kelley, the district court found that, "but for" Kelley's infringement, Rite–Hite would have made 80 more sales of its MDL–55; 3,243 more sales of its ADL–100; and 1,692 more sales of dock levelers, a bridging platform sold with the restraints and used to bridge the edges of a vehicle and dock. The court awarded Rite–Hite as a manufacturer the wholesale profits that it lost on lost sales of the ADL–100 restraints, MDL–55 restraints, and restraint-leveler packages. It also awarded to Rite–Hite as a retailer . . . reasonable royalty damages on lost ADL–100, MDL–55, and restraint-leveler sales caused by Kelley's infringing sales. Finally, prejudgment interest, calculated without compounding, was awarded. Kelley's infringement was found to be not willful.

On appeal, Kelley contends that the district court erred as a matter of law in its determination of damages. Kelley does not contest the award of damages for lost sales of the MDL–55 restraints; however, Kelley argues that the patent statute does not provide for damages based on Rite–Hite's lost profits on ADL–100 restraints because the ADL–100s are not covered by the patent in suit; lost profits on unpatented dock levelers are not attributable to demand for the '847 invention and, therefore, are not recoverable losses; and the court erred in calculating a reasonable royalty based as a percentage of ADL–100 and dock leveler profits. Rite–Hite and the ISOs challenge the district court's refusal to award lost retail profits and its award of prejudgment interest at a simple, rather than a compound, rate.

We affirm the damage award with respect to Rite–Hite's lost profits as a manufacturer on its ADL–100 restraint sales, affirm the court's computation of a reasonable royalty rate, [and] vacate the damage award based on the dock levelers.

DISCUSSION

I. Lost Profits on the ADL–100 Restraints

The district court's decision to award lost profits damages pursuant to 35 U.S.C. § 284 turned primarily upon the quality of Rite–Hite's proof of actual lost profits. The court found that, "but for" Kelley's infringing Truk Stop competition, Rite–Hite would have sold 3,243 additional ADL–100 restraints and 80 additional MDL–55 restraints. The court reasoned that awarding lost profits fulfilled the patent statute's goal of affording complete compensation for infringement and compensated Rite–Hite for the ADL–100 sales that Kelley "anticipated taking from Rite–Hite when it marketed the Truk Stop against the ADL–100." The court stated, "[t]he rule applied here therefore does not extend Rite–Hite's patent rights excessively, because Kelley could reasonably have foreseen that its infringement of the '847 patent would make it liable for lost ADL–100 sales in addition to lost MDL–55 sales." The court further reasoned that its decision would avoid what it referred to as the "whip-saw" problem, whereby an infringer could avoid paying lost profits damages altogether by developing a device using a first patented technology to compete with a device that uses a second patented technology and developing a device using the second patented technology to compete with a device that uses the first patented technology.

Kelley maintains that Rite–Hite's lost sales of the ADL–100 re-straints do not constitute an injury that is legally compensable by means of lost profits. It has uniformly been the law, Kelley argues, that to recover damages in the form of lost profits a patentee must prove that, "but for" the infringement, it would have sold a product covered by the patent in suit to the customers who bought from the infringer. Under the circumstances of this case, in Kelley's view, the patent statute provides only for damages calculated as a reasonable royalty. Rite–Hite, on the other hand, argues that the only restriction on an award of actual lost profits damages for patent infringement is proof of causation-in-fact. A patentee, in its view, is entitled to all the profits it would have made on any of its products "but for" the infringement. Each party argues that a judgment in favor of the other would frustrate the purposes of the patent statute. Whether the lost profits at issue are legally compensable is a question of law, which we review de novo.

Our analysis of this question necessarily begins with the patent statute. See General Motors Corp. v. Devex Corp., 461 U.S. 648, 653–54 (1983). Implementing the constitutional power under Article I, section 8, to secure to inventors the exclusive right to their discoveries, Congress has provided in 35 U.S.C. § 284 as follows: Upon finding for the claimant the court shall award the claimant damages adequate to compensate for the infringement, but in no event less than a reasonable royalty for the use made of the invention by the infringer, together with interest and costs as fixed by the court. 35 U.S.C. § 284 (1988). The statute thus mandates that a claimant receive damages "adequate" to compensate for infringement. Section 284 further instructs that a damage award shall be "in no event less than a reasonable royalty"; the purpose of this alternative is not to direct the form of compensation, but to set a floor below which damage awards may not fall. Thus, the language of the statute is expansive rather than limiting. It affirmatively states that damages must be adequate, while providing only a lower limit and no other limitation.

The Supreme Court spoke to the question of patent damages in General Motors, stating that, in enacting § 284, Congress sought to "ensure that the patent owner would in fact receive full compensation for 'any damages' [the patentee] suffered as a result of the infringement." *General Motors*, 461 U.S. at 654; *see also* H.R.Rep. No. 1587, 79th Cong., 2d Sess., 1 (1946) (the Bill was intended to allow recovery of "any damages the complainant can prove"); S.Rep. No. 1503, 79th Cong., 2d Sess., 2 (1946), (same). Thus, while the statutory text states tersely that the patentee receive "adequate" damages, the Supreme Court has interpreted this to mean that "adequate" damages should approximate those damages that will fully compensate the patentee for infringement. Further, the Court has cautioned against imposing limitations on patent infringement damages, stating: "When Congress wished to limit an element of recovery in a patent infringement action, it said so explicitly." *General Motors*, 461 U.S. at 653.

In *Aro Mfg. Co. v. Convertible Top Replacement Co.*, 377 U.S. 476 (1964), the Court discussed the statutory standard for measuring patent infringement damages, explaining: The question to be asked in determining damages is "how much had the Patent Holder and Licensee suffered by the infringement. And that question [is] primarily: had the Infringer not infringed, what would the Patentee Holder–Licensee have made?" 377 U.S. at 507. This surely states a "but for" test. In accordance with the Court's guidance, we have held that the general rule for determining actual damages to a patentee that is itself producing the patented item is to determine the sales and profits lost to the patentee because of the infringement. To recover lost profits damages, the patentee must show a reasonable probability that, "but for" the infringement, it would have made the sales that were made by the infringer.

Panduit Corp. v. Stahlin Bros. Fibre Works, Inc., 575 F.2d 1152, 197 U.S.P.Q. 726 (6th Cir.1978), articulated a four-factor test that has since been accepted as a useful, but non-exclusive, way for a patentee to prove entitlement to lost profits damages. The *Panduit* test requires that a patentee establish: (1) demand for the patented product; (2) absence of acceptable non-infringing substitutes; (3) manufacturing and marketing capability to exploit the demand; and (4) the amount of the profit it would have made. A showing under *Panduit* permits a court to reasonably infer that the lost profits claimed were in fact caused by the infringing sales, thus establishing a patentee's prima facie case with respect to "but for" causation. A patentee need not negate every possibility that the purchaser might not have purchased a product other than its own, absent the infringement. The patentee need only show that there was a reasonable probability that the sales would have been made "but for" the infringement. When the patentee establishes the reasonableness of this inference, *e.g.*, by satisfying the *Panduit* test, it has sustained the burden of proving entitlement to lost profits due to the infringing sales. The burden then shifts to the infringer to show that the inference is unreasonable for some or all of the lost sales.

Applying *Panduit*, the district court found that Rite–Hite had established "but for" causation. In the court's view, this was sufficient to prove entitlement to lost profits damages on the ADL–100. Kelley does not challenge that Rite–Hite meets the *Panduit* test and therefore has proven "but for" causation; rather, Kelley argues that damages for the ADL–100, even if in fact caused by the infringement, are not legally compensable because the ADL–100 is not covered by the patent in suit.

Preliminarily, we wish to affirm that the "test" for compensability of damages under § 284 is not solely a "but for" test in the sense that an infringer must compensate a patentee for any and all damages that proceed from the act of patent infringement. Notwithstanding the broad language of § 284, judicial relief cannot redress every conceivable harm that can be traced to an alleged wrongdoing. For example, remote consequences, such as a heart attack of the inventor or loss in value of shares of common stock of a patentee corporation caused indirectly by infringement are not compensable. Thus, along with establishing that a particular injury suffered by a patentee is a "but for" consequence of infringement, there may also be a background question whether the asserted injury is of the type for which the patentee may be compensated.

Judicial limitations on damages, either for certain classes of plaintiffs or for certain types of injuries have been imposed in terms of "proximate cause" or "foreseeability." Such labels have been judicial tools used to limit legal responsibility for the consequences of one's conduct that are too remote to justify compensation. The general principles expressed in the common law tell us that the question of legal compensability is one "to be determined on the facts of each case upon mixed considerations of logic, common sense, justice, policy and precedent."

We believe that under § 284 of the patent statute, the balance between full compensation, which is the meaning that the Supreme Court has attributed to the statute, and the reasonable limits of liability encompassed by general principles of law can best be viewed in terms of reasonable, objective foreseeability. If a particular injury was or should have been reasonably foreseeable by an infringing competitor in the relevant market, broadly defined, that injury is generally compensable absent a persuasive reason to the contrary. Here, the court determined that Rite–Hite's lost sales of the ADL–100, a product that directly competed with the infringing product, were reasonably foreseeable. We agree with that conclusion. Being responsible for lost sales of a competitive product is surely foreseeable; such losses constitute the full compensation set forth by Congress, as interpreted by the Supreme Court, while staying well within the traditional meaning of proximate cause. Such lost sales should therefore clearly be compensable.

Recovery for lost sales of a device not covered by the patent in suit is not of course expressly provided for by the patent statute. Express language is not required, however. Statutes speak in general terms rather than specifically expressing every detail. Under the patent statute, damages should be awarded "where necessary to afford the plaintiff full compensation for the infringement." *General Motors*, 461 U.S. at

654. Thus, to refuse to award reasonably foreseeable damages necessary to make Rite–Hite whole would be inconsistent with the meaning of § 284.

Kelley asserts that to allow recovery for the ADL–100 would contravene the policy reason for which patents are granted: "[T]o promote the progress of . . . the useful arts." U.S. CONST., art. I, § 8, cl. 8. Because an inventor is only entitled to exclusivity to the extent he or she has invented and disclosed a novel, nonobvious, and useful device, Kelley argues, a patent may never be used to restrict competition in the sale of products not covered by the patent in suit. In support, Kelley cites antitrust case law condemning the use of a patent as a means to obtain a "monopoly" on unpatented material.

These cases are inapposite to the issue raised here. The present case does not involve expanding the limits of the patent grant in violation of the antitrust laws; it simply asks, once infringement of a valid patent is found, what compensable injuries result from that infringement, i.e., how may the patentee be made whole. Rite–Hite is not attempting to exclude its competitors from making, using, or selling a product not within the scope of its patent. The Truk Stop restraint was found to infringe the '847 patent, and Rite–Hite is simply seeking adequate compensation for that infringement; this is not an antitrust issue. Allowing compensation for such damage will "promote the Progress of . . . the useful Arts" by providing a stimulus to the development of new products and industries.

Kelley further asserts that, as a policy matter, inventors should be encouraged by the law to practice their inventions. This is not a meaningful or persuasive argument, at least in this context. A patent is granted in exchange for a patentee's disclosure of an invention, not for the patentee's use of the invention. There is no requirement in this country that a patentee make, use, or sell its patented invention. If a patentee's failure to practice a patented invention frustrates an important public need for the invention, a court need not enjoin infringement of the patent. Accordingly, courts have in rare instances exercised their discretion to deny injunctive relief in order to protect the public interest. Whether a patentee sells its patented invention is not crucial in determining lost profits damages. Normally, if the patentee is not selling a product, by definition there can be no lost profits. However, in this case, Rite–Hite did sell its own patented products, the MDL–55 and the ADL–100 restraints.

Kelley next argues that to award lost profits damages on Rite–Hite's ADL–100s would be contrary to precedent. Citing *Panduit*, Kelley argues that case law regarding lost profits uniformly requires that "the intrinsic value of the patent in suit is the only proper basis for a lost profits award." Kelley argues that each prong of the *Panduit* test focuses on the patented invention; thus, Kelley asserts, Rite–Hite cannot obtain damages consisting of lost profits on a product that is not the patented invention.

Generally, the *Panduit* test has been applied when a patentee is seeking lost profits for a device covered by the patent in suit. However, *Panduit* is not the sine qua non for proving "but for" causation. If there are other ways to show that the infringement in fact caused the patentee's lost profits, there is no reason why another test should not be acceptable. Moreover, other fact situations may require different means of evaluation, and failure to meet the *Panduit* test does not *ipso facto* disqualify a loss from being compensable.

In any event, the only *Panduit* factor that arguably was not met in the present fact situation is the second one, absence of acceptable non-infringing substitutes. Establishment of this factor tends to prove that the patentee would not have lost the sales to a non-infringing third party rather than to the infringer. That, however, goes only to the question of proof. Here, the only substitute for the patented device was the ADL–100, another of the patentee's devices. Such a substitute was not an "acceptable, non-infringing substitute" within the meaning of *Panduit* because, being patented by Rite–Hite, it was not available to customers except from Rite–Hite. Rite–Hite therefore would not have lost the sales to a third party. The second Panduit factor thus has been met. If, on the other hand, the ADL–100 had not been patented and was found to be an acceptable substitute, that would have been a different story, and Rite–Hite would have had to prove that its customers would not have obtained the ADL–100 from a third party in order to prove the second factor of *Panduit*.

Kelley's conclusion that the lost sales must be of the patented invention thus is not supported. Kelley's concern that lost profits must relate to the "intrinsic value of the patent" is subsumed in the "but for" analysis; if the patent infringement had nothing to do with the lost sales, "but for" causation would not have been proven. However, "but for" causation is conceded here. The motive, or motivation, for the infringement is irrelevant if it is proved that the infringement in fact caused the loss. We see no basis for Kelley's conclusion that the lost sales must be of products covered by the infringed patent.

Kelley has thus not provided, nor do we find, any justification in the statute, precedent, policy, or logic to limit the compensability of lost sales of a patentee's device that directly competes with the infringing device if it is proven that those lost sales were caused in fact by the infringement. Such lost sales are reasonably foreseeable and the award of damages is necessary to provide adequate compensation for infringement under 35 U.S.C. § 284. Thus, Rite–Hite's ADL–100 lost sales are legally compensable and we affirm the award of lost profits on the 3,283 sales lost to Rite–Hite's wholesale business in ADL–100 restraints.

II. *Damages on the Dock Levelers*

Based on the "entire market value rule," the district court awarded lost profits on 1,692 dock levelers that it found Rite–Hite would have sold with the ADL–100 and MDL–55 restraints. Kelley argues that this award must be set aside because Rite–Hite failed to establish that the dock levelers were eligible to be included in the damage computation under the entire market value rule. We agree.

When a patentee seeks damages on unpatented components sold with a patented apparatus, courts have applied a formulation known as the "entire market value rule" to determine whether such components should be included in the damage computation, whether for reasonable royalty purposes, or for lost profits purposes. Early cases invoking the entire market value rule required that for a patentee owning an "improvement patent" to recover damages calculated on sales of a larger machine incorporating that improvement, the patentee was required to show that the entire value of the whole machine, as a marketable article, was "properly and legally attributable" to the patented feature. Subsequently, our predecessor court held that damages for component parts used with a patented apparatus were recoverable under the entire market value rule if the patented apparatus "was of such paramount importance that it substantially created the value of the component parts." We have held that the entire market value rule permits recovery of damages based on the value of a patentee's entire apparatus containing several features when the patent-related feature is the "basis for customer demand."

The entire market value rule has typically been applied to include in the compensation base unpatented components of a device when the unpatented and patented components are physically part of the same machine. The rule has been extended to allow inclusion of physically separate unpatented components normally sold with the patented components. However, in such cases, the unpatented and patented components together were considered to be components of a single assembly or parts of a complete machine, or they together constituted a functional unit.

In [*Paper Converting Machine Co. v. Magna–Graphics Corp.*, 745 F.2d 11, 223 U.S.P.Q. 591 (Fed.Cir.1984)], this court articulated the entire market value rule in terms of the objectively reasonable probability that a patentee would have made the relevant sales. Furthermore, we may have appeared to expand the rule when we emphasized the financial and marketing dependence of the unpatented component on the patented component. In Paper Converting, however, the rule was applied to allow recovery of profits on the unpatented components only because all the components together were considered to be parts of a single assembly. The references to "financial and marketing dependence" and "reasonable probability" were made in the context of the facts of the case and did not separate the rule from its traditional moorings.

Specifically, recovery was sought for the lost profits on sales of an entire machine for the high speed manufacture of paper rolls comprising several physically separate components, only one of which incorporated the invention. The machine was comprised of the patented "rewinder" component and several auxiliary components, including an "unwind stand" that supported a large roll of supply paper to the rewinder, a "core loader" that supplied paperboard cores to the rewinder, an "embosser" that embossed the paper and provided a special textured surface, and a "tail sealer" that sealed the paper's trailing end to the finished roll. Although we noted that the auxiliary components had "separate usage" in that they each separately performed a part of an entire rewinding operation, the components together constituted one functional unit, including the patented component, to produce rolls of paper. The auxiliary components derived their market value from the patented rewinder because they had no useful purpose independent of the patented rewinder. Similarly, our subsequent cases have applied the entire market value rule only in situations in which the patented and unpatented components were analogous to a single functioning unit.

Thus, the facts of past cases clearly imply a limitation on damages, when recovery is sought on sales of unpatented components sold with patented components, to the effect that the unpatented components must function together with the patented component in some manner so as to produce a desired end product or result. All the components together must be analogous to components of a single assembly or be parts of a complete machine, or they must constitute a functional unit. Our precedent has not extended liability to include items that have essentially no functional relationship to the patented invention and that may have been sold with an infringing device only as a matter of convenience or business advantage. We are not persuaded that we should extend that liability. Damages on such items would constitute more than what is "adequate to compensate for the infringement."

The facts of this case do not meet this requirement. The dock levelers operated to bridge the gap between a loading dock and a truck. The patented vehicle restraint operated to secure the rear of the truck to the loading dock. Although the two devices may have been used together, they did not function together to achieve one result and each could effectively have been used independently of each other. The parties had established positions in marketing dock levelers long prior to developing the vehicle restraints. Rite–Hite and Kelley were pioneers in that industry and for many years were primary competitors. Although following Rite–Hite's introduction of its restraints onto the market, customers frequently solicited package bids for the simultaneous installation of restraints and dock levelers, they did so because such bids facilitated contracting and construction scheduling, and because both Rite–Hite and Kelley encouraged this linkage by offering combination discounts. The dock levelers were thus sold by Kelley with the restraints only for marketing reasons, not because they essentially functioned together. We distinguish our conclusion to permit damages based on lost sales of the unpatented (not covered by the patent in suit) ADL–100 devices, but not on lost sales of the unpatented dock levelers, by emphasizing that the Kelley Truk Stops were devices competitive with the ADL–100s, whereas the dock levelers were merely items sold together with the restraints for convenience and business advantage. It is a clear purpose of the patent law to redress competitive damages resulting from infringement of the patent, but there is no basis for extending that recovery to include damages for items that are neither competitive with nor function with the patented invention. Promotion of the useful arts, see U.S. CONST., art. I, § 8, cl. 8, requires one, but not the other. These facts do not establish the functional relationship necessary to justify recovery under the entire market value rule. Therefore, the district court erred as a matter of law in including them within the compensation base. Accordingly, we vacate the court's award of damages based on the dock leveler sales.

NIES, CIRCUIT JUDGE, with whom ARCHER, CHIEF JUDGE, SMITH, SENIOR CIRCUIT JUDGE, and MAYER, CIRCUIT JUDGE join, dissenting-in-part.

The majority uses the provision in 35 U.S.C. § 284 for "damages" as a tool to expand the property rights granted by a patent. I dissent.

No one disputes that Rite–Hite is entitled to "full compensation for any damages suffered as a result of the infringement." *General Motors Corp. v. Devex Corp.*, 461 U.S. 648, 653–54, 103 S.Ct. 2058, 2062, 76 L.Ed.2d 211 (1983). "Damages," however, is a word of art. "Damages in a legal sense means the compensation which the law will award for an injury done." Recovery in Patent Infringement Suits: Hearings on H.R. 5231 [later H.R. 5311] Before the Committee on Patents, 79th Cong., 2nd Sess. 9 (1946) (statement of Conder C. Henry, Asst. Comm'r of Patents) (hereinafter "House Hearings"). Thus, the question is, "What are the injuries for which full compensation must be paid?".

The majority divorces "actual damages" from injury to patent rights. The majority holds that a patentee is entitled to recover its lost profits caused by the infringer's competition with the patentee's business in ADL-restraints, products not incorporating the invention of the patent in suit but assertedly protected by other unlitigated patents. Indeed, the majority states a broader rule for the award of lost profits on any goods of the patentee with which the infringing device competes, even products in the public domain.

I would hold that the diversion of ADL–100 sales is not an injury to patentee's property rights granted by the '847 patent. To constitute legal injury for which lost profits may be awarded, the infringer must interfere with the patentee's property right to an exclusive market in goods embodying the invention of the patent in suit. The patentee's property rights do not extend to its market in other goods unprotected by the litigated patent. Rite–Hite was compensated for the lost profits for 80 sales associated with the MDL–55, the only product it sells embodying the '847 invention. That is the totality of any possible entitlement to lost profits. Under 35 U.S.C. § 284, therefore, Rite–Hite is entitled to "damages" calculated as a reasonable royalty on the remainder of Kelley's infringing restraints.

PAULINE NEWMAN, CIRCUIT JUDGE, with whom CIRCUIT JUDGE RADER joins, concurring in part and dissenting in part.

The court today takes an important step toward preserving damages as an effective remedy for patent infringement. Patent infringement is a commercial tort, and the remedy should compensate for the actual financial injury that was caused by the tort. Thus I concur in the majority's result with respect to entitlement to damages for lost sales of the ADL–100.

Yet the court draws a new bright line, adverse to patentees and the businesses built on patents, declining to make the injured claimants whole. The majority now restricts en banc the patentee's previously existing, already limited right to prove damages for lost sales of collateral items?the so-called "convoyed" sales. Such remedy is now eliminated entirely unless the convoyed item is "functionally" inseparable from the patented item. The court thus propounds a legally ambivalent and economically unsound policy, authorizing damages for the lost sales of the ADL–100 but not those dock levelers that were required to be bid and sold as a package with the MDL–55 and the ADL–100.

The district court, in contrast, took a straightforward approach to the damages determination. The district court awarded compensatory damages for (1) Rite–Hite's lost sales of the MDL–55 and the ADL–100 models of truck restraint, recognizing the commercial and competitive relationships of these models and the infringing device; [and] (2) Rite–Hite's lost sales of 1,692 dock levelers that were bid and sold in packages with the truck restraints, recognizing that the dock leveler business was a significant factor in Kelley's infringing activity.

The majority affirms only the first of these areas of pecuniary injury ... I know of no law or policy served by eliminating recovery of actual damages when patents are involved. In holding that those injured by the infringement shall not be made whole, the value of the patent property is diminished. The majority's half-a-loaf award, wherein the patentee and the other plaintiffs are denied recovery of a significant portion or all of their proven damages, is an important policy decision.

Notes

1. The Dissenters. The complete dissenting opinions of Judges Nies and Newman, omitted here due to space limitations, are well worth reading in full. The opinion of Judge Nies was primarily directed towards the award of lost profits due to trade in goods not embodying the infringed patent. According to Judge Nies, the majority erred because "[p]atent 'damages' are limited to legal injury to property rights created by the patent, not merely causation in fact." 56 F.3d at 1557. In addition to mustering considerable case law supporting this position, Judge Nies offered the following policy argument, 56 F.3d at 1575:

It cannot be disputed that Congress intended that the patent grant provide an incentive to make investments in patented products during the patent term. If a patentee is rewarded with lost profits on its established products, the incentive is dulled if not destroyed. Why make the investment to produce and market a new drug if the patent on the new discovery not only protects the *status quo* in the market but also provides lost profits for the old?

In contrast, Judge Newman's dissenting opinion largely considered the issue of convoyed sales. In measuring lost profits, the *Rite–Hite* majority sought proof of damages "reasonably foreseeable . . . in the relevant market." Yet when it considered convoyed sales, the majority abandoned the "reasonable foreseeablity" test and adopted a test based on whether "unpatented components must function together with the patented components." Judge Newman advocated a consistent approach. Thus, under her view, foreseeable damage in the relevant market ought to have applied uniformly to the convoyed sales question as well. The United Kingdom has followed the approach advocated by Judge Newman. *Gerber Garment Tech. v. Lectra Sys.*, [1995] R.P.C. 383 (Pat. Ct.), aff'd [1997] R.P.C. 443 (CA).

2. *Rite–Hite* versus *Panduit*. Does *Rite–Hite* remain true to the *Panduit* test regarding acceptable noninfringing substitutes? After all, wouldn't the ADL–100 serve as an acceptable noninfringing substitute to the Truk'stop sales?

3. Competing Patents. Professor Adelman offered the following observation on *Rite–Hite*:

> Essentially, in *Rite–Hite*, we may view the fact pattern as one where Rite–Hite owns two competing patents. Thus, the value of each of them is dependent on the fact that the other is also owned by Rite–Hite. Had one been owned by a third party, the value of each patent would be substantially less. Indeed, each patent could be essentially valueless as Rite–Hite and the owner of the other patent could compete away their total value. As the '847 patent is more valuable than it otherwise would be because it is owned by Rite–Hite, and as Rite–Hite is suppressing its use in the automatic truck stop field, there is a strong patent policy argument against awarding Rite–Hite the profits lost to it owing to sales of a product using the '847 invention in the automatic truck stop area, an area where Rite–Hite deliberately chose not to exploit.

4 MARTIN J. ADELMAN, PATENT LAW PERSPECTIVES § 5.2[2] at n. 119 (2d ed. 1995). Do you agree? Other criticism of the decision may be found in Lisa C. Childs, Note, 27 LOY. U. CHI. L.J. 665 (1996); Robert J. Cox, *But How Far?* Rite–Hite Corp. v. Kelley Co.'s *Expansion of the Scope of Patent Damages*, 3 J. INTELL. PROP. L. 327 (1996).

4. A Companion Case. In *King Instruments Corp. v. Perego*, 65 F.3d 941, 36 U.S.P.Q.2d 1129 (Fed.Cir.1995), a Federal Circuit panel expanded upon the reasoning in *Rite–Hite*. This case involved two competitors in the market for automated cassette-loading machines. King, the plaintiff in an infringement action, did not commercialize its patented splicing technology. Tapematic, the adjudicated infringer, did, although the device it marketed was otherwise quite different from King's commercial embodiment. The court affirmed the award of lost profits damages based upon forty-nine sales completed by Tapematic. Of course, unlike King Instruments, Inc., the Rite–Hite Corporation did embody its patent, in that case in the MDL–100 restraint. Further, given the small role of the infringing technology in the marketed machine, the standard of "but for" causation seemed rather lower here than in *Rite–Hite*. Another Federal Circuit applying the reasoning of

King Instruments is *Hebert v. Lisle Corp.*, 99 F.3d 1109, 40 U.S.P.Q.2d 1611 (Fed.Cir.1996).

King Instruments is also notable for its discussion of two other significant points in favor of Judge Lourie's holding on the award of profits based on lost trade in competitive goods. First, the panel suggested that a contrary rule would require a patentee to prove that it embodied its own invention in order to obtain lost profits damages. According to the *King Instruments* panel, the creation of a new category of "reverse infringement" would create needless complexity in patent infringement proceedings. Second, the panel indicated that a commercialization requirement "would force patent owners to accept a reasonable royalty in cases where a reasonable royalty is inadequate compensation. Infringers would in effect receive the windfall of a retroactive compulsory license from the patent owner." 65 F.3d at 951, 36 U.S.P.Q.2d at 1136. Persuasive as the first point may be, does a reasonable royalty truly amount to a compulsory license given the availability of equitable relief? For more on the contrast between *Rite–Hite* and *King Instruments, see* Brent Rabowsky, Note, 70 S. Cal. L. Rev. 281, 318?31 (1996).

§ 17.2[b]   The Market Share Rule

BIC LEISURE PRODUCTS, INC. v. WINDSURFING INTERNATIONAL, INC.

United States Court of Appeals, Federal Circuit, 1993.
1 F.3d 1214, 27 U.S.P.Q.2d 1671.

Before Nies, Chief Judge, Smith, Senior Circuit Judge, and Rader, Circuit Judge.

Rader, Circuit Judge.

The United States District Court for the Southern District of New York awarded Windsurfing International, Inc. lost profits for BIC Leisure Products, Inc.'s infringement of U.S. Reissue Patent No. 31,167. The court refused to award lost profits for alleged price erosion.

Assuming BIC had not been in the market, Windsurfing did not show that BIC's customers would have purchased sailboards from Windsurfing and other manufacturers in proportion to their market shares. Therefore, this court reverses the award of lost profits based upon Windsurfing's market share. Otherwise, this court affirms.

Background

BIC infringed Windsurfing's Reissue Patent No. 31,167, which covers sailboards. Windsurfing seeks damages from BIC for the period from March 8, 1983 (the reissue date of Windsurfing's patent) to September 30, 1985 (the date the district court enjoined BIC from further infringement).

Windsurfing primarily manufactured and marketed sailboards embodying its patented invention for the "One–Design Class." The One–Design Class refers to a uniform competition class as defined by a sailboarding association. A sailboarding association sponsors regattas in which sailboarders compete against each other on boards of uniform weight and shape. Most of Windsurfing's sailboards fit within the weight and shape requirements for the One–Design competition class.

One–Design sailboards lost favor with most sailboarders, however, with the advent of faster, more maneuverable, and more versatile "funboards" and "wave boards." These newer boards had a lighter hull design. Despite the rising popularity of these newer boards in the early 1980s, Windsurfing decided to continue to concentrate on its One–Design boards.

Windsurfing licensed its patented technology extensively. Windsurfing licensed at least twelve companies in Europe. At least one of the European licensees granted sublicenses to other European manufacturers. Windsurfing also granted licenses in the United States. Eventually, Windsurfing licensed twelve companies in the United States. With few exceptions, Windsurfing charged 7.5% of net sales for the U.S. licenses. All of the U.S. licensees, as well as some of the European licensees, competed against Windsurfing in the United States.

Windsurfing manufactured its boards using a rotomolding process. During the early 1980s, many of Windsurfing's competitors reduced their production costs with a new blowmolding process. Instead of switching to the more efficient blowmolding process, Windsurfing invested one million dollars in an unsuccessful attempt to improve its rotomolding process. Windsurfing controlled 29.2% of the sailboard market in 1983, 25.6% in 1984, and 13.6% in 1985.

BIC began selling sailboards in 1981. BIC manufactured with the more efficient blowmolding process. BIC did not sell sailboards with the One Design hull form. Rather, BIC's sailboards differed from Windsurfing's products. BIC instead sold boards at the lower end of the market's price spectrum, reflecting its decision to target the entry level segment of the sailboard market.

In comparison, Windsurfing priced its sailboards at the upper end of the sailboard price spectrum. During the years covered by the damages period, U.S. sailboard dealers charged the following average prices:

1983		**1984**		**1985**	
Marker	837	Brockhaus	753	Mistral	804
Brockhaus	753	Mistral	741	Marker	774
Mistral	750	Marker	674	Brockhaus	750
Windsurfing	670	SAN/Romney	623	SAN	623
SAN/Romney	643	Windsurfing	589	Schutz	575
Alpha	574	Schutz	575	Windsurfing	571
Wayler	550	HiFly	527	HiFly	570
HiFly	518	Wayler	500	Wayler	500
SAN/Schaeffer	441	Alpha	450	O'Brien	477
O'Brien	436	O'Brien	412	Alpha	450
BIC	407	SAN/Schaeffer	388	AMF Inc.	380
AMF Inc.	377	AMF Inc.	384	BIC	312

Ten Cate	366	BIC	335	Ten Cate	253
AMF Mares	244	Ten Cate	299	AMF Mares	244
		AMF Mares	234		

The Patent and Trademark Office reissued Windsurfing's patent on March 8, 1983. On that date, BIC had 5,245 sailboards in its inventory and another 5,625 on order. BIC confirmed its purchase of the boards on order with a February 10, 1983 telex.

The district court applied the Panduit test to determine whether Windsurfing lost profits. The district court required Windsurfing to show (1) a demand for the patented product, (2) the absence of acceptable noninfringing substitutes, (3) its capacity to exploit the demand, and (4) the profits lost due to the infringement. The district court modified the Panduit test by presuming that Windsurfing would have captured a share of BIC's sales in proportion to Windsurfing's share of the sailboard market. Relying on *State Industries, Inc. v. Mor–Flo Industries, Inc.*, 883 F.2d 1573, 12 U.S.P.Q.2d 1026 (Fed.Cir.1989), *cert. denied*, 493 U.S. 1022 (1990), the district court awarded Windsurfing lost profits based upon its pro rata percentage of BIC's sales for each year of the damages period. In addition, the district court awarded Windsurfing lost royalties for the boards its licensees would have sold absent BIC's infringement. The court calculated the amount of lost royalties based upon a weighted average price of the boards sold by the licensees.

DISCUSSION

Lost Profits

The finding of the amount of damages for patent infringement is a question of fact on which the patent owner bears the burden of proof. Where the district court fixes the amount of damages, this court reviews that finding under the clearly erroneous standard of Federal Rule of Civil Procedure 52(a).

To recover lost profits as opposed to royalties, a patent owner must prove a causal relation between the infringement and its loss of profits. The patent owner must show that "but for" the infringement, it would have made the infringer's sales. An award of lost profits may not be speculative. Rather the patent owner must show a reasonable probability that, absent the infringement, it would have made the infringer's sales.

The district court clearly erred by failing to apply the "but for" test before awarding lost profits. The record in this case does not evince a reasonable probability that Windsurfing would have made its pro rata share of BIC's sales had BIC not been in the market. During the period in question, at least fourteen competitors vied for sales in the sailboard market with prices ranging from $234 to $837. BIC's boards sold for $312 to $407; Windsurfing's boards sold for $571 to $670—a difference of over $250 or about 60–80% above BIC's selling range. Because Windsurfing concentrated on the One Design class hull form and BIC did not, Windsurfing's boards differed fundamentally from BIC's boards.

The record contains uncontradicted evidence that demand for sailboards is relatively elastic. The record further contains uncontradicted evidence that the sailboard market's entry level, in which BIC competed, is particularly sensitive to price disparity. By purchasing BIC sailboards, BIC's customers demonstrated a preference for sailboards priced around $350, rather than One–Design boards priced around $600. Therefore, without BIC in the market, BIC's customers would have likely sought boards in the same price range.

Several manufacturers offered sailboards at prices much closer to BIC than to Windsurfing. At least two of Windsurfing's licensees, O'Brien and HiFly, sold boards resembling BIC's in the same distribution channels as BIC. On this record, Windsurfing did not show with reasonable probability that BIC's customers would have purchased from Windsurfing in proportion with Windsurfing's market share. The record shows rather that the vast majority of BIC's customers would have purchased boards from O'Brien or HiFly if BIC's boards had not been available. The district court erred in assuming that, without BIC in the market, its customers would have redistributed their purchases among all the remaining sailboards, including Windsurfing's One Design boards at a price $200 to $300 more than BIC's.

Moreover, Windsurfing's sales continued to decline after the district court enjoined BIC's infringement. This aspect of the record shows as well that Windsurfing did not capture its market share of the sales replacing BIC's market sales. According to the record, the principal beneficiary of BIC's exit appears to be O'Brien.

The district court applied the *Panduit* test for lost profits. Properly applied, the *Panduit* test is an acceptable, though not an exclusive, test for determining "but for" causation. The *Panduit* test, however, operates under an inherent assumption, not appropriate in this case, that the patent owner and the infringer sell products sufficiently similar to compete against each other in the same market segment. If the patentee's and the infringer's products are not substitutes in a competitive market, *Panduit*'s first two factors do not meet the "but for" test—a prerequisite for lost profits.

The first *Panduit* factor-demand for the patented product-presupposes that demand for the infringer's and patent owner's products is interchangeable. Under this assumption, evidence of sales of the infringing product may suffice to show *Panduit*'s first factor, "demand for the patented product." This analysis assumes that the patent owner and the infringer sell substantially the same product. In [*Gyromat Corp. v. Champion Spark Plug Co.*, 735 F.2d 549, 222 U.S.P.Q. 4 (Fed.Cir.1984)], for instance, the patent owner's and the infringer's products were similar in price and product characteristics. If the products are not sufficiently similar to compete in the same market for the same customers, the infringer's customers would not necessarily transfer their demand to the patent owner's product in the absence of the infringer's product. In such circumstances, as in this case, the first *Panduit* factor does not operate to satisfy the elemental "but for" test.

Similarly, the second *Panduit* factor-absence of acceptable, noninfringing alternatives-presupposes that the patentee and the infringer sell substantially similar products in the same market. To be acceptable to the infringer's customers in an elastic market, the alleged alternative "must not have a disparately higher price than or possess characteristics significantly different from the patented product." *Kaufman Co. v. Lantech, Inc.*, 926 F.2d 1136, 1142, 17 U.S.P.Q.2d 1828, 1832 (Fed.Cir. 1991) (citing *Gyromat*, 735 F.2d at 553). In *Kaufman*, for instance, the patent owner and the infringer sold substantially the same product. Thus Panduit 's second factor, properly applied, ensures that any proffered alternative competes in the same market for the same customers as the infringer's product. *See Yarway Corp. v. Eur–Control USA, Inc.*, 775 F.2d 268, 276, 227 U.S.P.Q. 352, 357 (Fed.Cir.1985) (alternative products did not possess features of the patent owner's and the infringer's products, nor compete in the same " 'special niche' or mini-market").

This court has held that a patent owner may satisfy the second *Panduit* element by substituting proof of its market share for proof of the absence of acceptable substitutes. This market share approach allows a patentee to recover lost profits, despite the presence of acceptable, noninfringing substitutes, because it nevertheless can prove with reasonable probability sales it would have made "but for" the infringement. Like *Panduit*'s second prong, however, this market share test also assumes that the patent owner and the infringer compete in the same market. In *State Industries*, for instance, the patent owner, infringer, and the other manufacturers sold substantially similar products. This similarity of products is necessary in order for market share proof to show correctly satisfaction of Panduit 's second factor.

The assumption underlying *Panduit, Gyromat*, and *State Industries* is not appropriate in this case. Instead, the record reveals that during the damages period the sailboard market was not a unitary market in which every competitor sold substantially the same product. Windsurfing and BIC sold different types of sailboards at different prices to different customers. As noted, their sailboards differed significantly in terms of price, product characteristics, and marketing channels. On the facts of this case, Windsurfing did not show "but for" causation under a correct application of Panduit or otherwise. The district court erred in awarding lost profits.

Moreover, Windsurfing itself set the value of its patent rights by licensing its technology to nearly every company supplying sailboards in the United States without competing itself in most sailboard submarkets. Windsurfing valued its patent in terms of licensing royalties, not in terms of profits it could make by excluding others from the market. *See Seymour v. McCormick*, 57 U.S. (How.) 480, 490, 14 L.Ed. 1024 (1854). Without evidence to support Windsurfing's claim to lost profits, this court reverses the district court's award.

With regard to royalties, Windsurfing is entitled to receive lost royalties (on amounts Windsurfing's licensees would have paid "but for" the infringement) and reasonable royalties (on amounts of any other BIC use, if any, of the patented invention). BIC challenges the methodology of the district court in calculating lost royalties per board, but this court concludes that the chosen methodology was within the court's discretion. On remand, the trial court may award damages based upon the lost royalties per board calculation.

Price Erosion

The district court evaluated the documentary and testimonial evidence on price erosion and found it too speculative to support an award of price erosion lost profits. This court finds nothing clearly erroneous in the district court's finding.

The record shows that other market forces, not BIC, forced Windsurfing to lower its prices. The record is replete with evidence that funboards, wave boards, and other designs replaced One Design boards as the sailboard of choice for many practitioners. Besides reducing the demand for One Design boards, consumer choices also caused many companies to discount their stock of One Design boards to make room for the newer boards.

Furthermore, Windsurfing licensed many competitors who produced boards at less cost. The more efficient blowmolding process allowed Windsurfing's competitors to cut prices. Windsurfing's own licensing policies exacerbated this problem. When the European market peaked in the early 1980s, Windsurfing's European licensees sold their excess inventory in the United States. The influx of European boards increased the supply of sailboards and further reduced prices. In light of these facts, the district court correctly found that Windsurfing failed to meet its burden of proof. Simply put, Windsurfing did not prove that it could have sold its boards at higher prices "but for" BIC's infringement.

Notes

1. BIC's "Market Share" of Future Federal Circuit Cases. In *Crystal Semiconductor Corp. v. TriTech Microelec. Int'l Inc.*, 246 F.3d 1336, 57 U.S.P.Q.2d 1953 (Fed.Cir.2001), the Federal Circuit explained:

> In *BIC Leisure*, this court required proper identification of the actual market affected by the infringement. This court explained: "[T]he patent owner and the infringer [must] sell products sufficiently similar to compete against each other in the same market segment." 1 F.3d at 1218. In other words, for lost profits based on the infringer's sales, a patentee must show that the infringing units do "not have a disparately higher price than or possess characteristics significantly different from the patented product." *Id.* at 1219. Similarly, to determine a patentee's market share, the record must accurately identify the market. This requires an analysis which excludes alternatives to the patented product with disparately different prices or significantly different characteristics.

With this introduction, the Federal Circuit then segmented the market and placed audio chips of a different quality in a different market category for assessment of lost profits. Is price always a reliable measure of a different market segment? Can't infringers always offer a lower price because their price does not include R & D expenses?

2. Price Erosion. As early as 1886, the Supreme Court opened the door for price erosion damages: "Reduction of prices, and consequent loss of profits, enforced by infringing competition, is a proper ground for awarding of damages. The only question is as to the character and sufficiency of the evidence in the particular case." *Yale Lock Mfg. Co. v. Sargent*, 117 U.S. 536, 551 (1886). Price erosion thus assumes that, without infringing competition, the patentee could have sustained a higher price and allows damages to compensate for the lower prices necessitated by the illicit competition. The Supreme Court, however, emphasizes "the character and sufficiency of the evidence." In the modern era of compensatory damages following *Rite–Hite*, these evidentiary considerations take on a distinctly economic flavor. The Federal Circuit explained:

> Moreover, in a credible economic analysis, the patentee cannot show entitlement to a higher price divorced from the effect of that higher price on demand for the product. In other words, the patentee must also present evidence of the (presumably reduced) amount of product the patentee would have sold at the higher price ... "[B]ut for" infringement, Crystal would have tried to charge at least 89? more per CODEC.

> Most of the CODECs Crystal sold were priced at under $10 per unit. A minimum 89¢ price increase would have translated to an approximate 10% increase in selling price. Because Crystal was competing in a competitive market, a 10% price increase would have likely caused customers to substitute the CODECs of other manufacturers for Crystal's CODECs. Crystal, however, presented no evidence of the elasticity of demand of the PC sound card CODEC market. Nor did Crystal make any estimates as to the number of sales it would have lost or kept had it increased its prices by 89¢ per unit. Thus, Crystal did not make a showing of "but for" causation of price erosion.

> Without economic evidence of the resulting market for higher priced CODECs, Crystal cannot have both lost profits and price erosion damages on each of those lost sales. The district court correctly denied Crystal's price erosion damages for lack of adequate record support.

Crystal Semiconductor Corp. v. TriTech Microelec. Int'l Inc., 246 F.3d 1336, 57 U.S.P.Q.2d 1953 (Fed.Cir.2001). Does this type of economic reasoning place a premium on economic experts in the damage phase of a trial?

§ 17.2[c] Availability of Non-infringing Substitutes

In *Panduit*, the U.S. Court of Appeals for the Sixth Circuit reasoned: "A product lacking the advantages of that patented can hardly be termed a substitute 'acceptable' to the customer who wants those advantages." This phrase emphasizes that the claimed invention will rarely have substitutes unless they encompass all the same advantages. In other words, the test for non-infringing substitutes is quite strict.

The marketplace, on the other hand, very often supplies several substitutes for every product—each with its own advantages and trade-offs. Thus, as the emphasis in damages law has shifted towards a compensation model, the requirements for "non-infringing substitutes" have reflected economic reasoning.

GRAIN PROCESSING CORP. v. AMERICAN MAIZE–PRODS.

United States Court of Appeals, Federal Circuit, 1999.
185 F.3d 1341, 51 U.S.P.Q.2d 1556.

The Federal Circuit explained at the outset that this case spanned over 18 years with more than eight federal court opinions—including four by the Federal Circuit. Much of the early litigation established that American Maize had infringed Grain Processing's patent. In response, American Maize adjusted its product. Grain Processing sued again. The central issue in the renewed litigation was the test for measuring the D.E. component of the claimed invention. At length, the Federal Circuit determined that Grain Processing's "Schoorl" test properly calculated the D.E. component of maltodextrins. Up to that time, American Maize had been using an alternate test that showed no infringement. With a finding of infringement, American Maize, within two weeks, shifted to a new way of making the product that avoided infringement. The trial court determined that this new alternative had always been available, though not actually in use in the marketplace. Based on this non-infringing alternative, the trial court awarded only a 3% royalty. The district court's 3% royalty rate yielded damages of approximately $2.4 million; Grain Processing sought lost profits of $35 million, which with applicable interest implied an award approaching $100 million. In a non-precedential opinion, the Federal Circuit remanded with the explanation that an acceptable non-infringing alternative must be on the market at the time of infringement. On remand, the trial court made additional findings that the substitute was available as a market substitute even if not literally on sale. This case considered the second appeal on this issue.

Before RADER, CIRCUIT JUDGE, FRIEDMAN, SENIOR CIRCUIT JUDGE, and BRYSON, CIRCUIT JUDGE.

RADER, CIRCUIT JUDGE.

The United States District Court for the Northern District of Indiana denied Grain Processing Corporation lost profits for American Maize–Products' infringement of U.S. Patent No. 3,849,194 (the '194 patent). The district court instead awarded Grain Processing a 3% royalty on American Maize's infringing sales. *Id.; see also Grain Processing Corp. v. American Maize–Products Co.,* 893 F.Supp. 1386, 1396 (N.D.Ind.1995) (*Grain Processing VI*), rev'd, Nos. 95–1506, 95–1507, 108 F.3d 1392 (Fed.Cir. Feb. 20, 1997) (nonprecedential) (*Grain Processing VII*). The district court found that American Maize proved that a noninfringing substitute was available, though not on the market or for sale, during the period of infringement. The court found further that this substitute was acceptable to all purchasers of the infringing product and concluded that American Maize rebutted the inference of "but for" causation for Grain Processing's alleged lost sales. Upholding the district court's findings and conclusions, this court affirms.

I.

The patent featured in this infringement suit involves maltodextrins, a versatile family of food additives made from starch. Commercial food manufacturers purchase hundreds of millions of pounds of maltodextrins annually from producers such as Grain Processing and American Maize.

Maltodextrins serve well as food additives because they are bland in taste and clear in solution. They do not affect the natural taste or color of other ingredients in food products. Maltodextrins also improve the structure or behavior of food products. For instance, they inhibit crystal growth, add body, improve binding and viscosity, and preserve food properties in low temperatures. Consequently, food manufacturers use maltodextrins in a wide variety of products such as frostings, syrups, drinks, cereals, and frozen foods.

Maltodextrins are starch hydrolysates that have a "dextrose equivalence" of less than 20. Dextrose equivalence (D.E.) is a percentage measurement of the "reducing sugars content" of the starch hydrolysate. D.E. reflects the degree to which the hydrolysis process broke down the starch and converted it into dextrose. Converting more starch into dextrose increases the D.E. of the resulting starch hydrolysate. Hence, pure starch has a D.E. of zero, pure dextrose a D.E. of 100. The D.E. value indicates functional properties of a maltodextrin. A 15 D.E. maltodextrin, for example, is slightly sweeter and more soluble than a 5 D.E. maltodextrin. On the other hand, the 5 D.E. maltodextrin has more prevalent binding, bodying, and crystal inhibiting properties.

Grain Processing is the assignee of the '194 patent, "Low D.E. Starch Conversion Products." The claimed invention represents improvements in the "heavily explored" field of starch hydrolysates. Claim 12, the sole claim on appeal, reads:

12.   A waxy starch hydrolysate having

a dextrose equivalent value between about 5 and about 25;

a descriptive ratio greater than about 2, said descriptive ratio being the quotient obtained by dividing the sum of the percentage of saccharides, dry basis, having a degree of polymerization of 1 to 6, by the dextrose equivalent value;

a monosaccharide content in the range of from about 0.1 percent by weight, to about 2.4 percent by weight, dry basis;

a dissaccharide content in the range of from about 1.3 percent to about 9.7 percent, by weight, dry basis; and being further characterized as capable of producing an aqueous solution of exceptional clarity and substantially complete lack of opaqueness when said hydrolysate is added to water.

Grain Processing has manufactured and sold a line of maltodextrins under the "Maltrin" brand name since 1969. The Maltrin line includes "Maltrin M100," a 10 D.E. maltodextrin. None of the Maltrin products, including M100, fall within claim 12 because they are all made from a non-waxy starch.

American Maize began selling maltodextrins in 1974. It made and sold several types of maltodextrins, including "Lo–Dex 10," a 10 D.E. waxy starch maltodextrin. American Maize sold Lo–Dex 10 during the entire time Grain Processing owned the '194 patent rights, from 1979 until the patent expired in 1991. During this time, however, American Maize used four different processes for producing Lo–Dex 10. The changes in American Maize's production processes, and the slight chemical differences in the Lo–Dex 10 from each process, are central to the lost profits issue in this appeal.

When Grain Processing accused American Maize of infringement, Grain Processing used the "Schoorl test" for measuring the D.E. of Lo–Dex 10. American Maize, on the other hand, used the "Lane–Eynon test," which it believed was the "industry standard," to measure D.E. The Schoorl test tends to yield a lower D.E. and therefore a higher D.R. than Lane–Eynon. Under the Lane–Eynon test, American Maize's measurements revealed that Lo–Dex 10 did not infringe claim 12, because all of its Lo–Dex 10 samples had a D.R. of less than 1.9. Grain Processing's Schoorl tests on the same samples, however, yielded a D.R. of greater than 2.

In 1990, Grain Processing tested commercial samples of American Maize's Process III Lo–Dex 10. Grain Processing again used the Schoorl test to measure D.E. Grain Processing's measurements showed that American Maize's Process III output had a D.R. value of greater than 1.9 and therefore infringed.

Because American Maize's Process III output consistently had a D.R. of less than 1.9 using Lane–Eynon, the district court ruled that it did not infringe. *Id.* Grain Processing appealed. This court reversed in a nonprecedential opinion. *Grain Processing V*, 21 USPQ2d 1474. Because the prosecution history of the '194 patent indicates that the inventor used the Schoorl test to measure D.E. of his invention, this court held that the Schoorl test, not Lane–Eynon, determines the relevant values in this case. *Id.* at 1477.

American Maize then adopted a fourth process (Process IV) for producing Lo–Dex 10. In Process IV, American Maize added a second enzyme, glucoamylase, to the reaction. Glucoamylase breaks down starch to a shorter average saccharide length. This shorter saccharide length yields a smaller D.R. without affecting D.E.

From the time American Maize began experimenting with the glucoamylase-alpha amylase combination, or the "dual enzyme method," it took only two weeks to perfect the reaction and begin mass producing Lo–Dex 10 using Process IV. According to the finding of the district court, this two-week development and production time is "practically instantaneous" for large-scale production. American Maize simply experimented with different combinations of glucoamylase and alpha amylase, along with pH, heat, and time of the reaction. American Maize did not change any equipment, source starches, or other ingredients from Process III. Glucoamylase has been commercially available and its effect in starch hydrolysis widely known since the early 1970's, before the '194 patent issued. American Maize had not used Process IV to produce Lo–Dex earlier because the high cost of glucoamylase makes Process IV more expensive than the other processes.

The parties agree that Process IV yielded only noninfringing Lo–Dex 10 and that consumers discerned no difference between Process IV Lo–Dex 10 and Lo–Dex 10 made by Processes I–III. American Maize used Process IV exclusively to produce Lo–Dex 10 from April 1991 until the '194 patent expired in November 1991, and then switched back to the cheaper Process III.

The district court commenced the damages portion of the trial on July 10, 1995. After a three day bench trial, the district court denied lost profits and determined that a 3% reasonable royalty was adequate to compensate Grain Processing. The court concluded that if Grain Processing had insisted on a rate greater than 3% in the hypothetical negotiations, American Maize instead would have chosen to invest in producing noninfringing Lo–Dex 10 with Process IV. The trial court determined that Grain Processing could not establish causation for lost profits, because American Maize "could have produced" a noninfringing substitute 10 D.E. maltodextrin using Process IV. "With infringing Lo–Dex 10 banned, the customers' substitute is non-infringing Lo–Dex 10." American Maize did not actually produce and sell this noninfringing substitute until April 1991, seven months before the '194 patent expired, but the district court nevertheless found that its availability "scotches [Grain Processing's] request for lost-profits damages."

Grain Processing appealed the district court's denial of lost profits, alleging that American Maize cannot escape liability for lost profits on the basis of "a noninfringing substitute that did not exist during, and was not developed until after, the period of infringement." This court reversed and remanded. This court noted that a product or process must be "available or on the market at the time of infringement" to qualify as an acceptable non-infringing substitute.

On remand, the district court again denied Grain Processing lost profits. The district court found that Process IV was "available" throughout the period of infringement. This factual finding, the district court explained, was not based merely on "the simple fact of switching [to Process IV]" but rather on several subsidiary factual findings regarding the technology of enzyme-assisted starch hydrolysis and the price and market structure for the patentee's and accused infringer's products. The trial court found that American Maize could obtain all of the materials needed for Process IV, including the glucoamylase enzyme, before 1979, and that the effects of the enzymes in starch hydrolysis were well known in the field by that time. American Maize did not make the substitution sooner because its test results using the Lane–Eynon method convinced it that it was not infringing.

II.

Upon proof of infringement, Title 35, Section 284 provides that "the court shall award [the patent owner] damages adequate to compensate for the infringement but in no event less than a reasonable royalty for the use made of the invention by the infringer." 35 U.S.C. § 284 (1998). To recover lost profits, the patent owner must show "causation in fact," establishing that "but for" the infringement, he would have made additional profits.

American Maize concedes that it did not make or sell Lo–Dex 10 from Process IV until 1991, after the period of infringement. However, an alleged substitute not "on the market" or "for sale" during the infringement can figure prominently in determining whether a patentee would have made additional profits "but for" the infringement. As this court stated in *Grain Processing VII*, "to be an acceptable non-infringing substitute, the product or process must have been available or on the market at the time of infringement." This statement is an apt summary of this court's precedent, which permits available alternatives—including but not limited to products on the market—to preclude lost profits damages.

In *Aro Manufacturing*, the Supreme Court stated that the statutory measure of "damages" is "the difference between [the patent owner's] pecuniary condition after the infringement, and what his condition would have been if the infringement had not occurred." *Aro Mfg. Co. v. Convertible Top Replacement Co.*, 377 U.S. 476, 507 (1964). Reconstructing the market, by definition a hypothetical enterprise, requires the patentee to project economic results that did not occur. To prevent the hypothetical from lapsing into pure speculation, this court requires sound economic proof of the nature of the market and likely outcomes with infringement factored out of the economic picture.

By the same token, a fair and accurate reconstruction of the "but for" market also must take into account, where relevant, alternative actions the infringer foreseeably would have undertaken had he not infringed. Without the infringing product, a rational would-be infringer is likely to offer an acceptable noninfringing alternative, if available, to compete with the patent owner rather than leave the market altogether. The competitor in the "but for" marketplace is hardly likely to surrender its complete market share when faced with a patent, if it can compete in some other lawful manner. Moreover, only by comparing the patented invention to its next-best available alternative(s)—regardless of whether the alternative(s) were actually produced and sold during the infringement—can the court discern the market value of the patent owner's exclusive right, and therefore his expected profit or reward, had the infringer's activities not prevented him from taking full economic advantage of this right. Thus, an accurate reconstruction of the hypothetical "but for" market takes into account any alternatives available to the infringer. *See Aro*, 377 U.S. at 507; MARTIN J. ADELMAN, PATENT LAW PERSPECTIVES § 5.2[2] (2d Ed.1998) ("[w]here an infringer demonstrates that it could have chosen to market a noninfringing alternative and that it would have done so had it known that it was infringing . . . the sales that it made of the infringing products were not sales that the patentee would otherwise have made. . . .").

Accordingly, this court in *Slimfold Manufacturing Co. v. Kinkead Industries, Inc.* held that an available technology not on the market during the infringement can constitute a noninfringing alternative. 932 F.2d 1453 (Fed.Cir.1991). In *Slimfold*, the patent owner (Slimfold) claimed lost profits on its bi-fold doors with a patented pivot and guide rod assembly. This court noted, however, that Slimfold did not show "that the alleged infringer [Kinkead] would not have made a substantial portion or the same number of sales had it continued with its old hardware or with the hardware utilized by any of the other companies." Id. at 1458. On the basis of this noninfringing substitute, which was not on the market at the time of infringement, this court affirmed the district court's denial of lost profits. This court determined that the record supported the district court's finding that this noninfringing "old hardware" was available to Kinkead at the time of the infringement. Specifically, Kinkead and others had used the substitute technology on other doors before the period of infringement. *See* id. Furthermore, consumers considered Kinkead's noninfringing alternative an acceptable substitute for the infringing doors. *See* id. Therefore, this court upheld the district court's award of a "small" royalty, rather than lost profits.

In *Zygo*, this court reviewed for clear error the district court's factual finding that the infringer's "SIRIS" interferometer was not an acceptable noninfringing substitute. *Zygo*, 79 F.3d at 1571. Like the accused infringer in the *Slimfold* case, the infringer in Zygo had "stopped marketing" the SIRIS when it began marketing the infringing interferometer. See id. In the words of this court, "[t]he central damages issue on appeal is whether . . . Wyko's SIRIS interferometer was . . . an acceptable noninfringing alternative. . . . " On that "central" point, this court noted "the insufficiency of the [district] court's findings" that the SIRIS interferometer was not acceptable, and observed that "the record evidence, while sparse, suggests a contrary conclusion." Therefore, this court remanded for additional factual findings. In addition to holding that the district court's decision lacked sufficient factual support, this court also opined: "[i]t is axiomatic . . . that if a device is not available for purchase, a defendant cannot argue that the device is an acceptable noninfringing alternative. . . . " Id. This statement beyond the premises necessary to resolve the legal issues in *Zygo* did not alter the standards for availability applied in the earlier *Slimfold* case and in subsequent cases. See *Gargoyles, Inc. v. United States*, 113 F.3d 1572 (Fed.Cir.1997) (denying lost profits because a substitute that was not on sale was "available" to the relevant consumer, the Army). Rather, at most it reflects a finding on the record in *Zygo* that availability of the substitute in that case depended on direct market sales.

Grain Processing asserts that permitting the infringer to show substitute availability without market sales, thereby avoiding lost profits, undercompensates for infringement. Section 284, however, sets the floor for "damages adequate to compensate for the infringement" as "a reasonable royalty." 35 U.S.C. § 284. Thus, the statute specifically envisions a reasonable royalty as a form of adequate compensation. While "damages adequate to compensate" means "full compensation," *General Motors*, 461 U.S. at 654, "full compensation" does not entitle Grain Processing to lost profits in the absence of "but for" causation. *Rite–Hite*. Moreover, although Grain Processing stresses that American Maize should not reap the benefit of its "choice" to infringe rather than use the more expensive Process IV, Grain Processing does not allege willful infringement and the record shows none. *See, e.g., Grain Processing VI*, 893 F.Supp. at 1391 (noting that American Maize eliminated the infringing product "practically instantaneous[ly]" upon becoming aware of infringement). To the extent that Grain Processing feels undercompensated, it must point out a reversible error in the district court's fact-finding, reasoning, or legal basis for denying lost profits or in its reasonable royalty determination.

III.

This court next turns to the district court's findings that Process IV was in fact "available" to American Maize for producing Lo–Dex 10 no later than October, 1979, and that consumers would consider Process IV Lo–Dex 10 an acceptable substitute. In this case, the district court did not base its finding that Process IV was available no later than October 1979 on speculation or possibilities, but rather on several specific, concrete factual findings, none of which Grain Processing challenges on appeal. The district court found that American Maize could readily obtain all of the materials needed for Process IV, including the glucoamylase enzyme, before 1979. The court also found that the effects of the enzymes in starch hydrolysis were well known in the field at that time. Furthermore, the court found that American Maize had all of the necessary equipment, know-how, and experience to use Process IV to make Lo–Dex 10, whenever it chose to do so during the time it was instead using Processes I, II or III. American Maize "did not have to 'invent around' the patent," the district court observed; "all it had to do was use a glucoamaylase enzyme in its production process."

Thus, with proper economic proof of availability, as American Maize provided the district court in this case, an acceptable substitute not on the market during the infringement may nonetheless become part of the lost profits calculus and therefore limit or preclude those damages.

Notes

1. Ripple Effects. Assume for a moment that *Grain Processing* will have a wide application, meaning that nearly every marketplace will feature some market alternatives that the infringer might have used "but for" infringement. With that assumption, *Grain Processing* has considerably reduced the risk of costly lost profits awards. Does this development in damages law thus give competitors an incentive to test the boundaries of a patent? Does this testing, in turn, both reduce the practical value of patent protection and provide a formula for increased litigation?

2. *Slimfold* and *Zygo*. *Slimfold*, it seems, could be distinguished from the facts of *Grain Processing*. In *Slimfold*, the non-infringing alternative had been on the market at one time, while *Grain Processing's* non-infringing alternative had never been on the market. The dicta in *Zygo* took a position different from both *Slimfold* and *Grain Processing:* if not for sale contemporaneous with the infringing product, the alternative was not available. What is the meaning of "available"? Does *Grain Processing's* economic theory definition further the goal of accurately compensating the wronged patentee?

3. Compensation vs. Deterrence again. *Grain Processing* relies heavily on the "but for" compensation model to justify its result. It then apparently limits any deterrence function of damages to instances of willful infringement which may justify enhanced damages. Is the Federal Circuit creating different standards for "innocent" infringers as opposed to willful infringers? Does § 284 of the Patent Act justify this distinction?

§ 17.2[d] Reasonable Royalties

In *Panduit*, Chief Judge Markey examined the standards for deriving a correct reasonable royalty, including the hypothetical negotiation test. The hypothetical negotiation test often obtains a very logical result by reference to an actual established royalty in the marketplace. Even if the patentee has not licensed the patented invention, a court may consider royalties on comparable patents or products in the market. *Mahurkar v. C.R. Bard, Inc.*, 79 F.3d 1572 (Fed.Cir.1996). Nonetheless a reasonable royalty may exceed an established royalty when, for instance, the record shows that widespread infringement artificially depressed the value of the license. *Nickson Indus. Inc. v. Rol Mfg. Co.*, 847 F.2d 795 (Fed.Cir.1988).

GEORGIA-PACIFIC CORP. v. UNITED STATES PLYWOOD CORP.

United States District Court, S.D. New York, 1970.
318 F.Supp. 1116, 166 U.S.P.Q. 235.
modified, 446 F.2d 295, 170 U.S.P.Q. 369.
cert. denied, 404 U.S. 870 (1971).

TENNEY, DISTRICT JUDGE.

A comprehensive list of evidentiary facts relevant, in general, to the determination of the amount of a reasonable royalty for a patent license may be drawn from a conspectus of the leading cases. The following are some of the factors mutatis mutandis seemingly more pertinent to the issue herein:

1.   The royalties received by the patentee for the licensing of the patent in suit, proving or tending to prove an established royalty.

"Going" Rate

2.   The rates paid by the licensee for the use of other patents comparable to the patent in suit.

3.   The nature and scope of the license, as exclusive or non-exclusive; or as restricted or non-restricted in terms of territory or with respect to whom the manufactured product may be sold.

4.   The licensor's established policy and marketing program to maintain his patent monopoly by not licensing others to use the invention or by granting licenses under special conditions designed to preserve that monopoly.

5.   The commercial relationship between the licensor and licensee, such as, whether they are competitors in the same territory in the same line of business; or whether they are inventor and promoter.

6.   The effect of selling the patented specialty in promoting sales of other products of the licensee; that existing value of the invention to the licensor as a generator of sales of his non-patented items; and the extent of such derivative or convoyed sales.

Market

7.   The duration of the patent and the term of the license.

8.   The established profitability of the product made under the patent; its commercial success; and its current popularity.

9.   The utility and advantages of the patent property over the old modes or devices, if any, that had been used for working out similar results.

10.   The nature of the patented invention; the character of the commercial embodiment of it as owned and produced by the licensor; and the benefits to those who have used the invention.

11.   The extent to which the infringer has made use of the invention; and any evidence probative of the value of that use.

12.   The portion of the profit or of the selling price that may be customary in the particular business or in comparable businesses to allow for the use of the invention or analogous inventions.

13.   The portion of the realizable profit that should be credited to the invention as distinguished from non-patented elements, the manufacturing process, business risks, or significant features or improvements added by the infringer.

14.   The opinion testimony of qualified experts.

15.   The amount that a licensor (such as the patentee) and a licensee (such as the infringer) would have agreed upon (at the time the infringement began) if both had been reasonably and voluntarily trying to reach an agreement; that is, the amount which a prudent licensee— who desired, as a business proposition, to obtain a license to manufac-

ture and sell a particular article embodying the patented invention—would have been willing to pay as a royalty and yet be able to make a reasonable profit and which amount would have been acceptable by a prudent patentee who was willing to grant a license.

The drawing of proper conclusions from conflicting evidence concerning the amount of a reasonable royalty has been said to call 'for the exercise of judicial discretion by the District Court.' *General Motors Corp. v. Dailey*, 93 F.2d 938, 942 (6th Cir.1937).

Notes

1. **Federal Circuit Recognition.** The *Georgia–Pacific* laundry list of appropriate factors is often used in reasonable royalty cases. *E.g., Unisplay, S.A. v. American Electronic Sign Co.*, 69 F.3d 512, 517 n. 7, 36 U.S.P.Q.2d 1540, 1546 n. 7 (Fed.Cir.1995); *SmithKline Diagnostics, Inc. v. Helena Laboratories Corp.*, 926 F.2d 1161, 1168, 17 U.S.P.Q.2d 1922, 1928 (Fed.Cir. 1991); *Sun Studs, Inc. v. ATA Equip. Leasing, Inc.*, 872 F.2d 978, 993, 10 U.S.P.Q.2d 1338, 1351 (Fed.Cir.1989).

2. **Reasonable Royalty Methodology.** In *Fromson v. Western Litho Plate & Supply Co.*, 853 F.2d 1568, 7 U.S.P.Q.2d 1606 (Fed.Cir.1988), the court mused on the "hypothetical negotiation" standard as follows:

> Like all methodologies based on a hypothetical, there will be an element of uncertainty; yet, a court is not at liberty, in conducting the methodology, to abandon entirely the statutory standard of damages "adequate to compensate" for the infringement. The royalty arrived at must be "reasonable" under all the circumstances; i.e., it must be at least a close approximation of what would be "adequate to compensate" for the "use made of the invention by the infringer." The methodology encompasses fantasy and flexibility; fantasy because it requires a court to imagine what warring parties would have agreed to as willing negotiators; flexibility because it speaks of negotiations as of the time infringement began, yet permits and often requires a court to look to events and facts that occurred thereafter and that could not have been known to or predicted by the hypothesized negotiators.

As has been said by the Supreme Court:

> At times the only evidence available may be that supplied by testimony of experts as to the state of the art, the character of the improvement, and the probable increase of efficiency or savings of expense.... This will generally be the case if the trial follows quickly after the issue of the patent. But a different situation is presented if years have gone by before the evidence is offered. Experience is then available to correct uncertain prophecy. Here is a book of wisdom that courts may not neglect. We find no rule of law that sets a clasp upon its pages, and forbids us to look within....

Sinclair Ref. Co. v. Jenkins Petroleum Process Co., 289 U.S. 689, 698–99 (1933) (citations omitted).

> Forced to erect a hypothetical, it is easy to forget a basic reality–a license is fundamentally an agreement by the patent owner not to sue the licensee. In a normal negotiation, the potential licensee has three

basic choices: forego all use of the invention; pay an agreed royalty; infringe the patent and risk litigation. The methodology presumes that the licensee has made the second choice, when in fact it made the third. Thus Western must be viewed as negotiating for the right to exclude competitors or to compete only with licensed competitors, a landscape far different from that created, post May 1965, by the infringement of Western and others.

Whatever royalty may result from employment of the methodology, the law is not without means for recognizing that an infringer is unlike a true "willing" licensee; nor is the law without means for placing the injured patentee "in the situation he would have occupied if the wrong had not been committed."

853 F.2d at 1575–76, 7 U.S.P.Q.2d at 1613–14.

3. A *Panduit* "Kicker?" In 1996, a United States District Court attempted to enhance a reasonable royalty award apparently to compensate the patent owner for the expenses of defending the patent. The Federal Circuit sustained the district court's reasonable royalty of 25.88%. To this amount, the district court added 9%. The Federal Circuit stated:

> To this reasonable royalty, however, the trial court added an additional 9%. It labeled this addition a "Panduit kicker," citing *Panduit Corp. v. Stahlin Bros. Fibre Works, Inc.*, 575 F.2d 1152, 197 U.S.P.Q. 726 (6th Cir.1978).
>
> Although one method for proving damages, the *Panduit* methodology does not include a "kicker" to account for litigation expenses or for any other expenses. In *Panduit*, the Sixth Circuit noted that the patentee had incurred more than $400,000 in litigation expenses battling with the infringer for over thirteen years.
>
> More important, *Panduit* does not authorize additional damages or a "kicker" on top of a reasonable royalty because of heavy litigation or other expenses. In sections 284 and 285, the Patent Act sets forth statutory requirements for awards of enhanced damages and attorney fees. The statute bases these awards on clear and convincing proof of willfulness and exceptionality. *Panduit* at no point suggested enhancement of a compensatory damage award as a substitute for the strict requirements for these statutory provisions. The district court's "kicker," on the other hand, enhances a damages award, apparently to compensate for litigation expenses, without meeting the statutory standards for enhancement and fees. Therefore, the district court abused its discretion in awarding a 9% "*Panduit* kicker."

Mahurkar v. C.R. Bard, Inc., 79 F.3d 1572, 1580–81, 38 U.S.P.Q.2d 1288, 1293–94 (Fed.Cir.1996). How then is a litigant to get full compensation in a reasonable royalty case for the expenses of litigation?

Shortly after the court's decision in *Mahurkar* the court may have reintroduced the idea of a "kicker" in *Maxwell v. J. Baker, Inc.*, 86 F.3d 1098, 39 U.S.P.Q.2d 1001 (Fed.Cir.1996), where the trial court instructed the jury to determine whether Maxwell was damaged in an amount in excess of the amount of the reasonable royalty and if so, by how much. The jury did so and the Federal Circuit affirmed. Should the law encourage such challenges to patents? For an argument that good faith challenges to patents perform an important function in properly regulating a patent system *see* Martin J. Adelman, *Property Rights Theory and Patent–Antitrust: The Role of Compulsory Licensing*, 52 N.Y.U. L. REV. 977 (1977) and 4 MARTIN J. ADELMAN, PATENT LAW PERSPECTIVES, § 5.2[3] at nn.135 and 152 (2d ed. 1995 & 1996).

§ 17.2[e]   Foreign Approaches

U.S. intellectual property lawyers have often criticized foreign courts as being overly conservative when awarding damages in patent cases. Recent trends in damages awards overseas may blunt some of these criticisms. Many foreign courts have become more generous in their damages awards, now attempting to approximate the financial situation the patentee would have enjoyed "but for" the infringement. The leading British decision of *Gerber Garment Technology v. Lectra Systems*, [1995] RPC 383, is exemplary of this approach.

The most notable changes have occurred in Japan. The Japanese patent system has traditionally been subject to severe criticism for the limited equitable and monetary relief available to patentees. Damages awards were often viewed as limited to the payment of minimal royalties. *See* Scott K. Dinwiddie, *A Shifting Barrier? Difficulties in Obtaining Patent Infringement Damages in Japan*, 70 WASH. L. REV. 833 (1995). Legislative and judicial developments have recently transformed this aspect of Japanese patent law. Reforms adopted by the Diet resulted in 1998 legislation clarifying that damages may be awarded based upon the patentee's lost profits, not just upon a conservative royalty amount. The October 12, 1998, judgment of the Tokyo District Court in *Smithkline & Beecham French Lab. Ltd. v. Fujimoto Seiyaku* resulted in a damages award based upon lost profits of $23.5 million. Given that acceptable noninfringing substitutes were probably available in the Japanese market during the period of infringement, the Tokyo District Court's award may have been greater than the amount available under U.S. patent law. Adjudicated infringers of Japanese patents can now expect to be subjected to increased liability in comparison to previous years.

Although German courts traditionally awarded patent claims a capacious scope, and even after the advent of the European Patent Convention are considered friendly to the patentee, the level of damage awards was formerly quite low. Several principles leads to this result: damages could only be awarded against infringers acting "with fault," a three-year statute of limitations applied, and limited discovery procedures indicated that the extent of the infringement was difficult to prove. More recent German Supreme Court cases have liberalized these strictures to some extent, allowing damages to be claimed under more generous unfair competition principles. *See generally* Jochen Pagenberg, *Assessment of Damages for Patent Infringement*, 14 INT'L REV. INDUS. PROP. & COPYRIGHT L. 85 (1983).

Those interested in European patent damages law should consider the work of a leading international intellectual property scholar, Professor Gunnar Karnell. His article, *Computation of Damages for Patent Infringement In Particular As Related To Extensions Outside The Scope of Patented Matter: A Comparative Law Overview*, appears in the first issue of INTERNATIONAL PATENT QUARTERLY.

Jurisdictions vary on the remedies available to applicants between the publication of their applications and the time of the patent grant. In particular, Article 67 of the European Patent Convention allows its contracting states considerable flexibility in the level of protection conferred. One implementation of Article 67 is Section 33 of the German patent statute, which provides:

Section 33—Rights Conferred by a Patent Application After Publication

(1) As from the publication [of the patent application], the applicant may request from any person who has used the subject of the application, although he knew or should have known that the invention used by him was the subject of the application, compensation reasonable under the circumstances; the claiming of further remedies shall not be permitted.

(2) The request for compensation shall not be admissible if the subject of the application is obviously unpatentable.

In *Open-End Spinning Machine (Offenend-spinnmaschine)*, Case No. X ZR 26/87 (1989) (English translation available at 21 INT'L REV. INDUS. PROP. & COPYRIGHT L. 241 (1990)), the German Federal Supreme Court set forth the following principles regarding Section 33:

a) It is not illegal to use the subject matter of a non-examined patent application that is merely laid open for public inspection.

b) A right to compensation can be demanded from the direct beneficiary and not, in addition, from the party who (as the legal representative or employee in charge) merely implements the use.

c) The method of the license analogy offers a suitable means for calculating the amount of reasonable compensation. It is not admissible to request an award of damages for actual losses nor surrender of user profits.

d) The right to demand disclosure—which is granted for the purpose of calculating the amount of compensation for use of the invention—does not, as a matter of principle, extend to disclosure of actual production and marketing costs.

See Wilfred Neuhaus, *The Claim for Compensation Under Section 33 of the German Patent Law in Practice*, 21 INT'L REV. INDUS. PROP. & COPYRIGHT L. 526 (1990). Article 32(1) of the dormant Community Patent Convention appears to follow German law, providing:

Compensation reasonable in the circumstances may be claimed from a third party who, in the period between the date of publication of a European patent application in which the Contracting States are designated and the date of publication of the mention of the grant of the European patent, has made any use of the invention which, after that period would be prohibited by virtue of the Community patent.

Some patent statutes are far more generous when providing protection following publication of their patent applications, however. Consider, for example, section 57(1) of the Australian Patents Act 1990:

> After a complete specification relating to an application for a standard patent grant has become open to public inspection and until a patent is granted on an application, the applicant has the same rights as he or she would have had if a patent for the invention had been granted on the day when the specification become open to public inspection.

The Australian statute goes on to provide that applicants may not start infringement proceedings until the patent is granted, and that accused infringers possess a defense regarding acts performed between publication and grant where "a patent could not validly have been granted to the applicant in respect of the claim (as framed when the act was done) that is alleged to have been infringed by the doing of the act." Australian Patents Act 1990 at § 57(3). What is your view of the appropriate level of protection for patentees following publication of the application, but prior to the grant of a patent?

§ 17.3 ENHANCED DAMAGES AND ATTORNEY FEES

The patent statute permits augmented damage awards in remarkably terse language, as follows:

§ 284. Damages

[T]he court may increase the damages up to three times the amount found or assessed.

§ 285. Attorney Fees

The court in exceptional cases may award reasonable attorney fees to the prevailing party.

The Federal Circuit explains that these provisions apply in instances of bad faith litigation and, more usually, in cases were the defendant has engaged in "willful infringement." *Beatrice Foods Co. v. New England Printing and Lithographing Co.*, 930 F.2d 1572, 18 U.S.P.Q.2d 1548 (Fed.Cir.1991). The next opinion presents the Federal Circuit's thinking on the concept of willful infringement and its remedial consequences.

READ CORP. v. PORTEC, INC.

United States Court of Appeals, Federal Circuit, 1992.
970 F.2d 816, 23 U.S.P.Q.2d 1426.

BEFORE NIES, CHIEF JUDGE, ARCHER, and MICHEL, CIRCUIT JUDGES.

NIES, CHIEF JUDGE.

Portec, Inc., appeals from the May 25, 1990, final judgment, entered upon a jury verdict, of the United States District Court for the District of

Delaware, Civil Action No. 88–29–JRR, holding Portec liable for infringement of U.S. Patent No. 4,197,194 (the '194 patent) and U.S. Design Patent No. 263,836 (the '836 patent), and awarding The Read Corporation and F.T. Read & Sons, Inc. (collectively Read) treble damages and attorney fees. We reverse the judgment with respect to liability for the enhancement of damages, vacate the award with respect to attorney fees, and remand for modification of the injunction and reconsideration of the award of Read's attorney fees in light of this opinion.

D C

Reversed
Vacate
atty fees

BACKGROUND

James L. Read is the president of Read and the named inventor in both the '194 and '836 patents. The '194 patent is directed to a portable loam screening apparatus for separating fine earth material from coarser materials. The '836 patent is directed to an ornamental design of such a screening apparatus.

Independent claim 2 of the '194 patent [is] at issue in this case. Claim 2 reads as follows:

> 2. A portable screening apparatus for separating coarse material from finer material comprising:
>
> a frame of generally rectangular cross section and having a tall end and a short joint [sic] by sides, said short end being closed from an upper edge of said short end to the ground and the lower portion of said tall end being completely open from the ground to a height sufficiently high to permit a payloader to collect the finer material from within the frame; said frame at said tall end having a width sufficient to accommodate the shovel of a payloader; a material separating shaker screen sloping downwardly from near the upper edge of said tall end to near the upper edge of said short end; a set of wheels mounted to one of said sides and movable relative to said frame from an operative position for transporting said apparatus to an inoperative position for resting said frame flush on the ground; and a trailer hitch mounted to the other of said sides.

As will become evident infra, critical to this case are the claim limitations requiring the short end to be closed "to the ground" and a set of wheels which are "movable relative to said frame" from "an operative position" to "an inoperative position for resting said frame flush on the ground."

U.S. Patent Application Serial No. 947,380, from which the '194 patent issued, was filed October 2, 1978, with 11 claims. Claim 2 as originally filed did not contain any wheels limitation, and required only that the short end be "closed." The examiner rejected all of the claims under 35 U.S.C. § 103 for obviousness in view of various combinations of references.

In response, Read added to claim 2 (as well as to the other independent claims), the "set of wheels" limitation. No amendment was made to the closed end limitation. In the remarks accompanying the amendment, Read stressed the nonobviousness of the claimed invention based on numerous differences from the prior art including the "closed" short end, which acts as a barrier between the coarse material and the finer material, and the wheels limitation, which allows the apparatus to be transported or stably set on the ground during screening operations.

The record shows that the examiner, in a telephonic interview, agreed to allow the claims if amended to include limitations more particularly pointing out the relationship of the width and height of the tall end portion of the frame to a payloader and the relation of where the short end's "closed" characteristics begin and end. Claim 2 and the other independent claims were thereafter amended, by examiner's amendment, to include, among other things, the requirement that the short end be closed "to the ground." The claims were subsequently allowed.

Read has been making screening devices in accordance with its invention since the late 1970's under the name "Read Screen–All." In December of 1984, officials from Portec met with James Read to discuss a possible acquisition of Read by Portec. Those discussions proved fruitless, and Portec began to consider whether it could produce a device to compete with the Read Screen–All.

In doing so, Portec obtained a written opinion by patent attorney Emory Groff, Jr., concerning the '194 and '836 patents in January of 1985. This opinion is very general, as it was prepared before Portec had done any significant development work. With respect to the '836 patent, Groff set forth the general test for design patent infringement, and noted that "[d]esign patents are generally narrowly construed by the courts." With respect to the '194 patent, Groff reviewed the patent and the file history, and concluded that "the limitations concerning the set of wheels, the hitch, the fully closed short end and the tall end opening extending to the ground are all critical limitations." After a brief discussion of the doctrine of equivalents, Groff concluded that "the claims of the patents could be circumvented to avoid infringement, however, whether or not the end result would produce an apparatus as efficient and commercially appealing as the Read devices, is questionable."

Nothing further was done by Portec concerning development of a portable screening device until late 1986. By that time, the popularity of the Read Screen?All had increased further, and Portec renewed its interest in designing a device to compete with the Screen–All. This interest resulted in several meetings between Portec engineer Gerald Dahlinger and patent attorney Brett Valiquet in January and February of 1987. Notes from those meetings indicate that Dahlinger and Valiquet discussed several possibilities for designing around the claims of the '194 patent, including "wheels which are not movable relative to the frame and not moving the frame onto the ground," and a "completely open short end."

Over the next several months, Portec developed design drawings for its proposed portable screening device. This screening device had two features designed to avoid infringement of the '194 patent: (1) the bottom of the short end ended about six inches from the ground; and (2) fixed wheels and a "footpad" attached to each side of the frame replaced the retractable wheels. The footpads were long metal bars which extended the entire length of the sides and which were movable relative to the frame by hydraulic cylinders. The footpads could be extended so as to lift the wheels off the ground, placing the weight of the device on the footpads.

Drawings of this design were given to Valiquet for an analysis of infringement of both the '194 and '836 patents. Valiquet concluded, in a written opinion dated September 25, 1987, that Portec's proposed device did not infringe either patent. With respect to the '194 patent, after discussing the details of the claims and of Portec's device, Valiquet stated: During prosecution before the U.S. patent office, Read was required by the patent office to add the limitation to his claims that the short end extends to the ground. Also, Read voluntarily added to his patent claims the concept of moving the frame so that it could be flush on the ground through use of movable wheels. Since these distinctions were added in view of prior art cited by the Examiner, Read cannot argue that Portec has any type of equivalent structure. With respect to the '836 patent, after discussing the details of various visual aspects of both the '836 design and Portec's proposed design, Valiquet concluded: In view of the forementioned visual distinctions and other probable visual distinctions not specifically mentioned herein, it is clear that the Portec unit will create a visually distinct and different impression than that shown in the drawing figures of the Read design patent. After preparing final drawings of its screening device, Portec sent these drawings to Valiquet, who, in a letter dated November 25, 1987, again confirmed his opinion of noninfringement. Portec began making its portable screening device shortly thereafter.

Read brought the present suit in January of 1988, charging Portec with infringement of the '836 patent and claims 2 and 7 of the '194 patent. Portec denied infringement and also asserted that the two patents were invalid on various grounds.

During pendency of the suit, Portec made several changes to its device in order to further distinguish it from that of the '194 and '836 patents. One of these changes arose from the discovery by Portec's customers that its device worked satisfactorily with only the front footpad (the one adjacent the hitch) lowered, so that at least part of the weight of the device remained on the wheels. Thus, Portec began making a new device which had only a single footpad located on the side adjacent to the hitch. The other changes were ornamental, designed to further make Portec's device, particularly the fender portion, look different from that of the '836 patent.

In response to interrogatories, the jury held each patent valid and infringed by each of Portec's devices, found that the infringement was willful, and found damages in the amount of $1,324,782. Read subsequently moved for and was granted treble damages and attorney fees. The district court entered judgment in favor of Read in the amount of $3,974,346 in damages plus $1,235,685.11 in attorney fees.

On appeal Portec challenges the district court's denial of JNOV on the issue of the award of enhanced damages and attorney fees.

DISCUSSION

Enhanced Damages

Under section 284 of Title 35, damages may be enhanced up to three times the compensatory award. An award of enhanced damages for infringement, as well as the extent of the enhancement, is committed to the discretion of the trial court. While no statutory standard dictates the circumstances under which the district court may exercise its discretion, this court has approved such awards where the infringer acted in wanton disregard of the patentee's patent rights, that is, where the infringement is willful. On the other hand, a finding of willful infringement does not mandate that damages be enhanced, much less mandate treble damages.

The paramount determination in deciding to grant enhancement and the amount thereof is the egregiousness of the defendant's conduct based on all the facts and circumstances. The court must consider factors that render defendant's conduct more culpable, as well as factors that are mitigating or ameliorating. In *Bott v. Four Star Corp.*, 807 F.2d 1567, 1572, 1 U.S.P.Q.2d 1210, 1213 (Fed.Cir.1986), three factors were identified for consideration in determining when an infringer "acted in [such] bad faith as to merit an increase in damages awarded against him":

(1) whether the infringer deliberately copied the ideas or design of another;

(2) whether the infringer, when he knew of the other's patent protection, investigated the scope of the patent and formed a good-faith belief that it was invalid or that it was not infringed; and

(3) the infringer's behavior as a party to the litigation.

The Bott factors are not all inclusive. In addition, other circumstances which courts appropriately have considered, particularly in deciding on the extent of enhancement, are:

(4) Defendant's size and financial condition. *St. Regis Paper Co. v. Winchester Carton Corp.*, 410 F.Supp. 1304, 1309, 189 U.S.P.Q. 514, 518 (D.Mass.1976) ("[D]ouble damages [appropriate]. If defendant were the giant and plaintiff the small independent, I would make it treble...."); *Bott v. Four Star Corp.*, 229 U.S.P.Q. 241, 254 (E.D.Mich.1985) ("[a] threefold increase in damages would severely affect [defendant's] financial condition."), vacated and remanded for clarification of damage amount, 807, F.2d 1567, 1 U.S.P.Q.2d 1210 (Fed.Cir.1986); *Lightwave Technologies, Inc. v. Corning Glass*

Works, 19 U.S.P.Q.2d 1838, 1849 (S.D.N.Y.1991) (Defendant "can withstand some increase in damages, but not treble damages."); *Kori Corp. v. Wilco Marsh Buggies and Draglines, Inc.*, 561 F.Supp. 512, 533, 217 U.S.P.Q. 1302, 1312 (E.D.La.1981) (Exemplary damages "should not unduly prejudice the defendants' non-infringing business."), *aff'd*, 761 F.2d 649, 225 U.S.P.Q. 985 (Fed.Cir.), *cert. denied*, 474 U.S. 902 (1985).

(5) Closeness of the case. *Modine Mfg. Co. v. The Allen Group*, 917 F.2d at 543, 16 U.S.P.Q.2d at 1626 (No abuse of discretion to award no enhanced damages on the ground that willfulness was "sufficiently close on the evidence."); *Crucible, Inc. v. Stora Kopparbergs Bergslags AB*, 701 F.Supp. 1157, 1164, 10 U.S.P.Q.2d 1190, 1196 (W.D.Pa.1988) ("[B]ecause the court still considers the [willfulness] question to be a close one . . . double, and not treble damages are appropriate.").

(6) Duration of defendant's misconduct. *Bott v. Four Star Corp.*, 229 U.S.P.Q. 241, 255 (E.D.Mich.1985) (For sales prior to the appellate court's affirmance of the liability judgment, damages increased by 20%; for sales after the affirmance, damages doubled.), *vacated and remanded for clarification of damage amount*, 807 F.2d 1567, 1 U.S.P.Q.2d 1210 (Fed.Cir.1986).

(7) Remedial action by the defendant. *Intra Corp. v. Hamar Laser Instruments, Inc.*, 662 F.Supp. 1420, 1439, 4 U.S.P.Q.2d 1337, 1351 (E.D.Mich.1987) (Damages only doubled because defendant "voluntarily ceased manufacture and sale of infringing systems during the pendency of this litigation. . . . "), *aff'd without opinion*, 862 F.2d 320 (Fed.Cir.1988), *cert. denied*, 490 U.S. 1021 [109 S.Ct. 1746, 104 L.Ed.2d 183] (1989).

(8) Defendant's motivation for harm. *American Safety Table Co. v. Schreiber*, 415 F.2d 373, 379, 163 U.S.P.Q. 129, 133 (2d Cir.1969) ("[D]efendants' infringing acts, although deliberate and with knowledge of plaintiff's rights, could not be termed pernicious due to prevailing 'economic pressure in the form of customer dissatisfaction.'"), *cert. denied*, 396 U.S. 1038 [90 S.Ct. 683, 24 L.Ed.2d 682] (1970).

(9) Whether defendant attempted to conceal its misconduct. *Russell Box Co. v. Grant Paper Box Co.*, 203 F.2d 177, 183, 97 U.S.P.Q. 19, 23 (1st Cir.) (Enhanced damages supported in part by findings "that the defendant had failed to preserve its records and had failed to cooperate as it should at the trial on the issue of damages."), *cert. denied*, 346 U.S. 821 (1953).

Use of these factors in patent cases is in line with punitive damage considerations in other tort contexts.

Inasmuch as a finding of willful infringement does not mandate enhancement of damages, the above factors taken together assist the trial court in evaluating the degree of the infringer's culpability and in determining whether to exercise its discretion to award enhanced damages and how much the damages should be increased. To enable appellate review, a district court is obligated to explain the basis for the award, particularly where the maximum amount is imposed. For the latter, the court's assessment of the level of culpability must be high.

In its award of enhanced damages, the district court here relied on Portec's "copying," the willful nature of Portec's infringement, and Portec's "manipulative" litigation strategy, which the court said was "reflective of the dubiousness of Portec's assertions that it produced its devices with a good faith belief in the innocence of its action."

Throughout its brief to this court, Read stresses Portec's "copying" of the Read Screen–All as evidence of willful and wanton infringement. The district court also characterized Portec's activity as "copying," and criticized Portec heavily for doing so. Such a characterization is unwarranted. Certainly the Read Screen–All served as the starting point for Portec's design efforts. And certainly the purpose of Portec's efforts was to make a device which would compete with the Read Screen–All. However, the undisputed evidence of record shows that Portec made specific changes deemed adequate by counsel to avoid infringement of both of Read's patents. We have often noted that one of the benefits of the patent system is the incentive it provides for "designing around" patented inventions, thus creating new innovations.

Of course, determining when a patented device has been "designed around" enough to avoid infringement is a difficult determination to make. One cannot know for certain that changes are sufficient to avoid infringement until a judge or a jury has made that determination. In the present case, the jury found that the changes made by Portec were not sufficient to avoid infringement of either patent, and we have herein reversed the judgment respecting infringement of the '836 patent and affirmed the judgment respecting infringement of the '194 patent. Portec is thus liable for damages caused by its miscalculation respecting infringement of the '194 patent. The question which must first be answered here with respect to enhanced damages is whether Portec proceeded without a reasonable belief that it would not be held liable for infringement.

Willfulness is a determination as to a state of mind. One who has actual notice of another's patent rights has an affirmative duty to respect those rights. That affirmative duty normally entails obtaining advice of legal counsel although the absence of such advice does not mandate a finding of willfulness. *See Kloster Speedsteel AB v. Crucible, Inc.*, 793 F.2d 1565, 1579, 230 U.S.P.Q. 81, 91 (Fed.Cir.1986) ("Though it is an important consideration, not every failure to seek an opinion of competent counsel will mandate an ultimate finding of willfulness."), *cert. denied*, 479 U.S. 1034, 107 S.Ct. 882, 93 L.Ed.2d 836 (1987). Those cases where willful infringement is found despite the presence of an opinion of counsel generally involve situations where opinion of counsel was either ignored or found to be incompetent. This precedent does not mean a client must itself be able to evaluate the legal competence of its attorney's advice to avoid a finding of willfulness. The client would not need the attorney's advice at all in that event. That an opinion is "incompetent" must be shown by objective evidence. For example, an attorney may not have looked into the necessary facts, and, thus, there would be no foundation for his opinion. A written opinion may be incompetent on its face by reason of its containing merely conclusory statements without discussion of facts or obviously presenting only a superficial or off-the-cuff analysis.

In the present case, Portec obtained at least two independent written detailed opinions of unrelated patent counsel and engaged in numerous conferences with its lawyers on the matter. The defenses put forth by Portec in this suit track defenses set forth in these opinions and required full trial, which supports their good faith. Despite these facts, the jury found that Portec had willfully infringed both the '194 and the '836 patents. The district court, in its opinion granting Read's motion for treble damages and attorney fees, discussed at length Portec's conduct relating to the willfulness issue. Reviewing the "evidence" which the district court relied on as allegedly showing the willfulness of Portec's conduct, as well as other evidence cited by Read in support of the jury verdict, we can only conclude that the jury's finding of willfulness is not supported by substantial evidence. No reasonable juror could find the asserted proof of willfulness rose to the quantum of clear and convincing evidence.

The district court indicated that Portec failed to heed the advice of its counsel. In support of this contention, the district court cites the January 1985 opinion of Groff as advising Portec that he "doubted" whether a device sufficiently modified to avoid infringement would be "as efficient and commercially appealing." This appears to be a misunderstanding of Groff's opinion. Groff stated unequivocally the patents "could be circumvented," but said it was questionable whether a device modified to avoid infringement would be as efficient or commercially appealing. However, the fact is that at the time Groff rendered his opinion, Portec had not yet begun design of any device, and thus Groff had no idea whether Portec could design a commercially acceptable device that avoided infringement.

The district court criticized the opinion of Valiquet because Valiquet admitted at trial that he performed no specific legal research prior to rendering the opinion. The district court was also of the view that Valiquet's opinion was incompetent because it failed to discuss infringement under the doctrine of equivalents. Further, the district court criticized Portec for not giving Groff's opinion to Valiquet.

None of these criticisms are justified. Valiquet was a patent attorney with many years of experience. Failure to perform legal research on the basic concepts of literal infringement, the doctrine of equivalents, and prosecution history estoppel does not per se make the opinion of a lawyer who specializes in patents incompetent.

Moreover, the district court was incorrect when it stated that Valiquet did not consider the doctrine of equivalents. Valiquet's opinion included the following: During prosecution before the U.S. patent office, Read was required by the patent office to add the limitation to his claims that the short end extends to the ground. Also, Read voluntarily added to his patent claims the concept of moving the frame so that is could be flush on the ground through use of movable wheels. Since these distinctions were added in view of prior art cited by the Examiner, Read cannot argue that Portec has any type of equivalent structure. The district court maintained that this portion of Valiquet's opinion was directed solely to the question of literal infringement. We disagree. The substance of this analysis with its reference to "prior art" and "equivalent structure" can only relate to infringement under the doctrine of equivalents.

Further, the failure to give the first lawyer's opinion to Valiquet is a plus, not a minus. Valiquet was not influenced thereby and was able to make his own independent evaluation.

The most important consideration, however, is that nothing in Valiquet's letter would alert a client to reject the letter as an obviously bad opinion. Indeed, his opinion on infringement of the '836 patent was on the mark. More importantly, the opinion was detailed not merely conclusory. On finalization of the drawings, Valiquet reviewed the matters again. Portec sought professional advice on making a competing device which avoided the patent. The monetary exposure of his client required no less from Valiquet than the soundest advice he could offer, not merely to avoid enhanced damages, but all damages. Counsel's opinion, in effect, has been treated inappropriately and unfairly as part of a scheme to avoid enhanced damages only.

Finally, the district court criticized Valiquet's September 25, 1987, opinion, because it was allegedly inconsistent with an "opinion" given in February of 1987. Specifically, the district court noted that in February, Valiquet and Dahlinger of Portec were discussing the use of a "completely" open short end to avoid infringement. In contrast, the September 25, 1987, opinion letter concluded that a device with only about a six-inch opening on the short end avoided infringement.

In February of 1987, Portec had developed no specific designs for a device. Whatever discussions Valiquet had with Dahlinger in February of 1987 can hardly be characterized as an "opinion" on the structure in issue; hand-written notes made during the discussions merely describe general avenues by which the '194 patent could be avoided. In fact, those notes describe other possibilities for avoiding infringement of the '194 patent, such as the use of a horizontal shaker screen. The fact that Portec later designed a device which incorporated some, but not all, of the design modifications first discussed by Valiquet and Dahlinger, and that Valiquet concluded that the resulting device was not an infringement, does not render his final opinion inconsistent.

In sum, upon review of the record before us, we hold that there is insufficient evidence from which a reasonable jury could find that

Portec's infringement was willful. Inasmuch as there is no infringement of the '836 patent, a finding of willful infringement with respect to that patent necessarily drops out of the case. That counsel's opinion turned out to be contrary to our judgment with respect to the '194 patent does not make his advice regarding that patent incompetent. Read cannot point to any substantial evidence which indicates that Portec did not have a good faith belief that it was not infringing, because it had successfully "designed around" the '194 patent. Thus, the factors of willful infringement and copying are not present.

The district court also relied upon instances of what it characterized as Portec's improper litigation strategy which the court stated demonstrated Portec's lack of a good faith belief in its defenses. Absent willful infringement, however, there is no basis in this case for enhanced damages. As indicated, bad faith behavior as a party to the litigation is a factor to be weighed in assessing the level of a defendant's culpability where an infringement is found willful. While dicta suggest that infringement damages may be enhanced solely by reason of misconduct during litigation, such dictum is contrary to our precedent that "[i]f infringement [is] . . . innocent, increased damages are not awardable for the infringement." Thus, we reverse the award of enhanced damages.

E.   Attorney Fees

With respect to making its award of attorney fees under 35 U.S.C. § 285, the district court again relied on the willfulness of Portec's infringement to find the case was exceptional. Thus, this award cannot stand. However, litigation misconduct may in itself make a case "exceptional." The district court found misconduct first by reason of Portec's creation, during litigation, of what the district court termed as an "aberrant model" of its device in order to avoid infringement of the '836 design patent. Even had we not reversed the finding of infringement of the '836 patent, this basis for enhancement would be meritless. Although Portec already had an opinion of noninfringement from its counsel on the device in suit, Portec made further design changes in its device in order to make sure that it had a noninfringing device. Such a "litigation strategy" should be encouraged, not viewed as misconduct.

The second example concerned a screening device referred to at trial as the "Hoehn device." Portec introduced evidence of the Hoehn device, in an attempt to show that the claims of the '194 patent were invalid, including two spatially-consecutive photographs showing the Hoehn device. Read discovered that part of the first photograph had been covered by the second photograph so that it could not be seen that the device in the first photograph had no hitch. The missing hitch seriously undermined the testimony which had already been presented by Portec concerning the chronology of the development of the Hoehn device. Portec asked the district court to allow it to present surrebuttal evidence to explain the absence of the hitch, but the district court denied its request, explaining that Portec should have presented this evidence in its case in chief.

We cannot say that the district court abused its discretion in not allowing Portec to present additional evidence to explain away the missing hitch on the Hoehn exhibit in connection with the issue of validity. On the other hand, where the question is improper conduct to support an award of attorney fees, we conclude that the evidence must be considered by the court before finding misconduct and that the finding that this incident constituted improper litigation strategy cannot stand. Accordingly, we remand for a re-determination by the district court whether Portec did engage in litigation misconduct and, if so, whether it was sufficiently culpable as to make the case exceptional. We point out that, when attorney fees under 35 U.S.C. § 285 are awarded solely on the basis of litigation misconduct, the amount of the award must bear some relation to the extent of the misconduct.

CONCLUSION

The judgment with respect to enhanced damages is reversed. The award of attorney fees is vacated and the case is remanded for modification of the injunction and for reconsideration of the award of attorney fees in light of this opinion.

Notes

1. The Search for a Safe Harbor. *Read* emphasizes the role of attorney opinion letters in the test for enhanced damages. This rule provides a steady source of employment for patent attorneys. Like drafting claims, drafting opinion letters demands considerable legal skill. Of course, patent owners want a letter that will immunize them against enhanced damages in any future infringement suit, but as attorneys realize, it is difficult to categorically exclude the prospect of infringement. Therefore, the opinion letter often creates numerous problems. In the event of litigation, the letter opens attorney work product to discovery and further excludes the author from serving as counsel in the case because he may be a witness. Moreover any hedging language in the letter will become a centerpiece of the patentee's infringement case. In light of these complications, commentators have urged that Congress or the Federal Circuit espouse, either directly or indirectly, a set of guidelines creating a "safe harbor" for individuals seeking to avoid the onus of willful infringement. *See* 4 MARTIN J. ADELMAN, PATENT LAW PERSPECTIVES, § 5.2[7] at n.97 (2d ed. 1995).

2. Willful Infringement Doctrine? Why should a court ever award enhanced damages for willful infringement where that infringement occurs only under the Doctrine of Equivalents? Would Congress do well to amend § 284 to limit judicial increases of damages awards to cases of literal infringement?

3. The "Exceptional" Requirement for Attorney Fees. In *Interspiro USA, Inc. v. Figgie International, Inc.*, 18 F.3d 927, 30 U.S.P.Q.2d 1070 (Fed.Cir.1994), the court further discussed the award of attorney fees under § 285:

> When considering a request for an award of attorney fees under 35 U.S.C.A. § 285, the trial judge undertakes a two-step inquiry: he or she must determine whether there is clear and convincing evidence that the

case is "exceptional," and if so, whether an award of attorney fees to the prevailing party is warranted.

18 F.3d at 933–34, 30 U.S.P.Q.2d at 1074. "Bad faith litigation, willful infringement, or inequitable conduct are among the circumstances which may make a case exceptional." *Mahurkar v. C.R. Bard, Inc.*, 79 F.3d 1572, 38 U.S.P.Q.2d 1288 (Fed.Cir.1996). Other sources of attorney fee awards include Federal Rule of Civil Procedure 11, *see Cambridge Prods., Ltd. v. Penn Nutrients, Inc.*, 962 F.2d 1048, 22 U.S.P.Q.2d 1577 (Fed.Cir.1992), the inherent power of the court, *see L.E.A. Dynatech, Inc. v. Allina*, 49 F.3d 1527, 33 U.S.P.Q.2d 1839 (Fed.Cir.1995), and, on appeal, Federal Rule of Appellate Procedure Rule 38, *see Finch v. Hughes Aircraft Co.*, 926 F.2d 1574, 17 U.S.P.Q.2d 1914 (Fed.Cir.1991).

4. Enhanced Damages and Attorney Fees Abroad. Foreign legal systems almost universally reject the notion of an award of punitive damages for patent infringement. They do routinely engage in the shifting of attorney fees to the winning party, however. These issues are taken up further in Chapter 18 of this casebook.

§ 17.4 MARKING

The Patent Act provides a significant incentive for patentees to give notice of their intellectual property rights on the patented device or its packaging. As set forth in 35 U.S.C. § 287:

> Patentees, and persons making or selling any patented article for or under them, may give notice to the public that the same is patented, either by fixing thereon the word "patent" or the abbreviation "pat.", together with the number of the patent, or when, from the character of the article, this can not be done, by fixing to it, or to the package wherein one or more of them is contained, a label containing a like notice. In the event of failure so to mark, no damages shall be recovered by the patentee in any action for infringement, except on proof that the infringer was notified of the infringement and continued to infringe thereafter, in which event damages may be recovered only for infringement occurring after such notice. Filing of an action for infringement shall constitute such notice.

The details of patent marking, as well as the consequences of failing to do so, are reviewed in the following opinion.

AMSTED INDUSTRIES INC. v. BUCKEYE STEEL CASTINGS CO.

United States Court of Appeals, Federal Circuit, 1994.
24 F.3d 178, 30 U.S.P.Q.2d 1462.

BEFORE PLAGER, LOURIE, and RADER, CIRCUIT JUDGES.

LOURIE, CIRCUIT JUDGE.

The '269 patent, which issued in the name of Stanley H. Fillion as inventor on May 23, 1972 and was assigned to Dresser Industries, is entitled "Combined Body Bolster Center Filler and Center Plate for Railway Cars" and claims a particular center plate in combination with several other components to form a railroad car underframe structure. The center plate component is the basis of the present dispute. Dresser made and sold the component center plate under the name "Low Profile" until 1985, at which time it sold the '269 patent and the Low Profile trademark to Amsted. Amsted thereafter began making and selling the Low Profile plate to rail car builders for assembly into the patented combination.

MARKING/NOTICE REQUIREMENT OF 35 U.S.C. § 287

1. Amsted's Cross–Appeal

Amsted cross-appeals from the district court's ruling that, because the patented articles were not marked, Amsted's recovery of damages was limited to the period after which it notified Buckeye of its infringement pursuant to 35 U.S.C. § 287.

The district court held that section 287 limited Amsted's recovery of damages because Amsted's customers, to whom Amsted sold one element of the patented combination with the expectation that they would use that element to make and sell the patented invention, were implied licensees who were "making or selling [the] patented article for or under [Amsted]" within the meaning of section 287. The court reasoned that "[t]he distribution or manufacturing arrangement of a patentee, unilaterally chosen by the patentee, cannot be allowed to relieve the patentee of its duty to mark under Section 287."

Amsted argues that section 287(a) does not so limit its damages. Amsted emphasizes that it never made the patented article and that its customers, who did make and sell the patented articles, did not do so "for or under" Amsted within the meaning of section 287(a). Amsted thus asserts that its recovery of damages should not have been predicated on marking or notice under section 287(a) and that it was entitled to damages from the beginning of Buckeye's infringement.

The question before us is the scope to be accorded the "for or under" language of section 287(a). This is an issue of statutory construction which we review for correctness as a matter of law. A licensee who makes or sells a patented article does so "for or under" the patentee, thereby limiting the patentee's damage recovery when the patented article is not marked. In view of the purpose of section 287, "to encourage the patentee to give notice to the public of the patent," there is no reason why section 287 should only apply to express licensees and not to implied licensees.

There is no dispute that Amsted impliedly authorized its customers to make, use, and sell the patented article. The record reveals that Amsted manufactured and sold its center plates for use in the patented combination, and that Amsted provided its customers with installation drawings which instruct how to assemble the center plate, along with other components, according to the teachings of the patent. Amsted argues that had it marked its center plate it would have violated 35 U.S.C. § 292 which prohibits the marking of an unpatented article. This is not persuasive. A marking such as "for use under U.S. X,XXX,XXX" would have sufficed. Moreover, Amsted could have sold its plates with a requirement that its purchaser-licensees mark the patented products "licensed under U.S. X,XXX,XXX." Such marking by either Amsted or its purchasers would have fulfilled the policy goal of notifying the public concerning the patent status of items in commerce. Thus, we conclude that Amsted's right to recover damages prior to actual notification is dependent upon compliance with the marking or notice requirements of section 287(a). Since there is no dispute that the patented articles sold by Amsted's customers were never marked, Amsted is precluded from recovering damages prior to the date that Buckeye, the accused infringer, "was notified of the infringement." Accordingly, the next issue before us is the date on which effective notice occurred.

Hold

2. *Proper Notice Under Section 287*

The parties dispute which of two letters written by Amsted to Buckeye, one dated January 10, 1986 and the other January 27, 1989, constituted effective statutory notice. The contents of these letters are not disputed. The 1986 letter stated in pertinent part:

> This is to advise you that Amsted ... has acquired a number of properties [from Dresser] ... including [the '269 patent]. ...

> It is our understanding that Dresser Industries actively sought to enforce its patent ... and those rights have been heretofore respected in the industry. AMSTED–ASF expects to continue to enforce those rights which it has acquired and similarly expects our industry to respect its patents.

> Accordingly, you should acquaint yourself with the ['269 patent] and refrain from supplying or offering to supply component parts which would infringe or contribute to the infringement of the patent[ ]. You should not offer to supply items which are copies of or designed to replace our LOW PROFILE center plate.

This letter was broadcast to a number of other companies, not only to Buckeye. It did not explicitly charge Buckeye with infringement of Amsted's '269 patent.

Amsted's 1989 letter stated in pertinent part:

> On January 10, 1986 I wrote to you and advised of AMSTED Industries' ownership and enforcement policy respecting the ['269 patent]. ...

> In our view [your center plate, a photocopy of which is attached,] or the intended application thereof to a freight car infringes the ['269 patent]. Accordingly we demand that you immediately cease and desist from any further unauthorized production and sales of such castings that ... include features covered by our patents. ...

We expect to . . . enforce our patent rights against your company should the matter remain unresolved.

Both parties agree that the 1989 was proper notice; the dispute is whether the 1986 letter so qualifies.

The jury found that the 1986 letter constituted statutory notice. In denying Buckeye's motion for JMOL on this issue, the court held that the notice requirement of section 287 does not require a specific charge of infringement and that, "[g]iven all the circumstances, the jury permissibly concluded that the 1986 letter notified Buckeye of [its] infringement." The court specifically pointed to evidence that Buckeye knew that it was infringing at the time it received Amsted's letter and evidence evincing Buckeye's "understanding" that the 1986 letter was a notice of infringement. Buckeye argues that the district court erred in denying its motion for JMOL on this issue because the 1986 letter did not constitute a notice of infringement under section 287 as a matter of law. Buckeye asserts that the statute requires a patentee to specifically charge an infringer with infringement and that a general communication which merely gives notice of the patent and the patentee's intention to enforce it is insufficient. Buckeye maintains that it was not notified of its infringement by Amsted until it received the 1989 letter and that Amsted was thus precluded from recovering damages under section 287 prior to that date.

Amsted argues that the notice provision does not require the patentee to identify an accused device, but only to inform the defendant of the type of product that would infringe. Amsted asks us to hold that the 1986 letter was sufficient notice in the context of what Buckeye knew at the time it received that letter and what Buckeye understood the letter to mean. Amsted emphasizes that Buckeye had known about the '269 patent for ten years and ultimately decided to copy it after numerous unsuccessful attempts to design around it. Amsted asserts that when Buckeye received the 1986 letter it knew it was infringing.

The question before us, the proper interpretation of the statutory language "notified of the infringement," is one which we review for correctness as a matter of law. Section 287(a) provides that absent marking, a patentee may not recover damages without proof that "the infringer was notified of the infringement." The Supreme Court in *Dunlap v. Schofield*, 152 U.S. 244, 14 S.Ct. 576, 38 L.Ed. 426 (1894), held that the "clear meaning" of this section is that a patentee cannot recover damages absent marking or notice to the "particular defendants by informing them of his patent and of their infringement of it." 152 U.S. at 247–48, 14 S.Ct. at 577. The Court further stated that notice "is an affirmative act, and something to be done by him." Because the plaintiffs in *Dunlap* offered no proof in support of their allegation that they had notified the defendants of the patent and of their infringement, the Court held that they could not recover damages. 152 U.S. at 248, 14 S.Ct. at 577. *Dunlap* thus established that notice must be an affirmative act on the part of the patentee which informs the defendant of his infringement. We regard *Dunlap* as highly persuasive, if not controlling, on the meaning of the notice requirement of section 287.

For purposes of section 287(a), notice must be of "the infringement," not merely notice of the patent's existence or ownership. Actual notice requires the affirmative communication of a specific charge of infringement by a specific accused product or device. The 1986 letter does not meet this standard. It is irrelevant, contrary to the district court's conclusion, whether the defendant knew of the patent or knew of his own infringement. The correct approach to determining notice under section 287 must focus on the action of the patentee, not the knowledge or understanding of the infringer. The 1986 letter was merely informational, of the kind that companies often send to others without intending to charge infringement. Just as such letters tend not to be threats sufficient to justify a declaratory judgment action, they also are not charges of infringement for "notice" purposes.

We thus conclude as a matter of law that the 1986 letter, which notified the whole industry, including Buckeye, only of Amsted's ownership of the patent and generally advised companies not to infringe, was not notice within the meaning of section 287. Amsted accordingly did not give Buckeye notice for purposes of section 287 until its 1989 letter, which specifically charged Buckeye with infringement and specified an infringing device. The district court thus erred as a matter of law in denying Buckeye's motion for JMOL on this issue. Amsted may recover damages only after it notified Buckeye of its infringement with the 1989 letter. We thus vacate the jury's damage award and remand for a recalculation of damages from the date of the 1989 letter.

Notes

1.   False Marking. 35 U.S.C.A. § 292 provides the unusual remedy of a *qui tam* action against entities that mark an article with a patent number "with the intent of counterfeiting or imitating the mark of the patentee, or of deceiving the public." Anyone may bring suit, and the fine of up to $500 per falsely marked article is split between the plaintiff and the United States Treasury. Courts have strictly construed the intent element of false marking, such that no violation occurs if the mismarking occurred in good faith, *Brose v. Sears, Roebuck and Co.*, 455 F.2d 763 (5th Cir.1972), or due to a mistake.

Another concern that may arise out of false marking is the threat of charges of an antitrust violation. A safe harbor of sorts appears to exist if the article is marked with a notice to the effect that the article is "[p]rotected by one or more of the following patents." At least one court has held that this sort of notice does not comprise a restraint on competition even if only one of the listed patents covers the product. *United States v. General Electric Co.*, 82 F.Supp. 753, 80 U.S.P.Q. 195 (D.N.J.1949). Given that many products are subject to protection to patents that may expire at different times, and that products are frequently redesigned, are you sympathetic to this holding? Or is it simply a convenient loophole?

2.   Patent Marking Estoppel. Several courts have held "that placing a patent number on a product will estop a manufacturer from denying that his product embodies the patent for purposes of liability for both patent infringement damages and patent license royalties." *Boyd v. Schildkraut Giftware Corp.*, 936 F.2d 76, 79, 19 U.S.P.Q.2d 1223, 1225 (2d Cir.1991) (citations omitted). The Federal Circuit has yet to discuss this equitable doctrine in a published opinion. At least one district court has declared that the doctrine is no longer extant, but on appeal the Federal Circuit expressly declined to address this holding one way or the other. *High Frequency Products, Inc. v. Wynn's Climate Systems, Inc.*, 91 F.3d 167 (Fed.Cir.1996) (nonprecedential).

3. Patents with both product and process claims. The Federal Circuit stated the rule in *Devices for Medicine* again in *American Medical Sys., Inc. v. Medical Eng'g Corp.*, 6 F.3d 1523, 28 U.S.P.Q.2d 1321 (Fed.Cir. 1993):

> The purpose behind the marking statute is to encourage the patentee to give notice to the public of the patent. The reason that the marking statute does not apply to method claims is that, ordinarily, where the patent claims are directed to only a method or process there is nothing to mark. Where the patent contains both apparatus and method claims, however, to the extent that there is a tangible item to mark by which notice of the asserted method claims can be given, a party is obliged to do so if it intends to avail itself of the constructive notice provisions of section 287(a).

6 F.3d at 1538–39, 28 U.S.P.Q.2d at 1332. Does this statement square with the holding in *Hanson v. Alpine Valley Ski Area, Inc.*, 718 F.2d 1075, 219 U.S.P.Q. 679 (Fed.Cir.1983)? In *Hanson*, the patent covered a method and apparatus for making artificial snow. The infringer, Alpine, sought to avoid damages because Hanson's licensee had not marked the patented snow-making machines. The Federal Circuit did not apply § 287:

> Alpine states that the Hanson patent also includes apparatus claims. The only claims that were found infringed in this case, however, were claims 1, 2, and 6 of the Hanson patent, which are drawn to "[t]he method of forming, distributing and depositing snow upon a surface. . . . "It is "settled in the case law that the notice requirement of this statute does not apply where the patent is directed to a process or method."

718 F.2d at 1083, 219 U.S.P.Q. at 685. Similarly, in *Crystal Semiconductor Corp. v. TriTech Microelec. Int'l Inc.*, 246 F.3d 1336, 57 U.S.P.Q.2d 1953 (Fed.Cir.2001), the Federal Circuit sustained damages on an unmarked process when the patentee could have marked an apparatus that operated the process. How can you reconcile *Hanson/Crystal Semiconductor* and *American Medical Systems*? If you reconcile them on the basis that the patentee in *Hanson* did not assert apparatus claims, only method claims, does this strict pleading rule accurately reflect the reasoning in *American Medical Systems* that concentrates on the need to supply notice whenever a tangible item presents the opportunity? Moreover in *Crystal Semiconductor* the patentee asserted both product and process claims.

4. Marking Abroad. The United States occupies a middle ground in its attitude towards the marking of patented articles. Most jurisdictions do not impose a marking requirement. Others appear to provide for marking as an affirmative right afforded by the patent grant, as indicated by Article 15 of the Patent Law of the People's Republic of China:

> The patentee has the right to affix a patent marking and to indicate the number of the patent on the patented product or on the packing of that product.

Still other regimes require marking. As indicated by Article 20 of the Chilean patent statute, failure to mark essentially renders the patent unenforceable:

> To have a right to the protection afforded by the law to industrial property, every product patented in the country must be clearly marked with the number and date of the patent, either on the article itself or its wrapper.

> The only exceptions to be made to this rule are the methods or processes that from their nature cannot possibly comply with it.

> On the expiry of the period of the monopoly the aforesaid marks must be suppressed. . . .

Given such varying requirements, multinational actors must be wary when embodying their patented inventions in different states.

REMEDIES EXERCISE

You work as an attorney in Detroit, Michigan. On November 15, 2001, you are contacted by Bob Battel, President of the Battel Toy Company and proprietor of U.S. Patent No. 9,876,543. The '543 patent is directed towards a miniature track and car system. Its embodiment, the Battel "Tot Wheels," is one of the most commercially successful toys in history. You know that Battel successfully enforced the '543 patent against a leading competitor, Angler–Preis Toys Unlimited, in a decision that was recently affirmed by the Federal Circuit. According to a newspaper article, Battel and Angler–Preis then settled the dispute for an undisclosed amount.

"Besides Battel and Angler–Preis," begins Mr. Battel, "there is only one other competitor in the car-and-track market, the Hasbeen Toy Company. Hasbeen sells a product called the 'Matchbook Racer Set.' Hasbeen's 'Matchbook Racer Set' is just like the one produced by Angler–Preis, so I am certain that Hasbeen also infringes the '543 patent. Before we bring suit against Hasbeen, I want to know what kind of remedies we can expect to obtain if we are ultimately successful.

"The '543 patent issued on January 1, 1995," Mr. Battel explains. "We began marketing 'Tot Wheels' the year before, on January 1, 1994. Since January 1, 1994, we have made annual sales of about 200,000 'Tot Wheels' units. We make a profit of about five dollars per unit. Further, we could have sold 'Tot Wheels' for another two dollars per unit, but competition from Hasbeen and Angler–Preis caused us to lower our price. Of course, that additional amount would have been pure profit for us. I understand that Hasbeen has sold approximately 150,000 'Matchbook Racer Sets' per year. I also suspect that they make a profit of about six dollars per unit on their sales.

"Within six months after we started marketing 'Tot Wheels'," Mr. Battel continues, "Hasbeen had came out with its 'Matchbook Racer Sets,' which was a total knock-off of our product. The day after the '543 patent issued, we sent Hasbeen a letter warning it about the patent and our intention to enforce it against the 'Matchbook Racer Set.' Hasbeen replied that it was studying the '543 patent. Later, on May 15, 1995, Hasbeen wrote and stated that it obtained an opinion from a patent attorney from the Washington, D.C. law firm of Beatum & Cheatum. According to this attorney, the '543 patent would have been obvious over a reference that hadn't been before the examiner, the Spielzeug patent.

"Fortunately for us, Angler–Preis also raised that defense," Mr. Battel concludes with glee. "But the Federal Circuit just said that the Spielzeug patent comprised nonanalogous art! We're really ready to sock it to Hasbeen. However, we decided to take on Angler–Preis first, and wrote Hasbeen a letter on June 1, 1995, saying that we would sue them once we were done with Angler–Preis. Hasbeen never altered its 'Matchbook Racer Set' despite our correspondence."

"I should also tell you that in addition to selling the basic 'Tot Wheels' set, which comes with a track and two cars," Mr. Battel notes, "we sell sets of additional cars, four to a pack. These sets come in different styles, like Formula One racers or funny cars, and are extremely popular. Our cars are especially designed to fit in the grooves of the 'Tot Wheels' track, although one can also just roll them along any surface. We sell about 100,000 sets of these additional cars each year, and guess that 80% of them are used in conjunction with the 'Tot Wheels' unit. We make a profit of two dollars per set on the additional cars. Hasbeen also maintains annual sales of about 25,000 additional sets of cars. None of our 'Tot Wheels' cars works with Hasbeen's 'Matchbook Racer Set', or vice versa."

You ask Mr. Battel about his manufacturing capabilities. "Well, our plant is currently capable of making about 300,000 'Tot Wheels' a year," Mr. Battel replies. "However, had our competitors respected our patent from the beginning, then we could have assuredly scaled up production to at least 500,000 units annually as early as 1998. We can easily make as many additional cars as you like-perhaps as many as five million a year."

Next, you inquire as to Battel's licensing policies. "Nobody ever approached us about licensing the '543 patent," Mr. Battel explains, "but we have licensed other patents in the toy industry. Our going rate varies from 10–15% of profits. You see, the toy industry is a real gold mine?profits here average around 20% of the sales price or so."

"We make nearly 70% of our annual sales during the holiday shopping season; that is, between Thanksgiving and December 31st," Mr. Battel notes in conclusion. "I realize that I have given you short notice, but do we have any options to protect our most profitable sales period? We want to stay on track for our shareholders this year, and not get beaten down the stretch by Hasbeen!"

What advice would you give to Mr. Battel regarding possible reme-dies against Hasbeen?

Chapter Eighteen

PATENT ENFORCEMENT

There is much to the making of a patent enforcement action beyond notions of infringement, defenses and remedies. This Chapter picks up on the themes developed in the preceding chapters to explore additional aspects of patent enforcement. Some of the issues presented here are unique to the patent law. Others lie on the border of civil procedure law but concern legal issues or fact patterns commonly encountered in patent litigation. We begin with a consideration of Chapter 26 of Title 35, which addresses the ownership and assignment of United States patents.

§ 18.1 OWNERSHIP AND ASSIGNMENT OF PATENT RIGHTS

The initial provision of Chapter 26, § 261, sets forth the elemental characteristic of patent rights—those of personal property—and also lays out rules governing the assignment of patents. The opinion which follows comprises the most significant Federal Circuit discussion of § 261, an opinion that has much to say about the nature of an issued patent as a property right.

FILMTEC CORP. v. ALLIED–SIGNAL INC.

United States Court of Appeals, Federal Circuit, 1991.
939 F.2d 1568, 19 U.S.P.Q.2d 1508.

Before PLAGER and LOURIE, CIRCUIT JUDGES, and FRIEDMAN, SENIOR CIRCUIT JUDGE.

PLAGER, CIRCUIT JUDGE.

Allied–Signal Inc. and UOP Inc. (Allied), defendants-appellants, appeal from the preliminary injunction issued by the district court in *FilmTec Corp. v. Allied–Signal, Inc.*, C.A. No. 89–0919–GT(M) (S.D. Cal. Mar. 1, 1990). The trial court enjoined Allied from "making, using or selling, and actively inducing others to make use or sell TFCL membrane in the United States, and from otherwise infringing claim 7 of United States Patent No. 4,277,344 ['344]." The injunction issued following the findings and conclusions of the district court reported in *FilmTec Corp. v. Allied–Signal, Inc.*, C.A. No. 89–0919–GT(IEG) (S.D.Cal. Feb. 22, 1990) (*FilmTec*). Because of serious doubts on the record before us as to who has title to the invention and the ensuing patent, we vacate the grant of the injunction and remand for further proceedings.

I. BACKGROUND

The application which ultimately issued as the '344 patent was filed by John E. Cadotte on February 22, 1979. The patent claims a reverse osmosis membrane and a method for using the membrane to reduce the concentration of solute molecules and ions in solution. Cadotte assigned his rights in the application and any subsequently issuing patent to plaintiff-appellee FilmTec Corp. (FilmTec). This assignment was duly recorded in the United States Patent and Trademark Office. Defendant-appellant Allied manufactured a reverse osmosis membrane and FilmTec sued Allied for infringing certain claims of the '344 patent.

John Cadotte was one of the four founders of FilmTec. Prior to founding FilmTec, Cadotte and the other founders were employed in various responsible positions at the North Star Division of Midwest Research Institute (MRI), a not-for-profit research organization. MRI was principally engaged in contract research, much of it for the United States (Government), and much of it involving work in the field of reverse osmosis membranes.

The evidence indicates that the work at MRI in which Cadotte and the other founders were engaged was being carried out under contract (the contract) to the Government "to provide research on In Situ–Formed Condensation Polymers for Reverse Osmosis Membranes." The contract provided that MRI

> agrees to grant and does hereby grant to the Government the full and entire domestic right, title and interest in [any invention, discovery, improvement or development (whether or not patentable) made in the course of or under this contract or any subcontract (of any tier) thereunder].

It appears that sometime between the time FilmTec came into being in 1977 (there is evidence that it was organized in the summer of 1977, and incorporated in September of that year) and the time Cadotte submitted his patent application in February of 1979, he made the invention that led to the '344 patent. As we will explain, just when in that period the invention was made is critical.

Cadotte left MRI in January of 1978. Cadotte testified that he conceived his invention the month after he left MRI. Allied disputes this, and alleges that Cadotte conceived his invention and formed the reverse osmosis membrane of the '344 patent earlier—in July of 1977 or at least by November of 1977 when he allegedly produced an improved membrane. Allied bases this on certain entries in the notebooks which Cadotte kept during this period. The trial judge found that "Cadotte's

1977 North Star notebook entries establish that he did [while still at MRI] combine the two chemicals which are claimed in the '344 patent."

However, because of its view of the issues, the trial court concluded it did not need to decide whether that combination resulted in the claimed invention. This was because in granting the preliminary injunction, the trial court concluded that as a matter of law even if the invention was made while Cadotte was employed at MRI, under the contract the Government could have no more than equitable title to the patent, which title cannot be raised as a defense by Allied. The district court stated

> that the [G]overnment's rights in an invention discovered by an employee while under contract are equitable, and are not available as a defense by the alleged infringer against the legal titleholder.

Cited for this proposition was *Sigma Eng'g Serv., Inc. v. Halm Instrument Co., Inc.*, 33 F.R.D. 129, 138 U.S.P.Q. 297 (E.D.N.Y.1963).

On the remaining issues raised, the trial judge ruled that: 1) Allied did not present clear and convincing evidence of Cadotte's intent to deceive the patent examiner; 2) Allied did not present clear and convincing evidence that the invention would have been obvious; 3) the Allied membrane is a literal infringement of claims 6 and 7 of the '344 patent; and 4) the issues of irreparable harm, balance of hardships, and public interest all weigh in favor of FilmTec.

II. ISSUES ON APPEAL

On appeal from the grant of the preliminary injunction, Allied argues that the trial court committed reversible error on each of five substantive issues. In Allied's view, the contract vested legal title to the invention in the Government and, therefore, FilmTec lacks standing to bring suit; Cadotte misled the patent examiner as to the Government's possible rights in the invention and the '344 patent is unenforceable; the '344 patent is invalid because the invention claimed would have been obvious; when the claims are properly read, the Allied membrane does not infringe the '344 patent; and finally, the district court misapplied the test for issuance of a preliminary injunction.

It is well settled in this court that a party seeking a preliminary injunction must establish a right thereto in light of four factors: 1) a reasonable likelihood of success on the merits; 2) irreparable harm; 3) the balance of hardships tipping in favor of the requesting party; and 4) that the issuance of an injunction is in the public interest. *Chrysler Motors Corp. v. Auto Body Panels of Ohio, Inc.*, 908 F.2d 951, 952, 15 USPQ2d 1469, 1470 (Fed.Cir.1990). The district court must balance each of these factors against the others and against the magnitude of the relief requested to determine whether a preliminary injunction should be granted or denied. We review the decision of the district court to determine "if there was an abuse of discretion, an error of law, or a serious misjudgment of the evidence."

III. Discussion

A.

We address first the question of title to the '344 patent. Because of its central importance to the resolution of this case, we requested and received supplemental briefing from the parties with regard to this issue. It is important to keep in mind that the issue before us is not who should ultimately be held to have title to the patent, but whether, in view of the state of the title, it can be said that FilmTec has a reasonable likelihood of success on the merits of that issue, sufficient to warrant the grant of the preliminary injunction.

Allied alleges that the evidence establishes that the contract between MRI and the Government grants to the Government "all discoveries and inventions made within the scope of their [i.e., MRI's employees] employment," and that the invention claimed in the '344 patent was made by Cadotte while employed by MRI. From this Allied reasons that rights in the invention must be with the Government and therefore Cadotte had no rights to assign to FilmTec. If FilmTec lacks title to the patent, FilmTec has no standing to bring an infringement action under the '344 patent. FilmTec counters by arguing that the trial court was correct in concluding that the most the Government would have acquired was an equitable title to the '344 patent, which title would have been made void under 35 U.S.C. § 261 (1988) by the subsequent assignment to FilmTec from Cadotte.

The parties agree that Cadotte was employed by MRI and that the contract between MRI and the Government contains a grant of rights to inventions made pursuant to the contract. However, the record does not reflect whether the employment agreement between Cadotte and MRI either granted or required Cadotte to grant to MRI the rights to inventions made by Cadotte. Allied argues that Cadotte's inventions were assigned nevertheless to MRI. Allied points to the provision in the contract between MRI and the Government in which MRI warrants that it will obligate inventors to assign their rights to MRI.

While this is not conclusive evidence of a grant of or a requirement to grant rights by Cadotte, it raises a serious question about the nature of the title, if any, in FilmTec. FilmTec apparently did not address this issue at the trial, and there is no indication in the opinion of the district court that this gap in the chain of ownership rights was considered by the court.

B.

Since property rights in an invention itself could not, under any conventional meaning of the term, be considered real property, they are by definition personal property. While early cases have pointed to the myriad ways in which patent rights—that is, property in patents—are closer in analogy to real than to personal property, the statutes establish as a matter of law that patents today have the attributes of personal property. And 35 U.S.C. § 261 makes clear that an application for patent as well as the patent itself may be assigned. Further, it is settled law that between the time of an invention and the issuance of a patent, rights in an invention may be assigned and legal title to the ensuing patent will pass to the assignee upon grant of the patent.

If an assignment of rights in an invention is made prior to the existence of the invention, this may be viewed as an assignment of an expectant interest. An assignment of an expectant interest can be a valid assignment. In such a situation, the assignee holds at most an equitable title.

Once the invention is made and an application for patent is filed, however, legal title to the rights accruing thereunder would be in the assignee (subject to the rights of a subsequent purchaser under § 261), and the assignor-inventor would have nothing remaining to assign. In this case, if Cadotte granted MRI rights in inventions made during his employ, and if the subject matter of the '344 patent was invented by Cadotte during his employ with MRI, then Cadotte had nothing to give to FilmTec and his purported assignment to FilmTec is a nullity. Thus, FilmTec would lack both title to the '344 patent and standing to bring the present action. *See* 28 U.S.C. § 1498 (1988).

The question of FilmTec's right to maintain the action against Allied should not be confused with the question of whether Allied could defend by arguing that title to the patent was in a third party—the Government—and therefore Allied has a good defense against any infringement suit. The plea in jus tertii (title in a third person) as it was known at common law was held in some early cases to be a good defense to a possessory action, although more recent cases reject the defense and allow recovery on a prior possession. But the issue here is not whether title lies in the Government or some other third party; it is rather whether FilmTec has made a sufficient showing to establish reasonable likelihood of success on the merits, which includes a showing that title to the patent and the rights thereunder are in FilmTec.

As noted, the district court was of the view that if the Government was the assignee from Cadotte through MRI, the Government would have acquired at most an equitable title, and that legal title would remain in Cadotte. (The legal title would then have passed to FilmTec by virtue of the later assignment, pursuant to § 261 of the statutes.) The district court's support for this proposition was the decision in the District Court for the Eastern District of New York in 1963, in the case of *Sigma Eng'g v. Halm Instrument*, 33 F.R.D. 129, 138 U.S.P.Q. 297.

But *Sigma*, even if it were binding precedent on this court, does not stretch so far. The issue in *Sigma* was whether the plaintiff, assignee of the patent rights of the inventors, was the real party in interest such as to be able to maintain the instant action for patent infringement. See FED.R.CIV.P. 12(b)(7). Defendant claimed that the inventors' employer had title to the invention by virtue of the employment contract which obligated the inventors to transfer all patent rights to inventions made while in its employ. As the court expressly noted, no such transfers were made, however, and the court considered any possible interest held by the employer in the invention to be in the nature of an equitable claim. Whatever it was, it was not sufficient to make the employer an indispensable party to the suit under the Rule, and defendant's motion to dismiss was denied.

In our case, the contract between MRI and the Government did not merely obligate MRI to grant future rights, but expressly granted to the Government MRI's rights in any future invention. Ordinarily, no further act would be required once an invention came into being; the transfer of title would occur by operation of law. If a similar contract provision existed between Cadotte and MRI, as MRI's contract with the Government required, and if the invention was made before Cadotte left MRI's employ, as the trial judge seems to suggest, Cadotte would have no rights in the invention or any ensuing patent to assign to FilmTec.

Because of the district court's view of the title issue, no specific findings were made on either of these questions. As a result, we do not know who held legal title to the invention and to the patent application and therefore we do not know if FilmTec could make a sufficient legal showing to establish the likelihood of success necessary to support a preliminary injunction.

C.

It is well established that when a legal title holder of a patent transfers his or her title to a third party purchaser for value without notice of an outstanding equitable claim or title, the purchaser takes the entire ownership of the patent, free of any prior equitable encumbrance. *Hendrie v. Sayles*, 98 U.S. 546, 549, 25 L.Ed. 176 (1879). This is an application of the common law bona fide purchaser for value rule.

Section 261 of Title 35 goes a step further. It adopts the principle of the real property recording acts, and provides that the bona fide purchaser for value cuts off the rights of a prior assignee who has failed to record the prior assignment in the Patent and Trademark Office by the dates specified in the statute. Although the statute does not expressly so say, it is clear that the statute is intended to cut off prior legal interests, which the common law rule did not.

Both the common law rule and the statute contemplate that the subsequent purchaser be exactly that—a transferee who pays valuable consideration, and is without notice of the prior transfer. The trial judge, with reference to FilmTec's rights as a subsequent purchaser, stated simply that "FilmTec is a subsequent purchaser from Cadotte for independent consideration. There is no evidence presented to imply that FilmTec was on notice of any previous assignment." *FilmTec* at 4. The court concluded that, even if § 35(b)(2) of the MRI contract automatically transferred title to the government, such assignment is not enforceable at law as it was never recorded.

Since this matter will be before the trial court on remand, it may be useful for us to clarify what is required before FilmTec can properly be considered a subsequent purchaser entitled to the protections of § 261. In the first place, FilmTec must be in fact a purchaser for a valuable consideration. This requirement is different from the classic notion of a purchaser under a deed of grant, where the requirement of consideration was a formality, and the proverbial peppercorn would suffice to have the deed operate under the statute of uses. Here the requirement is that the subsequent purchaser, in order to cut off the rights of the prior purchaser, must be more than a donee or other gratuitous transferee. There must be in fact valuable consideration paid so that the subsequent purchaser can, as a matter of law, claim record reliance as a premise upon which the purchase was made. That, of course, is a matter of proof.

In addition, the subsequent transferee/assignee—FilmTec in our case—must be without notice of any such prior assignment. If Cadotte's contract with MRI contained a provision assigning any inventions made during the course of employment either to MRI or directly to the Government, Cadotte would clearly be on notice of the provisions of his own contract. Since Cadotte was one of the four founders of FilmTec, and the other founders and officers were also involved at MRI, FilmTec may well be deemed to have had actual notice of an assignment. Given the key roles that Cadotte and the others played both at MRI and later at FilmTec, at a minimum FilmTec might be said to be on inquiry notice of any possible rights in MRI or the Government as a result of Cadotte's work at MRI. Thus once again, the key to FilmTec's ability to show a likelihood of success on the merits lies in the relationship between Cadotte and MRI.

CONCLUSION

In our view of the title issue, it cannot be said on this record that FilmTec has established a reasonable likelihood of success on the merits. It is thus unnecessary for us to consider the other issues raised on appeal concerning the propriety of the injunction. The grant of the preliminary injunction is vacated and the case remanded to the district court to reconsider the propriety of the preliminary injunction in light of the four *Chrysler* factors and for further proceedings consistent with this opinion.

Notes

1. The Patent Recording Statute. Section 261 closes with the provision: "An assignment, grant or conveyance shall be void as against any subsequent purchaser or mortgagee for a valuable consideration, without notice, unless it is recorded in the Patent and Trademark Office within three months from its date or prior to the date of such subsequent purchase or mortgage." Thus, the United States patent statute employs a "race-notice" recording statute akin to those provided by state laws governing real property. Unlike some of those state statutes, however, those transacting in patents obtain at least a three-month grace period. Does your understanding of the patent recording statute influence your thinking on United States adoption of a first-to-file regime for determining priority of invention?

2. Assignment as Statutory Bar. Why didn't Cadotte's assignments more than one year prior to the '344 patent critical date of February 22, 1978, constitute a statutory bar under § 102(b)? This answer was provided by the Federal Circuit early in its history:

> [T]he district court held that . . . an assignment or sale of the rights in the invention and potential patent rights is not a sale of "the invention" within the meaning of section 102(b). We agree. The few cases we have found on this issue have uniformly held that such a sale of patent rights does not come within the section 102(b) bar. Such a result comports with the policies underlying the on sale bar, and with the business realities ordinarily surrounding a corporation's prosecution of patent applications for inventors.

Moleculon Research Corp. v. CBS, Inc., 793 F.2d 1261, 1267, 229 U.S.P.Q. 805, 809 (Fed.Cir.1986) (citations omitted).

§ 18.2 STANDING

Section 281 of the United States patent statute succinctly tells us that "[a] patentee shall have remedy by civil action for infringement of his patent." We may also learn from § 100(d) that the term " 'patentee' includes not only the patentee to whom the patent was issued but also the successors in title to the patentee." But given the multiplicity of rights granted by a United States patent, as well as its spatial and temporal dimensions, determination of those parties who properly possess the right to sue for patent infringement within these contours is often a complex task. The best point of departure remains the century-old Supreme Court opinion in *Waterman v. Mackenzie*, a holding still frequently cited in the face of a variety of contemporary commercial arrangements regarding patent rights.

WATERMAN v. MACKENZIE

United States Supreme Court, 1891.
138 U.S. 252.

A complex series of transactions, reviewed in the opinion below, preceded this litigation. Originally, Lewis E. Waterman, the owner of a patent on a fountain pen, assigned the patent to his wife. Mrs. Waterman then assigned the patent to the firm of Asa L. Shipman's Sons, which in turn assigned the patent to Asa L. Shipman. Later, Mrs. Waterman attempted to both license the patent to her husband and to assign it back to him.

Litigation commenced when Lewis E. Waterman brought suit against James A. Mackenzie and Samuel R. Murphy for patent infringement. Among the defenses was that the plaintiff did not own the patent at suit. According to the defendants, the suit should be dismissed. The lower court agreed, allowing the defendant's plea and setting the stage for this opinion of the Supreme Court.

MR. JUSTICE GRAY, after stating the facts as above, delivered the opinion of the court.

Every patent issued under the laws of the United States for an invention or discovery contains 'a grant to the patentee, his heirs and assigns, for the term of seventeen years, of the exclusive right to make, use, and vend the invention or discovery throughout the United States and the territories thereof.' The monopoly thus granted is one entire thing, and cannot be divided into parts, except as authorized by those laws. The patentee or his assigns may, by instrument in writing, assign, grant, and convey, either (1) the whole patent, comprising the exclusive right to make, use, and vend the invention throughout the United States; or (2) an undivided part or share of that exclusive right; or (3) the exclusive right under the patent within and throughout a specified part of the United States. A transfer of either of these three kinds of interests is an assignment, properly speaking, and vests in the assignee a title in so much of the patent itself, with a right to sue infringers. In the second case, jointly with the assignor. In the first and third cases, in the name of the assignee alone. Any assignment or transfer, short of one of these, is a mere license, giving the licensee no title in the patent, and no right to sue at law in his own name for an infringement. In equity, as at law, when the transfer amounts to a license only, the title remains in the owner of the patent; and suit must be brought in his name, and never in the name of the licensee alone unless that is necessary to prevent an absolute failure of justice, as where the patentee is the infringer, and cannot sue himself. Any rights of the licensee must be enforced through or in the name of the owner of the patent, and perhaps, if necessary to protect the rights of all parties, joining the licensee with him as a plaintiff.

Whether a transfer of a particular right or interest under a patent is an assignment or a license does not depend upon the name by which it calls itself, but upon the legal effect of its provisions. For instance, a grant of an exclusive right to make, use, and vend two patented machines within a certain district is an assignment, and gives the grantee the right to sue in his own name for an infringement within the district, because the right, although limited to making, using, and vending two machines, excludes all other persons, even the patentee, from making, using, or vending like machines within the district. *Wilson v. Rousseau*, 4 How. 646, 686. On the other hand, the grant of an exclusive right under the patent within a certain district, which does not include the right to make, and the right to use, and the right to sell, is not a grant of a title in the whole patent-right within the district, and is therefore only a license. Such, for instance, is a grant of "the full and exclusive right to make and vend" within a certain district, reserving to the grantor the right to make within the district, to be sold outside of it. So is a grant of "the exclusive right to make and use," but not to sell, patented machines within a certain district. *Mitchell v. Hawley*, 16 Wall. 544. So is an instrument granting "the sole right and privilege of manufacturing and selling" patented articles, and not expressly authorizing their use, because, though this might carry by implication the right to use articles made under the patent by the licensee, it certainly would not authorize him to use such articles made by others. An assignment of the entire patent, or of an undivided part thereof, or of the exclusive right under the patent for a limited territory, may be either absolute or by way of mortgage, and liable to be defeated by non-performance of a condition subsequent, as clearly appears in the provision of the statute, that "an assignment, grant, or conveyance shall be void as against any subsequent purchaser or mortgagee for a valuable consideration without notice, unless it is recorded in the patent-office within three months from the date thereof." Rev. St. § 4898. Before proceeding to consider the nature and effect of the various instruments given in evidence at the hearing in the circuit court, it is fit to observe that, (as was assumed in the argument for the plaintiff,) by the law of the state of New York, where all the instruments were made and all the parties to them resided, husband and wife are authorized to make conveyances and contracts of and concerning personal property to and with each other, in the same manner and to the same effect as if they were strangers.

By the deed of assignment of February 13, 1884, the plaintiff assigned to Mrs. Waterman the entire patent-right. That assignment vested in her the whole title in the patent, and the exclusive right to sue, either at law or in equity, for its subsequent infringement.

The next instrument in order of date is the "license agreement" between them of November 20, 1884, by which she granted to him "the sole and exclusive right and license to manufacture and sell fountain pen-holders containing the said patented improvement throughout the United States." This did not include the right to use such pen-holders, at least if manufactured by third persons, and was therefore a mere license, and not an assignment of any title, and did not give the licensee the right to sue alone, at law or in equity, for an infringement of the patent. The plaintiff not having amended his bill, pursuant to the leave granted by the circuit court, by joining the licensor as a plaintiff, this point requires no further notice. Nor is it doubted that the circuit court rightly held that, if the plaintiff was entitled to recover only for infringements occurring between February 12 and November 25, 1884, his remedy was at law.

The remaining question in the case, distinctly presented by the plea, and adjudged by the circuit court, is of the effect of the deed of November 25, 1884, by which Mrs. Waterman assigned to the firm of Asa L. Shipman's Sons all her right, title and interest in the invention and the patent, with an express provision that the assignment should be null and void if she and her husband, or either of them, should pay at maturity a certain promissory note of the same date made by them, and payable to the grantees. This instrument, being a conveyance made to secure the payment of a debt, upon condition that it should be avoided by the subsequent payment of that debt at a time fixed, was a mortgage, in apt terms, and in legal effect. On the same day, the mortgagees assigned by deed to Asa L. Shipman all their title under the mortgage,

and the promissory note thereby secured, Both assignments were recorded in the patent-office within three months after their date, and the title
thereby acquired by Shipman was outstanding in him at the times of the
subsequent assignment of the patent-right by Mrs. Waterman to the
plaintiff, and of the filing of this bill. This last assignment was therefore
subject to the mortgage, though not in terms so expressed. By a mortgage of personal property, differing in this respect from a pledge, it is not
merely the possession or a special property that passes; but, both at law
and in equity, the whole title is transferred to the mortgagee, as security
for the debt, subject only to be defeated by performance of the condition,
or by redemption on bill in equity within a reasonable time, and the
right of possession, when there is no express stipulation to the contrary,
goes with the right of property. A mortgage of real estate has gradually,
partly by the adoption of rules of equity in courts of common law, and
partly by express provisions of statute, come to be more and more
considered as a mere security for the debt, creating a lien or incum-
brance only, and leaving the title in the mortgagor, subject to alienation,
levy on execution, dower, and other incidents of a legal estate; but the
rules upon the subject vary in different states, and a mortgage is every
where considered as passing the title in the land, so far as may be
necessary for the protection of the mortgagee, and to give him the full
benefit of his security. After the mortgagee has taken possession, the
mortgagor has no power to lease, and the mortgagee is entitled to have,
and is bound to account for, the accruing rents and profits, damages
against trespassers, timber cut on the premises, and growing crops. Even
against a mortgagor in possession, the mortgagee may obtain an injunction or damages for such cutting of timber as tends to impair the value
of the mortgage security, or as is not allowed by good husbandry or by
express or implied license from the mortgagee. A mortgagee of a lease-
hold or other personal property has the like right to an injunction to stay
waste by the mortgagor. The right of action against a stranger for an
injury to goods mortgaged, generally, though not always, depends upon
the right of possession. When the right of possession is in the mortgagor,
he is usually the proper party to sue. But even a mortgagee out of
possession may sometimes maintain an action for an injury to his
interest. And when the right of possession, as well as the general right of
property, is in the mortgage, the suit must be brought by the mortgagee,
and not by the mortgagor or any one claiming under a subsequent
conveyance from him. When it is provided by statute that a mortgage of
personal property shall not be valid against third persons, unless the
mortgage is recorded, a recording of the mortgage is a substitute for, and
(unless in case of actual fraud) equivalent to, a delivery of possession,
and makes the title and the possession of the mortgagee good against all
the world. A patent-right is incorporeal property, not susceptible of
actual delivery or possession; and the recording of a mortgage thereof in
the patent-office, in accordance with the act of congress, is equivalent to
a delivery of possession, and makes the title of the mortgagee complete
towards all other persons, as well as against the mortgagor. The right
conferred by letters patent for an invention is limited to a term of years,

and a large part of its value consists in the profits derived from royalties and license fees. In analogy to the rules governing mortgages of lands and of chattels, and with even stronger reason, the assignee of a patent by a mortgage duly recorded, whose security is constantly wasting by the lapse of time, must by held (unless otherwise provided in the mortgage) entitled to grant licenses, to receive license fees and royalties, and to have an account of profits or an award of damages against infringers. There can be no doubt that he is 'the party interested, either as patentee, assignee, or grantee,' and as such entitled to maintain an action at law to recover damages for an infringement; and it cannot have been the intention of congress that a suit in equity against an infringer to obtain an injunction and an account of profits, in which the court is authorized to award damages, when necessary to fully compensate the plaintiff, and has the same power to treble the damages as in an action at law, should not be brought by the same person. The necessary conclusion appears to us to be that Shipman, being the present owner of the whole title in the patent under a mortgage duly executed and recorded, was the person, and the only person, entitled to maintain such a bill as this; and that the plea, therefore, was rightly adjudged good. Decree affirmed.

Notes

1. The Federal Circuit Speaks. A significant discussion of licensee standing took place in the context of the *Rite–Hite Corp. v. Kelley Co.* decision, reprinted here in part in Chapter 17. Among the holdings of the trial court was that various Independent Sales Organizations, or ISOs, were exclusive licensees of the '847 patent and therefore possessed standing to join the patentee Rite–Hite in its suit against Kelley. The Federal Circuit discussed the matter as follows:

> Generally, one seeking money damages for patent infringement must have held legal title to the patent at the time of the infringement. A conveyance of legal title by the patentee can be made only of the entire patent, an undivided part or share of the entire patent, or all rights under the patent in a specified geographical region of the United States. A transfer of any of these is an assignment and vests the assignee with title in the patent, and a right to sue infringers. A transfer of less than one of these three interests is a license, not an assignment of legal title, and it gives the licensee no right to sue for infringement at law in the licensee's own name.

> Under certain circumstances, a licensee may possess sufficient interest in the patent to have standing to sue as a co-plaintiff with the patentee. Such a licensee is usually an "exclusive licensee." To be an exclusive licensee for standing purposes, a party must have received, not only the right to practice the invention within a given territory, but also the patentee's express or implied promise that others shall be excluded from practicing the invention within that territory as well. If the party has not received an express or implied promise of exclusivity under the patent, i.e., the right to exclude others from making, using, or selling the patented invention, the party has a "bare license," and has received

only the patentee's promise that that party will not be sued for infringement.

56 F.3d at 1551–52, 35 U.S.P.Q.2d at 1074–75. Applying these principles, the court concluded that the contracts at issue "were simply sales contracts between Rite–Hite and its independent distributors. They did not transfer any proprietary interest in the '847 patent and they did not give the ISO's the right to sue." Judge Newman authored a persuasive dissenting opinion, urging that:

> It is not necessary to decide the nuances of this contractual relationship, for the losses experienced at the sales level are compensable. If the ISOs were simply sales agents, as Kelley argues, then Rite–Hite is the seller of the goods. If these plaintiffs do not have "standing," as the majority states, because the lost sales were made by Rite–Hite, not the ISOs, then Rite–Hite is entitled to these damages. Thus, if compensation is not owed to the ISOs, it is owed to Rite–Hite.

56 F.3d at 1583, 35 U.S.P.Q.2d at 1100.

2. The Involuntary Plaintiff Technique. The third sentence of FED. R. CIV. P. 19(a) states: "If the person should join as a plaintiff but refuses to do so, the person may be made a defendant, or, in a proper case, an involuntary plaintiff." This phrasing leaves ample room for the *Waterman* rule. Recognizing *Waterman*, courts have recognized that a proper case includes instances where the patent owner is not subject to service of process. *See generally Katz v. Lear Siegler, Inc.*, 909 F.2d 1459, 1461–62, 15 U.S.P.Q.2d 1554 (Fed.Cir.1990); 7 CHARLES ALAN WRIGHT, ET AL., FEDERAL PRACTICE AND PROCEDURE § 1614 (1986).

3. Comparative Note. The German patent law also allows an exclusive licensee to assert patent infringement claims if its license is affected. *See* Kleiderbügel, Decision of the Bundesgerichtshof, Case No. X ZR (Dec. 20, 1994) (English translation available in 27 INT'L REV. INDUS. PROP. & COPYRIGHT L. 851 (1996)).

§ 18.3 PERSONAL JURISDICTION

Although the requirement of personal jurisdiction is hardly unique to this field, the intangible nature of intellectual property rights leads to conceptual difficulties in tying the tort of patent infringement to a particular location. In addition to resolving this issue, the Federal Circuit spoke in a robust voice on the application of personal jurisdiction standards to patent infringement actions in the following opinion.

BEVERLY HILLS FAN CO. v. ROYAL SOVEREIGN CORP.

United States Court of Appeals, Federal Circuit, 1994.
21 F.3d 1558, 30 U.S.P.Q.2d 1001.

Before NEWMAN, CIRCUIT JUDGE, SMITH, SENIOR CIRCUIT JUDGE, and PLAGER, CIRCUIT JUDGE.

PLAGER, CIRCUIT JUDGE.

Beverly is the current owner of U.S. Design Patent No. 304,229 (the '229 patent), which issued on October 24, 1989. That patent is directed to the design of a ceiling fan. Beverly is incorporated in Delaware and has its principal place of business in California.

Ultec is the manufacturer of a ceiling fan which Beverly alleges infringes the '229 patent. Ultec is incorporated in the People's Republic of China (PRC) and manufactures the accused fan in Taiwan. Royal imports into and distributes the accused fan in the United States. It is incorporated in New Jersey.

On December 11, 1991, Beverly filed suit against Ultec and Royal in the United States District Court for the Eastern District of Virginia. Beverly's complaint alleged in relevant part that both defendants are infringing and inducing infringement of the '229 patent by selling the accused fan to customers in the United States, including customers in Virginia; and that defendants are selling the accused fan to the Virginia customers through intermediaries.

Ultec and Royal subsequently filed a motion to dismiss for lack of personal jurisdiction pursuant to Rule 12(b)(2) of the Federal Rules of Civil Procedure. In support of their motion, defendants submitted several declarations. A first declaration was from James Cheng (the Cheng Declaration), the President of Ultec. In that declaration, Mr. Cheng stated that Ultec has no assets or employees located in Virginia; has no agent for the service of process in Virginia; does not have a license to do business in Virginia; and has not directly shipped the accused fan into Virginia. A second declaration was from T.K. Lim (the Lim Declaration), the President of Royal. In that declaration, Mr. Lim stated that Royal, as well, has no assets or employees in Virginia; has no agent for the service of process in Virginia; does not have a license to do business in Virginia; made a one-time sale of unrelated goods to Virginia in 1991 which represented less than three percent of Royal's total sales that year; and has not sold the accused fan to distributors or anyone else in Virginia.

Beverly then submitted several declarations in opposition to the motion. A first declaration was from Lyndal L. Shaneyfelt (the first Shaneyfelt Declaration), a private investigator. In that declaration, Mr. Shaneyfelt stated that, on December 4, 1991, he purchased one of the accused fans from the Alexandria, Virginia outlet of a company known as Builder's Square; that a manual accompanying the fan identified Royal as the source of the fan; that the fan was accompanied by a warranty which Royal would honor; and that Builder's Square has approximately six retail outlets located throughout Virginia. A second declaration was from Shelley A. Greenberg (the Greenberg Declaration), the President of Beverly. In that declaration, Mr. Greenberg stated that Beverly does a substantial amount of business in Virginia; that Beverly's Virginia customers include all six Builder's Square outlets; and that Beverly sells a commercial embodiment of the '229 patent to customers in Virginia through these outlets.

The trial court, after argument from the parties and consideration of their written submissions, ruled on the motion. The court correctly recognized that there were two limits to its jurisdictional reach: Virginia's long-arm statute and the Due Process Clause of the U.S. Constitution. The court found its analysis of the limits imposed by the Due Process Clause conclusive of the matter.

Relying on Supreme Court precedent as interpreted by the Fourth Circuit in *Chung v. NANA Development Corp.*, 783 F.2d 1124 (4th Cir.), *cert. denied*, 479 U.S. 948, 107 S.Ct. 431, 93 L.Ed.2d 381 (1986), the court concluded that the relevant inquiry was whether defendants' contacts with the forum were sufficiently purposeful that litigation in the forum could reasonably have been foreseen. The only purposeful contact the court considered relevant was the one-time shipment of unrelated goods referred to in the Lim Declaration. Finding that such contact was not sufficient to make litigation in Virginia reasonably foreseeable, the court granted the motion to dismiss. . . .

DISCUSSION

[W]e must disapprove the court's granting of the motion to dismiss. No additional development of the record is necessary for a decision on defendants' jurisdictional motion. The matter presents a pure question of law. The specific question on which the matter turns is whether the Due Process Clause of the Federal Constitution or specific limiting provisions in Virginia's long-arm statute preclude the exercise of jurisdiction in a case in which an alleged foreign infringer's sole contact with the forum resulted from indirect shipments through the stream of commerce.

As a preliminary matter, we consider whether we are bound to apply Fourth Circuit law to this question. As previously noted, the Fourth Circuit is where the case arose; under *Panduit Corp. v. All States Plastic Manufacturing Co.*, 744 F.2d 1564, 1574–75, 223 U.S.P.Q. 465, 471 (Fed.Cir.1984), we apply the law of the Fourth Circuit to procedural matters that are not unique to patent law. Beverly argues that we are not bound to apply Fourth Circuit law in this case because the issue here is intimately related to substantive patent law. Thus, argues Beverly, we are free to develop our own law on this issue.

Beverly is correct. Although in one sense the due process issue in this case is procedural, it is a critical determinant of whether and in what forum a patentee can seek redress for infringement of its rights. As we explain more fully below, the stream of commerce theory has achieved fairly wide acceptance in the federal courts. But even when followed, the theory comes in several variants. The regional circuits have not reached a uniform approach to this jurisdictional issue. *See, e.g., Max Daetwyler Corp. v. R. Meyer*, 762 F.2d 290, 226 U.S.P.Q. 305 (3d Cir.), cert. denied, 474 U.S. 980, 106 S.Ct. 383, 88 L.Ed.2d 336 (1985) (no jurisdiction found); *Honeywell, Inc. v. Metz Apparatewerke*, 509 F.2d 1137, 184 U.S.P.Q. 387 (7th Cir.1975) (jurisdiction found). Nor is there any apparent uniformity on the issue within the Fourth Circuit. The application of an assumed Fourth Circuit law, or for that matter, the law of any particular circuit, would thus not promote our mandate of achieving national uniformity in the field of patent law.

The creation and application of a uniform body of Federal Circuit law in this area would clearly promote judicial efficiency, would be consistent with our mandate, and would not create undue conflict and confusion at the district court level. Under circumstances such as these, we have held we owe no special deference to regional circuit law.

The Supreme Court stated in *International Shoe Co. v. Washington*, 326 U.S. 310, 66 S.Ct. 154, 90 L.Ed. 95 (1945), "due process requires ... that in order to subject a defendant to a judgment in personam, if he be not present within the territory of the forum, he have certain minimum contacts with it such that the maintenance of the suit does not offend 'traditional notions of fair play and substantial justice.' " Id. at 316, 66 S.Ct. at 158 (quoting *Milliken v. Meyer*, 311 U.S. 457, 463, 61 S.Ct. 339, 343, 85 L.Ed. 278 (1940)). Later cases have clarified that the minimum contacts must be "purposeful" contacts. Burger King Corp. v. Rudzewicz, 471 U.S. 462, 474, 105 S.Ct. 2174, 2183, 85 L.Ed.2d 528 (1985) (purposeful minimum contacts the 'Constitutional touchstone' of the due process analysis). The requirement for purposeful minimum contacts helps ensure that non-residents have fair warning that a particular activity may subject them to litigation within the forum. See Burger King, 471 U.S. at 472, 105 S.Ct. at 2182; *see also World–Wide Volkswagen Corp. v. Woodson*, 444 U.S. 286, 297, 100 S.Ct. 559, 567, 62 L.Ed.2d 490 (1980). Fair warning is desirable for non-residents are thus able to organize their affairs, alleviate the risk of burdensome litigation by procuring insurance and the like, and otherwise plan for the possibility that litigation in the forum might ensue.

Defendants argue that their contacts with Virginia were insufficient to give them warning that litigation in Virginia might ensue. We disagree. The allegations are that defendants purposefully shipped the accused fan into Virginia through an established distribution channel. The cause of action for patent infringement is alleged to arise out of these activities. No more is usually required to establish specific jurisdiction.

Defendants argue that the exercise of jurisdiction over them is foreclosed by the holding in *World–Wide Volkswagen*. In *World–Wide Volkswagen*, jurisdiction did not lie over an alleged foreign tortfeasor whose product was transported into the forum state through the unilateral actions of a third party having no pre-existing relationship with the tortfeasor. 444 U.S. at 298, 100 S.Ct. at 567. There was thus no purposeful contact by the tortfeasor with the forum, and thus no basis for exercising personal jurisdiction over the defendants. Here, by contrast, the allegations are that the accused fan arrived in Virginia through defendants' purposeful shipment of the fans through an established distribution channel. The Court in *World–Wide Volkswagen* specifically commented on the significance of this factual pattern: "[I]f the sale of a product of a manufacturer or distributor ... is not simply an isolated occurrence, but arises from the efforts of the [defendants] to serve, directly or indirectly, the market for its product ..., it is not unreasonable to subject it to suit." *Id.* at 297, 100 S.Ct. at 567. And "[t]he forum State does not exceed its powers under the Due Process Clause if it asserts personal jurisdiction over a corporation that delivers its products into the stream of commerce with the expectation that they will be purchased by consumers in the forum State." *Id.* at 297–98, 100 S.Ct. at 567.

Since the decision in *World–Wide Volkswagen,* lower courts have split over the exact requirements of the stream of commerce theory. In *Asahi Metal Industry Co. v. Superior Court,* 480 U.S. 102, 107 S.Ct. 1026, 94 L.Ed.2d 92 (1987), the Supreme Court reflected that split in the context of a case in which jurisdiction in California state courts was asserted for the purpose of requiring a Japanese corporation to indemnify a Taiwanese corporation on the basis of a sale made in Taiwan and a shipment of goods from Japan to Taiwan.

We need not join this debate here, since we find that, under either version of the stream of commerce theory, plaintiff made the required jurisdictional showing. When viewed in the light of the allegations and the uncontroverted assertions in the affidavits, plaintiff has stated all of the necessary ingredients for an exercise of jurisdiction consonant with due process: defendants, acting in consort, placed the accused fan in the stream of commerce, they knew the likely destination of the products, and their conduct and connections with the forum state were such that they should reasonably have anticipated being brought into court there.

Notwithstanding the existence of purposeful minimum contacts, a due process determination requires one further step. As Justice Stevens put it in his concurrence in *Asahi,* " 'minimum requirements inherent in the concept of "fair play and substantial justice" may defeat the reasonableness of jurisdiction even if the defendant has purposefully engaged in forum activities.' " In other words, even if the requisite minimum contacts have been found through an application of the stream of commerce theory or otherwise, if it would be unreasonable for the forum to assert jurisdiction under all the facts and circumstances, then due process requires that jurisdiction be denied.

In general, these cases are limited to the rare situation in which the plaintiff's interest and the state's interest in adjudicating the dispute in the forum are so attenuated that they are clearly outweighed by the burden of subjecting the defendant to litigation within the forum.

We conclude this is not one of those rare cases. Virginia's interests in the dispute are significant. Virginia has an interest in discouraging injuries that occur within the state. That interest extends to design patent infringement actions such as the one here.

Virginia also has a substantial interest in cooperating with other states to provide a forum for efficiently litigating plaintiff's cause of action. Beverly will be able to seek redress in Virginia for sales of the accused fan to consumers in these other states. These other states will thus be spared the burden of providing a forum for Beverly to seek redress for these sales. And defendants will be protected from harassment resulting from multiple suits.

That it is to plaintiff's advantage to adjudicate the dispute in the district court for the Eastern District of Virginia does not militate against its right to have access to that court. The court is part of the exclusive mechanism established by Congress for the vindication of patent rights. The fact that it has unique attributes of which plaintiff apparently has an interest in taking advantage does not change the case.

The burden on Royal does not appear particularly significant. Royal, being incorporated in New Jersey, is not located that far from Virginia. This is not a burden sufficiently compelling to outweigh Beverly's and Virginia's interests. Ultec, on the other hand, will be required to traverse the distance between its headquarters in the PRC and the district court in Virginia, and will also be required to submit itself to a foreign nation's judicial system. However, it is recognized that " 'progress in communications and transportation has made the defense of a lawsuit in a foreign tribunal less burdensome.' " *World–Wide Volkswagen*, 444 U.S. at 294, 100 S.Ct. at 565 (quoting *Hanson v. Denckla*, 357 U.S. 235, 251, 78 S.Ct. 1228, 1238, 2 L.Ed.2d 1283 (1958)). And Ultec, through its business dealings with Royal, cannot profess complete ignorance of the judicial system of the United States. Accordingly, we conclude that the burden on Ultec, as well, is not sufficiently compelling to outweigh Beverly's and Virginia's interests.

The final issue we must address is the applicability of Virginia's long-arm statute. Federal courts apply the relevant state statute when determining whether a federal court, sitting in a particular case, has personal jurisdiction over a defendant, even when the cause of action is purely federal. See Fed.R.Civ.P. 4(e)-(f).

Subsections A.3 and A.4 of the Virginia statute read:

A. A court may exercise personal jurisdiction over a person, who acts directly or by an agent, as to a cause of action arising from the person's:

3. Causing tortious injury by an act or omission in this Commonwealth;

4. Causing tortious injury in this Commonwealth by an act or omission outside this Commonwealth if he . . . derives substantial revenue from goods used or consumed or services rendered, in this Commonwealth.

Beverly first argues that subsection A.3, the "single act" provision of Virginia's long-arm statute, applies. That provision requires "an act or omission in this Commonwealth," i.e., a tortious act or omission within Virginia. But jurisdiction here cannot be based on a tortious omission, since active inducement of infringement requires the commission of an affirmative act. Nor is there support for finding such an affirmative act to have occurred in Virginia—there is nothing in the record suggesting that either defendant necessarily committed any affirmative act there.

The other relevant subsection of Virginia's long-arm statute, subsection A.4, also requires that a tortious injury occur in the state, but here the act or omission causing the injury can take place outside the state. The question, then, in determining whether subsection A.4 is applicable to the facts of this case, is whether a "tortious injury" occurred in the Commonwealth of Virginia.

Beverly contends that *Honeywell, Inc. v. Metz Apparatewerke*, 509 F.2d 1137, 184 U.S.P.Q. 387 (7th Cir.1975) supports jurisdiction over defendants. In Honeywell, plaintiff brought suit in the Northern District of Illinois against a U.S. retailer, two U.S. distributors, and the foreign manufacturer of a product the sale of which in Illinois was alleged to infringe Honeywell's patent. The district court, applying the Illinois statute, dismissed the suit against the foreign manufacturer. On appeal, the Seventh Circuit reversed, holding that Honeywell had suffered a tortious injury in Illinois and, under that state's statute, jurisdiction was proper.

The Honeywell decision can be read as holding that the injury occurred where infringing sales were made. Alternatively, however, Honeywell can also be read to mean that the situs of the injury is the situs of the intangible property interest, which is determined by where the patent owner resides (Honeywell's principal place of business was in Illinois). The law is unsettled on this question; the district courts have read the case both ways.

As noted, in a case such as this some courts consider the legal situs of an injury to intellectual property rights to be the residence of the owner of the interest. The theory is that, since intellectual property rights relate to intangible property, no particular physical situs exists. If a legal situs must be chosen, it is not illogical to pick the residence of the owner.

At first glance this rule may not seem illogical, but there are good arguments against it. Among the most important rights in the bundle of rights owned by a patent holder is the right to exclude others. This right is not limited to a particular situs, but exists anywhere the patent is recognized. It seems questionable to attribute to a patent right a single situs. A patent is a federally created property right, valid throughout the United States. Its legal situs would seem to be anywhere it is called into play. This point is illustrated by the fact that, when an infringement occurs by a sale of an infringing product, the right to exclude is violated at the situs where the sale occurs.

Other courts have avoided the problems created by the single-situs/place of residence idea, and found the situs of injury to intellectual property in an appropriate case to be the place of the infringing sale. Although economic harm to the interests of the patent holder is conceptually different from the tortious injury to the patent holder's right to exclude others, recognizing the relationship between these concepts permits the court to assess realistically the legal situs of injury for purposes of determining jurisdiction over the patent holder's infringement claim.

Economic loss occurs to the patent holder at the place where the infringing sale is made because the patent owner loses business there. This loss is immediate when the patent holder is marketing a competing product. Even if the patent holder is not, the loss may be no less real since the sale represents a loss in potential revenue through licensing or other arrangements. Furthermore, analysis of long-arm jurisdiction has its focus on the conduct of the defendant. Plaintiff's contacts with the forum—such as where the plaintiff resides—as a general proposition are not considered a determinative consideration. Additionally, a focus on the place where the infringing sales are made is consistent with other areas of intellectual property law—it brings patent infringement actions into line with the rule applied in trademark and copyright cases.

As we observed earlier in connection with the stream of commerce theory, we believe a uniform body of Federal Circuit law in this area would clearly promote judicial efficiency, would be consistent with our mandate, and would not create undue conflict and confusion at the district court level. Accordingly we hold that, in a case such as this, the situs of the injury is the location, or locations, at which the infringing activity directly impacts on the interests of the patentee, here the place of the infringing sales in Virginia.

We conclude that the "tortious injury" requirement of subsection A.4 has been met. The "act or omission outside this Commonwealth" requirement is likewise satisfied given our previous conclusion that defendants purposefully shipped the accused fan into Virginia through an established distribution channel.

This leaves the "substantial revenue" requirement. We conclude that this requirement is also satisfied. It can be inferred from plaintiff's allegations that defendants, by making through distribution channels ongoing and continuous shipments into Virginia, have derived substantial revenue, at least in absolute terms, from sales in Virginia. Although it is uncertain whether these sales have been substantial in percentage terms, the statute does not require that.

Furthermore, there is no requirement in subsection A.4 that the revenue derived have any connection to the pleaded causes of action. Royal derived revenue from the one-time sale referred to in the Lim Declaration. There is evidence in the record that this revenue was substantial given that the underlying sale represented something in the range of 3% of Royal's total sales in 1991. This revenue is relevant even though it resulted from the sale of unrelated goods.

For all the foregoing reasons, we conclude that the requirements of subsection A.4 have been satisfied, and that defendants were subject to personal jurisdiction under Virginia's long-arm statute.

CONCLUSION

The judgment granting the motion to dismiss for lack of jurisdiction is reversed.

REVERSED AND REMANDED

Notes

1. Criticizing *Beverly Hills Fan*. Are you a fan of the holding that a Chinese defendant must travel to Alexandria, Virginia, to defend itself before the notorious "Rocket Docket"? Does the court's quotation of *World-Wide Volkswagen*, with its reference to the conveniences afforded by modern artifacts, suffice to assuage your concerns that no excessive burdens would be involved in such an undertaking? The Federal Circuit's mandate against Ultec here suggests that the number of instances where the Federal Circuit's capacious jurisdictional standards would fall unfulfilled would be rare indeed.

2. A Universal Rule. Regarding *Beverly Hills Fan*'s discussion of the Virginia long-arm statute, perhaps the most important aspect of the court's ruling was its assertion of authority and selection of an ecumenical rule, at least with regard to the United States. One can readily observe that diverse rules could act to immunize alien patent infringers from suit. Consider, for example, a case where an alien sells infringing products in Maine to the detriment of a patent holder residing in Delaware. If the Maine court considered the situs of the harm to be the residence of the owner, while the Delaware court favored the place of the infringing acts as the appropriate situs, the patent holder would literally have nowhere to bring suit. These concepts are reviewed in David Wille, Note, *Personal Jurisdiction over Aliens in Patent Infringement Actions: A Uniform Approach Toward the Situs of the Tort*, 90 MICH. L. REV. 658 (1991).

3. Venue. Closely related to the subject of personal jurisdiction are the venue requirements of 28 U.S.C.A. § 1400(b), which provides:

> Any civil action for patent infringement may be brought in the judicial district where the defendant resides, or where the defendant has committed acts of infringement and has a regular and established place of business.

In *VE Holding Corp. v. Johnson Gas Appliance Co.*, 917 F.2d 1574, 16 U.S.P.Q.2d 1614 (Fed.Cir.1990), the Federal Circuit took a lengthy look at § 1400(b) on the occasion of the amendment of a related statute, § 1391(c). As noted by the court:

> In 1988 Congress adopted a new definition of "reside" as it applies to venue for corporate defendants. This case requires us to decide whether, by that amendment to § 1391(c) of chapter 87, Congress meant to apply that definition to the term as it is used in § 1400(b), and thus change this long-standing interpretation of the patent venue statute. The district courts addressing this question have arrived at conflicting results.

> This is a case of first impression. We hold that Congress by its 1988 amendment of 28 U.S.C.A. § 1391(c) meant what it said; the meaning of the term "resides" in § 1400(b) has changed....

As written, section 1400(b) dictates that venue is proper when either of two tests is satisfied: (1) the defendant resides in the judicial district, or (2) the defendant has committed acts of infringement and has a regular and established place of business in the judicial district. The Supreme Court in Fourco confirmed that for defendants that are corporations, "resides" meant the state of incorporation only. Section 1391(c), the general venue section which addressed the question of where corporations may be sued, and which contained language about the residence of corporations, did not supplement the specific provisions of § 1400(b).

[I]n 1988 Congress amended § 1391(c). The former one sentence subsection now consists of two sentences. The new second sentence of subsection (c) applies when a defendant corporation is amenable to federal jurisdiction in a state having several judicial districts. It prescribes which of them shall be the proper venue, and is not at issue in this case.

The new first sentence of amended § 1391(c) reads:

> (c) For purposes of venue under this chapter, a defendant that is a corporation shall be deemed to reside in any judicial district in which it is subject to personal jurisdiction at the time the action is commenced.

28 U.S.C.A. § 1391(c) (1988). The phrase "this chapter" refers to chapter 87 of title 28, which encompasses §§ 1391–1412, and thus includes § 1400(b). On its face, § 1391(c) clearly applies to § 1400(b), and thus redefines the meaning of the term "resides" in that section. * * *

In the case before us, the language of the statute is clear and its meaning is unambiguous. Absent extraordinary circumstances, our inquiry must end here. Section 1391(c) applies to all of chapter 87 of title 28, and thus to § 1400(b), as expressed by the words "For purposes of venue under this chapter." There can be no mistake about that.

After *VE Holding*, then, venue essentially lies in any judicial district where personal jurisdiction exists.

4. Declaratory Judgment Jurisdiction. The Declaratory Judgment Act provides for the quick and efficient resolution of disputes, particularly where a wronged party has not yet sued for relief. Declaratory judgment allows parties threatened with liability to adjudicate a contested matter promptly, limiting the unnecessary accrual of damages. As described in *Arrowhead Industrial Water, Inc. v. Ecolochem, Inc.*, 846 F.2d 731, 6 U.S.P.Q.2d 1685 (Fed.Cir.1988), this statute has found particular use with regard to patent-related matters:

> This appeal presents a type of the sad and saddening scenario that led to enactment of the Declaratory Judgment Act (Act), 28 U.S.C.A. § 2201. In the patent version of that scenario, a patent owner engages in a danse macabre, brandishing a Damoclean threat with a sheathed sword. Guerrilla-like, the patent owner attempts extra-judicial patent enforcement with scare-the-customer-and-run tactics that infect the competitive environment of the business community with uncertainty

and insecurity. Before the Act, competitors victimized by that tactic were rendered helpless and immobile so long as the patent owner refused to grasp the nettle and sue. After the Act, those competitors were no longer restricted to an in terrorem choice between the incurrence of a growing potential liability for patent infringement and abandonment of their enterprises; they could clear the air by suing for a judgment that would settle the conflict of interests. The sole requirement for jurisdiction under the Act is that the conflict be real and immediate, i.e., that there be a true, actual "controversy" required by the Act.

The Federal Circuit further discussed the standards for declaratory judgment jurisdiction in *Shell Oil Co. v. Amoco Corp.*, 970 F.2d 885, 23 U.S.P.Q.2d 1627 (Fed.Cir.1992):

Under the Declaratory Judgment Act, 28 U.S.C.A. § 2201 (1988),

[i]n a case of actual controversy within its jurisdiction, ... any court of the United States, upon the filing of an appropriate pleading, may declare the rights and other legal relations of any interested party seeking such declaration, whether or not further relief is or could be sought.

An actual controversy must be present before a declaratory judgment action is ripe for adjudication. To constitute an actual controversy, the plaintiff has the burden of establishing by a preponderance of the evidence, inter alia, that it has a reasonable apprehension that it will be sued. [The test for determining whether an actual controversy exists in a declaratory judgment suit in a patent case is two-pronged. First, the defendant's conduct must have created on the part of the plaintiff a reasonable apprehension that the defendant will initiate suit if the plaintiff continues the allegedly infringing activity. Second, the plaintiff must actually have either produced the device or have prepared to produce that device.] The test is an objective one, which in this case focuses on whether Amoco's conduct rose to a level sufficient to indicate an intent to enforce its patent. We must look for any express charges of infringement, and if none, then to the "totality of the circumstances."

For a discussion of another use of the Declaratory Judgment Act in this field, see Lawrence M. Sung, *Intellectual Property Protection or Protectionism? Declaratory Judgment Use by Patent Owners Against Prospective Infringers*, 42 Am. U. L. Rev. 239 (1992). What differences exist between patentee notice of infringement in terms of the marking statute and the Declaratory Judgment Act? *See Amsted Industries Inc. v. Buckeye Steel Castings Co.*, 24 F.3d 178, 30 U.S.P.Q.2d 1462 (Fed.Cir.1994).

5. Other Fora. Consideration of personal jurisdiction in federal courts should be accompanied by an overview of three additional fora for resolution of patent infringement suits.

The International Trade Commission. The United States International Trade Commission ("ITC") is an independent administrative agency which possesses jurisdiction over disputes arising under 19 U.S.C.A. § 1337, commonly referred to as "section 337." That statute prohibits unfair methods of competition and unfair acts, including patent infringement, in the importation of articles into the United States. If three of the six ITC Commissioners agree to institute a section 337 investigation, an ITC administrative law judge will conduct formal hearings to determine whether a violation of that statute has occurred.

ITC investigations ordinarily proceeds at a far brisker pace than litigation in district court. Additionally, jurisdiction is ordinarily much more readily obtained over foreign manufacturers in the ITC, which possesses national, *in rem* jurisdiction attaching to allegedly infringing imported articles. Standing may be a more complex matter, however. Plaintiffs must allege not only patent infringement, but importation of the accused technology and the existence or establishment of a domestic industry. Proof of these three elements establishes a violation of section 337. To redress violations, the ITC may issue exclusion orders and cease and desist orders, but is not empowered to award damages.

The ITC employs proceedings similar to those of a federal district court, but include a number of features with no counterpart to ordinary patent litigation. Among the more significant is that the ITC features a staff attorney who is a full party to the proceeding. The staff attorney represents the United States government in order to protect the public interest. ITC proceedings also involve the six ITC Commissioners, who must approve rulings of the administrative law judge. Finally, affirmative ITC decisions must be forwarded to the President of the United States for approval. Appeals of all final ITC decisions go to the Court of Appeals for the Federal Circuit. DONALD KNOX DUVALL, UNFAIR COMPETITION AND THE ITC (1996) presents a thorough overview of ITC proceedings.

Arbitration. Older cases have held that patent validity and infringement issues were without the scope of agreements to arbitrate. This situation changed considerably in 1982, when amendments to the Patent Act created § 294, entitled "Voluntary Arbitration." Section 294(a) renders arbitration clauses binding in the absence of independent equitable or legal grounds for contract revocation. Section 294(b) further specifies that arbitration of patent disputes, arbitrator awards, and confirmation of awards are governed by Title 9 of the United States Code. Section 294(c) states that arbitration awards are final and binding between the parties to the arbitration but shall not affect any other person. Sections (d) and (e) impose a requirement of Commissioner notification of arbitration awards.

Arbitration offers numerous advantages over federal district court. The parties may control the time and place of the hearings, select the arbitrators to include individuals with legal and technical expertise, and maintain the secrecy of the proceedings. Disadvantages attend arbitration as well: the arbitrator's award may be set aside by a court, albeit on limited grounds; these proceeding may proceed no more quickly than ordinary litigation, particularly where a jury is involved; and experience demonstrates that arbitrators tend to produce compromise awards, rather than decide exclusively in favor of one of the parties.

The U.S. Court of Federal Claims. Housed in the same building as the Federal Circuit is the Court of Federal Claims, formerly known as the Claims Court. Among the duties of that court is adjudication of suits under 28 U.S.C.A. § 1498, which provides in part:

Whenever an invention described in and covered by a patent of the United States is used or manufactured by or for the United States without license of the owner thereof or lawful right to use or manufacture the same, the owner's remedy shall be by action against the United States in the United States Court of Federal Claims for the recovery of his reasonable and entire compensation for such use and manufacture.

This statute renders the United States immune from suit for patent infringement in the district courts. As explained in *W.L. Gore & Associates, Inc. v. Garlock, Inc.*, 842 F.2d 1275, 6 U.S.P.Q.2d 1277 (Fed.Cir.1988)."The patentee takes his patent from the United States subject to the government's eminent domain rights to obtain what it needs from manufacturers and to use the same. The government has graciously consented, in the same statute, to be sued in the Claims Court for reasonable and entire compensation, for what would be infringement if by a private person."

Section 1498(a) litigation in the Court of Federal Claims are quite similar to a patent infringement lawsuit in a district court, although the remedy is set to the level of "reasonable and entire compensation." *Hughes Aircraft Co. v. United States*, 86 F.3d 1566, 39 U.S.P.Q.2d 1065 (Fed.Cir. 1996), *vac'd on other grounds*, 520 U.S. 1183, 117 S.Ct. 1466, 137 L.Ed.2d 680 (1997), discussed this damages concept further:

The government's unlicensed use of a patented invention is properly viewed as a taking of property under the Fifth Amendment through the government's exercise of its power of eminent domain and the patent holder's remedy for such use is prescribed by 28 U.S.C.A. § 1498(a). Under section 1498(a), the patent owner is entitled to its "reasonable and entire compensation for such use and manufacture." Because recovery is based on eminent domain, the proper measure is "what the owner has lost, not what the taker has gained." Generally, the preferred manner of reasonably and entirely compensating the patent owner is to require the government to pay a reasonable royalty for its license as well as damages for its delay in paying the royalty.

§ 18.4 FEDERAL CIRCUIT APPELLATE JURISDICTION

THE HOLMES GROUP, INC. v. VORNADO AIR CIRCULATION SYSTEMS, INC.

Supreme Court of the United States, 2002.
122 S.Ct. 1889, 62 U.S.P.Q.2d 1801.

JUSTICE SCALIA delivered the opinion of the Court.

In this case, we address whether the Court of Appeals for the Federal Circuit has appellate jurisdiction over a case in which the complaint does not allege a claim arising under federal patent law, but the answer contains a patent-law counterclaim.

I

Respondent, Vornado Air Circulation Systems, Inc., is a manufacturer of patented fans and heaters. In late 1992, respondent sued a competitor, Duracraft Corp., claiming that Duracraft's use of a "spiral grill design" in its fans infringed respondent's trade dress. The Court of Appeals for the Tenth Circuit found for Duracraft, holding that Vornado had no protectible trade-dress rights in the grill design. See *Vornado Air Circulation Systems, Inc. v. Duracraft Corp.,* 58 F.3d 1498 (1995) *(Vornado I).*

Nevertheless, on November 26, 1999, respondent lodged a complaint with the United States International Trade Commission against petitioner, The Holmes Group, Inc., claiming that petitioner's sale of fans and heaters with a spiral grill design infringed respondent's patent and the same trade dress held unprotectible in *Vornado I.* Several weeks later, petitioner filed this action against respondent in the United States District Court for the District of Kansas, seeking, *inter alia,* a declaratory judgment that its products did not infringe respondent's trade dress and an injunction restraining respondent from accusing it of trade-dress infringement in promotional materials. Respondent's answer asserted a compulsory counterclaim alleging patent infringement.

The District Court granted petitioner the declaratory judgment and injunction it sought. 93 F.Supp.2d 1140 (Kan.2000). The court explained that the collateral estoppel effect of *Vornado I* precluded respondent from relitigating its claim of trade-dress rights in the spiral grill design. It rejected respondent's contention that an intervening Federal Circuit case, *Midwest Industries, Inc. v. Karavan Trailers, Inc.,* 175 F.3d 1356 (C.A.Fed.1999), which disagreed with the Tenth Circuit's reasoning in *Vornado I,* constituted a change in the law of trade dress that warranted relitigation of respondent's trade-dress claim. The court also stayed all proceedings related to respondent's counterclaim, adding that the counterclaim would be dismissed if the declaratory judgment and injunction entered in favor of petitioner were affirmed on appeal.

Respondent appealed to the Court of Appeals for the Federal Circuit. Notwithstanding petitioner's challenge to its jurisdiction, the Federal Circuit vacated the District Court's judgment, 13 Fed.Appx. 961 (C.A.Fed.2001), and remanded for consideration of whether the "change in the law" exception to collateral estoppel applied in light of *TrafFix Devices, Inc. v. Marketing Displays, Inc.,* 532 U.S. 23, 121 S.Ct. 1255, 149 L.Ed.2d 164 (2001), a case decided after the District Court's judgment which resolved a circuit split involving *Vornado I* and *Midwest Industries.* We granted certiorari to consider whether the Federal Circuit properly asserted jurisdiction over the appeal.

II

Congress vested the Federal Circuit with exclusive jurisdiction over "an appeal from a final decision of a district court of the United States . . . if the jurisdiction *of that court* was based, in whole or in part, on [28 U.S.C. §] 1338. . . ." 28 U.S.C. § 1295(a)(1) (emphasis added). Section 1338(a), in turn, provides in relevant part that "[t]he district courts shall have original jurisdiction of any civil action arising under any Act of Congress relating to patents. . . ." Thus, the Federal Circuit's jurisdiction is fixed with reference to that of the district court, and turns on whether the action arises under federal patent law.

Section 1338(a) uses the same operative language as 28 U.S.C. § 1331, the statute conferring general federal-question jurisdiction, which gives the district courts "original jurisdiction of all civil actions *arising under* the Constitution, laws, or treaties of the United States." (Emphasis added.) We said in *Christianson v. Colt Industries Operating Corp.*, 486 U.S. 800, 808, 108 S.Ct. 2166, 100 L.Ed.2d 811 (1988), that "[l]inguistic consistency" requires us to apply the same test to determine whether a case arises under § 1338(a) as under § 1331.

The well-pleaded-complaint rule has long governed whether a case "arises under" federal law for purposes of § 1331. See, *e.g., Phillips Petroleum Co. v. Texaco Inc.*, 415 U.S. 125, 127–128, 94 S.Ct. 1002, 39 L.Ed.2d 209 (1974) *(per curiam).* As "appropriately adapted to § 1338(a)," the well-pleaded-complaint rule provides that whether a case "arises under" patent law "must be determined from what necessarily appears in the plaintiff's statement of his own claim in the bill or declaration.... " Christianson, 486 U.S., at 809, 108 S.Ct. 2166 (internal quotation marks omitted). The plaintiff's well pleaded complaint must "establis[h] either that federal patent law creates the cause of action or that the plaintiff's right to relief necessarily depends on resolution of a substantial question of federal patent law...." *Ibid.* Here, it is undisputed that petitioner's well pleaded complaint did not assert any claim arising under federal patent law. The Federal Circuit therefore erred in asserting jurisdiction over this appeal.

A

Respondent argues that the well-pleaded-complaint rule, properly understood, allows a counterclaim to serve as the basis for a district court's "arising under" jurisdiction. We disagree.

Admittedly, our prior cases have only required us to address whether a federal defense, rather than a federal counterclaim, can establish "arising under" jurisdiction. Nevertheless, those cases were decided on the principle that federal jurisdiction generally exists "only when a federal question is presented on the face of the *plaintiff's* properly pleaded complaint." *Caterpillar Inc. v. Williams*, 482 U.S. 386, 392, 107 S.Ct. 2425, 96 L.Ed.2d 318 (1987) (emphasis added). As we said in *The Fair v. Kohler Die & Specialty Co.*, 228 U.S. 22, 25, 33 S.Ct. 410, 57 L.Ed. 716 (1913), whether a case arises under federal patent law "cannot depend upon the answer." Moreover, we have declined to adopt proposals that "the answer as well as the complaint ... be consulted before a determination [is] made whether the case 'ar[ises] under' federal law...." *Franchise Tax Bd. of Cal. v. Construction Laborers Vacation Trust for Southern Cal.*, 463 U.S. 1, 10–11, n. 9, 103 S.Ct. 2841, 77 L.Ed.2d 420 (1983) (citing AMERICAN LAW INSTITUTE, STUDY OF THE DIVISION OF JURISDICTION BETWEEN STATE AND FEDERAL COURTS § 1312, pp. 188–194 (1969)). It follows that a counterclaim—which appears as part of the defendant's answer, not as part of the plaintiff's complaint—cannot serve as the basis for "arising under" jurisdiction.

Allowing a counterclaim to establish "arising under" jurisdiction would also contravene the longstanding policies underlying our precedents. First, since the plaintiff is "the master of the complaint," the well-pleaded-complaint rule enables him, "by eschewing claims based on federal law, . . . to have the cause heard in state court." *Caterpillar Inc., supra,* at 398–399, 107 S.Ct. 2425. The rule proposed by respondent, in contrast, would leave acceptance or rejection of a state forum to the master of the counterclaim. It would allow a defendant to remove a case brought in state court under state law, thereby defeating a plaintiff's choice of forum, simply by raising a federal counterclaim. Second, conferring this power upon the defendant would radically expand the class of removable cases, contrary to the "[d]ue regard for the rightful independence of state governments" that our cases addressing removal require. And finally, allowing responsive pleadings by the defendant to establish "arising under" jurisdiction would undermine the clarity and ease of administration of the well-pleaded-complaint doctrine, which serves as a "quick rule of thumb" for resolving jurisdictional conflicts.

For these reasons, we decline to transform the longstanding well-pleaded-complaint rule into the "well-pleaded-complaint-*or-counterclaim* rule" urged by respondent.

B

Respondent argues, in the alternative, that even if a counterclaim generally cannot establish the original "arising under" jurisdiction of a district court, we should interpret the phrase "arising under" differently in ascertaining the Federal Circuit's jurisdiction. In respondent's view, effectuating Congress's goal of "promoting the uniformity of patent law," Brief for Respondent 21, requires us to interpret §§ 1295(a)(1) and 1338(a) to confer exclusive appellate jurisdiction on the Federal Circuit whenever a patent-law counterclaim is raised.

We do not think this option is available. Our task here is not to determine what would further Congress's goal of ensuring patent-law uniformity, but to determine what the words of the statute must fairly be understood to mean. It would be difficult enough to give "arising under" the meaning urged by respondent if that phrase appeared in § 1295(a)(1)—the jurisdiction-conferring statute—*itself.* Even then the phrase would not be some neologism that might justify our adverting to the general purpose of the legislation, but rather a term familiar to all law students as invoking the well-pleaded-complaint rule. But the present case is even weaker than that, since § 1295(a)(1) does not itself *use* the term, but rather refers to jurisdiction under § 1338, where it is well established that "arising under any Act of Congress relating to patents" invokes, specifically, the well-pleaded-complaint rule. It would be an unprecedented feat of interpretive necromancy to say that § 1338(a)'s "arising under" language means one thing (the well-pleaded-complaint rule) in its own right, but something quite different (respondent's complaint-or-counterclaim rule) when referred to by § 1295(a)(1).

* * *

Not all cases involving a patent-law claim fall within the Federal Circuit's jurisdiction. By limiting the Federal Circuit's jurisdiction to cases in which district courts would have jurisdiction under § 1338, Congress referred to a well-established body of law that requires courts to consider whether a patent-law claim appears on the face of the plaintiff's well pleaded complaint. Because petitioner's complaint did not include any claim based on patent law, we vacate the judgment of the Federal Circuit and remand the case with instructions to transfer the case to the Court of Appeals for the Tenth Circuit.

It is so ordered.

JUSTICE STEVENS, concurring in part and concurring in the judgment.

The Court correctly holds that the exclusive jurisdiction of the Court of Appeals for the Federal Circuit in patent cases is "fixed with reference to that of the district court." It is important to note the general rule, however, that the jurisdiction of the court of appeals is not "fixed" until the notice of appeal is filed. See *Griggs v. Provident Consumer Discount Co.,* 459 U.S. 56, 58–59, 103 S.Ct. 400, 74 L.Ed.2d 225 (1982) *(per curiam)* ("The filing of a notice of appeal is an event of jurisdictional significance—it confers jurisdiction on the court of appeals and divests the district court of its control over those aspects of the case involved in the appeal").

Thus, if a case began as an antitrust case, but an amendment to the complaint added a patent claim that was pending or was decided when the appeal is taken, the jurisdiction of the district court would have been based "in part" on 28 U.S.C. § 1338(a), and therefore § 1295(a)(1) would grant the Federal Circuit jurisdiction over the appeal. Conversely, if the only patent count in a multi-count complaint was voluntarily dismissed in advance of trial, it would seem equally clear that the appeal should be taken to the appropriate regional court of appeals rather than to the Federal Circuit. Any other approach "would enable an unscrupulous plaintiff to manipulate appellate court jurisdiction by the timing of the amendments to its complaint." *Id.,* at 824, 108 S.Ct. 2166. To the extent that the Court's opinion might be read as endorsing a contrary result by reason of its reliance on cases involving the removal jurisdiction of the district court, I do not agree with it.

I also do not agree with the Court's statement that an interpretation of the "in whole or in part" language of § 1295(a)(1) to encompass patent claims alleged in a compulsory counterclaim providing an independent basis for the district court's jurisdiction would be a "neologism" that would involve "an unprecedented feat of interpretive necromancy," *ante,* at 1895. For there is well-reasoned precedent supporting precisely that conclusion. I am nevertheless persuaded that a correct interpretation of § 1295(a)(1) limits the Federal Circuit's exclusive jurisdiction to those cases in which the patent claim is alleged in either the original complaint or an amended pleading filed by the plaintiff. In my judgment, each of the three policies that the Court has identified as supporting the "well-pleaded-complaint" rule governing district court jurisdiction points in the same direction with respect to appellate jurisdiction.

First, the interest in preserving the plaintiff's choice of forum includes not only the court that will conduct the trial but the appellate court as well. A plaintiff who has a legitimate interest in litigating in a circuit whose precedents support its theory of the case might omit a patent claim in order to avoid review in the Federal Circuit. In some cases that interest would be defeated by a rule that allowed a patent counterclaim to determine the appellate forum.

Second, although I doubt that a rule that enabled the counterclaimant to be the occasional master of the appellate forum "would radically expand" the number of cases heard by the Federal Circuit, we must recognize that the exclusive jurisdiction of the Federal Circuit defined in § 1295(a)(1) does not comprise claims arising under the trademark and copyright laws, which are included in the district court's grant of jurisdiction under § 1338(a) As the instant litigation demonstrates, claims sounding in these other areas of intellectual property law are not infrequently bound up with patent counterclaims. The potential number of cases in which a counterclaim might direct to the Federal Circuit appeals that Congress specifically chose not to place within its exclusive jurisdiction is therefore significant.

Third, the interest in maintaining clarity and simplicity in rules governing appellate jurisdiction will be served by limiting the number of pleadings that will mandate review in the Federal Circuit. In his opinion in *Aerojet*, Chief Judge Markey merely held that a counterclaim for patent infringement that was "compulsory" and not "frivolous" or "insubstantial" sufficed to establish jurisdiction; he made a point of noting that there was no assertion in the case that the patent counterclaim at issue had been filed "to manipulate the jurisdiction of [the Federal Circuit]." 895 F.2d, at 738. The text of the statute, however, would not seem to distinguish between that counterclaim and those that are permissive, insubstantial, or manipulative, and there is very good reason not to make the choice of appellate forum turn on such distinctions. Requiring assessment of a defendant's motive in raising a patent counterclaim or the counterclaim's relative strength wastes judicial resources by inviting "unhappy interactions between jurisdiction and the merits."

There is, of course, a countervailing interest in directing appeals in patent cases to the specialized court that was created, in part, to promote uniformity in the development of this area of the law. But we have already decided that the Federal Circuit does not have exclusive jurisdiction over all cases raising patent issues. *Christianson*, 486 U.S., at 811–812, 108 S.Ct. 2166. Necessarily, therefore, other circuits will have some role to play in the development of this area of the law. An occasional conflict in decisions may be useful in identifying questions that merit this Court's attention. Moreover, occasional decisions by courts with broader jurisdiction will provide an antidote to the risk that the specialized court may develop an institutional bias.

In sum, I concur in the Court's judgment and join Parts I and II–A of its opinion.

JUSTICE GINSBURG, with whom JUSTICE O'CONNOR joins, concurring in the judgment.

For reasons stated by Chief Judge Markey, writing for a unanimous en banc Federal Circuit in *Aerojet–General Corp. v. Machine Tool Works, Oerlikon–Buehrle Ltd.*, 895 F.2d 736 (1990), I conclude that, when the claim stated in a compulsory counterclaim "aris[es] under" federal patent law and is adjudicated on the merits by a federal district court, the Federal Circuit has exclusive appellate jurisdiction over that adjudication and other determinations made in the same case.

The question now before this Court bears not at all on a plaintiff's choice of trial forum. The sole question presented here concerns Congress' allocation of adjudicatory authority among the federal courts of appeals. At that appellate level, Congress sought to eliminate forum shopping and to advance uniformity in the interpretation and application of federal patent law. *See generally* R. Dreyfuss, *The Federal Circuit: A Case Study in Specialized Courts*, 64 N.Y.U.L.REV. 1, 30–37 (1989).

The Court's opinion dwells on district court authority. See *ante,* at 1893–1894. But, all agree, Congress left that authority entirely untouched. I would attend, instead, to the unique context at issue, and give effect to Congress' endeavor to grant the Federal Circuit exclusive appellate jurisdiction at least over district court adjudications of patent claims. *See* R. Dreyfuss, 64 N.Y.U.L.REV., at 36.

In the instant case, however, no patent claim was actually adjudicated. For that sole reason, I join the Court's judgment.

Note

The Impact of *Vornado*. The Federal Circuit is frequently described as the court enjoying jurisdiction over all patent appeals in the United States. This statement has always been something of a shorthand, however. Depending upon the fashion in which the plaintiff styled its lawsuit, patent licensing disputes have been characterized as contract actions and therefore have been tried before state courts. *See, e.g., Genencor Int'l, Inc. v. Novo Nordisk A/S*, 766 A.2d 8 (Del.2000). The mechanism of diversity jurisdiction has also caused patent licensing suits to arrive before the regional circuit courts of appeal. *See, e.g., Scheiber v. Dolby Labs., Inc.*, 293 F.3d 1014, 63 U.S.P.Q.2d 1404 (7th Cir.2002).

Vornado appears to open another possibility for patent appeals to darken the doors of the regional circuit courts of appeals. Although it remains to be seen how frequently *Vornado* will be invoked in practice, the decision creates the possibility that the regional circuit courts will once again be required to adjudicate substantive issues of patent law. An issue of immediate interest is whether the regional circuit courts of appeal will approve of the considerable apparatus that *Markman* and its progeny have constructed around the process of claim interpretation. Another is whether the status of antitrust law will change following *Vornado*. Persistent commentary suggests that the Federal Circuit has applied antitrust principles more sparingly to patents than other courts of appeal might. What is clear is that the post-*Vornado* era is already upon us: the Federal Circuit began transferring cases to our courts of appeal shortly after the Supreme Court opinion issued. *See, e.g., Telecomm Technical Services, Inc. v. Siemens Rolm Communications, Inc.*, 295 F.3d 1249, 63 U.S.P.Q.2d 1606 (Fed.Cir.2002).

§ 18.5 THE SEVENTH AMENDMENT

The complexity of both the patent law and the technical subject matter which it addresses have rendered the role of the jury in patent enforcement actions a subject of great debate. The Supreme Court laid many of these issues to rest by substantially limiting the role of the jury in patent cases. But in so doing, it left open a number of procedural issues that the lower courts are beginning to address. The Supreme Court's *Markman* decision, provided below, is the starting point of this set of concerns.

MARKMAN v. WESTVIEW INSTRUMENTS, INC.

United States Supreme Court, 1996.
517 U.S. 370.

JUSTICE SOUTER delivered the opinion of the Court.

The question here is whether the interpretation of a so-called patent claim, the portion of the patent document that defines the scope of the patentee's rights, is a matter of law reserved entirely for the court, or subject to a Seventh Amendment guarantee that a jury will determine the meaning of any disputed term of art about which expert testimony is offered. We hold that the construction of a patent, including terms of art within its claim, is exclusively within the province of the court.

[In Part I of its opinion, deleted here, the Supreme Court reviewed the procedural history of the *Markman* litigation. Following the issuance of the Federal Circuit's *in banc* opinion, reprinted in this casebook in Chapter 15, Markman sought review and the Court granted certiorari.]

II

The Seventh Amendment provides that "[i]n Suits at common law, where the value in controversy shall exceed twenty dollars, the right of trial by jury shall be preserved.... " U.S. Const., Amdt. 7. Since Justice Story's day, *United States v. Wonson*, 28 F. Cas. 745, 750 (No. 16,750) (CC Mass. 1812), we have understood that "[t]he right of trial by jury thus preserved is the right which existed under the English common law when the Amendment was adopted." *Baltimore & Carolina Line, Inc. v. Redman*, 295 U.S. 654, 657, 55 S.Ct. 890, 891, 79 L.Ed. 1636 (1935). In keeping with our long-standing adherence to this "historical test,"

Wolfram, *The Constitutional History of the Seventh Amendment*, 57 Minn. L.Rev. 639, 640–643 (1973), we ask, first, whether we are dealing with a cause of action that either was tried at law at the time of the Founding or is at least analogous to one that was, *see, e.g., Tull v. United States*, 481 U.S. 412, 417, 107 S.Ct. 1831, 1835, 95 L.Ed.2d 365 (1987). If the action in question belongs in the law category, we then ask whether the particular trial decision must fall to the jury in order to preserve the substance of the common-law right as it existed in 1791.

A

As to the first issue, going to the character of the cause of action, "[t]he form of our analysis is familiar. 'First we compare the statutory action to 18th-century actions brought in the courts of England prior to the merger of the courts of law and equity.' "*Granfinanciera, S.A. v. Nordberg*, 492 U.S. 33, 42, 109 S.Ct. 2782, 2790, 106 L.Ed.2d 26 (1989) (citation omitted). Equally familiar is the descent of today's patent infringement action from the infringement actions tried at law in the 18th century, and there is no dispute that infringement cases today must be tried to a jury, as their predecessors were more than two centuries ago. *See, e.g., Bramah v. Hardcastle*, 1 Carp. P.C. 168 (K.B.1789).

B

This conclusion raises the second question, whether a particular issue occurring within a jury trial (here the construction of a patent claim) is itself necessarily a jury issue, the guarantee being essential to preserve the right to a jury's resolution of the ultimate dispute. In some instances the answer to this second question may be easy because of clear historical evidence that the very subsidiary question was so regarded under the English practice of leaving the issue for a jury. But when, as here, the old practice provides no clear answer, see infra, at 1391–1392, we are forced to make a judgment about the scope of the Seventh Amendment guarantee without the benefit of any foolproof test.

The Court has repeatedly said that the answer to the second question "must depend on whether the jury must shoulder this responsibility as necessary to preserve the 'substance of the common-law right of trial by jury.' " *Tull v. United States, supra*, at 426, 107 S.Ct., at 1840 (emphasis added) (quoting *Colgrove v. Battin*, 413 U.S. 149, 156, 93 S.Ct. 2448, 2452, 37 L.Ed.2d 522 (1973)); *see also Baltimore & Carolina Line, supra*, at 657, 55 S.Ct., at 891. " 'Only those incidents which are regarded as fundamental, as inherent in and of the essence of the system of trial by jury, are placed beyond the reach of the legislature.' " *Tull v. United States, supra*, at 426, 107 S.Ct., at 1840 (citations omitted); *see also Galloway v. United States*, 319 U.S. 372, 392, 63 S.Ct. 1077, 1088, 87 L.Ed. 1458 (1943).

The "substance of the common-law right" is, however, a pretty blunt instrument for drawing distinctions. We have tried to sharpen it, to be sure, by reference to the distinction between substance and procedure. We have also spoken of the line as one between issues of fact and law.

But the sounder course, when available, is to classify a mongrel practice (like construing a term of art following receipt of evidence) by using the historical method, much as we do in characterizing the suits and actions within which they arise. Where there is no exact antecedent, the best hope lies in comparing the modern practice to earlier ones whose allocation to court or jury we do know, seeking the best analogy we can draw between an old and the new.

C

"Prior to 1790 nothing in the nature of a claim had appeared either in British patent practice or in that of the American states," Lutz, Evolution of the Claims of U.S. Patents, 20 J. Pat. Off. Soc. 134 (1938), and we have accordingly found no direct antecedent of modern claim construction in the historical sources. Claim practice did not achieve statutory recognition until the passage of the Act of 1836, Act of July 4, 1836, ch. 357, § 6, 5 Stat. 119, and inclusion of a claim did not become a statutory requirement until 1870, Act of July 8, 1870, ch. 230, § 26, 16 Stat. 201; see 1 A. DELLER, PATENT CLAIMS § 4, p. 9 (2d ed.1971). Although, as one historian has observed, as early as 1850 "judges were ... beginning to express more frequently the idea that in seeking to ascertain the invention 'claimed' in a patent the inquiry should be limited to interpreting the summary, or 'claim,'" Lutz, supra, at 145, "[t]he idea that the claim is just as important if not more important than the description and drawings did not develop until the Act of 1870 or thereabouts." Deller, supra, § 4, at 9.

At the time relevant for Seventh Amendment analogies, in contrast, it was the specification, itself a relatively new development, H. DUTTON, THE PATENT SYSTEM AND INVENTIVE ACTIVITY DURING THE INDUSTRIAL REVOLUTION, 1750–1852, pp. 75–76 (1984), that represented the key to the patent. Thus, patent litigation in that early period was typified by so-called novelty actions, testing whether "any essential part of [the patent had been] disclosed to the public before," *Huddart v. Grimshaw*, Dav. Pat. Cas. 265, 298 (K.B.1803), and "enablement" cases, in which juries were asked to determine whether the specification described the invention well enough to allow members of the appropriate trade to reproduce it, *see, e.g., Arkwright v. Nightingale*, Dav. Pat. Cas. 37, 60 (C.P. 1785).

The closest 18th-century analogue of modern claim construction seems, then, to have been the construction of specifications, and as to that function the mere smattering of patent cases that we have from this period shows no established jury practice sufficient to support an argument by analogy that today's construction of a claim should be a guaranteed jury issue. Few of the case reports even touch upon the proper interpretation of disputed terms in the specifications at issue, *see, e.g., Bramah v. Hardcastle*, 1 Carp. P.C. 168 (K.B.1789); *King v. Else*, 1 Carp. P.C. 103, Dav. Pat. Cas., 144 (K.B.1785); *Dollond's Case*, 1 Carp. P.C. 28 (C.P. 1758); *Administrators of Calthorp v. Waymans*, 3 Keb. 710,

84 Eng. Rep. 966 (K.B.1676), and none demonstrates that the definition of such a term was determined by the jury. This absence of an established practice should not surprise us, given the primitive state of jury patent practice at the end of the 18th century, when juries were still new to the field. Although by 1791 more than a century had passed since the enactment of the Statute of Monopolies, which provided that the validity of any monopoly should be determined in accordance with the common law, patent litigation had remained within the jurisdiction of the Privy Council until 1752 and hence without the option of a jury trial. E. Walterscheid, *Early Evolution of the United States Patent Law: Antecedents* (Part 3), 77 J. Pat. & Tm. Off. Soc. 771, 771–776 (1995). Indeed, the state of patent law in the common-law courts before 1800 led one historian to observe that "the reported cases are destitute of any decision of importance.... At the end of the eighteenth century, therefore, the Common Law Judges were left to pick up the threads of the principles of law without the aid of recent and reliable precedents." Hulme, On the Consideration of the Patent Grant, Past and Present, 13 L.Q. Rev. 313, 318 (1897). Earlier writers expressed similar discouragement at patent law's amorphous character, and, a late as the 1830's, English commentators were irked by enduring confusion in the field. *See* Dutton, *supra,* at 69–70.

Markman seeks to supply what the early case reports lack in so many words by relying on decisions like *Turner v. Winter,* 1 T.R. 602, 99 Eng. Rep. 1274 (K.B.1787), and *Arkwright v. Nightingale,* Dav. Pat. Cas. 37 (C.P. 1785), to argue that the 18th-century juries must have acted as definers of patent terms just to reach the verdicts we know they rendered in patent cases turning on enablement or novelty. But the conclusion simply does not follow. There is no more reason to infer that juries supplied plenary interpretation of written instruments in patent litigation than in other cases implicating the meaning of documentary terms, and we do know that in other kinds of cases during this period judges, not juries, ordinarily construed written documents. The probability that the judges were doing the same thing in the patent litigation of the time is confirmed by the fact that as soon as the English reports did begin to describe the construction of patent documents, they show the judges construing the terms of the specifications. *See Bovill v. Moore,* Dav. Pat. Cas. 361, 399, 404 (C.P. 1816) (judge submits question of novelty to the jury only after explaining some of the language and "stat[ing] in what terms the specification runs"); *cf. Russell v. Cowley & Dixon,* Webs. Pat. Cas. 457, 467–470 (Exch.1834) (construing the terms of the specification in reviewing a verdict); *Haworth v. Hardcastle,* Webs. Pat. Cas. 480, 484–485 (1834) (same). This evidence is in fact buttressed by cases from this Court; when they first reveal actual practice, the practice revealed is of the judge construing the patent. *See, e.g. Winans v. New York & Erie R. Co.,* 21 How. 88, 100, 16 L.Ed. 68 (1859); *Winans v. Denmead,* 15 How. 330, 338, 14 L.Ed. 717 (1854); *Hogg v. Emerson,* 6 How. 437, 484, 12 L.Ed. 505 (1848); *cf. Parker v. Hulme,* 18 F. Cas. 1138 (No. 10,740) (CC ED Pa. 1849). These indications of our patent practice are the more impressive for being all of a piece with what we know about the analogous contemporary practice of interpreting terms within a land patent, where it fell to the judge, not the jury, to construe the words.

D

Losing, then, on the contention that juries generally had interpretive responsibilities during the 18th century, Markman seeks a different anchor for analogy in the more modest contention that even if judges were charged with construing most terms in the patent, the art of defining terms of art employed in a specification fell within the province of the jury. Again, however, Markman has no authority from the period in question, but relies instead on the later case of *Neilson v. Harford*, Webs. Pat. Cas. 328 (Exch.1841). There, an exchange between the judge and the lawyers indicated that although the construction of a patent was ordinarily for the court, id., at 349 (Alderson, B.), judges should "leav[e] the question of words of art to the jury," *id.*, at 350 (Alderson, B.); *see also id.*, at 370 (judgment of the court); *Hill v. Evans*, 4 De. G.F. & J. 288, 293–294, 45 Eng. Rep. 1195, 1197 (Ch. 1862). Without, however, in any way disparaging the weight to which Baron Alderson's view is entitled, the most we can say is that an English report more than 70 years after the time that concerns us indicates an exception to what probably had been occurring earlier. In place of Markman's inference that this exceptional practice existed in 1791 there is at best only a possibility that it did, and for anything more than a possibility we have found no scholarly authority.

III

Since evidence of common law practice at the time of the Framing does not entail application of the Seventh Amendment's jury guarantee to the construction of the claim document, we must look elsewhere to characterize this determination of meaning in order to allocate it as between court or jury. We accordingly consult existing precedent and consider both the relative interpretive skills of judges and juries and the statutory policies that ought to be furthered by the allocation.

A

The two elements of a simple patent case, construing the patent and determining whether infringement occurred, were characterized by the former patent practitioner, Justice Curtis. "The first is a question of law, to be determined by the court, construing the letters-patent, and the description of the invention and specification of claim annexed to them. The second is a question of fact, to be submitted to a jury." *Winans v. Denmead*, 15 How., at 338; *see Winans v. New York & Erie R. Co.*, 21 How., at 100; *Hogg v. Emerson*, supra, at 484; *cf. Parker v. Hulme*, *supra*, at 1140.

In arguing for a different allocation of responsibility for the first question, Markman relies primarily on two cases, *Bischoff v. Wethered*, 9 Wall. 812, 19 L.Ed. 829 (1870), and *Tucker v. Spalding*, 13 Wall. 453, 20

L.Ed. 515 (1872). These are said to show that evidence of the meaning of patent terms was offered to 19th-century juries, and thus to imply that the meaning of a documentary term was a jury issue whenever it was subject to evidentiary proof. That is not what Markman's cases show, however.

In order to resolve the *Bischoff* suit implicating the construction of rival patents, we considered "whether the court below was bound to compare the two specifications, and to instruct the jury, as a matter of law, whether the inventions therein described were, or were not, identical." 9 Wall., at 813 (statement of the case). We said it was not bound to do that, on the ground that investing the court with so dispositive a role would improperly eliminate the jury's function in answering the ultimate question of infringement. On that ultimate issue, expert testimony had been admitted on "the nature of the various mechanisms or manufactures described in the different patents produced, and as to the identity or diversity between them." *Id.*, at 814. Although the jury's consideration of that expert testimony in resolving the question of infringement was said to impinge upon the well-established principle "that it is the province of the court, and not the jury, to construe the meaning of documentary evidence," *id.*, at 815, we decided that it was not so. We said that

> "the specifications ... profess to describe mechanisms and complicated machinery, chemical compositions and other manufactured products, which have their existence in pais, outside of the documents themselves; and which are commonly described by terms of the art or mystery to which they respectively belong; and these descriptions and terms of art often require peculiar knowledge and education to understand them aright.... Indeed, the whole subject-matter of a patent is an embodied conception outside of the patent itself.... This outward embodiment of the terms contained in the patent is the thing invented, and is to be properly sought, like the explanation of all latent ambiguities arising from the description of external things, by evidence in pais." Ibid.

Bischoff does not then, as Markman contends, hold that the use of expert testimony about the meaning of terms of art requires the judge to submit the question of their construction to the jury. It is instead a case in which the Court drew a line between issues of document interpretation and product identification, and held that expert testimony was properly presented to the jury on the latter, ultimate issue, whether the physical objects produced by the patent were identical. The Court did not see the decision as bearing upon the appropriate treatment of disputed terms. As the opinion emphasized, the Court's "view of the case is not intended to, and does not, trench upon the doctrine that the construction of written instruments is the province of the court alone. It is not the construction of the instrument, but the character of the thing invented, which is sought in questions of identity and diversity of inventions." *Id.*, at 816 (emphasis added). *Tucker*, the second case proffered by Markman, is to the same effect. Its reasoning rested expressly on *Bischoff*, and it just as clearly noted that in addressing the ultimate issue of mixed fact and law, it was for the court to "lay down to the jury the law which should govern them." *Tucker, supra,* at 455.

If the line drawn in these two opinions is a fine one, it is one that the Court has drawn repeatedly in explaining the respective roles of the jury and judge in patent cases, and one understood by commentators writing in the aftermath of the cases Markman cites. Walker, for example, read *Bischoff* as holding that the question of novelty is not decided by a construction of the prior patent, "but depends rather upon the outward embodiment of the terms contained in the [prior patent]; and that such outward embodiment is to be properly sought, like the explanation of latent ambiguities arising from the description of external things, by evidence in pais." A. WALKER, PATENT LAWS § 75, p. 68 (3d ed. 1895). He also emphasized in the same treatise that matters of claim construction, even those aided by expert testimony, are questions for the court:

> "Questions of construction are questions of law for the judge, not questions of fact for the jury. As it cannot be expected, however, that judges will always possess the requisite knowledge of the meaning of the terms of art or science used in letters patent, it often becomes necessary that they should avail themselves of the light furnished by experts relevant to the significance of such words and phrases. The judges are not, however, obliged to blindly follow such testimony." *Id.,* § 189, at 173 (footnotes omitted).

Virtually the same description of the court's use of evidence in its interpretive role was set out in another contemporary treatise:

> "The duty of interpreting letters-patent has been committed to the courts. A patent is a legal instrument, to be construed, like other legal instruments, according to its tenor.... Where technical terms are used, or where the qualities of substances or operations mentioned or any similar data necessary to the comprehension of the language of the patent are unknown to the judge, the testimony of witnesses may be received upon these subjects, and any other means of information be employed. But in the actual interpretation of the patent the court proceeds upon its own responsibility, as an arbiter of the law, giving to the patent its true and final character and force." 2 W. ROBINSON, LAW OF PATENTS § 732, pp. 481–483 (1890) (emphasis added).

In sum, neither *Bischoff* nor *Tucker* indicates that juries resolved the meaning of terms of art in construing a patent, and neither case undercuts Justice Curtis's authority.

B

Where history and precedent provide no clear answers, functional considerations also play their part in the choice between judge and jury to define terms of art. We said in *Miller v. Fenton,* 474 U.S. 104, 114, 106 S.Ct. 445, 451, 88 L.Ed.2d 405 (1985), that when an issue "falls somewhere between a pristine legal standard and a simple historical fact, the fact/law distinction at times has turned on a determination that, as a matter of the sound administration of justice, one judicial actor is better positioned than another to decide the issue in question." So it turns out here, for judges, not juries, are the better suited to find the acquired meaning of patent terms.

The construction of written instruments is one of those things that judges often do and are likely to do better than jurors unburdened by training in exegesis. Patent construction in particular "is a special occupation, requiring, like all others, special training and practice. The judge, from his training and discipline, is more likely to give a proper interpretation to such instruments than a jury; and he is, therefore, more likely to be right, in performing such a duty, than a jury can be expected to be." *Parker v. Hulme*, 18 F. Cas., at 1140. Such was the understanding nearly a century and a half ago, and there is no reason to weigh the respective strengths of judge and jury differently in relation to the modern claim; quite the contrary, for "the claims of patents have become highly technical in many respects as the result of special doctrines relating to the proper form and scope of claims that have been developed by the courts and the Patent Office." Woodward, *Definiteness and Particularity in Patent Claims*, 46 MICH. L.REV. 755, 765 (1948).

Markman would trump these considerations with his argument that a jury should decide a question of meaning peculiar to a trade or profession simply because the question is a subject of testimony requiring credibility determinations, which are the jury's forte. It is, of course, true that credibility judgments have to be made about the experts who testify in patent cases, and in theory there could be a case in which a simple credibility judgment would suffice to choose between experts whose testimony was equally consistent with a patent's internal logic. But our own experience with document construction leaves us doubtful that trial courts will run into many cases like that. In the main, we expect, any credibility determinations will be subsumed within the necessarily sophisticated analysis of the whole document, required by the standard construction rule that a term can be defined only in a way that comports with the instrument as a whole. Thus, in these cases a jury's capabilities to evaluate demeanor, to sense the "mainsprings of human conduct," or to reflect community standards, are much less significant than a trained ability to evaluate the testimony in relation to the overall structure of the patent. The decisionmaker vested with the task of construing the patent is in the better position to ascertain whether an expert's proposed definition fully comports with the specification and claims and so will preserve the patent's internal coherence. We accordingly think there is sufficient reason to treat construction of terms of art like many other responsibilities that we cede to a judge in the normal course of trial, notwithstanding its evidentiary underpinnings.

C

Finally, we see the importance of uniformity in the treatment of a given patent as an independent reason to allocate all issues of construction to the court. As we noted in *General Elec. Co. v. Wabash Appliance Corp.*, 304 U.S. 364, 369, 58 S.Ct. 899, 902, 82 L.Ed. 1402 (1938), "[t]he limits of a patent must be known for the protection of the patentee, the encouragement of the inventive genius of others and the assurance that the subject of the patent will be dedicated ultimately to the public." Otherwise, a "zone of uncertainty which enterprise and experimentation may enter only at the risk of infringement claims would discourage invention only a little less than unequivocal foreclosure of the field," *United Carbon Co. v. Binney & Smith Co.*, 317 U.S. 228, 236, 63 S.Ct. 165, 170, 87 L.Ed. 232 (1942), and "[t]he public [would] be deprived of rights supposed to belong to it, without being clearly told what it is that limits these rights." *Merrill v. Yeomans*, 94 U.S. 568, 573, 24 L.Ed. 235 (1877). It was just for the sake of such desirable uniformity that Congress created the Court of Appeals for the Federal Circuit as an exclusive appellate courts for patent cases, H.R.Rep. No. 97–312, pp. 20–23 (1981), observing that increased uniformity would "strengthen the United States patent system in such a way as to foster technological growth and industrial innovation." Id., at 20.

Uniformity would, however, be ill served by submitting issues of document construction to juries. Making them jury issues would not, to be sure, necessarily leave evidentiary questions of meaning wide open in every new court in which a patent might be litigated, for principles of issue preclusion would ordinarily foster uniformity. *Cf. Blonder–Tongue Laboratories, Inc. v. University of Ill. Foundation*, 402 U.S. 313, 91 S.Ct. 1434, 28 L.Ed.2d 788 (1971). But whereas issue preclusion could not be asserted against new and independent infringement defendants even within a given jurisdiction, treating interpretive issues as purely legal will promote (though it will not guarantee) intrajurisdictional certainty through the application of stare decisis on those questions not yet subject to interjurisdictional uniformity under the authority of the single appeals court.

* * *

Accordingly, we hold that the interpretation of the word "inventory" in this case is an issue for the judge, not the jury, and affirm the decision of the Court of Appeals for the Federal Circuit.

It is so ordered.

Notes

1. **Problems With *Markman*?** In *Elf Atochem North America, Inc. v. Libbey–Owens–Ford Co.*, 894 F.Supp. 844, 37 U.S.P.Q.2d 1065 (D.Del.1995), a decision issued after the Federal Circuit's opinion in *Markman*, but prior to the issuance of the Supreme Court's decision, Judge McKelvie mused upon claim interpretation procedures as follows:

> The decision in Markman will undoubtedly change the face of patent litigation as it clearly did in this case. A number of procedural issues flow from this decision.

In the normal course of litigation, courts should endeavor to manage cases in such a way that all claims and issues in a civil action are presented for resolution in one trial. Moreover, in accordance with Congress's mandate in the Civil Justice Reform Act, this court schedules cases for trial within one year from the filing date of the complaint and generally schedules trials to last no more than two weeks.

The court's experience with this relatively rigid time frame shows that it promotes more efficient resolution of civil matters. For example, faced with firm and certain trial dates parties are often encouraged to settle rather than proceed to trial. Furthermore, and perhaps more importantly, this time frame assures parties that by a date certain they will have a final resolution of issues facing and affecting them as a result of litigation. Fixed trial time often leads parties to try only the core issues of their case, without wasting the court's and jury's time with issues upon which the party may have little chance of success.

In spite of this general practice, separate trials or staged resolution of issues may be worthwhile in certain circumstances. See Johns Hopkins Univ. v. CellPro, 160 F.R.D. 30, 33 (D.Del.1995). As this court noted, Federal Rule of Civil Procedure 42 provides that a court may order separate trials on claims or issues in an action when it is in the interests of efficient judicial administration. In CellPro, this court addressed claims for willful infringement and the resulting mischief which has become a consistent problem in patent cases. This court refused to order separate trials of liability, damages, and willful infringement because CellPro failed to satisfy the requirements of Rule 42.

In Markman, the Federal Circuit stated, in no uncertain terms, that it would have the final say as to the meaning of words in a claim of a patent, according no deference to decisions by the various United States District Court Judges. That is, in spite of a trial judge's ruling on the meaning of disputed words in a claim, should a three-judge panel of the Federal Circuit disagree, the entire case could be remanded for retrial on different claims.

As evidenced by this case and others pending in this court, in view of Markman, parties will now routinely move for the early resolution of the claim construction issue either under Federal Rule of Civil Procedure 56 or 12(b)(6). In a bench trial, the court can delay resolution of the claim construction issue until all of the evidence has been presented. However, in a jury trial, delaying resolution of this issue until trial may raise serious practical problems of how to adequately and fairly rule on these often difficult and vitally important issues at the close of the evidence while a jury waits. Moreover, in jury cases, it may be more efficient to put the case in a posture to have the Federal Circuit review the claim interpretation issue before trying the case to a jury, in order to avoid wasting two weeks or more of a citizen's time because the court erroneously instructed the jury on the meaning of a claim term. However, this approach could add significant time and expense to the ultimate resolution of the litigation.

Sensing the importance of claim construction on the outcome of patent cases, parties will likely seek ways to promptly bring the issue before the Federal Circuit. In cases where parties dispute facts surrounding the accused product, once the court resolves the meaning of claim terms the parties will seek an immediate interlocutory appeal to avoid the possibility of dual trials should the Federal Circuit reverse the trial court's claim construction on an appeal from a jury verdict. Where the parties do not dispute the facts surrounding the accused product, they may stipulate to the remaining issues on infringement and appeal to the Federal Circuit from a final order on that issue. In either situation, a case could be appealed to the Federal Circuit only months after the complaint is filed. This would be an unusual procedure for a district court to consistently face in patent cases.

Finally, it remains to be seen what the impact of the court's new role as arbiter of the meaning of disputed words in the claims of patents will have on a party's right to a jury trial on validity issues. For example, it is unclear how the issue of indefiniteness will be presented to a jury where this court instructs the jury on the meaning of vague words that commonly appear in patent claims, such as "substantially."

2.   The Approach of *Markman*. Does it make sense to interpret the Seventh Amendment with reference to the role that juries played in actions at common law in 1791? If so, was the appropriate analogy to modern claim interpretation the construction of patent specifications in England in 1791 as found by the Supreme Court; or the construction of statutes as found by the Federal Circuit? For an analysis of the Federal Circuit's opinion, see 5 MARTIN J. ADELMAN, PATENT LAW PERSPECTIVES (2d. Ed. 1995) at 7–228.42.

3.   The Reach of the Seventh Amendment. Should the Seventh Amendment apply to all questions involving issues at common law that are labeled fact, or only to so-called "historical facts"? Did the Court decide this question in *Markman*? Following *Markman*, what issues that arise in patent litigation are for juries under the Seventh Amendment?

4.   Choosing a Label. The Court in *Markman* set forth an important standard for deciding whether questions of judgment (sometimes labeled mixed questions of fact and law) should be labeled fact or law. Do you agree with the Court's approach to the labeling process? If not, why not? What do you make of the following analysis of the law/fact distinction and the Seventh Amendment written before the Supreme Court's *Markman* decision:

> For a variety of purposes, such as the appropriate standard of appellate review, it is important that courts classify issues as one of law or fact. Another reason to do so is to decide, as a matter of policy, whether to use juries to decide issues involving judgment. An issue of judgment classified as law would be for the judges, and one classified as fact would be for the jury. Federal Courts need not make the law/fact distinction as a matter of Seventh Amendment law. For example, Federal courts, in negligence actions, give the question of negligence to juries. Yet, there is no Seventh Amendment right to a trial by jury on the issue of negligence, because it is a question of judgment in view of underlying facts. Therefore, so called mixed questions are not historical facts and the judgment that their resolution calls for can be placed in the hands of judges without implicating the Seventh Amendment.

5 MARTIN J. ADELMAN, PATENT LAW PERSPECTIVES, § 7.6[2.–2] at n.172 (2d ed. 1996).

Even if you accept the above approach, you must ask whether the meaning of a term of art to one of skill in the art is a question of historical fact and not one of judgment. Consider the following:

> Significantly the Court did not believe that the question of the meaning of a word of art to one skilled in the art is one of historical fact, but rather a legal construct. The Court's approach is a restricted view of what is a historical fact. At first blush, the question of what a word of art meant would simply seem to be what did a certain class of people understand a word to mean at the critical time. It is very unlikely that they all understood it to mean X. The historical answer might be that 735 believed it to be X and 436 believed it to be Y. If classifying it as a historical fact would require that the majority rule prevails, then we must assume that the Court's classifying it as law meant that where the issue was in dispute, the question would be resolved by the exercise of judgment by judges rather than by majority rule.

5 MARTIN J. ADELMAN, PATENT LAW PERSPECTIVES, § 7.6[2.–2] at n.196 (2d ed. 1996).

5. The Doctrine of Equivalents. While the Federal Circuit determined that the question of equivalents is for the jury, the Supreme Court declined to review this holding on the theory that its resolution was not essential to its decision. As a practical matter unless the Supreme Court decides to specifically take up this question, trial courts will treat it as a question for the jury. However, do you think it is a question of judgment? If so, do you think it is the type of judgment that *Markman* suggests should be decided by judges?

6. The Federal Circuit Says No Damages Claim, No Jury. In *Tegal Corp. v. Tokyo Electron America, Inc.*, 257 F.3d 1331, 59 U.S.P.Q.2d 1385 (Fed.Cir.2001), the Federal Circuit held that where a patentee seeks only to enjoin the accused infringer, the Seventh Amendment right to a jury trial does not apply. Should the selection of remedies control the role of juries in patent cases?

7. Issues of Fact at the Supreme Court. In *Cooper Ind., Inc. v. Leatherman Tool Group, Inc.*, 532 U.S. 424 (2001), the Supreme Court held that the determination of punitive damages was not a factual one. As a result, a jury need not decide the issue. Does this holding suggest that the Court would decide that equivalency is a question of judgment and not fact?

§ 18.6 MULTINATIONAL PATENT ENFORCEMENT

A final patent enforcement topic of growing importance is that of multinational patent litigation. Treaties such as the Paris Convention, Patent Cooperation Treaty and TRIPS Agreement assist inventors in obtaining a series of parallel patents across the globe. But few conventions support patentees seeking to enforce their collections of patents against increasingly multinational infringers. The result is a fragmented scheme of world patent enforcement often plagued by burdensome litigation fees and inconsistent outcomes. This Chapter turns to this problem in its closing section, offering as well an overview of patent litigation overseas.

MARS, INC. v. KABUSHIKI–KAISHA NIPPON CONLUX

United States Court of Appeals, Federal Circuit, 1994.
24 F.3d 1368, 30 U.S.P.Q.2d 1621.

Before RICH and LOURIE, CIRCUIT JUDGES, and MILLS, DISTRICT JUDGE.

LOURIE, CIRCUIT JUDGE.

Mars Incorporated appeals from a judgment of the United States District Court for the District of Delaware granting the motion of Nippon Conlux Kabushiki–Kaisha to dismiss for lack of subject matter jurisdiction Mars' claim against Nippon Conlux alleging infringement of Mars' Japanese patent. Because the district court has neither original nor supplemental jurisdiction over Mars' claim, we affirm.

BACKGROUND

On October 2, 1992, Mars filed an action in the Delaware district court against Nippon Conlux, a company organized and operating under the laws of Japan, and certain officers and directors of Conlux U.S.A. Corporation, a U.S. subsidiary of Nippon Conlux. The complaint contained three separate causes of action relating to alleged infringement of Mars' U.S. Patent 3,918,565 and Japanese Patent 1557883, which patents are directed to electronic coin discriminators with programmable memories. The first two counts of the complaint charged Nippon Conlux and the individual defendants, respectively, with direct infringement and inducement of infringement of claims 2, 3, and 60 of the U.S. patent. The third count accused Nippon Conlux of infringement of the sole claim of the Japanese patent. Mars averred in its complaint that the district court possessed subject matter jurisdiction over the two counts alleging infringement of the U.S. patent under 28 U.S.C. §§ 1331, 1338(a) (1988), and "ancillary, pendent and supplemental jurisdiction" over the third count alleging infringement of the Japanese patent under 28 U.S.C. §§ 1338(b) (1988), 1367 (Supp. IV 1992).

Nippon Conlux moved to dismiss the third count based on a lack of subject matter jurisdiction, principles of international comity, and the doctrine of forum non conveniens. In granting the motion to dismiss, the court "assum[ed] without deciding" that it had subject matter jurisdiction over the disputed claim, but "declin[ed] to exercise that jurisdiction pursuant to its authority to decline to exercise supplemental jurisdiction and for reasons of comity." On July 1, 1993, the district court entered a final judgment pursuant to FED.R.CIV.P. 54(b), dismissing Mars' claim of infringement of the Japanese patent. Mars now appeals.

DISCUSSION

I. Choice of Law

When an issue before us pertains to a matter not unique to our exclusive appellate jurisdiction, our established practice has been to defer to the discernable law of the regional circuit in which the district court sits. Such deference, however, is inappropriate when an issue involves substantive questions coming exclusively within our jurisdiction, the disposition of which would have "a direct bearing on the outcome."

In this case, review of the propriety of the district court's dismissal for lack of jurisdiction necessarily requires consideration of facts and resolution of legal principles that "bear[ ] an essential relationship to matters committed to our exclusive control." The issue whether the district court had jurisdiction to hear Mars' claim of Japanese patent infringement "is of importance to the development of the patent law and is clearly a matter that falls within the exclusive subject matter responsibility of this court." Thus, we are not bound by the law of the Third Circuit in deciding this case. Notwithstanding that conclusion, "[w]e may, of course, look for guidance in the decisions of the [Third Circuit], as well as those of other courts."

Whether the trial court properly granted the motion to dismiss for lack of jurisdiction is a question of law. We address that question de novo. Moreover, when a party has moved to dismiss for lack of jurisdiction, we consider the facts alleged in the complaint as being correct. If these facts reveal any reasonable basis on which the non-movant might prevail, the motion will be denied.

In considering the jurisdictional issues presented in this appeal, we are guided by the "fundamental precept that federal courts are courts of limited jurisdiction. The limits upon federal jurisdiction, whether imposed by the Constitution or by Congress, must be neither disregarded nor evaded." A party seeking the exercise of jurisdiction in its favor bears the burden of establishing that such jurisdiction exists.

II. *Original Jurisdiction*

Mars maintains that the district court has original jurisdiction over the Japanese patent infringement claim pursuant to 28 U.S.C. § 1338(b),[2] which "is a jurisdictional statute, giving the district court jurisdiction to hear certain state or [other non-]federal unfair competition claims" when joined with a substantial and related claim under the patent laws. Mars contends that for purposes of section 1338(b), the term "unfair competition" should be broadly construed to cover all "business torts," including the infringement of a foreign patent.

Section 1338(b) was enacted to authorize a federal court to assume jurisdiction over a non-federal unfair competition claim joined in the same case with a federal cause of action arising from U.S. patent, copyright, plant variety protection, or trademark laws in an effort to avoid "piecemeal" litigation. See 28 U.S.C. § 1338(b) note; 1 JAMES W.

---

2. That subsection provides that [t]he district courts shall have original jurisdiction of any civil action asserting a claim of unfair competition when joined with a sub-stantial and related claim under the copyright, patent, plant variety protection or trade-mark laws. 28 U.S.C. § 1338(b) (1988).

MOORE ET AL., MOORE'S FEDERAL PRACTICE ¶ 0.62[6] (2d ed. 1993). However, being a jurisdictional provision, section 1338(b) creates no substantive basis for a claim of unfair competition. Thus, an asserted claim of unfair competition which a plaintiff seeks to join with a related claim under federal patent, copyright, plant variety protection, or trademark law must find a substantive basis in some other, independent source of law.

Here, Mars seeks to extend the scope of section 1338(b) to a claim of infringement of a Japanese patent, which it characterizes as a type of unfair competition. Mars, however, does not assert any state or federal basis for its claim of unfair competition. It does not even cite any Japanese precedent holding that patent infringement constitutes unfair competition under Japanese law. Nevertheless, Mars insists that infringement of a foreign patent is an act of unfair competition as a matter of United States law.

Whether an act constitutes the tort of "unfair competition" within the meaning of section 1338(b) is a question of law that we review de novo. In determining the breadth of the term "unfair competition" as it is used in section 1338(b), we bear in mind that when Congress borrows a common law term in a statute, absent a contrary instruction, it is presumed to adopt the term's widely accepted common law meaning.

The common law concept of "unfair competition" has not been confined to any rigid definition and encompasses a variety of types of commercial or business conduct considered "contrary to good conscience," *International News Serv. v. The Associated Press*, 248 U.S. 215, 240, 39 S.Ct. 68, 73, 63 L.Ed. 211 (1918), including acts of trademark and trade dress infringement, false advertising, dilution, and trade secret theft. However, infringement of patent rights, domestic or foreign, is not generally recognized as coming within the rubric of "unfair competition."

Unfair competition law and patent law have long existed as distinct and independent bodies of law, each with different origins and each protecting different rights. *Kewanee Oil Co. v. Bicron Corp.*, 416 U.S. 470, 480–82 (1974). The law of unfair competition generally protects consumers and competitors from deceptive or unethical conduct in commerce. Patent law, on the other hand, protects a patent owner from the unauthorized use by others of the patented invention, irrespective of whether deception or unfairness exists.

The distinction between the law of unfair competition and patent law is also evident in the general statutory framework enacted by Congress. Whereas patent law is completely preempted by federal law, see 35 U.S.C. §§ 1 through 376 (1988); U.S. Const. art. I, § 8, cl. 8, the law of unfair competition, despite some federal encroachment, see 15 U.S.C. § 1125(a) (1988), remains largely free from federal exclusivity. The provisions of Title 35 governing patents are not in pari materia with the state and federal provisions governing unfair competition. Moreover, section 1338(b) itself expressly sets a claim of unfair competition apart from a claim arising under U.S. patent law.

Although section 1338(b) does not make a comparable distinction between a claim of unfair competition and a claim arising under foreign patent law, that alone does not allow us to simply equate these dissimilar causes of action. Statutes purporting to confer federal subject matter jurisdiction must be narrowly construed, with ambiguities resolved against the assumption of jurisdiction. In the absence of clear evidence that a claim of infringement of a foreign patent was intended by Congress to qualify as a claim of unfair competition under section 1338(b), we are unable to read the statute as expansively as Mars urges. To interpret the term "unfair competition" in section 1338(b) in a manner inconsistent with the ordinary and usual sense of that word would impermissibly expand the jurisdiction of the district courts beyond that clearly envisioned or desired by Congress.

We hold as a matter of law that a claim of infringement of a foreign patent does not constitute a claim of unfair competition within the meaning of section 1338(b). Therefore, we conclude that the district court did not err in refusing to entertain Mars' claim of infringement of the Japanese patent under section 1338(b).

III. Supplemental Jurisdiction

Alternatively, Mars argues that the district court has jurisdiction over the Japanese patent infringement claim by authority of 28 U.S.C. § 1367. That provision confers on a district court, in an action in which it possesses original jurisdiction over a federal claim, "supplemental" jurisdiction to entertain certain non-federal claims contained in the same action that are not otherwise supported by original jurisdiction.

The fundamental principles of supplemental jurisdiction were addressed at length by the Supreme Court in *United Mine Workers of Am. v. Gibbs*, 383 U.S. 715, 86 S.Ct. 1130, 16 L.Ed.2d 218 (1966). In *Gibbs*, the Court delineated the constitutional limits of a federal court's authority to hear pendent non-federal claims. The Court stated that a federal court possesses the "power" to entertain a non-federal claim if it is joined with a related federal claim such that "the entire action before the court comprises but one constitutional 'case.' "*Id.* at 725, 86 S.Ct. at 1138. The Court further explained that the requisite relatedness between the federal and non-federal claims exists for jurisdictional purposes when the claims derive from a "common nucleus of operative fact," and as such, would ordinarily be expected to be tried in one proceeding. *Id.* In addition, the Court stated that when judicial power exists to hear a non-federal claim, the exercise of jurisdiction over that claim is discretionary with the trial court. *Id.* at 726, 86 S.Ct. at 1139.

Uncertainty respecting the scope of pendent and ancillary jurisdiction prompted Congress to provide the federal courts with express statutory authority to hear "supplemental" claims in actions commenced on or after December 1, 1990. *See* H.R.Rep. No. 734, 101st Cong., 2d Sess. 28 (1990); 28 U.S.C. § 1367 note. Enacted as part of the Judicial Improvements Act of 1990, Pub.L. 101–650, 104 Stat. 5089, section 1367 codified the basic principles articulated by the Supreme Court in *Gibbs* respecting the scope and exercise of supplemental jurisdiction. H.R.Rep. No. 734 at 29 n. 15. In cases in which a district court possesses original jurisdiction over a claim, subsection (a) confers on federal district courts supplemental jurisdiction to entertain all other claims "that are so related . . . that they form part of the same case or controversy under Article III of the United States Constitution." 28 U.S.C. § 1367(a). The relatedness requirement of section 1367(a) is satisfied by any claim meeting the "common nucleus of operative fact" test of *Gibbs*. Additionally, the statute reaffirms that the exercise of supplemental jurisdiction is within the discretion of the district court. 28 U.S.C. § 1367(c).

In the instant case, the district court assumed, without deciding, that it had the authority under section 1367(a) to hear the Japanese patent infringement claim, although it ultimately declined to exercise its jurisdiction. In making that assumption, the district court relied on *Ortman v. Stanray*, 163 U.S.P.Q. 331 (N.D.Ill.1969), *rev'd on other grounds*, 437 F.2d 231, 168 U.S.P.Q. 617 (7th Cir.1971), in which a district court held that it possessed supplemental jurisdiction over claims alleging foreign patent infringement brought in the same complaint as a claim alleging infringement of a U.S. patent.

In *Ortman*, a patent owner filed a complaint containing four separate causes of action for alleged infringement of its U.S., Canadian, Brazilian, and Mexican patents. The defendant moved to dismiss the three counts alleging infringement of the foreign patents for lack of jurisdiction. The motion was denied and the order was certified for appeal by the district court. On appeal, the Seventh Circuit affirmed the denial of the motion to dismiss, concluding that "[a]ll of the actions of defendant of which complaint is made are the result of defendant doing similar acts both in and out of the United States." *Ortman v. Stanray*, 371 F.2d 154, 158, 152 U.S.P.Q. 163, 166 (7th Cir.1967). Consistent with that holding, the district court on remand found jurisdiction on the basis that the "charges arising from the sale and manufacture of the same instrumentality in various countries clearly arise from 'a common nucleus of operative fact.' " 163 U.S.P.Q. at 334.

Although section 1367(a) was not at issue in *Ortman*, Mars maintains that the decision provides sufficient authority to support the district court's assumption that the two claims are so related that they form part of the same case or controversy. Mars contends that the U.S. and Japanese patents are "counterparts" of one another and that their claims are similar. Mars further asserts that the accused products in the U.S. and Japanese patent infringement claims against Nippon Conlux are the same or similar. Thus Mars insists that, as in *Ortman*, the similarities between the claims at issue are such that they constitute one case and would be expected to be tried in one proceeding.

The facts alleged in Mars' own complaint, however, belie the notion that the two claims are derived from a common nucleus of operative fact. Mars' claim respecting infringement of U.S. Patent 3,918,565 focuses exclusively on a device manufactured and designed by Nippon Conlux and marketed by Conlux U.S.A. in the United States as the "Premier Coin Changer." The Premier device incorporates an "E920" electronic coin discriminator that Mars asserts infringes claims 2, 3, and 60 of the '565 patent. All three claims are method claims directed to the electronic examination and identification of coins. In contrast, the sole claim of the Japanese Patent 1557883 is an apparatus claim that does not literally contain the limitations of claims 2, 3, and 60 of the U.S. patent, viz., those relating to the storage of first and second electrical signal values in programmable memory for comparison with a stored reference value, as disclosed in claims 2 and 60, or the limitation of claim 3 requiring the use of an electromagnetic field. Furthermore, the range of accused devices in Japan is much broader than in the United States. At least nine devices using five types of coin discriminators in addition to the E920 are accused of infringing the Japanese patent.

Although certain of the devices accused of infringing the Japanese patent may be similar to the Premier device, there are differences in the acts alleged in the two counts brought against Nippon Conlux. In one count, Mars charges Nippon Conlux with direct and induced infringement of Mars' U.S. patent in manufacturing the Premier device in Japan and causing it to be sold in the United States. In the other count, Nippon Conlux is charged only with direct infringement of Mars' Japanese patent.

Thus, in contrast to *Ortman*, neither "similar acts" nor the "same instrumentality" are at issue in the two remaining counts brought by Mars against Nippon Conlux in the Delaware district court. We conclude that the foreign patent infringement claim at issue here is not so related to the U.S. patent infringement claim that the claims form part of the same case or controversy and would thus ordinarily be expected to be tried in one proceeding. The respective patents are different, the accused devices are different, the alleged acts are different, and the governing laws are different. The assertion of supplemental jurisdiction over the Japanese infringement claim would in effect result in the trial court having to conduct two separate trials at one time.

Accordingly, we hold that the district court erred in assuming that it had "power" to hear the Japanese patent infringement claim under section 1367(a). Federal courts may not assume jurisdiction where none exists.

IV. Forum Non Conveniens

Mars has informed us that it may plead diversity jurisdiction under 28 U.S.C. § 1332(a)(2) by way of an amendment to the pleadings under 28 U.S.C. § 1653 if we hold that the district court does not have jurisdiction under section 1338(b) or 1367. In view of this "threat" and in the interest of judicial economy, we will address certain aspects of the district court's decision as they may apply to the possibility of future dismissal under the doctrine of forum non conveniens.

Although the district court did not directly rule on the forum non conveniens issue raised by Nippon Conlux below, it made a number of findings that are pertinent to the "public interest" factors that must be weighed in considering a motion for dismissal under that doctrine. Such factors include "the 'local interest in having localized controversies decided at home'; the interest in having the trial ... in a forum that is at home with the law that must govern the action; [and] the avoidance of unnecessary problems in conflict of laws, or in application of foreign laws." *Lacey v. Cessna Aircraft Co.*, 932 F.2d 170, 180 (3d Cir.1991).

In refusing to exercise jurisdiction over the Japanese patent infringement claim, the district court found that that claim would require the court to resolve complex issues of Japanese procedural and substantive law, a task further complicated by "having to agree on the proper translation of laws, documents and other communications." The court also found that general concerns respecting international comity counsel against exercising jurisdiction over a matter involving a Japanese patent, Japanese law, and acts of a Japanese defendant in Japan. *See Stein Assoc., Inc. v. Heat and Control, Inc.*, 748 F.2d 653, 658, 223 U.S.P.Q. 1277, 1280 (Fed.Cir.1984) ("Only a British court, applying British law, can determine ... infringement of British patents.").

Thus, the trial court has already made findings pertinent to a forum non conveniens analysis which may support dismissal in favor of adjudicating the Japanese patent infringement claim in a suitable forum in Japan. Those findings are not clearly erroneous; thus any attempt to replead jurisdiction based on diversity of citizenship at this point would seem ill-founded.

CONCLUSION

The district court lacks original jurisdiction over the Japanese patent infringement claim pursuant to 28 U.S.C. § 1338(b) because a claim of infringement of a foreign patent is not a claim of unfair competition within the meaning of that provision. In addition, the district court erred in assuming authority to hear the claim under its supplemental jurisdiction pursuant to 28 U.S.C. § 1367(a) because the claim is not so related to the U.S. patent infringement claim that it forms part of the same case or controversy under Article III of the U.S. Constitution.

AFFIRMED.

Notes

1. Comparative Approaches. The mid–1990's saw a virtual onslaught of plaintiffs petitioning courts worldwide to assume subject matter jurisdiction over patents issued abroad. Some tribunals overseas reached different conclusions than the Federal Circuit. In particular, the Dutch courts were receptive to the adjudication of pan-European infringement disputes. In the face of resistance from the English and other national European courts, as well as litigation strategies that would led the Dutch courts to decline jurisdiction over foreign patents, the consolidated multinational patent litigation technique pioneered by the Dutch jurists has grown dormant. For more on developments in the United States, the Netherlands and elsewhere, see Fritz Blumer, *Jurisdiction and Recognition in Transatlantic Patent Litigation*, 9 TEX. INTELL. PROP. L.J. 329 (2001).

2. Reconsidering Multinational Enforcement. The following commentary is drawn from John R. Thomas, *Litigation Beyond the Technological Frontier: Comparative Approaches to Multinational Patent Enforcement*, 27 LAW & POL'Y INT'L BUS. 277 (1996):

Stated most simply, the norms of international law provide each state with the power to control its own affairs within its own territory. Correspondingly, each state bears the responsibility of not interfering with the affairs of another. The adjudication of domestic patent rights in foreign courts has frequently been considered an example of such interference, as the resulting judgments have been presumed to divest individual nations of their inherent authority to control property rights of their own creation. This view has been defended on the grounds that patent rights have a significant effect upon the national order; one observer has suggested that "intellectual property rights can and do have profound effects on a country's economy and social fabric." Richard Arnold, *Can One Sue in England for Infringement of Foreign Intellectual Property Rights?*, 15 EUR. INTELL. PROP. REV. 243, 258 (1990). *See also Packard Instrument Co. v. Beckman Instruments, Inc.*, 175 USPQ 282, 284 (N.D.Ill.1972). To such commentators, the disposition of such matters as patent infringement should properly be considered a distinctly nationalistic one, requiring individual choices of law and technological policy. Such concerns would appear to increase when patent validity is contested, as a foreign court would be asked to rule on what could be seen as the sovereign grant of title.

[W]hatever the strength of the public law analogy, international trade dialogues and other recent events do much to support an argument that the patent law has been risen from its once obscure station. This rise in celebrity has sometimes been accompanied by a new tone of morality and nationalism; witness, for example, the response to pressures which the industrialized powers have placed upon developing countries to recognize patent protection for pharmaceuticals. To the extent that individual patents are no longer considered competitive tools to be brandished between private enterprises, but matters of profound public interest, concerns over sovereignty are felt more intensely, and jurisdictional analyses must proceed with more caution.

As compared with concerns over convenience, issues of sovereignty have largely been addressed through the act of state doctrine. An initial observation should be that the grant of a patent is less of a governmental act than a governmental reaction. Private parties initiate the process of patent prosecution by the filing of an application. Further, whether this application will ultimately mature into a granted patent or not is hardly a discretionary matter. World patent statutes instead establish that patents must be granted to applicants who fulfill the statutory conditions. Although these conditions vary greatly with each application, depending upon the scope of the claims, the teachings of the pertinent technological art, applicant activities and other factors, the determination of whether an individual patent should issue is technical and administrative in nature. While surely not every patent examiner would respond to a given application in an identical way, these individual differences in approach can occur as much within a single national patent office as among several different patent offices. They should hardly be considered a political act of central concern to a sovereign power.

A similar analysis should apply to patent litigation. Rarely, if ever, are fundamental principles of a nation's social order tested in the mundane process of patent infringement actions. Although undoubtedly "affected with a public interest," the level of this interest simply does not rise so greatly as in such disciplines as criminal or constitutional law. Patent infringement disputes remain affairs of private, commercial law, not providing an essential ordering of political conditions, setting forth the organization of the state, or dictating the relations between the role of individuals and the government in a fundamental way. Sovereign activity forms "merely ... the background to the dispute or in which the only governmental actions were the neutral application of the laws," circumstances in which courts have noted that the act of state doctrine does not apply.

But no matter what the level of sovereign interest of the granting state in a particular patent, it might certainly seem to exceed that of any foreign state. However, the interest of foreign states is not so negligible as might be supposed. In an era of increasing international commerce, global attention to intellectual property matters, and interconnection between national patent systems, all nations properly share concern over each issued patent. They do so, at a minimum, because even the mere publication of a foreign patent application directly impacts the availability of patent protection domestically. Not only do world patent systems allow foreign applications to serve as the basis for the domestic patent grant, they must devote considerable effort towards the interpretation of foreign patent instruments. Further, the technical information disclosed in a patent cannot be limited to a single set of borders, supporting the development of industries far from the confines of the patent-granting nation. And where domestic industry does not exist and economic or other conditions prevent its establishment, the existence of foreign patents may limit *de facto* the availability of technology locally as well. Thus, the issuance of a patent cannot be said to be a remote occurrence of scant consequence elsewhere.

So long as the force of a patent instrument remains tied to territorial boundaries, considerations of sovereignty and comity will continue to impact the international patent regime. But as stated so compellingly before, "there is no reason to invert a political limitation into a legal principle." Nicholas de Belleville Katzenbach, *Conflicts on an Unruly Horse: Reciprocal Claims and Tolerances in Interstate and International Law*, 65 YALE L.J. 1087, 1132 (1956). Rather than erect a proscription against foreign patent adjudication due to an assumed but unexamined sovereign interest, courts should be certain to review the precise nature of the patent grant and the extent to which their own resolution of a dispute would impinge upon areas of governmental concern. Doing so would assuredly ease the often unarticulated concerns which suggest application of the act of state or other comity-based doctrines.

If you have made it this far though this book, you are in a good position to judge the difficulties of applying foreign patent law for yourself. Do you agree with the position of the *Mars* court? Or is the Dutch approach superior?

3.   The Draft Hague Convention. The proposed Hague Conference on Private International Law Convention on Jurisdiction and the Recognition of Foreign Judgments represents the latest thinking on multinational civil litigation. The Hague Convention may become the first general treaty governing the recognition of foreign judgments with the United States as a party. Although the Convention concerns civil litigation generally, it holds important implications for patent litigation and in particular for jurisdictional issues. An early draft of proposed Article 12 in part reads:

Article 12 Exclusive jurisdiction

4.   In proceedings which have as their object the registration, validity, [or] nullity[, or revocation or infringement,] of patents, trade marks, designs or other similar rights required to be deposited or registered, the courts of the Contracting State in which the deposit or registration has been applied for, has taken place or, under the terms of an international convention, is deemed to have taken place, have exclusive jurisdiction. This shall not apply to copyright or any neighbouring rights, even though registration or deposit of such rights is possible.

5.   In relation to proceedings which have as their object the infringement of patents, the preceding paragraph does not exclude the jurisdiction of any other court under the Convention or under the national law of a Contracting State.

6.   The previous paragraphs shall not apply when the matters referred to therein arise as incidental questions.

How does this draft treaty language compare with the approach of the Federal Circuit in *Mars v. Conlux*? At the time this book goes to press, however, negotiations on the Hague Convention have apparently stalled. For more on the draft Hague Convention and its intellectual property ramifications, read the insightful Rochelle Dreyfuss, *An Alert to the Intellectual Property Bar: The Hague Judgments Convention*, 2001 Univ. Illinois L. Rev. 421.

4.   Comparative Note on Foreign Forum Shopping. Once a party has obtained patent protection in many different countries, it may ultimately need to consider using procedures to enforce them. The first step is ordinarily the selection of a litigation forum, or fora, in which to bring suit. This choice is ordinarily influenced by the availability of a particular defendant under national jurisdiction and venue laws. But in an era where even smaller commercial entities act multinationally, infringers are often amenable to suit in a number of countries. So the patentee often faces a choice between a number of different states in which to file suit.

The reader who has come with us this far possesses no small awareness of the substantive patent law of the United States and, secondarily, that of the world's other major patent regimes. An understanding of these principles should guide the choice of a favorable forum for patent enforcement. But equally important are the procedural elements that govern patent litigation within a particular jurisdiction. This Note cannot thoroughly review the traits of each of the world's legal systems, but instead will point to some of the chief distinctions between regimes that should influence would-be patent litigants. A laundry list of these factors follows.

Discovery. Nothing exists like United States discovery anywhere else in the world; but common law jurisdiction like the UK have more limited forms. Other jurisdictions, such as France, merely require that documents submitted to the court by one litigant be forward to the other party. The lack of discovery can significantly limit a patentee's options during a litigation, but does dramatically reduce the cost of patent enforcement.

Validity Determinations in the Judicial Forum. In nations such as Germany and Japan, courts must take patents as they find them. The defense of invalidity is not available in the judicial forum. Instead, an opposition or nullity proceeding must be instituted. These split proceedings often lead to delay and higher costs.

Procedural Complexity. Litigation in common law countries often features extensive pretrial motions, discovery, and other pre-trial preparation. Civil law jurisdictions feature a less adversarial trial system, with correspondingly less procedural law to navigate through.

Size of the Litigation Team. In the United States and United Kingdom, a virtual army of litigators is needed on a case of any complexity, comprising patent attorneys, solicitors and barristers. In other nations, such as the Napoleonic code countries, typically only two or three attorneys handle a particular cause.

The Availability of Immediate, Provisional Relief. Foreign legal systems offer several variations upon provisional proceedings for quick relief. Many of these would likely offend notions of due process in the United States, but can be used to great advantage by a patentee. These tools are particularly effective if a strong infringement case can be established.

As discussed above, the Netherlands features a "kort geding" summary proceeding which operates on extremely short notice to defendants: a hearing is usually scheduled within one month of notice to the court and to the defendant. The proceeding is usually quite informal; ordinary rules of evidence are suspended and the judge may choose not to hear the testimony of ordinary or expert witnesses. The judge will usually decide whether to issue an injunction within two weeks of the hearing.

Other nations, like Belgium and Taiwan, include even more drastic seizure proceedings. These comprise ex parte proceedings under which a court-appointed expert may enter an accused infringer's premises and seize infringements. Usually only a small deposit is required, and the patentee is often allowed to accompany this expert during the proceedings. Seizure proceedings offer a great chance to obtain evidence of the origin and quantity of any infringements.

Substantive Complexity. With its size and common law system, the United States patent law is likely the world's most complex. A host of subsidiary issues attend the basic determination of validity and infringement, and the statutory and case law shadings on this law is significant. Foreign patent law doctrine is often less elaborate. Most jurisdictions simply do not have as many sources of law as the United States or the willingness of United States society to devote so many resources towards the patent system. The German and British patent systems are the major exceptions to this trend; but as noted in Chapter 17, one British case on damages in patent cases largely cited United States law for lack of its own precedent in this area.

Sophistication of Courts in Patent Cases. Unlike the United States, many foreign jurisdictions feature specialized judges who decide patent cases. Owners of patents describing complex technologies often favor these courts. The contrast with the use of lay jurors in the United States could not be stronger. Note that the German courts enjoy a reputation for special expertise, in particular the Dusseldorf lower courts and the Tenth Senate of the Supreme Court.

Choosing a Litigator. Although all these variations among jurisdictions often leads to a great deal of strategizing, much of these efforts will be wasted without the appropriate individuals to assist in this decision and to implement the choices the patentee ultimately makes. Most of the factors which guide such decisions in the United States, such as the experience, reputation, and local connections of the counsel, also apply in abroad. It is often necessary to consider the English-language ability and the accessibility of the attorney. Because English is a common second language, the requirement of skill in this language often will not greatly limit the number of available counsel. But in particular countries and among older attorneys, it significantly decreases the number of available counsel. Further, United States attorneys should know that some of their foreign colleagues customarily work with a client only through intermediaries, such as junior associates, solicitors or local patent attorneys.

Costs. Many of these other factors lead into often the paramount consideration: costs. Additionally, many countries tie court fees to the amount in controversy. A litigation with a high dollar amount suggests the selection of another forum in order to decrease costs. Note that the prevailing party may decrease its costs because most jurisdictions require the losing party to pay at least some of the winning party's costs and attorney fees. Even in these so-called "British Rule" jurisdictions, however, the attorney fees that the loser must pay are often considerably less than the actual fees paid by the victor.

European Considerations. Although the European Union features a unified patent acquisition system, enforcement remains fragmented among the various national courts. Because significant distinctions remain among the procedural mechanisms existing in different jurisdictions, forum shopping has particular consequences here.

Traditional Approaches. The patent systems of Europe purport to be harmonized under the European Patent Convention. But many jurists cling to the traditional approaches of their national law prior to the adoption of the EPC. Thus, patentees still appear to enjoy a broad scope of patent protection in such jurisdictions as Germany and the Netherlands, while the UK typically serves as a more amenable forum for accused infringers.

Experience with the European Patent Convention may eliminate these differences over time, but for now these differences should not be discounted.

Additionally, defendants may employ so-called "**Euro defenses**" in patent infringement suits. These defenses arise out of the Treaty of Rome and other international agreements forming the European Common Market. Most important among these is the extension of the exhaustion principle to all Member States of the European Union. Thus, once a good subject to patent protection is sold within one Member State, it may be freely moved through the Common Market, even though other national patents would ordinarily block importation. As many of these defenses have no analog in the United States, consultation with competent local counsel is extremely important.

Enforcement Exercises

1.   Glaucon files a patent application on March 1, 2002 He then files a continuation application on July 10, 2005, including a specific reference to the 2002 application. The 2002 application goes abandoned on August 1, 2005. The PTO declares an interference between Glaucon's continuation application and an application filed by Cephalos on September 1, 2005. As a result of an October 1, 2008, decision, Glaucon prevails in the interference. A patent issues to Glaucon on November 10, 2008. *What is the expiration date of the Glaucon patent?*

2.   A patent issued to Carnap on June 1, 2002. Carnap assigns the patent to Frank for valuable consideration on September 1, 2002 Frank records the assignment at the PTO on January 15, 1998. On November 1, 2002, Carnap assigns the patent to Weissman for valuable consideration. Weissman never records the assignment. Neither Frank nor Weissman has knowledge of Carnap's assignment to the other. *Who possesses valid title to the Carnap patent?*

3.   Herder, a patentee, wishes to bring an infringement suit against Wolff. Herder possesses evidence that Wolff uses an infringing apparatus in Concord, New Hampshire. Herder resides in Bangor, Maine, while Wolff's place of residence is Montpelier, Vermont. Assume that the laws of Maine, New Hampshire and Vermont each include a long arm statute similar to that of the Commonwealth of Virginia as discussed in *Beverly Hills Fan. In which judicial districts does personal jurisdiction exist over Wolff under the various state long arm statutes?*

4.   Frege, a resident in the Eastern District of Michigan, is the owner of the '999 patent. She wishes to bring suit against the Whitehead Company. The Whitehead Company is a Delaware corporation, but does not otherwise conduct business there. Its corporate headquarters is located in the Southern District of California; additionally, it operates a manufacturing plant in the Northern District of Georgia. The Whitehead Company has established sales distributorships, and made extensive sales of products that Frege believes are within the scope of her patent claims, in every judicial district in the states of California, Florida, Georgia and Texas. *Where does venue lie in a patent infringement suit between Frege and the Whitehead Company?*

Chapter Nineteen

LICENSING, MISUSE AND PATENT–ANTITRUST

Title 35 directs that "patents shall have the attributes of personal property." 35 U.S.C.A. § 261. Among the chief attributes of personal property is alienability. Indeed, section 261 states expressly that, in addition to patents themselves, "applications for patent[s]" and "any [other] interest" in a patent are "assignable in law by an instrument in writing." Thus, the right to exclude itself may be transferred freely. In simple terms, ownership of exclusive rights in a patent is different from inventorship. Inventorship, as previously discussed, concerns who actually invented the claimed subject matter. 35 U.S.C.A. §§ 101, 116, 117, 118, 256. Ownership concerns who owns the legal title for, and consequently the right to exercise, the right to exclude defined by the patent. 35 U.S.C.A. §§ 110(d), 117, 118, 152, 261, 262.

As with other conveyances of property, a patent owner may convey the entire legal title or retain some rights after the transfer. Transfers of interests in patents take two forms, assignments and licenses. The sometimes difficult distinctions between these two forms of conveyance carry significant legal implications. The Supreme Court explained the distinction between an assignment, a conveyance of the right to exercise the right to exclude, and a license:

> The patentee or his assigns may, by instrument in writing, assign, grant, and convey, either (1) the whole patent, comprising the exclusive right to make use and vend the invention throughout the United States; or (2) an undivided part or share of that exclusive right; or (3) the exclusive right under the patent within and throughout a specified part of the United States. A transfer of . . . these three kinds of interests is an assignment, properly speaking, and vests in the assignee a title in so much of the patent itself, with a right to sue infringers. In the second case, jointly with the assignor. In the first and third cases, in the name of the assignee alone. Any assignment or transfer, short of one of these, is a mere license, giving the licensee no title in the patent, and no right to sue

1056

at law in his own name for infringement ... Any rights of the licensee must be enforced through or in the name of the owner of the patent. . . .

Whether a transfer of a particular right or interest under a patent is an assignment or a license does not depend upon the name by which it calls itself, but upon the legal effect of its provisions. For instance, a grant of an exclusive right to make, use, and vend two patented machines within a certain district is an assignment, and gives the grantee the right to sue in his own name for an infringement within the district, because the right, although limited to making, using, and vending two machines, excludes all other people, even the patentee, from making, using, or vending like machines within the district.

Waterman v. Mackenzie, 138 U.S. 252, 255–56 (1891).

This passage highlights some of the important implications of the distinction between an assignment and a license: First and foremost, assignees may enforce their exclusive rights in their own names without obtaining permission or cooperation from another. Licensees possess no rights to enforce the patent, though they may of course enforce the terms of their license agreement. In the most common assignment scenario, the first of *Waterman*'s three assignment options, inventors often assign all their rights to their corporate employer. In that case, the corporation can enforce the patent in its own name. In the second *Waterman* assignment option, joint owners have equal rights to enforce their exclusive rights and must have the cooperation of the other owners to bring an infringement suit. These joint owners, however, may use the invention without permission from the other owners. 35 U.S.C.A. § 261. In any event, the chief characteristic of an assignment is the unfettered right to enforce the patent.

Another distinction between an assignment and a license is a corollary of the first. An assignment confers jurisdiction to enforce patent rights in the federal district courts with an appeal to the Court of Appeals for the Federal Circuit. 28 U.S.C.A. § 1338. A license agreement, on the other hand, is a contract governed by ordinary principles of state contract law and enforced in state courts. *Power Lift, Inc. v. Weatherford Nipple–Up Sys., Inc.* 871 F.2d 1082, 10 U.S.P.Q.2d 1464 (Fed.Cir.1989). Thus a claim for failure to pay royalties under a patent license agreement arises out of state contract law and must be filed in a state court. *Schwarzkopf Dev. Corp. v. Ti–Coating, Inc.*, 800 F.2d 240, 231 U.S.P.Q. 47 (Fed.Cir.1986).

Finally, section 261 of title 35 applies the principle of real property recording acts to assignments. *Filmtec Corp. v. Allied–Signal Inc.*, 939 F.2d 1568, 19 U.S.P.Q.2d 1508 (Fed.Cir.1991). Specifically this provision voids an assignment when challenged by a later purchaser of the patent rights for value without notice of the first conveyance unless the initial assignment was recorded at the PTO within three months of the conveyance or before the later purchase. This rule puts a premium on recording any conveyance of patent rights which could be remotely construed as an assignment. Thus, as a precaution, even licenses are often recorded at the PTO. Otherwise a subsequent innocent buyer may acquire title to the patent if an unrecorded instrument is later construed as an assignment. However, although the bona fide purchaser for value rule applies to recorded assignments under § 261, it does not apply to licenses. Thus, one who obtains a license from the patent owner cannot protect its license via the "bona fide purchaser for value rule" from defects in the patent owner's title. *See Rhone–Poulenc Agro, S.A. v. DeKalb Genetics Corp.*, 284 F.3d 1323, 62 U.S.P.Q.2d 1188 (Fed.Cir. 2002).

Clearly the distinction between an assignment and a license has significant legal implications. To determine whether an conveyance constitutes an assignment or a license requires an examination of the intent of the parties to the agreement. An assignment should evince a clear intent to pass title to the patent, a clear intent to permit the transferee to bring suit to enforce the right to exclude. A license, on the other hand, is nothing more than a promise by the licensor not to sue the licensee, usually in exchange for the licensee's promise to pay royalties. Even if the license says "licensee has the right to make, use, or sell the invention," in reality these terms do not give the licensee the right to make, use, or sell. The reason is simple. Even the patent owner does not acquire from a patent any right to make, use, or sell an invention, but only the right to exclude others from making, using, or selling. Therefore, at most, a patent licensee receives an enforceable promise that the patent owner will not sue for infringement.

Licenses can take many forms, from a simple promise not to sue on a particular patent to a sweeping promise not to sue on any patent owned by the licensor. If the licensor also promises to license the patented technology solely to a single licensee, and none other, that licensee has an exclusive license. An exclusive licensee has received a promise that it alone may make, use, or sell the invention without facing an infringement suit. The right to enforce that exclusivity is, for all practical purposes, the same as an assignment. Indeed an exclusive licensee can sue a patent owner in federal court for infringing its own patent. *Yarway Corp. v. Eur–Control USA Inc.*, 775 F.2d 268, 227 U.S.P.Q. 352 (Fed.Cir.1985). An exclusive licensee has a property interest in the patent so close to ownership that it may sue for infringement, but only after joining the patent owner/licensor. Although technically unable to proceed without the patent owner, an exclusive licensee–to enforce its contract–can usually compel the patent owner to join as an involuntary plaintiff in an infringement suit. *Independent Wireless Tel. Co. v. Radio Corp.*, 269 U.S. 459, 472 (1926). The possibility that a license with royalty provisions might later be construed as exclusive and treated as an assignment explains why careful patent attorneys often record licenses at the PTO to avoid the innocent buyer rule.

A license is an affirmative defense against a suit for patent infringement. In addition to the standard contractual license agreements, license rights may also be implied without any written agreement by operation of law. Generally implied licenses protect sales or authorized uses of a patented invention. The classic example is the Supreme Court's decision in *United States v. Univis Lens Co.*, 316 U.S. 241 (1942). Under this implied license, the first authorized sale of an article embodying the patented invention exhausts the right to exclude for that article. Thus, the purchaser may use it, repair it, and even resell it without further fear of infringement suits from the patent owner. *Bandag, Inc. v. Al Bolser's Tire Stores, Inc.*, 750 F.2d 903, 223 U.S.P.Q. 982 (Fed.Cir.1984); *Standard Havens Prods. v. Gencor Indus.*, 953 F.2d 1360, 1375–76 (Fed.Cir.1991). Similarly full compensation creates an implied license. *Stickle v. Heublein, Inc.*, 716 F.2d 1550, 219 U.S.P.Q. 377 (Fed.Cir.1983). Thus, an infringer who has paid damages for infringement receives an implied license to use, repair, and resell the articles embodying the invention throughout their useful life.

Thus, licensing refers to the transfer of a set of rights short of full patent ownership. Individuals license patents for a variety of reasons, including the inability to exploit fully the patented technology, a need to obtain access to another's patented technology via cross-licensing, or simply a desire for additional revenues. As commercial activities increasingly concern intellectual property rights, those legal tenets governing licensing will enjoy an expanding role in the patent community. This Chapter considers the core principles of patent licensing, along with principles of the antitrust and patent misuse laws that restrain the transactional freedom of patent owners.

§ 19.1   THE TECHNOLOGY LICENSE AGREEMENT

The cases in this Chapter largely concern the legal effect of certain clauses in technology license agreements. However, a case-by-case review of each sort of covenant that makes up a technology license would be a time-consuming exercise indeed. The following discussion is intended to present an overview of the essentials of provisions that often find a place in technology license agreements.

Much like a patent claim itself, most technology license agreements begin with a **preamble**. The preamble ordinarily identifies the parties and sets forth various definitions to be used later in the license. It may often include various precatory recitals which may be given weight by a subsequent interpreter in order to determine the intentions of the parties.

The heart of the matter, the **granting clause**, transfers to the licensee specified legal rights, typically some subset of the right to make, use, sell, offer to sell or import into the United States technologies consistent with the licensed patents. 35 U.S.C.A. § 271(a). The granting clause should also set forth the duration of any licensed rights and indicate whether the license is exclusive or nonexclusive. Technology licenses often embrace trade secrets or know-how in addition to patents;

these should be identified as specifically as possible, perhaps through the use of technical specifications or drawings.

The parties may also wish to provide various **warranties**, of commercial utility, merchantability, or scope and validity of the licensed patents, for example. Note that Uniform Commercial Code § 2–312(3), which provides that "a seller who is a merchant regularly dealing in goods of the kind warrants that the goods shall be delivered free of the rightful claim of any third person by way of infringement," has no place in the typical technology license agreement, as such a contract is not one for the sale of goods. *See* UCC § 2–102. The UCC should not be ignored in the context of patent rights, however, given the increasing role of intellectual property in commercial transactions. *See* Robert P. Merges, *Intellectual Property and the Costs of Commercial Exchange: A Review Essay*, 93 MICH. L. REV. 1570 (1995).

Because a license does not immunize the licensee from the possibility of infringing another's intellectual property rights, or from other facing other tort liability, *see* William R. Norris, *Tort Liability That May Attach to Intellectual Property Licensing*, 61 J. PAT. OFF. SOC'Y 607 (1979), **indemnification clauses** also allow parties to balance risks and rewards. The extent of one party's liability may be expressed as a sum certain, *e.g., Hewlett–Packard Co. v. Bausch & Lomb Inc.*, 909 F.2d 1464, 15 U.S.P.Q.2d 1525 (Fed.Cir.1990) (reprinted here in Chapter 15), or the parties may agree to share the cost of litigation defense, *e.g., Ortho Pharm. Corp. v. Genetics Institute, Inc.*, 52 F.3d 1026, 34 U.S.P.Q.2d 1444 (Fed.Cir.1995).

Sublicensing clauses dictate such matters as which party may grant further licenses; to whom payments are due; and the effect of termination of the license on the sublicenses. From the perspective of the licensee, sublicensing clauses may have diminished in importance owing to the expansive interpretation of exhaustion principles by the Federal Circuit. For example, in *Unidisco, Inc. v. Schattner*, 824 F.2d 965, 3 U.S.P.Q.2d 1439 (Fed.Cir.1987), the court held that an exclusive licensee which lacked the right to sublicense could nonetheless sell the licenced product to an exclusive distributor. Nonetheless, provision for sublicensing is advisable both to avoid possible antitrust concerns and in the event third parties seek to employ the licensed product.

The possibility of employing alternative dispute resolution (ADR) or arbitration was reviewed briefly in Chapter 18. **ADR and arbitration clauses** should specify such matters as which disputes will be subject to arbitration, the place of the arbitration, the number of arbitrators, and the method of selection of arbitrators. As an alternative to specifying each rule, the license may simply place the arbitration process under the auspices of a designated association, such as the American Arbitration Association.

A licensor possesses no implied obligation to protect its licensee from infringement by third parties; indeed, it may tolerate as many infringers as it chooses. *See Water Technologies Corp. v. Calco Ltd.*, 576 F.Supp.

767, 220 U.S.P.Q. 603 (N.D.Ill.1983). As widespread, unchecked infringement may render a license meaningless, licensees often request that a license include a **third party infringement clause**. This provision typically obligates the licensor to invoke its patent rights against a third party engaged in infringing activity of sufficient magnitude. Such a clause is most important for nonexclusive licensees, for, as noted here in Chapter 18, exclusive licensees possess the ability to bring suit in the name of the patent owner.

Because a licensee may grant multiple nonexclusive licenses, licensees typically request that the license include a **most favored licensee** provision. This covenant allows a licensee to receive the benefits of a subsequent license with more favorable terms. Although most favored licensee provisions come in many flavors, well-drafted clauses will require the licensee to inform the licensor of subsequent licenses, *cf. Rothstein v. Atlanta Paper Co.,* 321 F.2d 90, 138 U.S.P.Q. 491 (5th Cir.1963), and will also describe how to evaluate whether a subsequent license is more or less favorable than those that came before it. Such an evaluation can be surprisingly difficult given the multiplicity of factors governing technology licenses, such as the amount of the royalty, scope of the transferred rights, cross licenses, duration of the agreement, and other licensor or licensee obligations. *See generally Studiengesellschaft Kohle, M.B.H. v. Hercules, Inc.,* 105 F.3d 629, 41 U.S.P.Q.2d 1518 (Fed.Cir.1997).

Best efforts clauses typically oblige the licensee to exercise its best efforts in commercializing a technology. Since *Wood v. Lucy, Lady Duff–Gordon,* 118 N.E. 214 (N.Y.1917), courts will imply a best efforts obligation when the economic success of the licensor rests solely upon licensee activities. Most licensors find the express statement of this obligation within a license advisable nonetheless. Unfortunately, most common is a broadly drafted clause that does not specify the required efforts, often leading to disputes and judicial resolutions based on little more than the court's sense of the equities of the arrangement. *See, e.g., Perma Research & Dev. v. Singer Co.,* 542 F.2d 111 (2d Cir.1976). Far more advisable are more detailed descriptions of the efforts to be expended, including project budgets, personnel and timetables. *See International Aluminum Window Corp. v. Ferri,* 72 So.2d 31, 101 U.S.P.Q. 131 (Fla.1954).

The often volatile nature of the technology marketplace should render **bankruptcy** of interest to both licensor and licensee. Most technology licenses comprise executory contracts, imposing continuing performance obligations on both parties. As such, a trustee in bankruptcy may assume or reject continued performance under the license. *See Lubrizol Enterprises, Inc. v. Richmond Metal Finishers, Inc.,* 756 F.2d 1043, 226 U.S.P.Q. 961 (4th Cir.1985). The United States Bankruptcy Code provides an exception, however, stating that licensees may continue to use the licensed intellectual property even though the licensor has filed for bankruptcy. 11 U.S.C.A. § 365(n).

Additionally, licensors ordinarily wish to terminate a license if the licensee becomes bankrupt, while the trustee in bankruptcy may wish to assign the license to another. *See* 11 U.S.C.A. § 365(c), (e)(2). "The long standing federal rule of law with respect to the assignability of patent license agreements provides that these agreements are personal to the licensee and not assignable unless expressly made so in the agreement." *Unarco Industries, Inc. v. Kelley Co.*, 465 F.2d 1303, 175 U.S.P.Q. 199 (7th Cir.1972). Therefore, the licensor possesses a strong interest in drafting the license in as terms as specific to the licensee as possible. Additionally, the licensor would be prudent to avoid such language as "licensee and its assigns" throughout the agreement.

For further discussion of technology licensing, see ROGER M. MILGRIM, MILGRIM ON LICENSING (2001); JAY DRATLER, JR., LICENSING OF INTELLECTUAL PROPERTY (2001); HARRY R. MAYERS & BRIAN G. BRUNSVOLD, DRAFTING PATENT LICENSE AGREEMENTS (3d ed. 1991).

§ 19.2   COMPULSORY LICENSING

The term "compulsory licensing" refers to a governmental requirement that a patent owner permit another to perform otherwise infringing acts at a mandated rate. "Compulsory licensing is a rarity in our patent system. . . . [I]t often has been proposed, but it has never been enacted on a broad scale. . . . Although compulsory licensing provisions were considered for possible incorporation into the 1952 revision of the patent laws, they were dropped before the final bill was circulated." *Dawson Chem. Co. v. Rohm & Haas Co.*, 448 U.S. 176, 215 (1980) (citations omitted). Nonetheless, compulsory licensing regimes exist under the Clean Air Act for air pollution control inventions, 42 U.S.C.A. §§ 1857(h)(6), 7608, the Atomic Energy Act for atomic energy inventions, 42 U.S.C.A. § 2183(g), and the Plant Variety Protection Act for new varieties of sexually reproduced plants, 7 U.S.C.A. § 2404. Congress also enacted legislation permitting the federal government and its contractors to employ patented technology in return for "reasonable and entire compensation," 28 U.S.C.A. § 1498 (a), as set by the Court of Federal Claims. United States courts have also created compulsory licenses in order to remedy antitrust violations.

Compulsory licensing schemes have met with far more favor abroad. Indeed, the considerable majority of world patent statutes allow for individuals to apply for state-regulated licenses under particular national patents. While it is fair to say that such schemes are more often discussed than invoked in practice, they can cast a shadow over licensing efforts and create obvious tensions between technology-producing nations and those who are primarily consumers of innovative technologies. Some of these tensions were addressed in the Paris Convention, which restricts the use of compulsory licenses. The most weighty restrictions are found in Article 5, Paragraph 4, which provides:

A compulsory license may not be applied for on the ground of failure to work or insufficient working before the expiration of a period of four years from the date of filing of the patent application or three years from the date of the grant of the patent, which period expires last; it shall be refused if the patentee justifies his inaction by legitimate reasons. Such a compulsory license shall be non-exclusive and shall not be transferable, even in the form of the grant of a sub-license, except with that part of the enterprise or goodwill which exploits such license.

The TRIPS Agreement saw the generation of even more exacting standards for the application of a compulsory licensing regime. Article 31 sets forth a long list of requirements that must be met for a Member to grant a compulsory license, including prior efforts by the proposed user to obtain authorization from the patentee; remuneration provided to the patentee; the possibility of terminating the compulsory license if the circumstances which led to its grant cease to exist and are unlikely to recur; and the availability of judicial review. For a thorough analysis of the application of both the Paris Convention and the TRIPS Agreement to an application for a compulsory license in Germany see the decision of the Bundesgerichtshof (Supreme Court of Germany) in case No. X ZR 26/92. An English translation of the Court's opinion is found at 28 INT'L REV. INDUS. PROP. & COPYRIGHT 242 (1997).

§ 19.3 LICENSEE ESTOPPEL

The formerly active state law principle of licensee estoppel barred individuals from attacking the validity of patents they had licensed from the patentee. Licensee estoppel ensured that patent owners could obtain revenue from their patents without fear of validity challenges by their contracting partners. In the seminal decision of *Lear, Inc. v. Adkins*, however, the United States Supreme Court held that licensee estoppel was preempted by the federal interest favoring free access to inventions, and thus the unhindered ability of licensees to mount challenges to patents. The ramifications of *Lear*, as well as its reach into contract law and other doctrines such as assignee estoppel, reach deep into the patent system.

LEAR v. ADKINS

United States Supreme Court, 1969.
395 U.S. 653, 162 U.S.P.Q. 1.

MR. JUSTICE HARLAN delivered the opinion of the Court.

In January of 1952, John Adkins, an inventor and mechanical engineer, was hired by Lear, Incorporated, for the purpose of solving a vexing problem the company had encountered in its efforts to develop a gyroscope which would meet the increasingly demanding requirements of the aviation industry. The gyroscope is an essential component of the navigational system in all aircraft, enabling the pilot to learn the direction and altitude of his airplane. With the development of the faster airplanes of the 1950's, more accurate gyroscopes were needed, and the gyro industry consequently was casting about for new techniques which would satisfy this need in an economical fashion. Shortly after Adkins was hired, he developed a method of construction at the company's California facilities which improved gyroscope accuracy at a low cost. Lear almost immediately incorporated Adkins' improvements into its production process to its substantial advantage.

The question that remains unsettled in this case, after eight years of litigation in the California courts, is whether Adkins will receive compensation for Lear's use of those improvements which the inventor has subsequently patented. At every stage of this lawsuit, Lear has sought to prove that, despite the grant of a patent by the Patent Office, none of Adkins' improvements were sufficiently novel to warrant the award of a monopoly under the standards delineated in the governing federal statutes. Moreover, the company has sought to prove that Adkins obtained his patent by means of a fraud on the Patent Office. In response, the inventor has argued that since Lear had entered into a licensing agreement with Adkins, it was obliged to pay the agreed royalties regardless of the validity of the underlying patent.

The Supreme Court of California unanimously vindicated the inventor's position. While the court recognized that generally a manufacturer is free to challenge the validity of an inventor's patent, it held that "one of the oldest doctrines in the field of patent law establishes that so long as a licensee is operating under a license agreement he is estopped to deny the validity of his licensor's patent in a suit for royalties under the agreement. The theory underlying this doctrine is that a licensee should not be permitted to enjoy the benefit afforded by the agreement while simultaneously urging that the patent which forms the basis of the agreement is void."

[T]he only issue open to us is raised by the court's reliance upon the doctrine of estoppel to bar Lear from proving that Adkins' ideas were dedicated to the common welfare by federal law. In considering the propriety of the State Court's decision, we are well aware that we are not writing upon a clean slate. The doctrine of estoppel has been considered by this Court in a line of cases reaching back into the middle of the 19th century. Before deciding what the role of estoppel should be in the present case and in the future, it is, then, desirable to consider the role it has played in the past.

A.

While the roots of the doctrine have often been celebrated in tradition, we have found only one 19th century case in this Court that invoked estoppel in a considered manner. And that case was decided before the Sherman Act made it clear that the grant of monopoly power to a patent owner constituted a limited exception to the general federal policy favoring free competition. *Kinsman v. Parkhurst*, 18 How. 289, 15 L.Ed. 385 (1856). Curiously, a second decision often cited as supporting the estoppel doctrine points clearly in the opposite direction. *St. Paul Plow Works v. Starling*, 140 U.S. 184, 11 S.Ct. 803, 35 L.Ed. 404 (1891), did not even question the right of the lower courts to admit the licensee's evidence showing that the patented device was not novel. A unanimous Court merely held that, where there was conflicting evidence as to an invention's novelty, it would not reverse the decision of the lower court upholding the patent's validity.

In the very next year, this Court found the doctrine of patent estoppel so inequitable that it refused to grant an injunction to enforce a licensee's promise never to contest the validity of the underlying patent. "It is as important to the public that competition should not be repressed by worthless patents, as that the patentee of a really valuable invention should be protected in his monopoly * * *." *Pope Manufacturing Co. v. Gormully*, 144 U.S. 224, 234, 12 S.Ct. 632, 636, 36 L.Ed. 414 (1892).

Although this Court invoked an estoppel in 1905 without citing or considering *Pope*'s powerful argument, *United States v. Harvey Steel Co.*, 196 U.S. 310, 25 S.Ct. 240, 49 L.Ed. 492, the doctrine was not to be applied again in this Court until it was revived in *Automatic Radio Manufacturing Co. v. Hazeltine Research, Inc.*, [339 U.S. 827, 70 S.Ct. 894 (1950)], which declared, without prolonged analysis, that licensee estoppel was "the general rule." 339 U.S., at 836, 70 S.Ct. at 899. In so holding, the majority ignored the teachings of a series of decisions this Court had rendered during the 45 years since *Harvey* had been decided. During this period, each time a patentee sought to rely upon his estoppel privilege before this Court, the majority created a new exception to permit judicial scrutiny into the validity of the Patent Office's grant. Long before *Hazeltine* was decided, the estoppel doctrine had been so eroded that it could no longer be considered the "general rule," but was only to be invoked in an ever narrowing set of circumstances.

III.

The uncertain status of licensee estoppel in the case law is a product of judicial efforts to accommodate the competing demands of the common law of contracts and the federal law of patents. On the one hand, the law of contracts forbids a purchaser to repudiate his promises simply because he later becomes dissatisfied with the bargain he has made. On the other hand, federal law requires, that all ideas in general circulation be dedicated to the common good unless they are protected by a valid patent. When faced with this basic conflict in policy, both this Court and courts throughout the land have naturally sought to develop an intermediate position which somehow would remain responsive to the radically different concerns of the two different worlds of contract and patent. The result has been a failure. Rather than creative compromise, there has been a chaos of conflicting case law, proceeding on inconsistent premises. Before renewing the search for an acceptable middle ground, we must reconsider on their own merits the arguments which may properly be advanced on both sides of the estoppel question.

A.

It will simplify matters greatly if we first consider the most typical situation in which patent licenses are negotiated. In contrast to the present case, most manufacturers obtain a license after a patent has issued. Since the Patent Office makes an inventor's ideas public when it issues its grant of a limited monopoly, a potential licensee has access to the inventor's ideas even if he does not enter into an agreement with the patent owner. Consequently, a manufacturer gains only two benefits if he chooses to enter a licensing agreement after the patent has issued. First, by accepting a license and paying royalties for a time, the licensee may have avoided the necessity of defending an expensive infringement action during the period when he may be least able to afford one. Second, the existence of an unchallenged patent may deter others from attempting to compete with the licensee.

Under ordinary contract principles the mere fact that some benefit is received is enough to require the enforcement of the contract, regardless of the validity of the underlying patent. Nevertheless, if one tests this result by the standard of good-faith commercial dealing, it seems far from satisfactory. For the simple contract approach entirely ignores the position of the licensor who is seeking to invoke the court's assistance on his behalf. Consider, for example, the equities of the licensor who has obtained his patent through a fraud on the Patent Office. It is difficult to perceive why good faith requires that courts should permit him to recover royalties despite his licensee's attempts to show that the patent is invalid.

Even in the more typical cases, not involving conscious wrongdoing, the licensor's equities are far from compelling. A patent, in the last analysis, simply represents a legal conclusion reached by the Patent Office. Moreover, the legal conclusion is predicated on factors as to which reasonable men can differ widely. Yet the Patent Office is often obliged to reach its decision in an ex parte proceeding, without the aid of the arguments which could be advanced by parties interested in proving patent invalidity. Consequently, it does not seem to us to be unfair to require a patentee to defend the Patent Office's judgment when his licensee places the question in issue, especially since the licensor's case is buttressed by the presumption of validity which attaches to his patent. Thus, although licensee estoppel may be consistent with the letter of contractual doctrine, we cannot say that it is compelled by the spirit of contract law, which seeks to balance the claims of promisor and promisee in accord with the requirements of good faith.

Surely the equities of the licensor do not weigh very heavily when they are balanced against the important public interest in permitting full and free competition in the use of ideas which are in reality a part of the public domain. Licensees may often be the only individuals with enough economic incentive to challenge the patentability of an inventor's discovery. If they are muzzled, the public may continually be required to pay tribute to would-be monopolists without need or justification. We think it plain that the technical requirements of contract doctrine must give way before the demands of the public interest in the typical situation involving the negotiation of a license after a patent has issued.

We are satisfied that *Automatic Radio Manufacturing Co. v. Hazeltine Research, Inc., supra,* itself the product of a clouded history, should no longer be regarded as sound law with respect to its 'estoppel' holding, and that holding is now overruled.

B.

The case before us, however, presents a far more complicated estoppel problem than the one which arises in the most common licensing context. The problem arises out of the fact that Lear obtained its license in 1955, more than four years before Adkins received his 1960 patent. Indeed, from the very outset of the relationship, Lear obtained special access to Adkins' ideas in return for its promise to pay satisfactory compensation.

Thus, during the lengthy period in which Adkins was attempting to obtain a patent, Lear gained an important benefit not generally obtained by the typical licensee. For until a patent issues, a potential licensee may not learn his licensor's ideas simply by requesting the information from the Patent Office. During the time the inventor is seeking patent protection, the governing federal statute requires the Patent Office to hold an inventor's patent application in confidence. If a potential licensee hopes to use the ideas contained in a secret patent application, he must deal with the inventor himself, unless the inventor chooses to publicize his ideas to the world at large. By promising to pay Adkins royalties from the very outset of their relationship, Lear gained immediate access to ideas which it may well not have learned until the Patent Office published the details of Adkins' invention in 1960. At the core of this case, then, is the difficult question whether federal patent policy bars a State from enforcing a contract regulating access to an unpatented secret idea.

Adkins takes an extreme position on this question. The inventor does not merely argue that since Lear obtained privileged access to his ideas before 1960, the company should be required to pay royalties accruing before 1960 regardless of the validity of the patent which ultimately issued. He also argues that since Lear obtained special benefits before 1960, it should also pay royalties during the entire patent period (1960—1977), without regard to the validity of the Patent Office's grant. We cannot accept so broad an argument.

Adkins' position would permit inventors to negotiate all important licenses during the lengthy period while their applications were still pending at the Patent Office, thereby disabling entirely all those who have the strongest incentive to show that a patent is worthless. While the equities supporting Adkins' position are somewhat more appealing than those supporting the typical licensor, we cannot say that there is enough of a difference to justify such a substantial impairment of overriding federal policy.

Nor can we accept a second argument which may be advanced to support Adkins' claim to at least a portion of his post-patent royalties, regardless of the validity of the Patent Office grant. The terms of the 1955 agreement provide that royalties are to be paid until such time as the "patent * * * is held invalid," § 6, and the fact remains that the question of patent validity has not been finally determined in this case. Thus, it may be suggested that although Lear must be allowed to raise the question of patent validity in the present lawsuit, it must also be required to comply with its contract and continue to pay royalties until its claim is finally vindicated in the courts.

The parties' contract, however, is no more controlling on this issue than is the State's doctrine of estoppel, which is also rooted in contract principles. The decisive question is whether overriding federal policies would be significantly frustrated if licensees could be required to continue to pay royalties during the time they are challenging patent validity in the courts.

It seems to us that such a requirement would be inconsistent with the aims of federal patent policy. Enforcing this contractual provision would give the licensor an additional economic incentive to devise every conceivable dilatory tactic in an effort to postpone the day of final judicial reckoning. We can perceive no reason to encourage dilatory court tactics in this way. Moreover, the cost of prosecuting slow-moving trial proceedings and defending an inevitable appeal might well deter many licensees from attempting to prove patent invalidity in the courts. The deterrent effect would be particularly severe in the many scientific fields in which invention is proceeding at a rapid rate. In these areas, a patent may well become obsolete long before its 17–year term has expired. If a licensee has reason to believe that he will replace a patented idea with a new one in the near future, he will have little incentive to initiate lengthy court proceedings, unless he is freed from liability at least from the time he refuses to pay the contractual royalties. Lastly, enforcing this contractual provision would undermine the strong federal policy favoring the full and free use of ideas in the public domain. For all these reasons, we hold that Lear must be permitted to avoid the payment of all royalties accruing after Adkins' 1960 patent issued if Lear can prove patent invalidity.

C.

Adkins' claim to contractual royalties accruing before the 1960 patent issued is, however, a much more difficult one, since it squarely raises the question whether, and to what extent, the States may protect the owners of unpatented inventions who are willing to disclose their ideas to manufacturers only upon payment of royalties. The California Supreme Court did not address itself to this issue with precision, for it believed that the venerable doctrine of estoppel provided a sufficient answer to all of Lear's claims based upon federal patent law. Thus, we do not know whether the Supreme Court would have awarded Adkins recovery even on his pre-patent royalties if it had recognized that previously established estoppel doctrine could no longer be properly invoked with regard to royalties accruing during the 17–year patent period. Our decision today will, of course, require the state courts to reconsider the theoretical basis of their decisions enforcing the contractual rights of inventors and it is impossible to predict the extent to which this reevaluation may revolutionize the law of any particular State in this regard. Consequently, we have concluded, after much consideration, that even though an important question of federal law underlies this phase of the controversy, we should not now attempt to define in even a limited way the extent, if any, to which the States may properly act to enforce the contractual rights of inventors of unpatented secret ideas. Given the difficulty and importance of this task, it should be undertaken only after the state courts have, after fully focused inquiry, determined the extent to which they will respect the contractual rights of such inventors in the future. Indeed, on remand, the California courts may well reconcile the competing demands of patent and contract law in a way which would not warrant further review in this Court.

The judgment of the Supreme Court of California is vacated and the case is remanded to that court for further proceedings not inconsistent with this opinion.

Notes

1. **Distinguishing *Lear*.** On at least one occasion, the Federal Circuit refused to extend the holding of *Lear* beyond the setting of licensor estoppel. In *Foster v. Hallco Mfg. Co.*, 947 F.2d 469, 20 U.S.P.Q.2d 1241 (Fed.Cir. 1991), the court considered whether the entrance of a consent decree concerning validity would estop a party from later asserting the invalidity of the patent. The court distinguished *Lear* as follows:

> The Supreme Court in Lear did not consider the policy concerns evoked when preserving the finality of a judgment, but only the policies involved in resolving the right of a patent licensee to challenge the validity of the licensed patent in a suit for royalties under the contract. That question puts at odds only the binding effect of contract provisions under state contract law and the federal patent policy favoring free use of ideas rightfully belonging to the public domain[.]

> The application of res judicata principles, thus, involves a public policy totally absent from Lear. We are aware of no court which has even suggested that Lear abrogates the application of res judicata principles based on a judgment imposed by the court after full litigation. Nevertheless, some courts, like the court here, have held that a consent judgment, unlike an imposed judgment, runs afoul of Lear even with respect to the same cause of action (i.e., a suit on the same device alleged to infringe the same patent) on the theory that Lear precludes parties from removing possible challenges to validity merely by their agreement.

> Moreover, the Federal Circuit has repeatedly expressed the view that there is a strong public interest in settlement of patent litigation. A binding consent judgment encourages patent owners to agree to settlement and to remove its force would have an adverse effect on settlement negotiations.

Thus, unlike Lear, where there was a conflict between federal patent policy and state law of contracts, here we have strong competing policies that do not implicate questions of the primacy of federal over state law. One policy seeks to outlaw restriction of challenges to validity of patents; the other favors the finality of judgments generally and the encouragement of settlements of litigation in particular, including settlements resulting in a consent judgment. In this light, we cannot conclude that the public policy expressed in Lear is so overriding that challenges to validity must be allowed when under normal principles of res judicata applicable to a consent judgment, such challenge would be precluded.

947 F.2d at 476–77, 20 U.S.P.Q.2d at 1246–47.

2.   Assignor Estoppel. In *Diamond Scientific Co. v. Ambico, Inc.*, 848 F.2d 1220, 6 U.S.P.Q.2d 2028 (Fed.Cir.1988), the court considered the closely related topic of assignor estoppel as follows:

In examining Lear, one important distinction between assignors and licensees becomes apparent—a distinction that cautions against the automatic application to assignment cases of the rationale underlying Lear and licensees. The public policy favoring allowing a licensee to contest the validity of the patent is not present in the assignment situation. Unlike the licensee, who, without Lear might be forced to continue to pay for a potentially invalid patent, the assignor who would challenge the patent has already been fully paid for the patent rights.

Assignor estoppel is an equitable doctrine that prevents one who has assigned the rights to a patent (or patent application) from later contending that what was assigned is a nullity. The estoppel also operates to bar other parties in privity with the assignor, such as a corporation founded by the assignor. See, e.g., *Stubnitz–Greene Spring Corp. v. Fort Pitt Bedding Co.*, 110 F.2d 192, 195–96 (6th Cir.1940). The estoppel historically has applied to invalidity challenges based on "novelty, utility, patentable invention, anticipatory matter, and the state of the art." *Babcock v. Clarkson*, 63 F. 607, 609 (1st Cir.1894).

The four most frequently mentioned justifications for applying assignor estoppel are the following: "(1) to prevent unfairness and injustice; (2) to prevent one [from] benefiting from his own wrong; (3) by analogy to estoppel by deed in real estate; and (4) by analogy to a landlord-tenant relationship." Cooper, *Estoppel to Challenge Patent Validity: The Case of Private Good Faith vs. Public Policy*, 18 Case W.Res. 1122 (1967). Although each rationale may have some utility depending on the facts presented by the particular case, our concern here is primarily with the first one.

Courts that have expressed the estoppel doctrine in terms of unfairness and injustice have reasoned that an assignor should not be permitted to sell something and later to assert that what was sold is worthless, all to the detriment of the assignee. Justice Frankfurter's dissent in Scott Paper explained that the doctrine was rooted in the notion of fair dealing. "The principle of fair dealing as between assignor and assignee of a patent whereby the assignor will not be allowed to say that what he has sold as a patent was not a patent has been part of the fabric of our law throughout the life of this nation." *Scott Paper v. Marcalus Mfg.*

Co., 326 U.S. 249, 260, 66 S.Ct. 101, 106, 90 L.Ed. 47 (Frankfurter, J., dissenting). "The essence of the principle of fair dealing which binds the assignor of a patent in a suit by the assignee, even though it turns out that the patent is invalid or lacks novelty, is that in this relation the assignor is not part of the general public but is apart from the general public." *Id.* at 261–62, 66 S.Ct. at 107. In other words, it is the implicit representation by the assignor that the patent rights that he is assigning (presumably for value) are not worthless that sets the assignor apart from the rest of the world and can deprive him of the ability to challenge later the validity of the patent. To allow the assignor to make that representation at the time of the assignment (to his advantage) and later to repudiate it (again to his advantage) could work an injustice against the assignee.

Our holding is that this is a case in which public policy calls for the application of assignor estoppel. We are, of course, not unmindful of the general public policy disfavoring the repression of competition by the enforcement of worthless patents. Yet despite the public policy encouraging people to challenge potentially invalid patents, there are still circumstances in which the equities of the contractual relationships between the parties should deprive one party (as well as others in privity with it) of the right to bring that challenge.

848 F.2d at 1224–25, 6 U.S.P.Q.2d at 2030–31. In her concurring opinion, Judge Newman added:

I write separately to state my belief that it is time to reaffirm the principle of assignor estoppel; that is, to reinstate assignor estoppel as the general rule rather than the exception. Such rule would place on the assignor/challenger the burden of proving that an apparently valid deed of assignment should not be enforced in accordance with the applicable laws of contracts and property transfers, rather than placing on the assignee the burden of proving that equity is on its side.

848 F.2d at 1227, 6 U.S.P.Q.2d at 2033. Do you agree? If the Federal Circuit were unhindered by binding Supreme Court precedent, how do you think that court would decide *Lear* today? For an argument that the argument for the *Lear* rule is stronger for assignor estoppel than for licensee estoppel, see 7 Martin J. Adelman, Patent Law Perspectives, § 12.4[3] at n.28 (2d ed. 1991).

3. No–Contest Clauses and Misuse. *Lear* renders unenforceable license provisions that purport to deny licensees the ability to contest the validity of a license patent. However, does the use of such provision constitute patent misuse? One court, *Bendix Corp. v. Balax, Inc.,* 471 F.2d 149, 176 U.S.P.Q. 33 (7th Cir.1972), refused to so hold. This casebook takes up the topic of patent misuse later in this chapter.

4. *Lear* and What is Owed. When a licensee successfully challenges the validity of the licensed patent, the question arises as to the point in time at which the licensee may cease paying royalties. The Federal Circuit considered this point in *Studiengesellschaft Kohle, M.B.H. v. Shell Oil Co.,* 112 F.3d 1561, 42 U.S.P.Q.2d 1674 (Fed.Cir.1997):

According to the 1987 licensing agreement, Shell agreed to pay SGK a 1.5% running royalty on the sale of any polypropylene, produced with a heavy metal catalyst as defined in claim 1 of the '698 patent, in excess of 450 million pounds per year. Further, as discussed above, this agreement obligated Shell to give a yearly accounting of its entire polypropylene production, specifying "the amount of Polypropylene produced which it considers as falling outside of the license." The agreement obligated Shell to provide SGK with sufficient information to allow independent evaluation of whether its production falls outside the scope of the license. The record shows that Shell breached this contract by producing polypropylene under the Seadrift Process, without either paying royalties or reporting the production as outside of the license.

Nothing in this license made payment of royalties contingent upon the validity of the '698 patent. Setting aside momentarily both federal patent law and policy, this contract—regardless of the patent's validity—obligates Shell to pay royalties on polypropylene produced in accordance with claim 1 of the '698 patent. In other words, contract law governs the enforcement of the license. Enforcement of these contract terms is not contingent upon validity of the patent which defines the subject matter of the license. Assuming that the Seadrift Process infringes claim 1 of the '698 patent and thus fits within the terms of the license, Shell breached the license by failing to pay royalties. Enforcement of the license, if the Seadrift Process infringes the '698 patent, would require Shell to pay back royalties.

With a patent licensing agreement at stake, this court examines the contract for rare, but potential, conflicts between state contract law and federal patent law. For example, in *Lear v. Adkins*, 395 U.S. 653, 23 L.Ed.2d 610, 89 S.Ct. 1902 (1969), the Supreme Court prevented the enforcement of a valid royalty payment agreement to facilitate a determination of patent validity. Specifically, the Supreme Court declined to estop a patent licensee from contesting the validity of the licensed patent. In tones that echo from a past era of skepticism over intellectual property principles, the Court in *Lear* feared that licensees may often be the only individuals with enough economic incentive to challenge the patentability of an inventor's discovery. If they are muzzled, the public may continually be required to pay tribute to would-be monopolists without need or justification. We think it plain that the technical requirements of contract doctrine must give way before the demands of the public interest. . . .

Lear, 395 U.S. at 670. Thus, in examining the interface between national patent policy and state contracts, the Supreme Court requires this court to consider "whether overriding federal policies would be significantly frustrated" by enforcing the license. *Id.*

This court encountered the *Lear* test when an assignor-inventor and his company sought to defend against an infringement action by challenging the validity of the assigned patents. *See Diamond Scientific Co. v. Ambico, Inc.*, 848 F.2d 1220, 6 U.S.P.Q.2d 2028 (Fed.Cir.1988). With careful consideration of the *Lear* test and policies, this court nonetheless estopped the assignor from challenging the validity of the patent:

> To allow the assignor to make that representation [of the worth of the patent] at the time of the assignment (to his advantage) and

later to repudiate it (again to his advantage) could work an injustice against the assignee.... Despite the public policy encouraging people to challenge potentially invalid patents, there are still circumstances in which the equities of the contractual relationships between the parties should deprive one party ... of the right to bring that challenge.

Diamond Scientific, 848 F.2d at 1224–25. Indeed, in several other settings, this court has distinguished Lear. *See, e.g., Foster v. Hallco Mfg. Co.*, 947 F.2d 469, 476–77, 20 U.S.P.Q.2d 1241, 1246–47 (Fed.Cir. 1991) (*Lear* does not bar enforcement of settlement agreement and consent decree); *Sun Studs, Inc. v. ATA Equip. Leasing, Inc.*, 872 F.2d 978, 991–93, 10 U.S.P.Q.2d 1338, 1349–51 (Fed.Cir.1989) (*Lear* does not bar enforcement of contract promise to share royalties); *Hemstreet v. Spiegel, Inc.*, 851 F.2d 348, 350–51, 7 U.S.P.Q.2d 1502, 1504 (Fed.Cir. 1988) (*Lear* does not bar enforcement of settlement agreement to pay royalties even if patent later held invalid).

As in *Diamond Scientific*, this court detects no significant frustration of federal patent policy by enforcing the 1987 license agreement between Shell and SGK, to the extent of allowing SGK to recover royalties until the date Shell first challenged the validity of the claims. First, as in *Diamond Scientific*, Shell executed a contractual agreement which produced significant benefits for the corporation and attested to the worth of the patent. Under the agreement (with its provision for Shell to notify SGK of all polypropylene production), Shell had the benefits of producing polypropylene insulated from unlicensed competition, insulated from investigations of infringement, and even insulated from royalties (until SGK's discovery of the Seadrift Process). To these benefits, Shell now seeks to add the benefit of abrogating its agreement and avoiding its breach of the contract. Following the reasoning of *Diamond Scientific*, this court must prevent the injustice of allowing Shell to exploit the protection of the contract and patent rights and then later to abandon conveniently its obligations under those same rights.

Just as important, however, Shell's apparent breach of its duty to notify under the agreement is itself more likely to frustrate federal patent policy than enforcement of the contract. As already noted, Lear focused on the "full and free use of ideas in the public domain." *Lear*, 395 U.S. at 674. By abrogating its notification duty, Shell delayed a timely challenge to the validity of the '698 patent and postponed the public's full and free use of the invention of the '698 patent. Shell enjoyed the protection of the license from 1987 until SGK became aware of the Seadrift Process. Upon SGK's discovery of its Seadrift process, Shell suddenly seeks the protection of the *Lear* policies it flaunted for many years. However, a licensee, such as Shell, cannot invoke the protection of the *Lear* doctrine until it (i) actually ceases payment of royalties, and (ii) provides notice to the licensor that the reason for ceasing payment of royalties is because it has deemed the relevant claims to be invalid. Other circuits addressing this issue have arrived at the same conclusion.

In this factual setting, therefore, enforcement of the license according to its terms, even if this entails a determination of whether the

Seadrift process infringes a now-invalidated patent, does not frustrate federal patent policy. Accordingly, this court remands this case to the district court for enforcement of the license (prior to the date Shell first challenged the validity of the claims) and, if necessary, computation of back royalties.

5. Further Reading. Rochelle Dreyfuss, *Dethroning* Lear: *Licensee Estoppel and the Incentive to Innovate*, 72 VA. L. REV. 677 (1986), presents a perceptive and critical analysis of *Lear v. Adkins*.

6. *Aronson v. Quick Point.* *Lear* left open the question of whether contracts for the payment of royalties based on secret technology as of the time of the grant, were enforceable. At least where no patent was ever obtained on the secret technology, the Supreme Court in *Aronson v. Quick Point Pencil Co.*, 440 U.S. 257, 201 U.S.P.Q. 1 (1979) said that such agreements were enforceable. Thus, secret technology that later goes into the public domain can support the payment of royalties for an indefinite period without running afoul of Lear. In essence, the Court concluded that, if one is foolish enough or unlucky enough to enter into a contract that requires payments, when none of your competitors are required to make payments, it was not the job of the Court to relieve you of your unfortunate bargain. The implications of Aronson are discussed at 7 MARTIN J. ADELMAN, PATENT LAW PERSPECTIVES, § 16.2[6.–2] at n.57 (2d ed. 1982).

§ 19.4 MISUSE AND PATENT–ANTITRUST

The detailed relationship between antitrust law and patent law is beyond the scope of this casebook. However, a violation of the antitrust laws by the patentee may constitute a defense to a suit for patent infringement under the equitable doctrine of patent misuse, at least until the adverse effects of the misuse are purged by the patentee. The patent misuse doctrine is not easy to understand because it provides a specific remedy for a litigant who brings a substantive misuse violation to the attention of the court during infringement litigation. These activities frequently are, but need not be antitrust violations.

The doctrinal development of substantive patent misuse began with a series of cases where the patent owner brought suit for contributory infringement against a manufacturer who was selling unpatented supplies, used by licensees of patented machines in violation of their license. The manufacturer defended on the ground that the patent owner was trying to monopolize an unpatented product. Hence, the court should not enforce the patent against it. The classic case was the decision of the Sixth Circuit written by Judge Taft (later President Taft and then Chief Justice Taft) in *Heaton–Peninsular Button–Fastener Co. v. Eureka Specialty Co.*, 77 F. 288 (6th Cir.1896). This opinion manifests a sophisticated approach to the economics of tying practices. The opinion recognized that permitting a patentee to control the supplies used in the operation of its patented machines merely measured the intensity of use of the patented machine and did not constitute improper monopolization and an unpatented product. However, this approach did not survive the passage of the Clayton Act for in 1917 the Supreme Court, while it did not rely on the Clayton Act, refused to enforce a patent against a contributory infringer who was selling movies used in connection with licensed patented projectors, *Motion Picture Patents Co. v. Universal Film Mfg. Co.*, 243 U.S. 502 (1917).

Motion Picture Patents was followed by a series of cases involving the refusal of courts to enforce patents against contributory infringers who were selling unpatented components that were either used with or were part of, but not the complete, patented combination or process. This line of cases culminated in *Mercoid Corp. v. Mid–Continent Investment Co.*, 320 U.S. 661 (1944) (Mercoid I) and *Mercoid Corp. v. Minneapolis–Honeywell Regulator Co.*, 320 U.S. 680 (1944) (Mercoid II). Mercoid I and II extended the doctrine against suits for contributory infringement to all unpatented components even if they were the essence of the patented combination or process. Moreover, they may have gone even further, precluding a suit for contributory infringement even if the patentee was not trying to control any unpatented component, but was merely trying to conveniently use a manufacturer of unpatented components as a collector of royalties for use of the patented combination.

However, all of these cases which discussed the patentee's extending his monopoly to unpatented components were suits against sellers of such components. Thus, the courts recognized no separate doctrine of patent misuse until 1942. However, defendants sued for contributory infringement could allege that the suit should fail because the lawsuit represented the patentee's attempt to monopolize unpatented components. Then the dam burst.

Meanwhile, two years before the Mercoid cases, the Supreme Court created the doctrine of patent misuse in the following decision.

MORTON SALT CO. v. G. S. SUPPIGER CO.

United States Supreme Court, 1942.
314 U.S. 488.

Mr. Chief Justice Stone delivered the opinion of the Court.

Respondent brought this suit in the district court for an injunction and an accounting for infringement of its Patent No. 2,060,645, of November 10, 1936, on a machine for depositing salt tablets, a device said to be useful in the canning industry for adding predetermined amounts of salt in tablet form to the contents of the cans.

Upon petitioner's motion, the trial court, without passing on the issues of validity and infringement, granted summary judgment dismissing the complaint. It took the ground that respondent was making use of the patent to restrain the sale of salt tablets in competition with its own sale of unpatented tablets, by requiring licensees to use with the patented machines only tablets sold by respondent. The Court of Appeals for the Seventh Circuit reversed, 117 F.2d 968, because it thought that respondent's use of the patent was not shown to violate § 3 of the

Clayton Act, 15 U.S.C. § 14, as it did not appear that the use of its patent substantially lessened competition or tended to create a monopoly in salt tablets. We granted certiorari because of the public importance of the question presented and of an alleged conflict of the decision below with *B. B. Chemical Co. v. Ellis*, 1 Cir., 117 F.2d 829, and with the principles underlying the decisions in *Carbice Corp. v. American Patents Development Corp.*, 283 U.S. 27, and *Leitch Mfg. Co. v. Barber Co.*, 302 U.S. 458.

The Clayton Act authorizes those injured by violations tending to monopoly to maintain suit for treble damages and for an injunction in appropriate cases. 15 U.S.C. §§ 1, 2, 14, 15, 26. But the present suit is for infringement of a patent. The question we must decide is not necessarily whether respondent has violated the Clayton Act, but whether a court of equity will lend its aid to protect the patent monopoly when respondent is using it as the effective means of restraining competition with its sale of an unpatented article.

Both respondent's wholly owned subsidiary and the petitioner manufacture and sell salt tablets used and useful in the canning trade. The tablets have a particular configuration rendering them capable of convenient use in respondent's patented machines. Petitioner makes and leases to canners unpatented salt deposition machines, charged to infringe respondent's patent. For reasons we indicate later, nothing turns on the fact that petitioner also competes with respondent in the sale of the tablets, and we may assume for purposes of this case that petitioner is doing no more than making and leasing the alleged infringing machines. The principal business of respondent's subsidiary, from which its profits are derived, is the sale of salt tablets. In connection with this business, and as an adjunct to it, respondent leases its patented machines to commercial canners, some two hundred in all, under licenses to use the machines upon condition and with the agreement of the licensees that only the subsidiary's salt tablets be used with the leased machines.

It thus appears that respondent is making use of its patent monopoly to restrain competition in the marketing of unpatented articles, salt tablets, for use with the patented machines, and is aiding in the creation of a limited monopoly in the tablets not within that granted by the patent. A patent operates to create and grant to the patentee an exclusive right to make, use and vend the particular device described and claimed in the patent. But a patent affords no immunity for a monopoly not within the grant, and the use of it to suppress competition in the sale of an unpatented article may deprive the patentee of the aid of a court of equity to restrain an alleged infringement by one who is a competitor. It is the established rule that a patentee who has granted a license on condition that the patented invention be used by the licensee only with unpatented materials furnished by the licensor, may not restrain as a contributory infringer one who sells to the licensee like materials for like use.

The grant to the inventor of the special privilege of a patent monopoly carries out a public policy adopted by the Constitution and laws of the United States, "to promote the Progress of Science and useful Arts, by securing for limited Times to * * * Inventors the exclusive Right * * *." to their "new and useful" inventions. United States Constitution, Art. I, § 8, cl. 8; 35 U.S.C. § 31. But the public policy which includes inventions within the granted monopoly excludes from it all that is not embraced in the invention. It equally forbids the use of the patent to secure an exclusive right or limited monopoly not granted by the Patent Office and which it is contrary to public policy to grant. It is a principle of general application that courts, and especially courts of equity, may appropriately withhold their aid where the plaintiff is using the right asserted contrary to the public interest. Respondent argues that this doctrine is limited in its application to those cases where the patentee seeks to restrain contributory infringement by the sale to licensees of competing unpatented article, while here respondent seeks to restrain petitioner from a direct infringement, the manufacture and sale of the salt tablet depositor. It is said that the equitable maxim that a party seeking the aid of a court of equity must come into court with clean hands applies only to the plaintiff's wrongful conduct in the particular act or transaction which raises the equity, enforcement of which is sought; that where, as here, the patentee seeks to restrain the manufacture or use of the patented device, his conduct in using the patent to restrict competition in the sale of salt tablets does not foreclose him from seeking relief limited to an injunction against the manufacture and sale of the infringing machine alone.

Undoubtedly "equity does not demand that its suitors shall have led blameless lives", *Loughran v. Loughran*, 292 U.S. 216,; but additional considerations must be taken into account where maintenance of the suit concerns the public interest as well as the private interests of suitors. Where the patent is used as a means of restraining competition with the patentee's sale of an unpatented product, the successful prosecution of an infringement suit even against one who is not a competitor in such sale is a powerful aid to the maintenance of the attempted monopoly of the unpatented article, and is thus a contributing factor in thwarting the public policy underlying the grant of the patent. Maintenance and enlargement of the attempted monopoly of the unpatented article are dependent to some extent upon persuading the public of the validity of the patent, which the infringement suit is intended to establish. Equity may rightly withhold its assistance from such a use of the patent by declining to entertain a suit for infringement, and should do so at least until it is made to appear that the improper practice has been abandoned and that the consequences of the misuse of the patent have been dissipated.

The reasons for barring the prosecution of such a suit against one who is not a competitor with the patentee in the sale of the unpatented product are fundamentally the same as those which preclude an infringement suit against a licensee who has violated a condition of the license by using with the licensed machine a competing unpatented article, or against a vendee of a patented or copyrighted article for violation of a condition for the maintenance of resale prices. It is the adverse effect upon the public interest of a successful infringement suit in conjunction with the patentee's course of conduct which disqualifies him to maintain the suit, regardless of whether the particular defendant has suffered from the misuse of the patent. Similarly equity will deny relief for infringement of a trademark where the plaintiff is misrepresenting to the public the nature of his product either by the trademark itself or by his label. The patentee, like these other holders of an exclusive privilege granted in the furtherance of a public policy, may not claim protection of his grant by the courts where it is being used to subvert that policy.

It is unnecessary to decide whether respondent has violated the Clayton Act, for we conclude that in any event the maintenance of the present suit to restrain petitioner's manufacture or sale of the alleged infringing machines is contrary to public policy and that the district court rightly dismissed the complaint for want of equity.

Reversed.

Notes

1. **Questioning Misuse.** Do you know of any other field of law where a defendant can ask the court to refuse to grant the plaintiff the relief it is entitled to because the plaintiff has taken some allegedly improper action that has harmed someone other than the defendant? If you find no parallel situation in any other field of law, what explains the need for this draconian doctrine in the law of patents? Are antitrust penalties too weak? For an argument that the doctrine of misuse represents an extraordinary level of hostility to the patent system *see* Martin J. Adelman, *Property Rights Theory and Patent–Antitrust: The Role of Compulsory Licensing*, 52 N.Y.U.L. Rev. 977, 1010–13 (1977); Martin J. Adelman, *The New World of Patents Created by the Court of Appeals for the Federal Circuit*, 20 U. Mich. J.L. Ref. 979, 1003–04 (1987); and Mark A. Lemley, *Irrationality of the Patent Misuse Doctrine*, 78 Cal. L. Rev. 1599 (1990).

2. **The Floodgates Open.** *Morton Salt* opened the floodgates to numerous misuse claims by accused infringers. Patent litigation was frequently marked by assertions that the patent owner was improperly extending its monopoly or engaging in conduct that amounted to an antitrust violation, even though the alleged infringer was itself unaffected by the challenged conduct. The majority of patent trials thus took on the flavor of antitrust trials.

The courts condemned a wide variety of practices in the name of patent misuse. For example, courts held that it was misuse for a patentee to insist on collecting royalties based on unpatented goods or processes as a condition of a patent license. Moreover, the mere collection of royalties on unpatented goods or processes was argued to be a misuse. Likewise, a patentee could not insist that a licensee take a license on more than one patent, but a license under multiple patents ultimately was found not to constitute misuse if the patentee did not insist on that form of licensee. Patentees could include a grant-back clause in a license, but whether a patentee may insist upon a grant-back clause was unclear. Clauses that precluded the licensee from competing with the patentee with a product or process not covered by the license were held to be a misuse even where the parties voluntarily agreed to such clauses.

Perhaps the key to understanding all of these cases is that any sort of leveraging by the patentee could invoke the misuse penalty: refusal to enforce the patent until the misuse is purged, even if the conduct is not an antitrust violation. In addition, any antitrust violations relating to the patent could support the misuse remedy whether or not grounded on the improper use of leverage. The modern approach to antitrust violations based on leverage is considered in *Jefferson Parish Hospital District No. 2 v. Hyde*, 466 U.S. 2 (1984).

The literature on patent misuse is voluminous. A good discussion of the misuse cases is found in 6 DONALD S. CHISUM, PATENTS § 19.04.

3. Congress Reacts to the Leveraging Theory. In 1952, Congress moved to overturn the extreme leveraging theory found in *Mercoid I and II* by passing § 271(d). However, as previously explained, the *Mercoid* opinions did not clearly state the precise nature of the conduct that the Court found offensive. Under one reading, the Court viewed the situation as that the patent owner attempted to collect royalties on unpatented components while simultaneously offering licenses to all potential contributory infringers, such that there was no attempt to monopolize such components. Another reading was that the Court simply believed that the patent owner was trying to monopolize the unpatented components. If the former, then Congress could have merely legislated that the mere collection of royalties without more was not a misuse; if the latter, then Congress intended that a patentee could monopolize an unpatented component. In the following opinion, the Court adopted the latter position in its interpretation of § 271(d).

DAWSON CHEMICAL CO. v. ROHM AND HAAS COMPANY

United States Supreme Court, 1980.
448 U.S. 176.

MR. JUSTICE BLACKMUN delivered the opinion of the Court.

This case presents an important question of statutory interpretation arising under the patent laws. The issue before us is whether the owner of a patent on a chemical process is guilty of patent misuse, and therefore is barred from seeking relief against contributory infringement of its patent rights, if it exploits the patent only in conjunction with the sale of an unpatented article that constitutes a material part of the invention and is not suited for commercial use outside the scope of the patent claims. The answer will determine whether respondent, the owner of a process patent on a chemical herbicide, may maintain an action for contributory infringement against other manufacturers of the chemical used in the process. To resolve this issue, we must construe the various provisions of 35 U.S.C. § 271, which Congress enacted in 1952 to codify certain aspects of the doctrines of contributory infringement and patent misuse that previously had been developed by the judiciary.

I

The doctrines of contributory infringement and patent misuse have long and interrelated histories. The idea that a patentee should be able to obtain relief against those whose acts facilitate infringement by others has been part of our law since *Wallace v. Holmes*, 29 F.Cas. 74 (No. 17,100) (CC Conn. 1871). The idea that a patentee should be denied relief against infringers if he has attempted illegally to extend the scope of his patent monopoly is of somewhat more recent origin, but it goes back at least as far as *Motion Picture Patents Co. v. Universal Film Mfg. Co.*, 243 U.S. 502 (1917). The two concepts, contributory infringement and patent misuse, often are juxtaposed, because both concern the relationship between a patented invention and unpatented articles or elements that are needed for the invention to be practiced.

Both doctrines originally were developed by the courts. But in its 1952 codification of the patent laws Congress endeavored, at least in part, to substitute statutory precepts for the general judicial rules that had governed prior to that time. Its efforts find expression in 35 U.S.C. § 271. Of particular import to the present controversy are subsections (c) and (d). The former defines conduct that constitutes contributory infringement; the latter specifies conduct of the patentee that is not to be deemed misuse.

A

The catalyst for this litigation is a chemical compound known to scientists as "3, 4–dichloropropionanilide" and referred to in the chemical industry as "propanil." In the late 1950's, it was discovered that this compound had properties that made it useful as a selective, "post-emergence" herbicide particularly well suited for the cultivation of rice.

Efforts to obtain patent rights to propanil or its use as a herbicide have been continuous since the herbicidal qualities of the chemical first came to light. The initial contender for a patent monopoly for this chemical compound was the Monsanto Company. In 1957, Monsanto filed the first of three successive applications for a patent on propanil itself. After lengthy proceedings in the United States Patent Office, a patent, No. 3,382,280, finally was issued in 1968. It was declared invalid, however, when Monsanto sought to enforce it by suing Rohm and Haas Company (Rohm & Haas), a competing manufacturer, for direct infringement.

Invalidation of the Monsanto patent cleared the way for Rohm & Haas, respondent here, to obtain a patent on the method of process for applying propanil. This is the patent on which the present lawsuit is founded. Rohm & Haas' efforts to obtain a propanil patent began in 1958. These efforts finally bore fruit when, on June 11, 1974, the United

States Patent Office issued Patent No. 3,816,092 (the Wilson patent) to Harold F. Wilson and Dougal H. McRay.

Petitioners, too, are chemical manufacturers. They have manufactured and sold propanil for application to rice crops since before Rohm & Haas received its patent. They market the chemical in containers on which are printed directions for application in accordance with the method claimed in the Wilson patent. Petitioners did not cease manufacture and sale of propanil after that patent issued, despite knowledge that farmers purchasing their products would infringe on the patented method by applying the propanil to their crops. Accordingly, Rohm & Haas filed this suit, in the United States District Court for the Southern District of Texas, seeking injunctive relief against petitioners on the ground that their manufacture and sale of propanil interfered with its patent rights.

The complaint alleged not only that petitioners contributed to infringement by farmers who purchased and used petitioners' propanil, but also that they actually induced such infringement by instructing farmers how to apply the herbicide. See 35 U.S.C. §§ 271(b) and (c). Petitioners responded to the suit by requesting licenses to practice the patented method. When Rohm & Haas refused to grant such licenses, however, petitioners raised a defense of patent misuse and counterclaimed for alleged antitrust violations by respondent. The parties entered into a stipulation of facts, and petitioners moved for partial summary judgment. They argued that Rohm & Haas has misused its patent by conveying the right to practice the patented method only to purchasers of its own propanil.

[The District Court granted summary judgment in favor of Dawson, holding that Rohm & Haas had misused its patent despite the enactment of § 271(d). Following a reversal by the Fifth Circuit, the Supreme Court granted certiorari.]

B

For present purposes certain material facts are not in dispute. First, the validity of the Wilson patent is not in question at this stage in the litigation. Second, petitioners do not dispute that their manufacture and sale of propanil together with instructions for use as a herbicide constitute contributory infringement of the Rohm & Haas patent.

As a result of these concessions, our chief focus of inquiry must be the scope of the doctrine of patent misuse in light of the limitations placed upon that doctrine by § 271(d). On this subject, as well, our task is guided by certain stipulations and concessions. The parties agree that Rohm & Haas makes and sells propanil; that it has refused to license petitioners or any others to do the same; that it has not granted express licenses either to retailers or to end users of the product; and that farmers who buy propanil from Rohm & Haas may use it, without fear of being sued for direct infringement, by virtue of an "implied license" they obtain when Rohm & Haas relinquishes its monopoly by selling the propanil. The parties further agree that §§ 271(d)(1) and (3) permit respondent both to sell propanil itself and to sue others who sell the same product without a license, and that under § 271(d)(2) it would be free to demand royalties from others for the sale of propanil if it chose to do so.

The parties disagree over whether respondent has engaged in any additional conduct that amounts to patent misuse. Petitioners assert that there has been misuse because respondent has "tied" the sale of patent rights to the purchase of propanil, an unpatented and indeed unpatentable article, and because it has refused to grant licenses to other producers of the chemical compound. They argue that § 271(d) does not permit any sort of tying arrangement, and that resort to such a practice excludes respondent from the category of patentees "otherwise entitled to relief" within the meaning of § 271(d). Rohm & Haas, understandably, vigorously resists this characterization of its conduct. It argues that its acts have been only those that § 271(d), by express mandate, excepts from characterization as patent misuse.

II

As we have noted, the doctrine of contributory infringement had its genesis in an era of simpler and less subtle technology. Its basic elements are perhaps best explained with a classic example drawn from that era. In *Wallace v. Holmes*, 29 F.Cas. 74 (No. 17,100) (CC Conn.1871), the patentee had invented a new burner for an oil lamp. In compliance with the technical rules of patent claiming, this invention was patented in a combination that also included the standard fuel reservoir, wick tube, and chimney necessary for a properly functioning lamp. After the patent issued, a competitor began to market a rival product including the novel burner but not the chimney. Under the sometimes scholastic law of patents, this conduct did not amount to direct infringement, because the competitor had not replicated every single element of the patentee's claimed combination. Yet the court held that there had been "palpable interference" with the patentee's legal rights, because purchasers would be certain to complete the combination, and hence the infringement, by adding the glass chimney. The court permitted the patentee to enforce his rights against the competitor who brought about the infringement, rather than requiring the patentee to undertake the almost insuperable task of finding and suing all the innocent purchasers who technically were responsible for completing the infringement. *Ibid.*

The *Wallace* case demonstrates, in a readily comprehensible setting, the reason for the contributory infringement doctrine. It exists to protect patent rights from subversion by those who, without directly infringing the patent themselves, engage in acts designed to facilitate infringement by others. This protection is of particular importance in situations, like the oil lamp case itself, where enforcement against direct infringers would be difficult, and where the technicalities of patent law make it relatively easy to profit from another's invention without risking a charge of direct infringement.

Although the propriety of the decision in *Wallace v. Holmes* seldom has been challenged, the contributory infringement doctrine it spawned has not always enjoyed full adherence in other contexts. The difficulty that the doctrine has encountered stems not so much from rejection of its core concept as from a desire to delimit its outer contours. In time, concern for potential anticompetitive tendencies inherent in actions for contributory infringement led to retrenchment on the doctrine. The judicial history of contributory infringement thus may be said to be marked by a period of ascendancy, in which the doctrine was expanded to the point where it became subject to abuse, followed by a somewhat longer period of decline, in which the concept of patent misuse was developed as an increasingly stringent antidote to the perceived excesses of the earlier period.

The contributory infringement doctrine achieved its high-water mark with the decision in *Henry v. A. B. Dick Co.*, 224 U.S. 1 (1912). In that case a divided Court extended contributory infringement principles to permit a conditional licensing arrangement whereby a manufacturer of a patented printing machine could require purchasers to obtain all supplies used in connection with the invention, including such staple items as paper and ink, exclusively from the patentee. The Court reasoned that the market for these supplies was created by the invention, and that sale of a license to use the patented product, like sale of other species of property, could be limited by whatever conditions the property owner wished to impose. *Id.*, at 31–32. The *A. B. Dick* decision and its progeny in the lower courts led to a vast expansion in conditional licensing of patented goods and processes used to control markets for staple and nonstaple goods alike.

This was followed by what may be characterized through the lens of hindsight as an inevitable judicial reaction. In *Motion Picture Patents Co. v. Universal Film Mfg. Co.*, 243 U.S. 502, 37 S.Ct. 416, 61 L.Ed. 871 (1917), the Court signalled a new trend that was to continue for years thereafter. The owner of a patent on projection equipment attempted to prevent competitors from selling film for use in the patented equipment by attaching to the projectors it sold a notice purporting to condition use of the machine on exclusive use of its film. The film previously had been patented but that patent had expired. The Court addressed the broad issue whether a patentee possessed the right to condition sale of a patented machine on the purchase of articles "which are no part of the patented machine, and which are not patented." *Id.*, at 508. Relying upon the rule that the scope of a patent "must be limited to the invention described in the claims," *id.*, at 511, the Court held that the attempted restriction on use of unpatented supplies was improper:

"Such a restriction is invalid because such a film is obviously not any part of the invention of the patent in suit; because it is an attempt, without statutory warrant, to continue the patent monopoly in this particular character of film after it has expired, and because to enforce it would be to create a monopoly in the manufacture and use of moving picture films, wholly outside of the patent in suit and of the patent law as we have interpreted it." *Id.*, at 518. By this reasoning, the Court focused on the conduct of the patentee, not that of the alleged infringer. It noted that as a result of lower court decisions, conditional licensing arrangements had greatly increased, indeed, to the point where they threatened to become "perfect instrument[s] of favoritism and oppression." *Id.*, at 515. The Court warned that approval of the licensing scheme under consideration would enable the patentee to "ruin anyone unfortunate enough to be dependent upon its confessedly important improvements for the doing of business." *Ibid.* This ruling was directly in conflict with *Henry v. A. B. Dick Co., supra*, and the Court expressly observed that that decision "must be regarded as overruled." 243 U.S., at 518, 37 S.Ct., at 421.

The broad ramifications of the *Motion Picture* case apparently were not immediately comprehended, and in a series of decisions over the next three decades litigants tested its limits. In *Carbice Corp. v. American Patents Corp.*, 283 U.S. 27 (1931), the Court denied relief to a patentee who, through its sole licensee, authorized use of a patented design for a refrigeration package only to purchasers from the licensee of solid carbon dioxide ("dry ice"), a refrigerant that the licensee manufactured. The refrigerant was a well-known and widely used staple article of commerce, and the patent in question claimed neither a machine for making it nor a process for using it. *Id.*, at 29. The Court held that the patent holder and its licensee were attempting to exclude competitors in the refrigerant business from a portion of the market, and that this conduct constituted patent misuse. It reasoned:

> "Control over the supply of such unpatented material is beyond the scope of the patentee's monopoly; and this limitation, inherent in the patent grant, is not dependent upon the peculiar function or character of the unpatented material or on the way in which it is used. Relief is denied because the [licensee] is attempting, without sanction of law, to employ the patent to secure a limited monopoly of unpatented material used in applying the invention." *Id.*, at 33–34.

Although none of these decisions purported to cut back on the doctrine of contributory infringement itself, they were generally perceived as having that effect, and how far the developing doctrine of patent misuse might extend was a topic of some speculation among members of the patent bar. The Court's decisions had not yet addressed the status of contributory infringement or patent misuse with respect to nonstaple goods, and some courts and commentators apparently took the view that control of nonstaple items capable only of infringing use might not bar patent protection against contributory infringement. This view soon received a serious, if not fatal, blow from the Court's controversial decisions in *Mercoid Corp. v. Mid–Continent Investment Co.*, 320 U.S. 661 (1944) (*Mercoid I*), and *Mercoid Corp. v. Minneapolis–Honeywell Regulator Co.*, 320 U.S. 680 (1944) (*Mercoid II*). In these cases, the Court definitely held that any attempt to control the market for unpatented goods would constitute patent misuse, even if those goods had no use outside a patented invention. Because these cases served as the point of departure for congressional legislation, they merit more than passing citation.

Both cases involved a single patent that claimed a combination of elements for a furnace heating system. Mid–Continent was the owner of the patent, and Honeywell was its licensee. Although neither company made or installed the furnace system, Honeywell manufactured and sold stoker switches especially made for and essential to the system's operation. The right to build and use the system was granted to purchasers of the stoker switches, and royalties owed the patentee were calculated on the number of stoker switches sold. Mercoid manufactured and marketed a competing stoker switch that was designed to be used only in the patented combination. Mercoid had been offered a sublicense by the licensee but had refused to take one. It was sued for contributory infringement by both the patentee and the licensee, and it raised patent misuse as a defense.

In *Mercoid I* the Court barred the patentee from obtaining relief because it deemed the licensing arrangement with Honeywell to be an unlawful attempt to extend the patent monopoly. The opinion for the Court painted with a very broad brush. Prior patent misuse decisions had involved attempts "to secure a partial monopoly in supplies consumed . . . or unpatented materials employed" in connection with the practice of the invention. None, however, had involved an integral component necessary to the functioning of the patented system. 320 U.S., at 665. The Court refused, however, to infer any "difference in principle" from this distinction in fact. *Ibid*. Instead, it stated an expansive rule that apparently admitted no exception: "The necessities or convenience of the patentee do not justify any use of the monopoly of the patent to create another monopoly. The fact that the patentee has the power to refuse a license does not enable him to enlarge the monopoly of the patent by the expedient of attaching conditions to its use. . . . The method by which the monopoly is sought to be extended is immaterial. . . . When the patentee ties something else to his invention, he acts only by virtue of his right as the owner of property to make contracts concerning it and not otherwise. He then is subject to all the limitations upon that right which the general law imposes upon such contracts. The contract is not saved by anything in the patent laws because it relates to the invention. If it were, the mere act of the patentee could make the distinctive claim of the patent attach to something which does not possess the quality of invention. Then the patent would be diverted from its statutory purpose and become a ready instrument for economic control in domains where the anti-trust acts or other laws not the patent statutes define the public policy." *Id.*, at 666.

Mercoid II did not add much to the breathtaking sweep of its companion decision. The Court did reinforce, however, the conclusion that its ruling made no exception for elements essential to the inventive character of a patented combination. "However worthy it may be, however essential to the patent, an unpatented part of a combination patent is no more entitled to monopolistic protection than any other unpatented device." 320 U.S., at 684.

What emerges from this review of judicial development is a fairly complicated picture, in which the rights and obligations of patentees as against contributory infringers have varied over time. We need not decide how respondent would have fared against a charge of patent misuse at any particular point prior to the enactment of 35 U.S.C. § 271. Nevertheless, certain inferences that are pertinent to the present inquiry may be drawn from these historical developments.

First, we agree with the Court of Appeals that the concepts of contributory infringement and patent misuse "rest on antithetical underpinnings." 599 F.2d, at 697. The traditional remedy against contributory infringement is the injunction. And an inevitable concomitant of the right to enjoin another from contributory infringement is the capacity to suppress competition in an unpatented article of commerce. Proponents of contributory infringement defend this result on the grounds that it is necessary for the protection of the patent right, and that the market for the unpatented article flows from the patentee's invention. They also observe that in many instances the article is "unpatented" only because of the technical rules of patent claiming, which require the placement of an invention in its context. Yet suppression of competition in unpatented goods is precisely what the opponents of patent misuse decry. If both the patent misuse and contributory infringement doctrines are to coexist, then, each must have some separate sphere of operation with which the other does not interfere.

Second, we find that the majority of cases in which the patent misuse doctrine was developed involved undoing the damage thought to have been done by *A. B. Dick*. The desire to extend patent protection to control of staple articles of commerce died slowly, and the ghost of the expansive contributory infringement era continued to haunt the courts.

III

The *Mercoid* decisions left in their wake some consternation among patent lawyers and a degree of confusion in the lower courts. Although some courts treated the *Mercoid* pronouncements as limited in effect to the specific kind of licensing arrangement at issue in those cases, others took a much more expansive view of the decision. Among the latter group, some courts held that even the filing of an action for contributory infringement, by threatening to deter competition in unpatented materials, could supply evidence of patent misuse. This state of affairs made it difficult for patent lawyers to advise their clients on questions of contributory infringement and to render secure opinions on the validity of proposed licensing arrangements. Certain segments of the patent bar eventually decided to ask Congress for corrective legislation that would restore some scope to the contributory infringement doctrine. With great perseverance, they advanced their proposal in three successive Congresses before it eventually was enacted in 1952 as 35 U.S.C. § 271.

A

The critical inquiry in this case is how the enactment of § 271 affected the doctrines of contributory infringement and patent misuse. Viewed against the backdrop of judicial precedent, we believe that the language and structure of the statute lend significant support to Rohm & Haas' contention that, because § 271(d) immunizes its conduct from the charge of patent misuse, it should not be barred from seeking relief. The approach that Congress took toward the codification of contributory infringement and patent misuse reveals a compromise between those two doctrines and their competing policies that permits patentees to exercise control over nonstaple articles used in their inventions.

Section 271(c) identifies the basic dividing line between contributory infringement and patent misuse. It adopts a restrictive definition of contributory infringement that distinguishes between staple and nonstaple articles of commerce. It also defines the class of nonstaple items narrowly. In essence, this provision places materials like the dry ice of the Carbice case outside the scope of the contributory infringement doctrine. As a result, it is no longer necessary to resort to the doctrine of patent misuse in order to deny patentees control over staple goods used in their inventions.

The limitations on contributory infringement written into § 271(c) are counterbalanced by limitations on patent misuse in § 271(d). Three species of conduct by patentees are expressly excluded from characterization as misuse. First, the patentee may "deriv[e] revenue" from acts that "would constitute contributory infringement" if "performed by another without his consent." This provision clearly signifies that a patentee may make and sell nonstaple goods used in connection with his invention. Second, the patentee may "licens[e] or authoriz[e] another to perform acts" which without such authorization would constitute contributory infringement. This provision's use in the disjunctive of the term "authoriz[e]" suggests that more than explicit licensing agreements is contemplated. Finally, the patentee may "enforce his patent rights against ... contributory infringement." This provision plainly means that the patentee may bring suit without fear that his doing so will be regarded as an unlawful attempt to suppress competition. The statute explicitly states that a patentee may do "one or more" of these permitted acts, and it does not state that he must do any of them.

In our view, the provisions of § 271(d) effectively confer upon the patentee, as a lawful adjunct of his patent rights, a limited power to exclude others from competition in nonstaple goods. A patentee may sell a nonstaple article himself while enjoining others from marketing that same good without his authorization. By doing so, he is able to eliminate competitors and thereby to control the market for that product. Moreover, his power to demand royalties from others for the privilege of selling the nonstaple item itself implies that the patentee may control the market for the nonstaple good; otherwise, his "right" to sell licenses for the marketing of the nonstaple good would be meaningless, since no one would be willing to pay him for a superfluous authorization.

Rohm & Haas' conduct is not dissimilar in either nature or effect from the conduct that is thus clearly embraced within § 271(d). It sells propanil; it authorizes others to use propanil; and it sues contributory infringers. These are all protected activities. Rohm & Haas does not license others to sell propanil, but nothing on the face of the statute requires it to do so. To be sure, the sum effect of Rohm & Haas' actions is to suppress competition in the market for an unpatented commodity. But as we have observed, in this its conduct is no different from that which the statute expressly protects.

The one aspect of Rohm & Haas' behavior that is not expressly covered by § 271(d) is its linkage of two protected activities—sale of propanil and authorization to practice the patented process—together in a single transaction. Petitioners vigorously argue that this linkage, which they characterize pejoratively as "tying," supplies the otherwise missing element of misuse. They fail, however, to identify any way in which this "tying" of two expressly protected activities results in any extension of control over unpatented materials beyond what § 271(d) already allows.

We find nothing in this legislative history to support the assertion that respondent's behavior falls outside the scope of § 271(d). To the contrary, respondent has done nothing that would extend its right of control over unpatented goods beyond the line that Congress drew. Respondent, to be sure, has licensed use of its patented process only in connection with purchases of propanil. But propanil is a nonstaple product, and its herbicidal property is the heart of respondent's invention. Respondent's method of doing business is thus essentially the same as the method condemned in the *Mercoid* decisions, and the legislative history reveals that § 271(d) was designed to retreat from *Mercoid* in this regard.

There is one factual difference between this case and *Mercoid* : the licensee in the *Mercoid* cases had offered a sublicense to the alleged contributory infringer, which offer had been refused. *Mercoid II*, 320 U.S., at 683, 64 S.Ct., at 280. Seizing upon this difference, petitioners argue that respondent's unwillingness to offer similar licenses to its would-be competitors in the manufacture of propanil legally distinguishes this case and sets it outside § 271(d). To this argument, there are at least three responses. First, as we have noted, § 271(d) permits such licensing but does not require it. Accordingly, petitioners' suggestion would import into the statute a requirement that simply is not there. Second, petitioners have failed to adduce any evidence from the legislative history that the offering of a license to the alleged contributory infringer was a critical factor in inducing Congress to retreat from the result of the *Mercoid* decisions. Third, petitioners' argument runs contrary to the long-settled view that the essence of a patent grant is the right to exclude others from profiting by the patented invention. If petitioners' argument were accepted, it would force patentees either to grant licenses or to forfeit their statutory protection against contributory infringement. Compulsory licensing is a rarity in our patent system, and we decline to manufacture such a requirement out of § 271(d).

V

Since our present task is one of statutory construction, questions of public policy cannot be determinative of the outcome unless specific policy choices fairly can be attributed to Congress itself. In this instance, as we have already stated, Congress chose a compromise between competing policy interests. The policy of free competition runs deep in our law. It underlies both the doctrine of patent misuse and the general principle that the boundary of a patent monopoly is to be limited by the literal scope of the patent claims. But the policy of stimulating invention that underlies the entire patent system runs no less deep. And the doctrine of contributory infringement, which has been called "an expression both of law and morals," *Mercoid I*, 320 U.S., at 677, 64 S.Ct., at 277 (Frankfurter, J., dissenting), can be of crucial importance in ensuring that the endeavors and investments of the inventor do not go unrewarded.

It is perhaps, noteworthy that holders of "new use" patents on chemical processes were among those designated to Congress as intended beneficiaries of the protection against contributory infringement that § 271 was designed to restore. We have been informed that the characteristics of practical chemical research are such that this form of patent protection is particularly important to inventors in that field. The number of chemicals either known to scientists or disclosed by existing research is vast. It grows constantly, as those engaging in "pure" research publish their discoveries. The number of these chemicals that have known uses of commercial or social value, in contrast, is small. Development of new uses for existing chemicals is thus a major component of practical chemical research. It is extraordinarily expensive. It may take years of unsuccessful testing before a chemical having a desired property is identified, and it may take several years of further testing before a proper and safe method for using that chemical is developed.

Under the construction of § 271(d) that petitioners advance, the rewards available to those willing to undergo the time, expense, and interim frustration of such practical research would provide at best a dubious incentive. Others could await the results of the testing and then jump on the profit bandwagon by demanding licenses to sell the unpatented, nonstaple chemical used in the newly developed process. Refusal to accede to such a demand, if accompanied by any attempt to profit from the invention through sale of the unpatented chemical, would risk forfeiture of any patent protection whatsoever on a finding of patent misuse. As a result, noninventors would be almost assured of an opportunity to share in the spoils, even though they had contributed nothing to the discovery. The incentive to await the discoveries of others might well prove sweeter than the incentive to take the initiative oneself.

Whether such a regime would prove workable, as petitioners urge, or would lead to dire consequences, as respondent and several amici insist, we need not predict. Nor do we need to determine whether the principles of free competition could justify such a result. Congress' enactment of § 271(d) resolved these issues in favor of a broader scope of patent protection. In accord with our understanding of that statute, we hold that Rohm & Haas has not engaged in patent misuse, either by its method of selling propanil, or by its refusal to license others to sell that commodity. The judgment of the Court of Appeals is therefore affirmed.

It is so ordered.

MR. JUSTICE STEVENS, dissenting.

This patentee has offered no licenses, either to competing sellers of propanil or to consumers, except the implied license that is granted with every purchase of propanil from it. Thus, every license granted under this patent has been conditioned on the purchase of an unpatented product from the patentee. This is a classic case of patent misuse. As Mr. Justice WHITE demonstrates in his dissenting opinion [omitted here], nothing in 35 U.S.C. § 271(d) excludes this type of conduct from the well-established misuse doctrine.

The Court may have been led into reaching the contrary, and in my view erroneous, conclusion by the particular facts of this case. It appears that it would not be particularly profitable to exploit this patent by granting express licenses for fixed terms to users of propanil or by granting licenses to competing sellers. Under these circumstances, the patent may well have little or no commercial value unless the patentee is permitted to engage in patent misuse. But surely this is not a good reason for interpreting § 271(d) to permit such misuse. For the logic of the Court's holding would seem to justify the extension of the patent monopoly to unpatented "nonstaples" even in cases in which the patent could be profitably exploited without misuse. Thus, for example, it appears that the Court's decision would allow a manufacturer to condition a long-term lease of a patented piece of equipment on the lessee's agreement to purchase tailormade—I.e., nonstaple—supplies or components for use with the equipment exclusively from the patentee. Whether all of the five Members of the Court who have joined today's revision of § 271(d) would apply their "nonstaple" exception in such a case remains to be seen.

Notes

1. Did *Dawson Chemical* Really Matter? The choice between the position of the dissenters and that of the majority was between giving the patentee the right to license the right to make and sell propanil at a nondiscriminatory royalty rate of its own choosing or giving the patentee a monopoly over propanil. In many cases a patentee would not be able to make any more money monopolizing the manufacture and sale of a product than licensing the product at a royalty rate of its own choosing. Nevertheless, for an analysis of the importance of this distinction see 8 Martin J. Adelman, Patent Law Perspectives, § 18.6[3.–4] at n.47 (2d ed. 1982). In any event do you agree with the majority as a matter of patent policy? What advantages accrue to patent owners if they are able to monopolize an unpatented component as permitted by the majority?

2.   Second Commercial Uses. What happens if a second commercial use is discovered for a component that otherwise meets the definition of Section 271(c)? Do you think Congress intended that the discovery of a second commercial use for an unpatented product would make the commercial practice followed by *Rohm & Haas* a misuse? If not, why do you believe Congress divided unpatented components into two categories and said that only where there is no other commercial use, beyond the specific use in the patented product or patented process, can a patentee monopolize an unpatented component?

3.   Tie–Outs. Section 271(d)(5) was not in the statute when the Supreme Court decided *Dawson Chemical*. It was added by the 1988 Patent Misuse Reform Act. The history of this legislation is reviewed in Richard Calkins, *Patent Law: the Impact of the 1988 Patent Misuse Reform Act and Noerr–Pennington Doctrine on Misuse Defenses and Antitrust Counterclaims*, 38 Drake L. Rev. 175 (1988–89). In 1993 the Indiana District Court applied section 271(d)(5) to tie-outs, i.e. provisions restricting licensees, as a condition of the grant of a patent license, from using competitive technology, *In re Recombinant DNA Technology*, 30 U.S.P.Q.2d 1881 (S.D.Ind.1993). Can one fairly read the language of section 271(d)(5) to cover tie-outs in addition to tie-ins? Assume that the answer is no, if you were the lawmaker, would you amend the language of section 271(d)(5) to cover tie-outs?

4.   Does § 271 (d) Immunize Antitrust Violations? In *In re Independent Serv. Org. Antitrust Litig.*, 203 F.3d 1322, 53 U.S.P.Q.2d 1852 (Fed.Cir.2000), the Federal Circuit in the course of discussing whether Xerox's refusal to either sell spare parts or license its intellectual property covering such spare parts violated the antitrust laws suggested that the answer is "yes". Do you agree? Remember that Section 271 (d) immunizes certain conduct against a charge of patent misuse. The statutory language says nothing about immunization against an antitrust violation. However, since all antitrust violations involving patents constitute patent misuse, can activities be immunized against a charge of patent misuse without also being immunized against an antitrust claim?

5.   Limited Licenses. A second broad area of possible limitations on patent licensing falls in the area of limited licenses. Limited licenses are licenses that permit the licensee to carry out only certain of the acts controlled by the licensed patent. For example, a license that permits the licensee to manufacture and sell a patented product, but only at a particular price or to particular customers. The Antitrust Division in the 1970s targeted various forms of limited patent licenses accusing them of illegality under the antitrust laws and thus also patent misuse since any violation of the antitrust laws causes any patent that facilitates that violation to be unenforceable under *Morton Salt*. This crusade against limited patent licenses ultimately collapsed under the weight of the Division's defeat in the following opinion.

UNITED STATES v. STUDIENGESELLSCHAFT KOHLE

United States Court of Appeals, District of Columbia Circuit, 1981.
670 F.2d 1122, 212 U.S.P.Q. 889.

Before ROBINSON, CHIEF JUDGE, MCGOWAN, SENIOR CIRCUIT JUDGE, and LOUIS F. OBERDORFER, UNITED STATES DISTRICT JUDGE.

OBERDORFER, DISTRICT JUDGE:

This is a civil antitrust enforcement action brought by the United States against Studiengesellschaft Kohle m.b.H. (S.K.) and its licensees. Essentially, the complaint challenged certain arrangements which granted an exclusive license to sell the product of a patented process as an unreasonable restraint of trade and an attempt to monopolize a part of trade or commerce in violation of Sections 1 and 2 of the Sherman Act, 15 U.S.C. §§ 1, 2. After a trial without a jury, the district court found that the license provisions in question, stripped of any patent law protection, violated Sections 1 and 2 of the Sherman Act. The court entered a decree enjoining defendant S.K. from enforcing any agreement limiting sales of the product of its process patent, and requiring defendant to license the patented process to all applicants at a reasonable royalty. This appeal followed. For reasons stated below, we reverse the judgment of the district court and remand with instructions that it enter judgment for the defendant.

I. FACTS

Between 1953 and 1954, Dr. Karl Ziegler, the Director of the Max Planck Institute in Mulheim, West Germany, developed a new process for the production of aluminum trialklys (ATAs), a catalytic agent and chemical reactant. For this and other related discoveries of organic-metallic catalysts and processes, Dr. Ziegler was awarded the 1963 Nobel Prize in Chemistry. He was also awarded with a number of U.S. patents on his process for producing ATAs.

Prior to Ziegler's invention, ATAs were known but had no commercial uses. Experience with the invention shows that ATAs produced by the Ziegler process cost an estimated 5% of what it cost to produce ATAs using the prior art. As the district court found, Ziegler's process "is so economical that no other process can be commercially competitive with it." Primarily as a result of these economies, the number of uses for ATAs increased dramatically. ATAs are now consumed in large quantities as a reactant in the manufacture of biodegradable household detergents and as a catalyst in the manufacture of synthetic rubber for tires. But since Ziegler did not discover the product ATAs, he was not awarded a patent on ATAs, but only on the process which he invented for their more economical manufacture.

In 1954 Dr. Ziegler concluded an agreement with Hercules Incorporated (formerly Hercules Powder Company) to exploit his process patents. Hercules had followed his research for a number of years and had previously expressed interest in obtaining licenses for the exploitation of his inventions. This Ziegler/Hercules agreement, designated by the parties as the "Technical Field Contract," granted Hercules a nonexclusive license to manufacture ATAs by the Ziegler process for use in Hercules' own manufacturing operations. It also granted to Hercules "an exclusive license to sell in the United States the aluminum trialkyl produced within the scope of the Technical Field." Ziegler's agreement with Hercules permitted him to grant nonexclusive licenses to a number of other manufacturers as long as they used, but did not sell, the ATAs manufactured pursuant to the license. Accordingly, Ziegler granted licenses to Ethyl Corporation (Ethyl), Continental Oil Co. (Conoco) and others to use his process to manufacture ATAs for internal use.

In 1959 Hercules entered into a joint venture with Stauffer Chemical Co. in an effort to exploit the exclusive license to manufacture ATAs for sale. Together they formed Texas Alkyls, Inc. (Texas); Stauffer contributed capital while Hercules contributed its exclusive license. This transaction purported to give Texas the exclusive right to sell ATAs in the United States, diluted only by licenses authorizing ATA users such as Conoco and Ethyl to manufacture ATAs for internal consumption. Several nonexclusive licensees sought licenses from Ziegler to use his patented process to produce ATAs for sale in competition with Texas, but he consistently denied these applications.

Ethyl was one such disappointed licensee. In 1959 it reacted to Ziegler's denial of its application for a license to sell by filing a declaratory judgment action in the United States District Court for Delaware challenging Ziegler's right to enforce the license provisions banning ATA sales by Ethyl. Before that case came to issue, the parties agreed that, whatever the outcome, Ethyl would be permitted to sell ATAs by right if the result was in favor of Ethyl, and if otherwise, according to the terms of a special license that would require Ethyl to pay Hercules an additional 2% royalty on sales of ATAs. The Delaware Court ultimately found that the license restrictions were a valid exercise of the monopoly power inherent in Ziegler's process patent. Ethyl Corp. v. Hercules Powder Co., 232 F.Supp. 453 (D.Del.1963). Ethyl took no appeal, but began selling ATAs, subject only to an obligation to pay the 2% royalty agreed upon in partial settlement of the Delaware litigation. Only Hercules and Ethyl have sold industrial quantities of ATAs since that time.

II.   THIS LITIGATION

On April 24, 1970, the United States filed the complaint in this case against Dr. Ziegler, Hercules, Stauffer, and Texas. After extensive discovery, defendants moved for summary judgment on the ground that the exclusive license to market ATAs manufactured by the Ziegler process was protected by the patent laws and thus immune from attack under the antitrust laws. The district court denied this motion, finding, contrary to the Delaware decision, that the patent laws did not protect the Ziegler licensing agreement. 426 F.Supp. 143, 149 (D.D.C.1976). The court emphasized that S.K. (which was substituted as a defendant upon the death of Dr. Ziegler) held a process patent and not a product patent. The court concluded that a restriction on sales of the product by the nonexclusive process licensees exceeded the scope of a process patent. According to the district court, Ziegler's

> "... patent claim gave him the right to exclude others from marketing, using, or selling his process. He therefore never had protection under the patent laws when he sought by whatever means to extend his process claim to restrict use or distribution of the unpatented product, the ATAs.... The holder of a process patent could not ... license several companies to use the process and attempt to limit the manner in which some of those companies decided to use the ultimate product."

426 F.Supp. at 148, 149 and n.3. Having denied defendants' motion for summary judgment, the court set the case for trial on the issue of whether the agreements limiting sales violated the Sherman Act.

With trial pending, defendants Hercules, Stauffer and Texas agreed to consent judgments and decrees. After a trial in which S.K. was the sole remaining defendant, the district court entered findings of fact and conclusions of law. The court found essentially four anticompetitive effects from the restrictions at issue: (1) the nonexclusive licensees, prospective sellers of ATAs, were excluded from the market, (2) the price of ATAs exceeded competitive levels, (3) the development of new uses for ATAs was retarded because of their supracompetitive price, and (4) trade in certain aluminum alkyls other than ATAs was restrained as a result of the restrictions on the Ziegler process. Without discussion of relevant authorities, the district court concluded that the agreements constituted an attempt to monopolize the sale of the ATAs in the United States in violation of Section 2 of the Sherman Act, 15 U.S.C. § 2, and were illegal restraints of trade under Section 1 of the Sherman Act, 15 U.S.C. § 1, both under a per se rule and as measured by the rule of reason. On March 15, 1979, the court entered an amended final decree that, inter alia, prohibited defendants from enforcing or granting limited licenses and mandated compulsory licensing at reasonable and nondiscriminatory rates of the Ziegler process, including the right to sell any ATAs so produced.

On appeal, the parties make a number of contentions, not all of which need be addressed in view of the conclusion we reach. Appellant renews its argument below in support of its motion for summary judgment that its conduct is protected by the patent laws because (1) it effected no greater restraint than the patent granted, and (2) it could have legally imposed a much greater restraint by granting Hercules an absolutely exclusive license to use the Ziegler process, thereby automatically vesting Hercules with the exclusive right to sell ATA's manufactured by that process. In addition, appellant argues that the restraints challenged here should be upheld as permissible quantity restrictions on the use of the process, citing *Q–Tips, Inc. v. Johnson & Johnson*, 109

F.Supp. 657 (D.N.J.1951), *aff'd*, 207 F.2d 509 (3d Cir.1953), *cert. denied*, 347 U.S. 935, 74 S.Ct. 630, 98 L.Ed. 1086 (1954). Finally, appellant argues that the government's failure to prove a relevant market is fatal to its claim under both Section 1 and Section 2.

The government grounds its position to the contrary on the summary judgment ruling by the district court below, that the agreements were designed to expand a legal monopoly of the process into an impermissible monopoly of the unpatented product. Arguing that a process patentee has no authority to control the sales of the unpatented product of the process, the government maintains that such an attempt is per se illegal as well as effecting an unreasonable restraint of trade. It also disagrees with the analogy to quantity limitations which defendant asserts, arguing that the license here restrains the use of the products and not the amount of the product which the licensee may produce. Finally, the government argues that it is not required to prove a relevant market, and that in any event the district court made adequate findings that ATAs constitute a relevant market. We conclude that, even assuming arguendo that ATAs constitute a relevant market and that the agreements are not defensible as quantity restrictions, the judgment must be reversed because defendant did not expand its monopoly or impose restraints beyond the scope of the monopoly which its patent gave it.

III.   ANALYSIS

B.

The district court treated the question of the interaction between the patent laws and the antitrust laws here in two stages: it first determined that the restriction imposed was outside the scope of the patent protection, then examined the unprotected restriction to determine if it constituted an attempt to monopolize or an unlawful restraint of trade. Although in the second step of its analysis the court purported to assess the reasonableness of the competitive effects of the restriction, in fact, its method of analysis had the effect of applying a per se rule. This is so because once the protection of the patent was removed, the license conditions, like the patent itself, inevitably had the effect of restricting competition.

Such a formalistic, two-step analysis forecloses adequate consideration of the fundamental fact that a patent by definition restrains trade, and in effect makes most exclusive patent licenses per se violations of the antitrust laws. But as the Supreme Court noted in *E. Bement & Sons v. National Harrow Co.*, 186 U.S. 70, 91, 22 S.Ct. 747, 755, 46 L.Ed. 1058 (1902); "(t)he very object of (the patent laws) is monopoly.... The fact that the conditions in the contract keep up the monopoly does not render them illegal." Thus, as appears more fully below, we conclude that a rule of reason rather than a per se rule applies here. Under our analysis, the protection of the patent laws and the coverage of the antitrust laws are not separate issues. Rather, the conduct at issue is illegal if it threatens competition in areas other than those protected by the patent, and is otherwise legal. The patentee is entitled to exact the full value of his invention but is not entitled to endanger competition in other areas by manipulating his patent monopoly. It was thus error to consider the scope of the patent protection irrespective of any competitive effects in the first phase of the case, and then rule separately on the anticompetitive effects of the arrangement without consideration of the protection of the patent.

If the four anticompetitive effects found by the district court are examined, it is clear that all of them were restraints on what the patent lawfully protects: ATAs manufactured by the Ziegler process. The effects as stated were (1) the exclusion from the market of potential sellers of ATAs manufactured by that process, (2) supracompetitive prices, (3) retarded development of new uses for ATAs because of supracompetitive prices, and (4) restraint on certain other aluminum alkyls which resulted from restrictions on the Ziegler process. None of these restraints go beyond what the patent itself authorizes. Such an exclusion of competitors and charging of supracompetitive prices are at the core of the patentee's rights, and are legitimate rewards of the patent monopoly. Similarly, the restraint on aluminum alkyls other than ATAs produced by the Ziegler process was a legitimate reward of the patent. All of these "anticompetitive effects" of the restriction on sales by licensees would have resulted from a conventional grant of an exclusive license to Hercules to practice the patented process. In fact, the anticompetitive effects of such an exclusive license would be even greater.

The government contends and the district court concluded that defendant's conduct in this case was an attempt to extend its monopoly of the process for making ATAs into a monopoly of the product, ATAs, which are themselves unpatented. As already noted previously, the defendant was not given a product patent on the ATAs because he did not invent them. S.K. thus has no right to prevent others from selling ATAs which are manufactured by another process. An attempt by defendant to expand its monopoly to cover such an unpatented product manufactured by another process would be an attempt to enlarge its monopoly beyond what the patent law gives it and would thus be subject to antitrust attack. For example, if S.K. had required its licensees to refrain from selling any ATAs, even if they were made by other processes, it might well be in violation of the antitrust laws. A requirement by defendant that any licensee who discovered an alternative process grant back to S.K. a license under that process might similarly be illegal, since such a license might dampen the incentive to invent around the patent. But S.K. did neither of these things. It merely restricted the sale of ATAs which were manufactured by its process. Such a restriction does not in any way operate to limit competition between ATAs manufactured pursuant to the Ziegler process and ATAs manufactured by other processes, now or hereafter available. Nor does this restriction make it less likely that such process will be discovered.

Defendant has thus sought nothing beyond what the patent itself gave it. The patent gives it the unlimited right to exclude others from utilizing its process. This process is, in fact, so superior to other processes that a monopoly over the process gives its holder a de facto monopoly over the product. But there is no danger that defendant can, by manipulating its process patent, "convert a process patent into a product patent." 426 F.Supp. at 149. S.K. has no monopoly over ATAs not produced by the Ziegler patent. Its monopoly of the product can continue only so long as its process remains "so superior to other processes that ATAs made by those other processes could not compete commercially . . ." The district court's ruling that Ziegler could not restrict sales of products made by the patented process, without a showing that trade in some article other than ATAs made by that process was restrained, amounted to a rule that restraints on sales by a process patentee, though not by a product patentee, are per se unlawful.

* * *

No functional difference between a process patent and a product patent supports the purely formal distinction the government urges. The government and the district court assume correctly that a process patent gives no power over products not manufactured by a patented process, such as unpatented salt, see *International Salt, supra*, or in this case, ATAs not manufactured by the Ziegler process. But the difference between a product patent and a process patent does not justify either the government's contention or the decision below that the process patentee has no more power over the product of his process than he does over the products not produced by that process. Ziegler did not invent ATAs, and thus he was not awarded any right to prevent others from making, using, or selling ATAs manufactured by a process other than his own. Any discoverer of an equally (or more) efficient process was and is free to compete in the market for ATAs despite S.K.'s patent. Ziegler's nonexclusive licensees are completely free to manufacture, use and sell any ATAs manufactured by a process not patented by Ziegler. Thus it is true, as the government asserts, that the sale of a product does not itself infringe a process patent, since the product may have been made by another process. This does not impair the patentee's right to impose restrictions in a license that affect products that were made by its process.

D.

The issue remains whether, having reversed the decision of the district court, we must remand for a new trial or whether we may judge the reasonableness of the restriction on sales by licensees on the basis of the findings and the record before us. We conclude, based on an examination of the restraint at issue and the findings and the record under the rule of reason, that a remand is unnecessary and inappropriate.

None of the anticompetitive effects of the challenged restriction found by the district court exceed the anticompetitive effects which the patent authorized. There is no basis in the record for a finding of other anticompetitive effects, and with one exception, which is discussed below, the government is unable to point to any other possible effect on competition. Finally, analysis of the arrangement itself demonstrates that it is no more restrictive than a legal exclusive license, and in fact has certain procompetitive effects not created by such a license.

As stated earlier, Dr. Ziegler lawfully could have licensed Hercules alone to practice the patented process. Such an exclusive license would, by definition, have given Hercules a monopoly over ATAs manufactured by his process, and would have effectively granted Hercules a monopoly over the sale of ATAs, since no other process is now commercially competitive with the Ziegler process. Exclusive licenses are tolerated because they normally threaten competition to no greater extent than is threatened by the patent itself. Equally important from the perspective of the rule of reason, many potential licensees might be unwilling to undertake the expense necessary to develop and promote a product but for assurances against attempts by later licensees to exploit the early licensee's development and promotion. See Adelman & Juenger, *[Patent–Antitrust: Patent Dynamics and Field of Use Licensing*, 50 N.Y.U. L.Rev. 273 (1975)] at 298–99; P. Areeda, Antitrust Analysis ¶ 411, at 585–86 (3d ed. 1981). An exclusive license protects licensees against such "free rider" problems, and thereby serves the interests of both the patentee and the public by facilitating more rapid and widespread use of new inventions.

The license restriction at issue here has similar virtues with somewhat fewer vices. It prevents other licensees from taking advantage of any promotional or developmental efforts by Hercules, but leaves them free to utilize the patented technology in their own operations. The prohibition on sales is thus a more narrowly tailored version of the exclusive license, having most of its benefits but fewer of its liabilities. The same considerations that lead courts to validate exclusive licenses lead us to approve the restriction at issue here.

This conclusion might not follow if the restriction here caused or threatened anticompetitive effects not present in an exclusive license. Price-fixing licenses create the possibility of using the patent to mask a cartel. Other impermissible market divisions by means of patent arrangements might give each competitor an economic incentive to continue the arrangement which insures its loyalty to the arrangement. But nothing in this record or the district court findings reveals or portends such effects.

A number of scholars have also noted that some patent arrangements, such as field-of-use restrictions, have a potential for facilitating market division by giving each participant a stake in the patent in the form of an exclusive territory, or by parceling out to each competitor exclusive access to particular customers. Thus, such agreements give potential competitors incentives to remain in cartels rather than turning to another product, inventing around the patent, or challenging its validity. See Adelman & Juenger, *supra*, at 305–08. In this case by contrast, only Hercules enjoys any advantage from the limitation on sales, and the advantage it enjoys is far less than the advantage which a conventional exclusive license would give it. All other competitors, bound as they are by the prohibition on sales, have every incentive to compete or challenge the defendant's patent and thereby become entitled to sell ATAs.

In addition, market division is a much more serious problem where the product restricted is also produced by other means. Each of the cases cited involved a product which was generic: other processes existed and competed with the patented process. If one of twenty competitors makes a slight improvement in existing technology and proceeds to divide the country into exclusive territories for the purpose of exploiting the patent, the danger that his competitors might abandon the existing technology in favor of the patented technology in order to divide markets is manifest. If the patentee invents a clearly superior technology, whether a product or process, and divides the country into exclusive territories, the case is completely different; there would be a de facto monopoly irrespective of whether the territories were divided. In such a case, as Professor Sullivan argues, "(v)irtue is not attacked, let alone undone. . . . competition is restricted to no greater degree by the assignment than is inherent in the patent grant itself." [L. SULLIVAN, HANDBOOK OF LAW OF ANTITRUST 534 (1977).] The commercial superiority of the Ziegler process is clear. The strength of the Ziegler patent and the inherent value of the process itself give the patentee a monopoly of all ATAs. The licensing arrangement adds nothing.

A patent license might also restrict competition by undermining incentives to attack the validity of the patent or to invent around it. The government briefly contends,without support from the record, that the restriction at issue here may have undermined Hercules' incentives to challenge the Ziegler patent. However, even if this were true, it would be functionally indistinguishable from the effect of a conventional exclusive license. See Adelman & Juenger, *supra*, at 299. And, as we have demonstrated, all other licensees have ample incentives to attack the validity of the patent. Indeed, the chief advocates of the theory that restraints that undermine incentives to challenge the patent should be illegal, Professors Adelman and Juenger, have directly and persuasively discounted the possibility of such a disincentive in this very case:

> This arrangement did not lessen incentives to attack the patent, since all other licensees presumably smarted under the prohibition against selling ... (T)he Government ... seemed to assert quite simply that since the unpatented products were "outside" the scope of the patent monopoly, the attempt to impose such restraints on sales must be illegal. As noted, such an approach sidesteps practical analysis of the issues.

Adelman & Juenger, *supra*, at 303.

Indeed, it may well be that striking down the restraint at issue here would itself injure competition. There is a reasonable likelihood that had the defendant been unable to issue licenses for internal use only, it would have issued only an exclusive license to Hercules. The record tends to show that Ziegler took his contract with Hercules seriously, and considered himself bound to refuse to grant any other licenses for sale. We should hesitate before we impose a legal rule that would force a patentee to follow the more anticompetitive route of a single exclusive license.

For these reasons, we are satisfied that under the principles which we have outlined, the district court would have no occasion on remand to receive further evidence or to make further findings before concluding that the Ziegler license arrangements were not unreasonable restraints of trade. Accordingly, we reverse the decision of the district court and remand with directions to enter judgment for defendant.

Notes

1. Facilitating Cartel Behavior. The court referred to a series of limited licenses that could facilitate cartel behavior among the various patent licensees. Can you design a limited licensing scheme using field, or territory, or price limitations, that a potential licensee would like to enter into because of the enhanced possibility that you could tacitly collude with your fellow licensees? In such circumstances would you be deterred by the need to pay a royalty to the patentee?

2. Discouraging Patent Challenges Through Licensing. Can you design a licensing scheme using limited licenses, such as licenses limited as to field, or territory, or price, that discourages competitors who enter into such licenses from (1) seeking to challenge the patent either through litigation challenging the validity of the licensed patent, or (2) through attempting to invent around the licensed patent?

3. Discouraging Patent Challenges Through Litigation Settlements. In an important case ongoing as this casebook goes to press, the Federal Trade Commission in *In re Schering–Plough Corporation, Upsher–Smith Laboratories, and American Home Products Corporation*, Docket No. 9297, alleged in its 2001 administrative complaint that Schering, the maker of K–Dur 20, a widely prescribed potassium chloride supplement, illegally paid Upsher and AHP millions of dollars to induce them to delay launching their generic versions of the drug. The agreements, and the subsequent delay of the generic being available to consumers, have been alleged to cost consumers more than $100 million. In an initial decision filed on June 27, 2002 , Administrative Law Judge D. Michael Chappell dismissed all allegations of anticompetitive conduct. The matter is now on appeal. The appeal brief filed by the Federal Trade Commission at http://www.ftc.gov/os/2002/08/scheringtrialbrief.pdf contains a detailed review of the issues involved in patent litigation settlements where the patentee pays the alleged infringer to terminate the litigation.

4. Justice Department Guidelines. On April 6, 1995, the Antitrust Division and the Federal Trade Commission issued "Antitrust Guidelines for the Licensing of Intellectual Property," 1995 WL 229332 (D.O.J.). The guidelines provide a useful insight into the thinking of the antitrust authorities regarding the licensing of intellectual property. The guidelines contain an analysis of various types of markets affected by intellectual property licensing such as goods markets, technology markets and research and development markets (innovation markets). They also contain an analysis of horizontal restraints, resale price maintenance, tying, exclusive dealing, cross-licensing and pooling, grantbacks as well as the acquisition of intellectual property rights.

5. Block Exemptions under the Treaty of Rome. The European Commission effective January 31, 1996, issued a block exemption for certain intellectual property agreements under the Treaty of Rome. For those students with a special interest in comparative patent-antitrust law, a careful study of this document is instructive. Documents relating to the European Union are readily accessible in the legal databases.

6. The Attitude of the Federal Circuit Towards Limited Patent Licenses. The Federal Circuit in the following case dealt with a limited license that permitted only one use of the purchased product. Given the focus of the Federal Circuit on the need for an anticompetitive effect and the important role of the "rule of reason," do you agree that the Federal Circuit is not about to declare any limited license a misuse that has not already been condemned by Supreme Court authority?

MALLINCKRODT INC. v. MEDIPART INC.

United States Court of Appeals, Federal Circuit, 1992.
976 F.2d 700, 24 U.S.P.Q.2d 1173.

Before NEWMAN, LOURIE, and CLEVENGER, CIRCUIT JUDGES.

NEWMAN, J.

This action for patent infringement and inducement to infringe relates to the use of a patented medical device in violation of a "single use only" notice that accompanied the sale of the device. Mallinckrodt sold its patented device to hospitals, which after initial use of the devices sent them to Medipart for servicing that enabled the hospitals to use the device again. Mallinckrodt claimed that Medipart thus induced infringement by the hospitals and itself infringed the patent.

The district court held that violation of the "single use only" notice can not be remedied by suit for patent infringement, and granted summary judgment of noninfringement.

The district court did not decide whether the form of the "single use only" notice was legally sufficient to constitute a license or condition of sale from Mallinckrodt to the hospitals. Nor did the district court decide whether any deficiencies in the "single use only" notice were cured by Mallinckrodt's attempted subsequent notice, the release of which was enjoined by the district court on the ground that it would harm Medipart's business. Thus there was no ruling on whether, if the initial notice was legally defective as a restrictive notice, such defect was cured in the subsequent notice. The district court also specifically stated that it was not deciding whether Mallinckrodt could enforce this notice under contract law. These aspects are not presented on this appeal, and the factual premises were not explored at the summary judgment proceeding from which this appeal is taken.

Instead, the district court held that no restriction whatsoever could be imposed under the patent law, whether or not the restriction was enforceable under some other law, and whether or not this was a first sale to a purchaser with notice. This ruling is incorrect, for if Mallinckrodt's restriction was a valid condition of the sale, then in accordance with *General Talking Pictures Corp. v. Western Electric Co.*, 304 U.S. 175, 37 U.S.P.Q. 357, *aff'd on reh'g*, 305 U.S. 124, 39 U.S.P.Q. 329 (1938), it was not excluded from enforcement under the patent law.

On review of these issues in the posture in which the case reaches us:

1. The movant Medipart did not dispute actual notice of the restriction. Thus we do not decide whether the form of the restriction met the legal requirements of notice or sufficed as a "label license", as Mallinckrodt calls it, for those questions were not presented on this motion for summary judgment.

2. Nor do we decide whether Mallinckrodt's enjoined subsequent notice cured any flaws in the first notice, for that issue was not reached by the district court.

We conclude, however, on Mallinckrodt's appeal of the grant of this injunction, that the notice was improperly enjoined.

3. We also conclude that the district court misapplied precedent in holding that there can be no restriction on use imposed as a matter of law, even on the first purchaser. The restriction here at issue does not per se violate the doctrine of patent misuse or the antitrust law. Use in violation of a valid restriction may be remedied under the patent law, provided that no other law prevents enforcement of the patent.

BACKGROUND

The patented device is an apparatus for delivery of radioactive or therapeutic material in aerosol mist form to the lungs of a patient, for diagnosis and treatment of pulmonary disease. Radioactive material is delivered primarily for image scanning in diagnosis of lung conditions. Therapeutic agents may be administered to patients suffering various lung diseases.

The device is manufactured by Mallinckrodt, who sells it to hospitals as a unitary kit that consists of a "nebulizer" which generates a mist of the radioactive material or the prescribed drug, a "manifold" that directs the flow of oxygen or air and the active material, a filter, tubing, a mouthpiece, and a nose clip. In use, the radioactive material or drug is placed in the nebulizer, is atomized, and the patient inhales and exhales through the closed system. The device traps and retains any radioactive or other toxic material in the exhalate. The device fits into a lead-shielded container that is provided by Mallinckrodt to minimize exposure to radiation and for safe disposal after use.

The device is marked with the appropriate patent numbers, and bears the trademarks "Mallinckrodt" and "UltraVent" and the inscription "Single Use Only". The package insert provided with each unit states "For Single Patient Use Only" and instructs that the entire contaminated apparatus be disposed of in accordance with procedures for the disposal of biohazardous waste. The hospital is instructed to seal the used apparatus in the radiation-shielded container prior to proper disposal. The hospitals whose activities led to this action do not dispose of the UltraVent apparatus, or limit it to a single use.

Instead, the hospitals ship the used manifold/nebulizer assemblies to Medipart, Inc. Medipart in turn packages the assemblies and sends them to Radiation Sterilizers Inc., who exposes the packages to at least 2.5 megarads of gamma radiation, and returns them to Medipart. Medipart personnel then check each assembly for damage and leaks, and place the assembly in a plastic bag together with a new filter, tubing, mouthpiece, and nose clip. The "reconditioned" units, as Medipart calls them, are shipped back to the hospitals from whence they came. Neither Radiation Sterilizers nor Medipart tests the reconditioned units for any residual biological activity or for radioactivity. The assemblies still bear the inscription "Single Use Only" and the trademarks "Mallinckrodt" and "UltraVent".

Mallinckrodt filed suit against Medipart, asserting patent infringement and inducement to infringe. Mallinckrodt also asserted other counts including trademark infringement, unfair competition under section 43(a) of the Lanham Trademark Act, and violation of Illinois unfair competition statutes. Both parties moved for summary judgment on all counts.

The district court granted Medipart's motion on the patent infringement counts, holding that the "Single Use Only" restriction could not be enforced by suit for patent infringement. The count also held that Medipart's activities were permissible repair, not impermissible reconstruction, of the patented apparatus. The court reserved for trial Mallinckrodt's counts of trademark infringement and unfair competition, and entered final judgment on the patent aspects in accordance with Fed. R. Civ. P. 54(b).

The district court also enjoined Mallinckrodt pendente lite from distributing a new notice to its hospital customers. The proposed new notice emphasized the "Single Use Only" restriction and stated that the purpose of this restriction is to protect the hospital and its patients from potential adverse consequences of reconditioning, such as infectious disease transmission, material instability, and/or decreased diagnostic performance; that the UltraVent device is covered by certain patents; that the hospital is licensed under these patents to use the device only once; and the reuse of the device would be deemed infringement of the patents.

Mallinckrodt appeals the grant of summary judgment on the infringement issue, and the grant of the preliminary injunction.

Mallinckrodt describes the restriction on reuse as a label license for a specified field of use, wherein the field is single (i.e., disposable) use. On this motion for summary judgment, there was no issue of whether this form of license gave notice of the restriction. Notice was not disputed. Nor was it disputed that sale to the hospitals was the first sale of the patented device. The issue that the district court decided on summary judgment was the enforceability of the restriction by suit for patent infringement. The court's premise was that even if the notice was sufficient to constitute a valid condition of sale, violation of that condition can not be remedied under the patent law.

Mallinckrodt states that the restriction to single patient use is valid and enforceable under the patent law because the use is within the scope of the patent grant, and the restriction does not enlarge the patent grant. Mallinckrodt states that a license to less than all uses of a patented article is well recognized and a valid practice under patent law, and that such license does not violate the antitrust laws and is not patent misuse. Mallinckrodt also states that the restriction here imposed is reasonable because it is based on health, safety, efficacy, and liability considerations and violates no public policy. Thus Mallinckrodt argues that the restriction is valid and enforceable under the patent law. Mallinckrodt concludes that use in violation of the restriction is patent infringement, and that the district court erred in holding otherwise.

Medipart states that the restriction is unenforceable, for the reason that "the Bauer trilogy and Motion Picture Patents clearly established that *no* restriction is enforceable under patent law upon a purchaser of a sold article." (Medipart's emphasis). The district court so held. The district court also held that since the hospitals purchased the device from the patentee, not from a manufacturing licensee, no restraint on the use of the device could lawfully be imposed under the patent law.

The district court described the cases sustaining field of use and other restrictions as "in tension" with the cases prohibiting restrictions such as price-fixing and tying, and with the cases holding that the patent right is exhausted with the first sale. The court stated that policy considerations require that no conditions be imposed on patented goods after their sale and that Mallinckrodt's restriction could not "convert [ ] what was in substance a sale into a license." As we shall discuss, on the premises of this summary judgment motion the court erred in its analysis of the law, for not all restrictions on the use of patented goods are unenforceable.

The enforceability of restrictions on the use of patented goods derives from the patent grant, which is in classical terms of property: the right to exclude. This right to exclude may be waived in whole or in part. The conditions of such waiver are subject to patent, contract, antitrust, and any other applicable law, as well as equitable considerations such as are reflected in the law of patent misuse. As in other areas of commerce, private parties may contract as they choose, provided that no law is violated thereby:

> [T]he rule is, with few exceptions, that any conditions which are not in their very nature illegal with regard to this kind of property, imposed by the patentee and agreed to by the licensee for the right to manufacture or use or sell the [patented] article, will be upheld by the courts.

E. Bement & Sons v. National Harrow Co., 186 U.S. 70, 91 (1902).

The district court's ruling that Mallinckrodt's restriction on reuse was unenforceable was an application of the doctrine of patent misuse, although the court declined to use that designation. The concept of patent misuse arose to restrain practices that did not in themselves violate any law, but that draw anticompetitive strength from the patent right, and thus were deemed to be contrary to public policy. The policy purpose was to prevent a patentee from using the patent to obtain market benefit beyond that which inheres in the statutory patent right.

The district court's holding that Mallinckrodt's restriction to single patent use was unenforceable was, as we have remarked, based on "policy" considerations. The district court relied on a group of cases wherein resale price-fixing of patented goods was held illegal, *viz. Bauer & Cie. v. O'Donnell*, 229 U.S. 1 (1913); *Straus v. Victor Talking Machine Co.*, 243 U.S. 490 (1917); *Boston Store of Chicago v. American Graphophone Co.*, 246 U.S. 8 (1918), ("the Bauer trilogy"), and that barred patent-enforced tie-ins, *viz. Motion Picture Patents Co. v. Universal Film Mfg. Co.*, 243 U.S. 502 (1917).

These cases established that price-fixing and tying restrictions accompanying the sale of patented goods were per se illegal. These cases did not hold, and it did not follow, that all restrictions accompanying the sale of patented goods were deemed illegal. In *General Talking Pictures* the Court, discussing restrictions on use, summarized the state of the law as follows:

> That a restrictive license is legal seems clear. *Mitchell v. Hawley*, 16 Wall. 544. As was said in *United States v. General Electric Co.*, 272 U.S. 476, 489, the patentee may grant a license "upon any condition the performance of which is reasonably within the reward which the patentee by the grant of the patent is entitled to secure"....
>
> The practice of granting licenses for restricted use is an old one, see *Rubber Company v. Goodyear*, 9 Wall. 788, 799, 800; *Gamewell Fire–Alarm Telegraph Co. v. Brooklyn*, 14 F. 255. So far as it appears, its legality has never been questioned.

305 U.S. at 127, 39 U.S.P.Q. at 330 .

In *General Talking Pictures* the patentee had authorized the licensee to make and sell amplifiers embodying the patented invention for a specified use (home radios). The defendant had purchased the patented amplifier from the manufacturing licensee, with knowledge of the patentee's restriction on use. The Supreme Court stated the question as "whether the restriction in the license is to be given effect" against a purchaser who had notice of the restriction. The Court observed that a restrictive license to a particular use was permissible, and treated the purchaser's unauthorized use as infringement of the patent, deeming the goods to be unlicensed as purchased from the manufacturer.

The Court, in its opinion on rehearing, stated that it

> [did not] consider what the rights of the parties would have been if the amplifier had been manufactured under the patent and had passed into the hands of a purchaser in the ordinary channels of trade.

305 U.S. at 127, 39 U.S.P.Q. at 330. The district court interpreted this reservation as requiring that since the hospitals purchased the Ultra-Vent device from the patentee Mallinckrodt, not from a manufacturing licensee, no restraint on the purchasers' use of the device could be imposed under the patent law. However, in *General Talking Pictures* the Court did not hold that there must be an intervening manufacturing licensee before the patent can be enforced against a purchaser with notice of the restriction. The Court did not decide the situation where the patentee was the manufacturer and the device reached a purchaser in ordinary channels of trade. 305 U.S. at 127, 39 U.S.P.Q. at 330.

The UltraVent device was manufactured by the patentee; but the sale to the hospitals was the first sale and was with notice of the restriction. Medipart offers neither law, public policy, nor logic, for the proposition that the enforceability of a restriction to a particular use is determined by whether the purchaser acquired the device from a manufacturing licensee or from a manufacturing patentee. We decline to make a distinction for which there appears to be no foundation. Indeed, Mallinckrodt has pointed out how easily such a criterion could be circumvented. That the viability of a restriction should depend on how the transaction is structured was denigrated as "formalistic line drawing" in *Continental T.V., Inc. v. GTE Sylvania, Inc.*, 433 U.S. 36, 57–59 (1977), the Court explaining, in overruling *United States v. Arnold, Schwinn & Co.*, 388 U.S. 365 (1967), that the legality of attempts by a manufacturer to regulate resale does not turn on whether the reseller had purchased the merchandise or was merely acting as an agent of the manufacturer. The Court having disapproved reliance on formalistic distinctions of no economic consequence in antitrust analysis, we discern no reason to preserve formalistic distinctions of no economic consequence, simply because the goods are patented.

The district court, holding Mallinckrodt's restriction unenforceable, described the holding of *General Talking Pictures* as in "some tension" with the earlier price-fixing and tie-in cases. The district court observed that the Supreme Court did not cite the *Bauer*, *Boston Store*, or *Motion Picture Patents* cases when it upheld the use restriction in *General Talking Pictures*. That observation is correct, but it should not be remarkable. By the time of *General Talking Pictures*, price-fixing and tie-ins were generally prohibited under the antitrust law as well as the misuse law, while other conditions were generally recognized as within the patent grant. The prohibitions against price-fixing and tying did not make all other restrictions per se invalid and unenforceable. Further, the Court could not have been unaware of the *Bauer* trilogy in deciding *General Talking Pictures*, because Justice Black's dissent is built upon those cases.

Restrictions on use are judged in terms of their relation to the patentee's right to exclude from all or part of the patent grant, see, e.g., W.F. Baxter, *The Viability of Vertical Restraints Doctrine*, 75 Calif. L. Rev. 933, 935 (1987) ("historically, legal prohibition began with [resale price control and tie-in agreements] and, with rare exceptions, now continues only with those devices"); and where an anticompetitive effect is asserted, the rule of reason is the basis of determining the legality of the provision. In *Windsurfing International, Inc. v. AMF, Inc.*, 782 F.2d 995, 228 U.S.P.Q. 562 (Fed.Cir.), *cert. denied*, 477 U.S. 905 (1986), this court stated:

> To sustain a misuse defense involving a licensing arrangement not held to have been per se anticompetitive by the Supreme Court, a factual determination must reveal that the overall effect of the license tends to restrain competition unlawfully in an appropriately defined relevant market.

Id. at 1001–1002, 228 U.S.P.Q. at 567 (footnote omitted). *See also Continental T.V. v. GTE Sylvania*, 433 U.S. at 58–59 (judging vertical restrictions under the rule of reason); *Business Electronics Corp. v. Sharp Electronics Corp.*, 485 U.S. 717, 735–36 (1988) (vertical non-price restraints are not per se illegal). The district court, stating that it "refuse[s] to limit *Bauer* and *Motion Picture Patents* to tying and price-fixing not only because their language suggests broader application, but because there is a strong public interest in not stretching the patent laws to authorize restrictions on the use of purchased goods", *Mallinckrodt*, 15 U.S.P.Q.2d at 1119 , has contravened this precedent.

In support of its ruling, the district court also cited a group of cases in which the Court considered and affirmed the basic principles that unconditional sale of a patented device exhausts the patentee's right to control the purchaser's use of the device; and that the sale of patented goods, like other goods, can be conditioned. The principle of exhaustion of the patent right did not turn a conditional sale into an unconditional one.

[Judge Newman then reviewed *Adams v. Burke*, 84 U.S. (17 Wall.) 453 (1874); *Keeler v. Standard Folding Bed*, 157 U.S. 659 (1895); *Providence Rubber Co. v. Goodyear*, 76 U.S. (9 Wall.) 788 (1870); and other cases of that era.]

Viewing the entire group of these early cases, it appears that the Court simply applied, to a variety of factual situations, the rule of contract law that sale may be conditioned. *Adams v. Burke* and its kindred cases do not stand for the proposition that no restriction or

1108   LICENSING, MISUSE & PATENT–ANTITRUST   Ch. 19

condition may be placed upon the sale of a patented article. It was error for the district court to derive that proposition from the precedent. Unless the condition violates some other law or policy (in the patent field, notably the misuse or antitrust law, *e.g., United States v. Univis Lens Co.*, 316 U.S. 241 (1942)), private parties retain the freedom to contract concerning conditions of sale. As we have discussed, the district court cited the price-fixing and tying cases as reflecting what the court deemed to be the correct policy, viz., that no condition can be placed on the sale of patented goods, for any reason. However, this is not a price-fixing or tying case, and the per se antitrust and misuse violations found in the *Bauer* trilogy and *Motion Picture Patents* are not here present. The appropriate criterion is whether Mallinckrodt's restriction is reasonably within the patent grant, or whether the patentee has ventured beyond the patent grant and into behavior having an anticompetitive effect not justifiable under the rule of reason.

Should the restriction be found to be reasonably within the patent grant, i.e., that it relates to subject matter within the scope of the patent claims, that ends the inquiry. However, should such inquiry lead to the conclusion that there are anticompetitive effects extending beyond the patentee's statutory right to exclude, these effects do not automatically impeach the restriction. Anticompetitive effects that are not per se violations of law are reviewed in accordance with the rule of reason. Patent owners should not be in a worse position, by virtue of the patent right to exclude, than owners of other property used in trade.

We conclude that the district court erred in holding that the restriction on reuse was, as a matter of law, unenforceable under the patent law. If the sale of the UltraVent was validly conditioned under the applicable law such as the law governing sales and licenses, and if the restriction on reuse was within the scope of the patent grant or otherwise justified, then violation of the restriction may be remedied by action for patent infringement. The grant of summary judgment is reversed, and the cause is remanded.

Notes

1. Federal Circuit Application of *Mallinckrodt*. Another decision, *B. Braun Medical Inc. v. Abbott Laboratories*, 124 F.3d 1419, 43 U.S.P.Q.2d 1896 (Fed.Cir.1997), provides a helpful summary and application of *Mallinckrodt*. There, Braun sold its patented valves to Abbott, but on the condition that the valves could be used only in certain applications. The parties were unable to agree on terms whereby Abbott could employ the valves in a so-called "extension set" application. After Abbott and its supplier subsequently developed a substitute valve for use in extension sets, Braun brought suit for patent infringement. The jury found that Braun had misused its patent after receiving the following instruction:

> [A] patent holder is not allowed to place restrictions on customers which prohibit resale of the patented product, or allow the customer to resell the patented product only in connection with certain products.... If you find, by a preponderance of the evidence, that Braun placed such

restrictions on its customers, including Abbott, you must find that Braun is guilty of patent misuse.

On appeal, Braun contended that the jury instruction contained legal error because, in essence, it made Braun automatically liable if any conditions were placed on its sales. The Federal Circuit panel first summarized its holding in *Mallinckrodt* as follows:

> In *Mallinckrodt*, we canvassed precedent concerning the legality of restrictions placed upon the post-sale use of patented goods. As a general matter, we explained that an unconditional sale of a patented device exhausts the patentee's right to control the purchaser's use of the device thereafter. The theory behind this rule is that in such a transaction, the patentee has bargained for, and received, an amount equal to the full value of the goods. See *Adams v. Burke*, 84 U.S. (17 Wall.) 453, 456–57, 21 L.Ed. 700 (1874); *Keeler v. Standard Folding–Bed Co.*, 157 U.S. 659, 663, 15 S.Ct. 738, 39 L.Ed. 848 (1895). This exhaustion doctrine, however, does not apply to an expressly conditional sale or license. In such a transaction, it is more reasonable to infer that the parties negotiated a price that reflects only the value of the "use" rights conferred by the patentee. As a result, express conditions accompanying the sale or license of a patented product are generally upheld. Such express conditions, however, are contractual in nature and are subject to antitrust, patent, contract, and any other applicable law, as well as equitable considerations such as patent misuse. Accordingly, conditions that violate some law or equitable consideration are unenforceable. On the other hand, violation of valid conditions entitles the patentee to a remedy for either patent infringement or breach of contract. This, then, is the general framework.

> In *Mallinckrodt*, we also outlined the framework for evaluating whether an express condition on the post-sale use of a patented product constitutes patent misuse. The patent misuse doctrine, born from the equitable doctrine of unclean hands, is a method of limiting abuse of patent rights separate from the antitrust laws. The key inquiry under this fact-intensive doctrine is whether, by imposing the condition, the patentee has "impermissibly broadened the 'physical or temporal scope' of the patent grant with anticompetitive effect." *Windsurfing Int'l, Inc. v. AMF, Inc.*, 782 F.2d 995, 1001–02, 228 U.S.P.Q. 562, 566 (Fed.Cir. 1986). Two common examples of such impermissible broadening are using a patent which enjoys market power in the relevant market, see 35 U.S.C. § 271(d)(5)(1994), to restrain competition in an unpatented product or employing the patent beyond its 17–year term. In contrast, field of use restrictions (such as those at issue in the present case) are generally upheld, see *General Talking Pictures*, 305 U.S. at 127, 39 U.S.P.Q. at 330, and any anticompetitive effects they may cause are reviewed in accordance with the rule of reason. See *Mallinckrodt*, 976 F.2d at 708, 24 U.S.P.Q.2d at 1179–80.

124 F.3d at 1426, 43 U.S.P.Q.2d at 1901–02. Concluding that the jury instruction was erroneous, the Federal Circuit remanded the matter to the district court to determine whether Braun's restriction exceeded the scope of the patent grant. If it did not, then Braun could not be guilty of patent

misuse. Otherwise, the Federal Circuit instructed the district court to evaluate the restriction under the rule of reason.

2. Limited Licenses at the Federal Circuit. Limited patent licenses granting rights to sell patented products at a price fixed by the patentee have never been expressly held to be either a misuse or an antitrust violation. In view of *Mallinckrodt* and *B. Braun Medical*, would you be willing to argue that such licenses constitute neither a misuse nor an antitrust violation? Can you think of any limited licenses that the Federal Circuit would categorize as a misuse or an antitrust violation?

3. *Mallinckrodt* and Patent Exhaustion. The propriety of the doctrine of international patent exhaustion, under which a sale abroad exhausts all rights under the domestic patent, is a major subject of international patent law. International exhaustion has been addressed in an important decision of the European Court of Justice, *Merck & Co Inc and Others v. Primecrown Limited and Others* (Joined Cases c 267–268/95), [1997] 1 C.M.L.R. 83, and of the Supreme Court of Japan, *Kabushiki Kaisha & Anor. v. BBS Kraftfahrzeug Technik A.G.*, case no. 95 (*o*) 1988 (July 1, 1997). It has not, however, been an important subject in the United States. Nevertheless since *Mallinckrodt* discusses at length the key cases dealing with domestic patent exhaustion, the following short discussion is included here.

A country incorporates patent exhaustion as part of its patent law if, even when the buyer and seller of a patented good seek to limit the implied license under the patent to use and sell, the sale nevertheless exhausts all patent rights. Often the imposed, but exhausted restriction is territorial in nature: for example, that licensee sales may be completed only in particular locations. Among others, Germany, the Netherlands and Italy take this approach. *See* Ulrich Schatz, *The Exhaustion of Patent Rights in the Common Market*, 2 INT'L REV. INDUS. PROP. & COPYRIGHT L. 1 (1972). If a country adopts the exhaustion doctrine for domestic sales, then it must decide whether to extend the doctrine to sales made outside of its territory. These European countries have decided not to extend patent exhaustion under their respective patent laws to international sales except to the extent patent exhaustion is required by the laws of the European Community.

The legal situation in the United States is more complex. The United States Supreme Court in *Keeler v. Standard Folding Bed Co.*, 157 U.S. 659 (1895), squarely held that the doctrine of domestic exhaustion formed a part of domestic patent law. The Court summed up the United States law on exhaustion in the following three paragraphs:

This brief history of the cases shows that in *Wilson v. Rousseau*, 4 How. at 688, and cases following it, it was held that as between the owner of a patent, on the one side, and a purchaser of an article made under the patent, on the other, the payment of a royalty once, or, what is the same thing, the purchase of the article from one authorized by the patentee to sell it, emancipates such article from any further subjection to the patent throughout the entire life of the patent, even if the latter should be by law subsequently extended beyond the term existing at the time of the sale, and that, in respect of the time of enjoyment, by those decisions the right of the purchaser, his assigns or legal representatives, is clearly established to be entirely free from any further claim of the patentee or any assignee; that in *Adams v. Burke*, 17 Wall. 453, it was held that as respects *the place* of enjoyment, and as between the purchaser of patented articles in one specified part of the territory and the assignee of the patent of another part, the right once legitimately acquired to hold, use, and sell will protect such purchaser from any further subjection to the monopoly; that in *Hobbie v. Jennison*, 149 U.S. 355, 13 Sup. Ct. 879, it was held that, as between assignees of different parts of the territory, it is competent for one to sell the patented articles to persons who intend, with the knowledge of the vender, to take them for use into the territory of the other.

     Upon the doctrine of these cases, we think it follows that one who buys patented articles of manufacture from one authorized to sell them becomes possessed of an absolute property in such articles, unrestricted in time or place. Whether a patentee may protect himself and his assignees by special contracts brought home to the purchasers is not a question before us, and upon which we express no opinion. It is, however, obvious that such a question would arise as a question of contract, and not as one under the inherent meaning and effect of the patent laws.

     The conclusion reached does not deprive a patentee of his just rights, because no article can be unfettered from the claim of his monopoly without paying its tribute. The inconvenience and annoyance to the public that an opposite conclusion would occasion are too obvious to require illustration.

157 U.S. at 666–67.

The Court's statement is among the earliest in the world adopting the proposition that the patent law grants only the right of first sale, and that further restrictions must be founded in contract and not on a limited patent license theory. The exhaustion doctrine of *Keeler* was apparently rejected by the Federal Circuit in *Mallinckrodt* because, in the view of the court, *General Talking Pictures* overruled *Keeler*. Do you agree with the Federal Circuit on this point? Even if you disagree, do you believe that the Federal Circuit's rejection of *Keeler* was sound as a matter of policy, even if wrong in law?

     4. Further Reading. The literature reflecting on *Mallinckrodt* is reviewed in Note, *Is The Patent Misuse Doctrine Obsolete?*, 110 HARV. L. REV. 1922 (1997). The Note reads *Mallinckrodt* as adopting the view that the only acts that will invoke the misuse remedy are acts that violate the antitrust laws. It then argues that there is a role for a substantive misuse doctrine. Do you agree, and if so, why? Perhaps *Mallinckrodt* applied the antitrust-only approach only to limited licenses, leaving other conduct such as leveraging as misuse violations, even if they are not antitrust violations so long as they are outside the language of Section 271 (d)(5).

     5. Misuse vis-a-vis Antitrust. While the previous materials have assumed that any behavior using patents that violates the antitrust laws invokes the penalty of patent misuse, they do not clearly distinguish between acts that merely invoke the misuse penalty and those that violate the antitrust laws and therefore invoke the misuse penalty. The following case contains an excellent discussion of this important distinction. It focused the debate on whether the law should recognize behavior that invokes only the misuse penalty, an approach that influenced the Federal Circuit's approach in *Mallinckrodt*.

USM CORP. v. SPS TECHNOLOGIES, INC.

United States Court of Appeals, Seventh Circuit, 1982.
694 F.2d 505, 216 U.S.P.Q. 959.

Before PELL, CIRCUIT JUDGE, STEWART, ASSOCIATE JUSTICE (RETIRED), and POSNER, CIRCUIT JUDGE.

POSNER, CIRCUIT JUDGE.

SPS, a manufacturer of industrial fasteners, owned a patent, issued in 1963, on a patch-type self-locking industrial fastener. In 1969 it sued USM, a competing manufacturer of fasteners, for infringement. After a trial on the issue whether USM had a valid license under the patent by virtue of a grant-back clause in a licensing agreement between the parties, the district court held that USM did not have a valid license. *Standard Pressed Steel Co. v. Coral Corp.*, 168 U.S.P.Q. 741 (N.D.Ill. 1971). The parties then settled the case by entry of a consent judgment in which USM acknowledged that the patent was valid and had been infringed. As part of the settlement SPS granted USM a license which allowed USM to continue using the patent but required it to pay royalties to SPS.

In 1974, three years after SPS's suit had been settled, USM brought the present suit, seeking to invalidate SPS's patent and get back the royalties it had paid since the settlement.... USM's suit not only challenges the validity of the patent but also alleges that certain terms that first appeared in the license agreement entered into at the termination of the first suit constitute patent misuse. * * * The remaining issue is whether SPS committed patent misuse by including a differential royalty schedule in the license agreement entered into as part of the settlement of the earlier suit. The agreement requires USM to remit to SPS 25 percent of any royalties it obtains by sublicensing SPS's patent, except that if USM should happen to sublicense any of four companies that SPS had previously licensed directly USM must remit 75 percent of the royalties obtained from the sublicensee(s).

The doctrine of patent misuse has been described as an equitable concept designed to prevent a patent owner from using the patent in a manner contrary to public policy. *Morton Salt Co. v. G.S. Suppiger Co.*, 314 U.S. 488 (1942). This is too vague a formulation to be useful; taken seriously it would put all patent rights at hazard; and in application the doctrine has largely been confined to a handful of specific practices by which the patentee seemed to be trying to "extend" his patent grant beyond its statutory limits. An early example was fixing the price at which the purchaser of the patented item could resell it. See *Bauer &*

Cie. v. O'Donnell, 229 U.S. 1 (1913). The courts reasoned (in rather a circular fashion, one must admit) that once the patent owner had given up title to the patented item his patent rights were at an end, and any further restriction on the purchaser would extend the patent beyond its statutory bounds. Similar thinking lies behind the most common application of the doctrine, which is to prevent the patent owner from requiring his licensees to buy an unpatented staple item used with the patented device—for example, ink with a mimeograph machine. See generally *Dawson Chem. Co. v. Rohm & Haas Co.*, 448 U.S. 176, 188–93 (1980).

Both examples—resale price maintenance and tying—suggest an overlap between misuse and antitrust principles. But although resale price maintenance by patentees was condemned as misuse shortly after *Dr. Miles Medical Co. v. John D. Park & Sons Co.*, 220 U.S. 373 (1911), held that the Sherman Act forbade resale price maintenance in nonpatent cases, see Bauer & Cie. v. O'Donnell, supra, and patent tie-ins were condemned as misuse shortly after the enactment of the tying provision (section 3) of the Clayton Act, 15 U.S.C. § 14, in 1914, see *Motion Picture Patents Co. v. Universal Film Mfg. Co.*, 243 U.S. 502, 517–18 (1917), in both instances the condemnation of the patentee's conduct was based on the doctrine of patent misuse rather than on antitrust law. More recently the doctrine has been used to forbid the patentee to require his licensees to pay royalties beyond the expiration of the patent, *Brulotte v. Thys Co.*, 379 U.S. 29 (1964), or to measure royalties by the sales of unpatented end products containing the patented item, *Zenith Radio Corp. v. Hazeltine Research, Inc.*, 395 U.S. 100, 133–40 (1969), or to require licensees not to make any items competing with the patented item, *Stewart v. Motrim, Inc.*, 192 U.S.P.Q. 410 (S.D.Ohio 1975).

As an original matter one might question whether any of these practices really "extends" the patent. The patentee who insists on limiting the freedom of his purchaser or licensee—whether to price, to use complementary inputs of the purchaser's choice, or to make competing items—will have to compensate the purchaser for the restriction by charging a lower price for the use of the patent. If, for example, the patent owner requires the licensee to agree to continue paying royalties after the patent expires, he will not be able to get him to agree to pay as big a royalty before the patent expires.

In all of these cases the patentee's total income may be higher—why else would he impose the restriction? But there is nothing wrong with trying to make as much money as you can from a patent. True, a tie-in can be a method of price discrimination. It enables the patent owner to vary the amount he charges for the use of the patent by the intensity of each user's demand for the patent (e.g., the mimeograph), as measured by the user's consumption of the tied product (e.g., the ink). *Heaton–Peninsular Button–Fastener Co. v. Eureka Specialty Co.*, 77 F. 288, 296 (6th Cir.1896); STIGLER, THE THEORY OF PRICE 210–11 (3d ed. 1966); BOWMAN, PATENT AND ANTITRUST LAW 55, 116–19 (1973). But since, as we shall see, there is no principle that patent owners may not engage in price discrimination, it is unclear why one form of discrimination, the tie-in, alone is forbidden.

But whether decided rightly or wrongly these are all cases where the license purports to enlarge the licensee's obligations beyond the limits of the patent grant. There is nothing of that sort here. But we must also consider whether the patent-misuse doctrine goes beyond these specific practices and constitutes a general code of patent licensing distinct from antitrust law.

The doctrine arose before there was any significant body of federal antitrust law, and reached maturity long before that law (a product very largely of free interpretation of unclear statutory language) attained its present broad scope. Since the antitrust laws as currently interpreted reach every practice that could impair competition substantially, it is not easy to define a separate role for a doctrine also designed to prevent an anticompetitive practice—the abuse of a patent monopoly. One possibility is that the doctrine of patent misuse, unlike antitrust law, condemns any patent licensing practice that is even trivially anticompetitive, at least if it has no socially beneficial effects. This might seem to explain cases such as *Duplan Corp. v. Deering Milliken, Inc.*, 444 F.Supp. 648, 697 (D.S.C.1977), *aff'd in relevant part*, 594 F.2d 979 (4th Cir.1979), which held that a patent tie-in agreement is misuse per se unless the patentee shows that he had some nonmonopolistic reason for the tie-in, such as protection of goodwill. To prove a tie-in prima facie unlawful under the antitrust laws all you have to show is that the defendant has some economic power in the market for the tying product, *United States Steel Corp. v. Fortner Enterprises, Inc.*, 429 U.S. 610 (1977), and *Duplan* eliminates this requirement in misuse cases. But if a patentee has no market power (and, of course, not every patent confers market power, *SCM Corp. v. Xerox Corp.*, 645 F.2d 1195, 1203 (2d Cir.1981)) he cannot use a tie-in to practice price discrimination, which presupposes market power. STIGLER, *supra*, at 211. Much less can he lever his way into a dominant position in the market for the tied product. The logical presumption in such a case is that the tie-in promotes efficiency—and there is no lack of hypotheses as to how it might do that. See BORK, THE ANTITRUST PARADOX 375–81 (1978). It is hard to understand why in these circumstances, where if any presumption is warranted it is that the tie-in promotes efficiency rather than reduces competition, the burden of proof on the issue of misuse should be shifted to the patentee.

But probably cases like *Duplan*—which was, like *Motion Picture Patents Co.*, *supra*, a tie-in case—are best understood simply as applications of the patent-misuse doctrine within its conventional, rather stereotyped boundaries. Outside those boundaries there is increasing convergence of patent-misuse analysis with standard antitrust analysis. See, e.g., *Carter–Wallace, Inc. v. United States*, 449 F.2d 1374, 1378–82 (Ct.Cl.1971); *Congoleum Indus., Inc. v. Armstrong Cork Co.*, 366 F.Supp. 220, 227–32 (E.D.Pa.1973), *aff'd*, 510 F.2d 334 (3d Cir.1975); *SCM Corp. v. Xerox Corp.*, 463 F.Supp. 983, 997–98 (D.Conn.1978) (the lengthy subsequent history of this case is irrelevant). One still finds plenty of statements in judicial opinions that less evidence of anticompetitive effect is required in a misuse case than in an antitrust case. See, e.g., *Transitron Electronic Corp. v. Hughes Aircraft Co.*, 487 F.Supp. 885, 892–93 (D.Mass.1980), aff'd, 649 F.2d 871 (1st Cir.1981). But apart from the conventional applications of the doctrine we have found no cases where standards different from those of antitrust law were actually applied to yield different results. For example, the issue in *Transitron* was whether patent misuse is a tort; the court held it was not.

If misuse claims are not tested by conventional antitrust principles, by what principles shall they be tested? Our law is not rich in alternative concepts of monopolistic abuse; and it is rather late in the day to try to develop one without in the process subjecting the rights of patent holders to debilitating uncertainty.

[The court then proceeded to analyze the particulars of USM's charge of patent misuse . . It found no misuse.]

Notes

1.   **Walker Process.** In *Walker Process Equipment, Inc. v. Food Machinery & Chem. Corp.*, 382 U.S. 172, 147 U.S.P.Q. 404 (1965) the Supreme Court held that a party injured by a patent that was obtained by fraud may recover treble damages under the Sherman Act so long as the patent covered a relevant market. The later requirement has made it difficult for those injured by patents obtained by fraud to recover treble damages. Should a patent be treated as a per se monopolization of a relevant market on the theory that any patent which has any value will result in an increased price for a covered product or process? *See* Martin J. Adelman, *Relevant Market Paradox—Attempted and Completed Patent Fraud Monopolization*, 28 OHIO STATE L.J. 289 (1977).

2.   **Patent Purchases.** Ordinarily the purchase of a patent or patents raises no antitrust concerns, but their purchase under certain circumstances can raise issues under the Sherman sections 1 and 2 and Clayton section 7, *SCM Corp. v. Xerox Corp.*, 645 F.2d 1195, 209 U.S.P.Q. 889 (2d Cir.1981). *See* 8 MARTIN J. ADELMAN, PATENT LAW PERSPECTIVES, § 18.11[4] at n.56 (2d ed. 1982).

3.   **Patent Skullduggery.** What if a patent on a patentable invention is obtain through manipulation by one party when a second party should rightfully have obtained the patent? Can an antitrust claim be built on such facts, *See Brunswick Corp. v. Riegel Textile Corp.*, 752 F.2d 261, 224 U.S.P.Q. 756 (7th Cir.1984) (Posner J.). For a similar approach, where the issue was antitrust injury, see Judge Rader's opinion in *Studiengesellschaft Kohle, M.B.H. v. Shell Oil Co.*, 112 F.3d 1561, 42 U.S.P.Q.2d 1674 (Fed.Cir. 1997). Neither *Brunswick* or *Studiengesellschaft Kohle* suggested that the patents in the wrong hands had additional value because of their ownership. However, if the alleged wrongful owner had additional competing patents, would you still agree with Judges Posner and Rader? For a general discussion of the differing value of patents depending on their ownership *see* Martin J. Adelman, *Property Rights Theory and Patent–Antitrust: The Role of Compulsory Licensing*, 52 N.Y.U. L. REV. 977, 995–8 (1977); 8 MARTIN J. ADELMAN, PATENT LAW PERSPECTIVES, § 17.3 at n.144 (2d ed. 1989).

4. How Should the Federal Circuit Deal With Misuse Cases?
The Federal Circuit does not have exclusive jurisdiction over patent-antitrust cases. They can be heard in any of the regional circuits. However, since
misuse is an equitable defense to a charge of patent infringement, what
constitutes substantive misuse is ordinarily a matter within the control of
the Federal Circuit. Should the Federal Circuit adopt the policy that no
conduct will be labeled a misuse unless there is Supreme Court authority
squarely holding that the challenged conduct is a misuse, or alternatively,
that the conduct is anticompetitive and therefore violates the antitrust laws?
Beyond the *Mallinckrodt* decision, the Federal Circuit may have adopted this
view in *Windsurfing International, Inc. v. AMF Inc.,* 782 F.2d 995, 228
U.S.P.Q. 562 (Fed.Cir.1986). However, in *Senza-Gel Corp. v. Seiffhart,* 803
F.2d 661, 231 U.S.P.Q. 363 (Fed.Cir.1986) the court appears to have stepped
away from it. For an analysis of these cases as well as the views of the
Justice Department on the need for anticompetitive conduct in misuse cases
see 8 MARTIN J. ADELMAN, PATENT LAW PERSPECTIVES, § 18.6[2.–3–2] at ns.21 and
22 (2d ed. 1989).

5. Patent Licensing Once More, the *Brulotte* Doctrine. In 1966
the Supreme Court decided that a patent license that provides for royalty
payments beyond the life of the patent is unenforceable. Thirty-six years
later the Seventh Circuit wrestled with whether there was any way for it not
to follow what it believed to be a decision wrong on its face. Studying the
court's opinion is a good way for students to review the subject matter of
this Chapter as the court makes every effort to find some doctrine that
would enable it to act sensibly. At the end of the day it said it could do
nothing more than follow *Brulotte* presumably hoping that the Supreme
Court will correct its mistake. Should the Seventh Circuit have simply
refused to follow *Brulotte,* thus forcing the Court to intervene or tacitly
admit that it was wrong in 1966?

SCHEIBER v. DOLBY LABORATORIES, INC.

United States Court of Appeals, Seventh Circuit, 2002.
293 F.3d 1014, 63 U.S.P.Q.2d 1404

Before POSNER, EVANS, AND WILLIAMS, CIRCUIT JUDGES.

POSNER, CIRCUIT JUDGE.

The plaintiff in a suit to enforce a patent licensing agreement
appeals to us from the grant of summary judgment to the defendants,
Dolby for short. Scheiber, the plaintiff, a musician turned inventor who
held U.S. and Canadian patents on the audio system known as "surround sound," sued Dolby in 1983 for infringement of his patents. The
parties settled the suit by agreeing that Scheiber would license his
patents to Dolby in exchange for royalties. The last U.S. patent covered
by the agreement was scheduled to expire in May 1993, while the last
Canadian patent was not scheduled to expire until September 1995.
During the settlement negotiations Dolby suggested to Scheiber that in
exchange for a lower royalty rate the license agreement provide that
royalties on all the patents would continue until the Canadian patent
expired, including, therefore, patents that had already expired. That way

Dolby could, it hoped, pass on the entire royalty expense to its sublicensees without their balking at the rate. Scheiber acceded to the suggestion and the agreement was drafted accordingly, but Dolby later refused to pay royalties on any patent after it expired, precipitating this suit. Federal jurisdiction over the suit is based on diversity of citizenship, because a suit to enforce a patent licensing agreement does not arise under federal patent law. E.g., *Jim Arnold Corp. v. Hydrotech Systems, Inc.*, 109 F.3d 1567, 1575 (Fed.Cir.1997).

Dolby argues that the duty to pay royalties on any patent covered by the agreement expired by the terms of the agreement itself as soon as the patent expired, because the royalties were to be based on Dolby's sales of equipment within the scope of the patents and once a patent expires, Dolby argues, there is no equipment within its scope. The argument would make meaningless the provision that Dolby itself proposed for continuing the payment of royalties until the last patent expired. Anyway the reference to equipment within the scope of the patent was clearly meant to *identify* the equipment on which royalties would be based (Dolby makes equipment that does not utilize Scheiber's patents as well as equipment that does) rather than to limit the duration of the obligation to pay royalties.

Dolby's principal argument is that the Supreme Court held in a decision that has never been overruled that a patent owner may not enforce a contract for the payment of patent royalties beyond the expiration date of the patent. The decision was *Brulotte v. Thys Co.*, 379 U.S. 29, 85 S.Ct. 176, 13 L.Ed.2d 99 (1964), dutifully followed by lower courts, including our own, in such cases as *Meehan v. PPG Industries, Inc.*, 802 F.2d 881, 883 (7th Cir.1986); *Virginia Panel Corp. v. MAC Panel Co.*, 133 F.3d 860, 869 (Fed.Cir.1997), and *Boggild v. Kenner Products*, 776 F.2d 1315, 1318–19 (6th Cir.1985). *Brulotte* involved an agreement licensing patents that expired at different dates, just like this case; the two cases are indistinguishable. The decision has, it is true, been severely, and as it seems to us, with all due respect, justly, criticized, beginning with Justice Harlan's dissent, 379 U.S. at 34, 85 S.Ct. 176, and continuing with our opinion in *USM Corp. v. SPS Technologies, Inc.*, 694 F.2d 505, 510–11 (7th Cir.1982). The Supreme Court's majority opinion reasoned that by extracting a promise to continue paying royalties after expiration of the patent, the patentee extends the patent beyond the term fixed in the patent statute and therefore in violation of the law. That is not true. After the patent expires, anyone can make the patented process or product without being guilty of patent infringement. The patent can no longer be used to exclude anybody from such production. Expiration thus accomplishes what it is supposed to accomplish. For a licensee in accordance with a provision in the license agreement to go on paying royalties after the patent expires does not extend the duration of the patent either technically or practically, because, as this case demonstrates, if the licensee agrees to continue paying royalties after the patent expires the royalty rate will be lower. The duration of the patent fixes the limit of the patentee's power to extract royalties; it is a detail whether he extracts them at a higher rate over a shorter period of time or a lower rate over a longer period of time.

This insight is not original with us. "The *Brulotte* rule incorrectly assumes that a patent license has significance after the patent terminates. When the patent term ends, the exclusive right to make, use or sell the licensed invention also ends. Because the invention is available to the world, the license in fact ceases to have value. Presumably, licensees know this when they enter into a licensing agreement. If the licensing agreement calls for royalty payments beyond the patent term, the parties base those payments on the licensees' assessment of the value of the license during the patent period. These payments, therefore, do not represent an extension in time of the patent monopoly.... Courts do not remove the obligation of the consignee to pay because payment after receipt is an extension of market power—it is simply a division of the payment-for-delivery transaction. Royalties beyond the patent term are no different. If royalties are calculated on post-patent term sales, the calculation is simply a risk-shifting credit arrangement between patentee and licensee. The arrangement can be no more than that, because the patentee at that time has nothing else to sell." Harold See & Frank M. Caprio, *The Trouble with Brulotte: the Patent Royalty Term and Patent Monopoly Extension*, 1990 UTAH L.REV. 813, 814, 851; to similar effect see Rochelle Cooper Dreyfuss, *Dethroning Lear: Licensee Estoppel and the Incentive to Innovate*, 72 VA. L.REV. 677, 709–12 (1986). "[T]he Supreme Court refused to see that typically such post-expiration royalties merely amortize the price of using patented technology." 10 PHILLIP E. AREEDA ET AL., ANTITRUST LAW §§ 1782c2–c3, pp. 505–11 (1996); cf. *Jahn v. 1–800–FLOWERS.com, Inc.*, 284 F.3d 807, 811–12 (7th Cir.2002).

These criticisms might be wide of the mark if *Brulotte* had been based on the interpretation of the patent clause of the Constitution, or of the patent statute or any other statute; but it seems rather to have been a free-floating product of a misplaced fear of monopoly ("a patentee's use of a royalty agreement that projects beyond the expiration date of the patent is unlawful per se. If that device were available to patentees, the free market visualized for the post-expiration period would be subject to monopoly influences that have no proper place there," 379 U.S. at 32–33, 85 S.Ct. 176) that was not even tied to one of the antitrust statutes. 10 AREEDA et al., *supra*, at §§ 1782c2, 1782c3, pp. 505, 511. The doctrinal basis of the decision was the doctrine of patent misuse, of which more later.

A patent confers a monopoly, and the longer the term of the patent the greater the monopoly. The limitation of the term of a patent, besides being commanded by the Constitution, see U.S. Const. art. I, § 8, cl. 8; *Bonito Boats, Inc. v. Thunder Craft Boats, Inc.*, 489 U.S. 141, 146, 109 S.Ct. 971, 103 L.Ed.2d 118 (1989), and necessary to avoid impossible tracing problems (imagine if some caveman had gotten a perpetual patent on the wheel), serves to limit the monopoly power conferred on the patentee. But as we have pointed out, charging royalties beyond the term of the patent does not lengthen the patentee's monopoly; it merely alters the timing of royalty payments. This would be obvious if the license agreement between Scheiber and Dolby had become effective a month before the last patent expired. The parties could have agreed that Dolby would pay royalties for the next 100 years, but obviously the royalty rate would be minuscule because of the imminence of the patent's expiration.

* * *

Now it is true that in *Aronson v. Quick Point Pencil Co.*, 440 U.S. 257, 99 S.Ct. 1096, 59 L.Ed.2d 296 (1979), a case decided some years after *Brulotte*, the Supreme Court upheld an agreement superficially similar to the one invalidated in *Brulotte* and at issue in the present case: a patent applicant granted a license for the invention it hoped to patent to a firm that agreed, if a patent were not granted, to pay the inventor-applicant royalties for as long as the firm sold products embodying the invention. The Court was careful to distinguish *Brulotte*, and not a single Justice suggested that any cloud had been cast over the earlier decision. Since no patent was granted, the doctrine of patent misuse could not be brought into play, and there was no other federal ground for invalidating the license. The Court emphasized that *Brulotte* had been based on the "leverage" that the patent had granted the patentee to extract royalties beyond the date of expiration, 440 U.S. at 265, 99 S.Ct. 1096, and that leverage was of course missing in *Aronson*.

If *Aronson* and *Brulotte* were inconsistent with each other and the Court had not reaffirmed *Brulotte* in *Aronson*, then we would have to follow *Aronson*, the later opinion, since to follow *Brulotte* in those circumstances would be to overrule *Aronson*. But the reaffirmation of *Brulotte* in *Aronson* tells us that the Court did not deem the cases inconsistent, and so, whether we agree or not, we have no warrant for declaring *Brulotte* overruled.

Scheiber argues further, however, that *Brulotte* has been superseded by a 1988 amendment to the patent statute which provides, so far as bears on this case, that "no patent owner otherwise entitled to relief for infringement ... shall be ... deemed guilty of misuse or illegal extension of the patent right by reason of his having ... conditioned the license of any rights to the patent or the sale of the patented product on the acquisition of a license to rights in another patent or purchase of a separate product" unless the patentee has market power in the market for the conditioning product (which is not argued here). 35 U.S.C. § 271(d)(5). The statute is doubly inapplicable to this case. It merely limits defenses to infringement suits, and Scheiber isn't suing for infringement; he's suing to enforce a license agreement. He can't sue for infringement; his patents have expired. Scheiber argues that since the agreement was in settlement of his infringement suit, the only effect of limiting the statute to such suits would be to dissuade patentees from settling them. Not so. Had Scheiber pressed his 1983 infringement suit against Dolby to judgment, he would not have obtained royalties beyond the expiration date of his patents, because Dolby had not as yet agreed to pay any royalties; there was no license agreement before the case was settled. The significance of the statute is that if some subsequent infringer should point to the license agreement with Dolby as a misuse of Scheiber's patent by reason of the tying together of different patents, Scheiber could plead the statute as a bar to the infringer's defense of patent misuse.

In any event, the new statutory defense is explicitly limited to tying, *Lasercomb America, Inc. v. Reynolds*, 911 F.2d 970, 976 and n. 15 (4th Cir.1990); *In re Recombinant DNA Technology Patent & Contract Litigation*, 850 F.Supp. 769, 775–77 (S.D.Ind.1994), normally of a nonpatented product to a patented product, as in a number of famous patent misuse cases, such as *Henry v. A.B. Dick Co.*, 224 U.S. 1, 32 S.Ct. 364, 56 L.Ed. 645 (1912), and antitrust tying cases, such as *International Business Machines Corp. v. United States*, 298 U.S. 131, 56 S.Ct. 701, 80 L.Ed. 1085 (1936); *Morton Salt Co. v. G.S. Suppiger Co.*, 314 U.S. 488, 62 S.Ct. 402, 86 L.Ed. 363 (1942), and *International Salt Co. v. United States*, 332 U.S. 392, 68 S.Ct. 12, 92 L.Ed. 20 (1947). The 1988 amendment limited the tying doctrine, in cases in which the tying product is a patent, to situations in which the patentee has real market power, not merely the technical monopoly (right to exclude) that every patent confers. *Virginia Panel Corp. v. MAC Panel Co., supra*, 133 F.3d at 869. There are multiple products here, and they are tied together in the sense of having been licensed as a package. The more exact term is bundling, because a single price is charged for the tied goods, rather than separate prices as in the canonical tying cases. *United States v. Microsoft Corp.*, 253 F.3d 34, 87, 96 (D.C.Cir.2001) (en banc) (per curiam); *Multistate Legal Studies, Inc. v. Harcourt Brace Jovanovich Legal & Professional Publications, Inc.*, 63 F.3d 1540, 1548 (10th Cir.1995). We may assume that the statute encompasses bundling. We can't find a case on the point, but certainly the statutory language encompasses it and the objections to tying and bundling, such as they are, are the same. (The naive objection is that they extend monopoly; the sophisticated objection is that they facilitate price discrimination.) But it is not the bundling of the U.S. and Canadian patents on which Dolby pitches its refusal to pay royalties; it is the duration of the royalty obligation. The objection would be the same if there were a single patent and the agreement required the licensee to continue paying royalties after the patent expired.

Brulotte called extending the royalty obligation beyond the term of the patent analogous to tying, 379 U.S. at 33, 85 S.Ct. 176, because the traditional objection to tying as we noted is that by telling the buyer that he can't buy the tying product unless he agrees to buy a separate product from the seller as well, the seller is trying to "lever" or "extend" his monopoly to the market for that separate product: only extending it in product space rather than in time. Yet if the seller tries to charge a monopoly price for that separate product, the buyer will not be willing to pay as much for the tying product as he would if the separate product, which he has to buy also, were priced at a lower rate.

Acquiring monopoly power in the tied-product market comes at the expense of losing it in the tying-product market. *Advo, Inc. v. Philadelphia Newspapers, Inc.*, 51 F.3d 1191, 1202–03 (3d Cir.1995); *Hirsh v. Martindale–Hubbell, Inc.*, 674 F.2d 1343, 1349 n. 19 (9th Cir.1982). Thus, as these cases and a tidal wave of legal and economic scholarship point out, the idea that you can use tying to lever your way to a second (or, in the post-expiration patent royalty setting, a longer and therefore greater) monopoly is economic nonsense, imputing systematic irrationality to businessmen. Congress seems to have recognized this in the 1988 amendment. But even if the amendment should therefore be interpreted to reject the rationale of the tying cases, and even though the rationale of *Brulotte* is materially identical to that of the discredited tying cases— the Court even invoked "leverage" (as it emphasized later in *Aronson*), saying that to "use that leverage [the power conferred by the monopoly] to project those royalty payments beyond the life of the patent is analogous to an effort to enlarge the monopoly of the patent," 379 U.S. at 33, 85 S.Ct. 176—and not a whit stronger (probably even weaker, since there is only one product), it would not follow that the statute had changed the rule of that case. Congress isn't constrained, as courts like to think they are, to rule logically. Most statutes are the product of compromise, and compromises need not cut at the logical joints of a controversy. There just is no evidence that Congress in the 1988 amendment wanted to go or did go beyond tying. Had it wanted to, it would have chosen different words. We are not literalists, but there must be some semantic handle on which to hang a proposed statutory interpretation, and there is none here, though we have found a district court case that did hold that the 1988 amendment had overruled *Brulotte*. *Sunrise Medical HHG, Inc. v. AirSep Corp.*, 95 F.Supp.2d 348, 457–59 (W.D.Pa. 2000).

Scheiber has another ground for disregarding *Brulotte* that deserves consideration (again a ground supported by a lone district court decision, *A.C. Aukerman Co. v. R.L. Chaides Construction Co.*, No. CIV. 88–20704 SW, 1993 WL 379548, at *6 (N.D.Cal. Sept.13, 1993), but one that misreads *Brulotte* as having been held in *Well Surveys, Inc. v. Perfo–Log, Inc.*, 396 F.2d 15, 17 (10th Cir.1968), to be inapplicable to package-licensing agreements that contain expired patents unless the licensees were coerced into making the agreements). The ground is that Dolby comes into court with "unclean hands" that should not be allowed to touch and stain the Supreme Court's decision. Scheiber points out that it was Dolby that asked him to stretch out the royalties until the last patent expired and that now seeks to get out of the obligation it not only accepted but volunteered to shoulder.

* * *

We needn't get deeper into this thicket of archaic distinctions, since it is apparent that to apply the doctrine of unclean hands in a case such as the present one would fatally undermine the policy of refusing enforcement to contracts for the payment of patent royalties after expiration of the patent. It would be (given the antimonopoly basis of *Brulotte*) inconsistent with the Supreme Court's rejection of the defense of in pari delicto ("equally at fault") in antitrust cases, *Perma Life Mufflers, Inc. v. International Parts Corp.*, 392 U.S. 134, 137–39, 88 S.Ct. 1981, 20 L.Ed.2d 982 (1968), since the effect of that rejection is to give a party to a contract that violates the antitrust laws a defense to a suit to enforce the contract even if he entered into the contract with full knowledge. We even said in *General Leaseways, Inc. v. National Truck Leasing Ass'n*, 744 F.2d 588, 597 (7th Cir.1984), in words that might have been uttered with the present case in mind, that "ever since the Supreme Court, in *Perma Life*, rejected the defense of in pari delicto in antitrust cases, it has been clear that whenever some maxim of equity (such as that to get equitable relief you must have 'clean hands') collides with the objectives of the antitrust laws, the equity maxim must give way." Later the Supreme Court equated "unclean hands" to in pari delicto. *McKennon v. Nashville Banner Publishing Co.*, 513 U.S. 352, 360, 115 S.Ct. 879, 130 L.Ed.2d 852 (1995); see also *Hartman Bros. Heating & Air Conditioning, Inc. v. NLRB*, 280 F.3d 1110, 1116 (7th Cir.2002).

What is true is that a contract that is voided on grounds of illegality—Dolby's defense to Scheiber's suit for the agreed-upon royalties—is ordinarily treated as rescinded, meaning that the parties are to be put back, so far as possible, in the positions they would have occupied had the contract never been made in the first place. *Cox v. Zale Delaware, Inc.*, 239 F.3d 910, 914 (7th Cir.2001); *United States v. Amdahl Corp.*, 786 F.2d 387, 392–93 (Fed.Cir.1986). For example, even if a contract is unenforceable because it violates the statute of frauds, the performing party can still claim the value of his performance, net of any payment received before the contract was rescinded, on a theory of quantum meruit, a type of restitution. See, e.g., *Clark v. United States*, 95 U.S. 539, 541–42, 24 L.Ed. 518 (1877); *Beanstalk Group, Inc. v. AM General Corp.*, 283 F.3d 856, 863–64 (7th Cir.2002). *Cox* and *Amdahl* involved contracts that were illegal, and not just unenforceable (there is nothing remotely "wrongful" about failing to memorialize in writing a contract that is enforceable only if so memorialized), yet quantum meruit would still have been available had the voiding party been unduly enriched by being able to walk away from the contract. But Scheiber is not arguing that if indeed the contract is unenforceable, as we believe it is, he is entitled to some form of restitution of the benefits received by Dolby under it as a result of Dolby's being allowed to use Scheiber's patents without paying the full price that they had agreed upon. Scheiber would be entitled to such relief only if the amount of royalties that Dolby did pay was less than the fair market value of Dolby's use of the patents, which of course it may not have been. In any event he makes no claim of quantum meruit.

Dolby was indeed entitled to summary judgment.

AFFIRMED.

Licensing Exercise

Gamma, which manufactures Product X using its patented process, offers a license for its process technology to every other manufacturer of Product X, each of which competes world-wide with Gamma in the manufacture and sale of X. The process technology does not represent an economic improvement over the available existing technologies. Indeed, although most manufacturers accept licenses from Gamma, none of the licensees actually uses the licensed technology. The licenses provide that each manufacturer has an exclusive right to sell Product X manufactured using the licensed technology in a designated geographic area and that no manufacturer may sell Product X, however manufactured, outside the designated territory.

If asked to draft the licenses between Gamma and its licensees, what licensing clauses would you recommend? What misuse and antitrust concerns would you raise before the President of Gamma?

*

Index

†

0–314–24637–1